MICROSOFT® OFFICE

FrontPage® 2003

Comprehensive Concepts and Techniques

Gary B. Shelly
Thomas J. Cashman
Jeffrey J. Quasney

THOMSON
COURSE TECHNOLOGY

COURSE TECHNOLOGY
25 THOMSON PLACE
BOSTON MA 02210

SHELLY CASHMAN SERIES®

Australia • Canada • Denmark • Japan • Mexico • New Zealand • Philippines • Puerto Rico • Singapore
South Africa • Spain • United Kingdom • United States

THOMSON
COURSE TECHNOLOGY

Microsoft Office FrontPage 2003 Comprehensive Concepts and Techniques

Gary B. Shelly
Thomas J. Cashman
Jeffrey J. Quasney

Executive Editor:
Cheryl Costantini

Senior Acquisitions Editor:
Dana Merk

Senior Product Manager:
Alexandra Arnold

Product Manager:
Reed Cotter

Editorial Assistant:
Selena Coppock

Print Buyer:
Laura Burns

Signing Representative:
Cheryl Costantini

Series Consulting Editor:
Jim Quasney

Director of Production:
Becky Herrington

Production Editor:
Deb Masi

Production Assistant:
Jennifer Quiambao

Development Editor:
Ginny Harvey

Copy Editor:
Mark Goodin

Proofreaders:
Lori Silfen
Lyn Markowicz

Interior Designer:
Becky Herrington

Cover Designer:
Richard Herrera

Illustrators:
Richard Herrera
Andrew Bartel

Compositors:
Jeanne Black
Andrew Bartel
Kellee LaVars

Indexer:
Cristina Haley

Printer:
Banta Menasha

Printed in the United States of America

2 3 4 5 6 7 8 9 10
BM 08 07 06 05 04

For more information, contact Course Technology
25 Thomson Place
Boston, Massachusetts 02210

Or find us on the World Wide Web at:
www.course.com

ISBN 0-619-25475-0

MICROSOFT® OFFICE

FrontPage® 2003

Comprehensive Concepts and Techniques

Contents

Project Three

Customizing and Managing Web Pages and Images

Table Feature

Creating a Stand-Alone Web Page Using a Layout Table

Project Four

Creating and Using Interactive Forms on the Web

Project Five

Using Frames to Display Database Results in Web Pages

Project Six

Using Subsites, the Database Interface Wizard, and Source Control

Layout Feature

Using a Tracing Image to Create a Web Page

Project Seven

Customizing Tables and Searching Web Sites

Project Eight

Working with Dynamic Web Templates, Layers, and Behaviors

Project Nine

Managing Web Sites on a Server

Multimedia Feature

Working with Multimedia Content in Web Pages

Appendix A

Microsoft FrontPage Help System

Appendix B

Speech and Handwriting Recognition

Appendix C

Appendix D

Changing Screen Resolution and Resetting the FrontPage Toolbars and Menus

Appendix E

Preface

The Shelly Cashman Series® offers the finest textbooks in computer education. We are proud of the fact that our series of Microsoft Office 4.3, Microsoft Office 95, Microsoft Office 97, Microsoft Office 2000, and Microsoft Office XP textbooks have been the most widely used books in education. With each new edition of our Office books, we have made significant improvements based on the software and comments made by the instructors and students. The *Microsoft Office FrontPage 2003* books continue with the innovation, quality, and reliability that you have come to expect from the Shelly Cashman Series.

In this *Microsoft Office FrontPage 2003* book, you will find an educationally sound, highly visual, and easy-to-follow pedagogy that combines a vastly improved step-by-step approach with corresponding screens. All projects and exercises in this book are designed to take full advantage of the FrontPage 2003 enhancements. The project material is developed to ensure that students will see the importance of learning FrontPage for future coursework. The popular Other Ways and More About features offer in-depth knowledge of FrontPage 2003, and the new Q&A feature offers students a way to solidify important Web page authoring and site management concepts. The Learn It Online page presents a wealth of additional exercises to ensure your students have all the reinforcement they need.

Objectives of This Textbook

Microsoft Office FrontPage 2003: Comprehensive Concepts and Techniques is intended for a full semester course or a major portion of a full-semester Web-related course that uses FrontPage 2003 to implement Web page and Web site designs. No experience with a computer is assumed, and no mathematics beyond the high school freshman level is required. The objectives of this book are:

- To teach the fundamentals of FrontPage 2003
- To acquaint students with the proper procedures to design and create Web pages suitable for course work, professional purposes, and personal use
- To illustrate the Web management features of FrontPage for Web sites located on a Web server.
- To introduce students to incorporating multimedia, such as flash movies, into Web pages
- To expose students to practical examples of the computer as a useful tool
- To develop an exercise-oriented approach that allows learning by doing
- To introduce students to new input technologies
- To encourage independent study and help those who are working alone

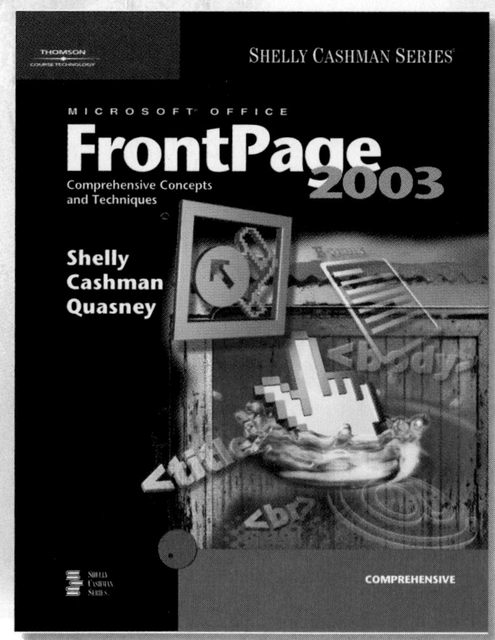

The Shelly Cashman Approach

Other Ways

1. Click image, in Voice Command mode, say "Position Absolutely"

More About

CGI Script Languages

On UNIX systems, most CGI scripts are written in C or Perl. On Windows systems, most CGI scripts are written in Visual Basic or Visual C++. To locate free CGI scripts, visit the FrontPage 2003 More About Web page (scsite.com/fp2003/more) and then click CGI Scripts.

Q&A

Q: Does FrontPage provide other methods to import files?

A: Yes. You can import an image simply by dragging the image from another Windows application to the Navigation or Folders view. You also may copy a file in Windows Explorer and paste it into the Folder List pane or the Contents pane while in Folders view.

Features of the Shelly Cashman Series *Microsoft Office FrontPage 2003* books include:

- **Project Orientation:** Each project in the book presents a practical problem and complete solution using an easy-to-understand methodology.
- **Step-by-Step, Screen-by-Screen Instructions:** Each of the tasks required to complete a project is identified throughout the project. Full-color screens accompany the steps.
- **Thoroughly Tested Projects:** Unparalleled quality is ensured because every screen in the book is produced by the author only after performing a step, and then each project must pass Course Technology's award-winning Quality Assurance program.
- **Other Ways Boxes and Quick Reference Summary:** The Other Ways boxes displayed at the end of many of the step-by-step sequences specify the other ways to perform the task completed in the steps. Thus, the steps and the Other Ways box make a comprehensive reference unit.
- **More About and Q&A Features:** These marginal annotations provide background information, tips, and answers to common questions that complement the topics covered, adding depth and perspective to the learning process.
- **Web Design Tips:** Web Design Tips boxed throughout the book emphasize important Web design concepts to help students as they design a Web site.
- **Integration of the World Wide Web:** The World Wide Web is integrated into the FrontPage 2003 learning experience by (1) More About annotations that send students to Web sites for up-to-date information and alternative approaches to tasks; (2) a FrontPage 2003 Quick Reference Summary Web page that summarizes the ways to complete tasks (mouse, menu, shortcut menu, and keyboard); and (3) the Learn It Online page at the end of each project, which has project reinforcement exercises, learning games, and other types of student activities.

Organization of This Textbook

Microsoft Office FrontPage 2003: Comprehensive Concepts and Techniques provides basic instruction on how to use FrontPage 2003. The material is divided into nine projects, a Table feature, a Layout feature, a Multimedia feature, five appendices, and a Quick Reference Summary.

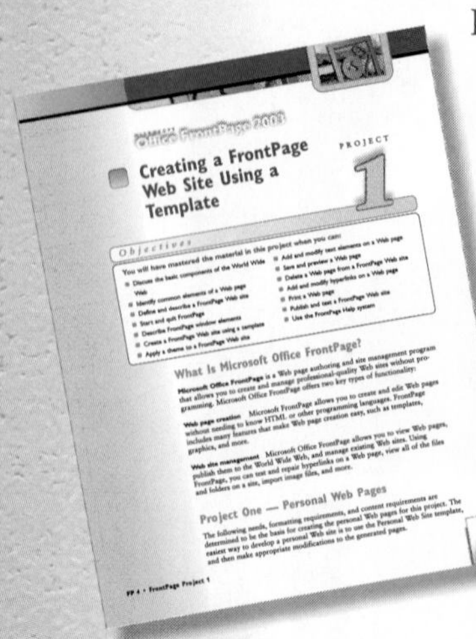

Project 1 — Creating a FrontPage Web Site Using a Template In Project 1, students are introduced to the basic components of the World Wide Web and of HTML, the FrontPage environment, and they learn how to use FrontPage templates. Students create a simple three-page Web site consisting of a Home page, a Professional Interests page, and a Favorite Links page. Topics include basic Web page editing and customization techniques; applying a theme using FrontPage commands and features; and saving, printing, and publishing the three pages to an available Web server. Students then can use a browser to view their own personal Web pages.

Project 2 — Adding a New Web Page to a Web Site In Project 2, students learn how to add a new page to an existing Web site and then how to customize that page. Topics include basic Web page design criteria; setting up the page background; inserting tables, images, and a Photo Gallery component; adding, replacing, and applying special formatting to text; and adding linked targets to the page. Students also learn how to preview the printout of a page.

Project 3 — Customizing and Managing Web Pages and Images In Project 3, students are introduced to techniques for using graphics and images in Web pages. Topics include opening an existing FrontPage Web site; displaying and using the Pictures toolbar to apply formatting to images; creating and applying a customized theme to a page; assigning a hyperlink to an image; creating an image map and assigning a URL to the image map hotspot; highlighting hotspots on an image map; copying and pasting from a Word document; inserting a hit counter, a shared border, and an AutoShapes drawing; using FrontPage reporting features; displaying and verifying the hyperlinks in a FrontPage Web site in a browser; and modifying the navigation structure of a Web site.

Table Feature — Creating a Stand-Alone Web Page Using a Layout Table In the Table feature, students are introduced to creating a stand-alone Web page and using layout tables to construct the layout of a Web page. Topics include creating a new stand-alone Web page; using a layout table to design a Web page; formatting layout cells in a layout table with rounded corners, shadows, and borders; and modifying the structure of a layout table.

Project 4 — Creating and Using Interactive Forms on the Web In Project 4, students are introduced to interactive forms. After learning the basics of forms, form handlers, and form data formats, students create a Web page with a form consisting of the most-used form fields. Topics include inserting a form in a Web page; inserting a table in a form; inserting a form in a table; creating a nested table; inserting radio buttons, drop-down menus, text boxes, and check boxes in a form; inserting a line drawing AutoShape; adjusting form field properties; assigning text as a form field label; and choosing a form handler to save results to a database. Students also will learn to manage files in Folders view and modify HTML code directly within FrontPage.

Project 5 — Using Frames to Display Database Results in Web Pages In Project 5, students are introduced to frames Web pages and the Database Results Wizard. Topics include how frames work; using a frames template; saving frames Web pages; creating an initial Web page for a frame; adjusting the size of frames; modifying properties of a frame and of a frames page; creating hyperlinks to pages in frames; using an existing Web page as the initial page in a frame; opening the target of a hyperlink in a different frame; printing Web pages in frames; and displaying the No Frames view. Students will learn how to use the Database Results Wizard and to create a custom SQL query. During the course of creating the frames Web page, students will import Web resources into an existing FrontPage Web site, demonstrating how to use FrontPage to manage preexisting related Web pages.

Project 6 — Using Subsites, the Database Interface Wizard, and Source Control In Project 6, students learn how to use the Database Interface Wizard to incorporate a database into their Web site, and how to use source control to coordinate development efforts. Topics include creating a folder; moving files and folders; converting a folder to a subsite; editing a subsite; using a default page as a hyperlink target; using the Database Interface Wizard to create Database Editor pages; applying a theme to a subsite; publishing a Web site and all subsites; enabling source control for a Web site; and checking files in and out using source control. Students also will learn how to view the Checkout Status report to determine which files are checked out, when they were checked out, and by whom.

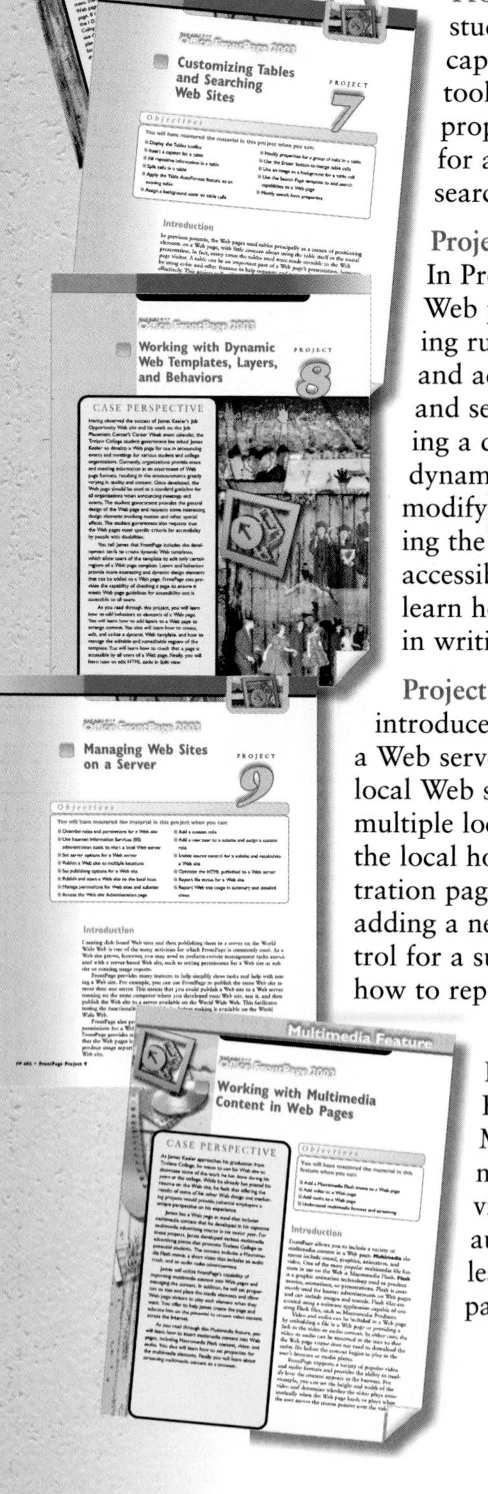

Layout Feature — Using a Tracing Image to Create a Web Page In the Layout Feature, students learn how to use a tracing image to develop a Web page and how to use inline frames to display one Web page within another Web page. Topics include adding a tracing image to a Web page; setting properties of a tracing image; inserting an inline frame into a Web page; setting properties of an inline frame; adding interactive buttons to a Web page; and designing interactive buttons. Students also learn how to add content to a Web page contained in an inline frame.

Project 7 — Customizing Tables and Searching Web Sites In Project 7, students learn how to customize tables in a Web page and how to add search capabilities to a FrontPage Web site. Topics include displaying the Tables toolbar; inserting a caption for a table; splitting cells in a table; modifying properties for a group of cells in a table; and using an image as a background for a table cell. Students also will learn to use the Search Page template to add search capabilities to a Web page and to modify search form properties.

Project 8 — Working with Dynamic Web Templates, Layers, and Behaviors In Project 8, students learn to use dynamic Web templates and add effects to a Web page using layers, DHTML effects, and behaviors. Topics include displaying rulers and a grid in Design view; displaying the DHTML Effects toolbar and adding DHTML effects to Web page elements; adding layers to a Web page and setting properties of layers; adding behaviors to Web page elements; creating a dynamic Web template; setting editable and non-editable regions of a dynamic Web template; creating a Web page using a dynamic Web template; modifying a dynamic Web template; checking the spelling on a Web page; checking the accessibility of a Web page for people with special needs; understanding accessibility guidelines; and correcting accessibility problems. Students also will learn how to edit HTML code in Split view and how to use IntelliSense to assist in writing HTML code.

Project 9 — Managing Web Sites on a Server In Project 9, students are introduced to the Web management features of FrontPage for Web sites located on a Web server. Topics include roles and permissions for a Web site; using IIS to start a local Web server; setting server options for a Web server; publishing a Web site to multiple locations; setting publishing options for a Web site; publishing a Web site to the local host; opening a Web site on the local host; accessing the Web site Administration page; managing permissions for Web sites and subsites; adding a custom role; adding a new user to a subsite and assigning a custom role; and enabling source control for a subsite. Students also will learn how to report file status for a Web site and how to report Web site usage in summary and detailed views.

Multimedia Feature — Working with Multimedia Content in Web Pages In this Multimedia Feature, students learn how to add Macromedia Flash movies, video, and audio to a Web page. Topics include adding a Macromedia Flash movie to a Web page and setting properties for the movie; embedding a video file in a Web page and setting properties for the video; embedding an audio file in a Web page and setting properties for the audio; and linking and streaming multimedia content. Students also will learn about plug-ins and the requirements for making certain that Web page visitors can use the multimedia content in a Web page.

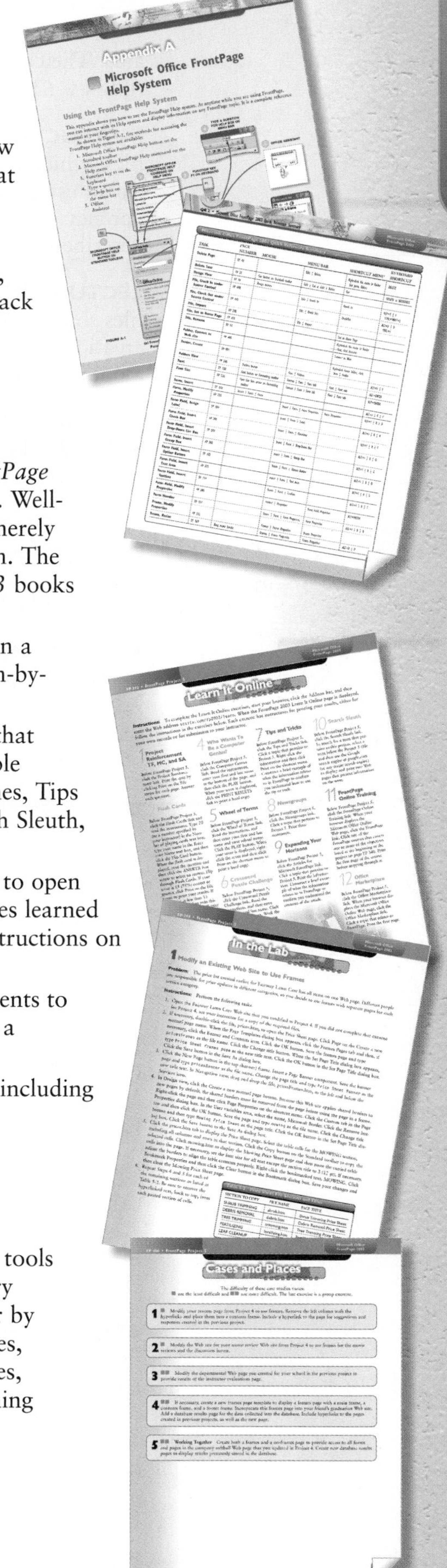

Appendices The book includes five appendices. Appendix A presents an introduction to the Microsoft FrontPage 2003 Help system. Appendix B describes how to use the speech and handwriting recognition capabilities of FrontPage 2003. Appendix C explains how to publish Web sites to a folder on a hard drive. Appendix D shows how to reset menus and toolbars. Appendix E summarizes the design tips that are introduced throughout the book.

Quick Reference Summary In Microsoft FrontPage 2003, you can accomplish a task in a number of ways, such as using the mouse, menu, shortcut menus, and keyboard. The Quick Reference Summary at the back of the book provides a quick reference to each task presented.

End-of-Project Student Activities

A notable strength of the Shelly Cashman Series *Microsoft Office FrontPage 2003* books is the extensive student activities at the end of each project. Well-structured student activities can make the difference between students merely participating in a class and students retaining the information they learn. The activities in the Shelly Cashman Series *Microsoft Office FrontPage 2003* books include the following.

- **What You Should Know** A listing of the tasks completed within a project together with the pages on which the step-by-step, screen-by-screen explanations appear.
- **Learn It Online** Every project features a Learn It Online page that contains 12 exercises. These exercises include True/False, Multiple Choice, Short Answer, Flash Cards, Practice Test, Learning Games, Tips and Tricks, Newsgroup usage, Expanding Your Horizons, Search Sleuth, Office Online Training, and Office Marketplace.
- **Apply Your Knowledge** This exercise usually requires students to open and manipulate a file on the Data Disk that parallels the activities learned in the project. To obtain a copy of the Data Disk, follow the instructions on the inside back cover of this textbook.
- **In the Lab** Three in-depth assignments per project require students to utilize the project concepts and techniques to solve problems on a computer.
- **Cases and Places** Five unique real-world case-study situations, including one small-group activity.

Instructor Resources CD-ROM

The Shelly Cashman Series is dedicated to providing you with all of the tools you need to make your class a success. Information on all supplementary materials is available through your Course Technology representative or by calling one of the following telephone numbers: Colleges and Universities, 1-800-648-7450; High Schools, 1-800-824-5179; Private Career Colleges, 1-800-347-7707; Canada, 1-800-268-2222; Corporations with IT Training Centers, 1-800-648-7450; and Government Agencies, Health-Care Organizations, and Correctional Facilities, 1-800-477-3692.

The Instructor Resources for this textbook include both teaching and testing aids. The contents of each item on the Instructor Resources CD-ROM (ISBN 0-619-20053-7) are described below.

INSTRUCTOR'S MANUAL The Instructor's Manual is made up of Microsoft Word files, which include detailed lesson plans with page number references, lecture notes, teaching tips, classroom activities, discussion topics, projects to assign, and transparency references. The transparencies are available through the Figure Files described below.

LECTURE SUCCESS SYSTEM The Lecture Success System consists of intermediate files that correspond to certain figures in the book, allowing you to step through the creation of an application in a project during a lecture without entering large amounts of data.

SYLLABUS Sample syllabi, which can be customized easily to a course, are included. The syllabi cover policies, class and lab assignments and exams, and procedural information.

FIGURE FILES Illustrations for every figure in the textbook are available in electronic form. Use this ancillary to present a slide show in lecture or to print transparencies for use in lecture with an overhead projector. If you have a personal computer and LCD device, this ancillary can be an effective tool for presenting lectures.

POWERPOINT PRESENTATIONS PowerPoint Presentations is a multimedia lecture presentation system that provides slides for each project. Presentations are based on project objectives. Use this presentation system to present well-organized lectures that are both interesting and knowledge based. PowerPoint Presentations provides consistent coverage at schools that use multiple lecturers.

SOLUTIONS TO EXERCISES Solutions are included for the end-of-project exercises, as well as the Project Reinforcement exercises.

TEST BANK & TEST ENGINE The ExamView test bank includes 110 questions for every project (25 multiple choice, 50 true/false, and 35 completion) with page number references and, when appropriate, figure references. A version of the test bank you can print also is included. The test bank comes with a copy of the test engine, ExamView, the ultimate tool for your objective-based testing needs. ExamView is a state-of-the-art test builder that is easy to use. ExamView enables you to create paper-, LAN-, or Web-based tests from test banks designed specifically for your Course Technology textbook. Utilize the ultra-efficient QuickTest Wizard to create tests in less than five minutes by taking advantage of Course Technology's question banks, or customize your own exams from scratch.

DATA FILES FOR STUDENTS All the files that are required by students to complete the exercises are included. You can distribute the files on the Instructor Resources CD-ROM to your students over a network, or you can have them follow the instructions on the inside back cover of this book to obtain a copy of the Data Disk.

ADDITIONAL ACTIVITIES FOR STUDENTS These additional activities consist of Project Reinforcement Exercises, which are true/false, multiple choice, and short answer questions that help students gain confidence in the material learned.

Online Content

Course Technology offers textbook-based content for Blackboard, WebCT, and MyCourse 2.1.

BLACKBOARD AND WEBCT As the leading provider of IT content for the Blackboard and WebCT platforms, Course Technology delivers rich content that enhances your textbook to give your students a unique learning experience.

MYCOURSE 2.1 MyCourse 2.1 is Course Technology's powerful online course management and content delivery system. MyCourse 2.1 allows nontechnical users to create, customize, and deliver Web-based courses; post content and assignments; manage student enrollment; administer exams; track results in the online grade book; and more.

Acknowledgments

The Shelly Cashman Series would not be the leading computer education series without the contributions of outstanding publishing professionals. First, and foremost, among them is Becky Herrington, director of production and book designer. She is the heart and soul of the Shelly Cashman Series, and it is only through her leadership, dedication, and tireless efforts that superior products are made possible.

Under Becky's direction, the following individuals made significant contributions to these books: Deb Masi, production editor; Jennifer Quiambao, production assistant; Ken Russo, senior Web and graphic designer; Richard Herrera, cover designer; Kellee LaVars, Andrew Bartel, Phillip Hajjar, and Kenny Tran, graphic artists; Michelle French, Jeanne Black, Andrew Bartel, and Kellee LaVars, QuarkXPress compositors; Mark Goodin, copy editor; Lori Silfen and Lyn Markowicz, proofreaders; and Cristina Haley, indexer.

We also would like to thank Kristen Duerr, executive vice president and publisher; Cheryl Costantini, executive editor; Dana Merk, senior acquisitions editor; Jim Quasney, series consulting editor; Alexandra Arnold, senior product manager; Marc Ouellette and Heather McKinstry, online product managers; Reed Cotter, product manager; and Selena Coppock, editorial assistant.

Gary B. Shelly
Thomas J. Cashman
Jeffrey J. Quasney

To the Student... Getting the Most Out of Your Book

Welcome to *Microsoft Office FrontPage 2003: Comprehensive Concepts and Techniques*. You can save yourself a lot of time and gain a better understanding of Microsoft Office FrontPage 2003 if you spend a few minutes reviewing the figures and callouts in this section.

1 Project Orientation

Each project presents a practical problem and shows the solution in the first figure of the project. The project orientation lets you see firsthand how problems are solved from start to finish using application software and computers.

2 Consistent Step-by-Step, Screen-by-Screen Presentation

Project solutions are built using a step-by-step, screen-by-screen approach. This pedagogy allows you to build the solution on a computer as you read through the project. Generally, each step is followed by an italic explanation that indicates the result of the step.

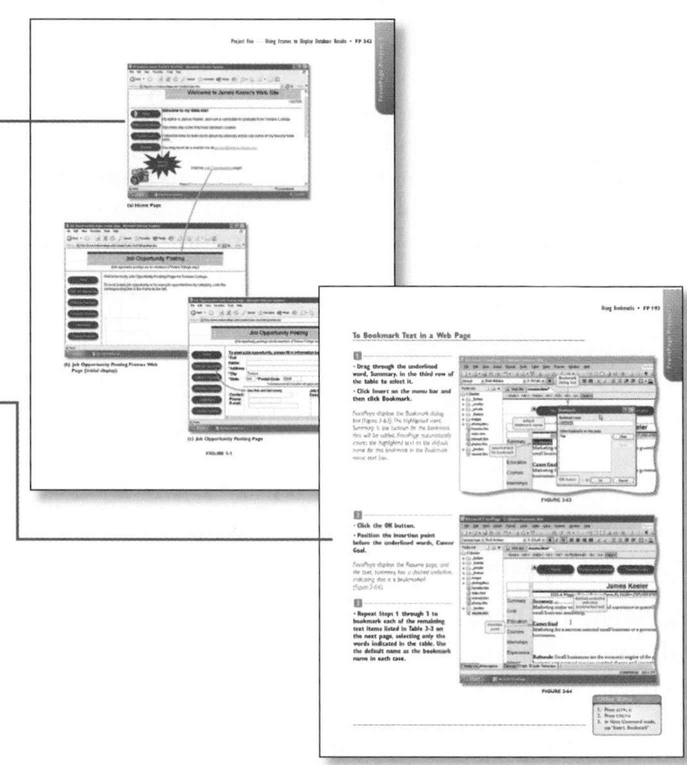

3 More Than Just Step-by-Step

More About and Q&A annotations in the margins of the book and substantive text in the paragraphs provide background information, tips, and answers to common questions that complement the topics covered, adding depth and perspective. When you finish with this book, you will be ready to use FrontPage to solve problems on your own.

4 Other Ways Boxes and Quick Reference Summary

Other Ways boxes that follow many of the step sequences and a Quick Reference Summary at the back of the book explain the other ways to complete the task presented, such as using the mouse, menu, shortcut menu, and keyboard.

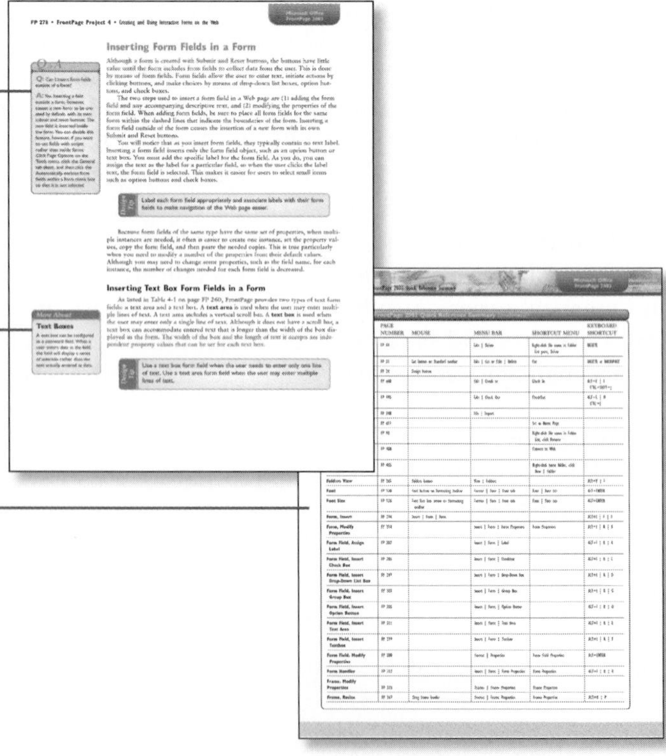

5 Emphasis on Getting Help When You Need It

The first project of each application and Appendix A show you how to use all the elements of the FrontPage Help system. Being able to answer your own questions will increase your productivity and reduce your frustrations by minimizing the time it takes to learn how to complete a task.

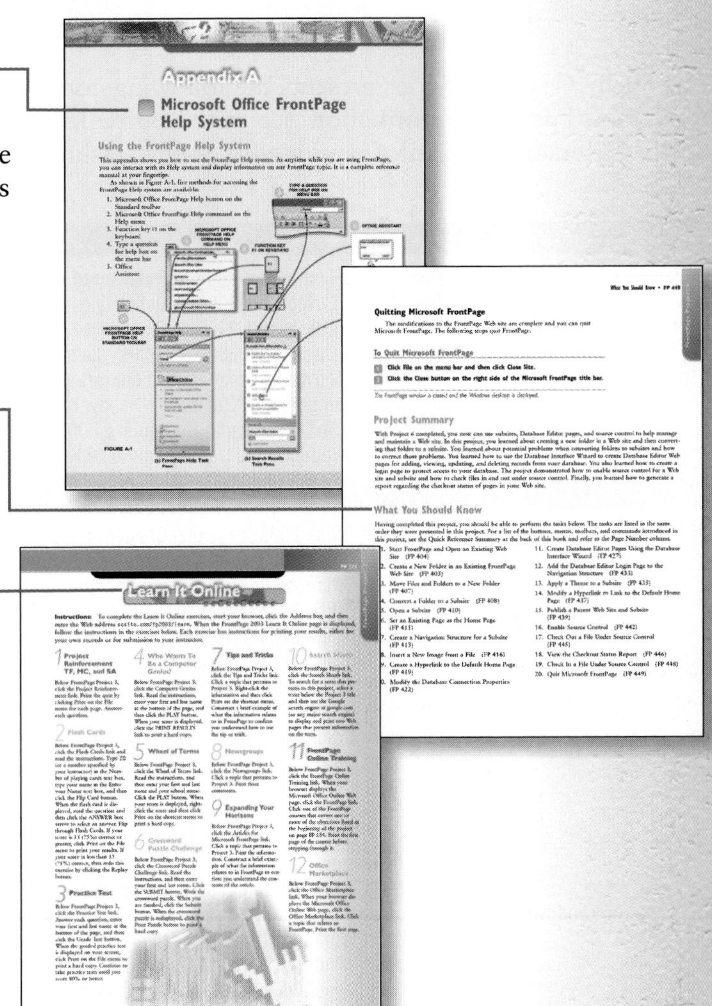

6 Review

After you successfully step through a project, a section titled What You Should Know summarizes the project tasks with which you should be familiar. Terms you should know for test purposes are bold in the text.

7 Reinforcement and Extension

The Learn It Online page at the end of each project offers reinforcement in the form of review questions, learning games, and practice tests. Also included are Web-based exercises that require you to extend your learning beyond the book.

8 Laboratory Exercises

If you really want to learn how to use the applications, then you must design and implement solutions to problems on your own. Every project concludes with several carefully developed laboratory assignments that increase in complexity.

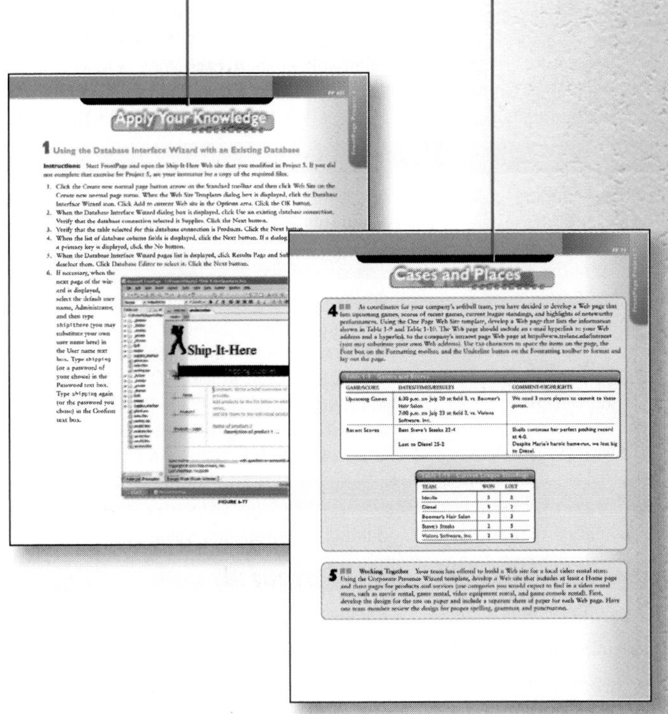

Shelly Cashman Series – Traditionally Bound Textbooks

The Shelly Cashman Series presents the following computer subjects in a variety of traditionally bound textbooks. For more information, see your Course Technology representative or call 1-800-648-7450. For Shelly Cashman Series information, visit Shelly Cashman Online at **scseries.com**

	COMPUTERS
Computers	Discovering Computers 2005: A Gateway to Information, Web Enhanced, Complete Edition Discovering Computers 2005: A Gateway to Information, Web Enhanced, Introductory Edition Discovering Computers 2005: A Gateway to Information, Web Enhanced, Brief Edition Discovering Computers 2005: Fundamentals Edition Teachers Discovering Computers: Integrating Technology in the Classroom 3e Exploring Computers: A Record of Discovery 4e Study Guide for Discovering Computers 2005: A Gateway to Information, Web Enhanced Essential Introduction to Computers 5e (40-pages)
	WINDOWS APPLICATIONS
Microsoft Office	Microsoft Office 2003: Essential Concepts and Techniques (5 projects) Microsoft Office 2003: Brief Concepts and Techniques (9 projects) Microsoft Office 2003: Introductory Concepts and Techniques (15 projects) Microsoft Office 2003: Advanced Concepts and Techniques (12 projects) Microsoft Office 2003: Post Advanced Concepts and Techniques (11 projects) Microsoft Office XP: Essential Concepts and Techniques (5 projects) Microsoft Office XP: Brief Concepts and Techniques (9 projects) Microsoft Office XP: Introductory Concepts and Techniques, Windows XP Edition Microsoft Office XP: Introductory Concepts and Techniques, Enhanced Edition (15 projects)[1] Microsoft Office XP: Advanced Concepts and Techniques (11 projects) Microsoft Office XP: Post Advanced Concepts and Techniques (11 projects)
Integration	Integrating Microsoft Office XP Applications and the World Wide Web: Essential Concepts and Techniques
PIM	Microsoft Office Outlook 2003: Introductory Concepts and Techniques • Microsoft Outlook 2002: Essential Concepts and Techniques
Microsoft Works	Microsoft Works 6: Complete Concepts and Techniques[2] • Microsoft Works 2000: Complete Concepts and Techniques[2]
Microsoft Windows	Microsoft Windows XP: Complete Concepts and Techniques[3] Microsoft Windows XP: Brief Concepts and Techniques Microsoft Windows 2000: Complete Concepts and Techniques (6 projects)[3] Microsoft Windows 2000: Brief Concepts and Techniques (2 projects) Microsoft Windows 98: Essential Concepts and Techniques (2 projects) Microsoft Windows 98: Complete Concepts and Techniques (6 projects)[3] Introduction to Microsoft Windows NT Workstation 4
Word Processing	Microsoft Office Word 2003[3] • Microsoft Word 2002[3]
Spreadsheets	Microsoft Office Excel 2003[3] • Microsoft Excel 2002[3]
Database	Microsoft Office Access 2003[3] • Microsoft Access 2002[3]
Presentation Graphics	Microsoft Office PowerPoint 2003[3] • Microsoft PowerPoint 2002[3]
Desktop Publishing	Microsoft Office Publisher 2003[2] • Microsoft Publisher 2002[2]
	PROGRAMMING
Programming	Microsoft Visual Basic.NET: Complete Concepts and Techniques[3] • Microsoft Visual Basic 6: Complete Concepts and Techniques[2] Programming in QBasic • Java Programming 2e: Complete Concepts and Techniques[3] • Structured COBOL Programming 2e
	INTERNET
Concepts	Discovering the Internet: Complete Concepts & Techniques[2]
Browser	Microsoft Internet Explorer 6: Introductory Concepts and Techniques • Microsoft Internet Explorer 5: An Introduction • Netscape Navigator 6: An Introduction
Web Page Creation and Design	Web Design: Introductory Concepts and Techniques • HTML: Complete Concepts and Techniques 2e[3] Microsoft Office FrontPage 2003[3] • Microsoft FrontPage 2002[3] • Microsoft FrontPage 2002: Essential Concepts and Techniques Java Programming: Complete Concepts and Techniques 2e[3] • JavaScript: Complete Concepts and Techniques 2e[2] • Macromedia Dreamweaver MX: Complete Concepts and Techniques[3]
	SYSTEMS ANALYSIS
Systems Analysis	Systems Analysis and Design 5e
	DATA COMMUNICATIONS
Data Communications	Business Data Communications: Introductory Concepts and Techniques 4e

[1]Available running under Windows XP or running under Windows 2000.
[2]Also available as an Introductory Edition, which is a shortened version of the complete book.
[3]Also available as an Introductory Edition, which is a shortened version of the complete book and also as a Comprehensive Edition, which is an extended version of the complete book.

MICROSOFT

Office FrontPage 2003

MICROSOFT OFFICE

FRONTPAGE

MICROSOFT
Office FrontPage 2003

Creating a FrontPage Web Site Using a Template

PROJECT 1

CASE PERSPECTIVE

As a Business and Technology major at Trelane College, you benefited from taking classes that included Web page authoring and other communications courses. After you developed the Trelane College Alumni Web site, the Alumni club president, Shirley Blair, was very impressed. She wanted to know if she might pass along your name to others who had an interest in Web site development. You wholeheartedly agreed, and she indicated that she already had a potential client for you. James Keeler, a close friend of hers, was looking for help in developing a personal Web site that he plans to use to promote his skills and knowledge as he approaches graduation. You told Shirley to have James contact you so you could set up a meeting to discuss his needs for the site.

At your first meeting, you explained to James that making a simple Web site was very easy to do with Microsoft FrontPage. Because he demonstrated a desire both to learn about Web page creation and eventually to maintain his own Web site, you thought it appropriate that he learn some basics about Web page construction and maintenance in an incremental fashion. By learning about the components of a Web page, then building an initial Web site, and later making modifications to the Web site, he would accomplish his goal of learning how to create and maintain his Web site. You explain to him that templates and themes included with FrontPage allow novices and those without artistic experience to create compelling Web sites quickly and with relative ease.

As you read through this project, you will learn about the fundamentals of how a Web page is constructed. You also will learn how to use FrontPage to create, save, print, and publish a Web site that includes several pages, text, and links.

Creating a FrontPage Web Site Using a Template

PROJECT

Objectives

You will have mastered the material in this project when you can:

- Discuss the basic components of the World Wide Web
- Identify common elements of a Web page
- Define and describe a FrontPage Web site
- Start and quit FrontPage
- Describe FrontPage window elements
- Create a FrontPage Web site using a template
- Apply a theme to a FrontPage Web site
- Add and modify text elements on a Web page
- Save and preview a Web page
- Delete a Web page from a FrontPage Web site
- Add and modify hyperlinks on a Web page
- Print a Web page
- Publish and test a FrontPage Web site
- Use the FrontPage Help system

What Is Microsoft Office FrontPage?

Microsoft Office FrontPage is a Web page authoring and site management program that allows you to create and manage professional-quality Web sites without programming. Microsoft Office FrontPage offers two key types of functionality:

Web page creation Microsoft FrontPage allows you to create and edit Web pages without needing to know HTML or other programming languages. FrontPage includes many features that make Web page creation easy, such as templates, graphics, and more.

Web site management Microsoft Office FrontPage allows you to view Web pages, publish them to the World Wide Web, and manage existing Web sites. Using FrontPage, you can test and repair hyperlinks on a Web page, view all of the files and folders on a site, import image files, and more.

Project One — Personal Web Pages

The following needs, formatting requirements, and content requirements are determined to be the basis for creating the personal Web pages for this project. The easiest way to develop a personal Web site is to use the Personal Web Site template, and then make appropriate modifications to the generated pages.

Needs: A group of related Web pages is referred to as a **Web site** in Microsoft Office FrontPage. For this site, the Web site will include three Web pages: a Home page, a Professional Interests page, and a Favorite Links page. The Home page introduces James Keeler to site visitors (Figure 1-1a); the Professional Interests page outlines his interests relating to his major and career goals (Figure 1-1b); and the Favorite Links page includes links to three Web sites, including his favorite site about music (Figure 1-1c). The Home page includes links to the other two pages in the FrontPage Web site. Once complete, you will publish the Web site to make it available for viewing on the World Wide Web.

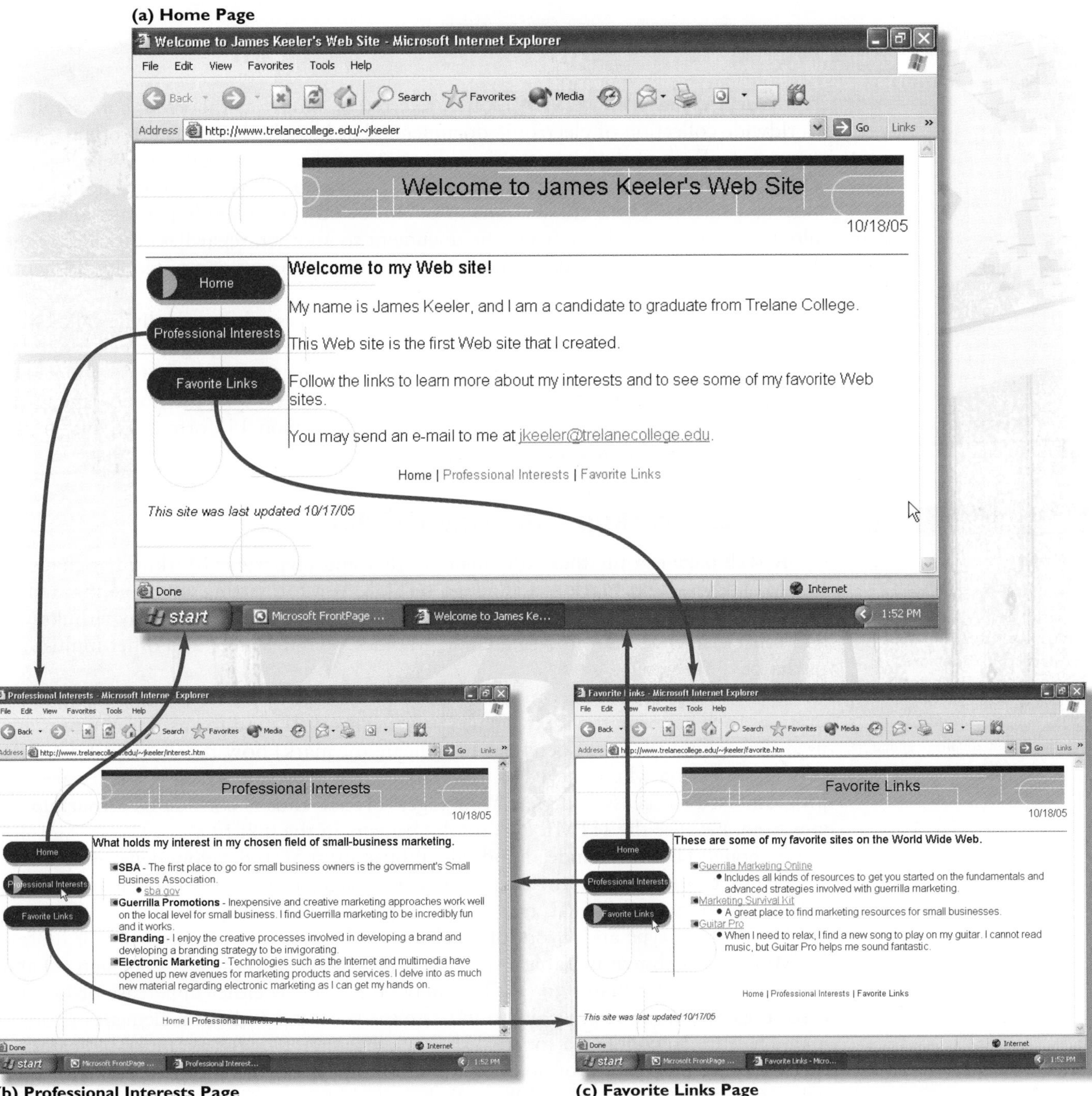

FIGURE 1-1

Formatting Requirements: To create the Web pages, you will use the Personal Web Site template included with Microsoft Office FrontPage. The Web pages then are formatted using the Microsoft Office FrontPage Capsules theme, which is just one of many complete themes that are available for immediate use. The Home page includes graphical hyperlinks to the other pages in this Web site.

Content Requirements: The Home page lists James Keeler's name, specifies his position as a student at Trelane College, and provides an e-mail address so visitors can contact him. The Professional Interests page includes a minimum of four topics that are associated directly with his major. The Favorite Links page includes links to at least three Web sites, one of which is a music-related site.

World Wide Web Basics

The **World Wide Web** (**WWW**), often referred to simply as the **Web**, consists of a worldwide collection of electronic documents that have built-in links to other related documents. Each of these electronic documents on the Web is called a **Web page**; a Web page can contain text, graphics, sound, and video, as well as connections to other documents. These connections to other documents, called hyperlinks or links, allow you to move quickly from one document to another, regardless of whether the documents are located on the same computer or on different computers in different countries.

A collection of related Web pages that you can access electronically is called a Web site. Most Web sites have a starting point, called a **home page**, which is similar to a book cover or table of contents for the site and provides information about the site's purpose and content. In a personal Web site, for example, the home page probably will list your name, your e-mail address, some personal information, and links to other information on your Web site.

More About

HTML

The World Wide Web Consortium (W3C) develops and updates common Web protocols. To learn more about the latest changes to HTML, visit the FrontPage 2003 More About Web page (scsite.com/fp2003/more) and then click W3C.

Hypertext Markup Language (HTML)

A Web page is a file that contains both text and Hypertext Markup Language (HTML). **Hypertext Markup Language** (**HTML**) is a formatting language that tells the browser how to display text and images; how to set up list boxes, hyperlinks, and other elements; and how to include graphics, sound, video, and other multimedia on a Web page.

HTML uses a set of special instructions called **tags** to define the characteristics of items such as formatted text, images, hyperlinks, lists, and forms. HTML tags are used throughout the text document to indicate (or mark) how these items should display and function when viewed as a Web page in a **browser**, which is a software program used to access and view Web pages. HTML thus is considered a **markup language**, because the HTML tags mark elements in the text file.

Although HTML includes hundreds of tags, most Web developers use only a small subset of these tags when building a Web page. Table 1-1 lists some of the more commonly used HTML tags and an explanation of their functions.

Defining the type and layout of an element on a Web page requires one or more HTML tags. As shown in Table 1-1, HTML tags begin with the less than sign (<) and end with the greater than sign (>). Tags may be entered as either uppercase or lowercase. Tags often are used in pairs to indicate the start and end of an element or format. The end tag contains a forward slash (/). The tag, <B>, for example, indicates the beginning of a section of bold text, and </B> indicates the end of a section of bold text. To display the text, World Wide Web, as bold text, you type the tags as follows:

```
<B>World Wide Web</B>
```

Table 1-1 Common HTML Tags

HTML TAG	FUNCTION
<HTML> </HTML>	Indicates the beginning and end of a Web document.
<HEAD> </HEAD>	Indicates the beginning and end of the header section of a Web document (used for the title and other document header information).
<TITLE> </TITLE>	Indicates the beginning and end of the Web page title. The title appears in the title bar of the browser, not in the body of the Web page itself.
<BODY> </BODY>	Indicates the beginning and end of the main section (body) of the Web page.
<Hn> </Hn>	Indicates the beginning and end of a section of text called a heading, which uses a larger font than normal text. In the tag, <Hn>, n indicates the size of the heading font; sizes range from <H1> through <H6>.
<P> </P>	Indicates the beginning of a new paragraph; inserts a blank line above the new paragraph. The end tag of </P> is optional. It will insert a blank line below the new paragraph, unless followed by a new paragraph.
<B> </B>	Indicates the beginning and end of a section of bold text.
<I> </I>	Indicates the beginning and end of a section of italic text.
<U> </U>	Indicates the beginning and end of a section of underlined text.
<UL> </UL>	Indicates the beginning and end of an unordered (bulleted) list
<OL> </OL>	Indicates the beginning and end of an ordered (numbered) list.
<LI> </LI>	Indicates that the item in the tag is an item within a list.
<HR>	Inserts a horizontal rule.
<A> </A>	Indicates the beginning and end of a hyperlink.
HREF="URL"	Indicates a hyperlink to a file in the location specified by the URL in quotation marks.
<IMG SRC="URL">	Inserts an inline image in the page. The URL in quotation marks specifies the location of the image.
<CENTER> </CENTER>	Indicates that the text, graphic, or other elements between the tags should display centered on the Web page.
<LEFT> </LEFT>	Indicates that the text, graphic, or other elements between the tags should display left-aligned on the Web page.
<RIGHT> </RIGHT>	Indicates that the text, graphic, or other elements between the tags should display right-aligned on the Web page.

You also can use tags in combination to apply multiple formatting features to text or other Web page elements. The tag

```
<CENTER><B>World Wide Web</B></CENTER>
```

for example, bolds and centers the words on the page. If you use HTML tags in combination, as in the example above, be sure to place the end tags in an order opposite that of the start tags.

Keywords included in HTML tags further define the appearance of the element created by the tag. Keywords take the form

```
keyword=value
```

where keyword is an HTML tag describing a characteristic of a Web page element and value is one of a range of numbers or words describing that characteristic. Instead of using the <CENTER> tag to center text on the page, for instance, you can use the keyword, <ALIGN>, and the value, <CENTER>. The tag, which you can use within another tag, might display as

```
<B ALIGN=CENTER>My Favorite Web Sites</B>
```

The tag tells the browser to display the text in bold and center the text on the page.

All of these elements are defined using HTML tags. The HTML used to create a Web page is called the **HTML source**, or **source code**. Figure 1-2 shows the HTML source for the Web page displayed in Figure 1-1c on page FP 5.

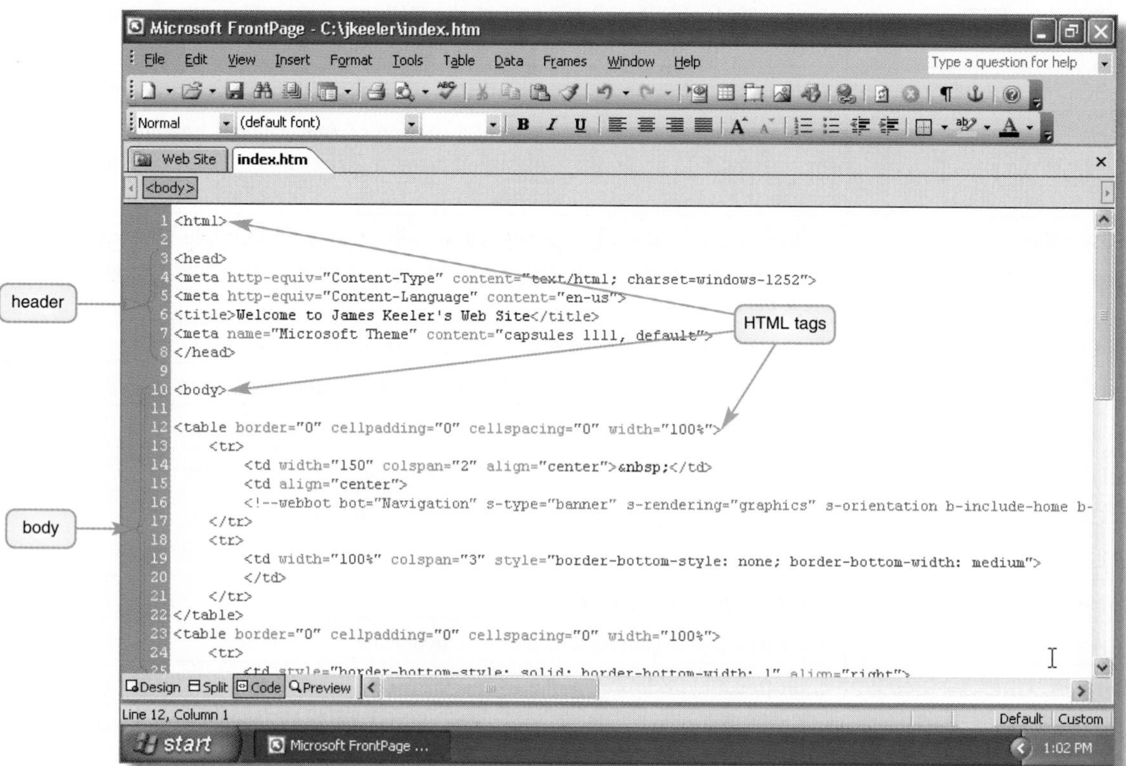

FIGURE 1-2

> *More About*
>
> **Viewing HTML Source Code**
>
> To see the HTML tags that FrontPage creates as you build a Web page, you can use the Show Code View button or the Show Split View button. These two views of the code allow you to display HTML tags and then edit them just as you would edit text using a word-processing program, utilizing standard editing commands such as cut, paste, find, and replace.

Most Web browsers allow you to view the HTML source for the Web page currently displayed in the browser window. If you are using Internet Explorer, for example, you can click the Source command on the View menu to display the HTML source.

Many HTML tags exist to help you design a Web page exactly as you want. Although a more detailed discussion of HTML is beyond the scope of this book, when using FrontPage to develop Web pages, you do not need to know every HTML tag. Instead, you simply determine the best way to convey the information and then make those changes on the Web page using FrontPage commands. FrontPage inserts the appropriate HTML code for you.

Web Browsers

You access and view Web pages using a software program called a Web browser. A **Web browser**, also called simply a browser, is a software program that requests a Web page, interprets the HTML codes and text used to create the page, and then displays the Web page on your computer screen. Today, the two more popular browsers are **Microsoft Internet Explorer** and **Netscape Navigator** (Figure 1-3a and 1-3b). Browsers have special buttons and other features to help you navigate Web sites.

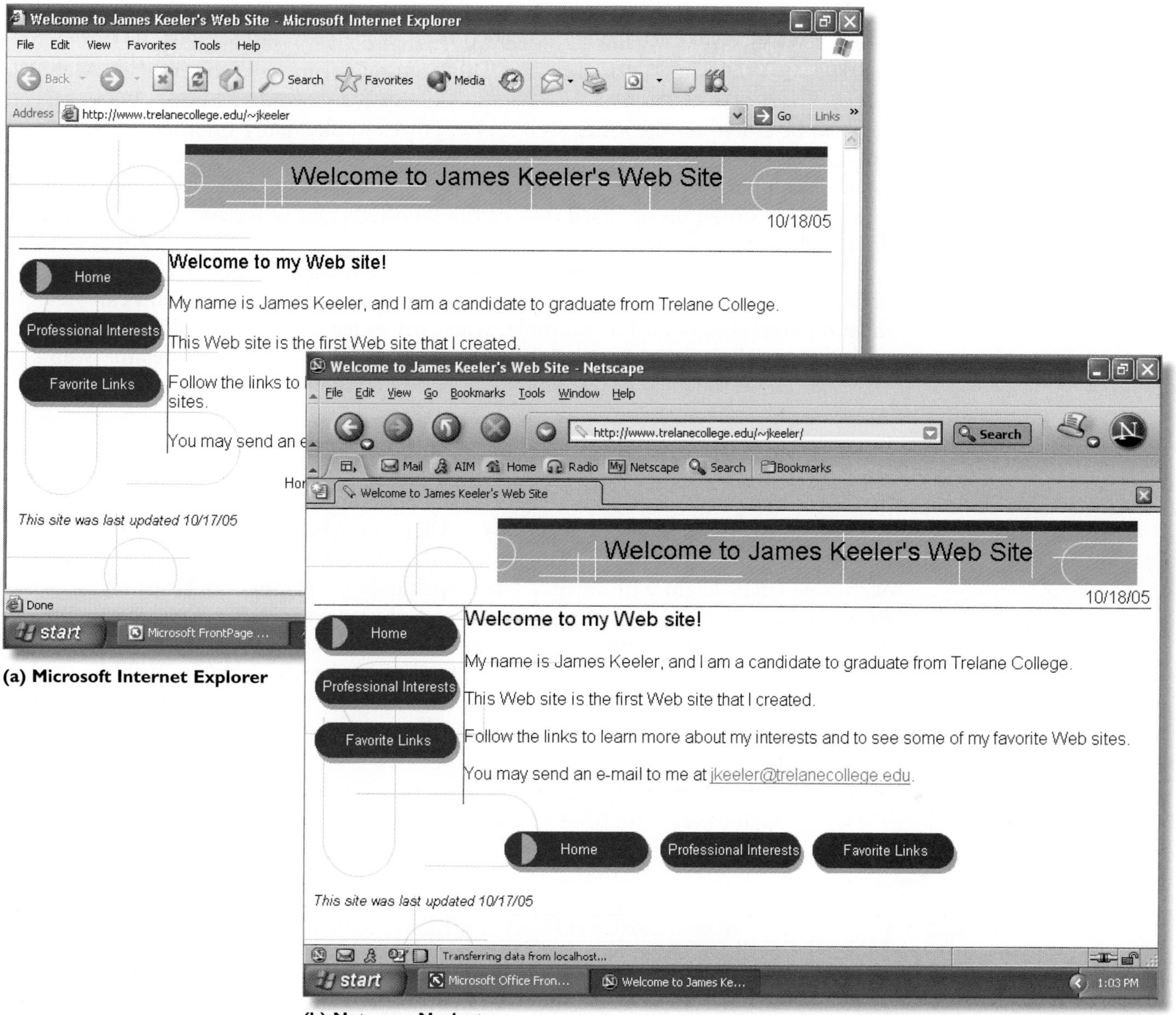

(a) **Microsoft Internet Explorer**

(b) **Netscape Navigator**

FIGURE 1-3

Different browsers will display the same Web page with slight variations. Netscape Navigator, for example, may display fonts, hyperlinks, tables, and other Web page elements in a manner different from Microsoft Internet Explorer. Some special features in a Web page may be available when using one browser, but may not work at all with a different browser. When developing a Web site, you should test the Web pages using Netscape Navigator, Microsoft Internet Explorer, and any other browsers your audience might use to ensure that the Web pages will be displayed correctly in the various browsers. FrontPage includes the capability of testing Web pages in a variety of browsers and screen resolutions.

As you develop a Web site, test the Web pages in as many browsers as your audience might use.

More About

Testing Web Pages in Browsers

When testing Web pages in various browsers, you may want to test the pages in several versions of the same browser (usually the two most recent versions). Consider whether you need to test the pages on both PC and Macintosh platforms.

The Web pages that comprise a Web site are stored on a server, called a Web server. A **Web server**, or **host**, is a computer that delivers (serves) requested Web pages. Every Web site is stored on and run from one or more Web servers; a Web server can have thousands of Web pages available for viewing. Multiple Web sites also can be stored on the same Web server. For example, many Internet service providers (ISPs) grant their subscribers storage space on a Web server for their personal or company Web sites. Each Web page on the Web site consists of one or more files that are stored on the hard disk of the Web server or other computer. ISPs are discussed later in this project.

A Web server runs **Web server software** that allows it to receive the requests for Web pages and sends the pages over the Internet to your browser, so you can view them on your computer. For example, when you enter a Web page address in your browser, your browser sends a request to the server; the server then uses the Web server software to fetch the Web page and send it to your browser.

Uniform Resource Locators (URLs)

Each Web page on a Web site has a unique address called a **Uniform Resource Locator** (**URL**). As shown in Figure 1-4, a URL consists of a protocol, a domain name, the path to a specific document, and the file name of the document. Most Web page URLs begin with http://. The **http** stands for **Hypertext Transfer Protocol**, which is the communications protocol used to transfer pages on the Web. The **domain name** identifies the Web server or computer on the Internet where the Web document is located. The **path** and **file name** indicate where the Web document is stored on the computer. In the URL shown in Figure 1-4, for example, the domain name is www.nationalgeographic.com, the path to the file is /ngm/, and the file name is index.htm.

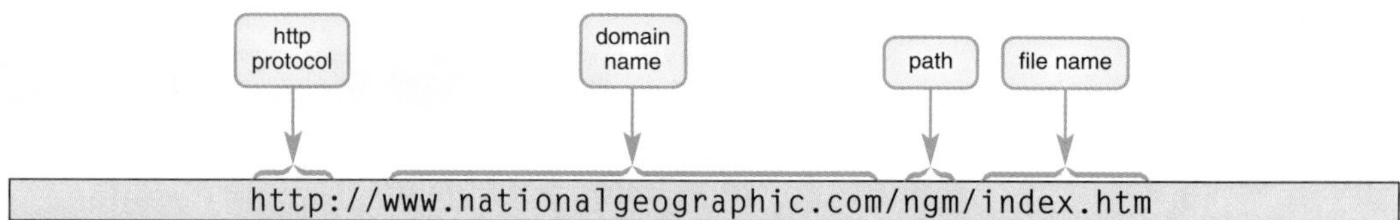

FIGURE 1-4

Each hyperlink on a Web page is associated with a URL, thus making it possible for you to navigate the Web using hyperlinks. When you click a hyperlink on a Web page, you are issuing a request to display the Web document specified by the URL. If, for example, you click a hyperlink associated with the URL, http://www.scsite.com/index.htm, your browser sends a request to the server whose domain name is www.scsite.com. The server then fetches the page named index.htm and sends it to your computer, where the browser displays it on your screen.

Elements of a Web Page

Although Web pages can be as distinctive and unique as the individuals who create them, almost every Web page has several basic features, or **elements**. Web page elements include basic features such as the background, text, hyperlinks, and images; and more advanced features such as forms, frames, and layers. As you begin to view Web pages through the eyes of a Web page developer, you will notice that most Web pages use variations on one or more of the elements identified in Figure 1-5.

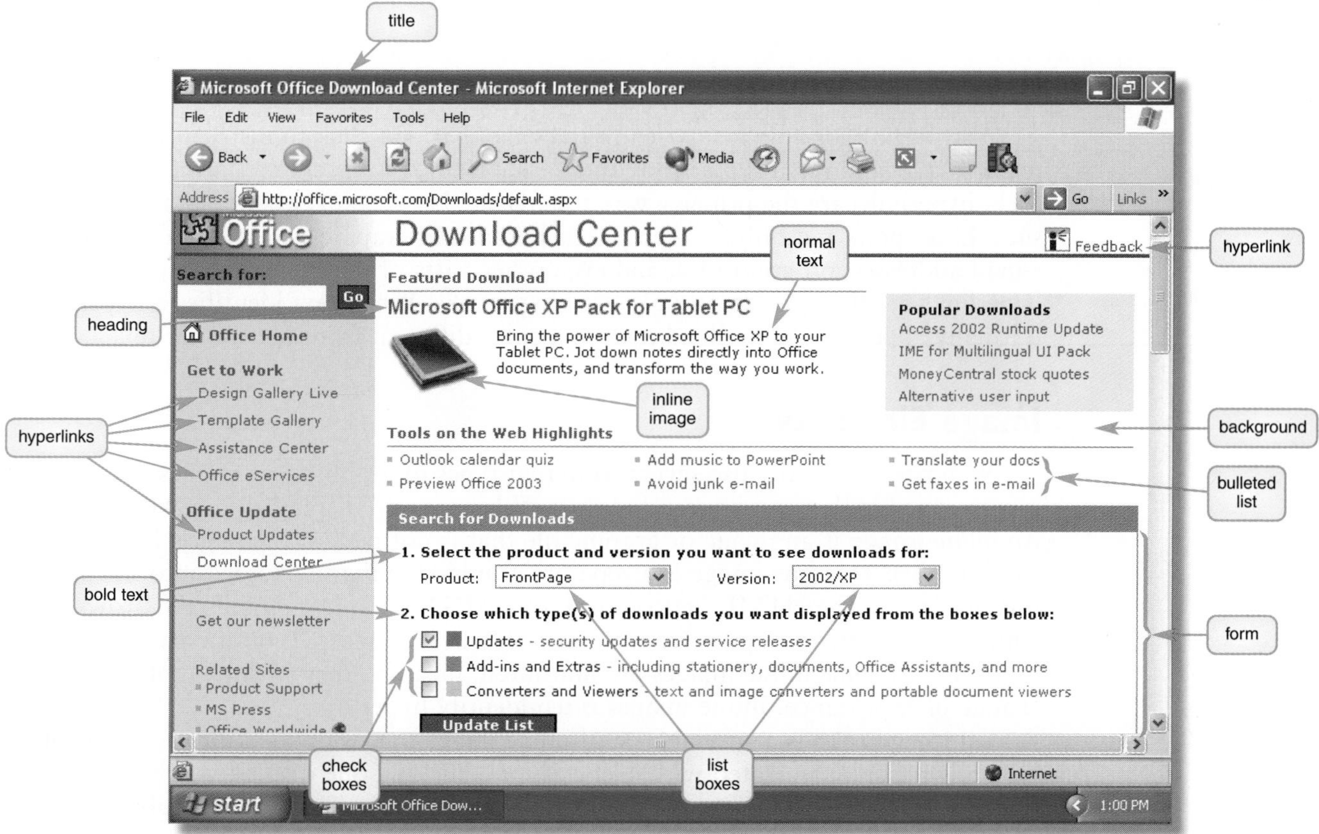

FIGURE 1-5

> *Design Tip*
>
> Many Web pages use common elements to which users are accustomed. When designing your page, consider using standard design elements such as a title, page banners, and link bars.

Window Elements

The **title** of a Web page is the text that appears on the title bar of the browser window when the Web page appears. The **background** of a Web page is either a solid color or a small graphic image that provides a backdrop against which the other elements display. Like the wallpaper in Windows, a background color or graphic can be **tiled**, or repeated, across the entire page.

Text Elements

On a Web page, the **body** contains the text that makes up the main content of a Web page, as opposed to the **header**, which contains the page title and other information about the page. The body of the Web page usually uses the default font format, known as **Normal text**. You also can format Normal text to display in color or in bold, italic, or underlined styles. **Headings** are used to separate different paragraphs of text or different sections of a Web page. Headings generally appear as a larger font size than normal text and usually are formatted with bold or italic styles.

Many Web pages present a series of text items as a **list**. Typically, lists are numbered or bulleted. A **numbered list** (also called an **ordered list**) presents an ordered list of items, such as the steps in this project. Numbers precede the items in a numbered list. A **bulleted list** (also called an **unordered list**) presents an unordered (unnumbered) list of items. Bulleted lists often use a small image called a **bullet** to mark each item in the list.

Hyperlink Elements

A **hyperlink**, or **link**, is an area of the page that you click to instruct the browser to go to a location in a file or to request a file from a Web server. On the World Wide Web, hyperlinks are the primary way to navigate between pages and among Web sites. Links point not only to Web pages, but also to graphics, sound, multimedia, e-mail addresses, program files, and even other parts of the same Web page. Text hyperlinks are the most commonly used hyperlinks. When text identifies a hyperlink, it usually appears as underlined text, in a color different from the regular text.

Image Elements

Web pages typically use several different types of graphics, or images. An **image** is a graphic file that can be inserted on a Web page and displayed in a Web browser. An **inline image** is an image or graphic file that is not part of the page's HTML file itself. Rather, an inline image is a separate graphic file that is merged into the page as it is displayed. The HTML file contains an <IMG SRC> tag that tells the browser which graphic file to request from the server, where to insert it on the page, and how to display it. Some inline images are **animated**, meaning they include motion and change in appearance. Inline images often identify hyperlinks.

An **image map** is a special type of inline image that is divided into sections, often with a hyperlink associated with each section. Clicking one of the hyperlinked sections, called a **hotspot**, instructs the browser to link to a Web page, graphic, sound, e-mail address, or other file.

As just described, the background of a Web page is the solid color, image, or pattern that serves as the backdrop on which text, images, hyperlinks, and other elements appear on the Web page. If you use an image for the background, the image repeats across and down the page.

Horizontal rules are lines that display across the page to separate different sections of the page. Although the appearance of a horizontal rule varies, many Web pages use an inline image as a horizontal rule.

Form, Table, Frame, and Layer Elements

A **form** is an area of a Web page that allows the viewer to enter data and information to be sent back to the Web server. Input elements within the form, such as **option buttons**, which allow for a single choice among several choices, or **text boxes**, which provide an area for the user to enter text, instruct the individual what items to enter and how to send them to the server.

A **table** is used to present text and graphics in rows or columns. The intersection of a row and a column is called a **cell**. The text or graphic within a cell often acts as a hyperlink. The border width of the table determines the width of the gridlines surrounding the cells. When the border width is greater than 0, gridlines surround the cells. When the border width is set to 0, gridlines are not displayed.

A **frame** allows Web page developers to divide the display area of the browser into sections, so the browser can display a different Web page in each frame. Web pages with frames have many possible applications. A table of contents for your Web site can be displayed in a smaller frame, for example, while different content pages appear in a separate main frame. Users can click hyperlinks in the smaller table of contents frame and display the linked page in the main frame.

A **layer** is a container you create on your Web page to hold text, graphics, or other content. Layers provide another dimension to Web pages beyond the horizontal and vertical. You can overlap layers, nest layers, and hide layers. You animate layers by assigning behaviors to layers.

FrontPage Web Sites

As previously defined, a collection of related Web pages that you can access electronically is called a Web site. A typical Web site contains one to several thousand Web pages, often with links to other pages in the same Web site and pages on separate Web sites.

In FrontPage, a group of related pages also is called a Web site. A **FrontPage Web site** consists of the Web pages, images, and other files, folders, and programs that make up the related content that will comprise the Web site. The Web pages in a FrontPage Web site usually are related by topic or purpose; most Web sites use a series of hyperlinks to connect the related pages. A Web site may consist of one or more FrontPage Web sites.

When working with a Web site in FrontPage, the Web site that currently is open is called the **current Web site**. Once created, a FrontPage Web site can be stored on the computer on which FrontPage is installed or on a Web server anywhere on the World Wide Web. Using FrontPage, you can upload and download a complete Web site to and from your computer and a Web server, or just upload the portions of the Web site that you have modified. Publishing involves sending, or uploading, copies of Web pages, image files, and other files, folders, and programs to a server where they then are made available on the World Wide Web. To publish a FrontPage Web site, you must have access to a Web server or other shared location to which you are allowed to upload files. As you complete this project, you will use FrontPage to develop and publish a personal Web site to the World Wide Web.

Plan to publish your Web site on a regular basis to keep content up-to-date after your Web site is up and running. Do not allow your content to become stale, or out-of-date.

Starting and Customizing FrontPage

To learn how to develop a Web site, this project starts FrontPage and then uses a template to create a personal Web site that introduces an individual, describes the person's professional interests, and lists links to several favorite Web sites. If you are stepping through this project on a computer and you want your screen to match the figures in this book, then you should change your computer's resolution to 800 × 600. For more information about how to change the resolution on your computer, see Appendix D. The steps on the next page start FrontPage.

To Start and Customize FrontPage

1

- **Click the Start button on the Windows taskbar, point to All Programs on the Start menu, point to Microsoft Office on the All Programs submenu, and then point to Microsoft Office FrontPage 2003 on the Microsoft Office submenu.**

Windows displays the Start menu, the All Programs submenu, and the Microsoft Office submenu (Figure 1-6).

FIGURE 1-6

2

- **Click Microsoft Office FrontPage 2003.**

Microsoft FrontPage 2003 is started. The document window is displayed in the default Page view of Design view (Figure 1-7). When you first start FrontPage, a blank page is displayed.

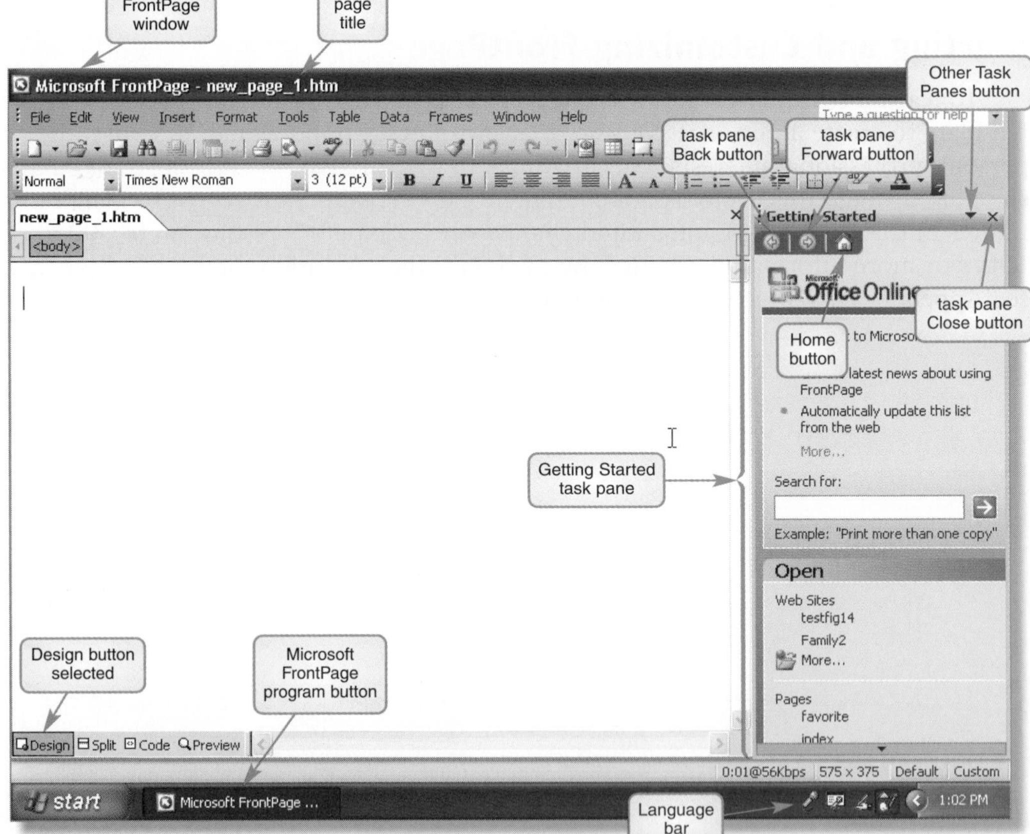

FIGURE 1-7

3

- **Click the Close button in the Getting Started task pane.**
- **If the Language bar shows and it indicates that the microphone is on, click the Microphone button to turn it off.**
- **To close the Language bar, right-click it to display a list of commands and then click Close the Language bar on the shortcut menu.**

The Getting Started task pane is closed, resulting in the maximum width for the new page. The Language bar disappears (Figure 1-8).

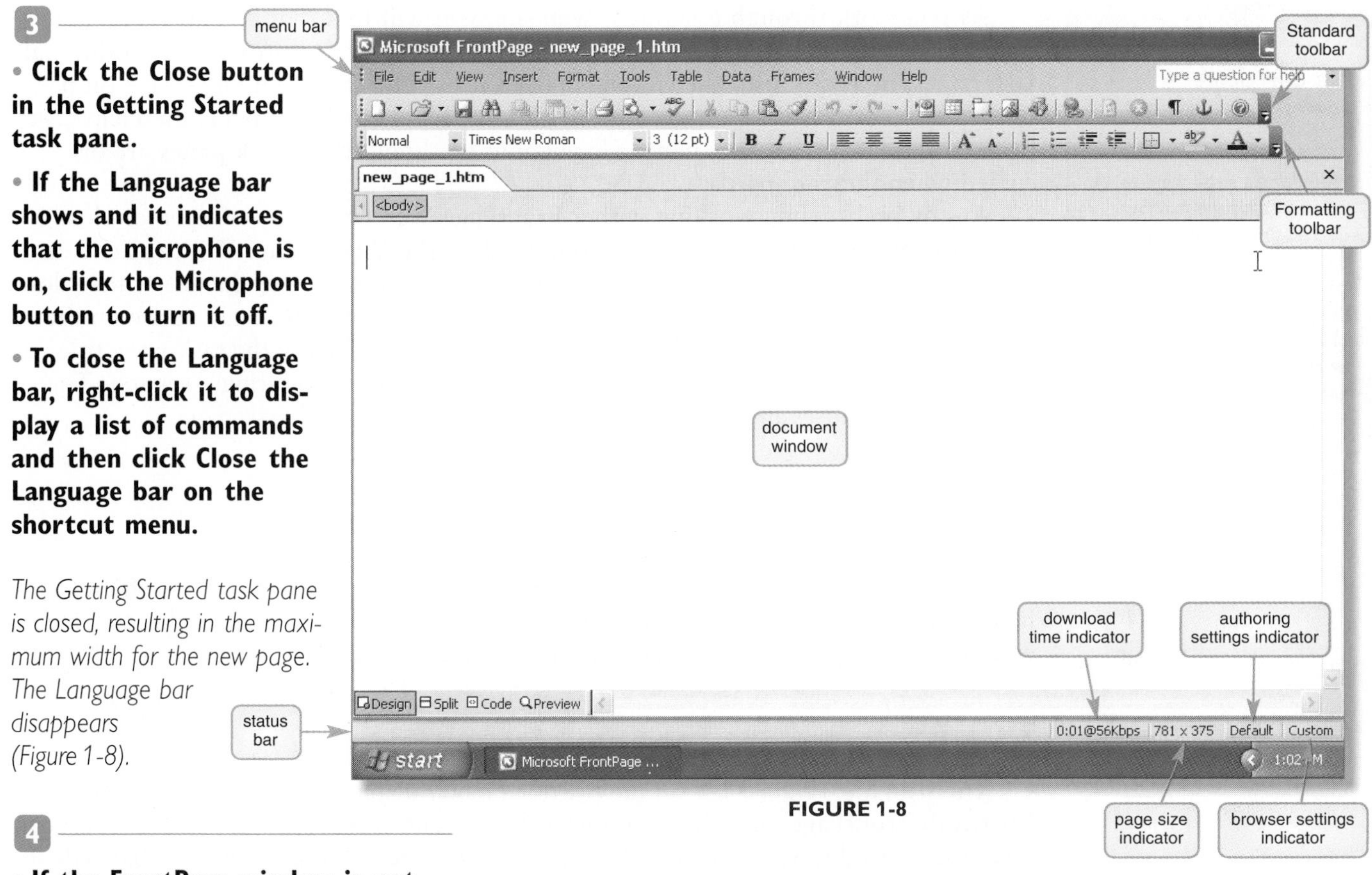

FIGURE 1-8

4

- **If the FrontPage window is not maximized, double-click its title bar to maximize it.**

Other Ways

1. Double-click Microsoft Office FrontPage icon on desktop
2. Click Start button on Windows taskbar, click Microsoft Office FrontPage 2003 on Start menu

The screen shown in Figure 1-8 illustrates how the FrontPage window looks the first time you start FrontPage after installation on most computers. If the Office Speech Recognition software is installed and active on your computer, then, when you start FrontPage, the Language bar is displayed on the screen. The **Language bar** allows you to speak commands and dictate text. It usually is located on the right side of the Windows taskbar next to the notification area and changes to include the speech recognition functions available in FrontPage. In this book, the Language bar is closed because it takes up computer resources and with the Language bar active, the microphone can be turned on accidentally, causing your computer to act in an unstable manner. For additional information about the Language bar, see page FP 19 and Appendix B.

As shown in Figure 1-7, FrontPage displays a task pane on the right side of the screen. A **task pane** is a separate window that enables users to carry out some FrontPage tasks more efficiently. When you start FrontPage, it displays the Getting Started task pane, which is a small window that provides commonly used links and commands that allow you to open files, create new files, or search Office-related topics on the Microsoft Web site. In this book, the Getting Started task pane is hidden to allow the maximum window space in the FrontPage window. When you start FrontPage, the FrontPage window is displayed the same way it displayed the last time you quit FrontPage. Thus, if the Getting Started task pane previously displayed on the right side of the window, then the task pane will be displayed when you start FrontPage.

Q: Can I change the position of the task pane?

A: Yes. When you first start FrontPage, a small window called a task pane may be docked on the right side of the screen. You can drag a task pane title bar to float the pane in your work area or dock it on either the left or right side of a screen, depending on your preference.

As you work through creating a Web site, you will find that certain FrontPage operations cause FrontPage to display a task pane. FrontPage provides 15 additional task panes, in addition to the Getting Started task pane shown in Figure 1-7 on page FP 14. Some of the more important ones are the Clipboard task pane, the Help task pane, and the Clip Art task pane. Throughout the book, these task panes are discussed when they are used.

At any point while working with a FrontPage Web site, you can open or close a task pane by clicking the Task Pane command on the View menu. You can activate additional task panes by clicking the Other Task Panes button to the left of the Close button on the task pane title bar (Figure 1-7) and then selecting a task pane on the Other Task Panes menu. The Back and Forward buttons below the task pane title bar allow you to switch between task panes that you opened during a session. The Home button causes FrontPage to display the Getting Started task pane.

The FrontPage Window

The FrontPage window consists of a variety of features to help you work efficiently. It contains a title bar, a status bar, a menu bar, toolbars, and a pane in the document window that displays different content, depending on the current view.

Title Bar

The **title bar** (Figure 1-8 on the previous page) displays the application name, Microsoft FrontPage, and the location of the current FrontPage Web site. If you open a Web site saved in the webpages folder on drive C, for example, the title bar will display the title, Microsoft FrontPage - C:\webpages, on the title bar.

Status Bar

The **status bar**, which is located at the bottom of the FrontPage window, consists of a message area, a download time indicator, an authoring settings indicator, and a browser settings indicator (Figure 1-8). As you are developing a page or Web site, the message area on the left side of the status bar displays information about file location, file name, hyperlinks, and more. The right side of the status bar includes indicators related to download times, page size, browser settings, and authoring features. The download time indicator displays the number of seconds it will take the page to download on the Web, based on a certain connection speed. The browser setting indicator displays the browser for which you are building the Web page. Double-clicking the browser settings indicator displays a dialog box that allows you to change the target browser and the target browser's capabilities. The authoring settings indicator displays information about which set of features you are allowed to use on Web sites created in FrontPage. You disable or enable more features by double-clicking the authoring settings indicator and changing the options in the Page Options dialog box.

Menu Bar

The **menu bar** displays the FrontPage menu names (Figure 1-8). Each name represents a menu of commands that allows you to create, retrieve, edit, save, print, and publish a FrontPage Web site. To display a menu, such as the Format menu, click the Format menu name on the menu bar. If you point to a command with an arrow on the right, a submenu appears, from which you can choose a command.

When you click a menu name on the menu bar, a **short menu** appears listing only basic or the most recently used commands (Figure 1-9a). If you wait a few seconds or click the arrows at the bottom of the short menu, the full menu appears. The **full menu** lists all the commands associated with a menu (Figure 1-9b). You also can display a full menu immediately by double-clicking the menu name on the menu bar. In this book, when you display a menu, you should always display the full menu using one of the following techniques:

1. Click the menu name on the menu bar and then wait a few seconds.
2. Click the menu name and then click the arrows at the bottom of the short menu.
3. Click the menu name and then point to the arrows at the bottom of the short menu.
4. Double-click the menu name on the menu bar.

Both short and full menus display some dimmed commands. A **dimmed command** appears gray, or dimmed, instead of black, which indicates it is not available for the current selection. A command with medium blue shading to the left of it on a full menu is called a **hidden command** because it does not appear on a short menu. As you use FrontPage, it automatically personalizes the short menus for you based on how often you use commands. That is, as you use hidden commands on the full menu, FrontPage unhides them and places them on the short menu.

More About

Short Menus

FrontPage allows you to turn off short menus and display all of the commands on each menu all the time. Click Tools on the menu bar and then click Customize. Click the Options tab, and then click the Always show full menus check box. To see full menus only after you click the double arrows, click the Show full menus after a short delay check box to remove the check mark. For other menu options, see Appendix D.

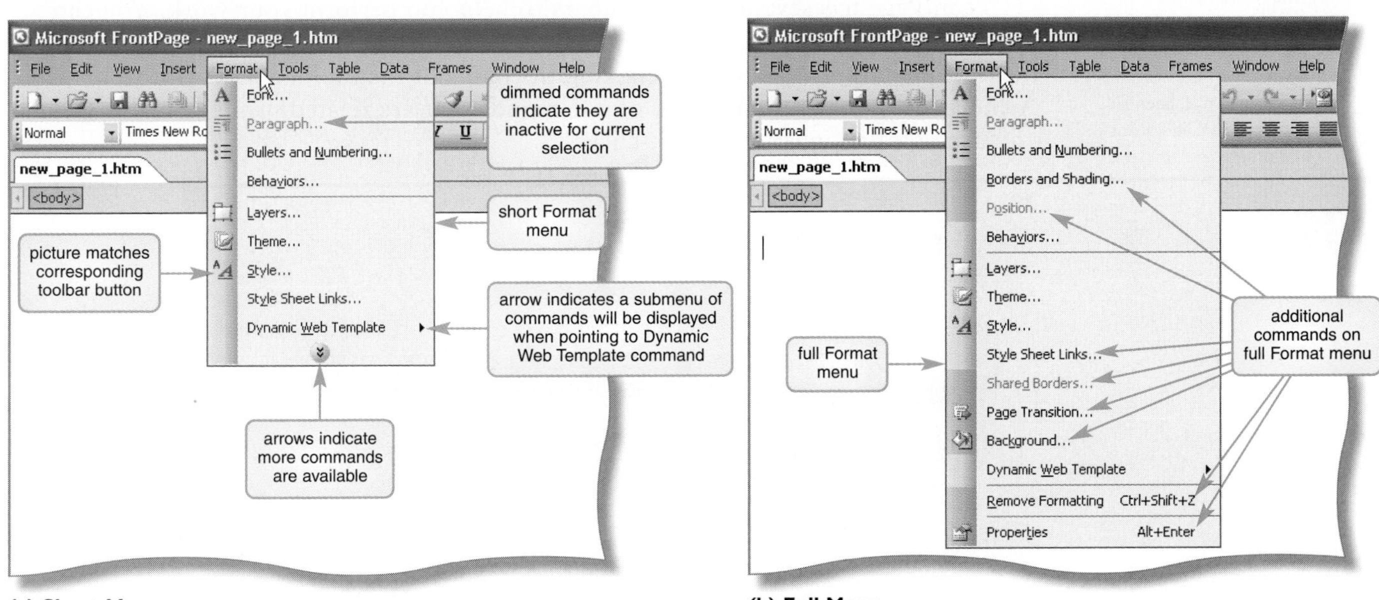

(a) Short Menu

(b) Full Menu

FIGURE 1-9

Toolbars

A **toolbar** consists of buttons that allow you to perform tasks more quickly than when using the menu bar. To save a Web page, for example, you can click the Save button on a toolbar, instead of clicking File on the menu bar and then clicking Save on the File menu. Each button uses a graphical representation to help identify the button's function.

More About

Sizing Toolbar Buttons

If you have difficulty seeing the small buttons on the toolbars, you can increase their size by clicking View on the menu bar, pointing to Toolbars, clicking Customize on the Toolbars submenu, clicking the Options tab, clicking the Large icons check box, and then clicking the Close button.

When you first start FrontPage, some of the buttons on the toolbars are dimmed (or grayed) to indicate that the toolbar buttons are inactive. When a button or command is **inactive**, the function performed by that button or command is not available. Once you have opened a Web page or a Web site, the buttons on the FrontPage toolbars are **active**, meaning you can use them to perform tasks in FrontPage. Figure 1-10a and Figure 1-10b show the buttons on each of the two toolbars that display when you open a Web page or Web site using FrontPage: the Standard toolbar and the Formatting toolbar. The book explains each button in detail when it is used.

STANDARD TOOLBAR The Standard toolbar (Figure 1-10a) contains buttons that execute commonly used commands such as Open, Print, Save, Cut, Copy, Paste, and many more. The Standard toolbar also contains a Microsoft Office FrontPage Help button that you can click to start **FrontPage Help**, which is a collection of reference materials, tips, and other assistance you can access at any time while using FrontPage.

More About

Toolbars

You can move a toolbar to any location on the screen. Drag the move handle (Figure 1-10a) to the desired location. Once the toolbar is in the window area, drag the title bar to move it. Each side of the screen is called a dock. You can drag a toolbar to a dock so it does not clutter the window.

FORMATTING TOOLBAR The Formatting toolbar (Figure 1-10b) contains buttons used to execute commonly used formatting commands that allow you quickly to change font, font size, and alignment. It also contains buttons, such as Bold, Italic, and Underline, which allow you to change text styles, and others that create lists and so on.

FrontPage has several other toolbars to help you perform your work. You can display a toolbar by right-clicking any toolbar to display a shortcut menu that lists the available toolbars and then clicking the name of the toolbar you want to display. A **shortcut menu** contains a list of commands that are related to the items to which you are pointing when you right-click.

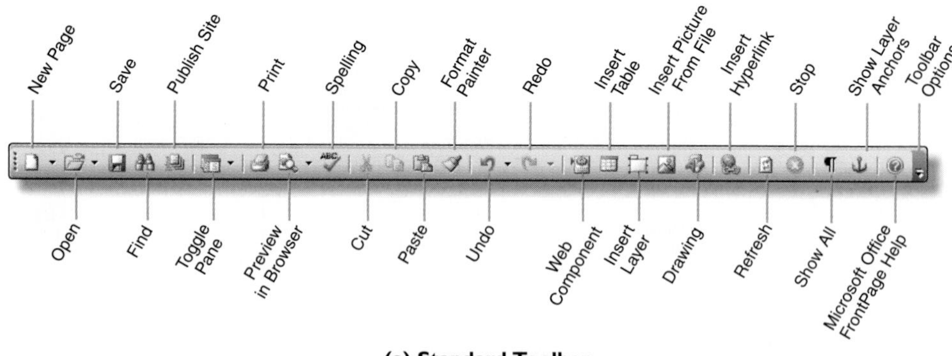

(a) Standard Toolbar

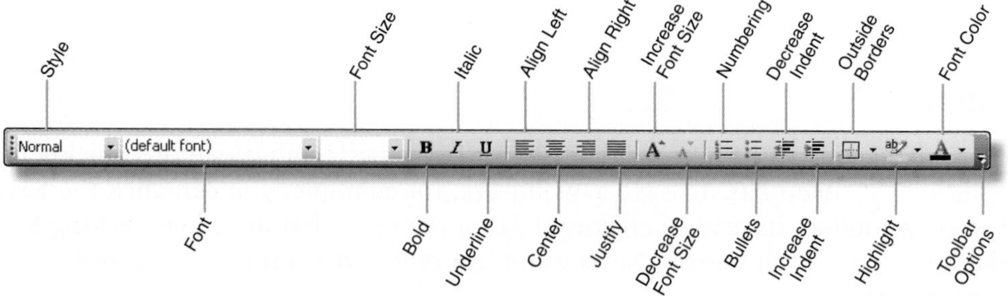

(b) Formatting Toolbar

FIGURE 1-10

More About

Resetting Toolbars

If your toolbars have a different set of buttons than shown in Figures 1-10a and 10b, it probably means that a previous user added or deleted buttons. To reset the toolbars to their default, see Appendix D.

Speech Recognition

With the **Office Speech Recognition software** installed and a microphone, you can speak the names of toolbar buttons, menus, menu commands, list items, alerts, and dialog box controls, such as OK and Cancel. You also can dictate cell entries, such as text and numbers. To indicate whether you want to speak commands or dictate cell entries, you use the Language bar. The Language bar can be in one of four states: (1) **restored**, which means it is displayed somewhere in the FrontPage window (Figure 1-11a); (2) **minimized**, which means it is displayed on the Windows taskbar (Figure 1-11b); (3) **hidden**, which means you do not see it on the screen but it will be displayed the next time you start your computer; or (4) **closed**, which means it is hidden permanently until you enable it. If the Language bar is hidden or closed and you want it to display, then do the following:

1. Right-click an open area on the Windows taskbar at the bottom of the screen.
2. Point to Toolbars and then click Language bar on the Toolbars submenu.

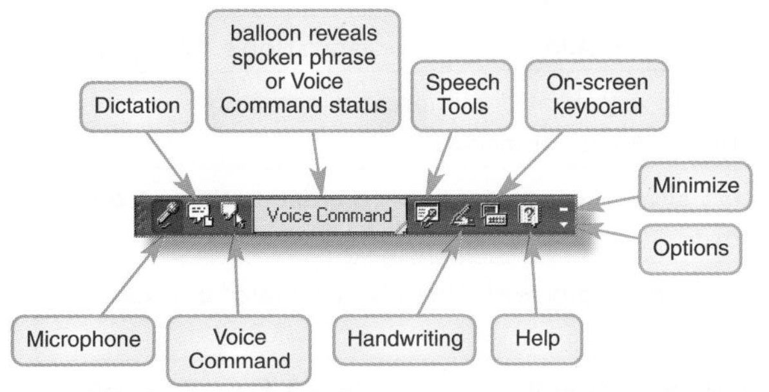

(a) Language Bar in FrontPage with Microphone Enabled

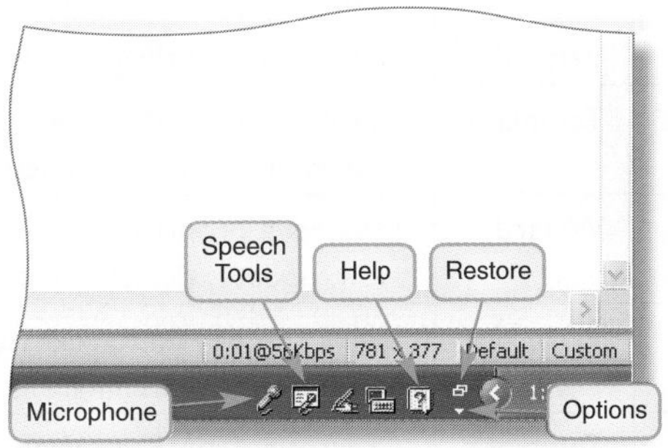

(b) Language Bar Minimized on Windows Taskbar

FIGURE 1-11

If the Language bar command is dimmed on the Toolbars submenu or if the Speech command is dimmed on the Tools menu, the Office Speech Recognition software is not installed.

In this book, the Language bar does not appear in the figures. If you want to close the Language bar so that your screen is identical to what you see in the book, right-click the Language bar, click Close the Language bar on the shortcut menu, and then click OK in the Language Bar dialog box.

Using a Template to Create a FrontPage Web Site

Designing a Web site is a complex process that requires you to make decisions concerning the structure of the Web site and the appearance and content of each Web page within the site. When developing a Web site composed of several pages, for example, you should use a consistent layout and design on each page. In addition, you should be sure to link appropriate pages using a navigation scheme that is easy to understand. To help simplify this process, FrontPage includes several wizards and preformatted Web sites that will help you create a set of pages for a Web site. These preformatted Web sites are called templates.

Before creating a Web site from scratch, lay out the navigation structure of your Web site and consider a template to alleviate a great deal of manual work when creating the Web site.

More About

Creating Templates

You can make a template from your own Web page. Click File on the menu bar and then click Save As. When the Save As dialog box is displayed, click FrontPage Template in the Save as type list. Click the Save button. If necessary, when the Save As Template dialog box is displayed, modify the Title, Name, and Description fields. Click the OK button.

A FrontPage **template** is a series of files and Web pages that are organized and formatted with a basic framework of content upon which you can base new pages and new FrontPage Web sites. You also can apply the formatting in a template to existing pages and Web sites. Each template consists of linked Web pages that already include basic elements such as headings, formatted text, images, and hyperlinks.

When you create a new Web site, you can choose to:

- Create an empty Web site or a Web site with one page
- Import a Web site from a Web server or your personal computer
- Create a Web site using a template or wizard

Table 1-2 outlines the options from which you can choose when creating a FrontPage Web site using a template.

Table 1-2 FrontPage Web Site Options

OPTION	TYPE	DESCRIPTION
One Page Web Site	Template	Creates a FrontPage Web site with a single page (a home page). Used to create a FrontPage Web site from scratch with no suggested content.
Corporate Presence Wizard	Wizard	Creates a FrontPage Web site with pages tailored to an organization's Web site.
Customer Support Web Site	Template	Creates a FrontPage Web site to help organizations improve a company's online customer support, particularly for software companies.
Database Interface Wizard	Wizard	Creates a FrontPage Web site that allows you to connect to a database, and then view, update, delete, or add records.
Discussion Web Wizard	Wizard	Helps the developer create a discussion group with threads, a table of contents, and full-text searching.
Empty Web Site	Template	Creates a FrontPage Web site with nothing in it. Used to create a FrontPage Web site from scratch with no suggested content.
Import Web Site Wizard	Wizard	Imports an existing Web site into a new FrontPage Web site. Starts the Import Web Site Wizard, which guides you through the process of importing an existing Web site.
Personal Web Site	Template	Creates a FrontPage Web site with Web pages about an individual's interests, photos, and favorite Web sites.
Project Web Site	Template	Creates a FrontPage Web site designed to support a project. The Web site includes pages for a list of members, a schedule, status, an archive, and discussions.
SharePoint Team Site	Template	Creates a Web site for team collaboration with a team events calendar, library for shared documents, task list, and contact list. Must be created on a Web server.

After you create a page or Web site using a template, you can customize the page or Web site. To reduce the editing work required to finish your Web site, you should choose the template closest to your desired site design and structure. Because FrontPage creates many files for a Web site, it is advisable to create the project using the computer's hard disk (typically drive C) rather than the floppy drive (A:). The following steps show how to use a template to create a FrontPage Web site on a hard disk.

To Use a Template to Create a FrontPage Web Site

1

- **Click File on the menu bar and then click Close.**

FrontPage closes the new_page_1.htm page.

2

- **Click the New Page button arrow on the Standard toolbar.**

FrontPage displays the New Page menu (Figure 1-12).

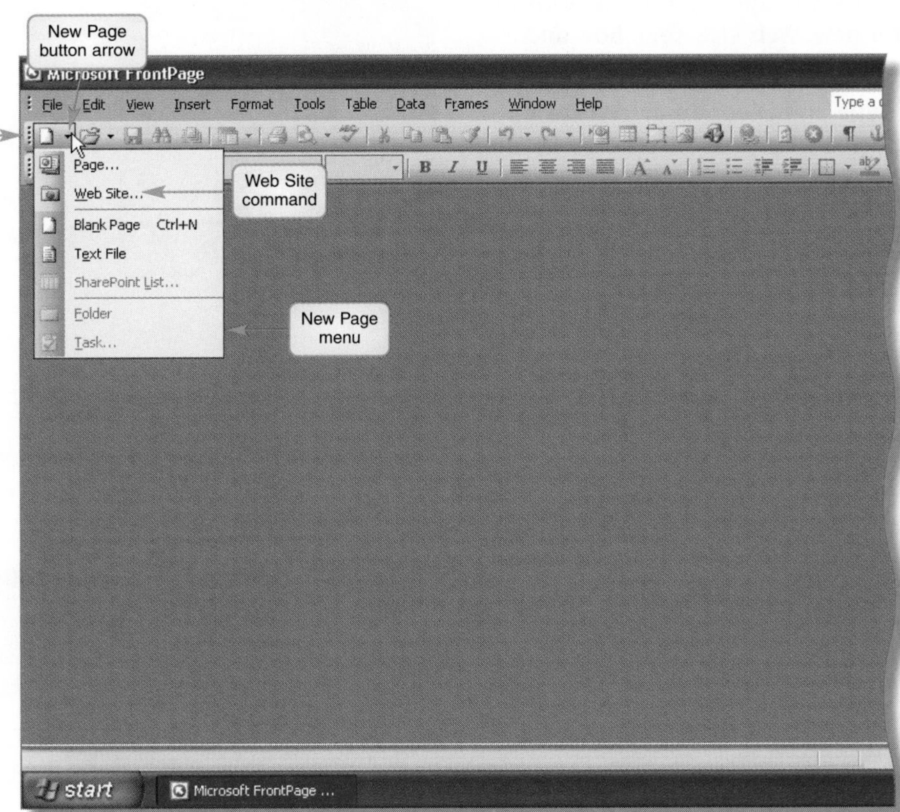

FIGURE 1-12

3

- **Click Web Site.**
- **When the Web Site Templates dialog box appears, click the Personal Web Site icon.**

The Web Site Templates dialog box is displayed, prompting you for information needed to create a new FrontPage Web site. The Personal Web Site icon is selected; the Description area describes the Web site the Personal Web Site template creates. The Specify the location of the new Web site text box indicates the location where FrontPage will store the new Web site (Figure 1-13).

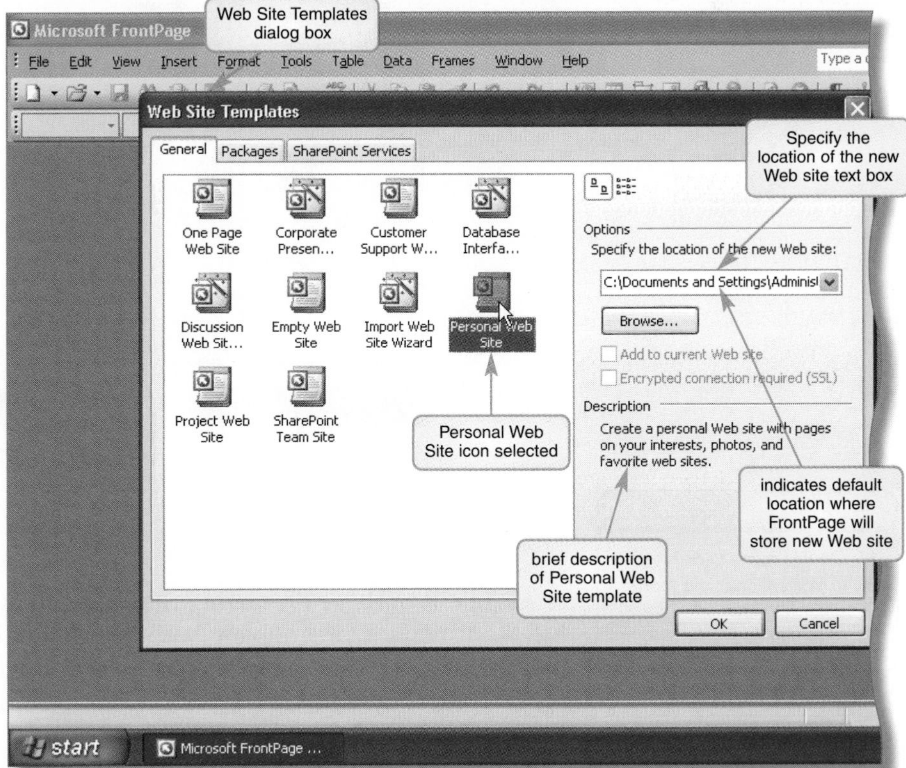

FIGURE 1-13

4

- **Click the Specify the location of the new Web site text box and select the default location text.**
- **Type** c:\jkeeler **or a location specified by your instructor in the text box.**

FrontPage displays the new location in the text box. FrontPage will save the new Web site in the jkeeler folder on drive C (Figure 1-14).

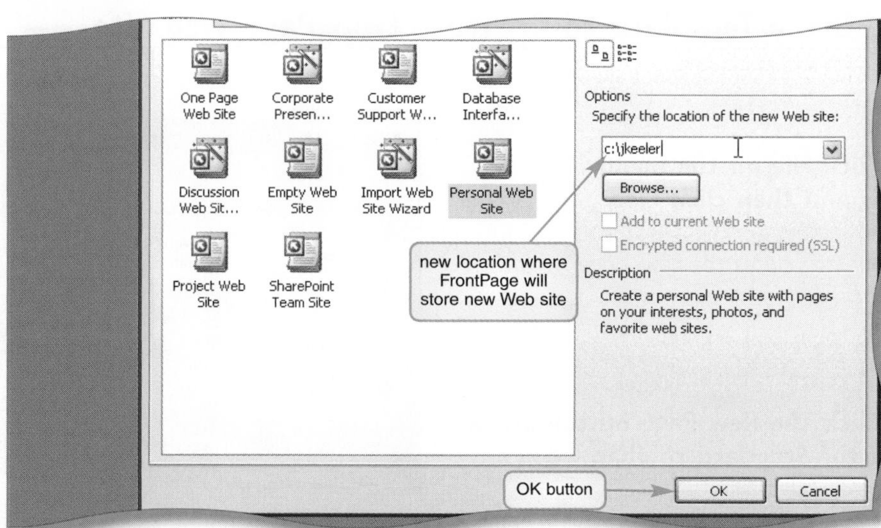

FIGURE 1-14

5

- **Click the OK button.**

FrontPage begins creating a set of folders and making copies of the Web pages in the Personal Web Site template for you to customize. When finished, the FrontPage window is displayed in Folders view with the Folder List pane open on the left side (Figure 1-15).

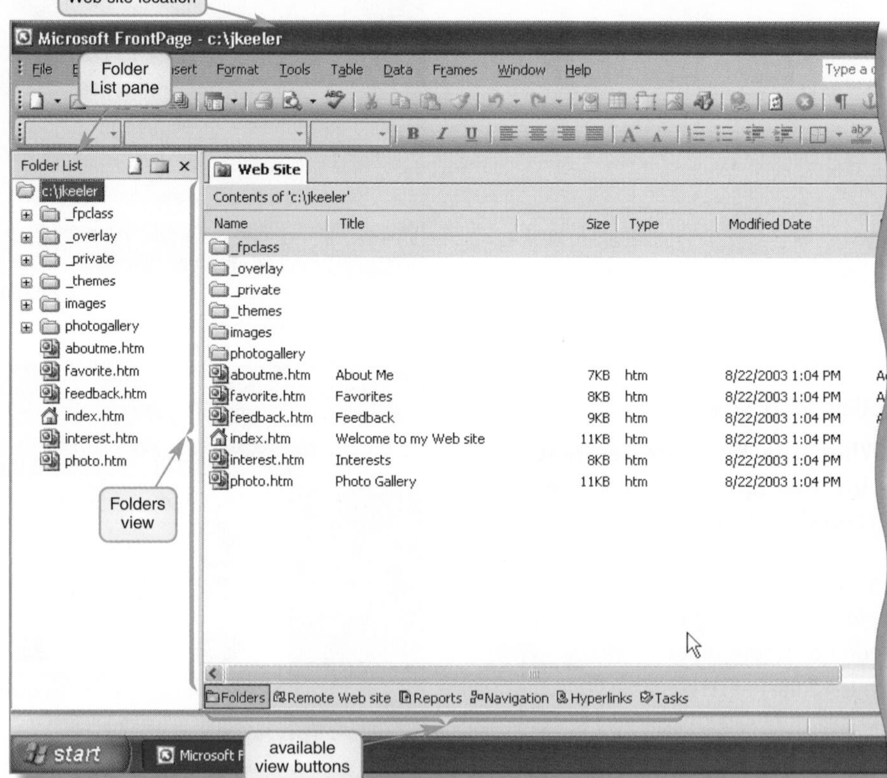

FIGURE 1-15

Other Ways

1. On File menu click New
2. In Voice Command mode, say "File, New"
3. Press ALT+F, N

While FrontPage is copying the Personal Web Site template pages, FrontPage briefly displays a Create New Web Site dialog box indicating that FrontPage is creating the new Web site in the folder, jkeeler, on drive C and the status of the copying process. As shown in Figure 1-15, when FrontPage creates a new Web site, the Folder List pane opens on the left side of the FrontPage window. The Folder List pane lists the name of all of the files and folders in the current FrontPage Web site. If it is not displayed, display the Folder List pane by using the Folder List command on the View menu or pressing ALT+F1.

Views

The document window shown in Figure 1-15 displays the Web Site tab in Folders view. The Web Site tab always is available when you are working on a Web site. FrontPage includes several types of views that display in the main FrontPage window. When you first create a new Web site, FrontPage is displayed in Folders view. A **view** provides a different way of looking at the information in your Web site, so you can manage your Web site effectively. The View menu contains commands that allow you to switch to different views of your Web site. You also can click the buttons at the bottom of the document window to switch to several different views. The selected view determines how the FrontPage window appears. For example, **Navigation view** displays a graphical representation of the Web site's **structure**, which is the set of relationships among the pages in a FrontPage Web site.

A Web site's structure defines the overall site organization and navigation, determining the pages that are linked, how many levels of pages exist, and so on. The structure of one Web site, for example, might be linear, with few levels; another site might use a hierarchical structure, with several levels of pages.

Q: Can I stop FrontPage from automatically opening the last Web site?

A: Yes. When FrontPage starts, it opens the last Web site you edited. To stop this behavior, click Options on the Tools menu. When the Options dialog box is displayed, click the General tab. Make certain that the Open last Web site automatically when FrontPage starts check box is cleared.

Design Tip

If your Web site's navigation structure is both well-designed and focused on your users, your visitors will be able to move to different locations on a page or to other pages in your Web site to find usable information quickly and easily.

Table 1-3 identifies the views available on the View menu and buttons at the bottom of the document window on the Web Site tab and provides a description of each view. All of the views appear on buttons at the bottom of the Web Site tab except for the Page view. Individual Page views for each page that is open appear in separate tabs to the right of the Web Site tab.

Table 1-3 Views on the View Menu

BUTTON	VIEW	DESCRIPTION
	Page	Used for creating, editing, and previewing Web pages. Page view displays Web pages in a manner similar to how they will be displayed in a Web browser.
	Folders	Displays a view of a Web site that shows how the content of the Web site is organized. Similar to Windows Explorer, Folders view allows you to create, delete, copy, and move folders.
	Remote Web Site	Allows you to view and publish the current Web site or portions of the current Web site to a Web server.
	Reports	Allows you to analyze a Web site's contents. You can calculate the total size of the files in your Web site, show which files are not linked to any other files, identify slow or outdated pages, group files by the task or person to whom the files are assigned, and so on.
	Navigation	Used to create, display, print, and change a Web site's structure and navigation. Navigation view also allows you to drag and drop pages into the Web site structure.
	Hyperlinks	Displays a list showing the status of the hyperlinks in the Web site. The list includes both internal and external hyperlinks, and graphically indicates whether the hyperlinks have been verified or whether they are broken.
	Tasks	Displays a list of the tasks required to complete or maintain a Web site.

Opening and Modifying a Web Page in Page View

When a Web site is opened, the path and name of the Web site appear on the title bar. When you create a new Web site, FrontPage automatically creates certain files and folders, such as Web pages, images, and other files in the Web site. The **Page view** displays a page currently being edited. FrontPage allows you to edit several pages at once by opening a tab for each page to the right of the Web Site tab.

Opening a Web Page in Page View

FrontPage allows you to open and modify text, images, tables, and other elements on each individual page in the current Web site. If the page is in the current Web site in any view or the Folder List pane, you can open the page by double-clicking the page's icon or file name. To open a Web page in Page view, for example, you simply double-click the file name of the page in the Folder List pane. After FrontPage displays the page in the document window, you can edit the page by selecting text, images, and other elements. The page being edited in Page view is referred to as the **active page** or **current page**. After you open a page, the document window displays the active page as a tabbed page. The file name of the active page, such as index.htm, appears in the tab at the top of the document window. The following step shows how to open a Web page in Page view.

To Open a Web Page in Page View

1

- **Double-click the file name, index.htm, in the Folder List pane.**

The Home page is displayed in the document window (Figure 1-16). The page contains placeholder text that you can edit to display your own message. A small pencil icon in the Folder List pane indicates that the Home page file, named index.htm, is open. The Design button is selected at the bottom of the document window, which indicates that the page is displayed in Design view. In Design view, you can edit the page. The tab at the top of the document window shows the name of the file opened for editing.

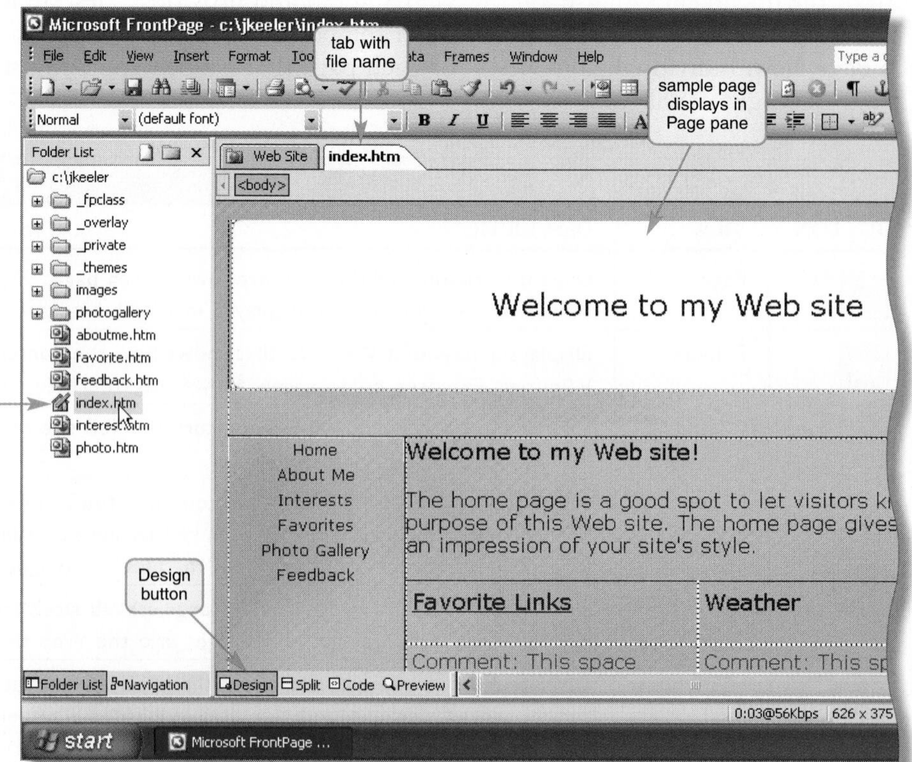

FIGURE 1-16

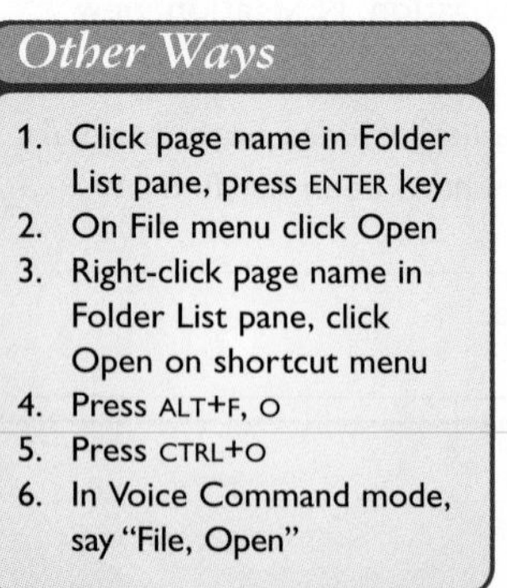

Other Ways

1. Click page name in Folder List pane, press ENTER key
2. On File menu click Open
3. Right-click page name in Folder List pane, click Open on shortcut menu
4. Press ALT+F, O
5. Press CTRL+O
6. In Voice Command mode, say "File, Open"

When a page is opened in the default Page view, the page appears in Design view. Design view is indicated by a button at the bottom of the Page view tab. There are four views in which to view a page while in Page view, including Design, Split, Code, and Preview. The Design view, which is the default button selected in Page view, is a **WYSIWYG** (**What You See Is What You Get**) design tool that displays a page as it will appear in a Web browser. As you create or modify a Web page in Design view, FrontPage displays the page as it will display on the Web, while generating the needed HTML code for you. If you insert an image on a page, for example, FrontPage automatically enters the proper HTML code (in this case, the <IMG> tag). Using FrontPage, you can insert text, images, hyperlinks, and other elements without having to type any HTML code.

As shown in Figure 1-16, the Folder List pane displays the pages and folders in the current Web site. When you first create a new Personal Web site, it contains six folders: _fpclass, _overlay, _private, _themes, images, and photogallery — included in the Personal Web Site template. The _fpclass, _overlay, and _themes folders include files used internally by FrontPage for special functionality. For example, the _themes folder contains files used for FrontPage themes, which are discussed in the next section. The **images folder** is a convenient place to store image files used in the FrontPage Web site. The _private folder holds files that you can use on the Web pages in the current Web site, but do not want people who are browsing your Web site to access individually. If you store a logo image in the _private folder, for example, you can use this on your Web pages, but others browsing your Web site cannot access the logo image. The **photogallery folder** is where FrontPage stores thumbnail images when a particular component, which is discussed later, is used. FrontPage also automatically creates a file named **index.htm**, which serves as the home page for your Web site.

Applying a Theme to a FrontPage Web Site

When developing a Web site that consists of many pages, you should maintain a consistent, professional layout and design throughout all of the pages. The pages in a Web site, for example, should use similar features such as background color, margins, buttons, and headings. To help you create pages with a cohesive and professional appearance, FrontPage includes a gallery of more than 75 preset themes. A **theme** is a unified set of design elements and color schemes for bullets, fonts, graphics, navigation bars, and other page elements.

Generate a sense of unity or familiarity within your Web site by utilizing a common graphic theme and a common color theme.

When applied to a Web site, a theme formats the Web page elements (images, backgrounds, text, and so on) so they share a consistent layout and design. You also have the option of applying themes to individual pages. The theme affects all aspects of a page's appearance, including text, color, and images, as follows:

- **Text:** A theme uses a unique set of fonts for the body text and headings.
- **Colors:** A theme uses a color scheme to set the color of body text, headings, hyperlinks, table borders, page background, and more.
- **Images:** A theme uses images (graphics) for several page elements, such as the background, bullets, horizontal rules, and more.

When you insert new elements on a page that uses a theme, FrontPage automatically formats those elements to match the theme. FrontPage also applies the theme automatically to any new pages you create in the Web site.

Each FrontPage template uses a default theme. When the Personal Web Site template was selected in the previous set of steps, FrontPage automatically applied a theme to the Web site. The following steps show how to preview the default theme used for the Web site and apply a new theme to the Web site.

To Apply a Theme to a FrontPage Web Site

1

- **Click Format on the menu bar (Figure 1-17).**

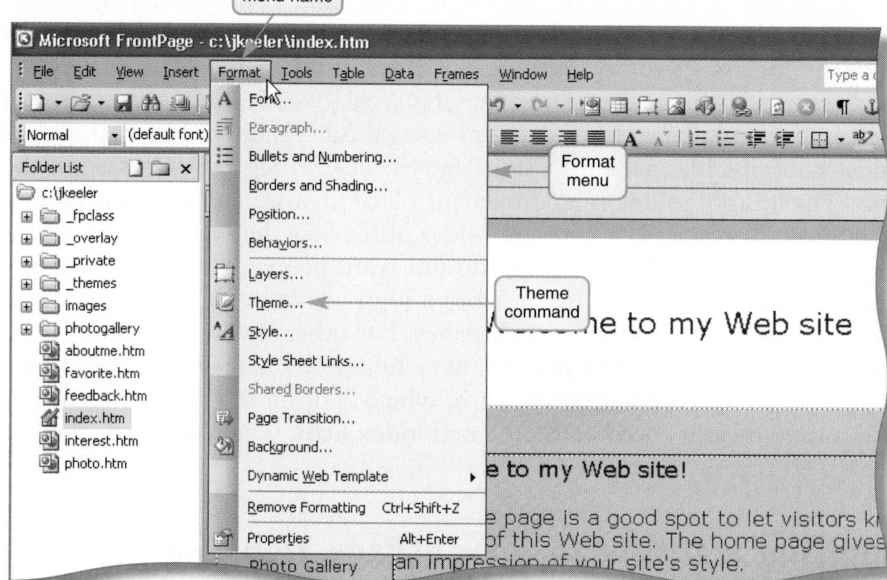

FIGURE 1-17

2

- **Click Theme.**
- **When the Theme task pane is displayed, click the Vivid colors check box to select it.**
- **Scroll to Capsules in the Select a theme list.**

The Theme task pane is displayed and the Vivid colors check box is selected (Figure 1-18). The Select a theme list allows you to preview a sample page of each theme in the list. The Select a theme list shows all of the themes provided with FrontPage.

FIGURE 1-18

3

- **Click the c:\jkeeler folder in the Folder List pane.**
- **Double-click Capsules in the Select a theme list.**

FrontPage displays the Microsoft FrontPage 2003 dialog box. The dialog box warns that the theme will be applied to all pages in the Web site (Figure 1-19). Selecting the c:\jkeeler folder ensures that all pages in the Web site receive the theme.

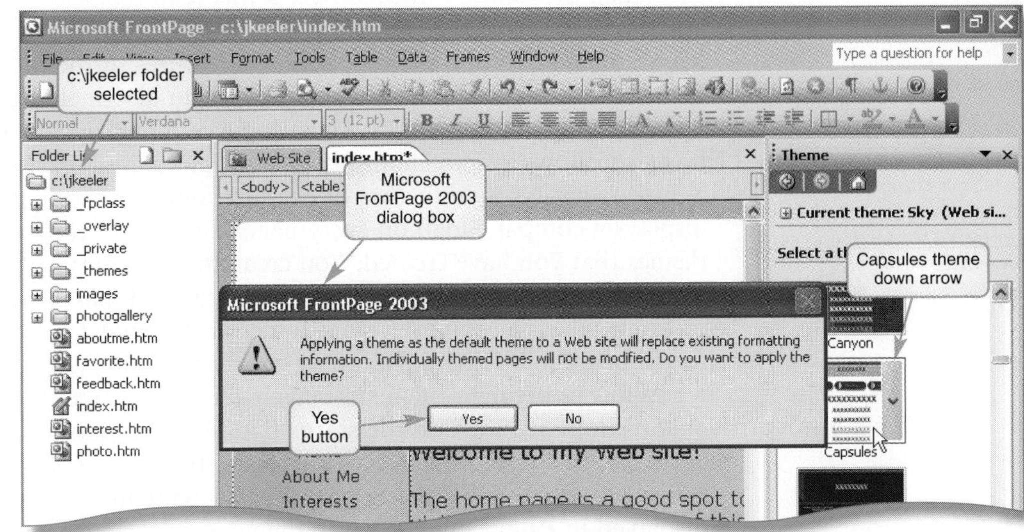

FIGURE 1-19

4

- **Click the Yes button.**

FrontPage displays a message on the status bar, indicating that FrontPage is applying the new theme to all pages in the Web site. When finished, FrontPage is displayed in Page view. The active page, index.htm, is displayed in the document window with the Capsules theme applied (Figure 1-20).

5

- **Click the Close button on the Theme task pane.**

FrontPage displays the index.htm page in Page view in the document window.

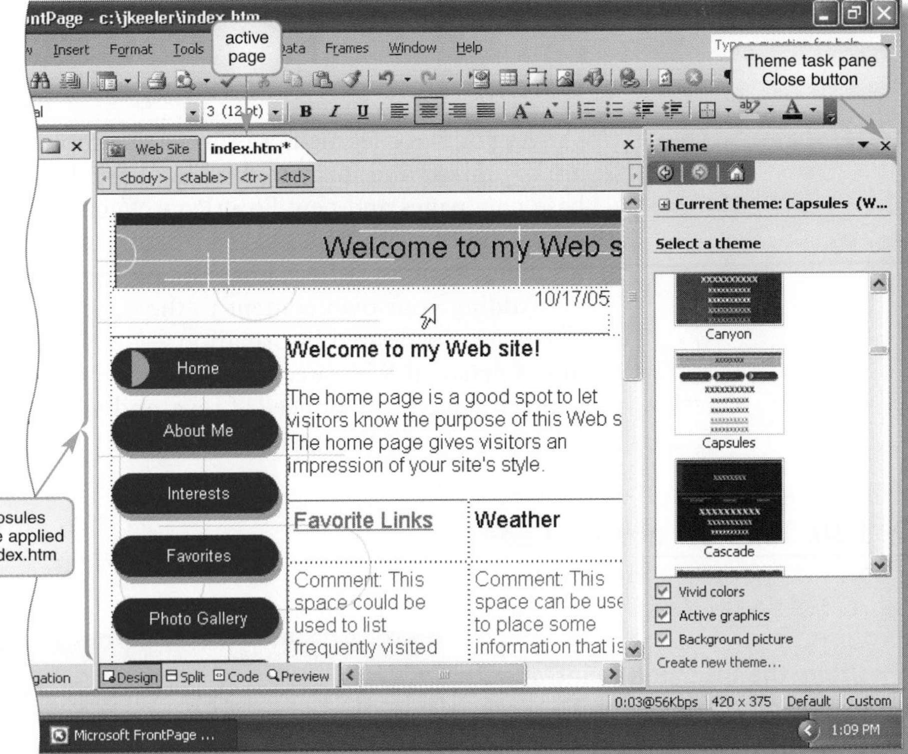

FIGURE 1-20

Other Ways

1. Press ALT+O, H
2. In Voice Command mode, say "Format, Theme"

The Theme task pane (Figure 1-18) contains options you can select to control how the current Web site uses themes. Selecting the Vivid colors check box changes the theme's normal set of colors to a brighter color scheme. Selecting the Active graphics check box animates certain graphic elements. Selecting the Background picture check box applies a textured background image to the pages in the current Web site.

Q: Can I modify one of the preset themes that are included with FrontPage?

A: Yes. However, you must save your changes as a new theme. The preset themes are protected so that you cannot overwrite them.

When the mouse is moved over a theme in the Select a theme list, a down arrow appears next to the theme (Figure 1-19 on the previous page). Clicking the arrow displays a menu that allows you to change features of the theme or apply the theme to one or more pages in the Web site. The menu also includes a Customize command and a Delete command. The Customize command displays the Customize Theme dialog box that allows you to change colors, graphics, and text in the theme. You can change a theme's background picture or heading font, for example, to create a new theme that displays a company logo on every page. The Delete command allows you to delete themes that you have created. You create new themes by clicking the Create new theme hyperlink at the bottom of the Theme task pane. As you saw in Step 3 on the previous page, selecting the main folder in the Folder List pane before applying the theme instructs FrontPage to apply the theme to every page in the current Web site.

While applying a theme to a Web site, FrontPage displays information about the operation in progress on the status bar. Depending on the number of pages in the Web site, this process can take anywhere from a few seconds to a few minutes. When FrontPage has applied the theme to every page in the current Web site, FrontPage is displayed in Page view. Once the theme is applied, FrontPage changes the background, fonts, and graphics used in the Web site. Applying the Capsules theme, for example, adds an oval pattern and colors to the white background (Figure 1-20 on the previous page).

Editing Text on a Web Page

As you have learned, a FrontPage template is a series of linked Web pages that are organized and formatted with a basic framework of content upon which you can base new pages and new FrontPage Web sites. To help you design your own Web page, the template Web pages include placeholders for basic page elements such as headings, formatted text, images, and hyperlinks.

Adding your own content to the page involves editing one or more placeholders to convey the desired information — or deleting them altogether. On the Home page of the personal Web site, for example, you will want to edit the text to introduce yourself, delete any unneeded text, and add new text to complete the page. The following steps edit text on a Web page.

To Edit Text on a Web Page

1

- **Position the insertion point at the beginning of the second paragraph, which begins with the text, The home page is a good spot... (Figure 1-21).**

FIGURE 1-21

2

• **Drag through the text to select it.**

The selected text is highlighted (Figure 1-22).

FIGURE 1-22

3

• **Type** `My name is James Keeler, and I am a candidate to graduate from Trelane College.` **(You may substitute your personal information here.)**

The new text replaces the selected text (Figure 1-23). The asterisk in the tab indicates changes made to the page are not yet saved.

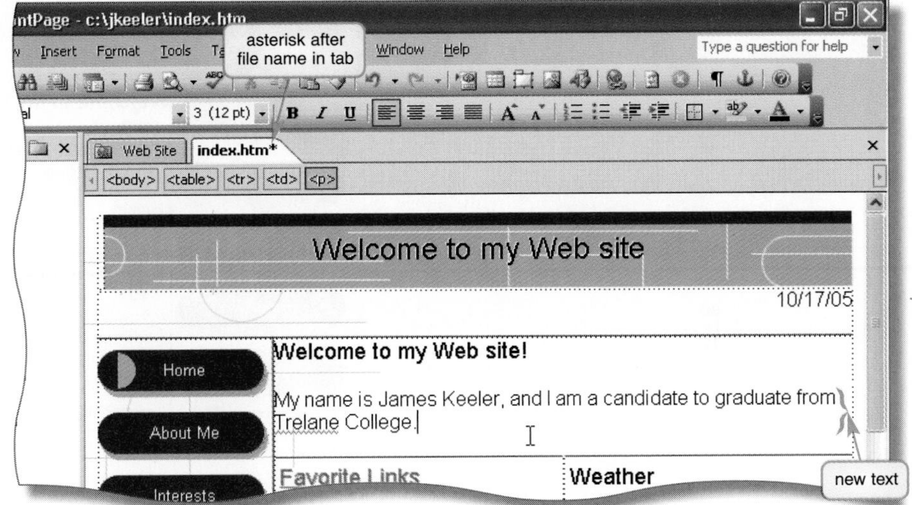

FIGURE 1-23

The previous steps edited a section of the placeholder text on the template page, which now displays the desired information. The other text sections remain unchanged.

Using FrontPage, you can edit and add text just as you would with word processing software. To begin editing, you position the insertion point where you want to make a change and then perform the desired action. You even can move around the text using your mouse or the arrow keys. If you make a mistake typing, you can use the BACKSPACE key or the DELETE key to correct the mistake. Use the Show All button on the Standard toolbar to toggle showing and hiding of hidden document formatting codes.

Adding New Text to a Web Page

If you want to include additional text beyond that contained in the template, you can add new text to the Web page. Just as you add new text to a word processing document, you add new text to a Web page by positioning the insertion point where you want the text to display and then typing the text. The following steps add text to a Web page.

To Add New Text to a Web Page

1

• **Press the ENTER key to start a new paragraph below the second paragraph.**

FrontPage displays the insertion point at the beginning of the new paragraph (Figure 1-24).

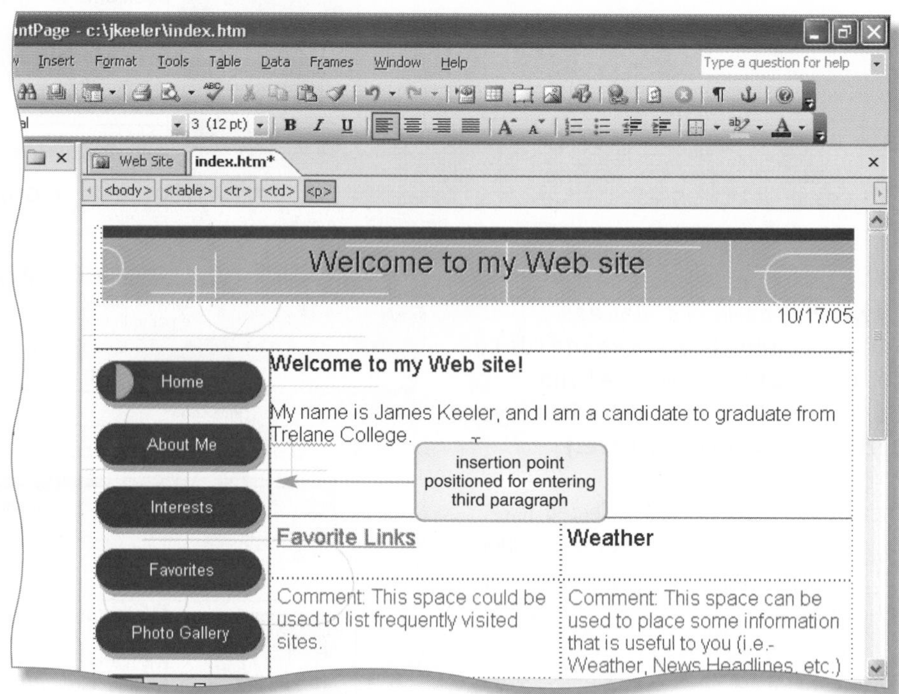

FIGURE 1-24

2

• **Type** `This Web site is the first Web site that I created.`

FrontPage displays the new text as the third paragraph on the Web page (Figure 1-25).

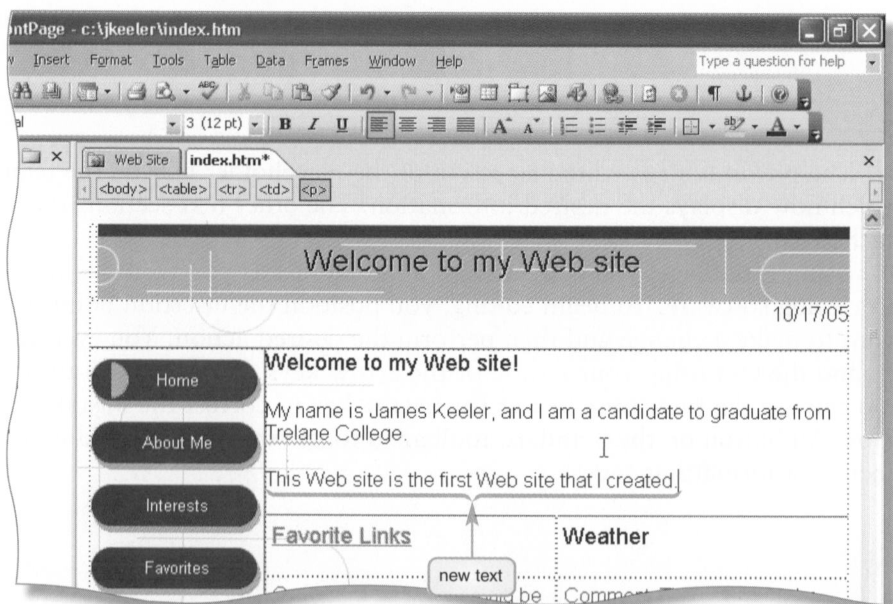

FIGURE 1-25

3

• **Press the ENTER key to start a new paragraph.**

• **Type** `Follow the links to learn more about my interests and to see some of my favorite Web sites.`

The inserted text automatically wraps to the next line as you type (Figure 1-26).

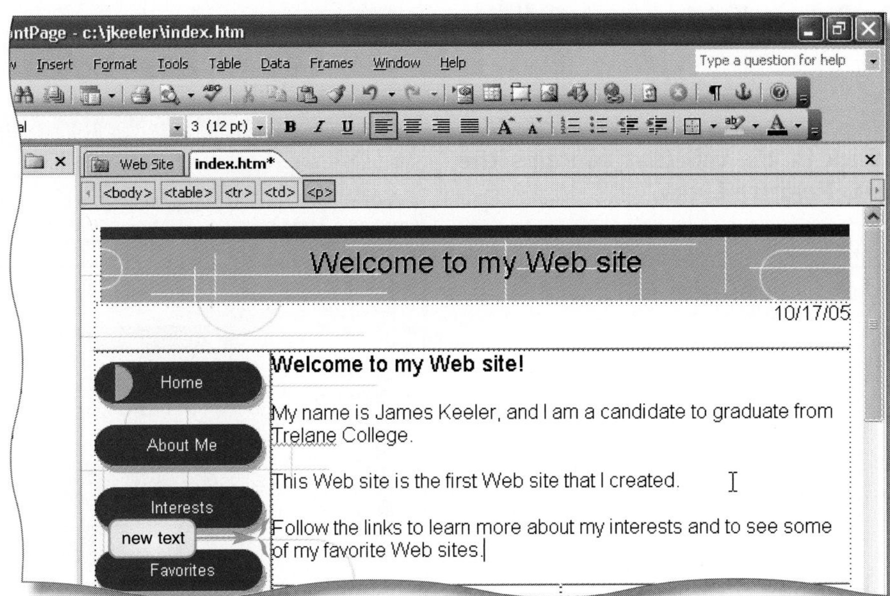

FIGURE 1-26

Editing and adding text on a Web page using FrontPage is similar to editing a word processing document. In the Design view of Page view, you can insert, delete, cut, copy, and paste text, just as you would with word processing software.

Design Tip

If the main content for your Web page is not already in a word processing document, consider first placing all of your content in one. You and other contributors can manage the content much easier in a common file format. When the content is ready to be made available on the Web, simply copy and paste the content from the document into the Web page in FrontPage.

As with many word processing applications, FrontPage automatically checks your spelling as you type and flags misspelled words with a red wavy underline. In the Home page, for example, the spell checker does not recognize the word, Trelane, and thus flags it with a red wavy underline. To add an unrecognized word to the spell checker dictionary, right-click the underlined word and then click Add to Dictionary on the shortcut menu. To correct a misspelled word, right-click the underlined word and then click the correct spelling on the shortcut menu.

Deleting Text Positioned with Tables

Often, cells in a table are used in a Web page to position textual elements. A table may contain only a single cell with text, may contain multiple cells containing text, or may contain another nested table. A table contained within another table is called a **nested** table. Although tables are discussed in a later project, the template used for this page incorporates tables to position some sections of text and also contains some nested tables. Because some of these tables and cells are not used in the Web site you are developing, they should be deleted. The steps on the next page select the tables and cells to be deleted.

To Select Tables and Cells

1

• **Click in the cell that contains the text, Favorite Links.**

FrontPage displays the insertion point at the end of the text (Figure 1-27).

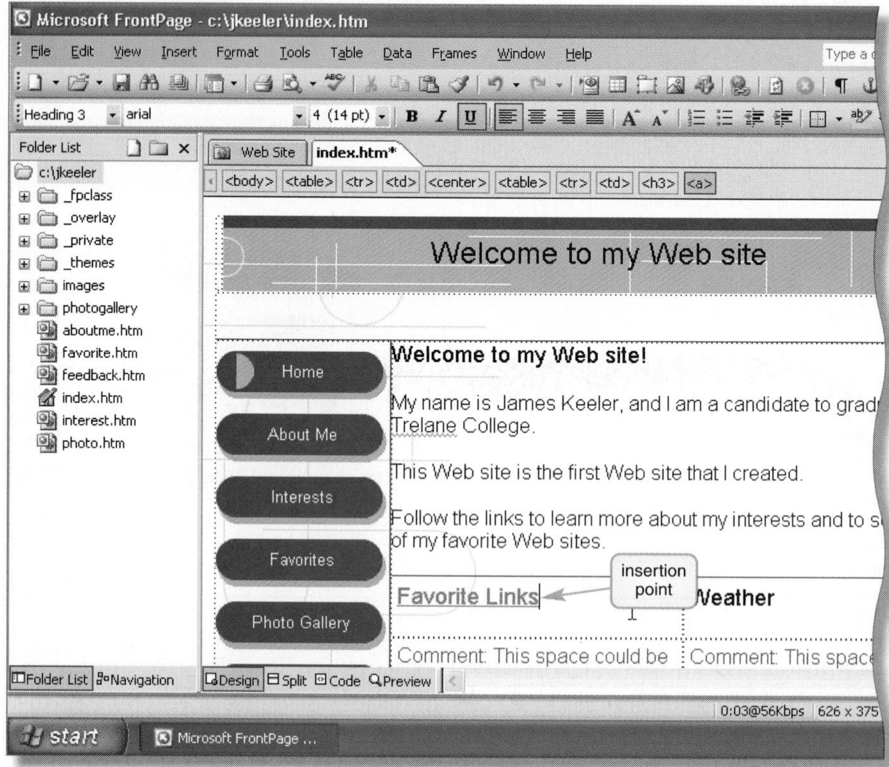

FIGURE 1-27

2

• **Click Table on the menu bar and then point to Select.**

FrontPage displays the Table menu and the Select submenu (Figure 1-28).

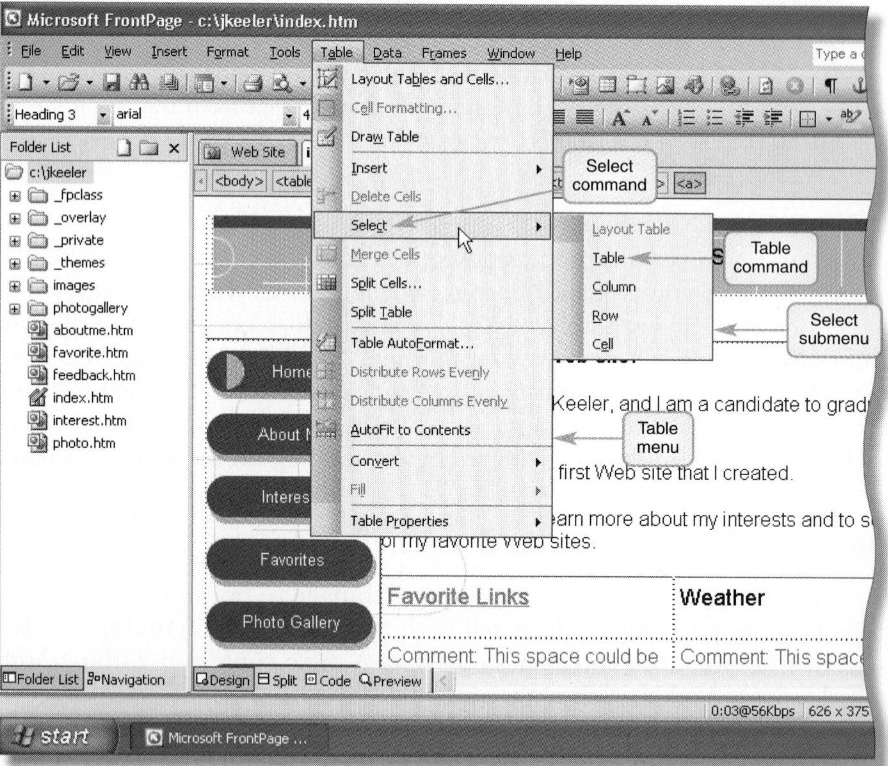

FIGURE 1-28

3

• **Click Table on the Select submenu.**

*The selected cells are highlighted (Figure 1-29). The **Quick Tag Selector** is displayed. It is a tool that makes it easier to select and edit tags.*

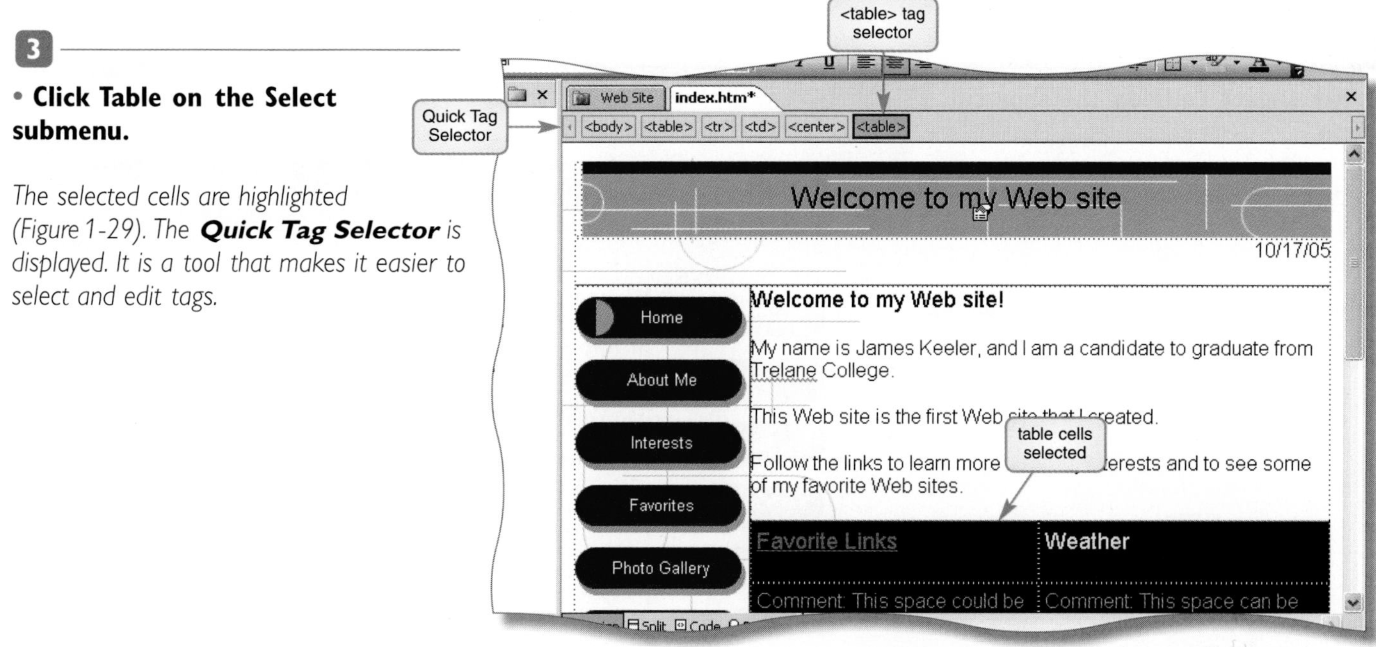

FIGURE 1-29

Other Ways

1. Click top-left cell in table, SHIFT+click bottom-right cell in table
2. Click cell in table, press ALT+A, press C, press T
3. Click cell in table, click rightmost <table> tag selector on Quick Tag Selector
4. Click cell in table, in Voice Command mode, say "Table, Select, Table"

You should exercise care in selecting the table cells you want to delete. Because tables often are nested, you inadvertently may select material that you want to keep. Figure 1-29 shows that the <table> tag selector in the Quick Tag Selector becomes highlighted when you select the table. The Quick Tag Selector shows the hierarchy of HTML tags that leads to the currently selected item in the Page view. Moving the mouse over a tag selector in the Quick Tag Selector displays a down arrow next to the tag selector. Clicking the arrow displays a menu that allows you to perform various actions on the tag, such as selecting the tag. Once it is verified that the selected cells and/or tables are correct, the following steps delete the selected table and cells in the table.

To Delete a Selected Table

1

• **Right-click one of the selected cells.**

FrontPage displays the shortcut menu (Figure 1-30).

FIGURE 1-30

2

• **Click Delete Cells on the shortcut menu.**

The selected cells are deleted (Figure 1-31).

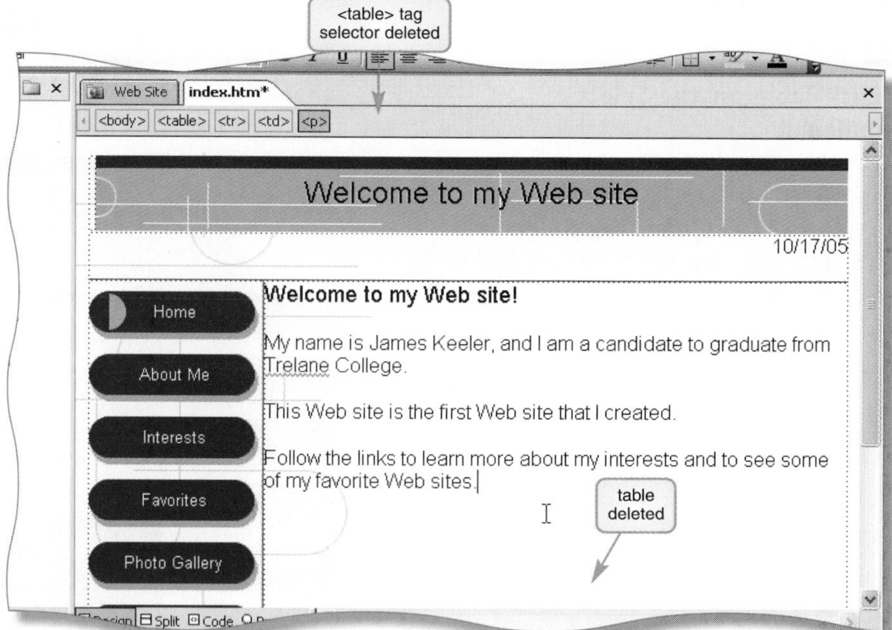

FIGURE 1-31

3

• **Use the scroll bar in Page view to scroll to the bottom of the Web page.**

The bottom of the Web page becomes visible (Figure 1-32).

FIGURE 1-32

Other Ways

1. Select table, on Table menu click Delete Cells
2. Select table, press ALT+A, press D
3. Select table, press DELETE key
4. In Voice Command mode, say "Table, Delete Cells"

Editing a Bulleted List

In the previous steps, you edited the file, index.htm, which FrontPage created as the default Home page. To complete the Web site, you need to edit the other pages in the Web site. The template for the Interests page, for example, includes a bulleted list of interests for customization.

Recall that a bulleted list is an unordered list of items, which usually uses small icons called bullets to indicate each item in the list. In Design view, you can edit the bulleted list on the Interests page, changing, adding, and deleting items as needed to customize it to your interests. The following steps edit the bulleted list.

To Edit a Bulleted List

1

• **Double-click the file name, interest.htm, in the Folder List pane.**

The Interests page is displayed in Design view in the document window (Figure 1-33). The template for the Interests page includes a bulleted list of items; a bullet image precedes each item in the list. In the Folder List, a small pencil is displayed on the icon next to the file name, interest.htm, to indicate that the file is open. Also, tabs at the top of the page indicate the pages currently opened for editing.

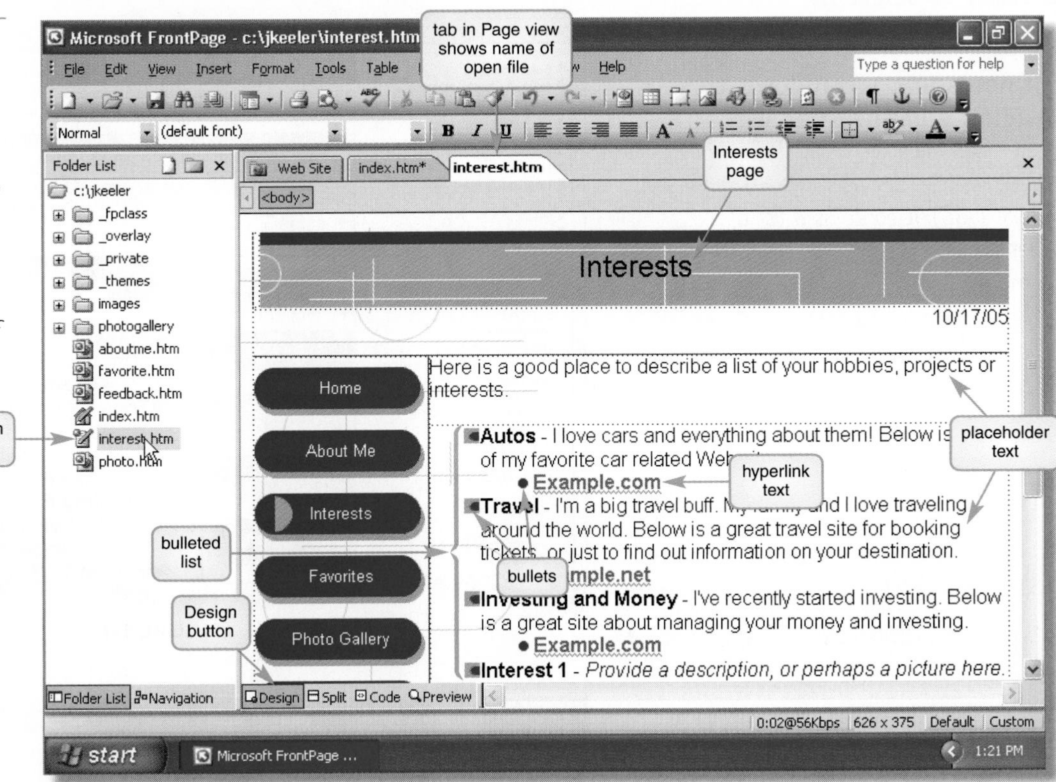

FIGURE 1-33

2

• **Drag through the first sentence of text that begins, Here is a good place, to select it.**

• **Type** `What holds my interest in my chosen field of small-business marketing.` **as the new text.**

The new text replaces the selected text (Figure 1-34).

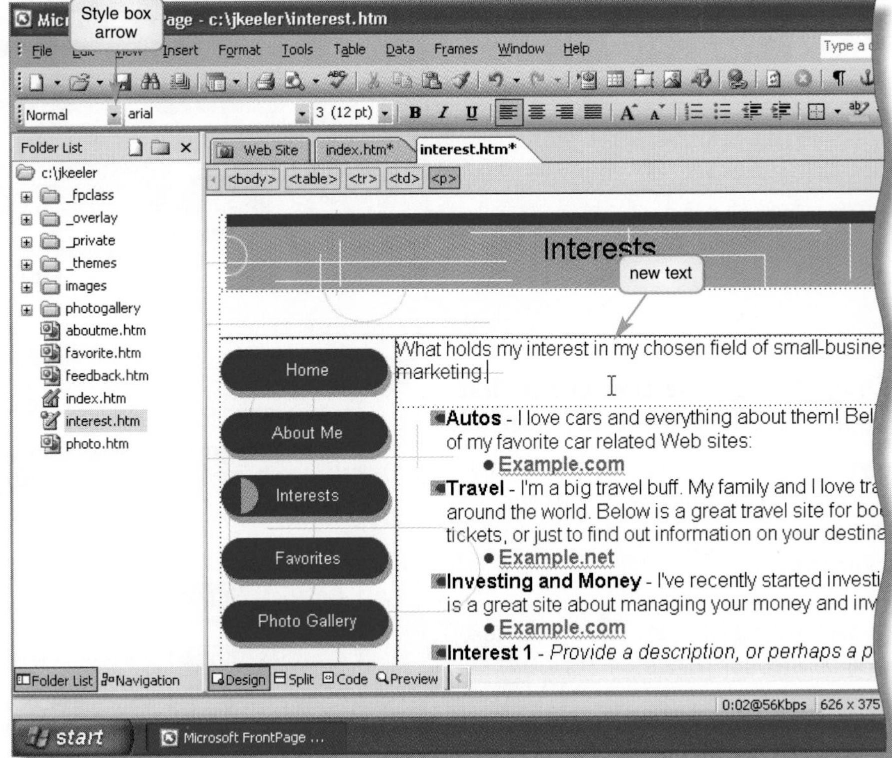

FIGURE 1-34

3

- **Drag through the text just entered to select it.**
- **Click the Style box arrow.**
- **If necessary, scroll down to Heading 3 in the Style list.**

FrontPage displays the Style list (Figure 1-35). It contains a list of styles for text, such as lists, headings, and normal text.

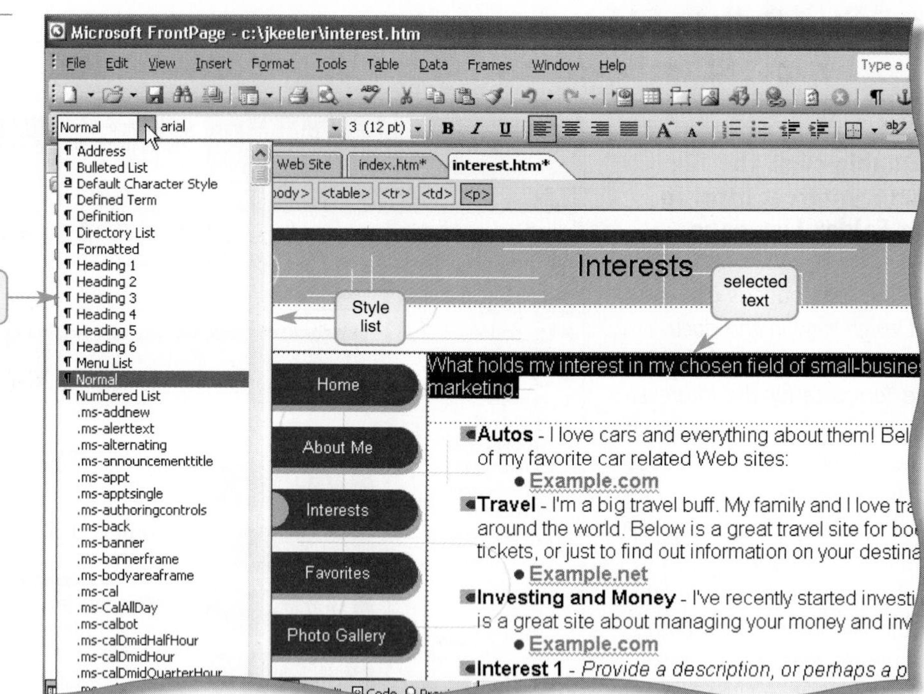

FIGURE 1-35

4

- **Click Heading 3 in the Style list.**

FrontPage displays the selected text with a style of Heading 3 (Figure 1-36).

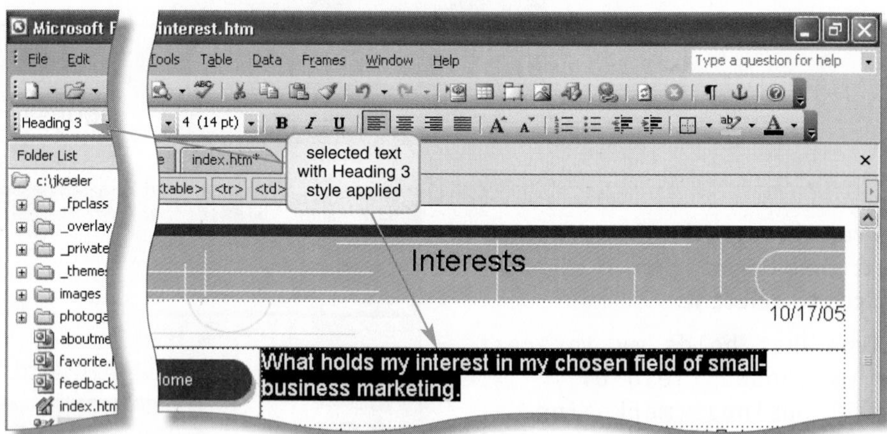

FIGURE 1-36

5

- **Drag through the text of the first line in the bulleted list to select it.**
- **Type** `SBA - The first place to go for small business owners is the government's Small Business Association.`

The new text replaces the placeholder text in the bulleted list (Figure 1-37).

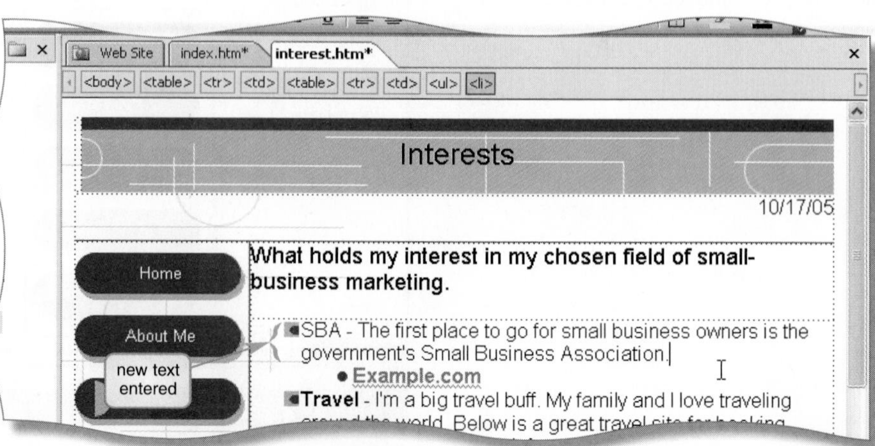

FIGURE 1-37

6

• **Drag through the first hyperlink to select it and then type** `sba.gov` **as the new link.**

The new text replaces the hyperlink text in the bulleted list (Figure 1-38). The actual hyperlink has not changed, but will be modified later in this project.

FIGURE 1-38

7

• **Drag through the remaining lines of text in the bulleted list and their respective hyperlinks.**

FrontPage scrolls the Web page as you drag through the text. The remaining bullets become visible (Figure 1-39).

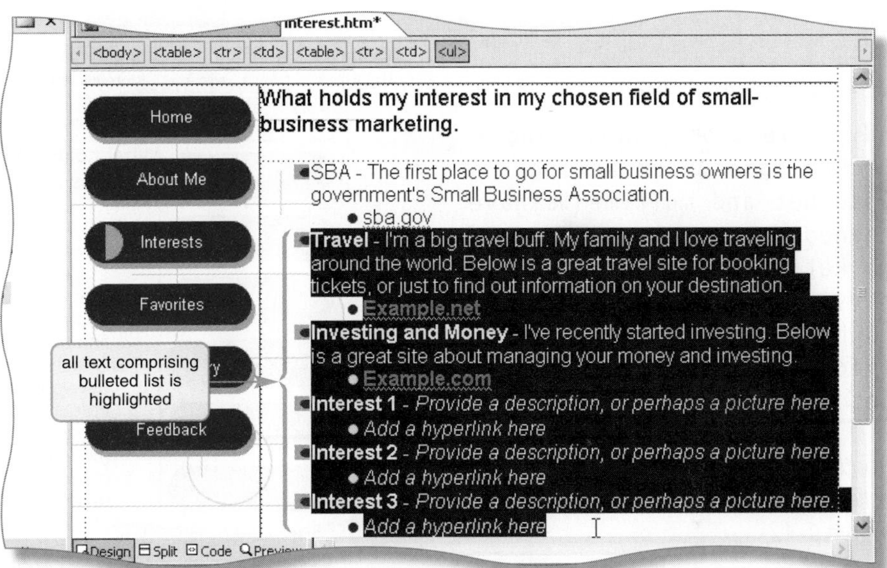

FIGURE 1-39

8

• **Type** `Guerrilla Promotions - Inexpensive and creative marketing approaches work well on the local level for small business. I find Guerrilla marketing to be incredibly fun and it works.`

• **Press the ENTER key.**

The new text replaces the placeholder text in the bulleted list (Figure 1-40). A third bullet is displayed below the last item in the list.

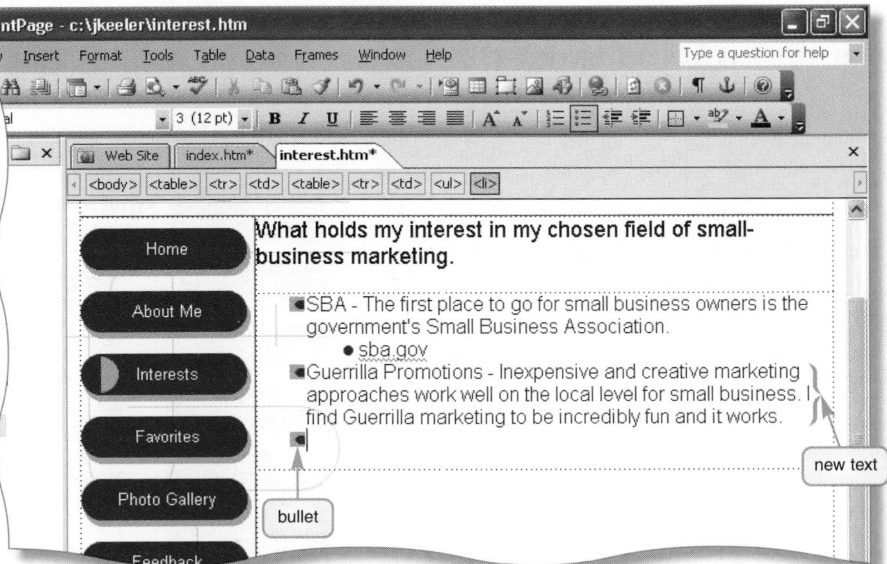

FIGURE 1-40

9

• **Type** Branding - I enjoy the creative processes involved in developing a brand and developing a branding strategy to be invigorating. **as the next item in the bulleted list.**

FrontPage displays the new text next to the bullet as the next item in the bulleted list (Figure 1-41).

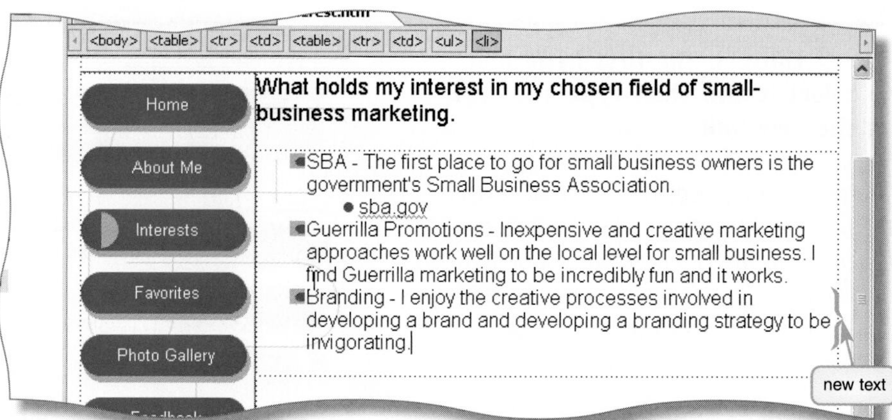

FIGURE 1-41

10

• **Press the ENTER key.**

• **Type** Electronic Marketing - Technologies such as the Internet and multimedia have opened up new avenues for marketing products and services. I delve into as much new material regarding electronic marketing as I can get my hands on.

FrontPage displays the new text next to the bullet as the last item in the bulleted list (Figure 1-42).

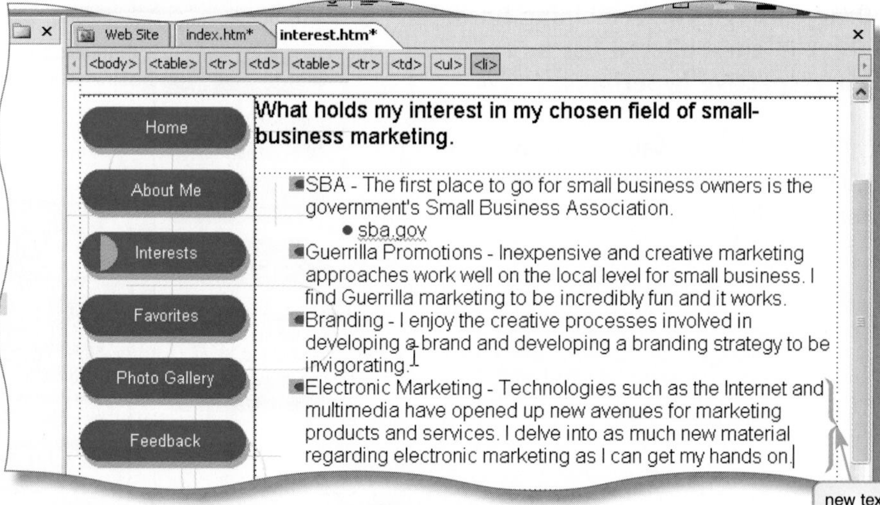

FIGURE 1-42

11

• **Select the acronym, SBA, just after the first bullet (Figure 1-43).**

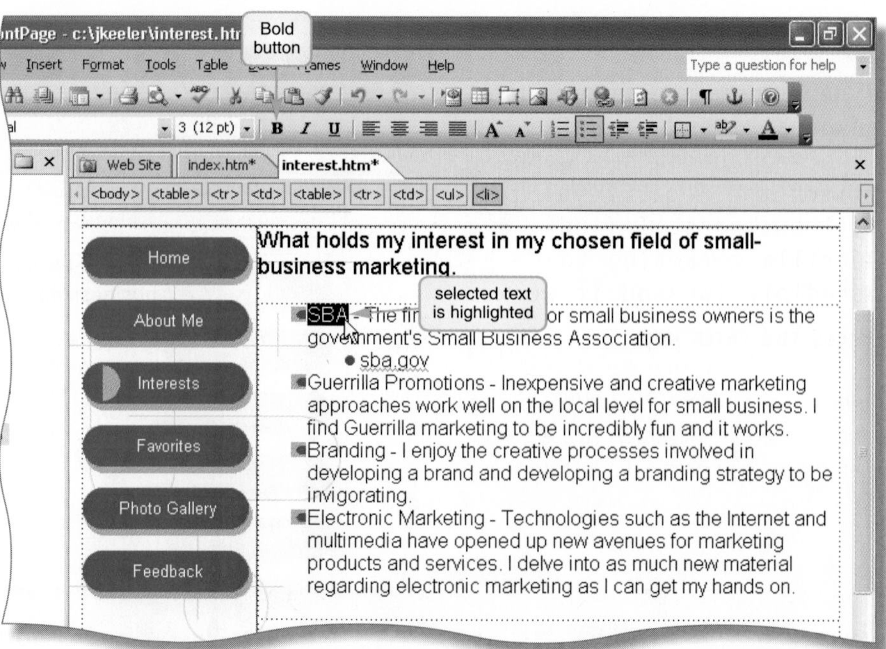

FIGURE 1-43

12

- **Click the Bold button on the Formatting toolbar.**
- **Select the phrase, Guerrilla Promotions, just after the second bullet.**

FrontPage displays the acronym SBA in bold text in the bulleted list (Figure 1-44). Guerilla Promotions is highlighted.

FIGURE 1-44

13

- **Repeat Step 12 to bold the words, Guerrilla Promotions, just after the second bullet; the word, Branding, just after the third bullet; and the words, Electronic Marketing, just after the fourth bullet.**

FrontPage displays the modified words in bold next to their respective bullets in the bulleted list (Figure 1-45).

FIGURE 1-45

The previous steps edited the items in a bulleted list, deleted some items, added two items to the list, and modified some text properties. As you add text and make edits to a Web page, FrontPage automatically generates HTML source code that defines how the Web page will display on the Web.

The heading of a Web page is used to set apart document or section titles. Web browsers recognize six levels of headings, Heading 1 through Heading 6. Heading 1 (H1) produces the largest text and Heading 6 (H6) the smallest. The Style list shown in Figure 1-35 on page FP 36 shows the six levels of headings among the styles that you can apply to text on a Web page. The first several styles listed in the style list include standard styles recognized by most browsers. The styles lower in the list represent special styles associated with the theme applied to the current Web page.

To see how your changes will be displayed on the Web, you can click the Preview button at the bottom of the document window to preview the Web page. Before previewing the page, however, you should save your work to retain any changes.

Saving a Web Page

FrontPage allows you to save a Web page to many different locations, including the current Web site, a different Web site, or a location on your computer or a network. The steps on the next page save the Web page to the current Web site.

To Save a Web Page

1

- **If necessary, scroll up and then click anywhere in the first paragraph of the Web page to unselect the last bold term.**

The asterisk in the interest.htm tab indicates that the page needs to be saved (Figure 1-46).

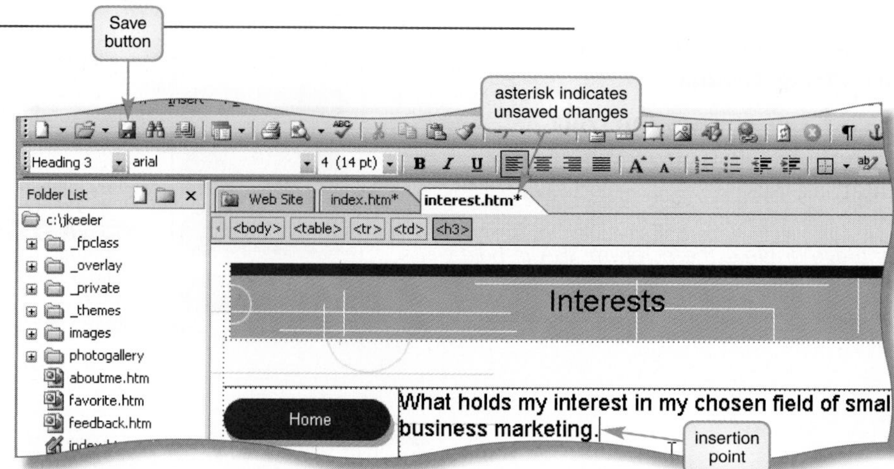

FIGURE 1-46

2

- **Click the Save button on the Standard toolbar.**

The Web page is saved in the jkeeler folder on drive C. Notice that the asterisk following the file name interest.htm in the tab has disappeared (Figure 1-47). The file name index.htm still has an asterisk, indicating that the page has changes that have not been saved yet.

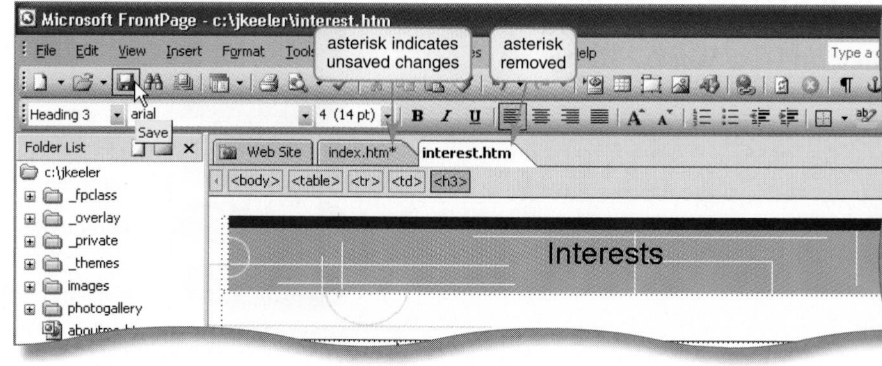

FIGURE 1-47

3

- **Click the index.htm tab at the top of the document window.**
- **Click the Save button on the Standard toolbar.**

Changes to the Home page are saved in the jkeeler folder on drive C (Figure 1-48).

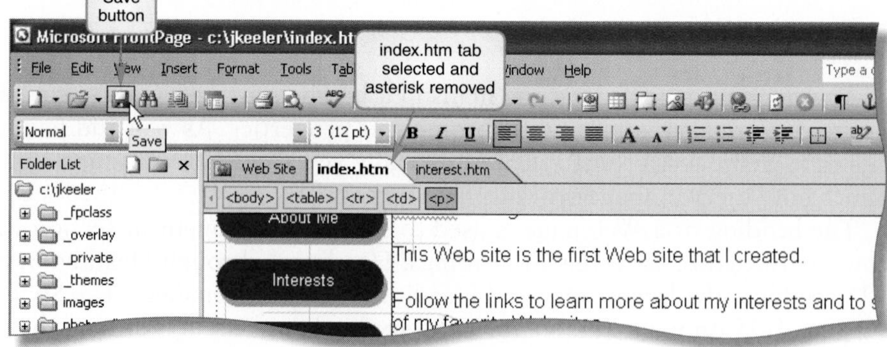

FIGURE 1-48

Other Ways

1. On File menu click Save
2. Press CTRL+S
3. In Voice Command mode, say "File, Save"
4. Press ALT+F, S

Clicking the Save button on the Standard toolbar saves the active page in HTML format, using the default file name, interest.htm. Because the Web page was opened from the current Web site, FrontPage saves the page without prompting you for a file name or file location. If you save a new Web page, clicking the Save button will cause FrontPage to display a Save As dialog box that prompts you to enter a file name. When you save a Web page, FrontPage also will prompt you to save any new images, sound files, or other objects to the same location as the page.

Once you have saved a Web page, you can preview how the page will display when viewed on the World Wide Web.

Previewing a Web Page in Preview View

Clicking the Preview button allows you to preview your page as it will display when viewed by a site visitor. Using Preview view is a useful method of quickly checking changes you make to a Web page. Preview view does not require you to save changes to the page before previewing, so if a change does not work as expected, you do not need to undo your change. Rather, you simply can close the page without saving it. You also can preview the page in Page view. The following steps show how to preview the page in Preview view.

To Preview a Web Page in Preview View

1

- **In Page view, click the Preview button at the bottom of the document window.**

FrontPage displays the Web page in Preview view in Page view (Figure 1-49). In Preview view, you can see how the page will display on the Web when viewed with a Web browser.

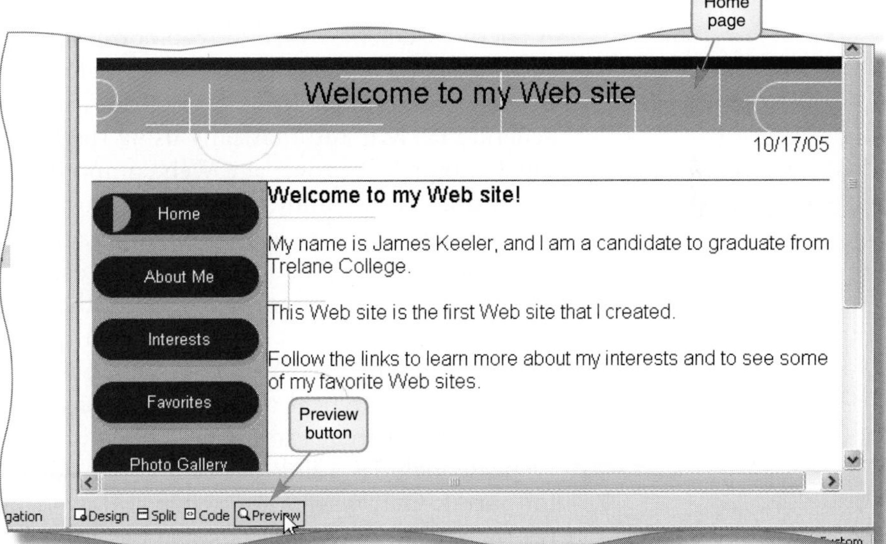

FIGURE 1-49

2

- **When you have finished viewing the Web page, click the interest.htm tab.**
- **When the interest.htm page appears, click the Preview button at the bottom of the document window.**

FrontPage displays the interest.htm Web page in Preview view (Figure 1-50).

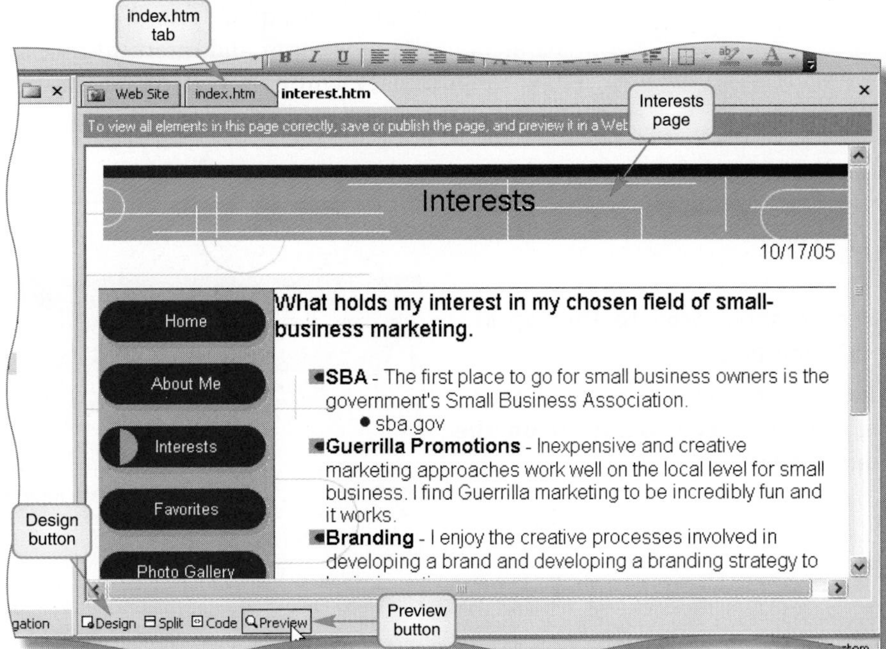

FIGURE 1-50

3

- **When you have finished viewing the Web page, click the index.htm tab.**
- **Click the Design button.**

The Web page appears in Design view in Page view. With FrontPage, most Web page development and design takes place in Design view of Page view.

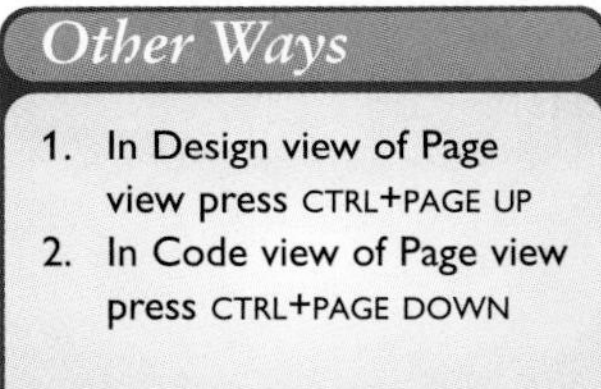

Other Ways

1. In Design view of Page view press CTRL+PAGE UP
2. In Code view of Page view press CTRL+PAGE DOWN

When you display a page in Preview view, a comment at the top of the document window may indicate that the page contains some elements that may need to be saved or published to preview correctly. Some elements, such as link bars, may not display properly until viewed on the Web. While it does not offer perfect viewing, using the Preview tab does eliminate the need to save a partially completed Web page continuously, preview it in your Web browser to test it, return to FrontPage to make changes, and so on.

Before you publish your Web site, you may want to add other elements to the page, such as a link bar or a graphical page banner. In FrontPage, you can add elements such as these using built-in FrontPage objects, called components.

Modifying Web Components

An active element, called a **Web component,** or just **component,** is a dynamic, built-in FrontPage object that is evaluated and executed when you save the page or, in some cases, when you display the page in a Web browser. Most Web components generate HTML automatically using the text, image files, and other items you supply. Examples of FrontPage Web components include a **Hit counter component** that keeps track of the number of visitors to a Web site and a **Photo Gallery component** that arranges a group of thumbnail images of photos on a page.

When working on a Web site, you easily can identify a component. Position the mouse pointer on the component and the shape of the pointer changes to look like a hand holding a written list.

A commonly used Web component is a link bar. In FrontPage, a **link bar** is a collection of graphical or textual buttons each containing a link to related Web pages in the current FrontPage Web site. The Capsules theme you applied to the Web site includes a link bar on the left side of the page. The link bar may be used for **parent-child navigation**, which allows you to move between the Home page (the parent) and the Interests page or Favorites page (the children), or for **same-level navigation**, which allows you to move back and forth between the Interests and Favorites pages. Another commonly used component is a **page banner**, which allows developers to add titles quickly to Web pages. The following steps modify the page banners in the index.htm and interest.htm pages. The page banner of the favorite.htm page will be updated later in this project.

To Modify a Page Banner

1

- **If necessary, scroll to the top of the Home page.**
- **Position the mouse pointer over the page banner component on the Home page.**

The mouse pointer changes shape to indicate that the designated item is a component (Figure 1-51).

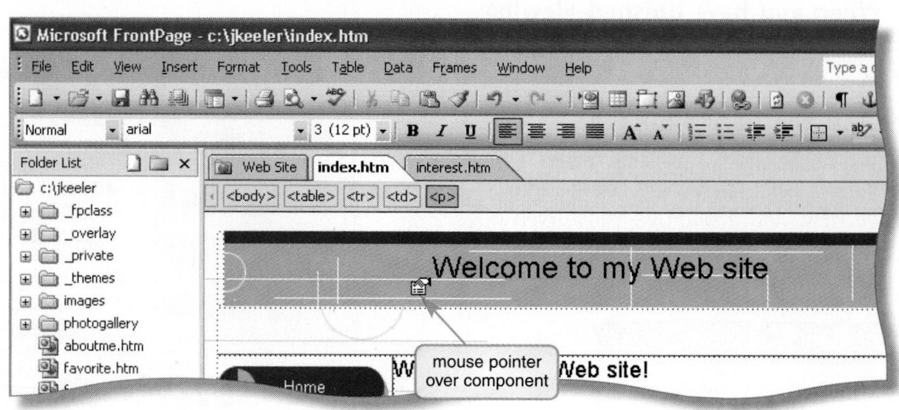

FIGURE 1-51

2

- **Right-click the page banner.**

FrontPage displays the shortcut menu (Figure 1-52).

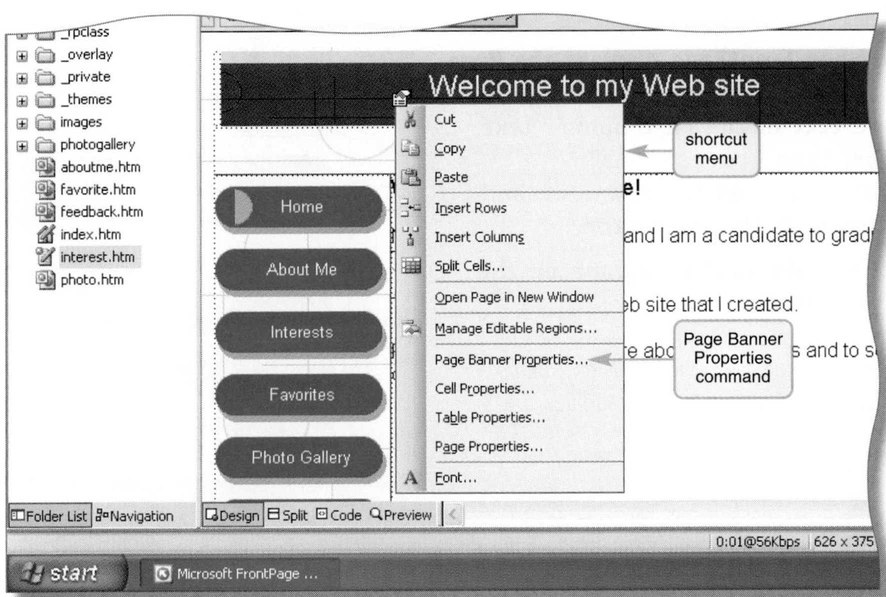

FIGURE 1-52

- **Click Page Banner Properties on the shortcut menu.**
- **When FrontPage displays the Page Banner Properties dialog box, select the text in the Page banner text box.**
- **Type** `Welcome to James Keeler's Web Site` **as the new text.**
- **If necessary, click Picture in the Properties area to select it.**

The new page banner text is entered (Figure 1-53).

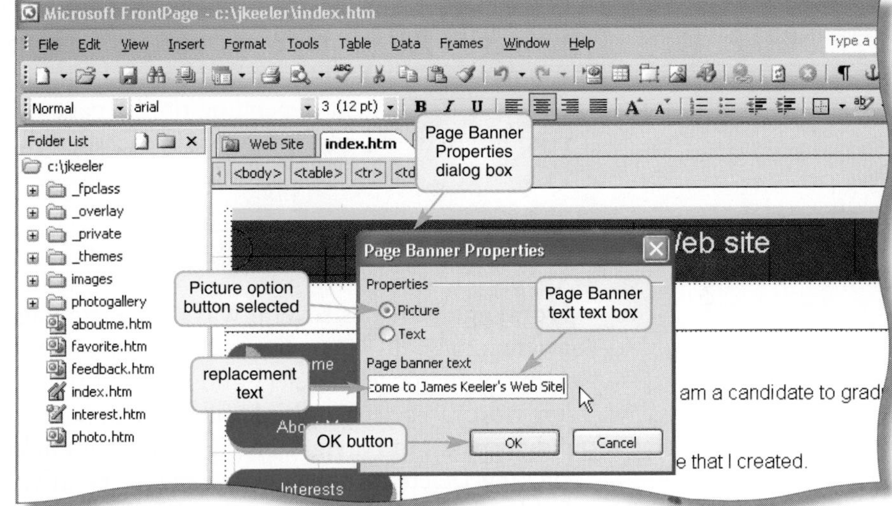

FIGURE 1-53

- **Click the OK button.**

FrontPage displays the modified page banner (Figure 1-54).

- **Click the interest.htm tab.**
- **Right-click the page banner.**
- **Click Page Banner Properties.**

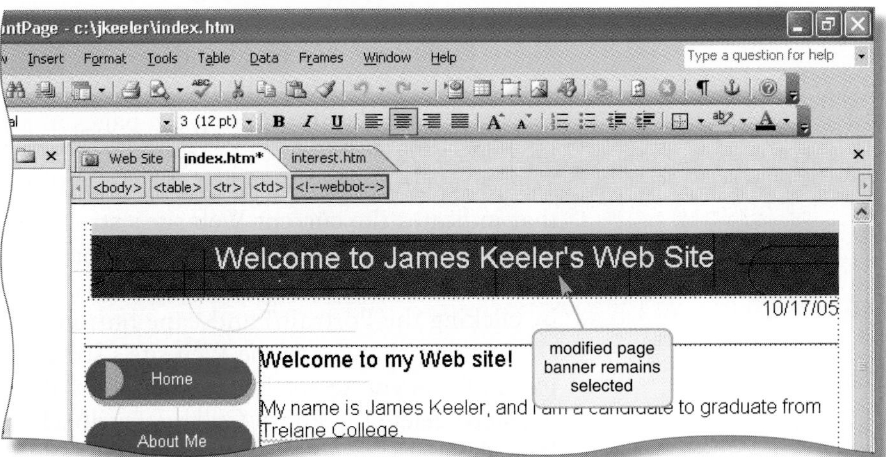

FIGURE 1-54

• **When FrontPage displays the Page Banner Properties dialog box, select the text in the Page banner text box, type** `Professional Interests` **as the new text, and then click the OK button.**

• **Click the first paragraph on the Web page.**

FrontPage displays the modified page banner and automatically modifies the text on the link button that links to the interest.htm page (Figure 1-55).

FIGURE 1-55

Other Ways

1. Double-click component to display Page Banner Properties dialog box

Different FrontPage components have different properties. The options that display in the component Properties dialog boxes vary, based on the properties of each specific component. Most FrontPage components change automatically in response to changes you make in the FrontPage Web site. The page banner just changed, for example, will display different text depending on the page title, on all pages where a page banner has been inserted and which have been included in your Web site navigation structure.

Deleting a Web Page from a Web Site

FrontPage provides several ways to delete pages from a current Web site. You can delete a page in Page view, for example, by selecting in the Folder List pane the file name of the page to delete and pressing the DELETE key. By holding down the CTRL key, you can select multiple files to delete at the same time. You also can delete individual pages in Navigation view by right-clicking the appropriate page icon and then clicking Delete on the shortcut menu. Finally, by selecting Navigation view in the Folder List pane, you can see a smaller Navigation pane in which you can select and delete individual pages. In this project, you will delete the Photo Gallery, Feedback, and About Me pages in Navigation view to create a Web site with three pages: a Home page, a Professional Interests page, and a Favorite Links page.

In FrontPage, **Navigation view** allows you to create, change, display, and print a Web site's structure and navigation. As previously discussed, a Web site's structure is the set of relationships among the pages in a FrontPage Web site; Navigation view includes a Navigation pane larger than the one displayed in the Folder List pane. This Navigation pane displays a graphical diagram similar to an organization chart that indicates the current Web site's structure. The Home page appears at the top (parent) level of the chart, and linked pages display at the lower (child) levels. You may choose to rotate the navigation structure to either a portrait or a landscape view by clicking the Portrait/Landscape button on the Navigation toolbar.

Making changes to the Web site's structure in Navigation view, such as deleting a page, allows you to see immediately how the change affects the structure. The following steps delete the Photo Gallery, Feedback, and About Me pages from the current Web site.

To Delete a Web Page from a Web Site

1

- **Click the Web Site tab.**
- **Click the Navigation button.**

FrontPage displays the current Web site in Navigation view, showing a graphical diagram of the Web site structure of the current Web site (Figure 1-56). A rectangular page icon represents each page in the Web site. The Folder List pane displays the file names for the pages in the Web site. The Navigation toolbar appears on the top-right of the Navigation pane. All buttons on the Formatting toolbar are dimmed, which indicates they currently are unavailable.

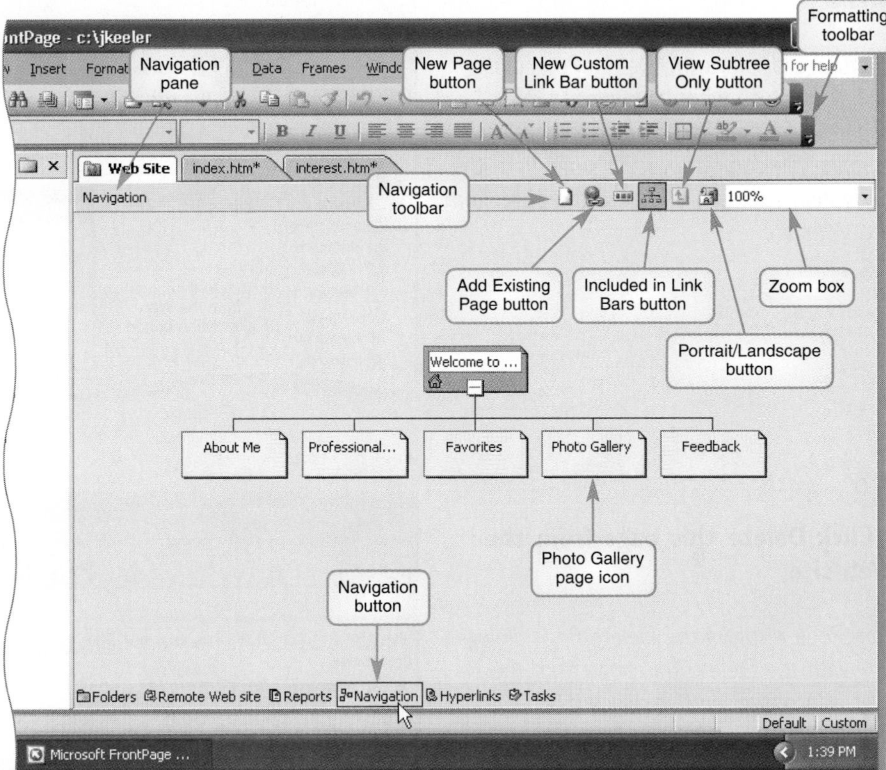

FIGURE 1-56

2

- **Right-click the Photo Gallery page icon.**

FrontPage displays a shortcut menu (Figure 1-57). The shortcut menu contains commands to manage individual pages within a FrontPage Web site.

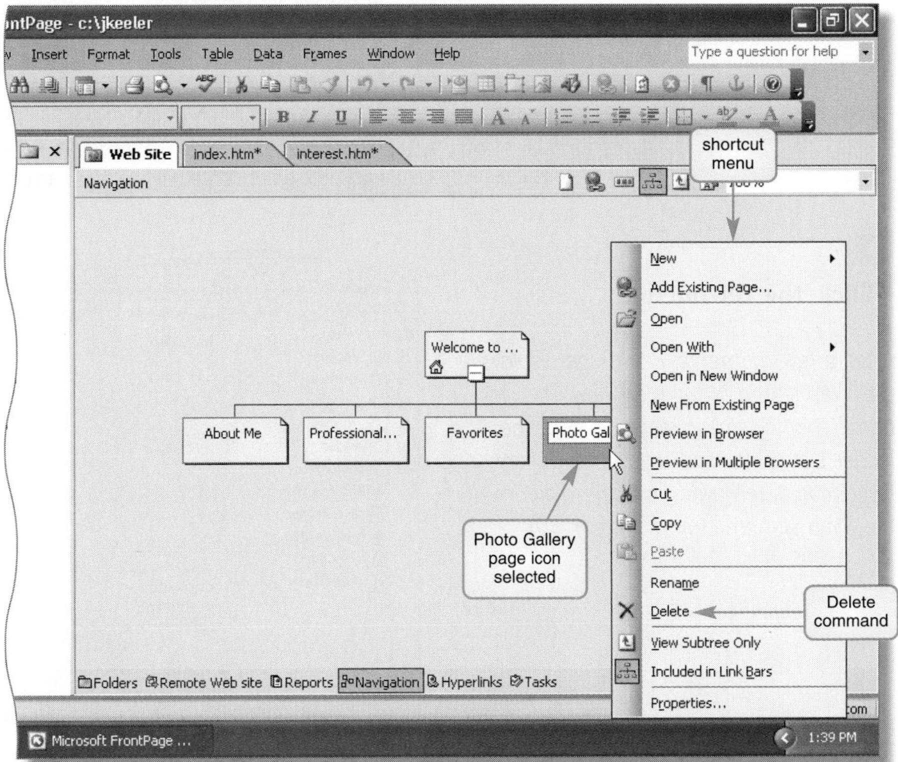

FIGURE 1-57

• **Click Delete on the shortcut menu.**

FrontPage displays the Delete Page dialog box, asking you what you want to do (Figure 1-58). The dialog box provides two options: you can remove this page from the navigation structure or delete the page from the Web site.

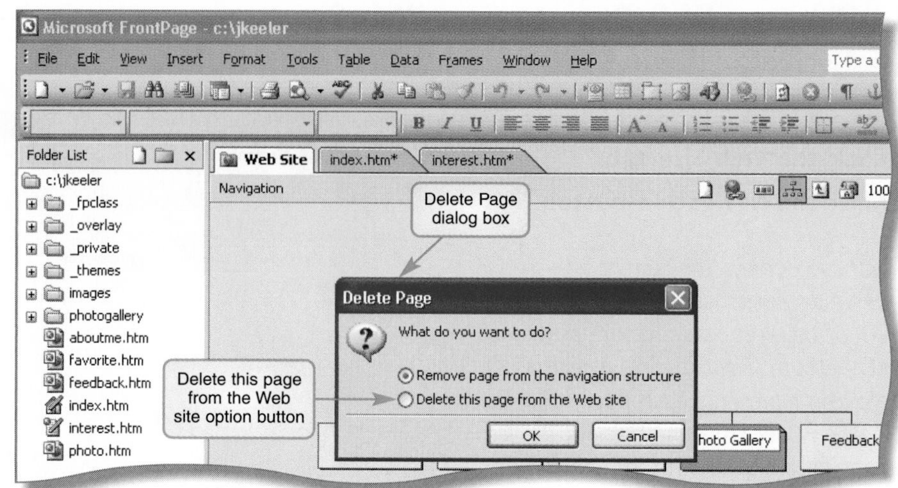

FIGURE 1-58

• **Click Delete this page from the Web site.**

FrontPage displays the Delete Page dialog box with the Delete this page from the Web site option button selected (Figure 1-59).

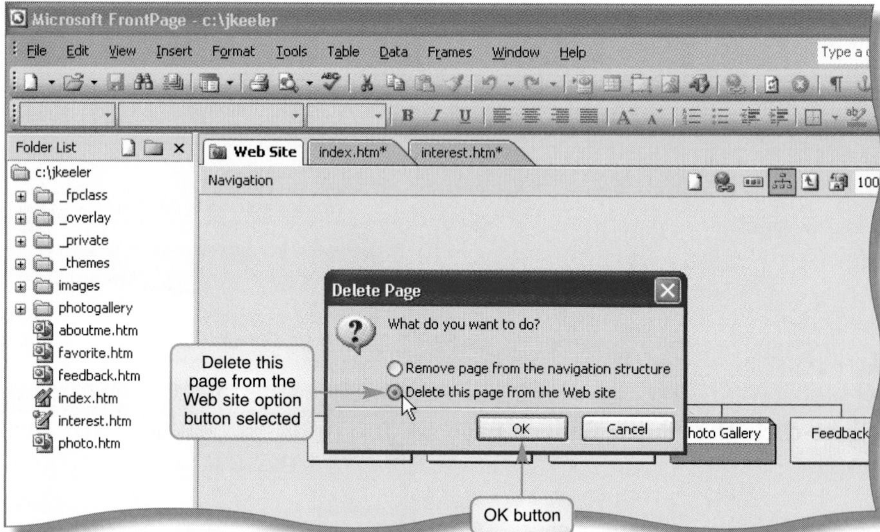

FIGURE 1-59

• **Click the OK button.**

After a few moments, FrontPage displays the Web site in Navigation view. The file name (photo.htm) is removed from the Folder List pane, and the Photo Gallery page icon is removed from the diagram of the Web site structure (Figure 1-60).

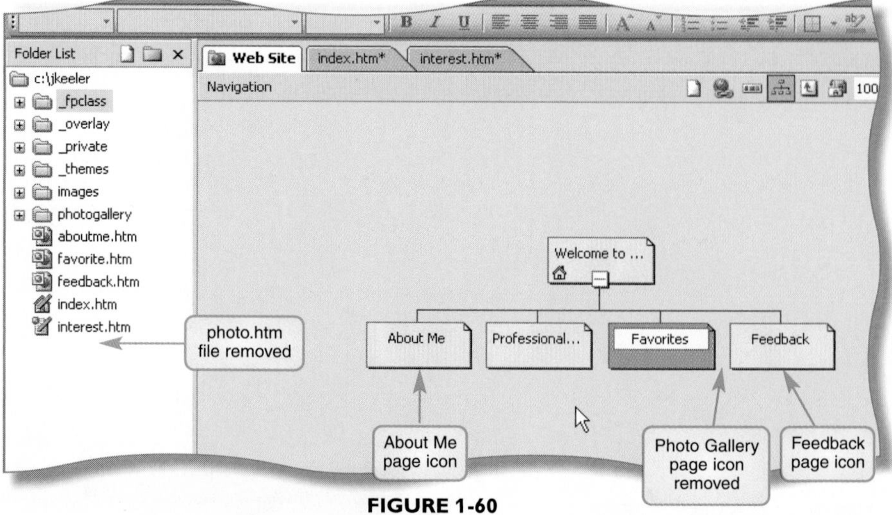

FIGURE 1-60

6

• **Repeat Steps 2 through 5 for the About Me page and the Feedback page.**

FrontPage displays the Web site in Navigation view with the About Me and the Feedback page icons removed. The file names aboutme.htm and feedback.htm are removed from the Folder List pane (Figure 1-61).

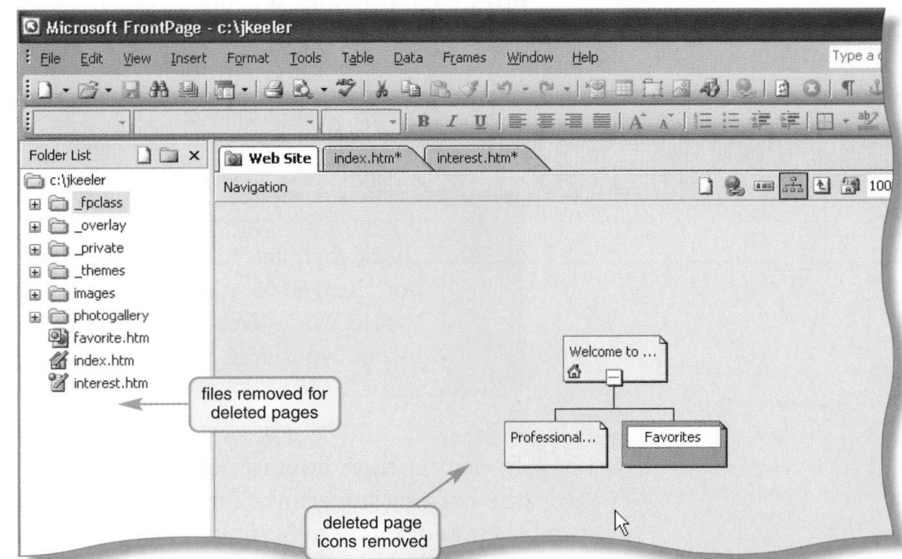

FIGURE 1-61

Other Ways

1. On Edit menu click Delete
2. Press ALT+E, O
3. Click file name in Folder List pane, press DELETE key
4. Right-click file name in Folder List pane, click Delete on shortcut menu
5. Click page icon in Navigation pane, press DELETE key
6. In Voice Command mode, say "Edit, Delete" or say "Delete"

If you choose to remove a Web page from the navigation structure, the Web page still exists on disk and can be linked to other pages. If you choose to delete a page from the Web site, as performed in the previous steps, the Web page is deleted from disk and removed from all link bars.

When you make changes to a Web site's navigation structure in Navigation view — for example, adding or deleting a page from the structure, or creating a new page — those changes are saved automatically when you switch to another view, such as Page view. You also can open files in Navigation view by double-clicking the page icon. Double-clicking the Favorites page icon, for example, will open the Favorites page so you can edit the final page in the current Web site.

Managing Hyperlinks on a Web Page

The final page to edit is the Favorites page, which contains hyperlinks to some of James Keeler's favorite Web sites. Because the Web site uses a template, the page already includes some placeholder hyperlinks. You can edit the links much like you edited the bulleted list on the Interests page.

Consider adding hyperlinks from key terms or phrases in the content on your page to other Web pages or external Web sites that include more information about the topic than you are willing to provide on your Web page.

Recall that a hyperlink, or link, is an area of the page that you click to instruct the browser to go to a location in a file or to request a file from a server. Often, a hyperlink consists of text or a picture that is associated with a URL that points to a page on the World Wide Web. Using FrontPage, you can create text or image links on your Web page. Adding a hyperlink to a Web page involves inserting text or an image on a Web page and then associating the text or image with a URL.

FrontPage provides several ways to associate a URL with the text or image on a Web page. You can type the URL, select a file within the current Web site or on your computer, or specify an e-mail link. You also can browse the Web to display the page to which you want to hyperlink; FrontPage automatically displays the URL in the appropriate text box.

> **Design Tip**
> If your Web page contains links to external Web sites, periodically check each link to be sure that the external Web site still exists or has not changed location. One of the more important elements of the World Wide Web is the ease of navigation to other sites through the use of hyperlinks.

To demonstrate how to manage hyperlinks on a Web page, the following steps edit the existing hyperlinks on the Favorites page and the Professional Interests page, and then add a new hyperlink. The page banner on the Favorites page also is changed to Favorite Links.

To Change a Hyperlink on a Web Page

1

- **Double-click the Favorites page icon in the Navigation pane.**

FrontPage displays the Favorites page in Page view (Figure 1-62). The vertical link bar consists of only three button links, because the Photo Gallery, About Me, and Feedback pages are deleted.

2

- **Right-click the page banner.**
- **Click Page Banner Properties.**
- **When FrontPage displays the Page Banner Properties dialog box, select the text in the Page banner text box, type** `Favorite Links` **as the new text, and then click the OK button.**

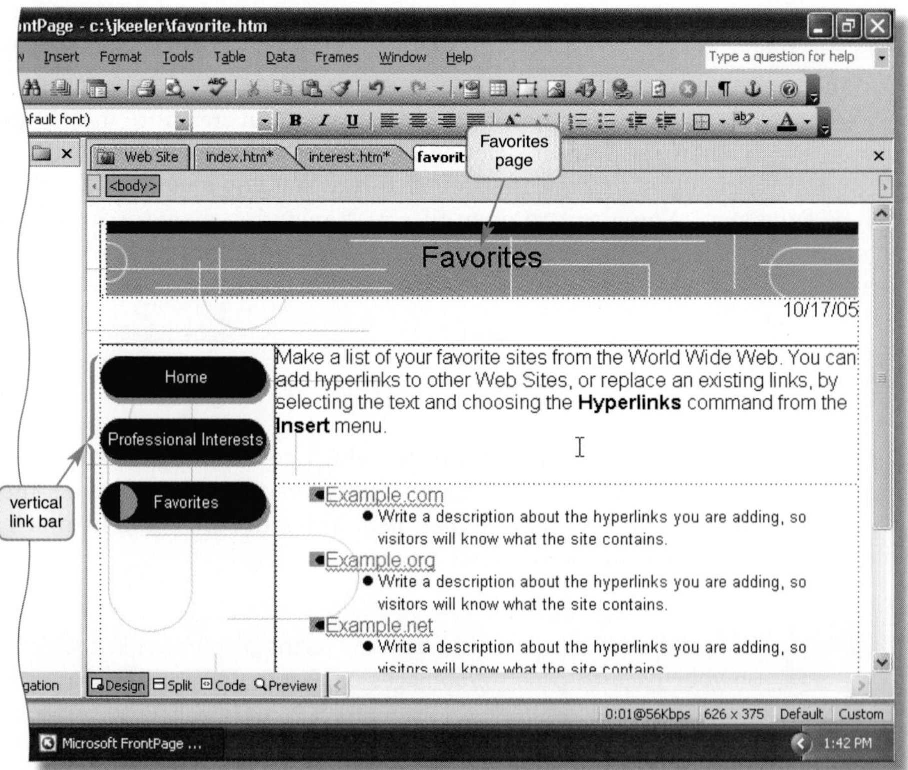

FIGURE 1-62

3

- **Select the first paragraph of text, which begins with, Make a list of your favorite sites.**
- **Click the Style box arrow on the Formatting toolbar and then click Heading 3.**
- **Type** `These are some of my favorite sites on the World Wide Web.`
- **Press the DELETE key once.**

The new text replaces the placeholder text and an extra blank line is deleted (Figure 1-63). The list entries are underlined, which identifies them as hyperlinks.

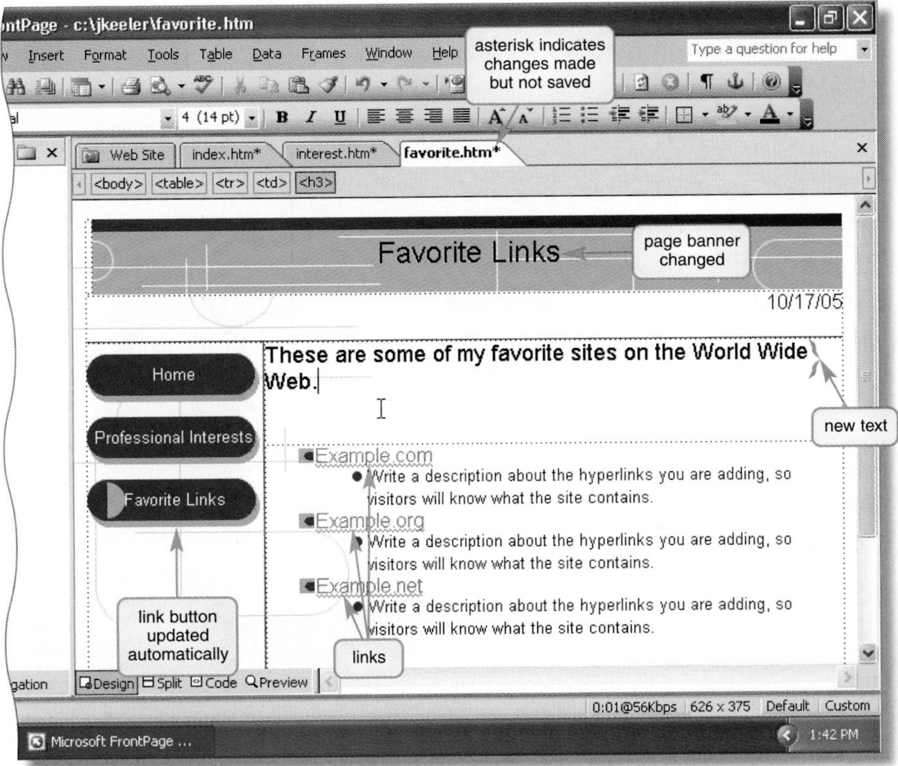

FIGURE 1-63

4

- **Right-click anywhere on the Example.com hyperlink.**

FrontPage displays a shortcut menu (Figure 1-64).

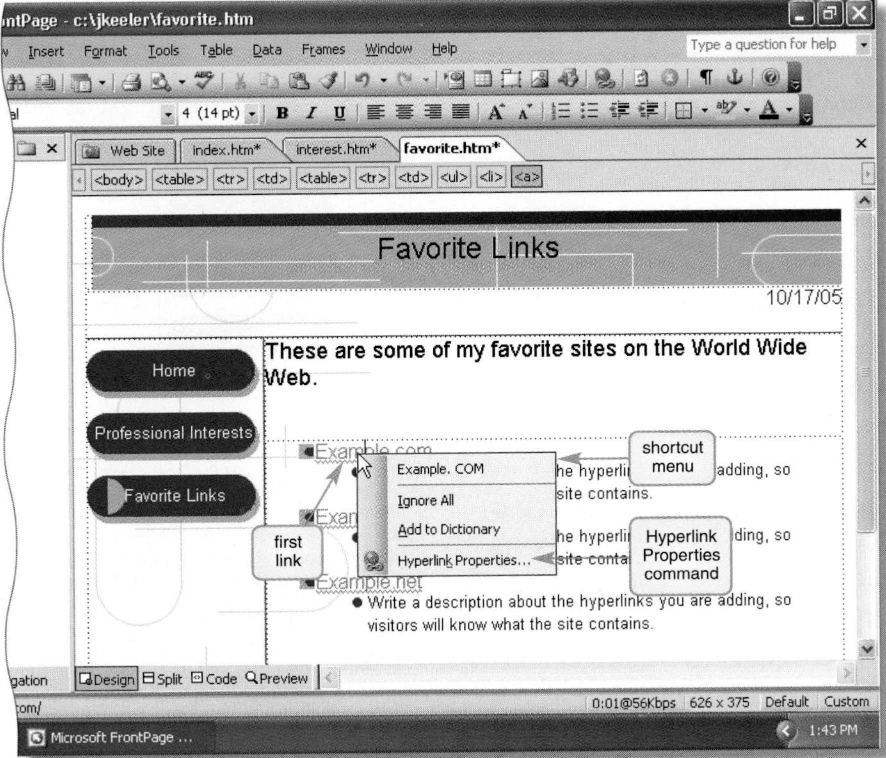

FIGURE 1-64

5

• **Click Hyperlink Properties on the shortcut menu.**

• **When FrontPage displays the Edit Hyperlink dialog box, select the text in the Text to display text box and then type** `Guerrilla Marketing Online` **as the new text.**

• **Select the text in the Address box and then type** `http://www.gmarketing.com/main.html` **as the new URL.**

FrontPage displays the Edit Hyperlink dialog box, with the new text to display for the hyperlink and the new URL, http://www.gmarketing.com/main.html, in the Address box (Figure 1-65). The Edit Hyperlink dialog box contains options that allow you to change the current URL and specify the URL of the Web resource to which you want to link.

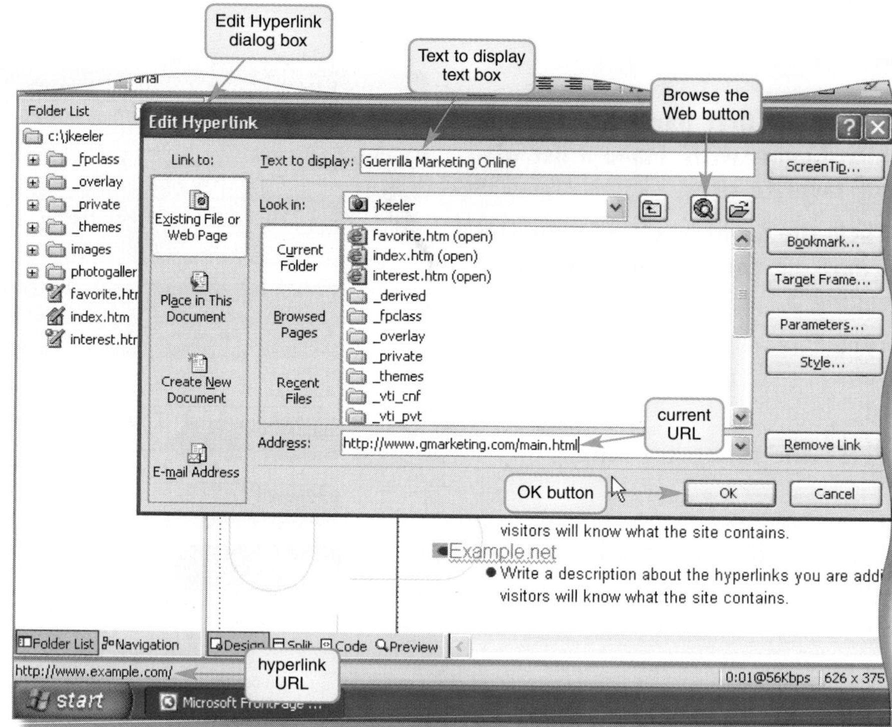

FIGURE 1-65

6

• **Click the OK button.**

FrontPage displays the new text for the hyperlink (Figure 1-66).

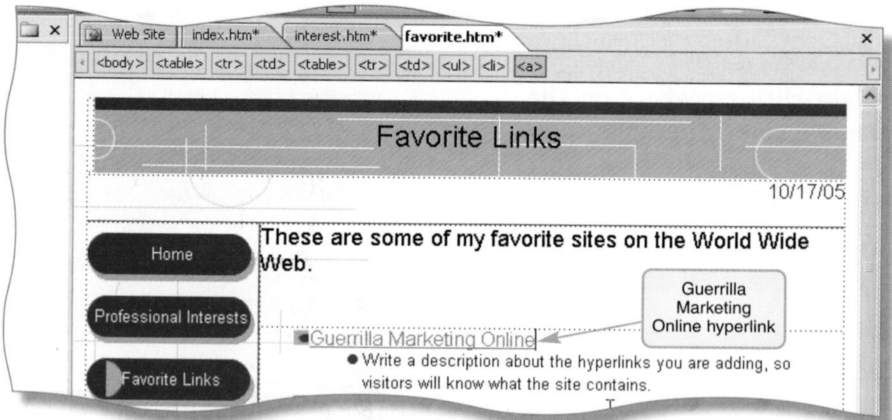

FIGURE 1-66

7

• **Below the first hyperlink, select the text that begins with, Write a description.**

• **Type** `Includes all kinds of resources to get you started on the fundamentals and advanced strategies involved with guerrilla marketing.`

The new text replaces the placeholder text (Figure 1-67).

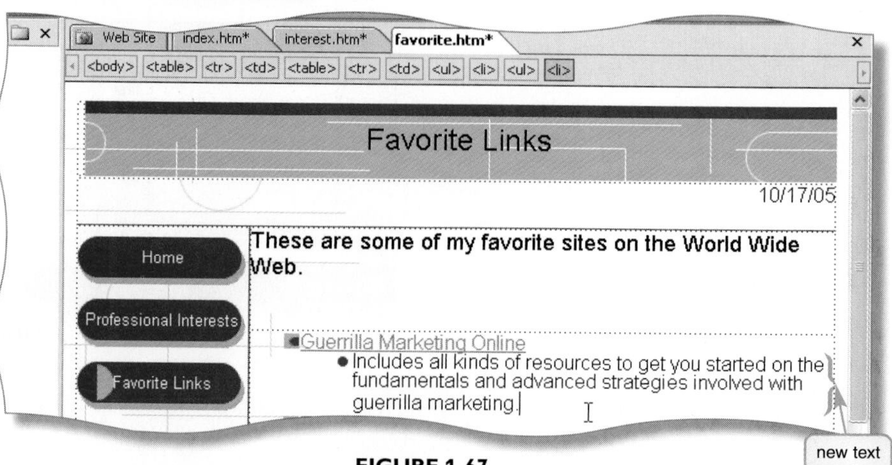

FIGURE 1-67

8

- **Repeat Steps 4 through 7 to replace the second hyperlink with the text** `Marketing Survival Kit` **that links to the URL** `http://www.marketingsurvivalkit.com` **and a description of** `A great place to find marketing resources for small businesses.`
- **Repeat Steps 4 through 7 to replace the third hyperlink with the text** `Guitar Pro` **that links to the URL** `http://www.guitarpro.com` **and a description of** `When I need to relax, I find a new song to play on my guitar. I cannot read music, but Guitar Pro helps me sound fantastic.`

The new text and hyperlinks replace the original placeholder text and hyperlinks (Figure 1-68).

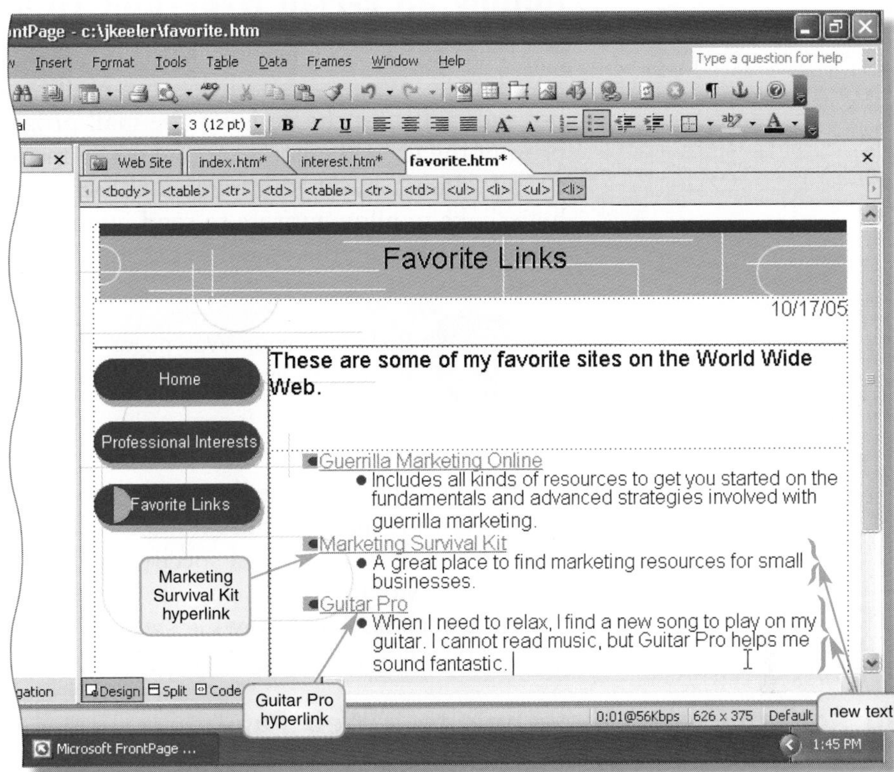

FIGURE 1-68

9

- **Click the Save button on the Standard toolbar to save changes.**
- **Click the interest.htm tab to view the Professional Interests page.**
- **Select the sba.gov link and then click the Insert Hyperlink button on the Standard toolbar.**
- **Type** `http://www.sba.gov` **as the address for the hyperlink.**

FrontPage displays the hyperlink (Figure 1-69).

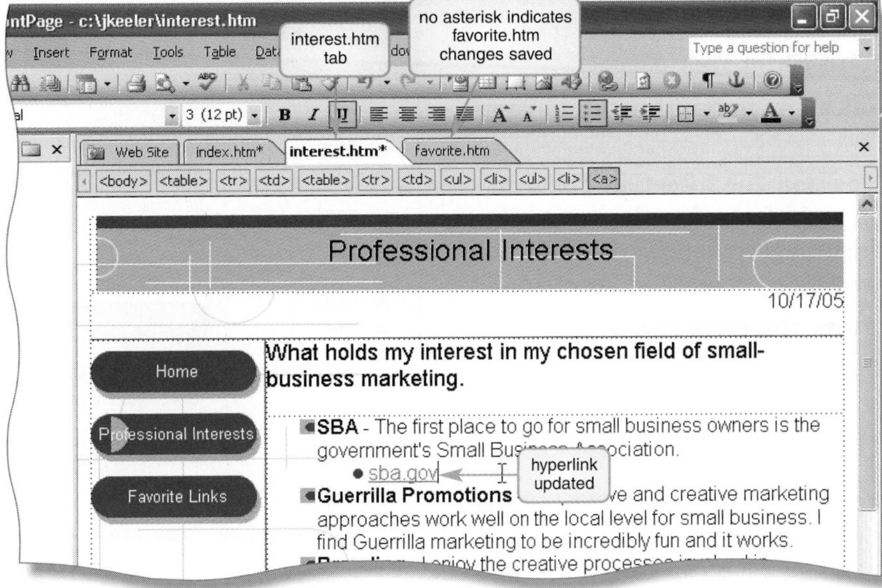

FIGURE 1-69

Other Ways

1. Click Insert Hyperlink button on Standard toolbar
2. Click hyperlink to select it, press CTRL+K
3. In Voice Command mode, say "Insert, Hyperlink"

You also can edit a URL by clicking the Browse the Web button in the Edit Hyperlink dialog box and browsing the Web to locate the Web resource to which you want to link. Once the desired page is displayed in the browser window, return to FrontPage with the browser still open and the browser automatically will return the URL of the current page to the Address box.

Adding an E-Mail Hyperlink to a Web Page

Using the Edit Hyperlink dialog box, you also can create e-mail hyperlinks on a Web page. When a user clicks an **e-mail hyperlink** on your Web page, the Web browser will start the designated e-mail program, such as Microsoft Outlook, and prompt the user to enter a message. The message automatically is addressed to the e-mail address specified in the e-mail hyperlink. Many Web pages include e-mail hyperlinks to allow visitors to send questions, comments, or requests via e-mail, simply by clicking the e-mail hyperlink.

Build into your Web pages simple and convenient ways for Web site visitors to interact with you or your organization.

E-mail hyperlinks use the **mailto protocol**, which is an Internet protocol used to send electronic mail. Because not all Web browsers and e-mail programs support the mailto protocol, you should specify the e-mail address somewhere on the Web page. The easiest way to do this is to use the e-mail address as the hyperlink text for the e-mail hyperlink. The following steps add an e-mail hyperlink to a Web page.

To Add an E-Mail Hyperlink to a Web Page

1

- **Click the Save button on the Standard toolbar to save the interest.htm Web page.**
- **Click the index.htm tab in Page view.**
- **Position the insertion point at the end of the fourth paragraph, which begins, Follow the links to learn more about.**
- **Press the ENTER key.**
- **Type** `You may send an e-mail to me at jkeeler@trelanecollege.edu.`

FrontPage displays the Home page in Page view (Figure 1-70). Using the e-mail address as the e-mail hyperlink text provides a quick way for users to identify your e-mail address.

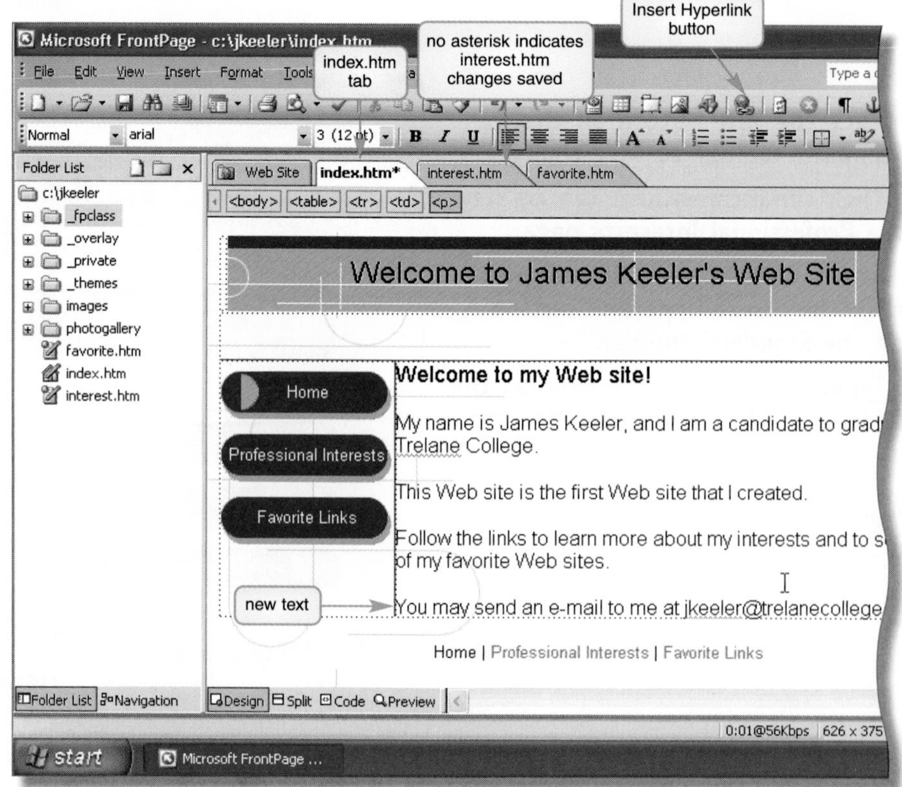

FIGURE 1-70

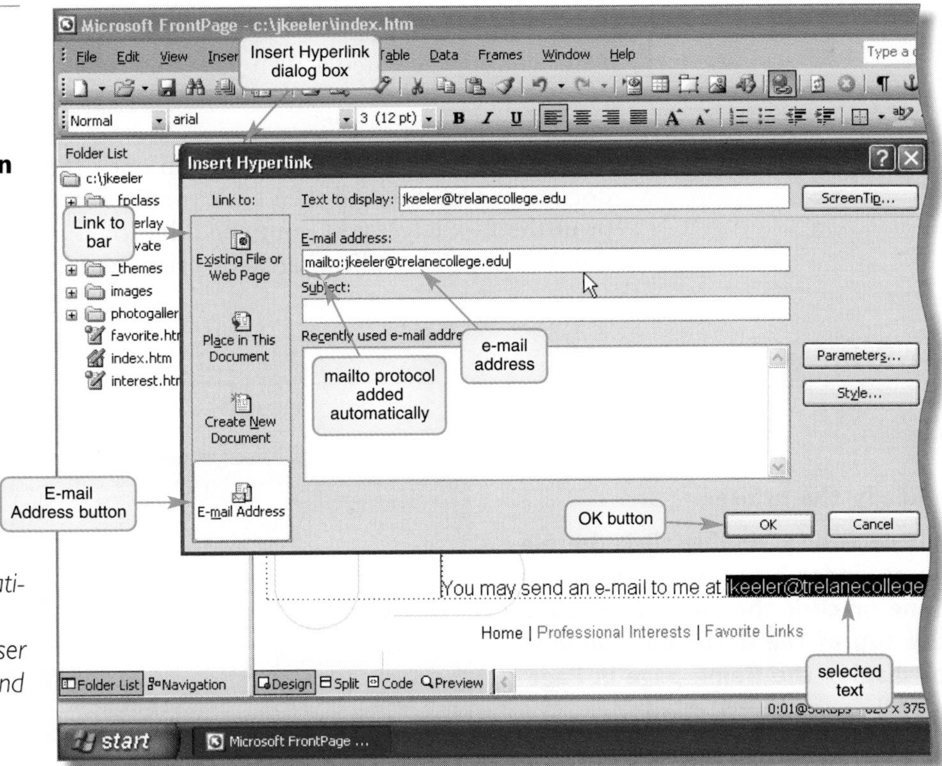

2

- **Drag through the text, jkeeler@trelanecollege.edu, to select it.**
- **Click the Insert Hyperlink button on the Standard toolbar.**
- **When FrontPage displays the Insert Hyperlink dialog box, click the E-mail Address button.**
- **Type** `jkeeler@trelanecollege.edu` **in the E-mail address text box.**

FrontPage displays the Insert Hyperlink dialog box and displays the complete e-mail hyperlink in the E-mail address text box (Figure 1-71). FrontPage automatically adds the mailto protocol before the e-mail address. It instructs the Web browser to start the designated e-mail program and address the message to the indicated e-mail address.

FIGURE 1-71

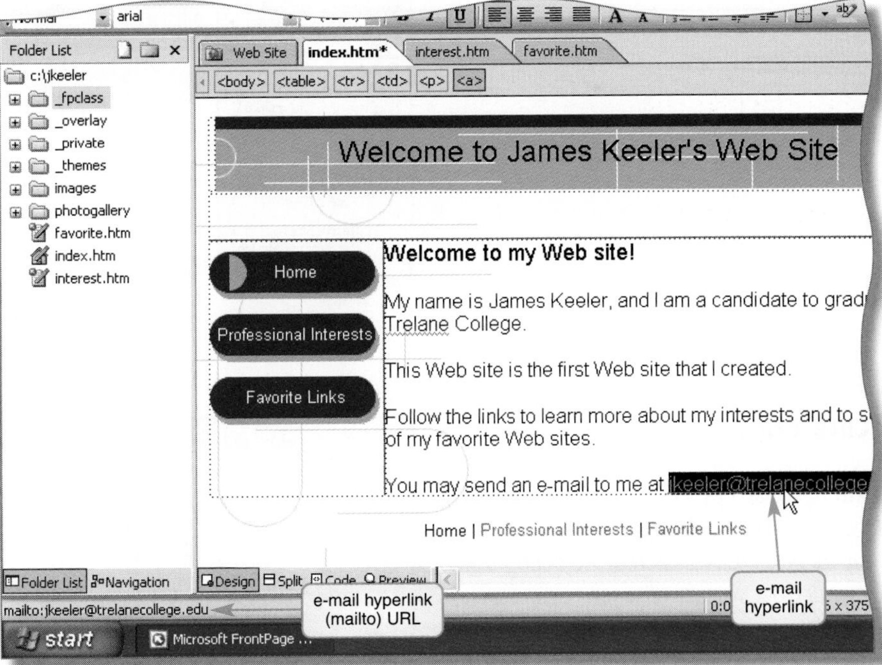

3

- **Click the OK button.**
- **Position the mouse pointer on the e-mail hyperlink.**

The e-mail hyperlink is displayed on the Home page. The URL for the e-mail hyperlink is displayed on the status bar, using the mailto protocol before the e-mail address, jkeeler@trelanecollege.edu (Figure 1-72).

4

- **Click the Save button on the Standard toolbar.**

The modified page is saved on disk as part of the current Web site. The asterisk in the tab of the modified page is removed.

FIGURE 1-72

You now have included two new types of text hyperlinks — hyperlinks to other Web pages on the Favorite Links and Professional Interests pages, and an e-mail hyperlink on the Home page.

Printing a Web Page Using FrontPage

After you have created a Web page and saved it on disk, you may want to print the page. A printed version of a document — in this case, a Web page — is called a **hard copy** or **printout**.

To print a page in Page view, you open the Web page so it is displayed in the document window and then click the Print button on the Standard toolbar. After you print the first page, you can open additional pages to print the remaining pages in the Web site. The following steps print the Home page of the personal Web site.

To Print a Web Page

1

- **Ready the printer.**
- **If necessary, double-click the file name, index.htm, in the Folder List pane or click the index.htm tab at the top of the document window to display the Home page in Page view.**
- **Click File on the menu bar.**

FrontPage displays the File menu (Figure 1-73).

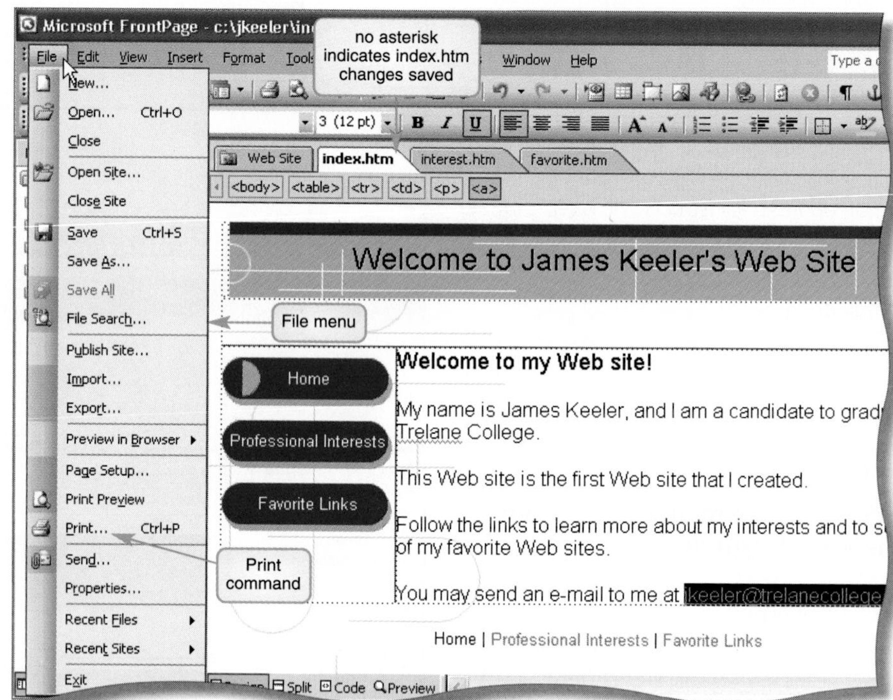

FIGURE 1-73

2

- **Click Print.**

FrontPage displays the Print dialog box (Figure 1-74). The All option button in the Print range area is selected, indicating that the entire document will print, regardless of its length.

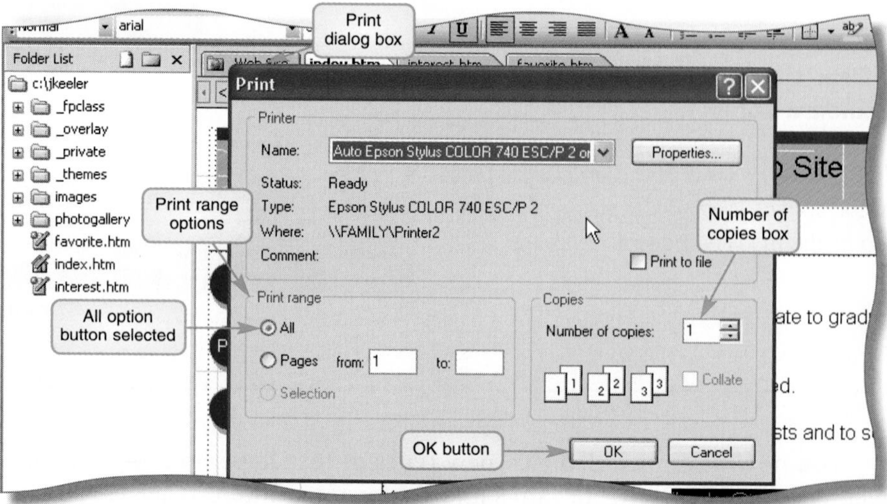

FIGURE 1-74

3

• **Click the OK button.**

The FrontPage message box is displayed momentarily, showing the status of the print process. The Home page is printed (Figure 1-75). FrontPage prints hyperlinks and images on the Web page as they are displayed in Design view of Page view.

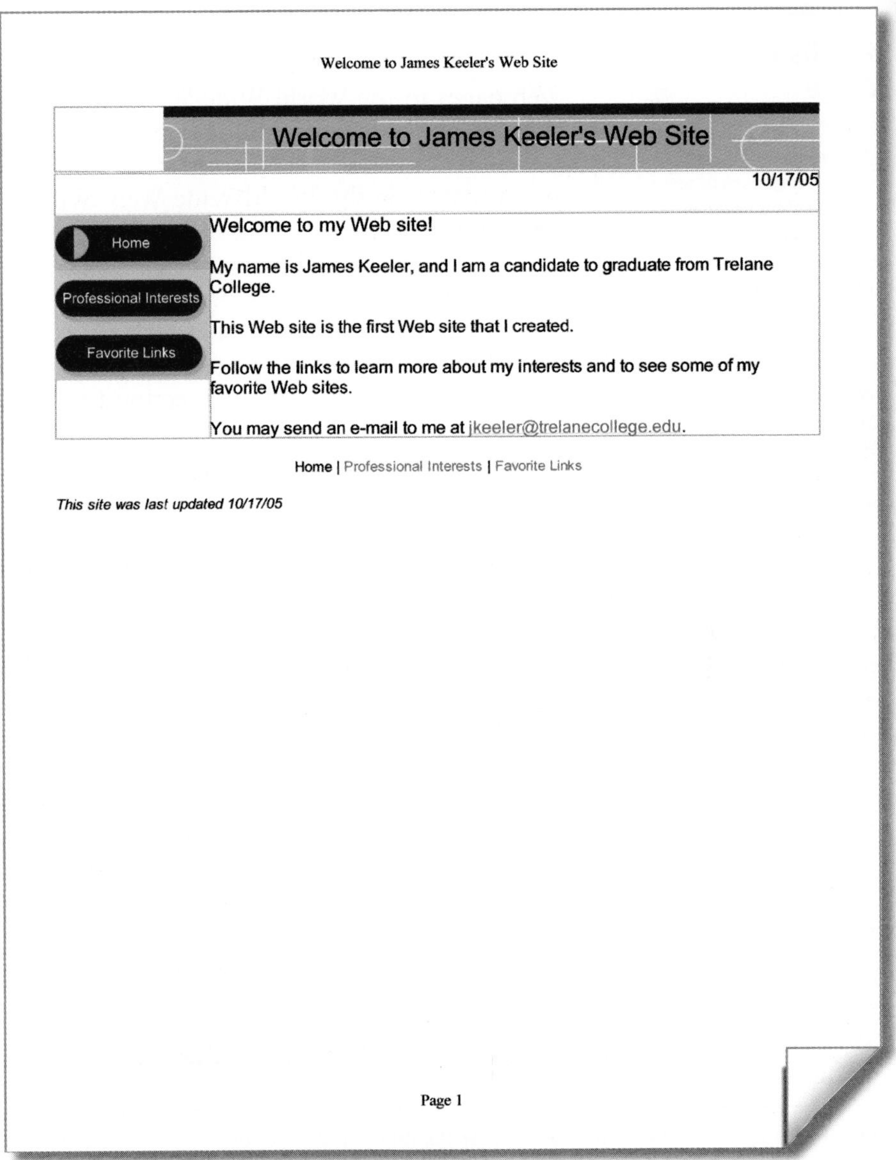

FIGURE 1-75

Other Ways

1. Click Print button on Standard toolbar
2. Press CTRL+P, click OK button
3. Press ALT+F, P
4. In Voice Command mode, say "File, Print"

The Print dialog box in Figure 1-74 provides many printing options. In the Print range area, the All option button instructs FrontPage to print the entire document. The Pages option button lets you print selected pages of a multiple-page document. The Number of copies box allows you to specify the number of copies to print.

To print the Web page as shown in Figure 1-75, the Web page must display in Page view Design view. FrontPage also allows you to print the HTML source for a home page. To print the HTML source for a home page, click the Code button to display the Web page in Code view and then print the page. You cannot, however, print a Web page in Page view Preview view. When the page appears in Preview view, FrontPage disables the printing function.

More About

Publishing a Web Page

FrontPage allows you to choose from options that allow you to publish only changed Web pages or publish all Web pages, which overwrites all previously published Web pages with the most recent versions. Click the Remote Web Site Properties button in Remote Web site view. When the Remote Web Site Properties dialog box is displayed, click the Publishing tab, and then select the desired options.

Publishing a FrontPage Web Site

If you have access to a Web server, FrontPage provides an easy way to publish your Web pages to the World Wide Web. As previously mentioned, **publishing a Web page** is the process of sending copies of Web pages, image files, multimedia files, and any folders to a Web server. Once saved on the Web server, the Web pages and files are available on the World Wide Web. With FrontPage, you use the Remote Web site view on the Web Site tab to manage the publishing process.

Many schools and companies provide a small amount of space on their Web servers for students and employees to publish personal Web pages and related files. For a modest fee, most Internet service providers (ISPs) also will provide space for publishing personal Web pages. An **Internet service provider** (**ISP**) is an organization that has a permanent connection to the Internet and provides temporary connections to individuals and companies for a fee. Some other Web-based services, such as Tripod, provide space on their Web servers for individuals to publish personal Web pages. To pay for the cost of maintaining these servers, these companies place advertisements at the top or bottom of your personal Web pages.

To publish your Web site to the World Wide Web, you will need access to an ISP or a Web server at your college, home, or office, preferably one with Microsoft FrontPage Server Extensions installed. Without FrontPage Server Extensions, some functionality in your Web site may not be available, such as most form handlers, hit counters, and other component features. With the server extensions, FrontPage will maintain your files and hyperlinks, comparing your local files with those on the server and updating any changes the next time you publish the Web site. Also, with the server extensions installed, FrontPage can publish your Web site using HTTP (Hypertext Transfer Protocol). Without the server extensions, your can publish your Web site using **FTP** (**File Transfer Protocol**), **WebDAV** (**Distributed Authoring and Versioning**), or a file system, such as the C: drive on your computer. Both HTTP and FTP are methods of transferring files over the Internet. Table 1-4 lists the types of servers to which FrontPage publishes Web sites and the situations in which you use each.

Table 1-4 Remote Web Server Types

TYPE	DESCRIPTION	WHEN TO USE
FrontPage or SharePoint Services	Allows for the greatest flexibility and functionality when publishing FrontPage Web sites. The server must be running FrontPage 2000 Server Extensions or later, or SharePoint Team Services 1.0 or later. To complete all of the projects in this book, you must publish the Web sites to a server that is running FrontPage Server Extensions 2002.	Used when a server supports the FrontPage Extensions or the server is a SharePoint server. When synchronizing files to a SharePoint server, some elements may not be transferred because SharePoint Team Services handles the functionality in a different manner than the FrontPage Server Extensions.
WebDAV	WebDAV (Distributed Authoring and Versioning) is a protocol for publishing and managing files on a Web server. WebDAV can allow you to work with a folder on a Web server in much the same way you work with a folder on a local hard disk. You must know the server name, user name, and password for the WebDAV site.	Used when a server does not support the FrontPage Server Extensions but does support WebDAV.
FTP	FTP (File Transfer Protocol) is a standard protocol for transferring files over the Web. You must know the server name, user name, and password for the FTP site.	Used when a server does not support the FrontPage Server Extensions but does support FTP.
File System	A local or networked folder.	Used to make backup copies of a Web site while maintaining the site's structure and allowing components to be used.

The following steps show how to publish a FrontPage Web site to a Web server that uses FrontPage Server Extensions. These steps work only if you have an account that grants you publishing rights on a Web server. To ensure that you publish your personal Web site successfully, be sure to substitute the URL of your own Web server when you see the URL, http://www.trelanecollege.edu/~jkeeler, in the following steps. If you do not know which URL or account information to use, see your instructor for more information. If you do not have access to a server, choose the File System Web server type in the steps below and then select an appropriate folder on your hard disk in which to publish the files. For information regarding publishing a FrontPage Web site to a file system, see Appendix C on page APP 23.

More About

Quick Reference

For more information, see the Quick Reference Summary at the back of this book, or visit the FrontPage 2003 Quick Reference Web page (scsite.com/fp2003/qr).

To Publish a FrontPage Web Site

1

- **If necessary, save any unsaved pages.**
- **Click the Publish Site button on the Standard toolbar.**
- **If necessary, click the Remote Web server type as directed by your instructor.**

FrontPage displays the Remote Web Site Properties dialog box and changes the view to Remote Web site on the Web Site tab (Figure 1-76). The Remote Web site location box displays the URL of the location where FrontPage will publish the current Web site.

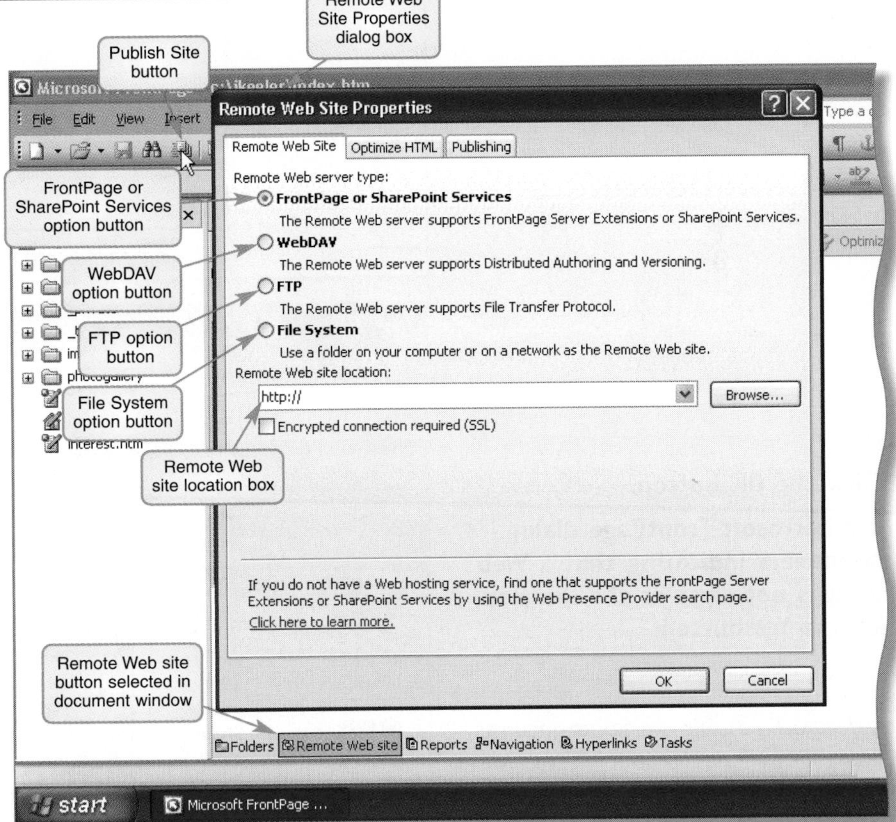

FIGURE 1-76

2

- **Click the Remote Web site location box and then type** `http://www.trelanecollege.edu/~jkeeler` **for the URL. Be sure to substitute your own URL when you see the URL, http://www.trelanecollege.edu/~jkeeler.**

FrontPage displays the destination URL in the Remote Web site location box (Figure 1-77).

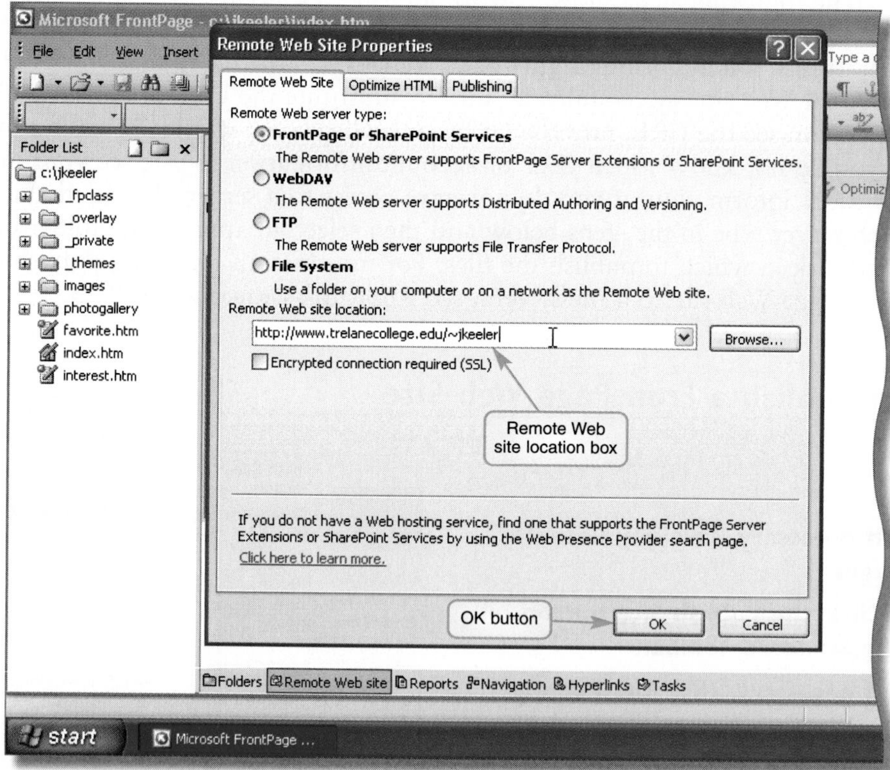

FIGURE 1-77

3

- **Click the OK button.**
- **If a Microsoft FrontPage dialog box appears indicating that a Web site does not exist at the location, click the Yes button.**

FrontPage displays the Connect to dialog box (Figure 1-78). This dialog box requests authorization information to allow you to publish your Web site to the server entered in the Remote Web site location box in Step 2.

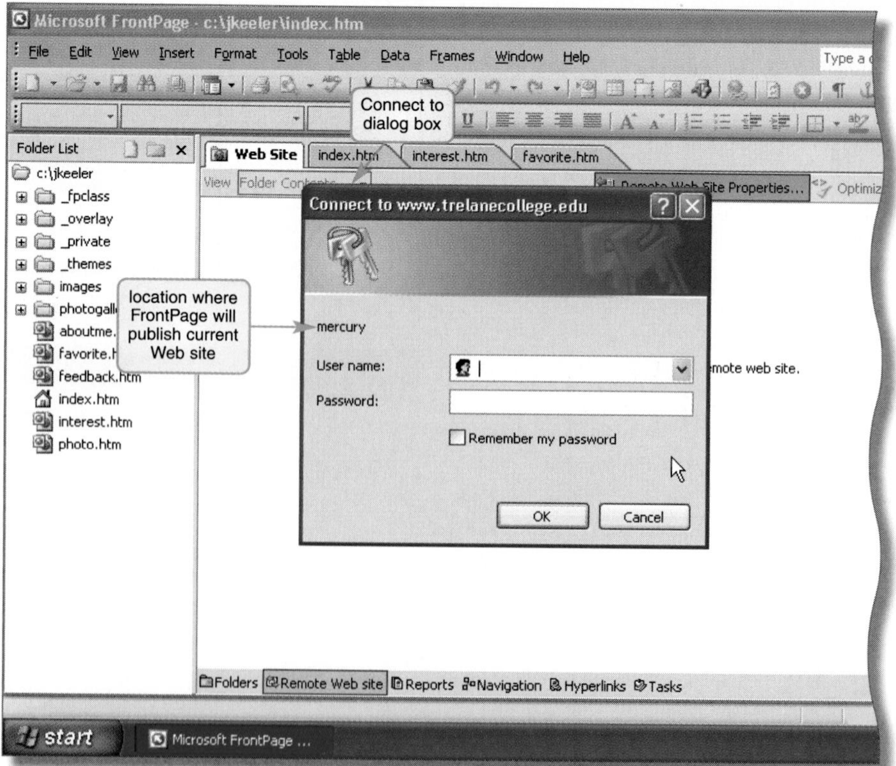

FIGURE 1-78

4

• **Type your name in the User name text box, and then type your password in the Password text box.**

FrontPage displays asterisks for the entered password for security purposes (Figure 1-79).

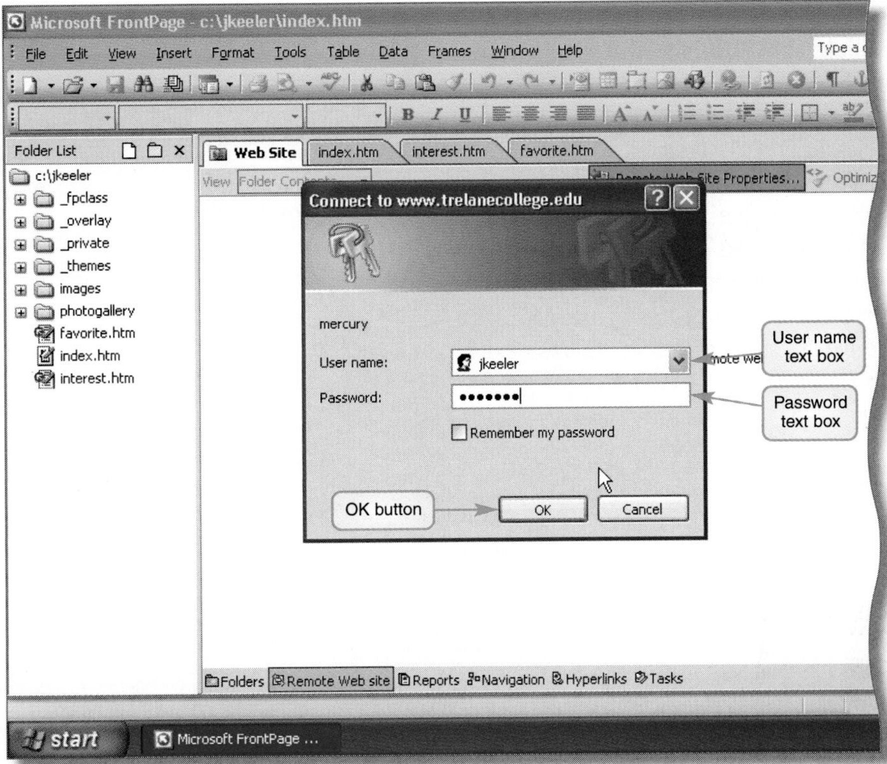

FIGURE 1-79

5

• **Click the OK button.**

The Web site appears in Remote Web site view and displays a list of files included in the current Web site and the Remote Web site (Figure 1-80). In Remote Web site view, FrontPage synchronizes files between this Web site and a remote site. Arrows indicate the files that are not yet on the remote Web site. The status area indicates the last time the Web site was published and includes hyperlinks and buttons that allow you to control the publishing process. If your Web server does not have the FrontPage Server Extensions installed, you will need to use another location to publish the Web site.

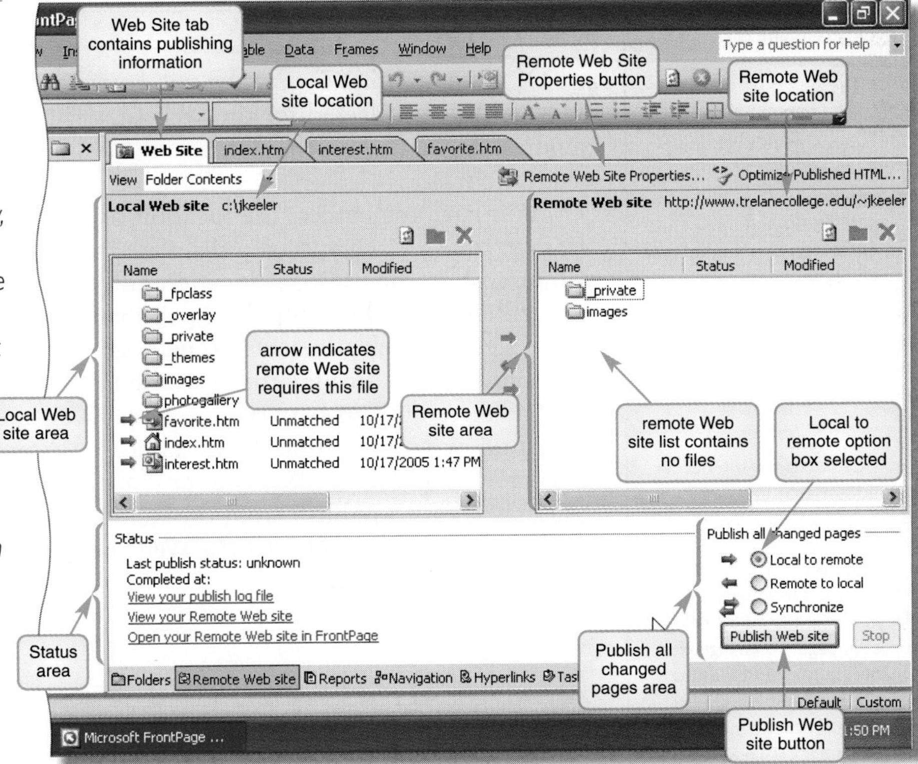

FIGURE 1-80

6

• **Click the Publish Web site button.**

A FrontPage dialog box displays a status bar indicating the progress of the file transfer. When FrontPage has finished publishing the Web site, the status area is updated and provides links you can click to view your published Web site and a log of files published. FrontPage updates the Remote Web site file list and removes the arrows next to the files in the Local Web site list (Figure 1-81).

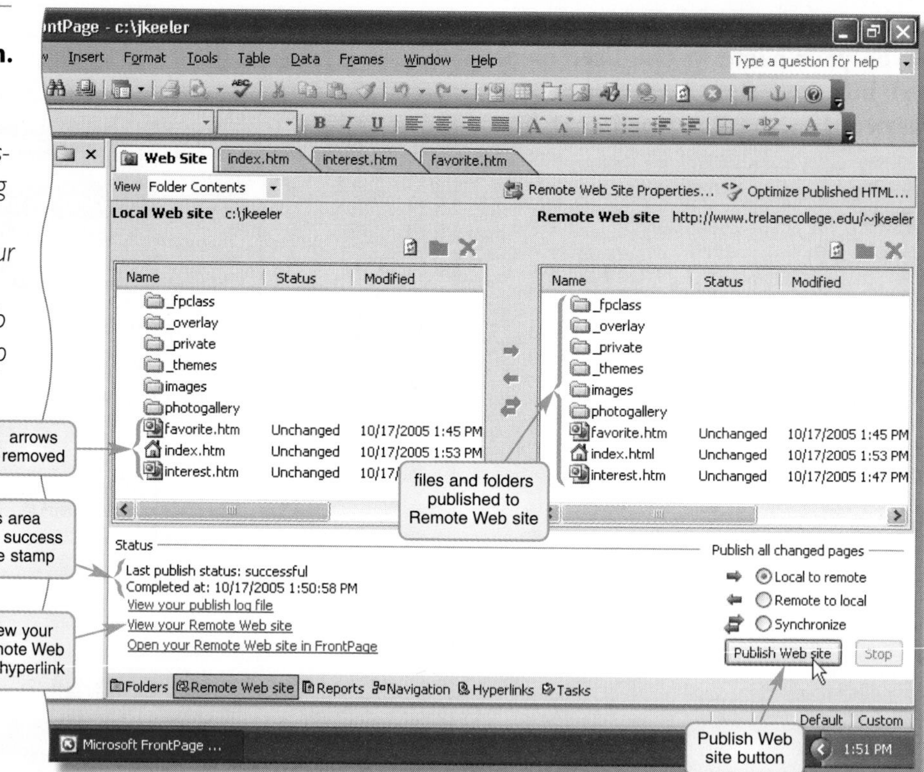

FIGURE 1-81

Other Ways

1. On File menu click Publish Site
2. Press ALT+F, U
3. Click Web Site tab at top of View pane, click Remote Web site button
4. In Voice Command mode, say "File, Publish Site"

Of the many files FrontPage will transfer, most of them contain elements in the Capsules theme selected for the Web site. The publishing process may take a few minutes, depending on the number of files in the Web site and the speed of your connection.

FrontPage remembers the location to which it published the current Web site, so the next time you click the Publish Site button on the Standard toolbar, FrontPage will publish to the previous location automatically. To publish to a new location or use a different method to publish, you can click the Remote Web Site Properties button in Remote Web site view. To manage the publishing process once the remote Web site is set up, display the Web site in Remote Web site view on the Web Site tab.

The three buttons between the Local Web site file list and the Remote Web site file list allow you to publish files selectively. You can publish files from the Local Web site to the Remote Web site or from the Remote Web site to the Local Web site. You may want to publish from the Remote Web site to the Local Web site if other FrontPage users are updating the Web site and you want to copy their changed files to your Local Web site.

Q&A

Q: Can I change the header and footer that print when FrontPage prints a Web page?

A: Yes. When you print a Web page, a header and footer are included by default on each page. To change the header or the footer, or to change the print margins, click File on the menu bar, and then click Page Setup before printing or previewing. When the Print Page Setup dialog box is displayed, you may enter new values for these items.

Testing the FrontPage Web Site

With the Web site published, it is available to anyone on the World Wide Web. You should take the time to test the newly published Web site to ensure the pages look as you expected and the hyperlinks work. The following steps test the personal Web site.

To Test a FrontPage Web Site

1

- **Click the View your Remote Web site link (see Figure 1-81).**

The Internet Explorer window is opened and displays the Home page of the Web site in the browser window (Figure 1-82).

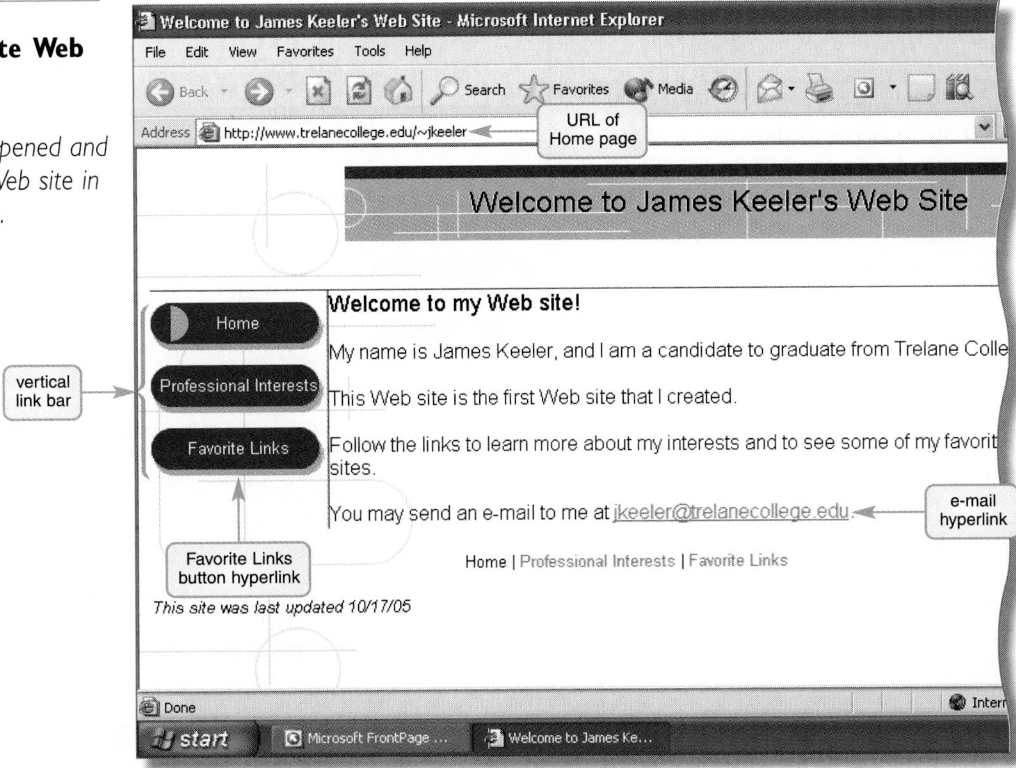

FIGURE 1-82

2

- **If necessary, click the Maximize button on the Internet Explorer title bar.**
- **Click the Favorite Links hyperlink on the link bar.**

The browser displays the Favorite Links page (Figure 1-83). The link bar displays the button hyperlink to the Favorite Links page in a different color than that of the button hyperlinks to the Home page and to the Professional Interests page. This is done to indicate that it links to the currently displayed page.

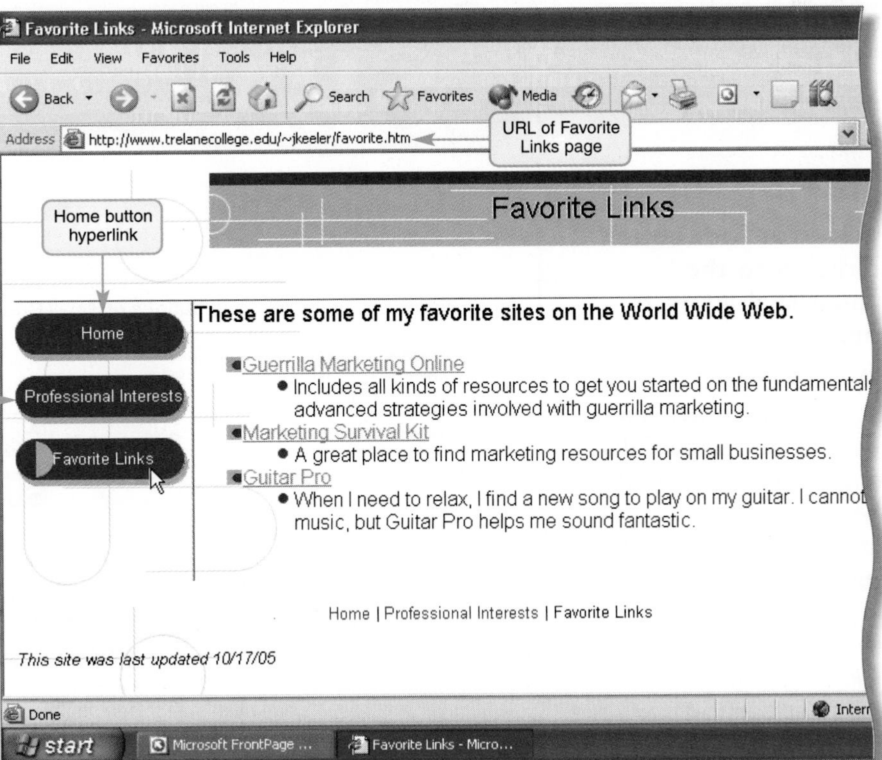

FIGURE 1-83

3

• **Click the Professional Interests button on the link bar.**

The browser displays the Professional Interests page (Figure 1-84). The link bar displays a button hyperlink to the Favorite Links page, which is located at the same level as the Professional Interests page. The link bar also includes a button hyperlink to the Home page, which is located at the parent level.

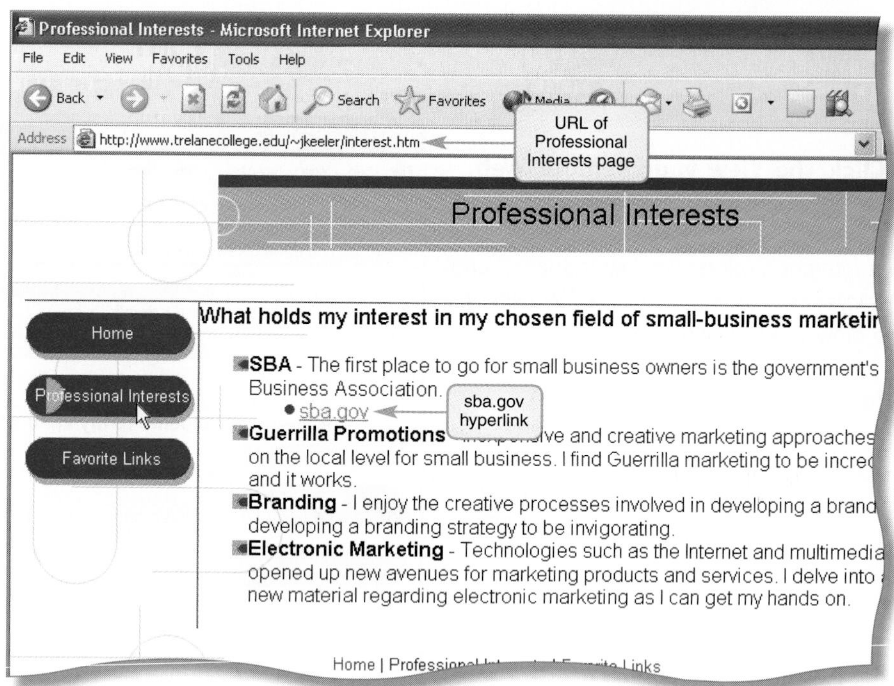

FIGURE 1-84

4

• **Click the sba.gov hyperlink.**

The Small Business Association home page is displayed in the Internet Explorer window (Figure 1-85).

5

• **Click the Back button to return to the Professional Interests page.**

• **After viewing all Web pages for accuracy and ensuring the hyperlinks function properly, click the Close button on the Internet Explorer title bar to close the browser.**

The Internet Explorer window is closed. The FrontPage window is displayed in Remote Web site view.

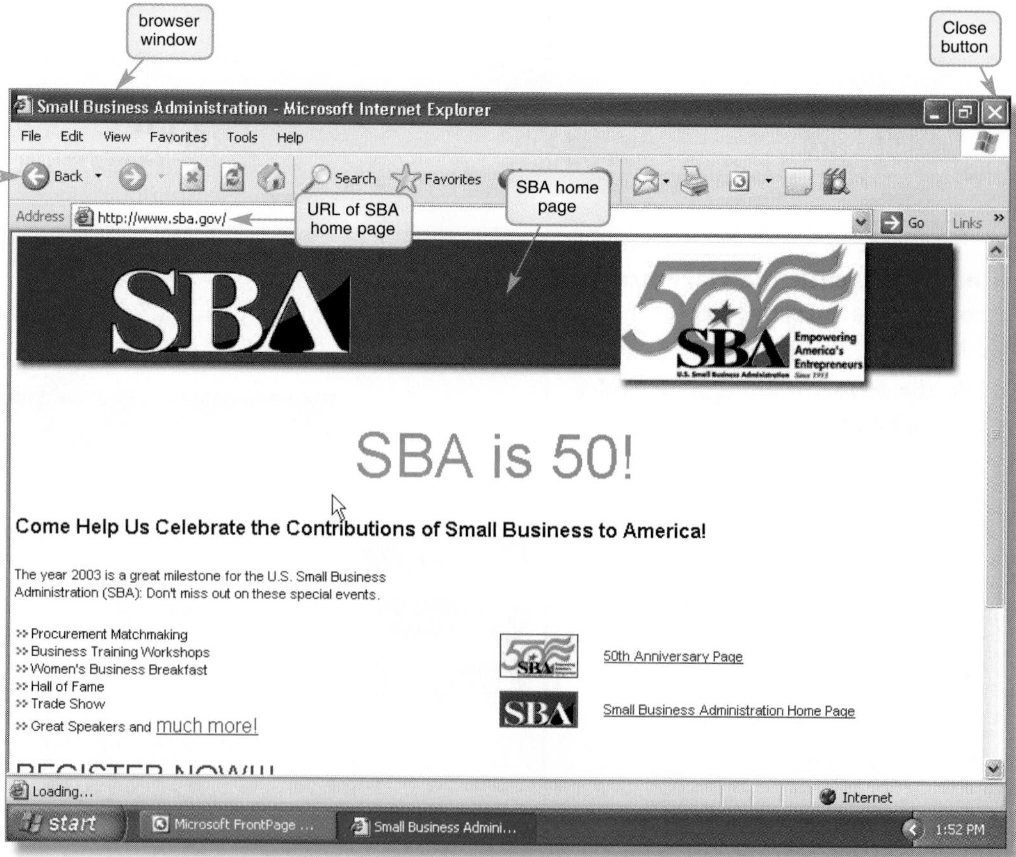

FIGURE 1-85

When you first link to your published Web site, the Web server displays a default Web page, called index.htm, in the URL in the Address bar. In your personal Web site, the Home page uses the file name, index.htm, and thus is displayed as the default page.

FrontPage Help System

At any time while you are using FrontPage, you can get answers to questions using the FrontPage Help system. You can activate the FrontPage Help system by using the Type a question for help box on the menu bar, by clicking the Microsoft Office FrontPage Help button on the Standard toolbar, or by clicking Help on the menu bar (Figure 1-86). Used properly, this form of online assistance can increase your productivity and reduce your frustrations by minimizing the time you spend learning how to use FrontPage.

The following section shows how to get answers to your questions using the Type a question for help box. Additional information on using the FrontPage Help system is available in Appendix A.

> *More About*
>
> **The FrontPage Help System**
>
> The best way to become familiar with the FrontPage Help system is to use it. Appendix A includes detailed information on the FrontPage Help system and exercises that will help you gain confidence in using it.

Obtaining Help Using the Type a Question for Help Box on the Menu Bar

The Type a question for help box on the right side of the menu bar lets you type free-form questions such as, how do I save or how do I create a template, phrases such as, save a Web page or print a Web page, or key terms such as, copy, save, or formatting. FrontPage responds by displaying a list of topics related to the question or terms you entered in the Search Results task pane. The following steps show how to use the Type a question for help box to obtain information on saving a Web page.

To Obtain Help Using the Type a Question for Help Box

1

• **Type** `save a Web page` **in the Type a question for help box on the right side of the menu bar (Figure 1-86).**

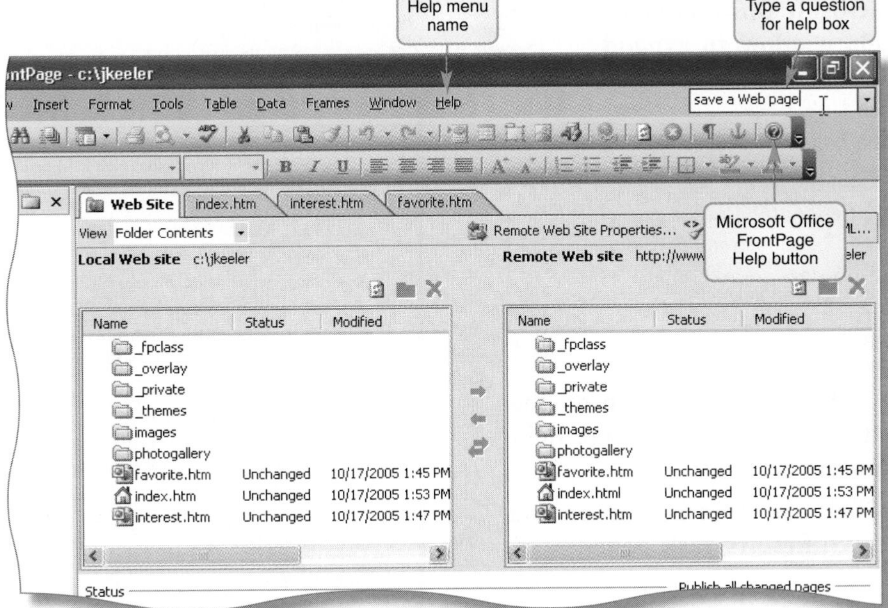

FIGURE 1-86

2

- **Press the ENTER key.**
- **If necessary, scroll the Search Results task pane, and then click the link Save a Web page.**

FrontPage displays the Search Results task pane with a list of topics related to the term, save. FrontPage found 30 search results (Figure 1-87). When the Save a Web page link is clicked, FrontPage opens the Microsoft Office FrontPage Help window on the right side of the screen.

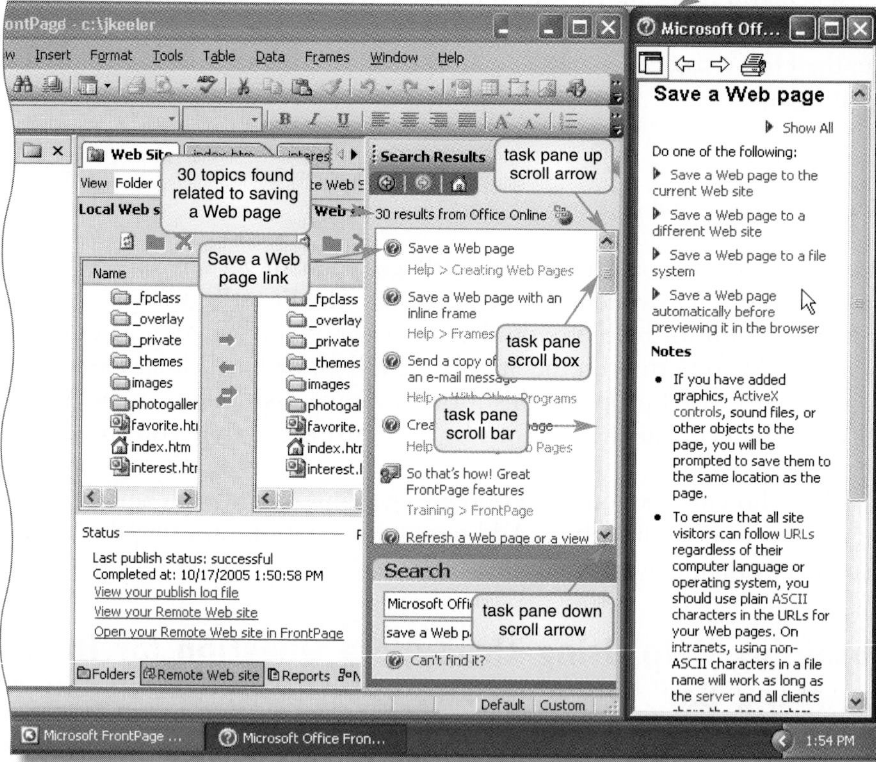

FIGURE 1-87

3

- **Double-click the Microsoft Office FrontPage Help title bar to maximize it.**
- **Click the Show All link on the right side of the Microsoft Office FrontPage Help window to expand the links in the window.**

FrontPage maximizes the Microsoft Office FrontPage Help window that provides Help information about saving Web pages to different locations (Figure 1-88). The links in the window are expanded.

4

- **Click the Close button on the Microsoft Office FrontPage Help window title bar.**
- **Click the Close button on the Search Results task pane.**

The Microsoft Office FrontPage Help window closes.

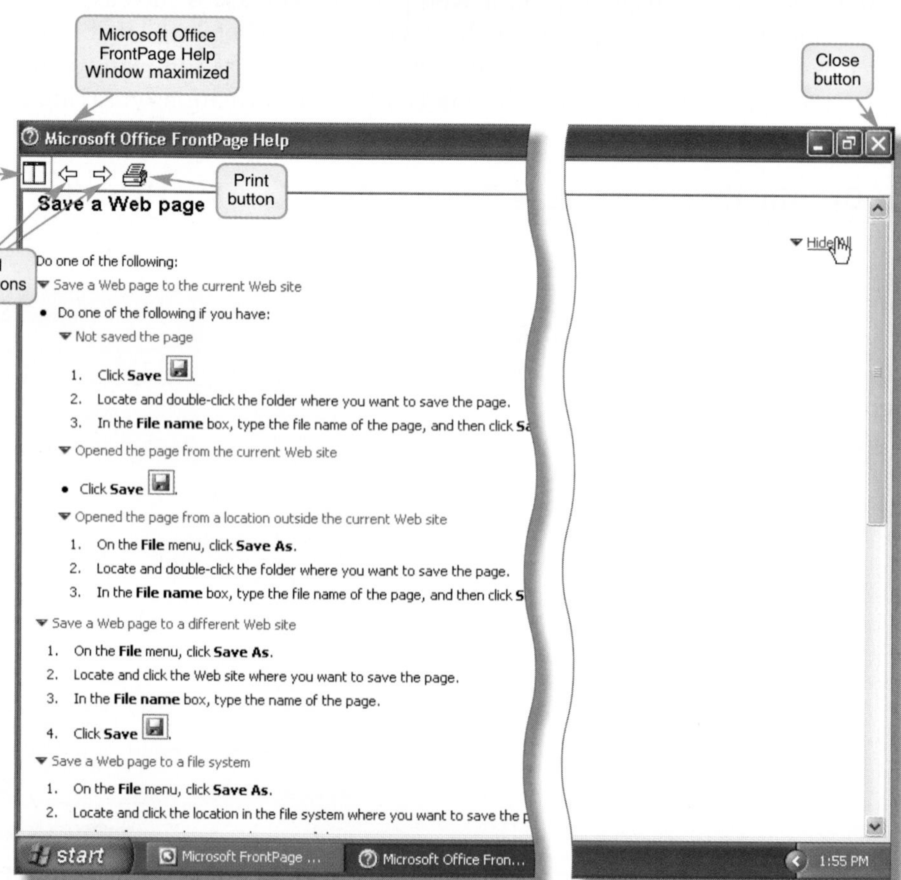

FIGURE 1-88

Use the buttons in the upper-left corner of the Microsoft Office FrontPage Help window (Figure 1-88) to navigate through the Help system, change the display, and print the contents of the window.

As you enter questions and terms in the Type a question for help box, FrontPage adds them to its list. Thus, if you click the Type a question for help box arrow (Figure 1-86 on page FP 63), FrontPage will display a list of previously entered questions and terms.

Closing a Web Site and Quitting FrontPage

After you have finished the steps in the project and developed and published the personal Web site, you can close the Web site and quit FrontPage. If you do not close a Web site in FrontPage, then FrontPage automatically opens the Web site the next time you start FrontPage. The following steps close the Web site and quit FrontPage.

More About

Quitting FrontPage 2003

Try to get into the habit of closing the last Web page or Web site that you work on before quitting FrontPage. FrontPage will open the last Web page or Web site that you worked on when it starts the next time.

To Close a Web Site and Quit FrontPage

1. **Click File on the menu bar and then click Close Site.**
2. **Click the Close button on the right side of the FrontPage title bar (see Figure 1-86).**
3. **If necessary, click the Close button on the Internet Explorer title bar to quit Internet Explorer.**

The FrontPage window closes.

Project Summary

With Project 1 complete, you developed a personal Web site and published the pages to a personal Web server. In this project, you learned the basic World Wide Web concepts, including HTML and the elements of a Web page. You learned how to create a FrontPage Web site using a template, to apply a theme, and to edit the placeholder text on a template page. You also learned how to modify a bulleted list, modify a FrontPage component, and edit and add hyperlinks on a Web page, including an e-mail hyperlink. You gained an understanding of how to use the view buttons in Page view to edit page layout and to preview a Web page. You learned how to use Navigation view to display and modify the structure of a Web site. Finally, you learned how to print Web pages, publish a Web site to the World Wide Web, and test the site in a browser.

What You Should Know

Having completed this project, you should be able to perform the tasks below. The tasks are listed in the same order they were presented in this project. For a list of the buttons, menus, toolbars, and commands introduced in this project, see the Quick Reference Summary at the back of this book and refer to the Page Number column.

1. Start and Customize FrontPage (FP 14)
2. Use a Template to Create a FrontPage Web Site (FP 21)
3. Open a Web Page in Page View (FP 24)
4. Apply a Theme to a FrontPage Web Site (FP 26)
5. Edit Text on a Web Page (FP 28)
6. Add New Text to a Web Page (FP 30)
7. Select Tables and Cells (FP 32)
8. Delete a Selected Table (FP 33)
9. Edit a Bulleted List (FP 35)
10. Save a Web Page (FP 40)
11. Preview a Web Page in Preview View (FP 41)
12. Modify a Page Banner (FP 42)
13. Delete a Web Page from a Web Site (FP 45)
14. Change a Hyperlink on a Web Page (FP 48)
15. Add an E-Mail Hyperlink to a Web Page (FP 52)
16. Print a Web Page (FP 54)
17. Publish a FrontPage Web Site (FP 57)
18. Test a FrontPage Web Site (FP 61)
19. Obtain Help Using the Type a Question for Help Box (FP 63)
20. Close a Web Site and Quit FrontPage (FP 65)

Learn It Online

Instructions: To complete the Learn It Online exercises, start your browser, click the Address bar, and then enter the Web address scsite.com/fp2003/learn. When the FrontPage 2003 Learn It Online page is displayed, follow the instructions in the exercises below. Each exercise has instructions for printing your results, either for your own records or for submission to your instructor.

1 Project Reinforcement TF, MC, and SA

Below FrontPage Project 1, click the Project Reinforcement link. Print the quiz by clicking Print on the File menu for each page. Answer each question.

2 Flash Cards

Below FrontPage Project 1, click the Flash Cards link and read the instructions. Type 20 (or a number specified by your instructor) in the Number of playing cards text box, type your name in the Enter your Name text box, and then click the Flip Card button. When the flash card is displayed, read the question and then click the ANSWER box arrow to select an answer. Flip through Flash Cards. If your score is 15 (75%) correct or greater, click Print on the File menu to print your results. If your score is less than 15 (75%) correct, then redo this exercise by clicking the Replay button.

3 Practice Test

Below FrontPage Project 1, click the Practice Test link. Answer each question, enter your first and last name at the bottom of the page, and then click the Grade Test button. When the graded practice test is displayed on your screen, click Print on the File menu to print a hard copy. Continue to take practice tests until you score 80% or better.

4 Who Wants To Be a Computer Genius?

Below FrontPage Project 1, click the Computer Genius link. Read the instructions, enter your first and last name at the bottom of the page, and then click the PLAY button. When your score is displayed, click the PRINT RESULTS link to print a hard copy.

5 Wheel of Terms

Below FrontPage Project 1, click the Wheel of Terms link. Read the instructions, and then enter your first and last name and your school name. Click the PLAY button. When your score is displayed, right-click the score and then click Print on the shortcut menu to print a hard copy.

6 Crossword Puzzle Challenge

Below FrontPage Project 1, click the Crossword Puzzle Challenge link. Read the instructions, and then enter your first and last name. Click the SUBMIT button. Work the crossword puzzle. When you are finished, click the Submit button. When the crossword puzzle is redisplayed, click the Print Puzzle button to print a hard copy.

7 Tips and Tricks

Below FrontPage Project 1, click the Tips and Tricks link. Click a topic that pertains to Project 1. Right-click the information and then click Print on the shortcut menu. Construct a brief example of what the information relates to in FrontPage to confirm you understand how to use the tip or trick.

8 Newsgroups

Below FrontPage Project 1, click the Newsgroups link. Click a topic that pertains to Project 1. Print three comments.

9 Expanding Your Horizons

Below FrontPage Project 1, click the Expanding Your Horizons link. Click a topic that pertains to Project 1. Print the information. Construct a brief example of what the information relates to in FrontPage to confirm you understand the contents of the article.

10 Search Sleuth

Below FrontPage Project 1, click the Search Sleuth link. To search for a term that pertains to this project, select a term below the Project 1 title and then use the Google search engine at google.com (or any major search engine) to display and print two Web pages that present information on the term.

11 FrontPage Online Training

Below FrontPage Project 1, click the FrontPage Online Training link. When your browser displays the Microsoft Office Online Web page, click the FrontPage link. Click one of the FrontPage courses that covers one or more of the objectives listed at the beginning of the project on page FP 4. Print the first page of the course before stepping through it.

12 Office Marketplace

Below FrontPage Project 1, click the Office Marketplace link. When your browser displays the Microsoft Office Online Web page, click the Office Marketplace link. Click a topic that relates to FrontPage. Print the first page.

Apply Your Knowledge

1 Modifying a Corporate Presence Web Site

Instructions: Start FrontPage. Open the file, index.htm, from the Project1/Apply1-1Ship-It-Here folder on the Data Disk. See the inside back cover of this book for instructions for downloading the Data Disk or see your instructor for information on accessing the files required in this book.

1. If necessary, close the new_page_1.htm page. If necessary, double-click the file index.htm in the Folder List pane to display the Ship-It-Here Home page in Page view.
2. Click the link bar component in the top-left of the page just below the image and above the Home banner to select it. Press the DELETE key three times to delete the link bar component and to move the graphic to the top of the page.
3. Click the fourth item in the bulleted list to select it and then type `The widest range of shipping materials at the lowest cost` as the new text.
4. Press the ENTER key to add a fifth item in the bulleted list and then type `Expert advice on protecting and insuring your goods` as the new text.
5. Select the heading, Our Mission, and then type `Our Destination` as the new text.
6. Scroll down. Position the insertion point after the word, Sales: in the Electronic mail section, and then type `manager@shipithereinc.com` as the e-mail hyperlink text. Create an e-mail hyperlink that sends e-mail to manager@shipithereinc.com.
7. Click the Preview button to preview the Web page. After you have previewed the page, click the Design button.
8. Print and then save the Web page.
9. Double-click the file products.htm in the Folder List pane to display the Products Web page in Page view.
10. Double-click the link bar component on the left side of the page. If necessary, edit the properties to include hyperlinks at the child level. Select the Home page check box and the Parent page check box.
11. Double-click the Products page banner component. To edit the page banner text, type `Shipping Supplies` as the new text.
12. If you have access to a Web server, publish the Web site and preview the Web site in your browser. Figure 1-89 shows the Web site as it should appear in the Web browser. Print and save the Web page, close the Web site, and then close FrontPage. Hand in the printouts to your instructor.

Apply Your Knowledge

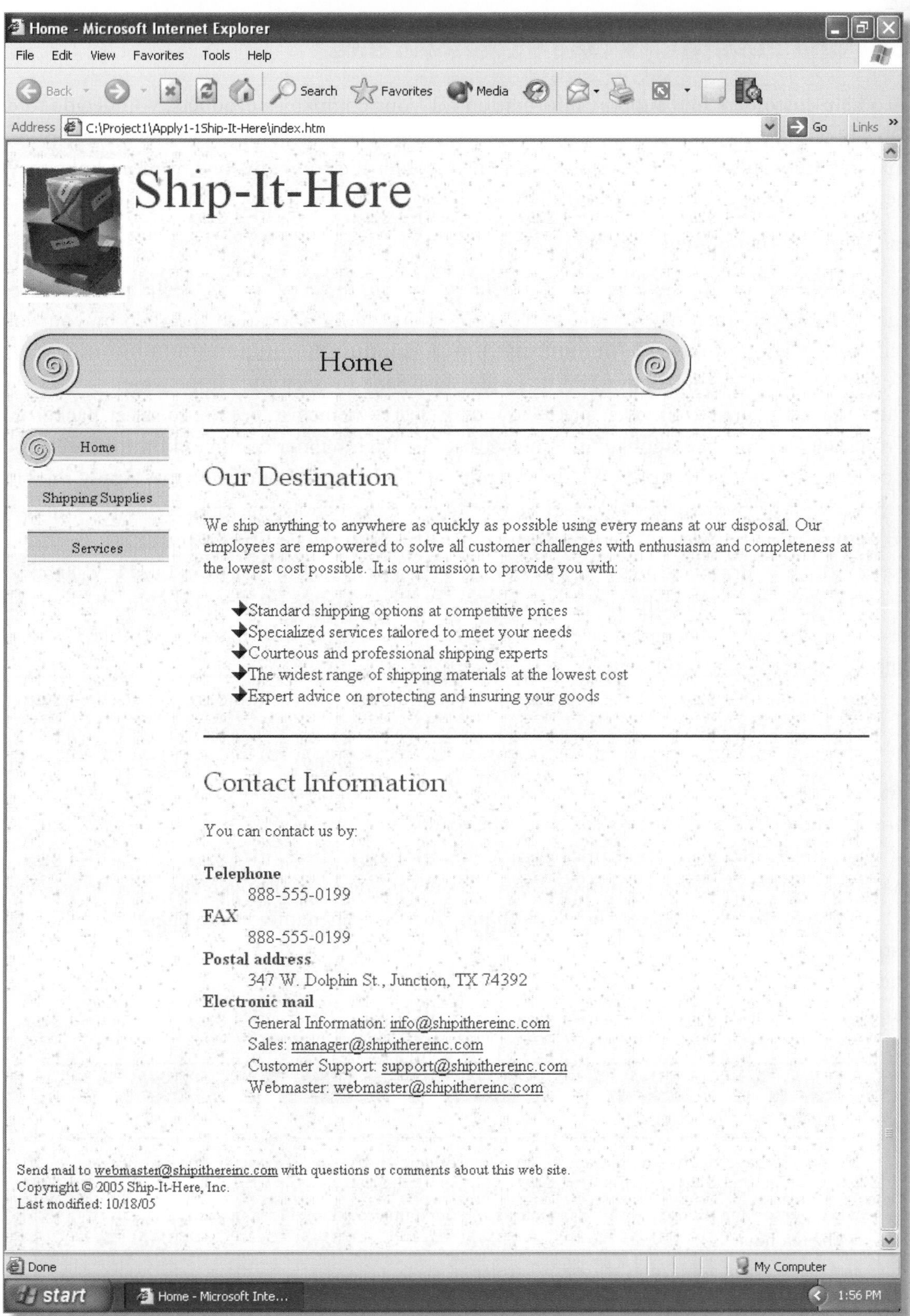

FIGURE 1-89

1 Creating and Modifying a One-Page Web Site

Problem: To help customers find support information for your company's products, you decide to develop a one-page Web site with commonly needed support information. The page should include a description of the company's quality philosophy, support options available through the company, one or more links to Web sites related to the products, and your contact information.

Instructions: Perform the following tasks.

1. Create a new Web site using the One Page Web Site template. In the Web Site Templates dialog box, click One Page Web Site and then type `C:\Project1\Lab1-1Whalen`, or a location specified by your instructor, in the Specify the location of the new Web site text box. Click the OK button.
2. Double-click the file name, index.htm, in the Folder List pane to open the Home page.
3. Apply the Industrial theme to the Web site. Below the Select a theme list, be sure to select Background picture.
4. When FrontPage has finished applying the theme, use the Page Banner command on the Insert menu to insert a page banner with the words Whalen Metals, or the name of your company. Apply the Heading 1 style to the title. Type the text in Table 1-5, or text of your own choosing, to describe the company's support and quality points of view. When you have finished typing the text, press the ENTER key.
5. Type `Whalen Metals` and then press the ENTER key. Type `Information on our Quality Programs:` and then press the ENTER key. Press the TAB key three times and then type the names of the three quality-centered Web sites separated by a TAB character. Press the ENTER key. Use the information in Table 1-6 to create hyperlinks for the company and each of the Web sites. Press the ENTER key.
6. Type `Sanjay Gupta, Director of Support Services` as the author name (or substitute your name and school). Press the ENTER key.
7. Type `Please e-mail questions and comments about our support and quality philosophy to sgupta@whalenmetals.com.` as the last line of text (or you can substitute your e-mail address).
8. Drag through the e-mail address text to select it. Create an e-mail hyperlink to the e-mail address, sgupta@whalenmetals.com (or you can substitute your e-mail address).
9. If you have access to a Web server, publish the Web site and preview the Web site in your browser (Figure 1-90). Save the Web page. Print the Web page, write your name on the page, and hand it in to your instructor.
10. Close the Web site.
11. Quit Internet Explorer and FrontPage.

Table 1-5 Support Options Description

SUPPORT INFORMATION
When you need help with your order or our products and services, contact one of our support specialists via e-mail, the Web, or telephone. We commit to getting you in touch with a live person for support within 30 minutes of your initial contact. Most issues are resolved within an hour. Whalen Metals practices a zero-defect quality management program. We take your concerns seriously and invite our customers to participate in our monthly quality meetings that include senior company management, vendors, and customers.

In the Lab

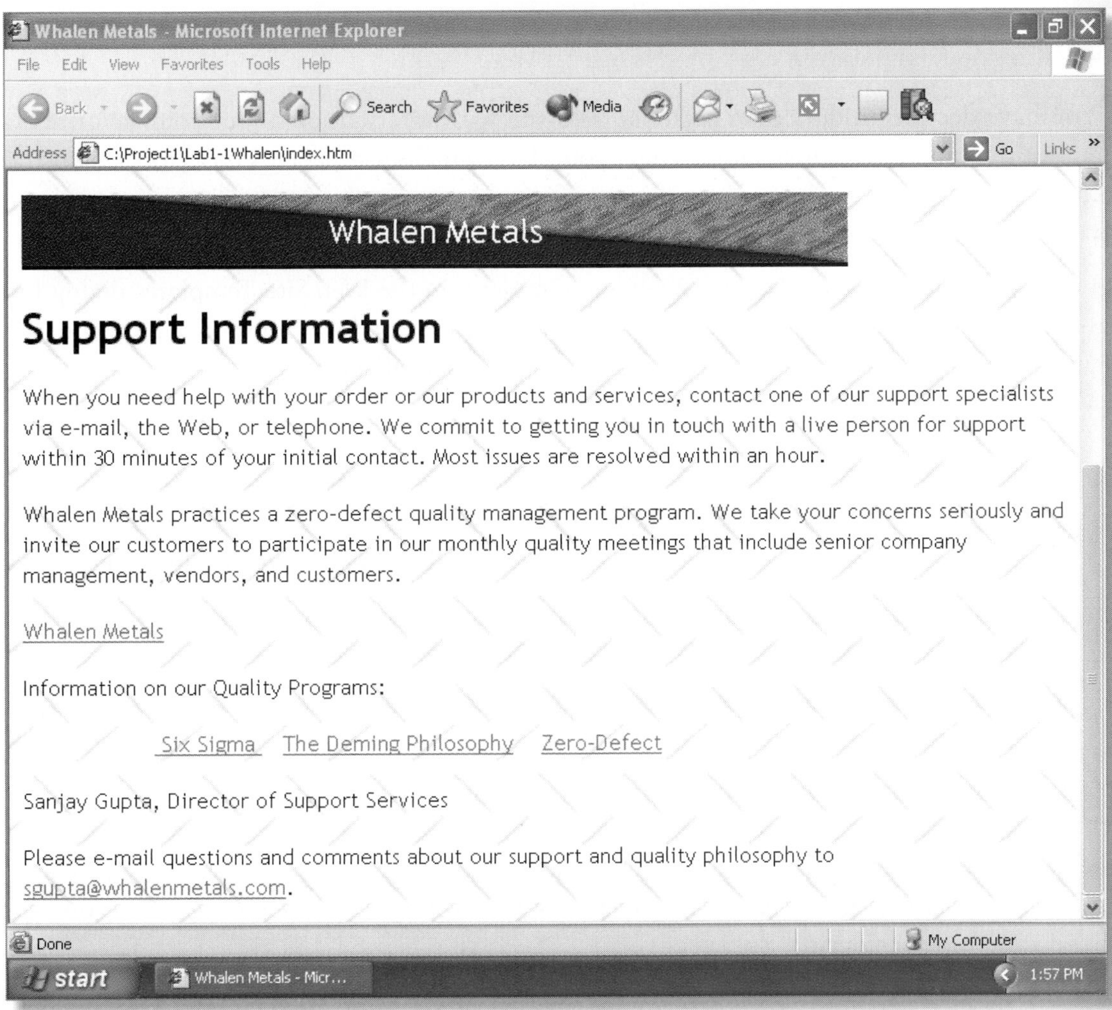

FIGURE 1-90

Table 1-6 Support Hyperlinks*

TEXT FOR HYPERLINK	URL FOR HYPERLINK
Whalen Metals	http://www.whalenmetals.com
Six Sigma	http://www.sixsigma.com
The Deming Philosophy	http://deming.eng.clemson.edu/pub/den/
Zero-Defect	http://www.philcrosby.com

* If you encounter an inoperative URL in the last three links, use the Google search engine, google.com, to find a similar Web page.

2 Creating and Modifying a Personal Web Site

Problem: You have decided to develop a personal Web site with information about your favorite hobby, running. In addition to an introductory Home page, you plan to include a page of links to sites on training, equipment, clubs, and other Web sites of interest.

Instructions: Perform the following tasks.

1. Create a new Web site using the Personal Web Site template. In the Web Site Templates dialog box, click Personal Web Site and then type `C:\Project1\Lab1-2Running`, or a location specified by your instructor, in the Specify the location of the new Web site text box. Click the OK button.
2. On the View menu, click Navigation. Delete the Interests, Feedback, and Photo Gallery pages from the Web site.
3. Double-click the index.htm page icon in the Folder List pane to open the Home page.
4. If necessary, apply the In Motion theme, or another theme of your choosing, to the Web site. Be sure to apply the theme to all pages in the Web site and to check Vivid colors, Active graphics, and Background picture.
5. Select and delete all table cells below Favorite Links and below Weather.
6. Double-click the page banner component. In the Page Banner Properties dialog box, select the text in the Page banner text text box and then type `Running My Way` as the new text.
7. Select the link bar and then edit the properties to add hyperlinks to child pages under Home. Remove the check mark from the Home page check box.
8. Delete the first paragraph of placeholder text.
9. Select the placeholder text in the second paragraph and then type `Looking for links to great running sites that I regularly read? Browse through my collection of favorite Web links to get information on great running resources.`
10. Save the Web page. Open the About Me page. Replace all placeholder text with information about yourself and the course for which you are doing this assignment. See your instructor for relevant course information.
11. Save the Web page. Open the Favorites page.
12. Select the first paragraph of placeholder text and then type `A topical listing of some of my favorite Web sites regarding running.`
13. Edit the bulleted list of hyperlinks to include the sites and URLs listed in Table 1-7. Use the underlined text as the hyperlink text and then type the descriptions in the placeholder text for each hyperlink. Include any other sites of interest to you. If necessary, for the descriptions, change the style to Bulleted List by selecting Bulleted List from the Style box on the Formatting toolbar before typing the text.
14. Save the Web page.
15. Print the Home page, About Me page, and Favorites page, write your name on the pages, and hand them in to your instructor.
16. If you have access to a Web server, publish the Web site. After you test the Web pages in your browser (Figures 1-91a and 1-91b on page FP 74), close your browser, close the Web site, and then quit FrontPage.

In the Lab

Table 1-7 Bulleted List Hyperlinks *

HYPERLINK TEXT AND DESCRIPTION	URL
Cool Running Race calendars, race results, news, and resources.	http://www.coolrunning.com
Runner's World Online companion to a popular running magazine.	http://www.runnersworld.com
CARA Chicago Area Runners Association home page.	http://www.cararuns.org
Onrunning.com News on the professional running world.	http://www.onrunning.com
RunningResearch News Companion site to a journal devoted to the latest research on training and nutrition.	http://www.rnnews.com

* If you encounter an inoperative URL, use the Google search engine, google.com, to find a similar Web page.

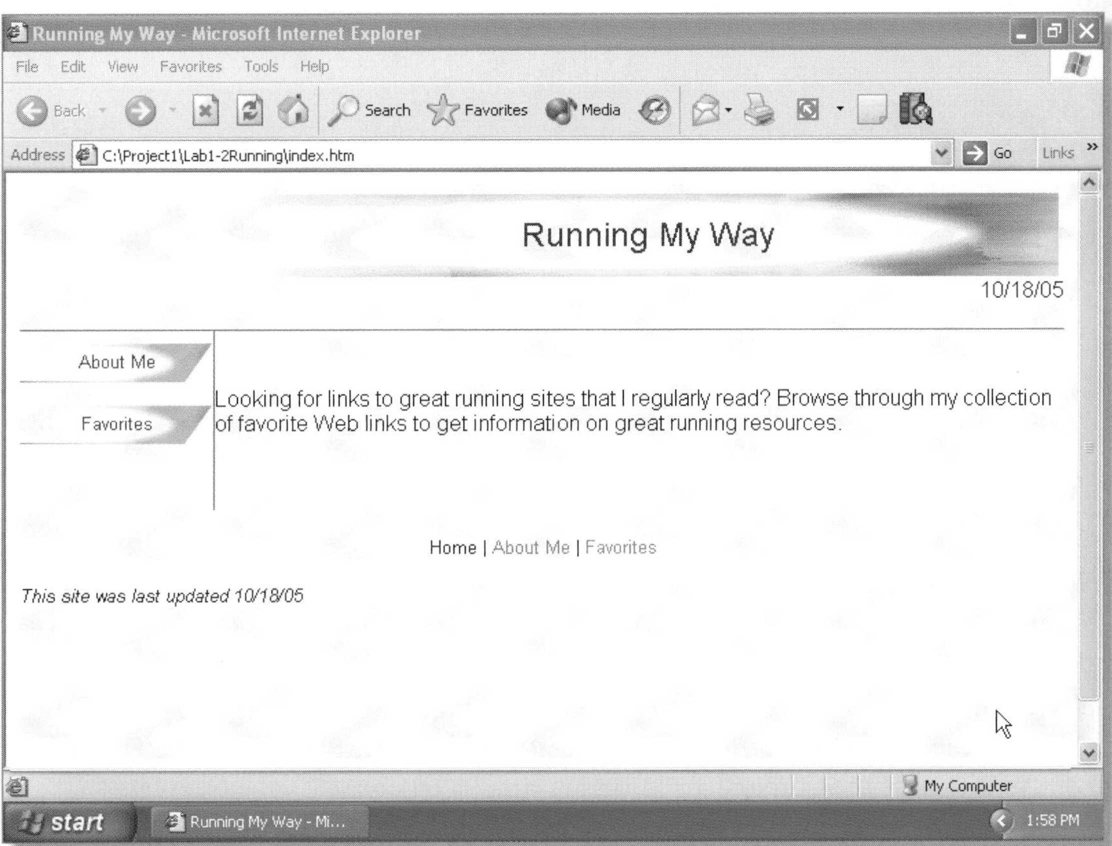

FIGURE 1-91a

(continued)

Creating and Modifying a Personal Web Site *(continued)*

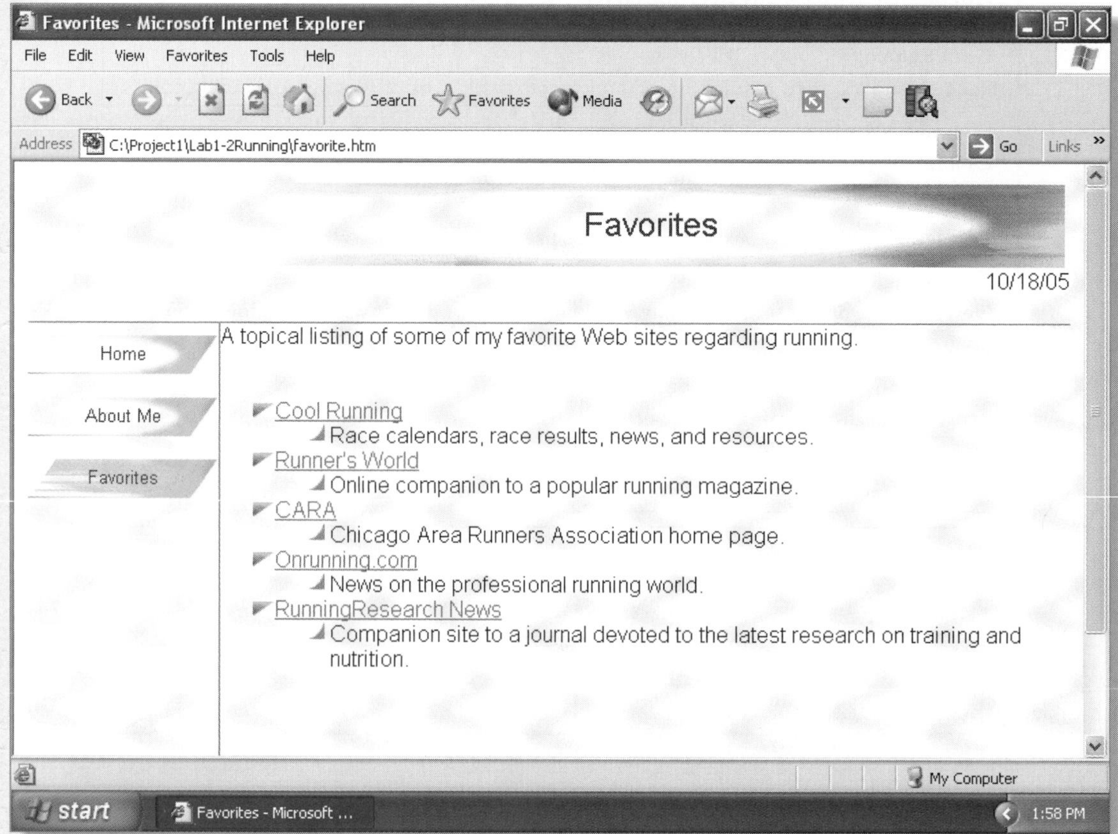

FIGURE 1-91b

3 Creating and Modifying a Corporate Presence Web Site

Problem: As the owner of Fairway Lawn Care, you want to develop a Web site that will provide customers with information about your lawn care services and your specialty landscaping services.

Instructions: Perform the following tasks.

1. Create a new Web site using the Corporate Presence Wizard template. In the Web Site Templates dialog box, click Corporate Presence Wizard and then type `C:\Project1\Lab1-3Fairway`, or a location specified by your instructor, in the Specify the location of the new Web site text box. Click the OK button.
2. When FrontPage displays the Corporate Presence Wizard dialog box, click the Next button. When prompted for information about the company, use the information in Table 1-8 to fill in the fields and choose which pages to include in your Web site. When you have finished, click the Finish button.
3. If necessary, when FrontPage is finished copying the template pages, click the Toggle Pane button arrow on the Standard toolbar and then click Folder List on the Toggle Pane button menu to display the Folder List pane. Open the Home page.

Table 1-8 Corporate Presence Web Site Field Information	
FIELD	INFORMATION
Main pages to include in Web Site	Products/Services
Home page information	Mission Statement
Products/Services information	0 Products 2 Services
Additional information	Capabilities list
What should appear at the top of each page	Page title Links to your main web pages
What should appear at the bottom of each page	E-mail address of your webmaster Date page was last modified
Under Construction icon	No
Full name of company	Fairway Lawn Care
Short version of name	Fairway
Company's street address	1056 Lexington Drive, Oxnard, WA 91933
Telephone and FAX numbers	888-555-3429 888-555-3430
E-mail address of your webmaster	webmaster@fairway.com
E-mail address for general information	info@fairway.com
Show Tasks View after Web site is uploaded	No

4. Open the Theme task pane by clicking Theme on the Format menu. Choose Checkers as the theme for the Web site. If necessary, click the Vivid colors, Active graphics, and Background picture check boxes. Close the Theme task pane.
5. Select the link bar component at the top of the page and then press the DELETE key. Press the BACKSPACE key twice.
6. Select the vertical link bar and, if necessary, edit the properties to include hyperlinks at the child level. Select the Home page check box and the Parent page check box.
7. Click the first paragraph to select it, click the Style box arrow on the Formatting toolbar, and then click Heading 3. Type `Welcome to Fairway Lawn Care!` as the new text.
8. Delete the header, Our Mission. Select the second paragraph. Type `We strive to meet our customers' goals of well-maintained and manicured lawns. Whether you need a one-time mowing for your home or need your corporate campus landscaped and maintained, we have the right plan for you. Call us anytime to work with our flexible planners and managers. Let us connect you with our satisfied clients, and you can hear about our many success stories!` as the new text.
9. Scroll down and select the third paragraph below the header, Contact Information. Press the DELETE key three times to delete the text and extra blank lines from the page.
10. Click the Code button. View and then print the HTML source code for the Home page. Click the Design button. Save and then print the Web page.

(continued)

Creating and Modifying a Corporate Presence Web Site *(continued)*

11. Open the Service 1 page by double-clicking the serv01.htm file in the Folder List pane. Double-click the page banner and replace the text in the Page banner text text box with Home Mowing.
12. Open the Service 2 page by double-clicking the serv02.htm file in the Folder List pane. Replace the text in the Page banner text text box with Business Services.
13. Open the Services page by double-clicking the services.htm file in the Folder List pane.
14. Select all of the text in the paragraph in the middle of the page. Type `Select the plan that is right for your property. We maintain your property as often as you like and in any manner you specify. Select a plan based on a weekly schedule and square footage, or work with us to develop a custom package that meets your needs and schedule.`
15. Select the two paragraphs below the paragraph entered in the previous step and delete them.
16. Print and save the Web page. The Web pages should display in the browser as shown in Figures 1-92a and 1-92b. Close the Web site and then close FrontPage. Hand in the printouts to your instructor.

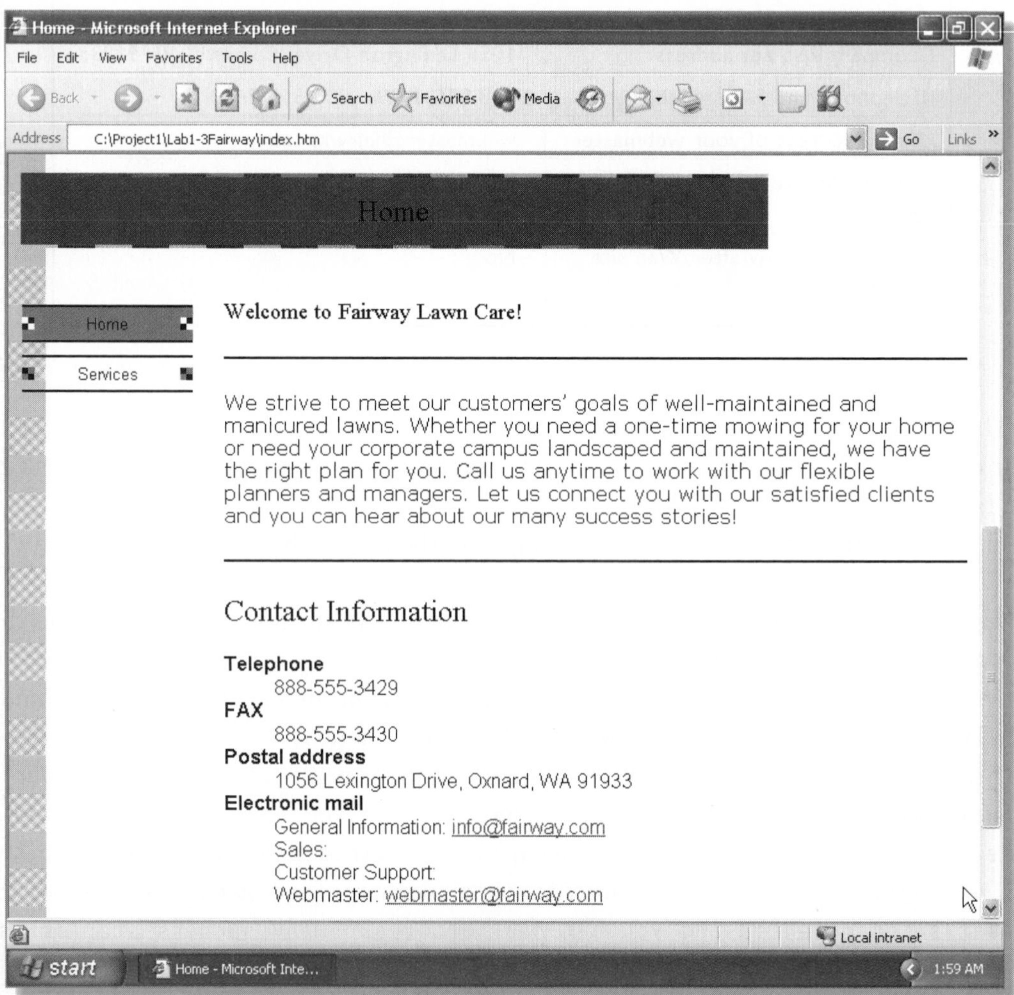

FIGURE 1-92a

In the Lab

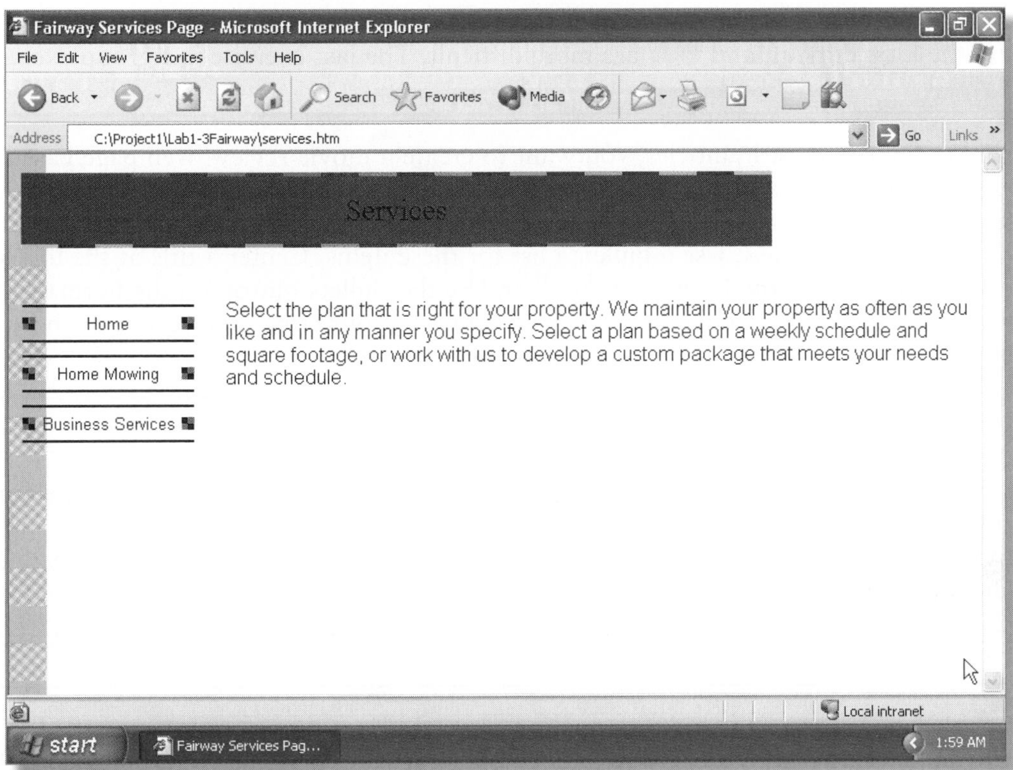
Fairway Services Page - Microsoft Internet Explorer
File Edit View Favorites Tools Help
Back Search Favorites Media
Address C:\Project1\Lab1-3Fairway\services.htm
Go Links
Services
Home
Home Mowing
Business Services
Select the plan that is right for your property. We maintain your property as often as you like and in any manner you specify. Select a plan based on a weekly schedule and square footage, or work with us to develop a custom package that meets your needs and schedule.
Local intranet
start
Fairway Services Pag...
1:59 AM

FIGURE 1-92b

Cases and Places

The difficulty of these case studies varies:
■ are the least difficult and ■■ are more difficult. The last exercise is a group exercise.

1 ■ Because of your interest in movies, you want to create a movie review Web page based on your personal reviews of movies you either like or dislike. Using the One Page Web Site template, develop a Web page that includes the following information about a movie of your choice: title, director, release year, studio, and a brief review. Use a bulleted list for these items. Center a title at the top of the page using the Center button on the Formatting toolbar. Use the Bullets button on the Formatting toolbar to add bullets to the items listed above. Include a hyperlink to your e-mail address at the bottom of the page. Optionally, apply a theme of your choice to the Web site.

2 ■ You want to make your resume available on the Web. Using the One Page Web Site template, create a text-only Home page that includes information about your educational history and work experience. Apply the theme of your choice to the Web site. Include a hyperlink to your e-mail address at an appropriate location in the resume.

3 ■■ In preparation for your friend's graduation from graduate school, you were asked to develop a Web site for him. Using the Personal Web Site template, develop a Web site that includes a Home page, an Interests page, and a History page (modify the Favorites page, including the page banner). Edit the link bar properties to include child level pages, and select the Home page check box and the Parent page check box. Edit the placeholder text to include your own new text. The Home page should include an e-mail hyperlink to your Web address as the creator of the site (webmaster). You also should include a link to the e-mail address of your friend. Delete unused pages and apply a theme of your choice.

Cases and Places

4 ■■ As coordinator for your company's softball team, you have decided to develop a Web page that lists upcoming games, scores of recent games, current league standings, and highlights of noteworthy performances. Using the One Page Web Site template, develop a Web page that lists the information shown in Table 1-9 and Table 1-10. The Web page should include an e-mail hyperlink to your Web address and a hyperlink to the company's intranet page Web page at http://www.trelanecollege.edu/intranet (you may substitute your own Web address). Use TAB characters to space the items on the page, the Font box on the Formatting toolbar, and the Underline button on the Formatting toolbar to format and lay out the page.

Table 1-9 Games and Scores

GAME/SCORE	DATES/TIMES/RESULTS	COMMENT/HIGHLIGHTS
Upcoming Games	6:30 p.m. on July 20 at field 3, vs. Boomer's Hair Salon 7:00 p.m. on July 23 at field 2, vs. Visions Software, Inc.	We need 3 more players to commit to these games.
Recent Scores	Beat Steve's Steaks 22-4 Lost to Diesel 25-2	Sheila continues her perfect pitching record at 4-0. Despite Mario's heroic home-run, we lost big to Diesel.

Table 1-10 Current League Standings

TEAM	WON	LOST
Ideolix	5	2
Diesel	5	2
Boomer's Hair Salon	3	3
Steve's Steaks	2	5
Visions Software, Inc.	2	5

5 ■■ **Working Together** Your team has offered to build a Web site for a local video rental store. Using the Corporate Presence Wizard template, develop a Web site that includes at least a Home page and three pages for products and services (use categories you would expect to find in a video rental store, such as movie rental, game rental, video equipment rental, and game console rental). First, develop the design for the site on paper and include a separate sheet of paper for each Web page. Have one team member review the design for proper spelling, grammar, and punctuation.

MICROSOFT Office FrontPage 2003

Adding a New Web Page to a Web Site

PROJECT 2

CASE PERSPECTIVE

James Keeler's personal Web site has gained attention and recognition from his friends and associates and has encouraged James to consider what he wants to see next. The current site consists primarily of text and hyperlinks. Because James describes himself as a visual person by nature, he wants to use the Internet's rich sources of unique images to enhance his Web pages to reflect his personality and activities. He wants to display photos of his school projects, some of his mentors, and a few of his favorite marketing ideas. He is concerned, however, that the significant amount of time it takes large pictures to download and display could discourage visitors from viewing his Web site. He wants to associate a brief, explanatory caption with each photo, but does not want to clutter the photo collection with too much text. He is unsure of the theme he selected for his Web pages because he thinks it might detract from the appeal of his photos.

You assure him that the photos can be added to his Web pages effortlessly, and using features that FrontPage provides will allow him to address all of his valid concerns, including the theme issue. Together, you plan the design of a new Web page that consists of a unique look and layout to add to his current Web site.

As you read through this project, you will learn about the processes involved in designing a well-planned Web page. You will learn how to manually add all of the Web page elements that were added automatically by the theme and template in the previous project. You will learn how to add a link bar and a Photo Gallery component to a Web page. Finally, you will learn how to publish changes to a Web site to a remote Web site.

Adding a New Web Page to a Web Site

PROJECT

Objectives

You will have mastered the material in this project when you can:

- List Web page design criteria
- Add a new Web page to an existing FrontPage Web site and rename the Web page
- Change the title and label of a Web page
- Change the theme and set the background color for a single Web page
- Insert a table in a Web page
- Merge cells in a table and change table properties
- Undo and redo actions in FrontPage
- Insert a clip art image in a Web page and replace an image
- Copy and paste items in a Web page
- Add a heading and normal text to a Web page
- Insert a horizontal rule
- Add a link bar and a Photo Gallery component to a Web page
- Print preview a Web page
- Save a Web page with embedded images
- Publish changes to an existing FrontPage Web site

Introduction

Every Web page designer wants to build a high-quality Web page that is attractive, that gets the attention of new visitors, that is admired by colleagues, and that even may be imitated. This appreciation does not come from complicated or overanimated designs, but from thoughtful planning, sensitivity to viewers, and careful attention to detail. You must have a thorough understanding of the diverse community of potential viewers and the goal that you want the Web page to accomplish.

Web page development consists of three phases: design, implementation, and maintenance. **Design** consists of understanding the audience, determining the purpose of the Web page, and then selecting and organizing the individual elements that, together, will achieve that purpose. **Implementation** consists of creating the HTML statements and organizing files and folders to give substance to the design. Sometimes the design and implementation tasks are separated, with a design group rendering the design and another group responsible for the implementation. **Maintenance** consists of keeping content up to date and correcting any problems on the Web page.

Designing a Web page is an **iterative process**. Typically, this means that you would perform some analysis concerning the requirements of the Web page and then call upon your creativity to arrive at a design that satisfies those requirements regarding function, and that also is attractive.

After a Web page is designed, it is a simple matter to create it using an HTML editor, such as Microsoft FrontPage. FrontPage has many rich features that will assist you in implementing Web page designs, from the simple to the complex. In this project, you will learn some of the criteria used to arrive at well-designed Web pages and then implement the design for the Photos page shown in Figure 2-1.

(a) Home Page

(b) Photos Page

FIGURE 2-1

Web Page Design Criteria

If you ask several experienced Web page designers what the criteria are for a good Web page design, you will get many different answers. Each designer will emphasize different elements that he or she thinks are important. A basic set of common criteria exists, however, on which all developers can agree.

When a Web page is well designed, the mechanics of the page almost disappear, enabling the users to concentrate on their research, exploration, or pleasure. Table 2-1 lists several important criteria with their associated guidelines for designing and developing Web pages. The list is by no means exhaustive.

Table 2-1 Criteria and Guidelines for Designing Web Pages

CRITERIA	GUIDELINES
Authentication	• Announce who is responsible for the existence of the Web page. • Name the sponsoring organization and author of the Web page. • Use clear, concise titles that identify or announce the purpose of the page. • List appropriate dates, such as the date written or the date the page was last changed. • List the sources for information or other data used on the Web page.
Aesthetics	• Ensure the Web page looks good and is easy to navigate. • Provide functionality and clear organization. • Select good metaphors to represent your concepts and ideas. • Use complementary color schemes. • Eliminate the use of too many animated graphics on a single page. • Avoid long paragraphs of plain text.
Performance	• Keep the pages relatively short. Long pages take time to display. • Web page design should be a compromise between many graphics versus speed of display. • Use the 7-second response rule when possible: A user will wonder if something is wrong after waiting about 7 seconds without a response.
Consistency	• Use the same colors, locations, and navigation techniques for all related pages. • Maintain a uniform look and feel for all related pages. • Utilize themes and templates to ensure consistency.
Validity	• As with any paper, story, or other literary piece, proofread the text for accuracy. • Verify all the hyperlinks to ensure they are valid. • Check the image, sound, or movie files used in the Web pages. • View the Web page using different browsers. Not every HTML trick or every file format is supported in all browsers.
Images	• Use alternate text in your Web page to provide support for text-only browsers. • Note the size of a large image next to a hyperlink so viewers can decide whether to download it. • Use thumbnail images to provide previews of larger images. • Use universally recognized images for items such as Forward and Back buttons. Remember that you have a global audience.
Hyperlinks	• Ensure that each Web page stands on its own; users can enter from any page of the Web site. • Provide hyperlinks to resources mentioned in the page. • Use clear navigation hyperlinks such as Next, Back, and Home. • At a minimum, always have a hyperlink to the site's Home page. • Limit the number of hyperlinks. • Avoid click here hyperlinks.
External files	• Note the type of file, such as .avi for compressed video files, or .jpg for image files. • Include a notation of the size of the file next to the hyperlink.

Each individual Web page should have one purpose or present one concept. Avoid splitting one concept into two parts simply to reduce the size of a page. Likewise, refrain from combining two unrelated ideas just to make a Web page larger.

To help you learn new tips and techniques, examine a number of well-designed pages. View the HTML source to see how other developers created the effects that interest you.

Design Tip

Each individual Web page should have one purpose or present one concept. Avoid splitting one concept into two parts simply to reduce the size of a page. Likewise, refrain from combining two unrelated ideas just to make a Web page larger. If information is designed to be read online, limit the pages to two screens, and provide links to additional information.

More About

Viewing HTML Code

In addition to using the HTML tab, you can click Reveal Tags on the View menu. This will display (or hide) HTML tags in Design view. Place your mouse cursor on any tag, and the details of the tag will appear in a ScreenTip.

Many HTML style guides are accessible on the Web. Style guides can contain rules, guidelines, tips, and templates that assist you in creating Web pages. Use any Web search engine and search for the keywords, html style guide. Your school or local library also may have an HTML style guide available.

Design Tip

Use the criteria outlined in Table 2-1 as a guide for designing Web pages.

Web Page Composition

Although not true of all Web pages, a typical Web page is composed of three common sections: the header, the body, and the footer (Figure 2-2). The **header** can contain text or images that identify the sponsoring site, the author, or the purpose of the page. Many business Web sites place an advertisement in the header area, because this is the first part of the Web page that shows in the browser's display area. The header also can contain hyperlinks to related pages at the Web site. The header is an important part of the Web page. Viewers evaluate your site from their first impression of the header information. An appealing header piques their interest, making them want to see what else is on the page.

The **body** of the Web page contains information and other materials that initially bring visitors to the Web page. The information is conveyed through combinations of text, images, animation, and hyperlinks.

FIGURE 2-2

Q: What is the difference between the <HEAD> or <BODY> tags and the Web page's header and body?

A: Do not confuse the header, body, and footer sections of a Web page with the <HEAD> and <BODY> tags in HTML, which are code segments. Information placed within a <HEAD> tag pair typically does not display on the Web page.

The **footer** of the Web page provides contact information and sometimes navigation controls. Here you probably can find the name and perhaps the e-mail address of the author of the Web page or other official contact person responsible for the Web site. Hyperlinks to other resources at the Web site, such as the Home page or Help information, also may be included in this section.

When designing a Web page, it is useful to divide the page into these three logical sections to ease the design process. You can focus your attention on completing one of the three sections, test it, and then proceed to the next one.

Designing the Web Page

Ideally, you create several Web page design alternatives and then discuss with other designers the merits and shortcomings of each. The leading contenders then are refined until a final design is agreed upon. In practice, however, often you will work alone and thus be responsible for these tasks yourself.

You can use several techniques, including brainstorming and word association, during the creative process. As with any artistic endeavor, form follows function. If something appears on the Web page, then it should serve some purpose. If something serves no purpose, then it should not be on the Web page.

More About

Web Page Design

Discover tips, tricks, and techniques for designing Web pages by perusing the numerous formal and informal Best of the Web sites. These sites contain links to outstanding Web pages. Use a search engine to find Best of the Web sites or visit the FrontPage 2003 More About page (scsite.com/fp2003/more) and then click Web Page Design.

Begin your Web page design with a single purpose in mind. If something appears on the Web page, then it should serve some purpose. If something serves no purpose, then it should not be on the Web page. Choose content that adds value, that is, content that is relative, informative, timely, accurate, and usable.

After your discussion with James, you design a Photos page, as illustrated in Figure 2-3. Although the pages previously created followed the typical page design, this one varies somewhat because it is composed primarily of pictures. Even so, you easily can identify the header and body sections and see that no footer section is used.

The header contains two images and a heading that identifies the page. The body of the page contains the desired photos arranged in a montage, each with descriptive information in the form of a ScreenTip. The navigation hyperlinks are on the left, consistent with the previous pages.

Notice the **notations** on the design document indicating special formatting requirements such as color, text size, and alignment. With the design of the page completed, you now can implement the design using FrontPage.

Adding a New Web Page to an Existing FrontPage Web Site

In Project 1 you learned that you can create a new FrontPage Web site in several ways. You can import an existing Web site from a Web server. You can use a template or wizard. Templates and wizards, such as the one used in Project 1, are great work-saving devices. As you develop customized Web sites, you will want to add new Web pages to the Web site when the need arises. To add a new Web page to an existing Web site, you start FrontPage and then open the original FrontPage Web site. The following steps start FrontPage.

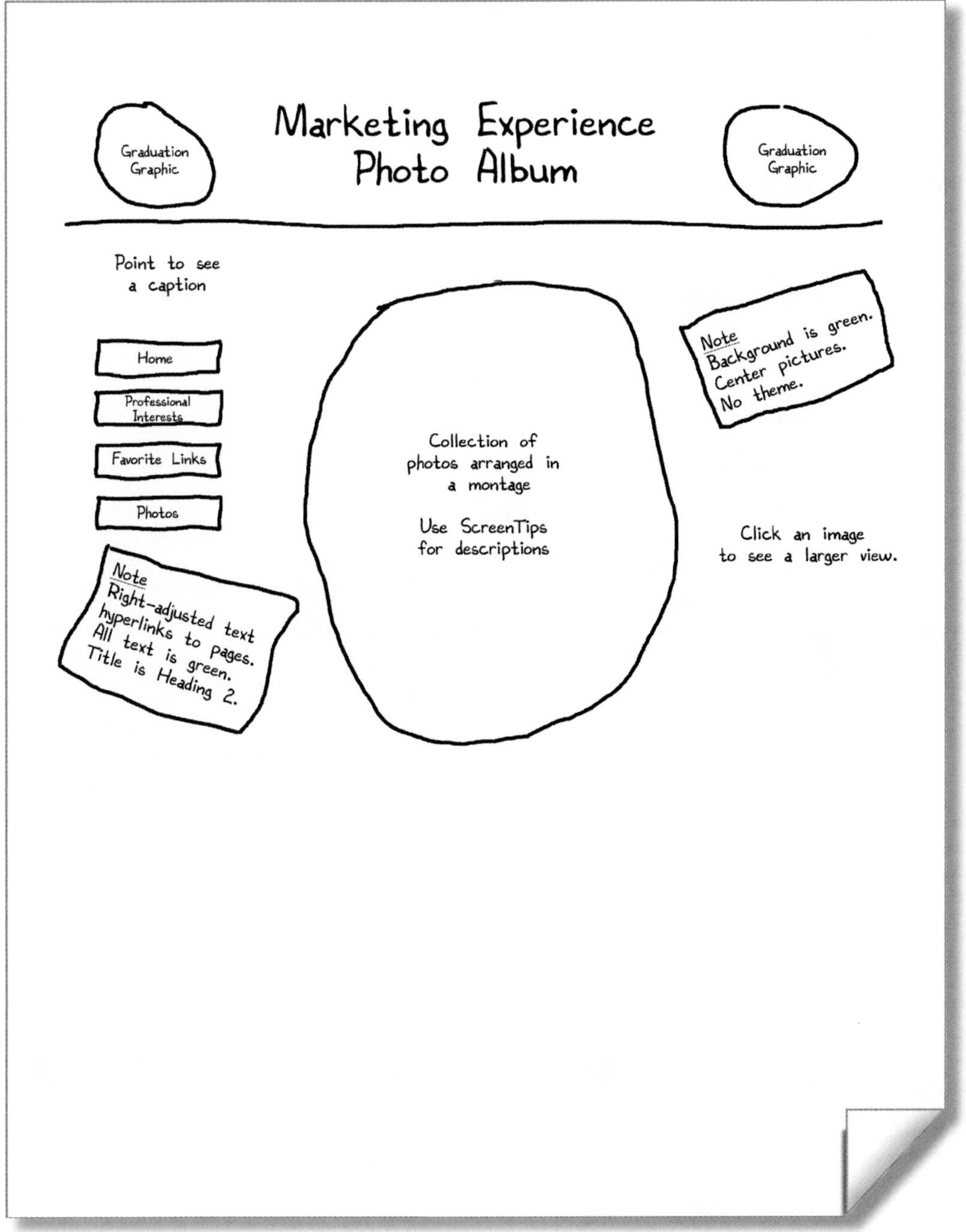

FIGURE 2-3

More About

The FrontPage Help System

Need Help? It is no further away than the Type a question for help box on the menu bar in the upper-right corner of the window. Click the box that contains the text, Type a question for help (Figure 2-4 on the next page), type `help`, and then press the ENTER key. FrontPage responds with a list of topics you can click to learn about obtaining help on any FrontPage-related topic. To find out what is new in FrontPage 2003, type `what is new in FrontPage` in the Type a question for help box.

To Start FrontPage

1. **Click the Start button on the Windows taskbar, point to All Programs on the Start menu, and then point to Microsoft Office on the All Programs submenu.**
2. **Click Microsoft Office FrontPage 2003 on the Microsoft Office submenu.**
3. **If FrontPage opened a Web site, click File on the menu bar and then click Close Site. If FrontPage opened a Web page, click File on the menu bar and then click Close.**

The FrontPage window is opened and an empty page is displayed. Alternatively, FrontPage may open the last Web page or Web site that was opened in FrontPage on the computer.

Opening an Existing FrontPage Web Site

The following steps open the FrontPage Web site created in Project 1. If you did not complete Project 1, see your instructor to obtain a copy of the completed project.

To Open an Existing FrontPage Web Site

1

- **Click the Open button arrow on the Standard toolbar.**

FrontPage displays the Open menu (Figure 2-4).

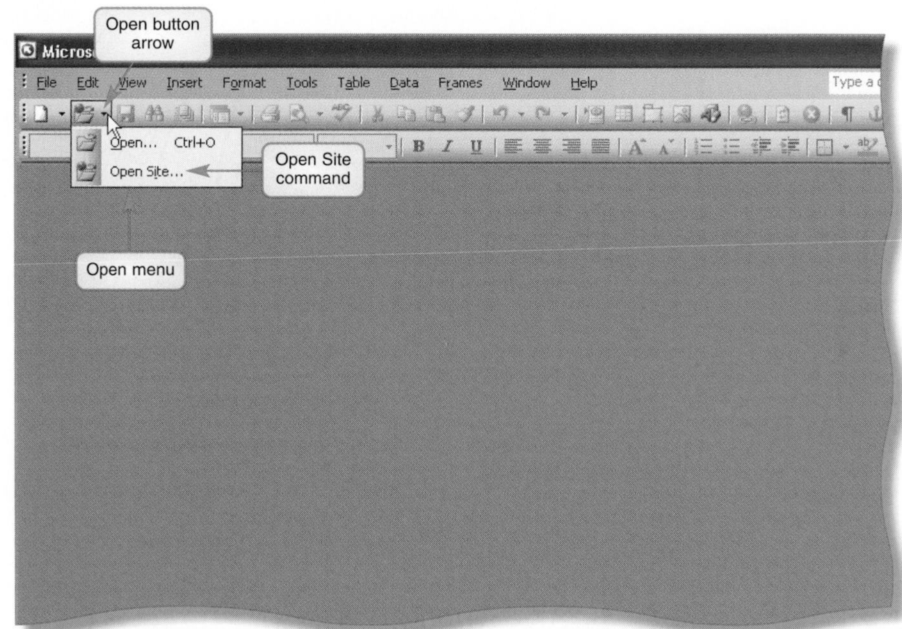

FIGURE 2-4

2

- **Click Open Site.**
- **If necessary, when the Open Site dialog box is displayed, click the Look in box arrow and select the folder location where you stored the Web site for Project 1 (e.g., C:\jkeeler).**

FrontPage displays the Open Site dialog box with the current folder selected (Figure 2-5). Use the drive and location that are appropriate for your environment. The new location is displayed in the text box.

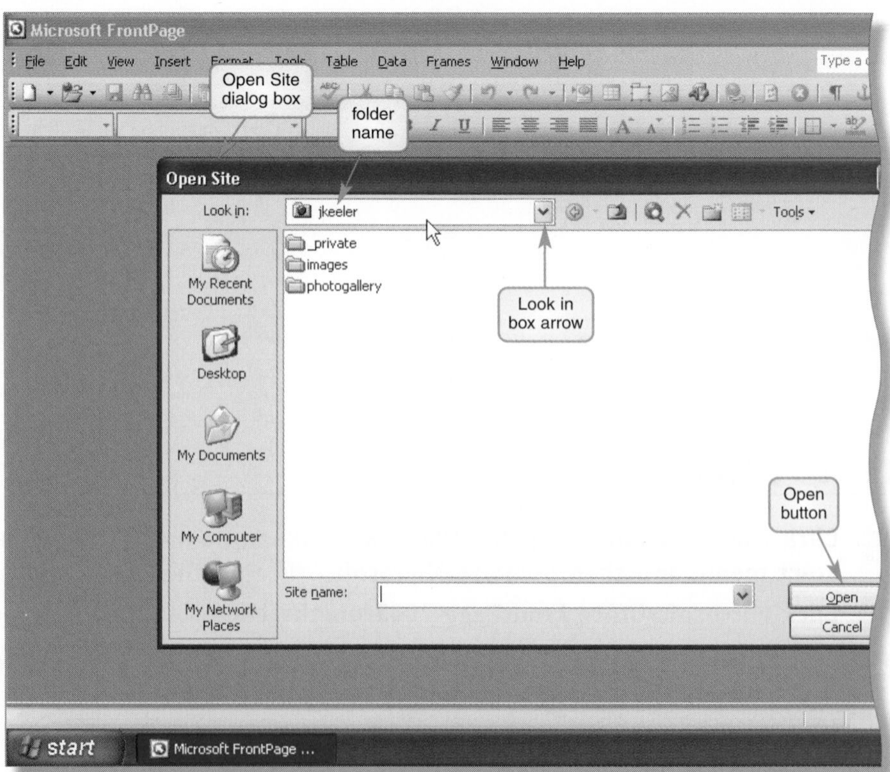

FIGURE 2-5

3

• **Click the Open button.**

• **Double-click index.htm in the Folder List pane.**

The previous Web site is loaded, and the file, index.htm, is displayed in Design view (Figure 2-6).

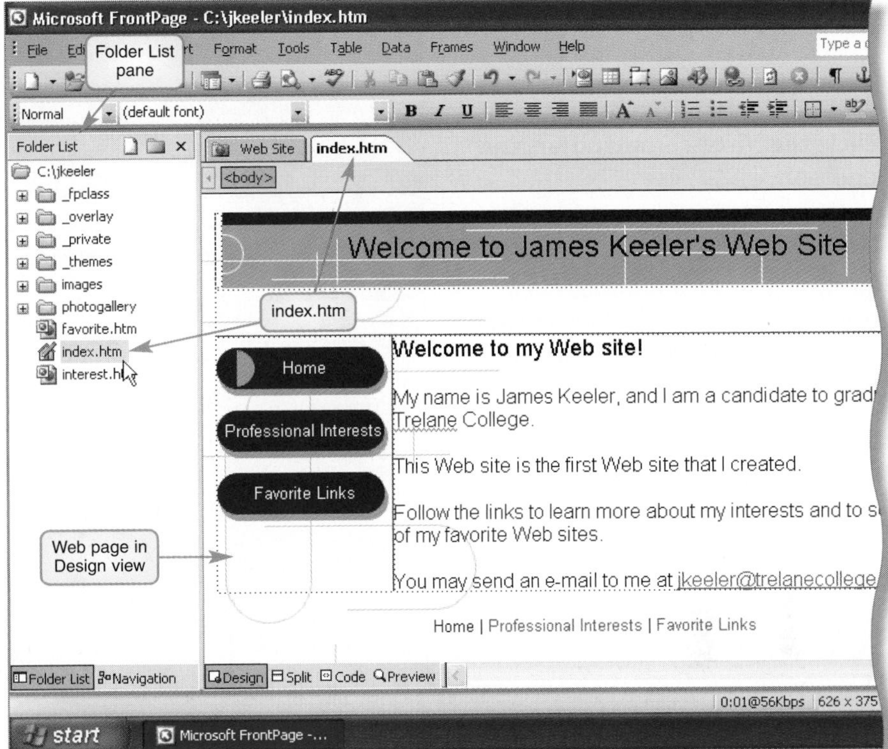

FIGURE 2-6

Other Ways

1. On File menu click Open Site
2. Press ALT+F, I
3. In Voice Command mode, say "File, Open Site"

Adding a New Web Page

The FrontPage toolbar contains the New Page button that you can use to add a new Web page to the current Web site. A new page can be added in Design, Folders, or Navigation view. If you are using link bars or banners in your Web site, as was done in Project 1, then you should add new pages after changing to Navigation view, and then indicate the location of the new page by selecting a page icon in the Navigation pane. The new page icon will be inserted as a child below the selected page icon. This allows the link bars to be updated correctly by FrontPage and preserves the visual relationship in the graphical tree diagram in the Navigation pane.

When a new page is added in Design view, FrontPage displays the new page just as it does when an existing Web site is first opened. Such a new page does not show in the Folder List pane until it has been saved. Adding a new page in Navigation view, however, causes that page to be saved and added to the Folder List as soon as the view is refreshed.

Because link bars will be used on this page, the page should be added in Navigation view. The steps on the next page insert a new page in Navigation view in the current FrontPage Web site.

To Add a New Web Page to an Existing Web Site

1

- **Click the View command on the menu bar.**
- **Click Navigation.**

FrontPage displays the Navigation view (Figure 2-7). The Home Page icon is identified by a small house figure in the lower-left corner of the icon.

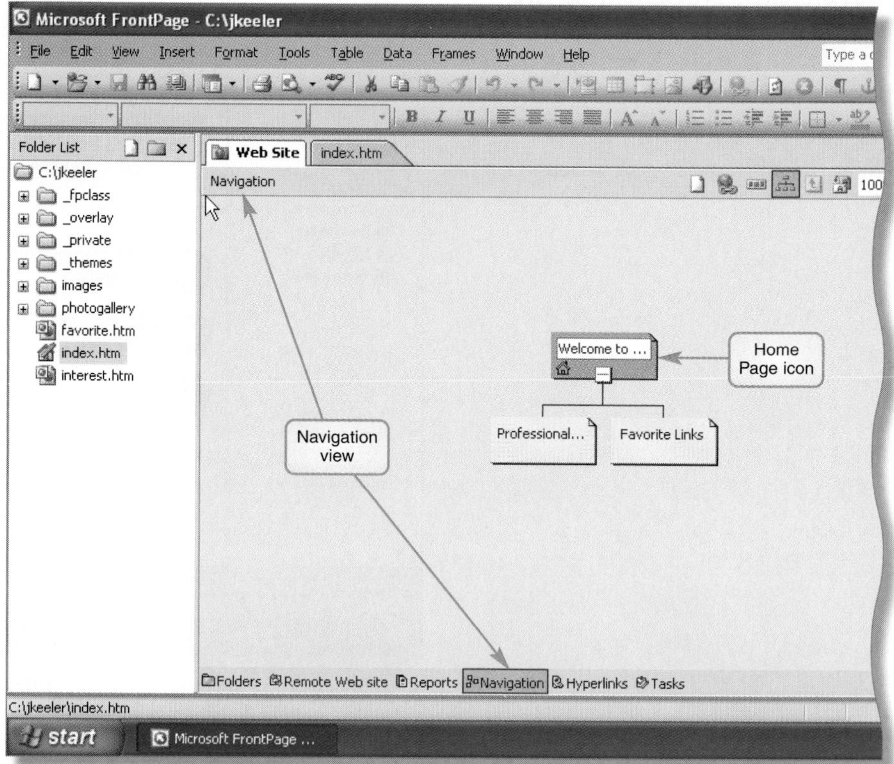

FIGURE 2-7

2

- **Right-click the Home Page icon.**
- **Point to the New command.**

FrontPage displays the New submenu (Figure 2-8).

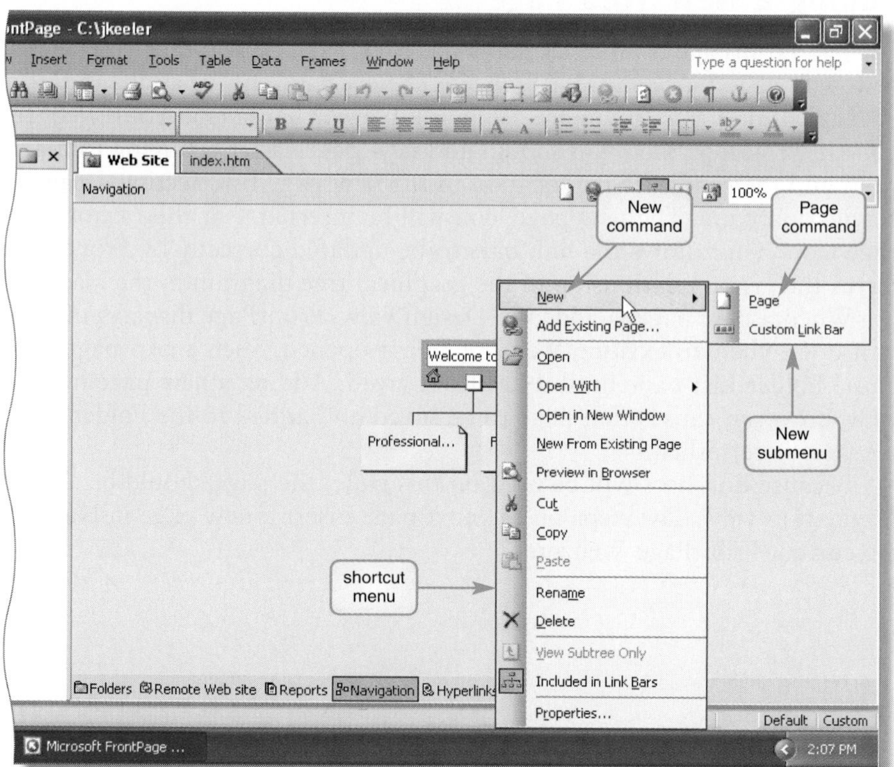

FIGURE 2-8

3

- **Click Page.**
- **When FrontPage adds the new page to the navigation structure, click View on the menu bar.**

FrontPage adds the new page to the navigation structure and displays the View menu (Figure 2-9).

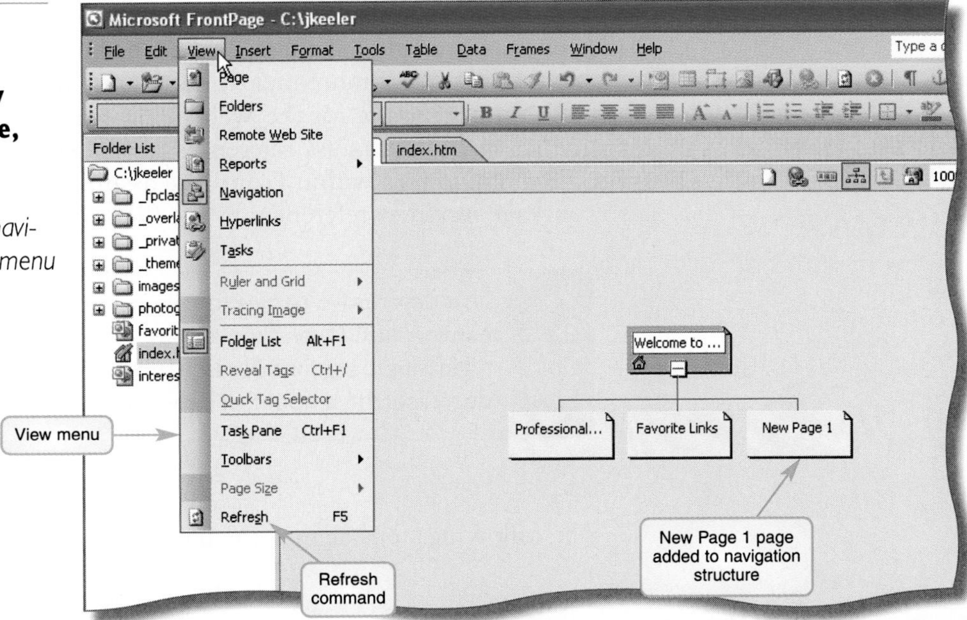

FIGURE 2-9

4

- **Click Refresh.**

FrontPage displays the new page in the Folder List pane as new_page_1.htm (Figure 2-10).

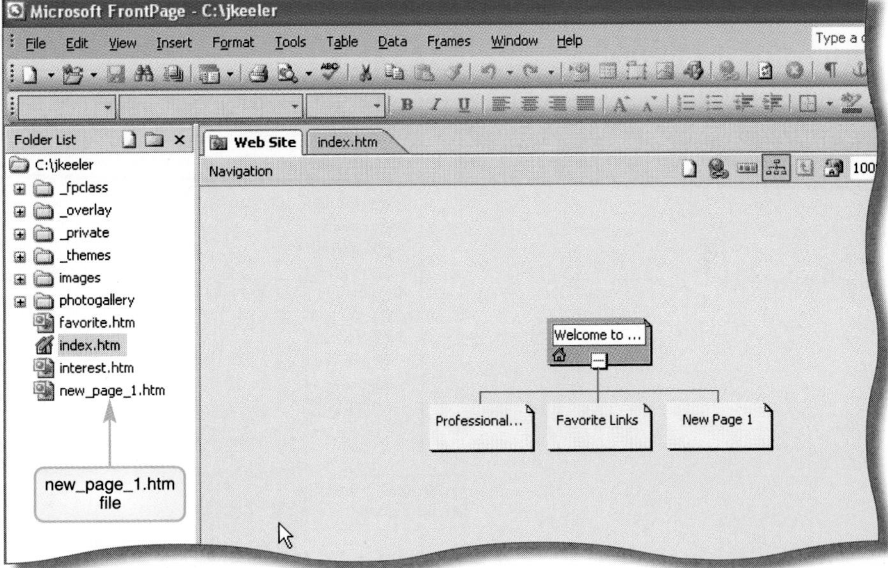

FIGURE 2-10

To control the location of the new Web page in the graphical tree diagram, you right-clicked a Web page icon to which the page was added. Because you right-clicked the top-level page, New Page 1 was added just below it, as shown in Figure 2-10. If you were to insert another page with the Home page selected, New Page 2 would be added on the same level as New Page 1. If you were to click New Page 1 and then click New Page, New Page 2 would be added below New Page 1, creating a three-level graphical tree diagram.

Other Ways

1. Click Create a new normal page button arrow on Standard toolbar, click Page
2. On the File menu click New
3. Right-click Folder List pane, click New
4. Press ALT+F, N
5. Press CTRL+N
6. In Voice Command mode, say "File, New"

Renaming a Web Page

Because a file name like new_page_1.htm is not very descriptive, you should rename the file with a more meaningful name. Because the new page is included in the navigation structure for the Web site, it was added to the Home page link bars automatically. Link bars use references to file names to locate the corresponding Web pages. Renaming files within FrontPage assures that such references are maintained, as FrontPage modifies references to the files automatically.

Design Tip

Use descriptive names for file names and maintain a standard for naming files. Over time and as your site includes more pages, a well-maintained organizational structure for the files in the Web site can decrease the amount of time spent on maintenance.

The following steps change the name of the newly created page.

To Rename a Web Page

1

- **Right-click the file name new_page_1.htm.**

FrontPage displays the shortcut menu (Figure 2-11).

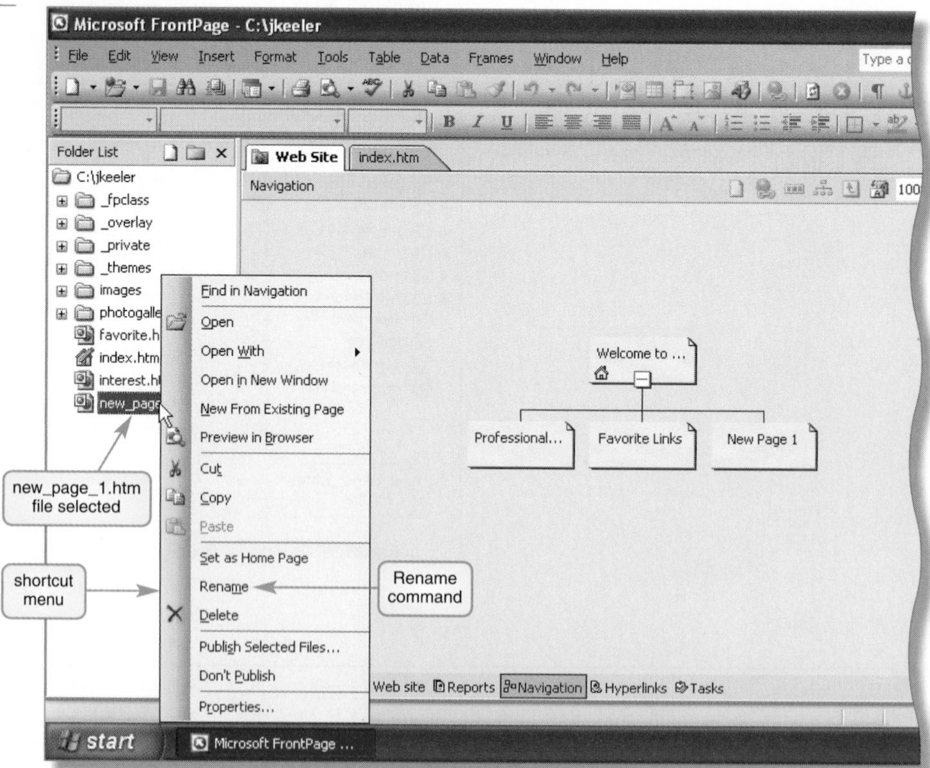

FIGURE 2-11

2

• **Click Rename on the shortcut menu.**

The new_page_1.htm file name is selected, and an edit text box is displayed around the file name (Figure 2-12).

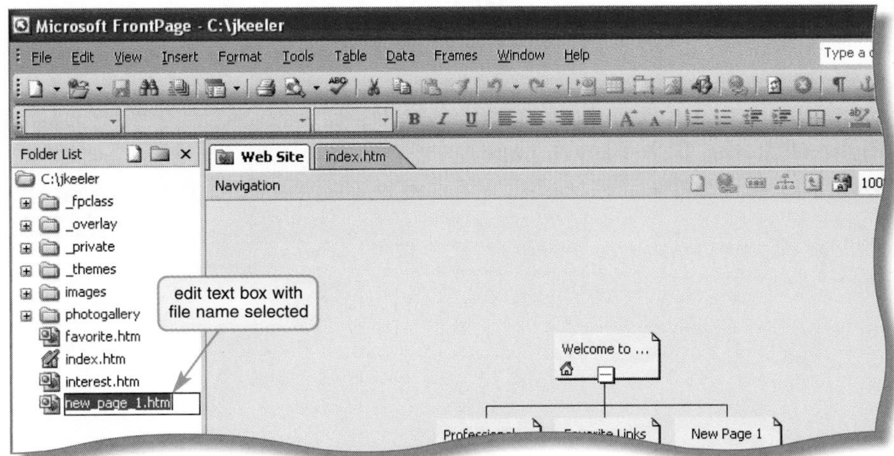

FIGURE 2-12

3

• **Type** `photos.htm` **as the new file name and then press the ENTER key.**

FrontPage displays a Rename dialog box during the renaming process and then closes it automatically after you press ENTER. The Folder List pane reflects the renamed file, photos.htm (Figure 2-13).

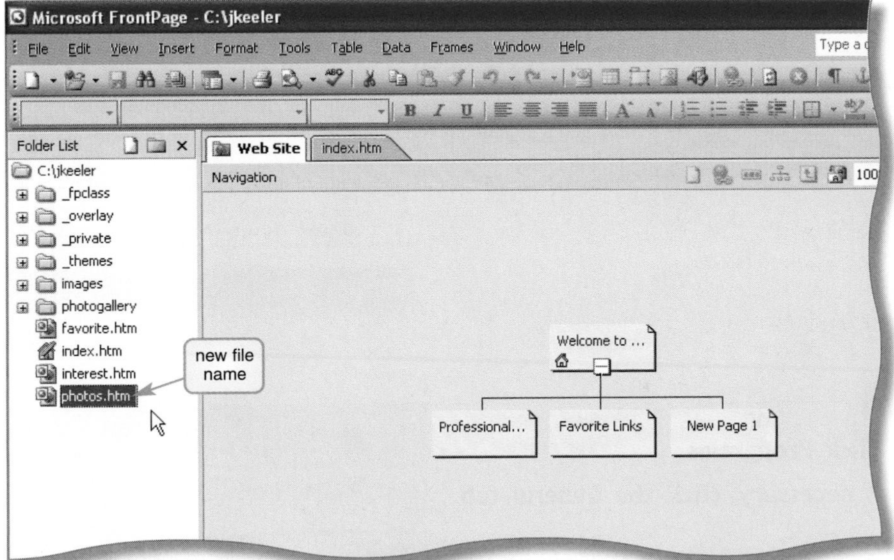

FIGURE 2-13

Other Ways

1. Click file name in Folder List pane to select it, click file name again, type new file name in edit text box

Changing the Title of a Web Page

The title of a Web page is displayed in the title bar of most browsers and in any bookmarks or favorites for that page. Although this is not the same as the page label, which is displayed in page banners and navigation bars created by FrontPage, the same text often is used by default. Each file, or page, in a Web site has its own title. The default title for a new page is New Page 1, corresponding to the default label of New Page 1 and the default file name of new_page_1.htm. You may change the title of a file without modifying its file name or label. Titles should reflect the name of the organization or purpose of the Web page.

The steps on the next page change the title of the newly created page to a name reflecting its purpose. This title will be placed on the title bar of browsers and in favorites or bookmark lists.

To Change the Title of a Web Page

1

- **Right-click the New Page 1 page icon.**

FrontPage displays the shortcut menu (Figure 2-14).

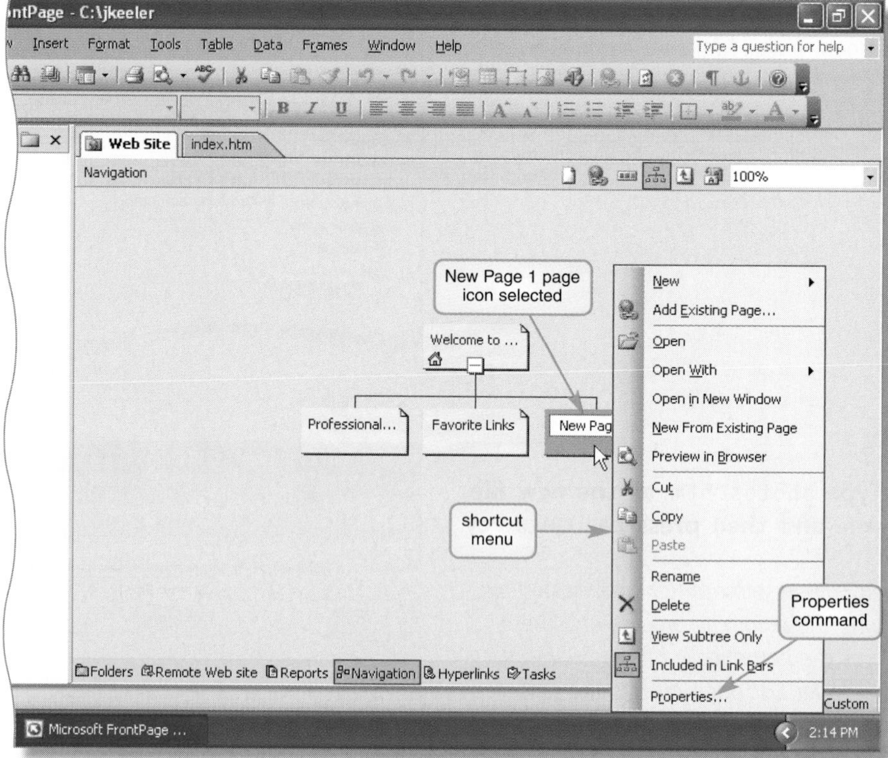

FIGURE 2-14

2

- **Click Properties.**
- **If necessary, click the General tab.**

The photos.htm Properties dialog box is displayed, and the default title is selected (Figure 2-15).

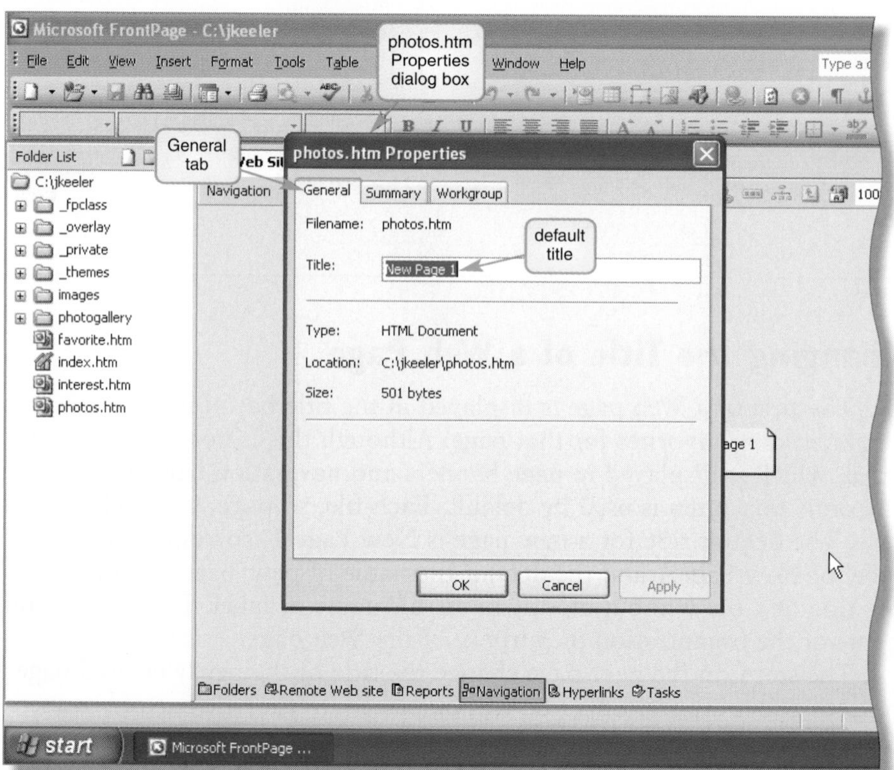

FIGURE 2-15

3

• **Type** `Marketing Experience` **in the Title text box.**

The new title replaces the old title (Figure 2-16).

4

• **Click the OK button.**

FrontPage closes the Page Properties dialog box. Although not visible at this point, the title has been changed.

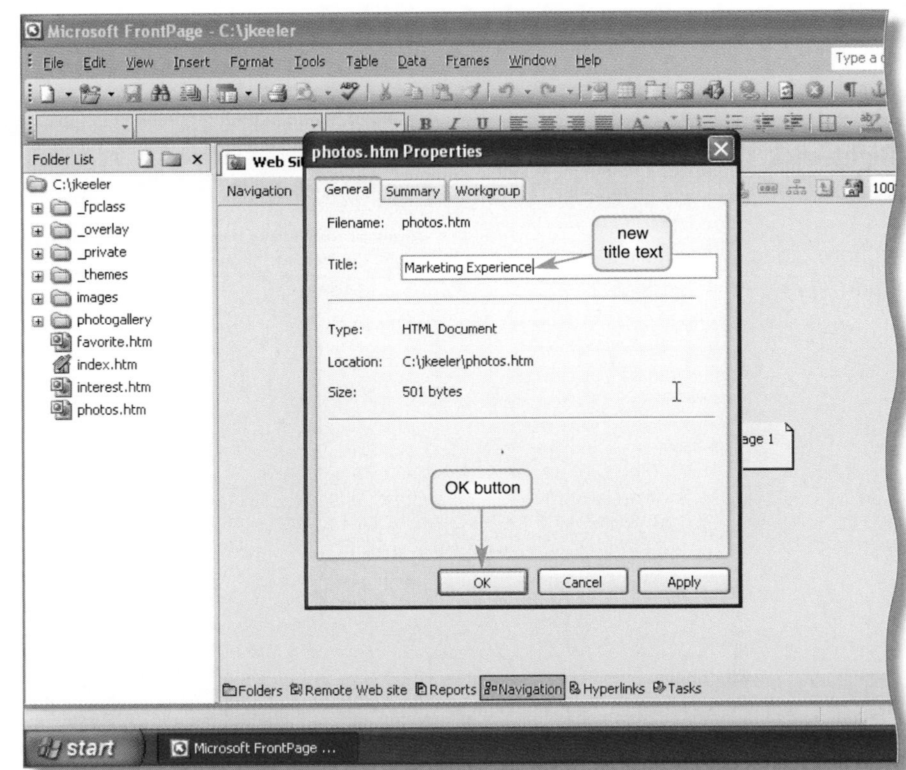

FIGURE 2-16

Other Ways

1. Right-click file name in Folder List pane, click Properties on shortcut menu, type new title in Title text box in General sheet in Properties dialog box
2. Right-click Page pane, click Properties on shortcut menu, type new title in Title text box in General sheet in Properties dialog box

Although FrontPage allows you to enter very long titles, browser title bars display approximately 80 to 90 characters, so keep this limitation in mind when entering the title.

Browser title bars display approximately 80 to 90 characters, so keep this limitation in mind when designing Web page titles.

Changing the Page Label of a Web Page

As you have seen, changing the title of a Web page did not affect the page label. FrontPage uses the page labels displayed in Navigation view as the labels for link bars. If you change a page title, you also may want the labels on corresponding link bars to match. You can change the text that is displayed on a link bar by changing the page labels in Navigation view.

The steps on the next page change the page label of the Photos page to indicate the content of the page in the labels of link bars.

To Change the Page Label of a Web Page

1

- **Right-click the New Page 1 page icon.**

FrontPage displays the shortcut menu (Figure 2-17).

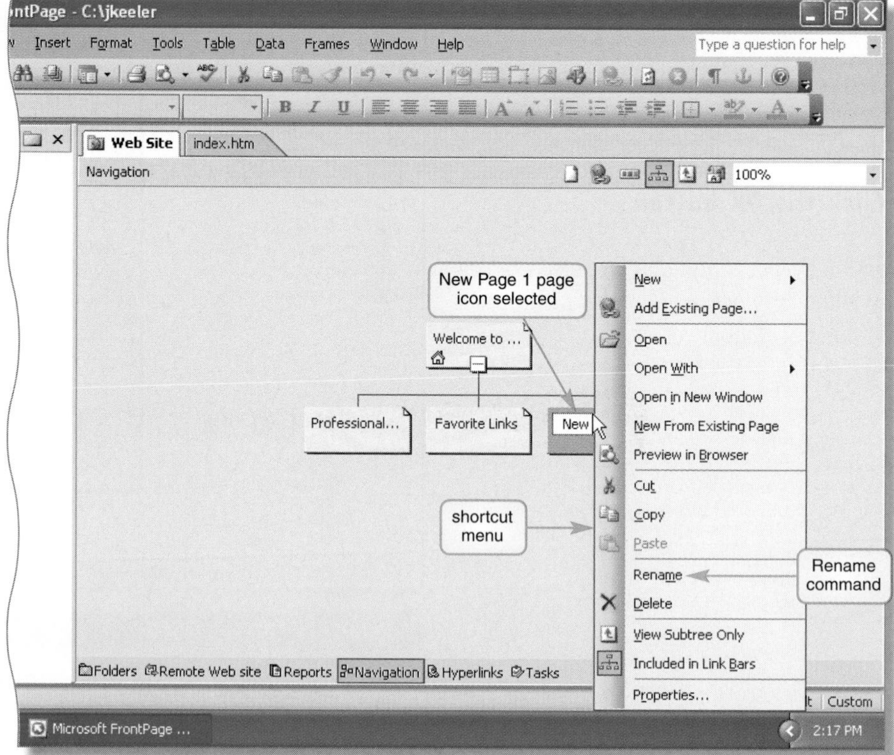

FIGURE 2-17

2

- **Click Rename.**

An edit text box is displayed around the default label, and the label is selected (Figure 2-18).

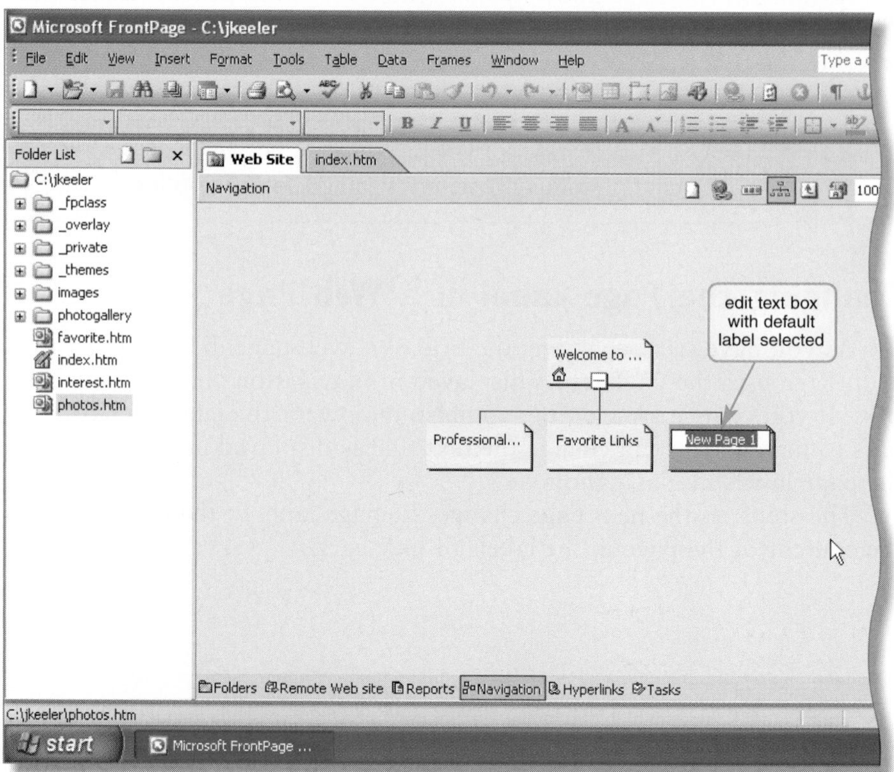

FIGURE 2-18

3

- **Type** `Photos` **in the edit text box.**
- **Press the ENTER key to save the new label.**

The edit text box closes, and the new label is displayed in the page icon (Figure 2-19). If a new label is longer than the room available in the page icon, then FrontPage displays ellipses to indicate that the label extends beyond the size of the icon.

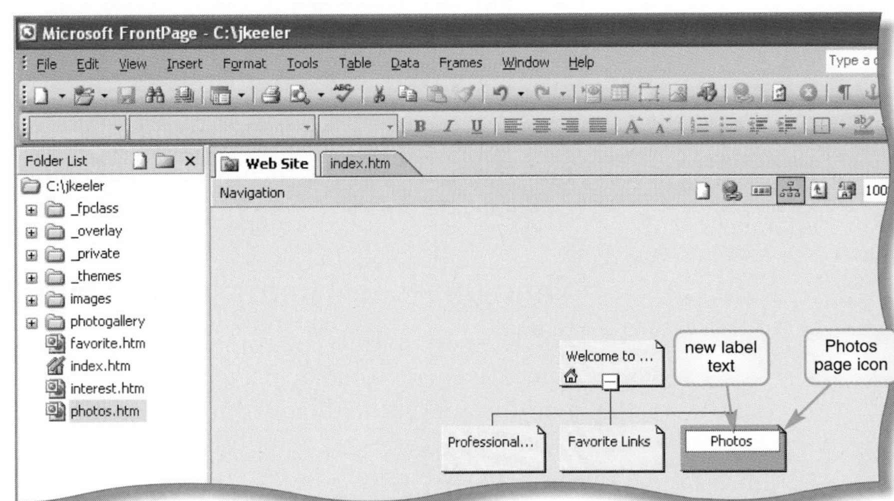

FIGURE 2-19

Other Ways

1. Click page icon to select, click text box, type new label

Editing the Web Page

The tasks required to create the Photos Web page consist of selecting the page background; inserting headings, images, and text; inserting a Photo Gallery component; and testing the page. In FrontPage, Web pages are edited in Design view. The following step edits the Photos page.

To Edit a Web Page in Design View

1

- **Double-click the Photos page icon in the Navigation pane.**

FrontPage opens the file photos.htm in Design view (Figure 2-20). The display area is empty; however, the theme for the Web site is applied to the page automatically.

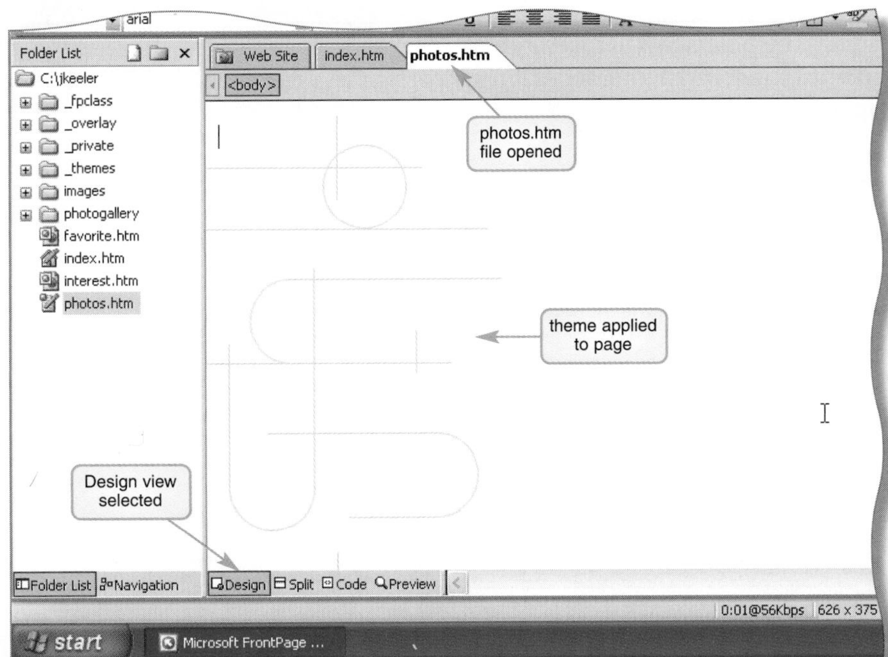

FIGURE 2-20

Other Ways

1. Double-click photos.htm file name in Folder List pane
2. Select page icon, click Design view icon
3. Right-click in Folder List and then click Open

With the page open in Design view, you can start customizing the Web page to implement the design shown in Figure 2-3 on page FP 87. Because this Web site had a theme applied before adding the new page, the theme is applied to the new page automatically. In this case, a background color with no theme applied is desired. The first step is to remove the current theme from only this page, but not from the rest of the Web site. After the theme has been removed, the default background color will be changed.

Changing the Theme for a Single Web Page

Themes typically are applied to an entire Web site, as was done in Project 1. In some cases, a particular page in a Web site might not be presented well with the current theme, yet the theme is attractive for the remainder of the Web site. With FrontPage, it is easy to apply a different theme, or no theme at all, to an individual page in a Web site.

Generate a sense of oneness within your Web site by utilizing consistent alignment, a common graphic theme, and a common color theme. Be judicious about whether a page properly fits within the chosen scheme.

The following steps remove the current theme from the Photos page.

To Change the Theme for a Web Page

1

- **Click Format on the menu bar and then click Theme.**
- **Scroll the Select a theme scroll bar until the No theme selection is displayed in the list.**

FrontPage displays the Theme task pane. The Select a theme area displays the currently selected theme at the top of the list and the No theme selection is displayed at the top of the All available themes section (Figure 2-21).

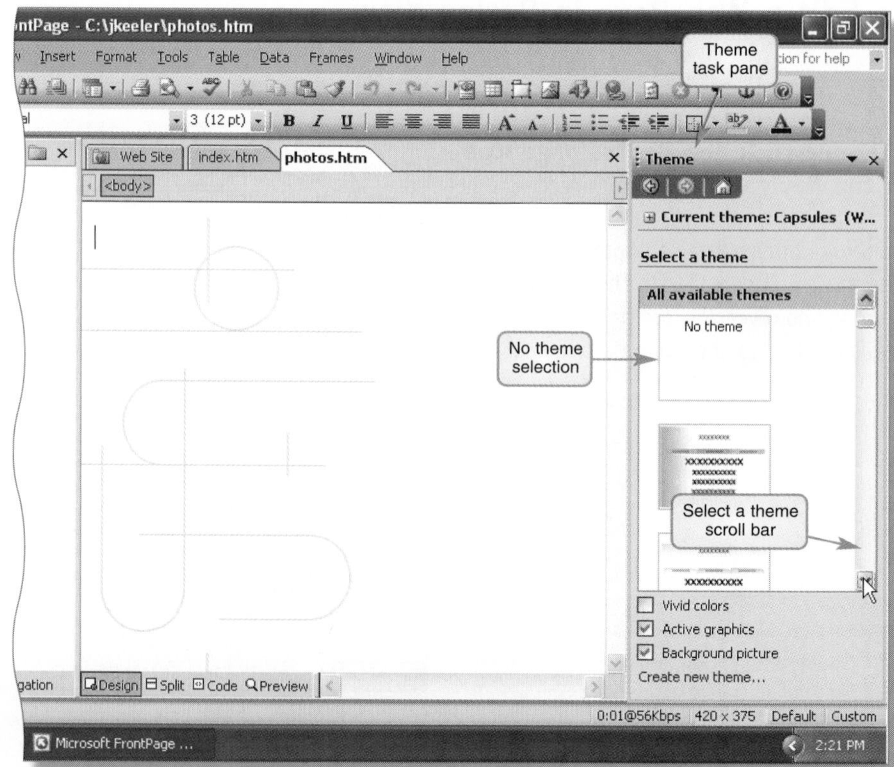

FIGURE 2-21

2

• **Click No theme.**

FrontPage displays the photos.htm page with no theme (Figure 2-22).

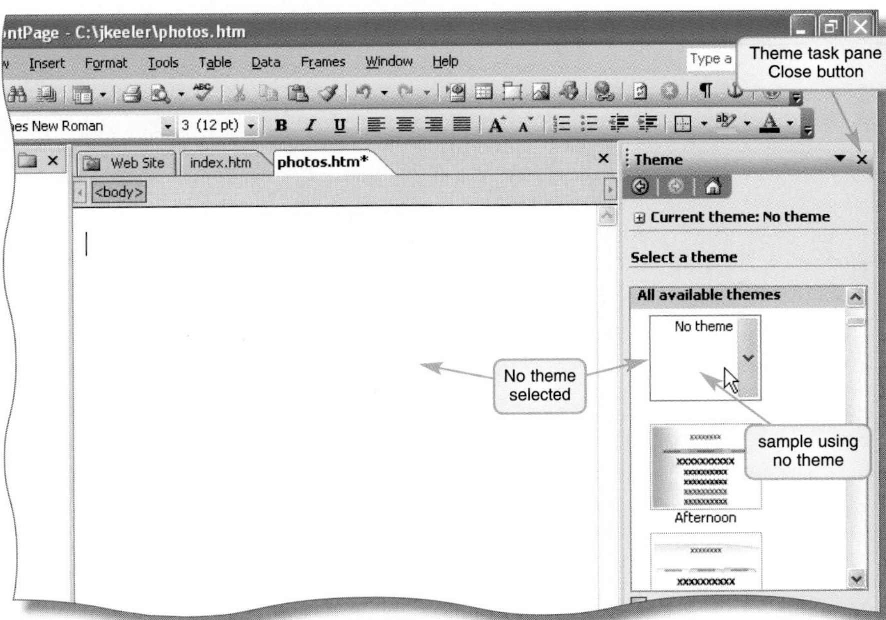

FIGURE 2-22

3

• **Click the Theme task pane Close button.**

FrontPage displays the Photos page with no theme applied (Figure 2-23).

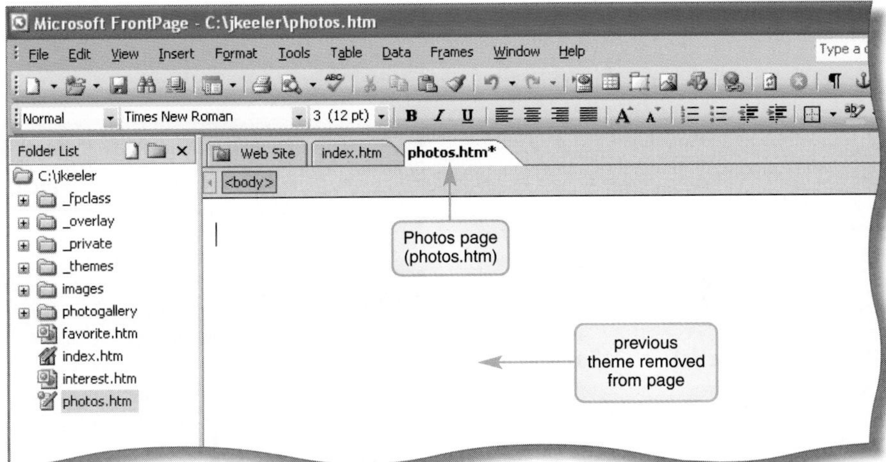

FIGURE 2-23

Other Ways

1. Press ALT+O, H
2. In Voice Command mode, say "Format, Theme"

Now that the Photos page no longer has the theme applied, you can change the default background and text colors.

Changing the Background Color of a Web Page

The background of a Web page can be a solid color, an image, or a pattern that is repeated across and down the page. You can select a color from within FrontPage, select an image or pattern stored on your local computer, or copy an image or pattern from any Web page on the World Wide Web.

Because the current theme was removed, FrontPage displays the Photos page in the default background color of white. According to the design, you are to use a solid color for the background. The steps on the next page change the background color of the Web page to a solid color.

To Change the Background Color

1

- **Click Format on the menu bar.**

FrontPage displays the Format menu (Figure 2-24). The Format menu contains commands to manage Web page formatting items such as themes, style sheets, and backgrounds.

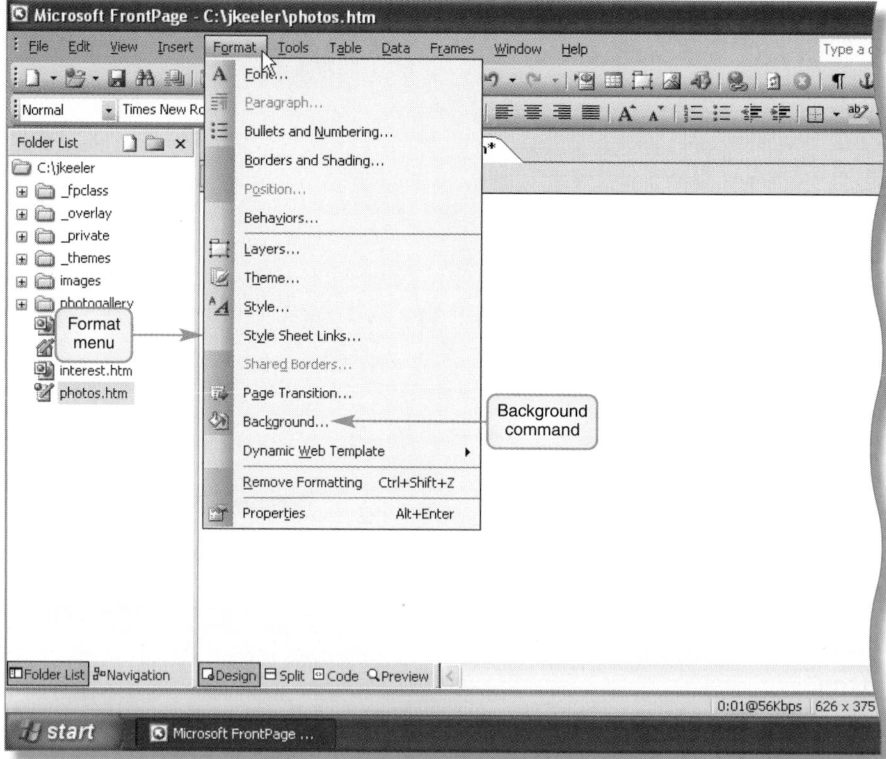

FIGURE 2-24

2

- **Click Background.**
- **If necessary, click the Formatting tab.**

FrontPage displays the Page Properties dialog box (Figure 2-25). The Formatting sheet contains settings to control the background image or color.

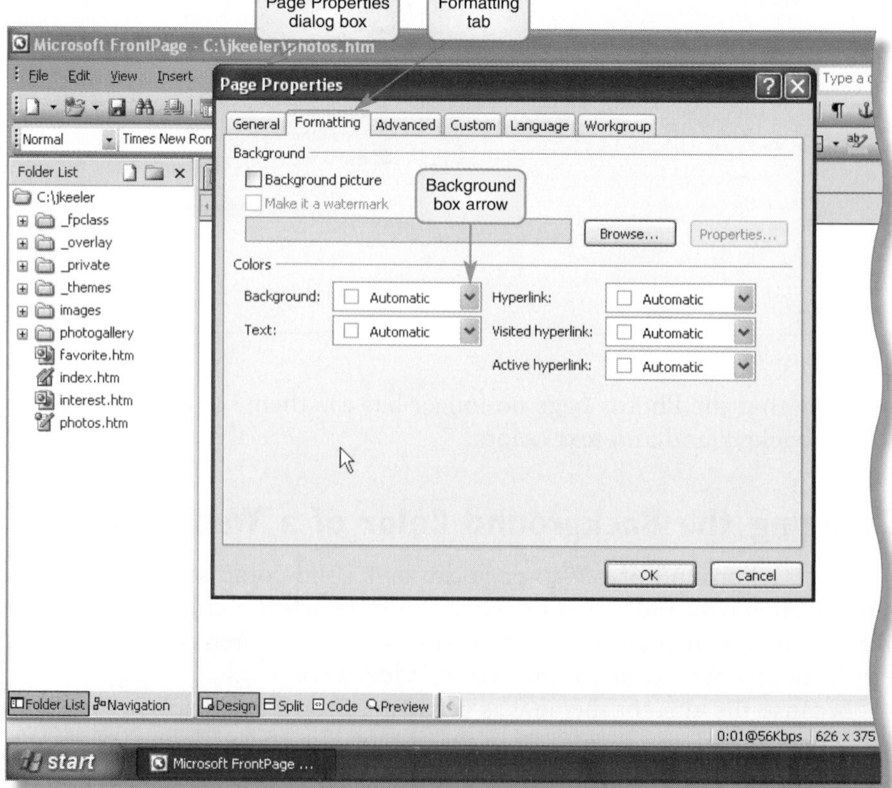

FIGURE 2-25

3

- **Click the Background box arrow.**

FrontPage displays a palette of available background colors (Figure 2-26).

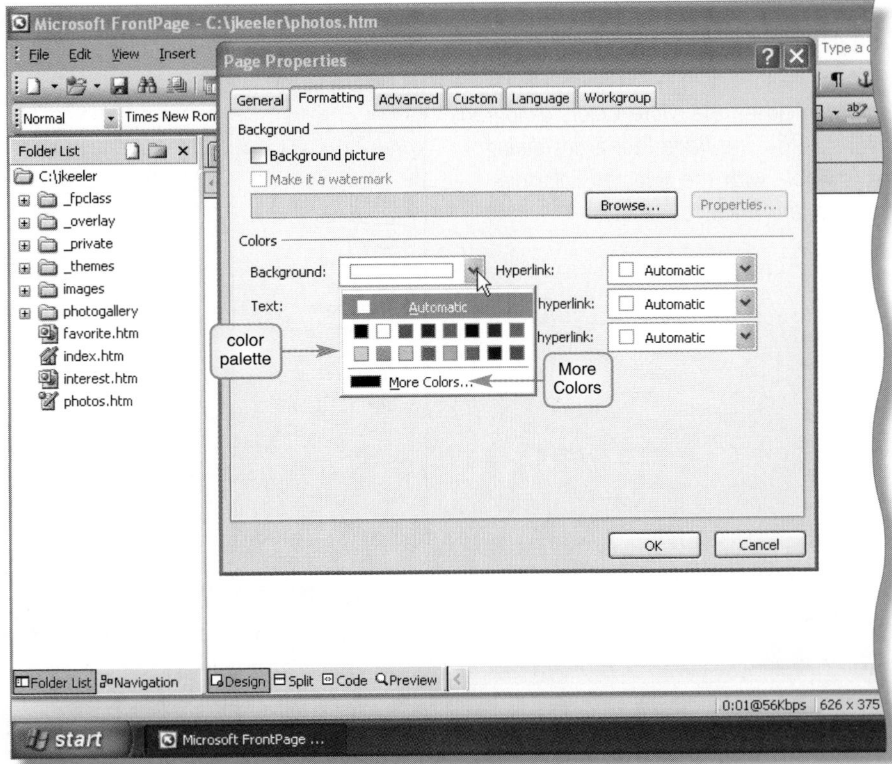

FIGURE 2-26

4

- **Click More Colors.**
- **Click the indicated color.**

FrontPage displays the More Colors dialog box (Figure 2-27). The selected color will display Hex={99,FF,CC} in the Value text box.

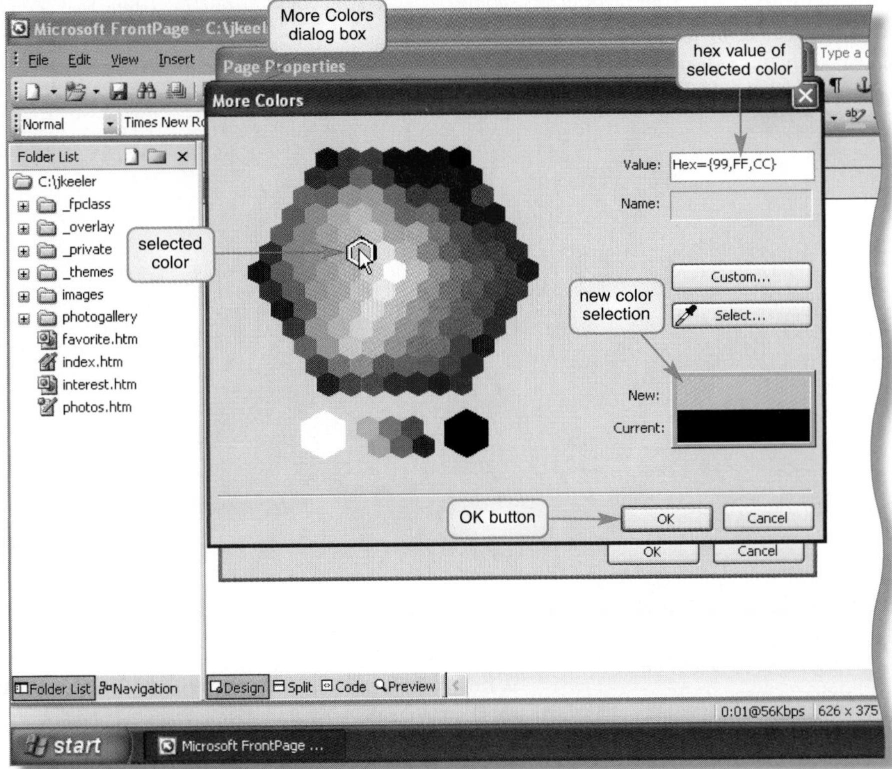

FIGURE 2-27

5

• **Click the OK button.**

FrontPage closes the More Colors dialog box (Figure 2-28). The Page Properties dialog box is visible with the selected color displayed in the Background box.

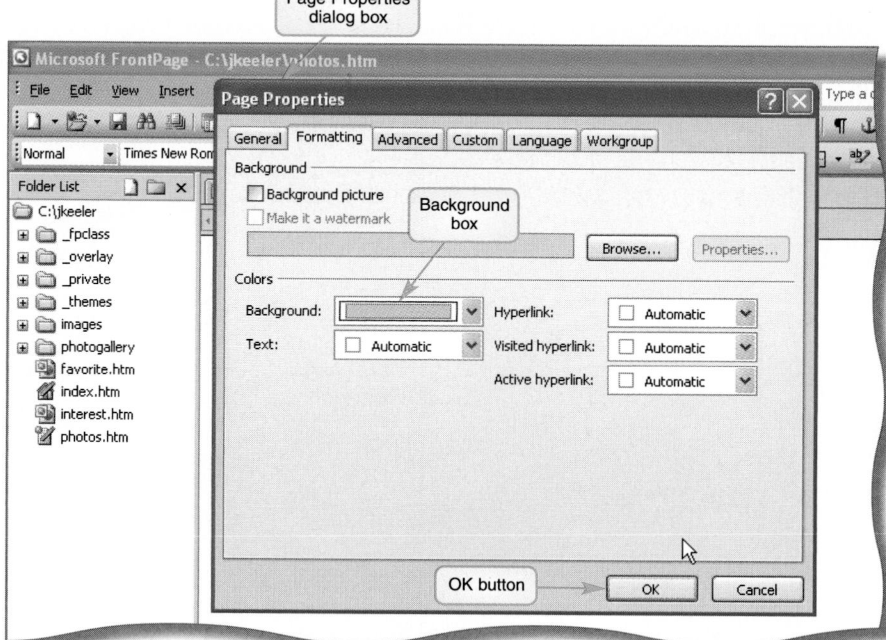

FIGURE 2-28

6

• **Click the OK button in the Page Properties dialog box.**

FrontPage closes the Page Properties dialog box (Figure 2-29). The Photos page is displayed with the selected color as the background color.

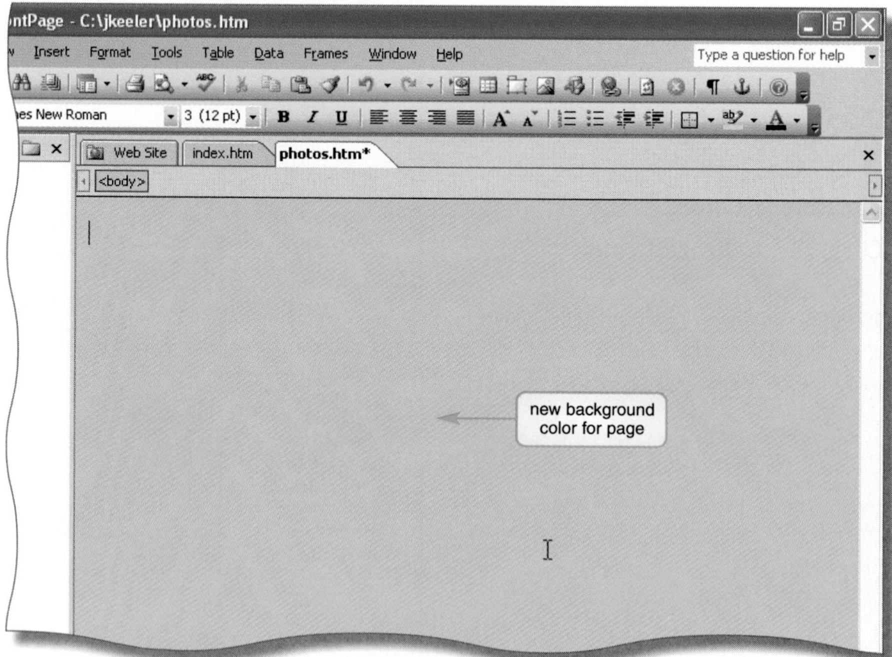

FIGURE 2-29

1. Right-click Web page, click Page Properties on shortcut menu, click Formatting tab
2. Press ALT+O, K, click Formatting tab
3. In Voice Command mode, say "Format, Background", click Formatting tab

When you click the Background box arrow, the color palette is displayed and allows you to select the color of your choice.

Selecting More Colors on the color palette displays a More Colors dialog box (Figure 2-27 on the previous page) with additional predefined colors available. For even more colors, click the Custom button in the More Colors dialog box to display a Color dialog box (Figure 2-30) in which you can mix your own color, save it as a custom color, and then use it as the background color.

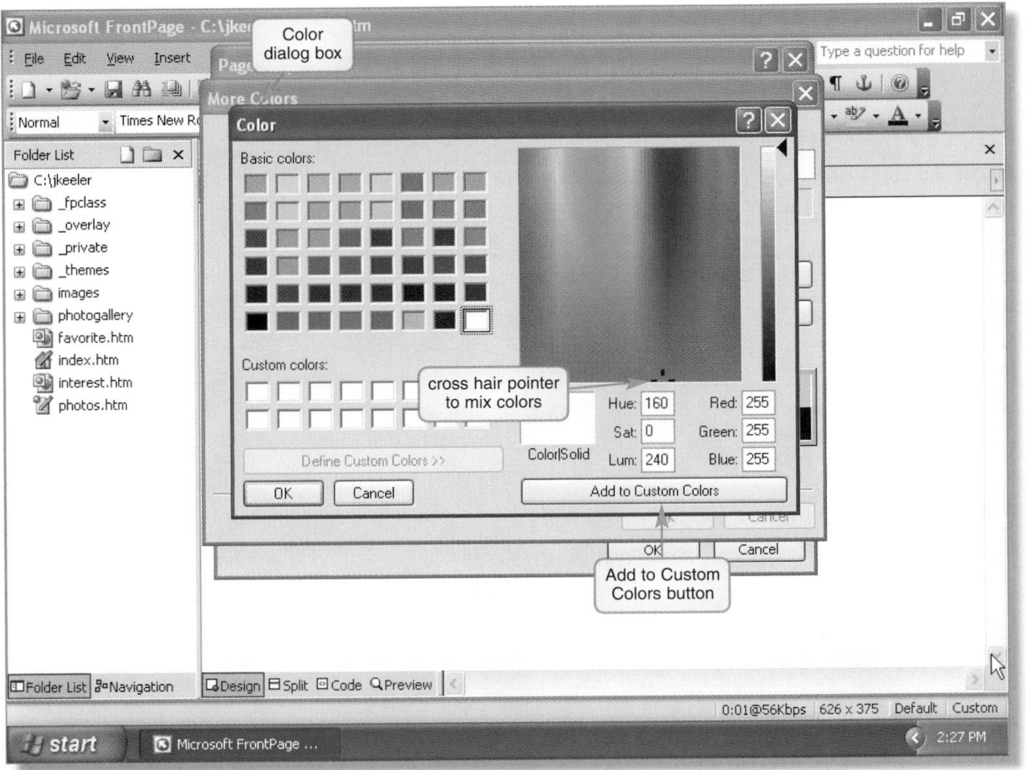

FIGURE 2-30

More About

Web Page Colors

FrontPage uses hue, saturation, and luminosity to specify colors. Hue represents a gradation of color, such as red or blue. Saturation is the amount of color in a hue. Luminosity is the brightness of a hue. Many sites offer help on selecting appropriate colors for Web pages. For more information about selecting colors for Web pages, visit the FrontPage 2003 More About page (scsite.com/fp2003/more) and then click Web Page Colors.

Inserting a Table in a Web Page

Tables are used frequently in applications to present information in a clear, concise format. Disciplines such as mathematics, engineering, and chemistry all take advantage of tables. A computer spreadsheet is laid out in the form of a table with rows and columns. Many different applications exist for which tables are an ideal solution.

An HTML table consists of one or more rows containing one or more columns. The intersection of a row and column is called a cell. Any Web page component, such as text or an image, can be placed in a cell.

Tables in a Web page help you to display any type of information that looks best in rows and columns, such as a list of products and their corresponding prices. In Web pages, tables also help you to accomplish special design effects, such as positioning of elements on a Web page.

More About

Tables

A table can have a different background color or image than the rest of the Web page. The Table Properties dialog box contains options that allow you to choose a different background color or an image file to display as a table background.

Design Tip

Before you create any table, sketch it on paper. Determine the number of rows and columns and the content that you will place in the cells. Calculate the overall width of the table and necessary width for each column.

You can create a table and insert your entire Web page in the cells. Using tables, you can define headings, sidebars, and captions and use other creative design techniques.

The Photos Web page will use a table with three rows and three columns to control the positioning of images, text, and the photo gallery (Figure 2-3 on page FP 87). The steps on the next page insert a table in a Web page.

To Insert a Table in a Web Page

1

• **Click the Insert Table button on the Standard toolbar.**

FrontPage displays the Insert Table grid (Figure 2-31). The grid is a graphical means of displaying the number of rows and columns used in a table. You can indicate how many rows and columns the table will have by clicking a cell on the grid.

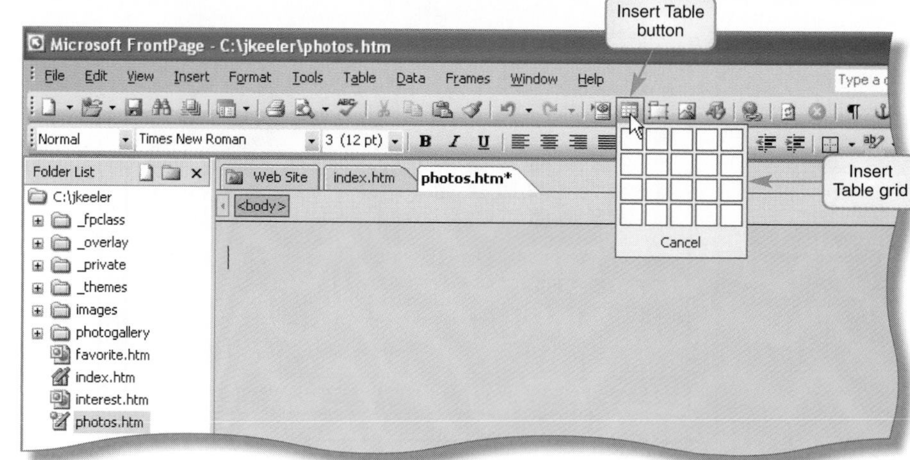

FIGURE 2-31

2

• **Point to the cell in the third row and third column to select nine squares in the grid.**

The nine squares are selected (Figure 2-32). This indicates a three-row table with three columns, for a total of nine cells.

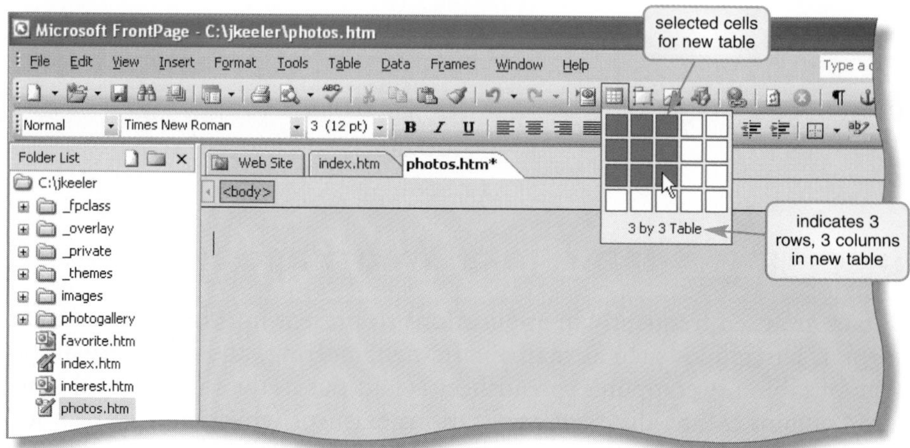

FIGURE 2-32

3

• **Click the cell in the third row and third column.**

FrontPage inserts a table in the Web page with three rows and three columns (Figure 2-33). The table extends across the width of the Web page. Each cell is the same size.

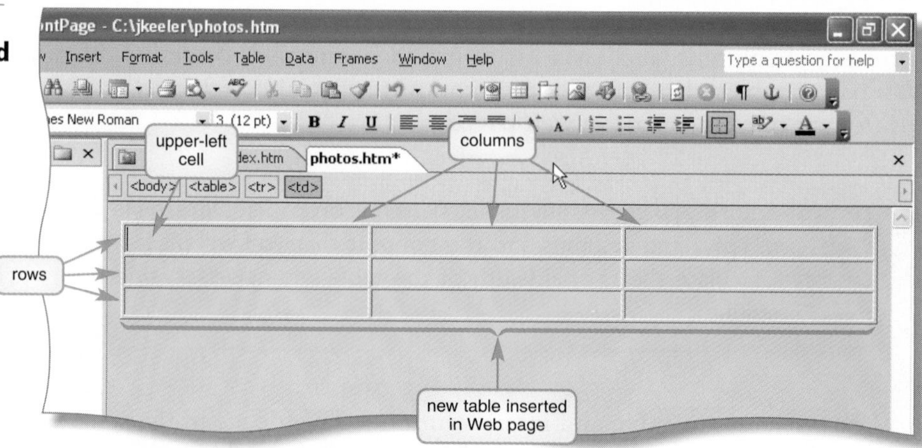

FIGURE 2-33

Other Ways

1. On Table menu click Insert, click Table
2. Press ALT+A, I, T
3. In Voice Command mode, say "Table, Insert, Table"

The Insert Table grid opens with only four rows and five columns. You can add more rows or columns simply by continuing to move the mouse through the grid. FrontPage automatically adds more rows and columns, and the Insert Table grid expands to accommodate the grid.

Extra rows can be added to the bottom of the table in the Web page by positioning the insertion point in the last column of the last row and then pressing the TAB key. You also can insert rows or columns anywhere in the table by positioning the insertion point and then clicking Insert on the Table menu and then clicking Rows or Columns. Doing so causes a dialog box to be displayed, allowing you to choose whether to insert rows or columns, the number to insert, and whether they should appear above or below the current insertion point. Finally, you can right-click any cell and then click Insert Rows on the shortcut menu to insert rows.

Merging Cells in a Table

When using a table to position items on a Web page, it is not unusual that some items span multiple cells in the table. By merging two or more cells in a table, you can set alignments that are more complex than just straight rows and columns.

The following steps merge cells in the table inserted in the previous set of steps.

To Merge Cells in a Table

1

- **Click the left cell in the middle row of the table.**
- **Hold down the SHIFT key and click the right cell in the middle row.**
- **Right-click one of the selected cells.**

The selected middle cells are highlighted, and a shortcut menu is displayed (Figure 2-34).

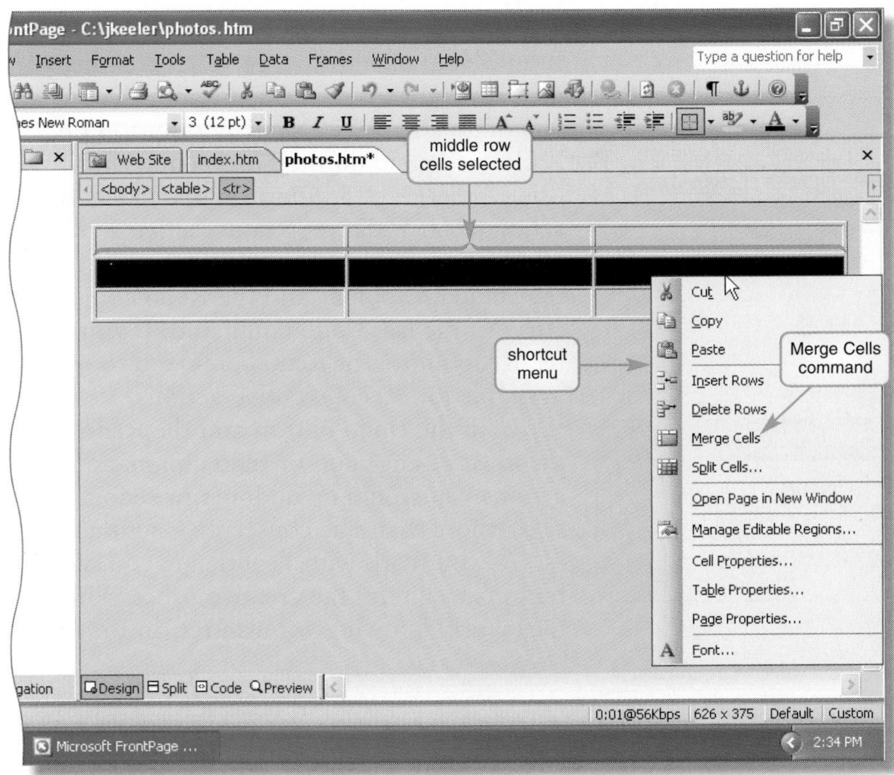

FIGURE 2-34

2

- **Click Merge Cells.**
- **Click the upper-left cell to remove the highlighting.**

The selected middle cells are merged into a single cell spanning three columns (Figure 2-35).

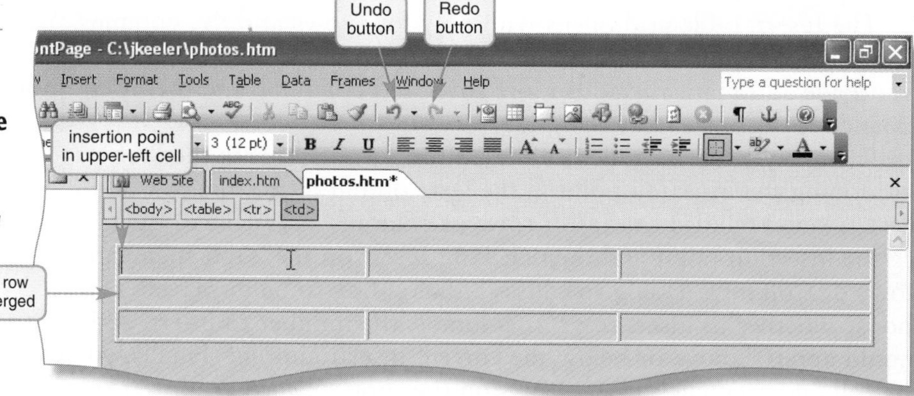

FIGURE 2-35

Other Ways

1. On Table menu click Merge Cells
2. Press ALT+A, M
3. In Voice Command mode, say "Table, Merge Cells"

In addition to using the SHIFT key to choose the final cell in a selection, you also can drag through the cells to select them. The shortcut menu shown in Figure 2-34 on the previous page indicates the commands available when working with tables and table cells. Merged cells can be split again using the Split Cells command on the shortcut menu.

Undoing and Redoing Actions

Even if you take great care when creating your Web pages, you may make mistakes or you may want to make an immediate change. FrontPage provides facilities to help you undo errors with the Undo button on the Standard toolbar (Figure 2-35) or the Undo command on the Edit menu. Thus, if you make a change or a mistake, undo it using either the Undo button or the Undo command. FrontPage will reverse your action as far back as 30 consecutive actions.

Also available for quick reversal of errors and changes are the Redo button on the Standard toolbar and the Redo command on the Edit menu. Redo reverses the effect of the last Undo command. If you decide the undo is incorrect, you can click the Redo button or Redo command to restore the last change you made. Redo is available for 30 consecutive actions.

Both the Undo button and the Redo button have arrows that allow you to see the most recent undo or redo commands, respectively. This allows you to see what actions you would be undoing or redoing before actually selecting them, and to select more than one consecutive action to undo or redo.

As you work with FrontPage, you will find that using the Undo and Redo buttons facilitates the creative process. You can add and rearrange items to see if they work, knowing you can return to a previous starting point with little effort.

Other Ways

1. Press ALT+E, U to undo
2. Press ALT+E, R to redo
3. Press CTRL+Z to undo
4. Press CTRL+Y to redo

Inserting an Image in a Web Page

Regardless of how impressive your written message, people always respond to images. The viewer's eye is drawn naturally to a picture before reading any text. The choice and quality of images you use largely determine whether someone will take the time to read your Web page or whether they will pass it by.

Much of the Web's success is due to its capability of presenting images. Because of the impact of images on the Web, it is important to master the image options necessary to include pictures in your Web pages.

Design Tip

When you design a Web page, do not limit your creativity to the print environment. Where appropriate, include color, photographs, animation, video, and sound clips.

Q&A

Q: What is the Clip Organizer?

A: One way to organize your clip art is to create a personal collection list using the Microsoft Clip Organizer. On the Insert menu, point to Picture, and then click Clip Art on the Picture submenu. When the Clip Art task pane displays, click Organize clips. You can create your own collections and even drag clips from one collection and drop them into other collections where you want them.

Along with the text heading, the Photos page has two images in the header. The table you inserted in earlier steps will be used to control the amount of horizontal spacing between the images and the text. The image on the left will be right-aligned in the left cell of the table. The image on the right will be left-aligned in the right cell of the table. The text, which is inserted later in the project, will be centered in the middle cell.

The goal of the images at the top of the page is to reflect the concept that the Photos page is like a computer-based photo album. Therefore, an image with an inviting cartoon caricature of a diploma is appropriate, reflecting that the pictures on the page relate to the author's academic experience. Refer to Table 2-1 on page FP 84 for criteria on the appropriate use of metaphors in your Web site designs.

FrontPage includes a library of ready-to-use images and photographs, called **clip art**, that you can insert into your Web pages. Some images probably are available on your local machine, but many more are accessible online. You also can use images from many different sources outside of FrontPage. You may use clip art from the FrontPage library or from the Data Disk to select an image for the Photos Web page.

To insert an image, you first position the insertion point at the desired location, and then select the image. The following steps insert an image in the Web page.

To Insert a Clip Art Image in a Web Page

1

- **If necessary, click the upper-left cell of the table to position the insertion point.**
- **Click Insert on the menu bar and then point to Picture.**

FrontPage displays the Insert menu and the Picture submenu (Figure 2-36).

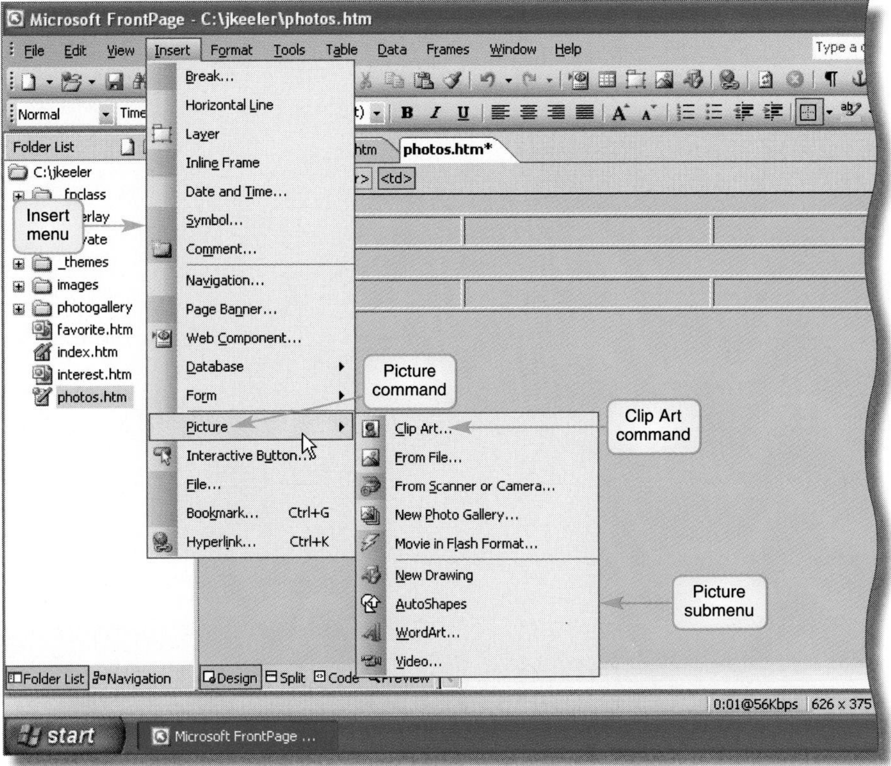

FIGURE 2-36

2

- **Click Clip Art.**
- **When the Clip Art task pane appears, type** `diploma` **in the Search for text box.**

FrontPage displays the Clip Art task pane (Figure 2-37). You can search for an image file or clip art file from your personal collections or collections from Office on your local computer, or from Microsoft collections on the World Wide Web.

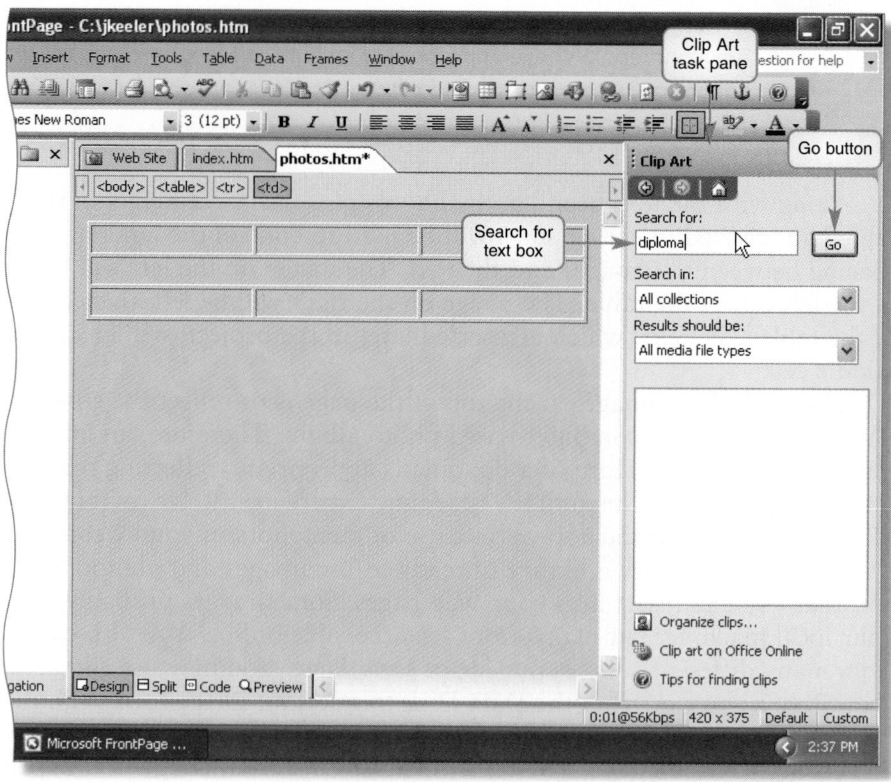

FIGURE 2-37

3

- **Click the Go button.**

FrontPage displays the results of your search as small sample preview images (Figure 2-38). Your sample images may be different.

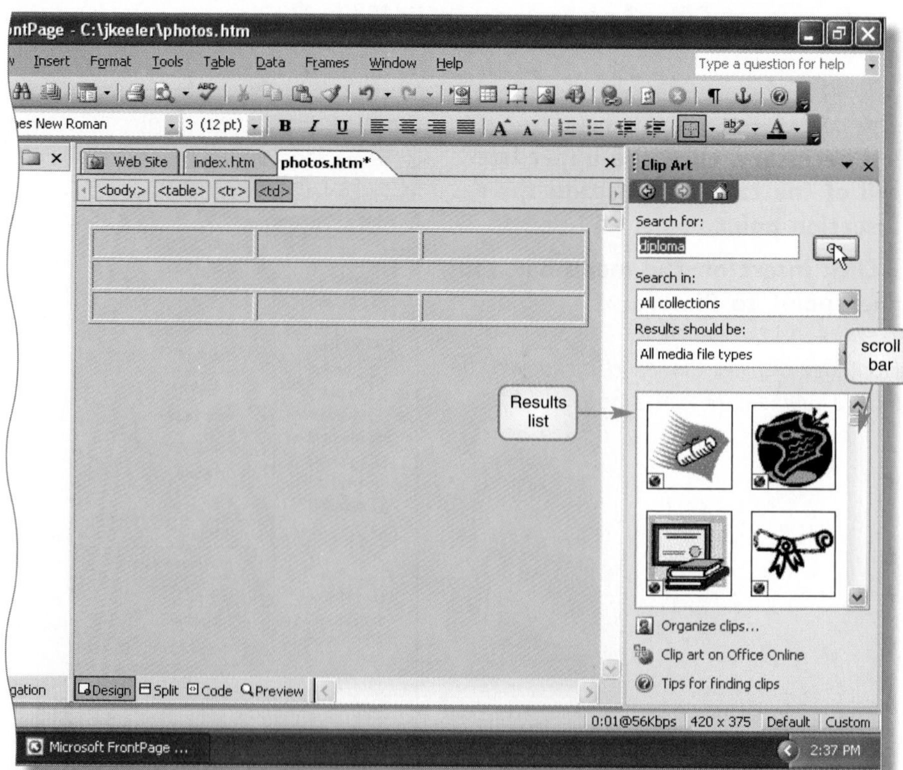

FIGURE 2-38

4

- **If necessary, scroll down the Results list until an image of a diploma is displayed, or another image of your choice.**

The image to be inserted is displayed (Figure 2-39).

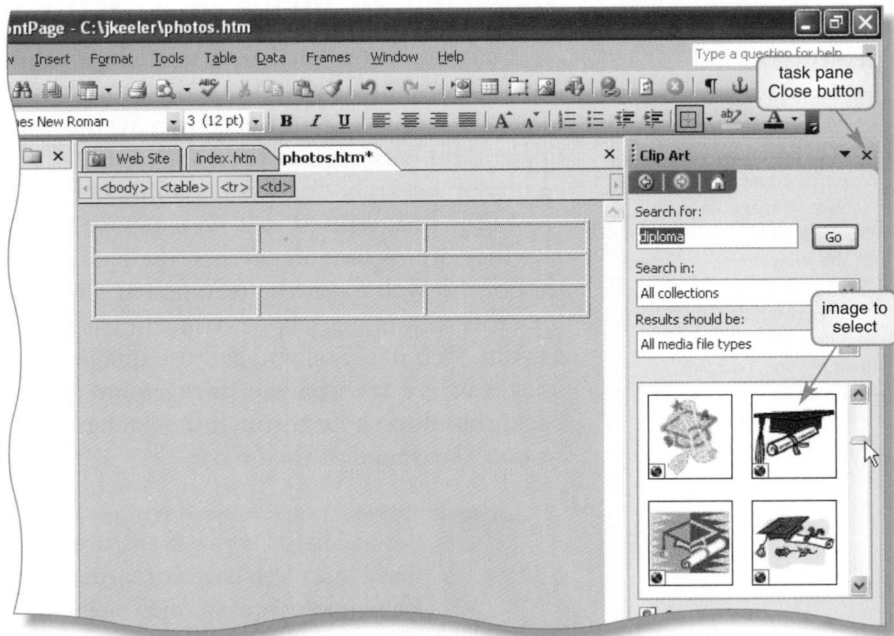

FIGURE 2-39

5

- **Point to the image.**
- **Click the box arrow and then click Insert on the shortcut menu to insert the clip art in the Web page.**
- **Click the Close button on the Clip Art task pane.**

When you point to the image, FrontPage displays a box arrow on its right. FrontPage inserts the clip art image into the upper-left cell of the table (Figure 2-40).

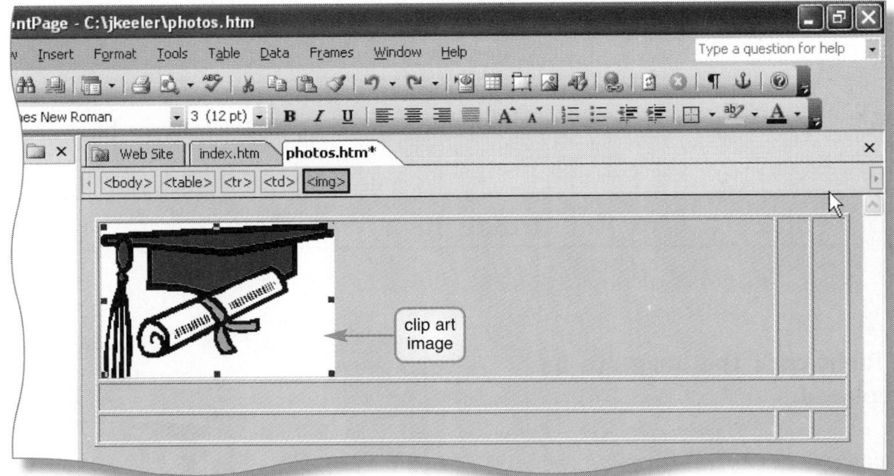

FIGURE 2-40

Other Ways

1. On Insert menu point to Picture, click Clip Art
2. On Insert menu point to Picture, click From File
3. Press ALT+I, P, C
4. Press ALT+I, P, F
5. In Voice Command mode, say "Insert, Picture, Clip Art"

As you can see in Figure 2-39, many samples of clip art may be available. By default, FrontPage searches both the World Wide Web and your local machine. Typically, the number of images on your local machine is limited. To obtain a large number of images, search the World Wide Web.

Design Tip

Before downloading photos or other media from the Web, ensure that they have no copyright restrictions or royalty charges that you cannot or will not pay. Royalty charges are fees to be paid to the creator or owner of the art for its use.

Replacing an Image in a Web Page

Once an image has been inserted into the Web page, you may decide that it is not as appealing as you originally thought. While many reasons to change an image may exist, replacing an image in a Web page is as easy as inserting the original image. You may replace the image simply by selecting a different image from the results of a search, or by using an image available on your local machine.

Many images used in a Web page may appear to be irregular in shape, when in fact they are rectangular. When the background color of the image is not the same as that of the Web page, the rectangular shape of the image becomes very obvious. To hide this rectangular shape, you can use images that have the same background color as your Web page, or you can use images that have a transparent background. Using images with a **transparent background** allows the color or image used in a Web page background to show through the background of the inserted image, thus hiding the rectangular shape of the image.

More About

Images

The more images your Web site contains, the longer it takes to download your Web pages. To count the total number of images in your Web site, point to Reports on the View menu, and then click Site Summary. In the Pictures row, the Count column lists the number of pictures in your Web site. Pictures located in hidden folders normally are not included in this report.

Design Tip

Using images with a transparent background allows the color or image used in a Web page background to show through the background of the inserted image, thus hiding the rectangular shape of the image. Cropping an image can eliminate distracting background elements and establish the focal point of the image. Discarding unwanted portions of an image also reduces its file size.

The following steps replace the image just inserted with a similar one from the local machine that has a transparent background.

To Replace a Clip Art Image in a Web Page

- **Right-click the image to be replaced.**

FrontPage displays a shortcut menu, and eight small boxes, called sizing handles, are displayed around the selected image (Figure 2-41).

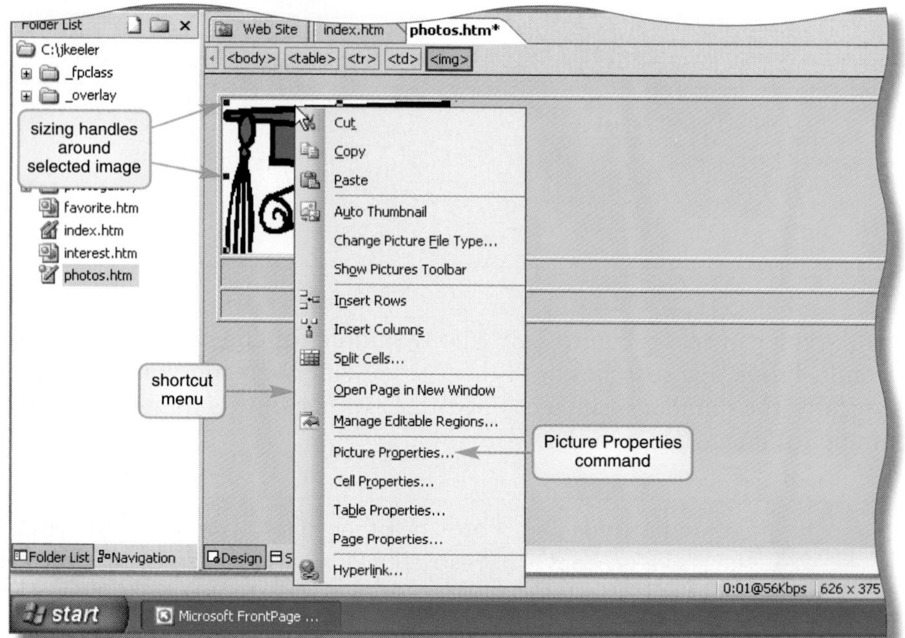

FIGURE 2-41

2

- **Click Picture Properties.**
- **If necessary, when the Picture Properties dialog box is displayed, click the General tab.**

FrontPage displays the Picture Properties dialog box. The name and location of the current image file are selected in the Picture text box (Figure 2-42).

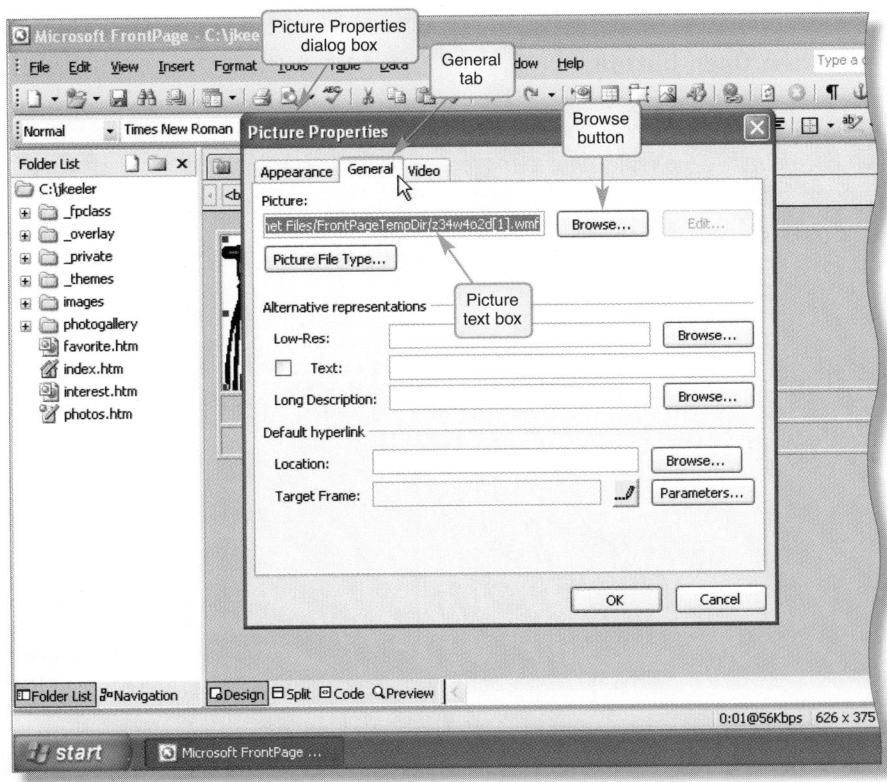

FIGURE 2-42

3

- **Click the Browse button.**
- **Insert the Data Disk in drive A.**
- **If necessary, when FrontPage displays the Picture dialog box, click the Look in box arrow and select the graduation.gif file in the Project2 folder.**

FrontPage displays the Picture dialog box with the graduation.gif file in the A:\Project2 folder selected (Figure 2-43). Use the drive and location that are appropriate for your environment.

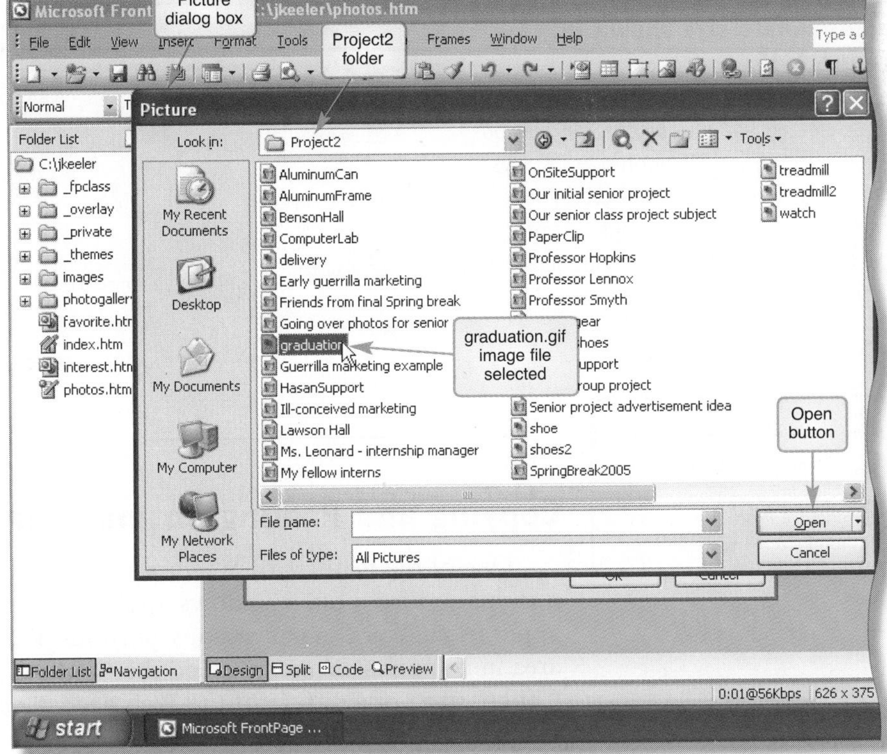

FIGURE 2-43

4

- **Click the Open button.**

FrontPage closes the Picture dialog box. FrontPage displays the replacement image file name and location in the Picture text box (Figure 2-44).

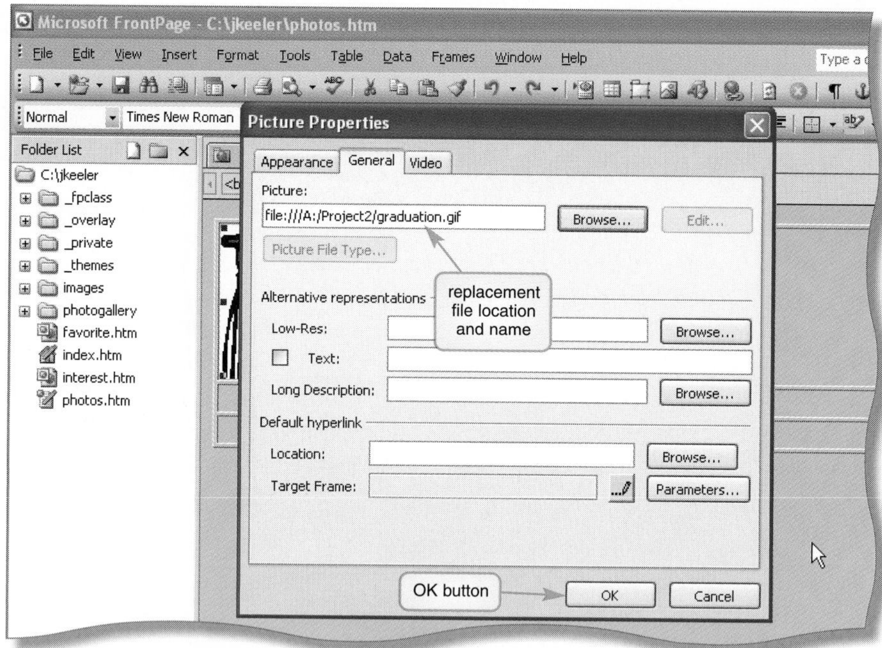

FIGURE 2-44

5

- **Click the OK button.**
- **Resize the replacement image by dragging the sizing handles to the approximate size shown in Figure 2-45.**

The selected image replaces the previous image (Figure 2-45). FrontPage displays sizing handles around the selected image. FrontPage changes the mouse pointer to a double-headed arrow when positioned on a sizing handle.

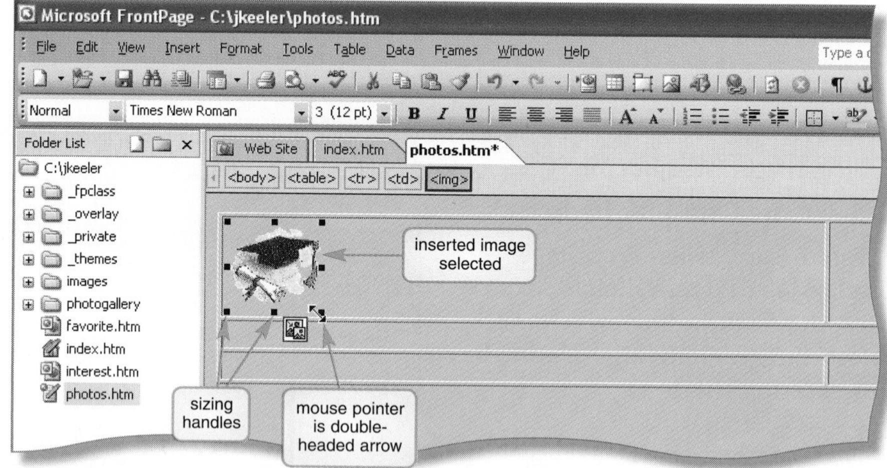

FIGURE 2-45

Other Ways

1. Open Pictures toolbar, click image, click Insert Picture From File button on Pictures toolbar

Copying and Pasting an Image in a Web Page

One of the features of Windows applications is the capability of copying information from one Windows application and inserting it in another Windows application. You can cut or copy portions of a Web page to a temporary storage area in computer memory, called the **Clipboard**, and then paste the contents of the Clipboard to other areas of the Web page. **Copy**, **Cut**, and **Paste** are useful when you want to move an item to another location or have the same item appearing several times in various places throughout the Web page. The clip art image you just inserted is to be inserted again, this time in the right cell of the table.

You can, of course, insert the clip art image using the steps previously shown for inserting an image. You also can copy the image to the Clipboard and then paste the image from the Clipboard to the Web page at the location of the insertion point. In this instance, the copy and paste operation would be more efficient, because you would have to maneuver through several windows to get the image from the Microsoft Clip Gallery or from an image on disk. The following steps copy and then paste the diploma image to another location in the Web page.

To Copy and Paste an Image in a Web Page

1

- **If necessary, click the clip art image to select it.**
- **Click Edit on the menu bar.**

The image is selected and the Edit menu is displayed (Figure 2-46). The Copy command copies a selected item to the Clipboard.

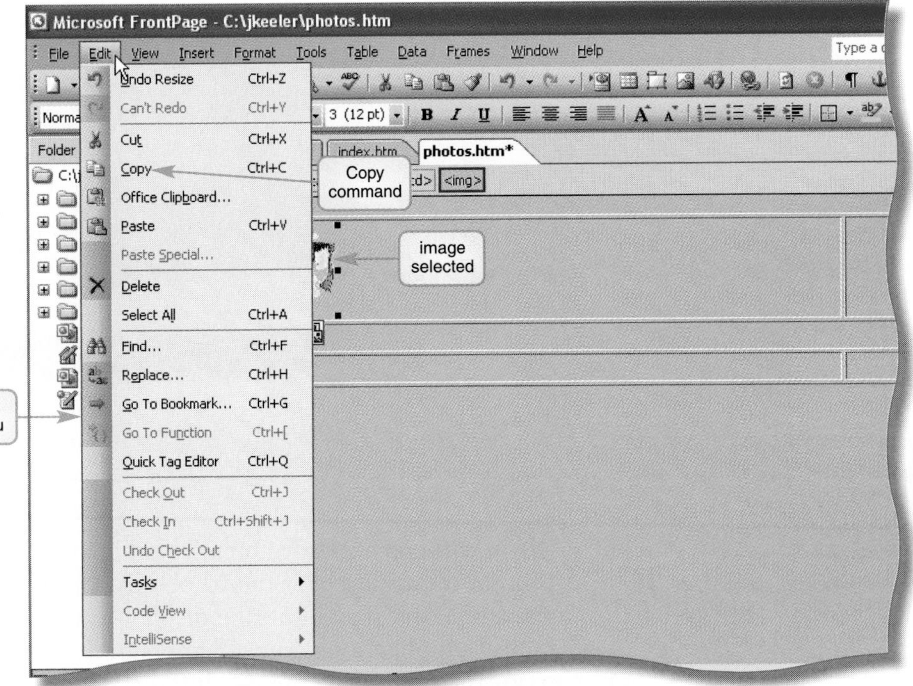

FIGURE 2-46

2

- **Click Copy and then click the upper-right cell of the table to position the insertion point.**
- **Click Edit on the menu bar.**

FrontPage displays the Edit menu (Figure 2-47). The image was copied to the Clipboard in the previous step. The Paste command inserts the contents of the Clipboard at the location of the insertion point.

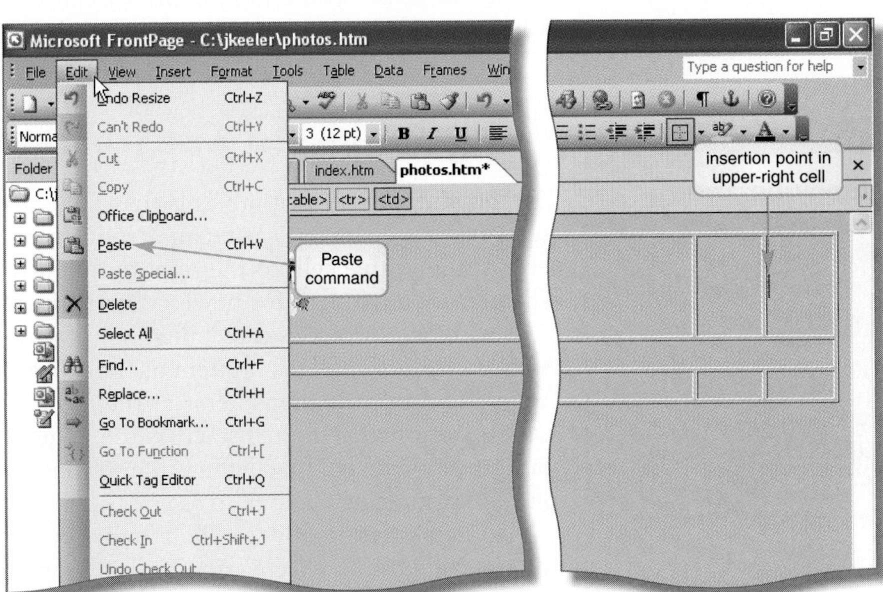

FIGURE 2-47

• **Click Paste.**

FrontPage copies the image on the Clipboard to the right table cell (Figure 2-48).

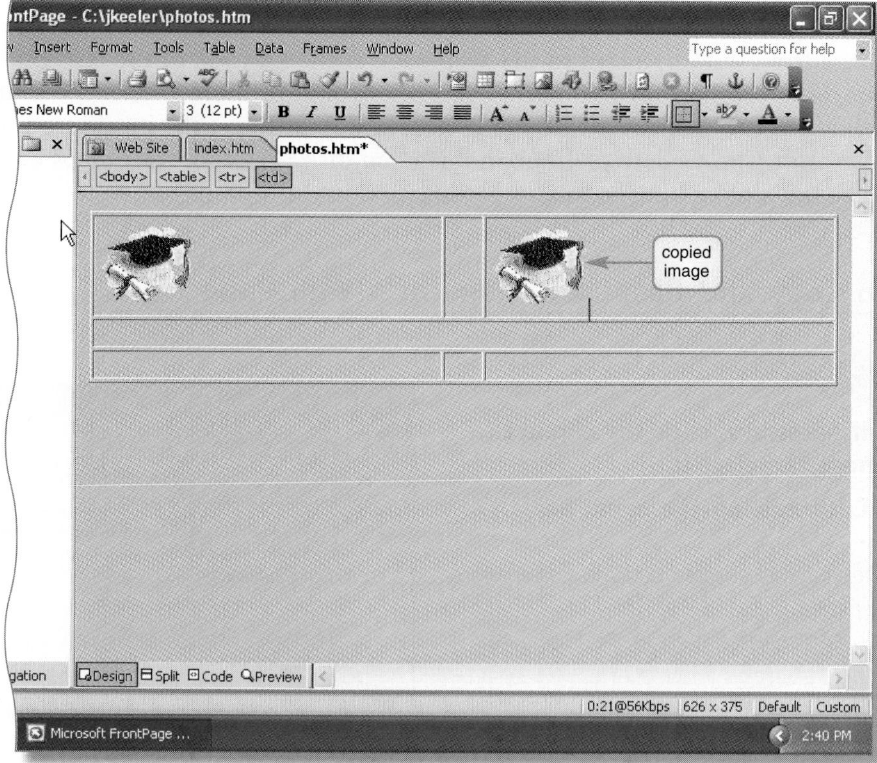

FIGURE 2-48

Other Ways

1. Press ALT+E, C to copy
2. Press ALT+E, P to paste
3. Press CTRL+C to copy
4. Press CTRL+V to paste
5. In Voice Command mode, say "Copy" to copy, or say "Paste" to paste

You can copy text or an entire table and then paste it in a similar fashion. Although the contents of the Clipboard can be inserted into other Windows applications, some objects will not be displayed as you would expect. Because many other Windows applications do not understand HTML, they cannot make an accurate copy of the three-row, three-column table if you were to try pasting it. You can, however, copy or cut and paste the clip art images and any text into other Windows applications, but you will lose any special formatting applied to the text. This again is because of the problem with translating HTML.

More About

Copying and Pasting

You can copy an image to a Web page by dragging the image from another Windows application to FrontPage. In addition to the Copy and Paste commands on the Edit menu, you also may use the shortcut keys, CTRL+C and CTRL+V.

Using Tables to Control Alignment on a Web Page

One advantage of using tables is that they allow you to control the arrangement of items on the Web page. You can arrange, or **align**, the current text or image to the left within a table cell, to the right within a table cell, or centered in the table cell. The default alignment for newly inserted items is left-aligned.

FrontPage provides three alignment buttons on the Formatting toolbar. The Align Left button aligns an item at the left margin of the page or table cell. The Align Right button aligns items at the right margin of the page or table cell. The Center button centers items across the page or in a table cell. You simply select the paragraph or image by clicking it, and then click the appropriate alignment button on the Formatting toolbar.

To demonstrate how to align items on a Web page, the clip art image inserted in the left cell will be selected and right-aligned in the cell, which results in the clip art image aligning at the right along with text that will follow later. The following steps align an item on a Web page.

To Align Items on a Web Page

1

- **If necessary, click the clip art image in the left cell to select it.**

FrontPage shows the clip art image as selected (Figure 2-49).

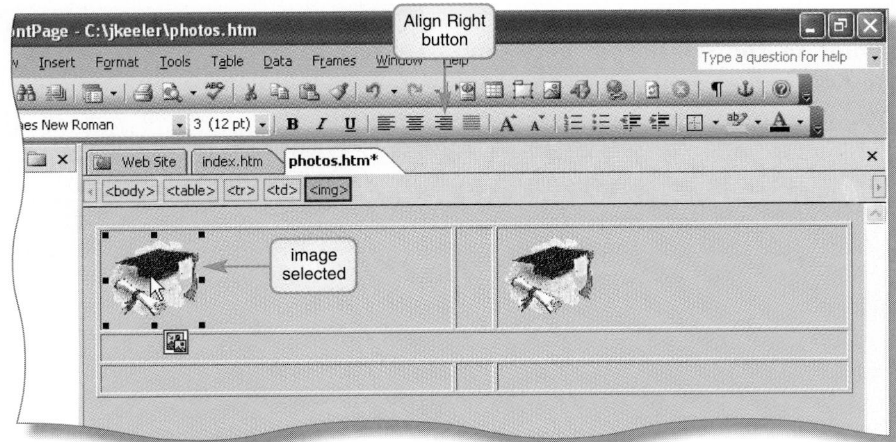

FIGURE 2-49

2

- **Click the Align Right button on the Formatting toolbar.**

FrontPage aligns the clip art image at the right margin of the table cell (Figure 2-50). The Align Right button on the Formatting toolbar is selected to denote that the image has been right-aligned.

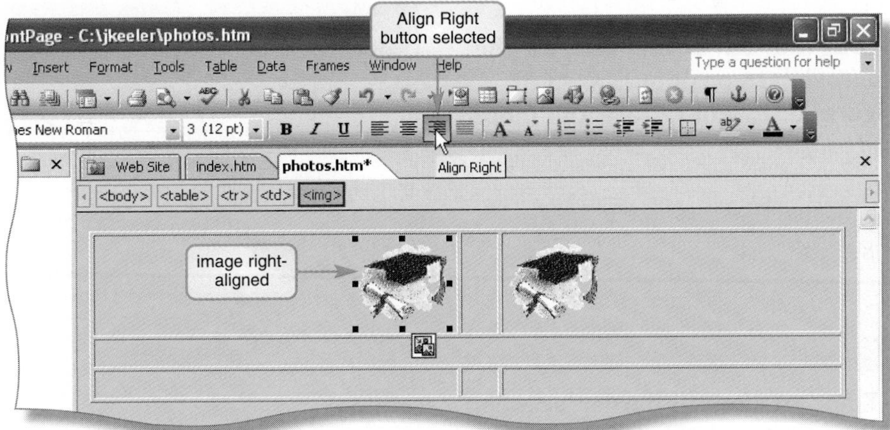

FIGURE 2-50

The image is right-aligned in the left table cell on the Web page. In later steps you use the Center button to center text and other items on the Web page.

Adjusting Table Borders

Another useful feature of tables is the capability of moving the outside borders of a table and the borders between individual cells, thus providing added flexibility in controlling spacing on the Web page.

You can adjust the borders of the table to control vertical and horizontal spacing. The bottom border can be dragged up or down to control vertical spacing. The right border can be dragged right or left to control horizontal spacing. The borders between cells also can be moved to control spacing within the table.

As shown in Figure 2-50, the clip art images do not consume all the space in their respective cells. You can adjust the borders between the cells to reduce the space in the two outside cells and increase the space in the center cell, thus providing more room for the heading. The steps on the next page adjust the borders of table cells.

To Adjust Table Cell Borders

1

- **Point to the cell border between the first and second cell in the top row.**

FrontPage changes the mouse pointer to a double-headed arrow (Figure 2-51).

FIGURE 2-51

2

- **Drag the cell border left, to the approximate position shown in Figure 2-52, and release the mouse button.**

The cell border moves to the left (Figure 2-52).

FIGURE 2-52

3

- **Point to the cell border between the second and third cell in the top row.**
- **Drag the cell border right, toward the left edge of the clip art image, so that the right cell is approximately the same size as the left cell.**

The cell border moves to the right (Figure 2-53).

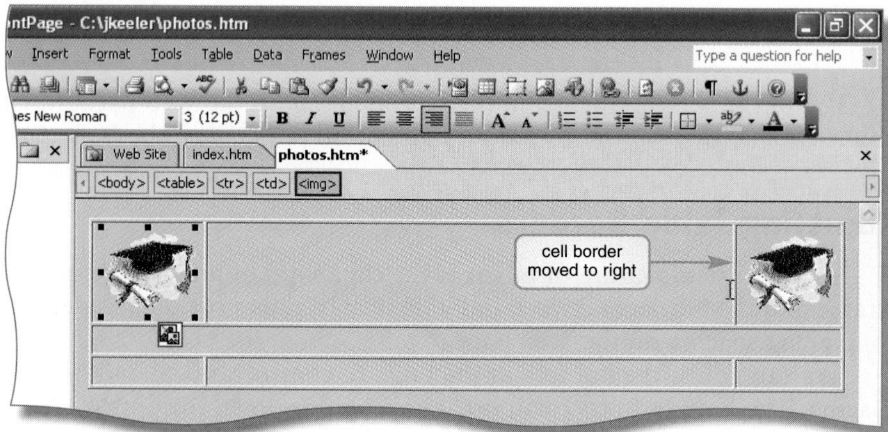

FIGURE 2-53

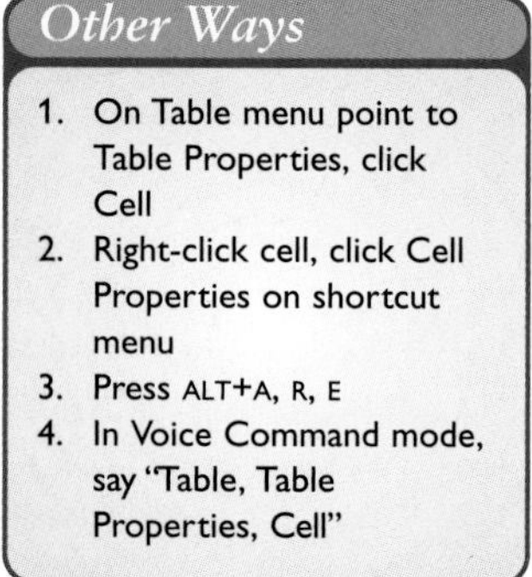

Other Ways

1. On Table menu point to Table Properties, click Cell
2. Right-click cell, click Cell Properties on shortcut menu
3. Press ALT+A, R, E
4. In Voice Command mode, say "Table, Table Properties, Cell"

Moving the cell to occupy the minimum width for the images allows more space in the center cell for the Photos page heading text. You should insert the images in the table cells before adjusting the cell borders so that you can see how much space is available. Adjusting table and cell borders is a powerful way of controlling spacing on a Web page.

Modifying Table Properties

A number of table properties can be adjusted to control how the table is displayed on a Web page. FrontPage allows you to adjust the horizontal alignment of the table with respect to the Web page. FrontPage also allows you to adjust the width of the table as a percentage of the entire page, or as a specified number of pixels. A **pixel**, short for **picture element**, is the smallest addressable element on your computer screen. Instead of dragging cell borders, you also may set the cell width directly by specifying the width as a percentage of the table, or as a specified number of pixels.

Tables and the individual cells are surrounded by a default table border. You can adjust the properties of the border, such as the width, color, and use of a 3-D shadow. When using a table for spacing purposes, you most likely will not want the table borders to be seen. You can turn off the border display and adjust other table properties by using the Table Properties command on the Table menu. The following steps modify table properties.

To Modify the Properties of a Table

1

- **If necessary, click one of the cells of the table.**
- **Click Table on the menu bar and then point to Table Properties.**

FrontPage displays the Table menu and Table Properties submenu (Figure 2-54). The Table menu contains commands to manage tables. The Table Properties submenu contains commands to access properties of tables or individual cells.

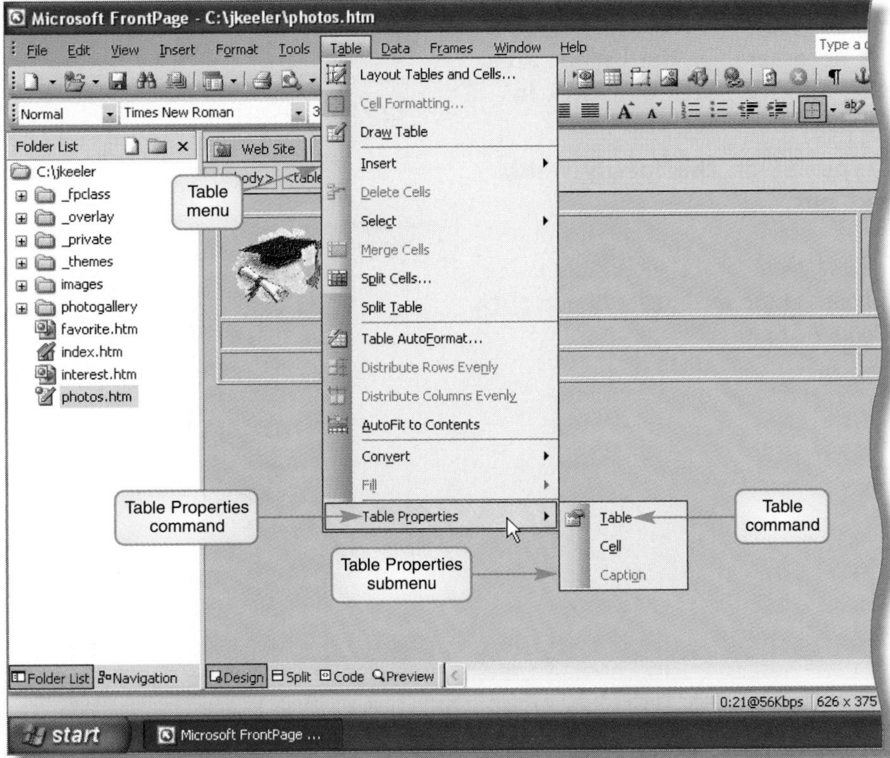

FIGURE 2-54

2

• **Click Table on the Table Properties submenu.**

• **When FrontPage displays the Table Properties dialog box, click the Alignment box down arrow in the Layout area.**

FrontPage displays the Table Properties dialog box (Figure 2-55). Options in this dialog box allow you to control various aspects of the table border and table background. The Alignment box in the Layout area allows you to control the horizontal alignment of the table on the Web page.

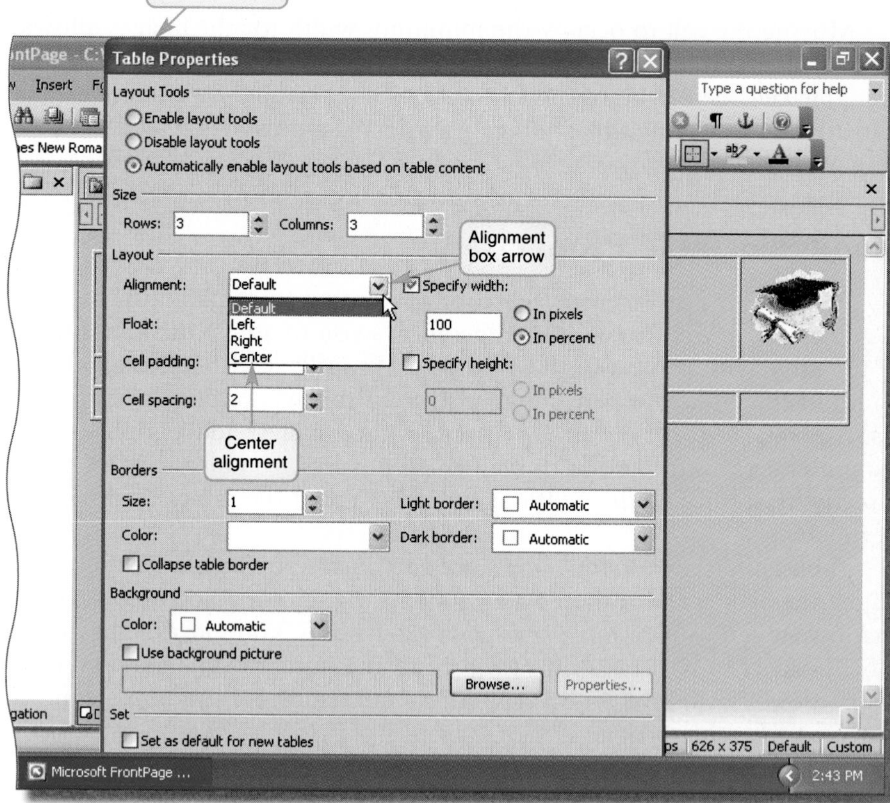

FIGURE 2-55

3

• **Click Center.**

• **If necessary, in the Layout area, click Specify width and click In pixels.**

• **Type** 688 **in the Specify width text box.**

The alignment for the table is set to Center and the width is set to 688 pixels (Figure 2-56).

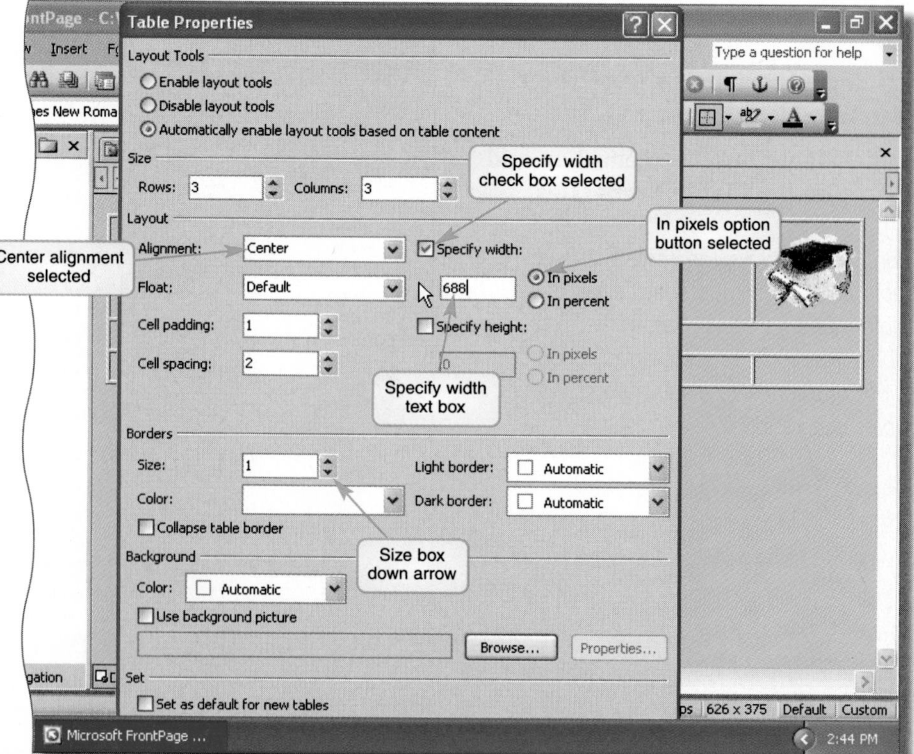

FIGURE 2-56

4

- **In the Borders area, click the Size box down arrow until zero (0) appears in the Size box.**

FrontPage displays zero (0) in the Size box, indicating that no visible border will be displayed around the table cells (Figure 2-57).

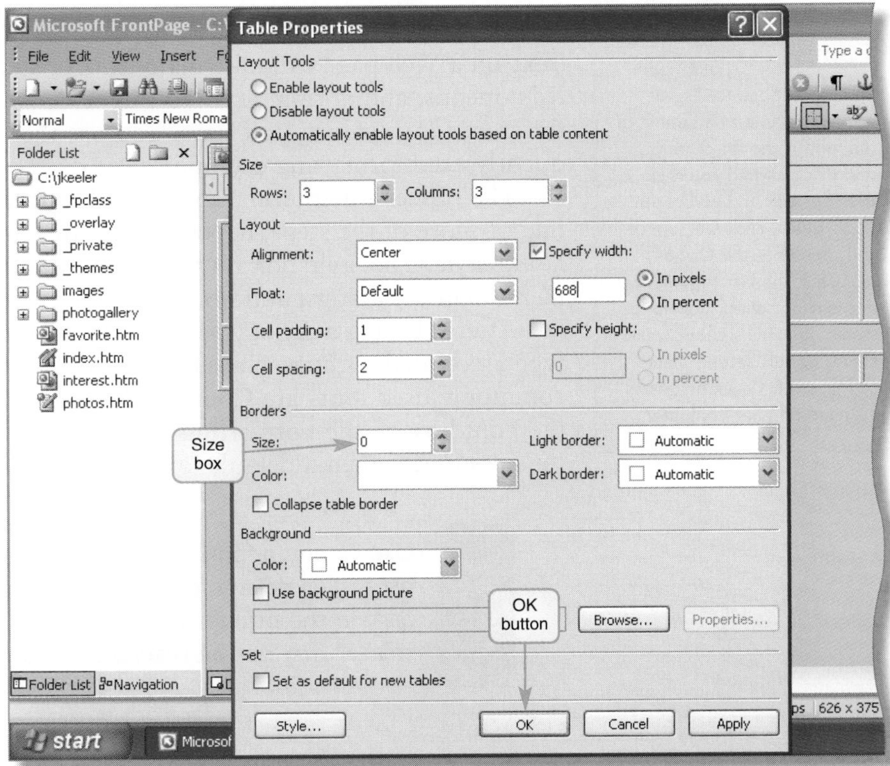

FIGURE 2-57

5

- **Click the OK button.**

The table width is set and the table border is replaced with dashed lines (Figure 2-58). These lines show you where the cell borders are and also indicate that no visible border is displayed when the browser displays the Web page.

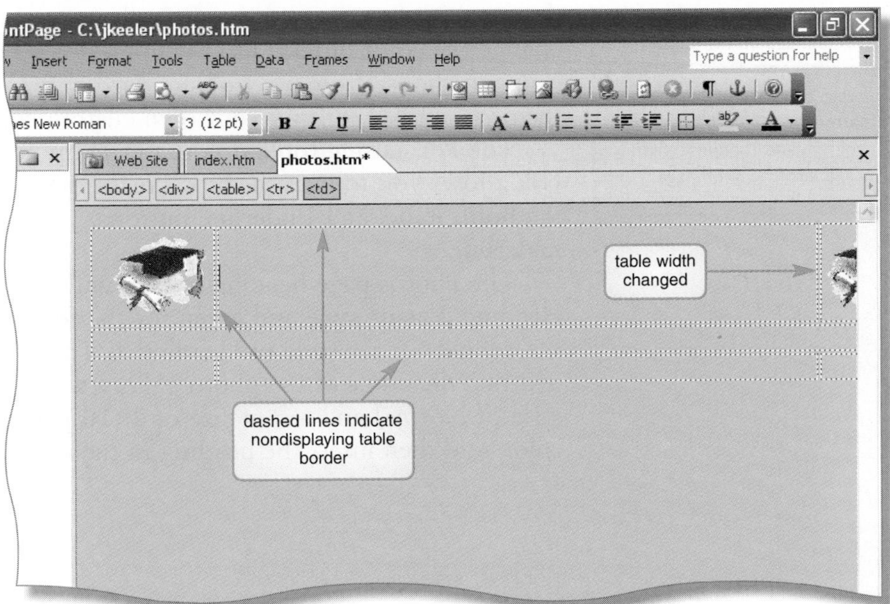

FIGURE 2-58

Other Ways

1. Right-click table, click Table Properties on shortcut menu
2. Press ALT+A, R, T
3. In Voice Command mode, say "Table, Table Properties, Table"

You have adjusted the borders around table cells and turned off the display of the table border. Now that the size of the center cell has been adjusted, the heading for the Web page can be inserted.

More About

Fonts

You can choose to display each font name as a sample of the font in the list of fonts that display when you click the Font box arrow. On the Tools menu, click Customize, and then click the Options tab. Click the List font names in their font check box so that it contains a check mark. Changing this setting affects all Microsoft Office programs installed on your computer.

Inserting a Heading in a Web Page

Text on a Web page can take many forms, such as a heading, ordered and unordered lists, menus, and normal text. To this text, you can apply special formatting such as different fonts, colors, and sizes. You use the Formatting toolbar for the more frequently used formatting options.

The process of entering text using FrontPage has several steps. You might skip one or more of the steps, depending on the current settings. The first step is to select a text style. The Style box on the Formatting toolbar contains styles such as lists, menu items, headings, and normal text.

After selecting a style, you may change the font type for the text or use the font type associated with the chosen style. A **font** is another name for character set. Some commonly used fonts are Courier, Helvetica, and Arial. You change the font using the Font box on the Formatting toolbar. If a font is not available on a Web site visitor's computer, then a default font is applied in the visitor's browser.

Design Tip

Use common fonts in your Web pages to increase the chances of overriding default font settings and allowing the visitor to view the page in the manner in which it was designed. Type that is 10 points or smaller may not be readable to many Web page visitors.

More About

Text Formatting

If the text formatting options in FrontPage do not provide the effect you desire, you can create an image of the formatted text using a graphics program and then insert the image into the Web page.

Next, you select a color for the text. The default color is black. A text color that complements the background color or image you have chosen is preferred so your text does not fade in and out as it moves across a background image or pattern. You do not want your page to be difficult to read because of poor color selection. To change the color of text, use the Font Color button arrow on the Formatting toolbar. You can choose from a set of standard colors or from a set that matches a theme if a theme is applied, or mix your own custom colors.

The Formatting toolbar contains many text-formatting options. The Font Size box allows you to increase or decrease the size of the characters in your text. Using the Bold, Italic, and Underline buttons, you can format certain text in bold, italic, or underline.

The Photos page heading, which will be placed in the center table cell, consists of Heading 2 as its style and green for the font color. The font and font size used are the default for the style of Heading 2. The heading also is centered in the cell. The text on either side of the photo gallery will use the same font color, but will have a style of Normal and a font size of 2 (10 pt). The following steps set the style and color, and then insert the heading in the center cell.

To Add a Heading to a Web Page

1

- **If necessary, click the top center table cell to position the insertion point.**
- **Click the Style box arrow.**
- **If necessary, scroll down to Heading 2 in the Style list.**

FrontPage displays the insertion point in the top center table cell. FrontPage also displays the Style list (Figure 2-59). It contains a list of styles available for use when developing Web pages.

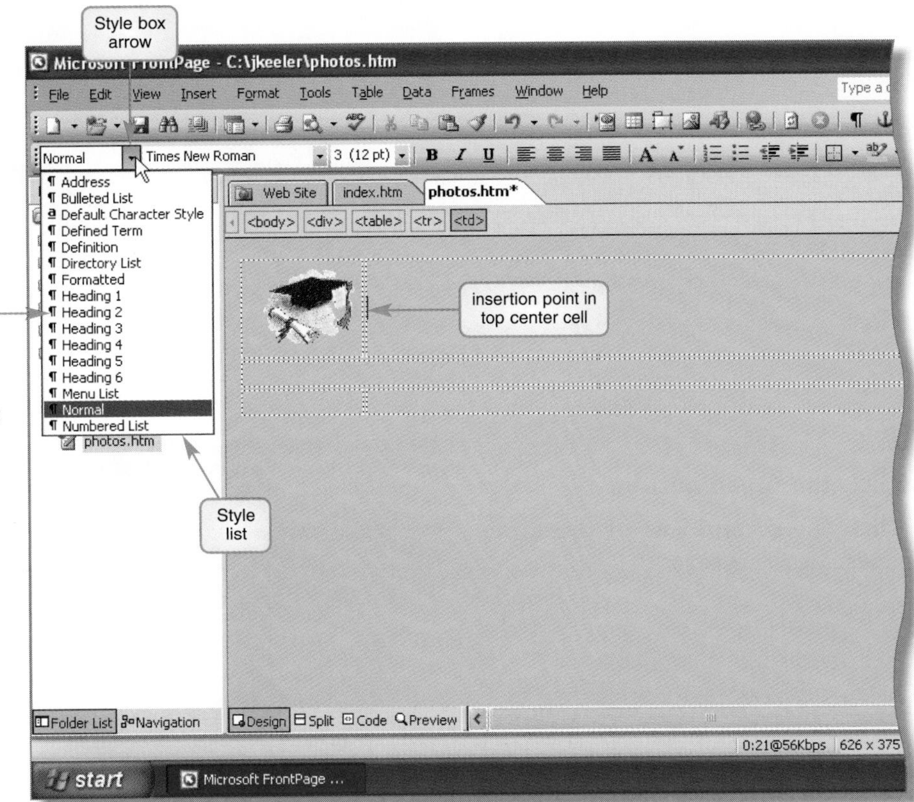

FIGURE 2-59

2

- **Click Heading 2.**
- **Click the Center button on the Formatting toolbar.**
- **Type** `Marketing Experience` **in the top center cell.**
- **Press SHIFT+ENTER.**
- **Type** `Photo Album` **to enter the remainder of the text.**

FrontPage displays the text centered in the top center table cell with a style of Heading 2 (Figure 2-60). The font and the font size associated with the style Heading 2 are displayed in the Font box and the Font Size box, respectively. The Bold button on the Formatting toolbar is selected automatically. Your font and font size may be different.

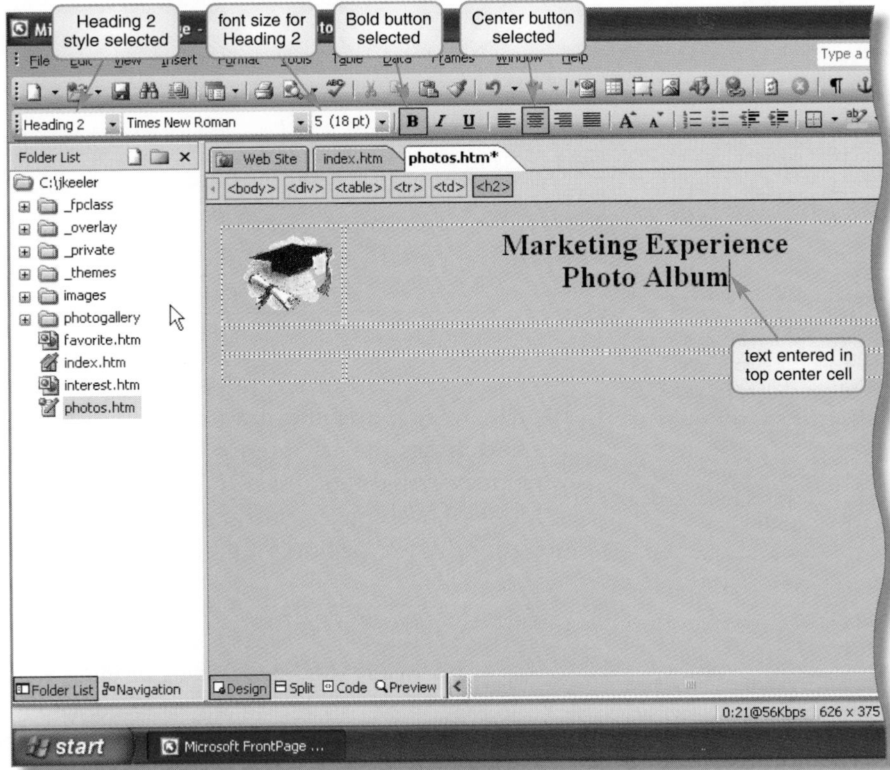

FIGURE 2-60

3

- **Drag through the text to select it.**
- **Click the Font Color button arrow.**

FrontPage displays the color palette (Figure 2-61).

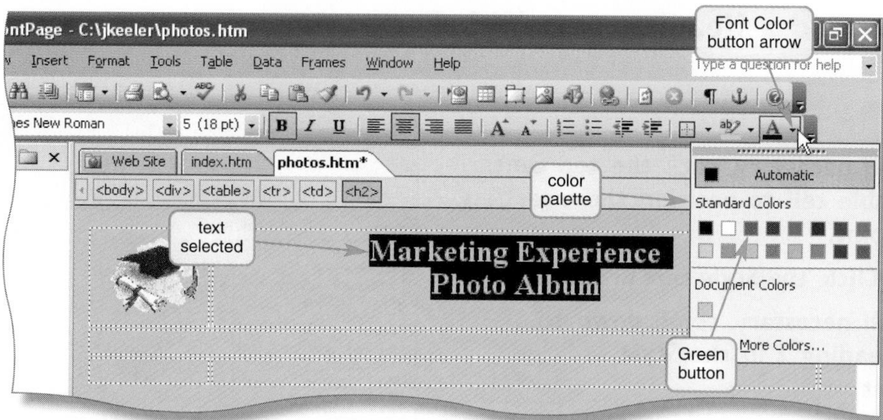

FIGURE 2-61

4

- **Click the Green button.**
- **Click the second row of the table to deselect the text.**

FrontPage displays the text centered in the top center cell with a color of green (Figure 2-62).

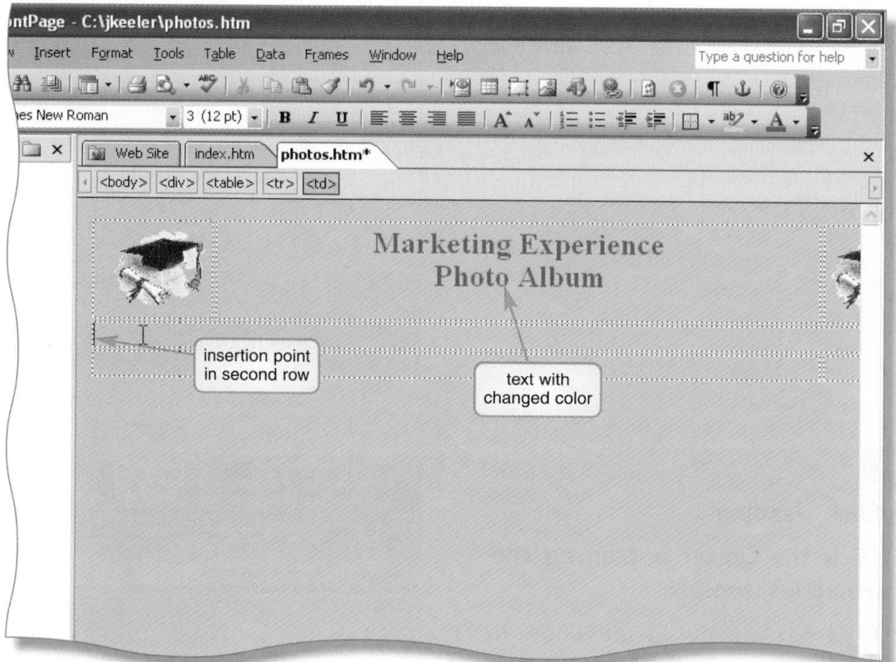

FIGURE 2-62

Other Ways

1. On Format menu click Font, click Font tab
2. Right-click text, click Font, click Font tab
3. Press ALT+ENTER
4. In Voice Command mode, say "Format, Font", click Font tab

Because the header is the part of the page that first-time viewers initially see in their browsers, it is important to format the header of the Web page so it is appealing and draws further interest. The body of the Web page keeps the viewer's attention when it is verbalized and formatted appropriately. It is customary to separate logical sections of Web pages, such as the header and body, using dividing elements called horizontal lines, or horizontal rules.

Design Tip

It is customary to separate logical sections of Web pages, such as the header and body, using dividing elements called horizontal lines, or horizontal rules. Use headers and footers on pages that comprise the main navigational structure of your site. Secondary pages need not fit a rigid design structure.

Inserting a Horizontal Rule

The use of elements such as a horizontal rule can add a special look to your pages, as well as provide the viewer with visual clues concerning the location of information on the Web page. Horizontal rules are used to break up the page into sections, and to separate elements on the page. A **horizontal rule** is a small, thin line that spans the entire Web page.

A horizontal rule will be used to separate the header section of the Web page from the body. The following steps insert a horizontal rule below the table cells containing the clip art images and heading.

To Add a Horizontal Rule to a Web Page

1

- **If necessary, click the second table row to position the insertion point.**
- **Click Insert on the menu bar.**

FrontPage displays the Insert menu (Figure 2-63). The Insert menu contains commands to insert various elements in the current Web page.

FIGURE 2-63

2

- **Click Horizontal Line.**
- **Press the DELETE key to remove the trailing blank line.**

FrontPage displays the horizontal rule in the middle row (Figure 2-64).

FIGURE 2-64

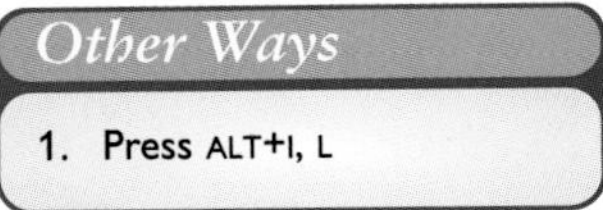
Other Ways

1. Press ALT+I, L

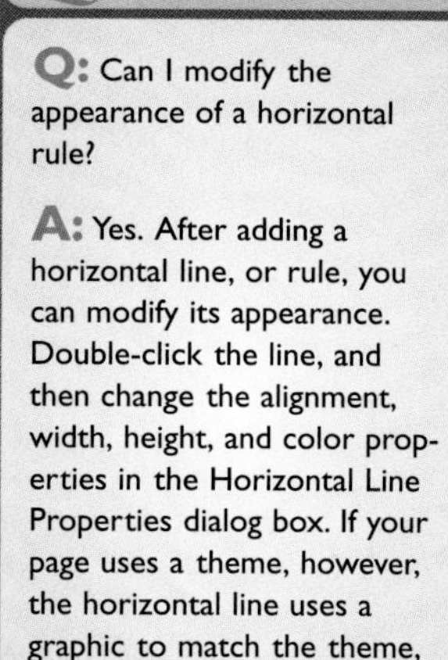

Q: Can I modify the appearance of a horizontal rule?

A: Yes. After adding a horizontal line, or rule, you can modify its appearance. Double-click the line, and then change the alignment, width, height, and color properties in the Horizontal Line Properties dialog box. If your page uses a theme, however, the horizontal line uses a graphic to match the theme, and you can change only the alignment of the line.

You can adjust the properties of the horizontal rule, such as the thickness and length, by right-clicking the horizontal rule and then clicking Horizontal Line Properties on the shortcut menu. The alignment of the horizontal rule also can be controlled using the Align Left, Center, and Align Right buttons on the Formatting toolbar.

Adding Normal Text to a Web Page

Notice in Figure 2-62 on page FP 122 that the style and font for new text reverted to the default values. This occurs whenever you move the insertion point with the mouse or arrow keys. You need to set the style, font, and color again in preparation for entering more text.

The steps for adding normal text are similar to the steps used previously to add the heading: set the style, and either use the associated font, font size, and color, or manually set these properties. According to the design, the text in the lower-left cell is to be aligned along the top edge of the cell, while the text in the right cell is to retain a default alignment. The following steps add the normal text that will be displayed on the Web page.

To Add Normal Text to a Web Page

1

• **Right-click the lower-left cell.**

FrontPage displays the shortcut menu (Figure 2-65).

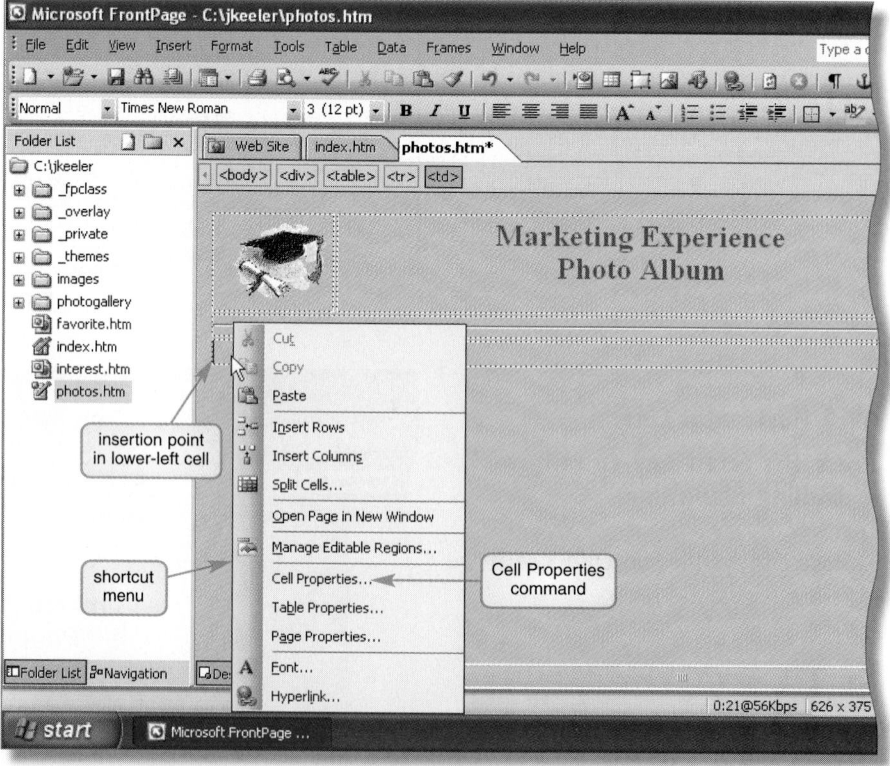

FIGURE 2-65

2

- **Click Cell Properties.**
- **When FrontPage displays the Cell Properties dialog box, click the Vertical alignment box arrow in the Layout area.**

FrontPage displays the Vertical alignment list showing the choices for vertical alignment in the cell (Figure 2-66).

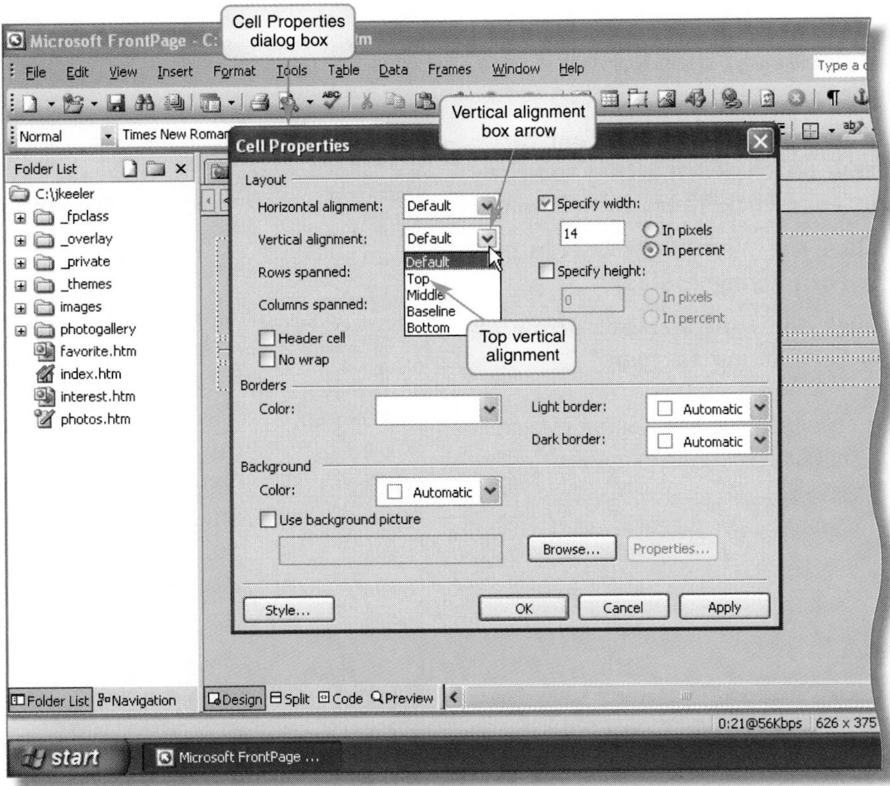

FIGURE 2-66

3

- **Click Top.**
- **Click the OK button.**

The Cell Properties dialog box closes (Figure 2-67). Although no change is visible, when an item is displayed in this cell, it will be aligned along the top cell edge.

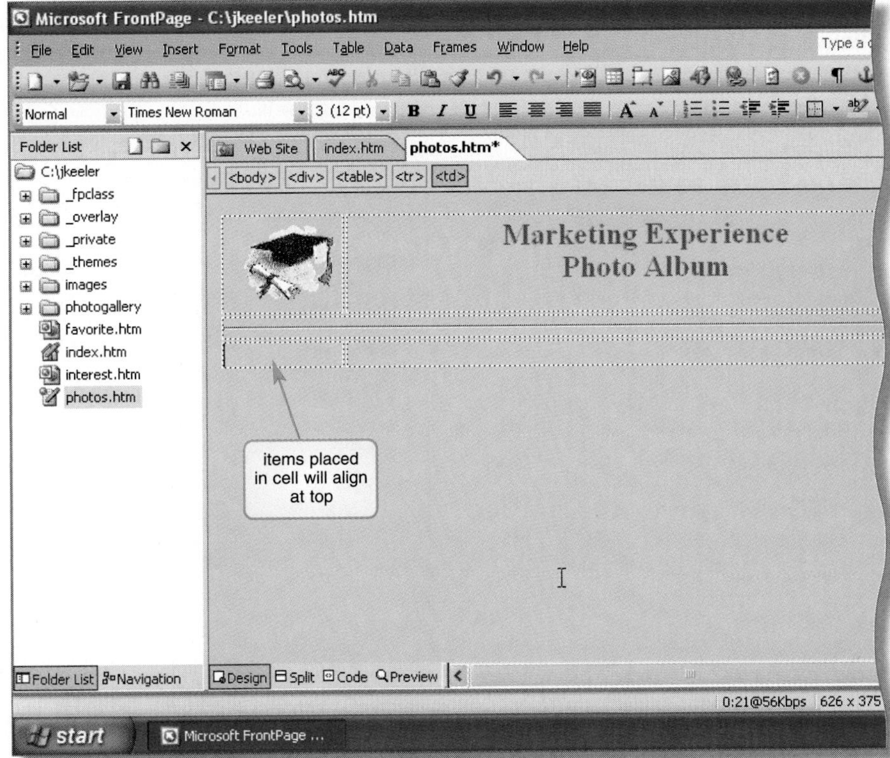

FIGURE 2-67

4

- **If necessary, click Normal in the Style list.**
- **If necessary, click the Font box arrow on the Formatting toolbar and then click Times New Roman.**
- **Click the Align Right button on the Formatting toolbar.**
- **Click the Font Size box arrow on the Formatting toolbar.**

The Style box indicates Normal style and the Font box indicates Times New Roman (Figure 2-68).

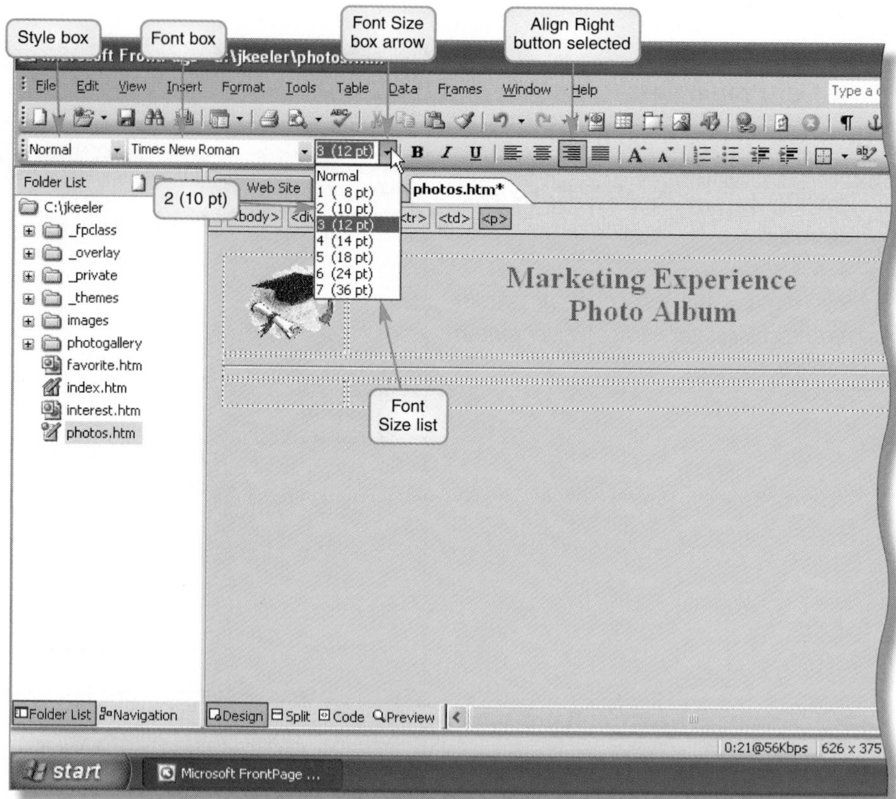

FIGURE 2-68

5

- **Click 2 (10 pt).**
- **Type** `Point to an image to see a caption` **in the lower-left cell.**

FrontPage displays the text entered right-aligned on the Web page (Figure 2-69).

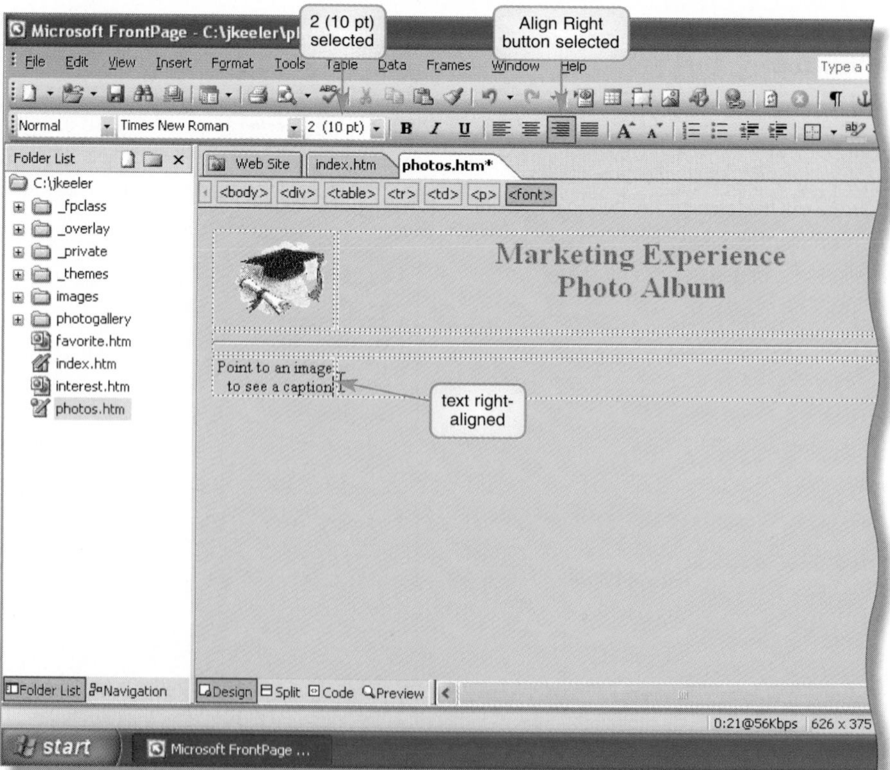

FIGURE 2-69

6

• **Drag through the entered text to select it.**

• **Click the Font Color button arrow on the Formatting toolbar and then click the Green button in the color palette.**

• **Click the bottom center cell to deselect the text.**

FrontPage displays the newly entered text with green as the font color (Figure 2-70).

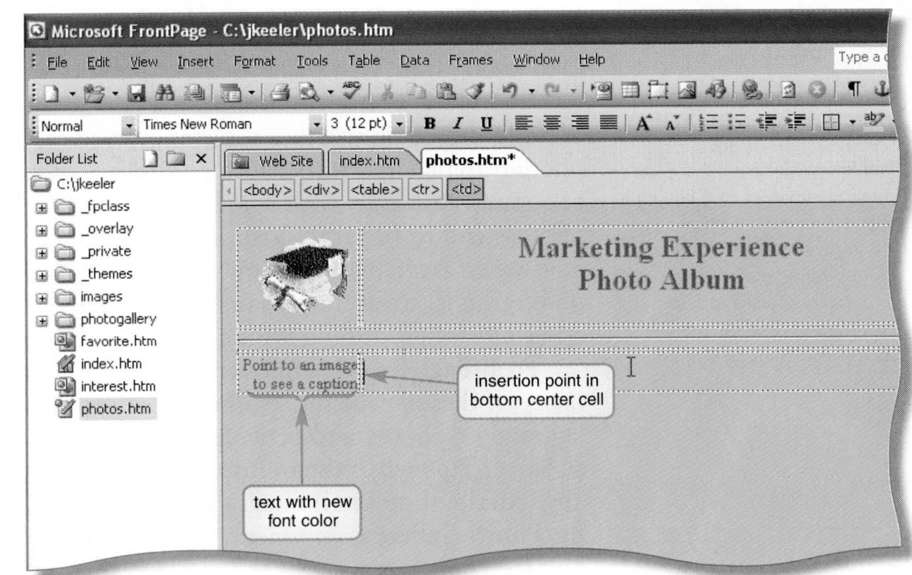

FIGURE 2-70

• **Click the lower-right cell to position the insertion point.**

• **If necessary, click Normal in the Style list and click Times New Roman in the Font list.**

• **Click the Font Size box arrow and then click 2 (10 pt).**

• **Type** `Click an image to see a larger view` **in the cell.**

• **Drag through the entered text to select it.**

• **Click the Font Color button arrow on the Formatting toolbar and then click the Green button in the color palette.**

• **Click the bottom center cell.**

FrontPage displays the newly entered text in Normal style, Times New Roman font, with a font size of 10 pt and a font color of green (Figure 2-71).

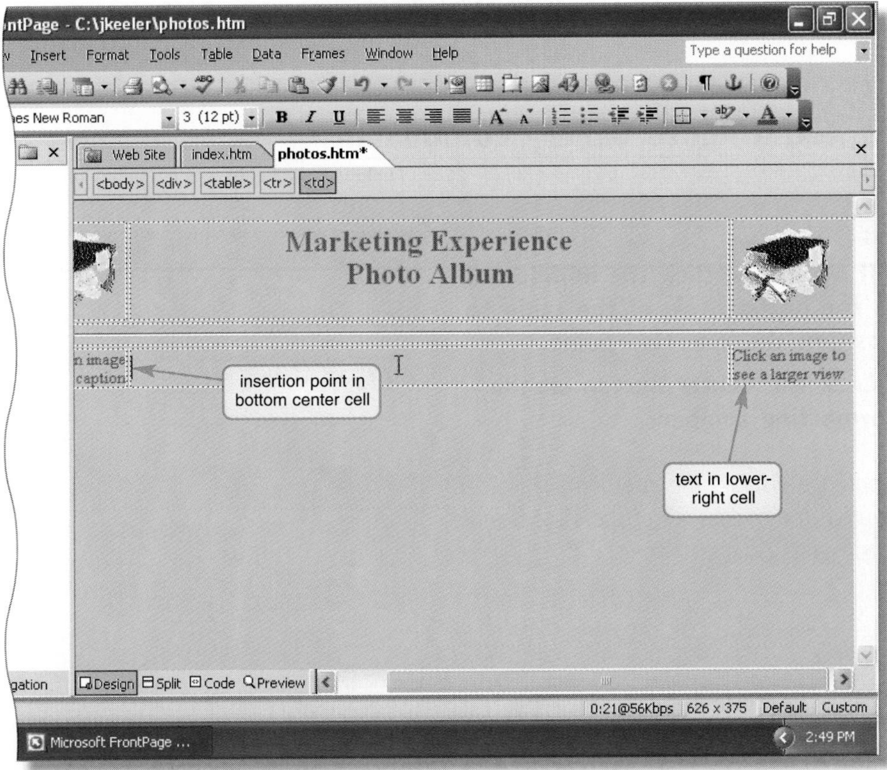

FIGURE 2-71

Other Ways

1. Select text, right-click text, click Font on shortcut menu
2. Select text, press ALT+ENTER
3. Select text, in Voice Command mode, say "Format, Font", click Font tab

---

You can see from the previous steps that the Formatting toolbar is very useful when entering text. You can change styles, fonts, font size, and other properties very quickly as you move through the body of the Web page.

More About

The Photo Gallery Component

The Photo Gallery component offers four layouts: Horizontal, Vertical, Montage, and Slideshow. You should examine each layout to determine which one is most appropriate for the photos you want to display.

Adding a Photo Gallery Component

One strength of Web pages is the capability to display images as well as text. Some information is better communicated in a textual form, while much fits the old adage of a picture being worth a thousand words. This is especially true when dealing with photographic clip art, because photos are meant to be seen, not just described. There are issues, however, with using photos in a Web page. First of all, the data files for photos tend to be large. Visitors to a Web page may not wait for the page to download when large pictures slow down the process. Also, when positioning text with photographs, it can be tedious and difficult to get an arrangement that is pleasing, especially when dealing with a large number of pictures.

FrontPage has a component called a Photo Gallery that presents solutions to many of these problems. A **Photo Gallery component** offers several customizable layouts for photos and provides for captions. The montage layout displays captions as ScreenTips when the mouse pointer rests on them. The pictures used in the layouts are actually thumbnail images of the original pictures, created automatically by using the Photo Gallery component. A **thumbnail image** is a small image that is a hyperlink to a larger version of the same picture. Using a thumbnail version of an image can speed up the time it takes to load a Web page, because only a smaller version is used. When you click the thumbnail image, the full-sized version of the file is loaded in your browser.

The following steps insert a Photo Gallery component.

To Add a Photo Gallery Component

1

- **If necessary, click the middle cell in the bottom row of the table to position the insertion point.**
- **Click the Center button on the Formatting toolbar.**

FrontPage displays the insertion point centered in the middle cell of the bottom table row (Figure 2-72).

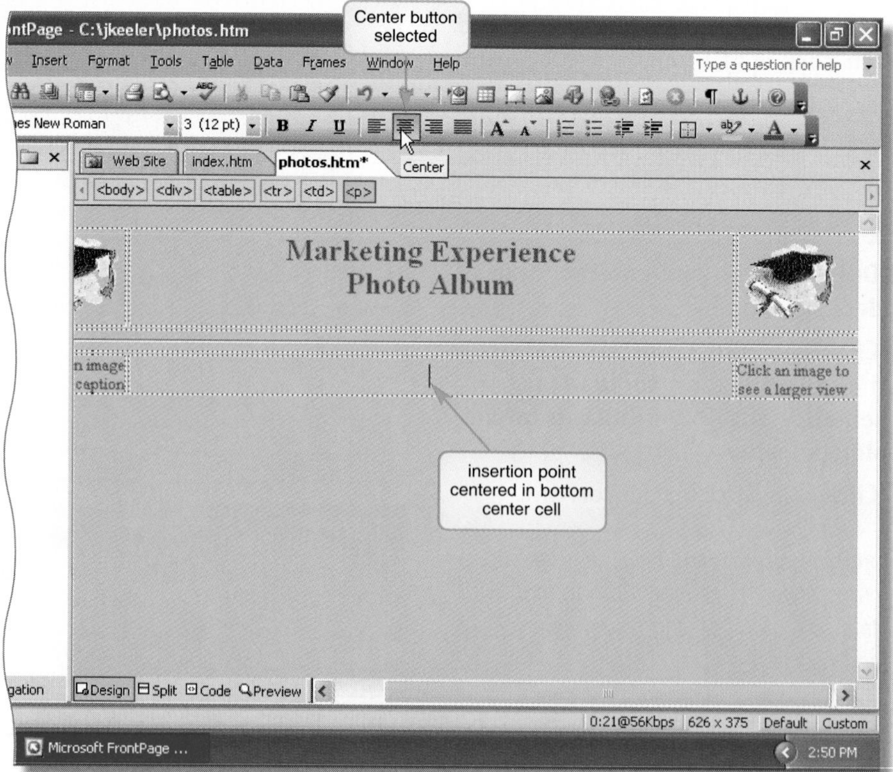

FIGURE 2-72

2

- **Click Insert on the menu bar.**

FrontPage displays the Insert menu (Figure 2-73).

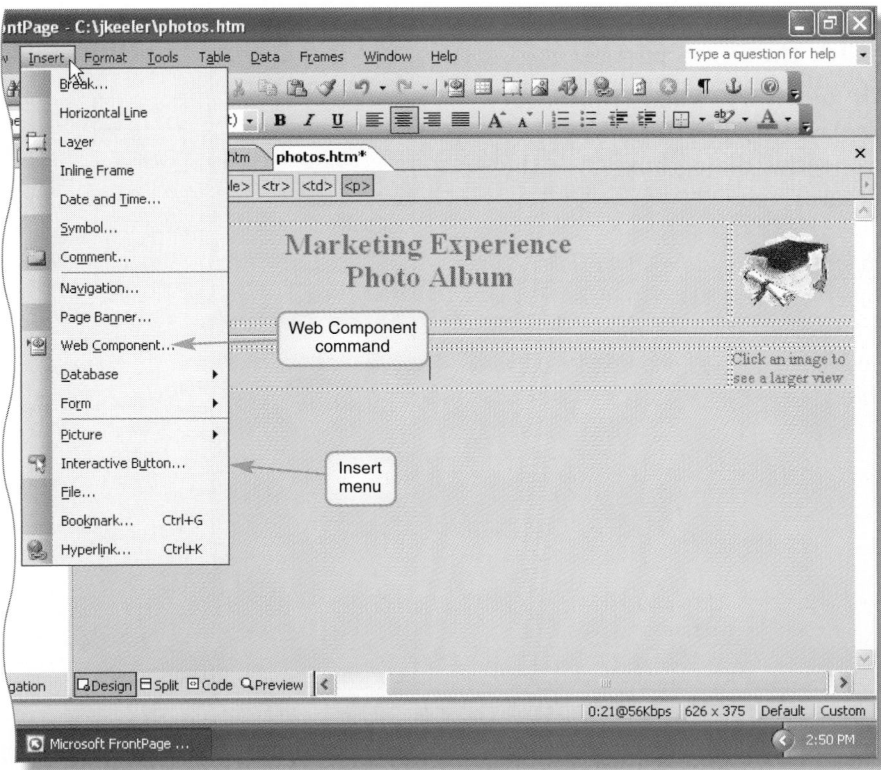

FIGURE 2-73

3

- **Click Web Component.**
- **When FrontPage displays the Insert Web Component dialog box, click Photo Gallery in the Component type list.**
- **Click the montage arrangement icon in the Choose a Photo Gallery Option list.**

FrontPage displays the Insert Web Component dialog box with the Photo Gallery component type and the montage option selected (Figure 2-74). FrontPage displays a brief description of the selected arrangement.

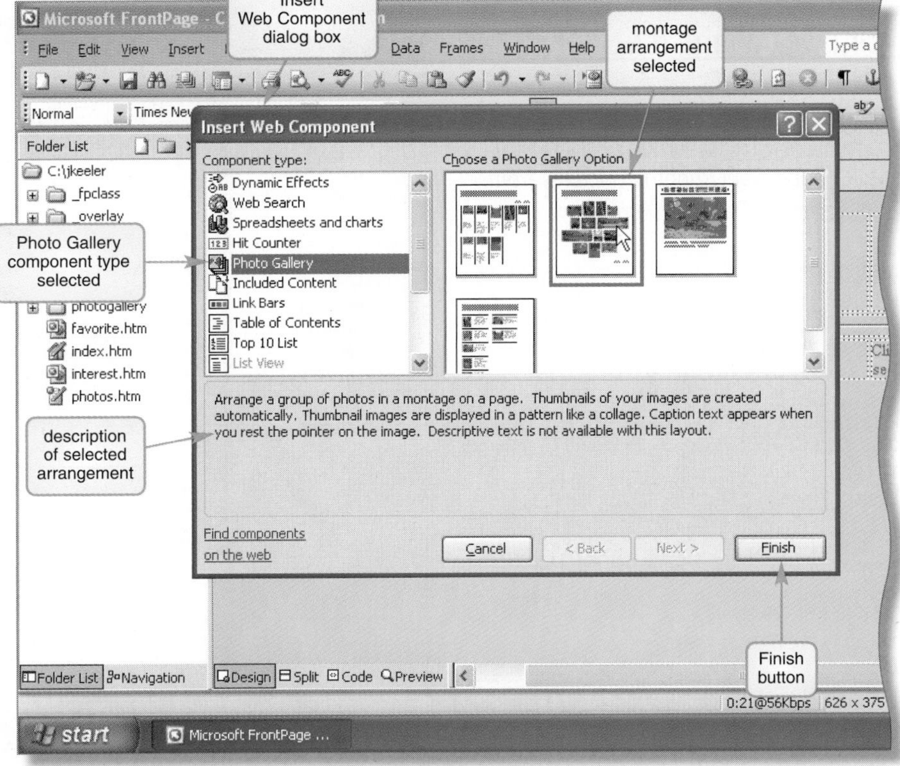

FIGURE 2-74

4

- **Click the Finish button.**
- **If necessary, when FrontPage displays the Photo Gallery Properties dialog box, click the Pictures tab.**

FrontPage displays the Photo Gallery Properties dialog box (Figure 2-75). The Pictures sheet contains settings to control the content, format, and text for a Photo Gallery.

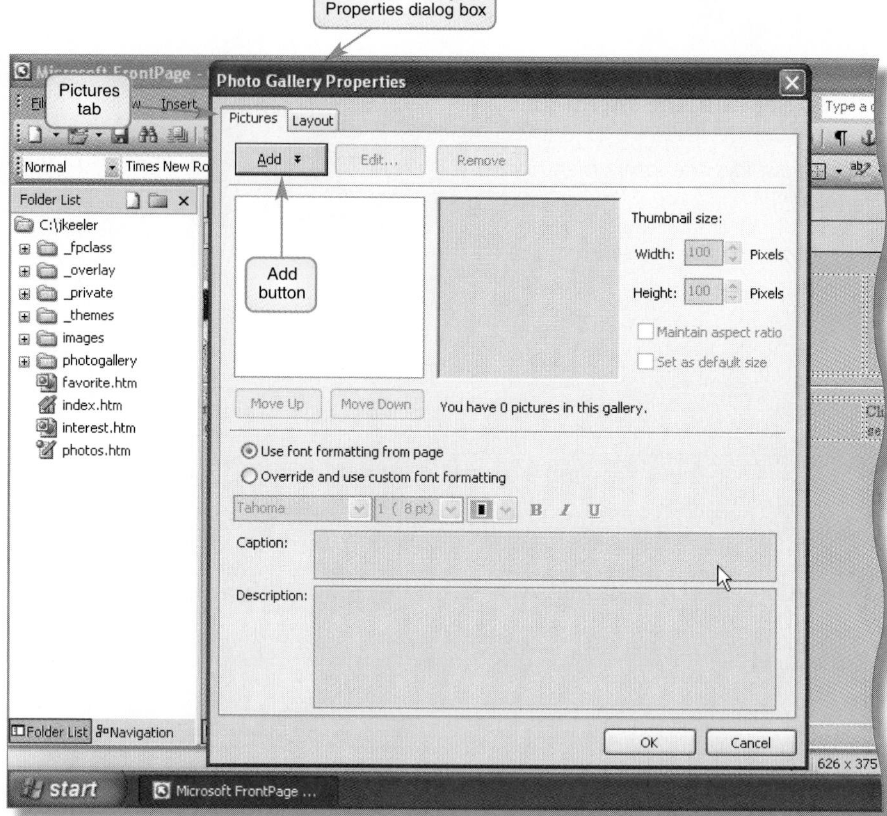

FIGURE 2-75

5

- **Click the Add button.**

FrontPage displays the Add menu (Figure 2-76). The commands on the Add menu enable you to obtain pictures from files, a scanner, or a camera.

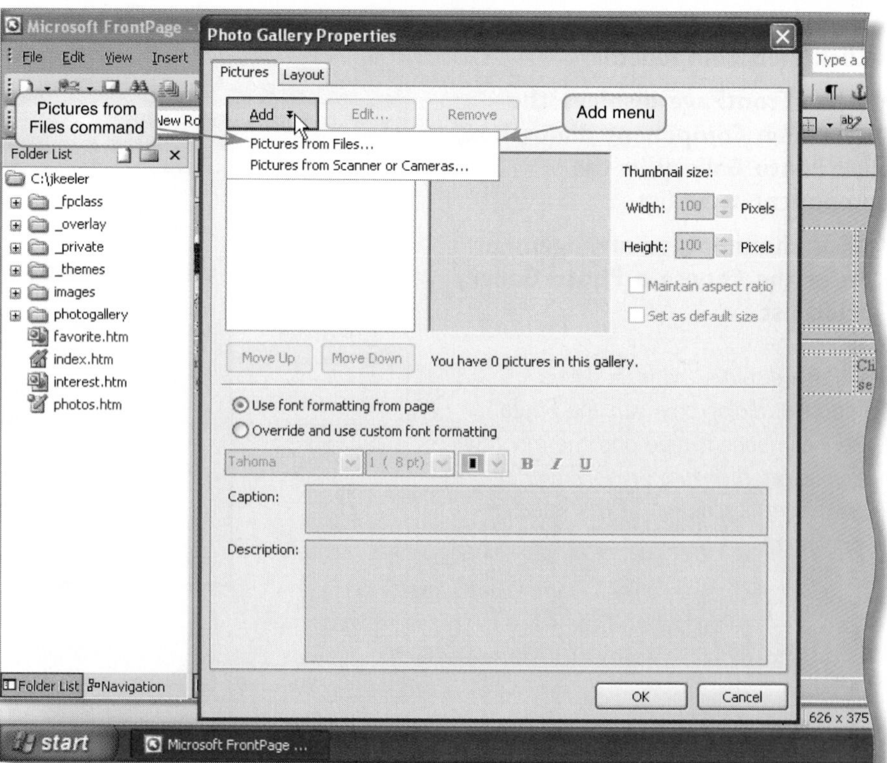

FIGURE 2-76

6

- **Click Pictures from Files.**
- **Insert the Data Disk in drive A.**
- **If necessary, when the File Open dialog box is displayed, click the Look in box arrow and select the Senior group project.jpg file in the Project2 folder.**

FrontPage displays the File Open dialog box (Figure 2-77). Use the drive and location that are appropriate for your environment.

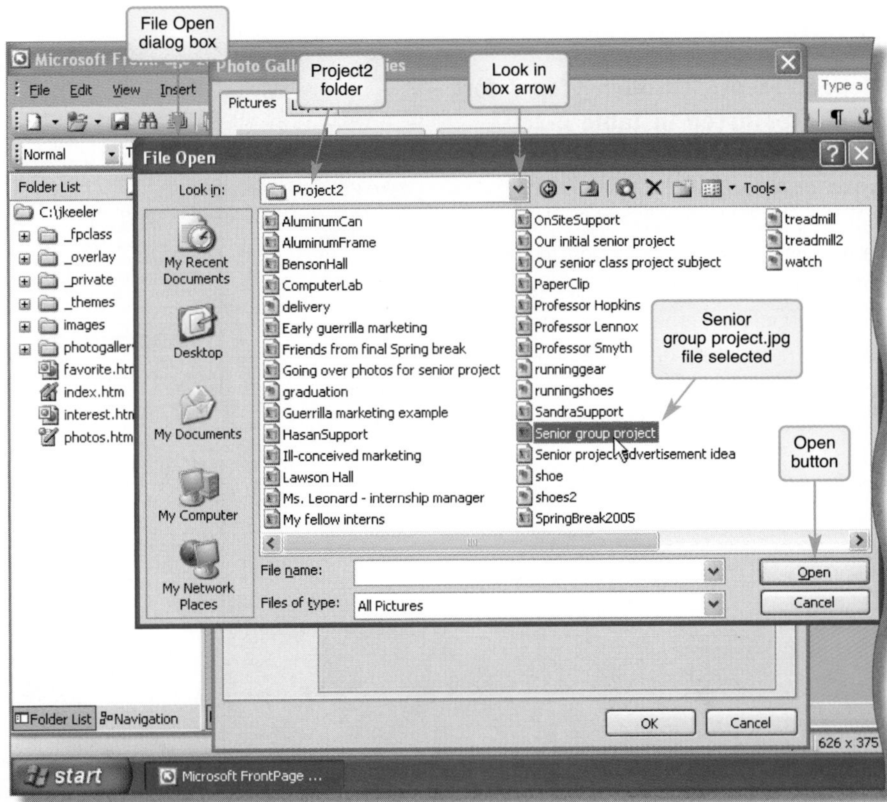

FIGURE 2-77

7

- **Click the Open button.**
- **When FrontPage closes the File Open dialog box and the Photo Gallery Properties dialog box again is visible, click the Caption text box and type** `Burning the midnight oil working on our Senior group project.` **in the text box.**
- **Verify that a check mark is displayed in the Maintain aspect ratio check box.**

The selected options for the Photo Gallery Properties dialog box are shown in Figure 2-78.

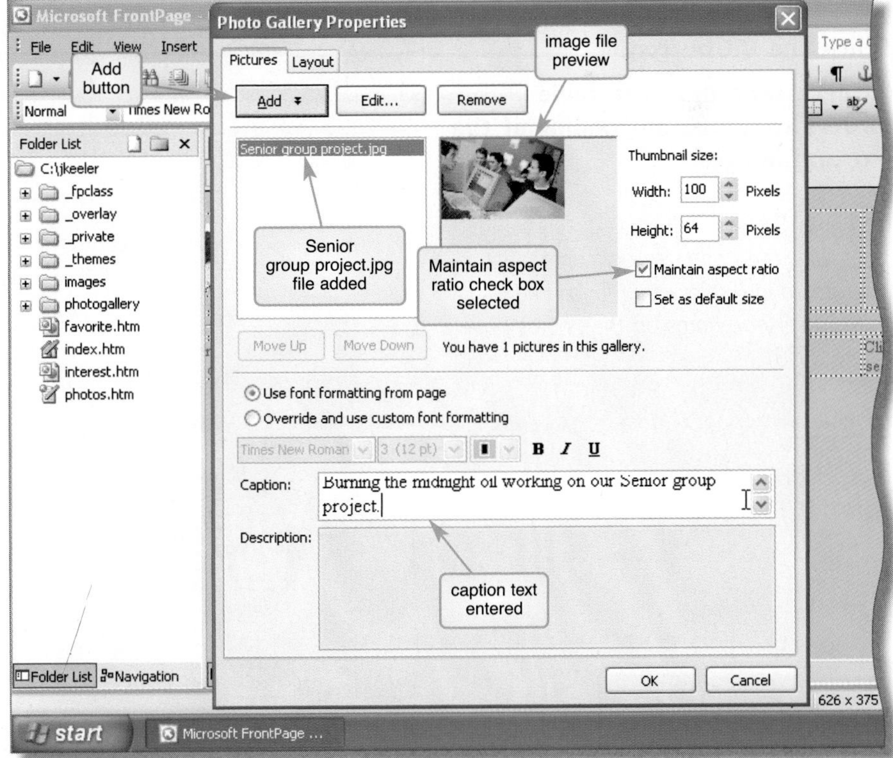

FIGURE 2-78

8

• **Repeat Step 5 through Step 7 for the photos listed in Table 2-2, typing the associated text for each photo caption.**

The remaining photos are added to the Photo Gallery list of photos (Figure 2-79). The Photo Gallery Properties dialog box indicates the number of pictures added.

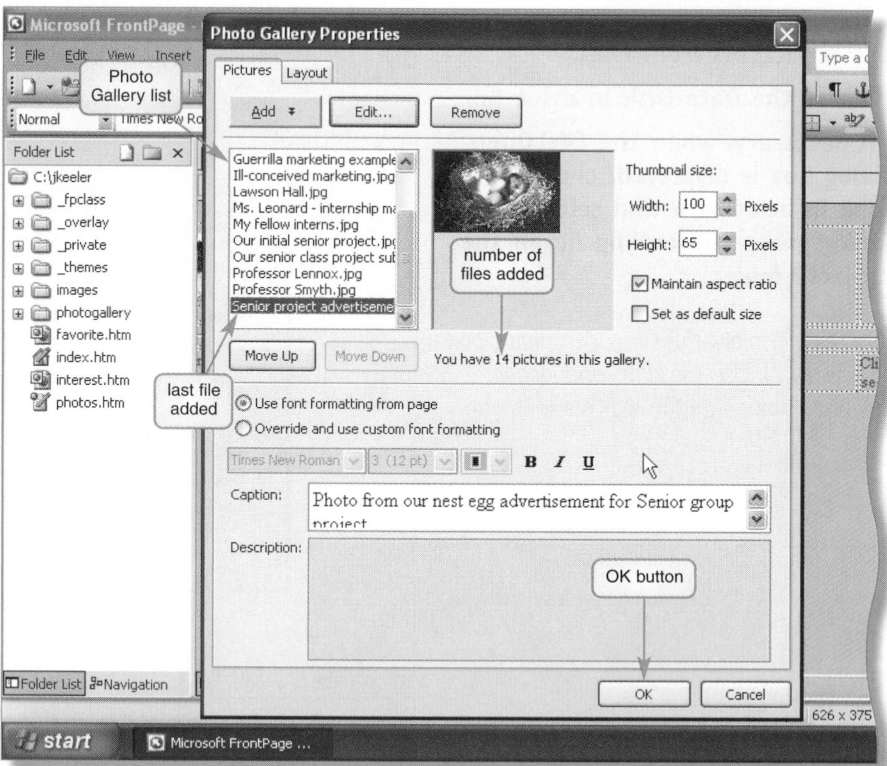

FIGURE 2-79

9

• **Click the OK button.**

• **If necessary, drag the table borders to adjust positioning of the text and images.**

The Photo Gallery Properties dialog box closes, and the Photo Gallery component generates and displays thumbnail images for the inserted photos on the Photos page (Figure 2-80).

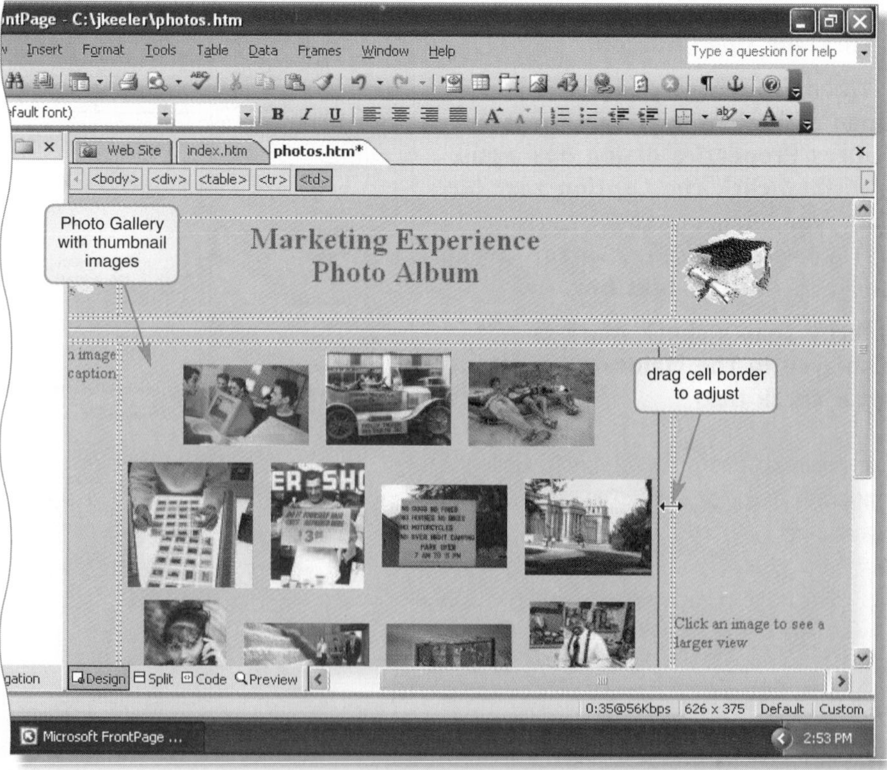

FIGURE 2-80

Other Ways

1. On the Insert menu point to Picture, click New Photo Gallery
2. Press ALT+I, P, P
3. In Voice Command mode, say "Insert, Picture, New Photo Gallery"

The thumbnail images are hyperlinks to their corresponding full-sized images. When a viewer clicks the thumbnail, the full-size image is displayed, much like a Web page would do. The browser, however, is displaying an image file, not a Web page, so hyperlinks are not available to navigate back to the previous page. The viewer must click the browser's Back button to display the previous page.

Table 2-2 Photo File Names and Captions

PHOTO FILE NAME	CAPTION
Senior group project.jpg	Burning the midnight oil working on our Senior group project.
Early guerrilla marketing.jpg	Early guerrilla marketing attempts were innovative.
Friends from final Spring break.jpg	Relaxing for a final time before we hit the real world.
Going over photos for senior project.jpg	Inspecting photos to use in our group project.
Guerrilla marketing example.jpg	Shocking or funny. Guerrilla marketing tactics serve to set you apart.
Ill-conceived marketing.jpg	A better alternative is to focus on positives.
Lawson Hall.jpg	Where I spent half of my life for the past four years.
Ms. Leonard - internship manager.jpg	Ms. Leonard was an ideal boss. Fair yet tough.
My fellow interns.jpg	My fellow interns take a late lunch last summer.
Our initial senior project.jpg	Starting at square one for our Senior group project.
Our senior class project subject.jpg	We eventually settled on a guerrilla marketing campaign for a local barber.
Professor Lennox.jpg	My mentor for my Senior year.
Professor Smyth.jpg	Professor Smyth was the department head and my advisor.
Senior project advertisement idea.jpg	Photo from our nest egg advertisement for Senior group project.

Inserting Link Bars on a Web Page

Q: Can I link to both internal and external pages with a link bar?

A: Yes. To create link bars with links both to internal pages and to pages external to your site, select the Bar with custom links bar type in the Insert Web Component dialog box.

As previously discussed, link bars are a commonly used component. The Capsules theme you applied to the Web site includes two link bars — a **vertical link bar** on the left-hand side of the page and a **horizontal link bar** on the bottom. Link bars typically are used for either child-level navigation, which allows you to move between the Home page (the parent) and the Professional Interests page or Favorite Links page (the children), or same-level navigation, which allows you to move back and forth between pages at the same level, such as the Professional Interests and Favorite Links pages. In the Personal Web site template, both link bars on a given page have the same navigation properties: links on the Home page are used for child-level navigation, and links on the child pages are set for same-level navigation. Each link bar also has an additional link to the Home page.

The steps on the next page insert a link bar component for the Photos page.

To Add a Link Bar Component

1

- **Position the insertion point at the end of the text in the lower-left cell of the table.**
- **Press the ENTER key.**
- **Click Insert on the menu bar.**

FrontPage displays the insertion point in the left cell of the bottom table row (Figure 2-81).

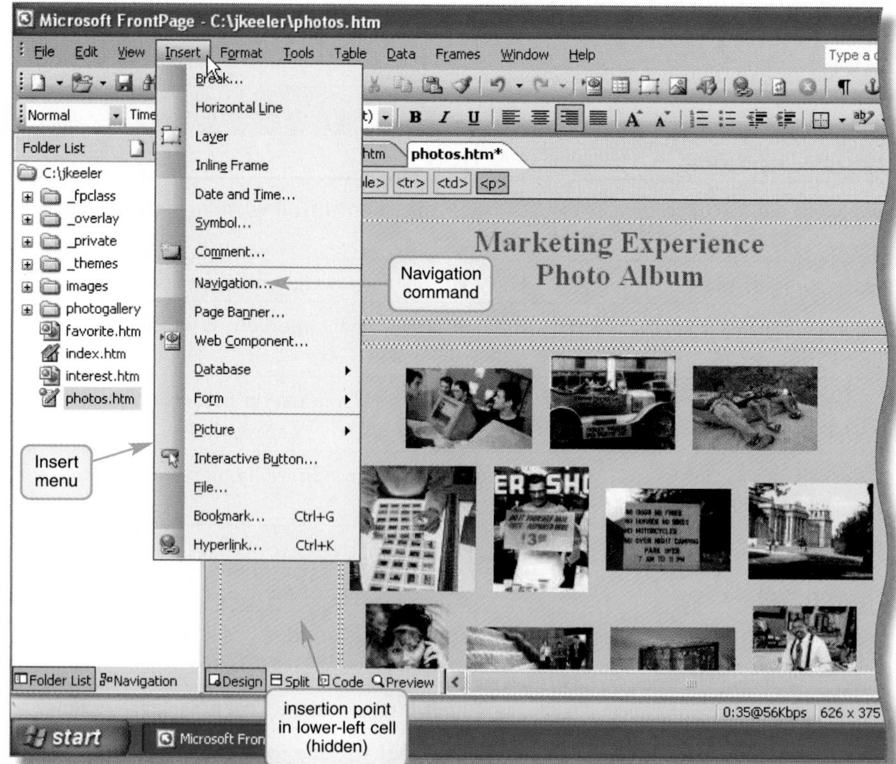

FIGURE 2-81

2

- **Click Navigation.**
- **When FrontPage displays the Insert Web Component dialog box, click Bar based on navigation structure in the Choose a bar type list.**

FrontPage displays the Insert Web Component dialog box with the Link Bars component type already selected (Figure 2-82). FrontPage displays a brief comment about the type of link bar to be added.

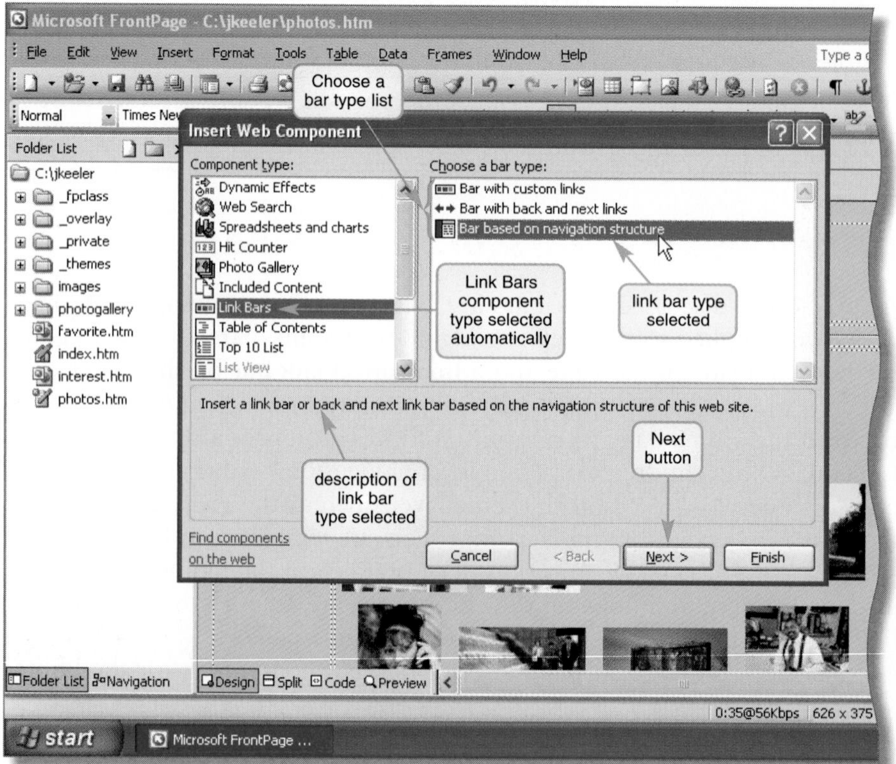

FIGURE 2-82

3

- **Click the Next button.**
- **If necessary, when FrontPage displays the Choose a bar style list in the Insert Web Component dialog box, scroll down, and then click the icon for a graphical style based on the Bars theme.**

FrontPage displays the Insert Web Component dialog box with a bar style selected based on the Bars theme (Figure 2-83). FrontPage displays a brief description of the selected style.

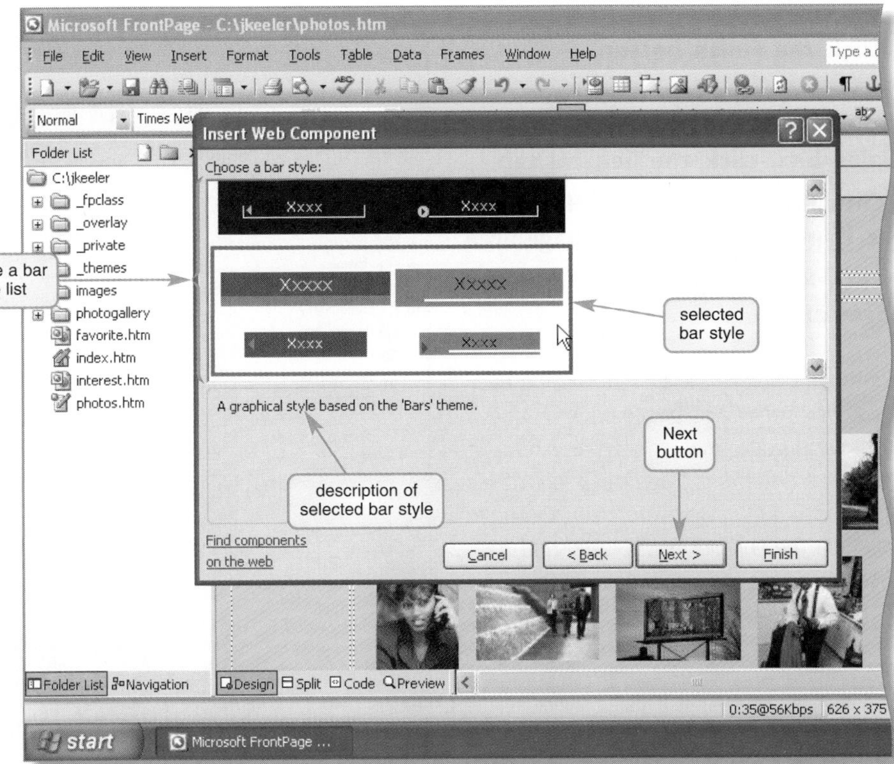

FIGURE 2-83

4

- **Click the Next button.**
- **When FrontPage displays the Choose an orientation list in the Insert Web Component dialog box, click the icon to insert the link bar with the links arranged vertically.**

FrontPage displays the Insert Web Component dialog box with a vertical link bar orientation selected (Figure 2-84). Some descriptive text indicates the arrangement to be used for the links.

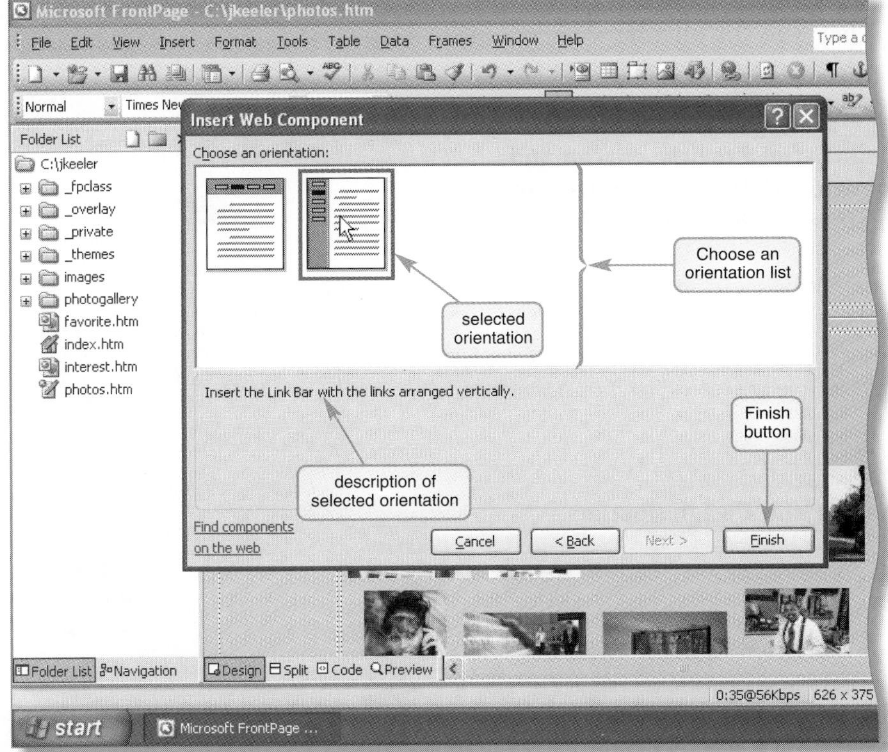

FIGURE 2-84

5

- **Click the Finish button.**
- **If necessary, when FrontPage displays the Link Bar Properties dialog box, click the General tab.**
- **Click Child pages under Home in the Hyperlinks to add to page area.**
- **Click Home page in the Additional pages area.**

FrontPage displays the Link Bar Properties dialog box with Child pages under Home and Home page selected (Figure 2-85). FrontPage displays a diagram to indicate hierarchical relationships between the page on which the link bar is displayed and the pages to which the link bar is linked.

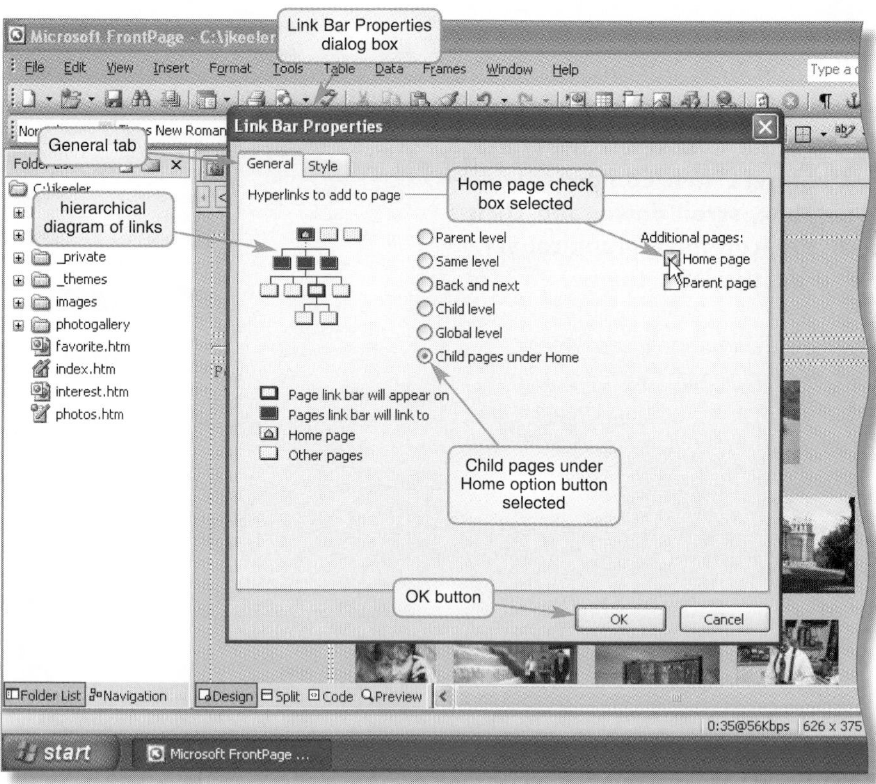

FIGURE 2-85

6

- **Click the OK button.**
- **If necessary, drag the cell borders to adjust positioning of the text.**
- **Click the Preview button and position the mouse pointer over a picture in the Photo Gallery.**

FrontPage displays the Photos page with a link bar based on the Bars theme (Figure 2-86). FrontPage displays the caption text for the indicated photo as a ScreenTip.

7

- **Click the Design button.**

FIGURE 2-86

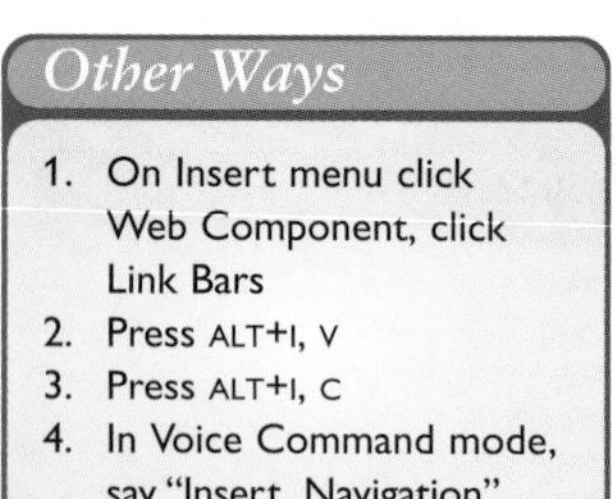

Other Ways

1. On Insert menu click Web Component, click Link Bars
2. Press ALT+I, V
3. Press ALT+I, C
4. In Voice Command mode, say "Insert, Navigation"

Because the Photos page was added to the Web site in Navigation view — thereby establishing a navigation structure with the Photos page as a child to the Home page — FrontPage was able to create the proper links for the link bar automatically.

In addition to the Home page, the link bar you just added also links to the other child pages in the Web site — the Professional Interests page and the Favorite Links page. If you delete one of these pages from the current Web site, the link bar component automatically removes links to the deleted page from the link bars on all pages in the current Web site.

Previewing and Printing a Web Page

In Project 1, you printed the Web page without previewing it on the screen. By previewing the Web page, you can see how it will look when printed without generating a printout, or hard copy. Previewing a Web page using the Print Preview command on the File menu can save time, paper, and the frustration of waiting for a printout only to discover it is not what you want. You must be using Design view to use print preview, as this command is not accessible when using the Preview tab.

You also can print the Web page while in print preview. The following steps preview and then print the Photos Web page.

To Preview and Print a Web Page

1

- **Ready the printer according to the printer instructions.**
- **Verify that the Design button is selected.**
- **Click File on the menu bar (Figure 2-87).**

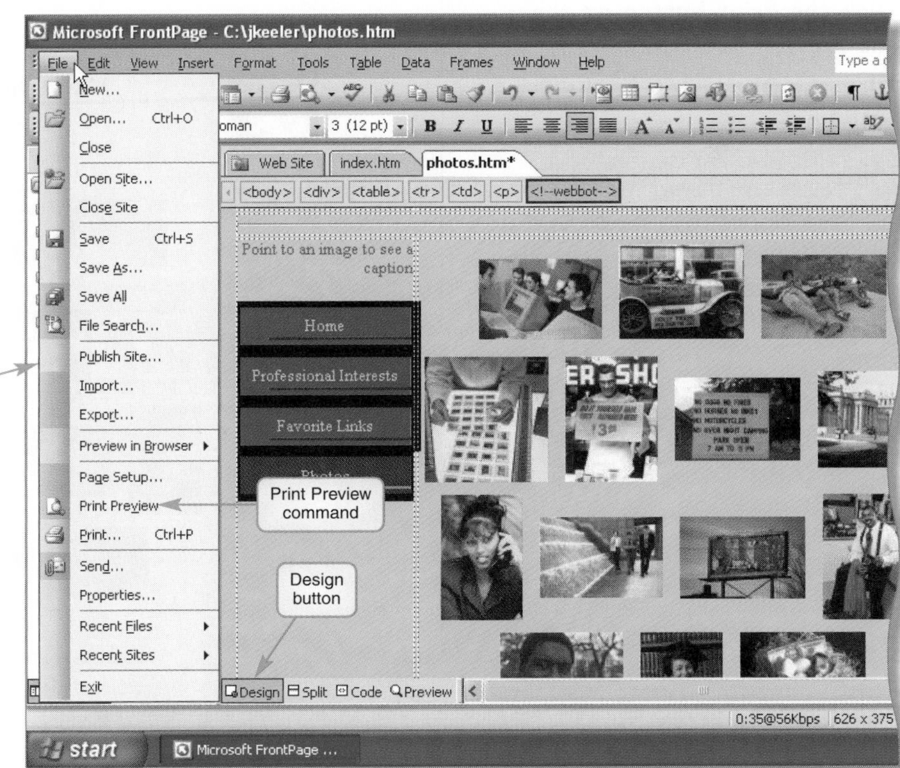

FIGURE 2-87

2

- **Click Print Preview.**

FrontPage displays a preview of the Web page in the preview pane and the mouse pointer changes to a magnifying glass when positioned over the image of the page (Figure 2-88). You may click on the image to zoom in for a closer view.

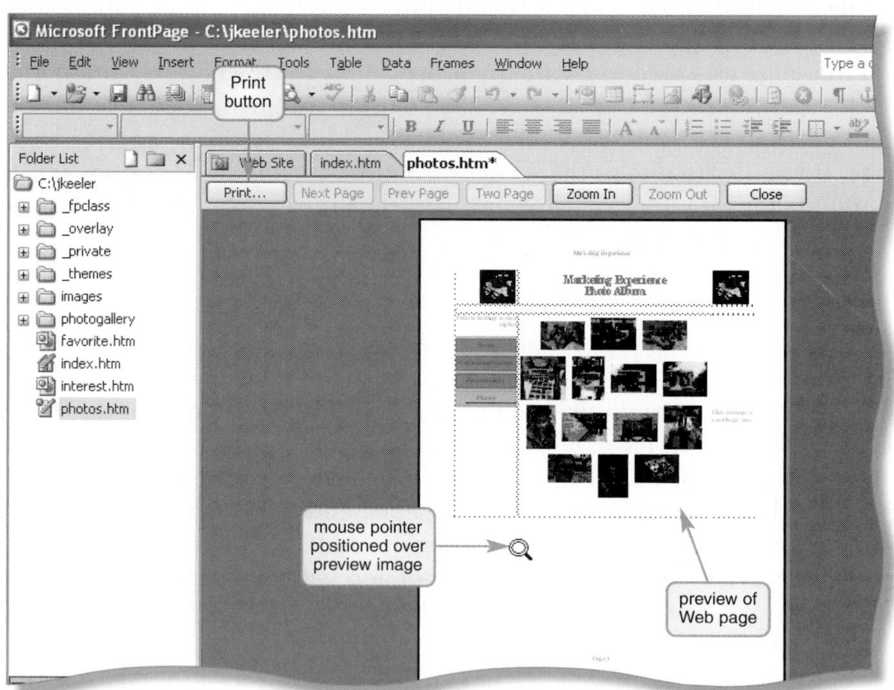

FIGURE 2-88

3

- **Click the Print button on the Print Preview toolbar.**
- **Click the OK button in the Print dialog box.**

FrontPage closes the preview pane and prints the Web page. When FrontPage completes the printing operation, retrieve the printout (Figure 2-89).

FIGURE 2-89

Other Ways

1. Press ALT+F, V
2. In Voice Command mode, say "File, Print Preview"

The Print Preview toolbar contains buttons to scroll through a multipage printout, to zoom in and out of the Web page, and to close the preview pane. You can use print preview to determine the page number of a particular page in a multipage printout and then print only that page. This allows you to print only the particular section of a long Web page on which you are working, thus saving time and paper.

Saving the Web Page and Embedded Images

Once you have finished editing the Web page, you should save it on disk. With the Photos page, the save operation consists of saving the HTML and the clip art images for the Web page. Neither the clip art images you inserted in earlier steps nor the thumbnail images created by FrontPage were physically inserted in the Photos page. FrontPage placed HTML instructions to include each clip art image file using an <IMG SRC=> tag. This tag has a reference to the file name containing the clip art image, but the image still must be saved with the Web page.

Because the thumbnail images are part of a Photo Gallery component, when the Photos page is saved, they are saved automatically in the photogallery folder in the current Web site. When the Photos Web page is saved, it contains only the HTML tags referencing the diploma clip art file and special commands referencing the Photo Gallery component. The original photo images are referenced by pages created by the Photo Gallery component in the photogallery folder. FrontPage saves the clip art and photo image files in the Web site folders as well. As a default, FrontPage saves the image files to the current folder. You may, however, want to have all images used in your Web page, except for the thumbnail images, stored in a folder separate from the actual Web page. Because FrontPage created an images folder when this new Web site was created, it makes sense to place the images in that folder. The following steps save the Photos page, along with the embedded image files.

To Save a Web Page and Embedded Images

1

• **Click the Save button on the Standard toolbar.**

FrontPage displays the Save Embedded Files dialog box (Figure 2-90). This dialog box shows the file names of the clip art images you inserted in the Web page.

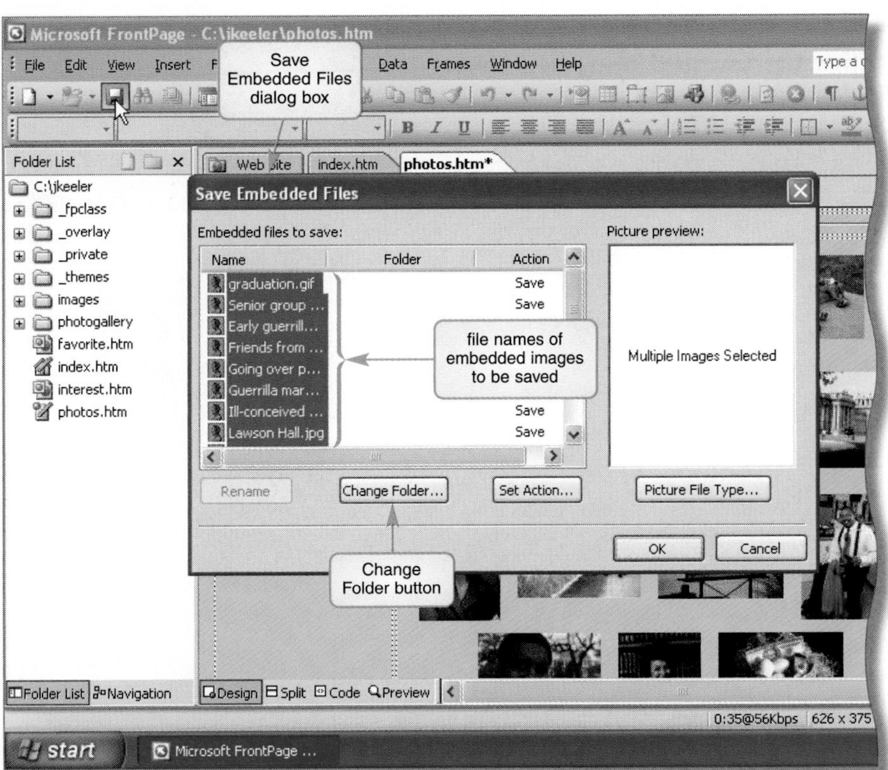

FIGURE 2-90

2

• **Click the Change Folder button.**

• **When FrontPage displays the Change Folder dialog box, click the images folder.**

FrontPage displays the Change Folder dialog box (Figure 2-91). The images folder is selected.

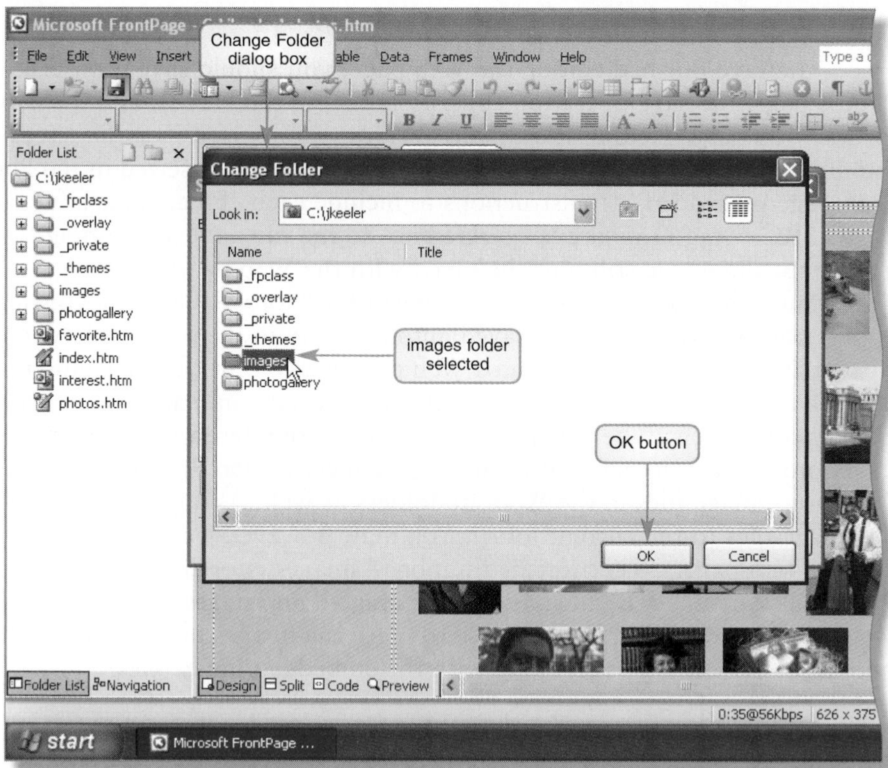

FIGURE 2-91

3

• **Click the OK button in the Change Folder dialog box.**

The Save Embedded Files dialog box indicates that the images folder will be used to store the images selected (Figure 2-92).

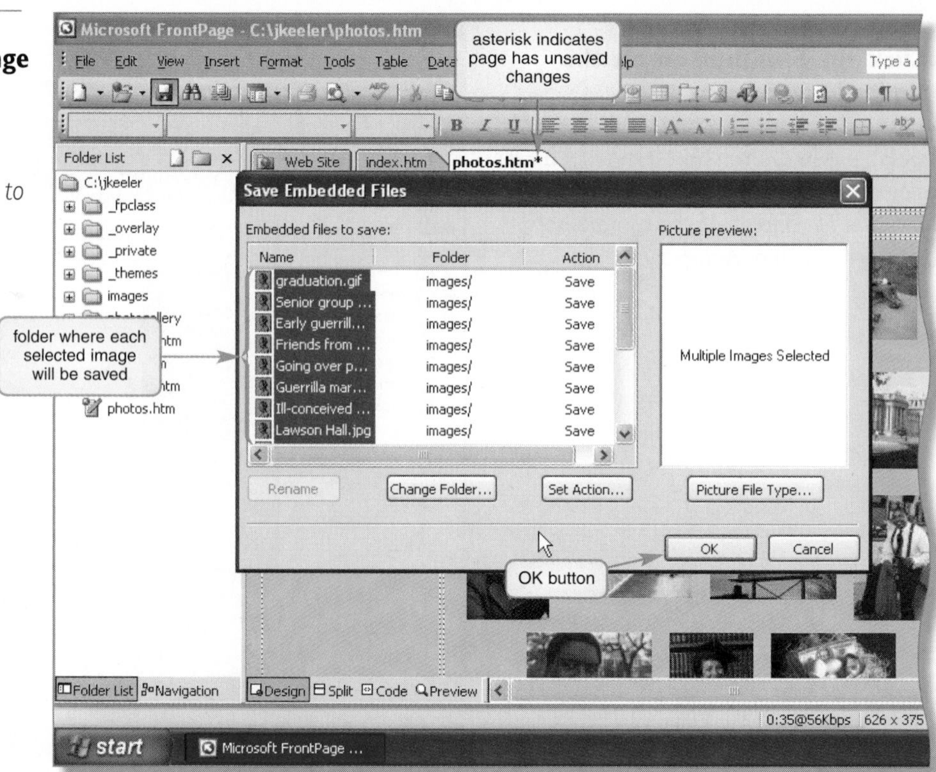

FIGURE 2-92

4

• **Click the OK button.**

The Save Embedded Files dialog box is closed and the Photos page and the clip art image files are saved (Figure 2-93).

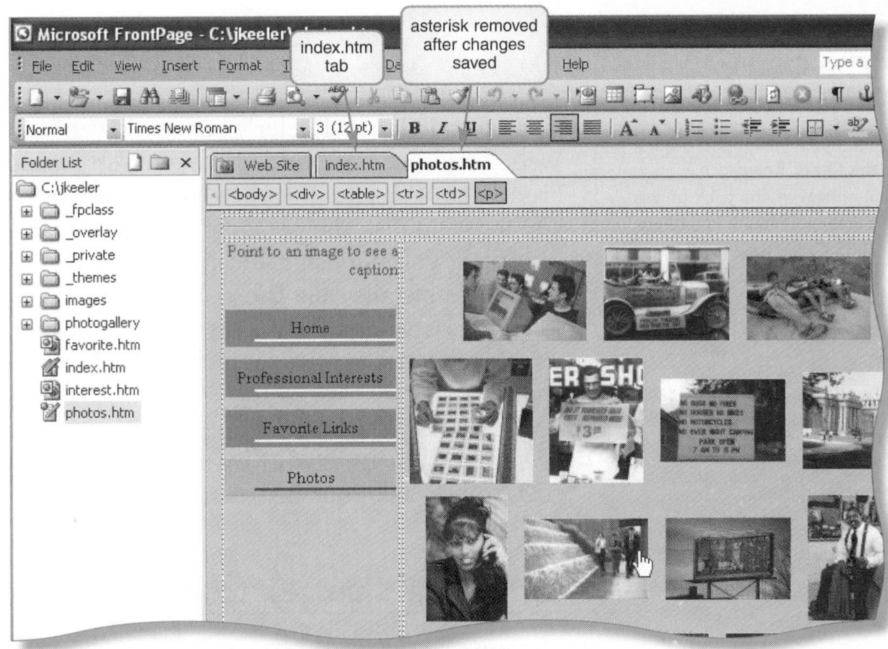

FIGURE 2-93

5

• **Click the index.htm tab to view the Home page.**

FrontPage displays the Home page with the link bar updated to include the Photos page (Figure 2-94).

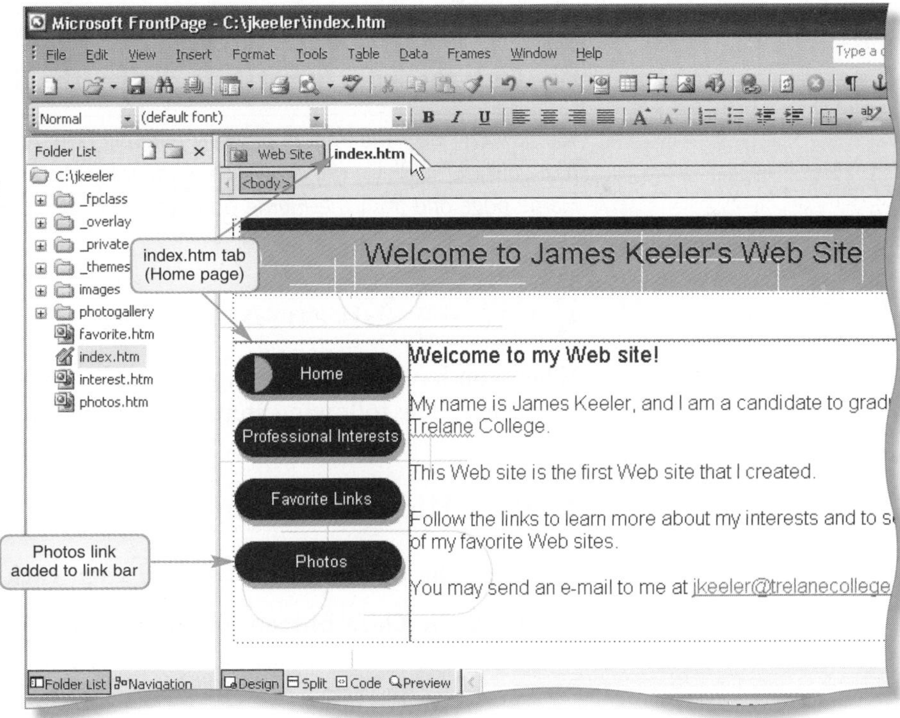

FIGURE 2-94

Other Ways

1. On File menu click Save
2. Press ALT+F, S
3. Press CTRL+S
4. In Voice Command mode, say "File, Save"

It is important that all clip art images be saved as part of the FrontPage Web site. These image files must be available when publishing the FrontPage Web site to a Web server. If you do not save them and then publish the FrontPage Web site, those <IMG SRC=> tags will be broken, because the files referenced by the tags will not be on the Web server. Thus, the Web page will not display properly.

More About

The Quick Reference

For more information, see the Quick Reference Summary at the back of this book, or visit the FrontPage 2003 Quick Reference Web page (scsite.com/fp2003/qr).

Publishing Changes to an Existing FrontPage Web Site

In Project 1, James Keeler's personal Web site was published on the World Wide Web. You since have added a new Web page and the accompanying image files to the FrontPage Web site. For these new items to be available on the World Wide Web, you must publish the personal Web site again.

When you publish a FrontPage Web site that has been published before, FrontPage installs only those parts of the Web site that are new or that have changed since the last time the Web site was published. This reduces the amount of data transfer that takes place, which is good for Web sites with many folders, Web pages, and files.

The following steps summarize how to publish changes to a FrontPage Web site. Be sure to substitute your own URL or an error will occur. If you do not know what URL to use, ask your instructor.

To Publish Changes to an Existing FrontPage Web Site

1. **Click the Publish Site button on the Standard toolbar. Because this Web site was published previously, FrontPage does not display the Publish Destination dialog box, but assumes that you want to publish to the same location.**
2. **If prompted, type your user name and password, and click the OK button.**
3. **Click the index.htm tab to display the Home page.**

You now can view the Photos page by entering http://www.trelanecollege.edu/~jkeeler/photos.htm (use your own URL) in any browser and pressing the ENTER key. Be sure to test the hyperlink to the Home page and from the Home page to the Photos page.

Quitting Microsoft FrontPage

When you have published James Keeler's Web site, you can quit Microsoft FrontPage. The following steps quit FrontPage.

To Quit Microsoft FrontPage

1. **Click File on the menu bar and then click Close Site.**
2. **Click the Close button on the FrontPage title bar.**

Project Summary

Project 2 introduced you to the essentials of Web page development. You learned about good design criteria. Using FrontPage, you created a new Web page providing your own original content. You removed an applied theme and changed the background color of the new Web page. You inserted a table and adjusted the table properties. Using appropriate images, you inserted clip art to enhance the appearance of the Web page and later replaced the clip art with a more suitable image. Then, you added text and learned how to change formats such as style, font, font size, and alignment. Next, you inserted horizontal rules. You inserted photographs in a Photo Gallery, including captions for each picture. You learned how to insert link bars for navigation, and then you previewed your Web page before printing. Finally, you saved a Web page along with the embedded image files and published the changes to your existing Web site.

What You Should Know

Having completed this project, you should be able to perform the tasks below. The tasks are listed in the same order they were presented in this project. For a list of the buttons, menus, toolbars, and commands introduced in this project, see the Quick Reference Summary at the back of this book and refer to the Page Number column.

1. Start FrontPage (FP 87)
2. Open an Existing FrontPage Web Site (FP 88)
3. Add a New Web Page to an Existing Web Site (FP 90)
4. Rename a Web Page (FP 92)
5. Change the Title of a Web Page (FP 94)
6. Change the Page Label of a Web Page (FP 96)
7. Edit a Web Page in Design View (FP 97)
8. Change the Theme for a Web Page (FP 98)
9. Change the Background Color (FP 100)
10. Insert a Table in a Web Page (FP 104)
11. Merge Cells in a Table (FP 105)
12. Insert a Clip Art Image in a Web Page (FP 107)
13. Replace a Clip Art Image in a Web Page (FP 110)
14. Copy and Paste an Image in a Web Page (FP 113)
15. Align Items on a Web Page (FP 115)
16. Adjust Table Cell Borders (FP 116)
17. Modify the Properties of a Table (FP 117)
18. Add a Heading to a Web Page (FP 121)
19. Add a Horizontal Rule to a Web Page (FP 123)
20. Add Normal Text to a Web Page (FP 124)
21. Add a Photo Gallery Component (FP 128)
22. Add a Link Bar Component (FP 134)
23. Preview and Print a Web Page (FP 137)
24. Save a Web Page and Embedded Images (FP 139)
25. Publish Changes to an Existing FrontPage Web Site (FP 142)
26. Quit Microsoft FrontPage (FP 142)

Learn It Online

Instructions: To complete the Learn It Online exercises, start your browser, click the Address bar, and then enter the Web address scsite.com/fp2003/learn. When the FrontPage 2003 Learn It Online page is displayed, follow the instructions in the exercises below. Each exercise has instructions for printing your results, either for your own records or for submission to your instructor.

1 Project Reinforcement TF, MC, and SA

Below FrontPage Project 2, click the Project Reinforcement link. Print the quiz by clicking Print on the File menu for each page. Answer each question.

2 Flash Cards

Below FrontPage Project 2, click the Flash Cards link and read the instructions. Type 20 (or a number specified by your instructor) in the Number of playing cards text box, type your name in the Enter your Name text box, and then click the Flip Card button. When the flash card is displayed, read the question and then click the ANSWER box arrow to select an answer. Flip through Flash Cards. If your score is 15 (75%) correct or greater, click Print on the File menu to print your results. If your score is less than 15 (75%) correct, then redo this exercise by clicking the Replay button.

3 Practice Test

Below FrontPage Project 2, click the Practice Test link. Answer each question, enter your first and last name at the bottom of the page, and then click the Grade Test button. When the graded practice test is displayed on your screen, click Print on the File menu to print a hard copy. Continue to take practice tests until you score 80% or better.

4 Who Wants To Be a Computer Genius?

Below FrontPage Project 2, click the Computer Genius link. Read the instructions, enter your first and last name at the bottom of the page, and then click the PLAY button. When your score is displayed, click the PRINT RESULTS link to print a hard copy.

5 Wheel of Terms

Below FrontPage Project 2, click the Wheel of Terms link. Read the instructions, and then enter your first and last name and your school name. Click the PLAY button. When your score is displayed, right-click the score and then click Print on the shortcut menu to print a hard copy.

6 Crossword Puzzle Challenge

Below FrontPage Project 2, click the Crossword Puzzle Challenge link. Read the instructions, and then enter your first and last name. Click the SUBMIT button. Work the crossword puzzle. When you are finished, click the Submit button. When the crossword puzzle is redisplayed, click the Print Puzzle button to print a hard copy.

7 Tips and Tricks

Below FrontPage Project 2, click the Tips and Tricks link. Click a topic that pertains to Project 2. Right-click the information and then click Print on the shortcut menu. Construct a brief example of what the information relates to in FrontPage to confirm you understand how to use the tip or trick.

8 Newsgroups

Below FrontPage Project 2, click the Newsgroups link. Click a topic that pertains to Project 2. Print three comments.

9 Expanding Your Horizons

Below FrontPage Project 2, click the Expanding Your Horizons link. Click a topic that pertains to Project 2. Print the information. Construct a brief example of what the information relates to in FrontPage to confirm you understand the contents of the article.

10 Search Sleuth

Below FrontPage Project 2, click the Search Sleuth link. To search for a term that pertains to this project, select a term below the Project 2 title and then use the Google search engine at google.com (or any major search engine) to display and print two Web pages that present information on the term.

11 FrontPage Online Training

Below FrontPage Project 2, click the FrontPage Online Training link. When your browser displays the Microsoft Office Online Web page, click the FrontPage link. Click one of the FrontPage courses that covers one or more of the objectives listed at the beginning of the project on page FP 82. Print the first page of the course before stepping through it.

12 Office Marketplace

Below FrontPage Project 2, click the Office Marketplace link. When your browser displays the Microsoft Office Online Web page, click the Office Marketplace link. Click a topic that relates to FrontPage. Print the first page.

Apply Your Knowledge

1 Modifying a Corporate Presence Web Site

Instructions: Start FrontPage. Open the Web site, Apply 1-1Ship-It-Here, that you modified in Project 1. If you did not complete this exercise for Project 1, see your instructor for a copy of the required files.

1. If necessary, double-click the file, index.htm, in the Folder List pane to display the Ship-It-Here Home page in Design view.
2. On the Format menu, click Theme. Scroll down until you see the theme Blends and select it, or another theme as directed by your instructor. Select Vivid colors, Active graphics, and Background picture. Apply the theme to all pages in the Web site.
3. Click the graphic in the upper-left corner of the page. On the Insert menu, point to Picture and then click Clip Art. Search on the Web for a graphic depicting packaging or shipping of your choice that fits the selected theme. Replace the current image with an image of your choice. Alternatively, you may use the image, delivery.gif, in the Project2 folder on the Data Disk. See the inside back cover of this book for instructions for downloading the Data Disk or see your instructor for information on accessing the files required in this book. Drag the sizing handles to size the image appropriately.
4. Select the first paragraph that begins, We ship anything, and change the font color to red, or a color of your choice, from the theme colors.
5. Select the text in the first paragraph under the Our Destination heading that reads, to anywhere as quickly as possible. Click the Italic button on the Formatting toolbar. Click the Font Color button arrow and change the text color to blue, or a color of your choice, from the current theme.
6. Select the text after each bullet and all remaining text that is the default color (black). Change the color of the selected text to green, or a color of your choice.
7. Click the Preview button to preview the Web page. When you have finished, click the Design button.
8. Print and save the Web page and then close FrontPage. Save the embedded images if prompted. Hand in the printout to your instructor.

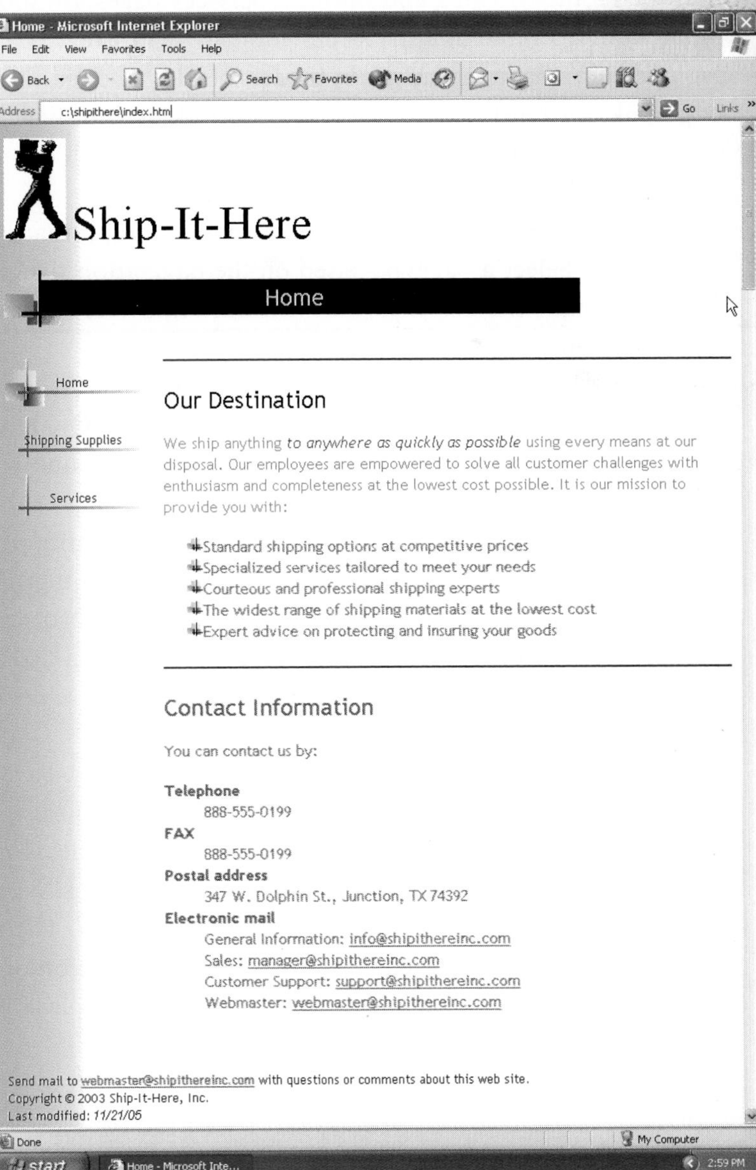

FIGURE 2-95

1 Modifying a Navigation Component on a Corporate Presence Web Site

Problem: The Fairway Lawn Care Web site that you began developing has an interesting and appropriate theme. Some of the pages, however, have no navigation bars — users can use only the Back button on their browsers to return to a previous Web page. You want to modify the Web site to include appropriate link bars for all pages.

Instructions: Perform the following tasks.

1. Open the Fairway Lawn Care Web site that you began in Project 1. If you did not complete that exercise for Project 1, see your instructor for a copy of the required files.
2. In the Folder List pane, double-click the file, serv01.htm, to open the Home Mowing page in Design view.
3. Click the Navigation command on the View menu to view the navigation structure of this Web site. Note that the Home Mowing and Business Services pages are shown on the same level, with the Services page as a parent to both. Double-click the Home Mowing page to display it in Design view.
4. Double-click the link bar text in the left border to open the Link Bar Properties dialog box. Note that the hyperlinks currently selected are for the child level, of which there currently are none. Furthermore, because this is a shared border, making changes here affects all other pages in the Web site. Click the Cancel button to close the Link Bar Properties dialog box.
5. Position the insertion point just before the paragraph that begins, This is a brief. On the Insert menu, click Navigation. Select a bar type based on the navigation structure. Click the Next button. Select a bar style using the page's theme. Click the Next button. Select a horizontal orientation for the link bar. Click the Finish button.
6. In the Link Bar Properties dialog box, select Back and next for hyperlinks to add to the page. Select Home page and Parent page as additional pages. Click the OK button.
7. If necessary, press the right-arrow key to deselect the link bar. Press the ENTER key. Save the changes to this page.
8. In the Folder List pane, double-click the file, serv02.htm, to open the Business Services page in Design view.
9. Position the insertion point just before the paragraph that begins, This is a brief. On the Insert menu, click Navigation. Select a bar type based on the navigation structure. Click the Next button. Select a bar style using the page's theme. Click the Next button. Select a horizontal orientation for the link bar. Click the Finish button. In the Link Bar Properties dialog box, select Back and next for hyperlinks to add to the page. Select Home page and Parent page as additional pages. Click the OK button. If necessary, press the right-arrow key to deselect the link bar. Press the ENTER key. Save the changes to this page.
10. Click the Preview tab to preview the changes made to this page. Note that the Business Services page has links for Back, Home, and Up. These link to the Home Mowing, Home, and Services pages, respectively. Click the Back button. The Home Mowing page opens. Note that the links here are almost the same, except for order and a Next button instead of a Back button. The Next button links to the Business Services page. The order and links on each page are due to the position of the page in the Web site's navigation structure.
11. Print and save the each changed Web page, and then close FrontPage. Hand in the printouts to your instructor.

In the Lab

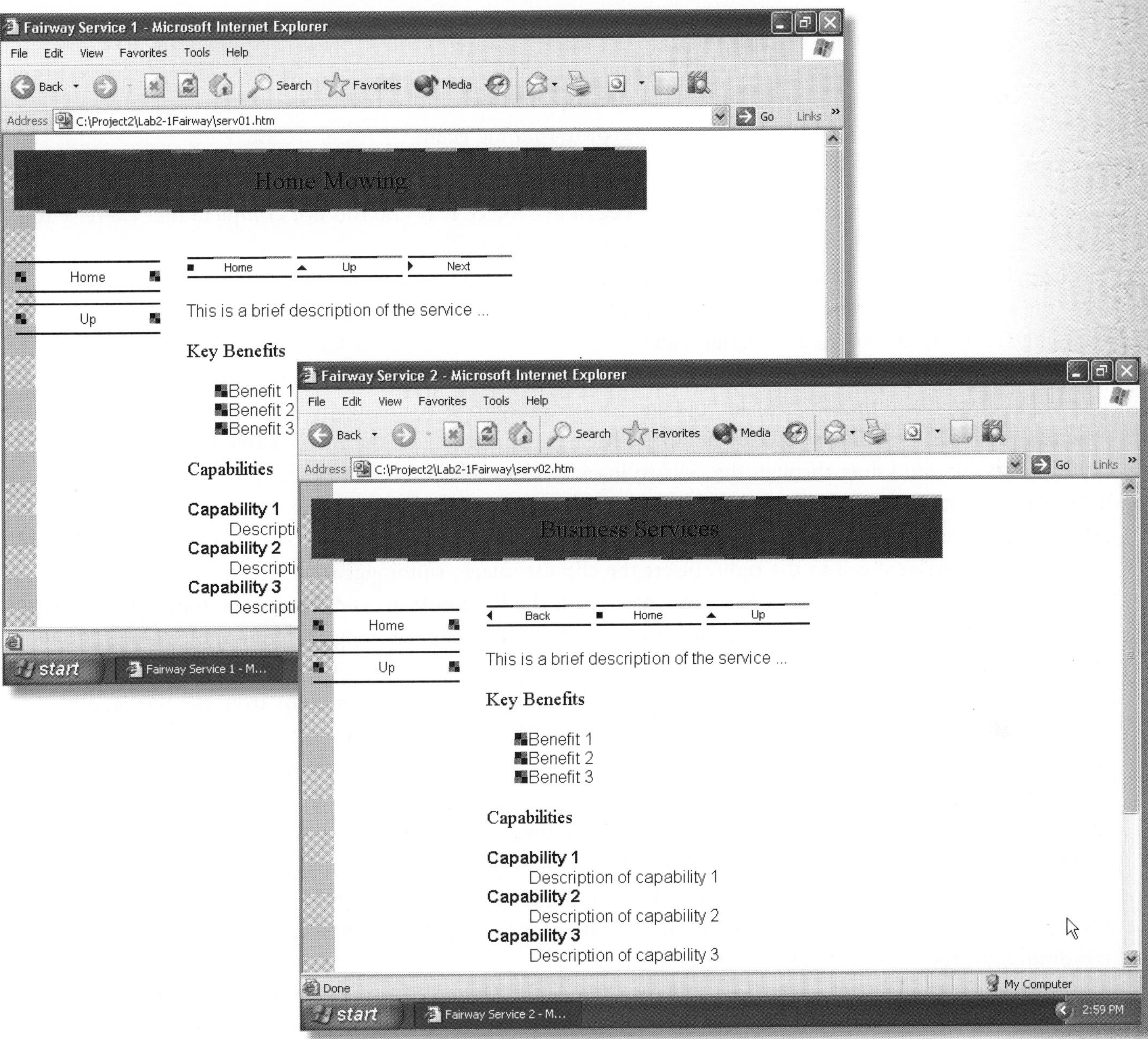

FIGURE 2-96

2 Modifying a Personal Web Site

Problem: Earlier, you created a personal Web site about your favorite Web sites. You have decided to add a page with links to Web pages about some of your favorite running gear.
Instructions: Perform the following tasks.

1. Open the Web site, Lab 1-2Running, that you began in Project 1. If you did not complete that exercise for Project 1, see your instructor for a copy of the required files.
2. In Navigation view, select the Home page. Right-click the Home page icon, click New, and then click Page.
3. Save the new page as gear.htm, change the page label to Running Gear, and change the page title to Running Gear. Open this page in Design view.
4. On the Insert menu, click Page Banner. When the Page Banner Properties dialog box appears, verify that Picture is selected and that the text in the Page banner text box is Running Gear. Click the OK button.
5. Position the insertion point below the newly added page banner. Click the Insert Table button on the Standard toolbar and drag through the cells to insert a 4×4 table.
6. Type `Some of my favorite` in the top row, first column of the table. Select the text and click the Bold button on the Formatting toolbar. Click the Align Right button. Change the font color to a color from the current theme. In the next cell to the right, insert the clip art image, runninggear.gif, from the Data Disk. Type `is:` in the top row, third column. Select the text, click the Bold button, and change the font color to match the text in the first cell. In the top row, fourth column, insert a clip art image of your choice representing running gear such as shoes, or you may use the file, runningshoes.gif, from the Data Disk.
7. Type `Watches:` in the left cell of the second row. Change the text color to a color from the theme, and make it bold and right-aligned. In the next cell to the right, insert a clip art image of your choice representing watches, or you may use the file, watch.gif, from the Data Disk. If necessary, resize the image to fit the page.
8. Type `Treadmills:` in the left cell of the third row. Change the text color to a color from the theme, and make it bold and right-aligned. In the next cell to the right, insert a clip art image of your choice representing a treadmill or other running equipment, or you may use the file, treadmill.gif, from the Data Disk. In the third column, insert another treadmill or running gear image of your choice, or you may use the file, treadmill2.gif, from the Data Disk.
9. Type `Shoes:` in the left cell of the bottom row. Change the text color to a color from the theme, and make it bold and right-aligned. In the next cell to the right, insert a clip art image of your choice representing a pedometer or other running gear, or you may use the file, shoe.gif, from the Data Disk. In the third column, insert another running gear image of your choice, or you may use the file, shoes2.gif, from the Data Disk. If necessary, resize the image to fit the page.
10. Merge the second and third cells of the second row into a single cell. Do the same for each following row.
11. Center the table alignment and specify the width as 80%. Drag the cell borders to align the text and images. Remove the table borders. Preview the Web page and adjust the alignment as needed to obtain a page similar to that shown in Figure 2-97.
12. Save the Web page. Save the embedded images to the images folder for the Web site. Print the changed Web pages and submit them to your instructor.

In the Lab

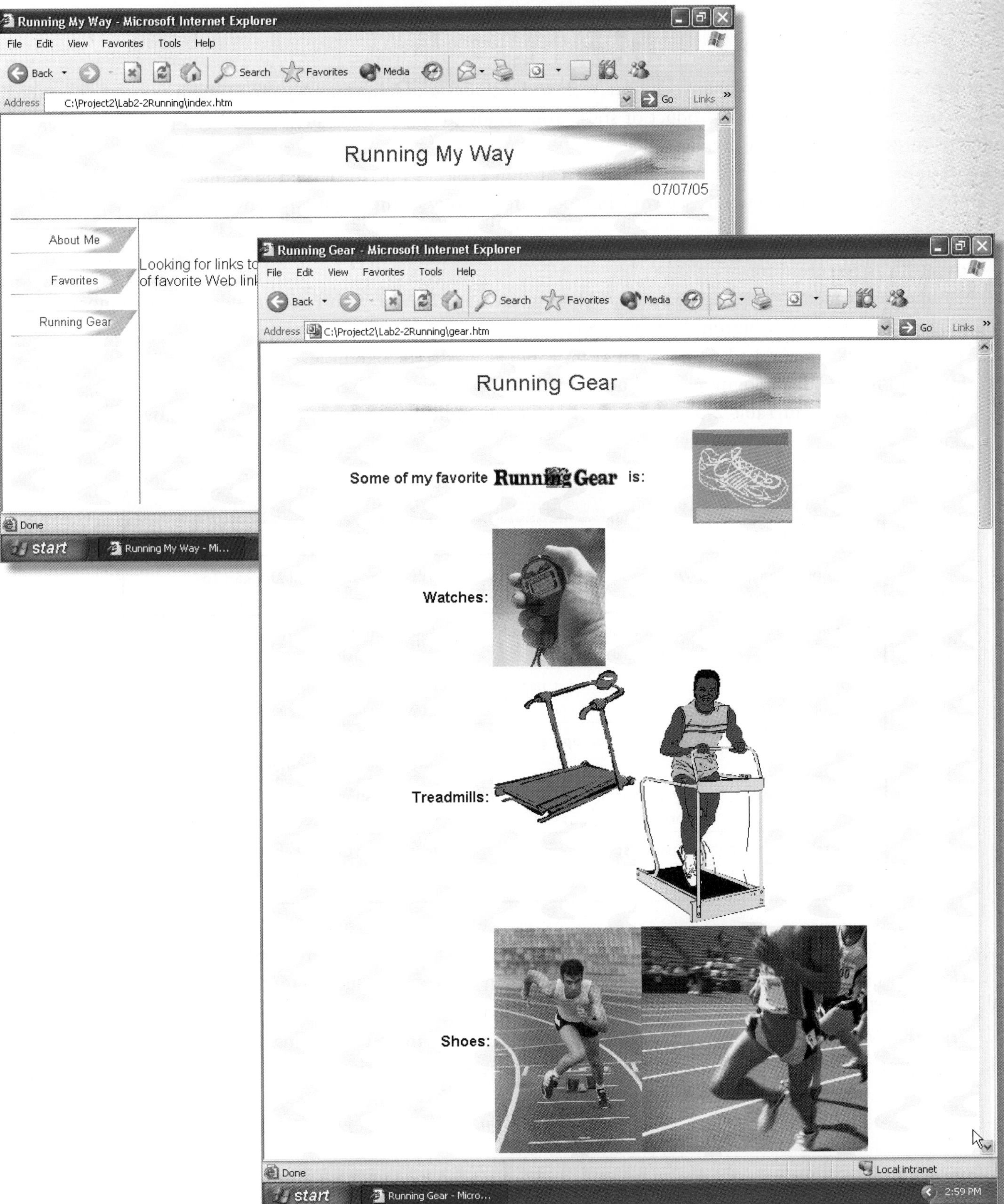

FIGURE 2-97

3 Adding a New Page and a Photo Gallery to a One-Page Web Site

Problem: Your one-page company support Web site includes a description of your company's support options, but no images of the company's product or staff. You decide to enhance the site by adding a page containing some pictures in an attractive layout.

Instructions: Using the support Web site you created in Project 1, perform the following tasks. If you did not complete this exercise in Project 1, see your instructor for a copy of the required Web site.

1. Add a new page to the current Web site navigation structure, with the current theme applied. Rename the page file as pictures.htm.
2. On the Insert menu, click Page Banner. Add a Picture Page Banner with Page banner text of Company Pictures. Click the OK button. Press the ENTER key.
3. Type, `go back to`. Add a link bar with a single hyperlink to the parent level.
4. Insert a Photo Gallery component. Choose the Slide Show layout. Insert the picture files, captions, and descriptions listed in Table 2-3, or personnel and product images and text of your own choosing (Figure 2-98).

Table 2-3 Support Image Files, Captions, and Descriptions

FILE NAME	CAPTION	DESCRIPTION
AluminumCan.jpg	Aluminum cans of any size and shape	We make any aluminum can to our customers' specifications.
AluminumFrame.jpg	From Aluminum framed housing...	Aluminum framed housing is our fastest growing business segment.
PaperClip.jpg	... to the smallest paperclip	But we still make the standards, such as paperclips and scissors.
SandraSupport.jpg	Billing and shipping support	24-hour support for our local and international customers alike.
HasanSupport.jpg	Hassan from specialty products support	Friendly support from people empowered to solve your problems.
OnSiteSupport.jpg	Specialists sent to your location	Industry veterans sent to your site for consulting or technical support.

5. Open the file, index.htm. At the end of the paragraph that begins, Whalen Metals practices a, type `Take a look at our` and then, after the text, insert a link bar with a hyperlink to the child level.
6. Save the Web pages and preview them by viewing them in your browser.
7. Print the Web pages, write your name on the pages, and give them to your instructor.
8. Close your browser and quit FrontPage. Save the embedded images if prompted.

In the Lab

FIGURE 2-98

Cases and Places

The difficulty of these case studies varies:
■ are the least difficult and ■■ are more difficult. The last exercise is a group exercise.

1 ■ In preparation for graduation, you created a text-only Web page in Project 1 to post your resume on the Web. Using that Web site, modify the text to use different font sizes for different sections, such as the title and section headings. Use bold and italics where appropriate. To position the various elements of your resume, cut and paste them into a table with no visible borders. Center the table on the Web page. Delete any bullets that remain after cutting and pasting the content to the table.

2 ■ You want to improve the appearance of the Web site you created for your movie review Web page from Project 1. Insert a two-column table with four rows per movie review. For each review, use one cell each in the left column for title, director, release year, and studio. In the right column, merge the corresponding four cells into one and place the review text for the movie in this merged cell. Do the same for all reviews completed.

3 ■ In preparation for an upcoming graduation for your friend, you were asked to develop a Web site for him. You created a personal Web site that includes a Home page, an Interests page, and a History page. Edit the History page to include a Photo Gallery of pictures from your friend's college life. Edit the caption text to provide brief descriptions of each photo. Use the exercise in Project 1 to develop the initial Web site.

4 ■■ Using clip art from the Web, enhance with appropriate images the company softball Web page that you created in Project 1. Include hyperlinks to several of your favorite sports-oriented Web sites. Use a table to position text, images, and hyperlinks. Cut and paste the existing text to insert it into the table. Apply an appropriate theme to the Web site.

5 ■■ **Working Together** You have decided to develop a Web site to promote your chosen career, and you want to illustrate it with appropriate images. Create a new Web site with at least a parent and two child pages. Apply an appropriate theme. On one child page, add links to various sites on the Web for this career choice. On another child page, place at least five clip art images from the Web, along with text describing each image, using appropriate fonts, font sizes, and colors. Insert these within a table to arrange a pleasing presentation. Modify each page's title and label to reflect their purpose. Add a navigation bar to each page. Let child pages link to each other, as well as to the parent page.

MICROSOFT
Office FrontPage 2003

Customizing and Managing Web Pages and Images

PROJECT 3

CASE PERSPECTIVE

An attractive photo collage enhances the layout of James Keeler's Photos Web page. Now, James wants to improve the visual appeal by using a lighter background and adding his favorite colors. He wants the Photos page to reflect the last date it was changed and have a counter for the number of visitors. He wants to add a graphical hyperlink on the Home page that links to the Photos page. James has created his resume in a Word document and plans to publish it to his Web site using hyperlinks to its various sections.

To manage his Web site properly, James requires a place to record ideas for new pages. He has visited Web sites with broken links and knows how frustrating it is as a visitor to be unable to navigate such a site. He needs the capability of determining whether any of the hyperlinks on his Web pages are broken. You know that FrontPage includes tools and features to help him easily change the hyperlinks, modify the theme of his choice, and incorporate data from other Office applications, such as his resume in Word. FrontPage has additional features that can help him plan and manage Web pages as well.

As you read through this project, you will learn how to customize Web pages using FrontPage's built-in themes. You also will learn about image formats used on the Web and how to enhance images for use on a Web page. You will learn how to create an image map and target a URL to the hotspot. You will learn how to insert bookmarks in a Web page to aid navigation. You also will learn how to copy text from a Word document and paste the text into a Web page. Finally, you will learn how to use FrontPage's reporting features and how to verify hyperlinks.

MICROSOFT

Office FrontPage 2003

Customizing and Managing Web Pages and Images

PROJECT

3

Objectives

You will have mastered the material in this project when you can:

- Discuss the types of images used on the Web
- Create and apply a custom theme
- Expand an existing table
- Add a hit counter
- Add a shared border and change the navigation structure of a Web site
- Copy and paste from a Word document
- Insert bookmarks into a Web page
- Display the Pictures toolbar
- Modify image properties
- Insert an AutoShapes drawing object in FrontPage
- Create an image map hotspot
- Use a graphical image as a hyperlink
- Use FrontPage to create and view reports
- Verify the hyperlinks in a FrontPage Web site

Introduction

With the widespread use of images, graphics, and animation, it is important to take the time to learn about the types of images used on the Web and master the graphics-editing features necessary to customize Web pages. Knowing the characteristics, advantages, and disadvantages of each type of image file can help you ascertain the best type of image to use for a particular situation.

Project 3 introduces you to customizing a Web page. You will learn how to create a transparent GIF image, an image map, and bookmarks. You also will see how easy it is in FrontPage to make significant changes to an existing theme. The project shows you how to create hotspots for an image map and copy text from a Word document directly into FrontPage.

Most of the pages developed in this project are customizations of previous work. The Home page will have two new links added, one of which is an image and one of which is an AutoShapes drawing (Figure 3-1a). The links navigate the user to the Photos page, which is modified to use a customized theme (Figure 3-1b). A new page contains a resume, the text of which is copied from a Word document (Figure 3-1c). The Resume page consists of several long sections of text. You insert bookmarks to allow a user to click a hyperlink at the top of the Resume page and immediately go to the corresponding section. A shared border is added to all the pages to consistently display the last date the pages were updated.

To help you in this process, the project presents some important concepts and definitions.

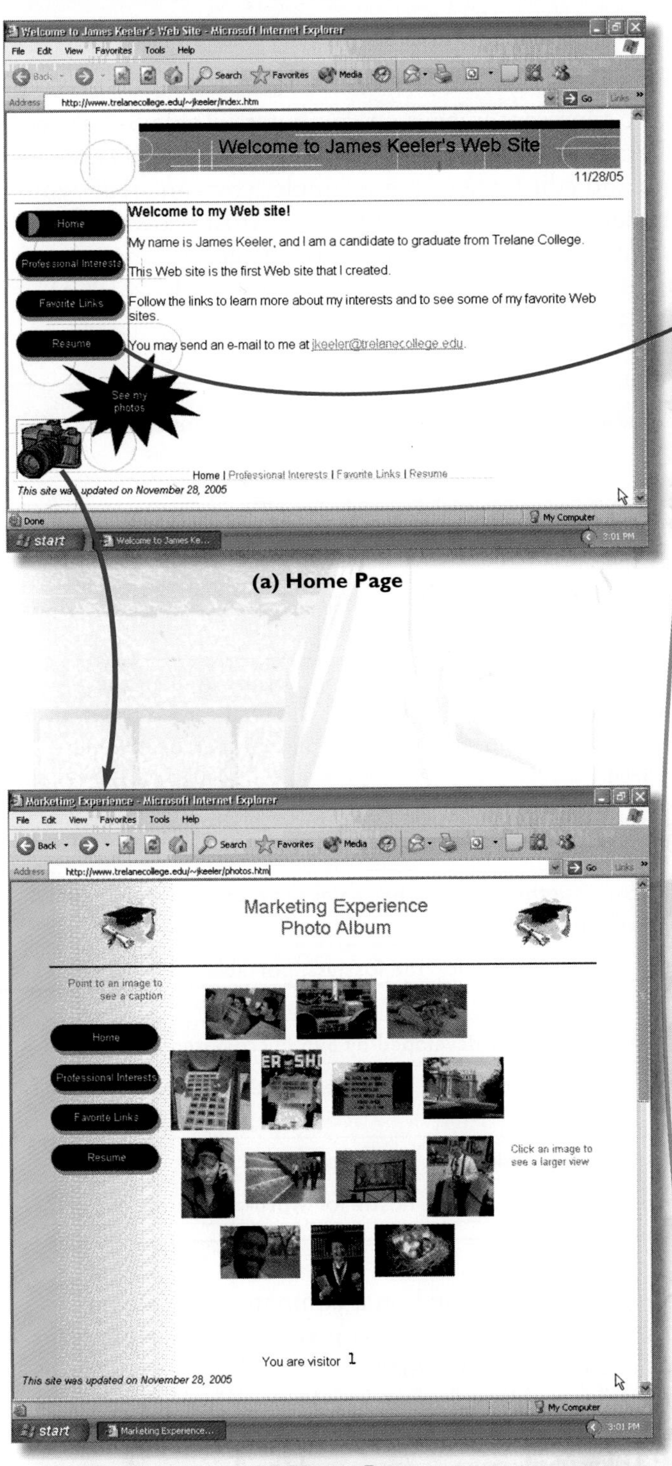

(a) Home Page

(b) Photos Page

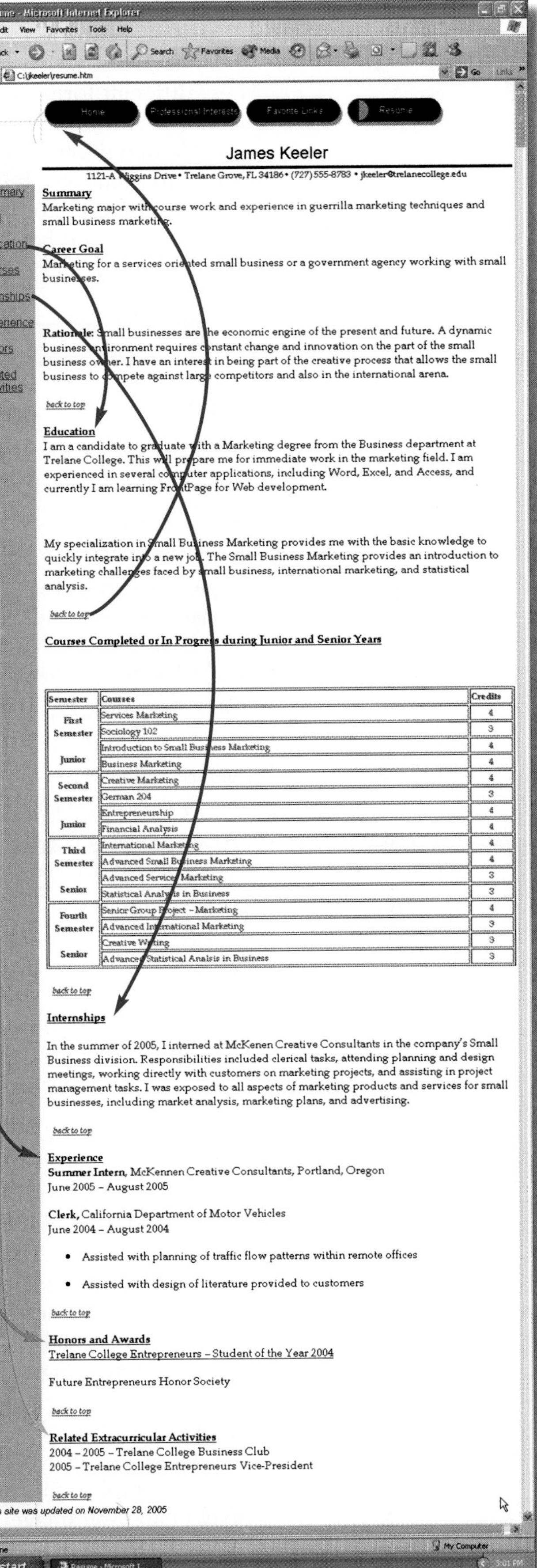

Semester	Courses	Credits
First Semester Junior	Services Marketing	4
	Sociology 102	3
	Introduction to Small Business Marketing	4
	Business Marketing	4
Second Semester Junior	Creative Marketing	4
	German 204	3
	Entrepreneurship	4
	Financial Analysis	4
Third Semester Senior	International Marketing	4
	Advanced Small Business Marketing	4
	Advanced Services Marketing	3
	Statistical Analysis in Business	3
Fourth Semester Senior	Senior Group Project – Marketing	4
	Advanced International Marketing	3
	Creative Writing	3
	Advanced Statistical Analsis in Business	3

(c) Resume Page

FIGURE 3-1

Image File Formats

Many different formats are used to represent images on computers. Table 3-1 shows some of the various image file formats. Numerous graphics editors and tools are available that allow you to create and edit images. For example, you can create your own custom buttons, bullets, dividers, and background images. Most browsers display only two types of image file formats: GIF and JPEG. FrontPage can import images in several other formats, including BMP, TIF, WMF, RAS, EPS, PCX, PCD, PNG, and TGA, and then convert them to GIF or JPEG images.

Table 3-1 Image File Formats

IMAGE FILE TYPE	DESCRIPTION
BMP	Windows bitmap file format — device-independent format, introduced with Windows 3.0 and increasingly supported by Windows applications.
EPS	Encapsulated PostScript file format — an extension of the PostScript file graphics format developed by Adobe Systems.
GIF	Graphic Interchange Format file format — a popular graphics exchange format used by the CompuServe Information Service and other online graphics sources. GIF is a licensed product for developers of commercial, for-profit software; however, for the nonprofit personal home page, a license agreement is not required.
JPEG	Joint Photographic Expert Group file format — used for true color, 24-bit photographic images scanned or digitized from films.
PCX	Paintbrush file format — used in Windows Paintbrush and other paint programs and supported by many desktop publishing and graphics programs.
PNG	Portable Network Graphics file format — a file format for the lossless, portable, well-compressed storage of raster images.
RAS	Sun Raster file format — the raster image file format developed by Sun Microsystems, Inc.
TGA	Targa file format — a photo-realistic image format designed for systems with a Truevision display adapter.
TIF (or TIFF)	Tagged Image File format — supported by many desktop publishing programs.
WMF	Windows Metafile format — a vector graphics format used mostly for word-processing clip art.

Q: Should I use the PNG file format in my Web pages?

A: FrontPage allows you to import many different image file formats, including the Portable Network Graphics (PNG) format. Although FrontPage does support the PNG file format, many Web browsers cannot display PNG pictures without a special plug-in. In general, it is better to use only GIF or JPEG images in your Web pages.

Regardless of the file type, an image is displayed on a computer screen using small points of color called pixels. As you have learned, a **pixel**, or **picture element**, is the smallest addressable point on the screen. An image is formed on the screen by displaying pixels of different color. The combined group of differently colored pixels makes up the image. The **image file** contains the information needed to determine the color for each pixel used to display the image.

The **bit resolution** of an image refers to the number of bits of stored information per pixel. With an **8-bit image**, 8 bits of information are stored for each pixel. Using the binary numbering system, you can represent up to 256 numbers using 8 bits. Thus, an 8-bit image can have a maximum of 256 colors, with each number representing a different color.

A **24-bit image** can have up to 16.7 million colors. These types of images have near-photographic quality. Each pixel, however, consumes three times the storage of a pixel in an 8-bit image, which results in a larger file size for an image with the same number of pixels.

GIF Image Files

GIF stands for **Graphic Interchange Format**. GIF files (GIFs) use 8-bit resolution and support up to 256 colors. GIF files support indexed color image types, line art, and grayscale images.

Special types of GIF files, called **animated GIFs**, contain a series of images that are displayed in rapid succession, giving the appearance of movement. Special animated GIF editors are available to combine the series of images and set the display timing.

The GIF89a format contains a **transparency index**. This index allows you to specify a transparent color, which causes the background of the Web page to show through the color that has been set as transparent. If you are using line art, icons, or images such as company logos, make sure they are in the GIF89a format. You then will be able to take advantage of the transparency index.

More About

Obtaining Images

You can browse the World Wide Web and select any image to insert on your Web page. Be sure that you have permission to use the image before placing it on your FrontPage Web page as some images on the Web are copyrighted.

Design Tip

GIF files are best suited for solid-colored images such as logos and illustrations. The 256-color limitation of GIF files makes them inappropriate for displaying photographs.

JPEG Image Files

JPEG stands for **Joint Photographic Expert Group**. The advantage to using JPEG files is the high color resolution. JPEG supports 24-bit resolution, providing up to 16.7 million possible colors. When including photographic images in your Web page, the images must use JPEG format because of the support for full color.

Design Tip

Each time a JPEG image is edited and saved, the image is compressed and decompressed, which degrades the image quality. You should make a copy of the original source image file and never alter the original image.

When you insert an image that is not in GIF or JPEG format, FrontPage automatically converts it to the GIF format if the image has eight or fewer bits of color. The image is converted automatically to JPEG format if the image has more than eight bits of color.

With FrontPage, you can import image files into the current FrontPage Web site, insert images in Web pages, align images with text, and create and edit image maps. The editing commands in FrontPage, such as crop, rotate, and resize, allow you to change the appearance of an image. In addition, you can change its brightness and contrast, make it black and white, or give the image beveled edges.

FrontPage can work with graphics editing programs such as the **Clip Art Gallery**, which is a tool for previewing and managing clip art, pictures, sounds, video clips, and animation. The Clip Art Gallery contains a collection of clip art and pictures you can insert into your Web pages. The Clip Art Gallery was used in Project 2 to create the Photos page.

More About

Photographic Images

Be careful when using photographic images with 24-bit color. Many computers do not have monitors and display adapters that support 24-bit color. If you change your Windows color setting to a lower bit resolution, you can preview a Web page to see how the images look before you publish the Web page.

Modifying an Existing Web Page

Because James wanted to change his original design for the Photos page once he saw it on the computer, you decide to use the theme currently used with the other pages, and then modify elements of the theme for this page only. Applying these modifications is a simple task with FrontPage.

To modify the Photos Web page, the original Web site first must be opened. The following steps open the Photos page in the personal Web site created in Project 2. If you did not complete Project 2, see your instructor for a copy of the files required to complete this project.

To Open an Existing Page in a FrontPage Web Site

1. **Click the Start button on the taskbar. Point to All Programs on the Start menu, point to Microsoft Office on the All Programs submenu, and then point to Microsoft Office FrontPage 2003.**
2. **Click Microsoft Office FrontPage 2003 on the Microsoft Office submenu.**
3. **If FrontPage opens a new_page_1.htm file, click Close on the File menu. If FrontPage opens another Web site, click Close Site on the File menu.**
4. **Click the Open button arrow on the Standard toolbar.**
5. **Click Open Site. If necessary, when FrontPage displays the Open Site dialog box, click the Look in box arrow and select the folder location where you stored the Web site for Project 2 (e.g., C:\jkeeler).**
6. **Click the Open button. Double-click photos.htm in the Folder List pane.**

The previous Web site is loaded, and the file, photos.htm, is displayed in Page view (Figure 3-2).

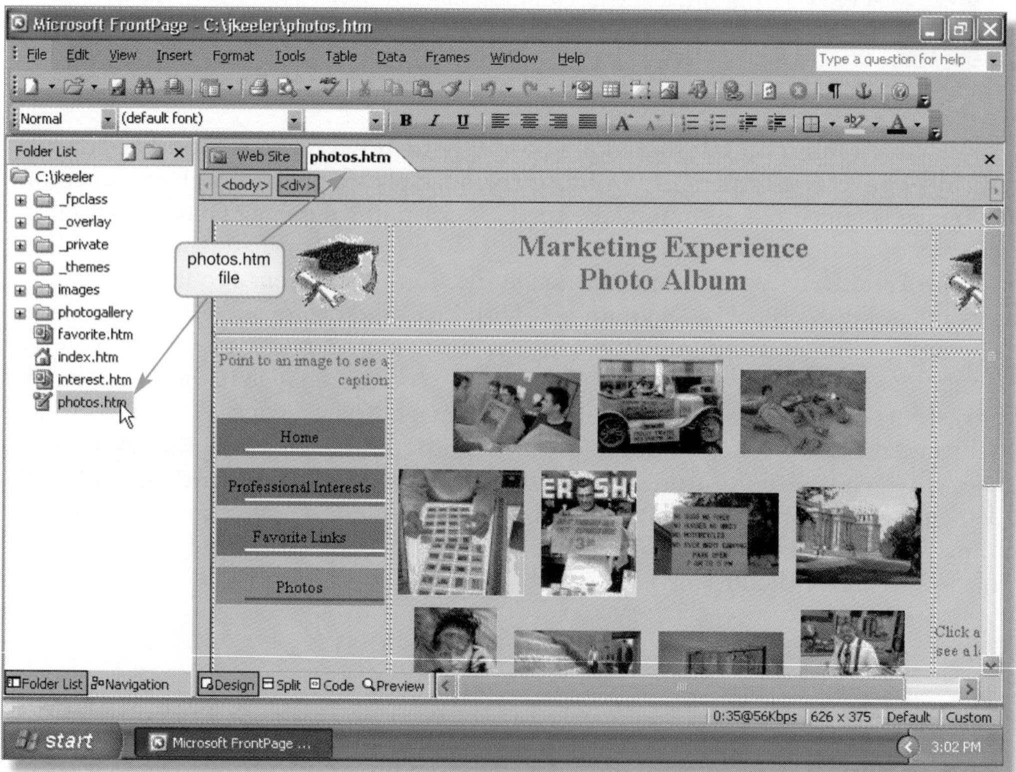

FIGURE 3-2

Creating and Applying a Customized Theme to a Web Page

Applying a theme to an existing Web page is essentially the same procedure used to apply a theme to a new Web site. When modifying a page that already contains certain graphic elements, such as a background color or image, be aware that applying a theme permanently alters such existing properties. In fact, once a theme has been applied, you cannot access the background properties of the page to apply an image or a color — they are under the control of the theme. You need to remove or modify the theme to make such changes. You effectively can remove the theme by applying a theme selection of No Theme to the Web page, as was done in Project 2. If you are not certain that you want to use a theme, you might want to make a backup copy of your FrontPage Web site by saving it in an alternate location before applying the theme.

A customized theme can be created easily by using an existing theme as a starting point, making changes to that theme, and then saving the modified theme with a new name. The following steps create and apply a customized theme to an existing Web page.

> *More About*
>
> **The FrontPage Help System**
>
> Need Help? It is no further away than the Type a question for help box on the menu bar in the upper-right corner of the window. Click the box that contains the text, Type a question for help, type `help`, and then press the ENTER key. FrontPage responds with a list of topics you can click to learn about obtaining help on any FrontPage-related topic. To find out what is new in FrontPage 2003, type `what is new in FrontPage` in the Type a question for help box.

To Create and Apply a Customized Theme

1

- **Click Format on the menu bar and then click Theme.**
- **If necessary, when FrontPage displays the Theme task pane, scroll down and point to Capsules in the Select a theme list.**
- **Click the Capsules theme arrow next to the Capsules theme preview.**

FrontPage displays the Theme task pane and displays the shortcut menu below the Capsules theme (Figure 3-3).

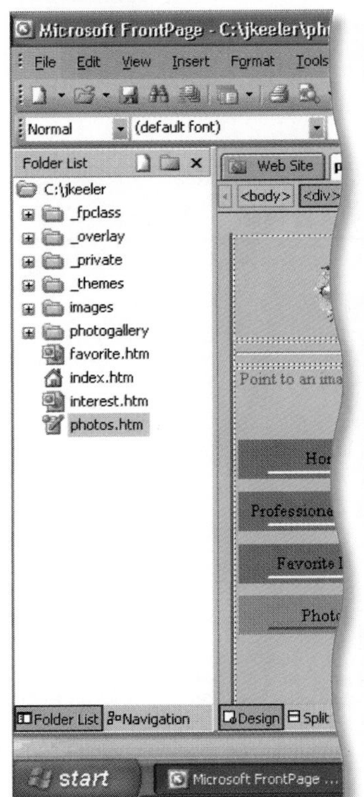

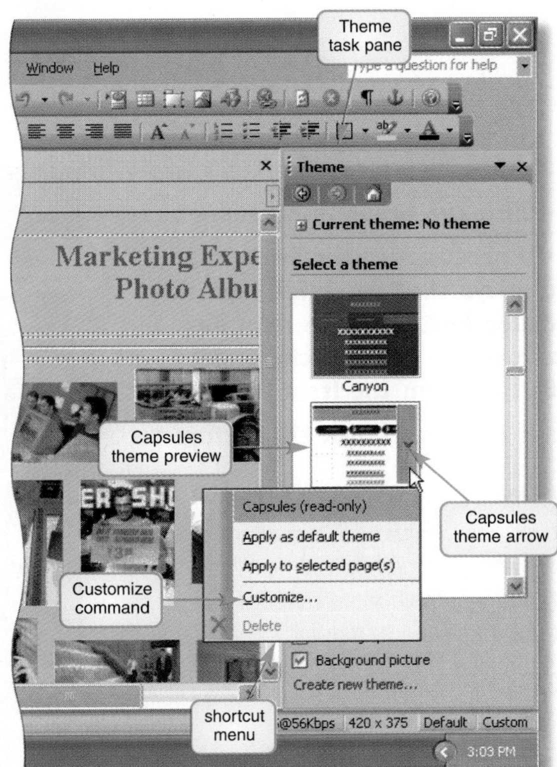

FIGURE 3-3

2

- **Click Customize.**

FrontPage displays the Customize Theme dialog box. The Preview of: Capsules area displays a sample page using the Capsules theme (Figure 3-4). FrontPage displays additional buttons that allow you to modify aspects of the theme and to save the modifications.

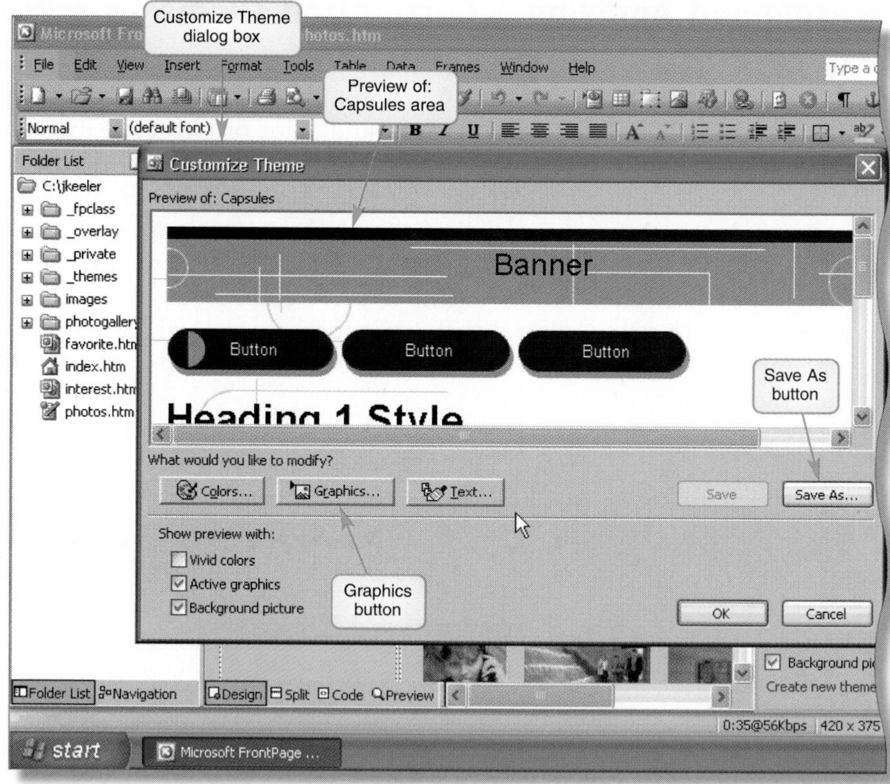

FIGURE 3-4

3

- **Click the Graphics button.**
- **If necessary, when FrontPage displays the Customize Theme dialog box, click the Item box arrow and select Background Picture from the Item list.**
- **If necessary, click the Picture tab.**

FrontPage displays the Customize Theme dialog box (Figure 3-5). FrontPage displays the item to modify in the Item list. FrontPage displays the current file used as the background picture for the theme in the Background Picture text box.

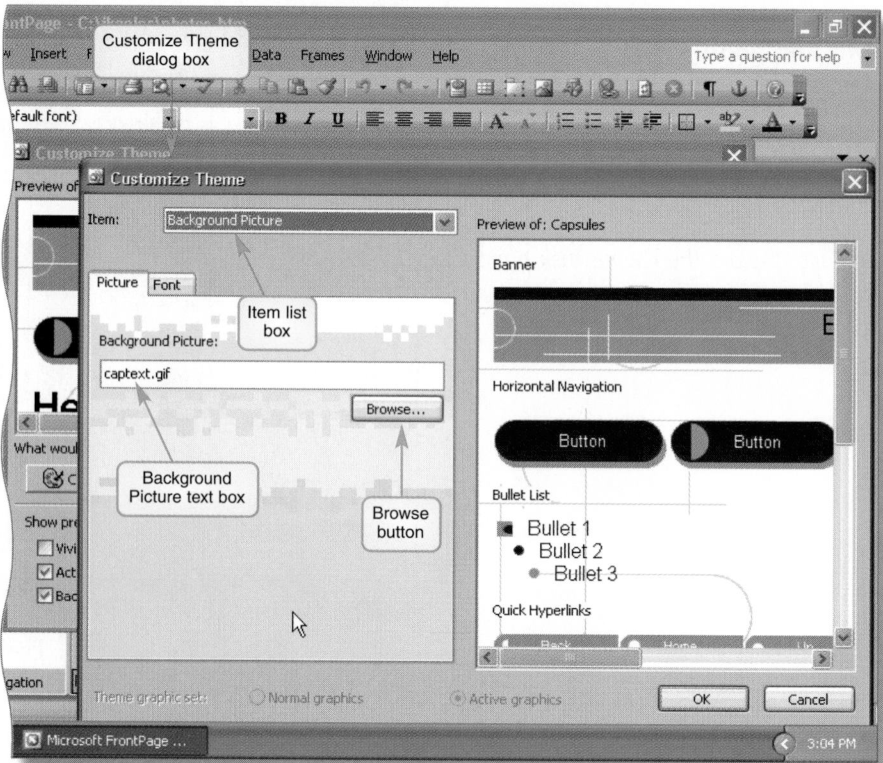

FIGURE 3-5

4

- **Click Browse.**
- **When FrontPage displays the Open File dialog box, select the newbackground file from the Project3 folder on the Data Disk.**

FrontPage displays the Open File dialog box (Figure 3-6).

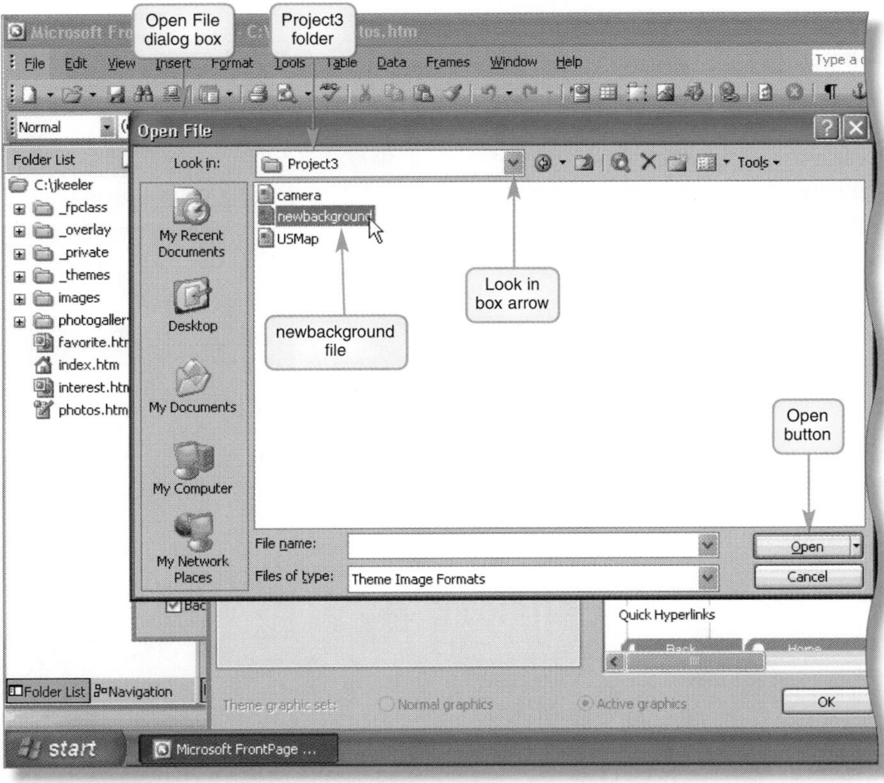

FIGURE 3-6

5

- **Click Open.**
- **Click the OK button.**
- **Click the Save As button.**
- **When FrontPage displays the Save Theme dialog box, type** `Capsules Green` **as the new theme title in the Enter new theme title text box.**

FrontPage displays a sample of the theme using the file, newbackground, as the background picture (Figure 3-7). FrontPage displays the new theme title in the Save Theme dialog box.

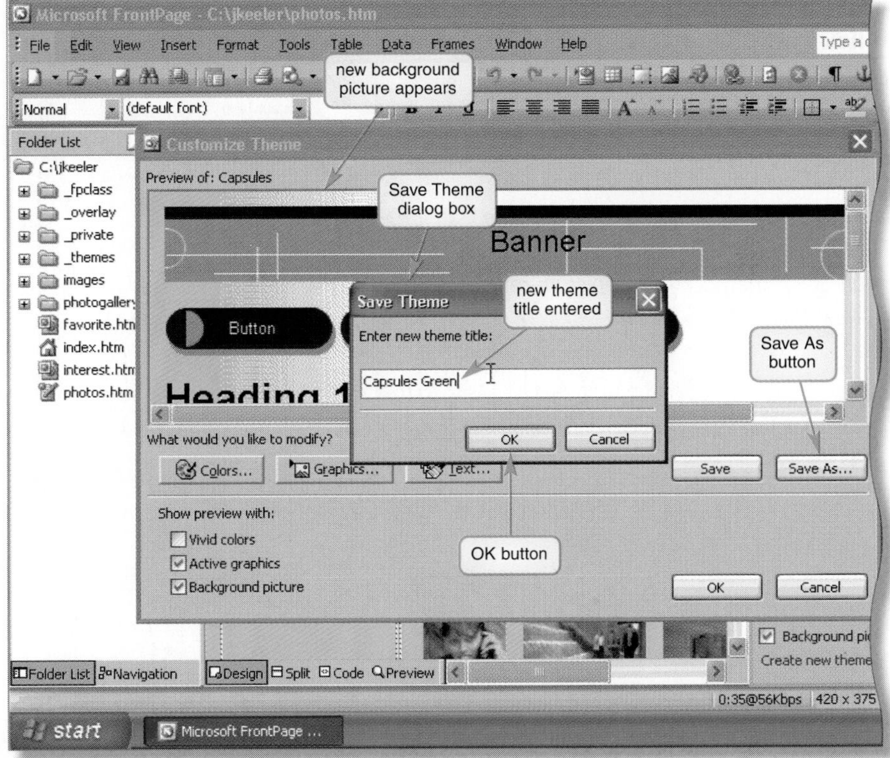

FIGURE 3-7

6

• **Click the OK button.**

FrontPage closes the Save Theme dialog box and saves the newly created theme. FrontPage displays the name of the new theme in the Preview of: area (Figure 3-8).

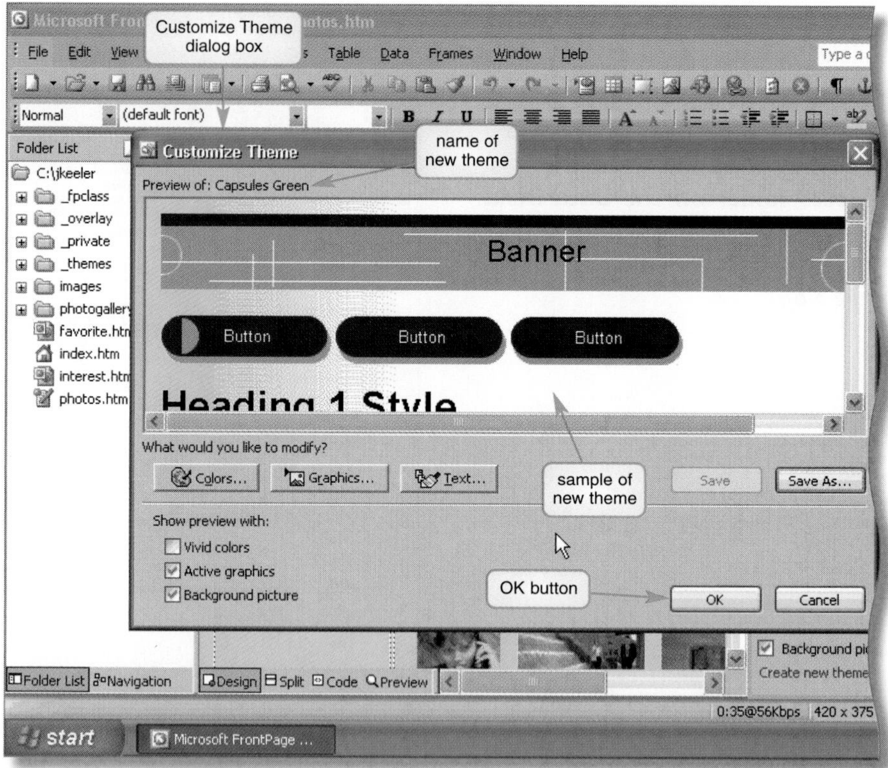

FIGURE 3-8

7

• **Click the OK button.**

• **If the Microsoft Office FrontPage dialog box appears, click the No button.**

FrontPage displays the new theme in the Select a theme list in the Theme task pane (Figure 3-9). The background picture reflects the new theme.

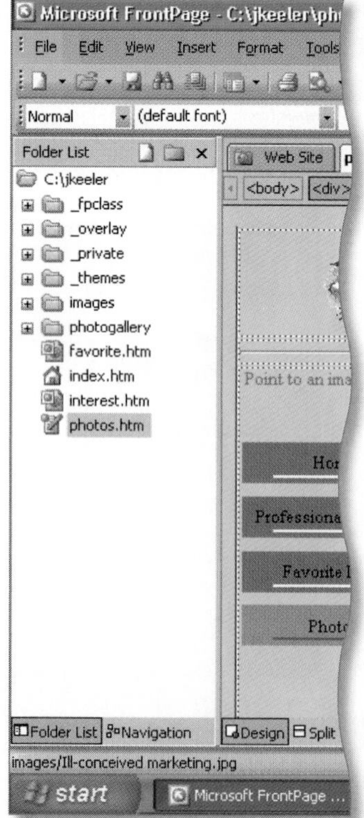

FIGURE 3-9

8

- **Click Vivid colors.**
- **Click the preview of the Capsules Green theme in the Select a theme list.**

FrontPage applies the theme to the photos.htm page (Figure 3-10).

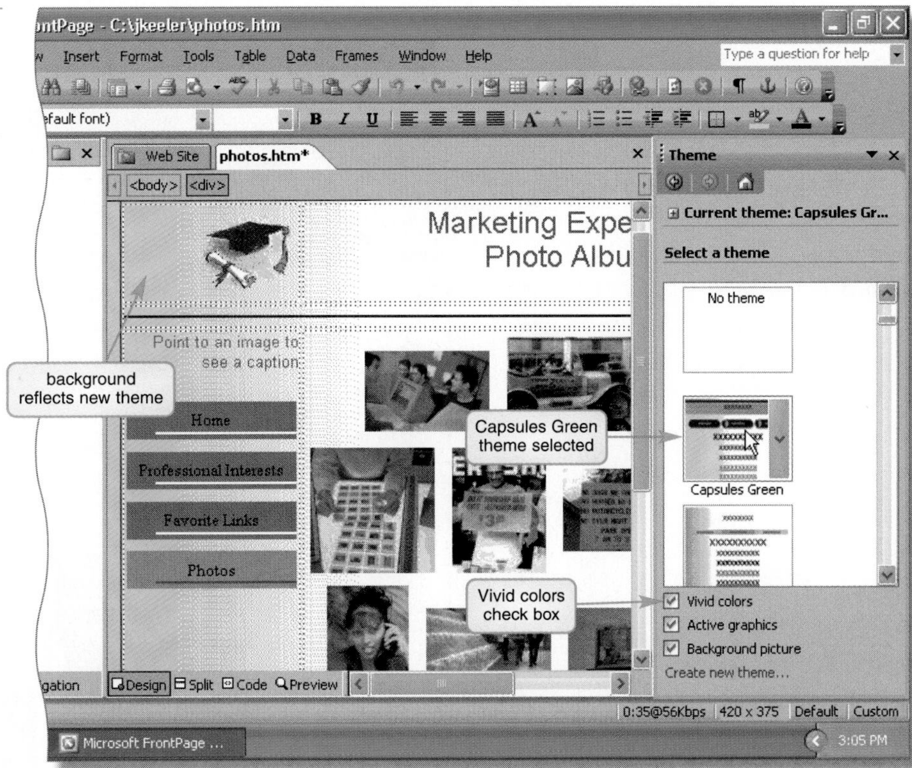

FIGURE 3-10

By saving changes to a theme as a new theme, the original theme remains unchanged. If you do not want a new theme, you simply may save the changes to the original theme.

Changing the Style of a Link Bar

When applying the new theme to the photos.htm Web page, FrontPage did not modify the link bar on the left side of the Web page to match the Capsules Green theme. To match the look of the other Web pages, the style of the link bar should be modified. The steps on the next page change the style of the link bar on the photos.htm page to match the style of the link bar on the other pages.

To Change the Style of a Link Bar

1

- **Right-click the link bar on the left side of the photos.htm Web page.**

FrontPage displays a shortcut menu (Figure 3-11).

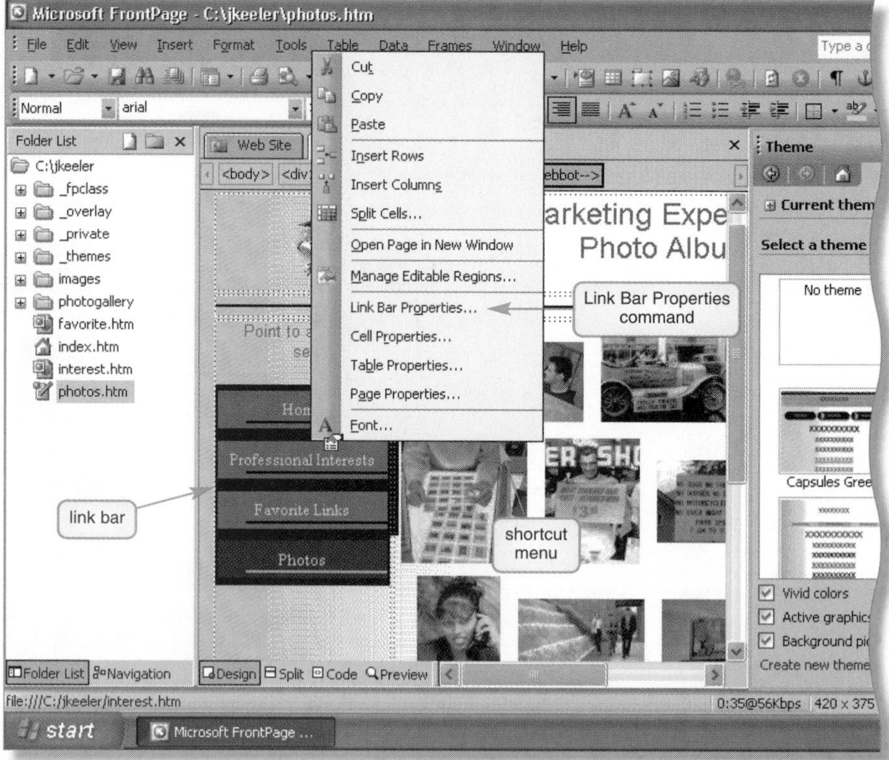

FIGURE 3-11

- **Click Link Bar Properties.**
- **If necessary, when FrontPage displays the Link Bar Properties dialog box, click the Style tab.**

FrontPage displays the Style sheet in the Link Bar Properties dialog box (Figure 3-12).

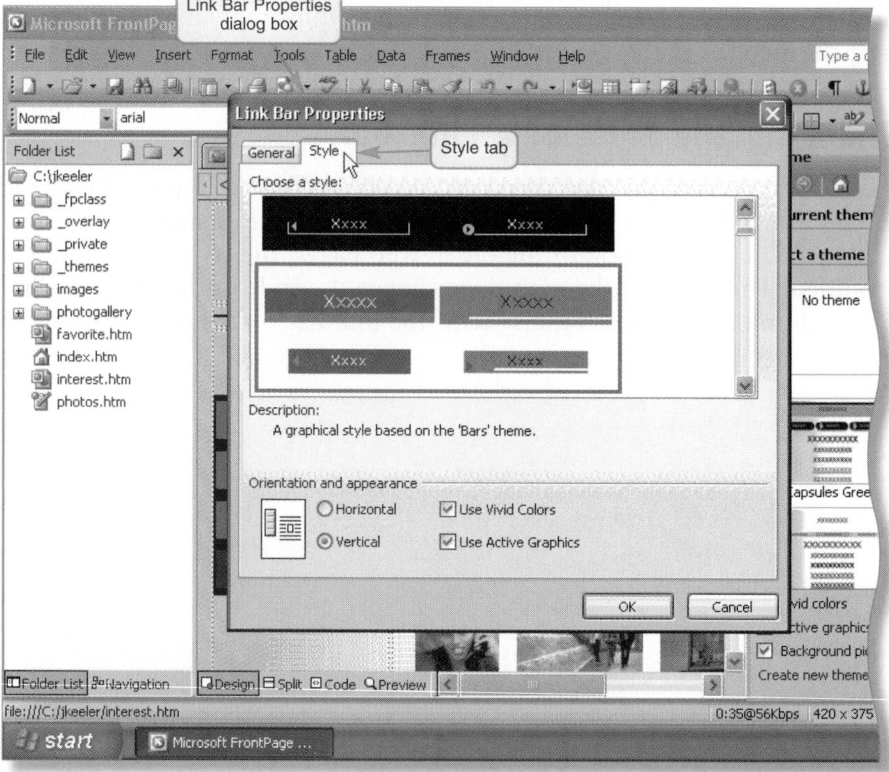

FIGURE 3-12

3

- **Scroll the Choose a style scroll bar up to display the Use Page's Theme style.**
- **Click the Use Page's Theme style.**

The Use Page's Theme style is selected in the Choose a style list box (Figure 3-13). The Use Page's Theme style indicates that the link bar should appear with the link bar style specified in the photos.htm page's style.

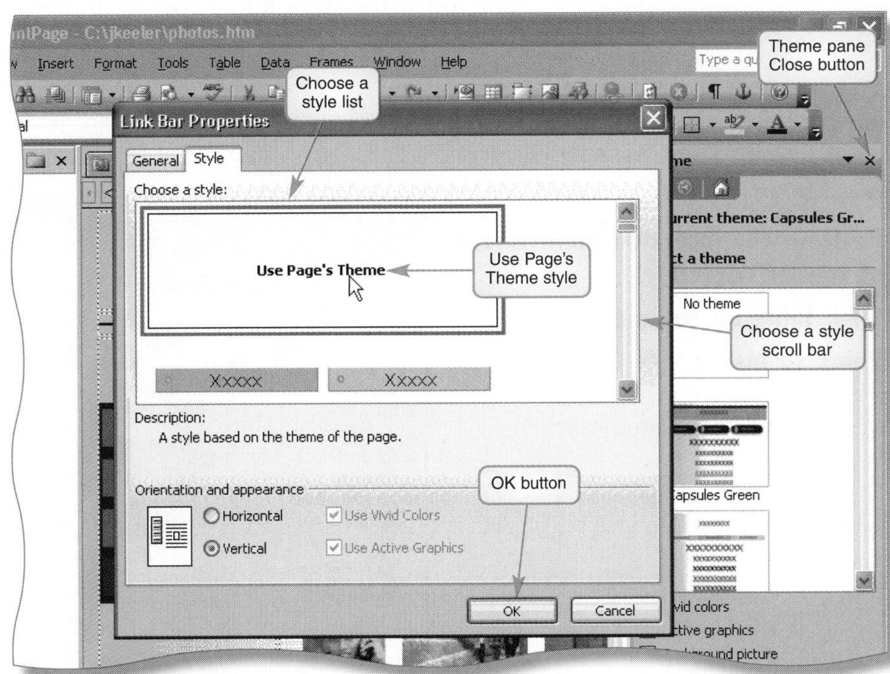

FIGURE 3-13

4

- **Click the OK button.**
- **Click the Close button on the Theme task pane.**

FrontPage displays the link bar using the Capsules Green theme's link bar style and closes the Theme task pane (Figure 3-14).

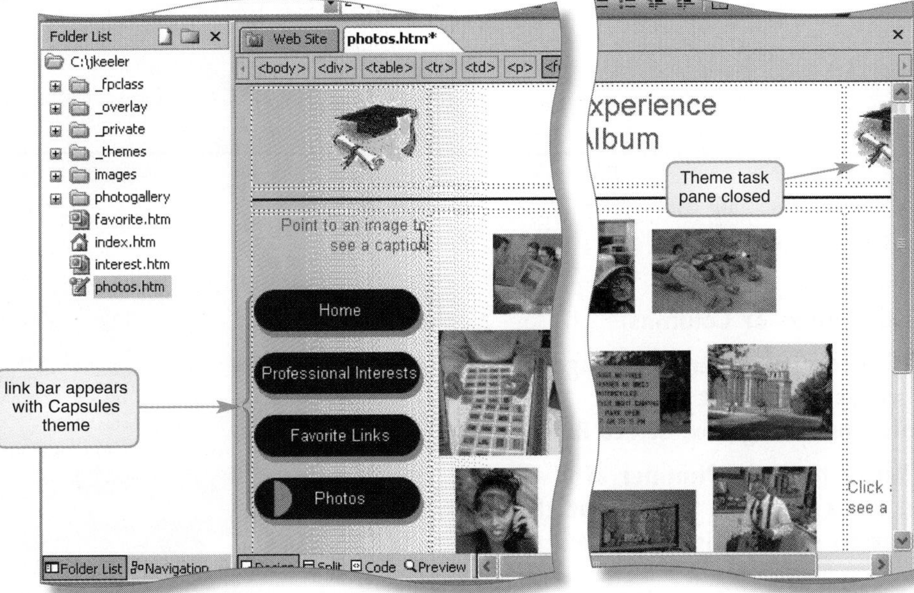

FIGURE 3-14

Expanding a Table

You may recall that tables often are used to position elements in a Web page. Items in the Photos page were placed within a table for this very reason. You already have learned how to merge table cells, and how to delete cells and even entire tables. As you make changes to the Web page, however, you may need additional rows, columns, or both, in your table. Rather than creating a new table with the required rows and columns, you can expand an existing table to accommodate new elements.

The following steps add a row to an existing table.

To Add a Row to a Table

1

- **Position the insertion point in the last row of the table.**
- **Click Table on the menu bar.**
- **Point to Insert.**

FrontPage displays the Insert submenu (Figure 3-15).

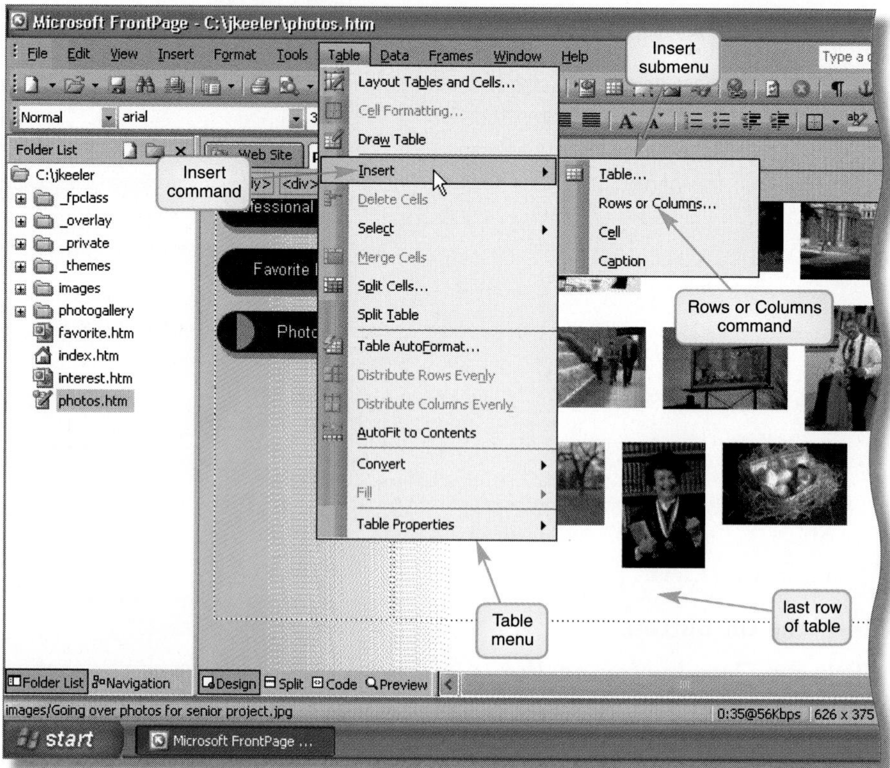

FIGURE 3-15

2

- **Click Rows or Columns.**
- **If necessary, when FrontPage displays the Insert Rows or Columns dialog box, select Rows.**
- **Verify that the Number of rows text box is set to 1 and that the location selected is Below selection.**

FrontPage displays the Insert Rows or Columns dialog box (Figure 3-16).

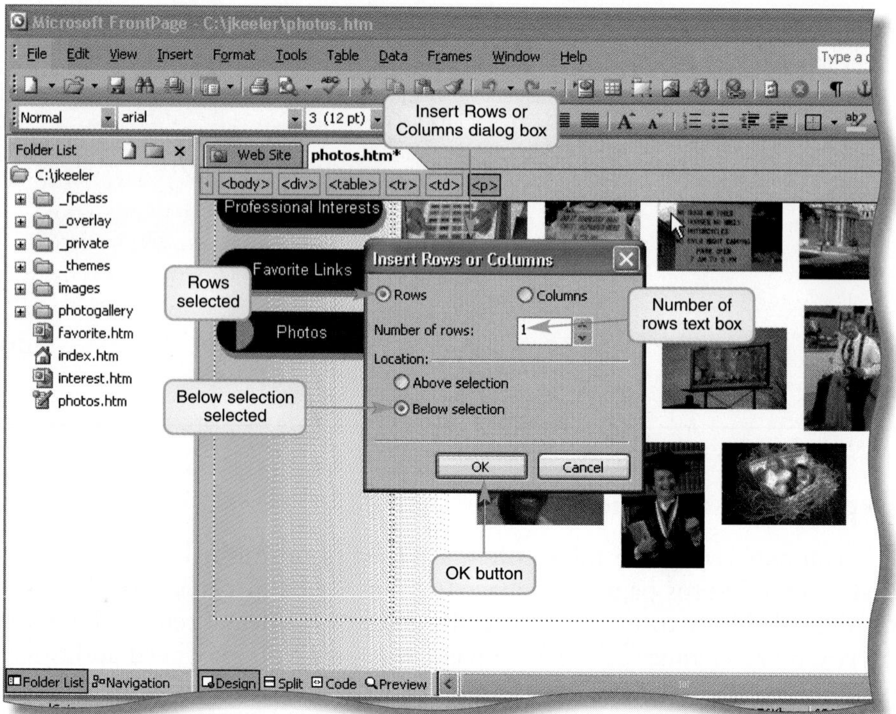

FIGURE 3-16

3

• **Click OK.**

• **Position the insertion point in the middle cell of the inserted row.**

The insertion point is positioned in the new row at the bottom of the table (Figure 3-17).

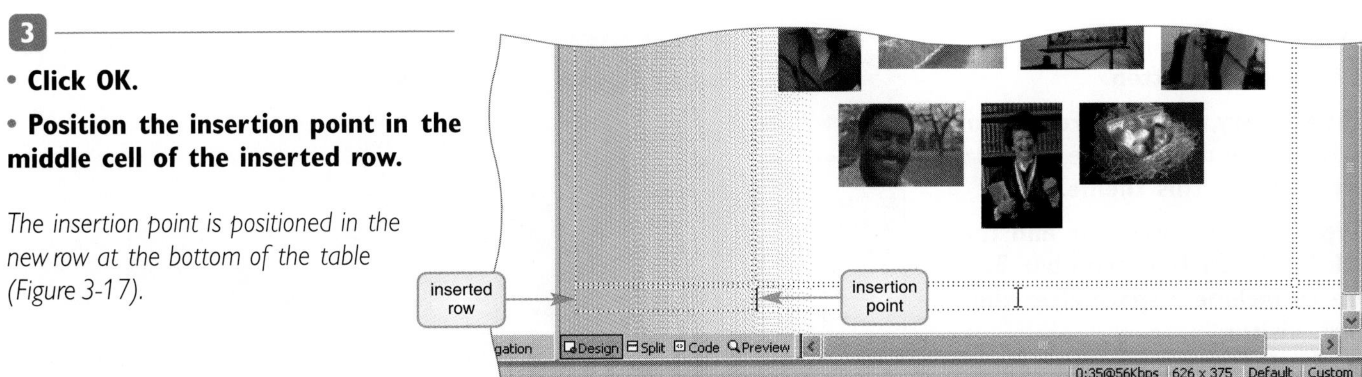

FIGURE 3-17

Other Ways

1. Right-click table, click Insert Rows
2. Press ALT+A, I, N
3. Click cell in table, in Voice Command mode, say "Table, Insert, Rows or Columns, OK"

Additional columns may be added to an existing table as easily as rows. Because FrontPage makes it easy to add or delete table rows and columns, you do not have to know the final dimensions of the table before you create it. You simply may modify the table size as needed.

Adding a Hit Counter Component

FrontPage provides a number of components that allow you to add common functionality to your pages easily. One feature often seen on Web pages is a hit counter. A **hit counter** is a component that displays a counter to indicate the number of times a Web page is accessed.

The following steps add a hit counter component to the Photos page.

To Add a Hit Counter

1

• **If necessary, position the insertion point in the middle cell of the last row inserted.**

• **Right-click the cell and then click Cell Properties on the shortcut menu.**

• **When FrontPage displays the Cell Properties dialog box, in the Layout area, select Center for Horizontal alignment and Middle for Vertical alignment.**

FrontPage displays the Cell Properties dialog box with Center selected for the Horizontal alignment and Middle for the Vertical alignment for the cell (Figure 3-18).

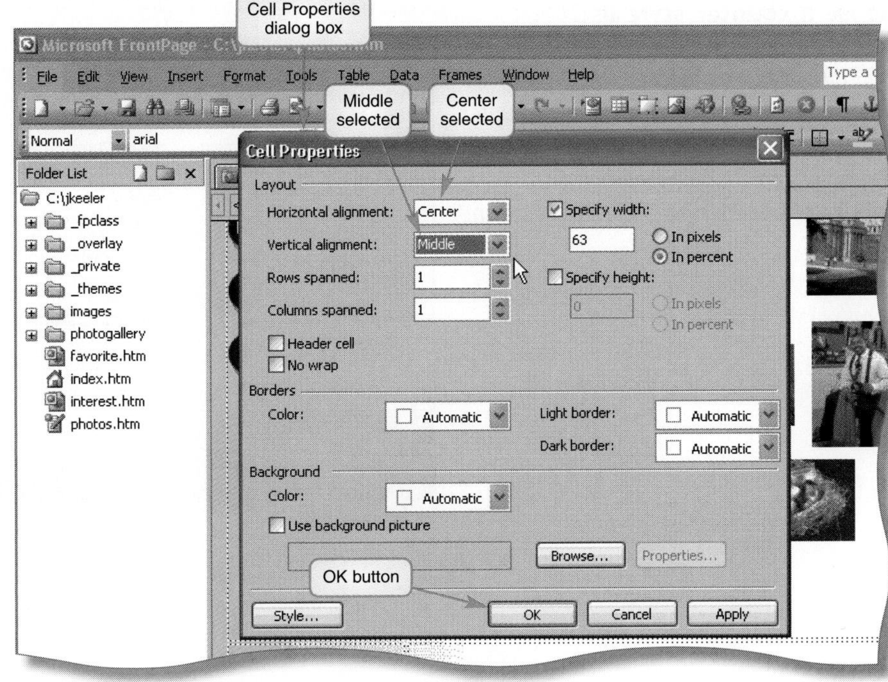

FIGURE 3-18

2

- **Click the OK button.**
- **If necessary, click the Font Color box arrow and select the Automatic font color for this theme.**
- **Type** `You are visitor` **and then click Insert on the menu bar. Be sure to include a space after the word, visitor.**

FrontPage inserts the text in the middle cell and displays the Insert menu (Figure 3-19).

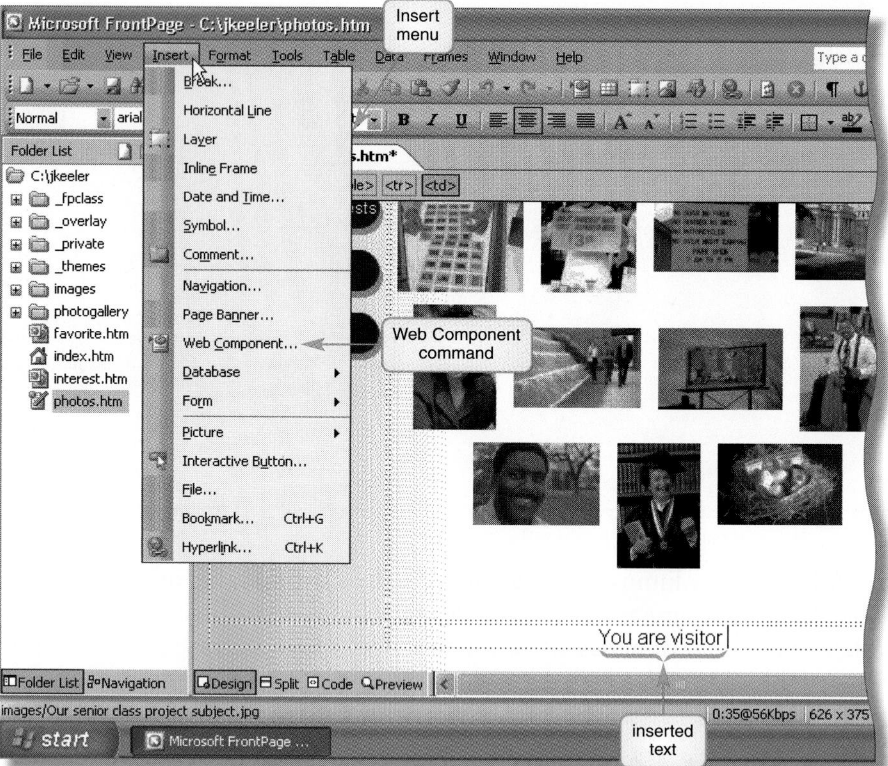

FIGURE 3-19

3

- **Click Web Component.**
- **When FrontPage displays the Insert Web Component dialog box, click Hit Counter in the Component type list.**
- **Click the second graphic in the Choose a counter style list.**

FrontPage displays the Insert Web Component dialog box with the Hit Counter component type and the counter style selected (Figure 3-20). FrontPage displays a brief description of a hit counter component.

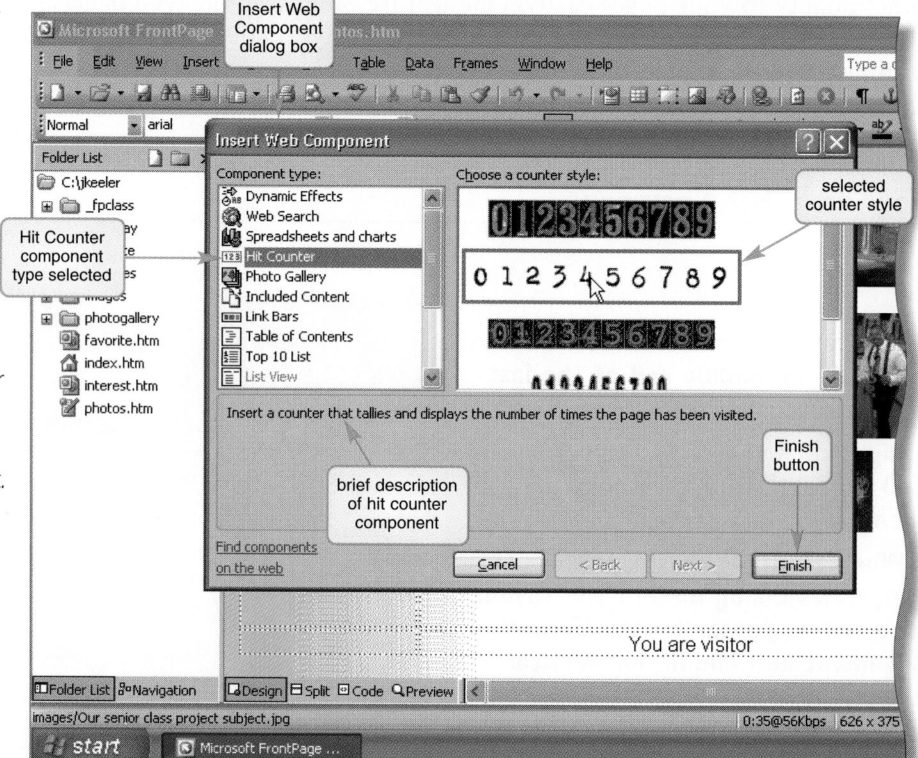

FIGURE 3-20

4

- **Click the Finish button.**
- **When FrontPage displays the Hit Counter Properties dialog box, verify that the second Counter Style is selected.**

FrontPage displays the Hit Counter Properties dialog box with the second Counter Style selected (Figure 3-21).

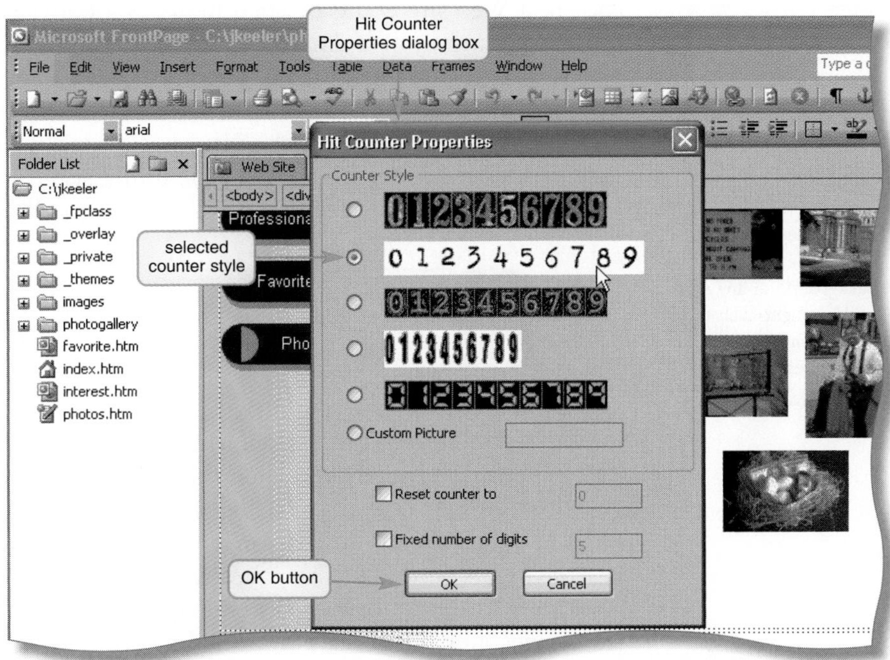

FIGURE 3-21

5

- **Click the OK button.**

FrontPage inserts a hit counter component (Figure 3-22). Placeholder text within square brackets indicates where the hit counter will be displayed when viewed on a Web server with the FrontPage Server Extensions installed.

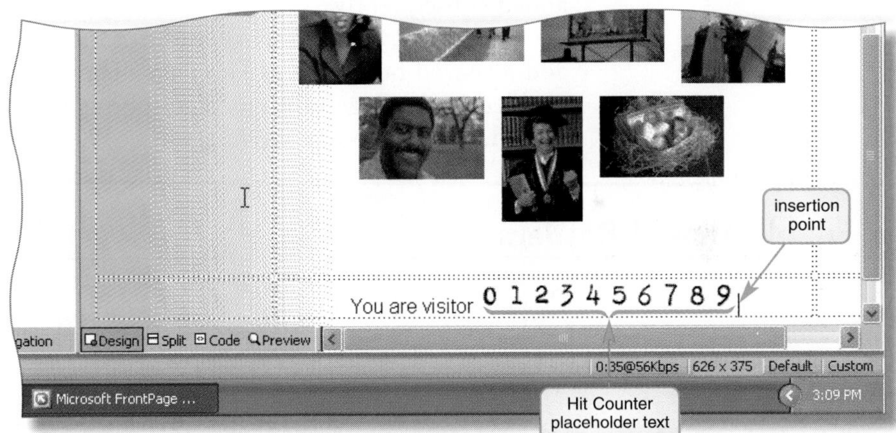

FIGURE 3-22

Other Ways

1. Press ALT+I, C
2. In Voice Command mode, say "Insert, Web Component"

When the page is viewed, either in a browser or on the Preview tab, the hit counter is displayed as a missing graphic with a textual description. To view the hit counter, the page must be published and viewed on a Web server containing the FrontPage Server Extensions. The program that actually increments and displays the graphic counter is a part of the FrontPage Server Extensions. The count itself is stored on the server in a file in the _private folder of the Web site.

Adding a Shared Border

Earlier, you learned that Web pages often have common sections that display similar, or sometimes identical, information on each page. An example of similar, but not identical, information might be link bars or page banners. In these cases, the same format and location are used on multiple pages, although the content may change from page to page. Identical information that might appear on multiple pages

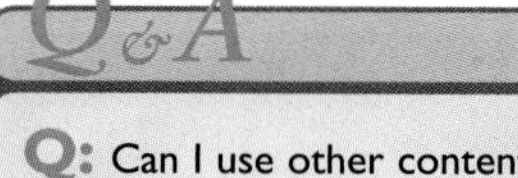

Q: Can I use other content and formatting besides text in a shared border?

A: Yes. Shared borders do not have to be plain text. You independently can assign a color or even an image to the background of any shared border. Right-click the shared border and then click Border Properties.

in a Web site could be such items as a copyright notice, an e-mail address for the page author, or a date indicating when the page was last updated. Rather than duplicating this identical information for each page, it would be much easier to enter or change it in one location and then have the information propagated to all pages automatically. Placing the information within a shared border does this. A shared border provides a means for including standard content at the top, bottom, left, or right edges of a page, or for all pages, in a Web site.

Design Tip: Use shared borders when multiple pages in a Web site contain identical information in the same location on the page.

The Home, Professional Interests, and Favorite Links pages each contain a line at the bottom indicating when the page was last changed. This line was inserted automatically as a result of using the Personal Web site template. Although each line displays the same information, the information is not in a shared border and could be changed on one of the pages without affecting the others, leaving the pages inconsistent. Additionally, when new pages are added to the Web site, such as the Photos page, they do not contain this line automatically. By removing this information from each individual page and inserting it into a shared border for all pages, the same information will appear on all pages currently in the Web and also on any new pages added subsequently.

By default, the Web page authoring settings in FrontPage do not allow you to add a shared border to a Web page. The capability to add shared borders must be enabled in the Page Options dialog box. The following steps turn on the ability to add shared borders to Web pages in a Web site.

To Enable Shared Borders

1

- **Click Tools on the menu bar.**

FrontPage displays the Tools menu (Figure 3-23).

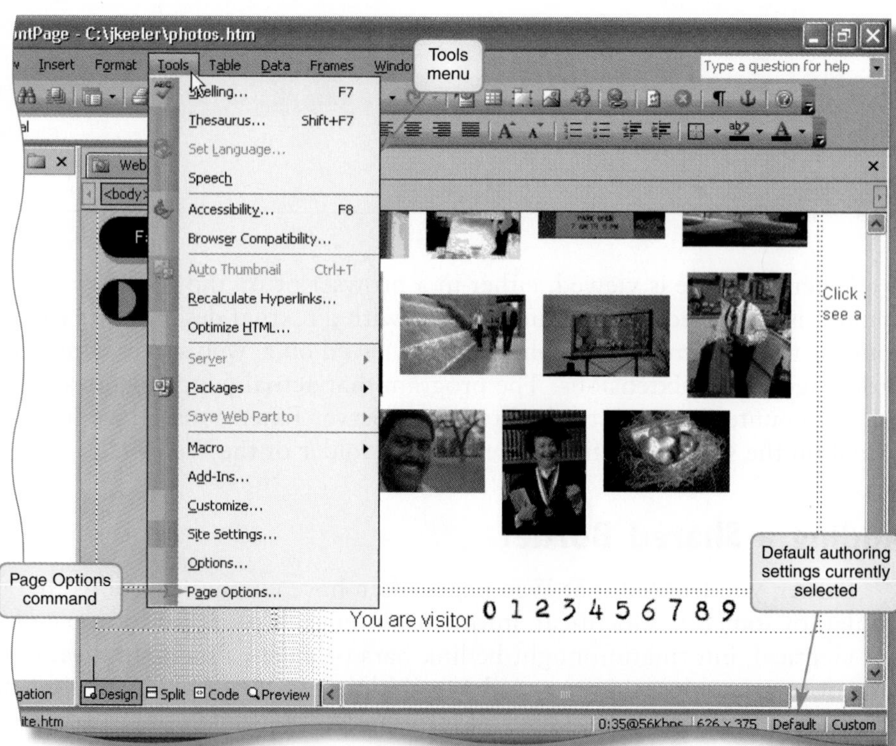

FIGURE 3-23

2

- **Click Page Options.**
- **If necessary, when the Page Options dialog appears, click the Authoring tab.**
- **Click Shared Borders.**

FrontPage displays the Page Options dialog box, and a check mark appears in the Shared Borders check box (Figure 3-24).

3

- **Click the OK button.**

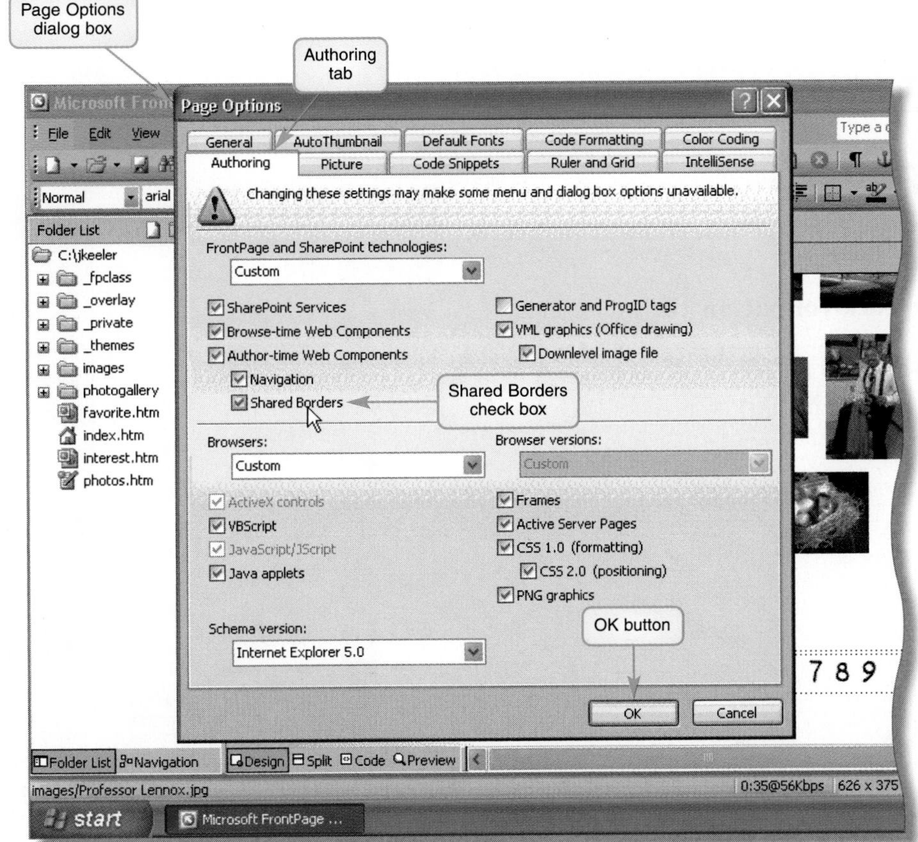

FIGURE 3-24

The Shared Borders option remains enabled for all Web pages and Web sites you create until you manually disable the option in the Page Options dialog box. After modifying the authoring settings, FrontPage displays Custom as the authoring settings in the status bar.

The steps on the next page place the date the pages were last updated into a shared border for all pages.

To Add a Shared Border

1

- **Position the insertion point below the table.**
- **Click Format on the menu bar.**

FrontPage displays the Format menu (Figure 3-25).

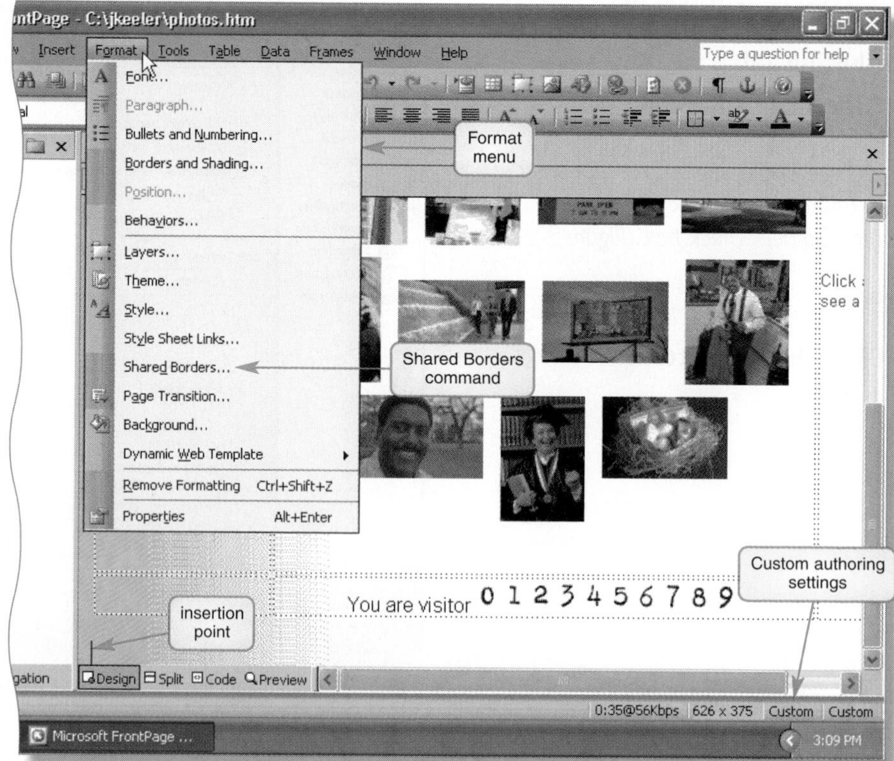

FIGURE 3-25

2

- **Click Shared Borders.**
- **When FrontPage displays the Shared Borders dialog box, verify that All pages is selected in the Apply to area.**
- **Click Bottom.**

FrontPage displays a dotted line across the bottom of the page preview graphic in the Shared Borders dialog box (Figure 3-26).

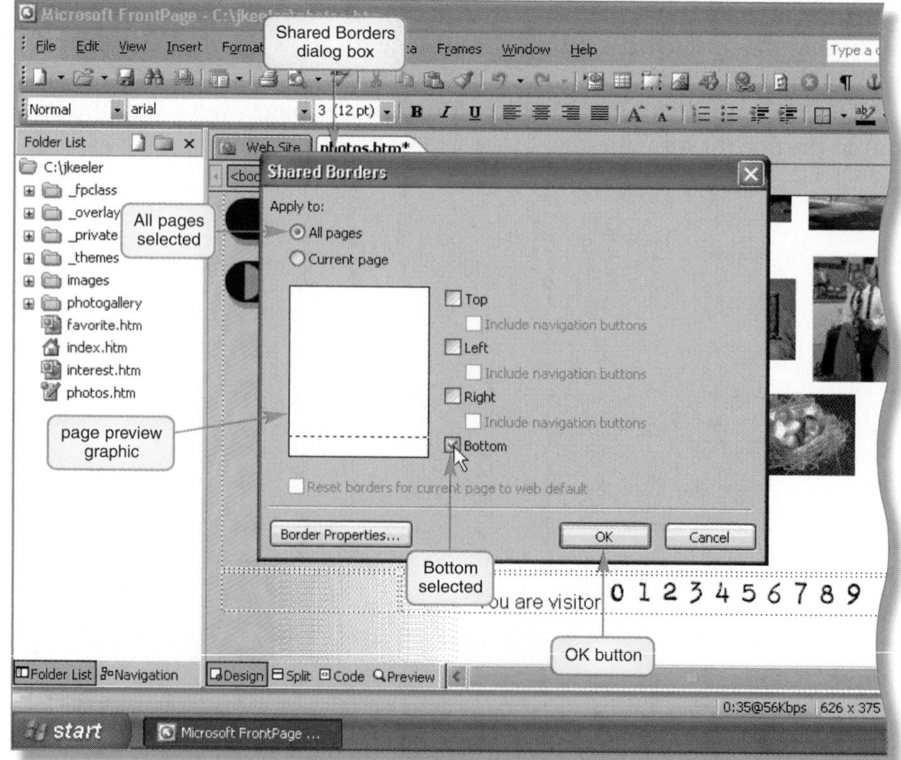

FIGURE 3-26

3

- **Click the OK button.**

A bottom shared border is inserted with a comment component as placeholder text (Figure 3-27).

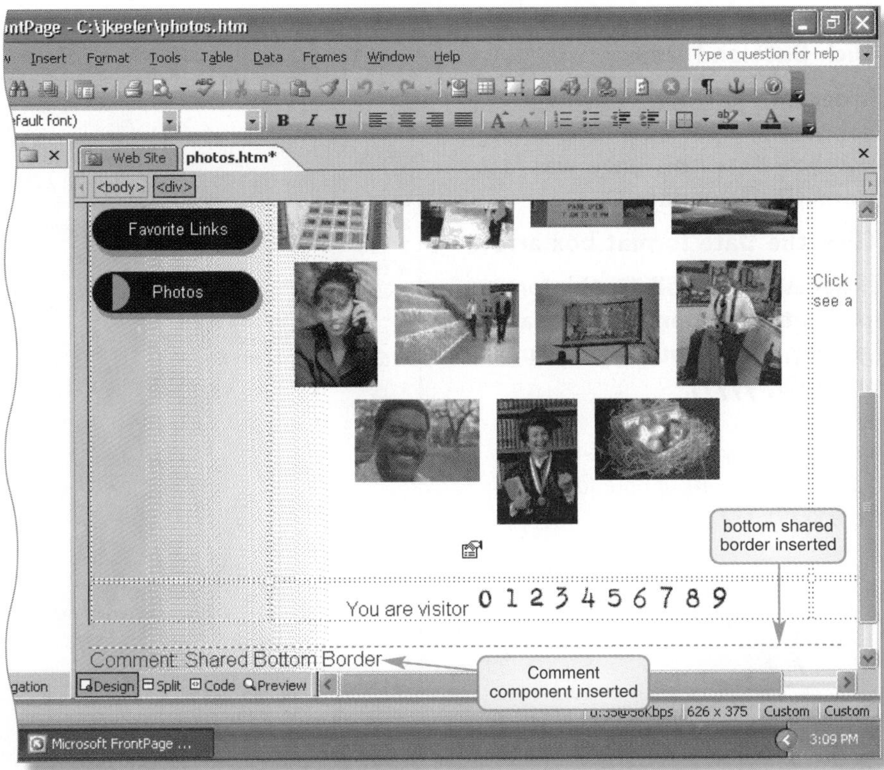

FIGURE 3-27

4

- **If necessary, scroll down to display the comment component.**
- **Click the comment component in the shared border to select it.**
- **On the Formatting toolbar, click the Font Size box arrow and select 2 (10 pt).**
- **Click the Italic button.**
- **Type** `This site was updated on` **and then click Insert on the menu bar. Be sure to include a space after the word, on.**

The replacement text replaces the comment component in the shared border and the Insert menu appears (Figure 3-28). Note that when the insertion point is placed within a shared border, the shared border appears as a rectangular area.

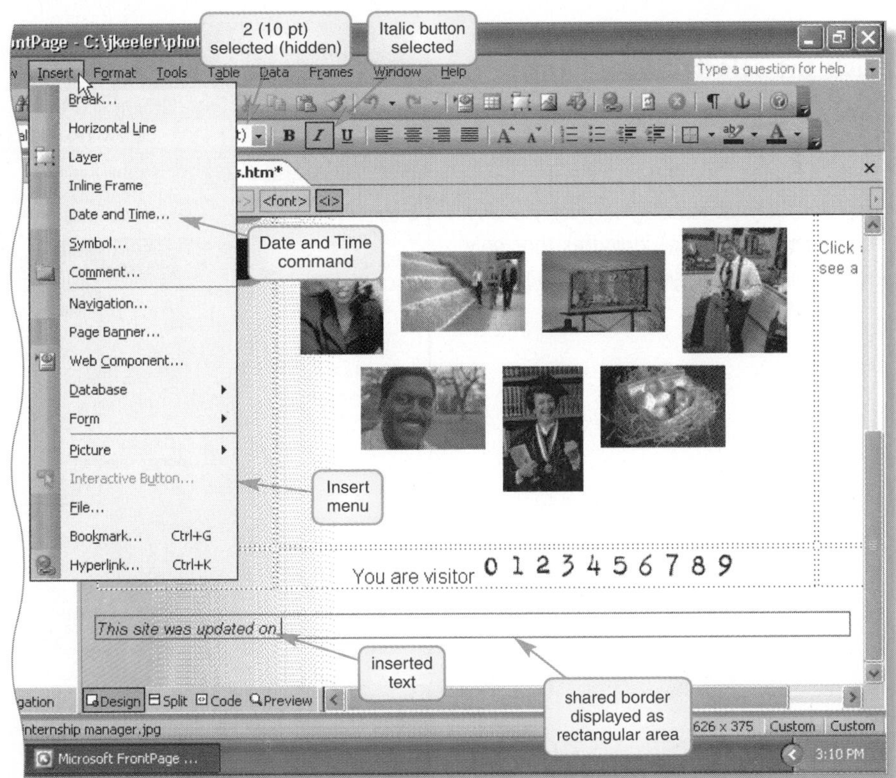

FIGURE 3-28

5

- **Click Date and Time.**
- **If necessary, when FrontPage displays the Date and Time dialog box, click Date this page was last automatically updated.**
- **Click the Date format box arrow.**
- **If necessary, scroll to the format representing a month name, a two-digit day, and a four-digit year (mmm dd, yyyy).**

FrontPage displays the Date and Time dialog box with a list of date formats (Figure 3-29).

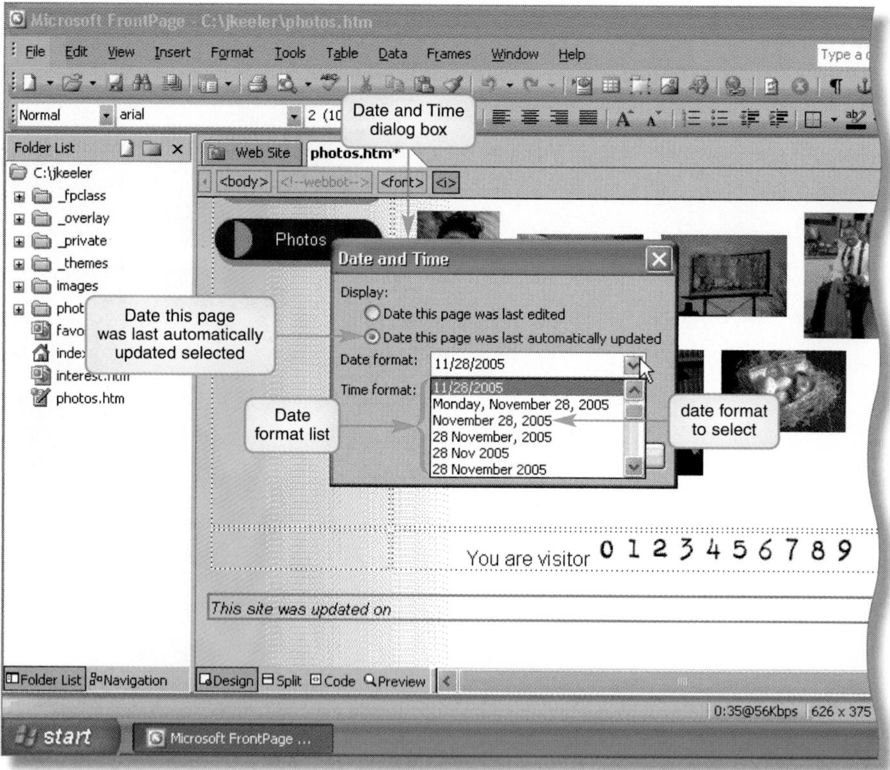

FIGURE 3-29

6

- **Click the selected date format.**
- **Verify that the Time format selected is (none).**

A long date format is selected (Figure 3-30). A time format of (none) indicates that only the date will be displayed, not a time.

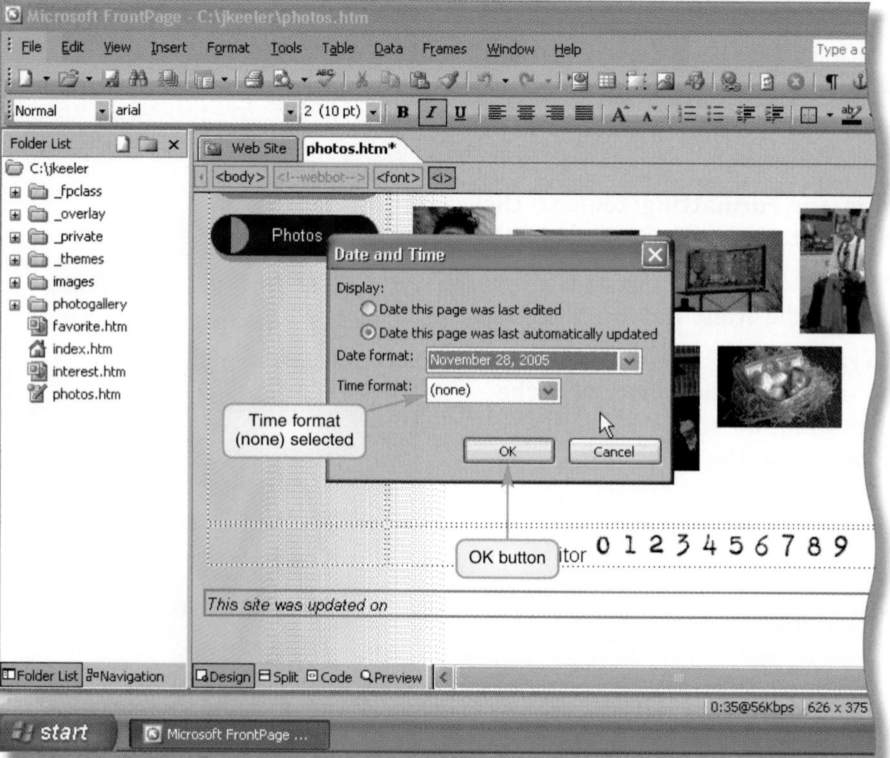

FIGURE 3-30

7

- **Click the OK button.**
- **Click the Save button on the Standard toolbar to save the changes to the page.**

FrontPage inserts a Date and Time component displaying the date that the page was last updated (Figure 3-31).

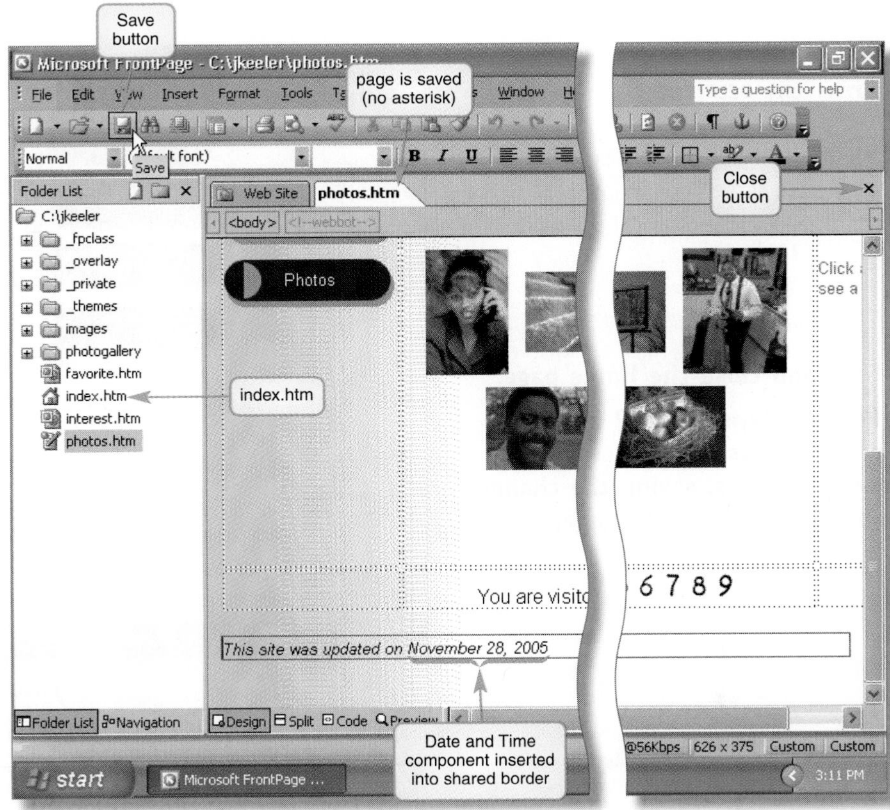

FIGURE 3-31

8

- **Click the Close button.**
- **Double-click the file name, index.htm, in the Folder List pane to open the Home page.**
- **If necessary, scroll down to the bottom of the page.**
- **Drag through the line above the shared border to select it.**

The line inserted by the Personal Web template, indicating the date that the page was last updated, is highlighted (Figure 3-32).

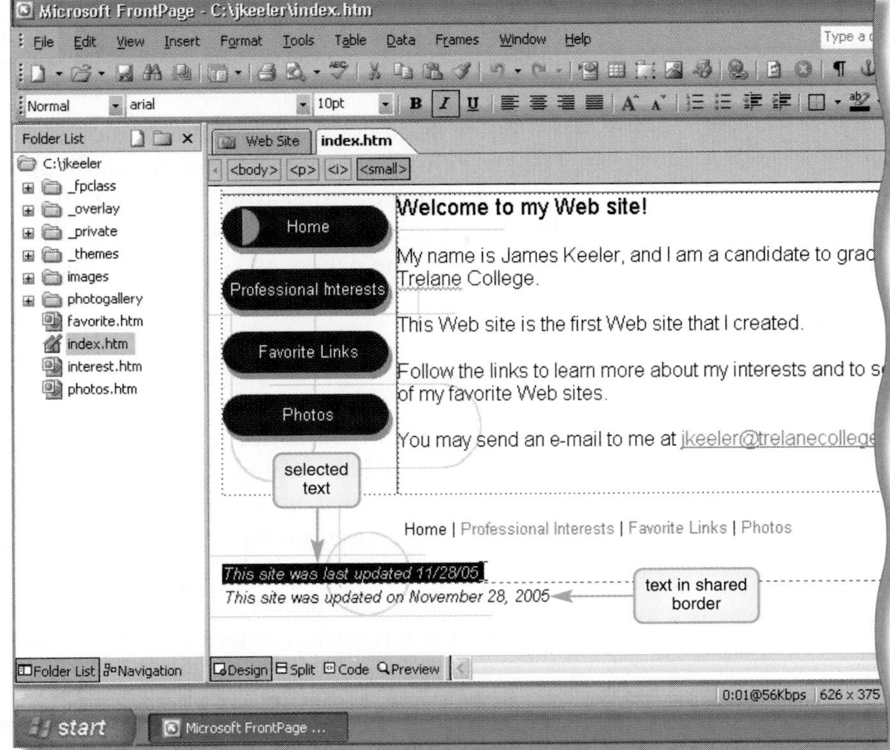

FIGURE 3-32

• **Press the DELETE key.**

FrontPage removes the duplicate line and only the shared border indicates the date that the page was last updated (Figure 3-33).

• **Save and close the Home page.**

• **Repeat Steps 8 and 9 for the Favorite Links and Professional Interests pages, saving the changes and then closing each page.**

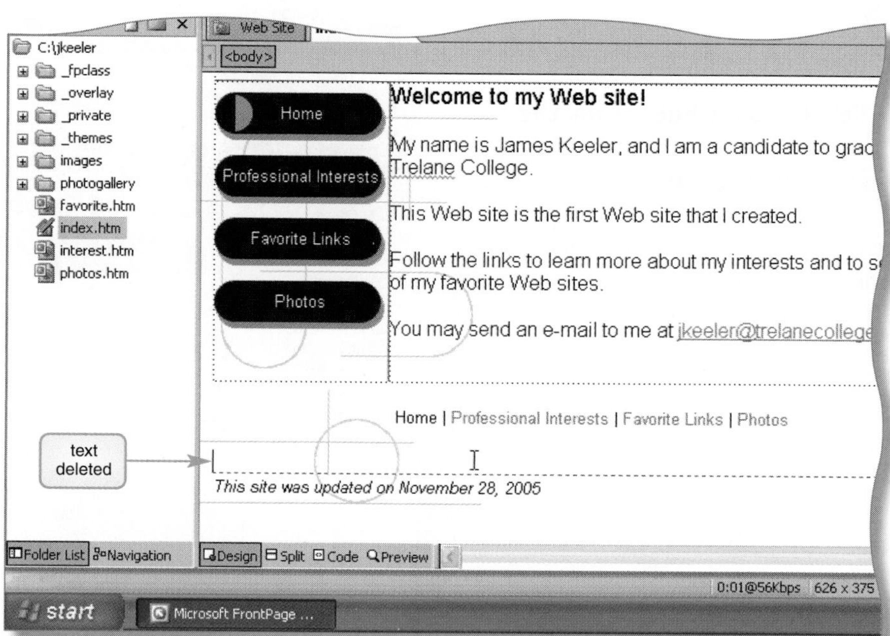

FIGURE 3-33

Other Ways

1. Press ALT+O, D
2. In Voice Command mode, say "Format, Shared Borders"

When a shared border is inserted, FrontPage automatically includes a comment component to identify the shared border while editing in FrontPage. A **comment component** is a component that displays text visible only in FrontPage, but not when the page is viewed in a browser or on the Preview tab. Because the date last updated must be visible in a browser, the comment component is replaced with normal text.

When adding a date and time component, you have a choice of two dates to use. The Date this page was last automatically updated option reflects the date the page was last changed, either from manual editing or from a change elsewhere in the Web site that caused automatic updating. The Date this page was last edited option yields the date that the page was last saved with FrontPage.

Modifying the Navigation Structure of a Web Site

Previously, when you added a new Web page, you did so in Navigation view, so that the page was added automatically to the navigation structure of the Web site. Recall that the navigation structure affects the links that display on link bars when the link bar type is Bar based on navigation structure. If the position of a page in the navigation structure is changed, the link bars may change as well. A new page added in Page view does not display added link bars of this type until the page is saved and added to the navigation structure of the Web site.

Creating a New Page in Page View

Recall that when a Web site has a theme applied, any new page will be displayed with the theme applied automatically. Because the shared border just added was applied to all pages, it also will be applied automatically to any new page.

The following step creates a new page in Page view.

To Add a New Page in Page View

1

• **Click the Create a new normal page button on the Standard toolbar.**

FrontPage creates a new page with the current theme applied and the shared border inserted (Figure 3-34).

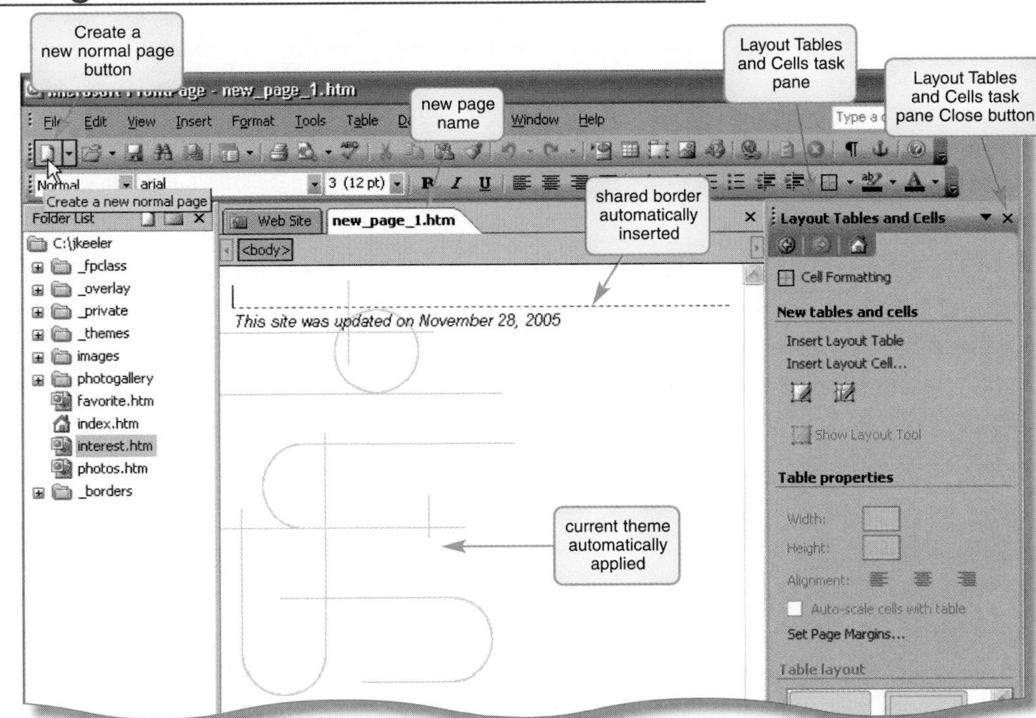

FIGURE 3-34

Although the new page has the theme of the current Web site applied, it has no hyperlinks to navigate to other pages in the Web site. A simple way to add such links is to add a Link Bar component with hyperlinks based on the navigation structure, as was done in Project 2.

The following steps add a Link Bar component to the new Web page.

To Add a Link Bar Component

1. **Click Insert on the menu bar and then click Navigation.**
2. **Click Bar based on navigation structure in the Choose a bar type area. Click the Next button.**
3. **Verify that Use Page's Theme is selected and then click the Next button.**
4. **Verify that the horizontal arrangement is selected and then click the Finish button.**
5. **Click Child pages under Home. Click Home page in the Additional pages area. Click the OK button.**
6. **Click the Center button on the Formatting toolbar.**
7. **Click the Close button on the Layout Tables and Cells task pane.**

The Link bar component is added, centered on the page (Figure 3-35 on the next page). A message appears indicating that the page must be added to the Navigation view for the hyperlinks to be displayed.

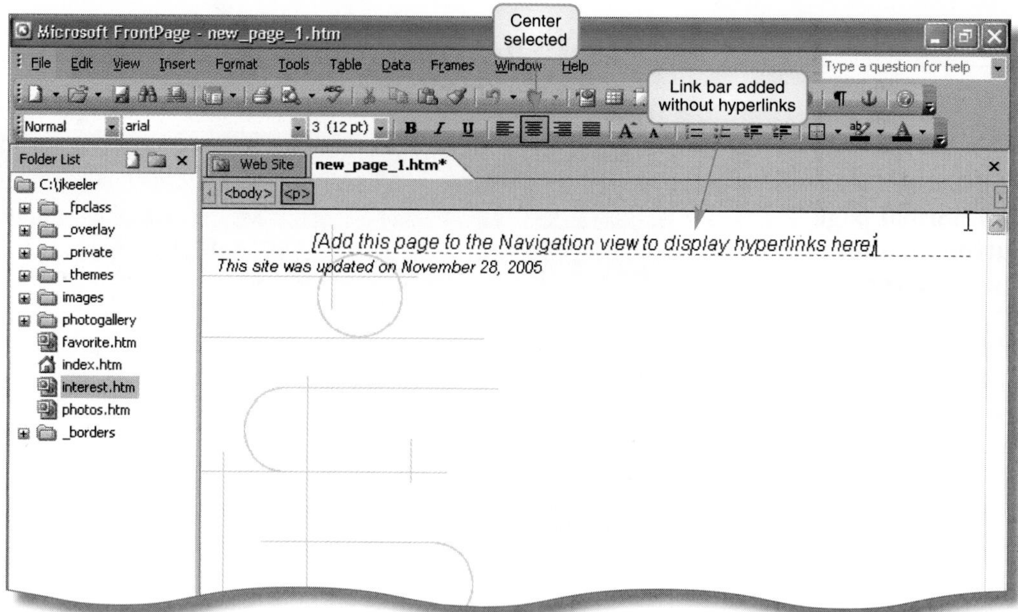

FIGURE 3-35

Modifying the Navigation Structure

When a new page was created in Page view, FrontPage automatically applied the theme and shared border. In order for a link bar based on the navigation structure to display hyperlinks, the page must be added to the navigation structure. Because visitors will access the Photos page only from the Home page, the Photo page's position in the navigation structure needs to be changed as well.

The following steps modify the navigation structure of the Web site.

To Modify the Navigation Structure

1

• **Click the Save button on the Standard toolbar.**

FrontPage displays the Save As dialog box with a default name and title for the new Web page (Figure 3-36).

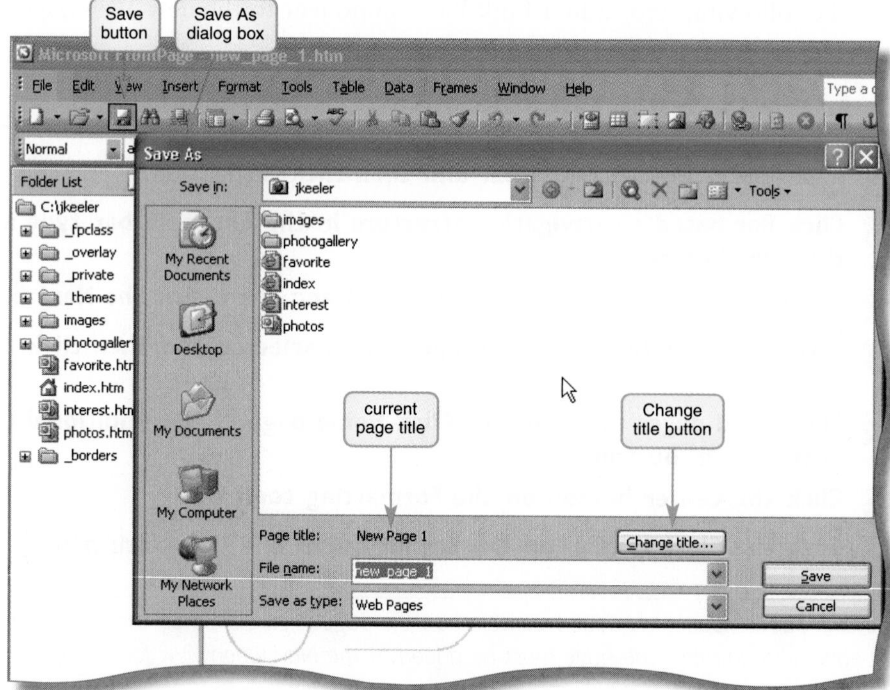

FIGURE 3-36

2

- **Click the Change title button.**
- **When FrontPage displays the Set Page Title dialog box, type** `Resume`**.**

FrontPage displays the Set Page Title dialog box with the new page title (Figure 3-37).

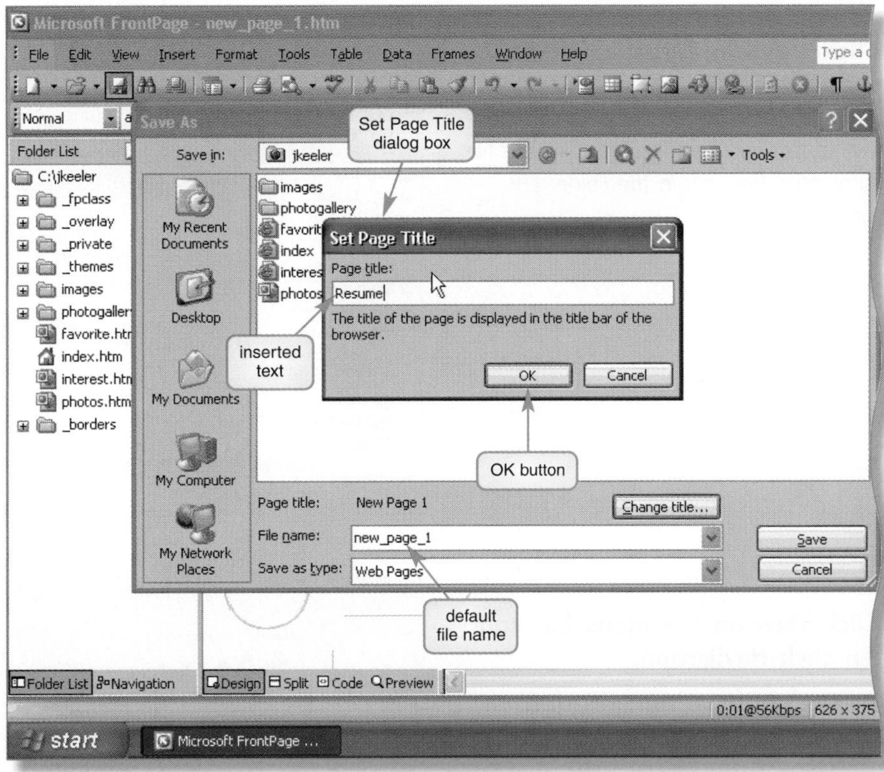

FIGURE 3-37

3

- **Click the OK button.**
- **Drag through the default file name and then type** `resume` **as the new file name.**

FrontPage closes the Set Page Title dialog box and displays the Save As dialog box with the new page title and new file name (Figure 3-38).

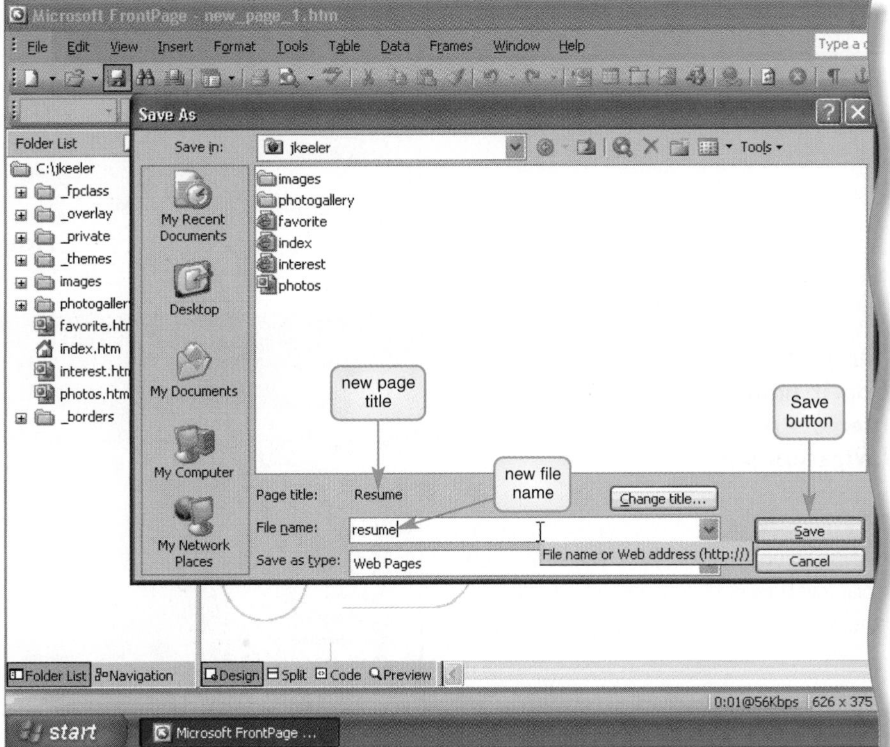

FIGURE 3-38

4

- **Click the Save button.**

FrontPage saves the new page with a file name of resume.htm (Figure 3-39). The file, resume.htm, appears in the Folder List pane.

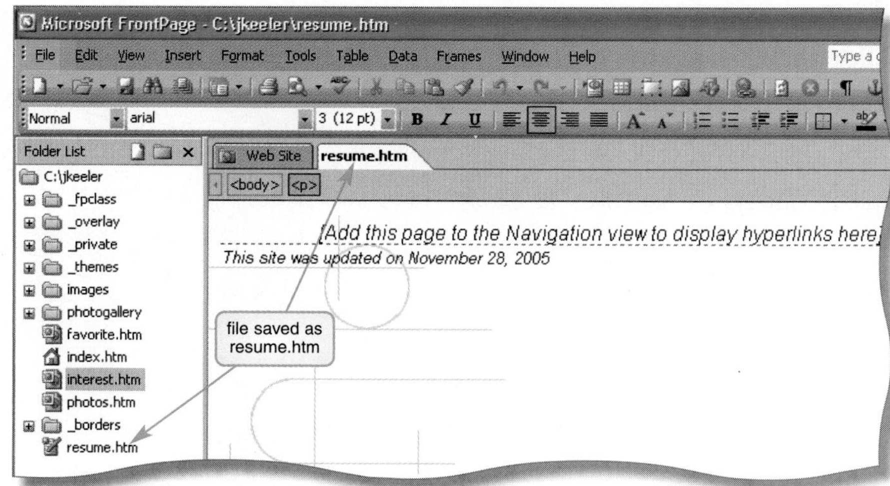

FIGURE 3-39

5

- **Click View on the menu bar and then click Navigation.**
- **Drag the file, resume.htm, from the Folder List pane and drop it under the Home page icon in the Navigation pane.**

The Resume page is added to the navigation structure of the Web site (Figure 3-40).

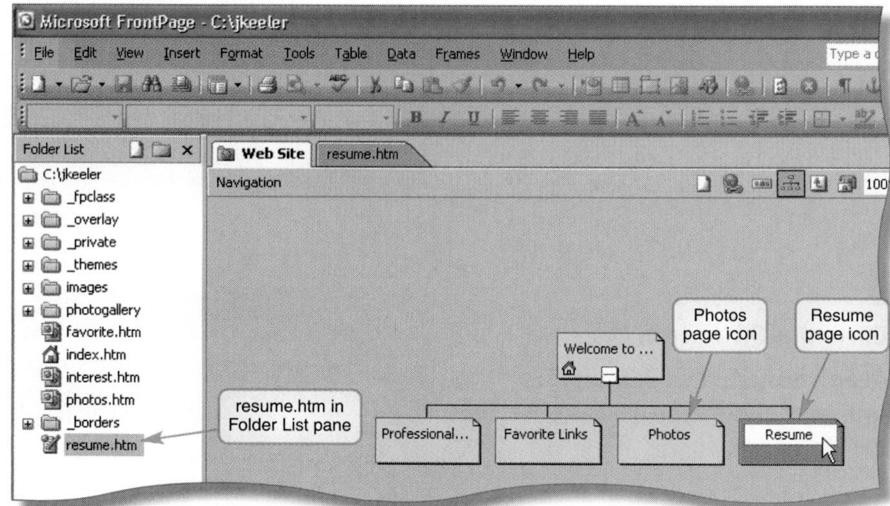

FIGURE 3-40

6

- **Drag the Photos page icon and drop it under the Professional Interests page icon in the Navigation pane.**

The Photos page no longer is displayed as a child page under the Home page and now is displayed as a child page under the Professional Interests page (Figure 3-41).

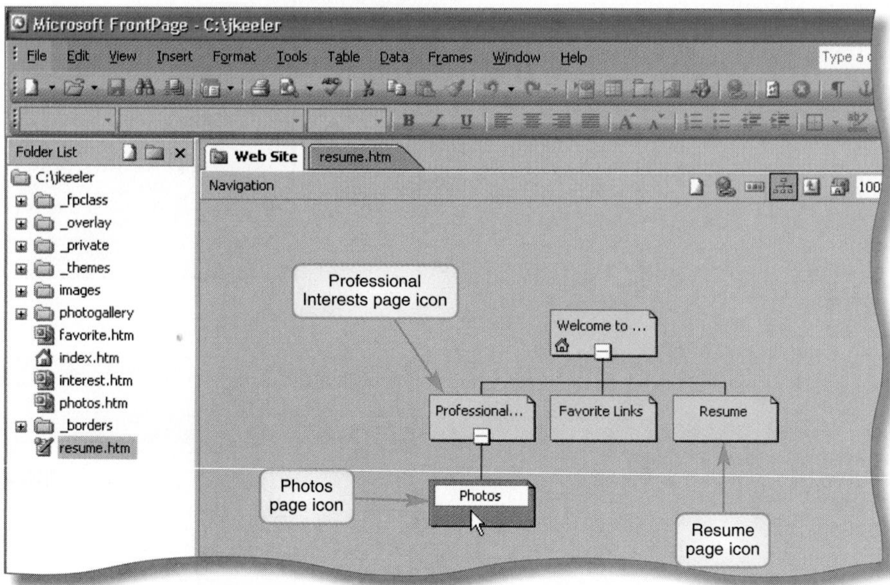

FIGURE 3-41

7

- **Double-click the Resume page file in the Folder List pane.**

FrontPage displays the Resume page in Page view with the link bar displaying hyperlinks to the Home page and to the child pages under the Home page (Figure 3-42).

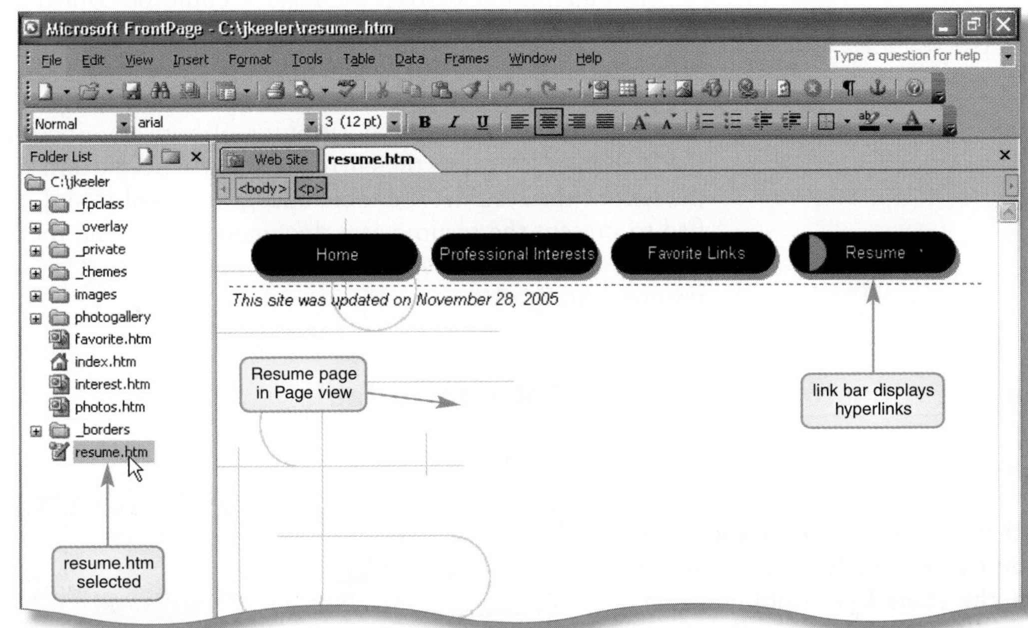

FIGURE 3-42

Other Ways

1. On View menu click Navigation
2. Press ALT+V, N
3. In Voice Command mode, say "Navigation"
4. In Voice Command mode, say "View, Navigation"

The Photos page also could be removed from the link bars by deleting it from the navigation structure. This would remove it from the navigation structure diagram displayed in Navigation view. By placing it under a page that does not link to child pages, the Photos page remains visible in the diagram but does not appear on any link bars. By placing the Resume page under the Home page, it appears on the link bars of other pages that link to the child pages under Home. These hyperlinks, as well as a link to the Home page, also are displayed on the Resume page.

Copy and Paste from a Word Document

You have learned that typing text in FrontPage is like typing text in a word processor. You also have learned that you can copy and paste items, such as images and text, in FrontPage. Images, text, or even tables can be copied and pasted from other Office applications into your Web pages just as easily.

The World Wide Web often is used for electronic publishing today. This means that sometimes people create Web pages to reflect what they previously produced only in a printed form, such as a resume, a scholarly paper, or even an entire book. Such a document already may exist in an electronic form, such as a Word document, but not in a form suitable for publication on the Web. Although a given word processor may allow saving a document as a Web page, the result may not appear exactly as desired. Rather than retyping a large amount of text, FrontPage allows copying the text from the document and pasting it in the Web page.

Design Tip

Copy and paste text from other documents into your Web page when the source application of the document cannot save the document in a suitable Web page format. Be sure to keep the Web page updated with any changes to the original document.

Although the text from the resume could be copied and pasted directly into a Web page, some thought should be given to the resulting presentation in a Web browser. Because the document will result in a long page, text hyperlinks should be used as an index to allow the user to navigate directly to sections of interest. A table will be used to control the positioning of both the document and the hyperlinks on the Web page. Because the current background pattern may distract the user from the text of the resume, the table background color and other properties will be modified to present the resume as a document overlaying the Web page.

The following steps create a table and modify it prior to incorporating the resume text.

To Use a Custom Background Color for a Table

1

- **If necessary, position the insertion point after the horizontal link bar, on the same line containing the horizontal link bar, on the Resume page.**
- **Click the Insert Table button on the Standard toolbar and drag through a 3 by 3 table.**

FrontPage displays the insertion point after the link bar (Figure 3-43).

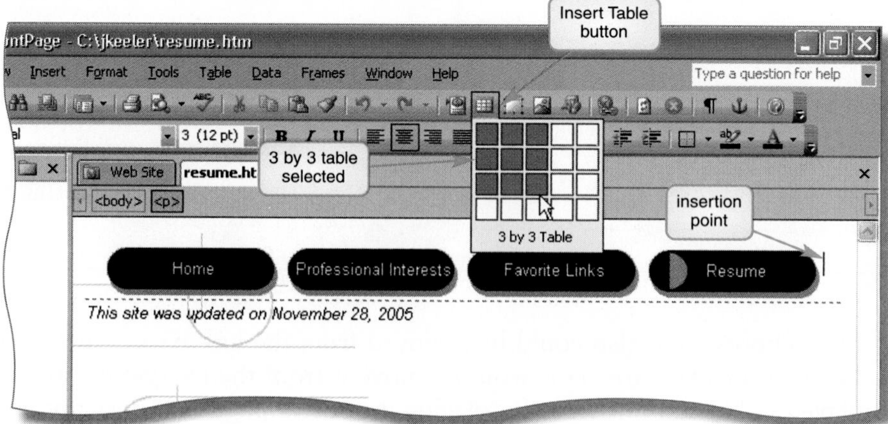

FIGURE 3-43

2

- **Release the mouse button.**
- **When FrontPage displays the new table, right-click the left cell of the bottom row.**
- **Click Table Properties on the shortcut menu.**
- **When FrontPage displays the Table Properties dialog box, select Center in the Alignment box in the Layout area and set Size to 0 in the Borders area.**

FrontPage displays the Table Properties dialog box with the alignment set to Center and the border size set to 0 (Figure 3-44).

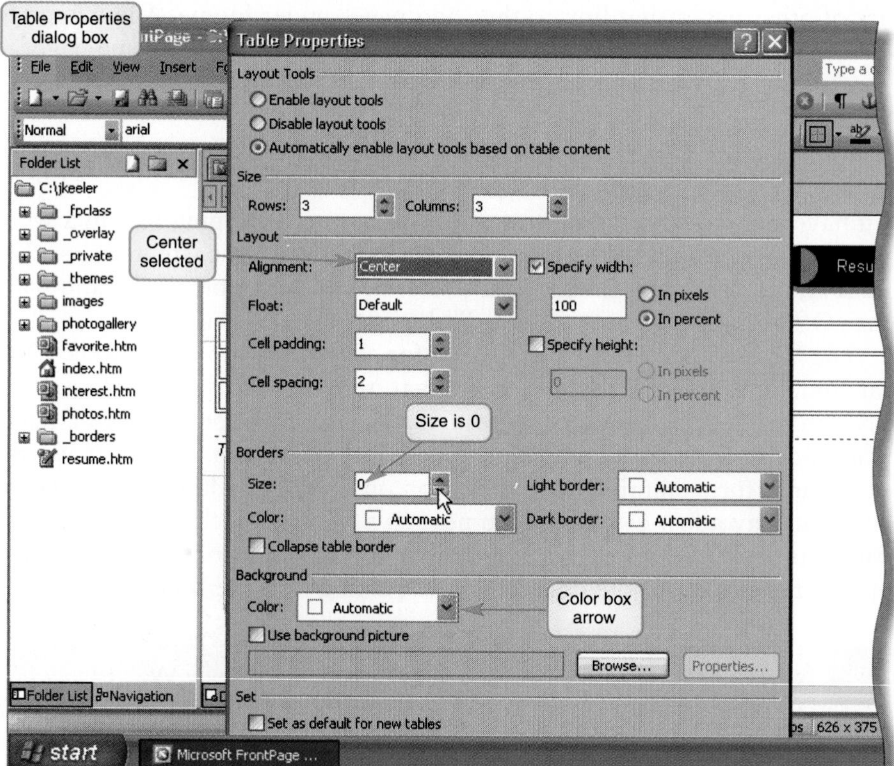

FIGURE 3-44

3

- **Click the Color box arrow in the Background area.**
- **Click More Colors.**
- **When FrontPage displays the More Colors dialog box, click the white hexagon to display a hex value in the Value text box.**
- **Drag through FF,FF,FF in the Value text box to select it.**
- **Type** `FC,FC,FC` **as the new hex value.**

FrontPage displays the new custom color hex value of FC,FC,FC (Figure 3-45).

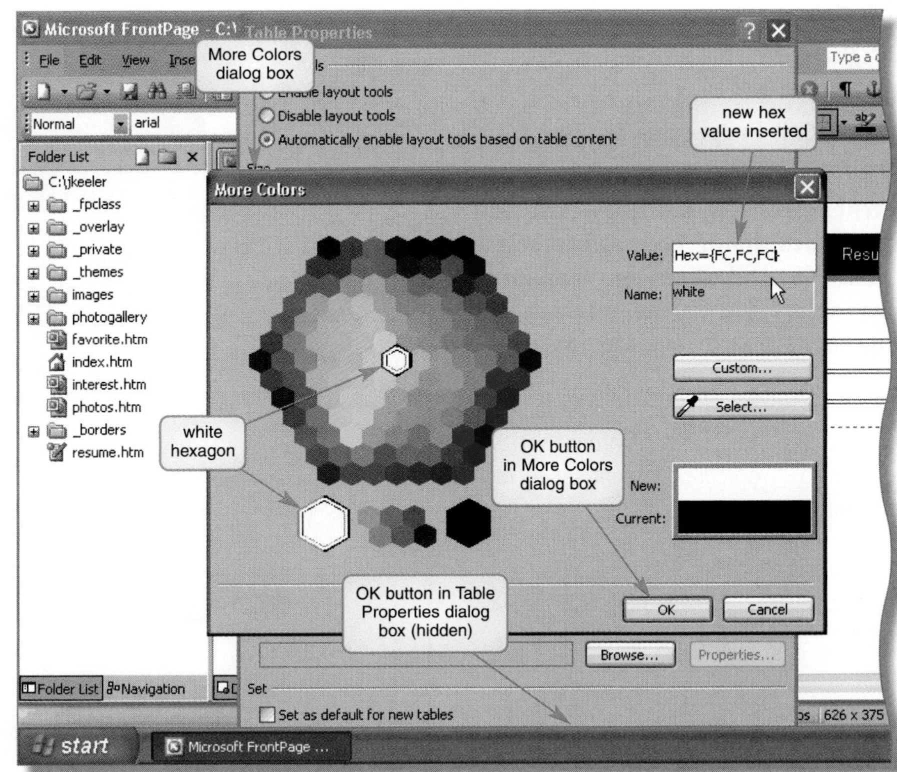

FIGURE 3-45

4

- **Click the OK button in the More Colors dialog box.**
- **Click the OK button in the Table Properties dialog box.**

FrontPage displays the table with a new background color and with dotted lines for cell borders, indicating that the borders are not displayed (Figure 3-46).

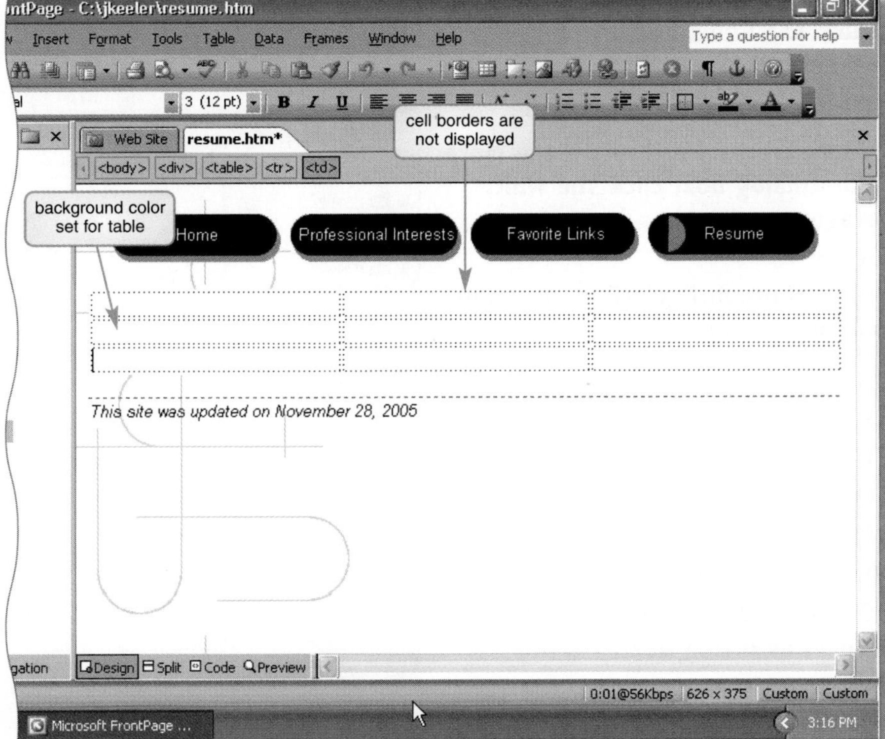

FIGURE 3-46

5

- **Right-click the left cell of the bottom row.**
- **Click Cell Properties on the shortcut menu.**
- **When FrontPage displays the Cell Properties dialog box, select Left in the Horizontal alignment box and then select Top in the Vertical alignment box in the Layout area.**

FrontPage displays the Cell Properties dialog box with the Horizontal alignment set to Left and the Vertical alignment set to Top (Figure 3-47).

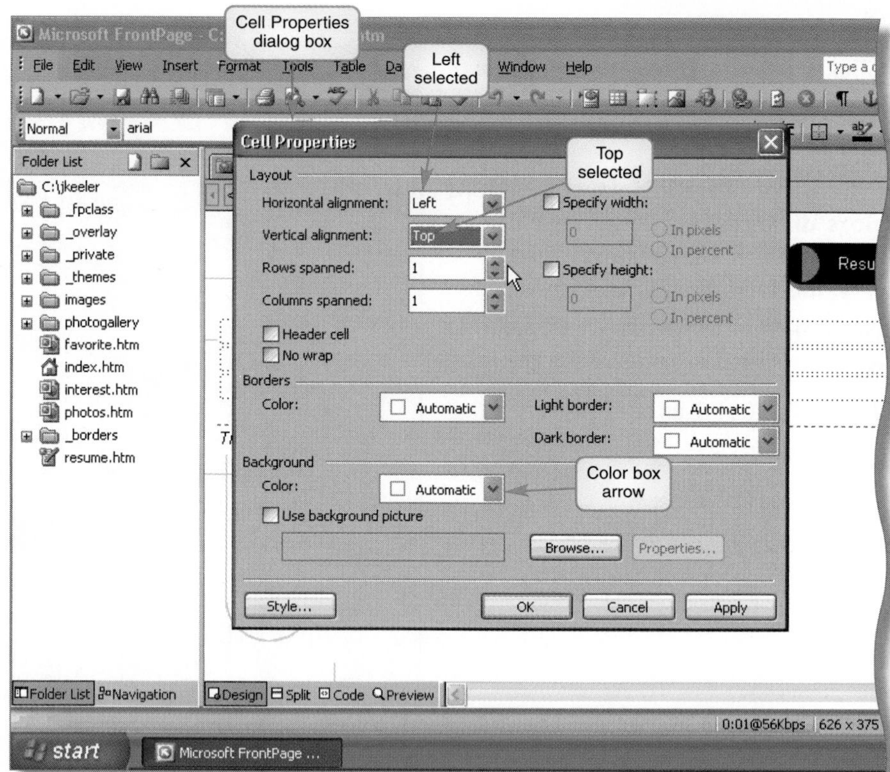

FIGURE 3-47

6

- **Click the Color box arrow in the Background area.**
- **Click More Colors.**
- **When FrontPage displays the More Colors dialog box, click the white hexagon to display a hex value in the Value text box.**
- **Drag through FF,FF,FF in the Value text box to select it.**

7

- **Type** `DF,DF,DF` **as the new hex value.**
- **Click the OK button in the More Colors dialog box.**
- **Click the OK button in the Cell Properties dialog box.**

FrontPage displays the cell with a background color different from that of the table (Figure 3-48).

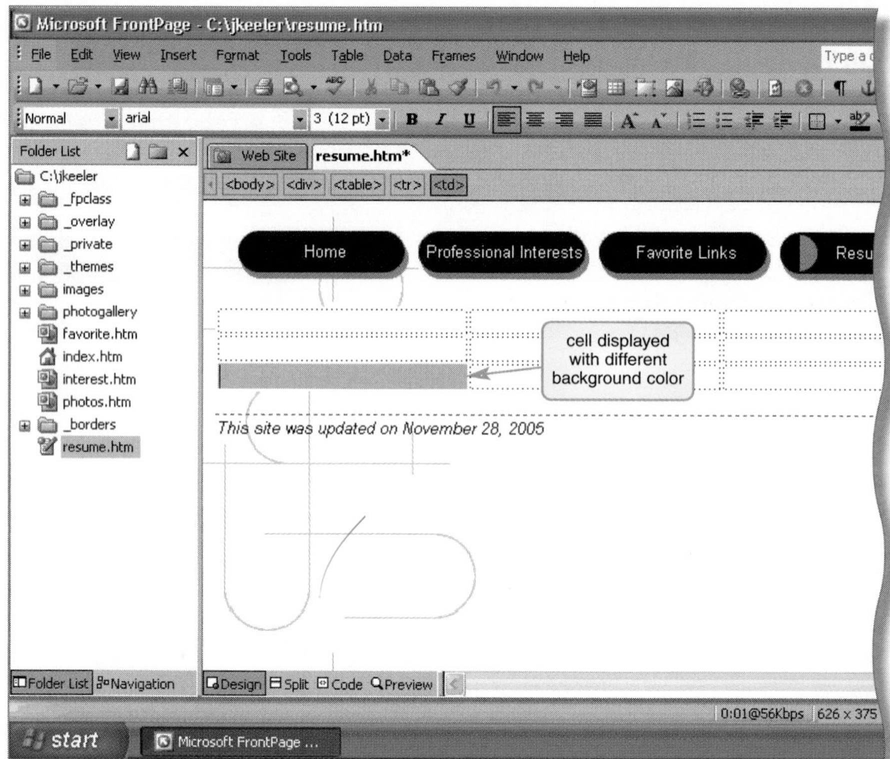

FIGURE 3-48

8

- **If necessary, click the Font Color arrow and select the Automatic font color for this theme.**
- **Type** `Summary` **and then press the ENTER key.**
- **Type each of the remaining text items listed in Table 3-2 on page FP 187, following each, except the last, with the ENTER key.**

The entered text appears in the lower-left cell (Figure 3-49). The cell expands as text is entered.

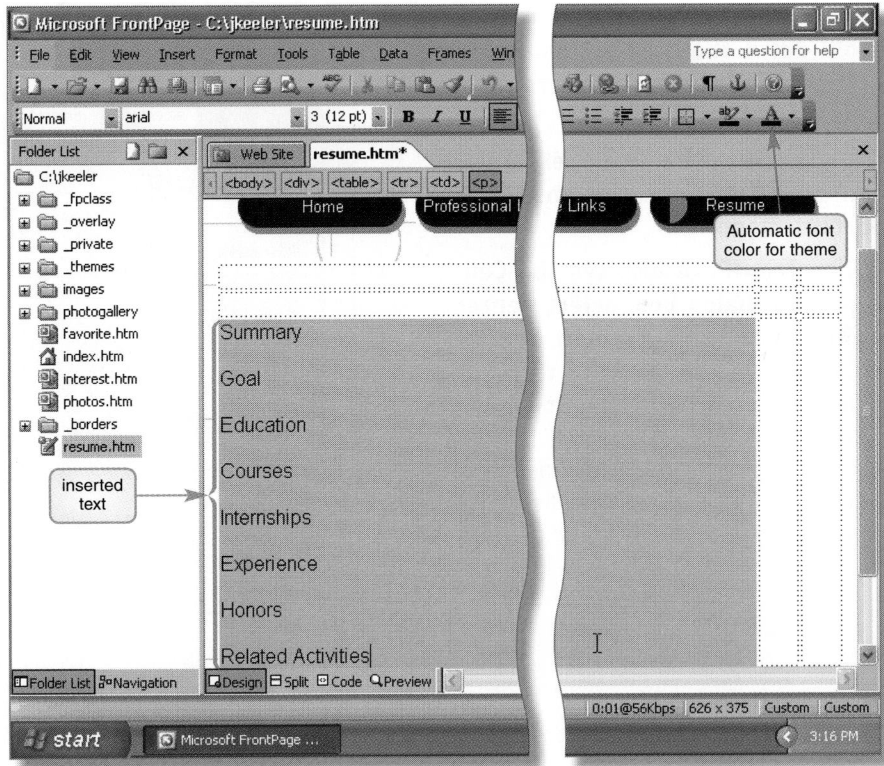

FIGURE 3-49

9

- **Drag the right borders of the left and middle columns to the left until they approximate those shown in Figure 3-50.**
- **Position the insertion point in the upper-right cell.**

Text longer than the column width automatically wraps (Figure 3-50).

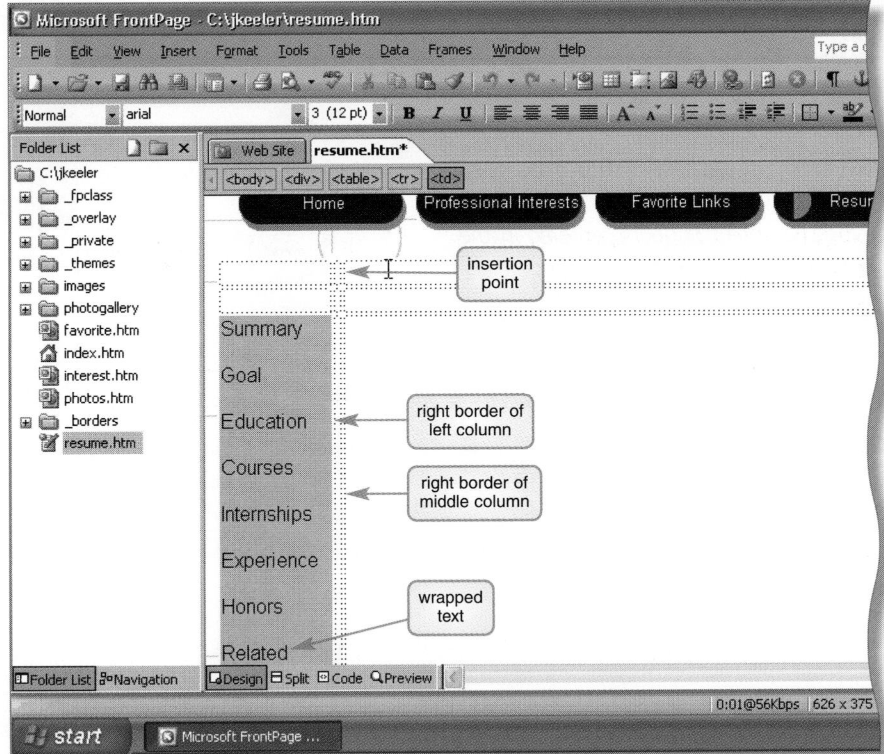

FIGURE 3-50

10

- **Hold down the SHIFT key and click the right cell in the second row to select both cells.**
- **Right-click the selected cells and then click Cell Properties on the shortcut menu.**
- **When FrontPage displays the Cell Properties dialog box, select Center in the Horizontal alignment box and then select Top in the Vertical alignment box in the Layout area.**

FrontPage displays the Cell Properties dialog box with the Horizontal alignment set to Center and the Vertical alignment set to Top (Figure 3-51).

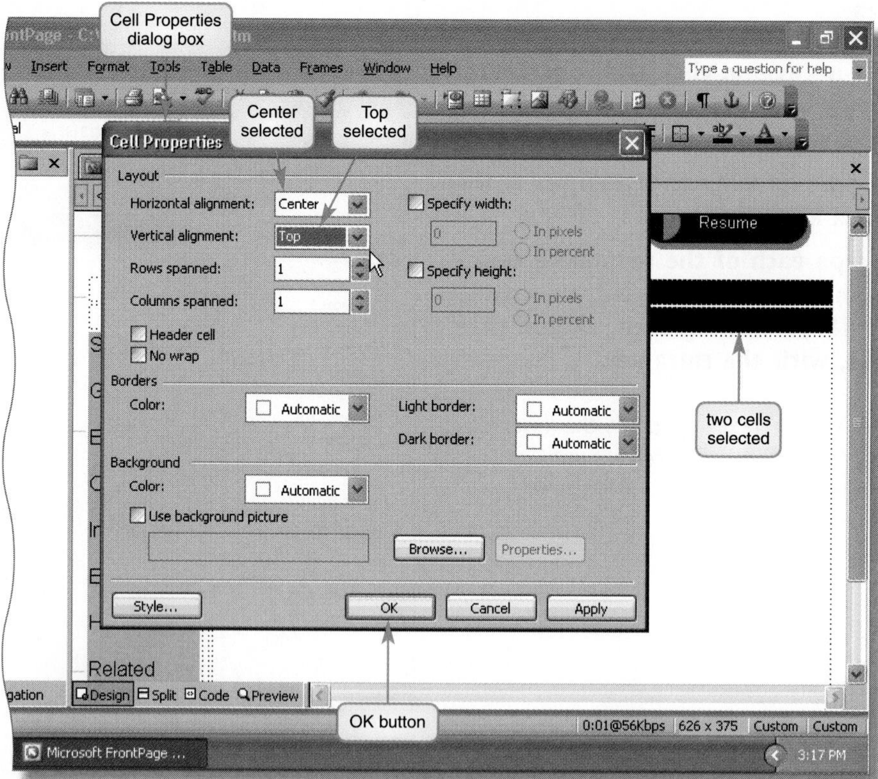

FIGURE 3-51

11

- **Click the OK button.**
- **Click the right cell in the middle row to position the insertion point.**
- **Click Format on the menu bar.**

The insertion point appears centered in the right cell of the middle row. FrontPage displays the Format menu (Figure 3-52).

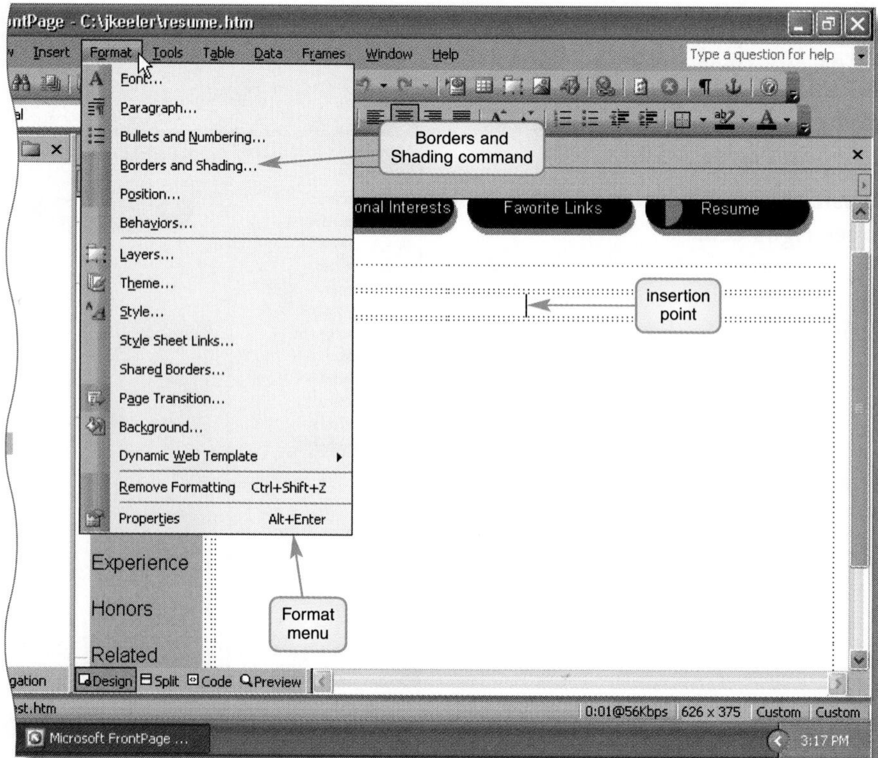

FIGURE 3-52

12

- **Click Borders and Shading.**
- **If necessary, when FrontPage displays the Borders and Shading dialog box, click the Borders tab.**
- **Click the top edge border button in the Preview area.**

FrontPage displays in the Preview area a graphic indicating where the new border will be applied (Figure 3-53).

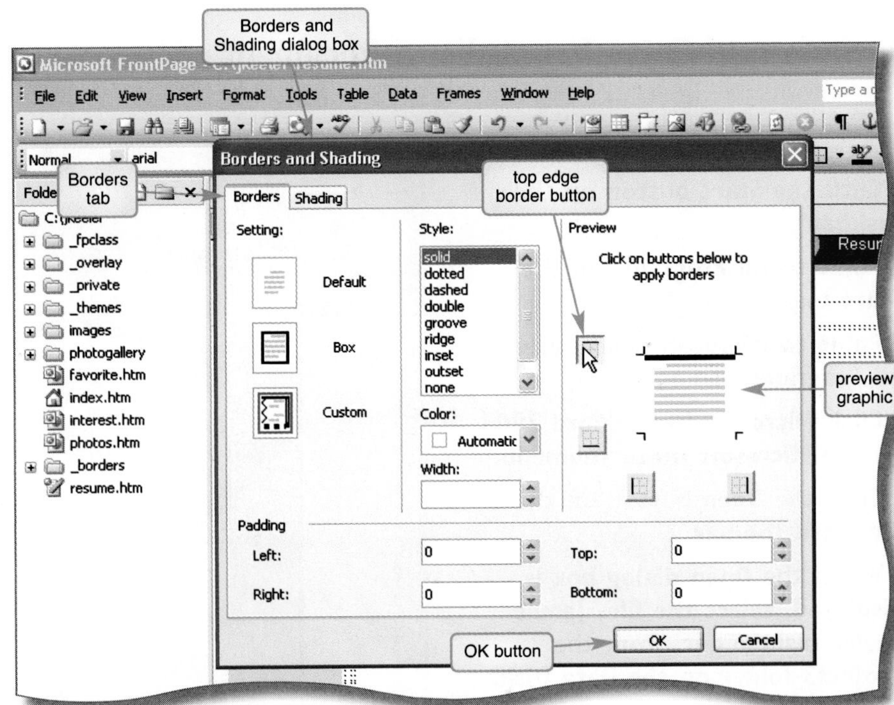

FIGURE 3-53

13

- **Click the OK button.**
- **Click the upper-right cell to position the insertion point.**

A top border is applied to the right cell of the middle row (Figure 3-54).

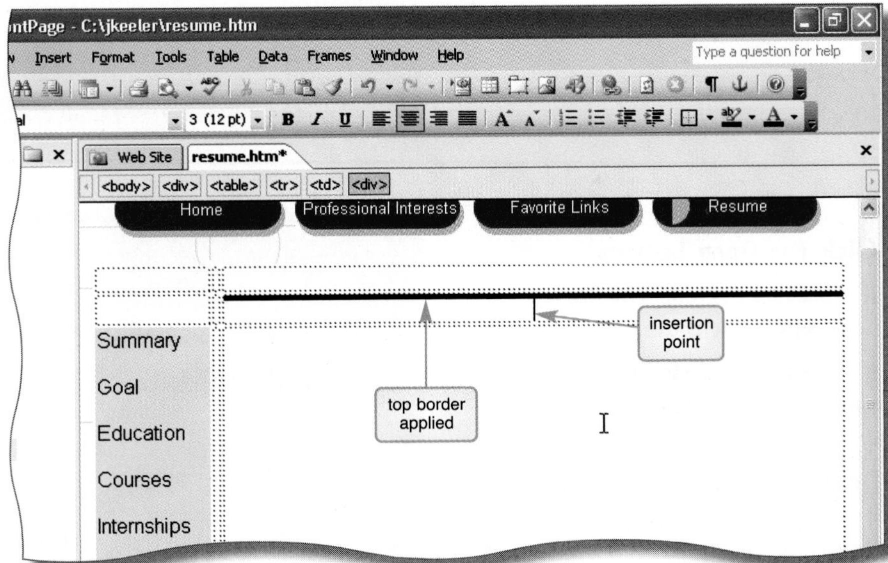

FIGURE 3-54

Other Ways

1. Press ALT+O, B
2. In Voice Command mode, say "Format, Borders and Shading"

Although the resume could be copied and pasted directly into a Web page, using the table you just inserted will make viewing and navigating easier and more pleasant for the user. Now that the table is prepared, the steps on the next page copy text from a resume in Word and paste it into the Web page.

Table 3-2 Text for Resume Index

TEXT	
Summary	Internships
Goal	Experience
Education	Honors
Courses	Related Activities

To Copy and Paste from a Word Document

1

- **Click the Start button on the taskbar.**
- **Point to All Programs on the Start menu.**
- **Point to Microsoft Office on the All Programs menu.**
- **Click Microsoft Office Word 2003 on the Microsoft Office submenu.**
- **Click the Open button on the Standard toolbar.**
- **When the Open dialog box is displayed, select the file, James Keeler resume.doc, from the Project3 folder on the Data Disk.**

Word displays the Open dialog box, with the Word document file, James Keeler resume.doc, selected (Figure 3-55).

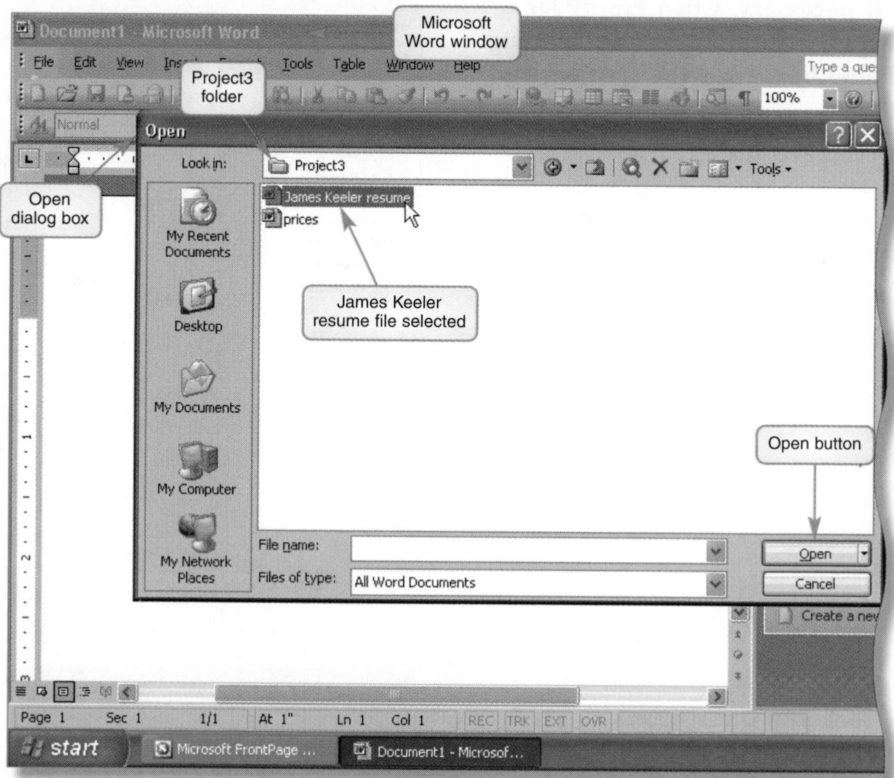

FIGURE 3-55

2

- **Click the Open button.**
- **If necessary, close the New Document task pane.**
- **If necessary, click View on the menu bar and then click Print Layout.**
- **Drag through the first line of text to select it and then press CTRL+C to copy it to the Office Clipboard.**

The Word document containing the resume is opened and is displayed in Print Layout view (Figure 3-56). The selected text is copied.

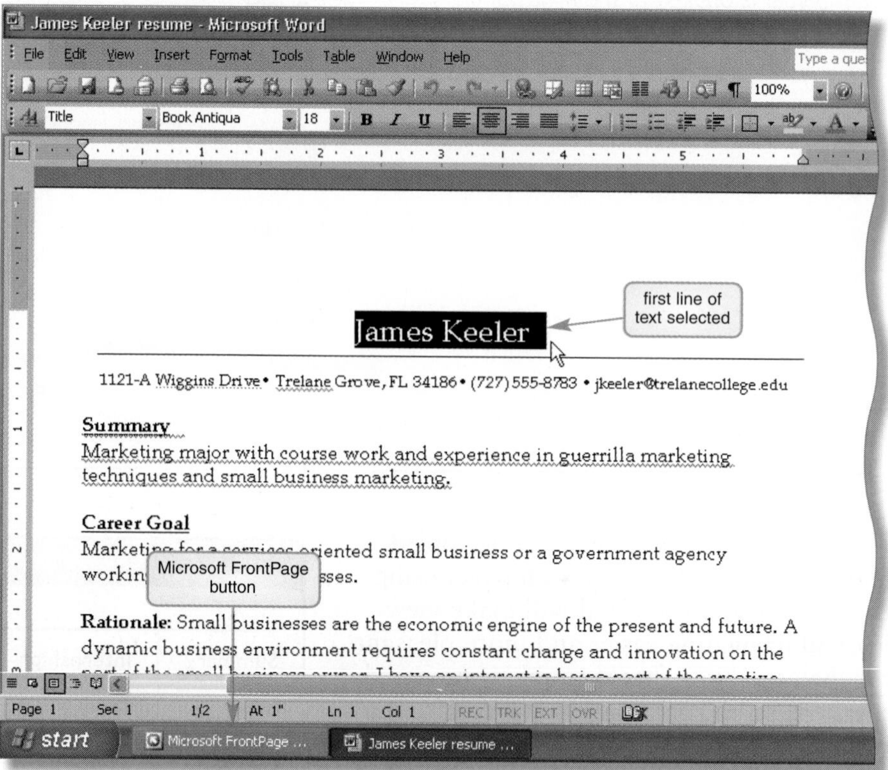

FIGURE 3-56

3

- **Click the Microsoft FrontPage button on the taskbar to switch to FrontPage.**
- **If necessary, click the upper-right cell to position the insertion point.**
- **Press CTRL+V to paste the copied text from Word into the Web page.**
- **Press the BACKSPACE key to delete the extra line.**
- **Select the text and change the font size to 5 (18 pt).**

FrontPage displays the pasted text in the Resume page in Page view (Figure 3-57).

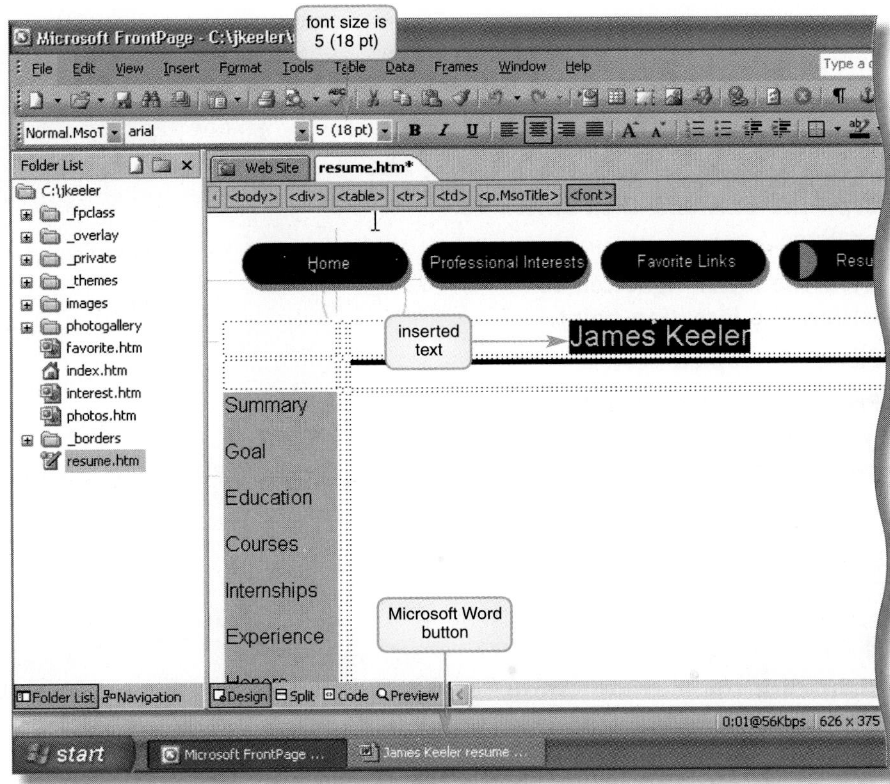

FIGURE 3-57

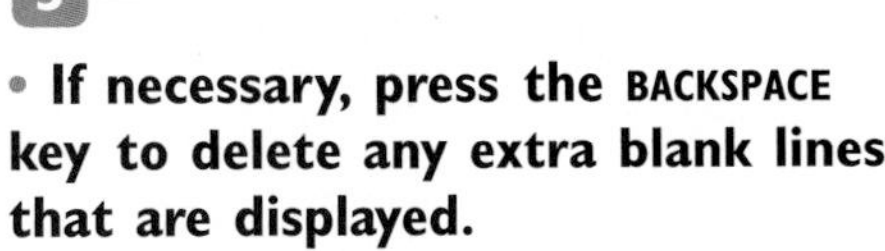

4

- **Click the Microsoft Word button on the taskbar to switch to Word and then drag through the second line of text to select it. Do not drag beyond the last letter in the line.**
- **Copy the text, switch to FrontPage, and then position the insertion point in the right cell of the middle row.**
- **Paste the copied text.**

5

- **If necessary, press the BACKSPACE key to delete any extra blank lines that are displayed.**

FrontPage displays the pasted text in the Resume page (Figure 3-58). The text may wrap if the width of the cell is not large enough.

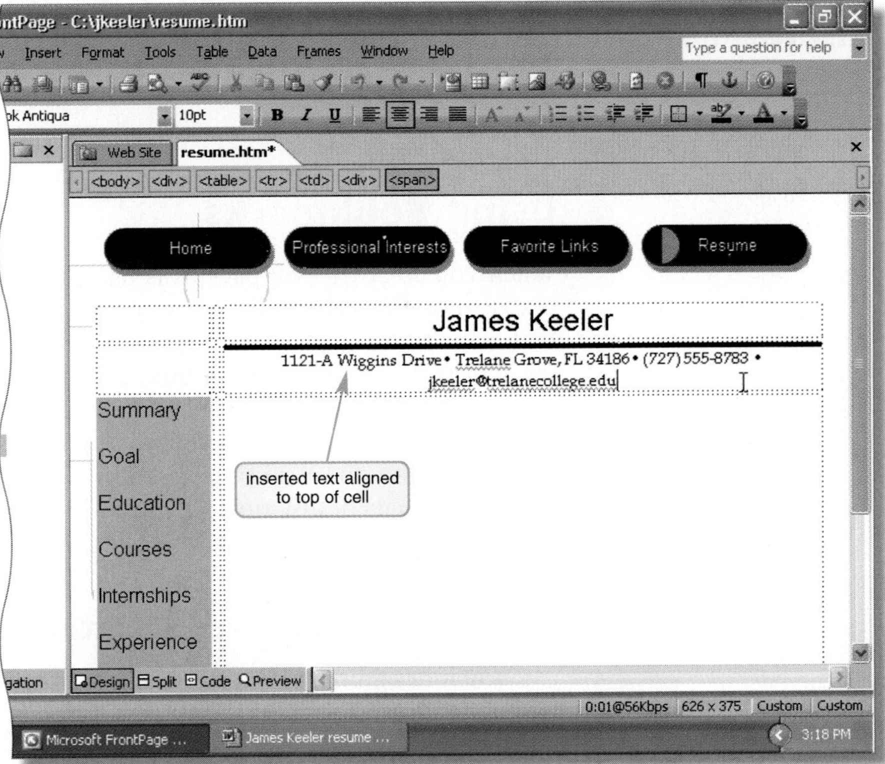

FIGURE 3-58

6

- **Switch to Word and then drag through the remaining text in the resume to select it, including the table.**
- **Copy the text and then switch to FrontPage.**
- **Click the lower-right cell to position the insertion point.**
- **Paste the copied text.**
- **Press the BACKSPACE key to delete any extra lines and spaces, but leave one blank line at the end.**

The remaining text is pasted in the Resume page (Figure 3-59).

FIGURE 3-59

- **Right-click the Microsoft Word button on the taskbar and then click Close on the shortcut menu.**
- **If a dialog box is displayed prompting you to save changes to the document, click No.**
- **If necessary, select all of the pasted text and then click the Font Color button on the Formatting toolbar to ensure that all pasted text has the same font color.**

Using Bookmarks

When you create a Web page, it is natural to assume that you may have to create one or more hyperlinks from that page to another page. The ability to link from one Web page to other pages of interest is one of the most basic and powerful features of the World Wide Web. Not all links are created for the same purpose or in the same manner, however. In Project 1, you created two types of links. One type provided an e-mail link, so users could e-mail the owner of the page. Another type provided a hyperlink from one Web page to another. You also can create a hyperlink that has a bookmark as its destination. A **bookmark** is a location, or selected text, that you have marked on a page.

Adding a Bookmarked Location

When designing a Web page, it is good to keep in mind how the user will interact with that page. If there are a number of links to relatively short pieces of information, and the user is likely to go back and forth from one page to another visiting these links, the best design may involve placing all of the information on a single Web page. This avoids having to reload each page as it is visited, which increases the perceived speed at which the pages can be reached. This approach must be balanced against having an overly large Web page, particularly if the user will not care to visit most of it. You also may want to link the user to a place in the Web page other than the top. This is a particular advantage when publishing a document as a Web page, because you have the ability to create hyperlinks to various sections of the document. These allow the user to move quickly from an index or table of contents to view the section of interest in the document. In a long document, particularly one containing a large amount of text, this prevents requiring the user to scroll down through the document in order to find the desired section. In both of these cases, using a bookmark can help accomplish the task.

Design Tip

If there are a number of links to relatively short pieces of information, and the user is likely to go back and forth from one page to another visiting these links, it may be better to place all of the information on a single Web page and use bookmarks to navigate to the short pieces of information.

The following steps bookmark a location in the current Web page.

To Bookmark a Location in a Web Page

1

- **Position the insertion point to the left of the horizontal link bar at the top of the page.**
- **Click Insert on the menu bar.**

The insertion point is positioned where the bookmark for this location is to be added. FrontPage displays the Insert menu (Figure 3-60).

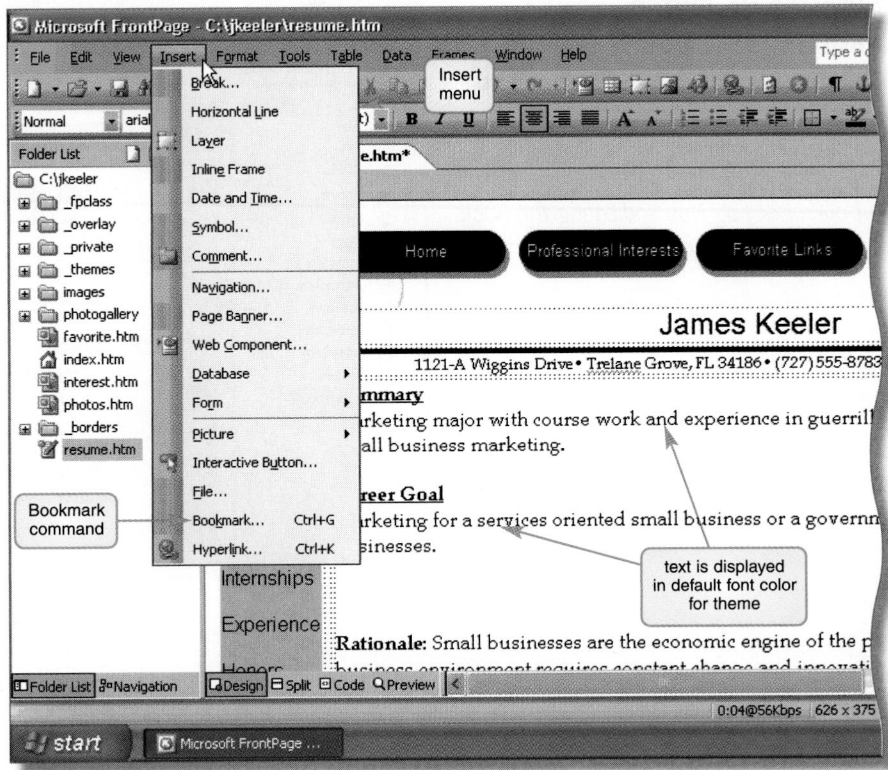

FIGURE 3-60

2

- **Click Bookmark.**
- **When FrontPage displays the Bookmark dialog box, type** Top **in the Bookmark name text box.**

FrontPage displays the Bookmark dialog box (Figure 3-61). The name of this bookmark is entered in the Bookmark name text box.

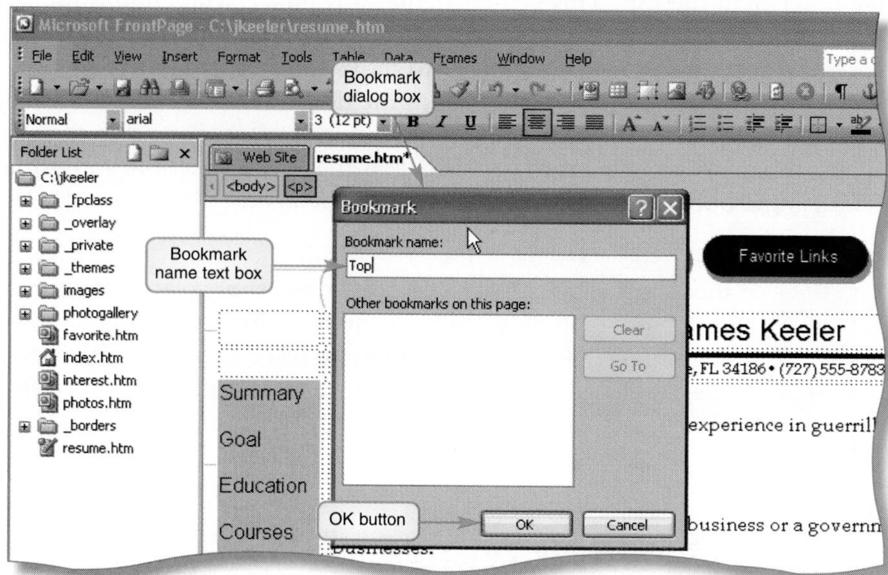

FIGURE 3-61

3

- **Click the OK button.**
- **Position the insertion point in the third row of the table, before the underlined word, Summary.**

FrontPage displays the Resume page with the bookmark flag icon, indicating the bookmarked location (Figure 3-62).

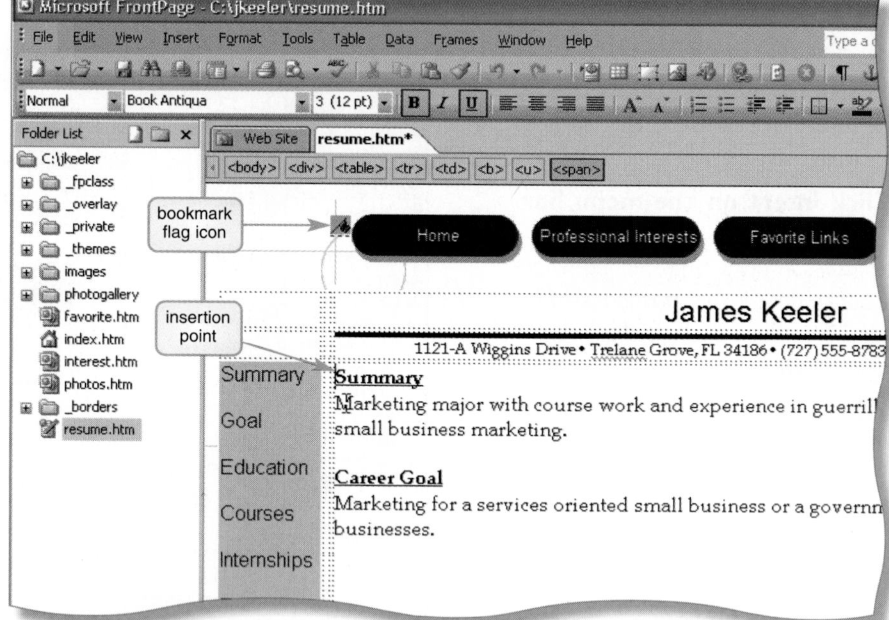

FIGURE 3-62

Adding Bookmarked Text

In FrontPage, if you bookmark a location or an image, a graphic flag icon indicates the presence of a bookmark. Text also can be bookmarked; however, it is displayed with a dashed underline. If the text was underlined previously, that underline is not removed and is displayed normally when the page is viewed. When editing the page, however, the original underline is not visible because the dashed underline, indicating a bookmark, obscures it.

The following steps add bookmarked text to the current Web page.

To Bookmark Text in a Web Page

1

- **Drag through the underlined word, Summary, in the third row of the table to select it.**
- **Click Insert on the menu bar and then click Bookmark.**

FrontPage displays the Bookmark dialog box (Figure 3-63). The highlighted word, Summary, is the location for the bookmark that will be added. FrontPage automatically inserts the highlighted text as the default name for this bookmark in the Bookmark name text box.

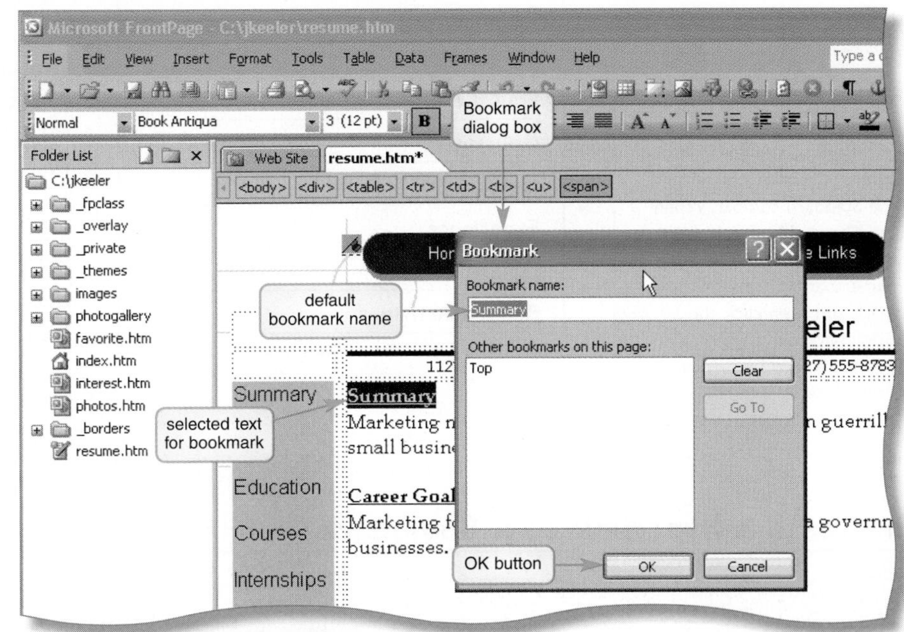

FIGURE 3-63

2

- **Click the OK button.**
- **Position the insertion point before the underlined words, Career Goal.**

FrontPage displays the Resume page, and the text, Summary, has a dashed underline, indicating that it is bookmarked (Figure 3-64).

3

- **Repeat Steps 1 through 3 to bookmark each of the remaining text items listed in Table 3-3 on the next page, selecting only the words indicated in the table. Use the default name as the bookmark name in each case.**

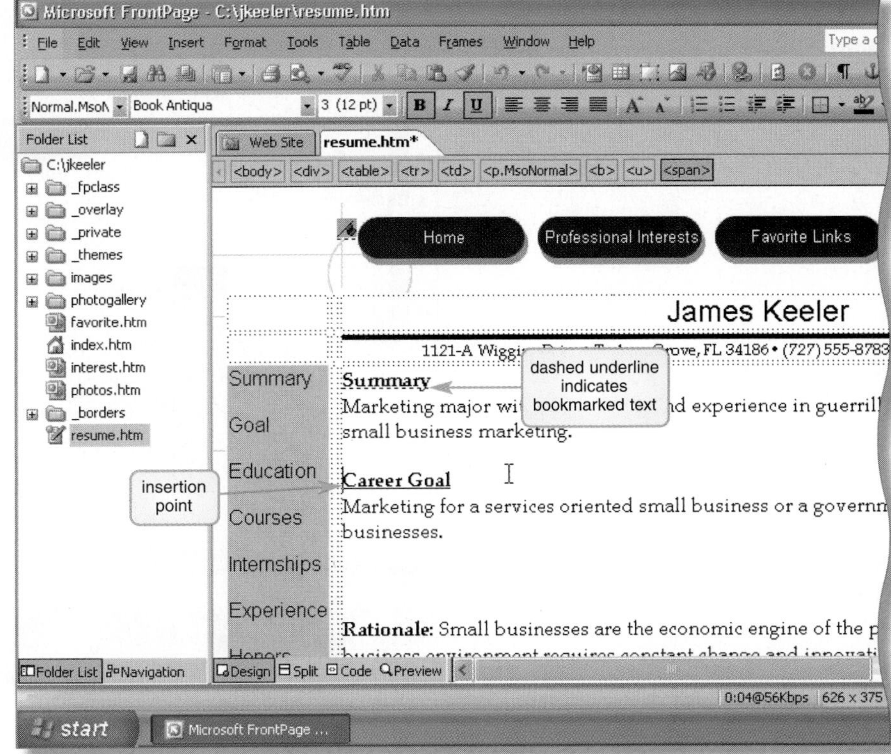

FIGURE 3-64

Other Ways

1. Press ALT+I, K
2. Press CTRL+G
3. In Voice Command mode, say "Insert, Bookmark"

More About

Hyperlinks to Bookmarks

Hyperlinks to bookmarks do not have to be located on the same Web page as the bookmarks. You easily can establish a hyperlink to a bookmark on another Web page. Click the Insert Hyperlink button on the Standard toolbar. When the Create Hyperlink dialog box displays, click the page name that contains the bookmark and then click the Bookmark button. When the Select Place in Document dialog box displays, click the desired bookmark.

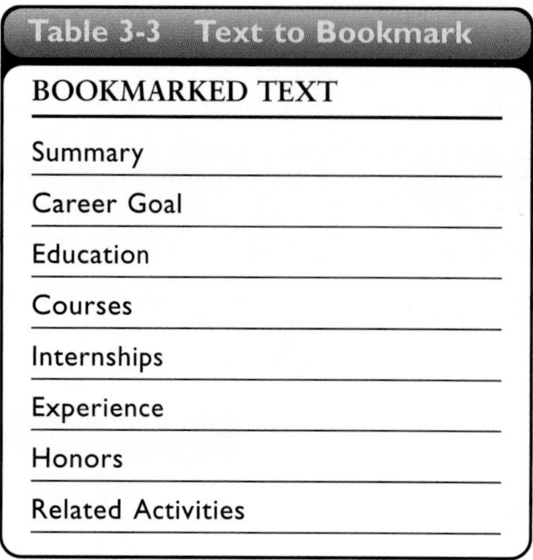

Table 3-3 Text to Bookmark

BOOKMARKED TEXT
Summary
Career Goal
Education
Courses
Internships
Experience
Honors
Related Activities

Adding Hyperlinks to Bookmarks

Once the bookmarks are identified, making hyperlinks to them is done in a similar fashion as the previous hyperlinks you have created. Hyperlink addresses that target a bookmark on a page, rather than just the page itself, have the same format as a URL addressing the page, with the addition of the bookmark. A pound sign (#) preceding the bookmark name identifies a bookmark in a URL, as shown in Figure 3-68 on page FP 196.

The following steps create text hyperlinks to bookmarks in the Web page.

To Create a Hyperlink to a Bookmark

1

- **Drag through the text, Summary, in the left column of the third row in the table.**
- **Right-click the selected text.**

The text, Summary, is selected and the shortcut menu is displayed (Figure 3-65).

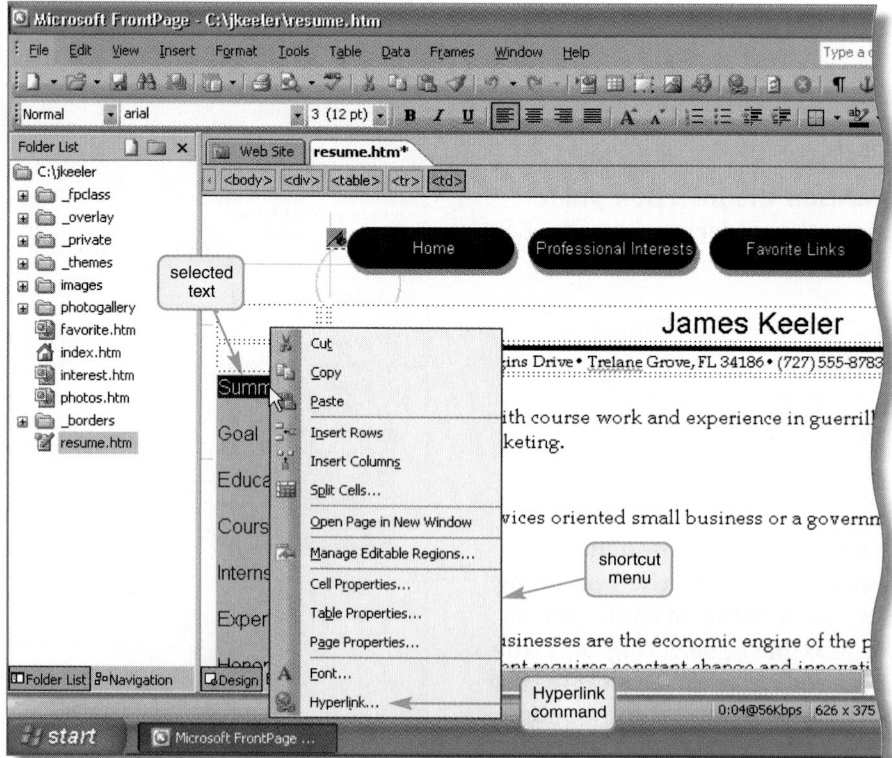

FIGURE 3-65

2

• **Click Hyperlink on the shortcut menu.**

FrontPage displays the Insert Hyperlink dialog box (Figure 3-66).

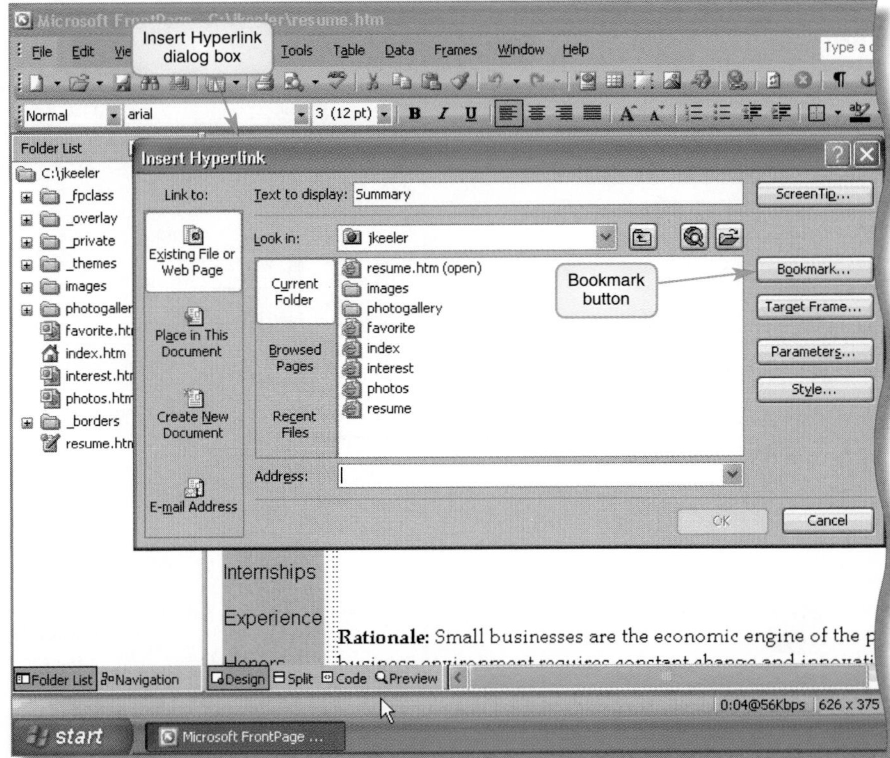

FIGURE 3-66

3

• **Click the Bookmark button.**

• **When FrontPage displays the Select Place in Document dialog box, click Summary in the list of bookmarks.**

The bookmark, Summary, is selected (Figure 3-67).

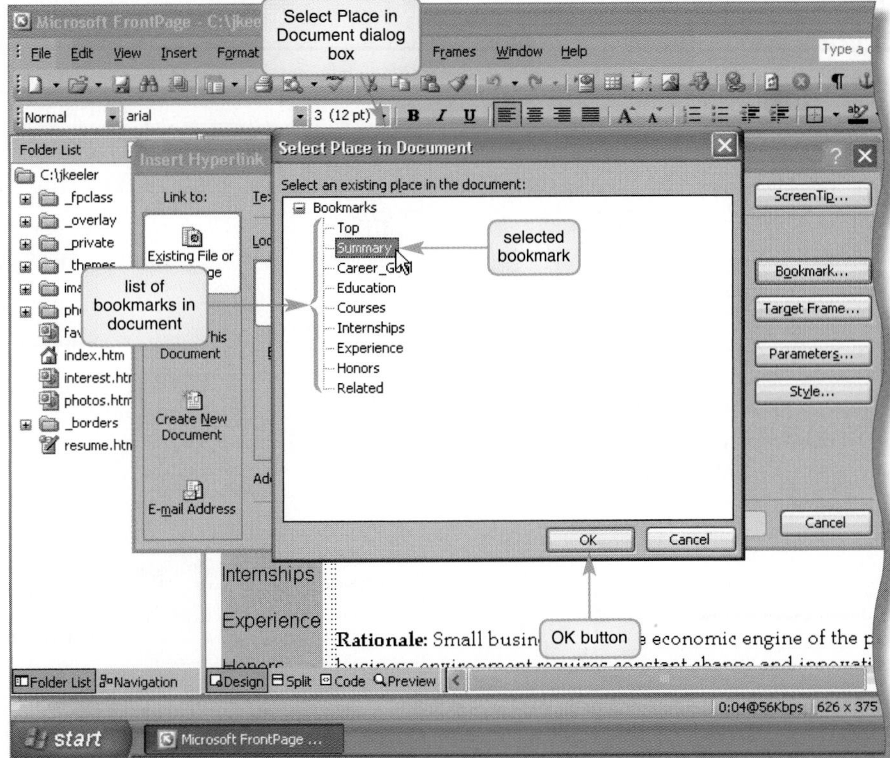

FIGURE 3-67

4

• **Click the OK button.**

The Select Place in Document dialog box is closed and the pound sign in the Address text box indicates that a bookmark will be used in the hyperlink (Figure 3-68).

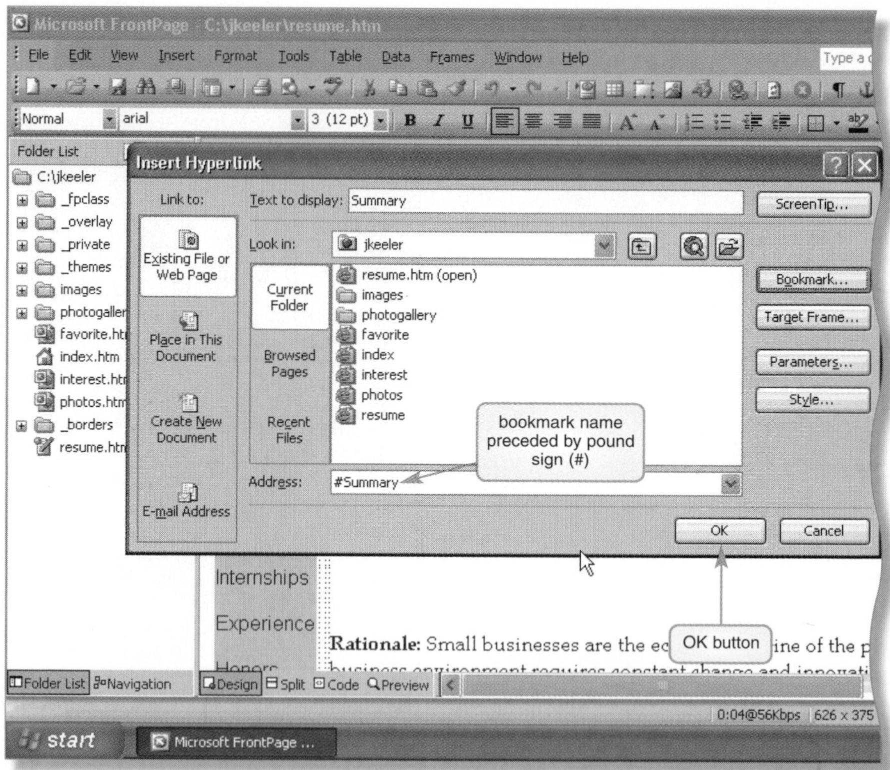

FIGURE 3-68

• **Click the OK button in the Insert Hyperlink dialog box.**

• **Point to the hyperlink, Summary.**

FrontPage displays the bookmark URL on the status bar (Figure 3-69). Because it links to a location on the same page, the full hyperlink address is not displayed.

• **Repeat Steps 1 through 5 to create hyperlinks to each of the remaining bookmarks, as listed in Table 3-4.**

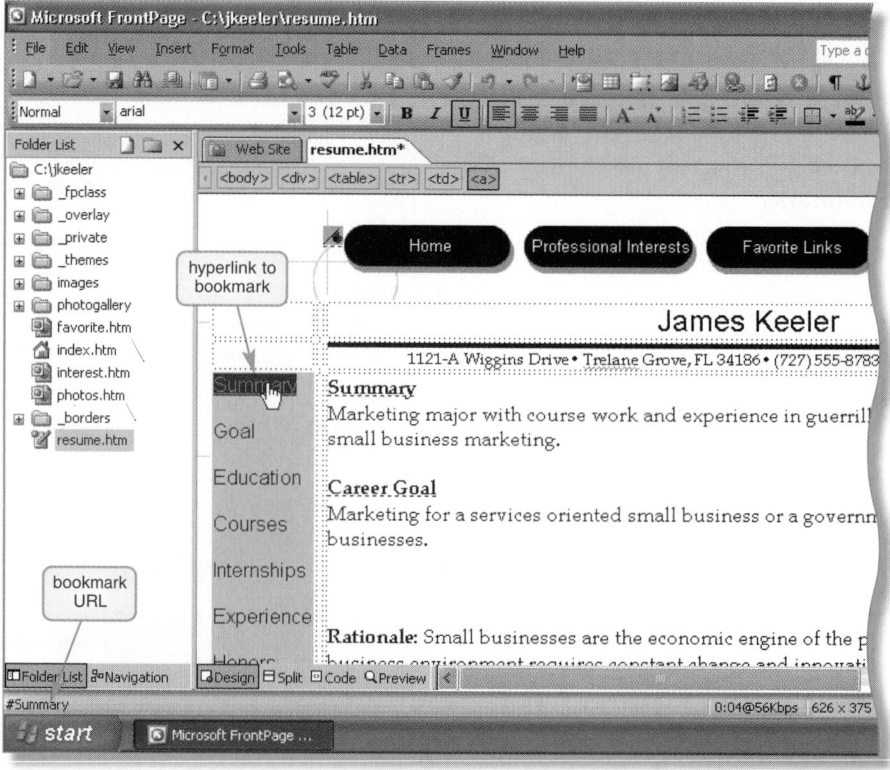

FIGURE 3-69

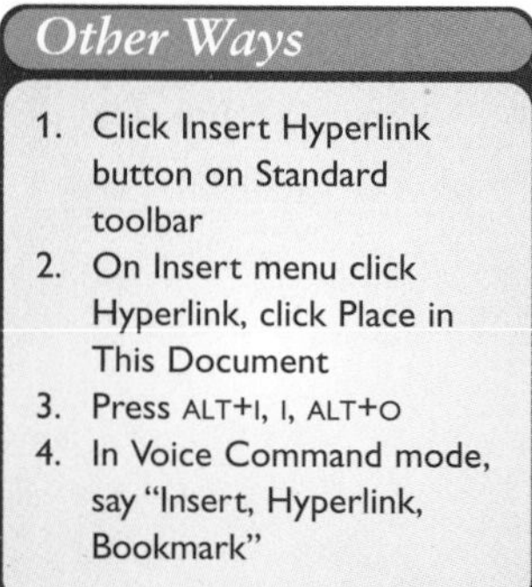

Other Ways

1. Click Insert Hyperlink button on Standard toolbar
2. On Insert menu click Hyperlink, click Place in This Document
3. Press ALT+I, I, ALT+O
4. In Voice Command mode, say "Insert, Hyperlink, Bookmark"

Once users have followed a hyperlink to a bookmark on the same Web page, they simply can scroll back to return to the previous location. If the page is very long or if the original hyperlink is not at the top of the page, however, it may be tedious for the users to find their way back. It is common to provide a back link to take the user back to the location that linked to the bookmark. Although using the Back button in the Web browser could achieve the same visible effect, there is a subtle difference. Using the browser's Back button to return removes the current page from the browser's list of recently visited links. By using a back link, the list of links the user has followed recently is preserved, even though a different page is not really loaded.

Use of a back link works if only one hyperlink targets a given bookmark. If multiple hyperlinks target the same bookmark, there is no way to determine the source of the hyperlink to which the user should be returned. Because all of the links that target your text bookmarks come from text near the top of the Web page, they may all target the same location for their back hyperlinks, the name at the top of the page. Use the following steps to create a back link for each of the text bookmarks.

Table 3-4 Bookmark Hyperlinks

HYPERLINKED TEXT	BOOKMARK
Summary	Summary
Career Goal	Goal
Education	Education
Courses	Courses
Internships	Internships
Experience	Experience
Honors	Honors
Related Activities	Related

To Create Back Hyperlinks

1

- **Position the insertion point in the first empty line after the paragraph beginning with Rationale, after the Career Goal bookmark.**
- **Click the Font Size box arrow and then click 2 (10 pt).**
- **Click the Italic button on the Standard toolbar.**
- **Type** `back to top` **as text for the back hyperlink.**

The text, back to top, is inserted (Figure 3-70).

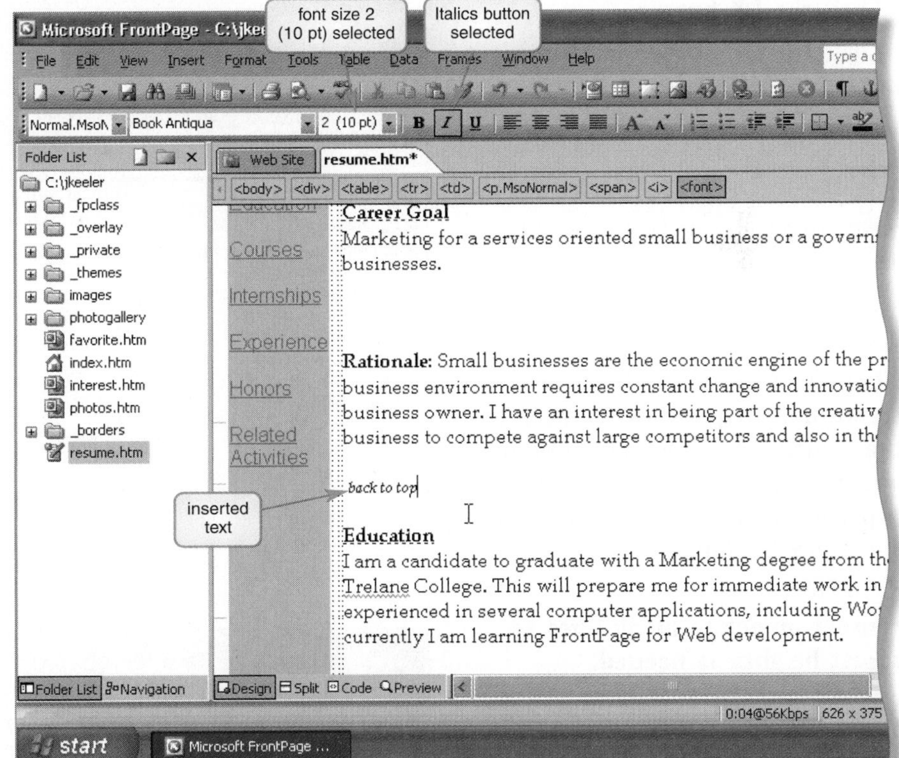

FIGURE 3-70

2

- **Drag through the text, back to top, to select it.**
- **Right-click the selected text and then click Hyperlink on the shortcut menu.**
- **When FrontPage displays the Insert Hyperlink dialog box, click the Bookmark button.**
- **When FrontPage displays the Select Place in Document dialog box, click Top in the list of bookmarks.**

The bookmark for the hyperlink is selected (Figure 3-71).

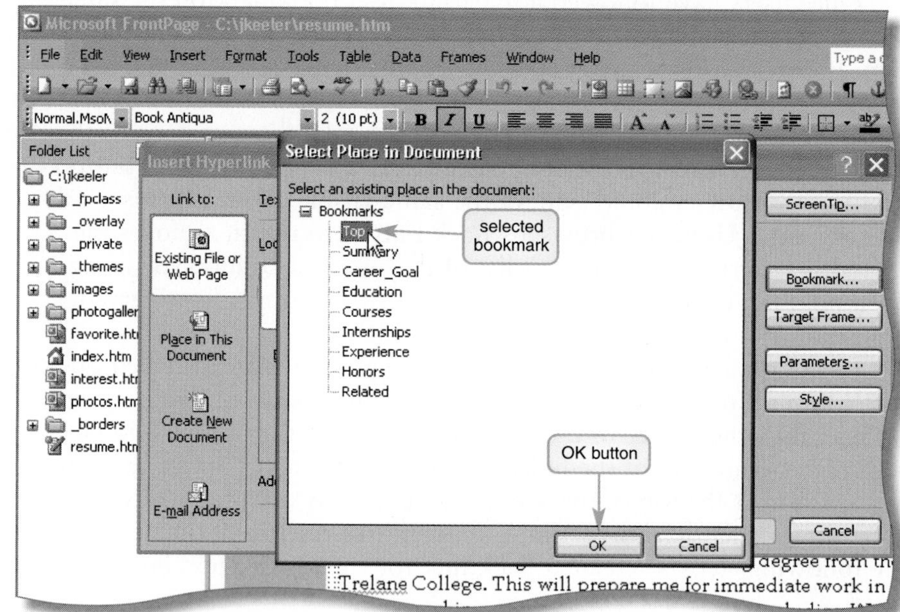

FIGURE 3-71

- **Click the OK button.**
- **Click the OK button in the Insert Hyperlink dialog box.**
- **Point to the hyperlink, back to top.**

FrontPage displays the bookmark URL on the status bar (Figure 3-72).

- **Copy and paste the hyperlink to create back hyperlinks for each of the remaining sections containing bookmarks. Do not create a back hyperlink in the cell containing the Summary bookmark at the top of the page.**
- **Insert or delete blank lines to adjust heights as needed.**
- **Save and close the Resume page.**

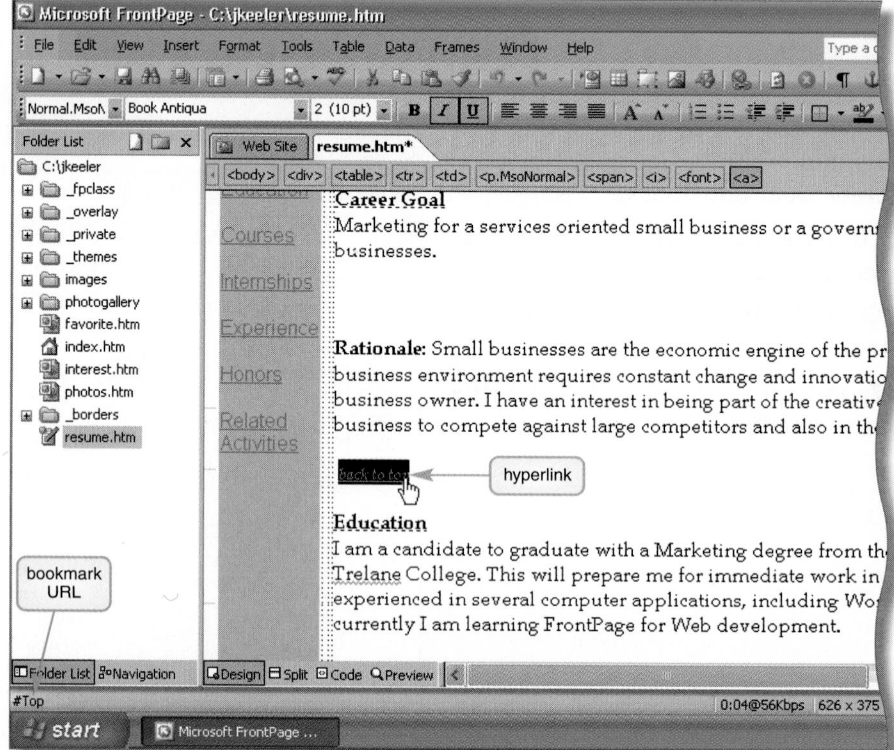

FIGURE 3-72

Because the back hyperlinks all reference the same location, the top of the page, the first back hyperlink was copied and pasted into multiple locations in the page. This saves time, rather than inserting the text and creating a hyperlink for each location separately.

Modifying an Image on a Web Page

Often, you want to use images that need some modification to be usable on a Web page. Typically, this has to do with the displayed size of the image, but also may include other properties, such as the image background or the size of the image file. FrontPage provides tools to modify these properties, thus making the images more useful.

Many images used on a Web page may appear to be irregular in shape when in fact they are rectangular. When the background color of the image is not the same as that of the Web page, the rectangular shape of the image becomes very obvious.

More About

The Pictures Toolbar

The Pictures toolbar provides a number of useful tools for images. Much as you can do with the Photo Gallery component, you can click the Auto Thumbnail button to create a thumbnail of a large image. The Auto Thumbnail button automatically inserts a hyperlink to the original, larger image.

Design Tip

To hide the rectangular shape common to all images, use images that have the same background color as the Web page, or use images that have a transparent background. Using images with a transparent background allows the color or graphic used in a Web page background to show through the background of the image, thus hiding the rectangular shape of the image.

Displaying the Pictures Toolbar

The Pictures toolbar contains a set of buttons that perform actions such as rotating the image and changing the brightness and contrast. The buttons on the Pictures toolbar may be active or inactive, depending on the type of image and its context. The Pictures toolbar can be hidden or displayed, depending on the setting on the View menu.

The following steps insert an image and display the Pictures toolbar.

To Insert an Image and Display the Pictures Toolbar

1

- **Double-click the file, index.htm, in the Folder List pane.**
- **Position the insertion point before the Home hyperlink on the bottom line.**
- **Press the ENTER key twice.**

FrontPage opens the Home page in Page view and inserts two additional blank lines (Figure 3-73).

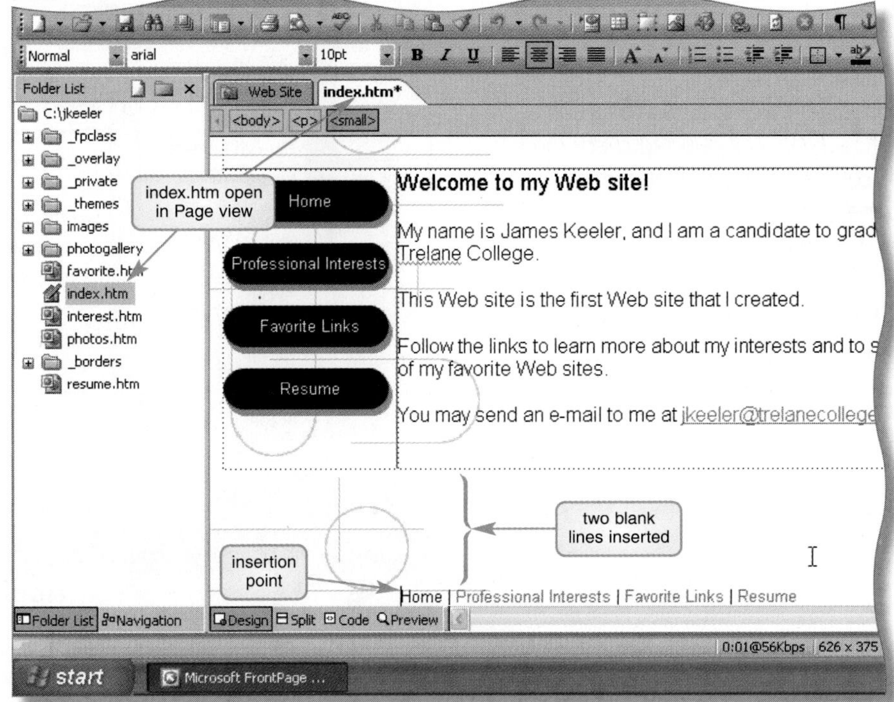

FIGURE 3-73

2

- **Click Insert on the menu bar and then point to Picture on the Insert menu.**
- **Click From File on the Picture submenu.**
- **When FrontPage displays the Picture dialog box, select the camera file from the Project3 folder on the Data Disk.**

FrontPage displays the Picture dialog box with the file, camera, selected (Figure 3-74).

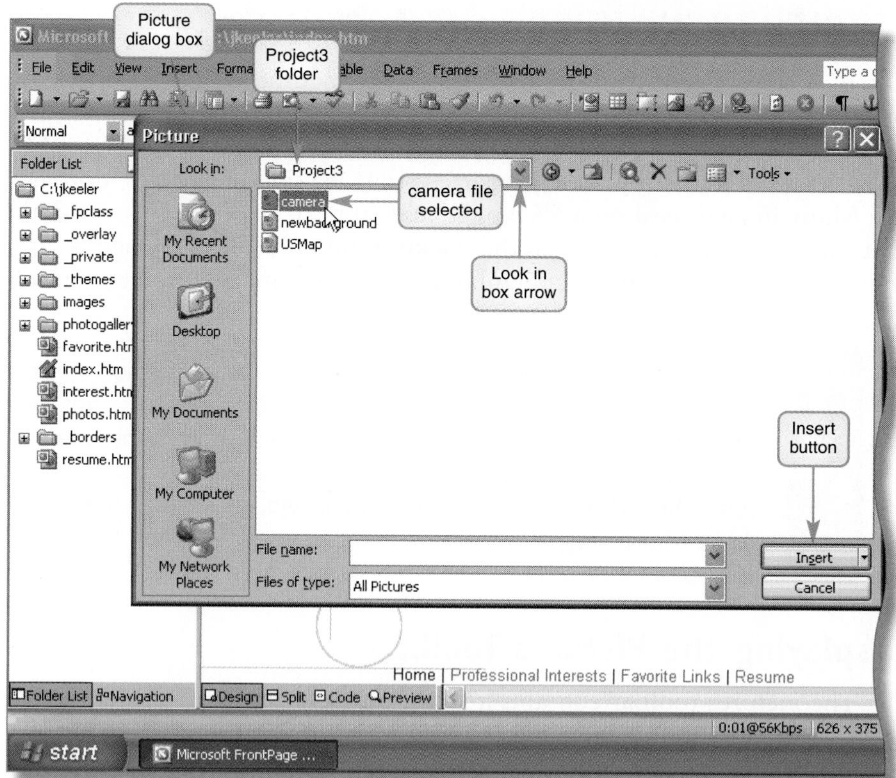

FIGURE 3-74

3

- **Click the Insert button.**
- **When the image is inserted, click the image to select it.**
- **Click View on the menu bar and then point to Toolbars on the View menu.**

FrontPage displays the Toolbars submenu (Figure 3-75). The selected check marks indicate the toolbars that currently are visible.

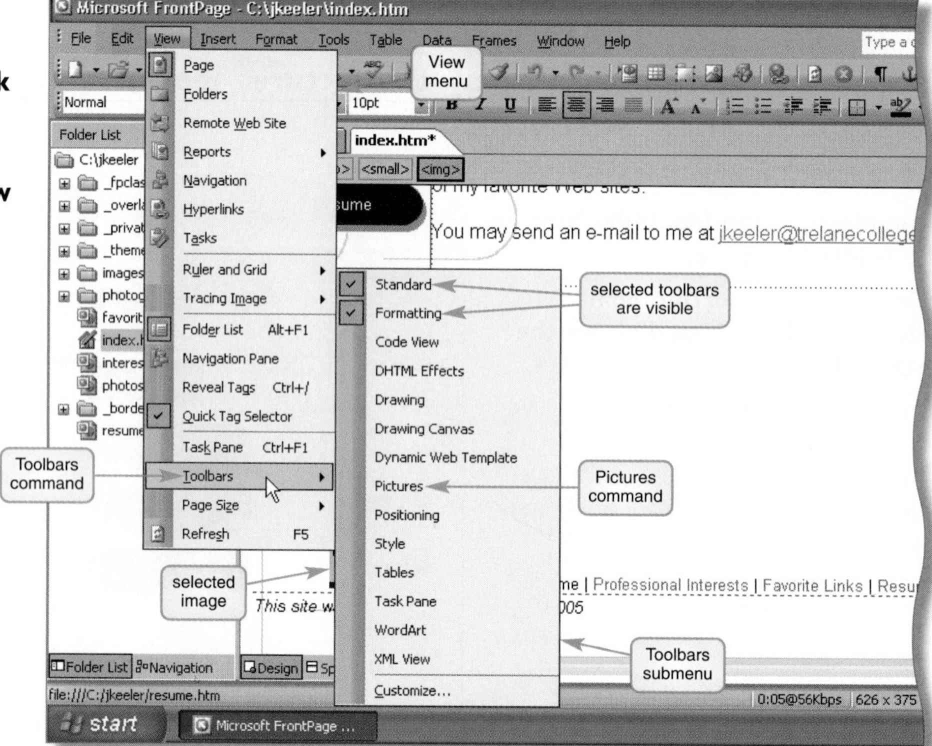

FIGURE 3-75

4

• **Click Pictures.**

FrontPage displays the Pictures toolbar (Figure 3-76).

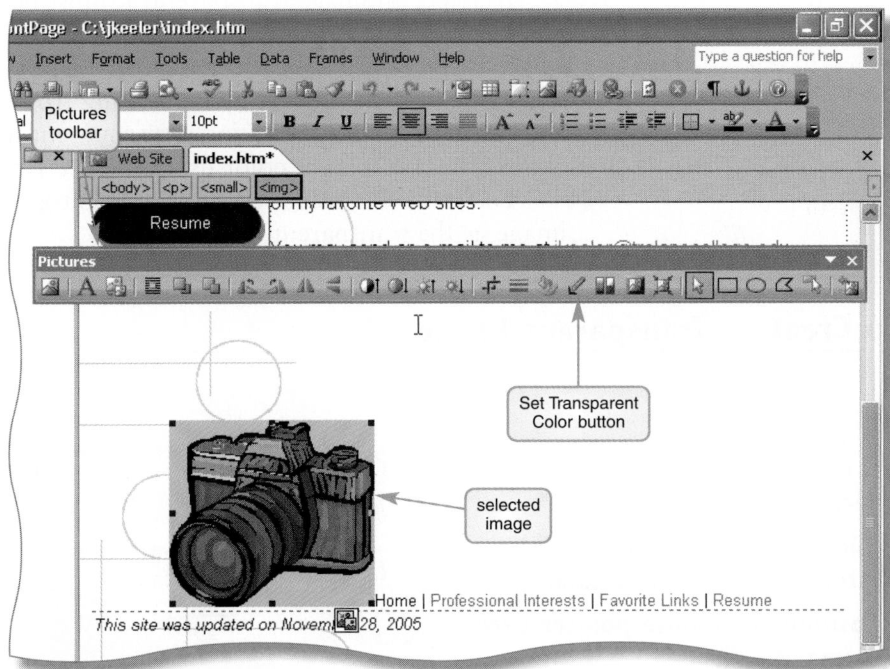

FIGURE 3-76

Other Ways

1. Press ALT+V, T, click Pictures
2. In Voice Command mode, say "View, Toolbars, Pictures"

By selecting an image and then selecting the Pictures toolbar on the Toolbars submenu, the Pictures toolbar is displayed only when an image is selected currently. If the image is deselected, the Pictures toolbar is not displayed. In order for the Pictures toolbar always to be visible on the screen, however, no image should be selected currently when the Pictures toolbar on the Toolbars submenu is chosen. In this case, the Pictures toolbar always will be displayed, whether or not an image is selected currently. All buttons are inactive, except the first, the Insert Picture From File button, until an image is selected.

Creating a Transparent Image

A **transparent image** sometimes is referred to as a **floating image** because it appears to float on the Web page. To make an image transparent, you select one of the colors in the image to be the **transparent color**. The background color or image of the page replaces the transparent color.

An image can have only one transparent color. If you select another transparent color, the first transparent color reverts to its original color. Use the Set Transparent Color button on the Pictures toolbar to make a selected color transparent. The mouse pointer changes to the Set Transparent Color pointer when the Set Transparent Color button is clicked and the mouse pointer is positioned over the image. You then click a color on the image to make it transparent.

Q&A

Q: Can I use a transparent color with an animated GIF image?

A: No. An animated GIF image consists of several images that display in rapid succession. GIF images that are animated will not allow you to select a transparent color.

Design Tip

To make an image transparent, select one of the colors in the image to be the transparent color. The transparent color is replaced by the background color, background design, or image of the page. An image can have only one transparent color.

To make an image transparent, it must be in the GIF file format. FrontPage asks you if you want to convert a JPEG image to GIF format when attempting to make a JPEG image transparent. Because GIF supports a maximum of only 256 colors, some image quality may be lost by converting from JPEG to GIF.

The procedure for making a transparent image is to select the image and then choose the transparent color using the Set Transparent Color pointer.

The following steps set the color light green around the sides of the camera image as the transparent color.

To Create a Transparent Image

1

- **If necessary, click the image to select it.**
- **Click the Set Transparent Color button on the Pictures toolbar.**
- **Position the mouse pointer over the image.**

FrontPage displays sizing handles around the image to indicate that it is selected (Figure 3-77). The mouse pointer changes to the Set Transparent Color pointer when positioned over the image.

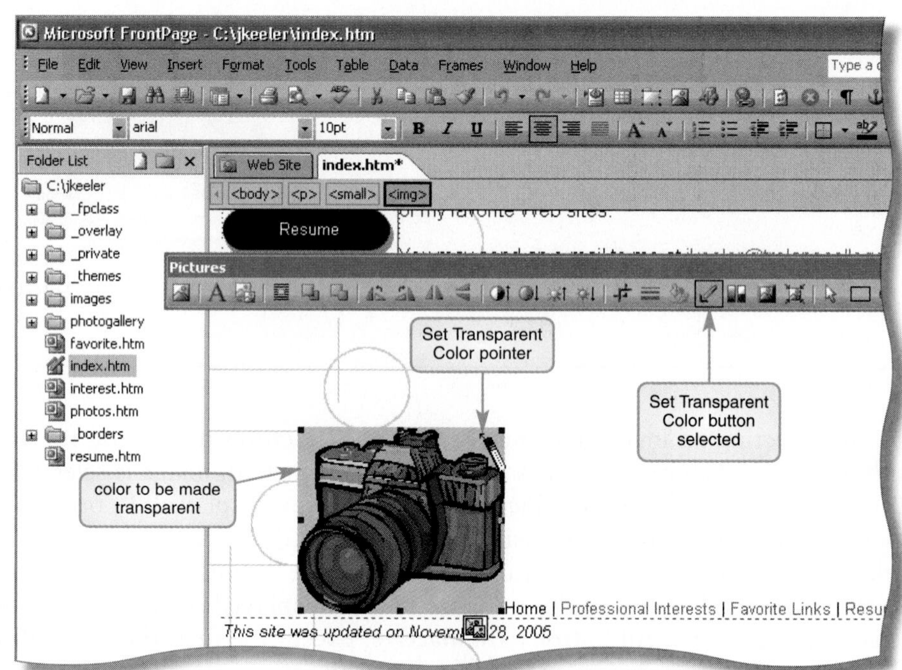

FIGURE 3-77

2

- **Click the light green color surrounding the image.**

The light green color becomes transparent and is replaced by the background (Figure 3-78). The mouse pointer is restored to the normal block arrow pointer and the Set Transparent Color button no longer is selected.

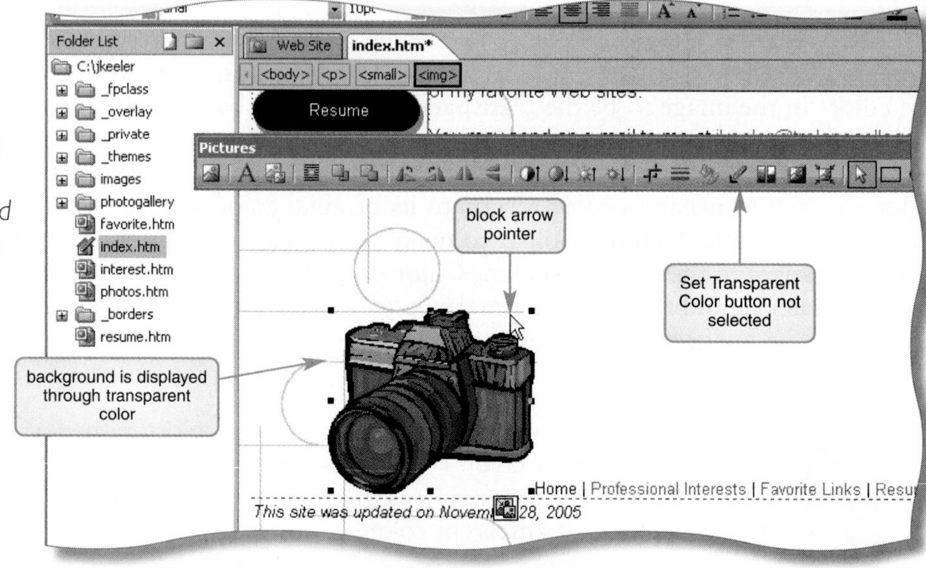

FIGURE 3-78

Other Ways

1. Click image, in Voice Command mode, say "Set Transparent Color"

Care must be exercised when selecting a color to be transparent. If the color appears in other sections of the image, it will become transparent in the other sections as well, and this might have an unexpected or undesirable effect. For example, if an image containing a face includes a purple background, the result of making white the transparent color could be a face with purple eyes and purple teeth.

Resizing and Resampling an Image

Sometimes an image for a Web page is too small or too large to fit within the space set aside for it in the Web page design. The image may be resized, shrinking or stretching it, by selecting the image and dragging its handles until it becomes the desired size. This was done in Project 2 with the book image on the Photos page. The width and height of the image also may be specified directly.

Resizing an image does not automatically change the size of the image file. It changes only the HTML tags for the image, so the browser actually does the shrinking or stretching when the image is displayed. This is an advantage for small images stretched to a larger size. The small image file takes less time to load than if the file contained the image at its larger size.

Conversely, for an image you have made smaller, the file still contains the image at its original size, and it still must be loaded even though the browser displays a smaller version of the image. To take advantage of the download performance brought about by a smaller image, the image must be resampled. **Resampling** an image stores the image in the file at its new size.

More About

Resampling an Image

Because resampling overwrites the image file in the images directory, you may want to make a backup copy of the original image file. If you save an unwanted change accidentally, you can retrieve the backup copy of the file and continue with your development.

Design Tip

When working with large image files, resample an image after adding the image to the page if the image is resized on the page. The resulting smaller file size allows the page to download faster.

Once an image has been resampled as a smaller size, it may appear better at the smaller size than before it was resampled. Once the resampled file is saved, trying to stretch it back to its original size typically results in a poorer-quality image. In both cases, this is due to the amount of information needed in the file to display the image at the given size. In the first case, too much information was provided for a smaller image. In the second, information that is needed for the larger displayed image was lost in the resampling. If you are going to resample an image but may need the larger version later, then make a backup copy.

Resampling an image becomes particularly important when inserting photographs, because the JPEG files usually are rather large. The photos used in the Photos page were not resampled, because FrontPage created the smaller thumbnail pictures for you.

Images can be resized and resampled as needed. The new images can be saved in the images folder of the project when the project is saved. If inserted images are not saved before resampling, the original images remain unchanged and are not included in the project. If the image is saved before resizing and resampling, then the saved version may be overwritten with the new one. The steps on the next page resize and resample the camera image for this project.

To Resize and Resample an Image

1

- **If necessary, click the image to select it.**
- **Use the sizing handles to resize the image to the approximate size illustrated in Figure 3-79.**

The image is resized using the sizing handles (Figure 3-79).

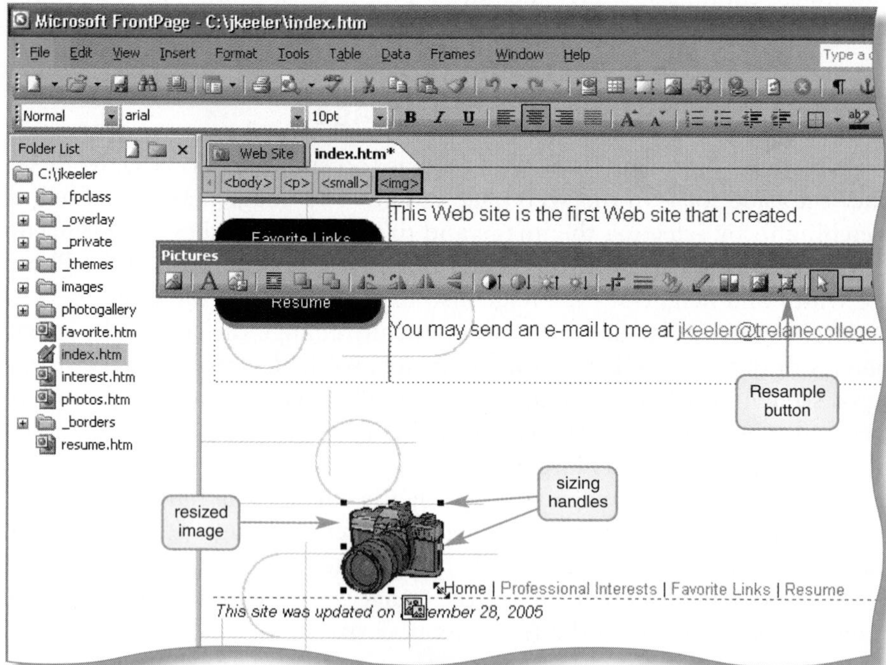

FIGURE 3-79

2

- **With the image still selected, click the Resample button on the Pictures toolbar.**

FrontPage displays the resized and resampled image (Figure 3-80).

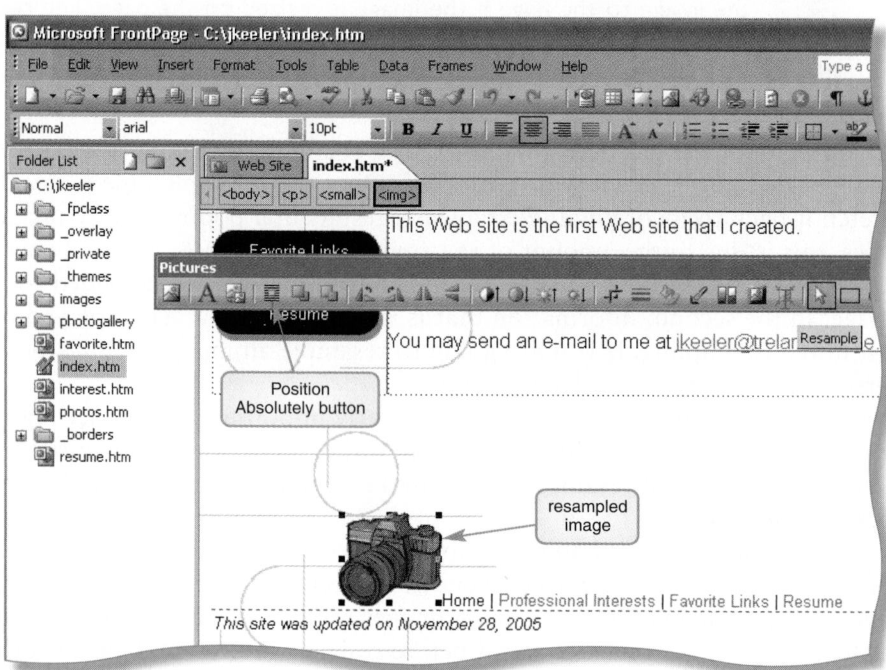

FIGURE 3-80

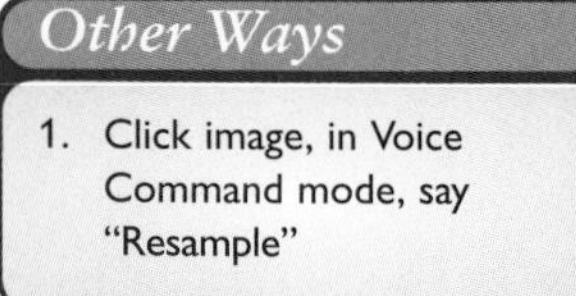

Other Ways

1. Click image, in Voice Command mode, say "Resample"

Once an image is resampled, it cannot be resampled again unless the size of the image is changed. The resample action can be undone, however, by clicking the Undo button.

Using Absolute Positioning with an Image

Although tables can be helpful in positioning elements on a Web page, at times even a table does not provide enough control over placement of an image. In other circumstances, using a table to position an image may prove to be difficult.

To provide more exact image placement, FrontPage supports absolute positioning for images. **Absolute positioning** refers to the ability to display page content at a specified distance from the upper-left corner of its container, which by default is the space that the Web page occupies in the browser. Unfortunately, due to differences in browsers and monitors, the results are not always consistent. Also, when an image is positioned absolutely, text and other items do not flow around the image. If a Web page's content changes, the image may need to be repositioned. Internet Explorer 6.0 and Netscape Navigator 6.0 both support absolute positioning; however, you should always verify the page in any browser that your Web site visitors are likely to use.

When designing a Web page that contains elements that are positioned absolutely, be sure to test the page with all browsers that Web page visitors use.

The following steps use absolute positioning with the camera image.

To Use Absolute Positioning with an Image

1

- **If necessary, click the image to select it.**
- **Click the Position Absolutely button on the Pictures toolbar.**
- **Position the mouse pointer over the edge of the image.**

The Position Absolutely button is selected and the pointer is displayed as a double two-headed arrow (Figure 3-81).

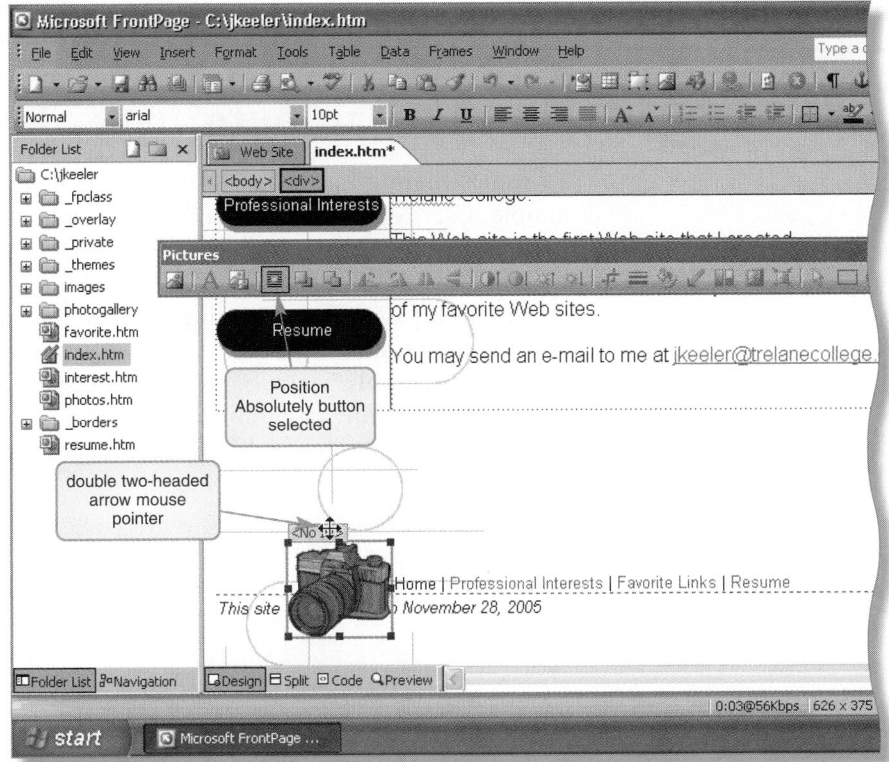

FIGURE 3-81

2

- **Drag the image to the approximate location illustrated in Figure 3-82.**
- **Click anywhere on the page off of the image to deselect the image.**

The image is repositioned (Figure 3-82).

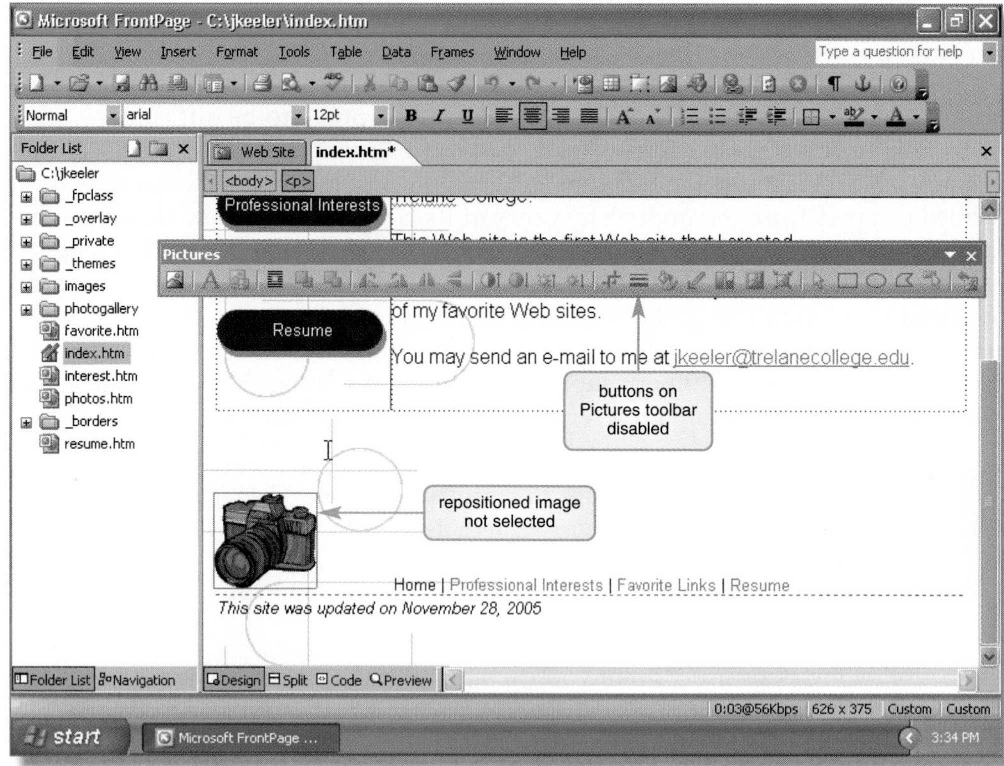

FIGURE 3-82

Other Ways

1. Click image, in Voice Command mode, say "Position Absolutely"

Inserting an AutoShapes Drawing Object

At times, finding just the right image can be time-consuming, even if it is rather simple. Users of other Microsoft Office products, such as Word and PowerPoint, are accustomed to adding drawings, as well as richly formatted text, directly to their documents. FrontPage supports drawing line graphics and rich text formatting within Web pages. The Drawing toolbar provides the ability to draw arrows, rectangles, lines, and other shapes. AutoShapes adds geometric shapes, block arrows, flowchart symbols, stars, banners, and other predrawn shapes. WordArt provides rich text formatting capabilities, such as shadowing and curving text.

The following steps add an AutoShapes object to a Web page.

To Add an AutoShapes Object

1

- **If necessary, click the Close button on the Pictures toolbar.**
- **If necessary, click View on the menu bar, point to Toolbars, and then click Drawing.**
- **Click the AutoShapes button on the Drawing toolbar.**
- **Point to Stars and Banners.**

FrontPage displays the Stars and Banners submenu (Figure 3-83).

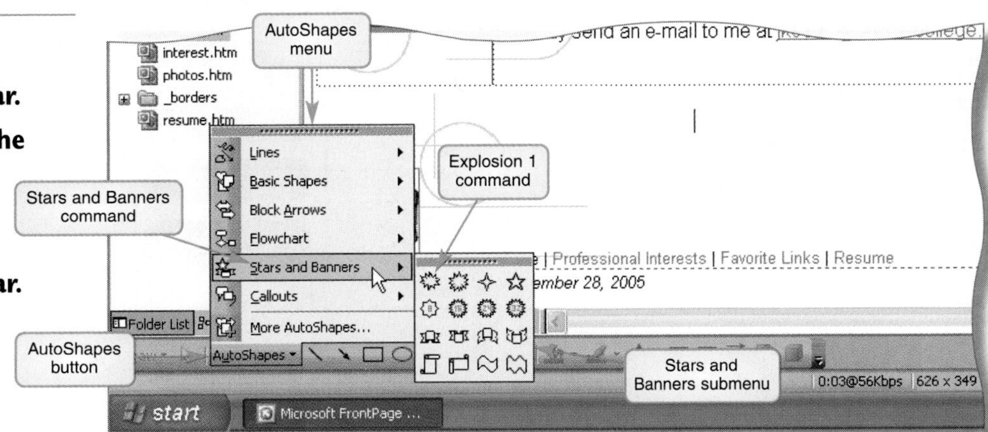

FIGURE 3-83

2

- **Click Explosion 1.**
- **Position the mouse pointer below the links bar.**

The mouse pointer changes to a cross hair (Figure 3-84).

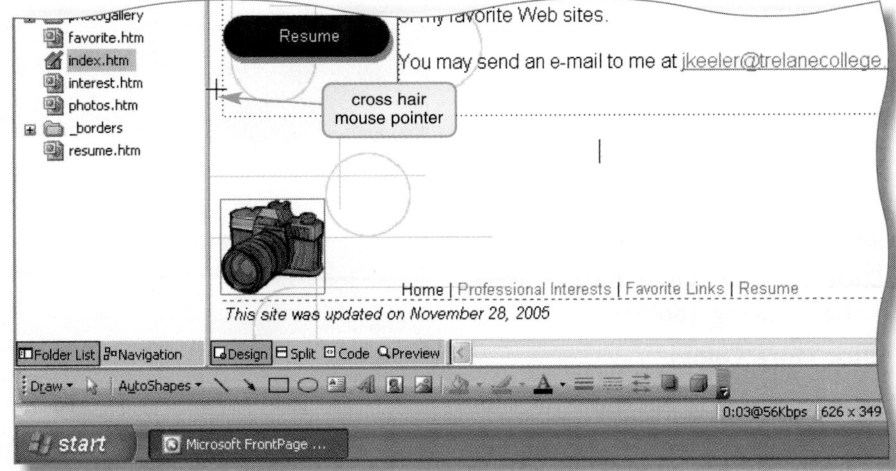

FIGURE 3-84

3

- **Drag the mouse pointer to the opposite corner to create a shape that is approximately the size shown in Figure 3-85.**
- **Release the mouse button.**
- **Right-click the shape and then click Add Text on the shortcut menu.**

The shape is drawn and a text box appears on the shape (Figure 3-85).

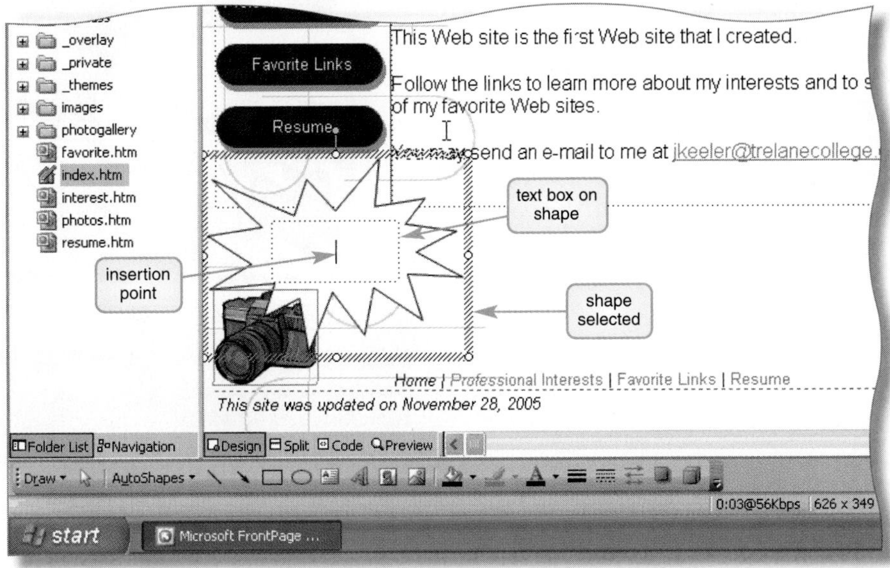

FIGURE 3-85

4

- **Click the Font Size button arrow on the Formatting toolbar and then select 2 (10 pt).**
- **Type** `See my photos` **in the text box on the shape.**
- **Drag through the text.**

FrontPage displays the entered text on the shape (Figure 3-86).

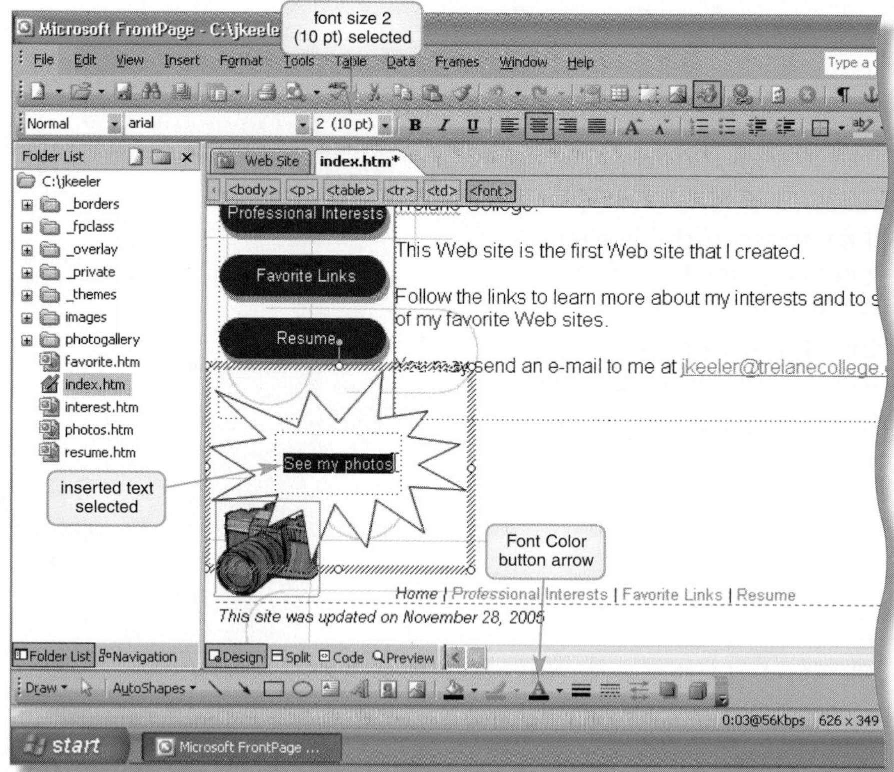

FIGURE 3-86

5

- **Click the Font Color button arrow on the Drawing toolbar.**
- **Click More Colors.**
- **When FrontPage displays the More Colors dialog box, click the title bar and drag the dialog box so it does not hide the text on the link bar buttons.**

FrontPage displays the More Colors dialog box. The dialog box is repositioned (Figure 3-87).

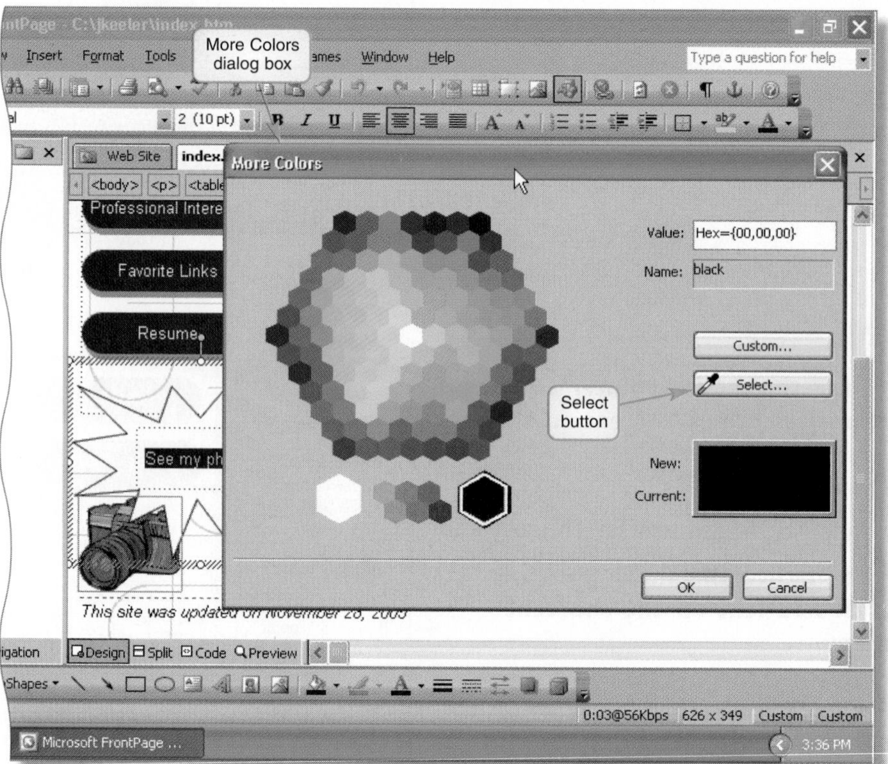

FIGURE 3-87

6

- **Click the Select button.**
- **Position the mouse pointer over the text on a Link Bar button so that the New area displays the same color as the Link Bar button text.**

FrontPage changes the mouse pointer to a dropper. The New area displays the color under the mouse pointer (Figure 3-88).

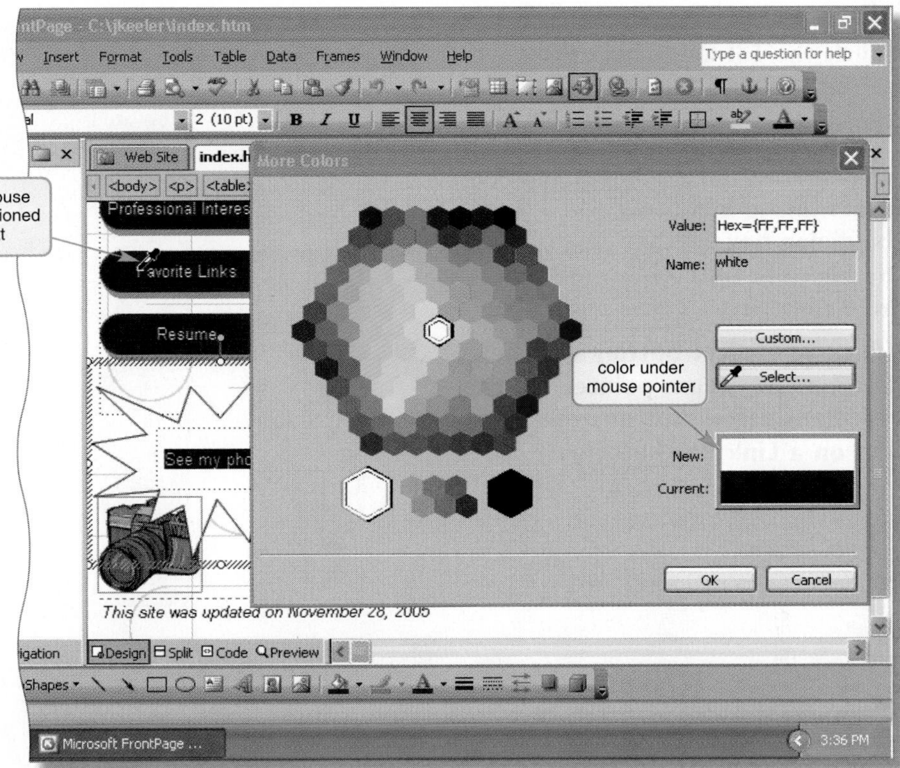

FIGURE 3-88

7

- **Click the mouse button.**
- **Click the OK button.**
- **Click the shape outside of the text box to deselect the text.**

FrontPage displays the text in the shape using the new color, which is white. Because white matches the background color of the shape, the text does not appear in the shape (Figure 3-89).

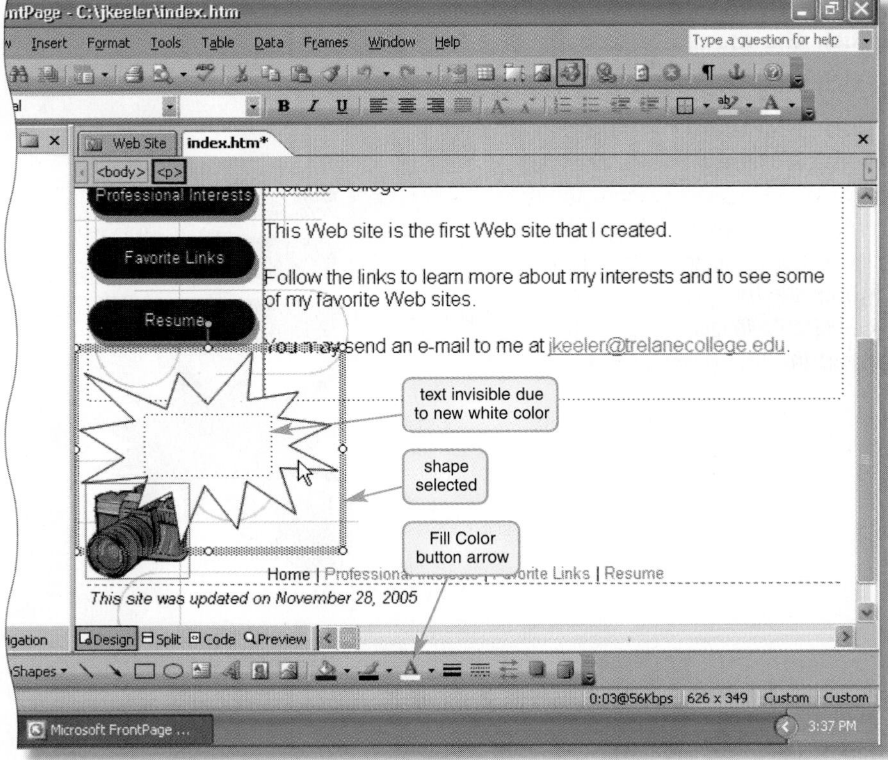

FIGURE 3-89

8

- **Click the Fill Color button arrow on the Drawing toolbar.**
- **Click More Fill Colors.**
- **When FrontPage displays the More Colors dialog box, drag the dialog box so that the Link Bar buttons are visible.**
- **Click the Select button and then position the mouse pointer over a Link Bar button, but not over the text on a Link Bar button.**

The mouse pointer is changed to a dropper and the New area displays the color under the mouse pointer (Figure 3-90).

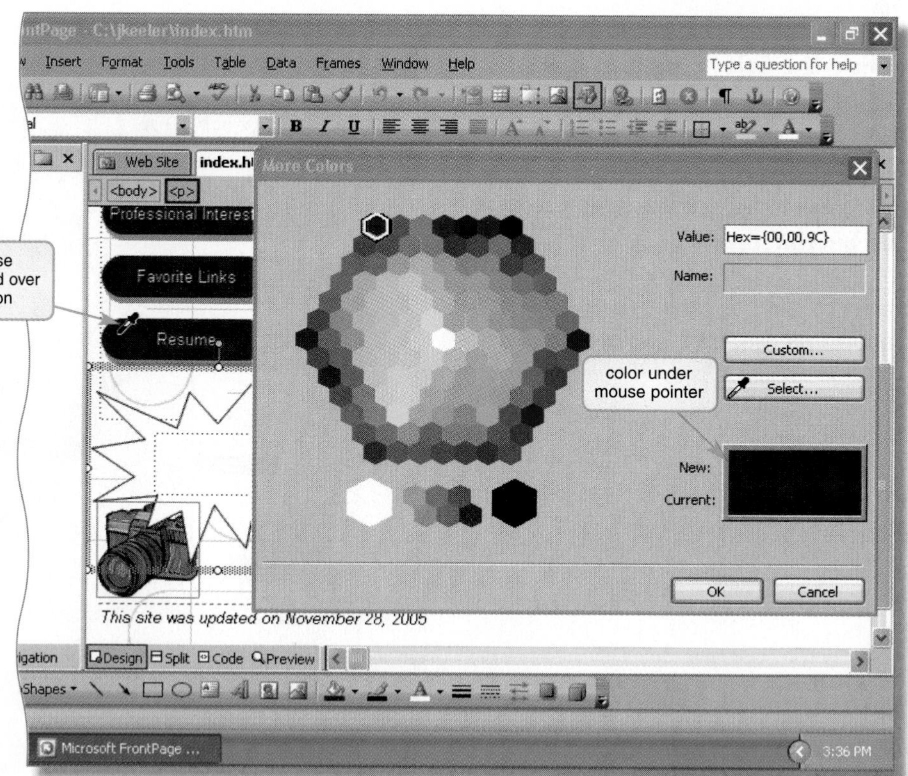

FIGURE 3-90

9

- **Click the mouse button.**
- **Click the OK button.**
- **Click the Line Color button arrow on the Drawing toolbar.**

FrontPage displays the shape using the selected color. The text appears because the background color of the shape no longer matches the color of the text (Figure 3-91).

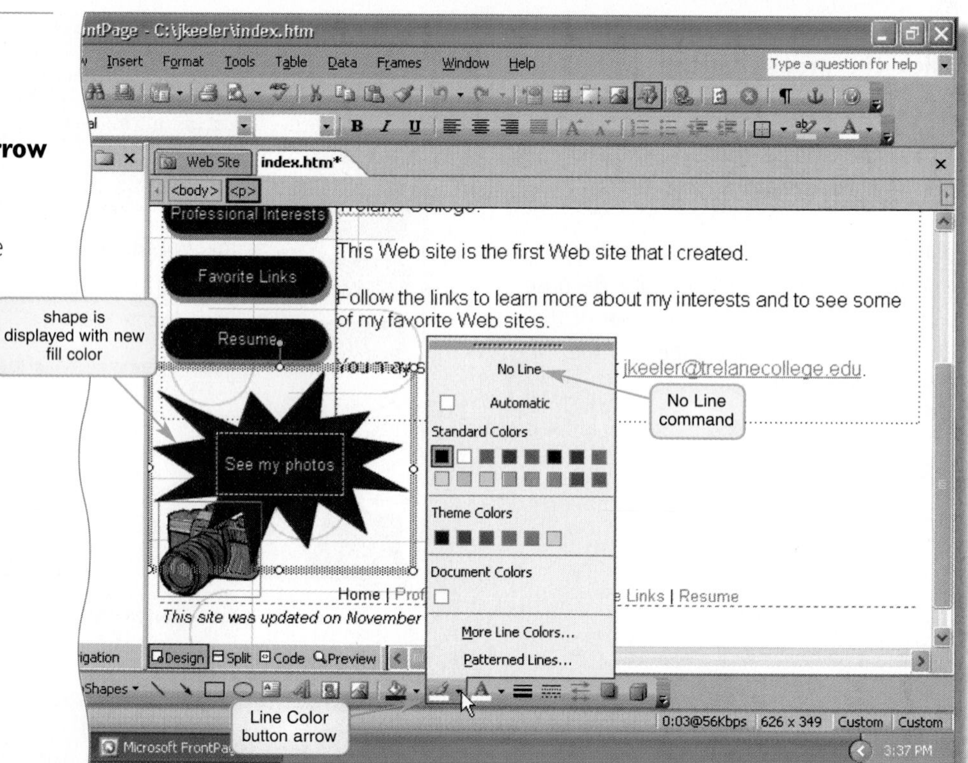

FIGURE 3-91

10

- **Click No Line.**
- **If necessary, resize the shape so that the text in the text box is fully visible.**
- **Position the pointer over the shape and then drag the shape to reposition it.**

The line around the shape is removed (Figure 3-92). When the mouse pointer is positioned over the shape, it becomes a double two-headed arrow, while if over the text, it becomes an I-beam.

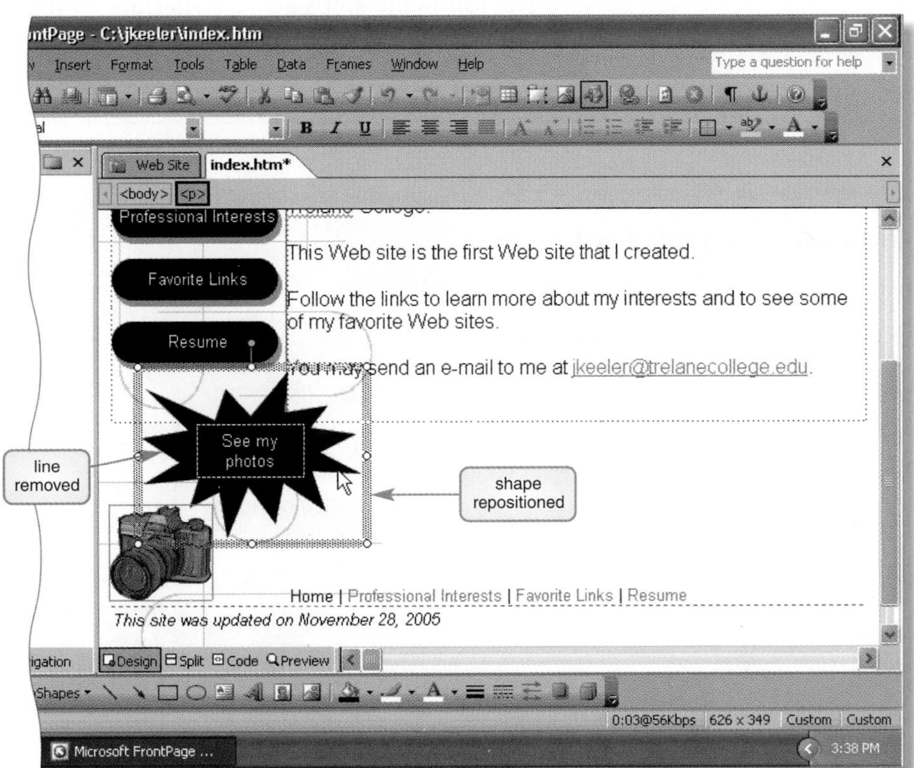

FIGURE 3-92

Other Ways

1. Press ALT+U, S, click shape
2. In Voice Command mode, say "AutoShapes, Stars and Banners, TAB, ENTER"

Besides simply creating line drawings and shapes, the Drawing toolbar includes tools to change drawing colors, add three-dimensional style effects, and add drop shadows.

These line-drawing graphics use a technology called VML (Vector Markup Language). **VML** is a way to describe images using curves, lines, and coordinates so that the instructions to draw the picture can be downloaded rather than the entire picture. A line drawing expressed in VML usually is much smaller than the same drawing stored as a GIF or JPEG file, and therefore can download more quickly.

Assigning a Hyperlink to an Image

Previous projects used text as hyperlinks, whether typed or created on a link bar. This project also will use images as hyperlinks. Now that the two images have the desired appearance, the next step is to make them function as hyperlinks.

Adding a hyperlink to the Explosion 1 shape can be accomplished in several ways. The text on the shape can be selected and assigned a hyperlink; however, this would require users to click the text, not just the shape, to activate the hyperlink.

As you have learned, many images used on a Web page may appear to be irregular in shape when in fact they are rectangular. When the Explosion 1 shape is selected, a rectangular box with sizing handles is displayed. A Web site visitor might think that clicking any area within the rectangle activates a hyperlink added to a shape. By adding a hyperlink to the shape itself, however, any location on the shape activates the hyperlink, while locations not on the shape but within the rectangular area do not. This is true even for irregular shapes, such as the Explosion 1 shape.

More About

Displaying Images

Current computers allow you to specify the bit resolution that your computer monitor will display. If the resolution is smaller than the bit resolution of an image, the image will not display properly. Right-click the desktop and then click Properties. When the Display Properties dialog box displays, click the Settings tab to see the current setting for your computer monitor.

The following steps add a hyperlink to the Explosion 1 AutoShape object.

To Add a Hyperlink to an AutoShapes Object

1

- **Right-click the Explosion 1 object.**

FrontPage displays a shortcut menu (Figure 3-93). Be sure to select the shape and not the text on the shape. If the Set AutoShape Defaults command does not appear on the shortcut menu, then the shape is not selected.

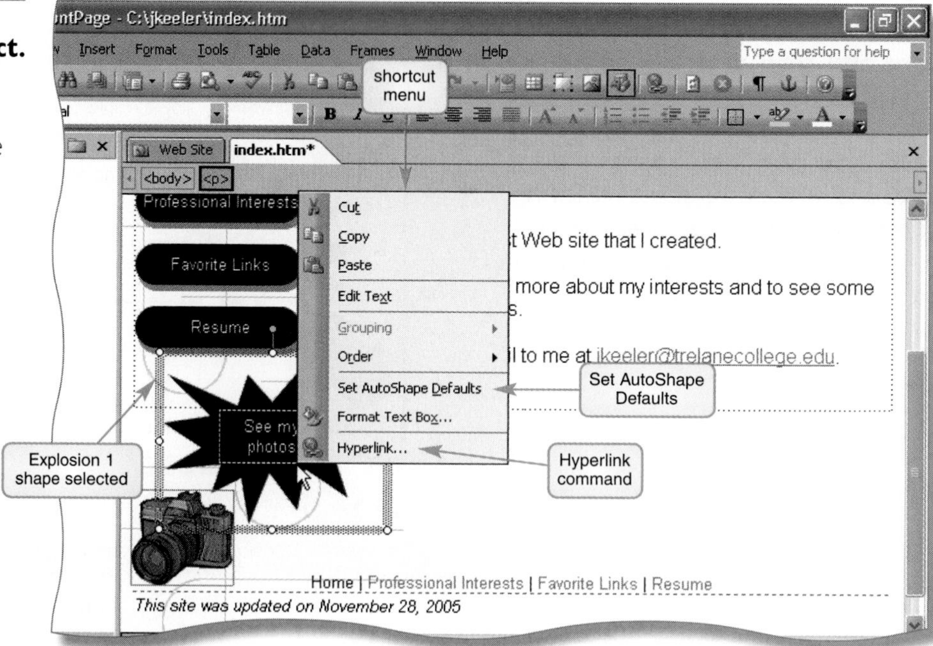

FIGURE 3-93

2

- **Click Hyperlink.**
- **If necessary, when the Insert Hyperlink dialog box appears, click the Existing File or Web Page button in the Link to bar.**
- **Select the file, photos, in the Web folder location (c:\jkeeler).**

3

- **Click the OK button.**
- **Click away from the shape to deselect it.**
- **Position the mouse pointer over the shape.**

FrontPage displays the new URL for the image hyperlink on the status bar (Figure 3-94). If the mouse pointer is positioned off of the shape, the URL does not appear.

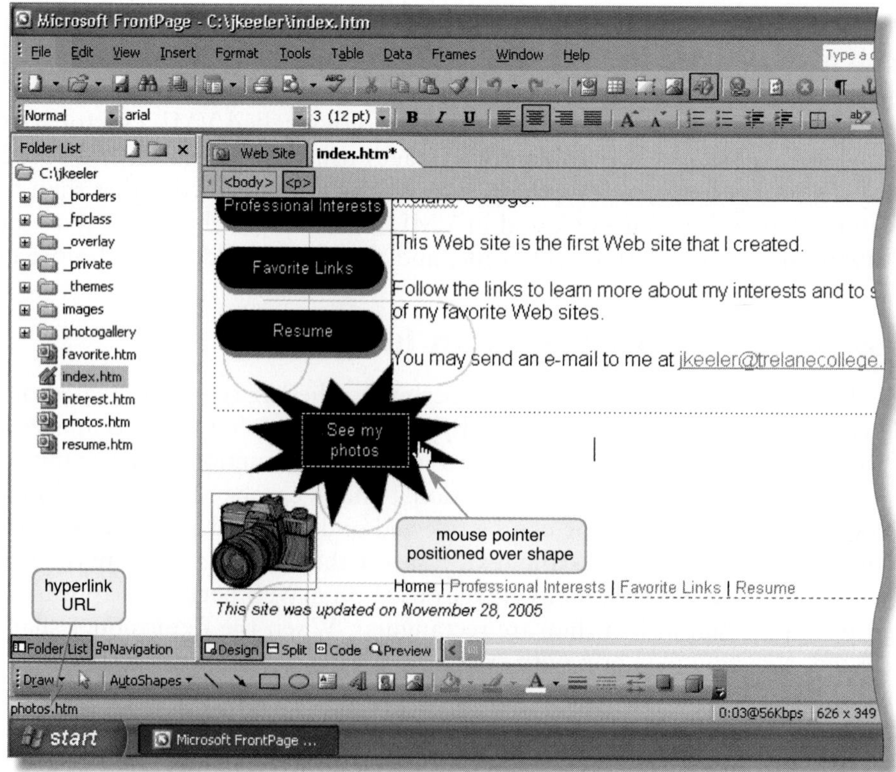

FIGURE 3-94

Adding a hyperlink to the camera image can be as simple as adding one to text. In such a case, any location within the rectangle encompassing the image will activate the hyperlink. To activate a hyperlink only from within the contours of the image, as was done with the AutoShape object, a hotspot must be defined first.

Image Maps

Rather than assign a hyperlink to an entire graphic, an image map may be used. An **image map** is a graphic image containing special areas called hotspots. A **hotspot** is a specially designated portion of the image that is set up as a hyperlink. Clicking a hotspot is the same as clicking a regular text hyperlink. The hotspot allows the Web page visitor to jump to the URL that is defined for that region of the image.

Image maps provide new ways to create interactive Web pages. They provide an alternative to plain text hyperlinks. They also allow the Web page designer to economize on images, because a single image can contain multiple hotspots and, thus, multiple hyperlinks. A well-designed image map gives the viewer clues about the destination of each hyperlink. For example, an art gallery might have an image containing a diagram of the various rooms in which different types of art are exhibited. Clicking a room displays another Web page containing images of related works of art. A college or university could have an image containing a map of the campus with hotspots defined for each building. Clicking a building would display another Web page describing the building.

When creating an image map, the use of a motif, or metaphor, for the images helps to guide the user. The image map typically replaces text hyperlinks and permits the user to navigate the Web site with less reading. For example, a campus map of different buildings might be used for obtaining navigation assistance. A bookshelf with books listing different topics might be used in a Help desk application.

When creating an image map, the use of a motif, or metaphor, for the images helps to guide the user. Consider image maps as a replacement for related text hyperlinks.

Defining Hotspots

To create an image map, the Web page designer first selects the image to use and then defines hotspots on the image. Finally, URLs are assigned to each hotspot.

Hotspots can be circles, rectangles, or irregularly shaped areas called polygons. Hotspots are designated using the hotspot buttons on the Pictures toolbar. For example, when the Rectangle button is clicked, the mouse pointer changes to a pencil pointer. To draw a rectangular hotspot, click and hold one corner of the desired rectangle, drag to the opposite corner, and then release the mouse button. The Insert Hyperlink dialog box automatically opens for specifying the target URL that will be assigned to the hotspot. Text can be added to an image and then hyperlinks created for the text, making it, in effect, a labeled rectangular hotspot. When adding hotspots other than as text, the Insert Hyperlink dialog box automatically appears. This is not true for text, because text may be added to an image without making it a hotspot.

The camera image only needs a single hotspot because it links only to the Photos page. Using an appropriate image, however, hotspots could be created to link to each page of interest in the Web site. The steps on the next page add a hotspot to the camera image.

More About

Image Map Hotspots

You can set a default hyperlink for any area on the image map that does not have a hotspot defined. Click the General tab in the Picture Properties dialog box.

To Add a Hotspot to an Image

1

- **If necessary, click the camera image to select it.**
- **If necessary, right-click anywhere on a toolbar and then click Pictures on the shortcut menu to display the Pictures toolbar.**

FrontPage displays the Pictures toolbar and the camera picture is selected (Figure 3-95).

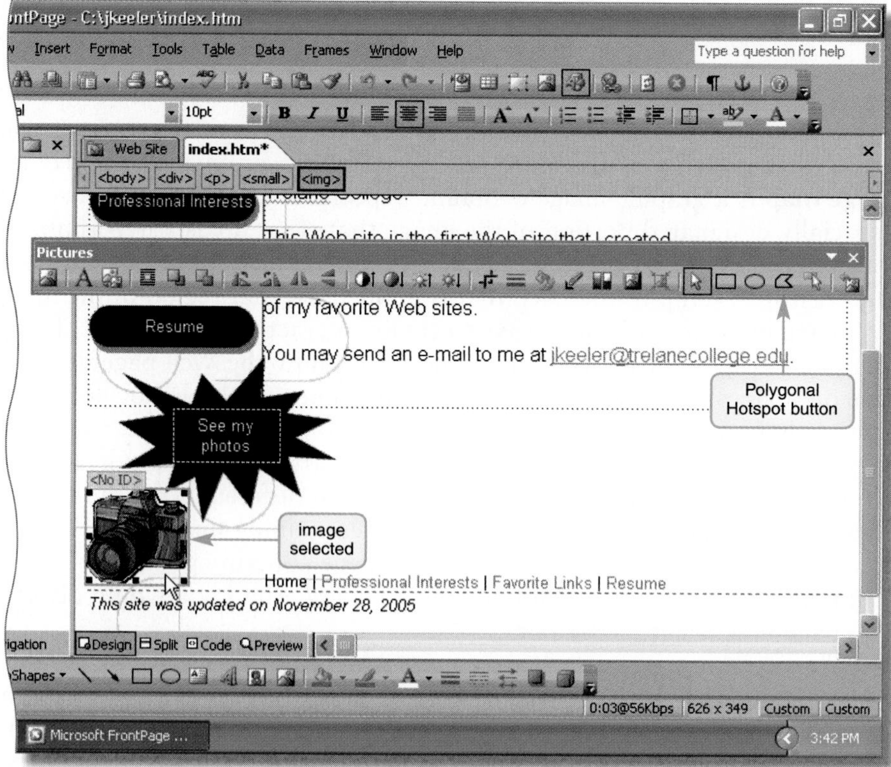

FIGURE 3-95

2

- **Click the Polygonal Hotspot button on the Pictures toolbar.**
- **Carefully draw around the perimeter of the camera image, using a single click to create a new edit point with each change of direction.**
- **When you have completed tracing around the perimeter, click the starting point to complete the hotspot.**
- **When FrontPage displays the Insert Hyperlink dialog box, click the file name, photos.**

FrontPage displays the Insert Hyperlink dialog box with the photos file selected (Figure 3-96).

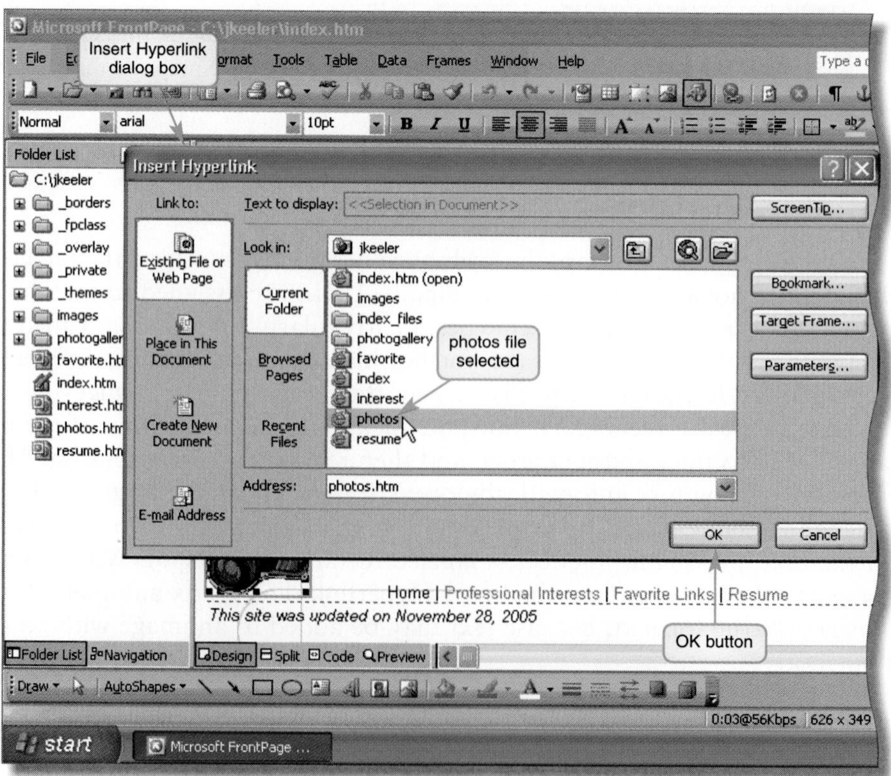

FIGURE 3-96

3

- **Click the OK button.**
- **Position the mouse pointer on the camera image.**

FrontPage displays the file name, photos.htm, on the status bar to indicate that the photos.htm file is the destination URL or the hyperlink (Figure 3-97).

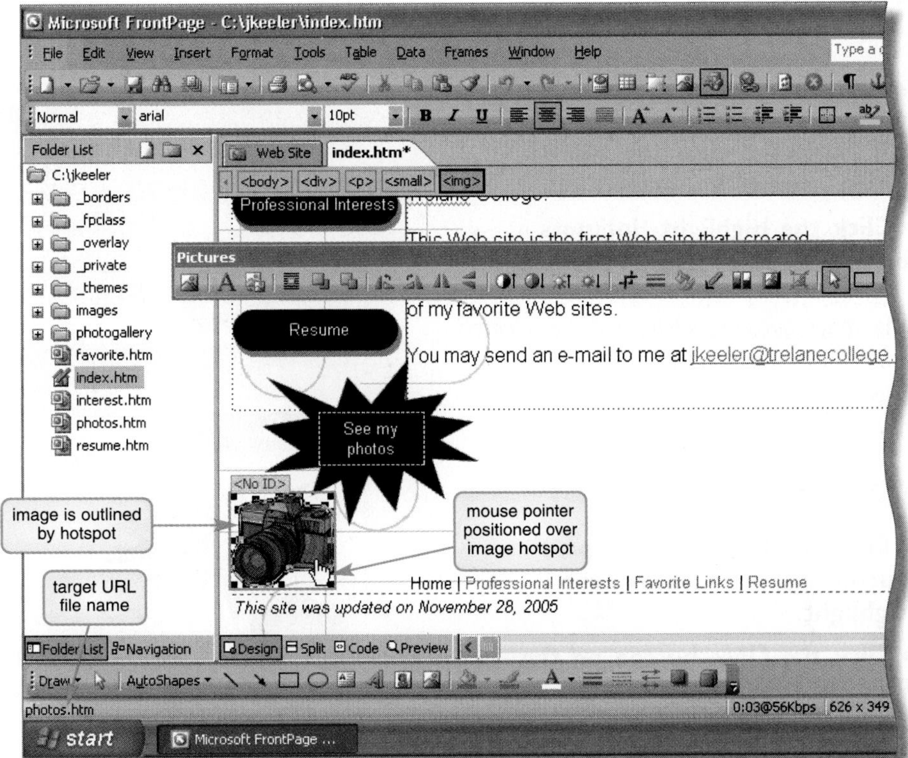

FIGURE 3-97

Other Ways

1. Click image, in Voice Command mode, say "Polygonal Hotspot"

The previous steps created a hotspot on an image map. Although this image contains only a single hotspot, it is an image map because the entire rectangular image was not used for the hyperlink. Image maps are an excellent way to present links visually in an intuitive and user-friendly fashion. Creating image maps is not hard to do, but requires some careful preparation.

Highlighting Image Map Hotspots

The hotspot on the camera image map is easy to find because there is only one and it has well-defined and intuitive boundaries. Some image maps do not have any text or image features associated with hotspots. Lines surrounding the hotspots are displayed when the image is selected. When multiple hotspots are used, or an image already has similar lines, the boundaries around each hotspot may be difficult to locate.

The Pictures toolbar includes the Highlight Hotspots button that toggles between displaying hotspots only and displaying the image and the hotspot. The steps on the next page highlight the hotspot on the camera image map.

More About

Highlighting Hotspots

When you highlight hotspots on an image, any hotspot currently not selected displays with a black outline. If a hotspot is selected, it displays as solid black.

To Highlight Hotspots on an Image Map

1

- **If necessary, click the camera image used as an image map.**
- **Click the Highlight Hotspots button on the Pictures toolbar.**

The image becomes white, and the selected hotspot is revealed as solid black (Figure 3-98). In this view, the hotspots readily are visible.

2

- **Click the Highlight Hotspots button again to remove the highlight.**
- **Click the Close button on the Pictures toolbar.**

FrontPage removes the highlight and closes the Pictures toolbar.

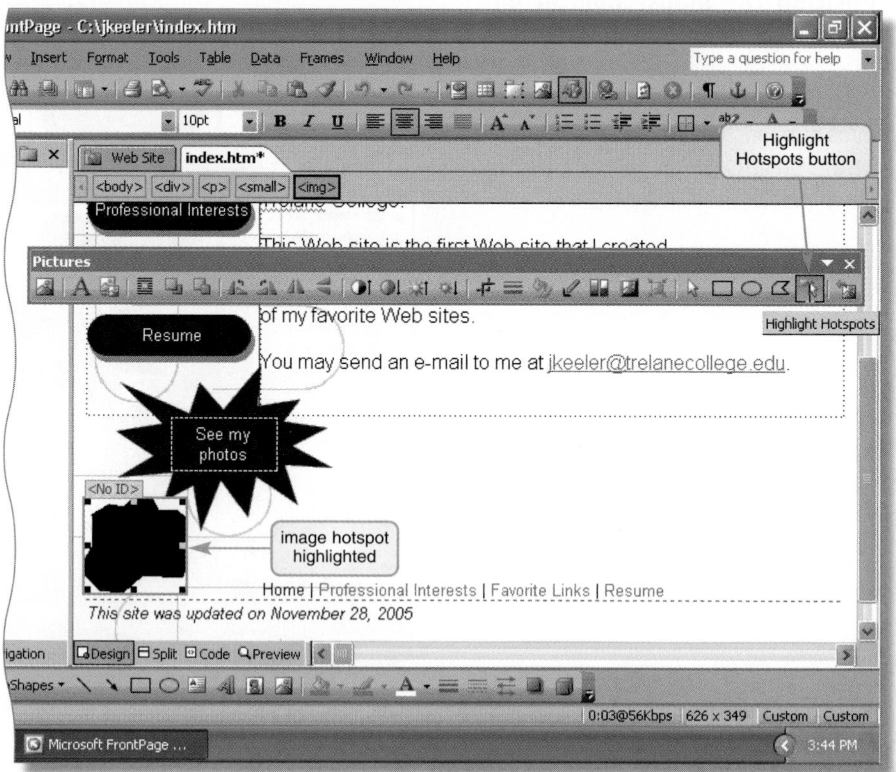

FIGURE 3-98

Other Ways

1. Click image, in Voice Command mode, say "Highlight Hotspot"

The Highlight Hotspots button is useful when image features make it difficult to see the hotspot outlines that are superimposed on the image.

More About

Hyperlinks View

If Hyperlinks view reveals a misspelled hyperlink in one of your Web pages, you can load the page in FrontPage by double-clicking the page icon in Hyperlinks view and then quickly correct the hyperlink.

Displaying the Hyperlinks in a FrontPage Web Site

In this and previous projects, links were created to other pages within a Web site, to Web sites not within the current Web site, and to an e-mail address. It is important to avoid having any of these hyperlinks point to nonexistent files. Hyperlinks that point to nonexistent files are referred to as **broken hyperlinks.**

Several reasons exist for encountering broken hyperlinks. The file that is the target of the hyperlink could have been deleted, renamed, moved to another folder, or moved to another Web server. The Web server on which the file resides could have had its Internet address changed, could be out of service for some period of time, or could be permanently out of service.

Avoid broken hyperlinks by testing the Web site before publishing the Web site, after publishing the Web site, and on a regular basis once the Web site is published.

Keeping track of broken hyperlinks in a small Web site such as James Keeler's is simple because it contains only a few hyperlinks. When developing very large Web sites, with many files and hyperlinks, however, it is very difficult to try to remember the pages that have hyperlinks, the targets where they link, and which hyperlinks are broken.

The Hyperlinks view in FrontPage alleviates this problem. For a given Web page, the Hyperlinks view displays in a graphical format the hyperlinks and their URLs, and indicates which hyperlinks are broken. The following steps display the Hyperlinks view and determine whether James Keeler's Web site has any broken hyperlinks.

To Display the Hyperlinks in a FrontPage Web Site

1

- **Make sure that you have saved all changes, saving the camera.gif file in the images folder when prompted to save the embedded image.**
- **If necessary, open the file index.htm in the Folder List pane.**

2

- **Click View on the menu bar and then click Hyperlinks.**
- **Click the plus sign on the interest.htm icon to display its links.**

FrontPage displays the Web site in Hyperlinks view (Figure 3-99). The plus sign on the interest.htm icon turns to a minus sign.

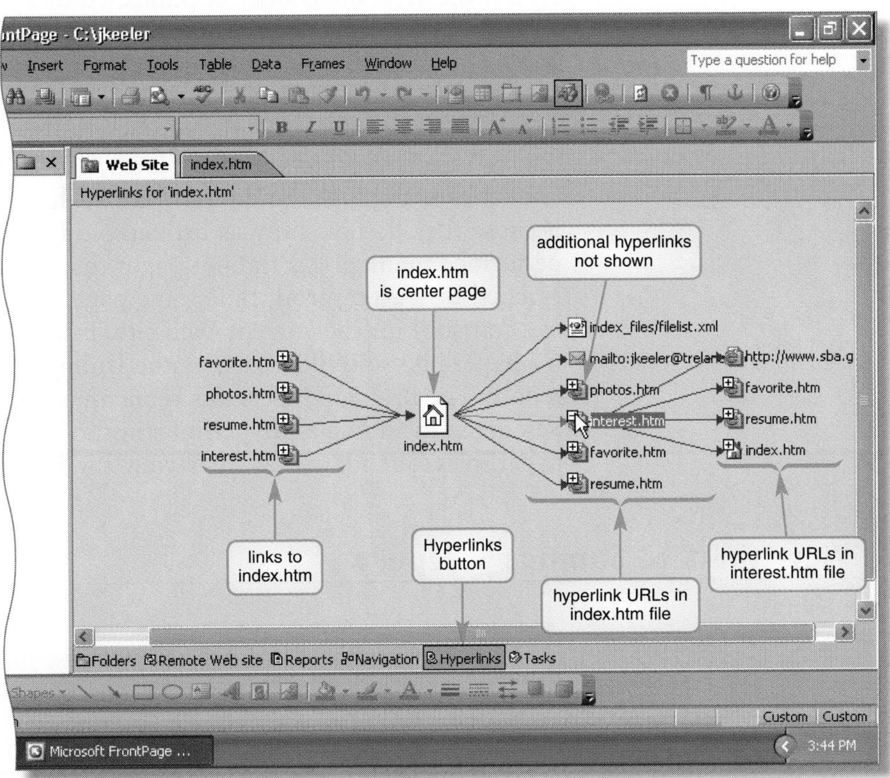

FIGURE 3-99

Other Ways

1. On View menu click Hyperlinks
2. Press ALT+V, H
3. In Voice Command mode, say "View, Hyperlinks"
4. In Voice Command mode, say "Hyperlinks"

The Hyperlinks view displays a graphical diagram of the hyperlinks in a center page. The **center page** is the page for which you want to see all hyperlinks, both to and from it, in the current FrontPage Web site. In this case it is the Home page, index.htm, which displays the hyperlinks shown in Figure 3-99. Hyperlinks exist from the Home page to the Photos page, the Professional Interests page, the Favorite Links page, and the Resume page, as well as a mailto: link. You also may see links to embedded script files or style sheets created by FrontPage. None of the hyperlinks is known to be broken. A broken hyperlink is displayed like any other hyperlink, except that it has as a broken line. A plus sign indicates additional hyperlinks that are not shown. You can view links on these pages by clicking the plus sign, as was done for the interest.htm file.

You can use Hyperlinks view to verify quickly which links, if any, are broken in the current FrontPage Web site.

Reporting on the Web Site

Even a relatively small Web site consists of many files and hyperlinks to possibly many more files, even to destinations outside of the Web site itself. Managing all of the pieces of a Web site can be a daunting task. FrontPage provides various reports to illustrate the status of the FrontPage Web site. FrontPage tracks many items in the Web site such as the number of picture files, broken hyperlinks, slow pages, recently added files, and so forth.

Viewing Reports on the Web Site

FrontPage provides a summary report on a variety of items such as uncompleted tasks and broken hyperlinks. FrontPage can generate many reports for a Web site, even if the Web site is not yet published to a server. The Web site must be opened on an appropriate server, however, to generate usage summary reports. Also, if you have made any changes to your Web pages, they should be saved before viewing reports or verifying hyperlinks.

Clicking through each file in Hyperlinks view to find broken hyperlinks displays only verified hyperlinks that are known to be broken. This can be a daunting and time-consuming task. Finding unverified hyperlinks could be even more difficult because they do not show as broken in Hyperlinks view. Another difficult task, if performed manually, is finding pages that no longer are linked and cannot be reached by starting from the Home page. The Site Summary report summarizes various statistics for the current Web site. From this report, you also can access reports for hyperlinks and files, such as the Unlinked Files report and the Broken Hyperlinks report. The Broken Hyperlinks report has multiple views available from the Site Summary, including all hyperlinks in the Web site, broken hyperlinks, and unverified hyperlinks. The following steps view the FrontPage Site Summary report.

To View the Site Summary Report

1

• **Click View on the menu bar and then point to Reports.**

FrontPage displays the View menu and Reports submenu (Figure 3-100). The selected check mark to the left of the Site Summary command on the Reports submenu indicates the report that currently is visible when in Reports view.

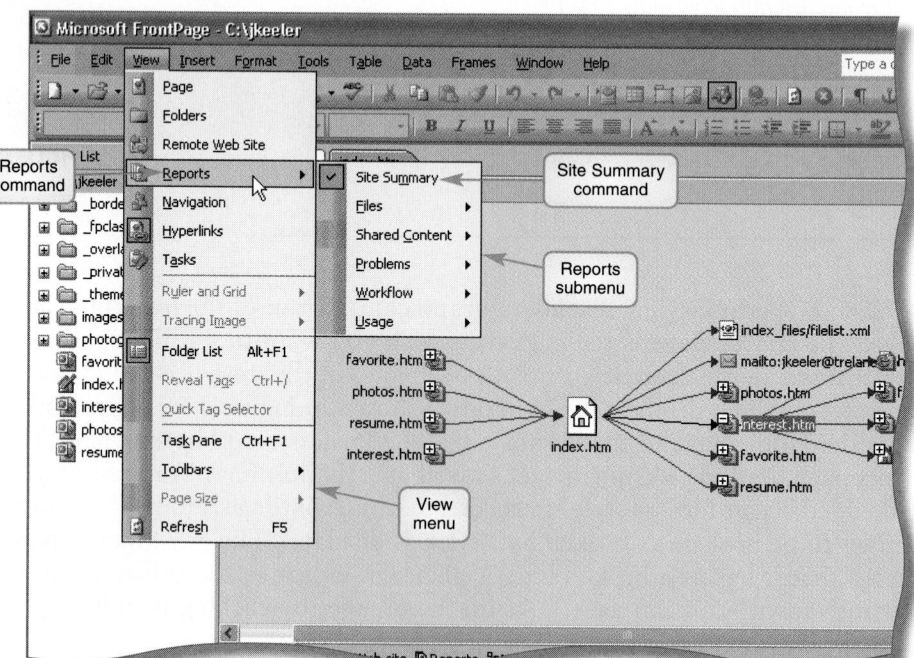

FIGURE 3-100

• **Click Site Summary.**

The FrontPage window switches to Reports view and the Site Summary report is displayed (Figure 3-101).

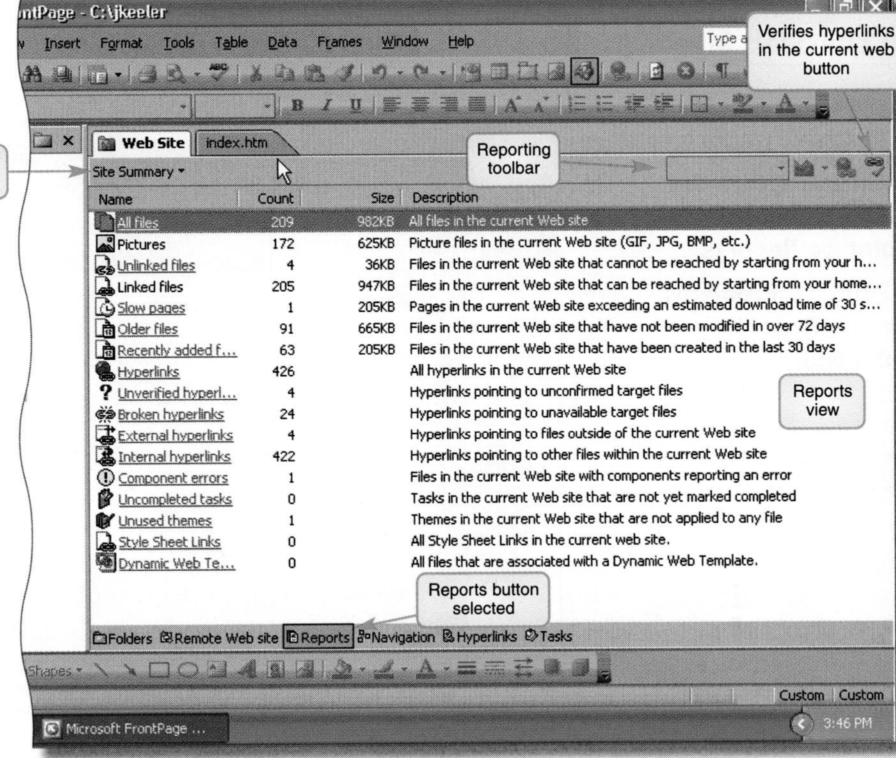

FIGURE 3-101

Other Ways

1. Click Reports on Reporting toolbar, click Site Summary
2. Press ALT+V, R, M
3. In Voice Command mode, say "View, Reports, Site Summary"

Verifying Hyperlinks

Just verifying that all hyperlinks in a Web site are correct is a critical and possibly time-consuming task. FrontPage provides a means of verifying that the hyperlinks to external destinations (destinations that are outside of the Web site) are valid.

Hyperlinks can be verified by using the Reporting toolbar. You need to be connected to the World Wide Web to verify external hyperlinks. The steps on the next page use the Reporting toolbar to verify hyperlinks in the Web site.

More About

Verifying Hyperlinks

Be aware that if you choose to verify the status of all the hyperlinks in the current Web site, it could take a significant length of time. FrontPage not only will verify hyperlinks to Web pages and bookmarks in the current Web site, but also will search the World Wide Web to make sure the other hyperlink targets specified in your current Web site exist.

To Use the Reporting Toolbar to Verify Hyperlinks in the Web Site

1

- **Click View on the menu bar and then point to Reports.**
- **Point to Problems on the Reports submenu.**

FrontPage displays the Problems submenu (Figure 3-102).

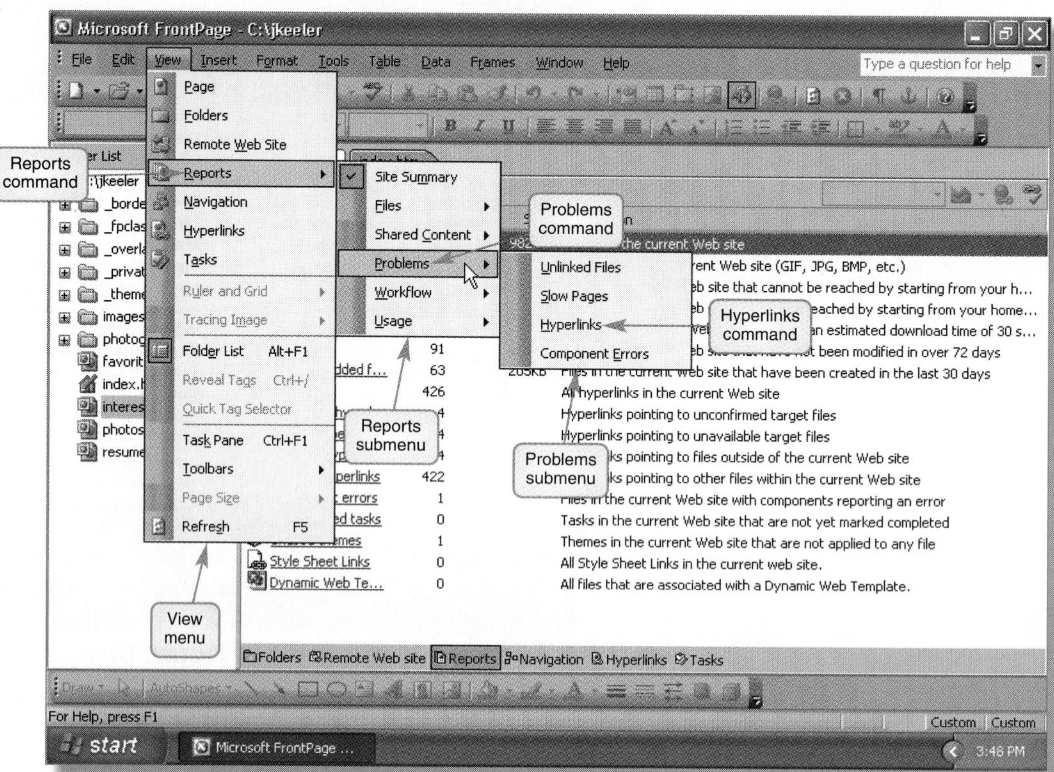

FIGURE 3-102

2

- **Click Hyperlinks.**

FrontPage displays the Reports View dialog box and the displayed report changes to the Hyperlinks report (Figure 3-103).

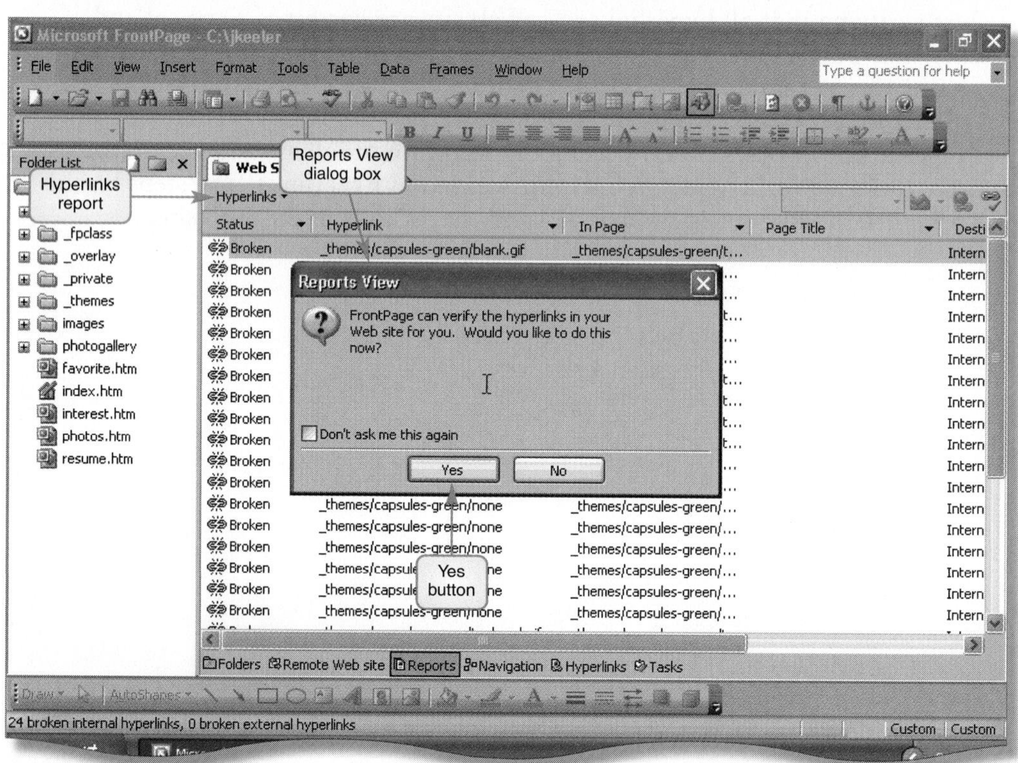

FIGURE 3-103

3

- **Click the Yes button.**

FrontPage verifies the hyperlinks and displays individual hyperlink results in the Broken Hyperlinks report (Figure 3-104). A count of broken internal and external hyperlinks is displayed on the status bar. Several of the hyperlinks in the new Capsules Green theme are broken, but the problems do not affect the Web site.

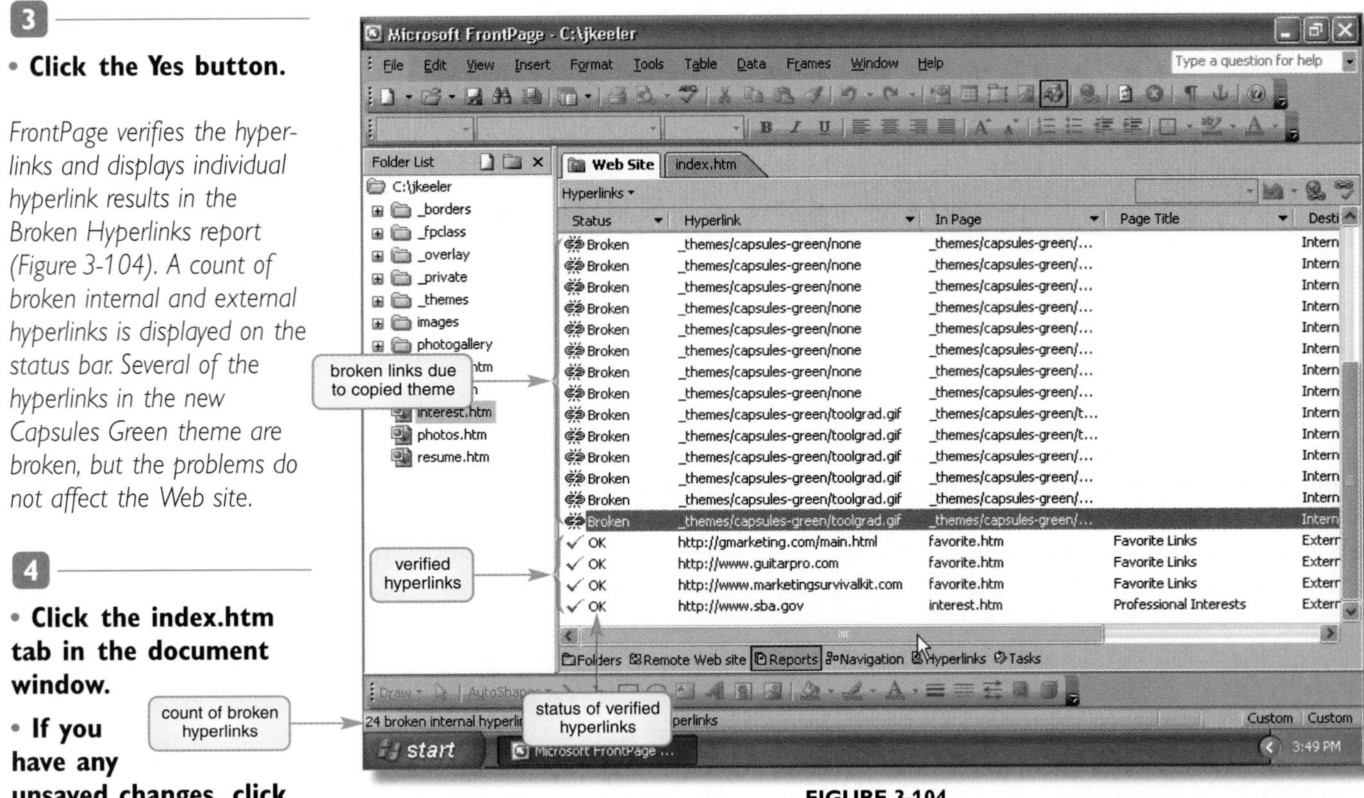

FIGURE 3-104

4

- **Click the index.htm tab in the document window.**
- **If you have any unsaved changes, click the Save button on the Standard toolbar.**

Other Ways

1. Press ALT+V, T, click Reporting
2. In Voice Command mode, say "View, Toolbars, Reporting"

After completing these modifications to the Web site, you should publish your changes. Remember, changes made locally do not appear to visitors to the Web site until those changes have been published.

To Publish Changes to an Existing FrontPage Web Site

1 **Click the Publish Web button on the Standard toolbar. Because this Web site was published previously, FrontPage does not display the Publish Destination dialog box, but assumes that you will publish to the same location.**

2 **If necessary, type your user name and password. Click the OK button.**

You now can view the changes by entering http://www.trelanecollege.edu/~jkeeler/index.htm (use your own URL) in any browser and pressing the ENTER key. Be sure to test the hyperlinks to the Photos and Resume pages and from those pages to the Home page.

More About

Quick Reference

For more information, see the Quick Reference Summary at the back of this book, or visit the FrontPage 2003 Quick Reference Web page (scsite.com/fp2003/qr).

Quitting Microsoft FrontPage

When you have published James Keeler's Web site, you can close the Web site and quit Microsoft FrontPage 2003. The steps on the next page close the Web site and quit FrontPage.

To Close a Web Site and Quit FrontPage

1. **Click File on the menu bar and then click Close Site.**
2. **Click the Close button on the right side of the FrontPage title bar.**

The FrontPage window closes and the Windows desktop is displayed.

Project Summary

Previously, you learned about essential Web page development. In Project 3, you learned how to customize your Web pages. You customized a theme, saved it for later reuse, and applied it to a single Web page. You learned about image file formats and customized images by creating a transparent image and resampling an image to change its file size. You created an image map and assigned a target URL to the hotspot. You copied text from a Word document and pasted it into a Web page. You inserted bookmarks in a Web page for easier navigation. You learned how to display the status of the hyperlinks used in the Web pages of the current FrontPage Web site. Finally, you learned how to use FrontPage reporting features and how to verify hyperlinks.

What You Should Know

Having completed this project, you should be able to perform the tasks below. The tasks are listed in the same order they were presented in this project. For a list of the buttons, menus, toolbars, and commands introduced in this project, see the Quick Reference Summary at the back of this book and refer to the Page Number column.

1. Open an Existing Page in a FrontPage Web Site (FP 158)
2. Create and Apply a Customized Theme (FP 159)
3. Change the Style of a Link Bar (FP 164)
4. Add a Row to a Table (FP 166)
5. Add a Hit Counter (FP 167)
6. Enable Shared Borders (FP 170)
7. Add a Shared Border (FP 172)
8. Add a New Page in Page View (FP 177)
9. Add a Link Bar Component (FP 177)
10. Modify the Navigation Structure (FP 178)
11. Use a Custom Background Color for a Table (FP 182)
12. Copy and Paste from a Word Document (FP 188)
13. Bookmark a Location in a Web Page (FP 191)
14. Bookmark Text in a Web Page (FP 193)
15. Create a Hyperlink to a Bookmark (FP 194)
16. Create Back Hyperlinks (FP 197)
17. Insert an Image and Display the Pictures Toolbar (FP 199)
18. Create a Transparent Image (FP 202)
19. Resize and Resample an Image (FP 204)
20. Use Absolute Positioning with an Image (FP 205)
21. Add an AutoShapes Object (FP 207)
22. Add a Hyperlink to an AutoShapes Object (FP 212)
23. Add a Hotspot to an Image (FP 214)
24. Highlight Hotspots on an Image Map (FP 216)
25. Display the Hyperlinks in a FrontPage Web Site (FP 217)
26. View the Site Summary Report (FP 218)
27. Use the Reporting Toolbar to Verify Hyperlinks in the Web Site (FP 220)
28. Publish Changes to an Existing FrontPage Web Site (FP 221)
29. Close a Web Site and Quit FrontPage (FP 222)

Learn It Online

Instructions: To complete the Learn It Online exercises, start your browser, click the Address bar, and then enter the Web address scsite.com/fp2003/learn. When the FrontPage 2003 Learn It Online page is displayed, follow the instructions in the exercises below. Each exercise has instructions for printing your results, either for your own records or for submission to your instructor.

1 Project Reinforcement TF, MC, and SA

Below FrontPage Project 3, click the Project Reinforcement link. Print the quiz by clicking Print on the File menu for each page. Answer each question.

2 Flash Cards

Below FrontPage Project 3, click the Flash Cards link and read the instructions. Type 20 (or a number specified by your instructor) in the Number of playing cards text box, type your name in the Enter your Name text box, and then click the Flip Card button. When the flash card is displayed, read the question and then click the ANSWER box arrow to select an answer. Flip through Flash Cards. If your score is 15 (75%) correct or greater, click Print on the File menu to print your results. If your score is less than 15 (75%) correct, then redo this exercise by clicking the Replay button.

3 Practice Test

Below FrontPage Project 3, click the Practice Test link. Answer each question, enter your first and last name at the bottom of the page, and then click the Grade Test button. When the graded practice test is displayed on your screen, click Print on the File menu to print a hard copy. Continue to take practice tests until you score 80% or better.

4 Who Wants To Be a Computer Genius?

Below FrontPage Project 3, click the Computer Genius link. Read the instructions, enter your first and last name at the bottom of the page, and then click the PLAY button. When your score is displayed, click the PRINT RESULTS link to print a hard copy.

5 Wheel of Terms

Below FrontPage Project 3, click the Wheel of Terms link. Read the instructions, and then enter your first and last name and your school name. Click the PLAY button. When your score is displayed, right-click the score and then click Print on the shortcut menu to print a hard copy.

6 Crossword Puzzle Challenge

Below FrontPage Project 3, click the Crossword Puzzle Challenge link. Read the instructions, and then enter your first and last name. Click the SUBMIT button. Work the crossword puzzle. When you are finished, click the Submit button. When the crossword puzzle is redisplayed, click the Print Puzzle button to print a hard copy.

7 Tips and Tricks

Below FrontPage Project 3, click the Tips and Tricks link. Click a topic that pertains to Project 3. Right-click the information and then click Print on the shortcut menu. Construct a brief example of what the information relates to in FrontPage to confirm you understand how to use the tip or trick.

8 Newsgroups

Below FrontPage Project 3, click the Newsgroups link. Click a topic that pertains to Project 3. Print three comments.

9 Expanding Your Horizons

Below FrontPage Project 3, click the Expanding Your Horizons link. Click a topic that pertains to Project 3. Print the information. Construct a brief example of what the information relates to in FrontPage to confirm you understand the contents of the article.

10 Search Sleuth

Below FrontPage Project 3, click the Search Sleuth link. To search for a term that pertains to this project, select a term below the Project 3 title and then use the Google search engine at google.com (or any major search engine) to display and print two Web pages that present information on the term.

11 FrontPage Online Training

Below FrontPage Project 3, click the FrontPage Online Training link. When your browser displays the Microsoft Office Online Web page, click the FrontPage link. Click one of the FrontPage courses that covers one or more of the objectives listed at the beginning of the project on page FP 154. Print the first page of the course before stepping through it.

12 Office Marketplace

Below FrontPage Project 3, click the Office Marketplace link. When your browser displays the Microsoft Office Online Web page, click the Office Marketplace link. Click a topic that relates to FrontPage. Print the first page.

Apply Your Knowledge

1 Customizing a Web Page Using AutoShapes and Color

Instructions: Start FrontPage. Open the Ship-It-Here Web site that you modified in Project 2. If you did not complete this exercise for Project 2, see your instructor for a copy of the required files.

1. If necessary, double-click the file, index.htm, in the Folder List pane to display the Ship-It-Here Home page in Page view.
2. On the Format menu, click Theme. When the Theme task pane appears, select the current Web site default theme in the Select a theme list and then click Customize on the shortcut menu. When the Customize Theme dialog box is displayed, click the Colors button.
3. If necessary, when the second Customize Theme dialog box is displayed, click the Color Schemes tab and, if necessary, scroll down and click the color scheme for Eclipse. Verify that Vivid colors is selected. Click the OK button.
4. Verify that Vivid colors and Active graphics are selected in the Customize Theme dialog box. If necessary, click Background picture so that it does not contain a check mark. Click Save As and save the new theme as Custom Eclipse, or a name of your choice. Click OK. Click the OK button in the Customize Theme dialog box. Apply the theme to all pages in the Web site.
5. Click the AutoShapes button on the Drawing toolbar. Point to Stars and Banners, and then click 5-Point Star. Position the mouse pointer centered under the links bar. Drag the mouse pointer to the opposite corner to create a small star shape. Release the mouse button. Click the Fill Color button arrow on the Drawing toolbar. Click Green on the color palette. Create two additional stars to the left and to the right of the original, positioned a little lower than the original star image.
6. Click the AutoShapes button on the Drawing toolbar, point to Stars and Banners, and then click Curved Down Ribbon. Position the mouse pointer under the star images. Drag the mouse pointer to the opposite corner to create a ribbon banner shape. Release the mouse button.
7. Right-click the ribbon shape. Click Add Text on the shortcut menu. Click the Font Size button arrow on the Formatting toolbar and then select 2 (10 pt). Type `International!` in the text box on the shape. Drag through the text and then click the Font Color button arrow on the Drawing toolbar. Click White on the color palette. Click the Fill Color button arrow on the Drawing toolbar and then click Red.
8. Click the Text Box button on the Drawing toolbar. Position the mouse pointer under the ribbon image. Drag the mouse pointer to the opposite corner to create a text box and then release the mouse button. Using font size 2 (10 pt), type `We now ship to over 100 countries overnight with the lowest rates in the business.` in the text box. If necessary, drag the sizing handles so all of the text is visible. Drag through the text and then click the Font Color button arrow on the Drawing toolbar. Click Red on the color palette. Click the text box to select it. Click the Fill Color button arrow. Click No Fill.
9. In the upper-left corner of the Web page, click the delivery man image to select it. If the Pictures toolbar is not displayed, point to Toolbars on the View menu and then click Pictures on the Toolbars submenu. When the Pictures toolbar is displayed, click the Set Transparent Color button. Click the white area on the image to make it transparent.
10. Click the Preview tab to preview the Web page. When you have finished, click the Normal tab.
11. Print and save the Web page. When prompted to save the modified image, save it in the images folder, overwriting the previous version. Close the Web site and then close FrontPage. When viewed in a Web browser, the Web page appears as shown in Figure 3-105.

Apply Your Knowledge

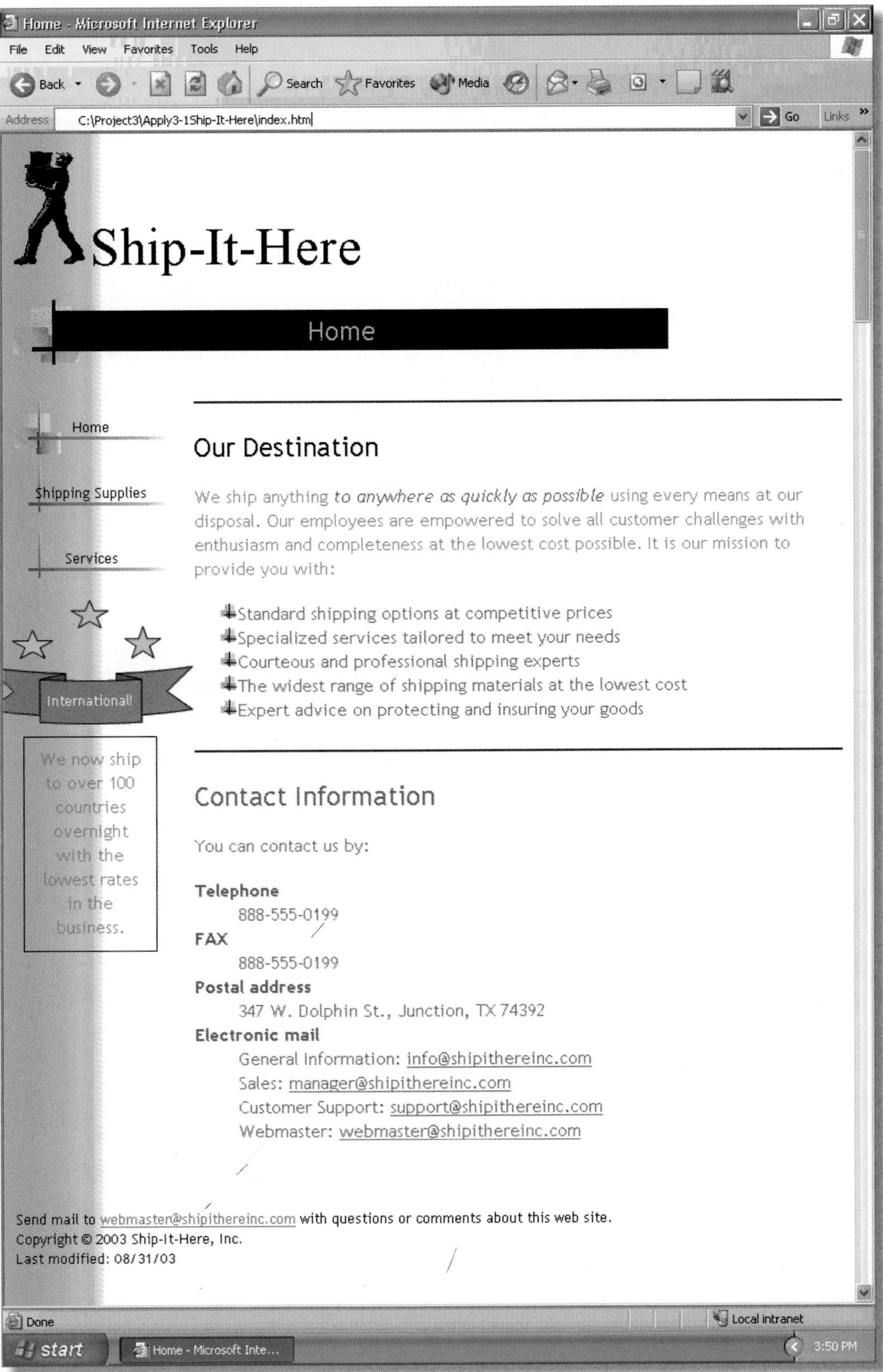

FIGURE 3-105

1 Adding Link Bars and Creating Bookmarks in a Table Copied from Word

Problem: The owner of Fairway Lawn Care wants to add a price list for various standard services. The list currently exists in a Word document. Because the list is rather long, you want to create hyperlinks that direct the visitor to the various sections of interest.

Instructions: Perform the following tasks.

1. Open the Lab2-2Fairway site that you modified in Project 2. If you did not complete that exercise for Project 2, see your instructor for a copy of the required files.
2. In Navigation view, add a new page under the Services page and then drag the new page icon to the left of the Home Mowing page icon. Right-click the New Page 1 icon and then click Rename on the shortcut menu. Type Price Sheet as the new page title. Double-click the Price Sheet icon to open the page in Page view. Rename the page as prices.htm in the Folder List pane.
3. Click the link bar on the left side of the page and press the DELETE key to delete the link bar. Click the line below the page title, click the Center button on the Formatting toolbar, and insert a link bar based on navigation structure. Use the page's theme as the link bar style and select a horizontal orientation for the bar. In the Link Bar Properties dialog box, select Back and next for hyperlinks. Select Home page and Parent page as additional pages. Click the OK button. If necessary, press the RIGHT ARROW key to deselect the link bar. Press the ENTER key.
4. Create a 2 by 3 table and, beginning with the upper-left cell, enter the hyperlink text from the first column in Table 3-5 into all the cells across the first row, and then the three columns of the second row. In the Table Properties dialog box, set the Alignment to Center, the border size to 0, and, if necessary, click Specify width so that it does not contain a check mark. Drag the table borders to prevent the text from wrapping. Position the insertion point after the table. On the Insert menu, click Horizontal Line.

Table 3-5 Hyperlink Text for Section Headings

HYPERLINK TEXT	SECTION HEADING
Mowing	MOWING
Shrub Trimming	SHRUB TRIMMING
Debris Removal	DEBRIS REMOVAL
Tree Trimming	TREE TRIMMING
Fertilizing	FERTILIZING
Leaf Cleanup	LEAF CLEANUP

5. Using Microsoft Word, open the file, prices.doc, on the Data Disk. See the inside back cover of this book for instructions for downloading the Data Disk or see your instructor for information on accessing the files required in this book. Click in the table and then click Table on the menu bar. Point to Select and then click Table on the Select submenu. Press CTRL+C to copy the table. Switch back to FrontPage. Position the insertion point under the horizontal line and then press CTRL+V to paste the copied table.
6. Click the page banner at the top of the page and then click the Center button on the Formatting toolbar.
7. Position the insertion point to the left of the horizontal link bar at the top of the page. Insert a bookmark. When the Bookmark dialog box is displayed, type `Top` in the Bookmark name text box. Click the OK button.
8. Select the section heading, MOWING, in the pasted table and insert a bookmark using the default name for the bookmark name. Select the text, Mowing, in the upper-left cell in the table above the horizontal line. Create a hyperlink to the MOWING bookmark. Repeat this process for each of the remaining section headings and the corresponding text in each cell of the top table as listed in Table 3-5.

In the Lab

9. Beginning with the second section heading, SHRUB TRIMMING, position the insertion point to the right of the bookmarked section heading. Insert a space, type `back to top`, and then insert spaces before this text to align it to the right side of the column. Select the text just inserted and insert a hyperlink to the Top bookmark. Copy and paste this hyperlink after each subsequent section heading, inserting spaces as needed to align the hyperlink to the right of the column.
10. Save the changes to this page. Preview the changes in your browser. Print the Web page, close the Web site, and then close FrontPage. The new Web page should be displayed in a browser as shown in Figure 3-106.

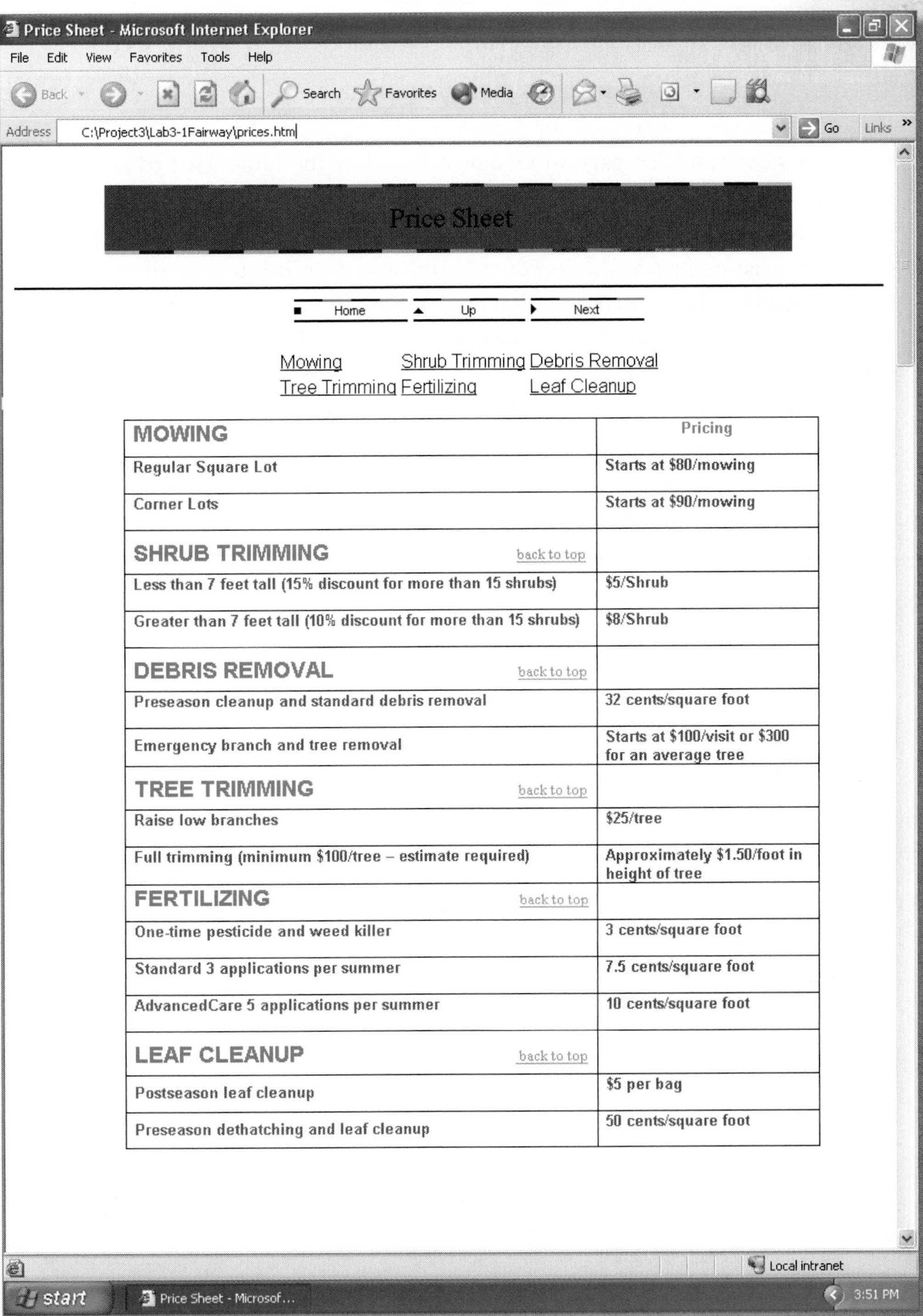

FIGURE 3-106

2 Expanding an Existing Table

Problem: Earlier, you added a Web page about running gear to your personal Web site; however, that page had none of the items common on the other pages, such as navigation links or the date last updated. You decide to add these items to your running gear Web page.

Instructions: Perform the following tasks.

1. Open the Web site Lab2-2Running that you modified in Project 2. If you did not complete that exercise for Project 2, see your instructor for a copy of the required files.
2. Open the gear.htm Web page in Design view. Click the table used to position elements on the page. Add a new row at the top and a new column at the left of the table. Merge the four rightmost cells in the top row just added. Merge the cells in rows two through five in the left column just added.
3. Click the page banner at the top of the page and drag it into the merged cells in the top row of the table. Delete the blank line remaining above the table.
4. In the merged cells of the left column, insert a vertical navigation bar with links to the Home page and children under Home. Adjust table cell widths as necessary and set the vertical alignment of the cell with the link bar to Top (see Figure 3-107).
5. Add a shared border for all pages at the bottom of the page. Type `This site was last updated on` in place of the comment component text and insert a Date and Time component for the date last updated. Edit the other pages in the Web site to remove similar information not in the shared border.
6. Save the changes to the Web pages. Print the running gear Web page, close the Web site, and then close FrontPage.

In the Lab

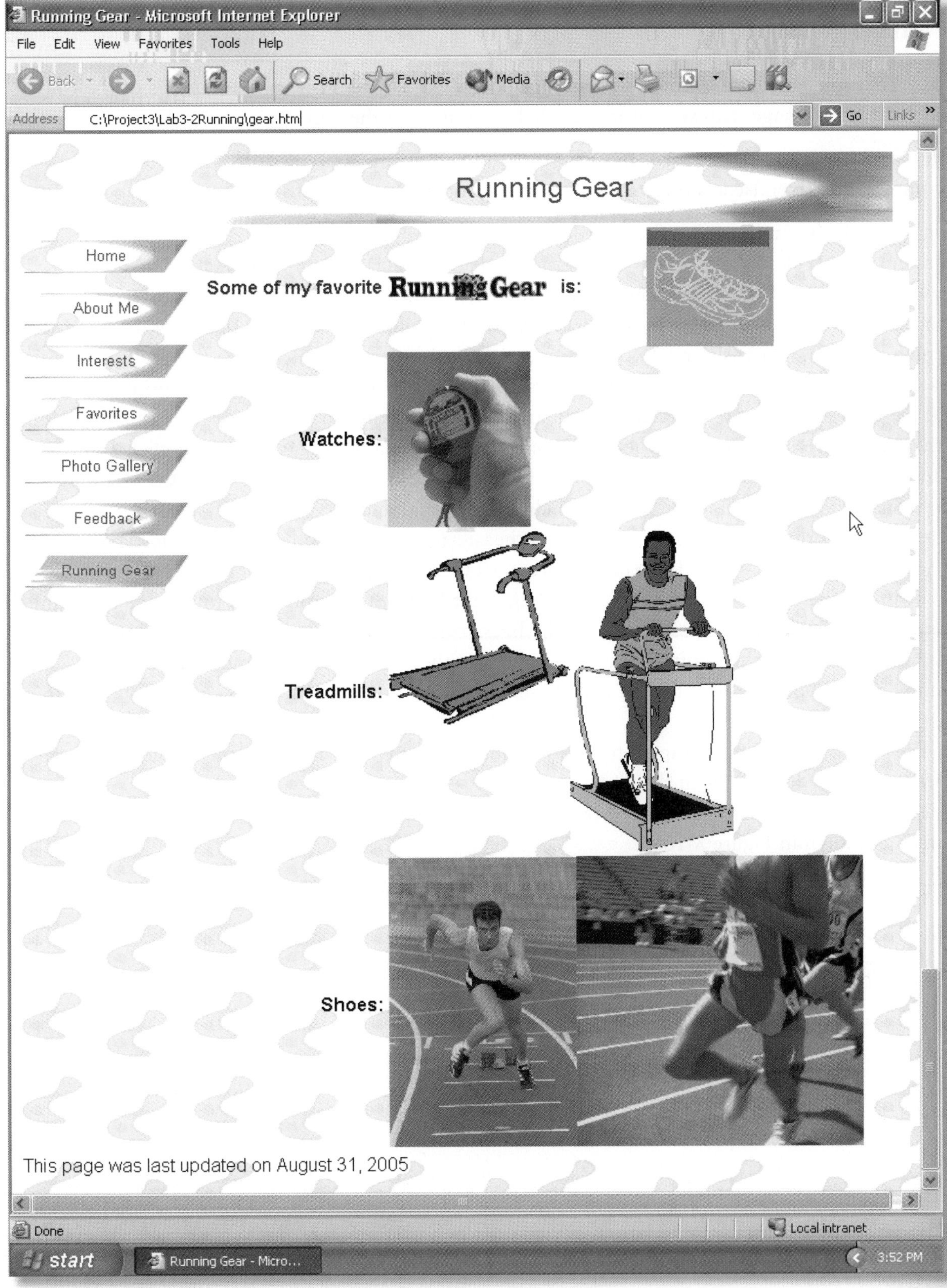

FIGURE 3-107

3 Creating an Image Map

Problem: The Whalen Metal support Web site includes links to pages for several regions of the United States. You decide to add an image map so visitors can click on a map of the regions.

Instructions: Using the support Web site that you modified in Project 2, perform the following tasks. If you did not complete this exercise in Project 2, see your instructor for a copy of the required files.

1. Open the Web site and position the insertion point after the link that reads, Zero-Defect. Press SHIFT+ENTER and then type `Click on a region to e-mail your regional support manager.`
2. Insert an image of a United States map using the file, USMap.gif, from the Project3 folder on the Data Disk, or another image as directed by your instructor. See the inside back cover of this book for instructions for downloading the Data Disk or see your instructor for information on accessing the files required in this book. Resize and move the image so that it fits appropriately on the Web page. Resample the image.
3. Click the map image, open the Pictures toolbar, and draw a polygonal hotspot approximately around the northeastern states. If necessary, when the Insert Hyperlink dialog box is displayed, click E-mail Address in the Link to area and type `dmartin@whalenmetals.com` as the e-mail address. Click the OK button.
4. Repeat Step 3 for the northwestern states, including Alaska, and type `smurrant@whalenmetals.com` as the e-mail address. Repeat Step 3 for the southeastern states, including Hawaii, and type `bbrown@whalenmetals.com` as the e-mail address. Click the Highlight Hotspots button on the Pictures toolbar to see the hotspot outlines. Click the Highlight Hotspots button again to remove the highlighting.
5. If necessary, click the image to select it. Set the background color as the transparent color for the image.
6. Add a shared border at the bottom of the page and apply it to all pages. Remove the comment component from the shared border. Move the name and e-mail information at the bottom of the page into the shared border.
7. Save the Web page. When prompted to save the image file, save the image in the images folder of the Web site. Verify all the hyperlinks in the Web site.
8. Preview the pages in your browser and then print the Web pages. The Web page should appear in your browser as shown in Figure 3-108.
9. Close your browser, close the Web site, and quit FrontPage.

In the Lab

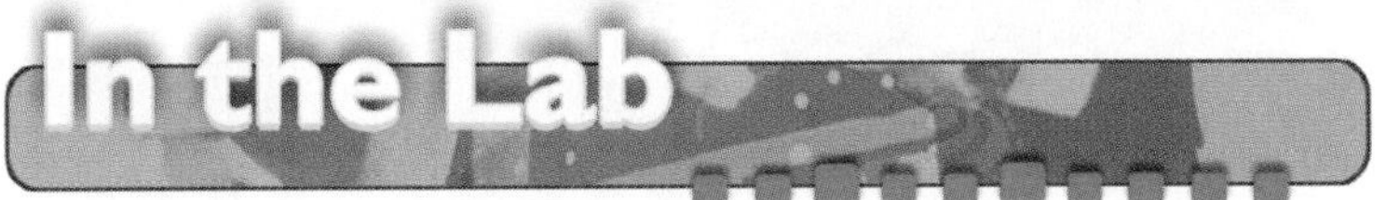

Whalen Metals - Microsoft Internet Explorer
File Edit View Favorites Tools Help
Back Search Favorites Media
Address C:\Project3\Lab3-3Whalen\index.htm
Go Links
Whalen Metals
Support Information
When you need help with your order or our products and services, contact one of our support specialists via e-mail, the Web, or telephone. We commit to getting you in touch with a live person for support within 30 minutes of your initial contact. Most issues are resolved within an hour.
Whalen Metals practices a zero-defect quality management program. We take your concerns seriously and invite our customers to participate in our monthly quality meetings that include senior company management, vendors, and customers. Take a look at our
Company Pictures
Whalen Metals
Information on our Quality Programs:
Six Sigma
The Deming Philosophy
Zero-Defect
Click on a region to e-mail your regional support manager.
ALASKA
Sanjay Gupta, Director of Support Services
Please e-mail questions and comments about our support and quality philosophy to sgupta@whalenmetals.com.
Done
Local intranet
start
Whalen Metals - Micr...
3:53 PM

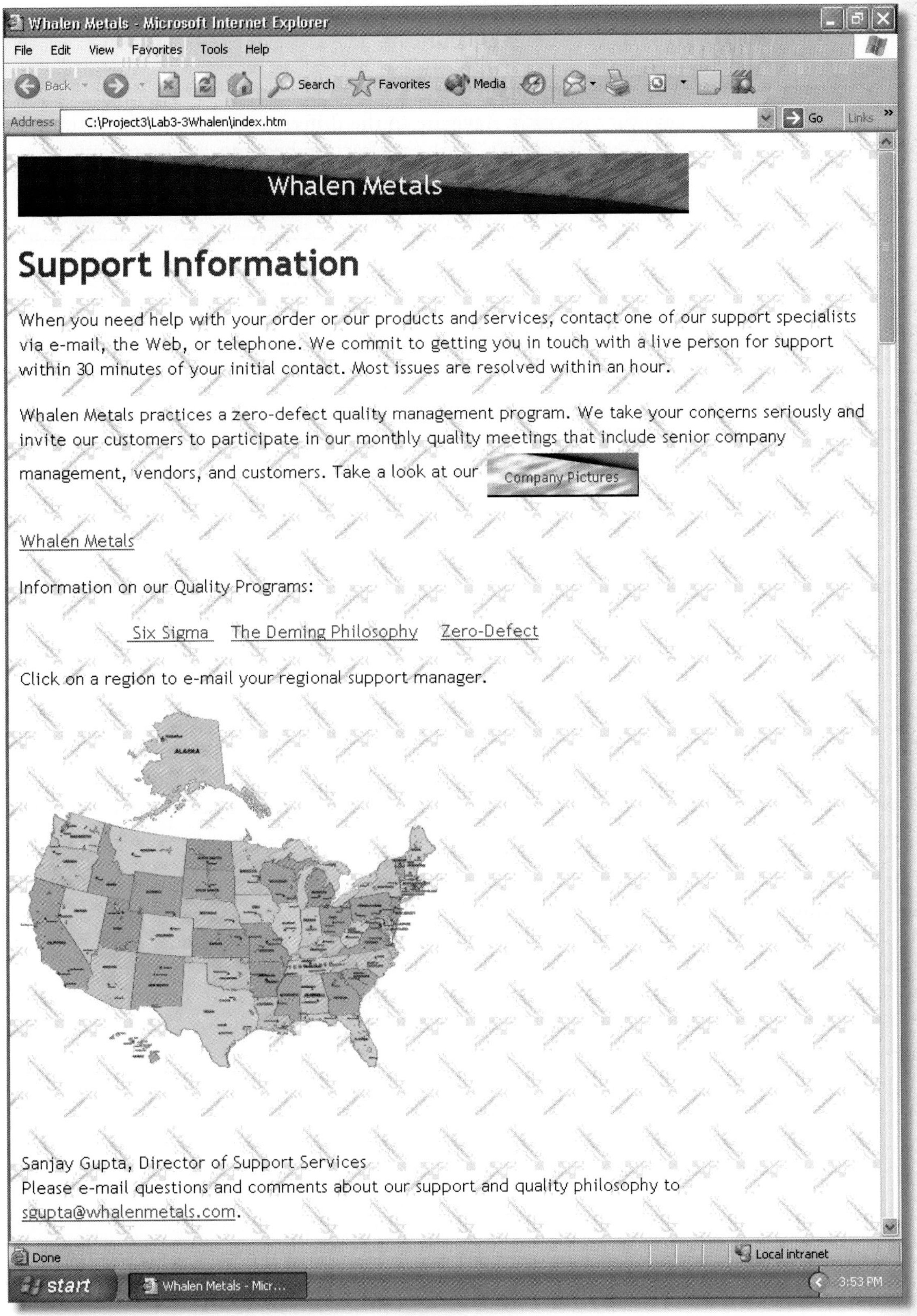

FIGURE 3-108

Cases and Places

The difficulty of these case studies varies:
■ are the least difficult and ■■ are more difficult. The last exercise is a group exercise.

1 ■ You want to make it easy for visitors to navigate to the different sections of the resume Web page that you created in Project 2. Create bookmarks for each section heading. Add a column to the left side of the table that contains the resume and then place hyperlinks in that column to each of the various bookmarked sections.

2 ■ Open the Web site that you created for your movie review Web page, and that you modified in Project 2. Add a shared bottom border for all pages and place in it your name, your e-mail address, and a date component for when the Web site was updated. Remove the portion of any Web page that already contains an e-mail address hyperlink.

3 ■■ Add a new page, titled Time Line, to the personal Web site that you created for your friend's graduation in Project 2. On the new page, draw a time line using AutoShapes, such as a rectangle, for each event of note, beginning with events listed on the History page. Use lines to connect each shape and use text and fill colors appropriately. Add a hyperlink from the rectangle for the first event (your friend starts school) to the Home page and make links for any other friends or events that have their own Web sites.

4 ■■ Modify the theme for the company softball Web page that you updated in Project 2. Search the Web for replacement graphics and modify the theme, replacing buttons, background picture, and bullets as needed. Add a marquee Web component to display announcements about upcoming games.

5 ■■ **Working Together** Develop a Web page that lists all of the instructors in your department at school. Include a brief description of the courses taught by each instructor under each instructor's name. Add bookmarks for each instructor, and at the top of the page, create links to each of the bookmarks. Check with the department for other enhancements, such as links to personal pages for each professor. Ask the department to supply you with any needed faculty photos and appropriate graphics.

MICROSOFT Office FrontPage 2003

Creating a Stand-Alone Web Page Using a Layout Table

CASE PERSPECTIVE

As James Keeler approaches his graduation, he plans to relinquish his extracurricular leadership positions to others. As president of the Future Entrepreneurs Honor Society, he must find a willing replacement to lead the club. James has decided to create a Web page that lists the requirements and duties for the president of the club. He has asked that you develop this page for him and provides you with a Word document that contains the content for the Web page.

The Webmaster for the school's extracurricular activities Web site provided the following guidelines. He wants only a single Web page that can be linked from one of the existing activities Web pages, and he has indicated that the design need not correspond to any of the templates included with FrontPage.

The design includes pages in which the content is surrounded by a thin border and is over a yellow background. Additionally, the borders have rounded corners and include a shadow outside the right and bottom border.

With your knowledge of FrontPage, you know that you quickly can create a Web page that meets the requirements of the design using layout tables and cells.

As you read through this Table feature, you will learn how to use layout tables to format a Web page. You will learn how to modify a layout table's structure to meet your needs. You will learn how to modify layout cells within a layout table and create effects such as shadowing and rounded corners.

Objectives

You will have mastered the material in this project when you can:

- Create a stand-alone Web page
- Use a layout table to design a Web page
- Format layout cells in a layout table with rounded corners, shadows, and borders

Introduction

Tables created using the Insert Table button on the Standard toolbar are useful for creating Web pages that are simple in format or contain tabular data. Templates provide another way to lay out the contents of a Web page. **Layout tables** provide a third method for creating the overall framework of a Web page's layout. Layout tables consist of layout cells arranged in rows and columns. **Layout cells** are the regions in the framework that include the content, such as text, images, or other elements.

Layout tables provide exact control over the location of content on Web pages. The use of layout tables provides the ability to create Web pages that resemble the layout of a newspaper page. Headers, a body, columns, and footers can be laid out precisely before or after content on the page is added. Content includes titles, images, text, and Web components. Figure 1 on the next page shows that the Web page developed in this project includes content in a header and the body. Empty columns and rows of layout cells surround and separate the content in a specific manner. The content for the body of the Web page is provided in a Word document.

The layout cells containing the header and body include formatting such as a shadow, rounded corners, and a background color. A layout cell also can include a header and footer. The cells containing the title and body in Figure 1 include rounded corners, a shadow on the right and bottom of the second cell, and a background color. The layout cells that surround these cells do not include formatting and appear as empty space on the Web page, but in fact are a part of the formatting because they provide the positioning for the cells that include the content.

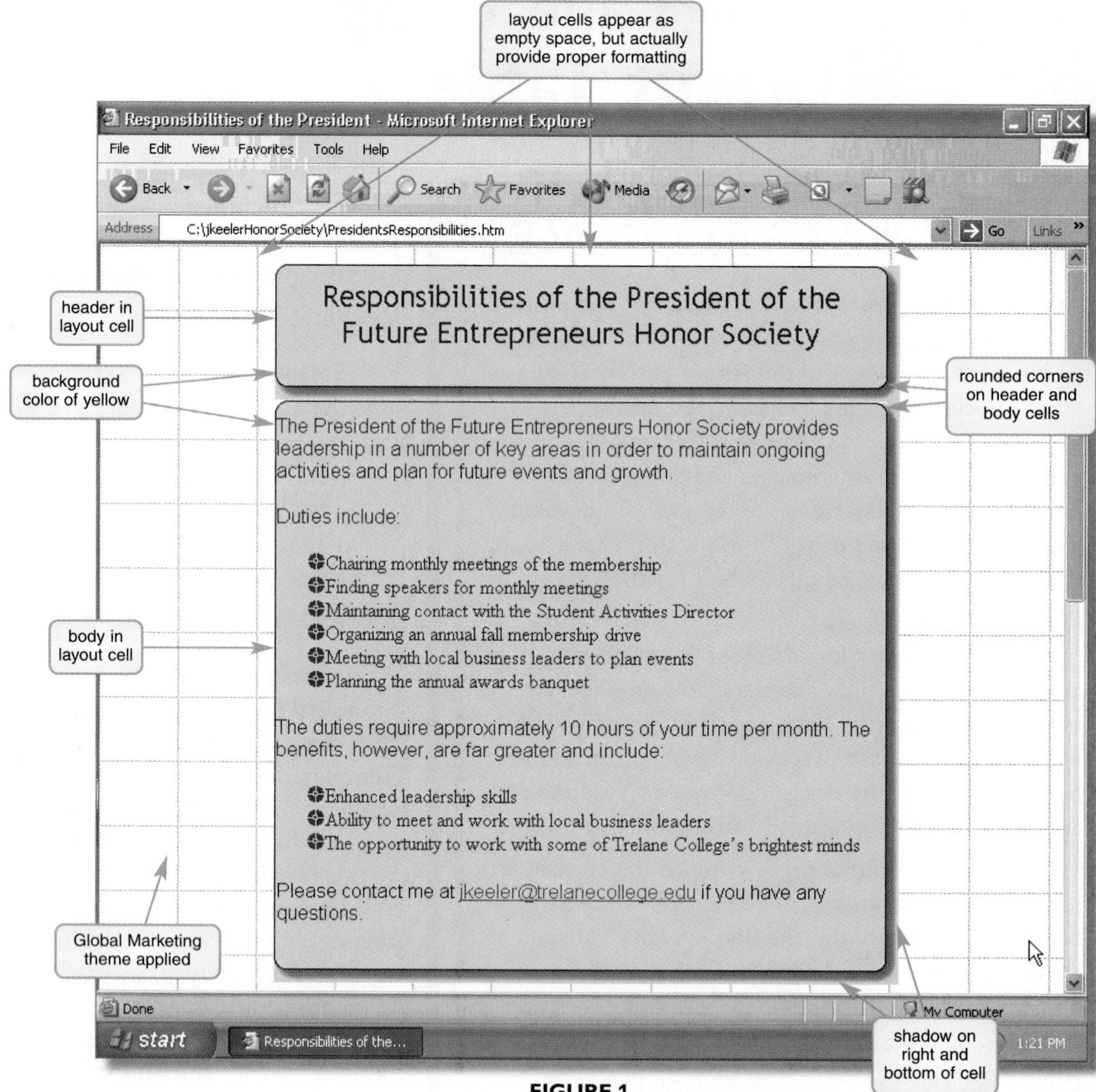

FIGURE 1

Creating a Web Page with a Layout Table

The previous projects in this book discussed the development of Web sites. FrontPage also provides for the development of individual Web pages that can be published as individual pages or incorporated into a Web site at a later time. The following steps start FrontPage and create a new Web page.

More About

Creating a New Web Page

Use the New command on the File menu to create a new page using the New task pane. The New task pane allows you to choose a template for the new page or to create a new page from an existing Web page.

To Start FrontPage and Create a New Web Page

1. **Click the Start button on the Windows taskbar, point to All Programs on the Start menu, and then point to Microsoft Office on the All Programs submenu.**
2. **Click Microsoft Office FrontPage 2003 on the Microsoft Office submenu.**
3. **If FrontPage has opened a previously opened Web site, click File on the menu bar and then click Close Site.**
4. **If a new Web page named new_page_1.htm is not displayed in Design view, click the Create a new normal page button on the Standard toolbar to create a new Web page.**
5. **If a task pane appears, click the Close button on the task pane.**

The FrontPage window is opened and an empty page is displayed. The Web Site tab is not displayed because only a Web page is opened in FrontPage.

Adding a Layout Table to a Web Page

FrontPage provides eleven predefined layout tables. When using a layout table, you select the layout table that most closely resembles the overall design of the Web page. A layout table may include a header, a footer, one or more columns, corners, and cells on the left or right of the layout table. Each area may contain content or be used simply to provide positioning of other elements of the Web page. After adding the predefined layout table to the Web page, FrontPage allows for the modification of the layout cells that compose the layout table. FrontPage also allows you to add additional layout cells, merge layout cells, or remove layout cells from the layout table.

The Web page developed in this feature, President's Responsibilities Web page, requires a header and a body. The Centered Header, and Centered Body layout table provides the necessary framework for the required content. The steps on the next page add a theme to the new_page_1.htm Web page and then add the Centered Header, and Centered Body layout table to the new_page_1.htm Web page.

Q&A

Q: Can I nest the layout table templates?

A: No. While standard tables can be nested, you can apply only one layout table template to a Web page. That is, you cannot embed a layout table template from the Layout Tables and Cells task pane within another layout table.

To Add a Layout Table to a Web Page

1

- **Click Format on the menu bar.**
- **Click Theme.**
- **When FrontPage displays the Theme task pane, scroll to Global Marketing in the Select a theme list.**

The Theme task pane is displayed (Figure 2).

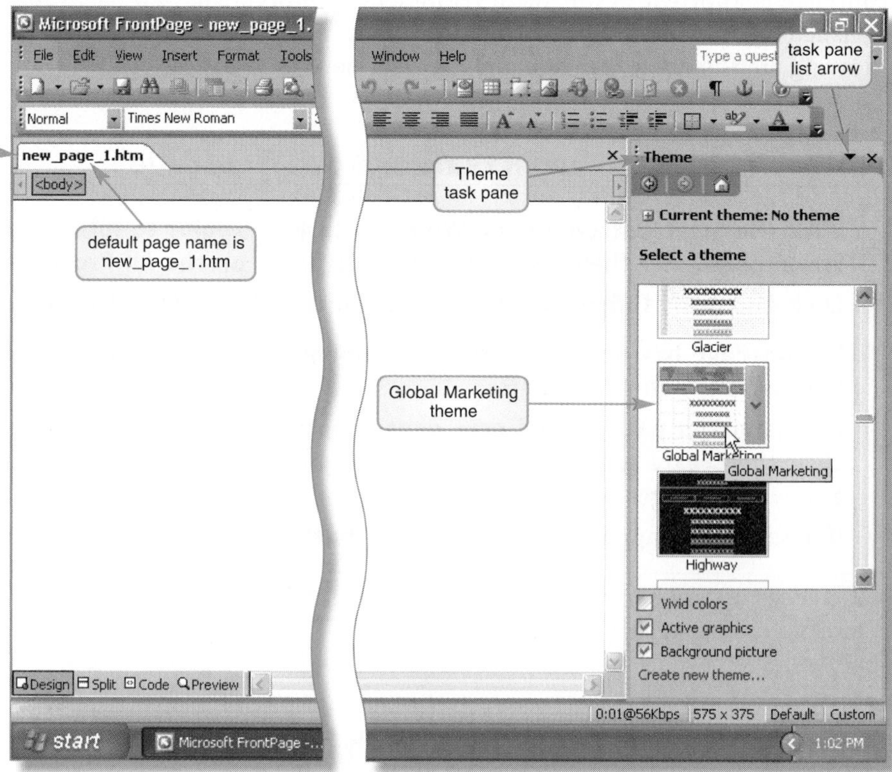

FIGURE 2

2

- **Click Global Marketing in the Select a theme list.**
- **Click the task pane list arrow.**

FrontPage applies the selected theme to the Web page and displays the task pane menu (Figure 3).

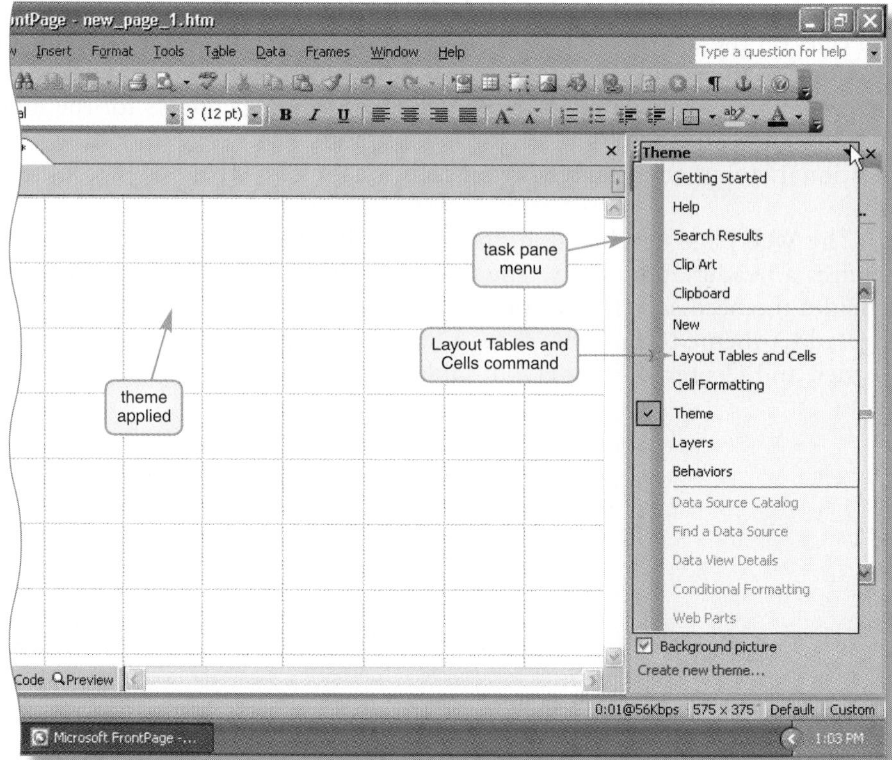

FIGURE 3

3

- **Click Layout Tables and Cells.**

FrontPage displays the Layout Tables and Cells task pane (Figure 4).

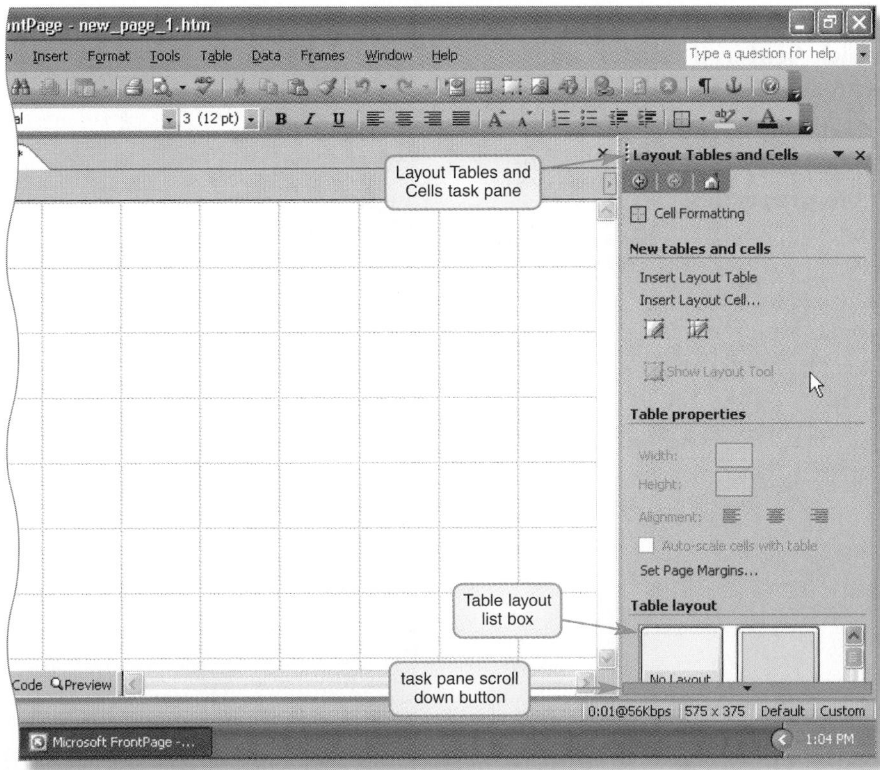

FIGURE 4

4

- **Click the task pane down scroll arrow to scroll through the task pane.**
- **Use the scroll bar on the Table layout list to scroll through the Table layout list until the Centered Header, and Centered Body table layout appears.**

FrontPage displays the lower portion of the Layout Tables and Cells task pane. The Centered Header, and Centered Body table layout appears in the Table layout list (Figure 5).

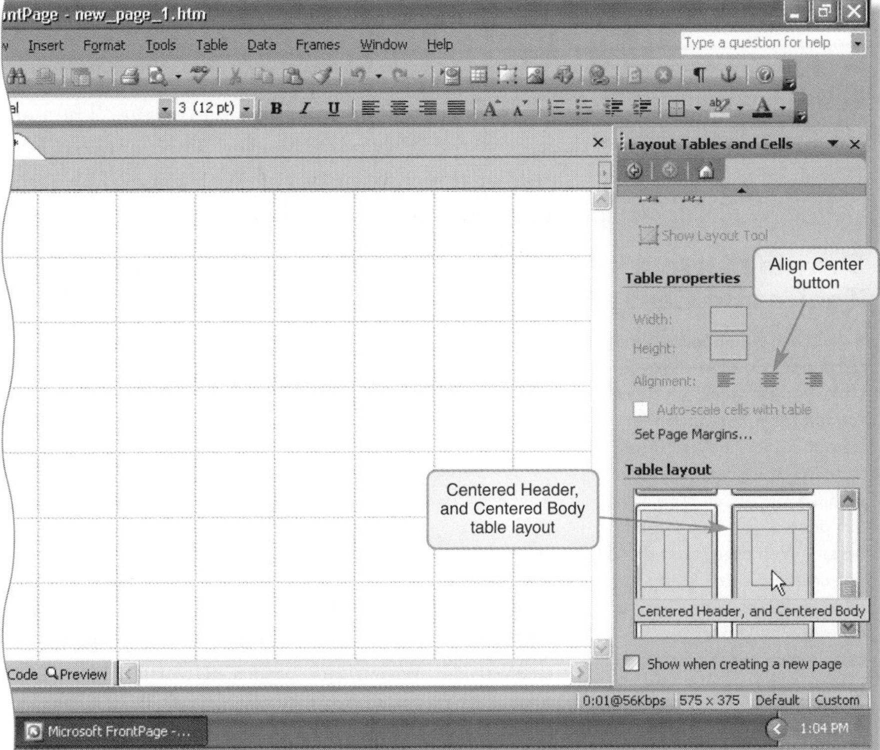

FIGURE 5

5

- **Click Centered Header, and Centered Body.**
- **Click the Align Center button in the Table properties area.**

FrontPage adds the layout table and layout cells to the Web page. Height and width labels appear in the layout cells (Figure 6). The table dimensions may vary depending on your screen resolution.

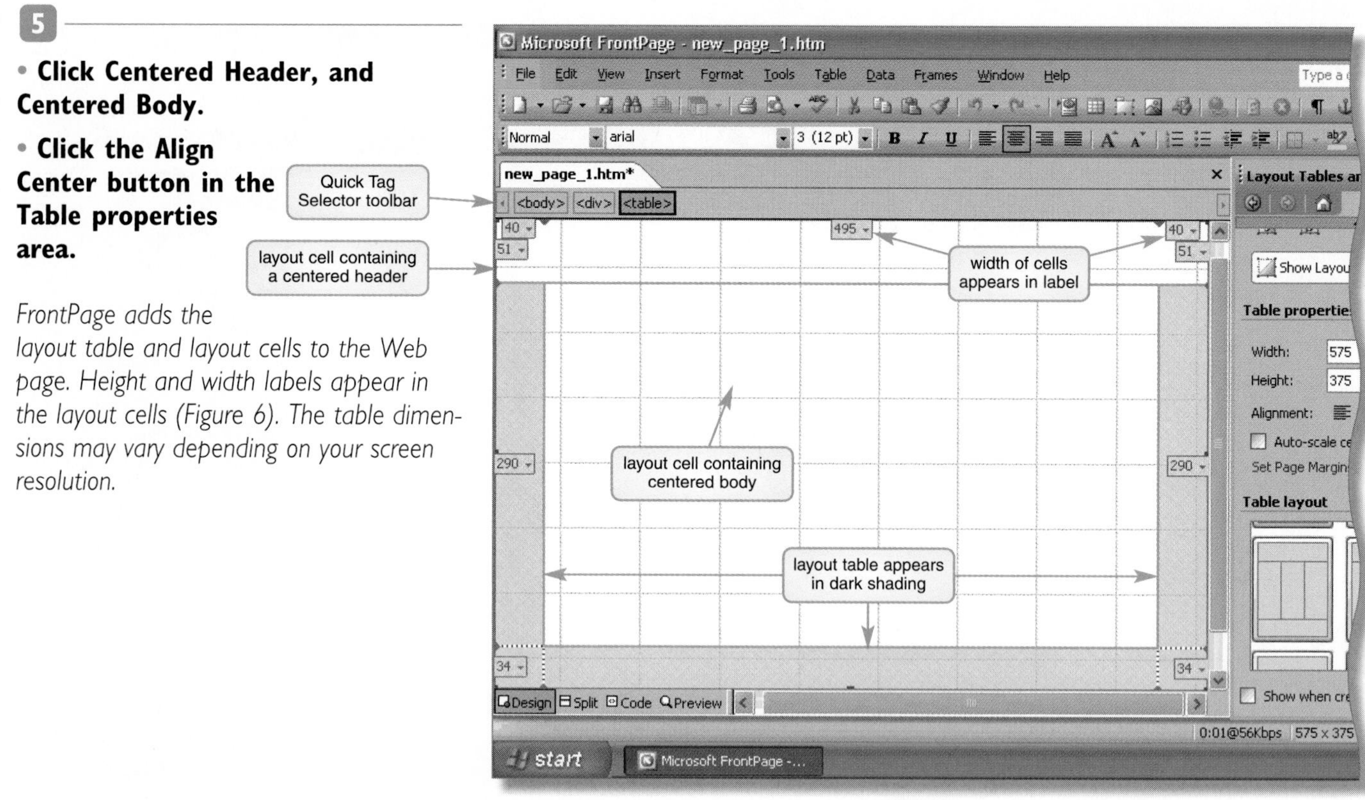

FIGURE 6

In Figure 6, the Design view indicates the areas, or layout cells, that should contain the content of the Web page. The centered header layout cell provides an area for a Web page header. The centered body layout cell provides an area for the rest of the content of the Web page. The remainder of the layout table appears as gray cells, indicating that content should not be added to these areas of the Web page. Each layout cell includes labels that indicate the height and width of the layout cell. Clicking the label displays a shortcut menu that allows you to modify the dimensions and behavior of the layout cell. The layout table's Alignment property is changed to center so that the entire layout table appears centered in the Web page visitor's browser no matter what the screen resolution or browser window size.

More About

Drawing Layout Tables and Cells

If you wish to embed a layout table within another layout table, you can click the Draw Layout Table button in the Layout Tables and Cells task pane and then draw the table within a layout cell. You also can draw a new layout table on any Web page, even those not created with a layout table template. Similarly, you can draw additional layout cells by clicking the Draw Layout Cell button in the Layout Tables and Cells task pane.

Formatting Layout Cells with Rounded Corners, Borders, and Shadows

Once a layout table is added to a page, you can customize the size and position of the layout cells. As you have learned, graphics and images provide a method for drawing a Web page user's attention to content and serve to provide a unified look and feel to the pages within a Web site. FrontPage also allows you to add graphic effects to layout cells. Layout cells may include a background color, rounded corners, a header, a footer, margins, borders, and shadows.

Resizing Layout Cells

In order to give the President's Responsibilities Web page a more balanced appearance, the centered header layout cell should be resized to match the width of the centered body layout cell. The following steps resize the centered header layout cell to match the width of the centered body layout cell.

To Resize a Layout Cell

1

- **In Design view, use the scroll bar to scroll the Web page to the top of the Web page.**
- **Click the centered header layout cell.**
- **Click the <td> tag selector in the Quick Tag Selector toolbar.**

FrontPage displays a bold border around the centered header layout cell. The <td> quick tag is selected in the Quick Tag Selector toolbar (Figure 7).

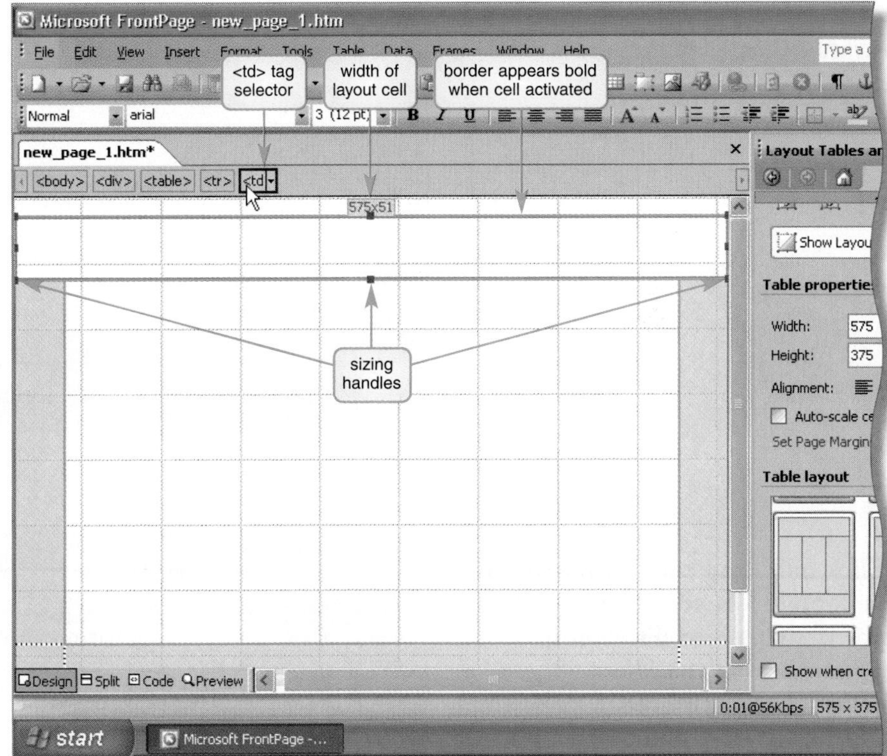

FIGURE 7

2

• **Position the mouse pointer over the left border of the centered header layout cell until the mouse pointer appears as the table repositioning pointer.**

The mouse pointer changes to a table repositioning pointer to indicate that the layout cell now can be modified by dragging the mouse pointer (Figure 8).

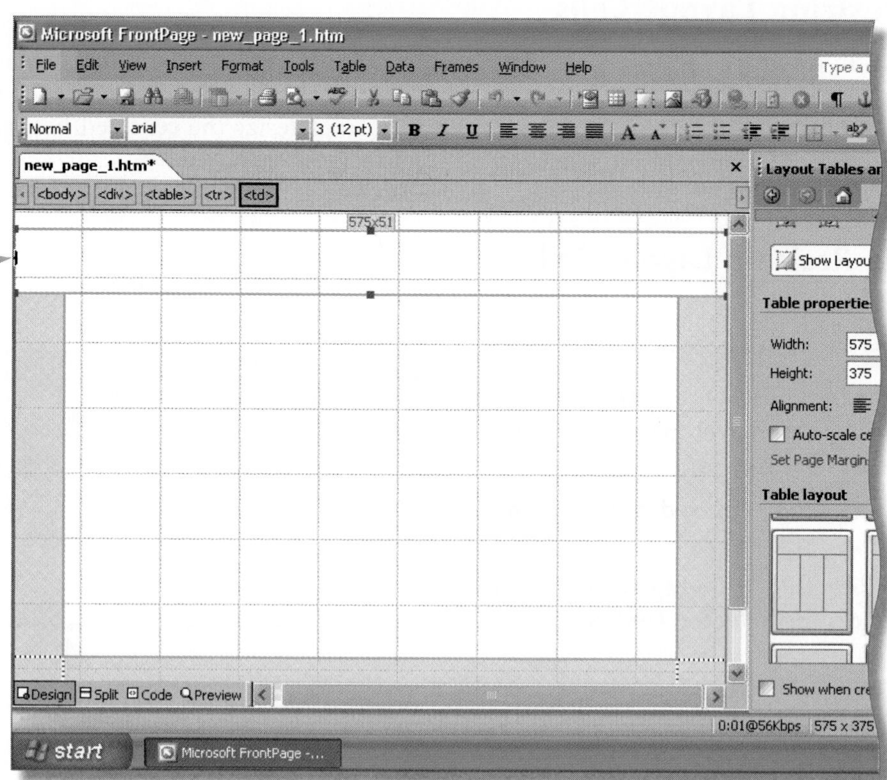

FIGURE 8

3

• **Click and drag the left border of the centered header layout cell until it snaps into position in alignment with the left border of the centered body layout cell, and then release the mouse button.**

The left border of the centered header layout cell appears aligned with the left border of the centered body layout cell (Figure 9).

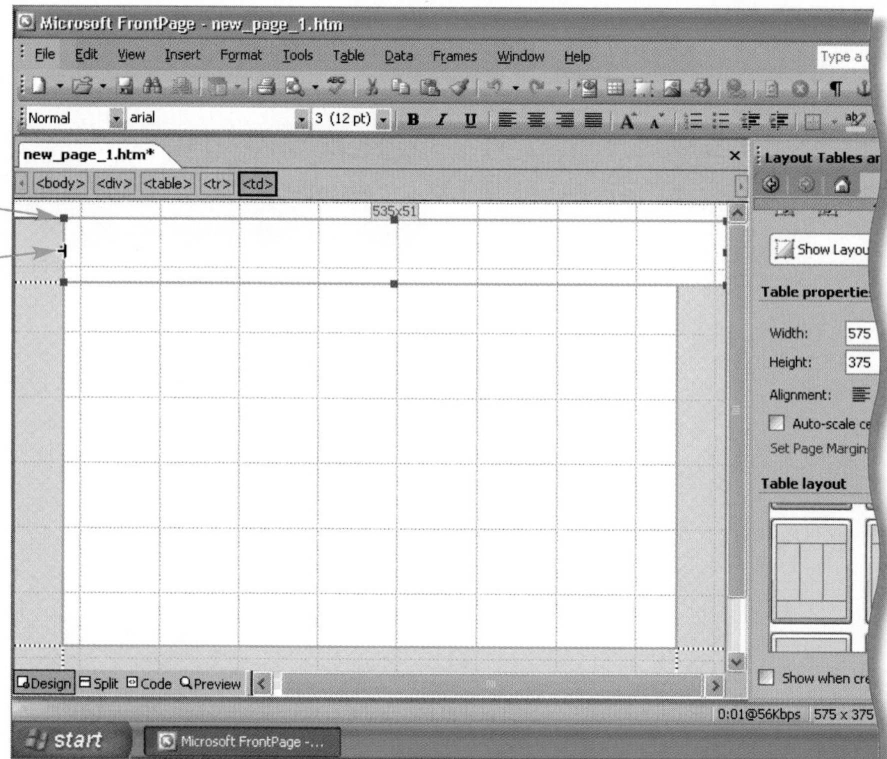

FIGURE 9

4

- **Repeat Step 3 for the right border of the centered header layout cell.**
- **If necessary, use the task pane up scroll arrow to scroll to the top of the task pane.**

The centered header layout cell appears as shown in Figure 10.

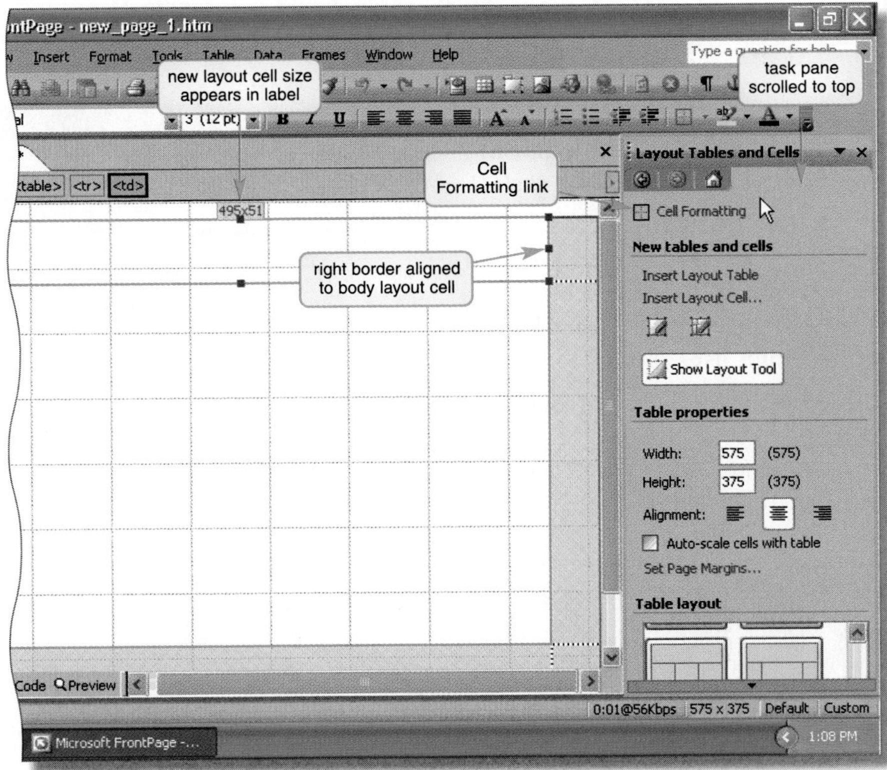

FIGURE 10

Other Ways

1. Click the layout cell border

As shown in Step 3 of the previous set of steps, the layout cell border can be resized to an exact pixel position, or it can snap to the size of an adjacent layout cell. As the size of the layout cell changes, FrontPage updates the label on the layout cell that indicates the size in pixels of the layout cell.

Changing the Background Color of a Layout Cell

Both layout cells in the Web page require a new background color, rounded corners, a border, and a shadow. When working with layout cells, the best practice is to format one cell at a time until you achieve the desired effect for that cell. The first step in applying the custom formatting to the Web page is to apply a background color to the centered header layout cell. The steps on the next page change the alignment for the text that will be added to the layout cell and then apply a yellow background to the layout cell.

More About

Formatting Multiple Layout Cells

FrontPage allows you to select multiple layout cells. You cannot, however, format the selected cells at the same time. You must select each cell individually to format it. If you want to copy and paste layout cell formatting, you can switch to Code view and carefully copy and paste the HTML code for the layout cells.

To Change the Background Color of a Layout Cell

1

- **Click the Cell Formatting link in the Layout Tables and Cells task pane.**
- **When FrontPage displays the Cell Formatting task pane, click the VAlign box arrow and select Middle in the VAlign list.**
- **Click the BgColor box arrow.**

FrontPage displays the Cell Formatting task pane. The VAlign property of the centered header layout cell appears as Middle. FrontPage displays a color palette from which a background color can be selected (Figure 11).

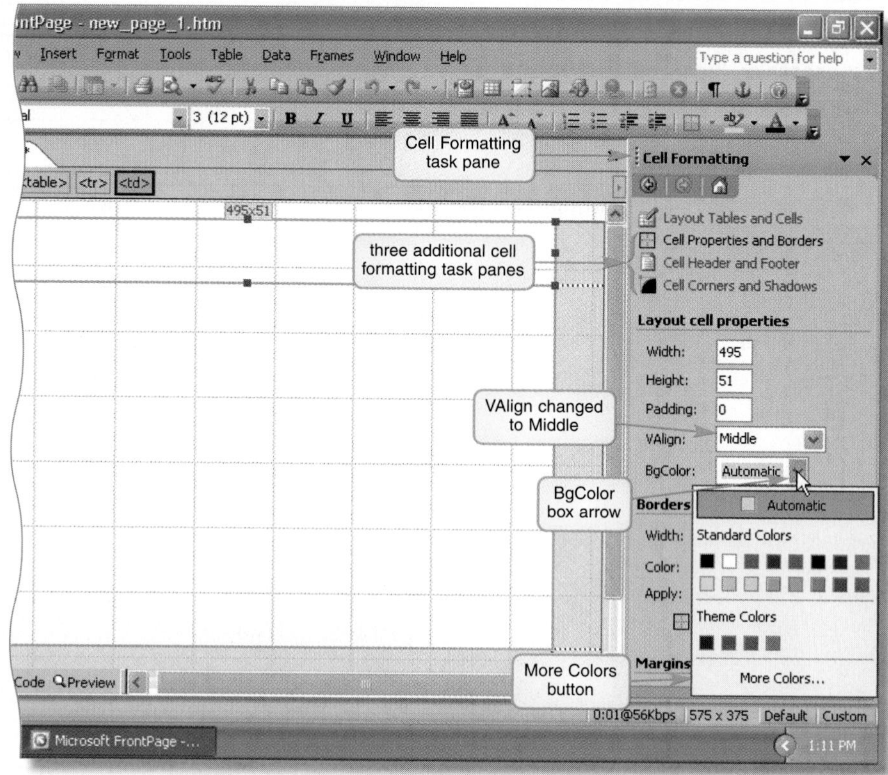

FIGURE 11

2

- **Click More Colors.**
- **When FrontPage displays the More Colors dialog box, select the yellow color with the hex value of {FF,FF,CC} and then click the OK button.**

The centered header layout cell appears with a yellow background (Figure 12).

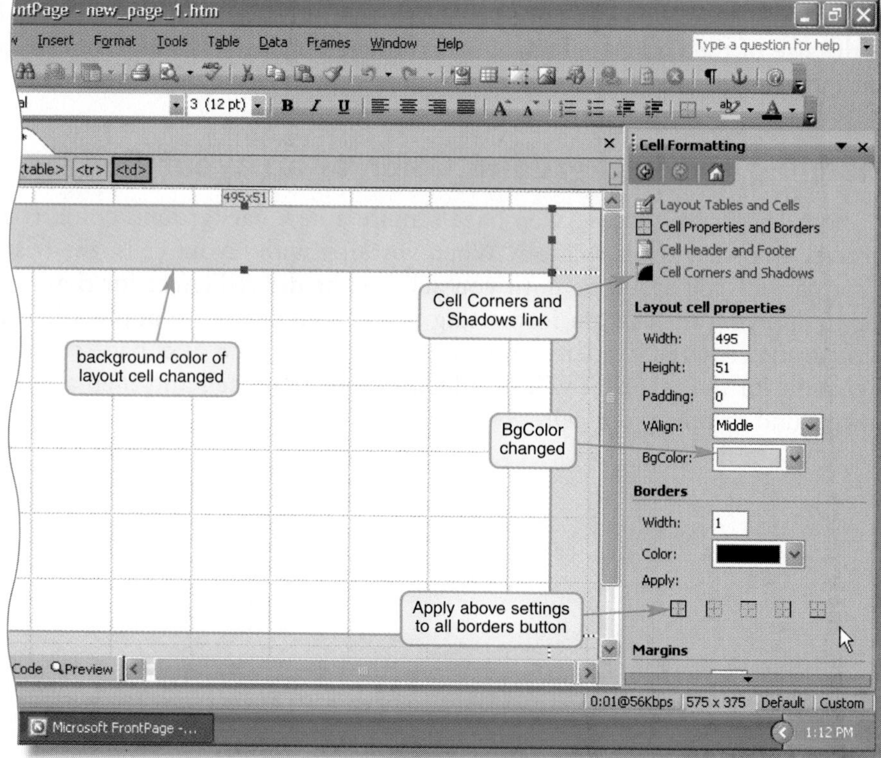

FIGURE 12

The centered header layout cell now includes a yellow background color. As shown in Figure 12, the Cell Formatting task pane also allows you to modify the width and height of the layout cell by specifying the number of pixels in the Width and Height text boxes. You can apply **padding** to the cell, which specifies the number of pixels between the content in the layout cell and the layout cell's border. The next step is to apply the remaining formatting to the layout cell, including rounded corners, a border, and shadows.

More About

Layout Cell Padding

If you attempt to add too many elements to a layout cell, such as padding, headers, footers, shading, and rounded corners, the cell may not be large enough to accommodate all of the elements. FrontPage displays an error message when it cannot fit an element that you are attempting to add. If you receive such an error, resize or reformat your layout cells or table.

Adding Corners, Borders, and Shadows to a Layout Cell

Layout cells allow you to add enhanced formatting that cells in a standard table do not allow. In Project 2, a table was added to a Web page to contain images and other content. The cells in the table provided very little flexibility in the formatting as compared with layout cells. When you select a layout cell, all of the options on the Cell Formatting task pane become available to you, including cell headers and footers, borders, rounded corners, and shadows. The following steps add single-pixel, black borders to all four sides, ten-pixel rounded corners to all four corners, and a ten-pixel shadow to the bottom and right of the centered header layout cell.

To Add Corners, Borders, and Shadows to a Layout Cell

1

- **Click the Apply above settings to all borders button in the Borders area.**
- **Click the Cell Corners and Shadows link at the top of the task pane.**

The Cell Corners and Shadows options are displayed in the Cell Formatting task pane (Figure 13).

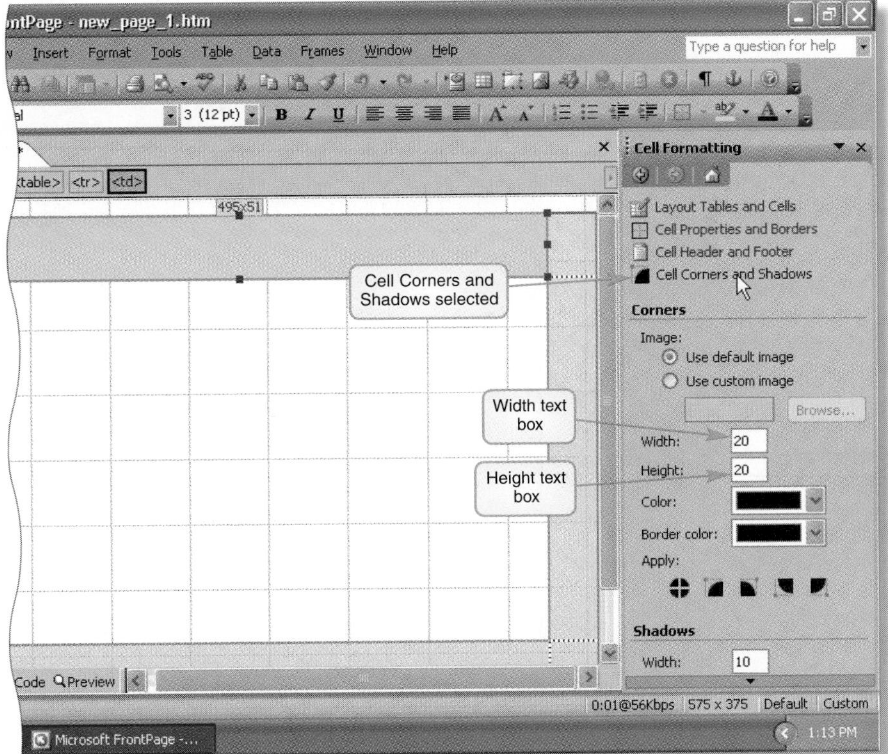

FIGURE 13

2

- **Type** 10 **in the Width text box in the Corners area.**
- **Type** 10 **in the Height text box in the Corners area.**
- **Click the Color box arrow.**

The Height and Width for the corners appear as 10. FrontPage displays the color palette for selecting the color of the corners that will be added to the layout cell (Figure 14).

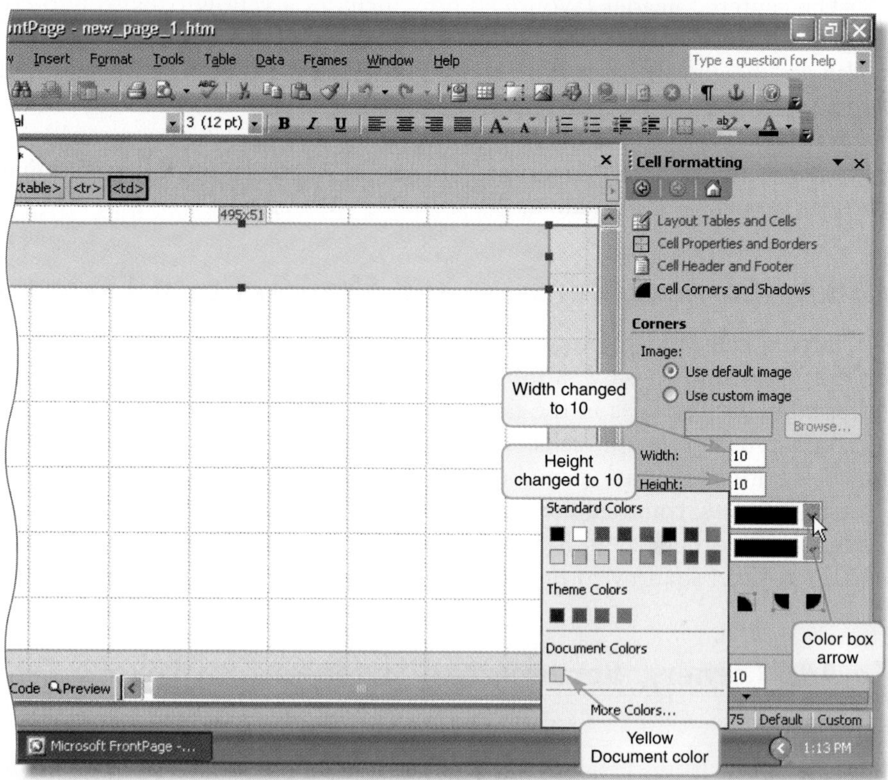

FIGURE 14

3

- **Click the yellow color in the Document Colors area.**
- **Click the Apply above settings to all corners button in the Corners area of the task pane.**

FrontPage adds corners to the centered header layout cell as shown in Figure 15.

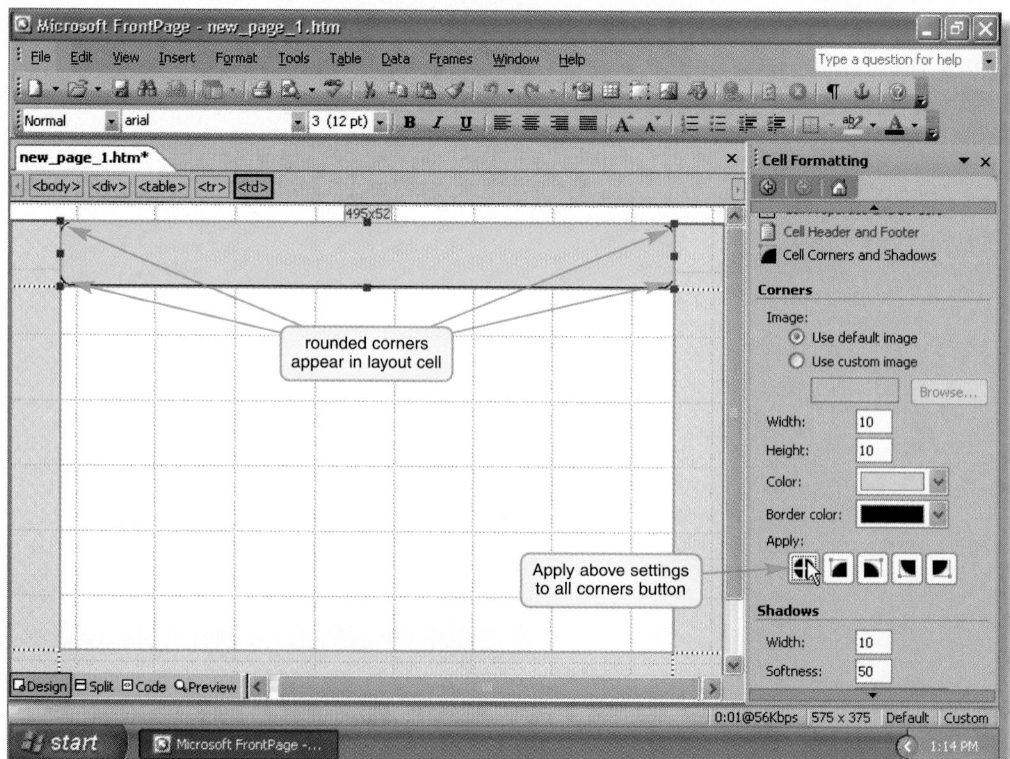

FIGURE 15

4

- **Click the task pane down scroll arrow so that the bottom of the task pane appears.**
- **Click the Apply above settings to bottom and right shadows button in the Shadows area.**

FrontPage adds a shadow to the bottom and right sides of the centered header layout cell (Figure 16).

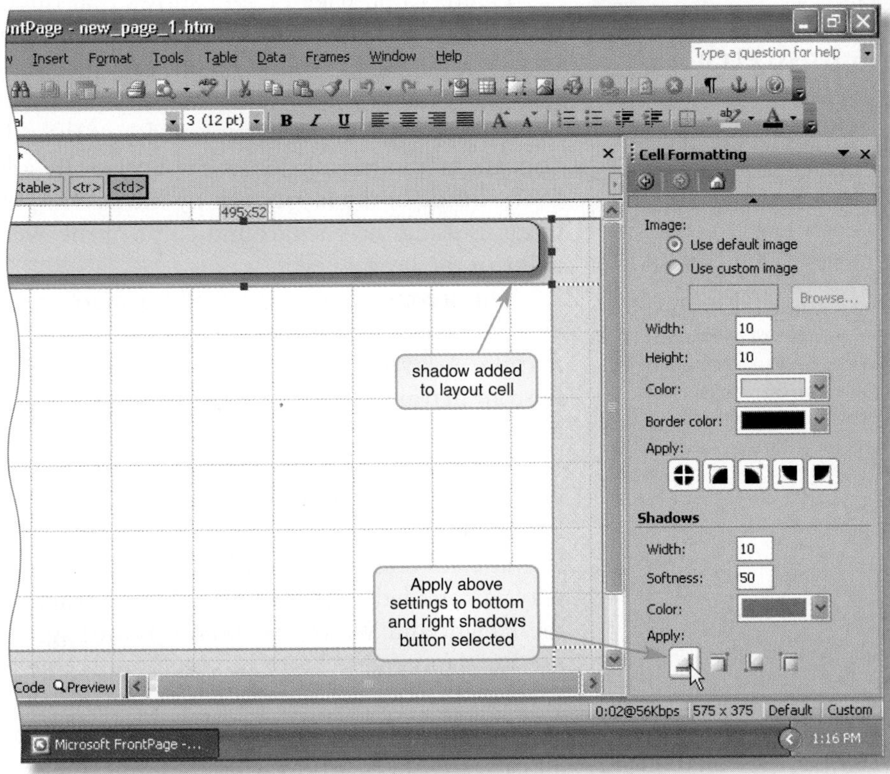

FIGURE 16

5

- **Click anywhere in the centered header layout cell and type** `Responsibilities of the President of the` **and then press SHIFT+ENTER.**
- **Type** `Future Entrepreneurs Honor Society.`
- **Select Heading 2 in the Style box on the Formatting toolbar.**
- **Click the Center button on the Formatting toolbar.**
- **Click the Apply above settings to bottom and right shadows button twice in the Shadows area in the Cell Formatting task pane.**

The text appears in the centered header layout cell as shown in Figure 17. FrontPage extends the shadow to the portion of the cell that was extended by the newly added text.

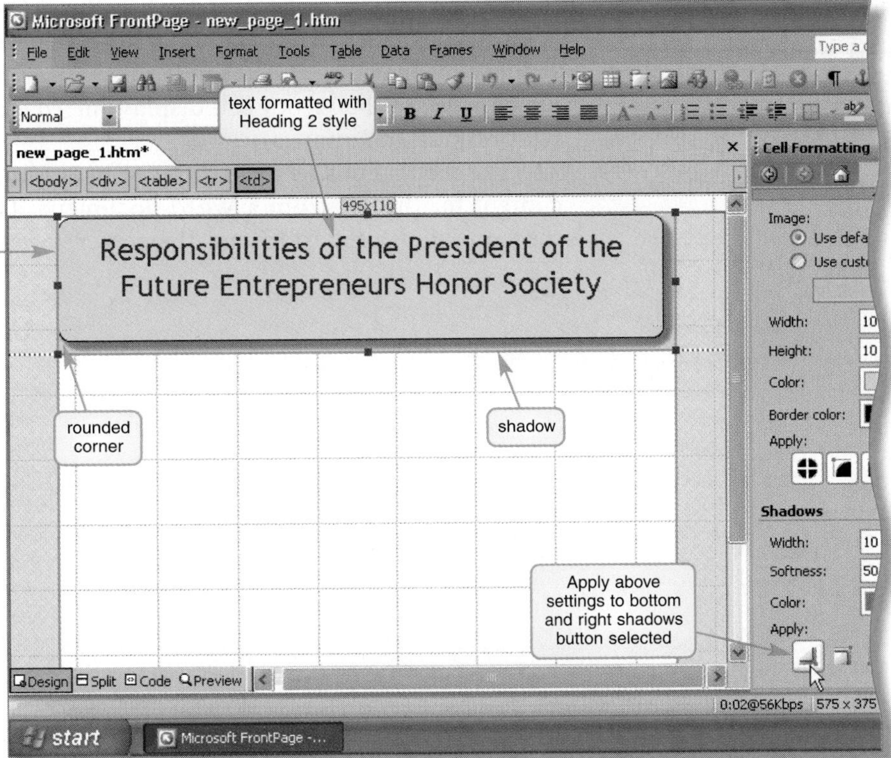

FIGURE 17

More About

Autostretch

You can assign the autostretch property to one cell in a layout table by selecting the layout cell, clicking the down arrow in the column width or row height label, and then clicking Make Column Autostretch or Make Row Autostretch. The row or column will change size as the table changes size, such as when the user resizes the browser window.

More About

Rounded Corners

You can use rounded corners on just the top of a layout cell to make the layout cell appear as a tab. By adding consecutive cells in this manner across the top of a layout table, you can give the appearance of several tabs or pages.

Figure 13 on page FP 243 shows that the Cell Formatting task pane includes three different views. The first view is the Cell Properties and Borders view. This view allows modification of the overall layout cell, including width, height, padding, alignment, and background color. Additionally, you can add borders and margins to the cell. A **border** appears on one or more sides of the cell as a line of the chosen color. A **margin** appears as an area outside of the border. By adding a margin, the border moves closer to the inside of the layout cell by the size in pixels of the margin. FrontPage displays margins using the background color of the Web page, rather than the background color of the layout cell.

The second view of the Cell Formatting task pane is the Cell Header and Footer view. A layout cell header appears at the top of the layout cell, but below any top margin. A layout cell footer appears at the bottom of the layout cell, but above any bottom margin. A cell header or footer can be assigned a color and a border and may include cell padding.

The third view of the Cell Formatting task pane is the Cell Corners and Shadows view. The corners of a layout cell appear in the header or footer of a layout cell if a header or footer is selected for the layout cell. Otherwise, the corners appear in the layout cell's content area, which is not in the margin area. By default, FrontPage displays a rounded, colored area for the corner that is the height and width specified in the Height and Width text boxes. FrontPage also allows you to specify an image to use for the corners. You can specify only one image, meaning that if you select several corners, they all will appear with the same image. FrontPage rotates the image in the appropriate manner to display the image properly for each corner. The Apply area allows you to specify which corners of the layout cell should display the corner image.

The Shadows area allows you to place a colored shadow around the layout cell. Like the corners, the shadow appears on the content area of the layout cell and not the margin. By adding a shadow, therefore, FrontPage makes the content area of the layout cell smaller to accommodate the shadow. You adjust the intensity of the shadow by changing the Softness text box. FrontPage also allows you to specify which sides of the layout cell display the shadow, the color of the shadow, and the width of the shadow.

The next step is to format the centered body layout cell and copy and paste the content for the cell from a Word document. The second layout cell is formatted using the same steps used to format the centered header layout cell.

To Format and Add Content to the Second Layout Cell

- **Click anywhere in the centered body layout cell.**
- **Use the up scroll arrow of the task pane to scroll to the top of the task pane.**
- **Click the Cell Properties and Borders link.**
- **Click the BgColor box arrow to display the BgColor list, and then click the yellow color in the Document Colors area.**

- **Click the Apply above settings to all borders button in the Borders area.**
- **Click the Cell Corners and Shadows link at the top of the task pane.**
- **If necessary, click the Color box arrow and then click the yellow color in the Document Colors area.**

- **Click the Apply above settings to all corners button in the Corners area of the task pane.**
- **Click the task pane down scroll arrow so that the bottom of the task pane appears.**
- **Click the Apply above settings to bottom and right shadows button in the Shadows area.**

The centered body layout cell appears with a background color, a border, rounded corners, and a shadow (Figure 18).

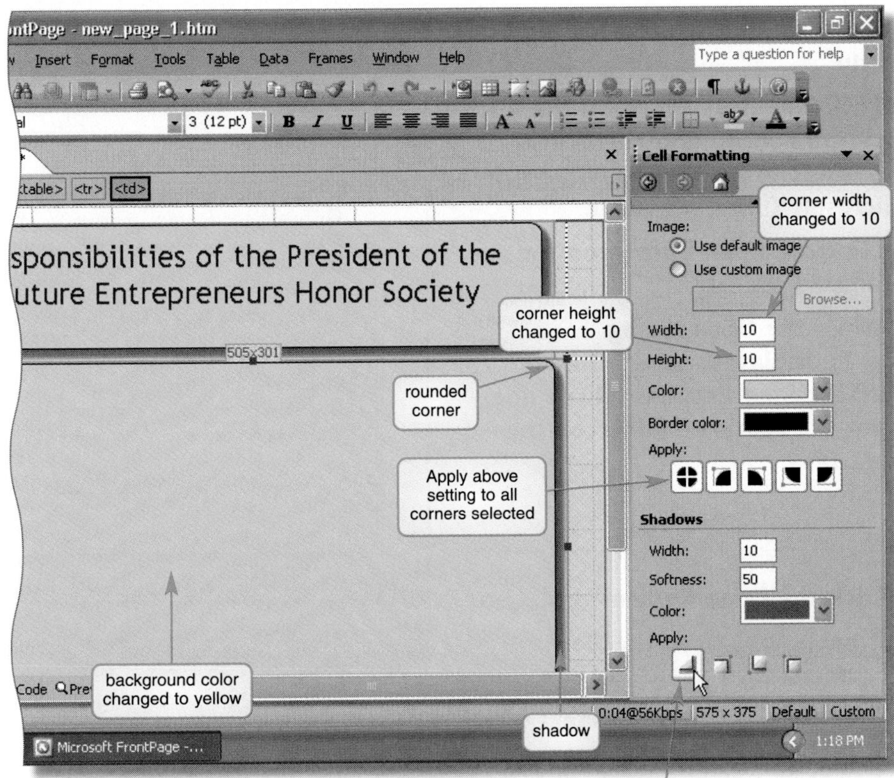

FIGURE 18

4

- **Click the Start button on the taskbar.**
- **Point to All Programs on the Start menu.**
- **Click Microsoft Office on the All Programs menu and then click Microsoft Office Word 2003 on the Microsoft Office submenu.**
- **Click the Open button on the Standard toolbar.**
- **When the Open dialog box is displayed, select the file, FEHSPresidentResponsibilities.doc, from the Feature1 folder on the Data Disk.**

5

- **Click the Open button.**
- **If necessary, close the New Document task pane.**
- **Drag through all of the text after the first line in the document to select it and then press CTRL+C to copy it to the Office Clipboard.**
- **Click the Close button on the Microsoft Word title bar.**

6

- **If necessary, click the Microsoft FrontPage button on the taskbar to switch to FrontPage.**
- **If necessary, click the centered body layout cell to position the insertion point.**
- **Press CTRL+V to paste the copied text from Word into the Web page.**

FrontPage pastes the contents of the Word document into the centered body layout cell. FrontPage formats the text and bullets according to the settings for the Global Marketing theme (Figure 19).

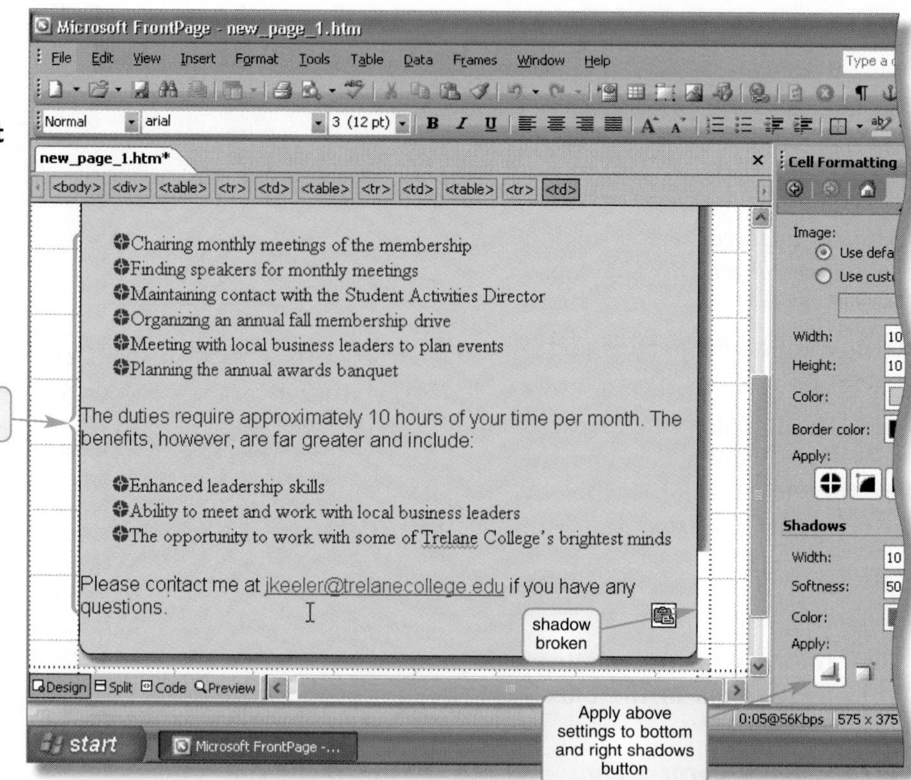

FIGURE 19

7

• **Click the Apply above settings to bottom and right shadows button twice in the Shadows area.**

FrontPage extends the shadow to the portion of the cell that was extended by the newly added text (Figure 20).

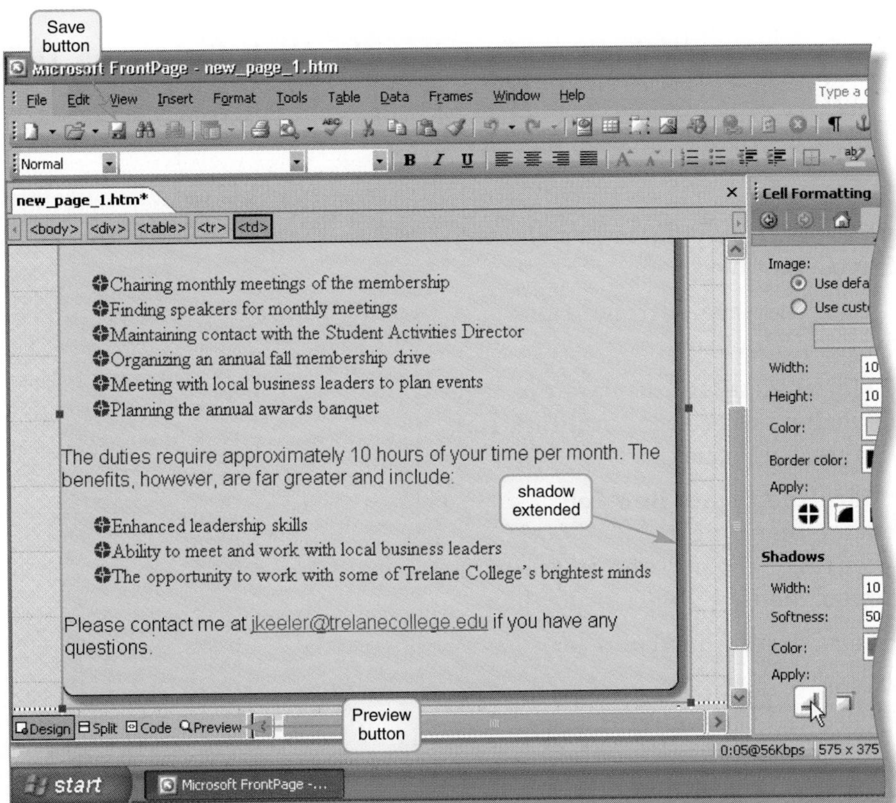

FIGURE 20

As shown in Figure 19, as the added content changes the layout cell's size, the shadow size does not change. By reapplying the shadow in the last step, the shadow is extended across the full height of the layout cell. Because a theme is applied to the Web page, FrontPage automatically formats the newly added text so that it requires no additional formatting.

> *More About*
>
> **The Quick Reference**
>
> For more information, see the Quick Reference Summary at the back of this book, or visit the FrontPage 2003 Quick Reference Web page (scsite.com/fp2003/qr).

Previewing and Saving the Web Page

After you have finished the steps in this feature and developed the Web page, you can preview the Web page in Preview view and quit FrontPage. The steps on the next page save the Web page, preview the Web page, and quit FrontPage.

To Save the Web Page, Preview the Web Page, and Quit FrontPage

1

- **Click the Close button on the Cell Formatting task pane.**
- **Click the Save button on the Standard toolbar.**
- **When FrontPage displays the Save As dialog box, select Local Disk (C:) in the Save in box.**
- **Click the Create New Folder button and type** `jkeelerHonorSociety` **in the Name box in the New Folder dialog box.**
- **Click the OK button.**
- **Type** `PresidentsResponsibilities` **in the File name text box and then click the Save button.**
- **When the Save Embedded Files dialog box appears, click the Change Folder button and select C:\jkeelerHonorSociety\images as the folder for the embedded images by clicking the Create New Folder button in the Change Folder dialog box.**
- **Click the OK button in the Save Embedded Files dialog box.**

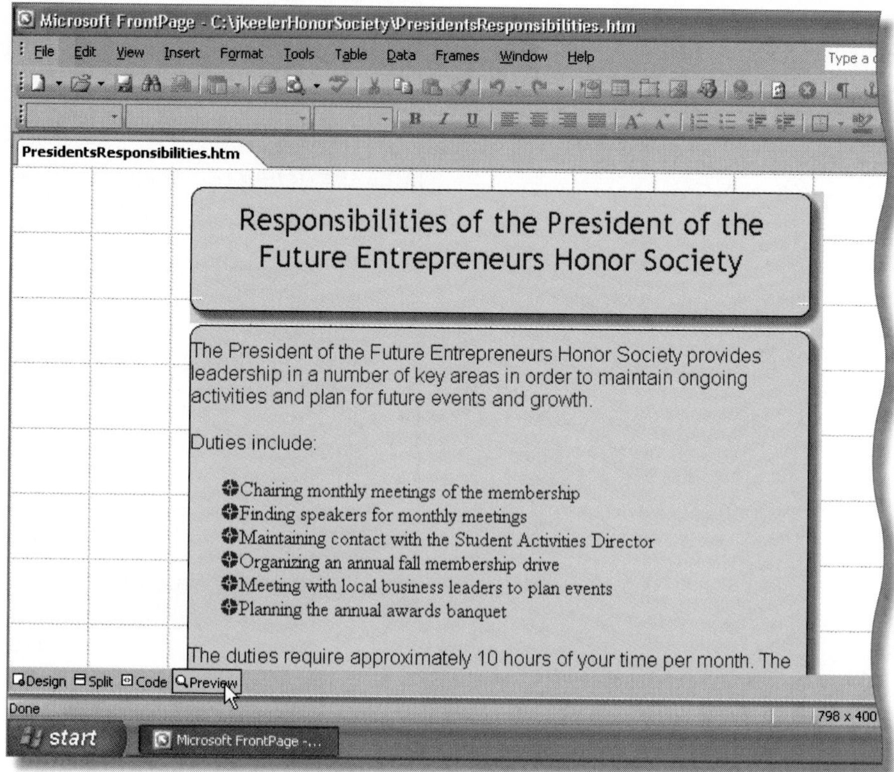

FIGURE 21

2

- **After FrontPage saves the files, click the Preview button.**
- **When the Web page appears in Preview view, use the scroll bar to view the entire page.**

FrontPage displays the completed Web page in Preview view (Figure 21).

3

- **Click the Design button to return to Design view.**
- **Click File on the menu bar and then click Close.**

FrontPage closes the Web page.

4

- **Click the Close button on the right side of the FrontPage title bar.**

The FrontPage window closes.

After saving the Web page, the files and folder created with the Web page can be added to a Web site or distributed to another Web site developer so that he or she can include the Web page in another site. FrontPage does not provide the capability to publish an individual Web page to a server.

Feature Summary

This Table feature introduced you to using layout tables and layout cells to position content on a Web page. Layout tables allow you to position content precisely in columns and rows. Layout cells include enhanced design elements such as rounded corners, shadows, borders, and background colors. By combining the functionality of layout tables and layout cells, you learned how to create sophisticated layouts for Web page content.

What You Should Know

Having completed this feature, you should be able to perform the tasks below. The tasks are listed in the same order they were presented in this feature. For a list of the buttons, menus, toolbars, and commands introduced in this feature, see the Quick Reference Summary at the back of this book and refer to the Page Number column.

1. Start FrontPage and Create a New Web Page (FP 235)
2. Add a Layout Table to a Web Page (FP 236)
3. Resize a Layout Cell (FP 239)
4. Change the Background Color of a Layout Cell (FP 242)
5. Add Corners, Borders, and Shadows to a Layout Cell (FP 243)
6. Format and Add Content to the Second Layout Cell (FP 247)
7. Save the Web Page, Preview the Web Page, and Quit FrontPage (FP 250)

In the Lab

1 Creating a Web Page with a Centered Header, and Centered Body Layout Table

Problem: Fairway Lawn Care runs a summer special each year during slow work periods. Create a Web page advertisement that promotes the summer special.

Instructions: Perform the following tasks.

1. Create a new Web page and apply the Compass theme to the page.
2. Open the Layout Tables and Cells task pane and apply the Centered Header, and Centered Body layout table to the Web page. Center the layout table.
3. Select the centered header layout cell. Add a 1-pixel border to the layout cell. Change the background color of the layout cell to Fuchsia. Add rounded corners and a shadow to the layout cell. Type the text in the layout cell as shown in Figure 22. Center the text and apply the Heading 1 style. Make sure the shadow on the cell extends through the entire length and width of the cell.
4. Select the centered body layout cell. Add a 1-pixel border to the layout cell and add rounded corners and a border to the layout cell. Add 10 pixels of padding to the cell. Type the text in the layout cell as shown in Figure 22. The text at the top of the cell has a style of Heading 3. Resize the centered body layout cell so that the text fits the cell appropriately.
5. Preview the Web page in your browser. Save the Web page as SummerSpecial.htm in the Feature1\LabSF1-1FairwayLawnCare folder on the Data Disk or your hard drive. Save the embedded images in a new images subfolder.

In the Lab

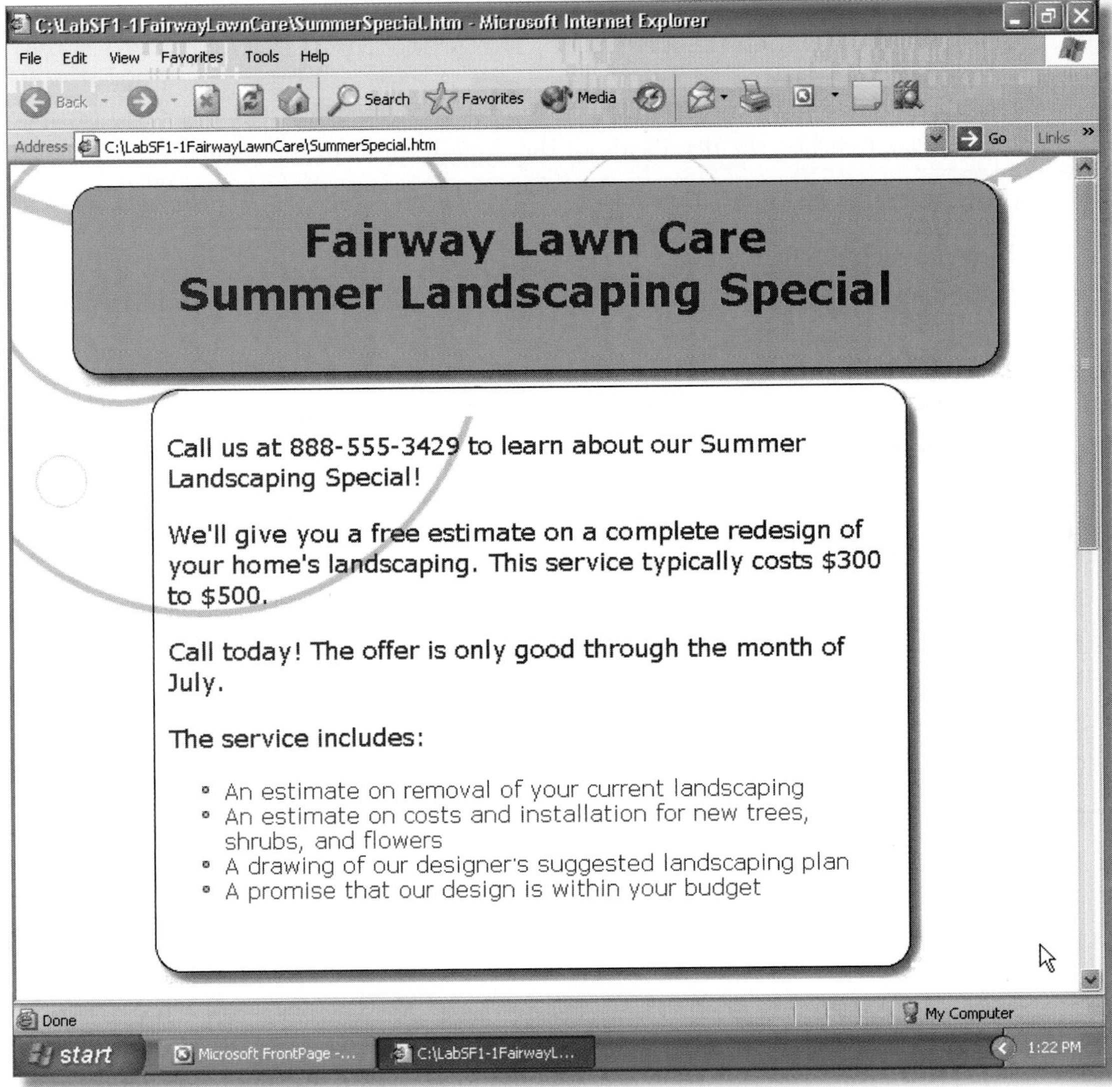

FIGURE 22

In the Lab

2 Creating a Web Page with a Header, Footer, and 3 Columns Layout Table

Problem: You are hosting a running seminar and need to provide details about the event to prospective attendees. Create a Web page that lists the details about the three sessions of the seminar.

Instructions: Perform the following tasks.

1. Create a new Web page and apply the Echo theme to the page.
2. Open the Layout Tables and Cells task pane and apply the Header, Footer, and 3 Columns layout table to the Web page. Center the layout table.
3. Add the content to the five layout cells as shown in Figure 23. Format the header layout cell with the Heading 2 style for line 1 and the Heading 3 style for line 2. Set the VAlign property of the header layout cell to Bottom. Center the text in the cell.
4. Center the content in the footer layout cell. Provide a link for your e-mail address using the word, me. Set the VAlign property for the footer cell to Middle.
5. For each of the three column layout cells, format the background to a gray color. Set the Padding to 5. Set the first line of each layout cell to the style of Heading 3. Add a 1-pixel black border to each layout cell.
6. Preview the Web page in your browser. Save the Web page as MarathonTraining.htm in the Feature1\LabSF1-2RunningMyWaySeminar folder on the Data Disk or your hard drive.

In the Lab

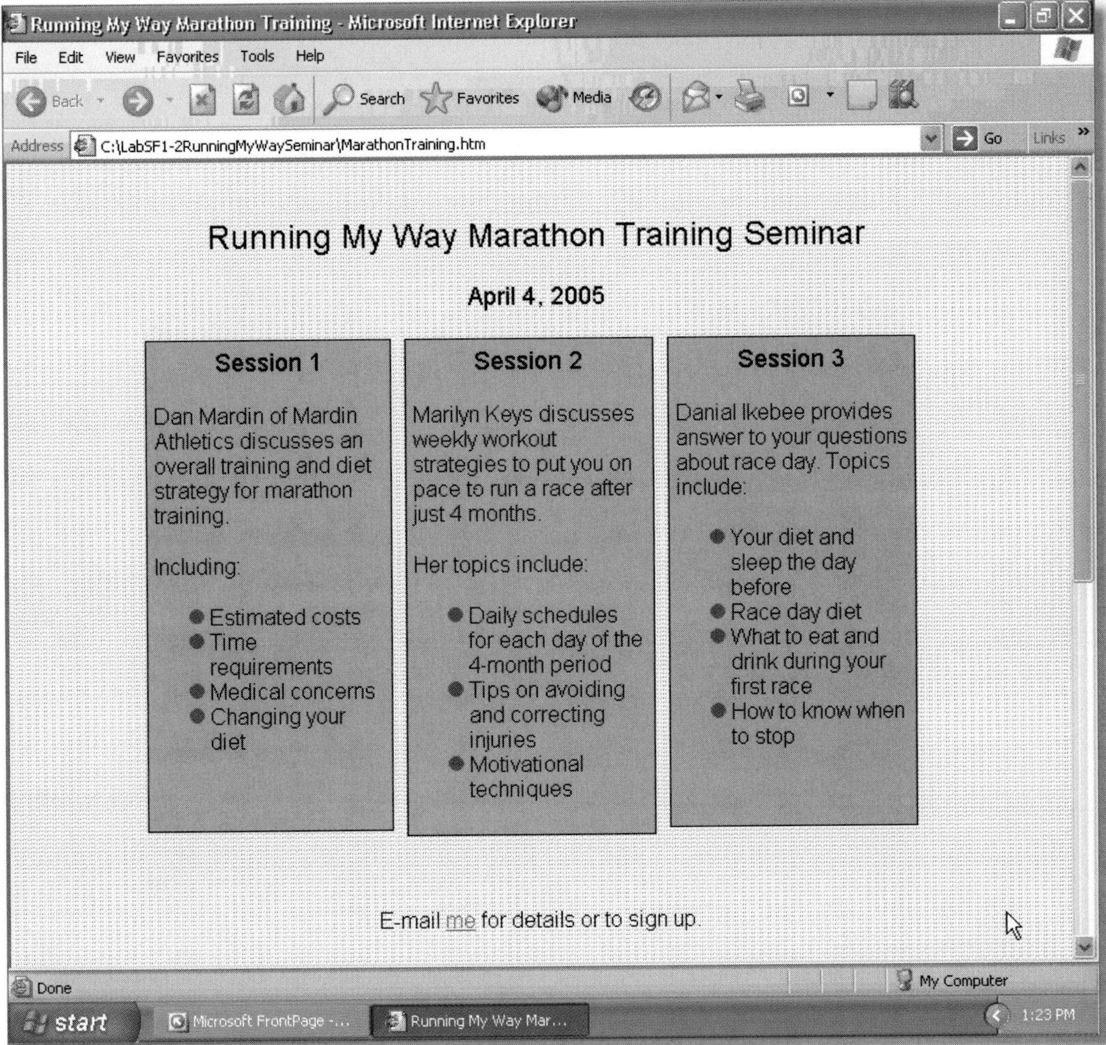

FIGURE 23

MICROSOFT
Office FrontPage 2003

Creating and Using Interactive Forms on the Web

PROJECT

CASE PERSPECTIVE

James Keeler's Web site offers visitors several interesting Web pages, including a photo gallery and his resume. He now is ready to begin some of the planned enhancements to his site; specifically, he wants to add a page that allows visitors to place free job opportunity listings. James has found that he and his classmates routinely share job possibilities by word of mouth or by e-mail. He wants to consolidate this loose sharing of information into a Web page. James is unclear about how he is to implement this task and the impact on future tasks of organizing and displaying the results. He wants to collect the information in a format more structured than an e-mail message, and he does not want to receive large amounts of data via e-mail and then have to sort and post it manually. Using a form would provide consistency and completeness in data collection. He has seen other Web sites that accept information by having visitors complete a form and he would like to do the same. He also wants to know how he can increase awareness of this service to potential users.

You assure James that by using features of FrontPage, the information visitors enter into a form can be added automatically to a database. Later, he can use the database to sort, select, and post the job opportunities. Finally, you suggest some ideas for promoting his free service by using the Web site itself.

As you read through this project, you will learn about the fundamentals of how data is submitted on a Web page and how to save the submitted data. You also will learn how to use FrontPage to create a form that includes text boxes, drop-down boxes, check boxes, option buttons, and text areas. Finally, you will learn how to edit HTML code directly within FrontPage.

MICROSOFT
Office FrontPage 2003

Creating and Using Interactive Forms on the Web

PROJECT

4

Objectives

You will have mastered the material in this project when you can:

- Describe forms and types of form fields
- Describe available form handlers
- Describe the methods and format used to submit form data
- Manage files in Folders view
- Modify a page title in Folders view
- Copy and paste a page banner and a link bar
- Hide the Folder List pane
- Insert a form in a Web page and a table
- Insert a table, text box, text area, and check box in a form
- Insert a line drawing AutoShape in a table
- Create a nested table
- Insert a drop-down box, group box, and option button in a form
- Modify form button properties
- Choose a form handler
- Modify HTML code directly in FrontPage

Introduction

You have created Web pages that go in one direction: from you to your reader. Most of the flow of information over the Web uses this technique. A Web server sends the majority of Web pages to your computer for viewing without any way for you to send information or data back to the Web server.

Methods do exist, however, for providing feedback and interaction with Web pages. Special HTML objects, called forms, provide two-way communication between you and a Web server. Using forms, you can order products, do banking, engage in live conversations, leave comments or suggestions, and use Web search engines. Forms make a Web page interactive. Users can respond to a Web site by filling in forms and submitting them.

Project Four — Creating and Using an Interactive Form

In this project, you will learn how to use forms and form fields by creating the Job Opportunity Posting page that links from the James Keeler Home page (Figure 4-1a). The Job Opportunity Posting page (Figure 4-1b) will be used to collect information from individuals wanting to post job opportunities about which they have read or heard that may be of interest to James and his friends. When the visitor clicks the Send button in the form, that information is sent to a database, as illustrated by the receipt of a Confirmation page in Figure 4-1c. A hyperlink to the Job Opportunity Posting page from the Home page also will be added (Figure 4-1a). Before creating the Job Opportunity Posting page, you should familiarize yourself with some important concepts and definitions concerning forms.

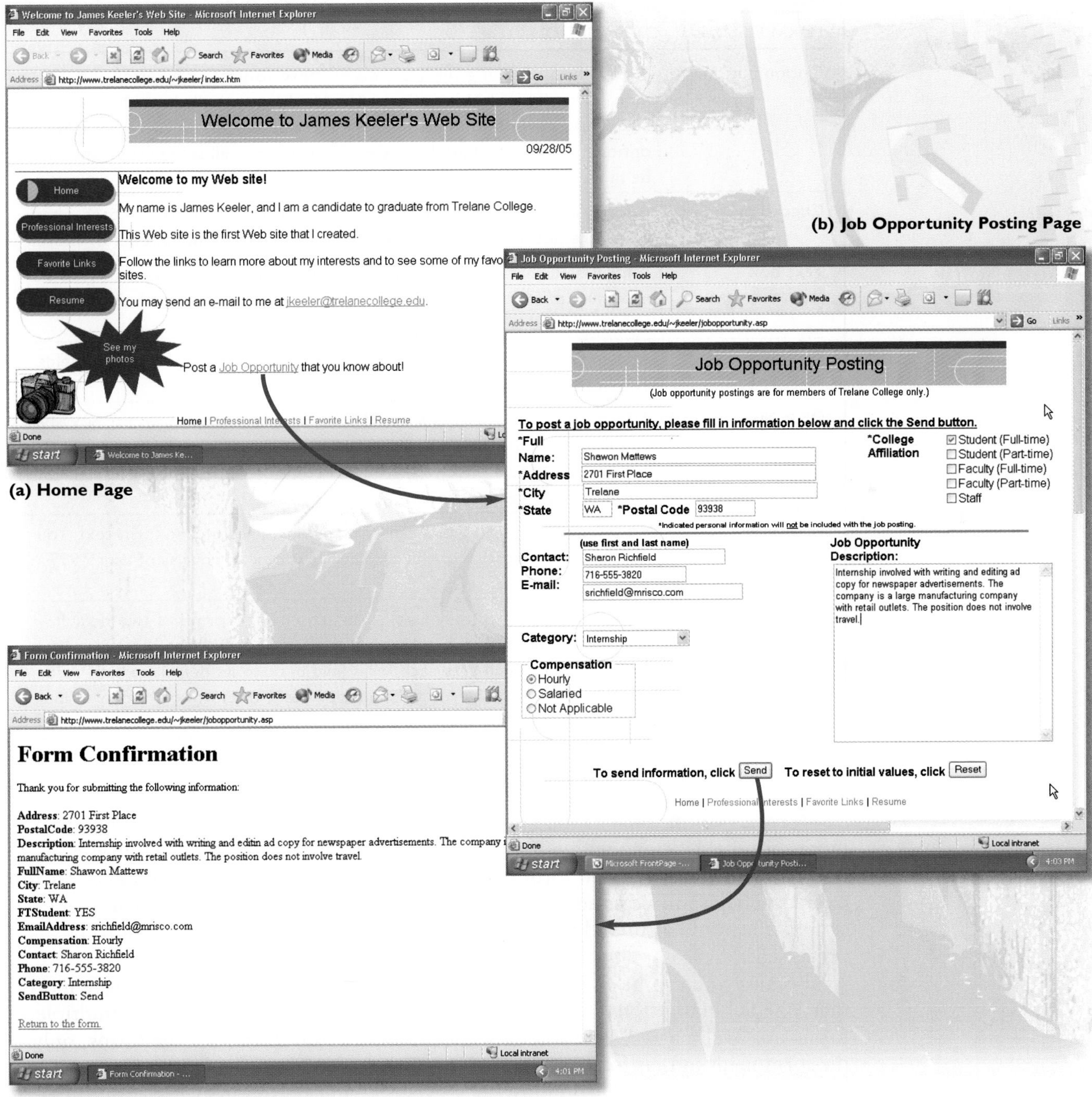

FIGURE 4-1

HTML Forms

Two components are required to send data using forms: (1) a Web page containing the form, and (2) a form handler. A **form** is a collection of input fields in a Web page that enables a user to enter data and send it to be processed on the Web server by a form handler. The **form fields** can be text boxes, check boxes, option buttons, drop-down list boxes, or buttons. Table 4-1 lists commonly used form fields and briefly describes each field type.

Table 4-1 Common FrontPage Form Fields

FORM FIELD	DESCRIPTION
Option button	A form field used in groups of two or more to present a set of one or more mutually exclusive options, one of which typically is set by default. Selecting a new option button in the form deselects the currently selected option button. For multiple sets on a single form, all sets except one must be in a group box.
Check box	A form field you can select by clicking a box. Unlike option buttons, check boxes are not mutually exclusive, so you can choose none, one, or more.
Text box	A form field that allows you to enter alphanumeric text. You can type a maximum of 500 characters. If you type nothing in the text box, only the text box name is sent to the server.
Group box	A form field that provides a border to surround a group of related fields. The border may include a title.
Drop-down box	A form field that presents a list of selections in a drop-down list box style. You can use it to present a wide variety of choices — more than option buttons can handle effectively. You can configure a drop-down box to allow single or multiple selections.
Text area	A form field in which users can type multiple lines of free-form text. You can set the properties of the scrolling text box to consist of up to 999 columns and 999 rows.
Push button	A form field that typically invokes an action. Each form has two default buttons: a Submit button, which sends a form to the Web server, and a Reset button, which sets each form field back to its default setting. Additional buttons can be used to submit or reset the form or invoke scripts. An Advanced button also can display HTML content on its face.

A typical form, such as the one created in this project, is composed of one or more form fields, along with a Submit button and a Reset button. The **Submit button** sends the completed form to the Web server for processing. The **Reset button** clears the fields and sets them back to their original default conditions. The user simply fills in the form and then clicks the Submit button to send the data to be processed.

Because you can have more than one form in a Web page, you could have more than one Submit button in a Web page. You must use caution when using multiple forms in a Web page. When you click the Submit button for one of the forms, only the form fields in that form are sent to the Web server. Form fields that are not part of that form are ignored. You must click every Submit button in every form to send each separate collection of data entered in each form back to the Web server.

Use caution when using multiple forms in a Web page. In general, develop a design in such as manner that the main area of the Web page contains only one form.

Some applications might require several forms in a Web page. This allows you to have the same Web page return one of several potential sets of data and process the data differently depending on which Submit button the user clicks. Whenever a user clicks the Submit button, the server processes the data in the form using a form handler.

Q&A

Q: Can CGI scripts be used without a form?

A: Yes. You do not need a form to use a CGI script. You can use a hyperlink that points to a CGI script to generate dynamic Web pages based on real-time data.

Form Handlers

A form handler provides a means of collecting information entered on a form. A **form handler** is a program that resides on the server and is executed when a user submits a form using the Submit button. A form handler normally is not visible to a user viewing a Web page.

Form handler programs are highly dependent on the computer operating system and Web server software. Because of this, writing form handler programs can be a complex process and requires advanced programming skills.

You can use one of several available techniques when deciding how to handle the form data. Several standard techniques are available on the Web. In addition, FrontPage has several form handlers included in the **FrontPage Server Extensions**, a set of programs and scripts that support authoring in FrontPage and extend the functionality of a Web server. Table 4-2 describes the standard Web techniques as well as the Server Extensions available with FrontPage. The most popular way of handling forms is the **Common Gateway Interface**, or **CGI**. In addition to the standard techniques, you can have the data e-mailed to an e-mail address or placed into a file or database.

Table 4-2 Standard and FrontPage Form Handlers

FORM HANDLER	DESCRIPTION
CGI	Common Gateway Interface — A standard method of extending Web server functionality by executing programs or scripts on a Web server in response to Web browser requests.
ISAPI	Internet Server Application Program Interface — A Web server application development interface developed by Process Software and Microsoft Corporation that can be used in place of CGI.
NSAPI	Netscape Server Application Program Interface — A Web server application development interface developed by Netscape Communications Corporation.
ASP	Active Server Page — A method of creating programs that execute on a Web server, first available on the Microsoft Internet Information Server 3.0.
Discussion Form Handler	A FrontPage form handler that allows users to participate in an online discussion. The Discussion Form Handler collects information from a form, formats it into an HTML page, and adds the page to a table of contents and text index.
Registration Form Handler	A FrontPage form handler that allows users to register themselves automatically for access to a service implemented as a World Wide Web site. The Registration Form Handler adds the user to the service's authentication database, then gathers optional information from the form and stores it in one of many supported formats.
Save Results Form Handler	A FrontPage form handler that gathers information from a form and stores it in one of a selection of formats or sends the information to an e-mail address.

More About

CGI Script Languages

On UNIX systems, most CGI scripts are written in C or Perl. On Windows systems, most CGI scripts are written in Visual Basic or Visual C++. To locate free CGI scripts, visit the FrontPage 2003 More About Web page (scsite.com/fp2003/more) and then click CGI Scripts.

CGI Scripts

CGI is a universal way to execute programs on a Web site. CGI programs can be written in one of several available programming languages, such as Perl, Java, or Visual Basic. These programs frequently are called **CGI scripts**.

CGI scripts begin executing after the user supplies data by filling in form fields and then clicking the Submit button. The browser sends the data fields from the form to the Web server. The name of the CGI script is stored in the form. The CGI script processes the data and sends back a confirmation Web page.

The CGI script can perform many different functions with the data, including retrieving or updating data from a database, storing data in a series of data files, or executing other programs. When finished, the CGI script usually returns information to the browser in the form of a new HTML document indicating the status of the form processing.

You can choose a form handler that appends the data to a data file, sends the data to an e-mail address, or immediately processes the data with a user-supplied CGI program. If you use the FrontPage handlers rather than a custom form handler, such as a CGI script, a server that has the FrontPage Server Extensions installed is required. Regardless of the technique you choose to process the data, two basic formats, or methods, are used to send data for processing: Get and Post.

More About

Get and Post

Other related information about forms data, such as the length of the data string and the Internet address of the computer sending the data, is available in environment variables. To understand more about Get and Post methods, visit the FrontPage 2003 More About Web page (scsite.com/fp2003/more) and then click Get and Post.

Get and Post Methods

The creator of the Web page form assigns names to the form fields (for example, Full Name or City). When the user enters values or selects form fields, and then clicks the Submit button, the data is sent in plain ASCII text in a name=value format, with the name of the field first, followed by an equal sign, and then followed by the data the user entered in the field. Values that have embedded spaces have those spaces replaced with plus (+) signs, to indicate that this text is concatenated together to form a single value. Names cannot have spaces in them; so when assigning a name to a field, uppercase and lowercase letters, along with underscores, are used to make the names more readable. Figure 4-2 shows the format of the collection of name=value pairs from a sample form. Each name=value pair is separated by an ampersand (&).

```
Name=Jose+Hernandez&Address=2532+Allan+Dr.&City=San+Jose&State=CA&ZipCode=
94375&Employee=Yes&Phone=202-555-8392&Email=jhernandez@isp.com&SendButton=Send
```

FIGURE 4-2

The way in which the form handler reads the information depends on which one of the two methods is used to send the form. The **Get method** stores the name=value pairs in an environment variable called QUERY_STRING. The form handler program must contain instructions to access the QUERY_STRING environment variable in order to read the name=value pairs.

The **Post method** reads the name=value pairs as input directly to the form handler from a standard input stream. A **stream** is similar to a data file. Most programs have a standard input stream and a standard output stream automatically defined when they are compiled.

Post is the preferred method, as most programs can be written to read from the standard input stream with little effort and remain portable across different computer platforms. Reading environment variables can require sets of instructions that are unique to each computer platform, requiring more programming effort to migrate the programs from one computer system to another.

Design Tip

In general, the Post method is the preferred method to handle forms. Use the Get method when you want to use special features provided by the Get method.

Regardless of the method you choose to handle the form, the steps to use the form remain the same: you fill in the form by typing data in the text boxes, clicking option buttons and check boxes, and selecting items from lists. You then send the data in the form by clicking the Submit button. A default Web page normally is returned, confirming the receipt of the data by the form handler. You can supply a customized Web page containing the confirmation information.

More About

Form Design

Form design can be done most readily by freehand sketching. If the design has to be stored on a computer or sent via e-mail, however, and you do not have access to a scanner, you can do a comparable job using a tool such as Microsoft Word. For tips on form design, visit the FrontPage 2003 More About Web page (scsite.com/fp2003/more) and then click Form Design.

Designing a Form

This project requires the design and creation of a form in a Web page to obtain useful information from potential job opportunity posters, such as their name and address, their status with the school, and the job opportunity they want to post. Figure 4-3 illustrates the design for the Job Opportunity Posting Web page. The form data will be sent to an Access database on the server by a FrontPage form handler, so a server with the FrontPage Server Extensions installed is required for this project.

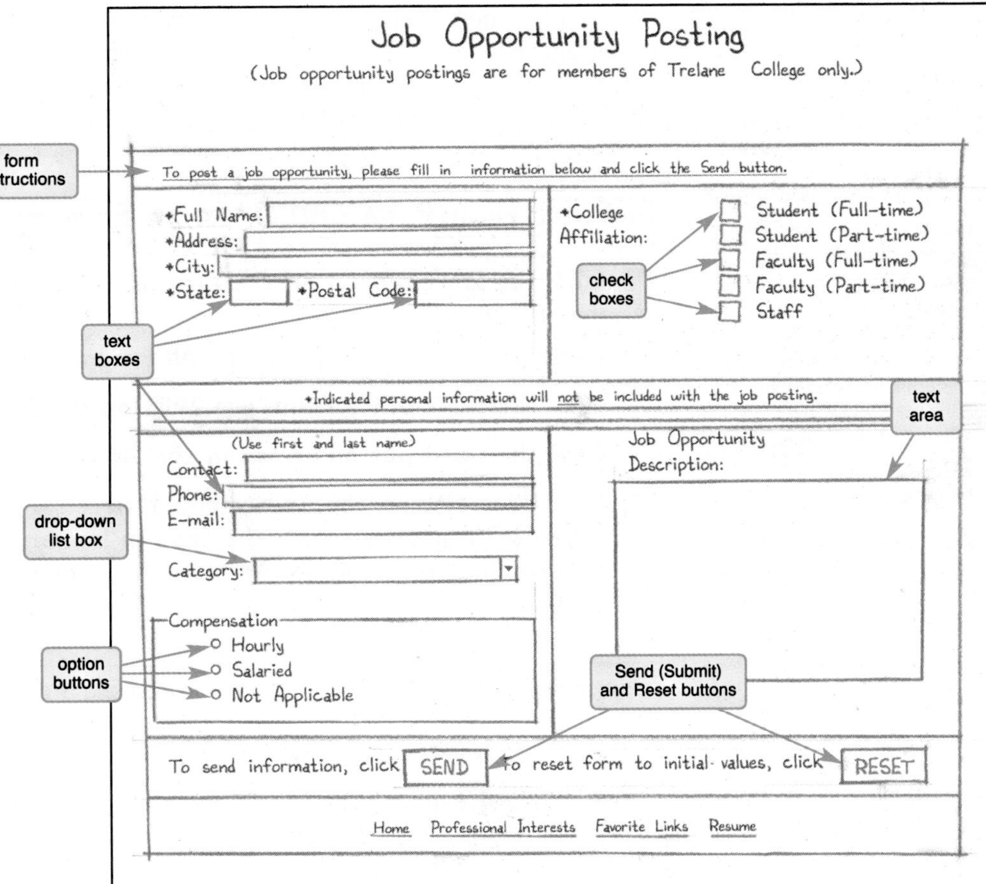

FIGURE 4-3

The form shown in Figure 4-3 on the previous page consists of two logical sections. The purpose of each section is to obtain a certain type of information. The number and purpose of the sections in your form design depends on the types of information you are requesting and any design concerns and issues for the Web page.

When designing a form for a Web page, typically you lay out the input fields in the order you would read a book — from left to right and top to bottom. You can use tables to organize and control the spacing of the form fields in the Web page.

Design Tip

When designing a form for a Web page, typically you lay out the input fields in the order you would read a book — from left to right and top to bottom. You can use tables to organize and control the spacing of the form fields in the Web page.

Adding Web Pages

Before beginning any work on a form, you first must add a new page to the James Keeler FrontPage Web site. Additionally, you will need to add a hyperlink from an existing page to the new page. Often, the hyperlink is from the Home page, as it is in this project.

To add a new Web page, you need to start FrontPage and then open the original FrontPage Web site. The following steps start FrontPage and open James Keeler's FrontPage Web site updated in Project 3. If you did not complete Project 3, see your instructor for a copy of the files required to complete this project.

More About

The FrontPage Help System

Need Help? It is no further away than the Type a question for help box on the menu bar in the upper-right corner of the window. Click the box that contains the text, Type a question for help, type `help`, and then press the ENTER key. FrontPage responds with a list of topics you can click to learn about obtaining help on any FrontPage-related topic. To find out what is new in FrontPage 2003, type `what is new in FrontPage` in the Type a question for help box.

To Start FrontPage and Open an Existing Web Site

1. **Click the Start button on the taskbar. Point to All Programs on the Start menu.**
2. **Point to Microsoft Office on the All Programs submenu.**
3. **Click Microsoft Office FrontPage 2003 on the Microsoft Office submenu.**
4. **Click the Open button arrow on the Standard toolbar.**
5. **Click Open Site on the Open menu. If necessary, when FrontPage displays the Open Site dialog box, click the Look in box arrow and select the folder location where you stored the Web site for Project 3 (e.g., C:\jkeeler).**
6. **Click the Open button.**

The previously created FrontPage Web site is loaded and is displayed in Folders view (Figure 4-4).

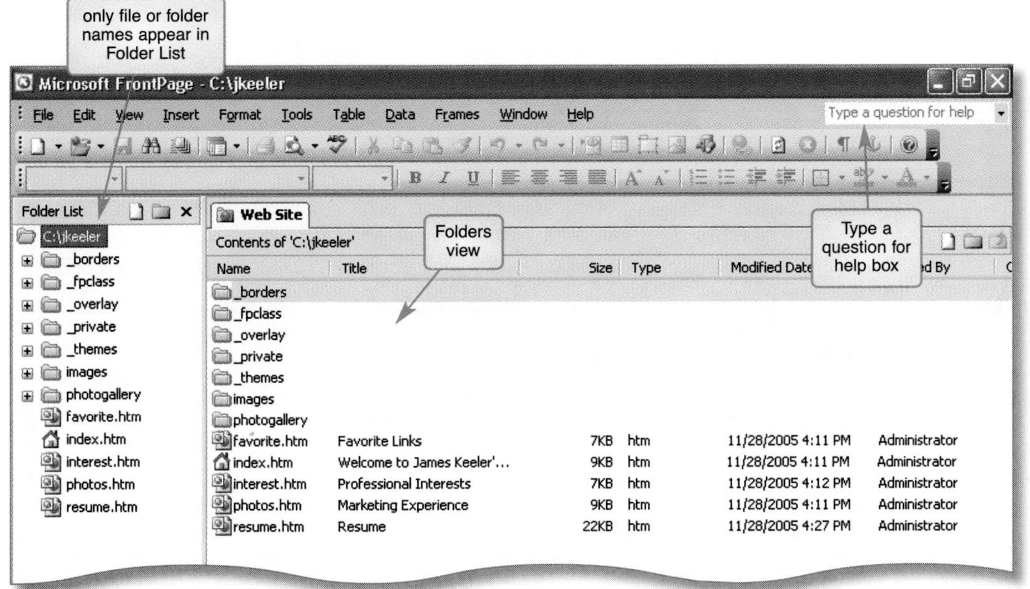

FIGURE 4-4

FrontPage has several ways in which you can manage the files in your FrontPage Web site. The Folder List pane displays the files included in the current Web site. Operations on these files, such as renaming or deleting files, can be performed in the Folder List pane, as previously demonstrated. Another view, Folders view, allows for similar file management and displays additional information about files in the current Web site, such as file size, title, when the file was last modified, and who last modified it. The Folder List pane is a subset of the more expanded Folders view.

Adding and Renaming a Web Page in Folders View

While viewing the Web site in Folders view, you can add a new page to a FrontPage Web site. Adding a page in this view causes the page to be saved and added to the list of files in the Web site as soon as you rename the new page or change views. When you add a new page in Folders view, FrontPage supplies a default name and title for the page and allows you to change the name of the new page immediately. You also can change the name later. The Folder List pane includes three buttons at the top of the pane. The New Page button adds a new Web page to the current Web site. The New Folder button adds a new folder to the current Web site. The Close button closes the pane. Adding a new page in any view other than Navigation or Folders view automatically changes the view to Page view. For a new page created in another view to be displayed in Folders view, you must save it before switching to Folders view.

The steps on the next page add and rename a new Web page in Folders view.

To Add and Rename a Web Page in Folders View

1

- **Right-click on an empty area of the Folders view.**
- **Click the New command on the shortcut menu.**

FrontPage displays a shortcut menu (Figure 4-5).

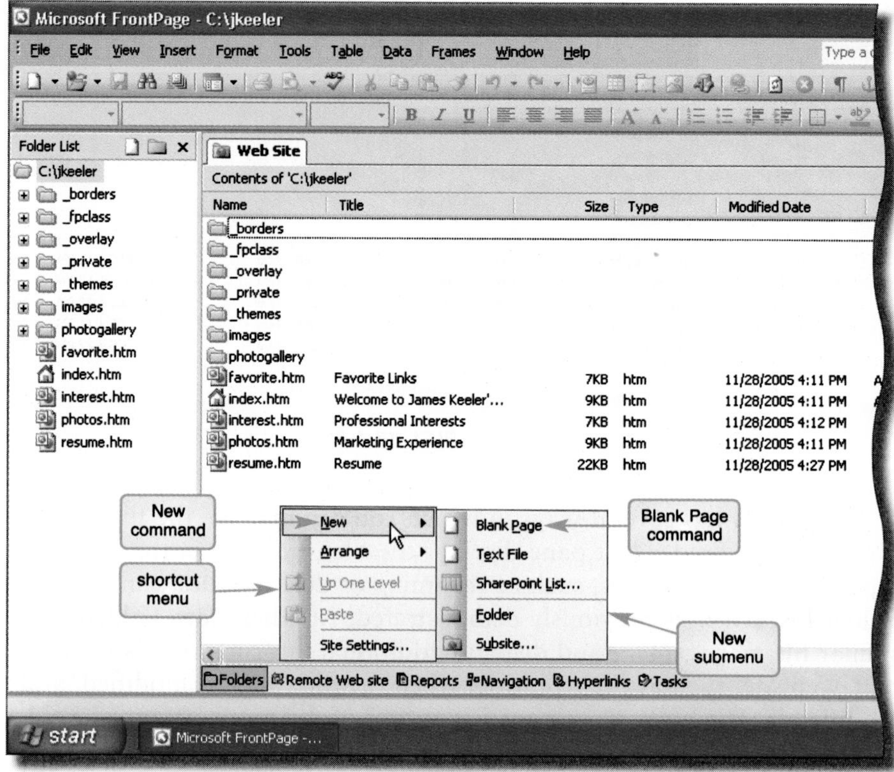

FIGURE 4-5

2

- **Click Blank Page on the New submenu.**

A new file is added to the Web site and is displayed in Folders view. The name of the new file is highlighted (Figure 4-6).

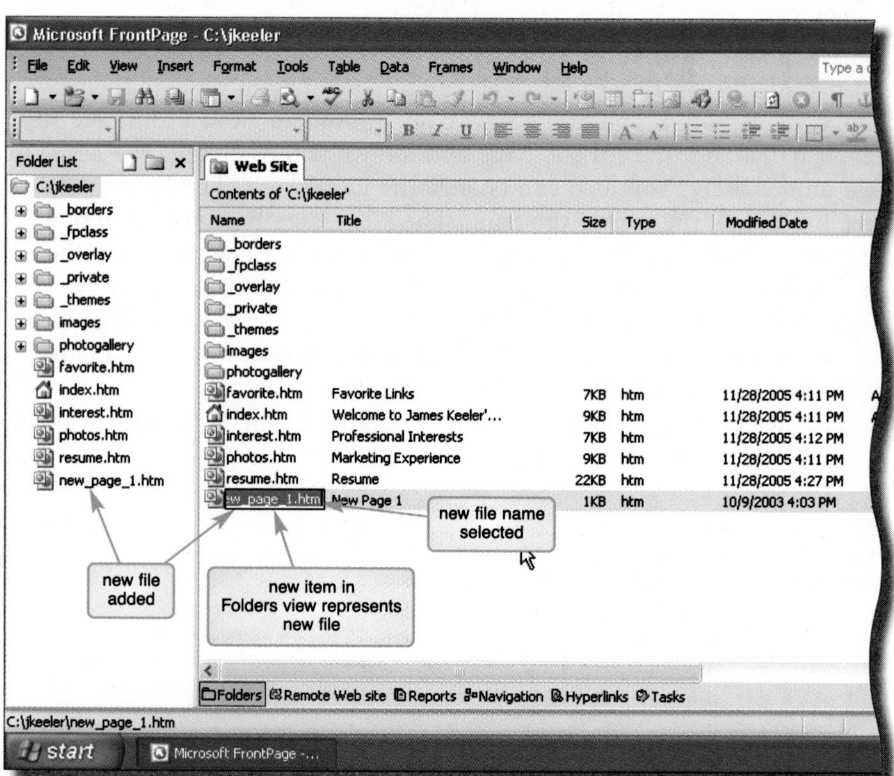

FIGURE 4-6

3

- **Type** `jobopportunity.asp` **as the new file name and then press the ENTER key.**
- **If the Microsoft Office FrontPage dialog box is displayed, click the Yes button.**

The file name changes to jobopportunity.asp (Figure 4-7). This page later will have code added by FrontPage that requires the .asp extension.

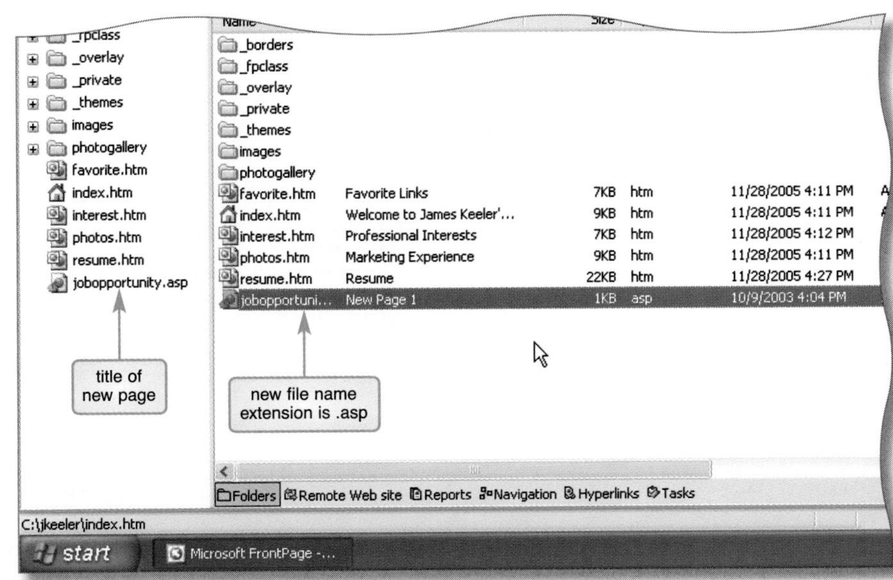

FIGURE 4-7

> **Other Ways**
>
> 1. Click file name to select it, click file name, type new file name
> 2. Right-click file name in Folders List pane, click Rename on shortcut menu, type new file name

Adding a new page in this manner causes FrontPage to use the supplied file name as the default title for the new Web page. You likely will want to change the title, as the title is displayed on the title bar of the Web browser when the page is viewed.

The following steps modify the title of a Web page in Folders view.

To Modify a Page Title in Folders View

1

- **Right-click on the new file in Folders view and then click Properties on the shortcut menu.**
- **When the jobopportunity.asp Properties dialog box is displayed, type** `Job Opportunity Posting` **in the Title text box.**

FrontPage displays the jobopportunity.asp Properties dialog box. The new title appears in the Title text box (Figure 4-8).

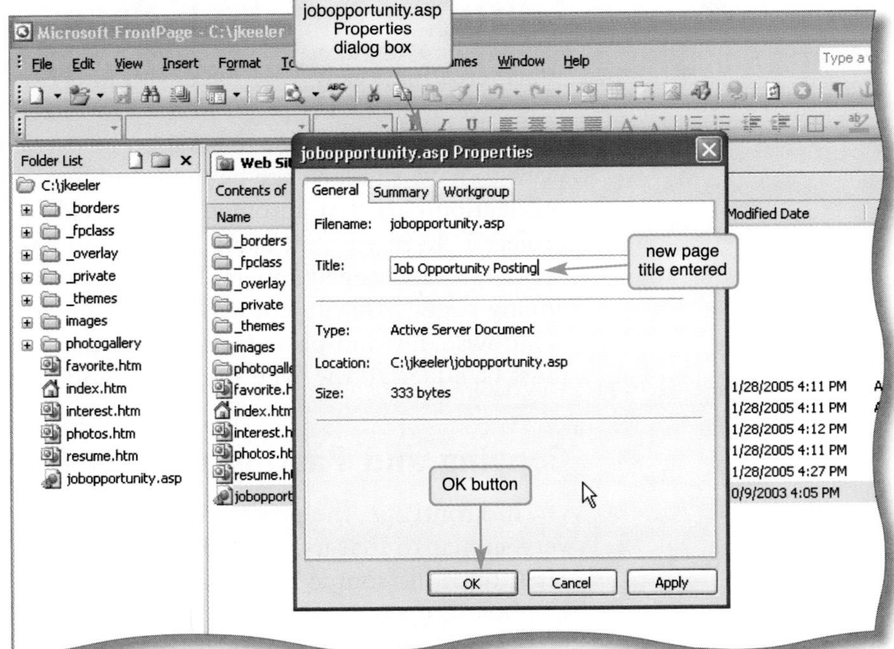

FIGURE 4-8

2

• **Click the OK button.**

FrontPage displays the new title for the page in Folders view (Figure 4-9).

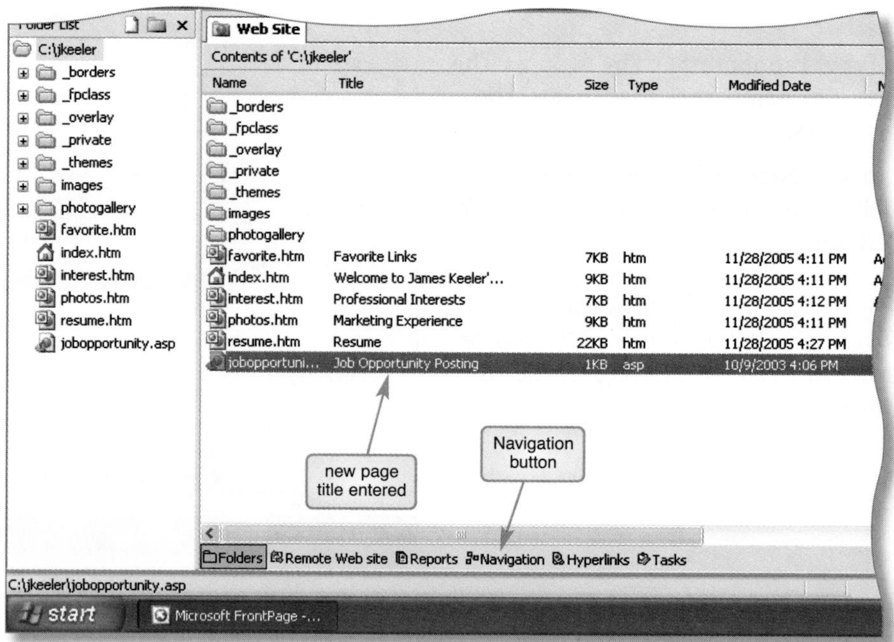

FIGURE 4-9

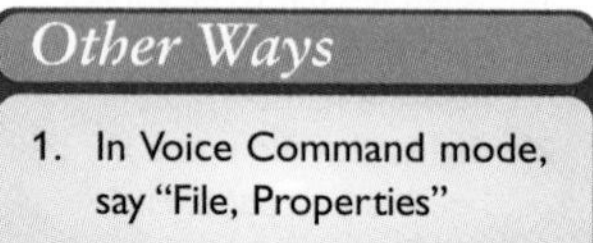

Other Ways

1. In Voice Command mode, say "File, Properties"

If necessary, you can rename a file in Folders view safely at any time. When renaming a file, FrontPage determines if other pages reference the current file name and, if they do, FrontPage prompts for permission to update any such links accordingly.

Editing a New Web Page

When creating a new Web page, you likely will want some similarity between the new page and existing pages in the FrontPage Web site. Using a theme allows certain aspects, such as the color scheme, to be carried over to new pages. You also may want to have similar page banners and hyperlinks on each page. FrontPage provides Navigation bars that automatically provide continuity in hyperlinks, as was done in Project 1. Even without using Navigation bars, you can copy elements, such as hyperlinks and page banners, from one Web page to another. To maintain continuity among pages, you can copy the page banner from James Keeler's Home page using Windows copy-and-paste features; for the banner to be displayed, however, the page must be added to the Web site's navigation structure.

Copying and Pasting Objects from Another Web Page

In FrontPage, the procedure to copy objects from one Web page to another is very similar to that used earlier to copy text from a Word document to a Web page. First, open the source Web page, select the object to be copied, place it on the Clipboard, open the target Web page, and then paste the copied object into the target Web page.

The following steps summarize how to add the Job Opportunity Posting Web page to the navigation structure of the Web site, and then copy the Home page banner, paste it into the Job Opportunity Posting Web page, and modify the page banner text.

To Copy and Paste a Page Banner

1. **Click the Navigation button. Drag and drop the file, jobopportunity.asp, from the Folder List below the Resume page icon.**
2. **Double-click the Home page icon to display the Home page in Page view.**
3. **When the Home page is displayed, click the page banner to select it. Press CTRL+C to copy the page banner.**
4. **Double-click the file, jobopportunity.asp, in the Folder List. Click the Center button on the Formatting toolbar. Press CTRL+V to paste the copied page banner.**
5. **Hold down the SHIFT key and then press the ENTER key.**
6. **Select a font size of 2 (10 pt). Type** `(Job opportunity postings are for members of Trelane College only.)` **as text centered below the page banner. Press the ENTER key.**

Figure 4-10 shows the page, jobopportunity.asp, with the pasted page banner and new text.

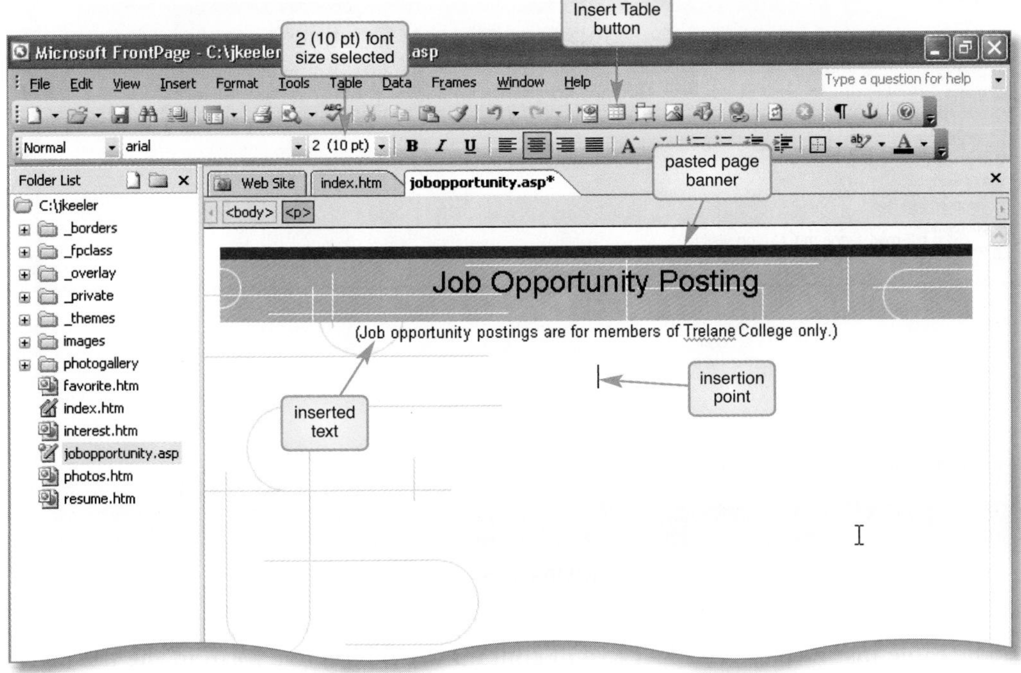

FIGURE 4-10

This project uses tables to control spacing of objects in the Web page. In this case, one table contains the form and a link bar with hyperlinks to other pages, while additional tables are used within the form to position form fields and text. Although no name is associated with a given table in FrontPage, it can be helpful for discussion to reference them by the order in which they are created. The banner and text inserted earlier are not in a table, so the next table to add is the first table for this page, or table-T1. The steps on the next page summarize how to add a table, table-T1, to the Job Opportunity Posting page.

To Add a Table to a Web Page

1. **If necessary, position the insertion point below the text below the page banner. Click the Insert Table button on the Standard toolbar and then drag to select two rows and one column (2 by 1 table). Release the mouse button.**
2. **Right-click the table and then click Table Properties on the shortcut menu. When the Table Properties dialog box is displayed, type** 0 **in the Size box in the Borders area and then click the OK button.**

Figure 4-11 shows the FrontPage window after the insert table operation is completed. The table is displayed on the Web page with two rows and one column.

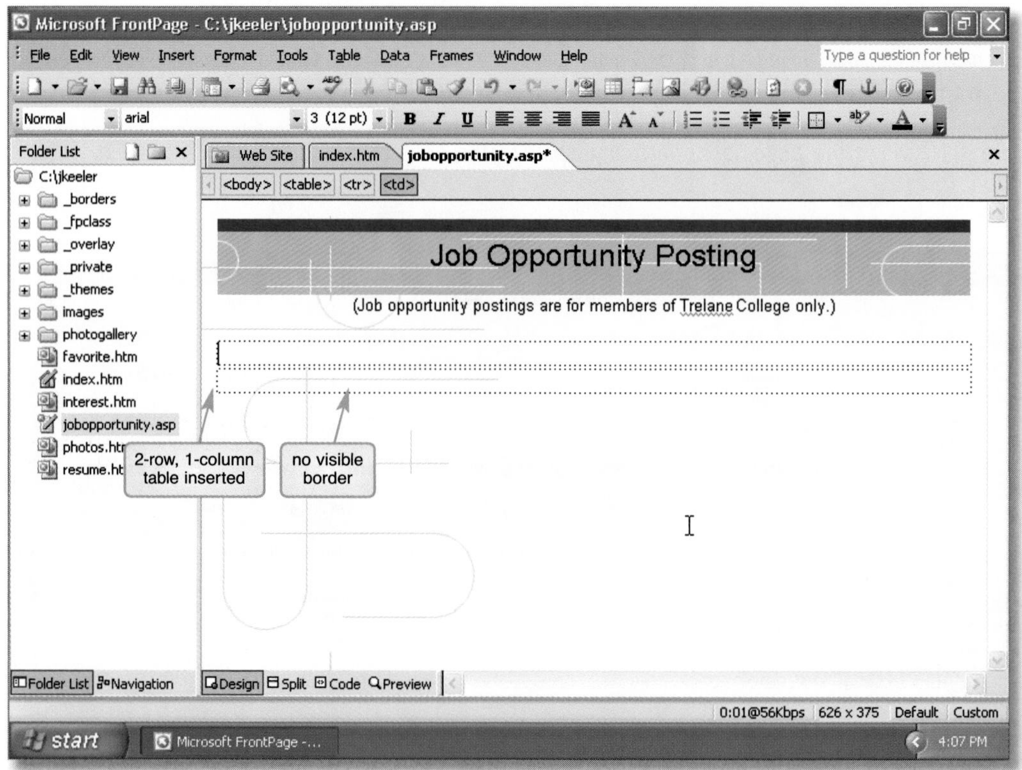

FIGURE 4-11

The table just inserted, table-T1, will contain the interactive form in the top row and the link bar hyperlinks to other pages in this Web site in the bottom row. Copying and pasting the link bar from the Home page to the Job Opportunity Posting page is done in a similar manner as copying and pasting the page banner.

The following steps copy and paste the link bar from the Home page to the Job Opportunity Posting page.

To Copy and Paste a Link Bar from a Web Page

1

- **Click the index.htm tab at the top of the Page pane.**
- **If necessary, scroll down and then select the link bar at the bottom of the page.**

The Home page is displayed and the link bar is selected (Figure 4-12).

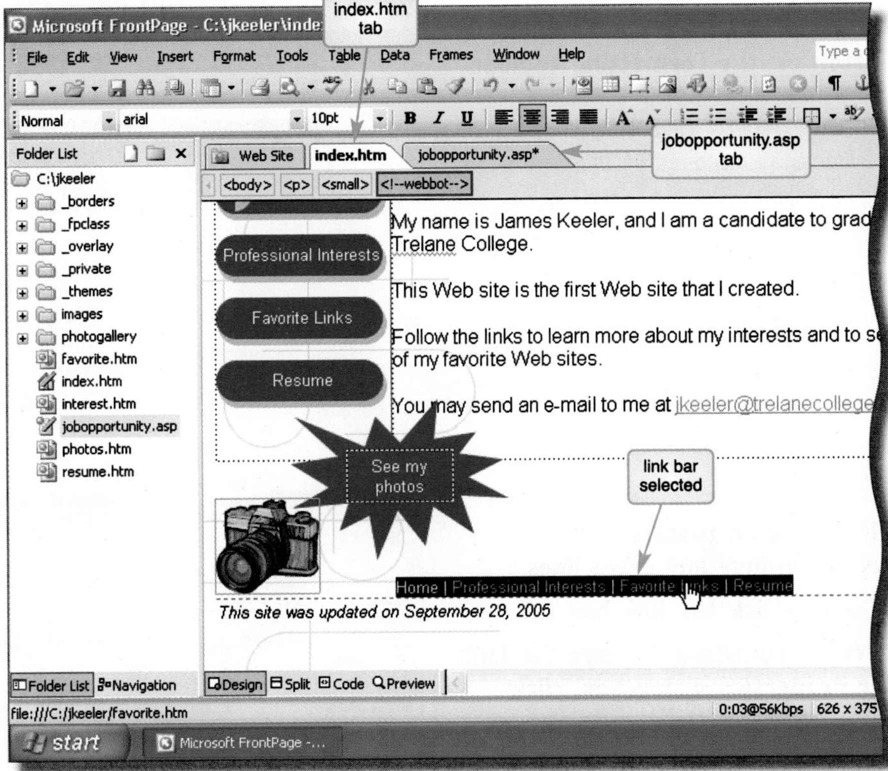

FIGURE 4-12

2

- **Press CTRL+C to copy the selected component.**
- **Click the jobopportunity.asp tab to display the Job Opportunity Posting page.**
- **Click in the bottom row of table-T1 to position the insertion point.**

The Link Bar component is copied, and the insertion point is positioned in the bottom row of table-T1 on the Job Opportunity Posting page (Figure 4-13).

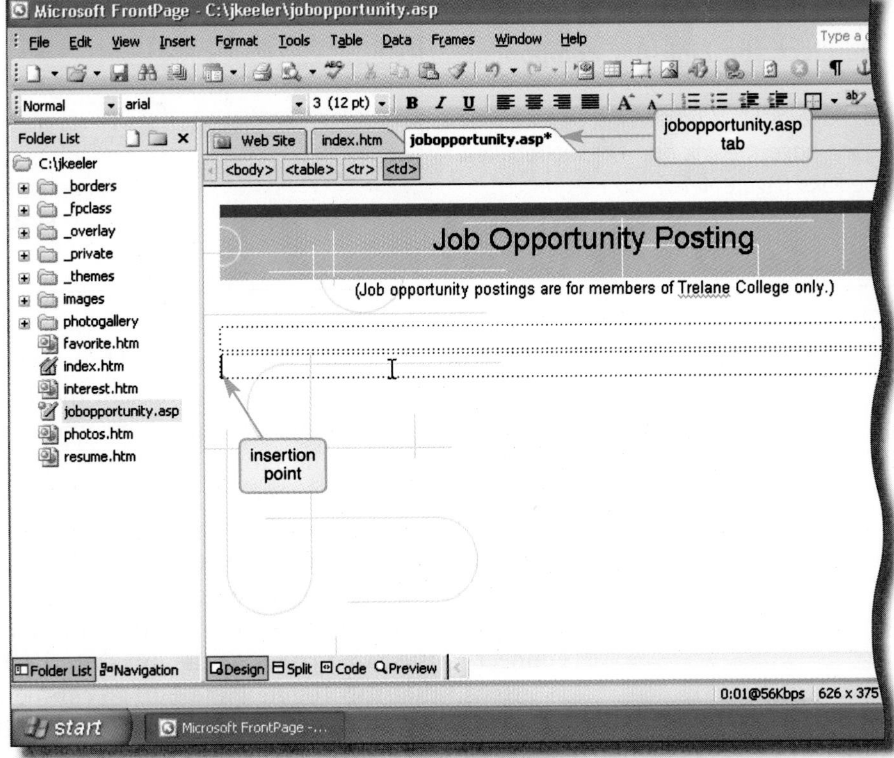

FIGURE 4-13

3

- **Press CTRL+V to paste the copied link bar.**
- **If necessary, click the Center button on the Formatting toolbar.**

FrontPage displays the copied link bar with the Home link centered on the page (Figure 4-14).

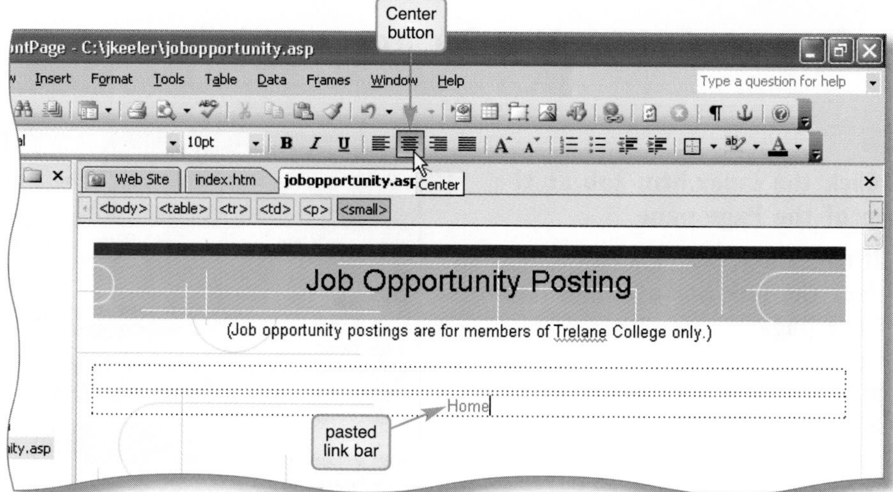

FIGURE 4-14

4

- **If necessary, press the BACKSPACE key to remove any extra lines.**
- **Double-click the link bar.**
- **When FrontPage displays the Link Bar Properties dialog box, click Parent level in the Hyperlinks to add to page area.**
- **Verify that Home page is selected in the Additional pages area.**
- **Click the OK button.**
- **Deselect the Link Bar component.**

FrontPage displays on the Job Opportunity Posting page the link bar with the required hyperlinks (Figure 4-15).

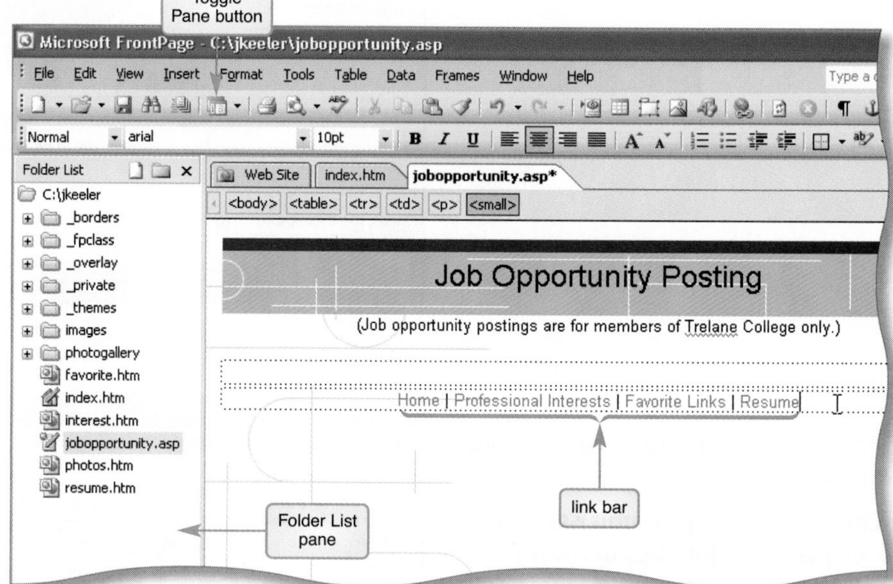

FIGURE 4-15

A copy of the link bar from the Home page is pasted into the Job Opportunity Posting page. The Link Bar component displays hyperlinks based on the position of the page in the Web site navigation structure and the selection of hyperlinks to relative pages. Because the Home page link bar is set to display hyperlinks to the Home page and child-level pages (Professional Interests, Favorite Links, Resume), the link bar retained those properties when pasted into the Job Opportunity Posting page. No child-level pages exist for the Job Opportunity Posting page, however. The child-level pages for the Home page are at the parent level for the Job Opportunity Posting page. Consequently, you modified the Link Bar properties accordingly so the links connect to the same pages as the links on the Home page.

Recall that the Toggle Pane button can be used to display or hide the Folder List pane. Hiding the Folder List pane provides additional space for editing the page. When the form fields and text are added later, having a larger area for editing the page will make positioning such elements easier. The following step hides the Folder List pane.

To Hide the Folder List Pane

1

- **Click the Toggle Pane button on the Standard toolbar.**

FrontPage displays the current page in Page view with the Folder List pane hidden (Figure 4-16). This button is a toggle, so repeating the same step redisplays the Folder List pane.

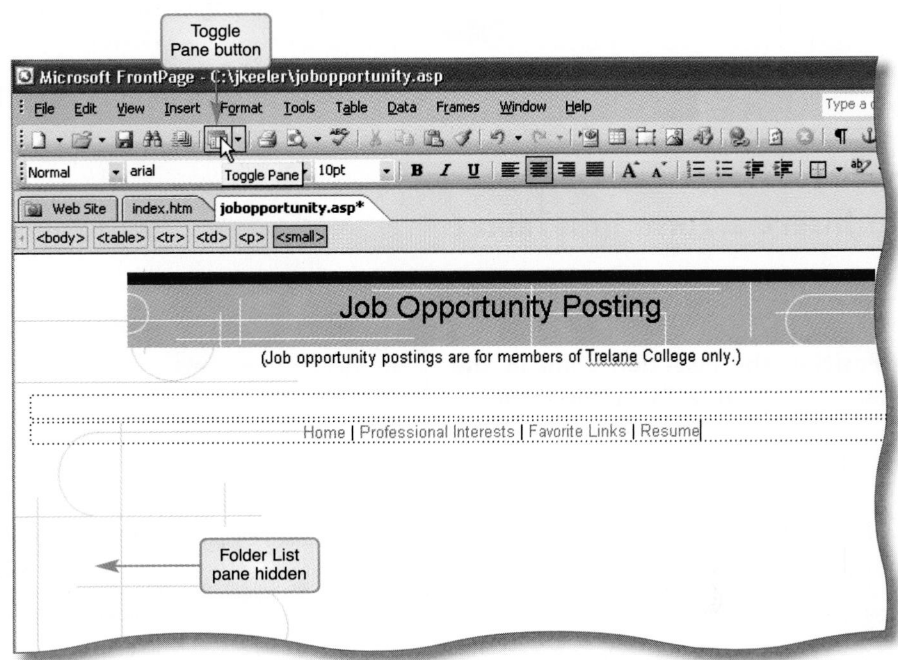

FIGURE 4-16

Other Ways

1. Click the Toggle Pane button arrow on Standard toolbar, click Folder List
2. Click the Close button at the top of the Folder List pane
3. On View menu click Folder List
4. Press ALT+V, E
5. In Voice Command mode, say "View, Folder List"

With the page banner, table-T1, and the link bar added, this page now is ready to have the form and form fields added to it, which will provide the mechanism for feedback from the user.

Inserting a Form in a Web Page

You learned that a form typically consists of one or more form fields along with Submit and Reset buttons. FrontPage automatically creates the Submit and Reset buttons when you insert a form in the Web page. You also can create a new form by inserting any of the form fields outside of an existing form. Within any one form in a Web page, you may have many form fields, but you will have only one Submit button and only one Reset button.

Inserting a Form in a Table

Although FrontPage automatically creates a form when you insert the first form field in the Web page, you also can insert a form before inserting any form fields. In both cases, FrontPage inserts a form HTML tag in the Web page, along with the HTML tags describing the form field you inserted, if any. Additional form fields subsequently can be added to the existing form. A form can be added to a Web page without using a table. Using a table, however, allows you to control the positioning of text relative to a form, whether the text is external to the form or within the form.

Although not required, inserting a new form into a table allows you to control positioning of the form on the Web page.

The following steps insert a form in table-T1 on the Job Opportunity Posting page.

To Insert a Form in a Table

1

• **Position the insertion point in the first row of table-T1 in the form.**

FrontPage displays the insertion point in the first row of the table on the Job Opportunity Posting page (Figure 4-17).

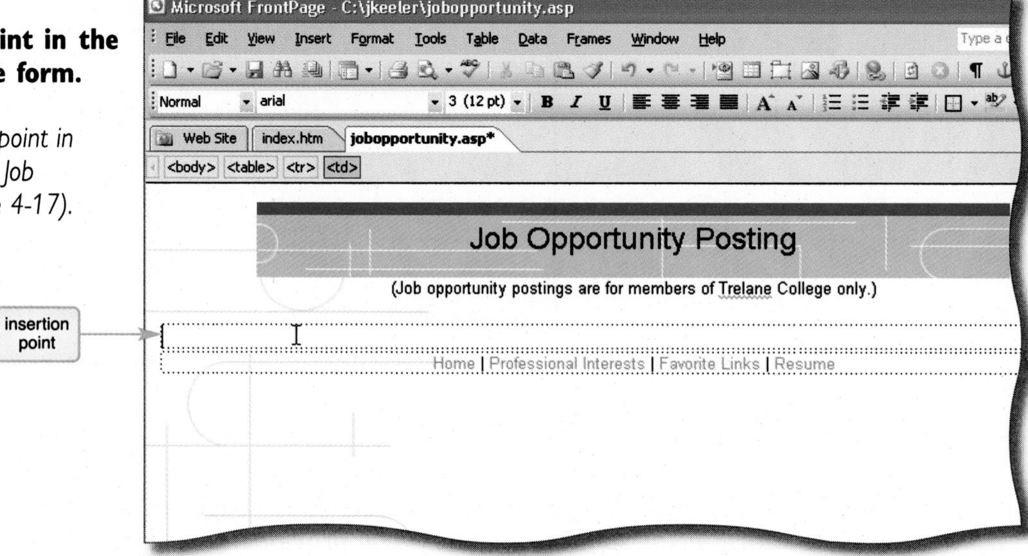

FIGURE 4-17

2

• **Click Insert on the menu bar and then point to Form.**

The Form submenu displays the form fields that you can add to a page (Figure 4-18).

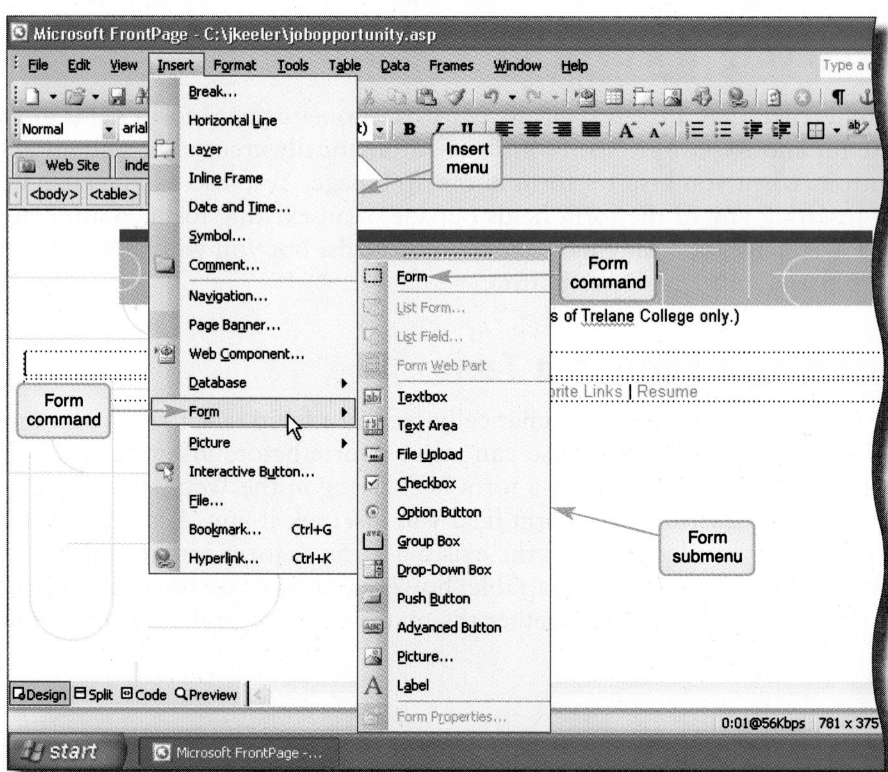

FIGURE 4-18

3

- **Click Form on the Form submenu.**

A form is inserted in the first row of table-T1 (Figure 4-19). FrontPage adds the Submit and Reset buttons automatically.

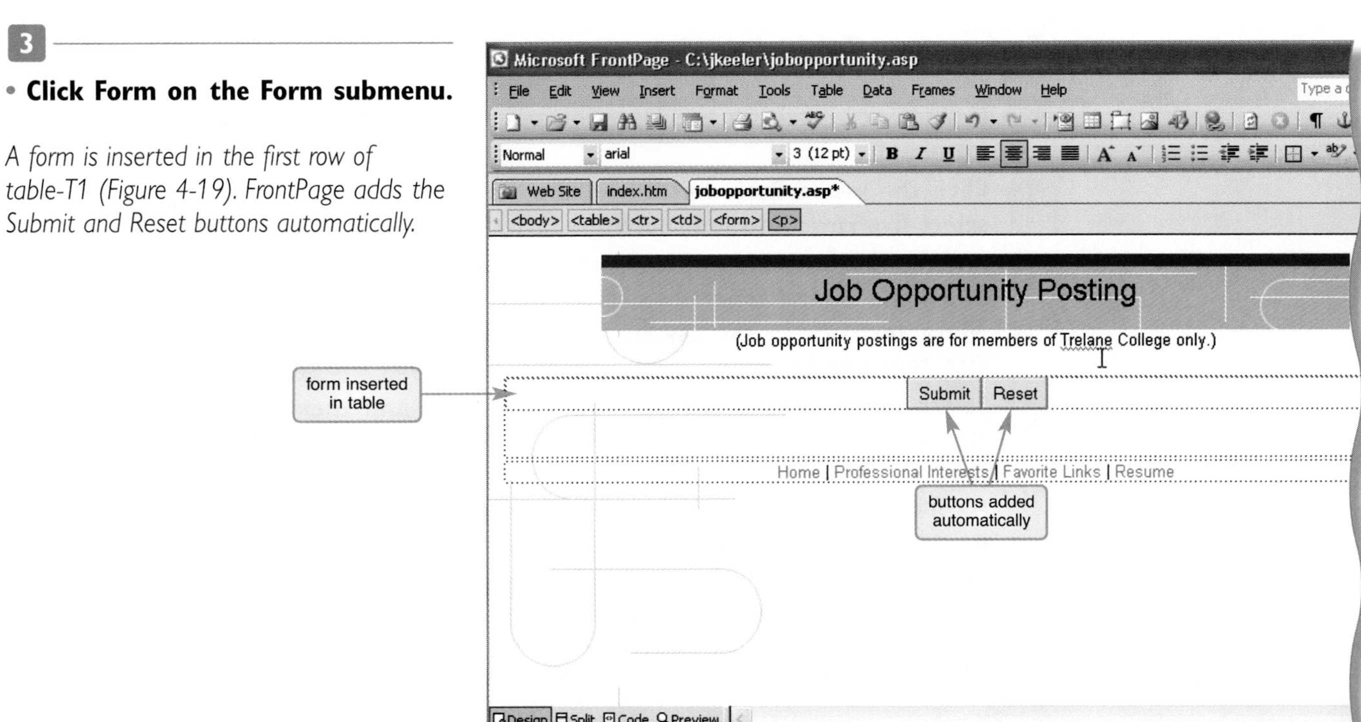

FIGURE 4-19

Other Ways

1. Press ALT+I, R, F
2. In Voice Command mode, say "Insert, Form", click Form

Inserting a Table in a Form

The use of a table to contain the form allows better positioning of the form with respect to text outside the form. Within the form, a table also is useful to position text and form fields. A table allows a physical grouping of related fields and text, although it does not affect the function of the form in the collection of data. In each cell of the second table, table-T2, you will place several form fields and, in one case, an additional table. To ensure that table-T2 is part of the form, you must insert the form in the Web page before inserting the table.

Although not required, inserting a new table into a form allows you to control positioning of the elements of the form, such as text and form fields.

If you insert the table first, followed by the form, the form location is inside one of the table cells, as was done with table-T1. Inserting form fields in another table cell (table-T1) would insert another form, complete with its own Submit and Reset buttons. In this form, you want the user to be able to send all the information he or she enters by clicking only one Submit button. Remember that each Submit button controls only those fields within the same form. The steps on the next page summarize how to insert a table, table-T2, in the form just created.

To Insert a Table in a Form

1. **If necessary, position the insertion point before the Submit button in the form.**
2. **Click the Insert Table button on the Standard toolbar and then drag to select five rows and four columns (5 by 4 table). Release the mouse button.**
3. **Right-click the table and then click Table Properties on the shortcut menu. When the Table Properties dialog box is displayed, type** 99 **in the Specify width text box in the Layout area. Verify In percent is selected. Type** 0 **in the Size text box in the Borders area and then click the OK button.**
4. **Select all columns of the top row, right-click, and then click Merge Cells on the shortcut menu. Follow the same steps to merge the columns of each of the bottom three rows into single columns. Adjust column widths in the second row as shown in Figure 4-20.**
5. **Position the insertion point in the row below the Submit button and then press the BACKSPACE key to delete the extra line. Click the Save button on the Standard toolbar to save the changes.**

Figure 4-20 shows the form with the table, table-T2, added and with the indicated adjustments made.

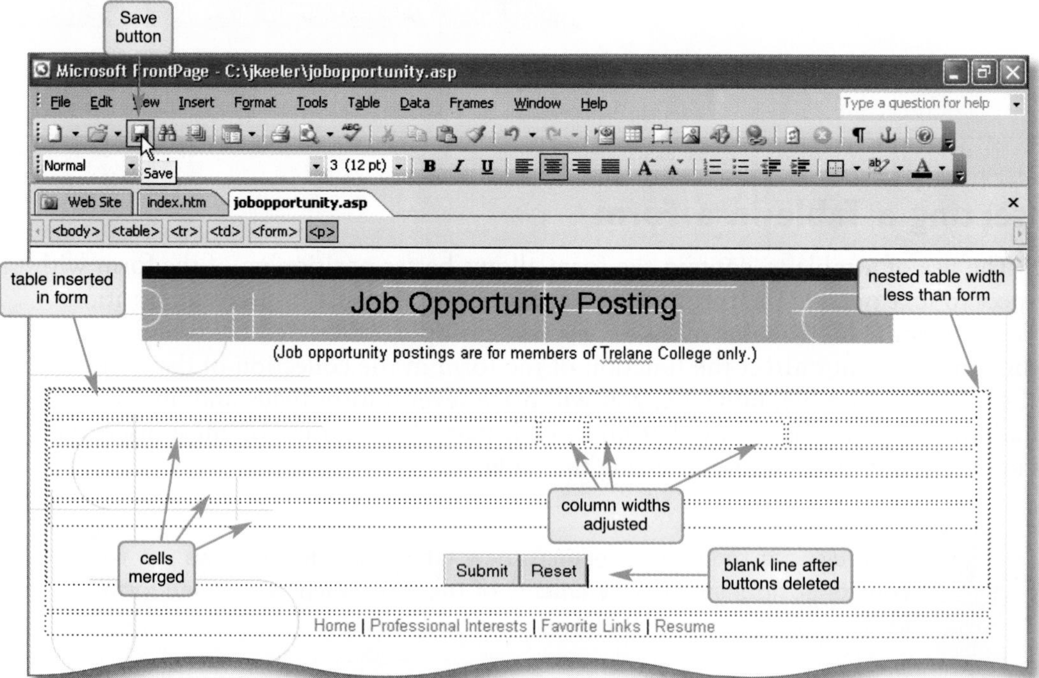

FIGURE 4-20

Inserting Text in a Form

Forms often include text for descriptive reasons, such as giving a user instructions on the actions he or she should take. Inserting text in a form is as simple as positioning the insertion point and then typing. Using tables, as in this project, is helpful for controlling the position of the text. The following steps summarize how to insert descriptive text in the form just created.

To Insert Text in a Form

1. **Position the insertion point in row 1 of table-T2. Click the Underline button and then the Bold button on the Formatting toolbar. Type** `To post a job opportunity, please fill in information below and click the Send button.` **in the first row.**
2. **Position the insertion point in row 2 and column 3 of table-T2. Click the Bold button. Type** `*College Affiliation` **and then, if necessary, drag the right cell border to the left, to wrap the text onto two lines. Right-click the cell and then click Cell Properties on the shortcut menu. In the Cell Properties dialog box, set the Horizontal alignment to Left and the Vertical alignment to Top for the cell. Click the OK button.**
3. **Position the insertion point in row 3 of table-T2. Click the Bold button. Select a font size of 1 (8 pt) in the Font Size list. Type** `*Indicated personal information will not be included with the job posting.` **in row 3. Select the word, not, in the sentence just entered and then click the Underline button. Click the Center button on the Formatting toolbar to center the text.**
4. **Position the insertion point before the Submit button. Click the Bold button. Type** `To send information, click` **and then press the SPACEBAR to include a space between the last word and the button.**
5. **Position the insertion point between the Submit button and the Reset button. Press the SPACEBAR four times to insert four spaces. Click the Bold button. Type** `To reset to initial values, click` **and then press the SPACEBAR to include a space between the last word and the Reset button. If necessary, click the Center button on the Standard toolbar to center the line.**

Figure 4-21 shows the form with the added text and with the last line centered.

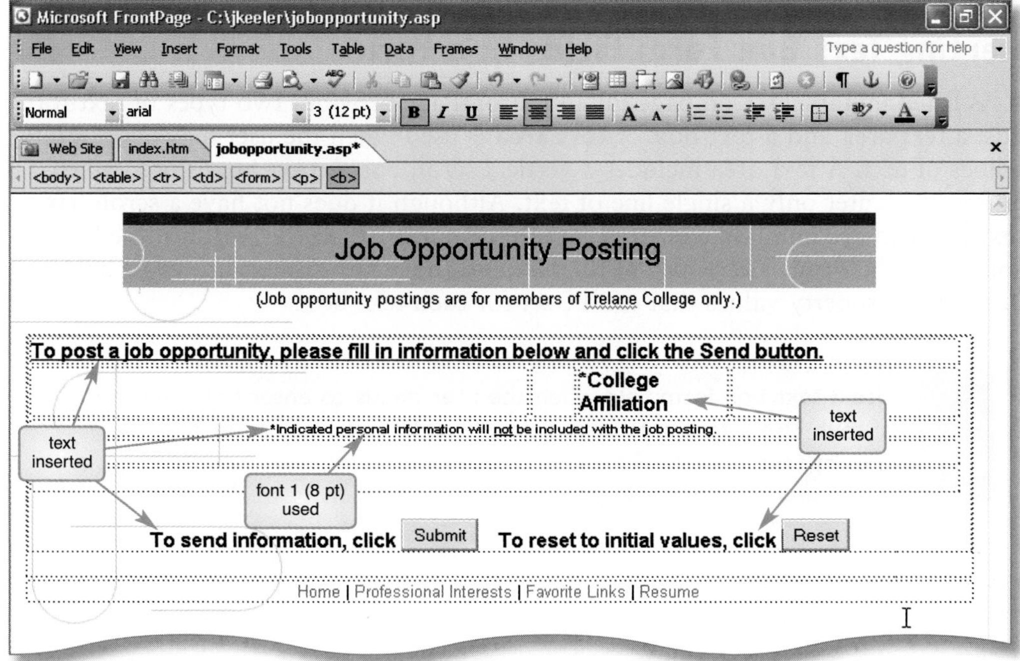

FIGURE 4-21

Inserting Form Fields in a Form

Q&A

Q: Can I insert form fields outside of a form?

A: Yes. Inserting a field outside a form, however, causes a new form to be created by default, with its own submit and reset buttons. The new field is inserted inside the form. You can disable this feature, however, if you want to use fields with scripts rather than inside forms. Click Page Options on the Tools menu, click the General tab, and then click the Automatically enclose form fields within a form check box so that it is not selected.

Although a form is created with Submit and Reset buttons, the buttons have little value until the form includes form fields to collect data from the user. This is done by means of form fields. Form fields allow the user to enter text, initiate actions by clicking buttons, and make choices by means of drop-down list boxes, option buttons, and check boxes.

The two steps used to insert a form field in a Web page are (1) adding the form field and any accompanying descriptive text, and (2) modifying the properties of the form field. When adding form fields, be sure to place all form fields for the same form within the dashed lines that indicate the boundaries of the form. Inserting a form field outside of the form causes the insertion of a new form with its own Submit and Reset buttons.

You will notice that as you insert form fields, they typically contain no text label. Inserting a form field inserts only the form field object, such as an option button or text box. You must add the specific label for the form field. As you do, you can assign the text as the label for a particular field, so when the user clicks the label text, the form field is selected. This makes it easier for users to select small items such as option buttons and check boxes.

Label each form field appropriately and associate labels with their form fields to make navigation of the Web page easier.

Because form fields of the same type have the same set of properties, when multiple instances are needed, it often is easier to create one instance, set the property values, copy the form field, and then paste the needed copies. This is true particularly when you need to modify a number of the properties from their default values. Although you may need to change some properties, such as the field name, for each instance, the number of changes needed for each form field is decreased.

Inserting Text Box Form Fields in a Form

More About

Text Boxes

A text box can be configured as a password field. When a user enters data in the field, the field will display a series of asterisks rather than the text actually entered as data.

As listed in Table 4-1 on page FP 260, FrontPage provides two types of text form fields: a text area and a text box. A **text area** is used when the user may enter multiple lines of text. A text area includes a vertical scroll bar. A **text box** is used when the user may enter only a single line of text. Although it does not have a scroll bar, a text box can accommodate entered text that is longer than the width of the box displayed in the form. The width of the box and the length of text it accepts are independent property values that can be set for each text box.

Use a text box form field when the user needs to enter only one line of text. Use a text area form field when the user may enter multiple lines of text.

The following steps insert a text box form field in a form.

To Insert a Text Box Form Field in a Form

1

- **Position the insertion point in the second row and first column of table-T2.**
- **Right-click the cell and then click Cell Properties on the shortcut menu.**
- **In the Cell Properties dialog box, set the Horizontal alignment to Left and the Vertical alignment to Top for the cell.**
- **Click the OK button.**
- **Click the Bold button.**
- **Type `*Full Name:` and then press the SPACEBAR one time.**

FrontPage displays the inserted text in the second row and first column of the table in the form on the Web page (Figure 4-22).

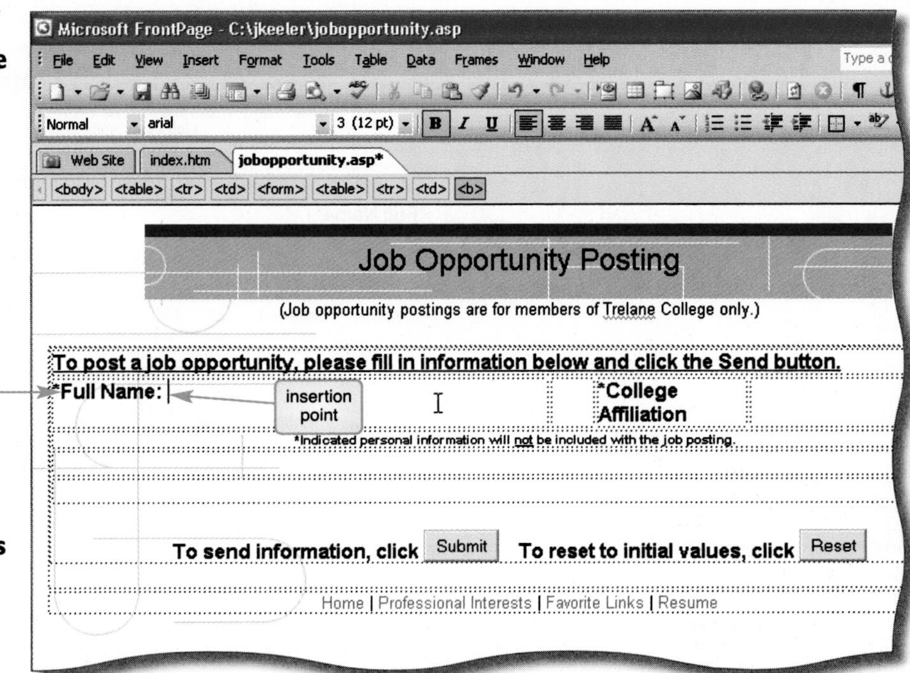

FIGURE 4-22

2

- **Click Insert on the menu bar and then point to Form.**

FrontPage displays the Form submenu (Figure 4-23).

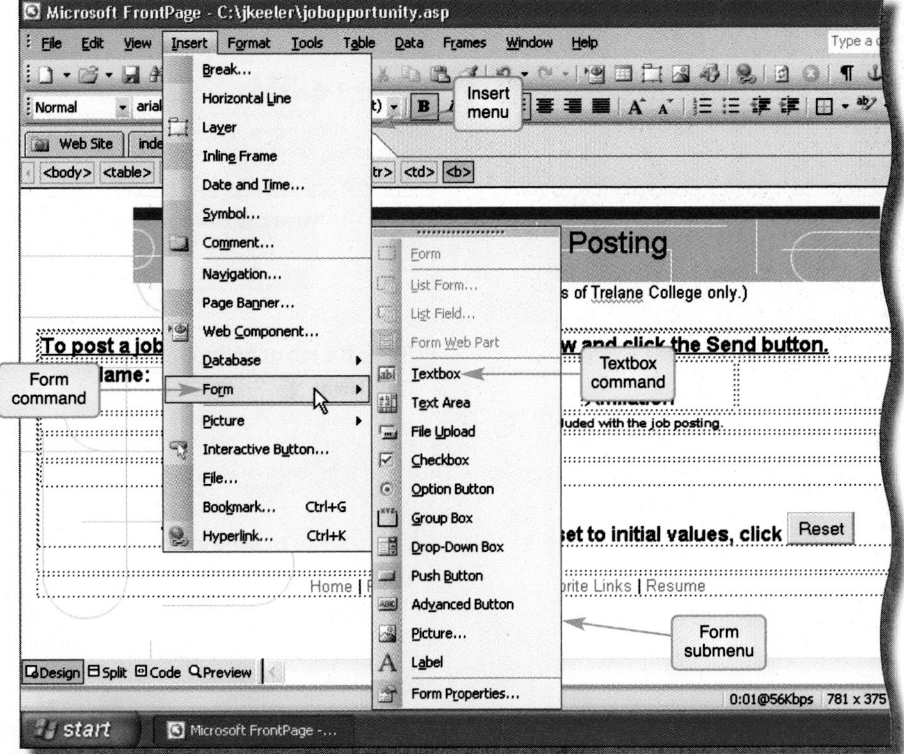

FIGURE 4-23

3

- **Click Textbox.**

A text box form field is inserted in the form with a default length (Figure 4-24).

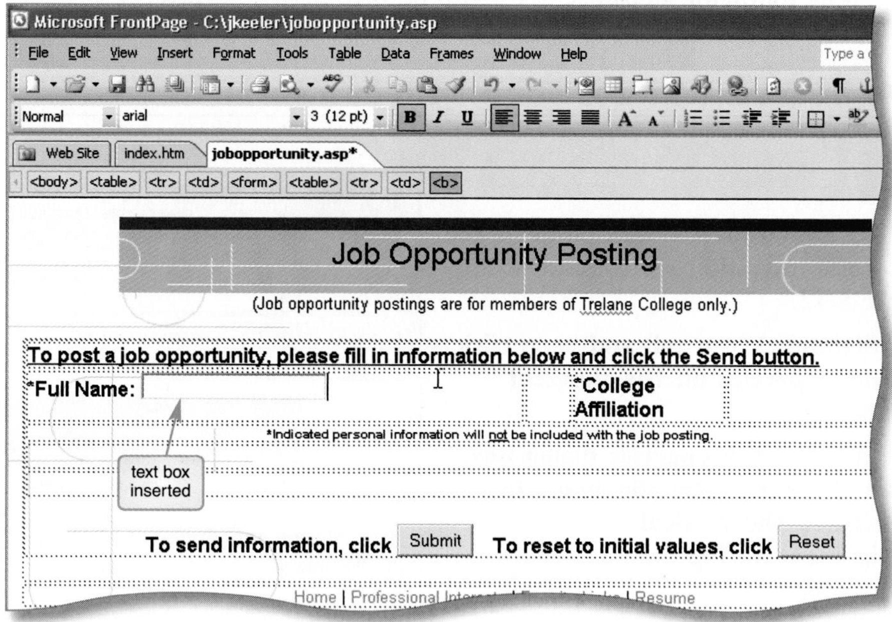

FIGURE 4-24

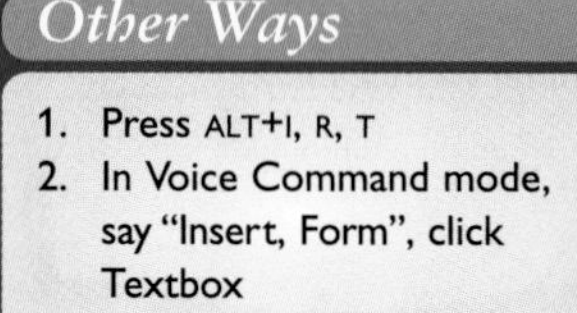

Other Ways

1. Press ALT+I, R, T
2. In Voice Command mode, say "Insert, Form", click Textbox

A text box is inserted in the form. The text box form field has a default set of properties, several of which must be modified. The following steps describe how to modify the properties of a text box form field.

To Modify the Properties of a Text Box Form Field

1

- **Right-click the text box.**

The text box form field is selected and a shortcut menu is displayed (Figure 4-25).

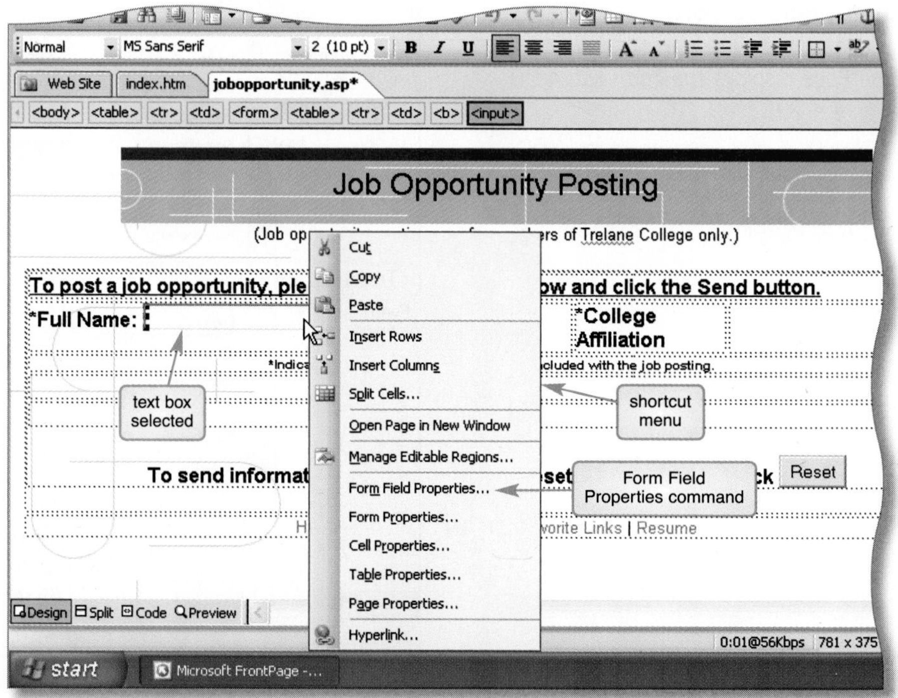

FIGURE 4-25

2

- **Click Form Field Properties.**
- **When FrontPage displays the Text Box Properties dialog box, type** `FullName` **in the Name text box, type** `50` **in the Width in characters text box, and then type** `1` **in the Tab order text box.**

FrontPage displays the Text Box Properties dialog box as shown in Figure 4-26. Because the Name property cannot contain spaces, it is a common practice to use a combination of uppercase and lowercase letters to distinguish each word in a field name.

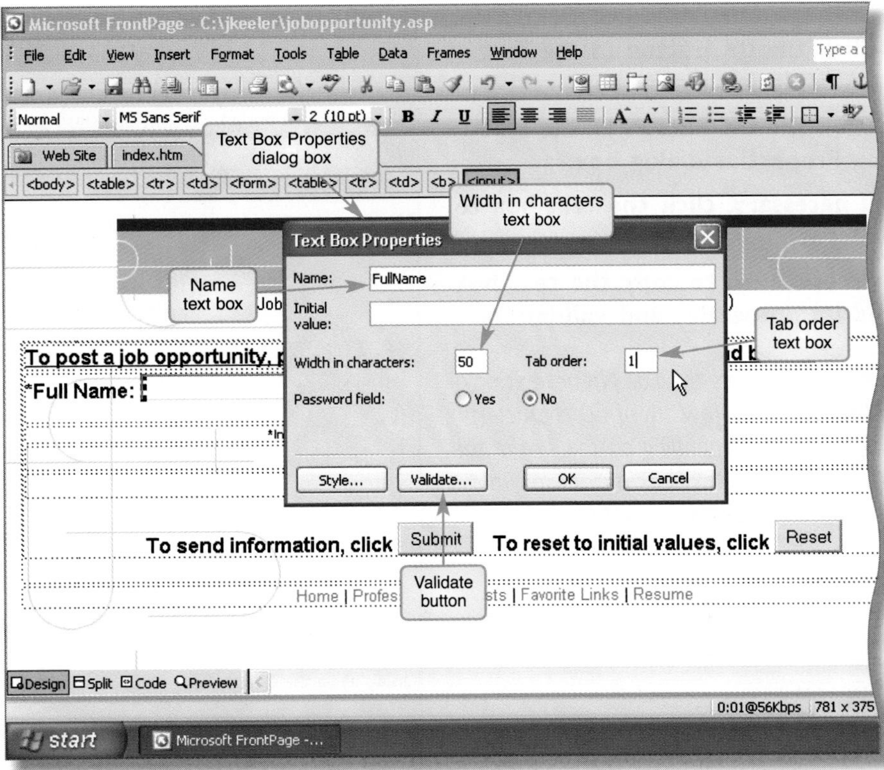

FIGURE 4-26

3

- **Click the Validate button.**
- **When FrontPage displays the Text Box Validation dialog box, click Required in the Data length area and then type** `Full Name` **in the Display name text box.**

FrontPage displays the Text Box Validation dialog box with the changes indicated (Figure 4-27). With Required selected, an error is displayed, using the Display name, if the user enters no data in this form field.

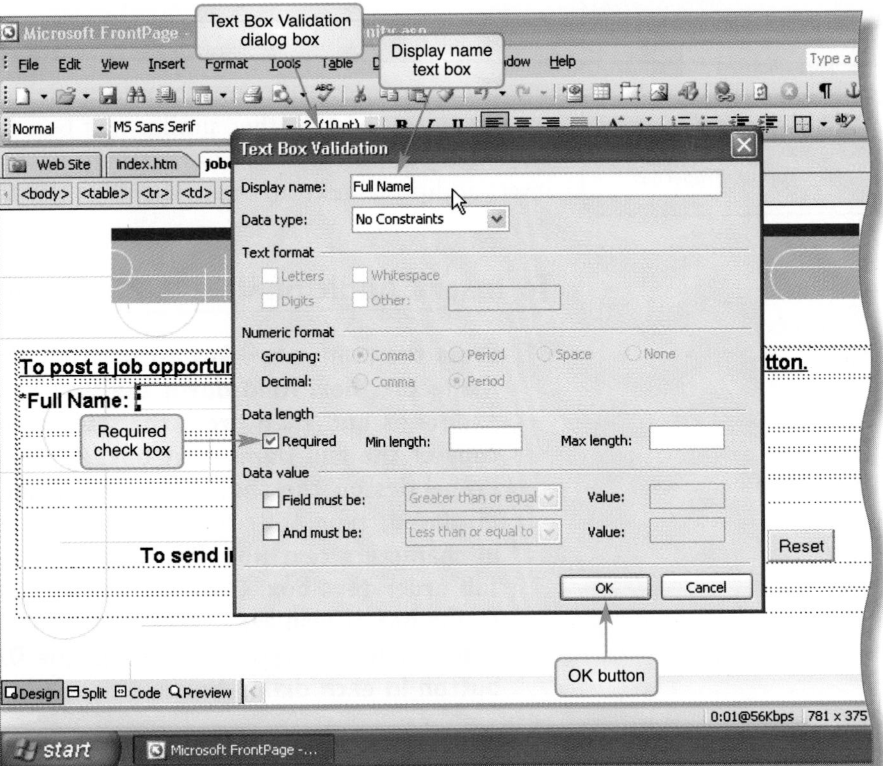

FIGURE 4-27

4

- **Click the OK button in the Text Box Validation dialog box.**
- **Click the OK button in the Text Box Properties dialog box.**
- **If necessary, click the text box to select it.**
- **Press CTRL+C to copy the text box and its properties and validations.**

FrontPage displays the Full Name text box in the form, with a width of 50 characters (Figure 4-28). Depending on the size of the first column, the text box may or may not wrap to a line below its caption.

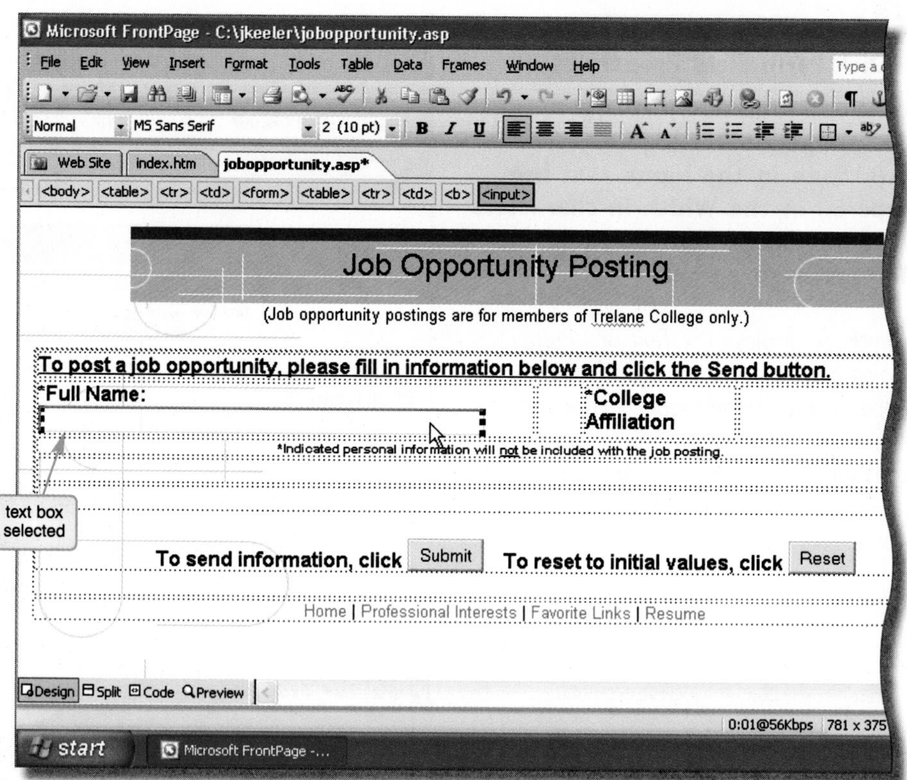

FIGURE 4-28

Other Ways

1. On Format menu click Properties
2. Press ALT+O, T
3. Press ALT+ENTER
4. In Voice Command mode, say "Format, Properties"

The properties of the text box form field have been modified successfully. The form requires several other similar text box form fields to collect the information needed about potential job opportunity posters. The following steps describe how to insert additional text box form fields in the Job Opportunity Posting Web page.

To Insert Additional Text Box Form Fields

1 **Press the RIGHT ARROW key to position the insertion point after the Full Name text box. Hold down the SHIFT key and then press the ENTER key. Type** `*Address` **and then press the SPACEBAR five times. Press CTRL+V to paste a copy of the Full Name text box. Right-click the text box. Click Form Field Properties on the shortcut menu. When the Text Box Properties dialog box is displayed, type** `Address` **in the Name text box. Verify that 50 is in the Width in characters text box. Press the TAB key three times and then type** `2` **in the Tab order text box. Click the Validate button. When the Text Box Validation dialog box is displayed, verify that the Required check box in the Data length area is selected. Type** `Address` **in the Display name text box. Click the OK button in each dialog box.**

2 **Press the RIGHT ARROW key to position the insertion point after the Address text box. Hold down the SHIFT key and then press the ENTER key. Type** `*City` **and then press the SPACEBAR twelve times. Press CTRL+V to paste a copy of the Full Name text box. Right-click the text box. Click Form Field Properties on the shortcut menu. When the Text Box Properties dialog box is displayed, type** `City` **in the Name text box. Press the TAB key and then type** `Trelane` **in the Initial value text box. Verify that 50 is in the Width in characters text box. Press the TAB key twice and then type** `3` **in the Tab order text box. Click the Validate button. When the Text Box Validation dialog box is displayed, verify that the Required check box in the Data length area is selected. Type** `City` **in the Display name text box. Click the OK button in each dialog box.**

3 **Press the RIGHT ARROW key to position the insertion point after the City text box. Hold down the SHIFT key and then press the ENTER key. Type** `*State` **and then press the SPACEBAR eleven times. Press CTRL+V to paste a copy of the Full Name text box. Right-click the text box. Click Form Field Properties on the shortcut menu. When the Text Box Properties dialog box is displayed, type** `State` **in the Name text box. Press the TAB key and then type** `WA` **in the Initial value text box. Press the TAB key and then type** `3` **in the Width in characters text box. Press the TAB key and then type** `4` **in the Tab order text box. Click the Validate button. When the Text Box Validation dialog box is displayed, verify that the Required check box in the Data length area is selected. Type** `State` **in the Display name text box. Select Text in the Data type drop-down list. Click Letters in the Text format area. In the Data length area, type** `2` **in the Min length text box and then type** `2` **in the Max length text box. In the Data value area, click Field must be, if necessary select Greater than or equal to in the drop-down list, and type** `AA` **in the Value text box. Click And must be, if necessary select Less than or equal to in the drop-down list, and type** `ZZ` **in the Value text box. Click the OK button in each dialog box.**

4 **Press the RIGHT ARROW key to position the insertion point after the State text box. Press the SPACEBAR two times. Type** `*Postal Code` **and press the SPACEBAR one time. Press CTRL+V to paste a copy of the Full Name text box. Right-click the text box. Click Form Field Properties on the shortcut menu. When the Text Box Properties dialog box is displayed, type** `PostalCode` **in the Name text box. Press the TAB key and then type** `93938` **in the Initial value text box. Press the TAB key and then type** `10` **in the Width in characters text box. Press the TAB key and then type** `5` **in the Tab order text box. Click the Validate button. When the Text Box Validation dialog box is displayed, verify that the Required check box in the Data length area is selected. Type** `Postal Code` **in the Display name text box. Select Text in the Data type drop-down list. In the Text format area, click Letters, click Digits, click Other and type a hyphen (**`-`**) in the Other text box. In the Data length area, type** `5` **in the Min length text box and type** `10` **in the Max length text box. Click the OK button in each dialog box.**

5 **If necessary, drag the cell borders to widen or shorten the current cell to the maximum size of the largest text box. Click the Save button on the Standard toolbar to save your changes.**

The Web page appears as shown in Figure 4-29 on the next page. The labels, properties, and validations for the form fields in this table are listed in Table 4-3 on the next page.

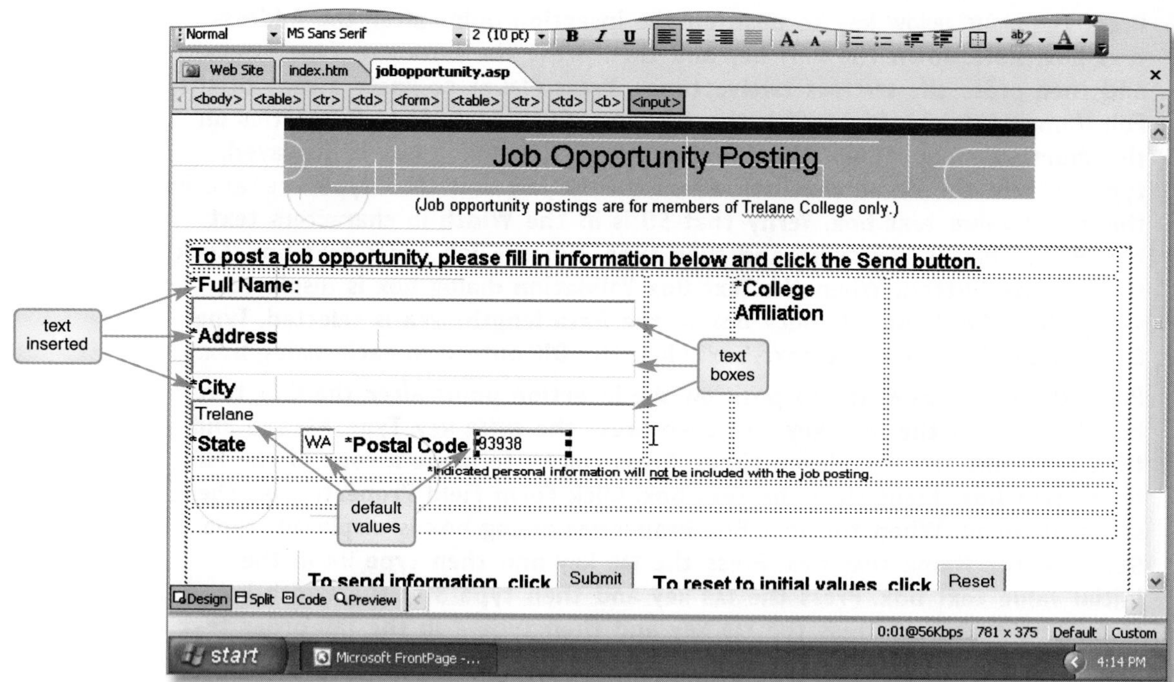

FIGURE 4-29

Table 4-3 Labels, Properties, and Validations for Text Box Form Fields in Table-T2

LABEL	PROPERTY VALUES TO SET	VALIDATIONS TO SET
*Full Name:	Name=FullName Width=50 Tab order=1	Display name=Full Name In Data length area, click Required
*Address	Name=Address Width=50 Tab order=2	Display name=Address In Data length area, click Required
*City	Name=City Initial value=Trelane Width=50 Tab order=3	Display name=City In Data length area, click Required
*State	Name=State Initial value=WA Width=3 Tab order=4	Display name=State Data type=Text In Text format area, click Letters In Data length area, click Required, Min length=2, Max length=2 In Data value area, click Field must be, select Greater than or equal to, set Value to AA; check And must be, select Less than or equal to, set Value to ZZ
*Postal Code	Name=PostalCode Initial value=93938 Width=10 Tab order=5	Display name=Postal Code Data type=Text In Text format area, click Digits, click Letters, click Other; in Other text box, type a hyphen (-) In Data length area, click Required, Min length=5, Max length=10

Several text boxes have been entered in the Web page. The values typed in the Name text box in the Form Field Properties dialog box will be the name portion of each name=value pair that is sent to the Web server to be processed. Even if a user types nothing in the text box, the name is returned to the server when the user submits the form. You should keep track of the names you use, so you do not duplicate any of the names in later form field properties.

You can toggle between Design view and Preview view to see how the fields are aligned. Use the SPACEBAR and the table cell borders to adjust the text boxes to be displayed as desired in the Web page. You also may preview the page in your browser as you adjust page elements, if you save the page between changes.

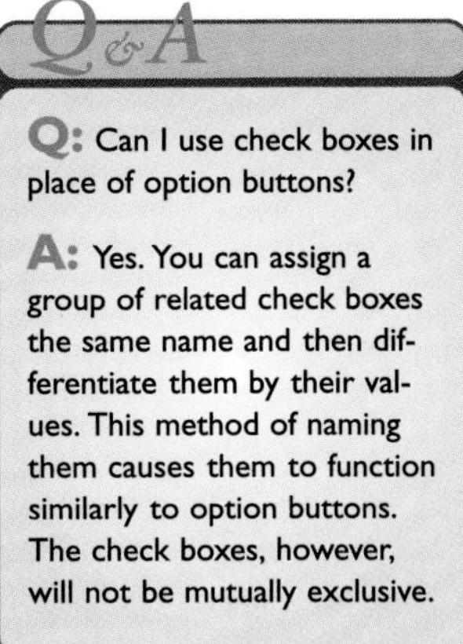

Inserting Check Boxes in a Form

As listed in Table 4-1 on page FP 260, inserting a check box in a form allows a user to choose none, one, or more than one choice from a set of options. Unlike option buttons, check boxes are not mutually exclusive; that is, selecting one check box does not deselect another check box. When the user submits the form, the name=value pair for each selected check box is sent to the server. If a check box is not selected, nothing is returned for that check box. The following steps insert a check box form field in the form.

To Insert a Check Box Form Field in a Form

1

- **Position the insertion point in the fourth column of the second row of table-T2.**
- **Right-click the cell and then click Cell Properties on the shortcut menu.**
- **When FrontPage displays the Cell Properties dialog box, in the Layout area, select Left for the Horizontal alignment and Top for the Vertical alignment for the cell.**

FrontPage displays the Cell Properties dialog box (Figure 4-30). The layout for the cell is set to align to the top and left.

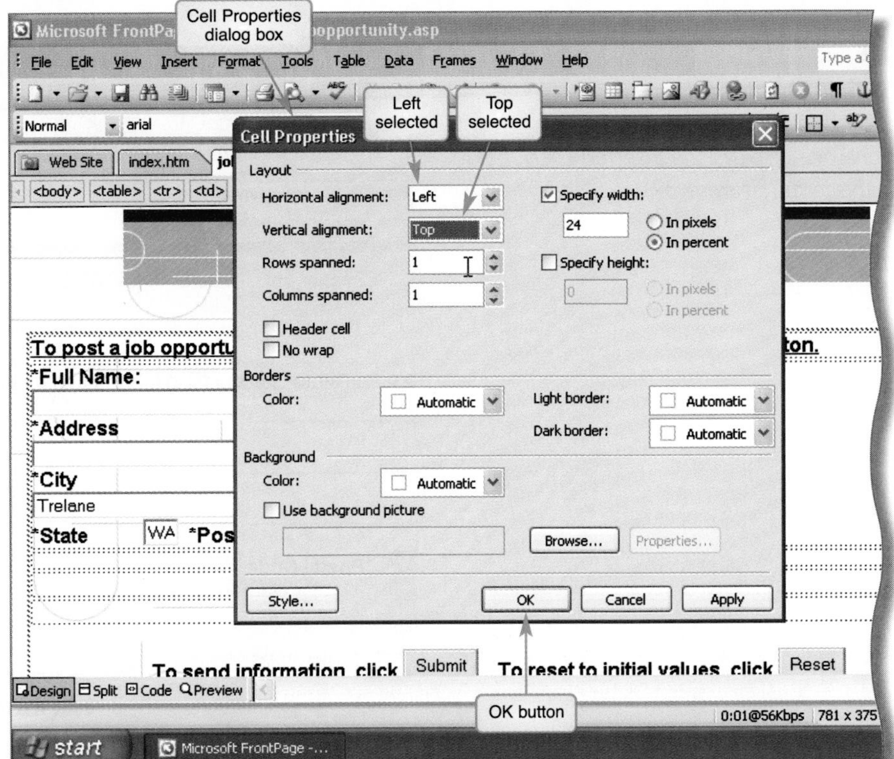

FIGURE 4-30

2

- **Click the OK button.**
- **Click Insert on the menu bar and then point to Form.**

FrontPage displays the Form submenu (Figure 4-31).

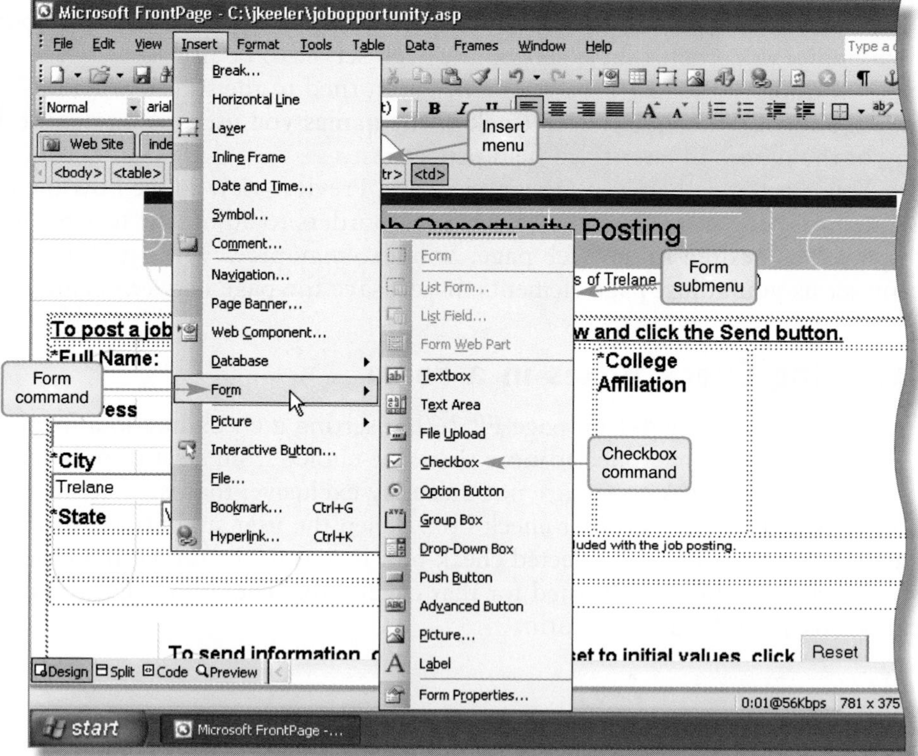

FIGURE 4-31

3

- **Click Checkbox.**

FrontPage displays the inserted check box in the form (Figure 4-32).

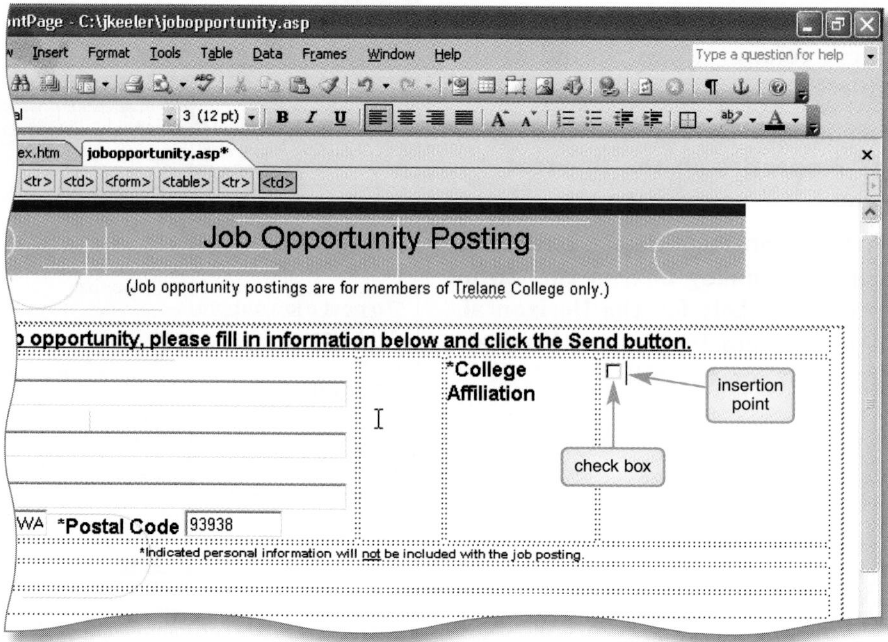

FIGURE 4-32

Other Ways

1. Press ALT+I, R, C
2. In Voice Command mode, say "Insert, Form", click Checkbox

A check box has been added to the form; next, a label will be added to inform the user what he or she is checking. The following steps add text to the form and assign the text as a label for the check box.

To Assign Text as a Label for a Check Box

1

- **Type** Student (Full-time) **to the right of the check box.**
- **Hold down the SHIFT key and then press the ENTER key.**

FrontPage displays the inserted check box and its label text in the form (Figure 4-33).

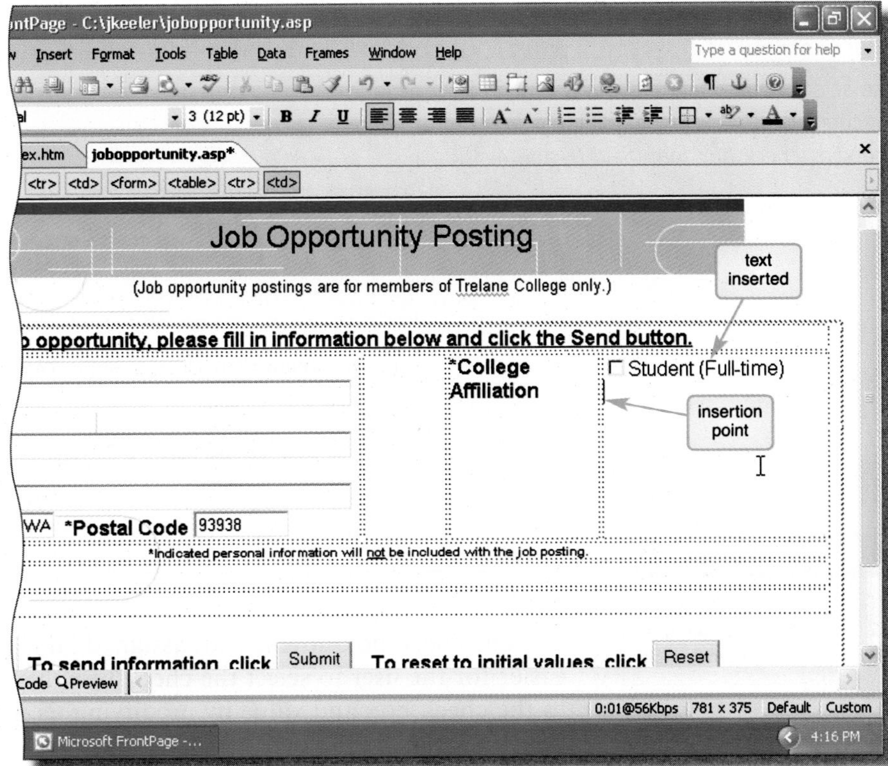

FIGURE 4-33

2

- **Drag through both the check box and the text to select them together.**
- **Click Insert on the menu bar and then point to Form.**

FrontPage displays the Form submenu (Figure 4-34).

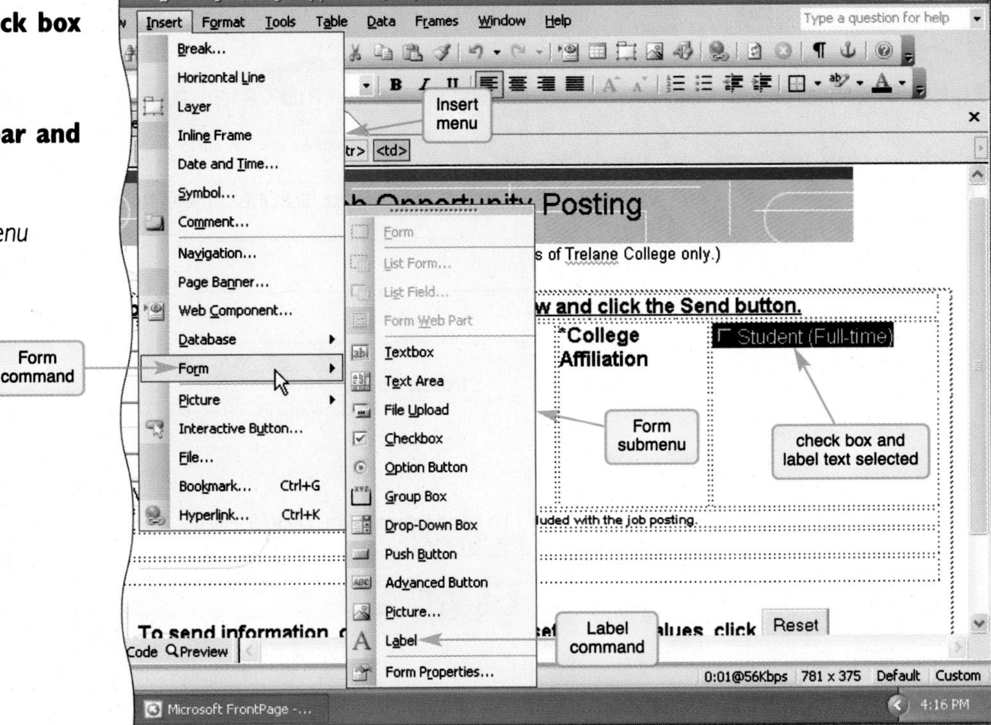

FIGURE 4-34

3

- **Click Label.**
- **Press the RIGHT ARROW key to deselect the text.**

The selected text now has a box around it, indicating that it is a label for the corresponding check box form field (Figure 4-35).

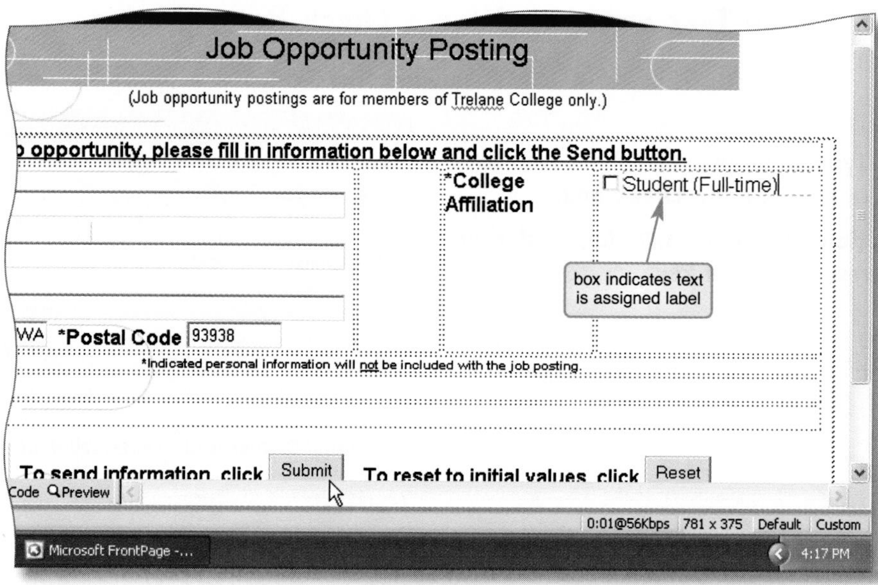

FIGURE 4-35

Other Ways

1. Press ALT+I, R, A
2. In Voice Command mode, say "Insert, Form", click Label

The check box now has an assigned label to describe the option and to make it easier for the user to select the check box. Next, a particular data name will be given to the check box and value by modifying its properties. The following steps modify the check box properties.

To Modify the Properties of a Check Box Form Field

1

- **Right-click the check box.**

FrontPage displays the check box form field as being selected and a shortcut menu is displayed (Figure 4-36).

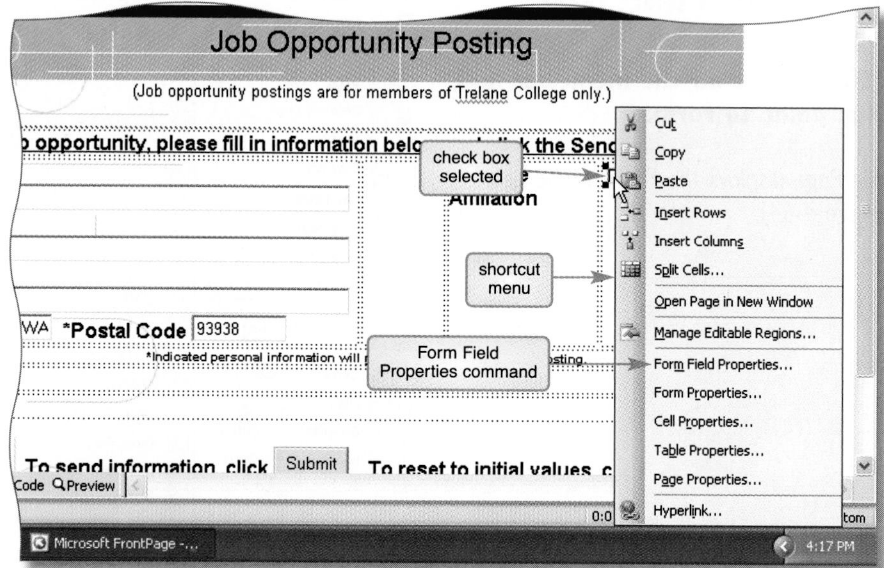

FIGURE 4-36

2

- **Click Form Field Properties.**
- **When FrontPage displays the Check Box Properties dialog box, type** `FTStudent` **in the Name text box and then type** `YES` **in the Value text box.**
- **If necessary, click Checked in the Initial state area to select it.**
- **Type** 6 **in the Tab order text box.**

FrontPage displays the Check Box Properties dialog box as shown in Figure 4-37.

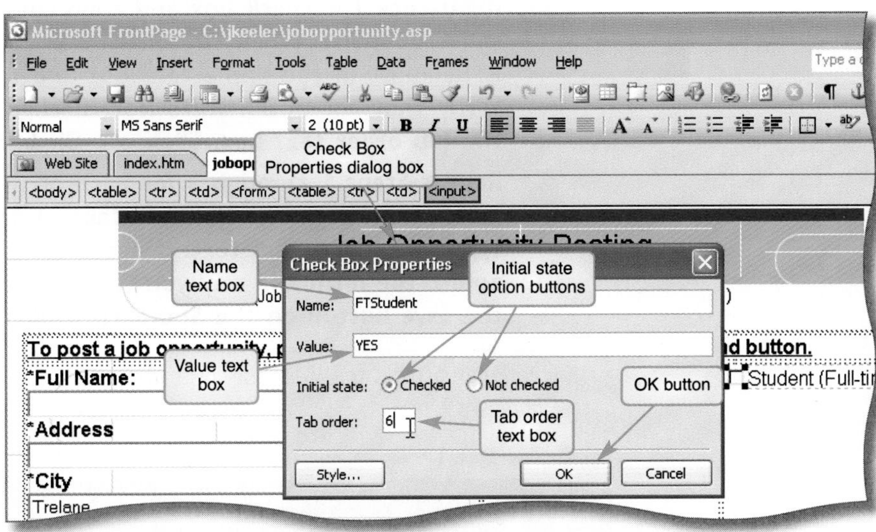

FIGURE 4-37

3

- **Click the OK button.**

The dialog boxes are closed and the check box and its label are displayed in the form (Figure 4-38). The check box initially is selected.

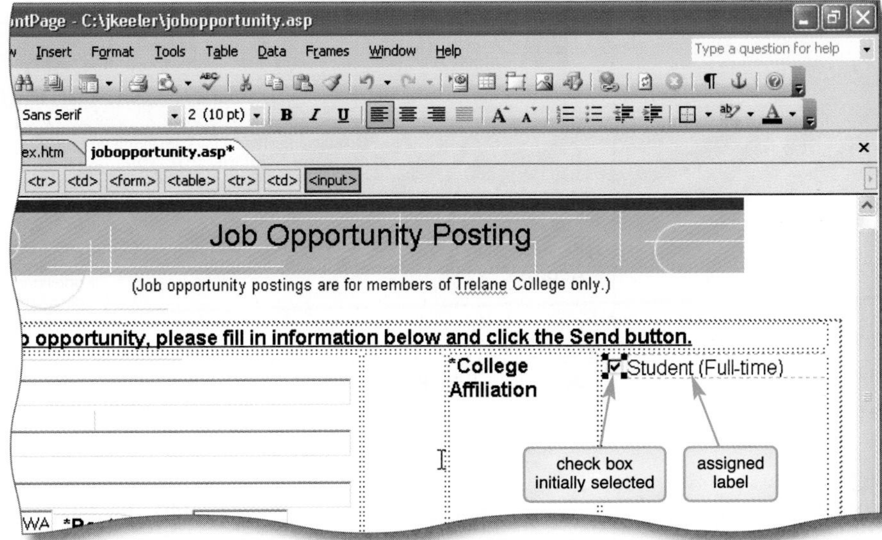

FIGURE 4-38

Other Ways

1. On Format menu click Properties
2. Press ALT+O, T
3. Press ALT+ENTER
4. In Voice Command mode, say "Format, Properties"

Four other check boxes must be inserted to complete this area of the form. The following steps insert the additional check boxes.

To Insert Additional Check Box Form Fields

1. **Click below the check box to position the insertion point. Click Insert on the menu bar, point to Form, and then click Checkbox on the Form submenu.**
2. **Type** `Student (Part-time)` **to the right of the check box. Hold down the SHIFT key and then press the ENTER key. Drag through both the check box and the text to select them. Be sure to select only the check box and text, not the previous label. Click Insert on the menu bar, point to Form, and then click Label on the Form submenu.**

3 **Right-click the check box and then click Form Field Properties on the shortcut menu. When the Check Box Properties dialog box is displayed, type** PTStudent **in the Name text box and then type** YES **in the Value text box. Verify that the Initial state Not checked option button is selected. Type** 7 **in the Tab order text box. Click the OK button.**

4 **Repeat Steps 1 through 3 for each of the remaining check boxes using the labels and properties listed in Table 4-4. Do not press the ENTER key after typing the last label text. If necessary, drag table borders and columns to adjust the form the way you want it to be displayed in the Web page. Click the Save button on the Standard toolbar to save your changes.**

FrontPage displays the Web page with the additional check boxes and labels as shown in Figure 4-39.

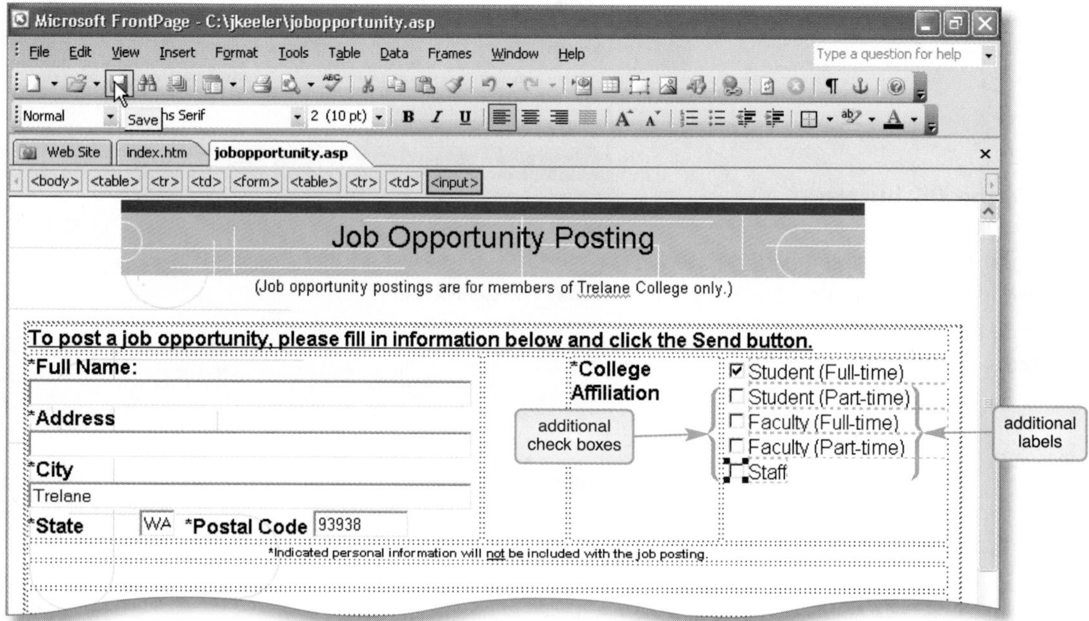

FIGURE 4-39

Table 4-4 Labels and Properties for Check Boxes

LABEL	NAME	VALUE	INITIAL STATE	TAB ORDER
Student (Full-time)	FTStudent	YES	Checked	6
Student (Part-time)	PTStudent	YES	Not checked	7
Faculty (Full-time)	FTFaculty	YES	Not checked	8
Faculty (Part-time)	PTFaculty	YES	Not checked	9
Staff	Staff	YES	Not checked	10

Check boxes have been inserted in a form and assigned labels, and their properties modified successfully. Notice that the Check Box Properties dialog box shown in Figure 4-37 on the previous page contains no Validate button. Check boxes only can be checked or unchecked, and cannot be required, so no data needs validation.

Inserting a Line Drawing AutoShape in a Table

Depending on your Web page design, you may want more than just text to direct the user's attention. In addition to text, you can insert other objects in a form, such as pictures or line art, in the same manner as you would with any other Web page. Being in a form has no particular effect on these objects.

For this Web page, a line is used to separate the personal information that will not be published from the contact and descriptive information that will be published in the job opportunity posting.

The following steps insert a line drawing AutoShape object in a table.

> *More About*
>
> **AutoShape Drawings**
>
> To draw an AutoShape while keeping its default proportions, press and hold the SHIFT key while you draw the object. To resize an AutoShape while keeping its default proportions, press and hold the CTRL key while you resize the object.

To Insert a Line Drawing AutoShape in a Table

1

- **Position the insertion point in the fourth row of table-T2.**
- **Click the Center button on the Formatting toolbar.**

The insertion point is centered in the fourth row of table-T2 (Figure 4-40).

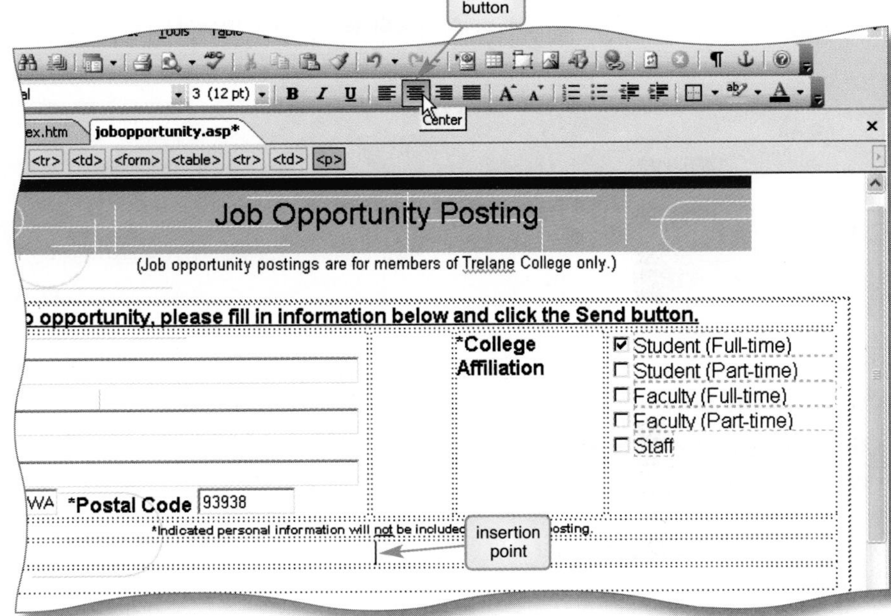

FIGURE 4-40

2

- **If necessary, click View on the menu bar, click Toolbars, and then click Drawing on the Toolbars submenu to display the Drawing toolbar.**
- **Click the Line button on the Drawing toolbar.**
- **Position the mouse pointer at the left side of the fourth row of table-T2.**
- **Hold down the SHIFT key.**
- **Click the mouse button and then drag a horizontal line drawing across the width of the fourth row.**
- **Release the mouse button and the SHIFT key.**

A straight line is drawn in the fourth row of the table (Figure 4-41). Holding down the SHIFT key ensures that the line is straight.

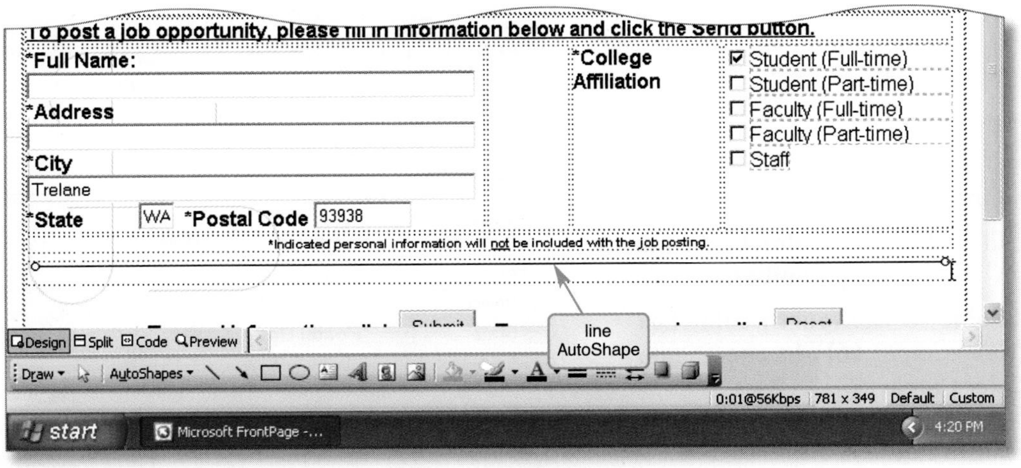

FIGURE 4-41

3

- **Right-click the line drawing and then click AutoShape on the shortcut menu.**
- **If necessary, when FrontPage displays the Format AutoShape dialog box, click the Layout tab.**
- **Click Relative in the Positioning style area.**

A positioning style of Relative is selected for the line AutoShape (Figure 4-42).

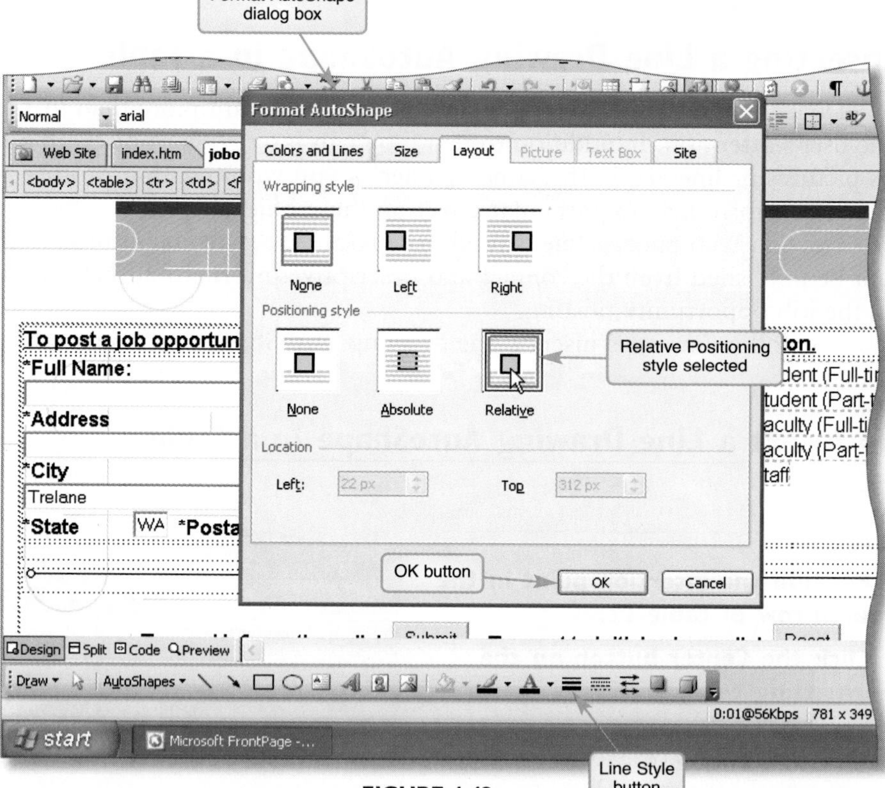

FIGURE 4-42

4

- **Click the OK button.**
- **Click the Line Style button on the Drawing toolbar.**

FrontPage displays the Line Style menu (Figure 4-43).

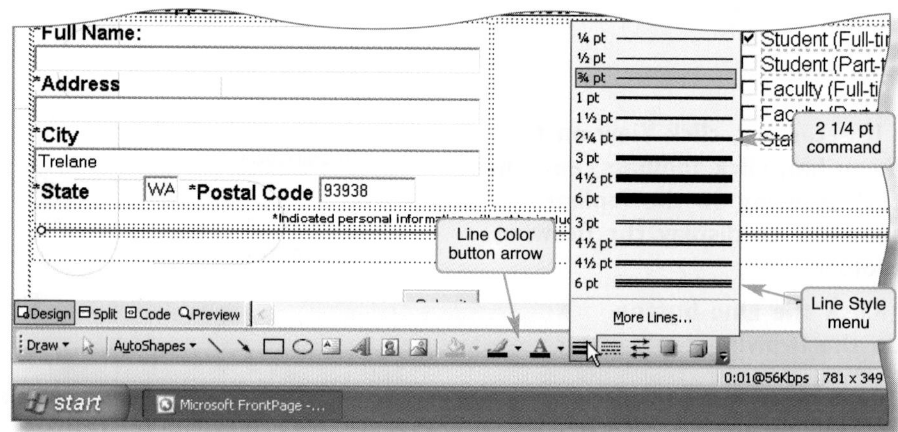

FIGURE 4-43

5

- **Click 2¼ pt.**
- **Click the Line Color button arrow on the Drawing toolbar.**
- **Point to the fourth color box (Hex={33,99,66}) in the Theme Colors area.**

FrontPage displays the colors for the current theme below the standard colors (Figure 4-44).

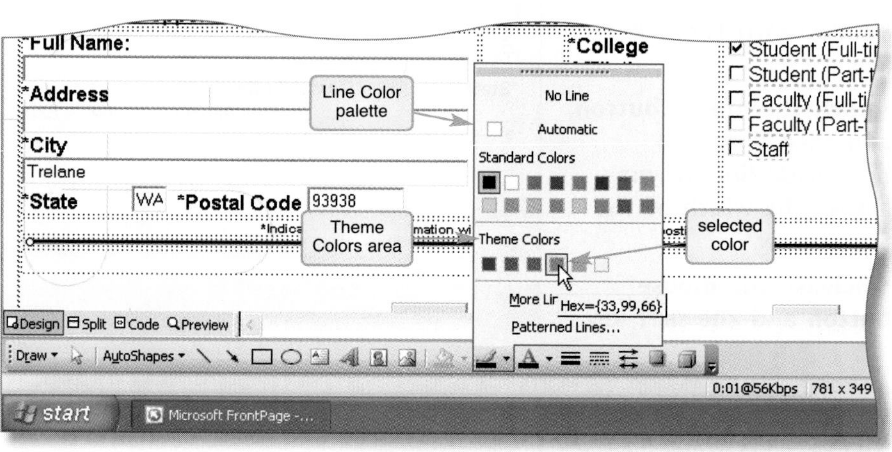

FIGURE 4-44

6

- **Click the fourth color box (Hex={33,99,66}) in the Theme Colors area.**
- **If necessary, drag the ends of the line drawing to adjust the width to be just less than the width of the table.**
- **Click the Save button to save the changes.**

The line AutoShape is centered in the fourth row of the table and is displayed in the new color (Figure 4-45).

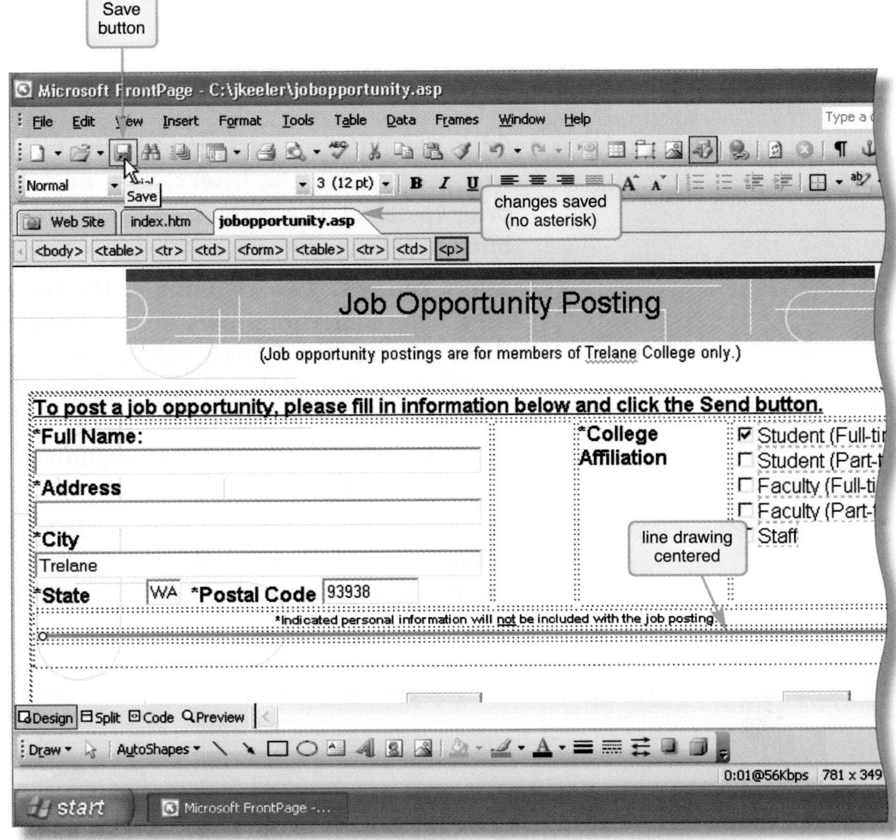

FIGURE 4-45

Other Ways

1. Click AutoShapes button on Drawing toolbar, point to Lines, click Line on Lines submenu
2. On Insert menu point to Picture, click AutoShapes on Picture submenu, click Lines button on AutoShapes toolbar, click Line on Lines submenu
3. Press ALT+U, L
4. In Voice Command mode, say "Insert, Picture, AutoShapes"

Because the line drawing has a positioning style of None, the table widens if the line is drawn wider than the current table width.

Creating a Nested Table

The next step in the design of this Web page is to create a third table, table-T3, to help control positioning of additional elements in the form. You will insert the table within a cell of table-T2 to create a **nested table**. You saw an example of a nested table in Project 3, where a table was imported into the project as part of a Word document. In this case, you will create the nested table by inserting a table in an existing table. The steps on the next page summarize how to create a nested table.

Design Tip

Before working with nested tables, sketch out the design on paper to be sure you have a good idea of how to draw the table in Design view. Calculate the necessary widths and heights of the columns and rows and the size of the overall table.

To Create a Nested Table

1 **Click the fifth row of table-T2 (the row below the line) to position the insertion point. Click the Insert Table button on the Standard toolbar and then drag to select three rows and four columns (3 by 4 table). Release the mouse button.**

2 **Select the first two columns in the bottom row of the table and merge the cells. Select all three rows in the third column and merge the cells. Select all three rows in the fourth column and merge the cells. Select all four columns in the first row. Right-click the selected cells and then click Cell Properties on the shortcut menu. In the Layout area of the Cell Properties dialog box, select Left for the Horizontal alignment and select Top for the vertical alignment. Click the OK button.**

3 **Right-click the table and then click Table Properties on the shortcut menu. When the Table Properties dialog box is displayed, type** 0 **in the Size box in the Borders area. Click the OK button. Click the second column in the second row.**

Figure 4-46 shows the FrontPage window after the nested table is inserted.

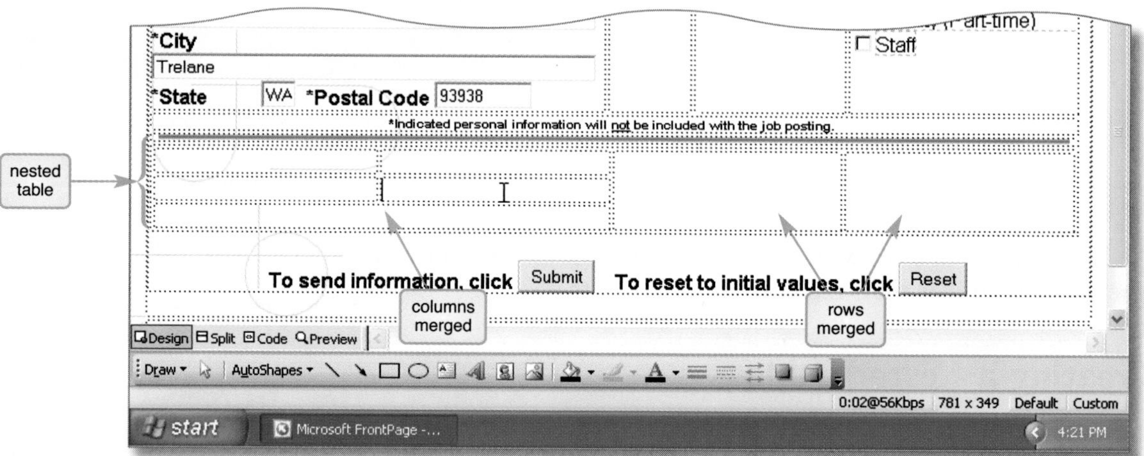

FIGURE 4-46

> *More About*
>
> **Positioning Form Fields**
>
> As you insert form fields in a form, it is best to preview the page in a browser to verify the form field positioning. This advice is especially true for wide text fields that cannot be wrapped. They may appear on a different line during editing, yet appear on the same line in the browser.

As you can see, creating a nested table is no different from making any other table, except that the entire new table is located within a cell of an existing table.

As Figure 4-1b on page FP 259 illustrates, three additional text boxes are yet to be added to the form. As discussed earlier, tables often are used to align elements in a Web page. The previous text boxes were aligned by pressing the SPACEBAR after the accompanying label text. The new text boxes will not require additional spaces for alignment. Instead, these text boxes are aligned by placing the labels in one cell of the table and then placing the text boxes in an adjacent cell. By adjusting the position of the cell borders, you can obtain the required alignment.

While you can use spaces to separate labels from form fields, consider using table cells to separate the items. By adjusting the position of the cell borders, you can obtain the required alignment.

The following steps insert and align the label text and text box elements in a nested table.

To Insert and Align Elements in a Nested Table

1. **Position the insertion point in the first row and the first column of table-T3. Click the Bold button on the Formatting toolbar. Hold down the SHIFT key and then press the ENTER key.**

2. **Type** `Contact:` **and then hold down the SHIFT key and press the ENTER key. Type** `Phone:` **and then hold down the SHIFT key and press the ENTER key. Type** `E-mail:` **as the last label.**

3. **Position the insertion point in the first row and the second column of table-T3. Click the Bold button on the Formatting toolbar. Click the Font Size box arrow and then click 2 (10 pt). Type** `(use first name and last name)` **and then hold down the SHIFT key and press the ENTER key.**

4. **Insert a text box form field. Right-click the text box. Click Form Field Properties on the shortcut menu. When the Text Box Properties dialog box is displayed, type** `Contact` **in the Name text box, type** `29` **in the Width in characters text box, and then type** `11` **in the Tab order text box.**

5. **Click the Validate button. When the Text Box Validation dialog box is displayed, click Required in the Data length area and then type** `Contact Name` **in the Display name text box. Click the OK button in the Text Box Validation dialog box. Click the OK button in the Text Box Properties dialog box. Press CTRL+C to copy the text box. Press the RIGHT ARROW key.**

6. **Hold down the SHIFT key and then press the ENTER key. Press CTRL+V to insert a copy of the text box. Right-click the text box. Click Form Field Properties on the shortcut menu. When the Text Box Properties dialog box is displayed, type** `Phone` **in the Name text box, type** `20` **in the Width in characters text box, and then type** `12` **in the Tab order text box.**

7. **Click the Validate button. When the Text Box Validation dialog box is displayed, type** `Phone Number` **in the Display name text box and then select Text in the Data type list. Click Digits, click Whitespace, and click Other in the Text format area; then type** `(-)` **(a left parenthesis, a hyphen, and a right parenthesis) in the Other text box. In the Data length area, verify that the Required check box is not selected. Click the OK button in the Text Box Validation dialog box and then click the OK button in the Text Box Properties dialog box. Press the RIGHT ARROW key.**

8. **Hold down the SHIFT key and then press the ENTER key. Press CTRL+V to insert a copy of the text box. Right-click the text box. Click Form Field Properties on the shortcut menu. When the Text Box Properties dialog box is displayed, type** `EmailAddress` **in the Name text box, type** `33` **in the Width in characters text box, and then type** `13` **in the Tab order text box. Click the OK button.**

9. **Drag the right border of the cell in the first column to align the text and form fields. Click the Save button on the Standard toolbar.**

FrontPage displays the Web page as shown in Figure 4-47 on the next page. The properties and validations for the text boxes in this table are listed in Table 4-5 on the next page.

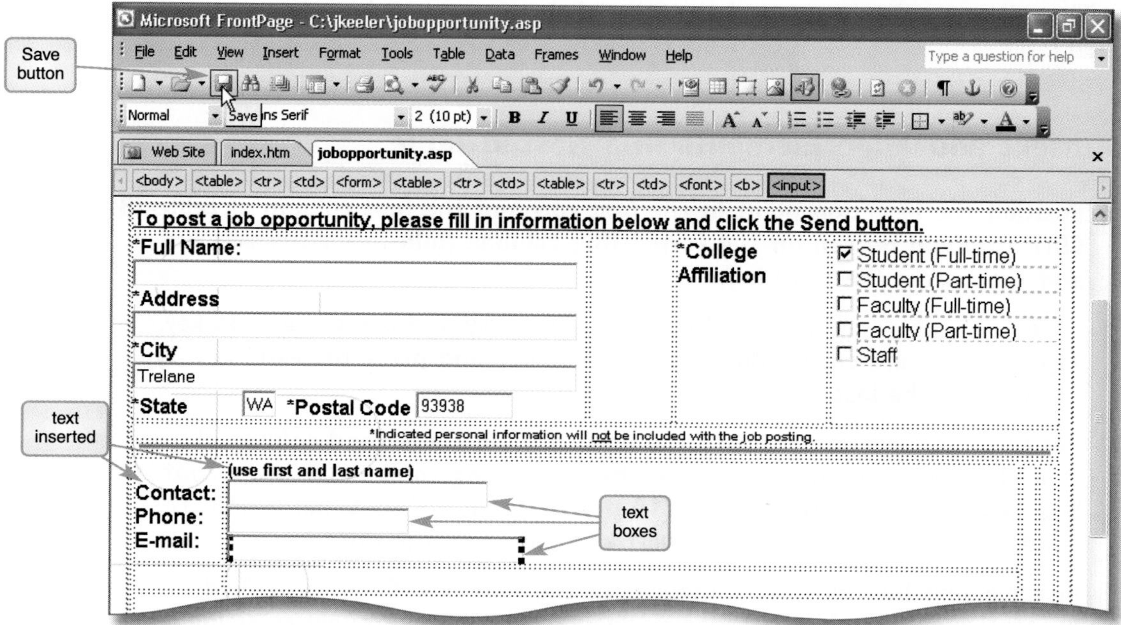

FIGURE 4-47

Table 4-5 Properties and Validations for Text Box Form Fields in Table-T3

TEXT BOX	PROPERTY VALUES TO SET	VALIDATIONS TO SET
Contact	Name=Contact Width=29 Tab order=11	Display name=Contact Name In Data length area, click Required
Phone	Name=Phone Width=20 Tab order=12	Display name=Phone Number Select Text in the Data type list In Other text box, type (-) (a left parenthesis, a hyphen, and a right parenthesis) In Data length area, deselect Required
E-mail	Name=EmailAddress Width=33 Tab order=13	

More About

Drop-Down List Boxes

Drop-down list boxes are useful for presenting a large number of choices in a small space. The choices are not displayed unless the user clicks the list box arrow. When the user selects a choice, the list of choices is hidden once again. You can alter the properties of a menu to allow the selection of more than one choice. This method is an alternative to using a group of check boxes.

The next section of the form contains a drop-down list box so a job opportunity poster can indicate the job type category for the job opportunity that he or she wants to submit.

Inserting a Drop-Down List Box in a Form

As listed in Table 4-1 on page FP 260, a drop-down list box is useful when you have a variety of choices — more than option buttons can handle effectively.

With a drop-down list box, you give the drop-down list box a name and then add choices to the list. You can order the list choices from the most frequently occurring choice to the least frequently occurring choice, alphabetically, or in another sequence.

Use a drop-down list when you need to provide the user with a variety of choices. Use option buttons for a variety of choices when the user has only a few choices.

When the user makes a selection and clicks the Submit button, the list name and the value associated with the selected choice are sent. You can select a default choice that is returned automatically if the user makes no selection. You also can make an item that is descriptive only and cannot be selected by the user, forcing him or her to make a selection. The following steps show how to insert a drop-down list box form field in a form.

To Insert a Drop-Down List Box Form Field in a Form

1

- **Position the insertion point in the second row and first column of table-T3, the second table in the form.**
- **Click the Bold button on the Formatting toolbar.**
- **Type `Category:` and then position the insertion point in the second row and second column of table-T3.**

FrontPage displays the inserted text in the second row and first column of the third table in the form (Figure 4-48). The column widens, if necessary, to accommodate the text.

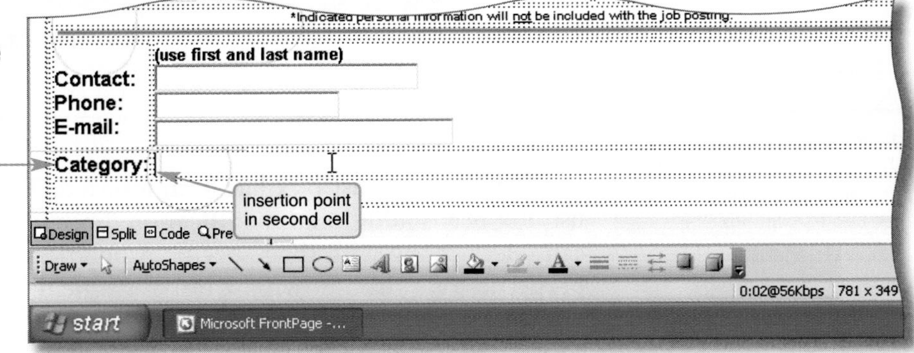

FIGURE 4-48

2

- **Click Insert on the menu bar and then point to Form.**

FrontPage displays the Form submenu (Figure 4-49).

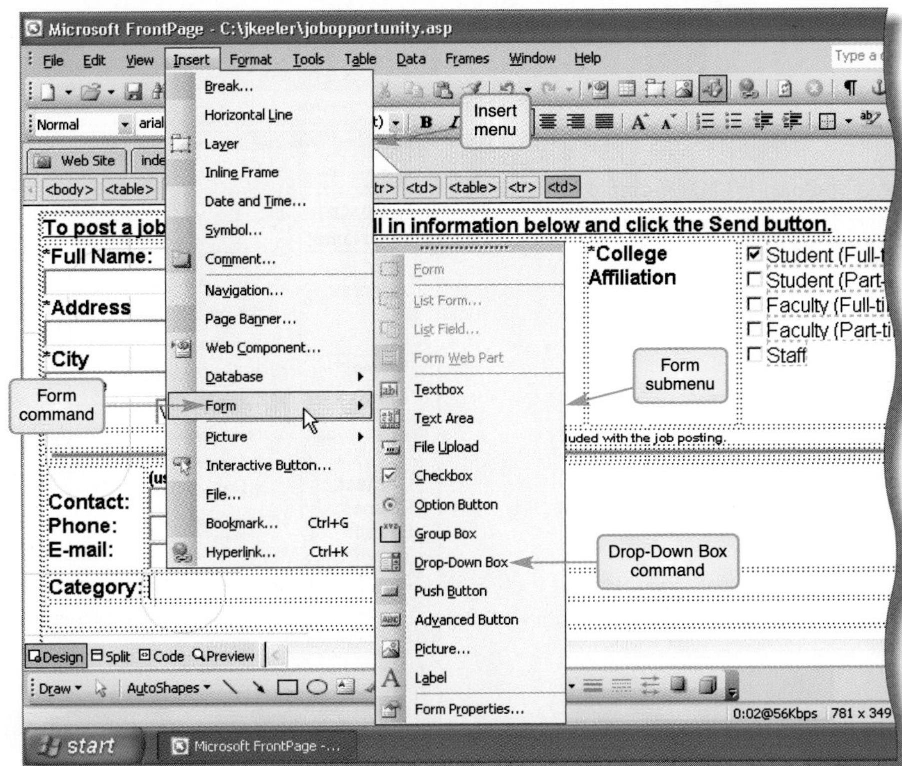

FIGURE 4-49

3

• **Click Drop-Down Box.**

A drop-down list box is inserted in the form with a default size (Figure 4-50).

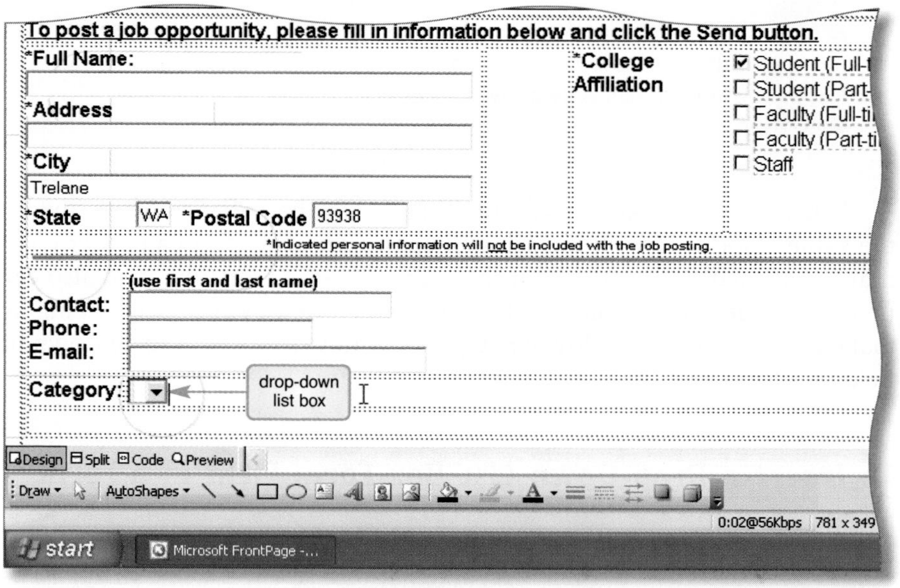

FIGURE 4-50

Other Ways

1. Press ALT+I, R, D
2. In Voice Command mode, say "Insert, Form", click Drop-Down Box

A drop-down list box has been inserted. To be useful, however, the drop-down list box needs additional modification. Specifically, it needs the choices that the user can select, along with their specific properties. The following steps modify the properties of a drop-down list box form field.

To Modify the Properties of a Drop-Down List Box Form Field

1

• **Right-click the drop-down list box.**

The drop-down list box form field is selected and a shortcut menu is displayed (Figure 4-51).

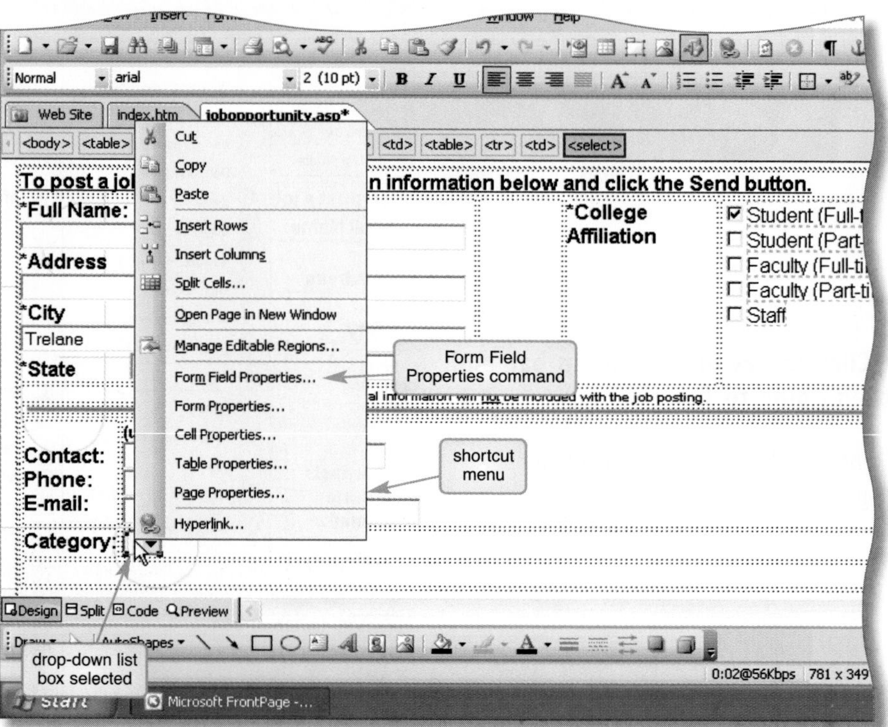

FIGURE 4-51

2

- **Click Form Field Properties.**
- **When the Drop-Down Box Properties dialog box is displayed, drag through the text D1 and then type** `Category` **in the Name text box.**

FrontPage displays the Drop-Down Box Properties dialog box (Figure 4-52).

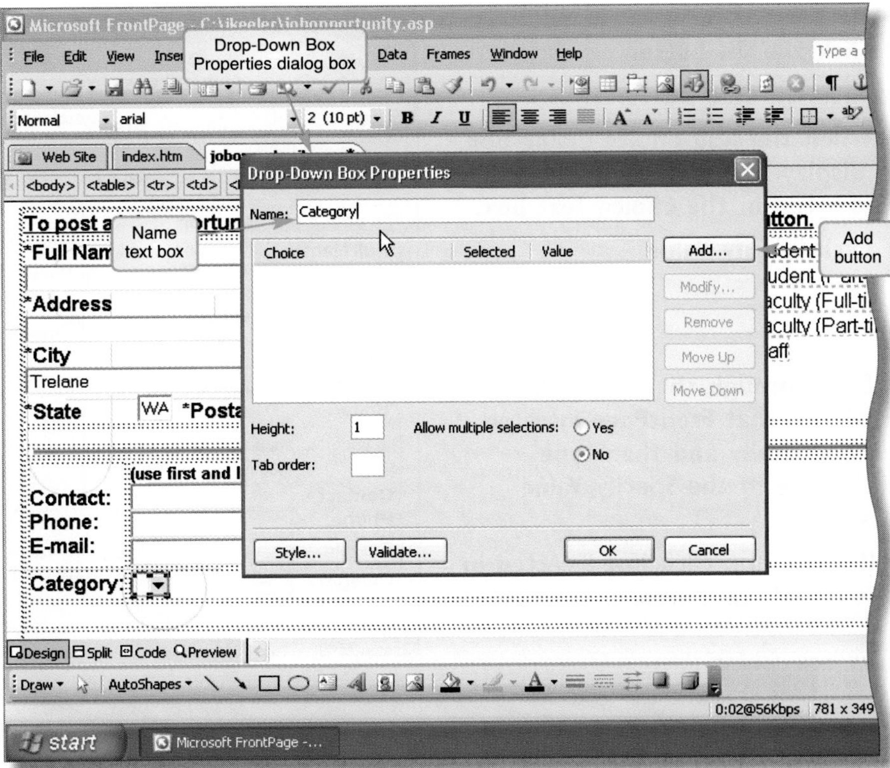

FIGURE 4-52

3

- **Click the Add button.**
- **When the Add Choice dialog box is displayed, type** `Select Position Type` **in the Choice text box.**
- **If necessary, click Not selected in the Initial state area.**

FrontPage displays the Add Choice dialog box as shown in Figure 4-53.

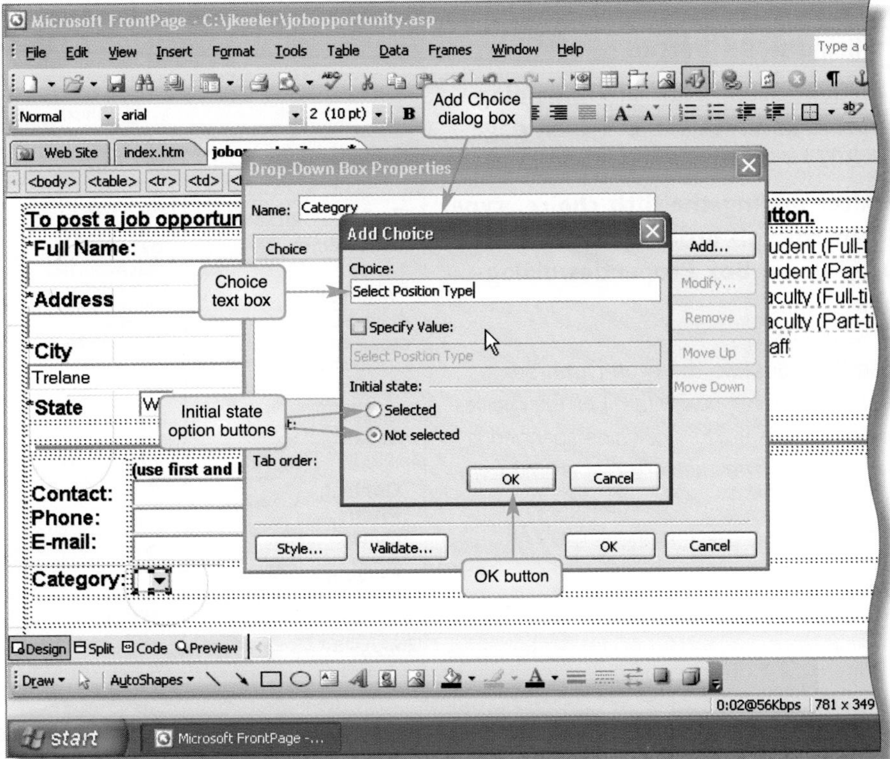

FIGURE 4-53

4

- **Click the OK button.**
- **Click the Add button.**
- **When the Add Choice dialog box is displayed, type** `Full-time Position` **in the Choice text box.**
- **Click Specify Value.**

- **Drag through the text, Full-time Position, that FrontPage inserted automatically and then type** `FullTime` **in the Specify Value text box.**
- **If necessary, click Not Selected in the Initial state area.**

FrontPage displays the Add Choice dialog box with the second choice entered (Figure 4-54).

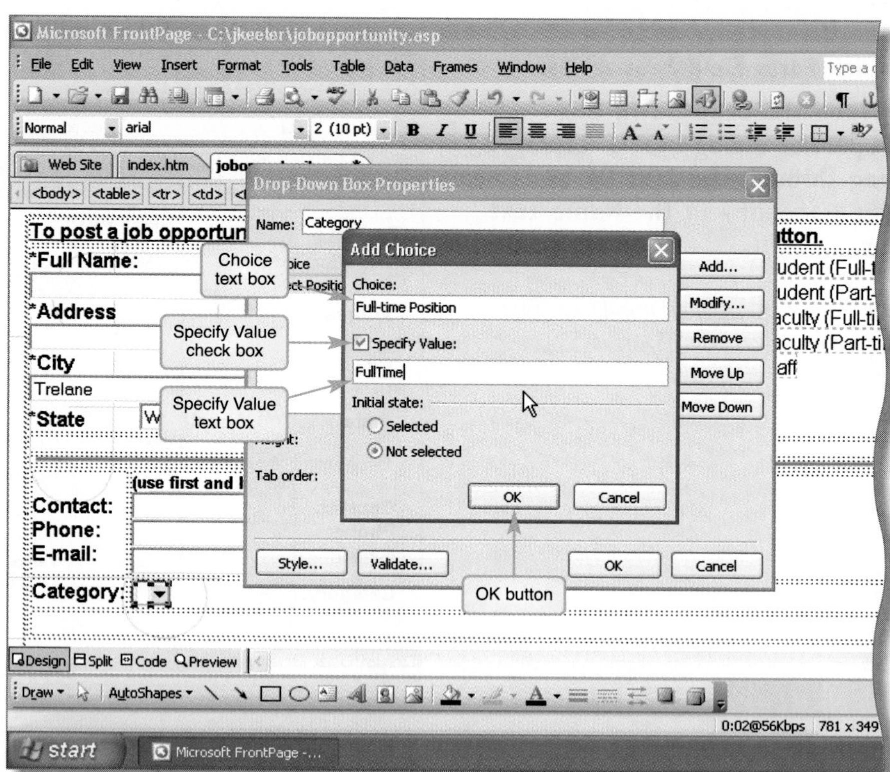

FIGURE 4-54

6

- **Click the OK button.**
- **Repeat Step 4 for the remaining choices listed in Table 4-6 on page FP 302.**
- **After adding the fifth choice, type** 14 **in the Tab order text box in the Drop-Down Box Properties dialog box.**

FrontPage displays the Drop-Down Box Properties dialog box with all of the choices added (Figure 4-55). The value specified is the value sent to the server when the form is submitted. If no value is specified, the choice name is used as the value.

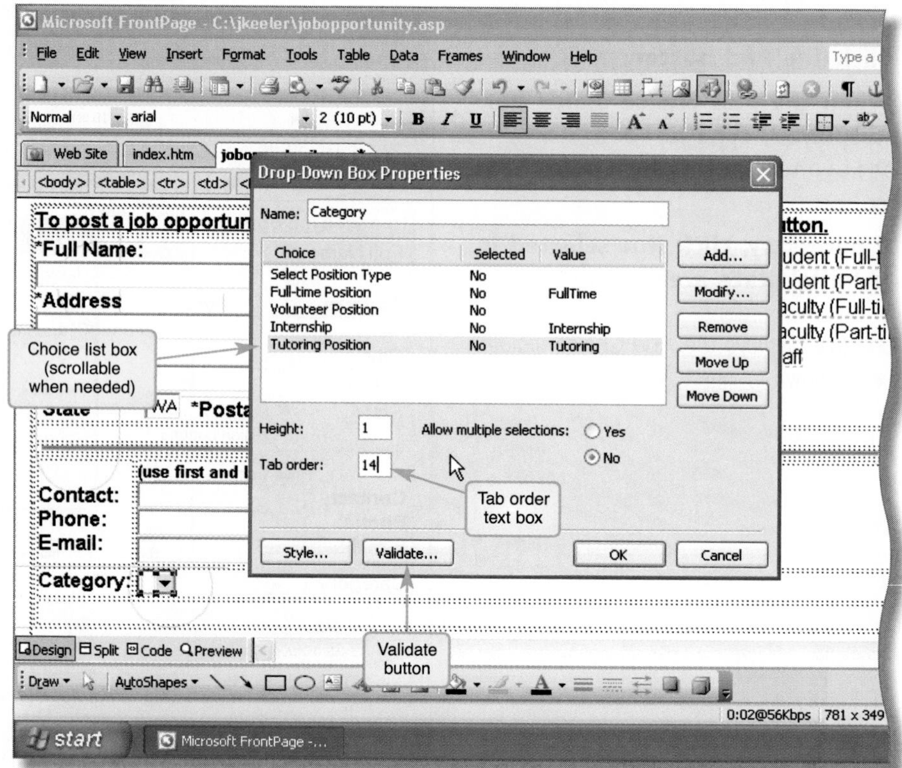

FIGURE 4-55

7

- **Click the Validate button.**
- **When the Drop-Down Box Validation dialog box is displayed, click Data required.**
- **Click Disallow first choice.**
- **Type** `Job Category` **in the Display name text box.**

FrontPage displays the Drop-Down Box Validation dialog box with the changes indicated (Figure 4-56). Selecting Disallow first choice sets the first choice, Select Position Type, as a descriptive field that a user cannot select.

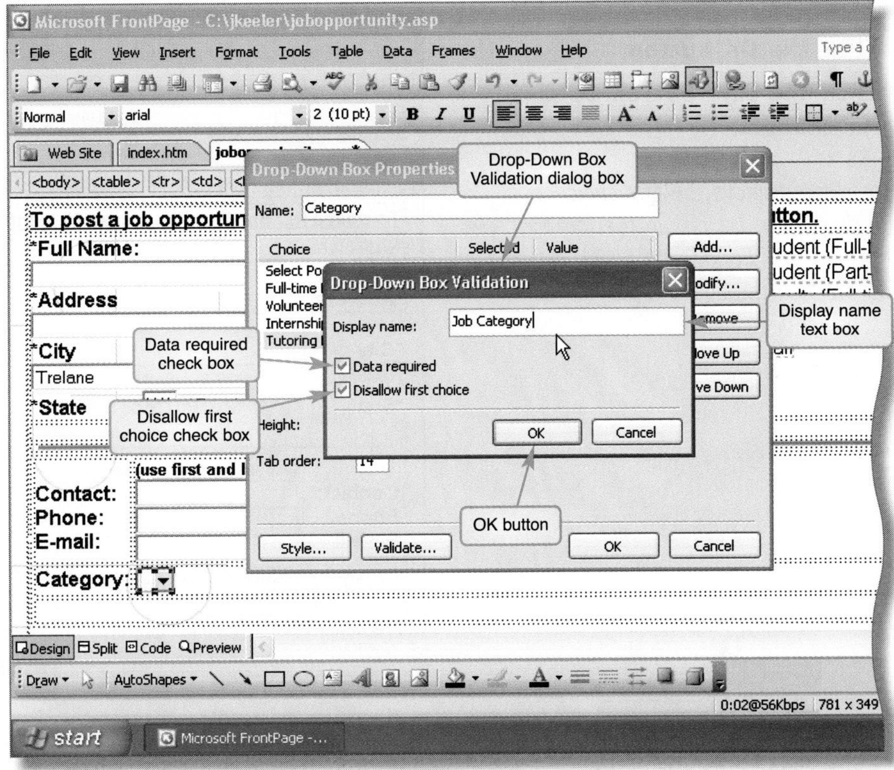

FIGURE 4-56

8

- **Click the OK button.**
- **Verify that the Allow multiple selections No option button is selected.**

The Drop-Down Box Validation dialog box is closed, and the choices are displayed in the Choice list box in the Drop-Down Box Properties dialog box (Figure 4-57).

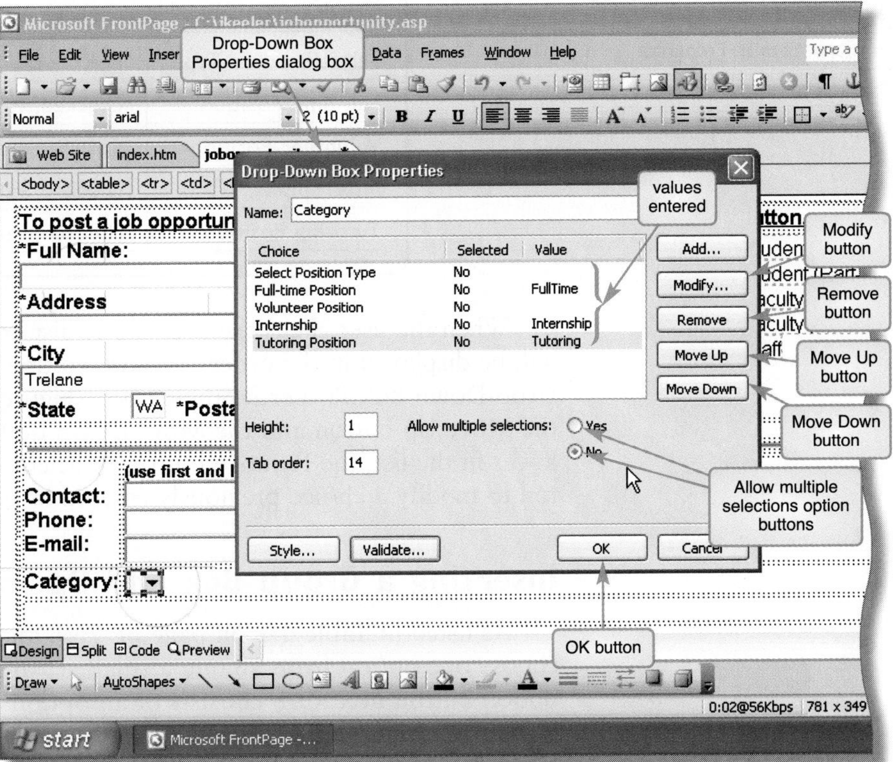

FIGURE 4-57

9

- **Click the OK button.**
- **Click the Save button to save your changes.**

FrontPage displays the first choice in the drop-down list box in the form (Figure 4-58). Periodically saving changes as you proceed through the project is recommended.

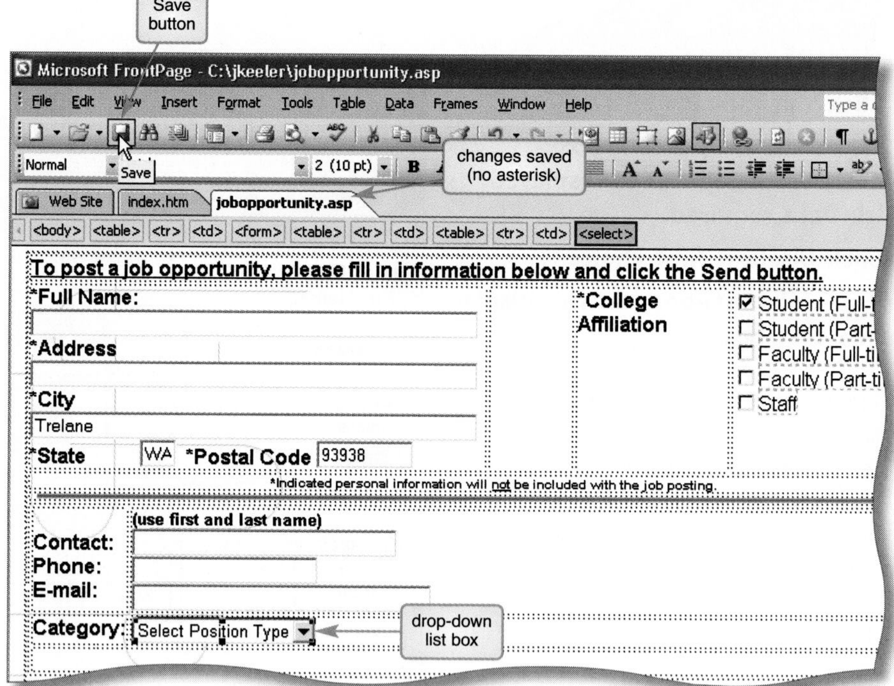

FIGURE 4-58

Other Ways

1. On Format menu click Properties
2. Press ALT+O, T
3. Press ALT+ENTER
4. In Voice Command mode, say "Format, Properties"

Table 4-6 Choices for Category Drop-Down Box Form Field

CHOICE TEXT BOX	SPECIFY VALUE	INITIAL STATE
Select Position Type	not checked	Not selected
Full-time Position	checked, value=FullTime	Not selected
Volunteer Position	not checked	Not selected
Internship	checked, value=Internship	Not selected
Tutoring Position	checked, value=Tutoring	Not selected

When the user clicks the drop-down list box arrow, the choices just entered will be displayed in the order you entered them. You can modify the choices in the Drop-Down Box Properties dialog box (Figure 4-57 on the previous page) by using the Move Up button and the Move Down button to move a given choice higher or lower in the list, the Remove button to delete a choice altogether, and the Modify button to modify a choice previously entered by changing its name, value, or initial state.

Inserting a Group Box and Option Buttons in a Form

As listed in Table 4-1 on page FP 260, an **option button** is useful when you must choose one option from among a small set of mutually exclusive options. Each option button in a form consists of an option button and a corresponding label. As indicated earlier, text can be assigned as the label for a form field so that clicking the text is like clicking the form field.

Related option buttons are defined in a group. A **group box** is a titled border that surrounds a group of related fields. Option buttons not contained within a group box are considered the default group in a form; that is, they are mutually exclusive. Therefore, to have more than a single group of option buttons, a form must have at least one group box.

Design Tip

Always place options buttons in a group box. Use option buttons when the user must choose one option from among a small set of mutually exclusive options.

The process of inserting option buttons begins with the insertion of the group box, if one is needed. Even if only one group of option buttons is used, a group box can provide a visual clue that the option buttons are related.

The following steps insert a group box form field in a form.

To Insert a Group Box Form Field in a Form

1

- **Position the insertion point in the third row and first column of table-T3, the nested table you just created.**
- **Click Insert on the menu bar and then point to Form.**

FrontPage displays the Form submenu (Figure 4-59).

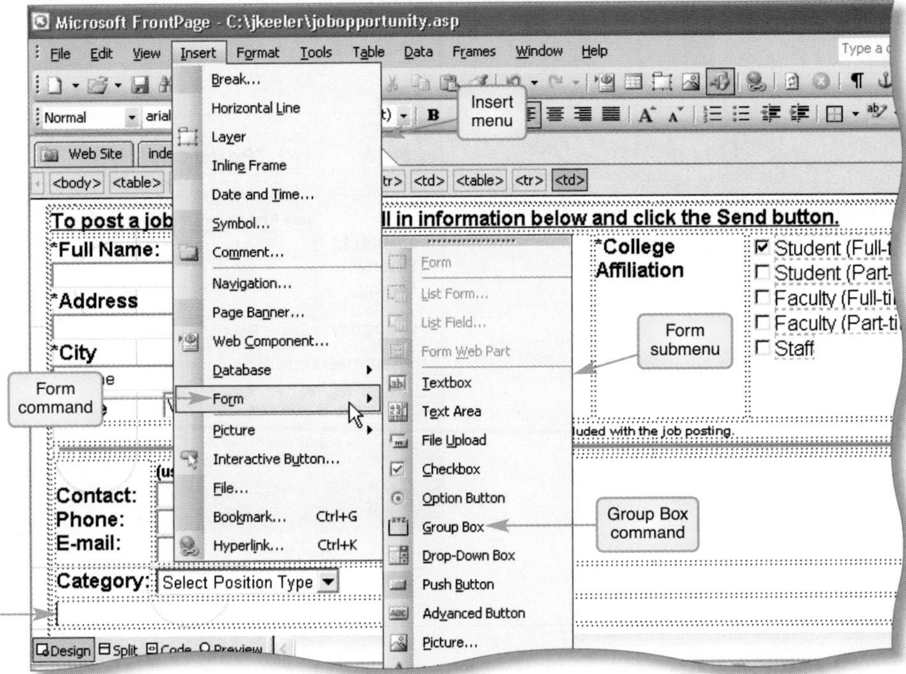

FIGURE 4-59

2

- **Click Group Box.**
- **Drag the right border of the cell to the left so that the form fields take up the width of the cell.**

FrontPage displays the group box in the form (Figure 4-60).

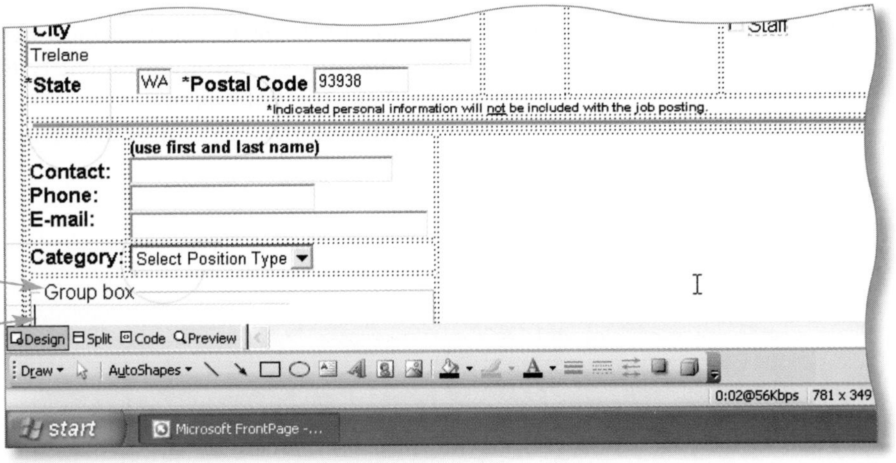

default title

Group box

FIGURE 4-60

Other Ways

1. Press ALT+I, R, G
2. In Voice Command mode, say "Insert, Form", click Group Box

You should change the default title for the group box to reflect the purpose of the option button choices. The following step modifies the title of a group box form field.

To Modify the Title of a Group Box Form Field

1

- **Drag through the group box title text to select it.**
- **Click the Bold button on the Formatting toolbar and then type** `Compensation` **as the new title.**

FrontPage displays the new title for the group box (Figure 4-61).

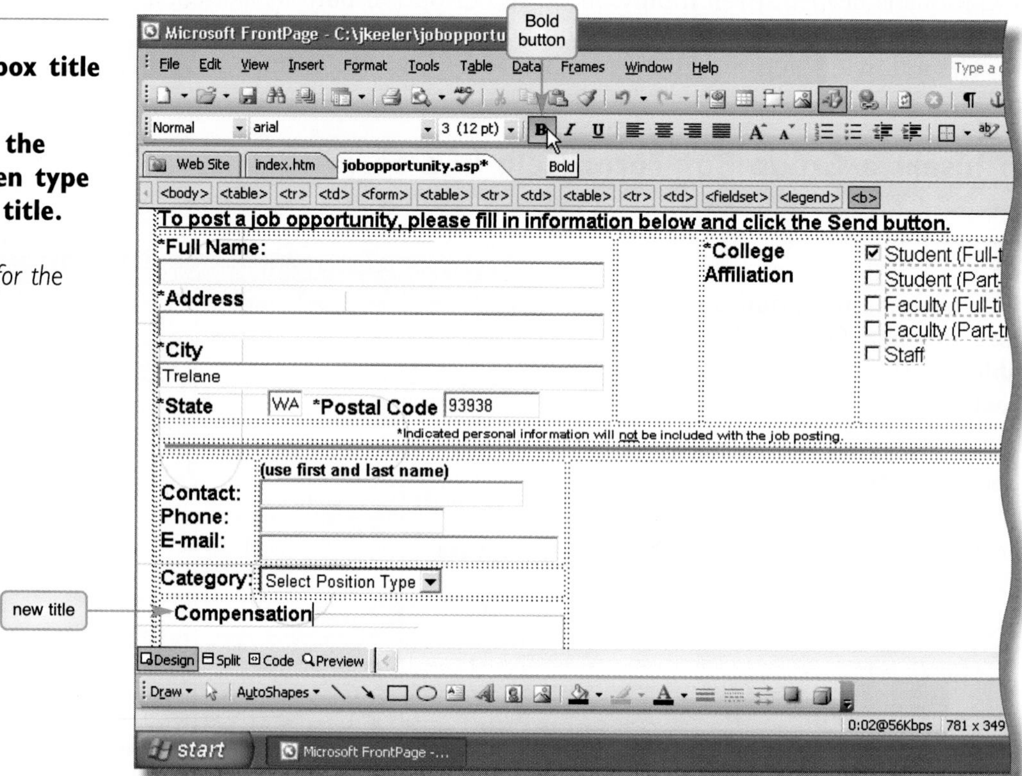

FIGURE 4-61

Other Ways

1. On Format menu click Properties
2. Press ALT+O, T
3. Press ALT+ENTER
4. In Voice Command mode, say "Format, Properties"

After adding a group box, the next step is to add option buttons. You should add labels to each option button for the same reasons that you added a label to a check box: to make the choice easier for the user to select and to indicate which of the mutually exclusive options that option button represents. You then adjust the properties of the option button and identify the value that is sent to the Web server when a user clicks the Submit button.

The following steps insert an option button form field in a group box.

To Insert an Option Button Form Field in a Group Box

1

- **Position the insertion point in the group box.**
- **Click Insert on the menu bar and then point to Form.**

FrontPage displays the Form submenu (Figure 4-62).

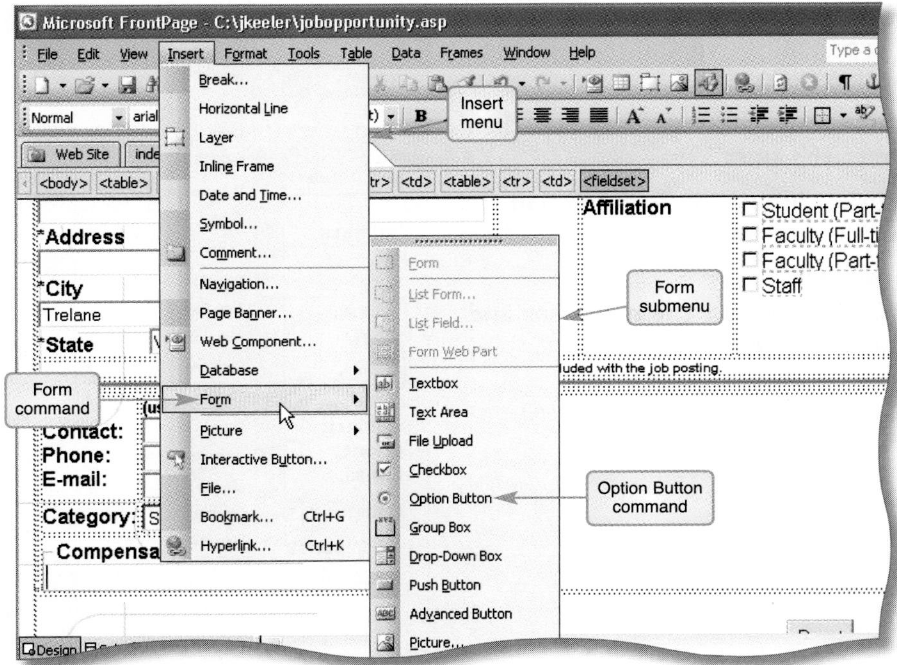

FIGURE 4-62

2

- **Click Option Button.**

FrontPage displays the inserted option button in the form (Figure 4-63).

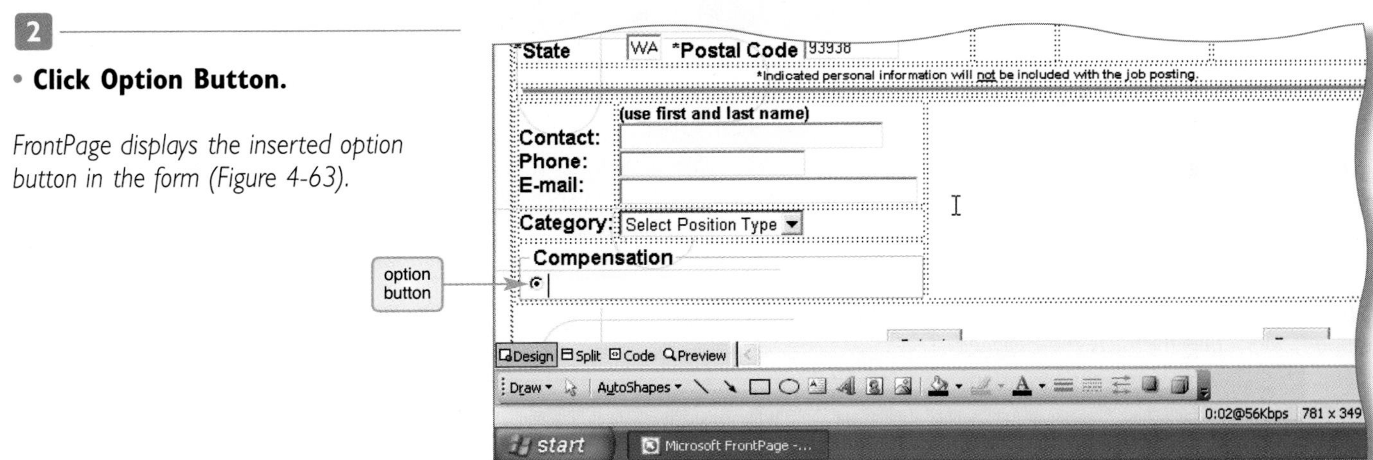

FIGURE 4-63

Other Ways

1. Press ALT+I, R, O
2. In Voice Command mode, say "Insert, Form", click Option Button

Recall that inserting a form field inserts only the form field object, as with this option button. You must provide a label for each form field you insert. Furthermore, just typing text next to the form field does not assign the text as a label for the field. You explicitly have to assign the text entered as the label for the field. The steps on the next page assign a label to the option button.

To Assign a Label to an Option Button Form Field

1

- **Type** `Hourly` **to the right of the option button.**
- **Hold down the SHIFT key and then press the ENTER key.**
- **Drag through both the option button and the text to select them together.**
- **Click Insert on the menu bar and then point to Form.**

FrontPage displays the Form submenu (Figure 4-64).

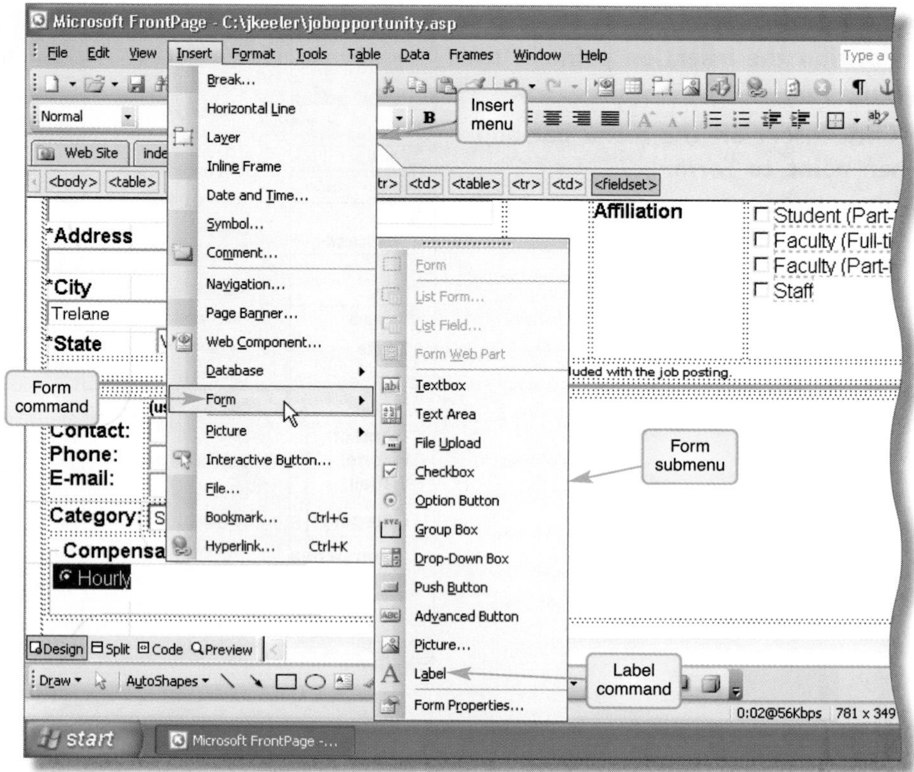

FIGURE 4-64

2

- **Click Label.**
- **Click to the right of the label text to deselect it.**

FrontPage displays the text with a box around it, indicating that it is the assigned label for the corresponding option button form field (Figure 4-65).

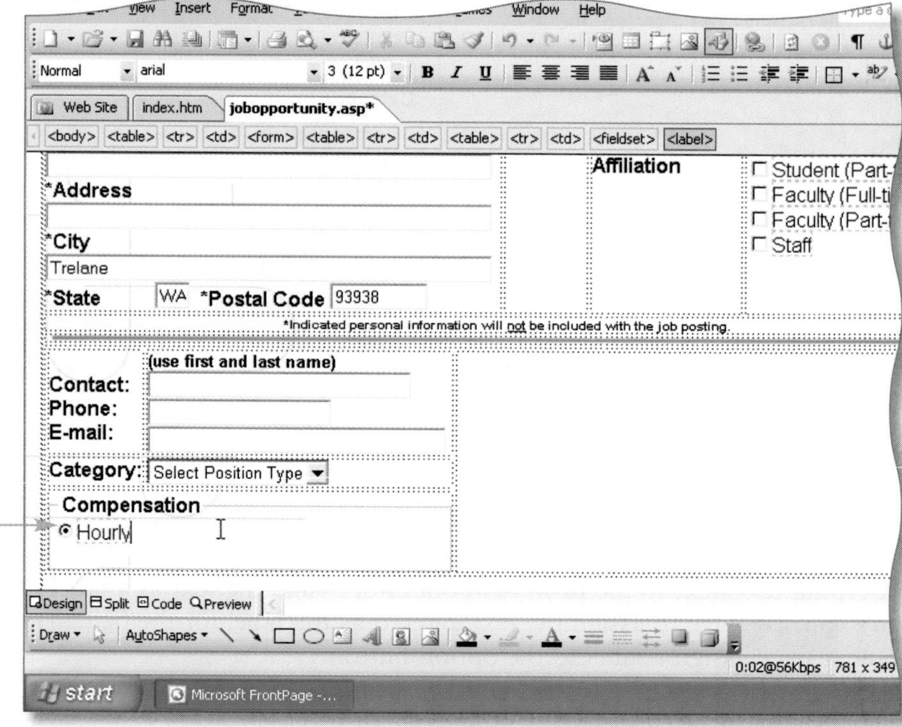

FIGURE 4-65

Other Ways

1. Press ALT+I, R, A
2. In Voice Command mode, say "Insert, Form", click Label

Finally, you need to modify some properties of the option button, such as the value that is returned when the option button is selected, whether the option button is selected by default (initial state), and the group name with which the option button is associated. Remember that option buttons are mutually exclusive; that is, selecting any option button in a given group deselects all of the others in that same group. The following steps modify the properties of an option button form field.

To Modify the Properties of an Option Button Form Field

1

- **Right-click the option button.**

The option button form field is selected and a shortcut menu is displayed (Figure 4-66).

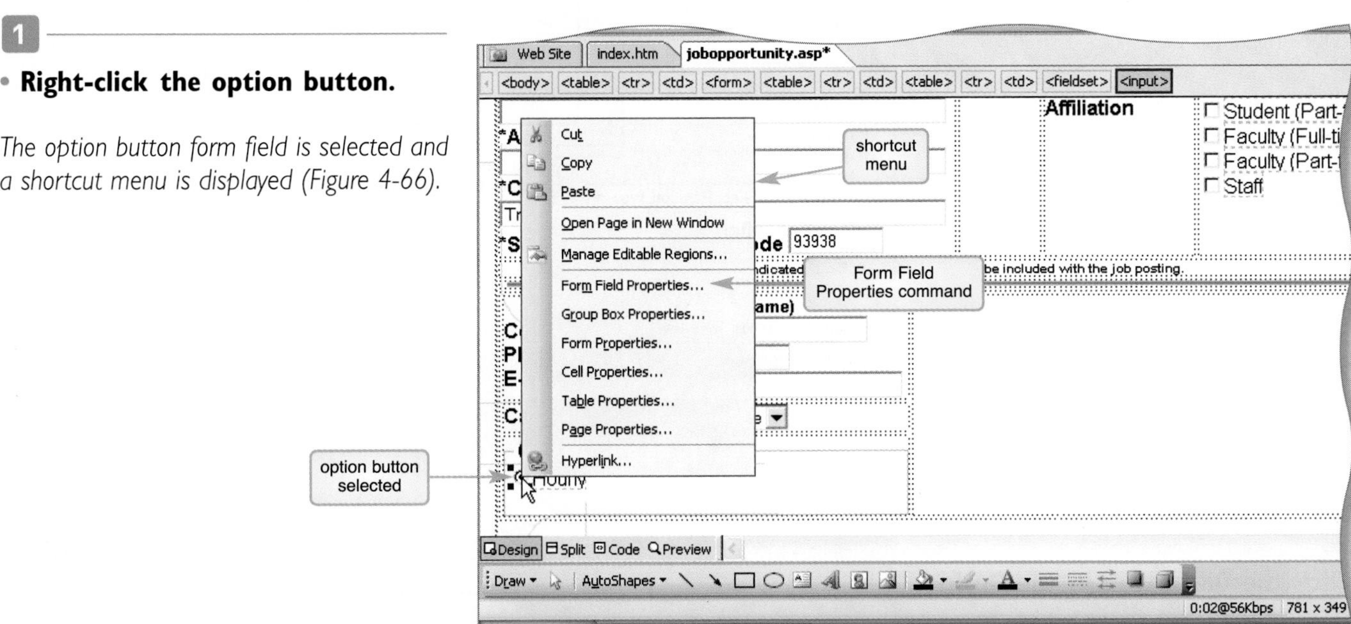

FIGURE 4-66

2

- **Click Form Field Properties.**
- **When the Option Button Properties dialog box is displayed, type** `Compensation` **in the Group name text box, press the TAB key, and then type** `Hourly` **in the Value text box.**
- **If necessary, click Not selected in the Initial state area to select it.**
- **Type** `15` **in the Tab order text box.**

FrontPage displays the Option Button Properties dialog box (Figure 4-67). The Group name, Compensation, automatically is used for all option buttons in the same group.

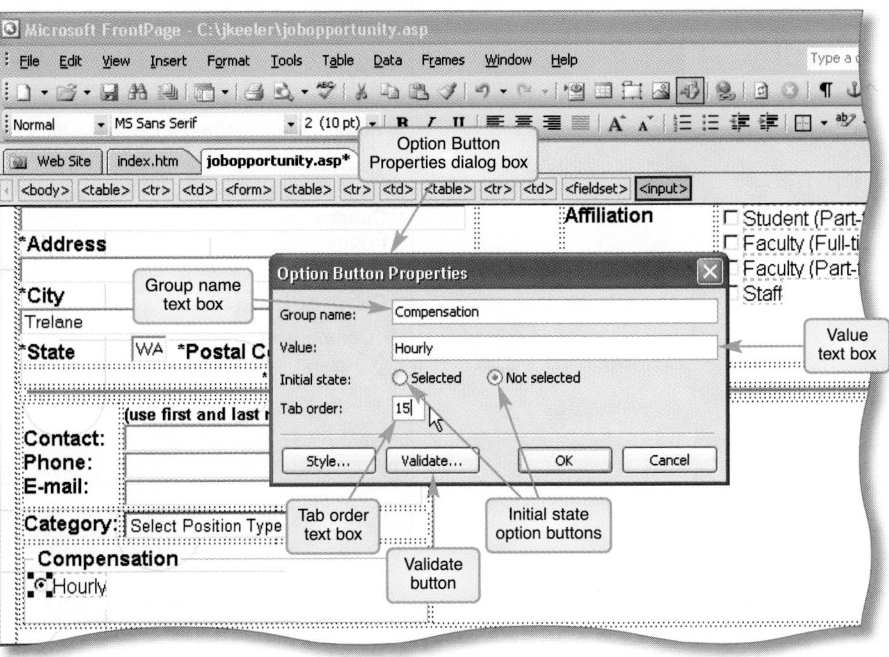

FIGURE 4-67

3

- **Click the Validate button.**
- **When the Option Button Validation dialog box is displayed, click Data required and then type** `Compensation` **in the Display name text box.**

FrontPage displays the Option Button Validation dialog box with the indicated changes (Figure 4-68).

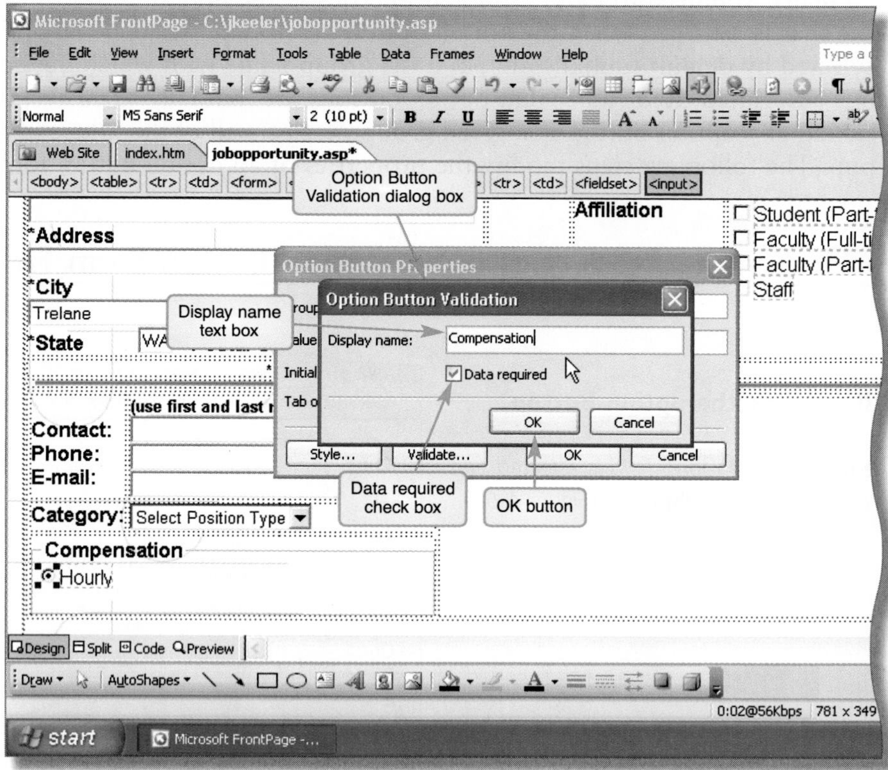

FIGURE 4-68

4

- **Click the OK button in the Option Button Validation dialog box.**
- **Click the OK button in the Option Button Properties dialog box.**

The option button and its label are displayed (Figure 4-69).

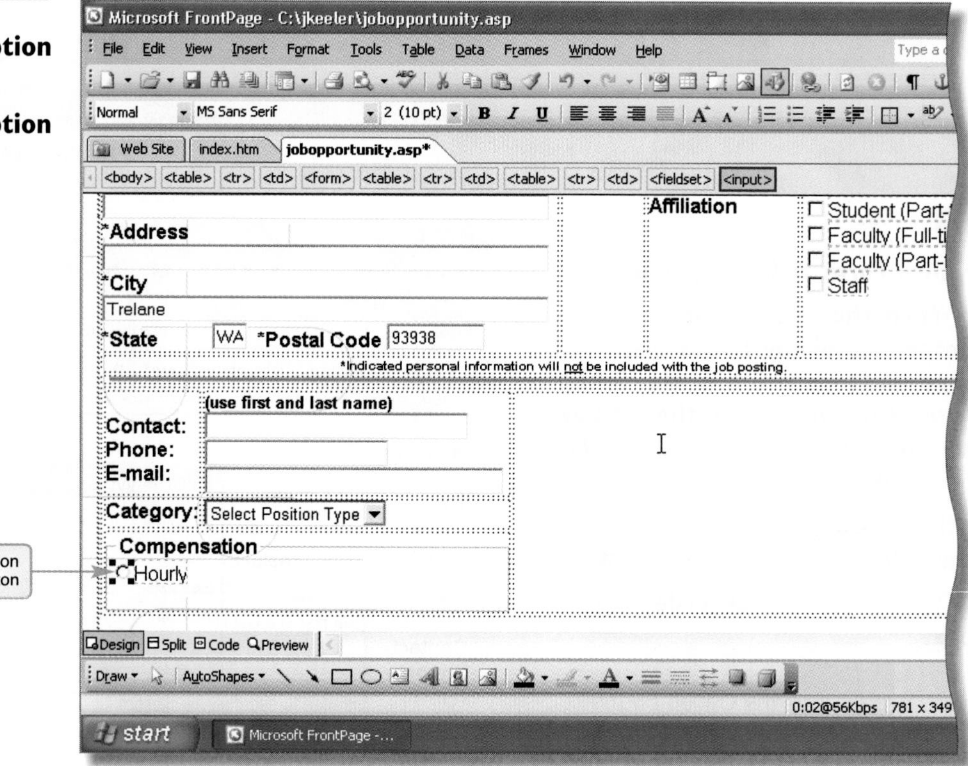

FIGURE 4-69

5

- **For each of the option button fields listed in Table 4-7 on the next page, insert the option button, assign its label, and modify its properties accordingly. Leave the Groupname as Compensation and make sure that the field is required.**
- **Click the OK button.**

The dialog boxes are closed and all of the Compensation group option buttons and their assigned labels are displayed in the form (Figure 4-70).

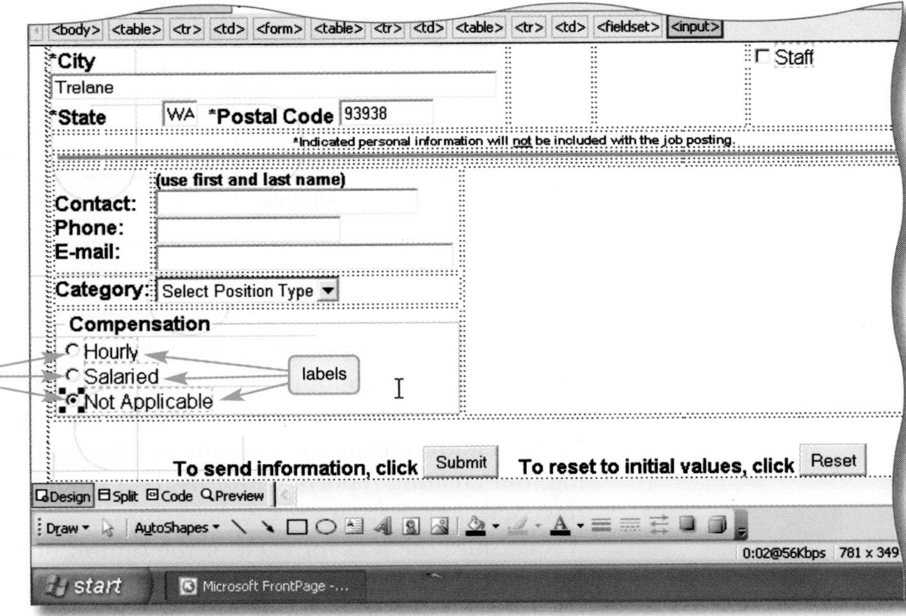

FIGURE 4-70

6

- **Click the border of the group box and then use the sizing handles to drag the right border to the left.**
- **Click the Save button to save your changes.**

The group box is sized proportionately to the contents (Figure 4-71).

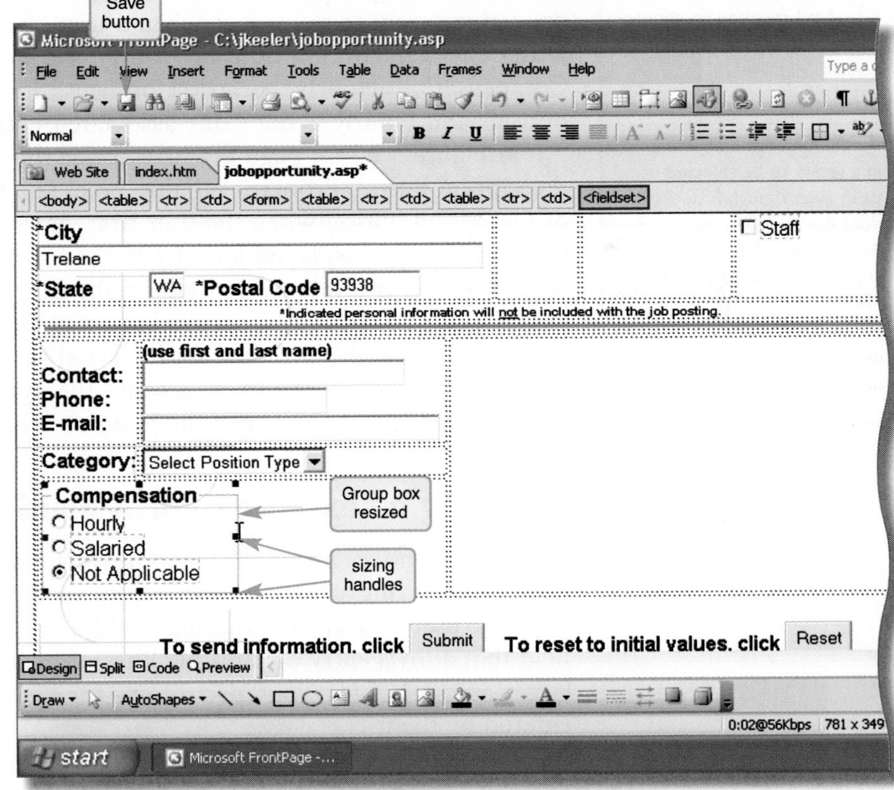

FIGURE 4-71

Other Ways

1. On Format menu click Properties
2. Press ALT+O, T
3. Press ALT+ENTER
4. In Voice Command mode, say "Format, Properties"

Table 4-7 Option Button Fields for Compensation Group

LABEL	VALUE	INITIAL STATE	TAB ORDER
Hourly	Hourly	Not selected	15
Salaried	Salaried	Not selected	16
Not Applicable	N/A	Selected	17

The option buttons have been inserted in the form. The values for each option button — as entered in the Value text box — will be sent to the form handler when the user clicks the Submit button. In this form, the values of the option buttons are the same as the button labels. Codes could have been used (eliminating any space characters) to reduce the amount of data sent back to the form handler for processing, but creating reports with this data would require subsequent interpretation of the codes.

Because the text for each of the option buttons was assigned as a label, the user can click the text and the option button is selected. This makes selection a little easier for users and can reduce data entry time.

Q: Am I required to choose one option button as the default selection?

A: You always should choose one option button in a group to be selected initially, even though FrontPage does not force you to do so. Because option buttons in a group are mutually exclusive, preselecting one button reduces confusion for your users and may reduce their data entry time.

Because these option buttons all are in the same group (in this case, the Compensation group), a user can select only one option button at a time, and only one value is sent to the server when a user clicks the Submit button. For example, if a user clicks the option button, Hourly, the name=value pair sent for processing is Compensation=Hourly, because Compensation is the name of the group of option buttons and Hourly is the value associated with the Hourly option button.

In Figure 4-67 on page FP 307, notice the two options in the Initial state area of the Option Button Properties dialog box. The Initial state option indicates the state of the option button when the user first views the Web page. Selected means the option button is displayed initially in the form as active. Not selected means the option button is displayed initially in the form as inactive.

You should choose an option button as the default value, typically the one chosen most frequently, and then set its initial state to Selected. This saves the user some time when filling out the form because the option button most frequently chosen is active already, so the user can move on to other fields.

Inserting a Text Area Form Field in a Form

The text boxes inserted earlier allow the user to enter only a single line of text. If you are collecting a textual description, such as a job opportunity, then you want to offer the user a means of entering multiple lines of text. A text area is a single form field that allows entry of multiple lines of text. A text area not only accommodates a larger amount of text, but also allows for easier reading and reviewing of the text entered by the user.

The following steps insert a text area form field in the form.

To Insert a Text Area Form Field in a Form

1

- **If necessary, drag the right border of the third column of table-T3 to the left as shown in Figure 4-72.**
- **Position the insertion point in the first row and the fourth column of table-T3, the nested table.**
- **Click the Bold button on the Formatting toolbar.**
- **Type** `Job Opportunity.`
- **Hold the SHIFT key and then press the ENTER key and type** `Description:`
- **Hold the SHIFT key and then press the ENTER key.**

FrontPage displays the entered text aligned to the top and left in the cell (Figure 4-72).

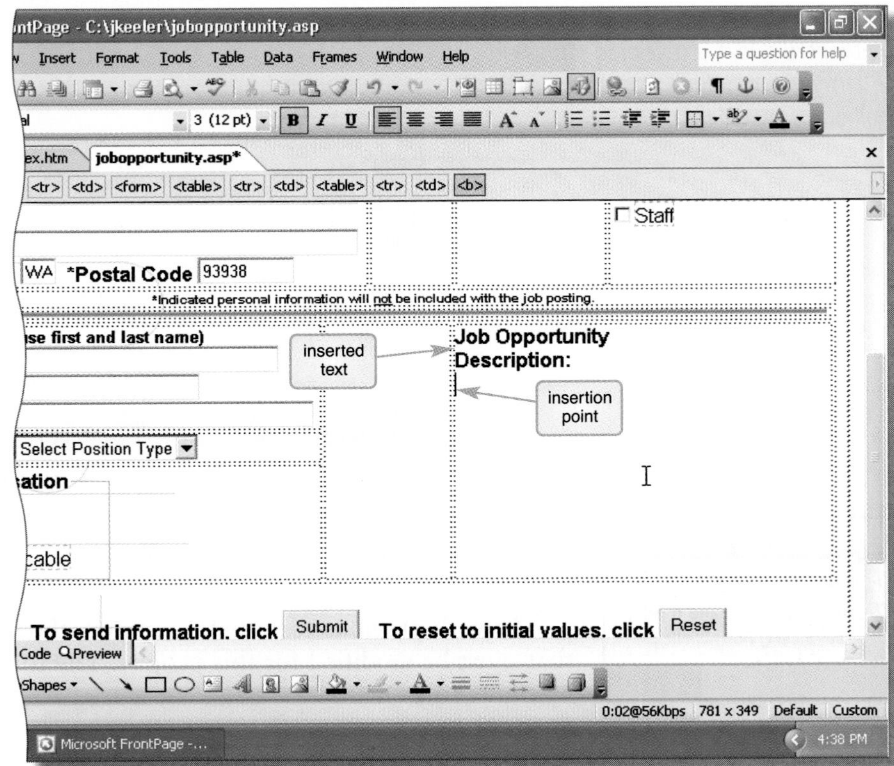

FIGURE 4-72

2

- **Click Insert on the menu bar and then point to Form.**

FrontPage displays the Form submenu (Figure 4-73).

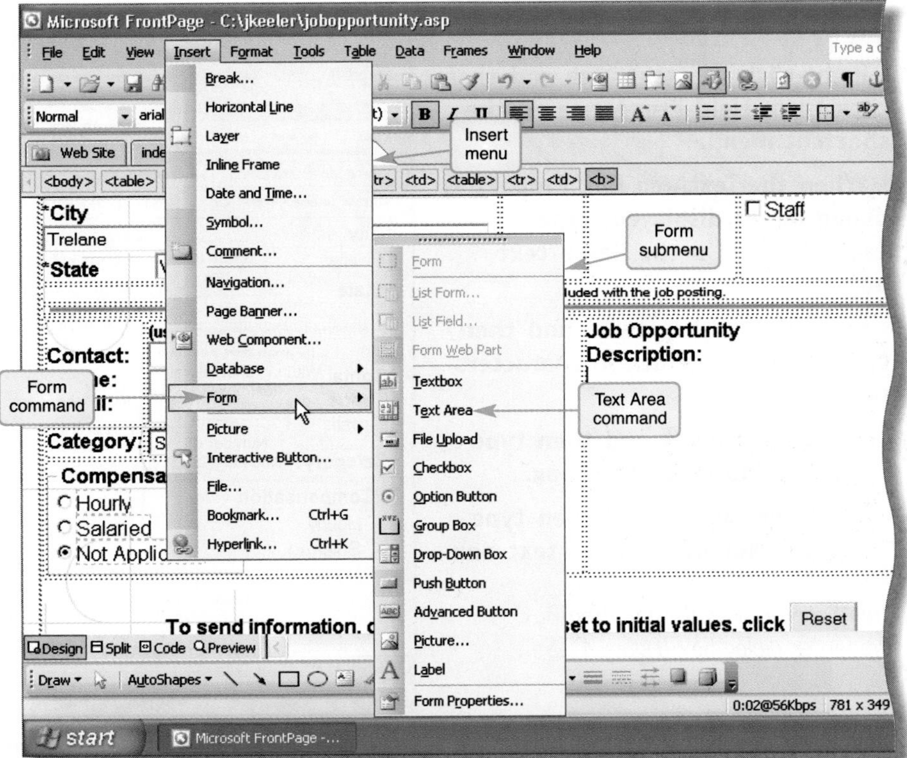

FIGURE 4-73

3

- **Click Text Area on the Form submenu.**

FrontPage displays a text area form field in the form with a default size and a vertical scroll bar (Figure 4-74).

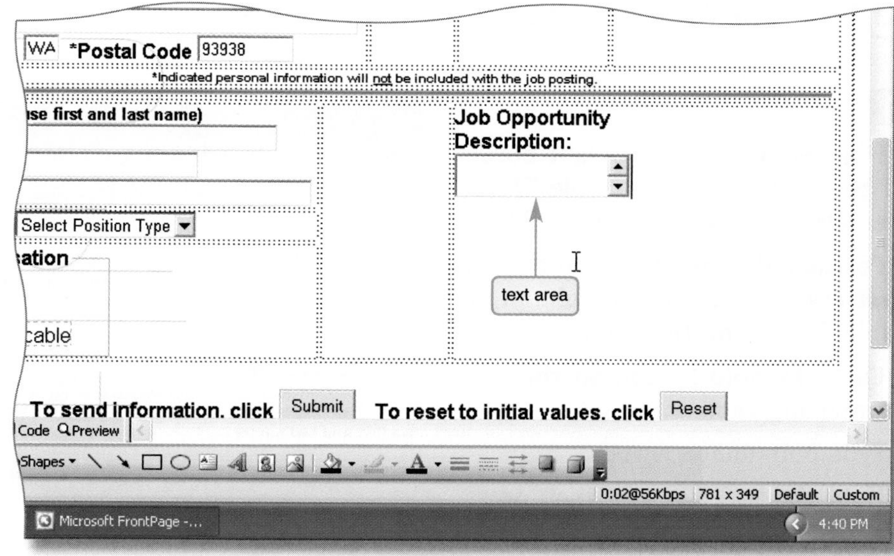

FIGURE 4-74

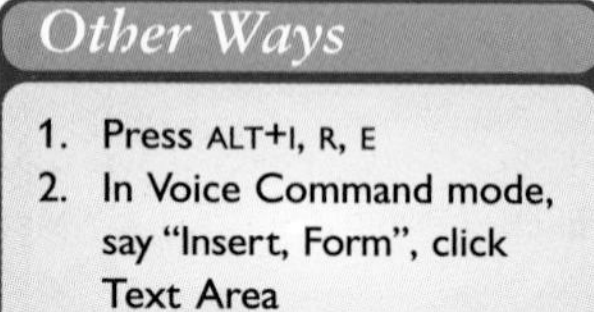

Other Ways

1. Press ALT+I, R, E
2. In Voice Command mode, say "Insert, Form", click Text Area

As with previous form fields entered, the text area has a default set of properties that must be modified for this project. The following steps modify the properties of a text area form field.

To Modify the Properties of a Text Area Form Field

1

- **Right-click the text area and then click Form Field Properties on the shortcut menu.**
- **When the TextArea Box Properties dialog box is displayed, type** `Description` **in the Name text box.**
- **Press the TAB key twice and then type** 37 **in the Width in characters text box.**
- **Press the TAB key and then type** 18 **in the Tab order text box.**
- **Press the TAB key and then type** 15 **in the Number of lines text box.**

FrontPage displays the TextArea Box Properties dialog box (Figure 4-75).

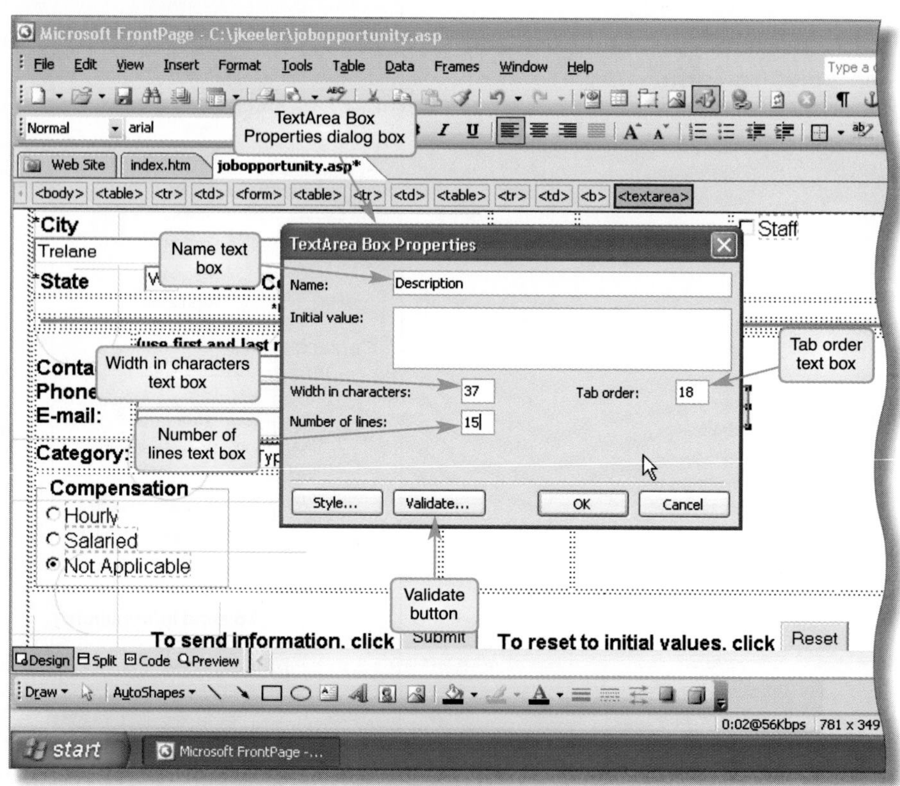

FIGURE 4-75

2

- **Click the Validate button.**
- **When the Text Box Validation dialog box is displayed, click Required in the Data length area, and then type** `Job Opportunity Description` **in the Display name text box.**

FrontPage displays the Text Box Validation dialog box (Figure 4-76).

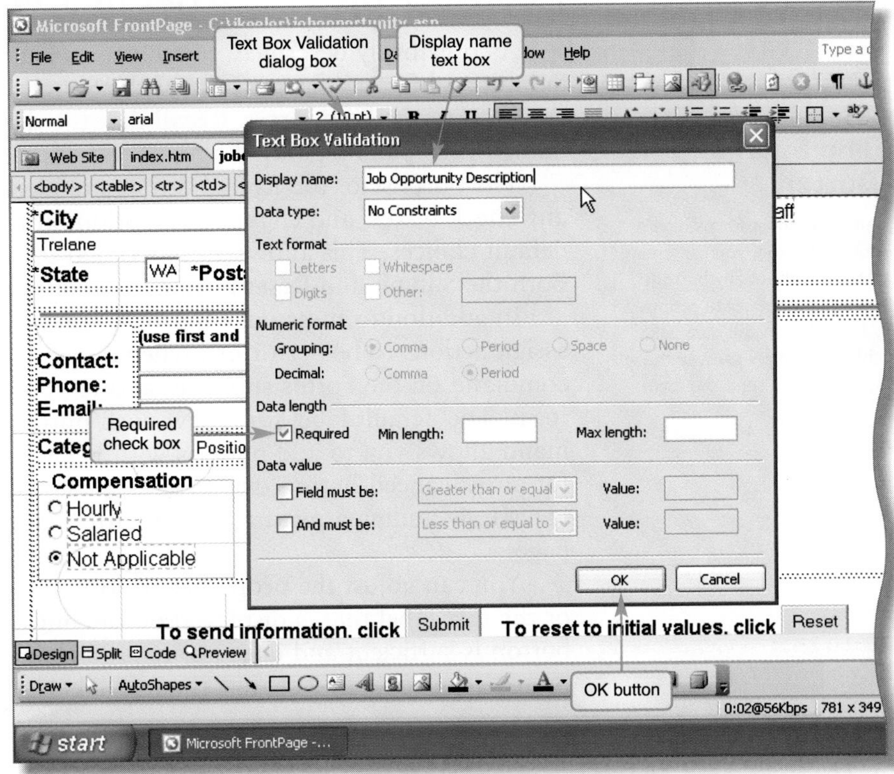

FIGURE 4-76

3

- **Click the OK button in the Text Box Validation dialog box.**
- **Click the OK button in the TextArea Box Properties dialog box.**
- **If necessary, drag cell borders to adjust widths.**

FrontPage displays the text area form field with the new size (Figure 4-77).

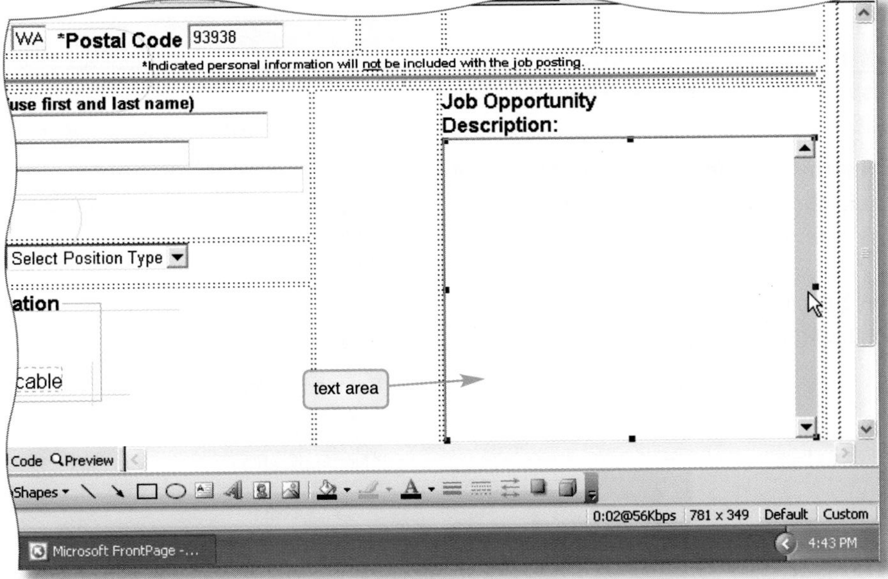

FIGURE 4-77

Other Ways

1. On Format menu click Properties
2. Press ALT+O, T
3. Press ALT+ENTER
4. In Voice Command mode, say "Format, Properties"

You can change the size of a text area by modifying its properties, as done here, or by selecting the text area and dragging the sizing handles to the required size.

The form is almost complete. The last two steps are to adjust the properties of the Submit and Reset buttons as needed and to adjust the properties of the form itself.

Modifying the Properties of a Push Button Form Field

More About

The Submit Button

Although most forms have a Submit button, you can create a form without any buttons by using appropriate scripts. After filling in the data fields, the user simply presses the ENTER key to send the form data.

As previously described, two buttons usually are displayed in every form — Submit and Reset. The purpose of the Submit button is to send the data entered in the form to the Web server. Recall that the data to be sent is in the form of name=value pairs separated by ampersands (&).

The purpose of the Reset button is to clear any data typed in text boxes, clear any check boxes, and change any option buttons and selected items back to the default choices. This allows an individual to clear his or her changes and start over. Both the Submit and Reset buttons are considered push buttons.

In addition to these push buttons, you can add other buttons to the form and assign actions to be performed when a user clicks those buttons. The Push Button command on the Forms submenu allows you to add other regular buttons to the form. The default label for a new push button is Button. The Advanced Button command allows you to add buttons with HTML as the button label. The default label for an Advanced Button displays, Type Here, and initially is selected. You can insert HTML, including a picture, as the button label just as you would insert it in a Web page.

You can adjust the properties of form buttons, such as the data value they return or the text label that is displayed on the button. In some cases, the default label on a button is sufficient and does not require changes. The following steps modify form button properties and change the text labels of the buttons.

To Modify the Properties of a Push Button Form Field

1

- **If necessary, scroll down to display the Submit and Reset buttons.**
- **Right-click the Submit button and then click Form Field Properties on the shortcut menu.**

The Submit button is selected and the shortcut menu is displayed (Figure 4-78).

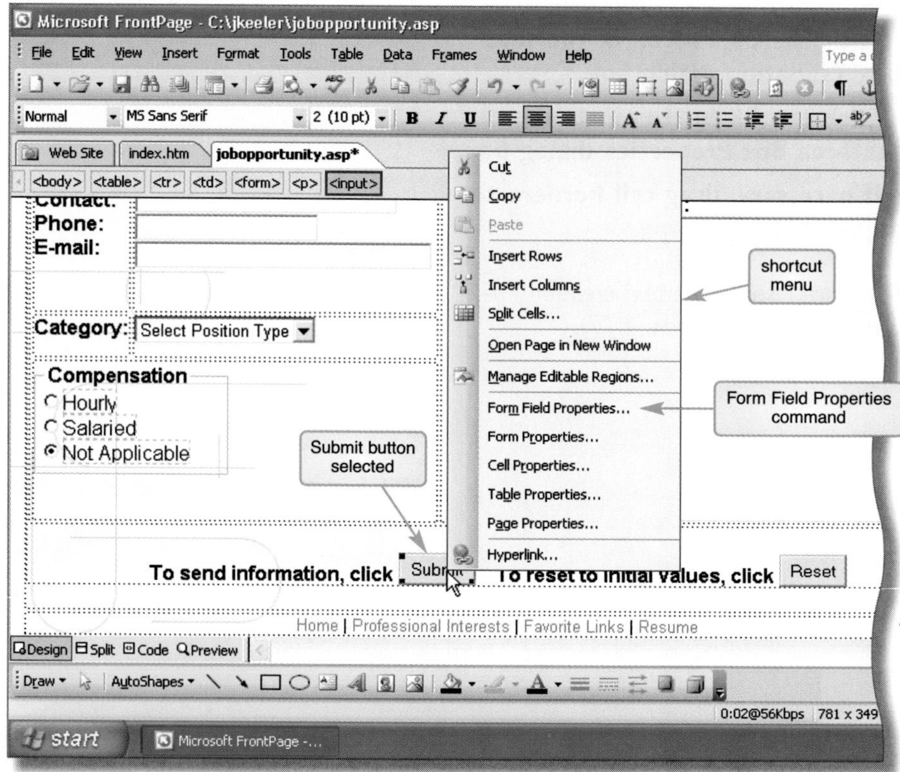

FIGURE 4-78

2

- **Click Form Field Properties.**
- **When the Push Button Properties dialog box is displayed, type** SendButton **in the Name text box.**
- **Drag through the text, Submit, in the Value/label text box and then type** Send **in the text box.**
- **Type** 19 **in the Tab order text box.**

FrontPage displays the Push Button Properties dialog box. The new name and label text are displayed and the tab order is set to 19 (Figure 4-79).

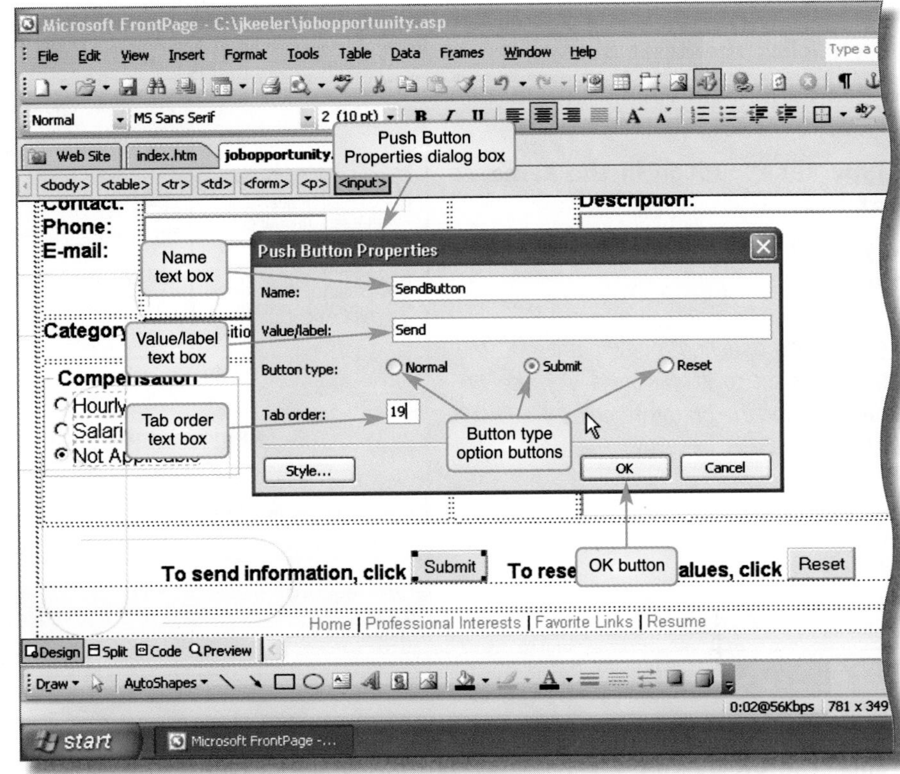

FIGURE 4-79

3

- **Click the OK button.**

FrontPage displays the new text label in the button (Figure 4-80).

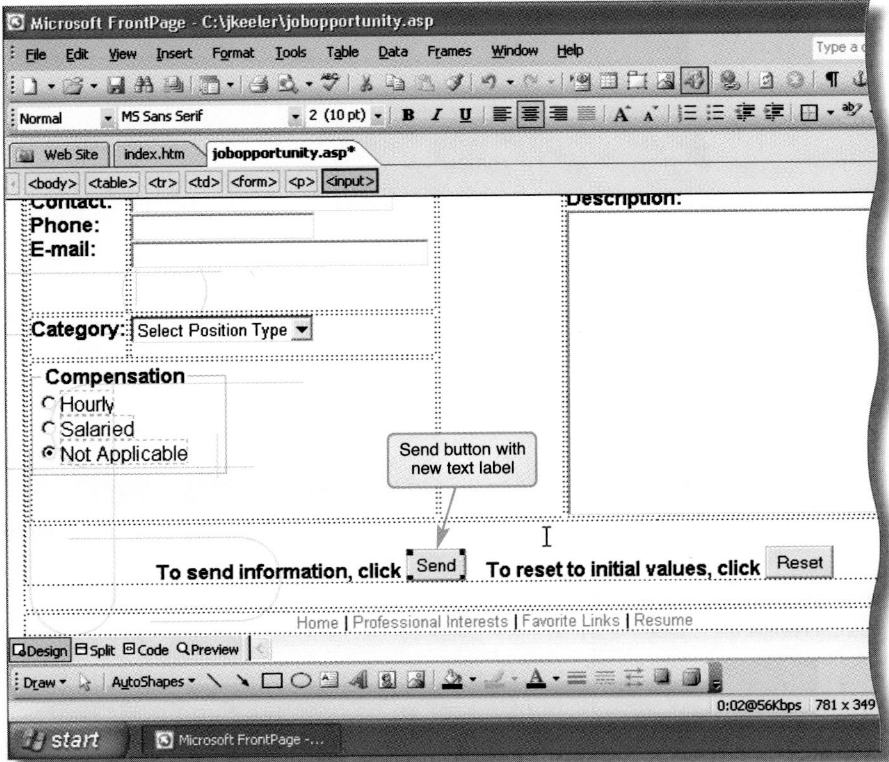

FIGURE 4-80

4

- **Right-click the Reset button.**
- **Click Form Field Properties on the shortcut menu.**
- **Type** `ResetButton` **in the Name text box.**
- **Type** `20` **in the Tab order text box.**

The button is assigned a new name and the tab order is set to 20 (Figure 4-81). The value/label for the button remains unchanged.

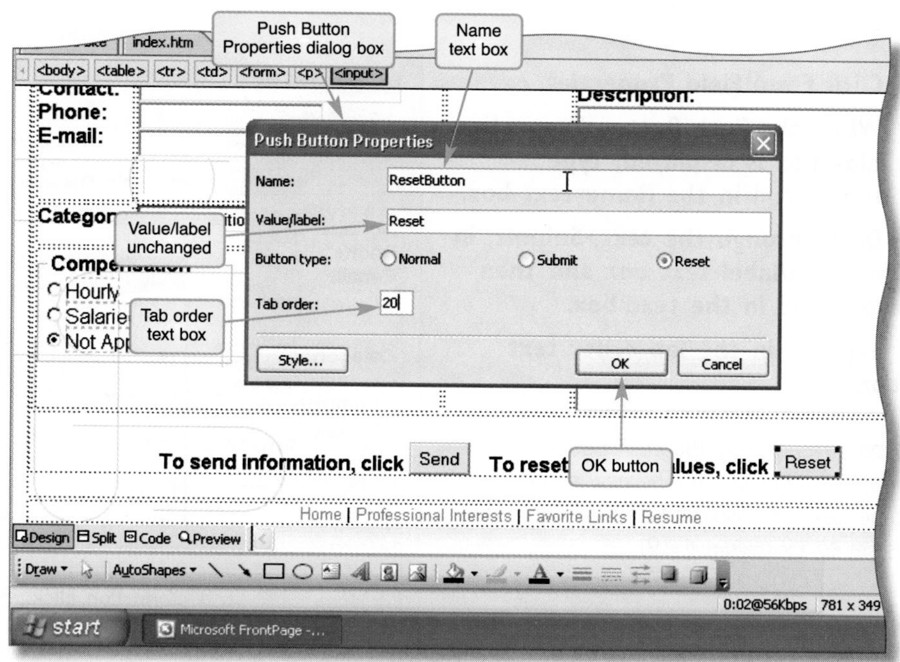

FIGURE 4-81

5

- **Click the OK button.**

FrontPage displays the completed form (Figure 4-82).

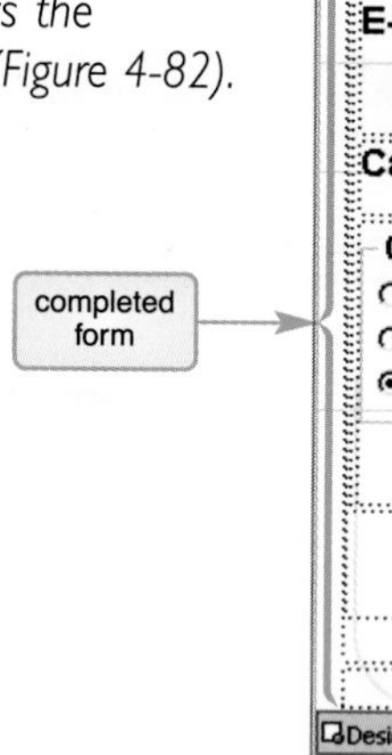

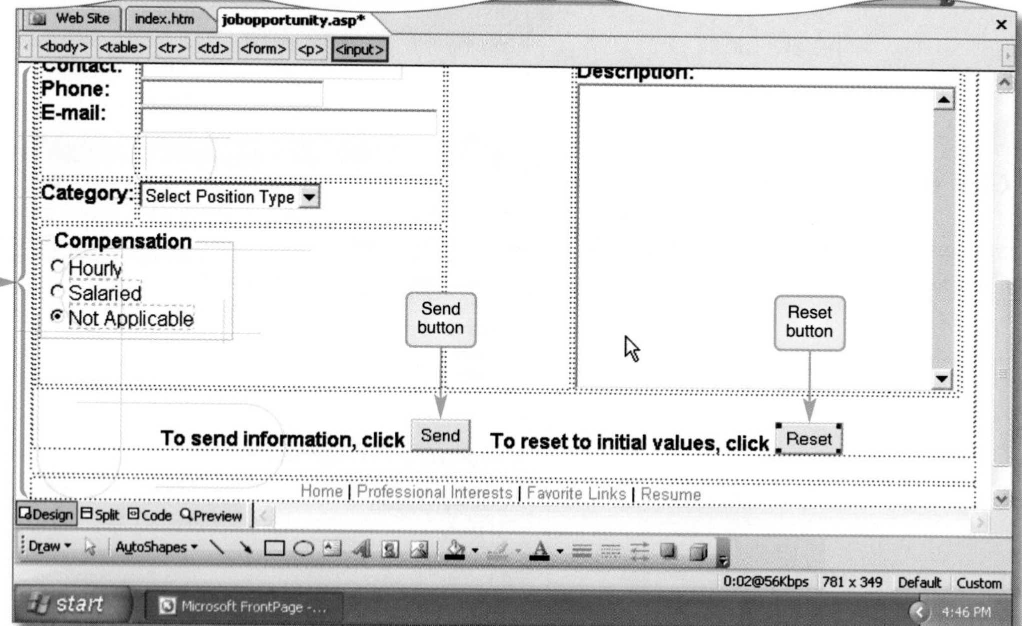

FIGURE 4-82

Other Ways

1. On Format menu click Properties
2. Press ALT+O, T
3. Press ALT+ENTER
4. In Voice Command mode, say "Format, Properties"

In the Push Button Properties dialog box shown in Figure 4-81, you can set a button type to be Normal, Submit, or Reset. You can use the Normal type to add other buttons to the form and then assign a script to be run if a user clicks the Normal button. Be sure to give the button a name and label that correctly indicate its purpose.

When a user clicks the Submit button, this sends the form and initiates the form handler. When the form has been designed completely, you must decide how the form should be handled when a user clicks the Submit button.

Choosing the Form Handler for the Form

After a user fills out the form and clicks the Submit button, the form data is sent back to the Web server, where an appropriate form handler is invoked to process the form data. Table 4-2 on page FP 261 lists several types of form handlers you can use to process form data.

Recall that the form data for the Job Opportunity Posting page is to be sent to a database. You can let FrontPage create the database or you can provide the name of an existing database. FrontPage can insert ASP (Active Server Page) scripts to enable the Web page to access the database. **Scripts** are program statements inserted in the Web page, typically intended for execution on the Web server. To use Active Server Pages, the page must have a file extension of .asp and the server also must support Active Server Pages.

More About

Active Server Pages

Using Active Server Pages (ASP) has become a popular way to process information from Web pages and to make Web pages dynamic. To learn more about Active Server Pages, visit the FrontPage 2003 More About Web page (scsite.com/fp2003/more) and then click Active Server Pages.

Setting the Form Properties and Form Handler

FrontPage provides several ways to store form data entered by users. By default, form information is saved to a text file. With FrontPage, you also can create a form that saves form results in a different file format, sends form results in an e-mail message, submits information to a database, or saves form results using a custom or FrontPage form handler, as listed in Table 4-2.

In this project, the form will submit information to an Access database. A database organizes data into tables. A **table** is a means of organizing data into columns and rows within a database.

To submit information to a database, FrontPage must establish a connection to an existing database or to a newly created database. A **connection** is an object that provides a path to a database. FrontPage then must use a valid table name from the database and insert the information into that table.

The following steps modify the form properties and choose a form handler.

Q&A

Q: Where can I learn more about databases?

A: Database terminology may seem confusing at first, but it does not have to be. To learn more about database terminology, visit the FrontPage 2003 More About Web page (scsite.com/fp2003/more) and then click Database Terminology.

To Modify Form Properties and Set a Form Handler

1

- **Right-click the form.**

FrontPage displays a shortcut menu (Figure 4-83). The Form Properties command allows you to change the form handler, as well as set other form properties.

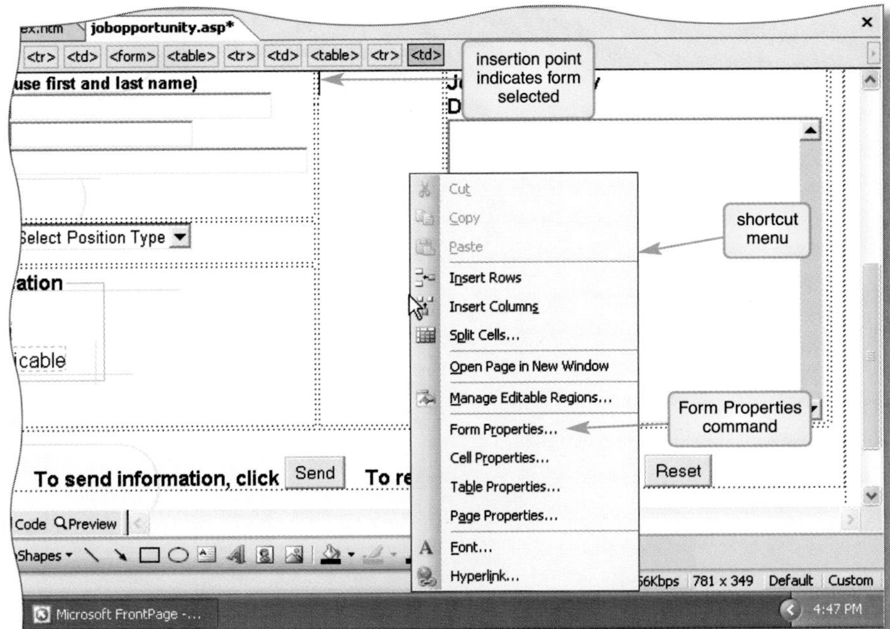

FIGURE 4-83

2

• **Click Form Properties.**

FrontPage displays the Form Properties dialog box (Figure 4-84). The Form Properties dialog box contains text boxes and option buttons that control what type of form handler you want to use to store form data.

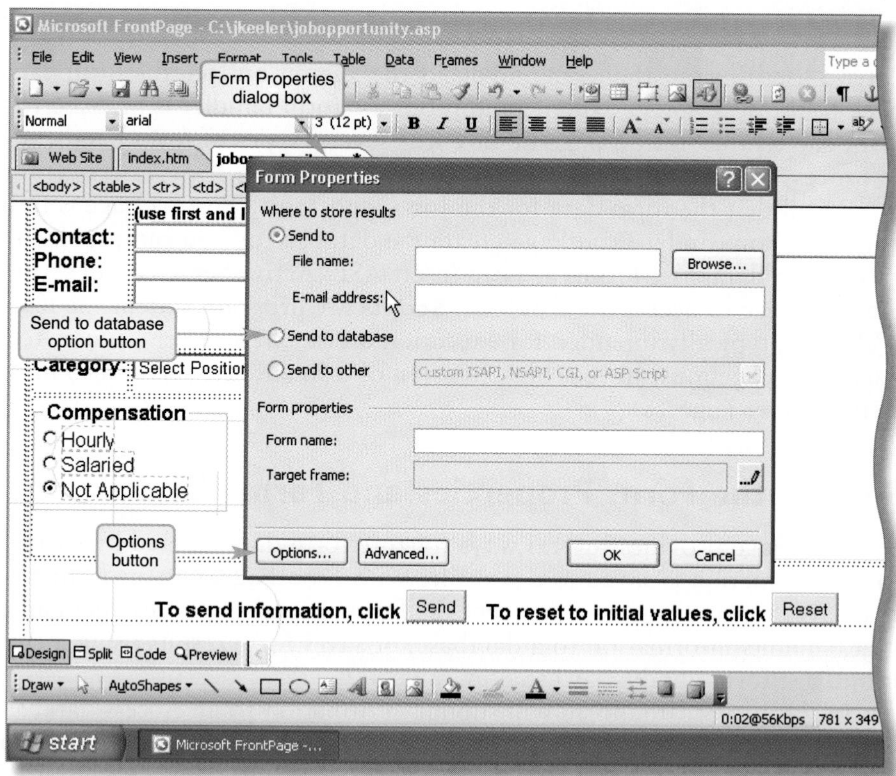

FIGURE 4-84

3

• **Click Send to database.**

FrontPage displays the Form Properties dialog box with the above changes (Figure 4-85).

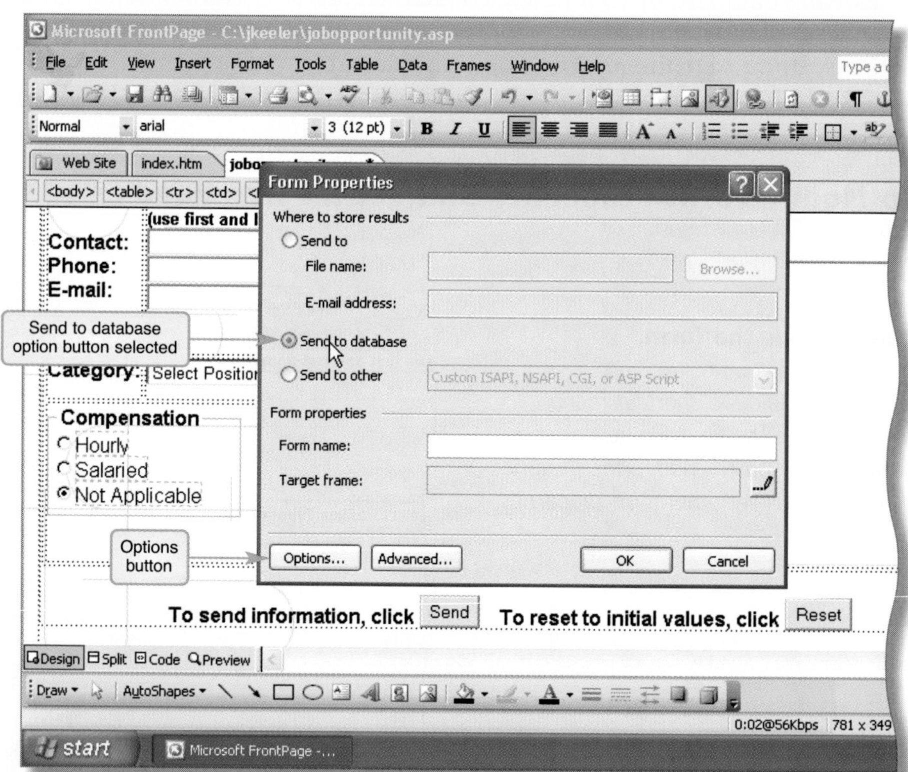

FIGURE 4-85

4

- **Click the Options button.**
- **If necessary, when the Options for Saving Results to Database dialog box is displayed, click the Database Results tab.**

FrontPage displays the Options for Saving Results to Database dialog box with the Database Results sheet selected (Figure 4-86).

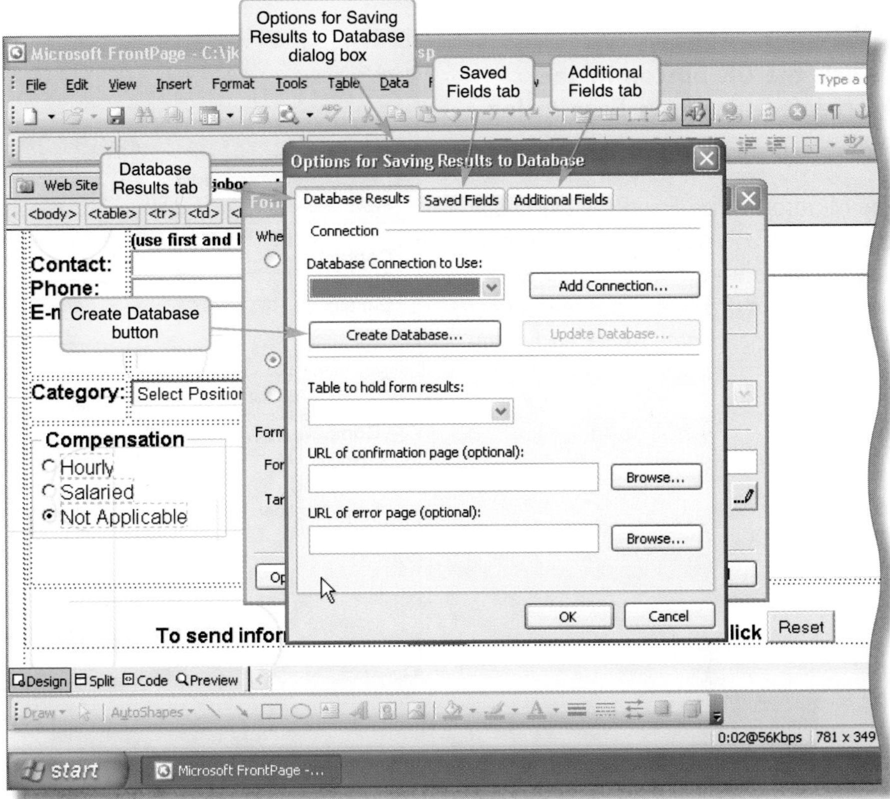

FIGURE 4-86

5

- **Click the Create Database button.**

A Microsoft Office FrontPage dialog box is displayed indicating FrontPage has created a database for you using the page name as the name for the database connection (Figure 4-87).

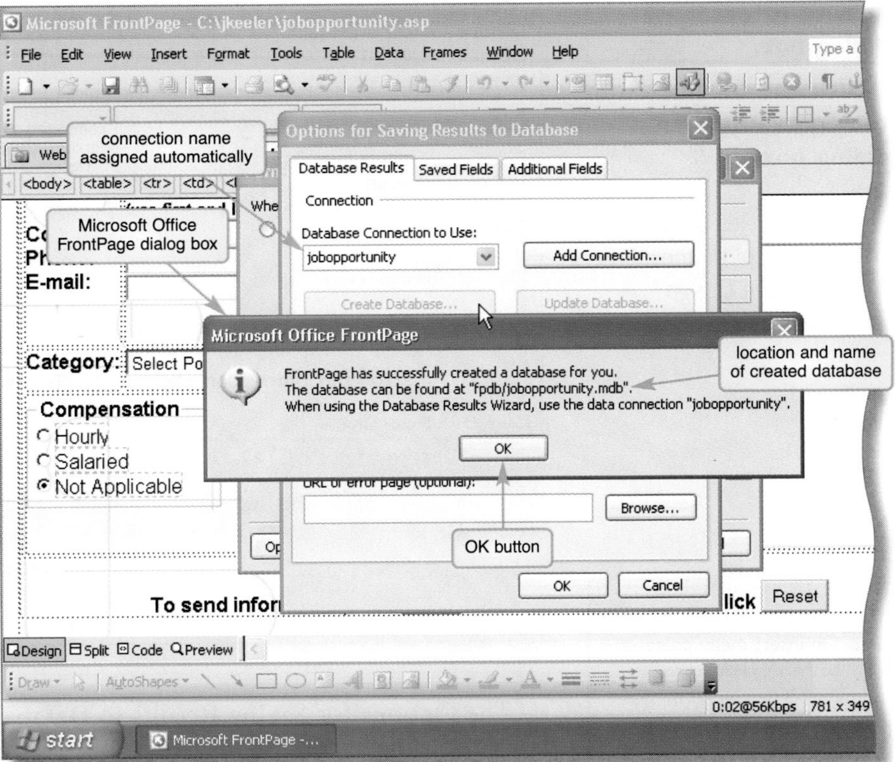

FIGURE 4-87

6

- **Click the OK button in the Microsoft Office FrontPage dialog box.**

The Microsoft Office FrontPage dialog box is closed. FrontPage created a table in the new database with a default name of Results (Figure 4-88). A corresponding entry exists in the new database for each form field.

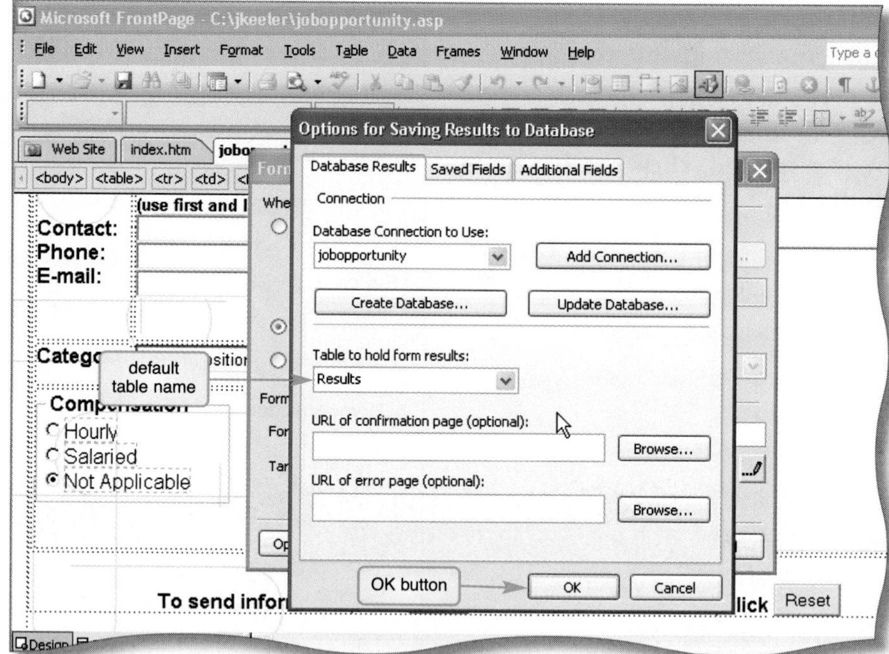

FIGURE 4-88

7

- **Click the OK button in the Options for Saving Results to Database dialog box.**
- **Click the OK button in the Form Properties dialog box.**

The dialog boxes close and FrontPage displays the completed page in Design view (Figure 4-89).

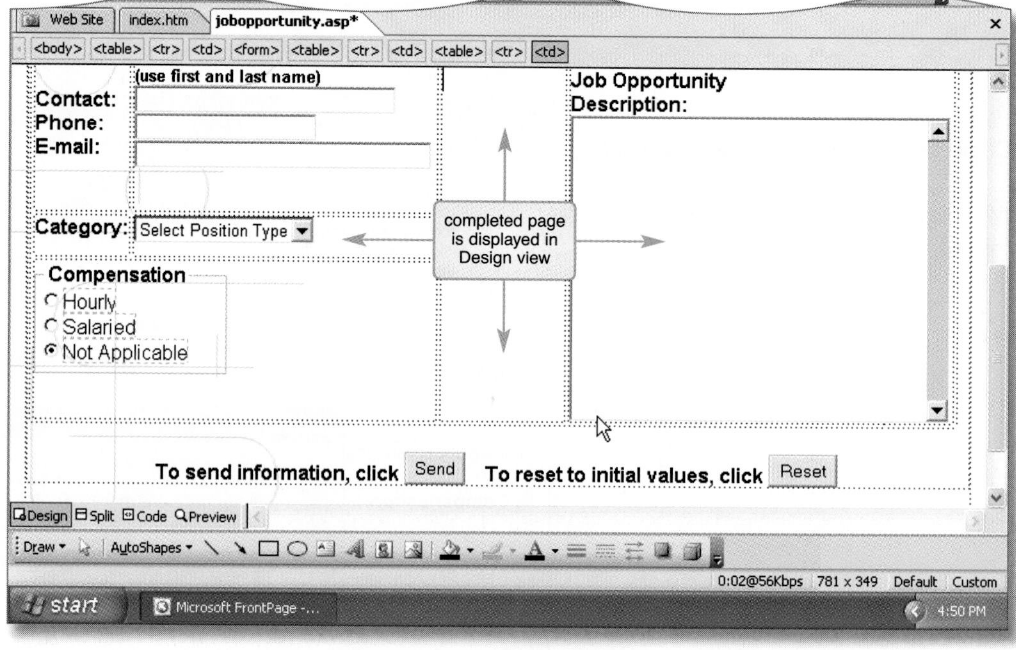

FIGURE 4-89

Other Ways

1. On Insert menu point to Form, click Form Properties on Form submenu
2. Right-click form, click Form Properties
3. Press ALT+I, R, R
4. In Voice Command mode, say "Insert, Form", click Form Properties

The Options for Saving Results to Database dialog box shown in Figure 4-86 on the previous page contains several tabbed sheets. In addition to specifying the database connection and table to use, the Database Results sheet allows you to specify a customized confirmation page be returned to the user after he or she submits the form and a customized failure page if an error occurs. Because FrontPage provides default pages, both are optional. The Saved Fields sheet allows you not only to choose which form fields actually are saved, but also to change the field column names in the database. The Additional Fields sheet provides similar capabilities for additional information, such as the date and time the form was submitted, browser type, remote computer name, and user name.

Modifying HTML Code Directly

More About

HTML Code

For resources to help you understand HTML better, visit the FrontPage 2003 More About Web page (scsite.com/fp2003/more) and then click HTML.

The World Wide Web is a vast resource of information that is largely unstructured. To find information of interest, a Web user typically performs a search using a search engine. A **search engine** is software that indexes, or organizes, a portion of the information available on the Web. That organization of information focuses on text supplied within the indexed Web pages themselves. Some search engines use whatever text they find near the top of your Web page. Others utilize special HTML tags to define keywords and a description for the page. Meta tags are one category of these special HTML tags.

A **meta tag** can contain keywords or a description of the content of the page. Recall that HTML tags have the form <tag name> and that some HTML tags can contain keyword-value pairs in the form keyword=value. Meta tags are of this variety. Most meta tags have the format

```
<META name="name of meta tag" content="descriptive content for meta tag">
```

and are not case-sensitive with respect to the tag name or keywords. By appropriately organizing the content of your Web page and inserting some of these tags, you increase the likelihood that users of search engines will locate your site more readily.

Design Tip

Include meta tags as part of your design. Choose targeted meta tags that succinctly describe the use and content of the Web page. The use of common words in meta tags decreases the chance that a Web user will find your page using a search engine.

Modifying HTML Code on the HTML Sheet

Not all search engines use the same information from your Web pages for indexing. Most search engines retrieve the text contained in the Web page title. Some search engines use information within meta tags and some only use text near the top of your page. You may use meta tags for the search engines that support their use and insert a comment for those that do not.

A comment in HTML code has the format

```
<!– comment text goes here –>
```

with all text between the <!– and the –> ignored by the browser.

The steps on the next page modify the HTML code directly in FrontPage to insert meta tags and comments in the Job Opportunity Posting Web page.

To Modify HTML Code and Insert Meta Tags

1

- **Click the Code button.**
- **If necessary, scroll toward the top of the Web page until the form <head> tag is displayed.**
- **Position the insertion point at the beginning of the line below the <title> tag.**

FrontPage displays the HTML source for the Job Opportunity Posting Web page (Figure 4-90). Notice that FrontPage automatically includes some meta tags in each Web page it creates. Your tags and HTML code may appear somewhat different.

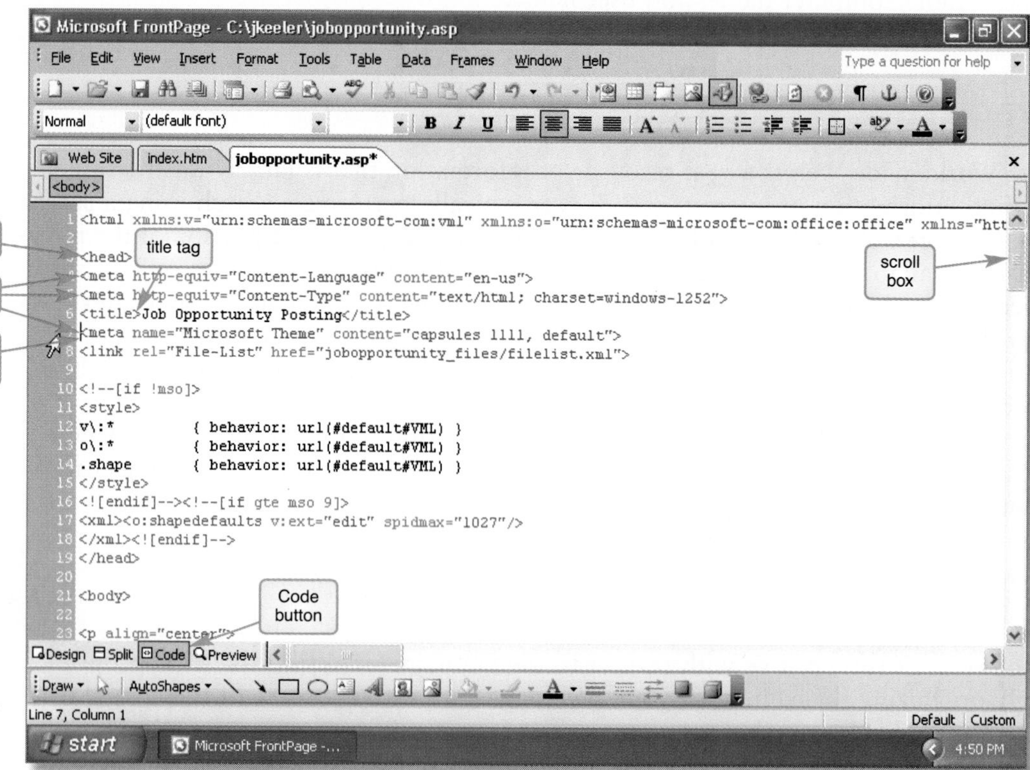

FIGURE 4-90

2

- **Type** `<meta name="description" content="Members of Trelane College may post Job Opportunities at the Web site of James Keeler.">` **and then press the ENTER key.**

FrontPage displays the entered meta tag (Figure 4-91). FrontPage does not display the entire meta tag as it extends beyond the right edge of the screen.

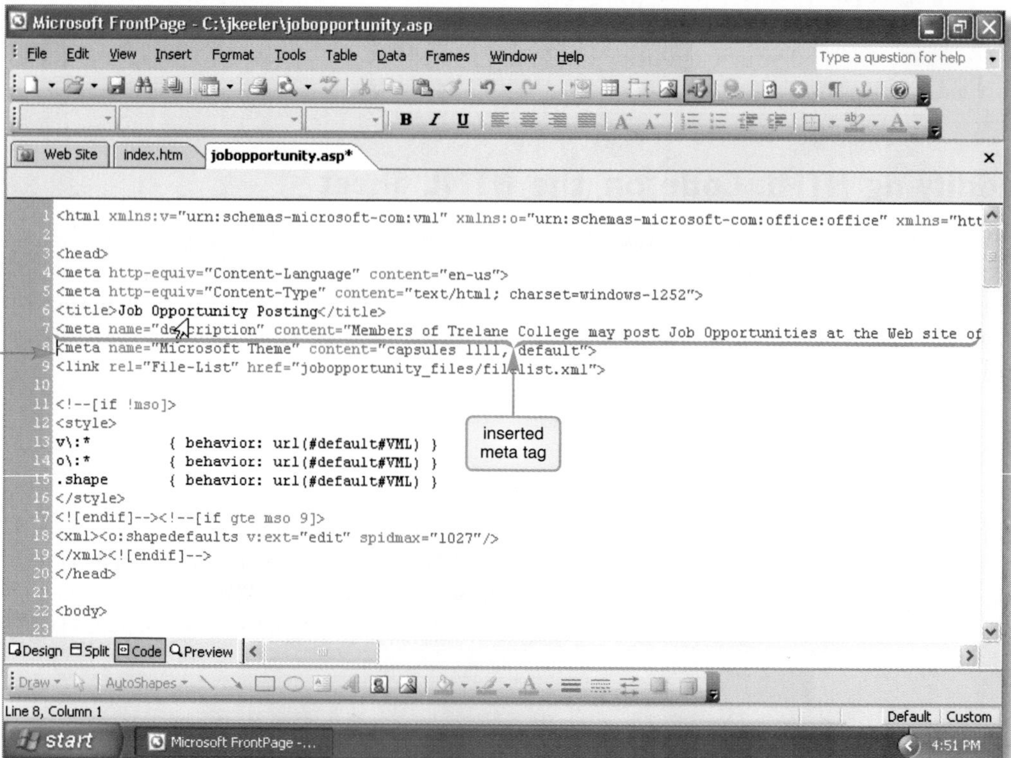

FIGURE 4-91

3

• **Type** <meta name="keywords" content="Job Opportunity Postings, Trelane College, James Keeler"> **and then press the ENTER key.**

FrontPage displays the meta tag for keywords for this Web page (Figure 4-92). When using meta tags, use distinctive keywords for each Web page and limit the number to approximately ten keywords.

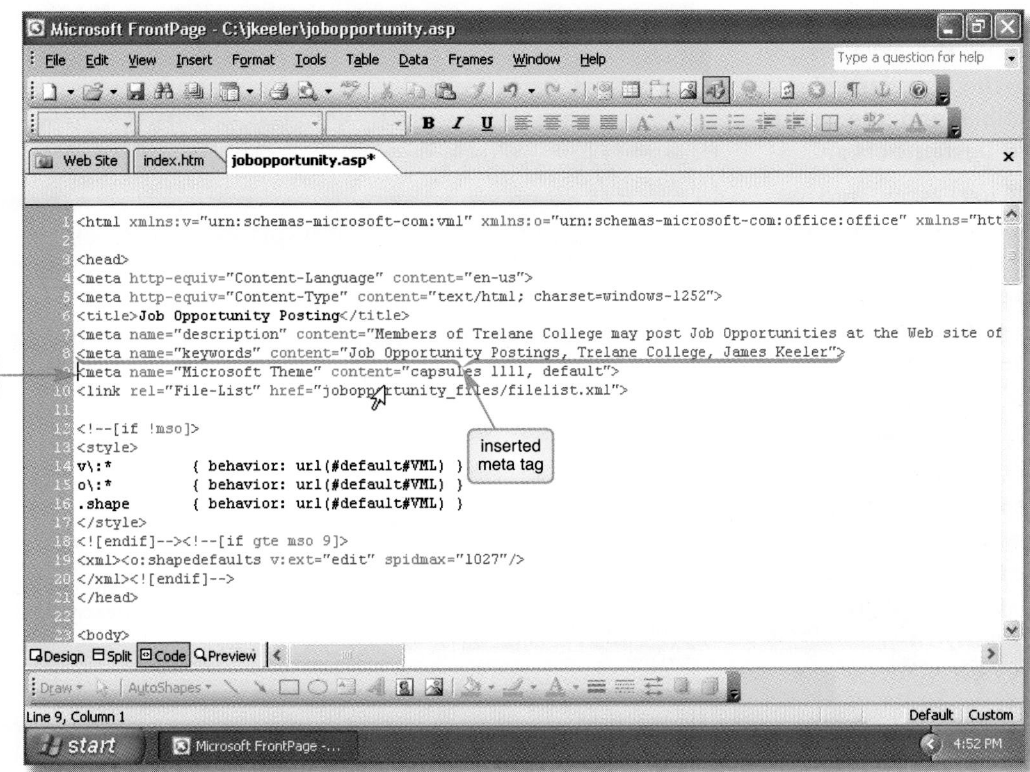

FIGURE 4-92

4

• **Type** <!– Members of Trelane College may post Job Opportunities at the Web site of James Keeler.–> **and then press the ENTER key.**

FrontPage displays the entered comment (Figure 4-93). Comments are for information only and do not represent executable code statements.

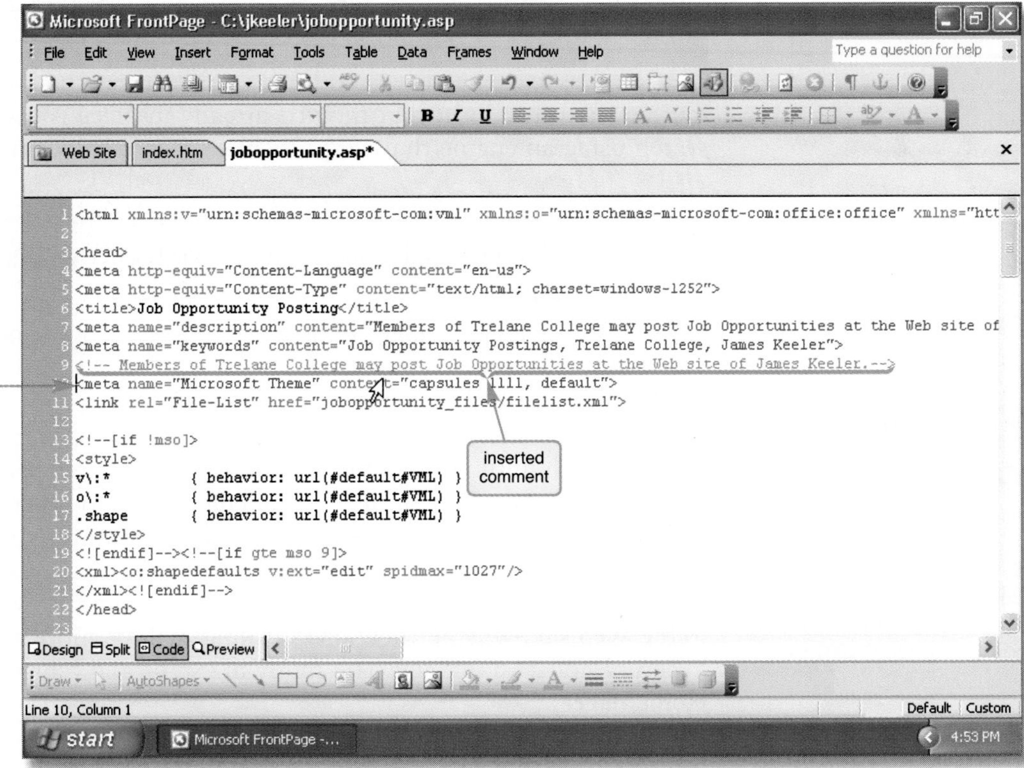

FIGURE 4-93

5

- **Click the Save button on the Standard toolbar and then click the Design button.**
- **If necessary, add spaces after the labels and in front of the text boxes if the text boxes do not align properly in Preview view.**
- **If necessary, adjust the right border of the cell containing the Full Name, Address, City, State, and Postal Code text boxes so that the text boxes align properly in Preview view.**

The HTML view is closed and the Web page is displayed in Design view (Figure 4-94).

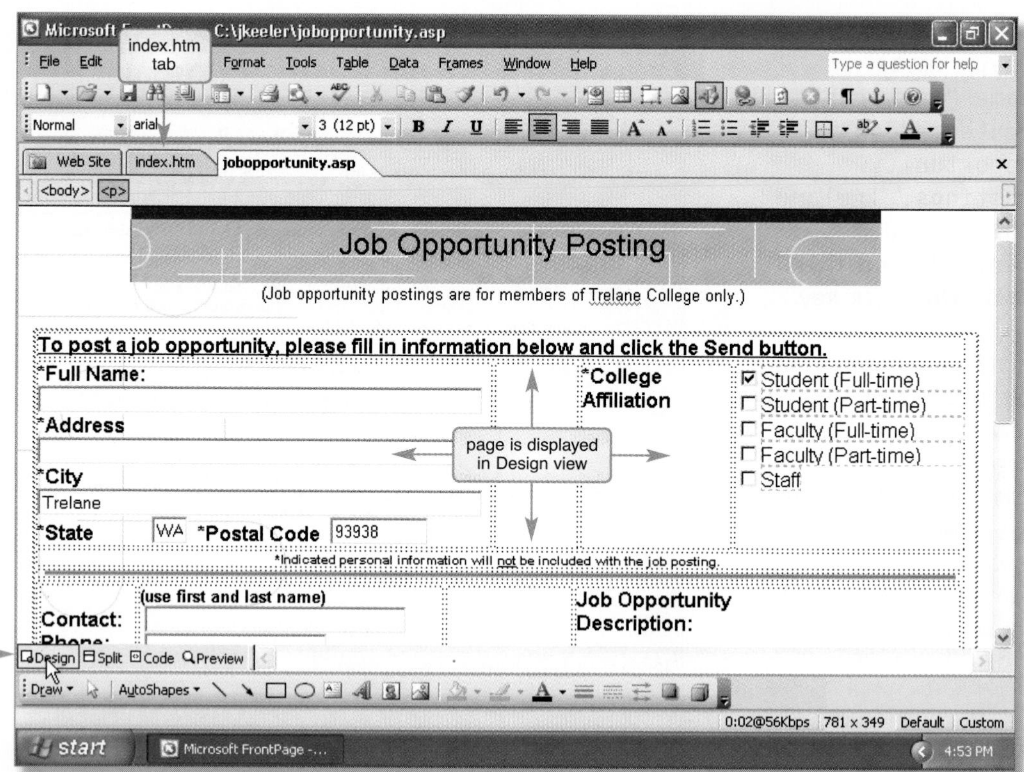

FIGURE 4-94

The Web page has been modified so that it may be indexed by search engines more effectively. Given that the title already in place is Job Opportunity Posting, a search using an engine that supports meta tags would return a search result such as:

> Job Opportunity Posting
>
> Members of Trelane College may post Job Opportunities at the Web site of James Keeler.
>
> http://www.trelanecollege.edu/~jkeeler/jobopportunity.asp

More About

Quick Reference

For more information, see the Quick Reference Summary at the back of this book, or visit the FrontPage 2003 Quick Reference Web page (scsite.com/fp2003/qr).

You have provided descriptive text and keywords for search engines that may index the Web site. The Web site is not indexed, however, and will not be displayed on any search until you manually submit the page to a search engine, requesting that the page be indexed, or until a search engine that looks for Web sites (usually called a **spider** or **crawler**) finds the site and indexes it automatically.

Another simple and obvious means to publicize the existence of the new Job Opportunity Posting page is to provide a link from the Web site Home page. Visitors to the Web site, whether new or returning, will be more aware of the new page if the hyperlink for it is obvious. The following steps add a link for the new page to the Home page.

To Add a Hyperlink to a Page

1. **Click the tab, index.htm, to display the Home page.**
2. **Position the insertion point below the last line of text that begins, You may send. If necessary, click the Center button on the Formatting toolbar.**
3. **Click the Bold button on the Formatting toolbar and then type** `Post a Job Opportunity that you know about!`
4. **Drag through the words, Job Opportunity. Click the Insert Hyperlink button on the Standard toolbar. When the Insert Hyperlink dialog box is displayed, click the file jobopportunity.asp (open) and then click the OK button. Click the page to deselect the hyperlink. Click the Save button on the Standard toolbar.**

The Home page displays a hyperlink to the Job Opportunity Posting page (Figure 4-95).

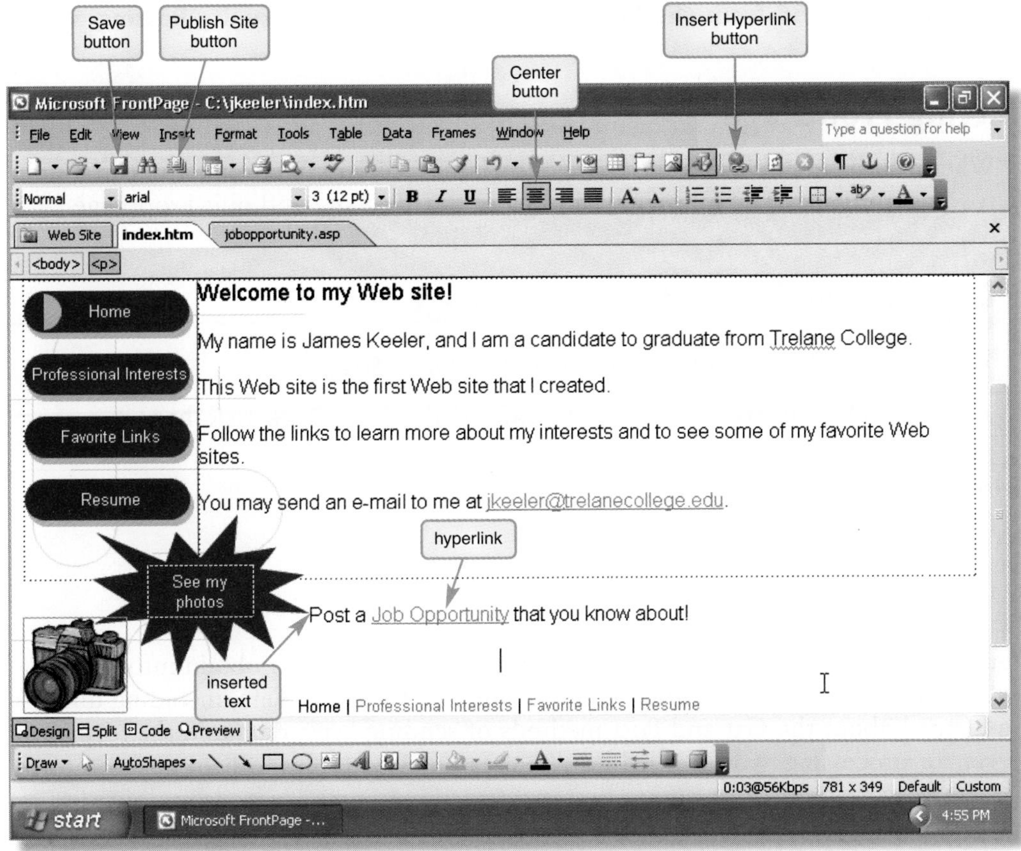

FIGURE 4-95

After saving the Web page on disk, you should publish the changes to the Web site.

Publishing Changes to a FrontPage Web Site

In Project 3, changes to James Keeler's Web site were published on the World Wide Web. Because you have made additional changes to the FrontPage Web site, you must publish the FrontPage Web site again.

When you publish a FrontPage Web site that has been published before, FrontPage adds and updates only those parts of the Web site that are new or have changed since the last time the Web site was published. This reduces the amount of data transfer that takes place and speeds the publishing of a Web site with many folders, Web pages, and files.

The following steps publish changes to a FrontPage Web site. Be sure to use your own URL or an error will occur. If you do not know what URL to use, ask your instructor.

To Publish Changes to a FrontPage Web Site

1. **Click the Publish Site button on the Standard toolbar.**
2. **To view the Job Opportunity Posting page, type** `http://www.hcc.edu/~jkeeler/jobopportunity.asp` **(or use your own URL) in any browser and then press the ENTER key. Be sure to test the hyperlinks to the other pages in the Web site and from the Home page to the Job Opportunity Posting page.**

Quitting FrontPage

When you have published the changes to James Keeler's Web site, you can quit Microsoft FrontPage. The following steps close the Web site and quit FrontPage.

To Close a Web Site and Quit FrontPage

1. **Click File on the menu bar and then click Close Site.**
2. **Click the Close button on the right side of the FrontPage title bar.**

The FrontPage window closes and the Windows desktop is displayed.

Project Summary

Having completed Project 4, you now are ready to create interactive forms and use them to obtain information from the users of your Web pages. In this project, you learned about forms and form handlers, including different types of form handlers. You learned about the Get and Post methods of sending form data and the format in which form data is sent to a server for processing. You learned how to create nested tables to help position form elements. You learned how to insert form fields such as option buttons, text boxes, text areas, drop-down list boxes, and check boxes in a form. You learned how to adjust the properties of the different types of form fields. You learned how to adjust the properties of the form and specify the form handler to be used to process the data from the form. Finally, you learned how to insert meta tags to help identify the page to Web search engines.

What You Should Know

Having completed this project, you should be able to perform the tasks below. The tasks are listed in the same order they were presented in this project. For a list of the buttons, menus, toolbars, and commands introduced in this project, see the Quick Reference Summary at the back of this book and refer to the Page Number column.

1. Start FrontPage and Open an Existing Web Site (FP 264)
2. Add and Rename a Web Page in Folders View (FP 266)
3. Modify a Page Title in Folders View (FP 267)
4. Copy and Paste a Page Banner (FP 269)
5. Add a Table to a Web Page (FP 270)
6. Copy and Paste a Link Bar from a Web Page (FP 271)
7. Hide the Folder List Pane (FP 273)
8. Insert a Form in a Table (FP 274)
9. Insert a Table in a Form (FP 276)
10. Insert Text in a Form (FP 277)
11. Insert a Text Box Form Field in a Form (FP 279)
12. Modify the Properties of a Text Box Form Field (FP 280)
13. Insert Additional Text Box Form Fields (FP 282)
14. Insert a Check Box Form Field in a Form (FP 285)
15. Assign Text as a Label for a Check Box (FP 287)
16. Modify the Properties of a Check Box Form Field (FP 288)
17. Insert Additional Check Box Form Fields (FP 289)
18. Insert a Line Drawing AutoShape in a Table (FP 291)
19. Create a Nested Table (FP 294)
20. Insert and Align Elements in a Nested Table (FP 295)
21. Insert a Drop-Down List Box Form Field in a Form (FP 297)
22. Modify the Properties of a Drop-Down List Box Form Field (FP 298)
23. Insert a Group Box Form Field in a Form (FP 303)
24. Modify the Title of a Group Box Form Field (FP 304)
25. Insert an Option Button Form Field in a Group Box (FP 305)
26. Assign a Label to an Option Button Form Field (FP 306)
27. Modify the Properties of an Option Button Form Field (FP 307)
28. Insert a Text Area Form Field in a Form (FP 311)
29. Modify the Properties of a Text Area Form Field (FP 312)
30. Modify the Properties of a Push Button Form Field (FP 314)
31. Modify Form Properties and Set a Form Handler (FP 317)
32. Modify HTML Code and Insert Meta Tags (FP 322)
33. Add a Hyperlink to a Page (FP 325)
34. Publish Changes to a FrontPage Web Site (FP 326)
35. Close a Web Site and Quit FrontPage (FP 326)

Learn It Online

Instructions: To complete the Learn It Online exercises, start your browser, click the Address bar, and then enter the Web address `scsite.com/fp2003/learn`. When the FrontPage 2003 Learn It Online page is displayed, follow the instructions in the exercises below. Each exercise has instructions for printing your results, either for your own records or for submission to your instructor.

1 Project Reinforcement TF, MC, and SA

Below FrontPage Project 4, click the Project Reinforcement link. Print the quiz by clicking Print on the File menu for each page. Answer each question.

2 Flash Cards

Below FrontPage Project 4, click the Flash Cards link and read the instructions. Type 20 (or a number specified by your instructor) in the Number of playing cards text box, type your name in the Enter your Name text box, and then click the Flip Card button. When the flash card is displayed, read the question and then click the ANSWER box arrow to select an answer. Flip through Flash Cards. If your score is 15 (75%) correct or greater, click Print on the File menu to print your results. If your score is less than 15 (75%) correct, then redo this exercise by clicking the Replay button.

3 Practice Test

Below FrontPage Project 4, click the Practice Test link. Answer each question, enter your first and last name at the bottom of the page, and then click the Grade Test button. When the graded practice test is displayed on your screen, click Print on the File menu to print a hard copy. Continue to take practice tests until you score 80% or better.

4 Who Wants To Be a Computer Genius?

Below FrontPage Project 4, click the Computer Genius link. Read the instructions, enter your first and last name at the bottom of the page, and then click the PLAY button. When your score is displayed, click the PRINT RESULTS link to print a hard copy.

5 Wheel of Terms

Below FrontPage Project 4, click the Wheel of Terms link. Read the instructions, and then enter your first and last name and your school name. Click the PLAY button. When your score is displayed, right-click the score and then click Print on the shortcut menu to print a hard copy.

6 Crossword Puzzle Challenge

Below FrontPage Project 4, click the Crossword Puzzle Challenge link. Read the instructions, and then enter your first and last name. Click the SUBMIT button. Work the crossword puzzle. When you are finished, click the Submit button. When the crossword puzzle is redisplayed, click the Print Puzzle button to print a hard copy.

7 Tips and Tricks

Below FrontPage Project 4, click the Tips and Tricks link. Click a topic that pertains to Project 4. Right-click the information and then click Print on the shortcut menu. Construct a brief example of what the information relates to in FrontPage to confirm you understand how to use the tip or trick.

8 Newsgroups

Below FrontPage Project 4, click the Newsgroups link. Click a topic that pertains to Project 4. Print three comments.

9 Expanding Your Horizons

Below FrontPage Project 4, click the Expanding Your Horizons link. Click a topic that pertains to Project 4. Print the information. Construct a brief example of what the information relates to in FrontPage to confirm you understand the contents of the article.

10 Search Sleuth

Below FrontPage Project 4, click the Search Sleuth link. To search for a term that pertains to this project, select a term below the Project 4 title and then use the Google search engine at google.com (or any major search engine) to display and print two Web pages that present information on the term.

11 FrontPage Online Training

Below FrontPage Project 4, click the FrontPage Online Training link. When your browser displays the Microsoft Office Online Web page, click the FrontPage link. Click one of the FrontPage courses that covers one or more of the objectives listed at the beginning of the project on page FP 258. Print the first page of the course before stepping through it.

12 Office Marketplace

Below FrontPage Project 4, click the Office Marketplace link. When your browser displays the Microsoft Office Online Web page, click the Office Marketplace link. Click a topic that relates to FrontPage. Print the first page.

Apply Your Knowledge

1 Sending Form Results with E-mail

Instructions: Start FrontPage. Open the Ship-It Here Web site that you modified in Project 3. If you did not complete this exercise for Project 3, see your instructor for a copy of the required files.

1. If necessary, open the Folder List pane. If necessary, double-click the file, serv01.htm, in the Folder List pane to display the Ship-It-Here Service 1 page in Page view.
2. Select the text that begins, This is a brief description, through the text that ends, Description of capability 3, and then press the DELETE key. Click Insert on the menu bar, point to Form, and then click Form on the Form submenu. When the form is displayed, type `To receive a copy of our weekly e-mail newsletter, please provide the following information.` and then press the ENTER key.
3. Type `Name:` followed by a space. Click Insert on the menu bar, point to Form, and then click Textbox on the Form submenu. Right-click the text box and then click Form Field Properties on the shortcut menu. When the Text Box Properties dialog box is displayed, type `Name` in the Name text box, type `40` in the Width in characters text box, and then type `1` in the Tab order text box. Click the Validate button. When the Text Box Validation dialog box is displayed, click Required in the Data length area and then type `Name:` in the Display name area. Click the OK button in the Text Box Validation dialog box. Click the OK button in the Text Box Properties dialog box.
4. Press the RIGHT ARROW key to deselect the text box and to position the insertion point after the text box. Hold down the SHIFT key and then press the ENTER key. Type `E-mail:` and then click Insert on the menu bar. Point to Form and then click Textbox on the Form submenu. Right-click the text box and then click Form Field Properties on the shortcut menu. When the Text Box Properties dialog box is displayed, type `Email` in the Name text box, type `40` in the Width in characters text box, and then type `2` in the Tab order text box. Click the Validate button. When the Text Box Validation dialog box is displayed, click Required in the Data length area and then type `E-mail address` in the Display name area. Click the OK button in both dialog boxes.
5. Press the RIGHT ARROW key to deselect the text box and to position the insertion point after the text box. Press the ENTER key. Click the Center button on the Formatting toolbar. Position the insertion point between the Submit and Reset buttons. Press the SPACEBAR five times.
6. Right-click the form and then click Form Properties on the shortcut menu. When the Form Properties dialog box is displayed, drag through the default file name in the File name text box in the Where to store results area and then press the DELETE key. Type `newsletter@ship-it-here.com` in the E-mail address text box (you may substitute your own e-mail address). Click the Options button. When the Saving Results dialog box is displayed, click the E-mail Results tab and then type `Subscribe to newsletter` in the Subject line text box. Verify that the Form field name check box is not selected for this text box. Type `E-mail` in the Reply-to-line text box. Verify that the Form field name check box is selected for this text box. Click the OK button in the Saving Results dialog box. Click the OK button in the Form Properties dialog box. If a Microsoft Office FrontPage dialog box is displayed, click the No button.
7. Double-click the page banner. When the Page Banner Properties dialog box is displayed, drag through the text in the Page banner text box. Type `Get Newsletter` in the text box. Click the OK button. Click the Save button on the Standard toolbar to save your changes. If a Confirm Save dialog box is displayed, click the Yes button.
8. Double-click the file, services.htm, in the Folder List pane to display the Ship-It-Here services page in Page view. Select the text that begins, Comment: Write a, through the text that ends, description pages., and then

(continued)

Apply Your Knowledge

Sending Form Results with E-mail *(continued)*

press the DELETE key twice. Drag to select the hyperlink, Name of service 1 and then type `Subscribe to Newsletter`. If necessary, drag through the new text, click the Insert Hyperlink button on the Standard toolbar, and create a hyperlink to the serv01.htm page in the Web site. Drag to select the text, Description of service 1 ..., and then type `Get our weekly newsletter to keep up to date on services, events, and our seasonal shipping specials`. Click the Save button on the Standard toolbar to save your changes.

9. Click the Preview tab to preview the Web page (Figure 4-96). When you have finished, click the Design button to return to Design view.
10. Print the Web pages. Close the Web site, quit FrontPage, and hand in the printouts to your instructor.

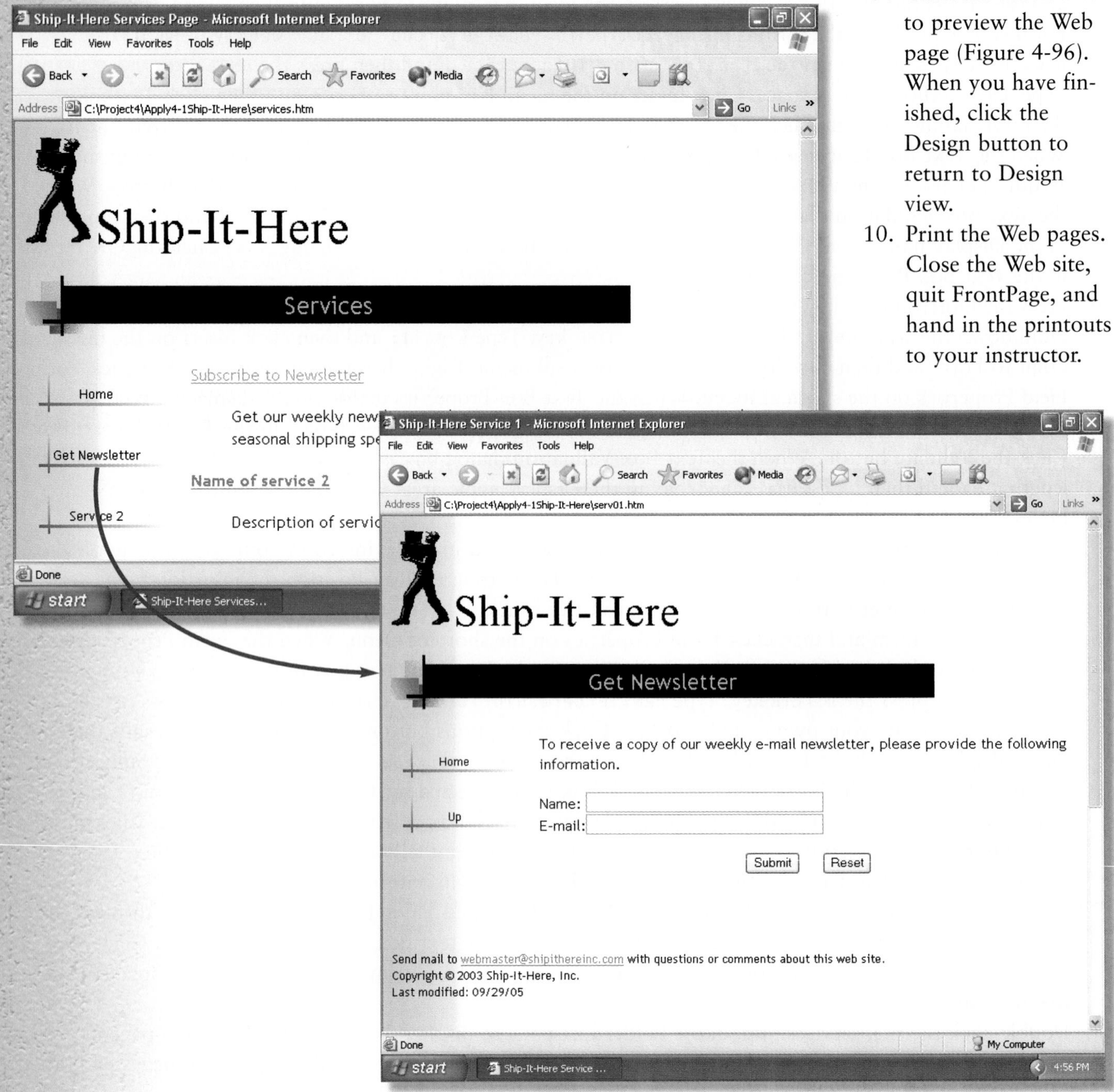

FIGURE 4-96

1 Adding a Frequently Asked Questions (FAQ) Page to a Web Site

Problem: Fairway Lawn Care often gets e-mail messages asking questions about its services. To reduce the number of e-mails asking common questions, the owner wants to add a Frequently Asked Questions (FAQ) page to the Web site.

Instructions: Perform the following tasks.

1. Open the Fairway Lawn Care Web site that you modified in Project 3. If you did not complete that exercise for Project 3, see your instructor for a copy of the required files.
2. If necessary, double-click the file, index.htm, to display the Home page in Design view. Scroll down and then select the text in the line that reads, Contact Information. Click Bookmark on the Insert menu. When the Bookmark dialog box is displayed, click the OK button.
3. Position the insertion point after the word, Sales:, and then type `sales@fairway.com`. Select the text and insert an e-mail hyperlink. Save the changes to the Home page.
4. Click File on the menu bar and then click the New command. When the New task pane is opened, click More page templates in the New page area.
5. When the Page Templates dialog box is displayed, click the Frequently Asked Questions icon. Click the OK button.
6. Select the paragraph that begins with Comment and delete the paragraph. Select the bookmarked text, Table of Contents, and then type `Frequently Asked Questions` as the new text.
7. Scroll the page down and select the text for bullet number 1, How do I ...? and then type `How do I sign up for home mowing services?` as the new hyperlink text. Repeat this process for each of the remaining hyperlinks as listed in Table 4-8.
8. If necessary, scroll down to the bookmark that reads, How do I ... ?, select the text, and then type `How do I sign up for home mowing services?` as the replacement text. Select the text below the bookmark, [This is the answer to the question.], and then type `Contact us by mail, phone, fax, or e-mail so that we can come out and provide a monthly service price. See the addresses and phone numbers listed on our Home page.` Select the text, Home page, and create a hyperlink to the Home page, index.htm. Repeat this process for each of the remaining bookmarks as listed in Table 4-9 on the next page.
9. Delete the three lines of text at the bottom of the page that begin, Author information.

Table 4-8 Replacement Hyperlink Text

BULLET NUMBER	HYPERLINK TEXT	NEW HYPERLINK TEXT
1	How do I ...?	How do I sign up for home mowing services?
2	Where can I find ...?	Where can I find prices on tree trimming?
3	Why doesn't...?	Why can't I order services online?
4	Who is ... ?	Who owns and manages Fairway Lawn Care?
5	What is ... ?	What is the difference between home and business services?
6	When is ... ?	When do seasonal prices take effect?

(continued)

Adding a Frequently Asked Questions (FAQ) Page to a Web Site *(continued)*

Table 4-9 Replacement Bookmarks and Text

OLD BOOKMARK TEXT	NEW BOOKMARK TEXT	TEXT BELOW BOOKMARK	HYPERLINKED TEXT
How do I ...?	How do I sign up for home mowing services?	Contact us by mail, phone, fax, or e-mail so that we can come out and provide a monthly service price. See the addresses and phone numbers listed on our Home page.	Home page Hyperlinked to index.htm
Where can I find ...?	Where can I find prices on tree trimming?	See Tree Trimming on our Price Sheet.	Tree Trimming Hyperlinked to bookmark prices.htm#Tree_Trimming
Why doesn't...?	Why can't I order services online?	We are working on it! Our Web pages are new, but we hope to have online order processing soon.	
Who is ... ?	Who owns and manages Fairway Lawn Care?	Sheila Farnel started the company in 1998 after not being able to find quality services for her home or her employer's property.	
What is ... ?	What is the difference between home and business services?	Business owners receive preferential treatment in the event of rescheduling due to bad weather or other circumstances. Business services generally are on a 7-day mowing schedule while home mowing occurs approximately every 10 days.	
When is ... ?	When do seasonal prices take effect?	For the most part, May 1st begins the summer season and October 1st marks the beginning of the fall/winter season. These dates generally change depending on first and last frost.	

10. Save the page as FAQ.htm and add it to the navigation structure below the Home page and to the right of the Services page. Double-click the FAQ page and then double-click the page banner. Type `FAQ` in the Page banner text box and then click the OK button. Double-click the link bar on the left side of the page and add a hyperlink to the parent page (Figure 4-97).
11. Preview the changes in your browser. Print the Web page, and then quit FrontPage. Write your name on the printout and hand it in to your instructor.

In the Lab

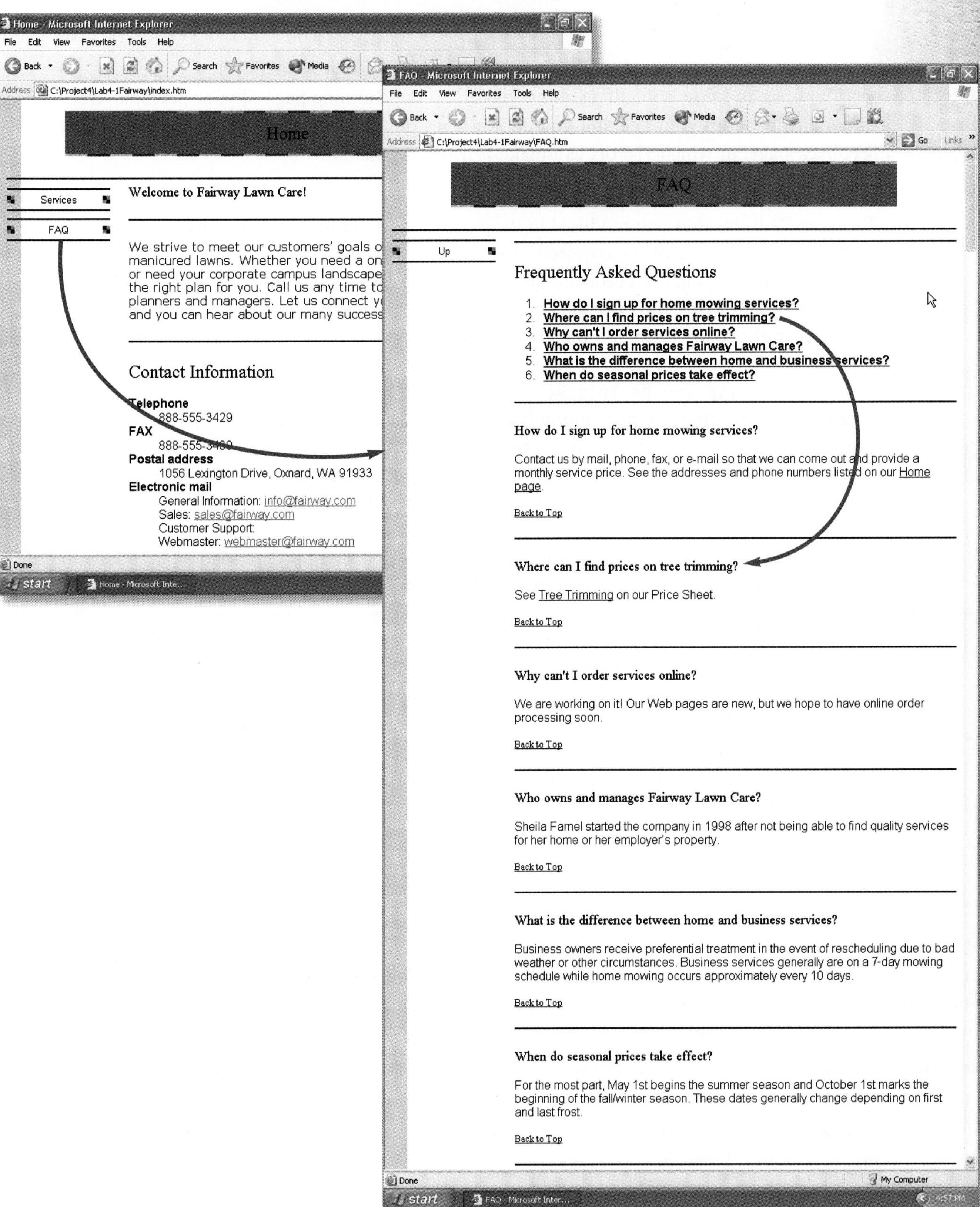

FIGURE 4-97

2 Adding a Feedback Form to a Web Site

Problem: You would like to know something about visitors to the Running page of your personal Web site and receive their comments about your site, but you do not want the comments to be public. You decide to incorporate a Feedback page, in which visitors can make private comments.

Instructions: Perform the following tasks.

1. Open the Running Web site that you modified in Project 3. If you did not complete that exercise for Project 3, see your instructor for a copy of the required files.
2. Create a new normal page using the Feedback Form page template.
3. Select the paragraph that begins with Comment and delete the paragraph and the line following the paragraph. Select the text above the form and then type `Tell me about your favorite running-related Web sites and race experiences. See if your favorites can make the Top Ten list! Also, you can comment on the links you see on this Web site.`
4. Select the word Complaint after the first option button and type `Improvement` as the new label. Select the text, What do you want to comment on?, and type `Subject` as the new text. Select the drop-down box that contains the term, Web Site, and press the DELETE key to delete the box. Select the word, Other, and press the DELETE key to delete the text. Drag the text box that was next to the word, Other, to the left side of the Web page.
5. Right-click the Subject text box and select Form Field Properties on the shortcut menu. Click the Validate button and then click the Required check box in the Data length area. Type `Subject` in the Display name text box.
6. Change the tab order of each form field. Starting with the first option button, assign 1 as the tab order and proceed to assign each form field a consecutive number. The Clear Form button should have a tab order of 13.
7. Save the Web page as feedback.htm. If necessary, in Navigation view, add the page below the Home page (Figure 4-98).
8. Print the Feedback and Home Web pages, write your name on the pages, and submit them to your instructor. Close the Web site and then quit FrontPage.

3 Adding a Guest Book to a Web Site

Problem: Your Whalen Metal support Web site provides information about quality and support services to customers, but does not provide a means of response from them. You would like visitors to be able to discuss various support issues. You decide to add a public guest book to your Web site where visitors can make comments and read comments made by others.

Instructions: Using the Whalen Metals Web site you modified in Project 3, perform the following tasks. If you did not complete this exercise in Project 3, see your instructor for a copy of the required files.

1. Open the Home page for the Web site and position the insertion point after the graphic hyperlink that reads, Company Pictures. Press the ENTER key.
2. Type `Please visit our Guest Book page and share your comments about our approach to quality and customer support.`
3. Create a new normal page using the Guest Book page template.

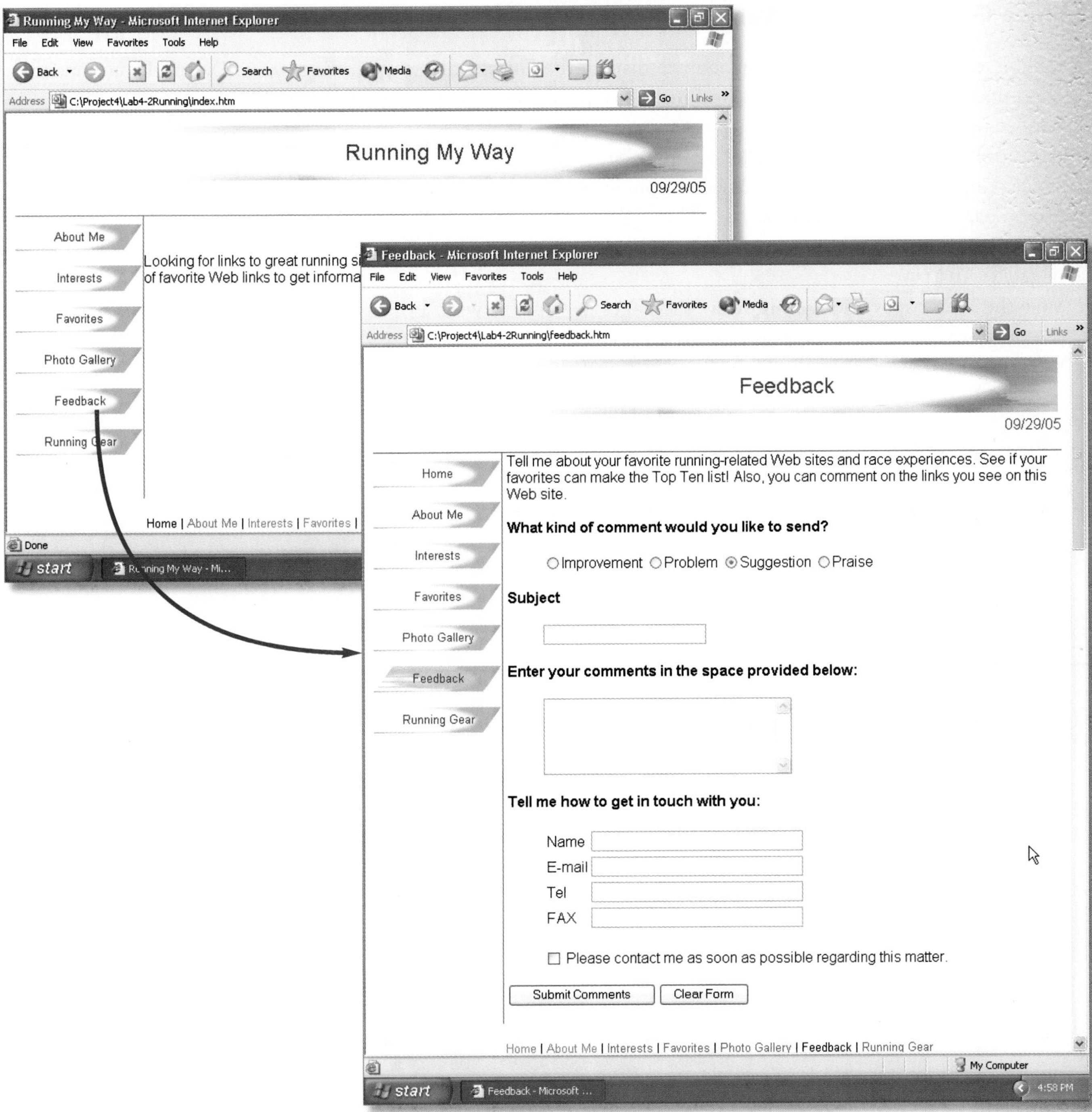

FIGURE 4-98

4. On the new page, delete the text, We'd like to know what you think about our web site. Position the insertion point to the right of the text area. Press the ENTER key.
5. Type `URL of your company's Web site` followed by a space. Insert a text box and modify the form field properties. Type `URL` in the Name text box and `40` in the Width in characters text box. Click the OK button.
6. Delete the three lines of text at the bottom of the page that begin, Author information. Save the page as guestbook.htm. In Navigation view, add the page below the Company Pictures page.

(continued)

Adding a Guest Book to a Web Site *(continued)*

7. Double-click the Guest Book page icon to display the Guest Book page in Page view. Delete the comment component at the top of the page and insert a page banner component. Type `Guest Book` as the page banner text (see Figure 4-99).
8. After the text that ends, with other visitors., press the ENTER key and then type `Back to` followed by a space. Copy and paste the Link Bar component from the Home page. Modify the link bar to link to the Home page. Save your changes.
9. Open the Home page in Page view. Select the text, Guest Book, and make a hyperlink to the Guest Book page.
10. Save the Web pages and then preview the pages in your browser. Print the Web pages, write your name on the printouts, and hand them in to your instructor.
11. Close your browser, close the Web site, and quit FrontPage.

Whalen Metals - Microsoft Internet Explorer

Address C:\Project4\Lab4-3Whalen\index.htm

Whalen Metals

Support Information

When you need help with your order or our products and services, contact one of our support specialists via e-mail, the Web, or telephone. We commit to getting you in touch with a live person for support within 30 minutes of your initial contact. Most issues are resolved within an hour.

Whalen Metals practices a zero-defect quality management program. We take your concerns seriously and invite our customers to participate in our monthly quality meetings that include senior company management, vendors, and customers. Take a look at our Company Pictures

Please visit our Guest Book page and share your comments about our approach to quality and customer support .

Whalen Metals

Information on our Quality Programs:

Six Sigma The Deming Philosophy

Click on a region to e-mail your regional support man

Sanjay Gupta, Director of Support Services
Please e-mail questions and comments about our supp
sgupta@whalenmetals.com.

Guest Book - Microsoft Internet Explorer

Address C:\Project4\Lab4-3Whalen\guestbook.htm

Guest Book

Please leave your comments in this public guest book so we can share your thoughts with other visitors.

Back to Home

Add Your Comments

URL of your company's Web site:

Submit Comments Clear Comments

After you submit your comments, you will need to reload this page with your browser in order to see your additions to the log.

Please e-mail questions and comments about our support and quality philosophy to sgupta@whalenmetals.com.

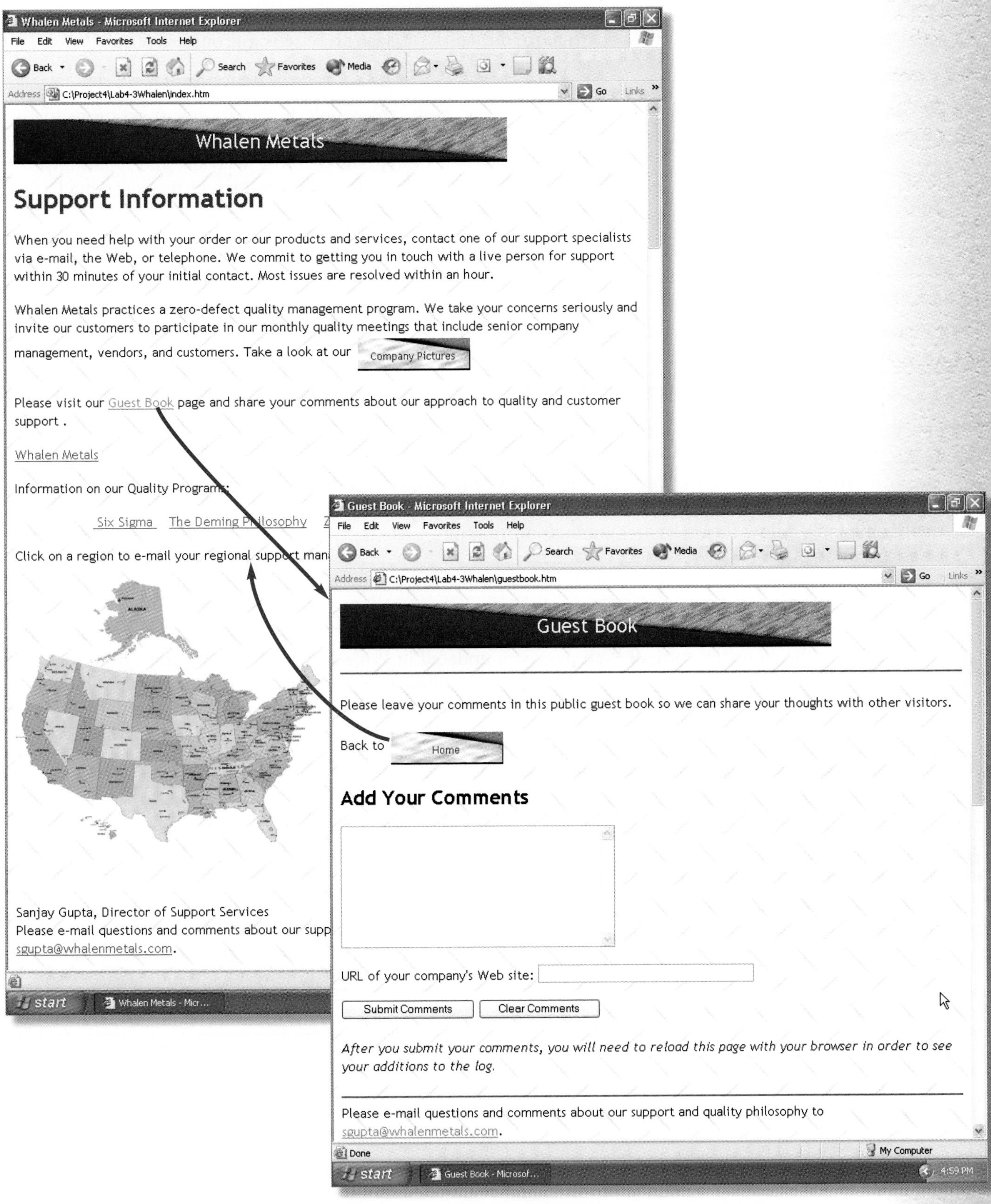

FIGURE 4-99

Cases and Places

The difficulty of these case studies varies:
■ are the least difficult and ■■ are more difficult. The last exercise is a group exercise.

1 ■ In Project 3, you modified your resume Web page. Now, you would like to receive suggestions for improvement as well as responses from potential employers. Add a new page with a feedback form and a hyperlink from the resume to the new page. Verify all hyperlinks in the Web site and repair any broken hyperlinks that appear on the Broken hyperlinks report. Have the results sent to your e-mail address.

2 ■ The Web site for the movie review Web site you modified in Project 3 has your reviews for several movies. Allow class members or other visitors to post their reviews by adding a discussion forum to your Web site.

3 ■■ Add a new page to the Web site you created for your friend's graduation. Use a form to collect memories from your friend's college career and save the results to a database. On the new page, collect the visitors' names, relationship (instructor, friend, or associate) to your friend, and have a text area for their comments. Allow them to enter contact information, such as a mailing address, telephone number, or e-mail address.

4 ■■ Modify the company softball Web page you updated in Project 3. Add a discussion forum for players to comment on the latest game. Add a form to collect names and e-mail addresses for addition to a notification list for upcoming games. Store the collected information in a database. Verify the external hyperlinks added earlier and replace any hyperlinks that appear on the Broken hyperlinks report.

5 ■■ **Working Together** Modify the instructor Web page you created for your department at school in Project 3 to include an instructor evaluation page using a form. Use drop-down list boxes to allow students to select the instructor, course, and term. Use option buttons for the expected grade from the instructor, whether the instructor's course was required, and whether the department is the student's major area. Present a list of evaluation questions or statements and option buttons to determine the student's response. Provide a text area for general comments and record the results to a database. Use nested tables to help control positioning of elements in the form.

MICROSOFT
Office FrontPage 2003

Using Frames to Display Database Results in Web Pages

PROJECT

5

CASE PERSPECTIVE

Students at Trelane College visit James Keeler's Job Opportunity Posting Web page to read and post job opportunities. The Web page receives numerous hits. James stores the job postings in a database. His Web site is almost complete, with only one remaining item on his task list, which is to create pages that display results from the database to the user. James plans to have a separate page for each of the categories of job opportunities (Full-time Positions, Volunteer Positions, Internships, and Tutoring Positions). He wants to be sure he does not include too many hyperlinks on his Home page and does not want to confuse his users by directing them to many different pages.

You assure James that creating pages to retrieve and display information to users is easy to accomplish and that a simple solution to make sure that too many links are not included on his Home page is to use a single hyperlink for job opportunity postings. Users can be directed from the Home page to a frames page that allows them to place and view job opportunities. Viewing a frames page gives users the feeling of viewing only a single page with an area that changes depending on the action desired.

As you read through this project, you will learn how to incorporate frames and framesets into your Web page designs. You will learn how to modify frame properties and frame page properties, how to create and display no-frames HTML code, and how to use database results in your Web pages. You will learn how to use the Database Results Wizard to create custom SQL queries to retrieve information from a relational database. Finally, you will learn how to print pages with frames from FrontPage.

Using Frames to Display Database Results in Web Pages

PROJECT

Objectives

You will have mastered the material in this project when you can:

- Describe frames pages and explain how they work
- Use the Database Results Wizard
- Use a custom SQL query
- Use a frames page template
- Save a frames page
- Set an existing Web page as the initial page in a frame
- Modify the size of a frame
- Create a new Web page for the initial page in a frame
- Modify the properties of a frame
- Modify the properties of a frames page
- Import files into an existing FrontPage Web site
- Create hyperlinks to pages in a frame
- Create a hyperlink to a whole page
- Display the No Frames view
- Print framed Web pages

Introduction

As you learned in Project 4, Web pages increasingly use forms and other methods to allow users to interact with the Web pages and provide data that can be collected and stored for future use. A major reason to collect data from users is to organize the data and then allow other users to view it. In creating the Job Opportunity Posting page, for example, you allowed users to enter job opportunities in a form that submitted that data to an Access database. In Project 5, you will learn how to create Web pages that can retrieve and display the data to users who want to browse through the job opportunities.

Typically, a Web page displays a particular view of stored data to a user, not all of the data stored in the database. A **view** is a subset of data presented in a specific context. A view arranges the data in some order and can make only certain fields visible; the physical organization of the database, however, is not affected. Each particular view of data often is presented on a single Web page. A user might request to see only those job opportunity postings that are for tutoring positions, for example. The view of the data would define which job opportunities are appropriate to display on the page.

Up to this point, you have created single Web pages with links to other single Web pages. When a user views a single Web page, the page display fills the entire browser window. Clicking a link to a different Web page replaces the previous Web page in the browser window.

Using frames gives you the ability to divide the browser window into multiple regions, or panes. A **frame** is an independent region within a browser window that can act independently of other regions in the window. Each frame can be given a unique URL, so it can load information independently of the other frames, and each frame also can be given a unique name, so it can be targeted by other URLs. In addition, each frame can be set to resize dynamically if the user changes the window's size, or it can have its sizing disabled, ensuring a constant frame size.

With frames, a Web page designer has greater flexibility in page design. Frames allow the designer to display several Web pages in the same browser window, with each Web page appearing in its own frame. For example, if the pages in a Web site share many of the same links, creating and maintaining these links for each page involves a lot of duplication. With frames, you can create a Web page to display the common links in one frame and display the linked target Web pages in another frame. Some typical uses of frames include displaying a table of contents consisting of hyperlinks in one frame and displaying the corresponding Web pages in another; placing a list of products for sale in one frame and displaying the accompanying descriptions and details in another; and placing a list of vocabulary words in one frame and displaying their definitions in another.

Design Tip

With frames, a Web page designer has greater flexibility in page design. Frames allow the designer to display several Web pages in the same browser window, with each Web page being displayed in its own frame. With frames, you can create a Web page to display the common links in one frame and display the linked target Web pages in another frame.

With frames, a Web page author can place elements the user always should see, such as copyright notices and title graphics, in a static frame that does not change. As the user navigates through the site, the static frame's contents remain fixed, even as new pages are displayed in adjoining frames. Placing frames side by side also allows a user to enter a query and view the answer in the same browser window, with one frame holding the query form and another displaying the results. You also can place hyperlinks for selecting different views of data in one frame, with the selected view of the data in another.

More About

Designing Frames Pages

Although most modern browsers support frames, some users either may not have the latest browser version or may not like to use frames. To appeal to the broadest audience, you may want to offer an alternative set of pages for your site that do not use frames. That way, users can choose the format they want to employ for viewing your site.

Although most Web browsers support frames, some users of your site may have browsers that do not support frames or may prefer a no-frames version. Developers of Web sites that use frames often create an alternative set of pages without frames to display to those users.

Although most Web browsers support frames, some users of your site may have browsers that do not support frames or may prefer a no-frames version. When designing with frames, consider the creation of an alternative set of pages without frames to display to those users.

Project Five — Using Frames to Display Database Results

In this project, you will learn how to create a view of data from a database and then display that view in a framed Web page. Microsoft FrontPage provides a Database Results Wizard that simplifies the process of defining the view of the data and displaying those database results into a Web page. You will learn how to query the database using a custom SQL query. You then will learn how to create frames and display Web pages within a frame, including those providing a view of database results.

Creating and Using Frames

Creating framed Web pages is more complex than creating regular pages without frames. To create framed Web pages, you first create a frames page in HTML. A **frames page**, also called a **frame definition file** or a **frameset document**, contains the layout of the frames on the Web page and specifies an initial Web page to display in each frame. To create a frames page, you use a combination of three HTML tags: <FRAMESET>, <FRAME>, and <NOFRAMES>. A **frameset** is used to define the layout of the frames when displayed on the screen. A pair of <FRAMESET> tags contains the content and structure of each frame. Within each pair of <FRAMESET> tags, the <FRAME> tag defines what Web page content is displayed in each frameset. A pair of <NOFRAMES> tags is used to specify alternate text that is displayed on the page if a user's browser does not support frames.

To facilitate this process, Microsoft FrontPage includes several ready-to-use frame templates, each of which contains a variety of frames of various sizes. Recall from Project 1 that a template is one or more Web pages that have been organized and formatted with a basic framework of content on which new Web pages can be built. You can select from one of the templates and customize it to suit your needs — and even save the customized version as a new template. In addition, you can resize the existing frames in the template or add new frames using the mouse and/or special key combinations.

In this project, you will learn how to create a frames page to display the job opportunity results pages (Figures 5-1a through 5-1g on page FP 344). The pages use frames to display the Job Opportunity Posting request form and views of the job opportunities retrieved from the database, as well as a common page banner and common hyperlinks. Before you begin creating the results pages, however, you should familiarize yourself with some important concepts and definitions relating to frames.

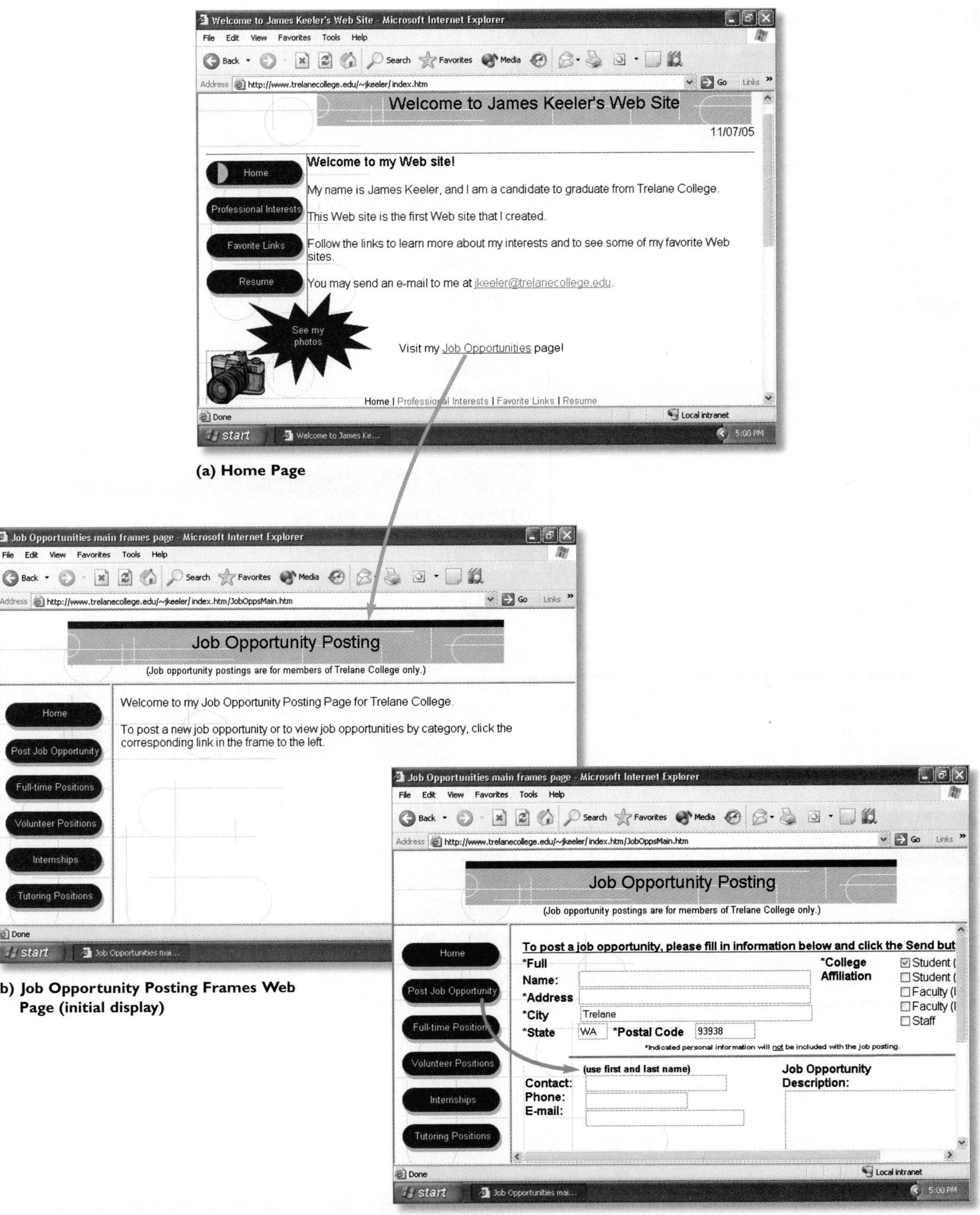

(a) Home Page

(b) Job Opportunity Posting Frames Web Page (initial display)

(c) Job Opportunity Posting Page

FIGURE 5-1

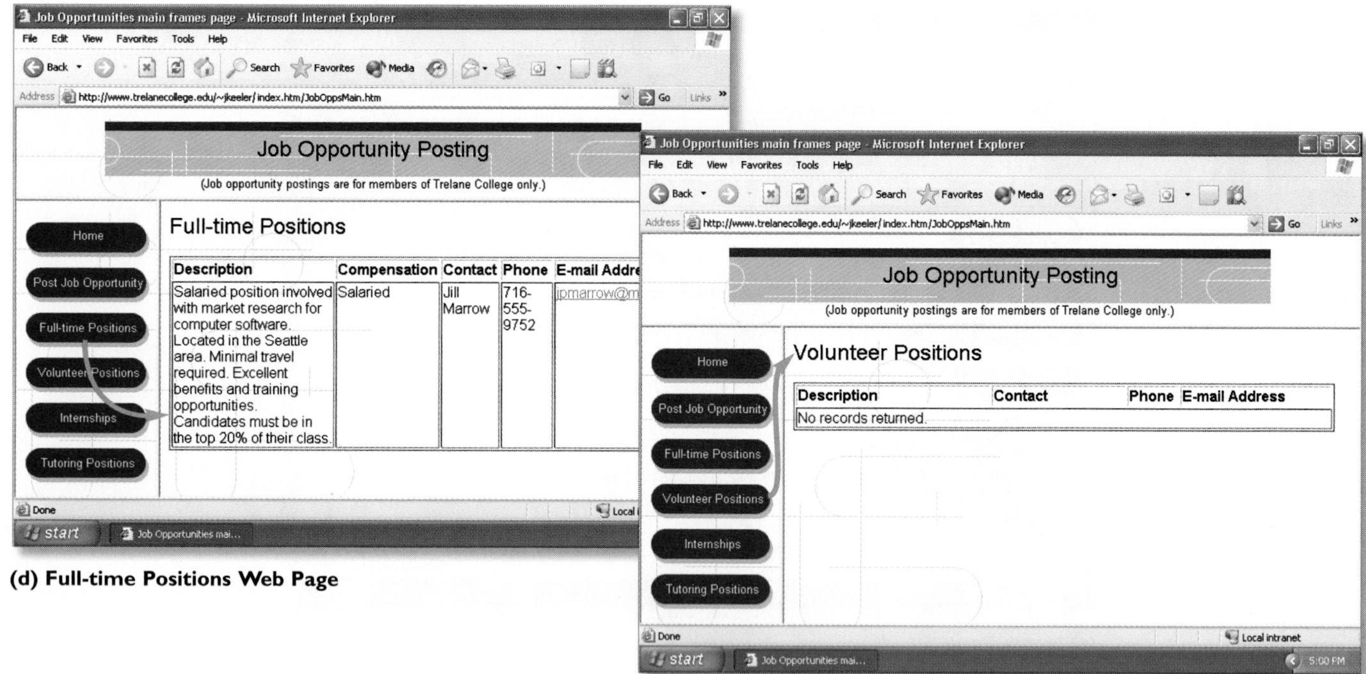

(d) Full-time Positions Web Page

(e) Volunteer Positions Web Page

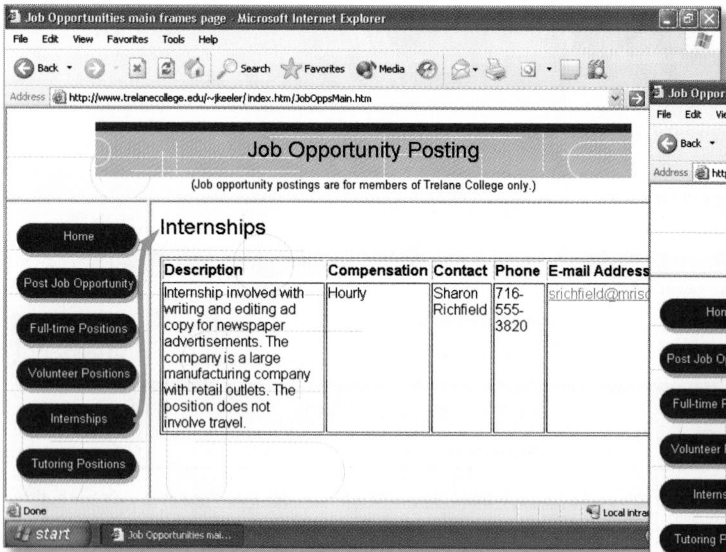

(f) Internships Web Page

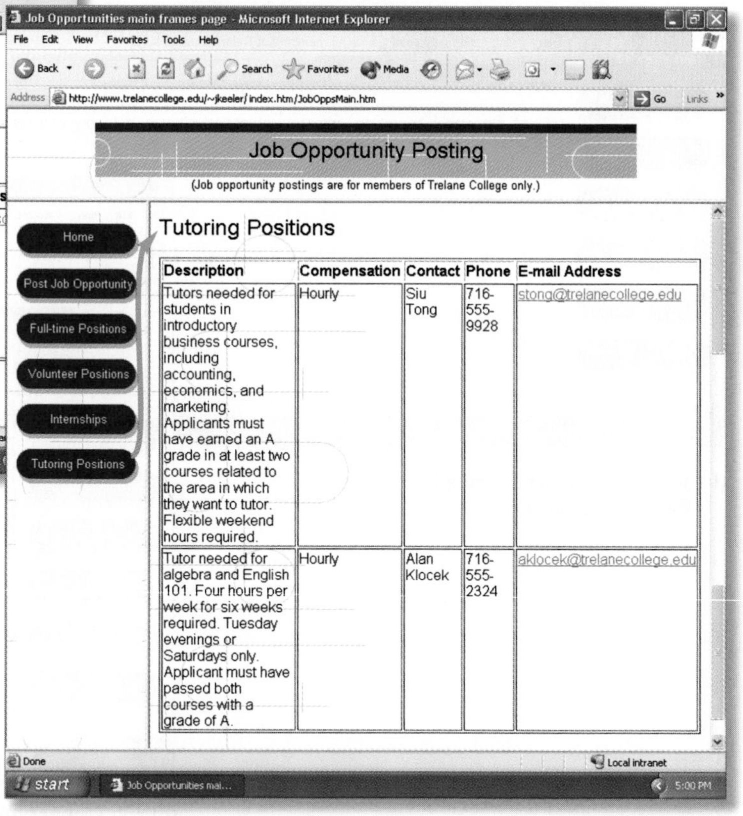

(g) Tutoring Positions Web Page

FIGURE 5-1 *(continued)*

Using Frames Pages

As previously noted, a frames page contains the layout of the frames on the Web page and specifies an initial Web page to display in each frame. The frames page itself contains little or no visible content; instead, it serves as a container that holds two or more frames and specifies which pages to display and how to display them. For example, in a frame page with two frames, a table of contents page may be set as the initial page for the left frame, while another initial page is displayed in the right frame. When the user clicks a hyperlink in the left frame, the selected Web page is displayed in the right frame, replacing the initial page in that frame. The table of contents displayed in the left frame remains the same. The user can select another hyperlink from the table of contents and the corresponding Web page replaces the page currently in the right frame.

Designing the Frames Page

In this project, the frames page allows users to navigate easily between the form page used to post a new job opportunity and the four database results pages that display views of the job opportunities by category. The frames page — which is named the Job Opportunity Posting main page — includes three frames, shown in Figures 5-2a and 5-2b.

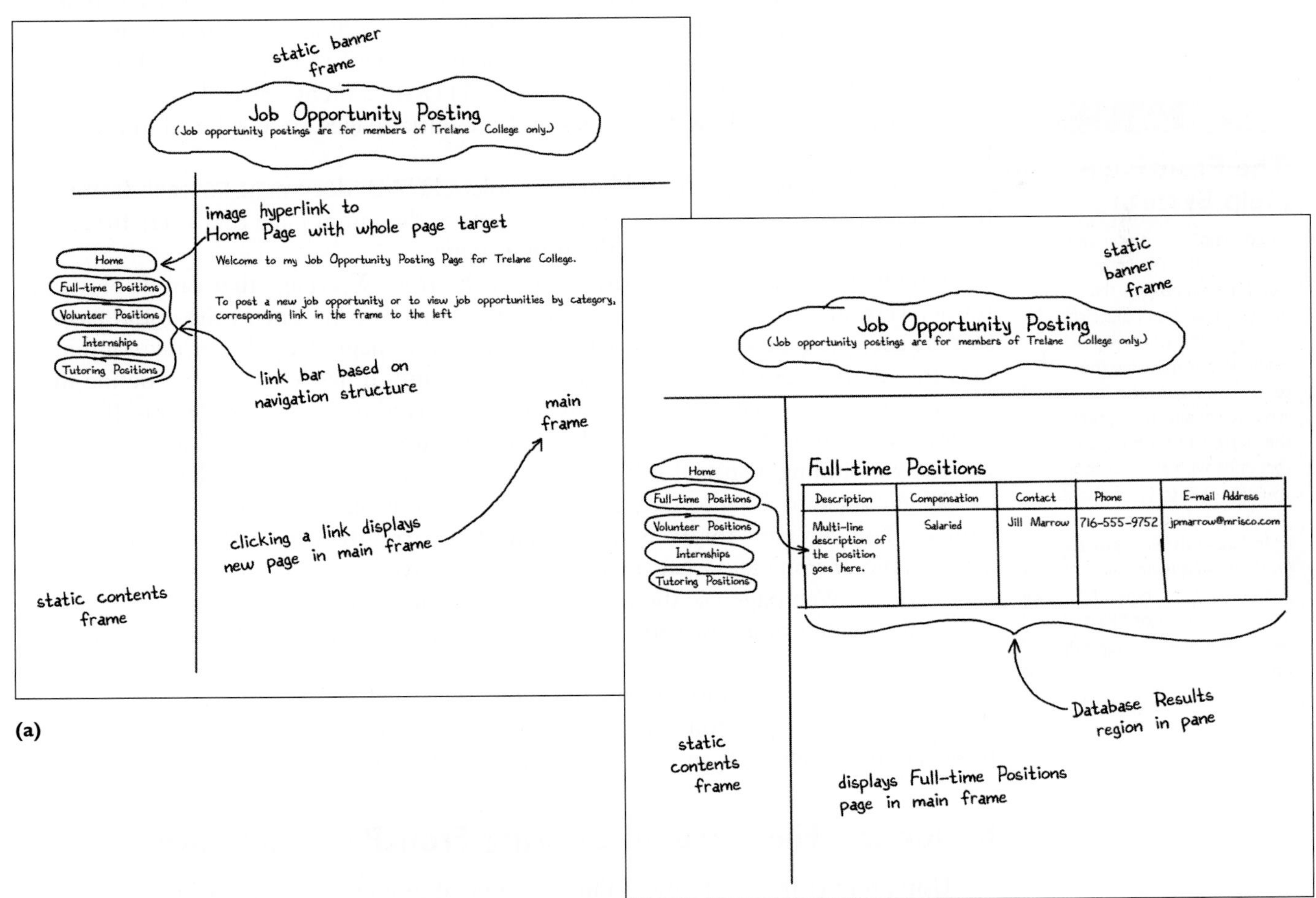

FIGURE 5-2

The top frame contains a common banner heading similar to the one used with other pages in the Web site. The contents of the top banner frame will remain the same, or static, while the frames page is displayed.

The left frame contains a table of contents type list of hyperlinks to the Job Opportunity Posting form page and the various database results Web pages. The contents of the left frame remain static while the frames page is displayed. At the top of the left contents frame is a hyperlink to the Home page. Clicking this hyperlink displays the Home page, replacing the entire frames Web page.

The right, or main, frame initially contains a welcome page with instructions for the user. The contents of this frame change depending on which hyperlink a user clicks in the left frame.

The Web page design in Figure 5-2b on the previous page illustrates the general design used for each database results Web page. Altogether, nine Web pages will be used to implement this design: the frames page, the three initial Web pages, shown in Figure 5-2a on the previous page, four pages for views of the database results, and one form page for collection of data. With the design of the page completed, you now can implement the design using Microsoft FrontPage.

Using Frames in a FrontPage Web Site

Implementing frames in a FrontPage Web site requires the creation and coordination of links between multiple Web pages. As previously noted, you first must create a frames page. The frames page contains the HTML tags describing the number, sizes, and properties of the frames and defining the initial page to display in each frame. The frames page itself usually has little other HTML content; instead, it serves as a container that defines how the frames and the initial pages are displayed in the browser window.

Next, you must create or add one complete HTML document for each frame in the frames page. The Web page for each frame is the initial page that users first see in each frame when they display the frames page.

Finally, you must create hyperlinks to each target Web page that can display in a frame. Typically, you would include these hyperlinks within one of the initial pages, so that users can click a hyperlink to view the target page. Each hyperlink contains tags that define the URL of the target Web page and, if needed, tags that define the frame in which the page should be displayed, referred to as a **target frame**. If desired, you can opt to specify a default target frame for all links within a particular frame by including a special base target tag in the header section of the frames page.

When deciding how to target Web pages when using frames, you have several choices. You can have the Web page replace the currently displayed Web page in the same frame or you can target the page to be displayed in a different frame. You also can have the Web page use the entire browser window. Finally, you can have the Web page appear in a new browser window, keeping the original browser window's contents intact.

You can create the initial pages and target pages before or during the creation of the frames page. With FrontPage, the frames page template has buttons that allow you to select an existing page or create a new page as the initial page to display in a frame.

More About

The FrontPage Help System

Need Help? It is no further away than the Type a question for help box on the menu bar in the upper-right corner of the window. Click the box that contains the text, Type a question for help, type `help`, and then press the ENTER key. FrontPage responds with a list of topics you can click to learn about obtaining help on any FrontPage-related topic. To find out what is new in FrontPage 2003, type `what is new in FrontPage` in the Type a question for help box.

Importing Files into an Existing FrontPage Web Site

Using frames in a Web site can involve a great amount of effort. Because the content of each frame is a complete Web page, if you are the only person performing the development work, you have to create the frames page, the initial page for each frame, and possibly any target pages for which you have hyperlinks in the initial pages.

The Job Opportunities section of the Web site in this project uses nine different Web pages within frames. In order for you to complete the project within a reasonable amount of time, four of the nine Web pages are available on the Data Disk. See the inside back cover of this book for instructions for downloading the Data Disk or see your instructor for information on accessing the files required in this book.

Four files from the Data Disk will be imported into the FrontPage Web site. Next, a new page for one of the database results views will be created. Finally, a frames page with three frames will be created, the initial pages for the frames in the frames page defined, and an existing page for use in a frame modified.

The following steps start FrontPage and then open the FrontPage Web site from Project 4. If you did not complete Project 4, see your instructor for a copy of the required files.

Q: Does FrontPage provide other methods to import files?

A: Yes. You can import an image simply by dragging the image from another Windows application to the Navigation or Folders view. You also may copy a file in Windows Explorer and paste it into the Folder List pane or the Contents pane while in Folders view.

To Start FrontPage and Open an Existing Web Site

1. **Click the Start button on the taskbar. Point to All Programs on the Start menu.**
2. **Point to Microsoft Office on the All Programs submenu.**
3. **Click Microsoft Office FrontPage 2003 on the Microsoft Office submenu.**
4. **Click the Open button arrow on the Standard toolbar.**
5. **Click Open Site on the Open menu. If necessary, when FrontPage displays the Open Site dialog box, click the Look in box arrow and select the folder location where you stored the Web site for Project 4 (e.g., C:\jkeeler).**
6. **Click the Open button.**

The previously created FrontPage Web site is loaded and is displayed in Folders view (Figure 5-3).

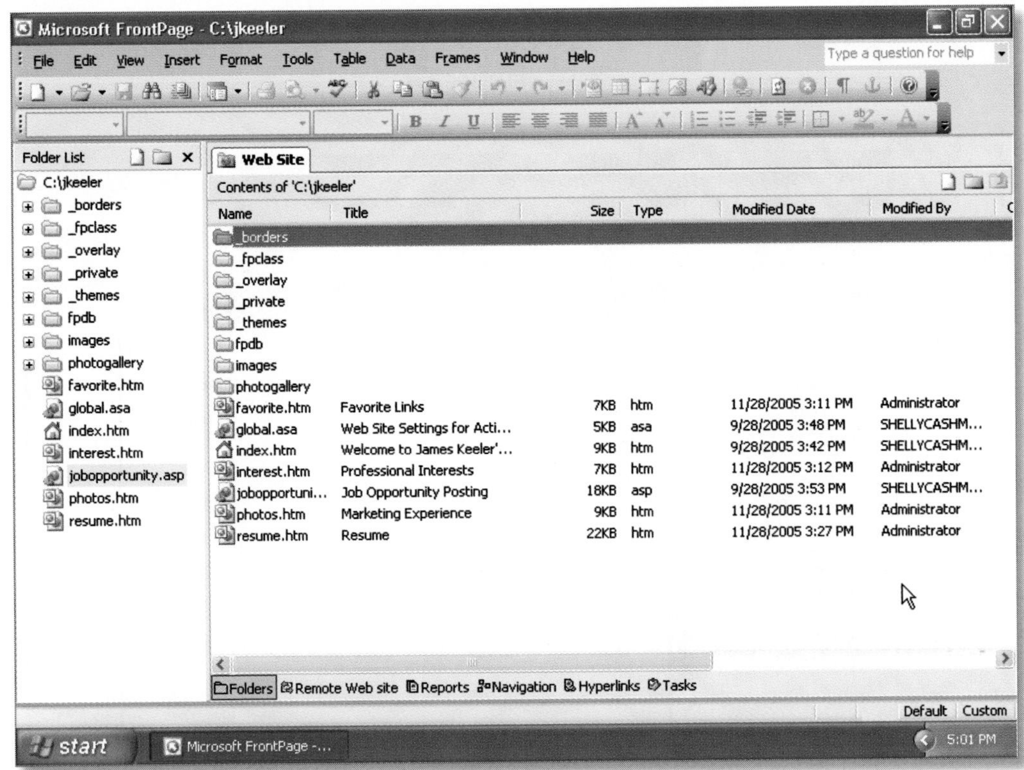

FIGURE 5-3

As the development of the Job Opportunities section of the Web site begins, the four Web pages from the Data Disk must be imported into the current FrontPage Web site. The files cannot simply be copied into the Web folder, as FrontPage may not recognize and include the pages automatically. The Import command is used to import existing Web pages into a current Web site.

The following steps import existing Web pages into the current FrontPage Web site.

To Import Files into an Existing FrontPage Web Site

1

- **Insert the Data Disk in drive A.**
- **If necessary, select the C:\jkeeler folder in the Folder List pane.**
- **Click File on the menu bar.**

FrontPage displays the File menu (Figure 5-4).

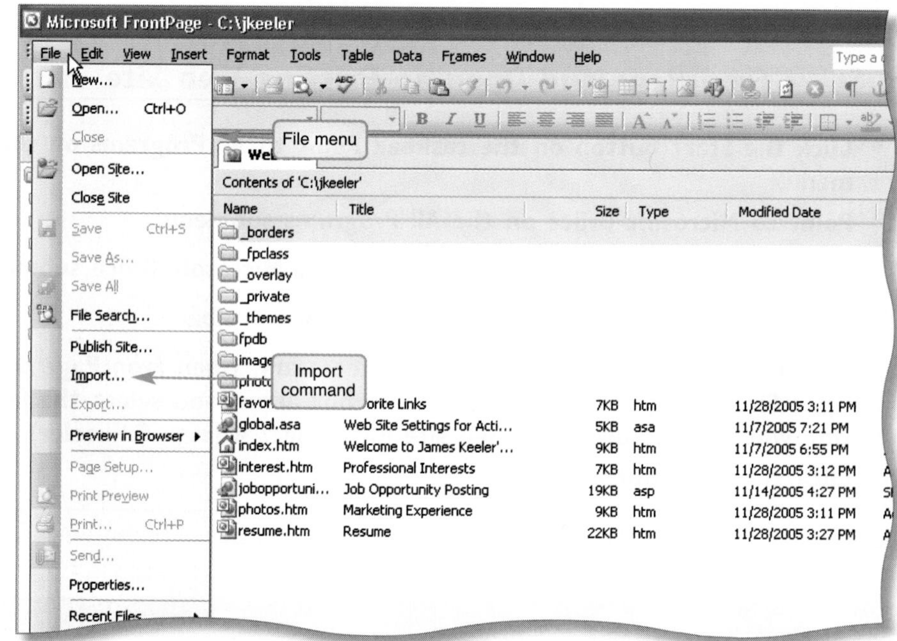

FIGURE 5-4

2

- **Click Import.**

FrontPage displays the Import dialog box (Figure 5-5). Buttons are available for importing files or entire folders from your local machine or for importing pages from the Web site.

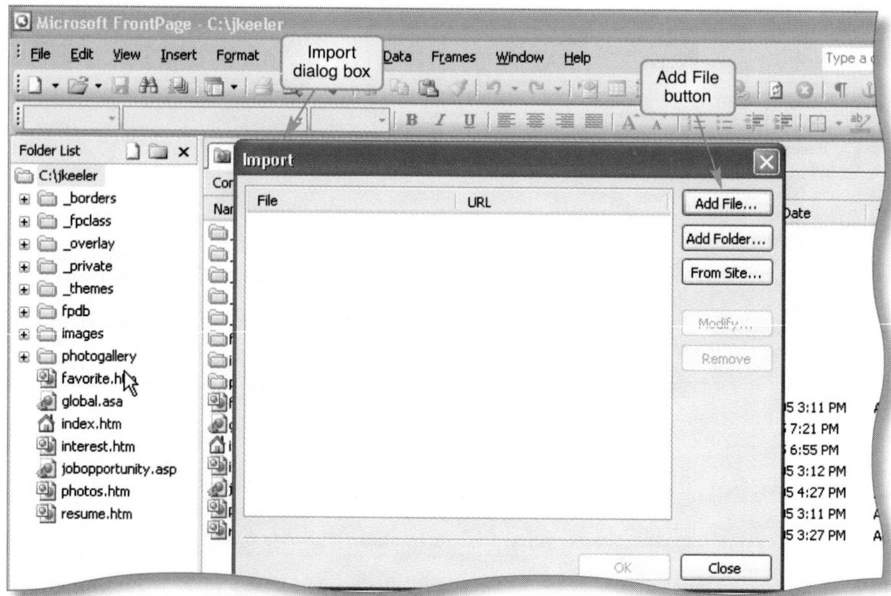

FIGURE 5-5

3

- **Click the Add File button.**
- **If necessary, when FrontPage displays the Add File to Import List dialog box, insert the Data Disk, click the Look in box arrow, and then click 3½ Floppy (A:).**
- **If necessary, double-click the Project5 folder.**
- **Hold down the CTRL key and select the files JobOpsBanner, Internship.asp, Tutoring.asp, and Volunteer.asp.**

FrontPage displays the Add File to Import List dialog box (Figure 5-6). The four selected files in the Project5 folder are highlighted.

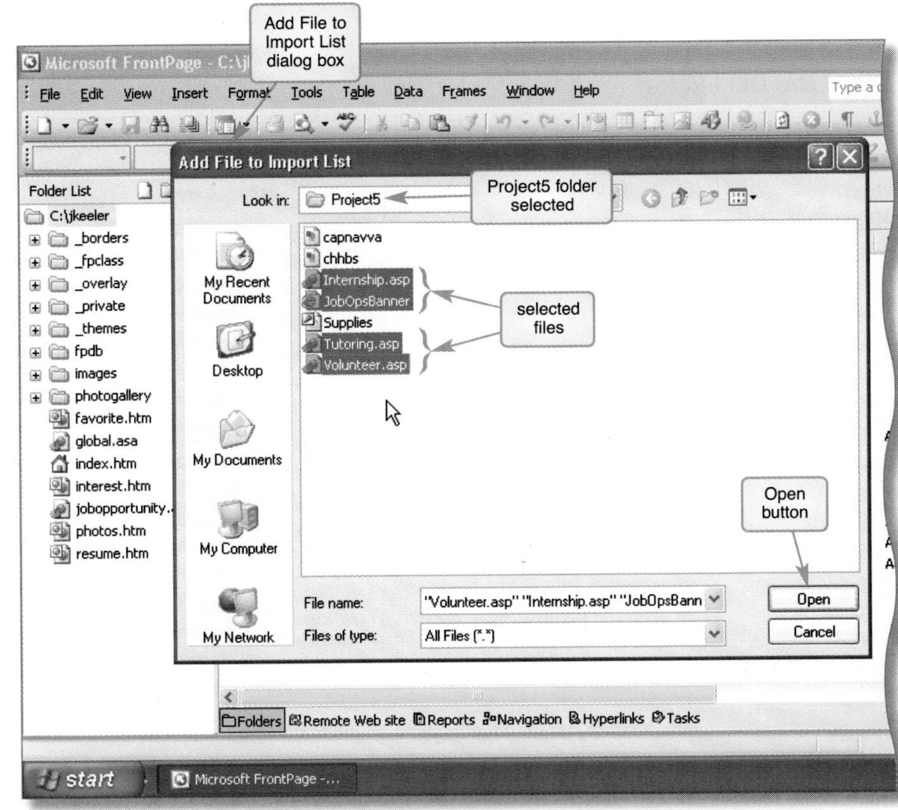

FIGURE 5-6

4

- **Click the Open button.**

The files to be imported into the Web site are displayed in the Import dialog box (Figure 5-7).

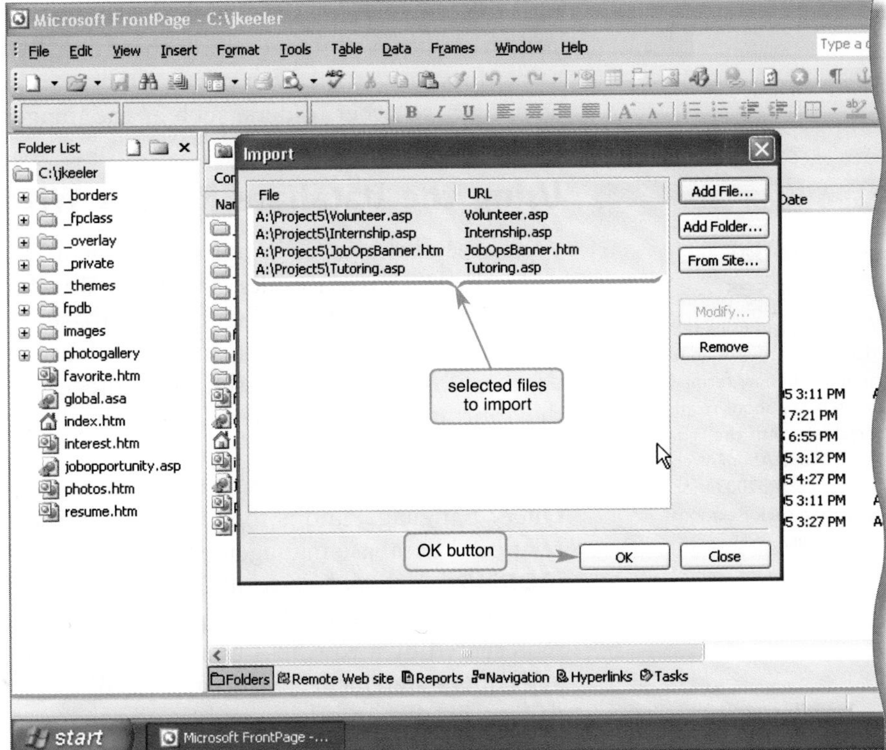

FIGURE 5-7

5

• **Click the OK button.**

FrontPage closes the Import dialog box, and displays the imported files in the Folder List pane (Figure 5-8).

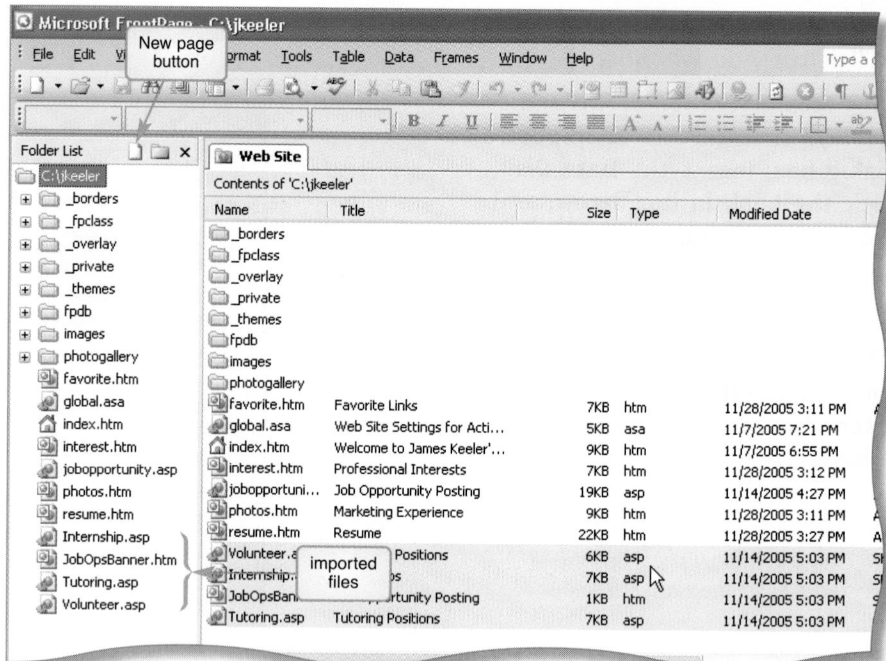

FIGURE 5-8

Figure 5-8 shows the Folder List pane after the existing files have been imported into the current Web site. Using the Import command, you can import not only Web page files, but also images and other files. By default, all files are imported into the same directory as the Web pages. Once you import the files, you can move files, such as images, to other folders, such as the images folder.

More About

Relational Databases

Designing and using relational databases requires an understanding of new terms. To learn more about relational databases, visit the FrontPage 2003 More About Web page (scsite.com/fp2003/more) and then click Relational Databases.

Using the Database Results Wizard

Three of the pages imported include a Database Results region that was created using the Database Results Wizard. A **Database Results region** is an area on a Web page where data retrieved from a database will appear. In this project, the results pages retrieve and display a subset of data from the job opportunities placed in the database by category: full-time, volunteer, internship, or tutoring. The pages select the appropriate job opportunities to display by querying the database with a statement written in SQL.

SQL (pronounced as separate letters, es-que-el), is an abbreviation for Structured Query Language, and is the most widely used language for communicating with a relational database management system. A **relational database management system** (**RDBMS**), such as Microsoft Access, helps users manage data by modeling the data as tables. Each data field is represented by a column and each entry, or record, is represented by a row, in a manner similar to a spreadsheet. Special keywords in the SQL query statement instruct the RDBMS to select the desired columns (fields) of data to display and then display only those rows (records) where a specified field or fields contain specific values.

A SELECT statement defines which columns of data are selected for display. For example, if you wanted to select the Description and Category columns, you would write the SELECT statement, SELECT Description, Category. To select all columns in the database, you can use an asterisk in the SELECT statement, SELECT *.

Additionally, the WHERE clause is used to limit rows selected to only those containing specific data values. For example, the clause, WHERE (Category='Tutoring'), limits the selected records to those where the category field contains the value 'Tutoring'.

Design Tip

If you do not understand the structure of a database or do not have access to the structure of a database, work with a database administrator (DBA) or a developer familiar with the database structure when designing the queries used to gather data from the database.

More About

SQL

If you want to do any work with modern databases, you will need to learn how to formulate database queries using SQL statements. To learn more about SQL, visit the FrontPage 2003 More About Web page (scsite.com/fp2003/more) and then click SQL.

In addition to retrieving data stored in a database, SQL can perform other functions. One capability is to create a temporary field constructed from one or more fields from the database and other constant data. In this project, you will create a custom SQL query to combine the e-mail address field and the appropriate HTML code in a temporary field called email, so that e-mail addresses appear as hyperlinks in the Database Results region on the page.

An additional page is needed to display the full-time job opportunities. The following steps use the Database Results Wizard to create a page with a Database Results region containing a custom SQL query.

To Create a Database Results Region and Custom SQL Query

1

- **Click the New Page button at the top of the Folder List pane.**
- **When the new file appears in the Folder List pane, type** `FullTime.asp` **as the new page name.**

A new normal page is created and the name is changed to FullTime.asp (Figure 5-9).

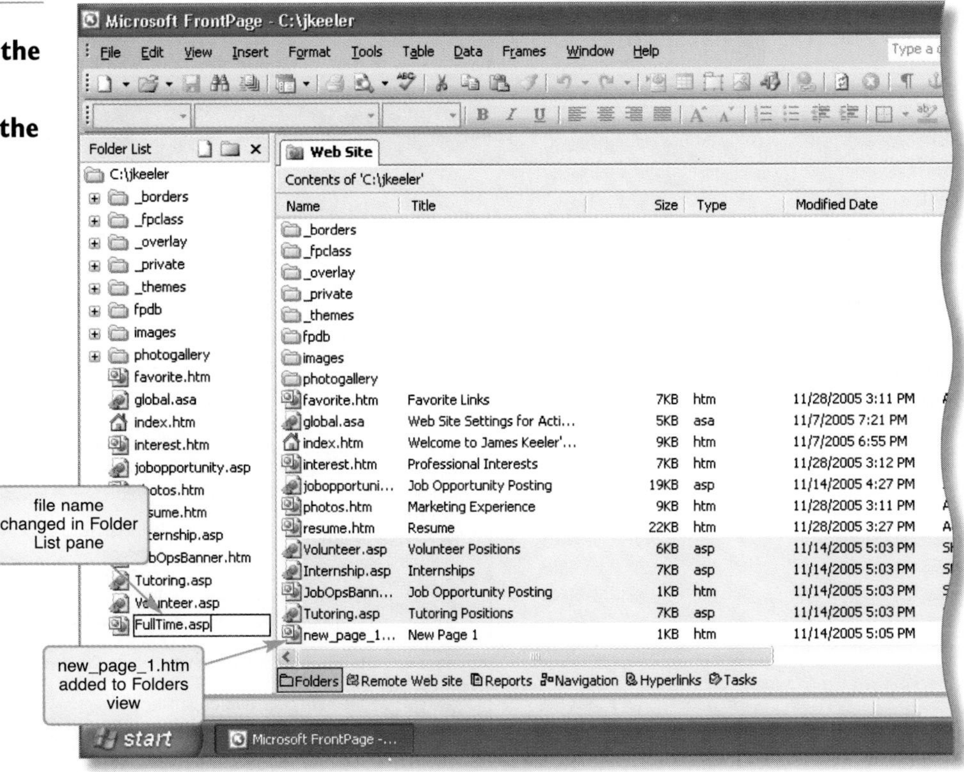

FIGURE 5-9

2

- **Press the ENTER key.**
- **Click on the title of the new page and leave the mouse steady until the text box appears around the page title.**

A text box appears around the page title, allowing you to edit the page name in Folders view (Figure 5-10).

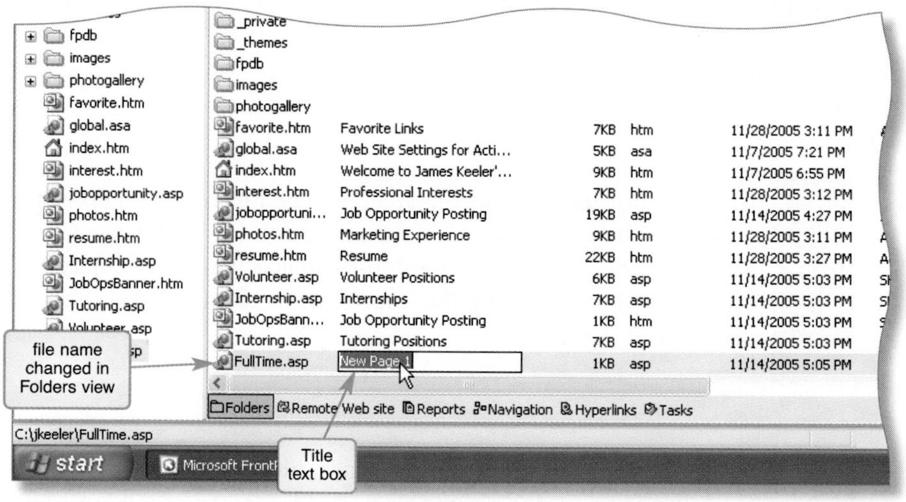

file name changed in Folders view

Title text box

FIGURE 5-10

3

- **Type** `Full-time Positions` **as the page title.**

The new page title appears in the text box (Figure 5-11).

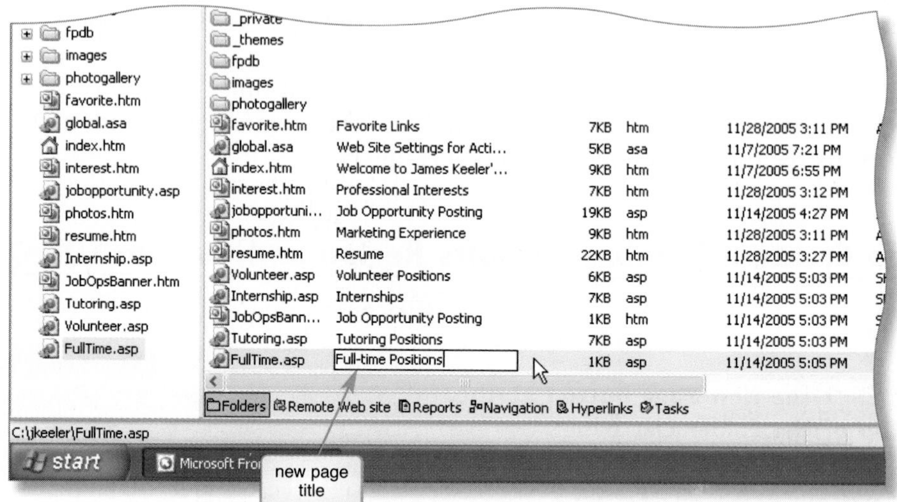

FIGURE 5-11

4

- **Press the ENTER key.**

FrontPage displays the new page title in Folders view (Figure 5-12).

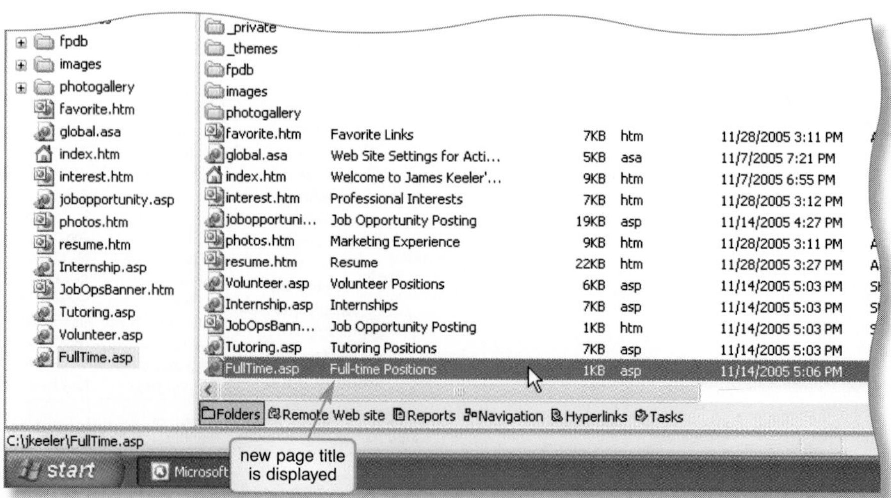

FIGURE 5-12

5

- **Double-click the FullTime.asp page in the Folder List pane to open the page in Design view.**
- **If necessary, position the insertion point at the top of the new page, click 5 (18 pt) in the Font Size box, select the Arial font in the Font box, type** `Full-time Positions`**, and then press the ENTER key.**
- **Click Insert on the menu bar and then point to Database.**

The new heading appears at the top of the Web page. FrontPage displays the Insert menu and the Database submenu (Figure 5-13).

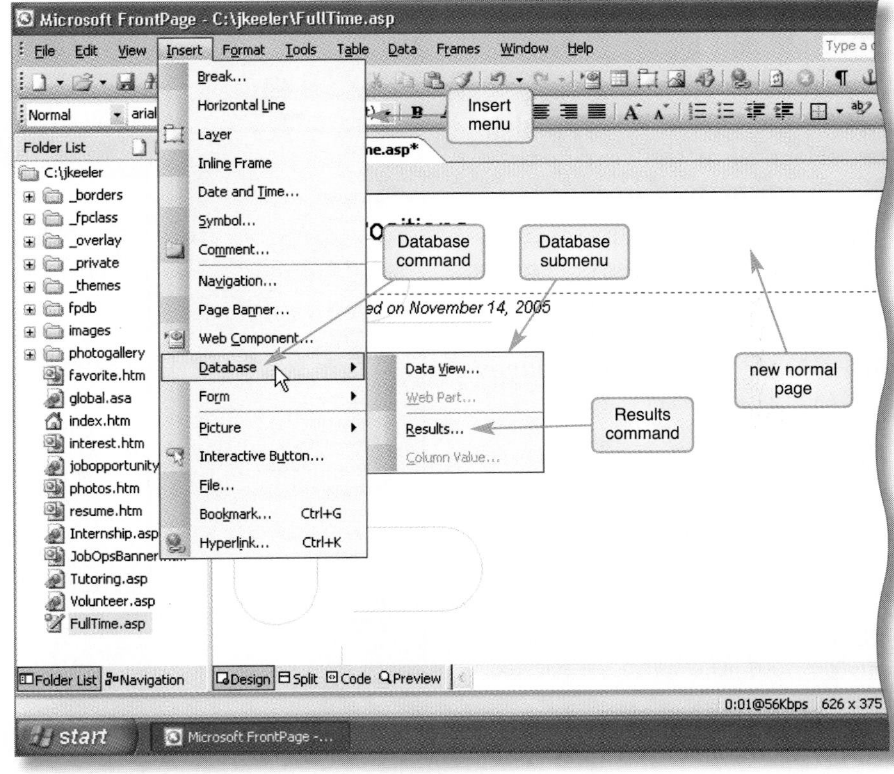

FIGURE 5-13

6

- **Click Results.**
- **When FrontPage displays the first page of the Database Results Wizard dialog box, click the Next button.**
- **When FrontPage displays the next page of the Database Results Wizard dialog box, click Custom query.**

FrontPage displays the Database Results Wizard dialog box with the Custom query option button selected (Figure 5-14).

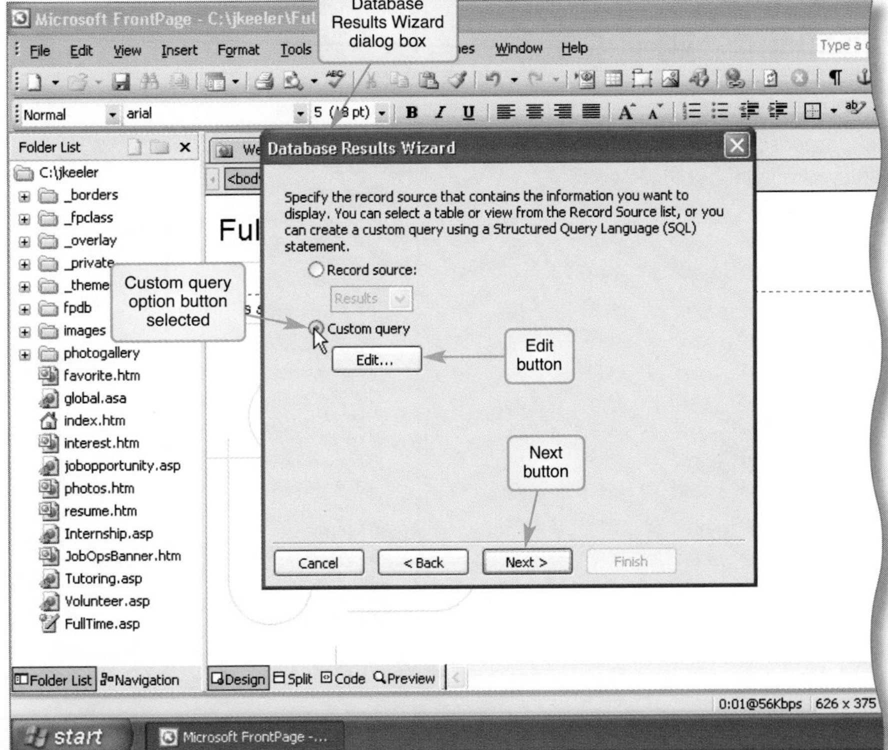

FIGURE 5-14

7

- **Click the Edit button.**
- **If necessary, when FrontPage displays the Custom Query dialog box, select all of the text in the SQL Statement text area.**
- **Type** `SELECT Description, Compensation, Contact, Phone, ('<a href=' & Chr$(34) & 'mailto:' & EMailAddress & Chr$(34) & '>' & EMailAddress & '</a>') as email FROM Results WHERE (Category = 'FullTime').`

FrontPage displays the Custom Query dialog box with the custom SQL statement entered (Figure 5-15). You can click the Verify Query button to verify that the query references valid fields within the selected database.

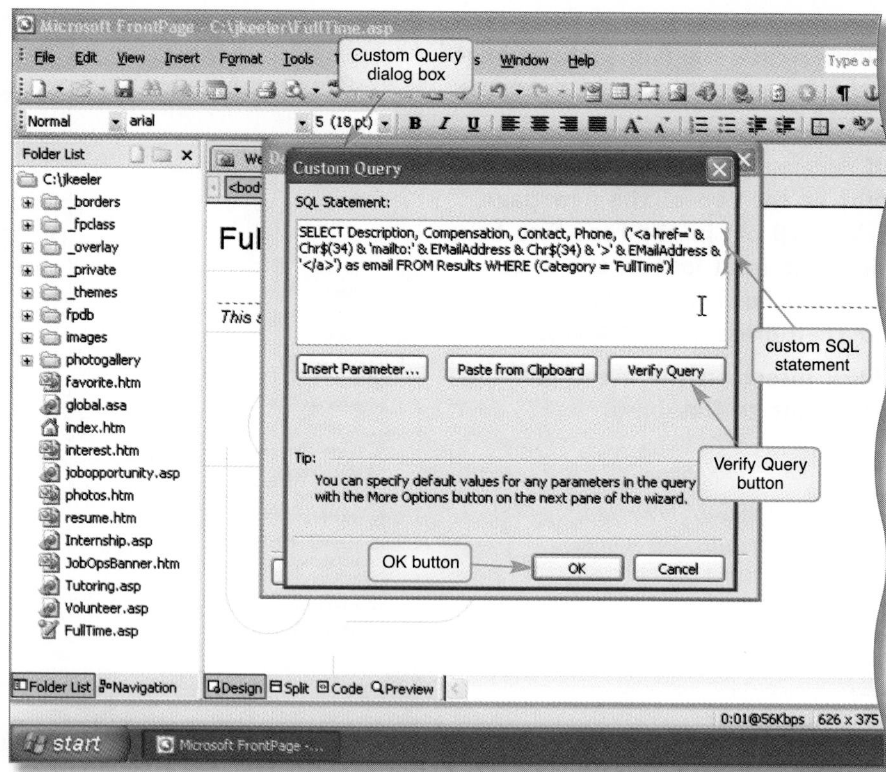

FIGURE 5-15

8

- **Click the OK button.**

The Custom Query dialog box is closed and the Database Results Wizard dialog box is displayed (Figure 5-16).

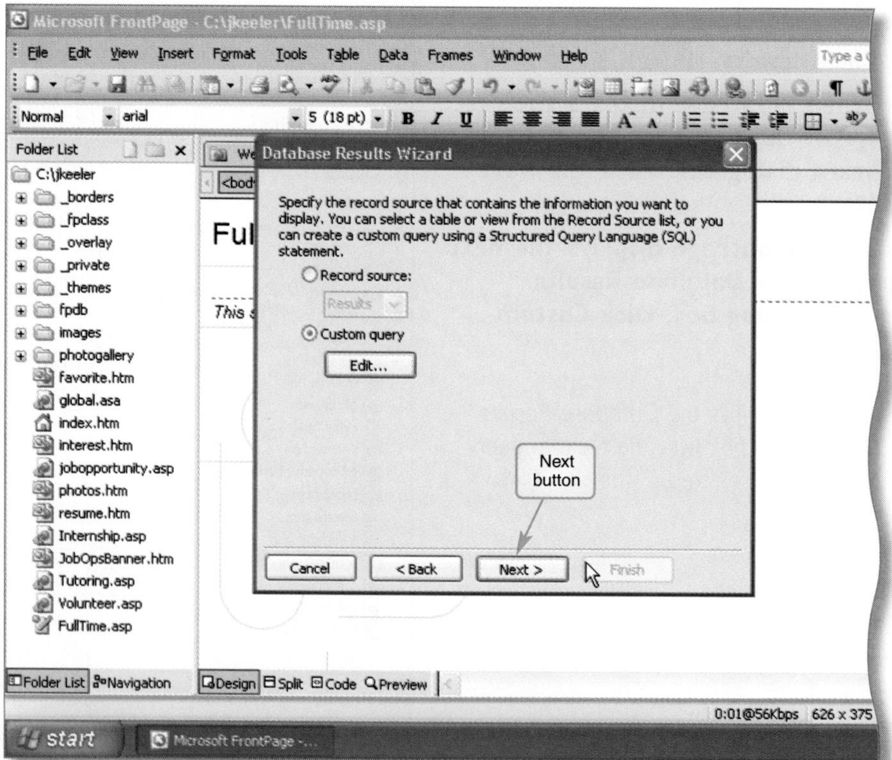

FIGURE 5-16

9

• **Click the Next button.**

FrontPage displays the next page of the Database Results Wizard dialog box (Figure 5-17). The fields to display in the database results are listed in order. If necessary, use the scroll bar to view the fields.

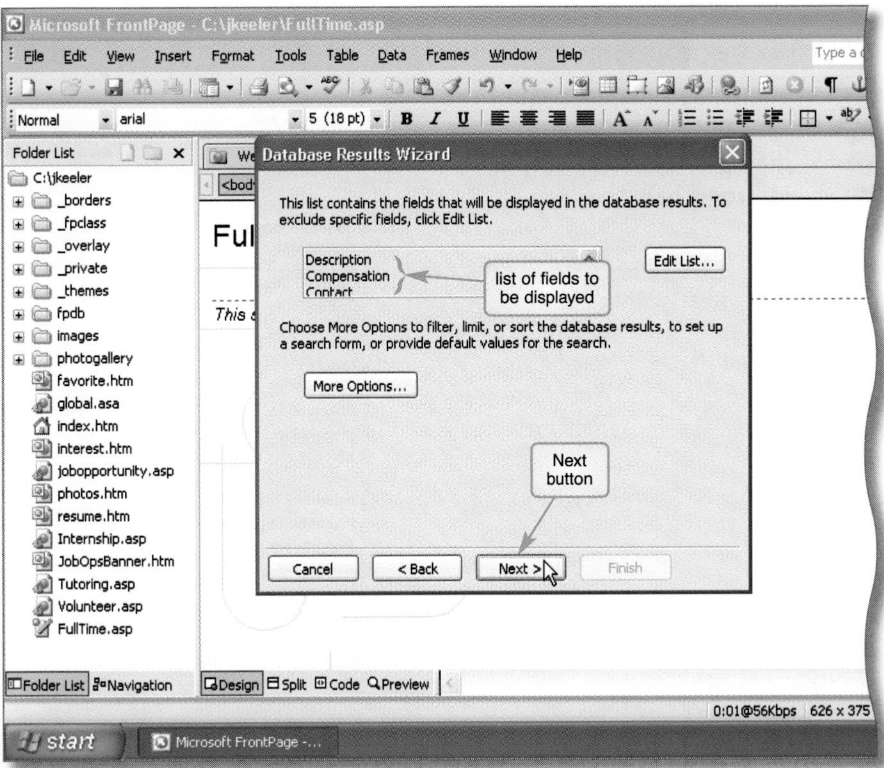

FIGURE 5-17

• **Click the Next button.**

FrontPage displays the next page of the Database Results Wizard dialog box (Figure 5-18). By default, FrontPage selects formatting options to display table borders, expand the table to page width, and include a header row with column labels. A preview graphic of the resulting table is displayed.

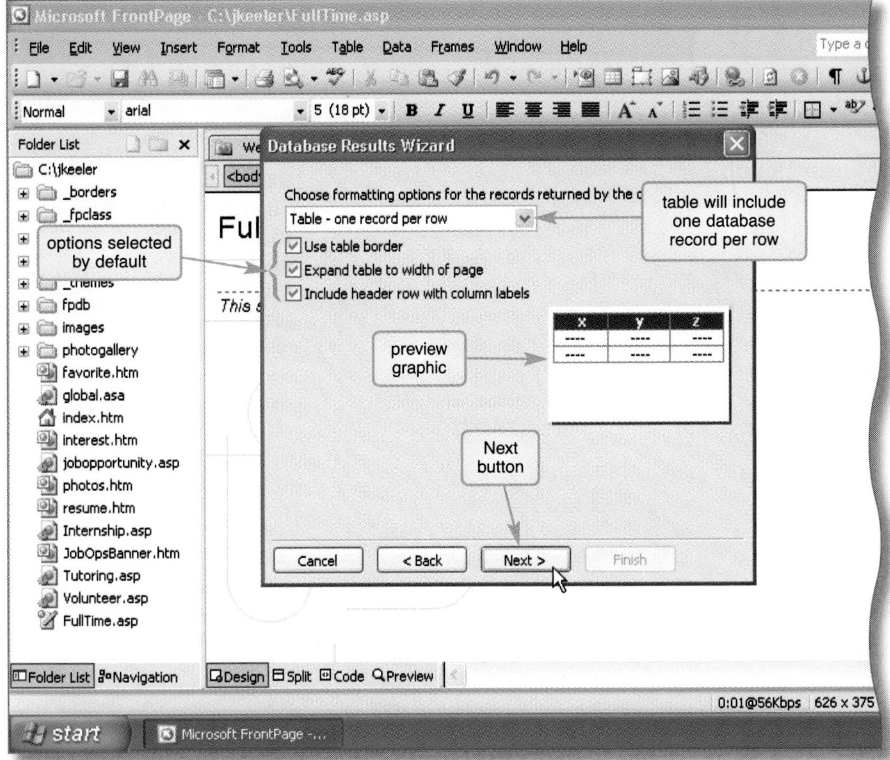

FIGURE 5-18

11

- **Click the Next button.**
- **When FrontPage displays the next page of the Database Results Wizard dialog box, select Display all records together.**

FrontPage displays the next page of the Database Results Wizard dialog box (Figure 5-19). If you expect a large number of records to satisfy the selection criteria in the custom SQL query, you can opt to return the records in smaller groups.

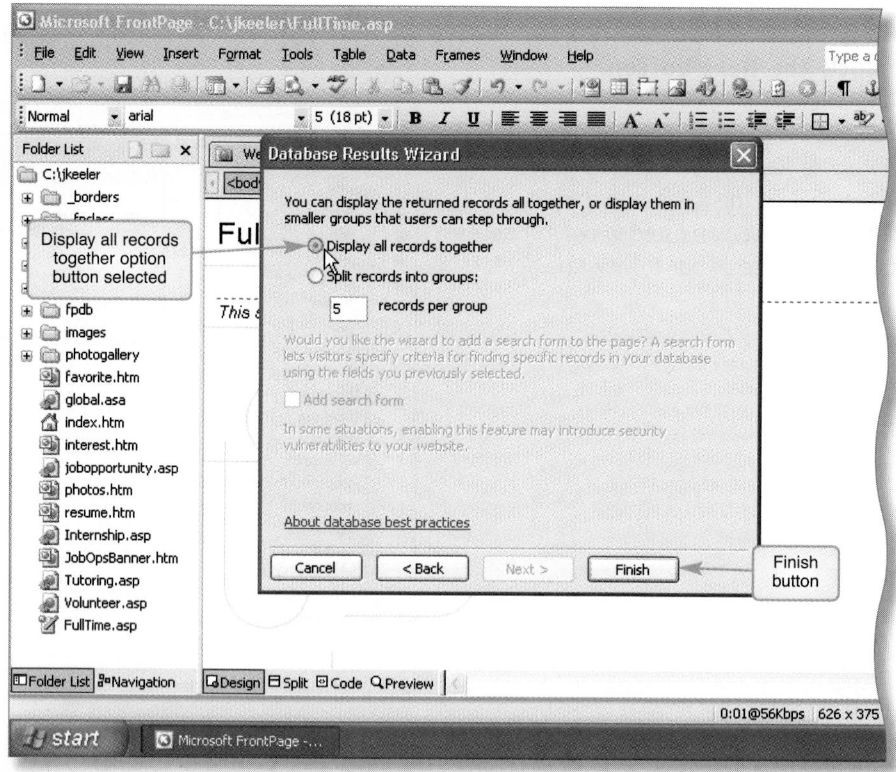

FIGURE 5-19

12

- **Click the Finish button.**
- **Select the text in the column heading, email, and then type** `E-mail Address` **as the new column heading.**

FrontPage displays a Database Results region as a table with default column headings derived from the field names (Figure 5-20). The last column heading is changed from the default. FrontPage automatically inserts database column value components as placeholders for displayed records.

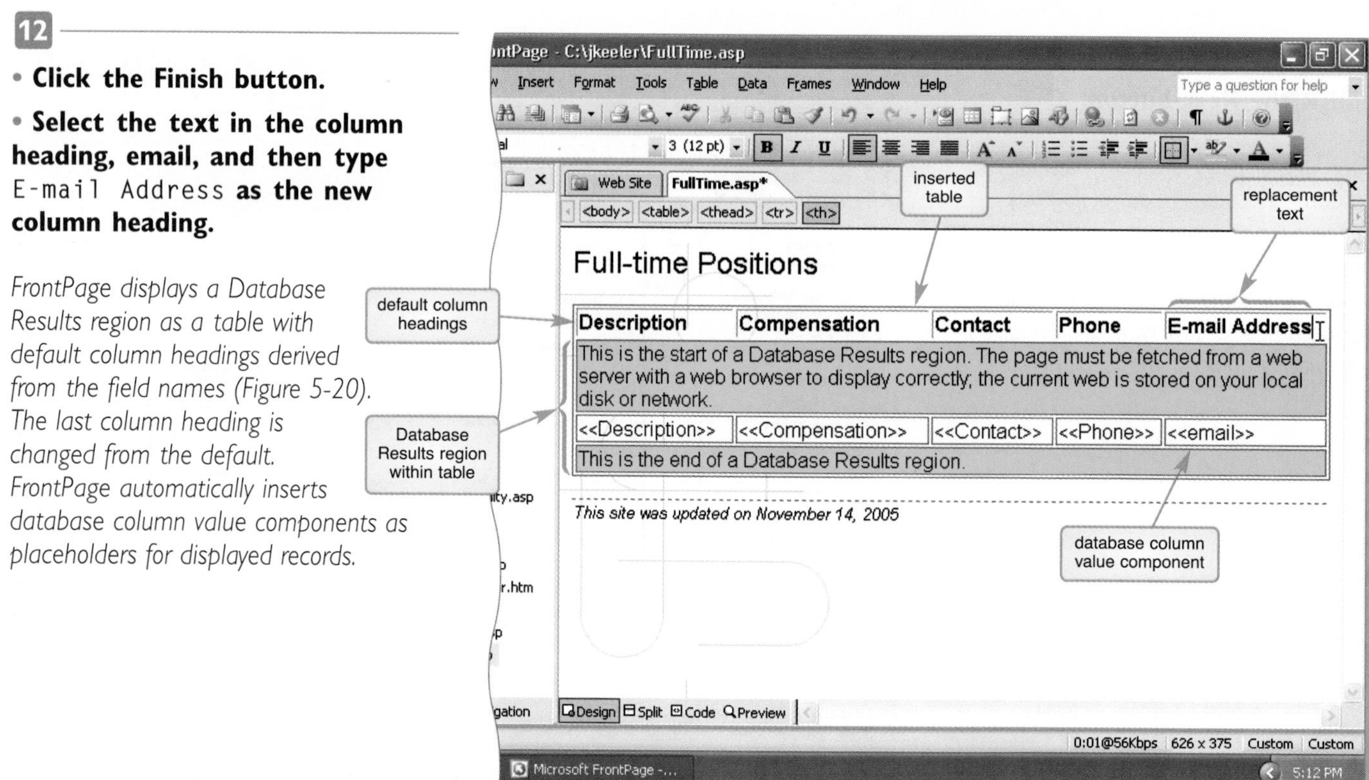

FIGURE 5-20

13

- **Right-click the database column value component, <<email>>.**

The database column value component, <<email>>, is selected (Figure 5-21).

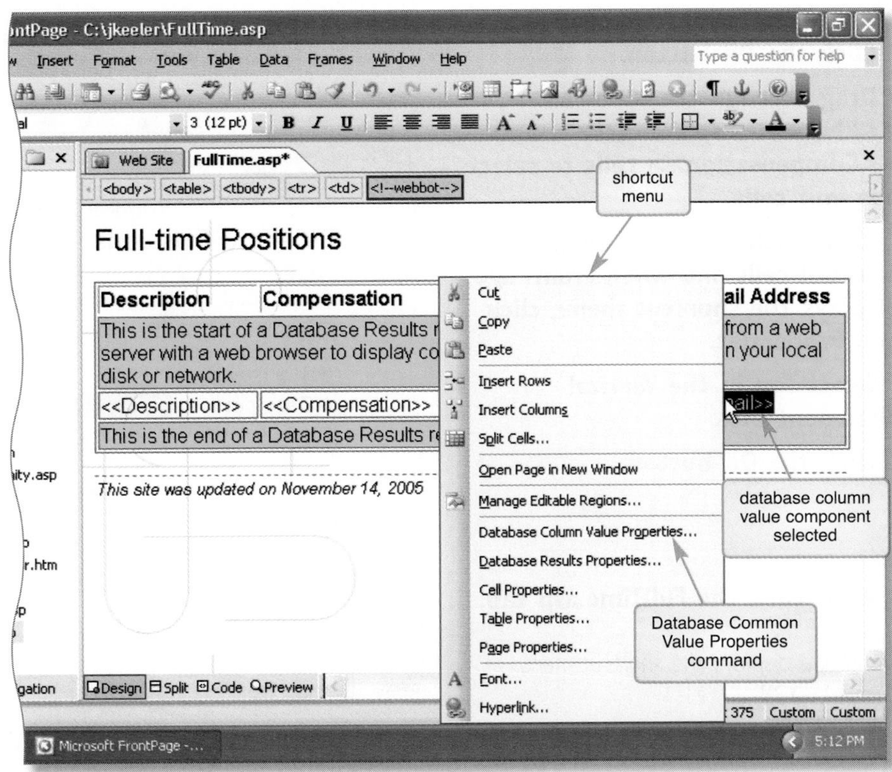

FIGURE 5-21

14

- **Click Database Column Value Properties.**
- **When FrontPage displays the Database Column Value dialog box, click Column value contains HTML.**

FrontPage displays the Database Column Value dialog box (Figure 5-22). The database column value, <<email>>, is set to display formatted HTML when the page is viewed in a browser.

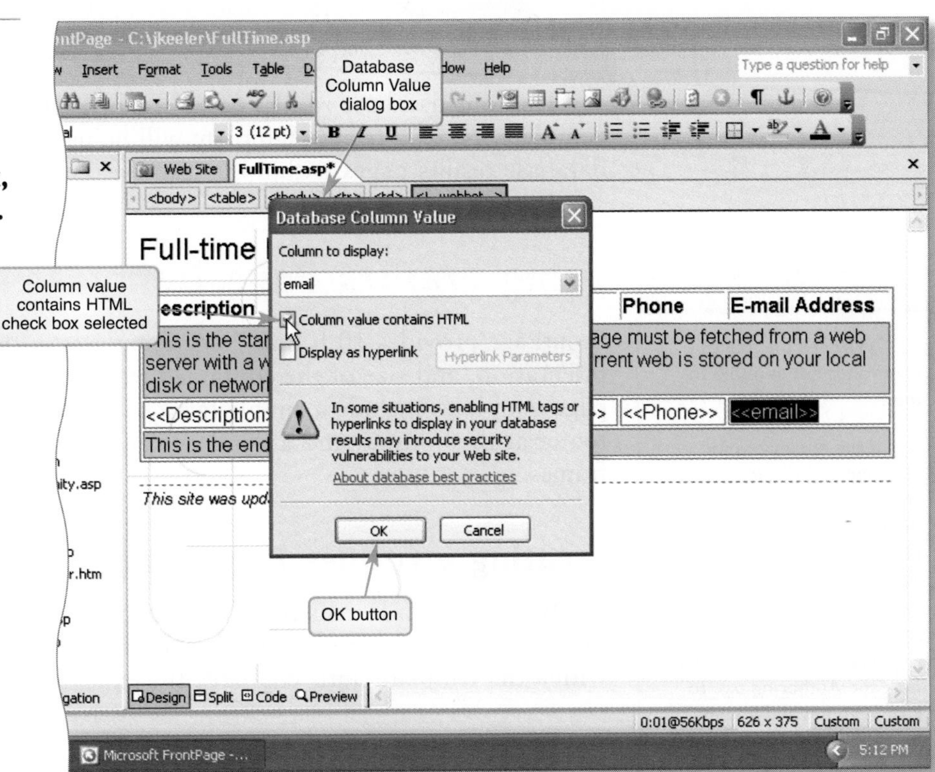

FIGURE 5-22

15

- **Click the OK button.**
- **Drag through the <<email>>, <<Phone>>, <<Contact>>, and <<Compensation>> cells to select the four cells.**
- **Right-click anywhere on the selected cells and when FrontPage displays the shortcut menu, click Cell Properties.**
- **Select Top in the Vertical alignment box.**
- **Click the OK button.**

16

- **Right-click the FullTime.asp tab.**

FrontPage displays the shortcut menu (Figure 5-23).

17

- **Click Save.**

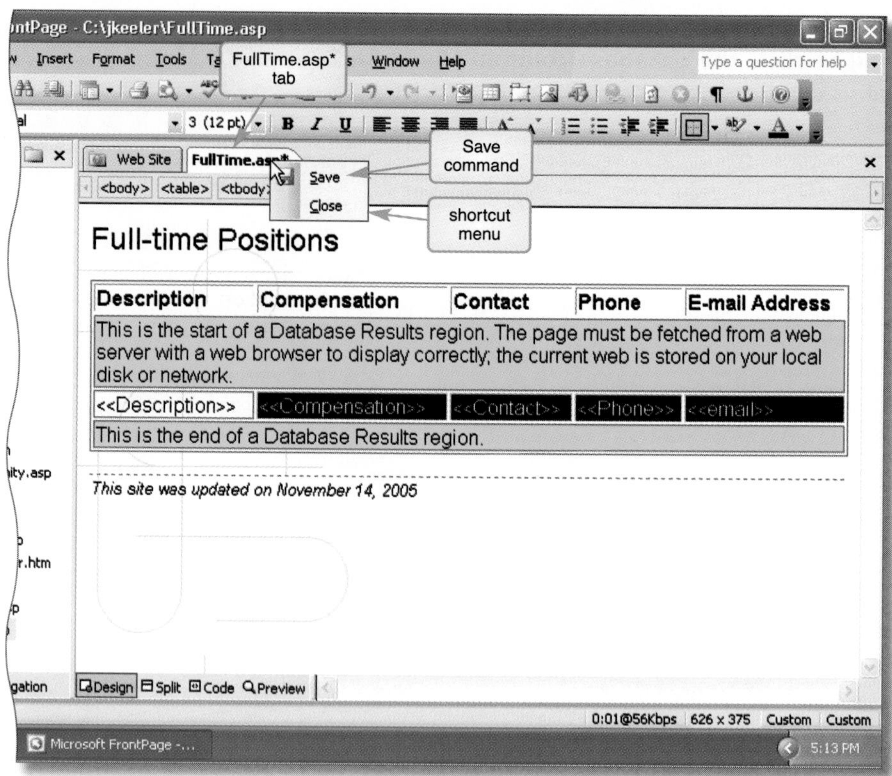

FIGURE 5-23

The four database results pages used to retrieve data from the database now are complete. Next, a frames template will be used to create a frames page that displays database results pages within the frames.

Q&A

Q: Why are the frames commands not available to me?

A: If the commands for inserting or using frames appear dimmed on menus or the Frames Pages tab is not displayed in the Page Templates dialog box, check for browser compatibility. On the Tools menu of FrontPage, click Page Options, and then click the Authoring tab. To enable frames and frames pages, click the Frames check box to select it. In addition, verify that you have not selected a target browser that does not support frames.

Using Frames Page Templates

FrontPage provides 10 frames page templates with each varying in the number, orientation, and size of the contained frames. The layouts provided in the frames page templates include a simple table of contents, a small header at the top, a small footer at the bottom, and a window split into any number of horizontal or vertical frames.

Creating a Frames Page Using a Frames Page Template

When using a frames page template, you should choose a template that best satisfies your design requirements. You then can alter the size and number of frames within the template until you have the exact size and number of frames you need.

Use FrontPage's built-in frames templates when designing a Web page with frames. If you cannot find a template to match your intended design, then choose the closest template to the design you have in mind and alter the frames in the Web page.

When you select a frames page template, FrontPage opens a new document and places the template within the new document. The following steps create a frames page using a frames page template.

To Create a Frames Page Using a Frames Page Template

1

- **Click the Close button on the Design view window.**
- **Click the Create a new normal page button arrow.**

FrontPage displays the Create a new normal page menu (Figure 5-24).

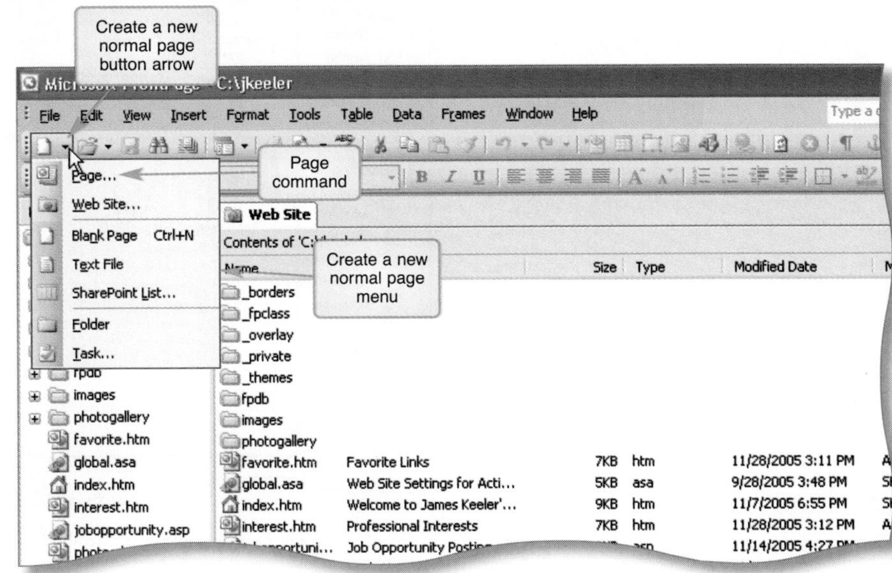

FIGURE 5-24

2

- **Click Page.**

FrontPage displays the Page Templates dialog box (Figure 5-25).

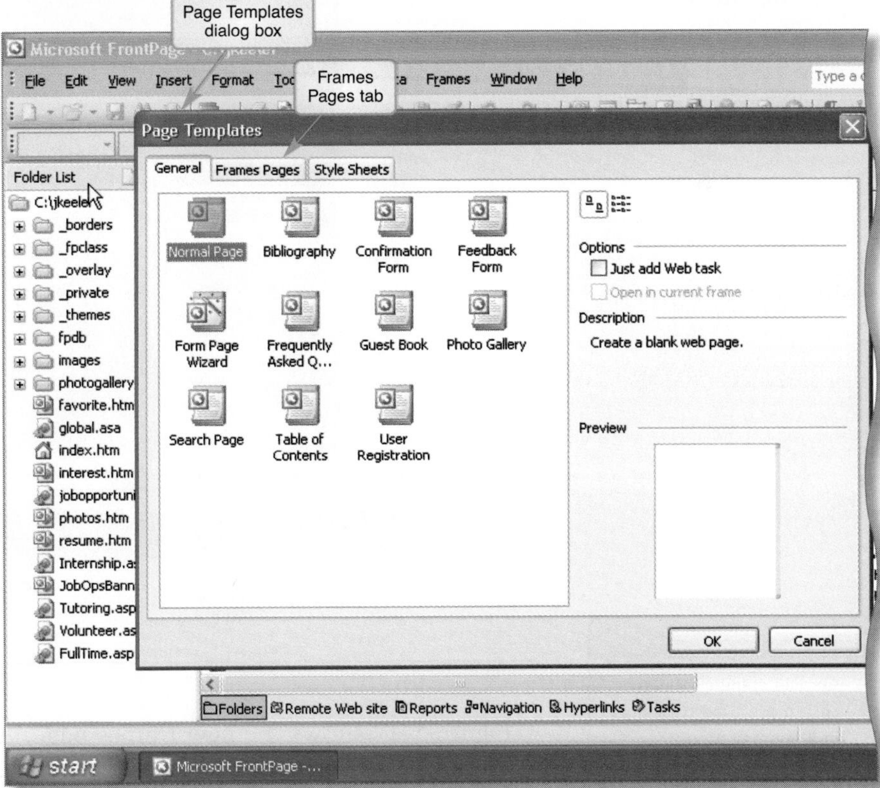

FIGURE 5-25

3

- **Click the Frames Pages tab.**
- **If necessary, click the Banner and Contents icon.**

FrontPage displays the Frames Pages sheet (Figure 5-26). Each frames page template is displayed as an icon with a descriptive name below. A description of the selected frames template is displayed in the Description area and a preview of the frames page is displayed in the Preview area.

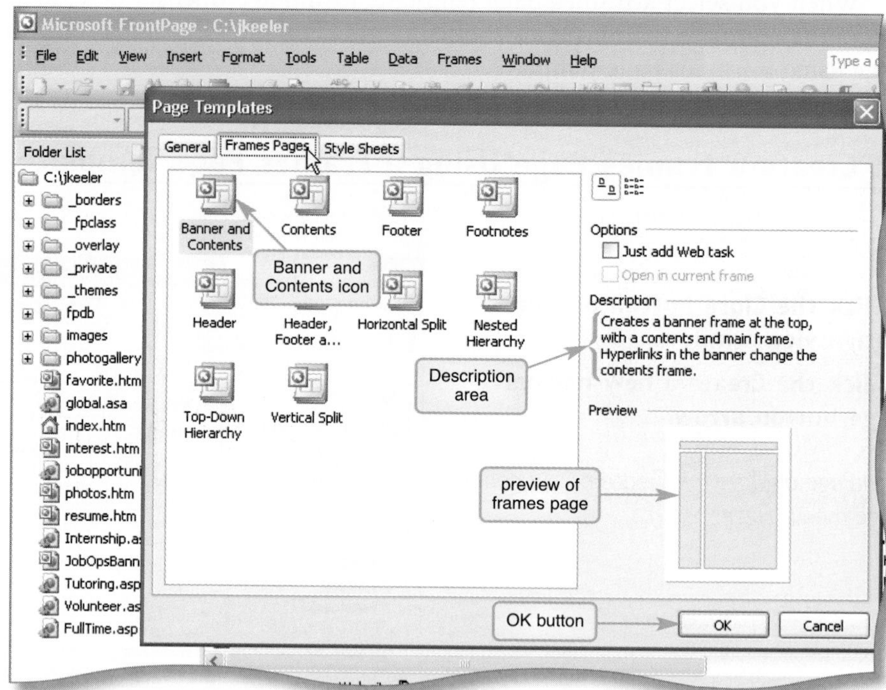

FIGURE 5-26

4

- **Click the OK button.**

FrontPage displays a new frames page with three frames: a banner frame, a contents frame, and a main frame (Figure 5-27).

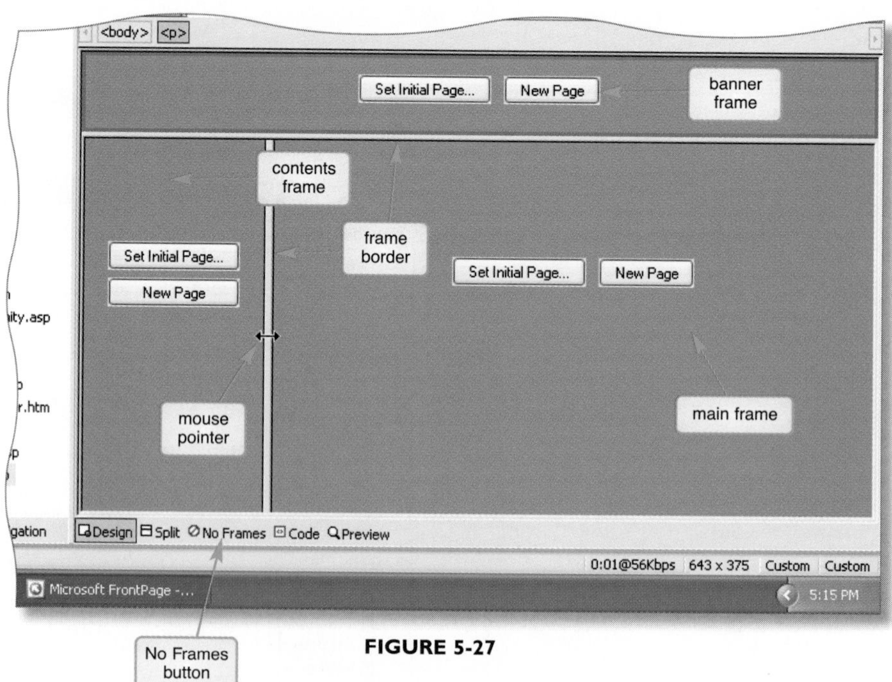

FIGURE 5-27

Other Ways

1. On File menu click New, click more page templates in New task pane
2. Press ALT+F, N, P
3. In Voice Command mode, say "File, New, Page or Web, Page Templates, Frames Pages"

Figure 5-27 shows the new frames page. As you have learned, each frame within the frames page will display a separate Web page. Within each frame are two buttons you use to define which page is displayed in each frame initially. The Set Initial Page button allows you to select a preexisting Web page as the initial Web page for that frame. The page can be from the current FrontPage Web site, another Web page on the Web server where the frames page will be published, or any page on the World Wide Web. The New Page button allows you to create a new Web page, directly in the frame, to be displayed as the initial Web page for that frame.

Notice the blue highlighted border surrounding the top frame shown in Figure 5-27. The blue highlighted border indicates the current active frame. Any steps you perform — such as defining special formats, inserting objects, or saving a file — are performed on the Web page in the active frame. You can change the active frame simply by clicking the desired frame. The highlighted border will surround the frame you clicked to indicate that it is the current active frame.

As shown in Figure 5-27, an additional button is displayed at the bottom of the window. The No Frames button displays the Web page that the user sees if the browser does not support frames.

More About

Frames Template Descriptions

The description for a selected frames template usually will indicate when hyperlinks in one frame affect the contents of another frame. Typically, the frame or frames that will contain the hyperlinks, as well as the target frame, all are identified in the frames page description.

Saving the Frames Web Page

You now are ready to create the initial Web pages that will be displayed in each frame. Before you begin, however, you should save the frames page.

As you work on pages in a Web site, FrontPage keeps track of whether or not you saved a file. If you create an initial Web page and then try to save it, you are prompted twice — once to save the initial Web page and once to save the frames page. This happens every time you try to save, until you finally save the frames page. Saving the frames page first prevents the second prompt from appearing, saving you time and reducing confusion over which page you are saving.

Before you can save the frames Web page, you must select it to make it the active page. You can select the frames page to be the current active page by clicking any of the frames borders. The blue highlighted border will surround the entire window, indicating that the frames page is the current active page. The following steps save the frames page.

To Save the Frames Web Page

1

• **Click the border between any of the frames to select the frames page as the current active page.**

The highlighted border surrounds the entire frames page (Figure 5-28).

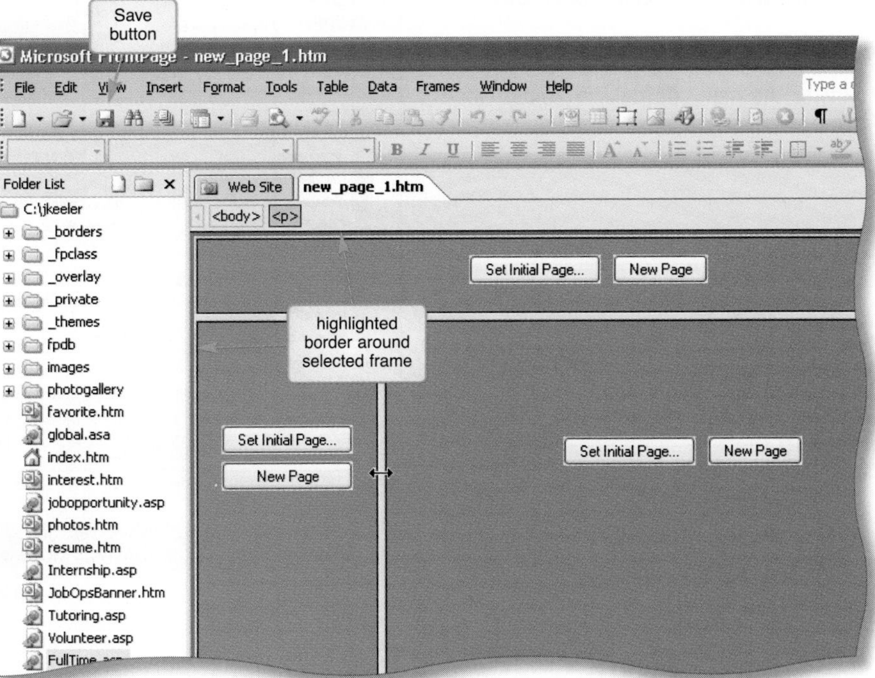

FIGURE 5-28

2

- **Click the Save button.**

FrontPage displays the Save As dialog box with a default file name and page title for the new frames page (Figure 5-29). A graphic map indicates the frames page as the frame to be saved.

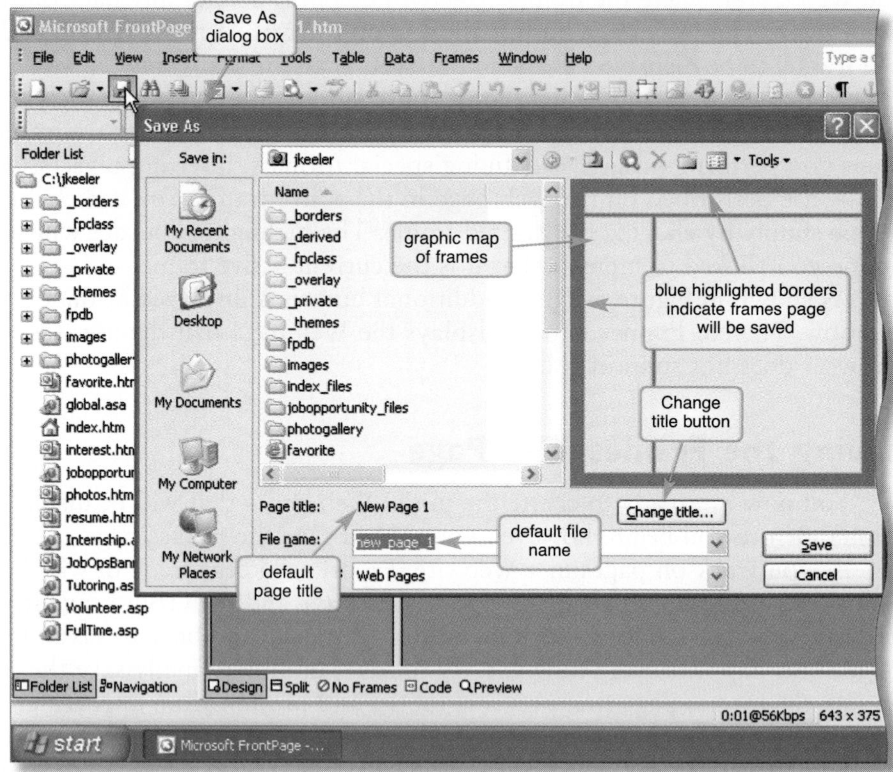

FIGURE 5-29

3

- **Click the Change title button.**
- **When FrontPage displays the Set Page Title dialog box, type** `Job Opportunities main frames page` **in the Page title text box.**

FrontPage displays the Set Page Title dialog box with the new title for the frames page displayed (Figure 5-30).

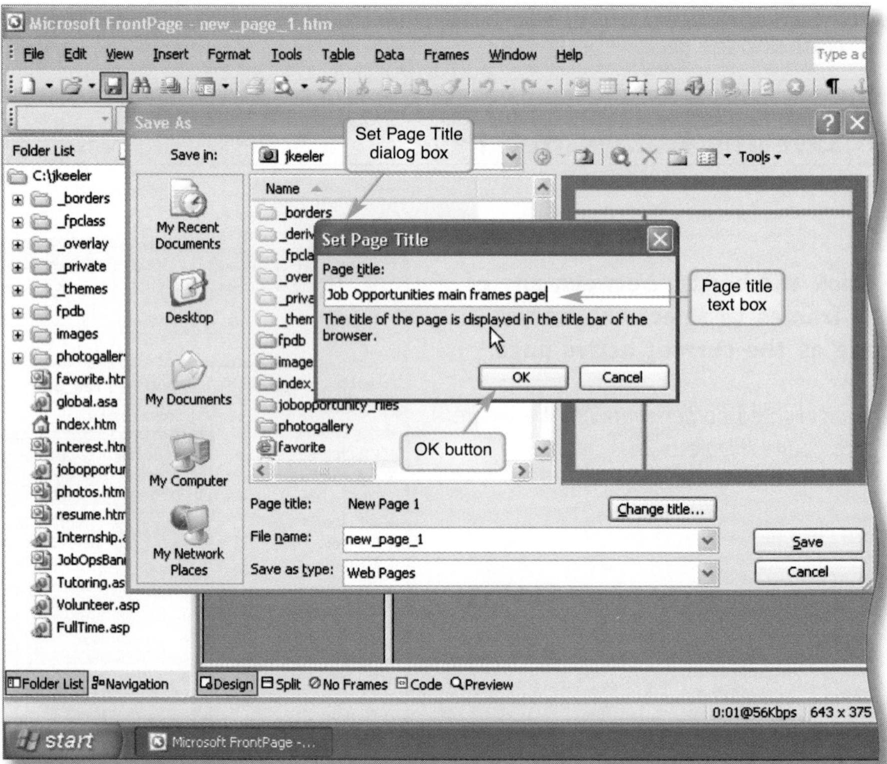

FIGURE 5-30

4

- **Click the OK button.**
- **Drag through the file name in the File name text box, and then type** `JobOppsMain` **as the new file name.**

FrontPage closes the Set Page Title dialog box. The page title is set to Job Opportunities main frames page and the file name is set to JobOppsMain.htm (Figure 5-31).

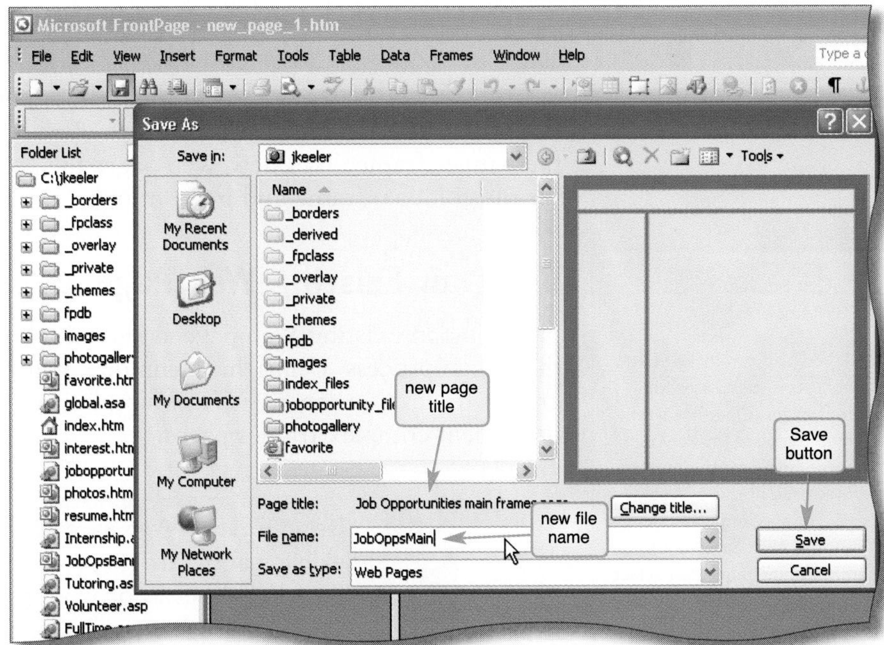

FIGURE 5-31

5

- **Click the Save button.**

The frames Web page is saved using the file name, JobOppsMain.htm (Figure 5-32).

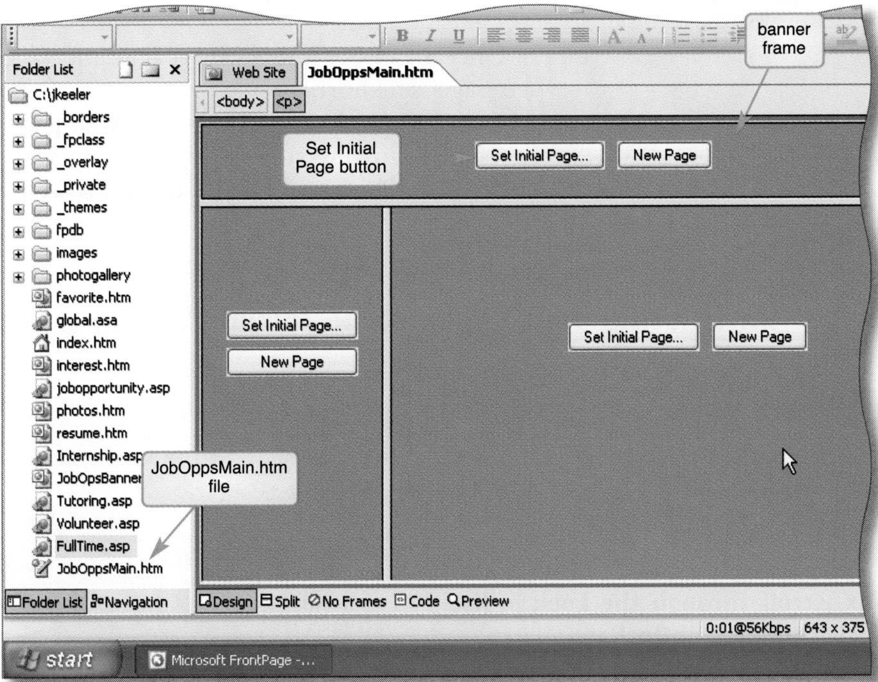

FIGURE 5-32

With the frames page saved, FrontPage will not prompt you to save it every time you save one of the other Web pages you develop in this project. The next step is to set the initial Web page to appear in the banner frame.

Setting an Initial Page to Appear in a Frame

You can set an initial page to appear in a frame by selecting an existing Web page or creating a new Web page within the frames page.

In this project, an existing Web page will be set as the initial page to appear in the banner frame. Two new Web pages then will be created to use as the initial pages for the contents frame and main frame.

Q&A

Q: Can I develop my own frame templates?

A: Yes. You can make your own custom templates for frames pages. Open a current frames template, make your changes, and save the current frames page not as a Web page, but as a template file. To do so, click Save As on the File menu, and then select FrontPage template from the Save as type list before saving the file. To learn more about custom frame templates, visit the FrontPage 2003 More About Web page (scsite.com/fp2003/more) and then click Frame Templates.

Using an Existing Web Page as the Initial Page in a Frame

Using an existing Web page as the initial page in a frame provides flexibility in the design process. Using this technique, you can assign different individuals or work groups to develop the Web pages simultaneously, thus reducing the time it takes to implement complex frames pages.

Design Tip

Use an existing Web page as the initial page in a frame to provide flexibility in the design process. Using this technique, you can assign different individuals or work groups to develop the Web pages simultaneously, thus reducing the time it takes to implement complex frames pages.

Once all of the initial Web pages and target Web pages exist, creating the frames Web page is a short, simple process. Simply select a template, arrange the frame borders if necessary, identify the initial Web pages, and then save and test the frames page. The following steps set an existing Web page as the initial page in a frame, and remove the shared border from the Web site so that the shared border is not displayed in the frames.

To Set an Existing Web Page as the Initial Page in a Frame

1

- **Click the Set Initial Page button in the top frame.**
- **If necessary, when FrontPage displays the Insert Hyperlink dialog box, scroll through the Look in list until the file, JobOpsBanner.htm, appears.**
- **Click the file, JobOpsBanner.htm.**

FrontPage displays the Insert Hyperlink dialog box (Figure 5-33). The banner frame becomes the current active frame. The JobOpsBanner.htm file name appears in the Address box.

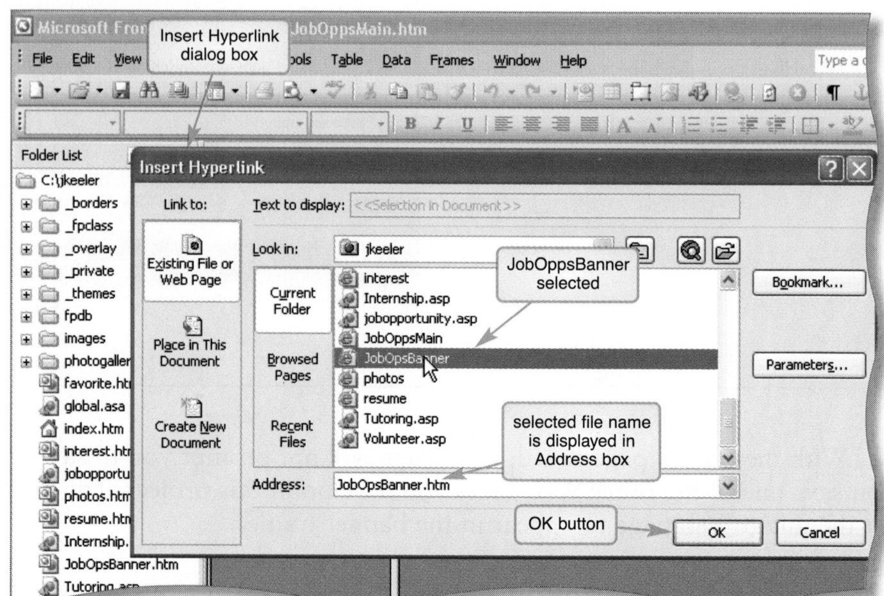

FIGURE 5-33

2

- **Click the OK button.**
- **Click Format on the menu bar and then click Shared borders.**
- **Click Bottom to deselect the shared border and then click the OK button.**

FrontPage displays the JobOpsBanner.htm file in the banner frame (Figure 5-34). The banner image will not appear until the page has been added to the Navigation view.

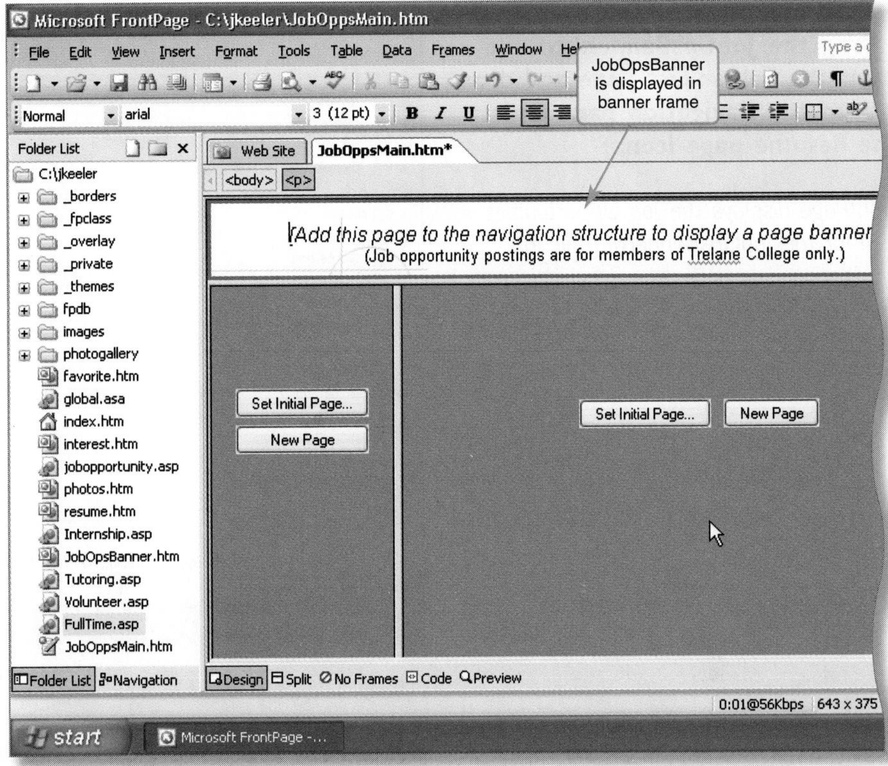

FIGURE 5-34

3

- **Click View on the menu bar and then click Navigation.**

FrontPage displays the current Web site in Navigation view (Figure 5-35). The file, JobOpsBanner.htm, is selected in the Folder List pane.

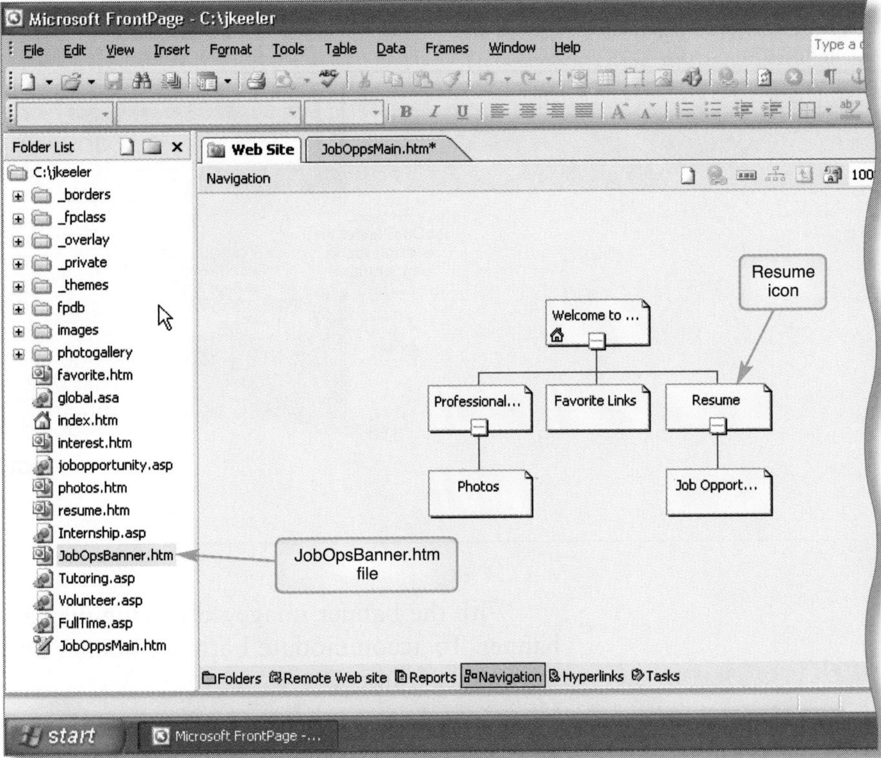

FIGURE 5-35

4

• **Drag the JobOpsBanner.htm file from the Folder List pane and drop it into the Navigation pane under the Resume page icon.**

FrontPage displays the Job Opportunities icon for the JobOpsBanner.htm file in Navigation view under the Resume icon (Figure 5-36).

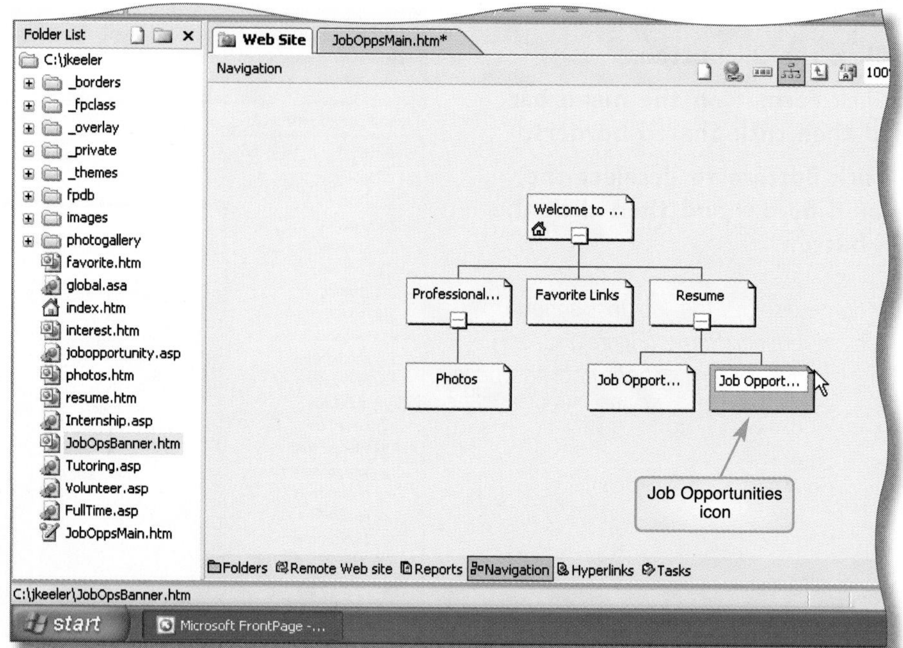

FIGURE 5-36

5

• **Click the JobOppsMain.htm tab.**

FrontPage displays the frames page in Design view. The banner frame displays the file, JobOpsBanner.htm, with a banner image (Figure 5-37).

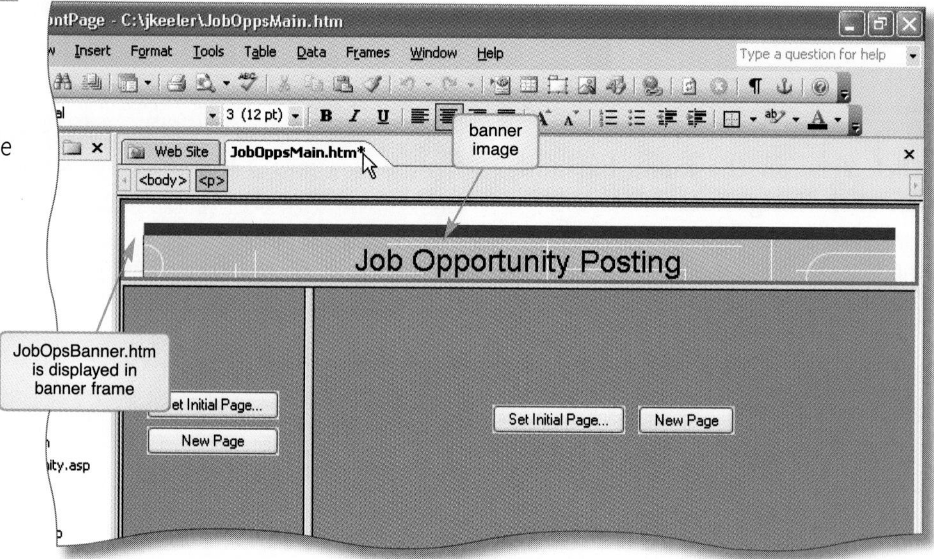

FIGURE 5-37

With the banner image now being displayed, you cannot see the text below the banner. To accommodate both the banner and the text, you can modify the size of the banner frame.

Modifying the Size of a Frame

You can modify the size of a frame by dragging the frame border to set the frame to the desired height or width. In this project, the size of the banner frame will be increased so the text and banner image appear without the need for a scroll bar. The following step modifies the size of a frame.

To Modify the Size of a Frame

1

- **Point to the horizontal frame border below the banner frame.**
- **Drag the border down until the text in the banner frame is visible.**

The frame border has been dragged to modify the frame size (Figure 5-38). To determine the appropriate size, you should preview the Web page in a browser.

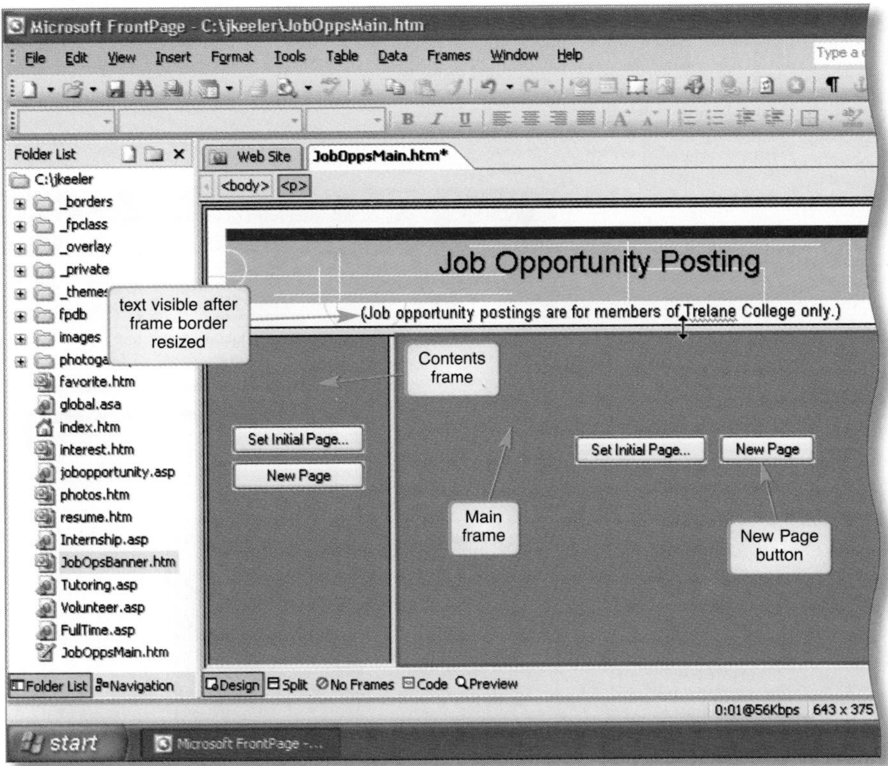

FIGURE 5-38

Other Ways

1. On Frames menu click Frame Properties, type new size values
2. Right-click frame, click Frame Properties on shortcut menu, type new size values
3. Press ALT+R, P
4. In Voice Command mode, say "Frames, Frame Properties"

You can decrease the size of a frame in the same fashion — simply by dragging the frame border until the frame is the desired size.

You do not have to save this Web page, JobOpsBanner.htm, because you have not changed it since you imported it into the Web site in previous steps. You have changed the frames page, however, and should save these changes. The following step saves the changes to the frames page.

To Save Changes to the Frames Page

1 **Click the Save button on the Standard toolbar.**

Creating a New Web Page for the Initial Page in a Frame

Creating a new Web page to use as the initial page for a frame is just like creating any other new Web page. With a frames page template, you indicate that you want to create a new Web page as the initial page for that frame by clicking the New Page button in the desired frame. You then create the Web page. All the objects and text inserted in the page will appear in that frame only. The step on the next page creates the initial Web page that will appear in the main frame when the user first displays the frames page.

To Create a New Web Page for the Initial Page in a Frame

1. **Click the New Page button in the main frame.**

FrontPage displays a new Web page in the main frame with the current theme applied (Figure 5-39). The main frame is the current active frame and the insertion point is located in the new Web page.

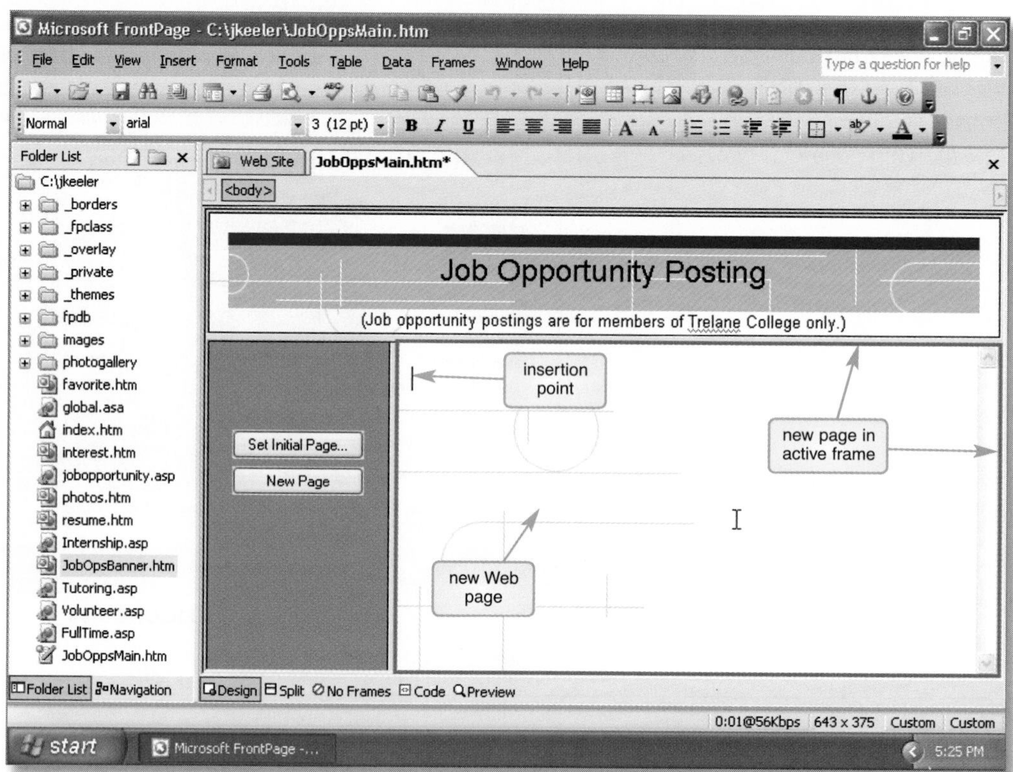

FIGURE 5-39

You now can modify this Web page just as you modified Web pages in previous projects. The following steps insert text in the initial page for the main frame.

To Insert Text in the Initial Page for the Main Frame

1. **If necessary, click the Web page in the main frame to position the insertion point.**
2. **Type** `Welcome to my Job Opportunity Posting Page for Trelane College.` **and then press the ENTER key.**
3. **Type** `To post a new job opportunity or to view job opportunities by category, click the corresponding link in the frame to the left.` **to enter the remaining text.**

FrontPage displays the main page in the frames page with the added text (Figure 5-40).

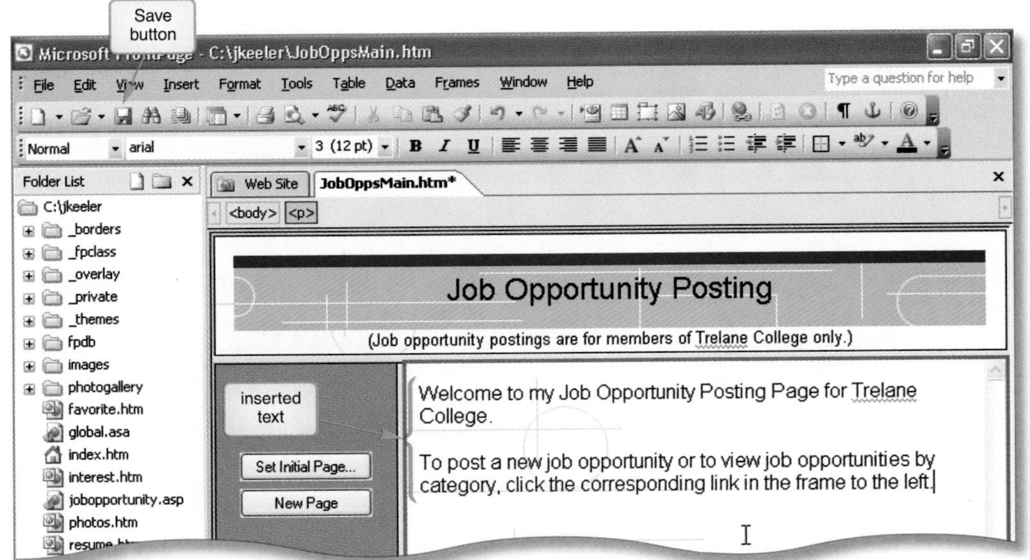

FIGURE 5-40

The initial page for the main frame is complete. Because the Web page was created rather than imported, you should save it before continuing. In general, you should save your work periodically. Although FrontPage prompts you to save changes when you close a page or quit FrontPage, any unsaved pages can be lost due to outside factors, such as an unexpected loss of power. Another reason for saving a frame page is that you must save it first before you can use it as a target for a hyperlink in another frame.

Saving the Initial Page for a Frame

In the previous steps, the initial page for the main frame was created directly in the frame. This Web page now must be saved in the FrontPage Web site. When the Save button is clicked, FrontPage saves the Web page in the current active frame by default. The following steps save the initial page for a frame.

To Save the Initial Page for the Main Frame

1

• **Click the Save button on the Standard toolbar.**

FrontPage displays the Save As dialog box (Figure 5-41). FrontPage displays a graphic map with the current active frame high-lighted to indicate which Web page will be saved. You should save the page using a file name that represents the function of the initial page.

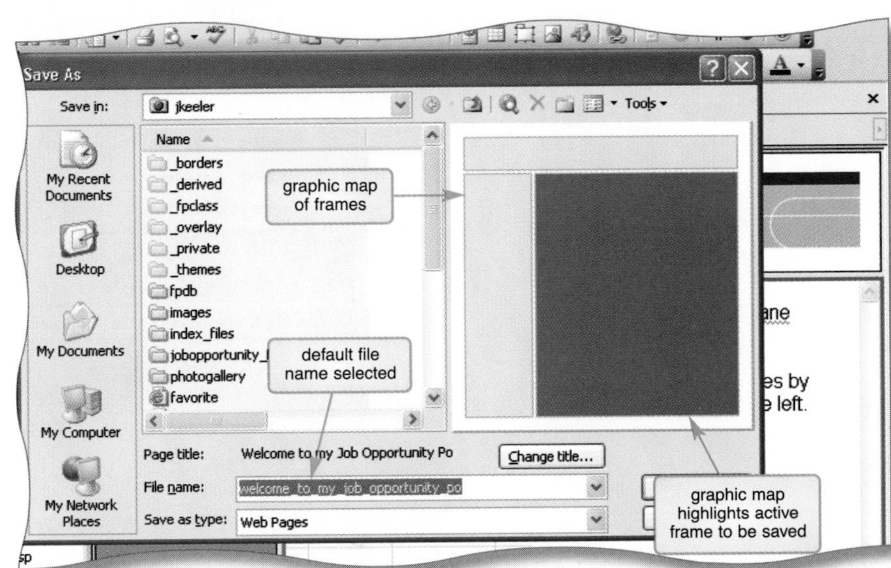

FIGURE 5-41

2

- **Type** `JobOppsWelcome` **in the File name text box.**

FrontPage displays the new file name in the File name text box (Figure 5-42).

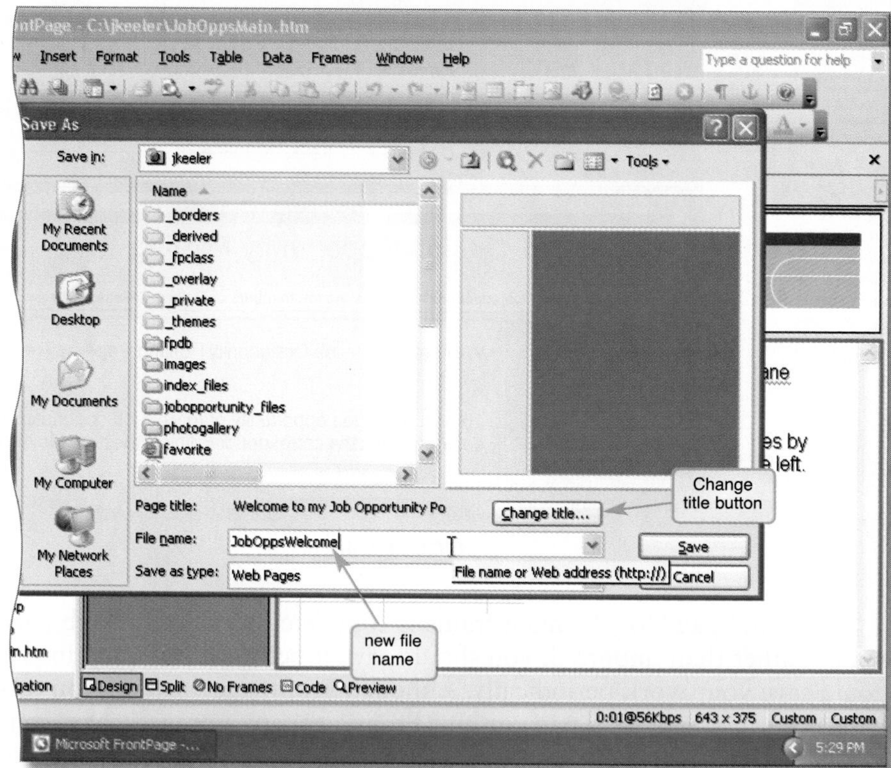

FIGURE 5-42

3

- **Click the Change title button.**
- **When FrontPage displays the Set Page Title dialog box, type** `Welcome to my Job Opportunity Posting Page` **in the Page title text box.**

FrontPage displays the new title in the Page title text box (Figure 5-43).

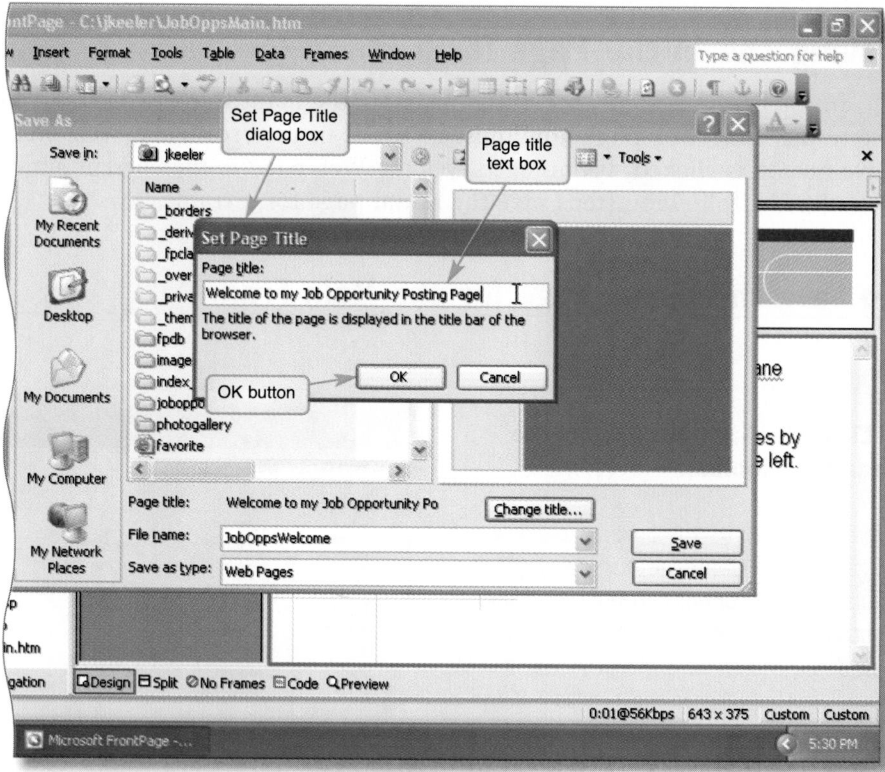

FIGURE 5-43

4

• **Click the OK button.**

The page title in the Save As dialog box is set to Welcome to my Job Opportunity Posting Page (Figure 5-44).

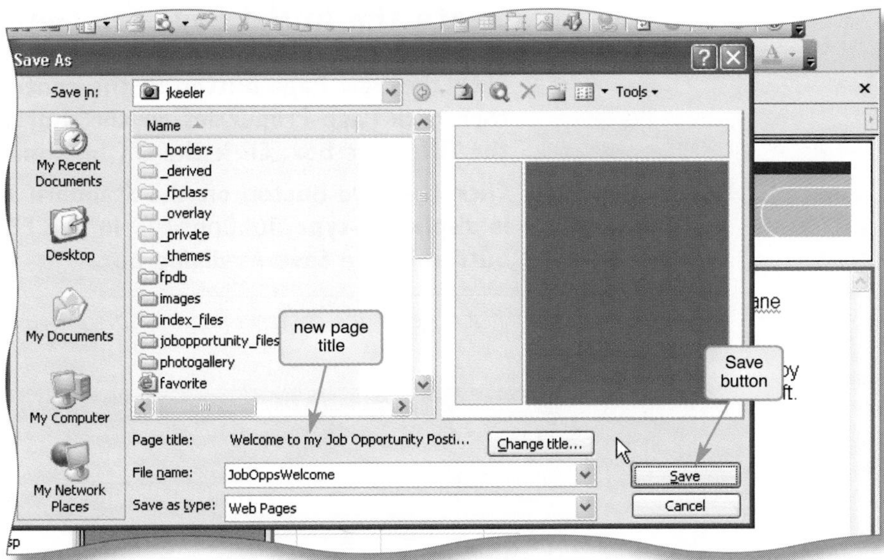

FIGURE 5-44

5

• **Click the Save button.**

The initial page for the main frame is saved as JobOppsWelcome.htm (Figure 5-45).

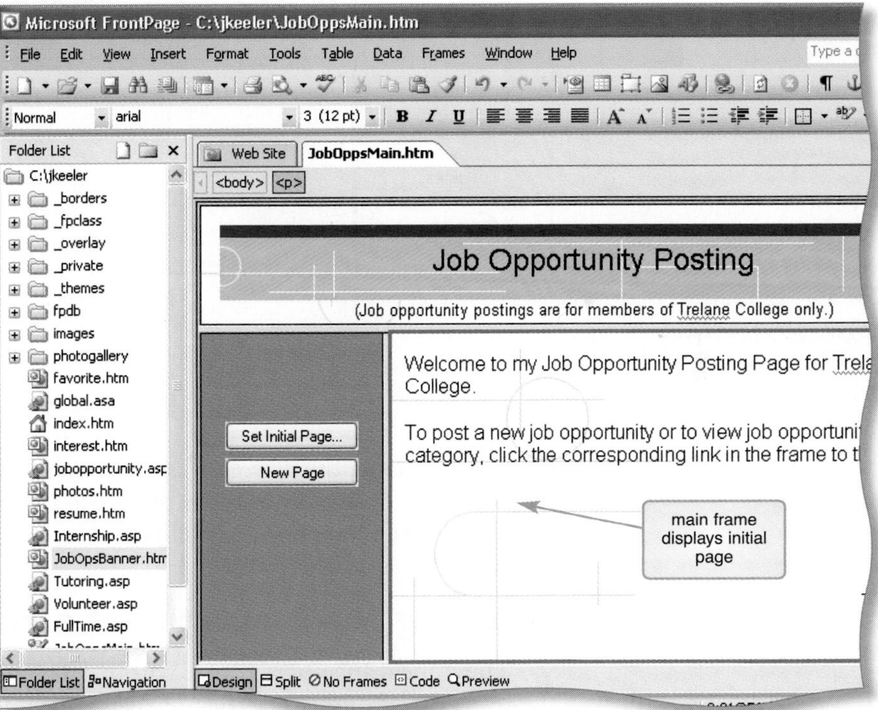

FIGURE 5-45

One of the initial pages for a frame now has been created, directly within the frame itself. To create the other initial Web pages, you will follow steps similar to the preceding steps. The next page to be created is the contents page, which will appear as the initial page for the contents frame. According to the design, this page will contain a table of contents with hyperlinks to the other target pages. The steps on the next page create the initial page for the contents frame.

To Create the Initial Page for the Contents Frame

1. **Click the New Page button in the contents frame. Right-click the page and then click Page Properties on the shortcut menu. Type** `Contents Page` **in the Title text box. Click the OK button.**
2. **Click the Save button on the Standard toolbar. When the Save As dialog box is displayed, type** `JobOppsTOC` **in the File name text box. Click the Save button in the Save As dialog box.**

The initial page for the contents frame is saved (Figure 5-46).

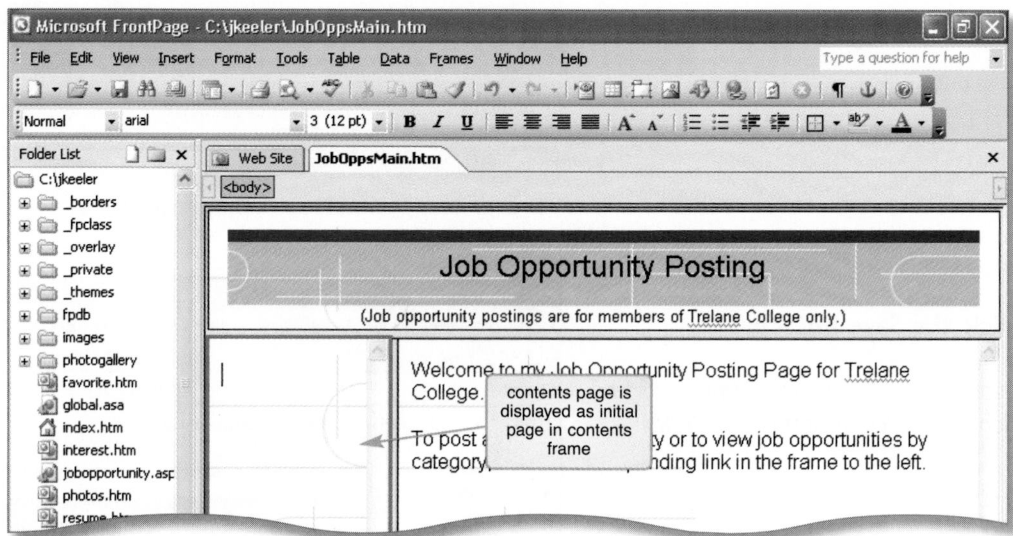

FIGURE 5-46

Modifying Properties of Frames and Frames Pages

In previous steps, the size of a frame was modified by dragging its border. While this sets the initial size of the frame, you also can set other properties such as whether a frame is resizable or has a scroll bar.

Modifying the Properties of a Frame

The appearance of a frame within a frames page is defined by both properties of the frame itself and properties of the frames page. When modifying frame properties, you should make decisions about frame properties carefully because they can affect the ability of the user to see all of the frame content.

Some decisions, such as whether the frame should be displayed with scroll bars, are made on a frame-by-frame basis. Some frames do not need scroll bars, while other frames, even in the same frames page, may need them. A frame can be set to always show scroll bars, never show scroll bars, or show them only if needed.

Other decisions, such as allowing the user to resize the frame in a browser, are made for multiple frames together, even though the property value is set for an individual frame. For example, if one frame is set to be resizable and the frames around it are not resizable, then the setting for that one frame has no effect.

Design Tip

Carefully consider the set of features that you add to each frame, such as whether the user can resize the frame, the initial size of the frame, and whether the frame includes scroll bars. Take into consideration your user's browser and screen resolution when making these decisions.

The following steps modify the properties of a frame.

To Modify the Properties of a Frame

1

- **Right-click the contents frame.**

FrontPage displays the shortcut menu (Figure 5-47).

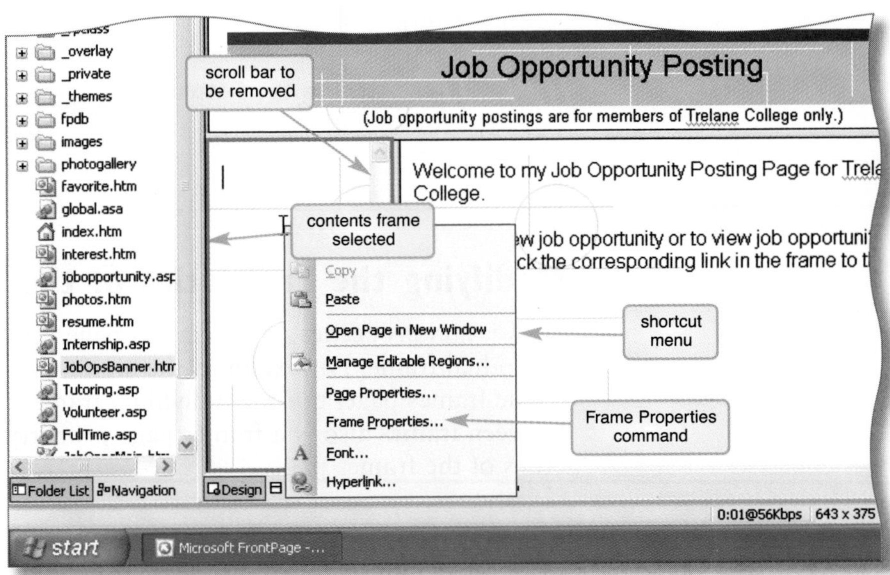

FIGURE 5-47

2

- **Click Frame Properties.**
- **When FrontPage displays the Frame Properties dialog box, click the Show scrollbars box arrow in the Options area and then click Never.**
- **If necessary, click Resizable in browser.**

FrontPage displays the Frames Properties dialog box with the changes (Figure 5-48). Selecting Never on the Show scrollbars list indicates that scroll bars never will appear in the contents frame.

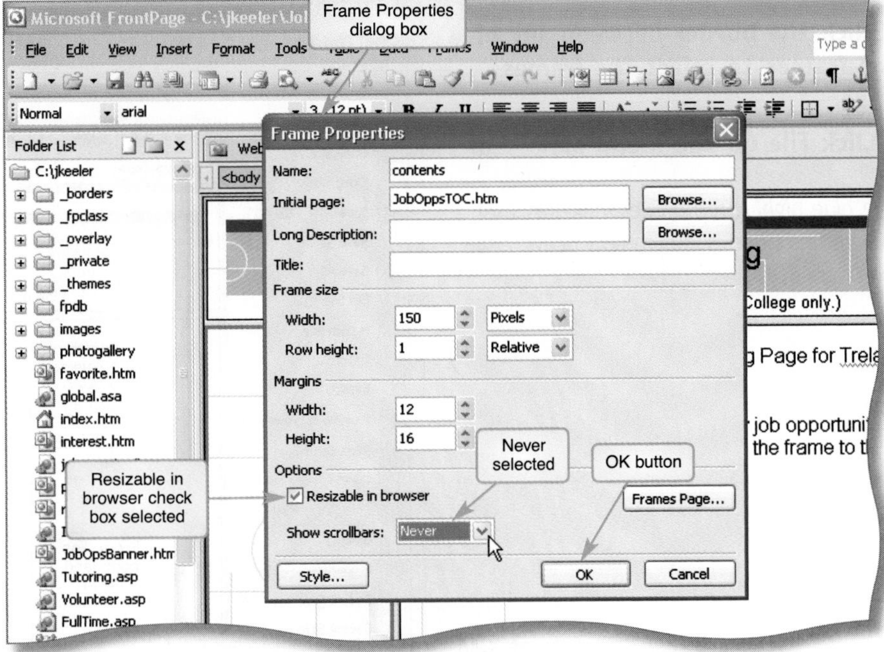

FIGURE 5-48

3

- **Click the OK button.**

FrontPage displays the contents frame without scroll bars (Figure 5-49).

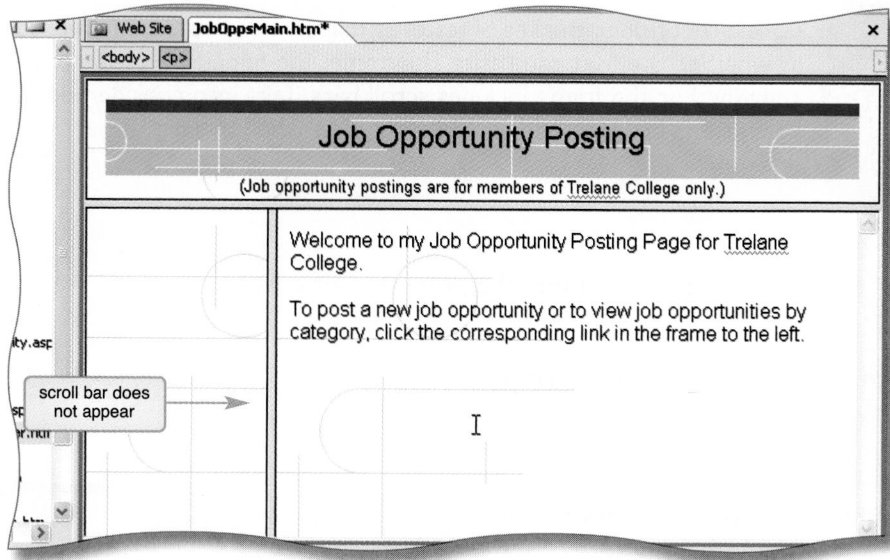

FIGURE 5-49

Modifying the Properties of the Frames Page

Certain properties of the frames page itself also affect the appearance of each individual frame. For example, the amount of spacing between frames is a property of the frames page, not the individual frames. Whether or not borders are displayed between frames also is a frames page property. The following steps modify the properties of the frames page.

To Modify the Properties of the Frames Page

1

- **Click the border between any of the frames to select the frames page.**
- **Click File on the menu bar.**

The blue highlighted border indicates that the frames page is the current active page (Figure 5-50).

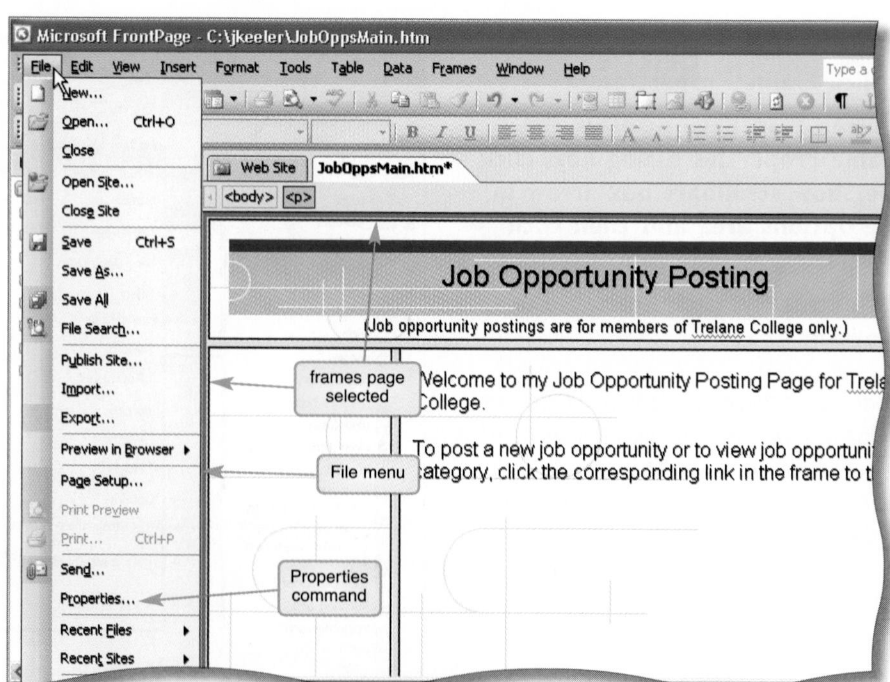

FIGURE 5-50

2

• **Click Properties.**

FrontPage displays the Page Properties dialog box (Figure 5-51).

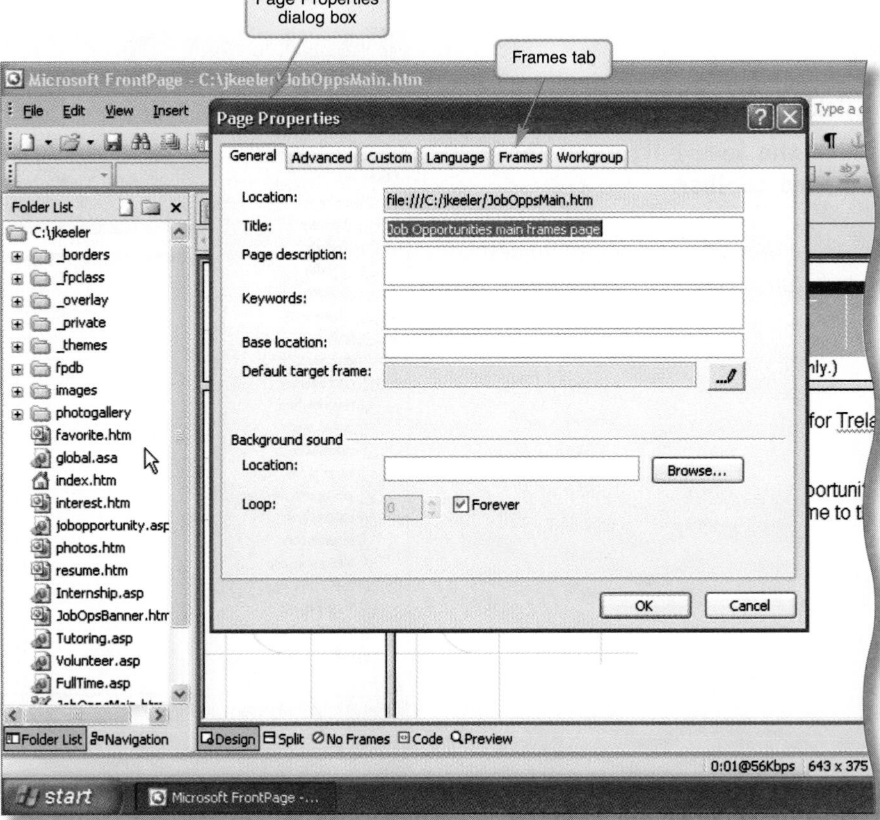

FIGURE 5-51

3

• **Click the Frames tab.**

• **If necessary, type** 1 **in the Frame Spacing box.**

FrontPage displays the Frames sheet (Figure 5-52). The spacing between frames is set to 1 and borders are set to be displayed.

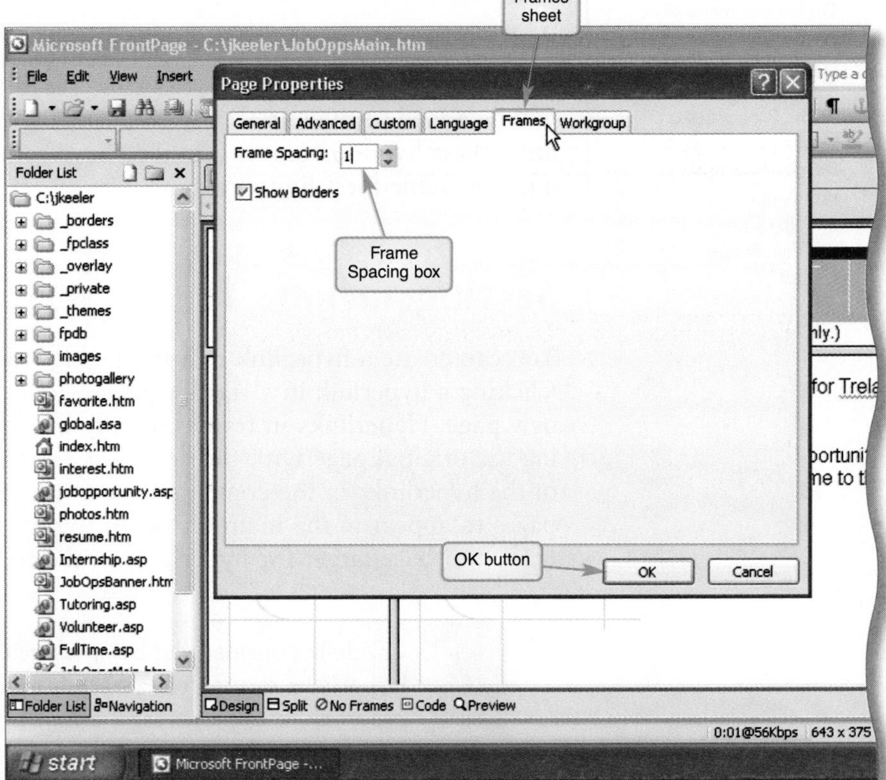

FIGURE 5-52

- **Click the OK button.**
- **Click the Save button on the Standard toolbar.**

FrontPage displays the modified frames page (Figure 5-53).

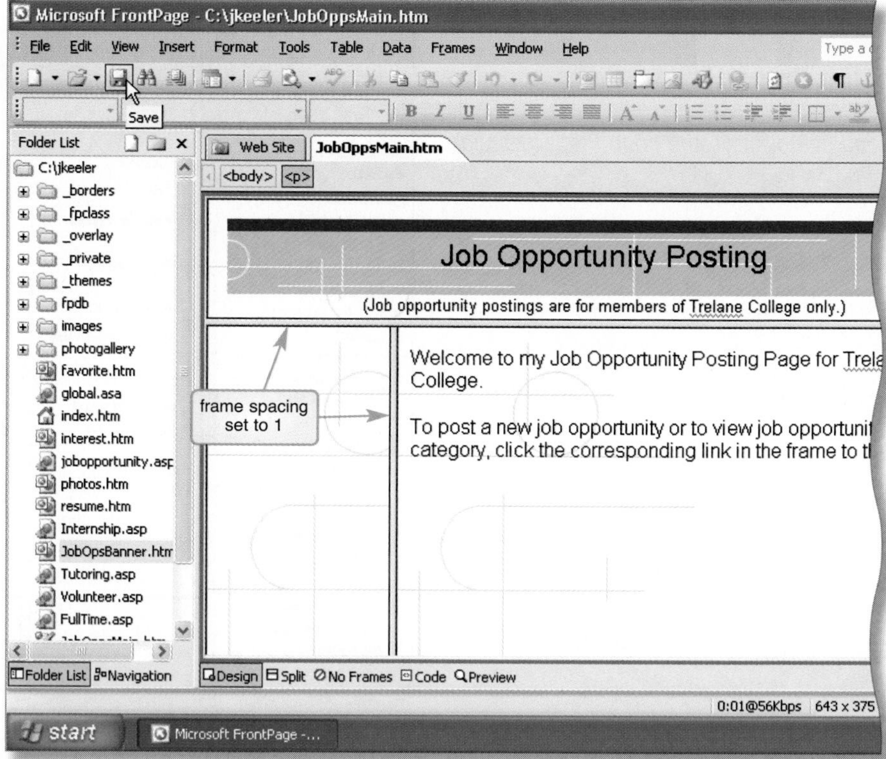

FIGURE 5-53

Other Ways

1. On Frames menu click Frame Properties, click Frames Page button
2. Right-click frame, click Frame Properties on shortcut menu, click Frames Page button
3. Press ALT+F, I
4. In Voice Command mode, say "File, Properties, Frames"

In the previous steps, the initial page for the contents frame was created and the frame and frames page properties were set to affect how it appears. Next, hyperlinks will be added to the initial page to allow users to navigate to new pages. Before creating these hyperlinks, it is useful to have some background regarding the choices for a target frame for a hyperlink.

Setting Targets for Hyperlinks in Frames

You can create a hyperlink in a frame page just as you would in any other page. Clicking a hyperlink in a regular page causes the current page to be replaced with a new page. Hyperlinks in frames usually display the new pages in another frame, leaving the original page with the hyperlink unaffected. In this project, for instance, most of the hyperlinks in the contents page in the contents frame will cause target Web pages to appear in the main frame. In this example, the main frame is considered the default or base target for hyperlinks in the contents frame.

Design Tip

Carefully consider the behavior of each hyperlink in a frame. Hyperlinks may target a default frame, the same frame as the hyperlink, the entire page, a new browser window, or the parent frame. Consider whether targeting a link to another frame may cause unwanted behavior, such as the nesting of one framed page within another.

The frame target for a hyperlink also can be set to display a page in frames or windows other than the default target. As shown in Table 5-1, you also can set a frame to display a Web page in the same frame; in a different frame; in the entire browser window, thus replacing the frames page; or in a new browser window. The available choices for a target frame are predefined frame settings that are understood by all Web browsers that support frames.

More About

Frame Borders

If you do not want the borders between frames to be visible when the frames page is displayed, click Properties on the File menu, and then, if necessary, click the Frames tab on the Page Properties dialog box. Click the Show Borders check box to clear it.

Table 5-1 Common Settings for Frame Targets

FRAME TARGET	DESCRIPTION
Page Default	Specifies that the linked page should be displayed in the default target frame for the active page. This is the recommended method of specifying target frames for hyperlinks.
Same Frame	Sets the target frame of the hyperlink to the same frame that contains the hyperlink. This setting overrides the page's default target frame.
Whole Page	Sets the target frame of the hyperlink to the entire Web browser window.
New Window	Specifies that a new Web browser window should be launched on the user's desktop, and the target page should be displayed in the new Web browser window.
Parent Frame	Specifies that the linked page should be displayed in the frame that contains the current frameset tag. This is an advanced feature.

Q&A

Q: Can one or more hyperlinks in a frame have a different target frame than the others?

A: Yes. A hyperlink in a frame still can target a location other than the one identified in a base target tag. The HTML code for the individual hyperlink overrides the base target tag with a target value of its own. When editing properties of a hyperlink, you can use the common target settings for the frame target provided by FrontPage, or you can supply a custom target. To learn more about using the target tag in HTML, visit the FrontPage 2003 More About Web page (scsite.com/fp2003/more) and then click HTML Target Tag.

Creating Hyperlinks to Pages in Frames

The purpose of the contents page in the contents frame is to present the user with a list of hyperlinks to different Web pages in the job opportunities section of the Web site. As noted earlier, these hyperlinks can link to Web pages in the same FrontPage Web site, to other Web pages on the same Web server, or to any Web page on the World Wide Web. For these hyperlinks, the target Web pages will appear in the main frame.

The frames page template you selected sets the main frame as the base target for hyperlinks in the contents frame. Figure 5-54 shows the HTML code in the header section of the contents frame. The base target tag in each frame sets the default target for hyperlinks in this frame. Because the main frame is set as the default or **base target** for the contents frame, you do not need to set the main frame as the target for each link within the frame. Therefore, a Link bar component can be used to create hyperlinks that use the default target frame. The steps on the next page create a Link bar component in the contents page that targets the default frame.

```
<html>

<head>
<meta http-equiv="Content-Type" content="text/html; charset=windows-1252">
<title>Contents Page</title>
<base target="main">
<!--mstheme--><link rel="stylesheet" type=text/css"
href="_themes/capsules/caps1111.css"><meta name="Microsoft Theme" content="capsules
1111, default">
<meta name="Microsoft Border" content="none, default">
</head>

<body>

</body>

</html>
```

base target tag sets main frame as default target

FIGURE 5-54

To Create a Link Bar Targeting the Default Frame

1. **If necessary, click the contents frame to position the insertion point. Click Insert on the menu bar and then click Navigation. When FrontPage displays the Insert Web Component dialog box, click Bar based on navigation structure in the Choose a bar type list. Click the Next button. When FrontPage displays the Choose a bar style list in the Insert Web Component dialog box, verify that the Use Page's Theme icon is selected and then click the Next button. When the Choose an orientation list is displayed in the Insert Web Component dialog box, click the second icon to insert the link bar with the links arranged vertically. Click the Finish button.**

2. **If necessary, when the Link Bar Properties dialog box appears, click the General tab. Verify that child level is selected in the Hyperlinks to add to page area and that no pages are selected in the Additional pages area. Click the OK button. Click the Save button on the Standard toolbar.**

3. **Double-click the file, jobopportunity.asp, in the Folder List pane to open the Job Opportunity Posting page in Design view. Delete the page banner and all text above the form, including the blank line above the form. Click the Save button on the Standard toolbar. Close the Job Opportunity Posting page.**

4. **Click View on the menu bar and then click Navigation. Right-click the Job Opportunity Posting icon. Click Rename on the shortcut menu. Type** `Post Job Opportunity` **as the new page label and then press the ENTER key. Drag and drop the file, JobOppsTOC.htm, below the Job Opportunities icon. Drag and drop the Post Job Opportunity icon below the Contents Page icon.**

5. **Drag the file, FullTime.asp, from the Folder List pane and drop it below the Contents Page icon to the right of the Post Job Opportunity icon. Drag the file, Volunteer.asp, from the Folder List pane and drop it below the Contents Page icon to the right of the Full-time icon. Drag the file, Internship.asp, from the Folder List pane and drop it below the Contents Page icon to the right of the Volunteer icon. Drag the file, Tutoring.asp, from the Folder List pane and drop it below the Contents Page icon to the right of the Internship icon.**

6. **Click the JobOppsMain.htm tab to display the JobOppsMain.htm page in Design view. If necessary, drag the right border of the contents frame to adjust the size of the frame to accommodate the link bar. Click the Save button on the Standard toolbar.**

FrontPage displays the link bar in the contents frame (Figure 5-55).

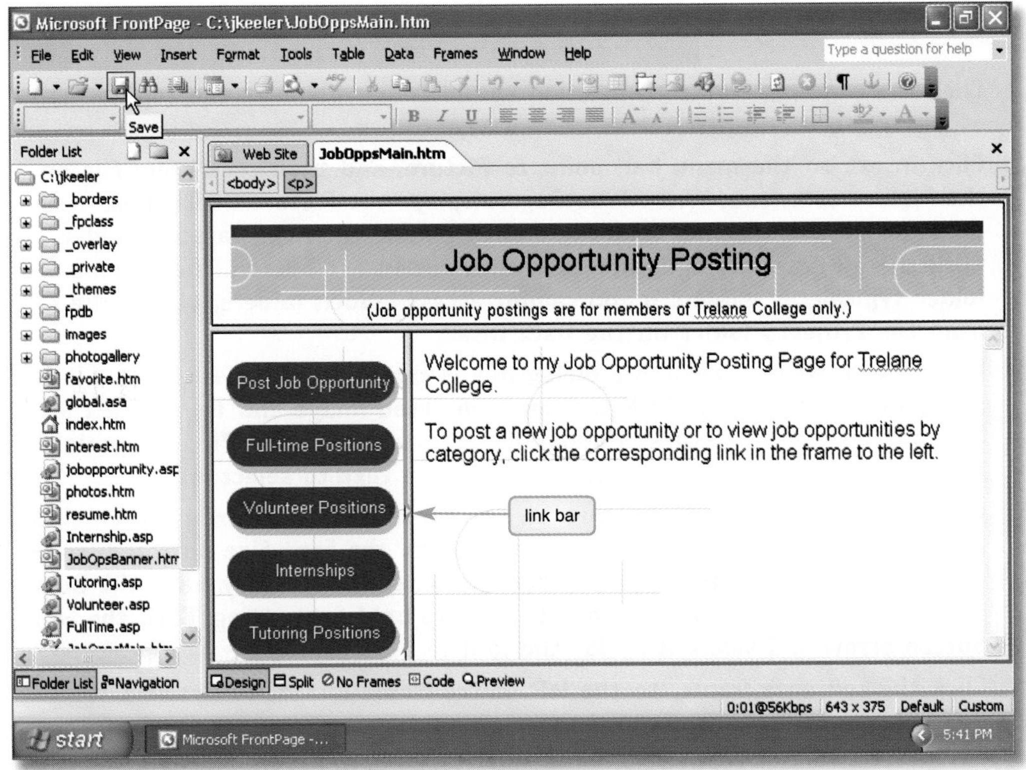

FIGURE 5-55

The contents page now contains a link bar with hyperlinks to all of the pages that the user can choose to display in the main frame. To complete the contents page, one more hyperlink must be created to the Home page.

Creating a Hyperlink to a Whole Page

As listed in Table 5-1 on page FP 377, a hyperlink in a frame can be used to display a Web page in an entire browser window, instead of in a frame. This is the purpose of the hyperlink for the Home page. Because the link bar hyperlinks use the default main frame as the target, you cannot use the link bar to link to the Home page and display it in the entire browser window. If you did, the Home page would appear in the main frame, instead of replacing the frames page, causing a cascading effect that is not desired. To avoid displaying its target Web page in the frame, the Home page hyperlink must indicate a target of a whole page.

Because you will not use the link bar to link to the Home page, you first must insert an image identical to those used in the link bar. Because the Capsules theme is used for this page, the images used in the link bar are available in the capsules folder within the _themes folder in this Web site. The steps on the next page insert an image from the current theme used in this Web site.

To Insert an Image from the Current Theme

1. **Click the contents frame to position the insertion point at the top and left of the frame.**
2. **Click Insert on the menu bar, point to Picture, and then click From File on the Picture submenu. When FrontPage displays the Picture dialog box, double-click the _themes folder and then double-click the capsules folder. Click the file, capnavva.gif, and then click the Insert button. The _themes folder typically is hidden. If you cannot access hidden folders, obtain the file from the Project5 folder on the Data Disk.**
3. **If necessary, when the Picture dialog box is closed, hold down the SHIFT key and press the ENTER key. Click the newly inserted image and then click the Text button on the Pictures toolbar. If necessary, open the Pictures toolbar. Type** `Home` **as the label text. Drag through the text to select it.**
4. **Click the Font Color button arrow on the Formatting toolbar and then click [white] on the color palette. If necessary, click the Font Size button arrow on the Formatting toolbar and then click 2 (10 pt). If necessary, click the Bold button on the Formatting toolbar to remove bold formatting. Click the Font button arrow and select Arial for the font.**
5. **Click the contents frame, to the left of the Home image, to deselect the image.**

FrontPage displays the inserted image in the contents frame (Figure 5-56).

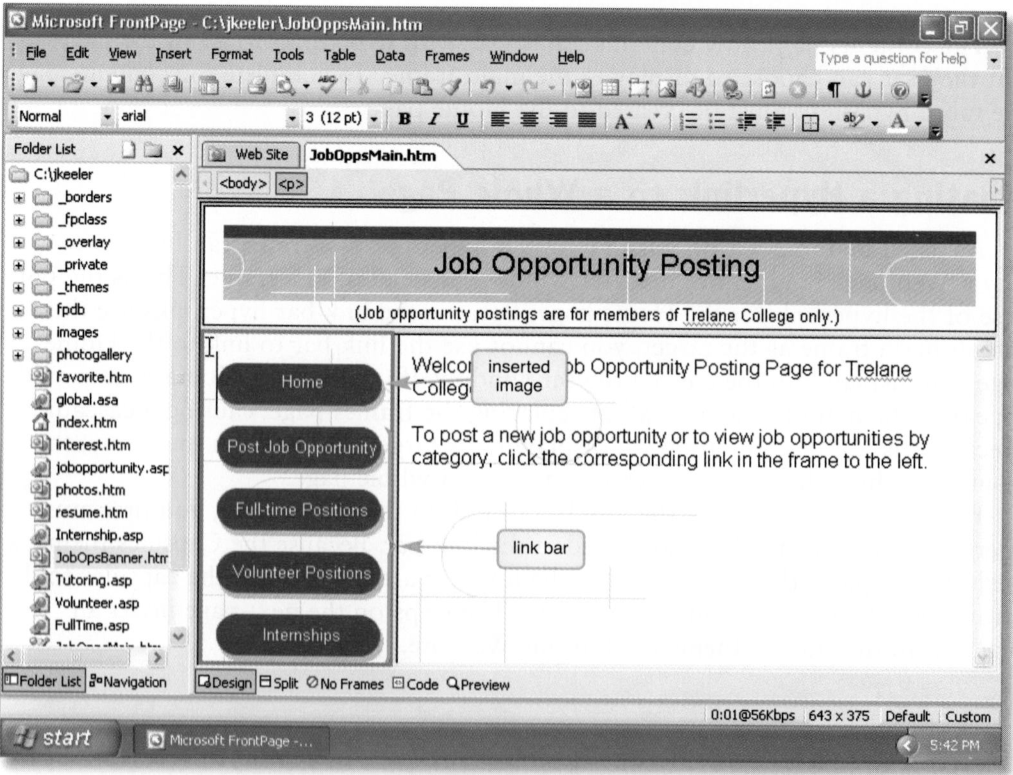

FIGURE 5-56

Now that the image has been placed in the page, a hyperlink can be inserted that links to the Home page and targets the whole frames page, not just a single frame. The following steps create a hyperlink with the target frame set as a whole page.

To Create a Hyperlink to a Whole Page

1

- **Right-click the Home image, not the text, and then click Hyperlink on the shortcut menu.**
- **When FrontPage displays the Insert Hyperlink dialog box, click index.htm and then point to the Target Frame button.**

FrontPage displays the Insert Hyperlink dialog box (Figure 5-57). The file, index.htm, is selected as the linked page.

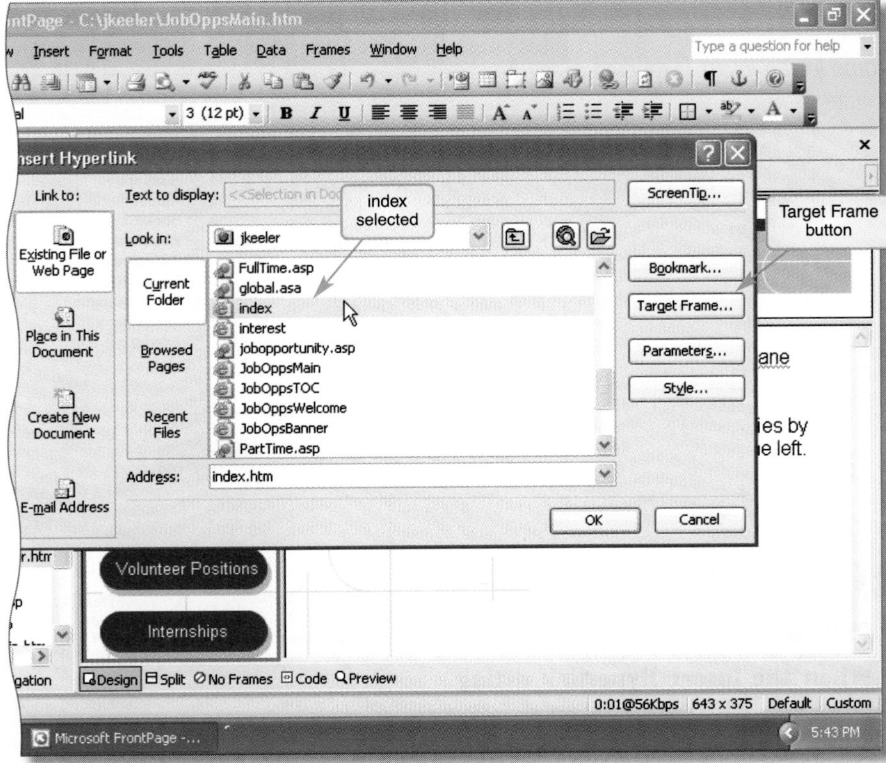

FIGURE 5-57

2

- **Click the Target Frame button.**
- **When FrontPage displays the Target Frame dialog box, click Whole Page in the Common targets area.**

FrontPage displays the Target Frame dialog box (Figure 5-58). When Whole Page is selected, FrontPage automatically enters _top in the Target setting text box.

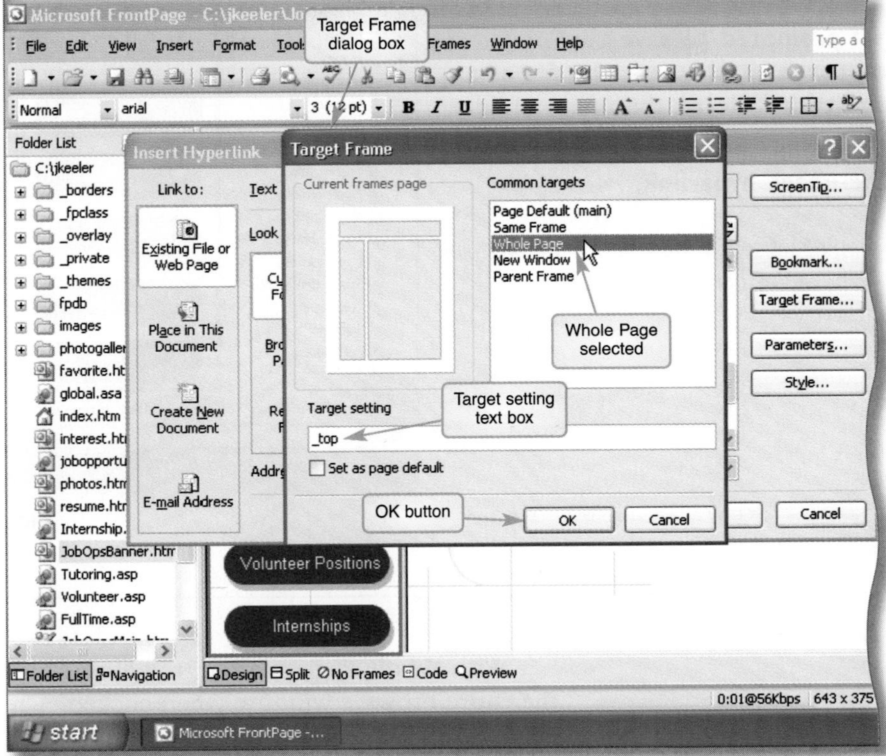

FIGURE 5-58

3

- **Click the OK button.**

The Target Frame dialog box closes. FrontPage displays the selected target frame in the Insert Hyperlink dialog box (Figure 5-59).

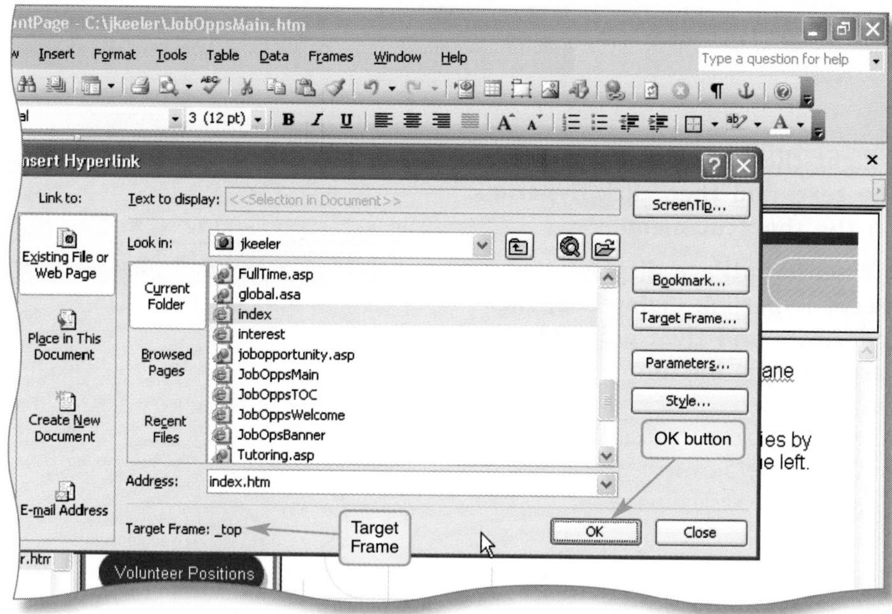

FIGURE 5-59

4

- **Click the OK button.**
- **When the Insert Hyperlink dialog box closes, click the contents frame, to the left of the Link bar component, to deselect the image.**
- **Click the Save button on the Standard toolbar.**
- **If prompted to save the capnavva.gif file, save the file as an embedded file to the images folder.**
- **Position the mouse pointer over the image hyperlink.**

FrontPage displays the URL for the hyperlink on the status bar (Figure 5-60).

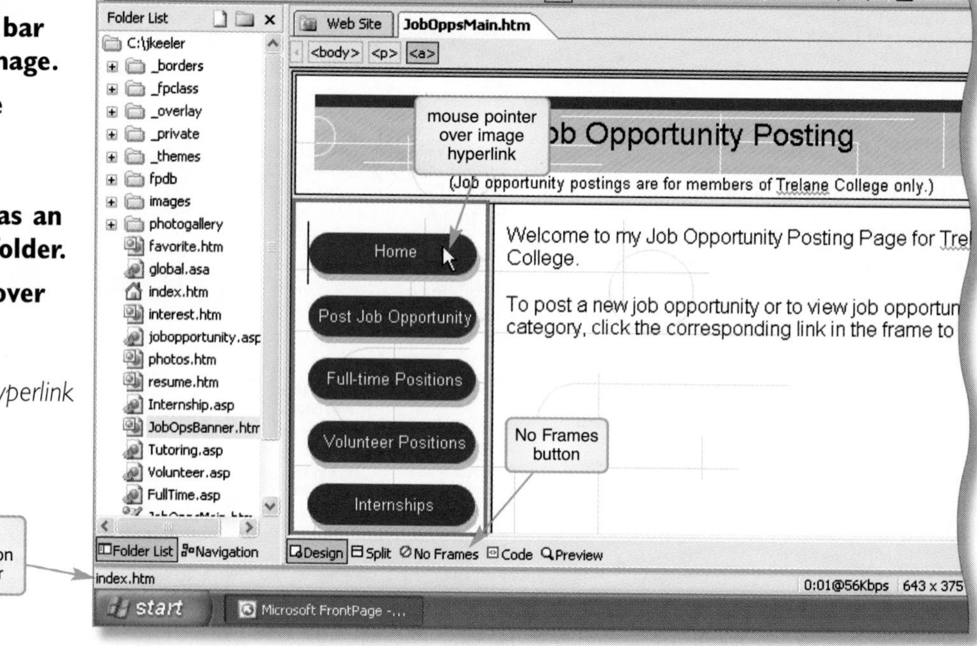

FIGURE 5-60

With Whole Page selected, the Home hyperlink now displays the Home page in the entire browser window when clicked. The Current frames page area, shown in the Target Frame dialog box in Figure 5-58 on the previous page, displays a map of the frames page. When specifying a target frame using the Target Frame dialog box, you can click the target frame in this map or type the name of the target frame in the Target setting text box. The name of that frame then appears in the Target setting field.

Click Set as page default at the bottom of the Target Frame dialog box in Figure 5-58 to make the selected target frame the default for all hyperlinks on the current active Web page.

All of the initial pages and hyperlinks to pages in the frames page have been created. The frames page is almost complete. Next, you will view the HTML code in the No Frames view, to view what is displayed to users with browsers that do not support frames.

More About

No Frames View

HTML code inserted into the No Frames View is displayed only in browsers that do not accommodate frames pages. Browsers that are frames-compatible do not display this view. To allow your users to select whether to view frames, include a hyperlink on the frames page to a version of your page that does not use frames.

Displaying the No Frames View

Initially, only the Netscape Navigator 2.0 browser supported frames. Since then, support for frames has been added to virtually all modern browsers. It is possible, however, that some users still use older versions of browsers that do not support frames. If a user displays a frames page in a browser that does not support frames, special no-frames HTML code is displayed instead.

The **no-frames HTML code** is contained inside the frames Web page and usually advises a user that his or her browser does not support frames. The no-frames HTML can define a complete, no-frames Web page and supply hyperlinks to other no-frames versions of the Web pages used in your frames page. You can customize the no-frames HTML code by displaying the No Frames view. The following steps display the No Frames view.

To Display the No Frames View

1

- **Click the No Frames tab at the bottom of the FrontPage window.**

FrontPage displays the Web page in No Frames view (Figure 5-61). A message is displayed to the user, stating that the page uses frames, which the user's browser does not support.

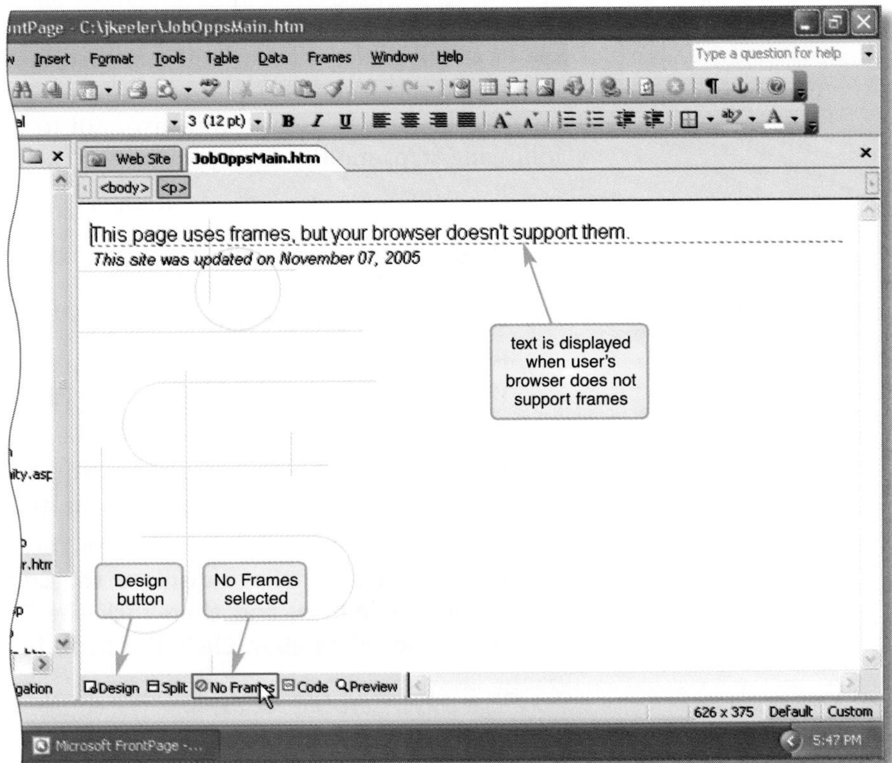

FIGURE 5-61

2

• **Click the Design button.**

FrontPage redisplays the Web page in Design view (Figure 5-62).

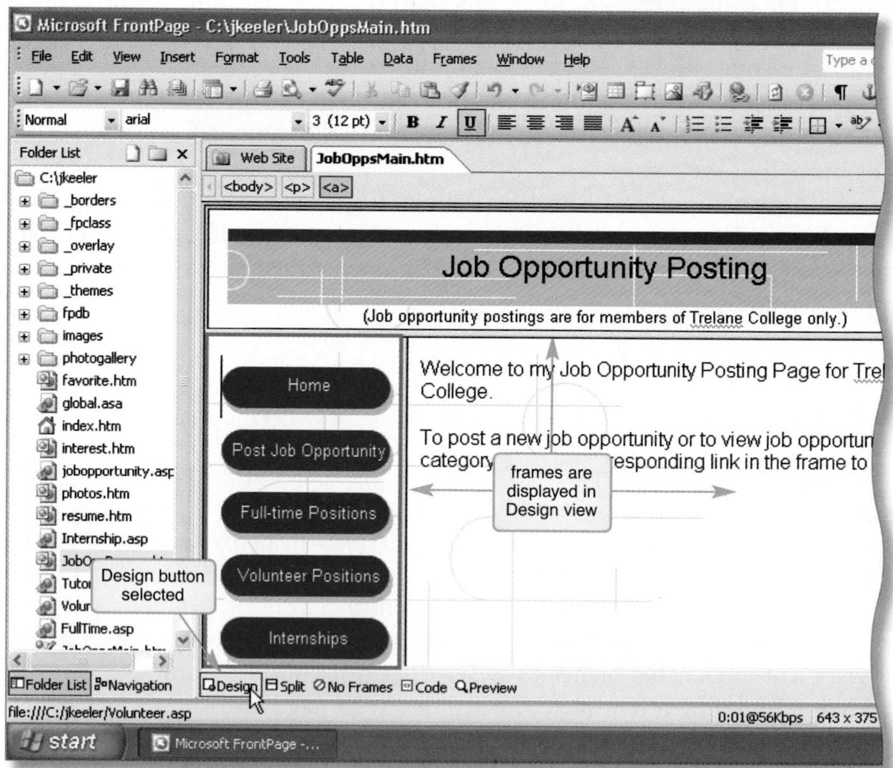

FIGURE 5-62

You can edit the no-frames HTML code as you would any other Web page. This feature is becoming less important as the use of the older browsers diminishes.

Now that you have a completed frames page, you must modify the hyperlink on the Home page. Recall that you modified the original Job Opportunity Posting page, jobopportunity.asp, to incorporate it into a frame. The hyperlink on the Home page links to the page jobopportunity.asp, not to the frames page, JobOppsMain.htm. The following steps modify the hyperlink on the Home page to link to the frames page.

To Modify a Hyperlink to Link to a Frames Page

1. **Double-click the index.htm file in the Folder List pane to display the Home page in Design view.**
2. **If necessary, scroll down, and drag through the text, Post a, and then type** `Visit my` **as the replacement text.**
3. **Drag through the text, Opportunity, in the hyperlink and then type** `Opportunities` **as the replacement text.**
4. **Right-click the hyperlink and then click Hyperlink Properties on the shortcut menu. When FrontPage displays the Edit Hyperlink dialog box, click the file, JobOppsMain.htm, and then click the OK button. Click the Save button on the Standard toolbar. Click the hyperlink to remove the selection.**

FrontPage displays the URL for the hyperlink on the status bar (Figure 5-63).

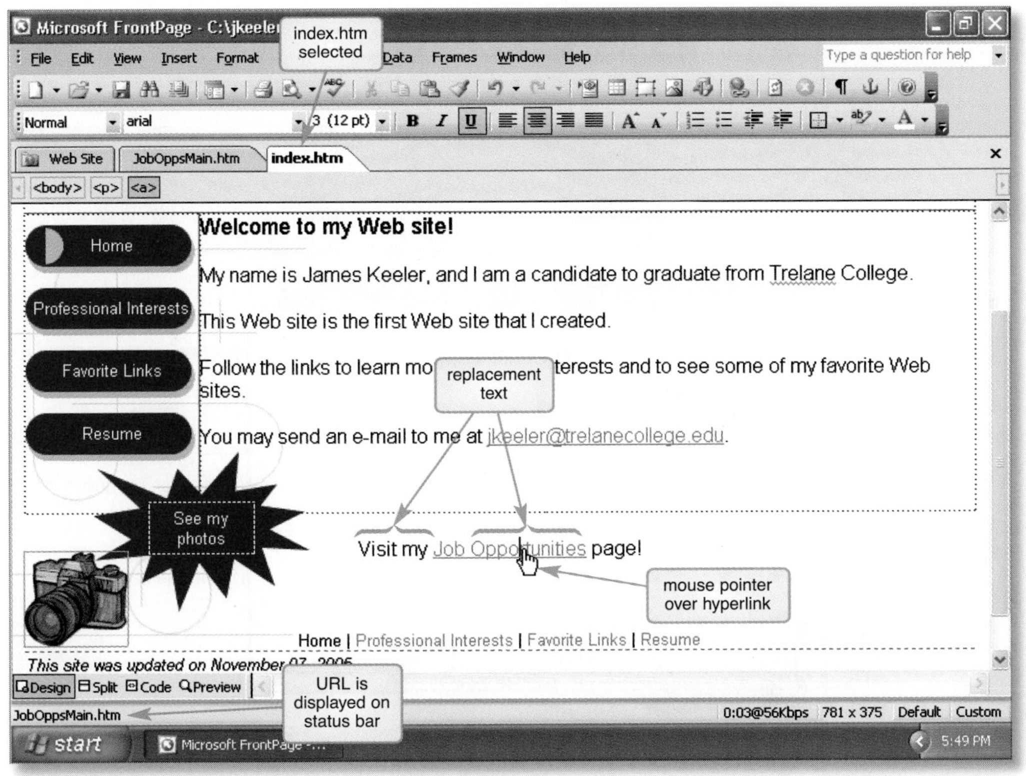

FIGURE 5-63

Printing Web Pages in Frames

Once all of the pages in the frames have been saved, you can print them. You cannot print the entire frames page at one time, however. Instead, you must print each individual Web page in a frame. You do this by clicking the frame containing the desired Web page to make it the active frame, and then printing that individual Web page.

FrontPage and most browsers do not support printing multiple frames at the same time. For this reason, when designing a Web page with frames, try to combine a region of information that a user may want to print within a single frame, rather than requiring that a user print multiple frames.

To display the different Web pages in the main frame so you can print them, the hyperlinks in the contents frame must be clicked. The steps on the next page print all the separate pages that appear in the Job Opportunities frames page.

To Print the Web Pages in Frames

1

- **Ready the printer.**
- **Click the JobOppsMain.htm tab.**
- **Click the banner frame.**
- **Click File on the menu bar and then click Print.**

The banner frame becomes the active frame and the Print dialog box is displayed (Figure 5-64).

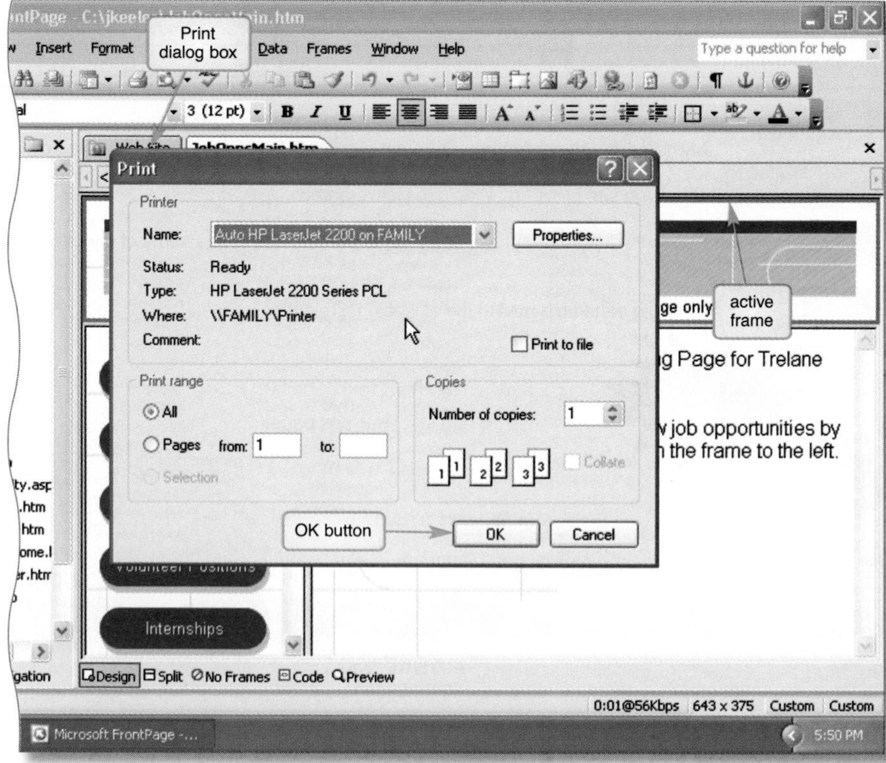

FIGURE 5-64

2

- **Click the OK button.**
- **Click the contents frame to make it the current active frame.**

The Web page in the top frame prints and the contents frame becomes the active frame (Figure 5-65).

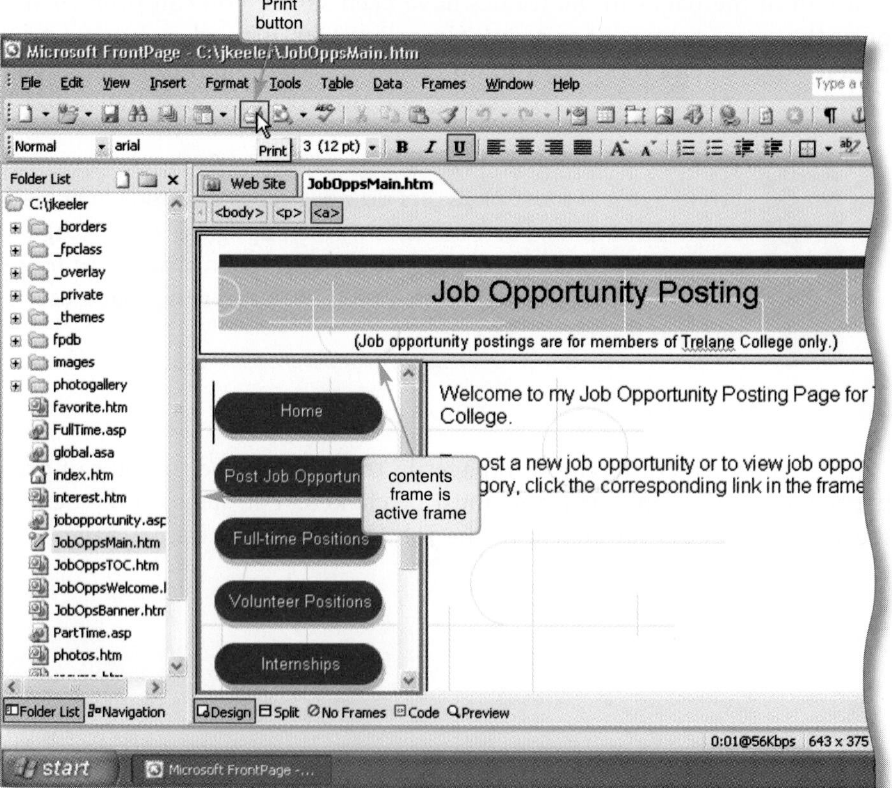

FIGURE 5-65

3

- **Click the Print button.**
- **Click the main frame to make it the current active frame.**

The Web page in the contents frame prints and the main frame becomes the active frame (Figure 5-66). FrontPage displays the Job Opportunity Posting Welcome page in the main frame.

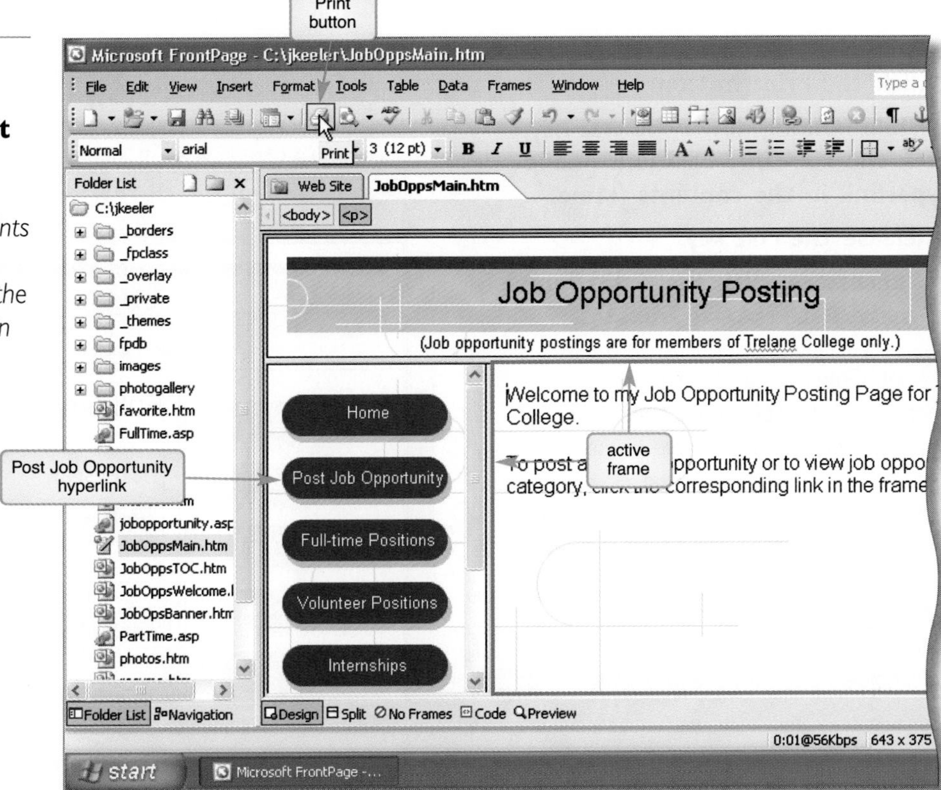

FIGURE 5-66

4

- **Click the Print button.**
- **While holding down the CTRL key, click the Post Job Opportunity image hyperlink in the contents frame.**
- **Release the CTRL key.**
- **If necessary, click the right frame to make it the active frame.**

The Job Opportunity Posting Welcome page prints and the modified Job Opportunity Posting Web page is displayed in the main frame (Figure 5-67). Earlier, the page banner was removed from this page because it would be redundant with the banner frame contents.

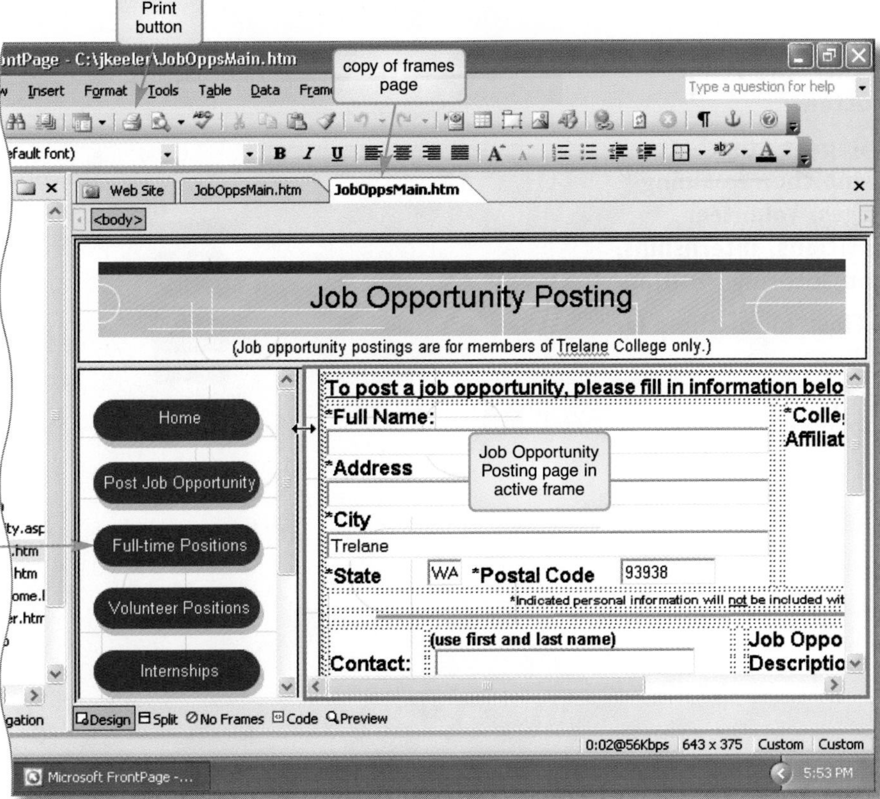

FIGURE 5-67

5

- **Click the Print button.**
- **While holding down the CTRL key, click the Full-time Positions image hyperlink in the contents frame.**
- **Release the CTRL key.**
- **If necessary, click the right frame to make it the active frame.**

The Job Opportunity Postings page is printed and the Full-time Positions Web page is displayed in the main frame (Figure 5-68). Pages displaying database results must be retrieved from a Web server to display actual data. Until the Web site is published, the database column value placeholders appear instead of data.

FIGURE 5-68

6

- **Click the Print button.**
- **Repeat Step 5 to print the remaining pages, Volunteer Positions, Internships, and Tutoring Positions.**
- **Close all of the pages.**

When the printer stops, retrieve the printouts (Figure 5-69).

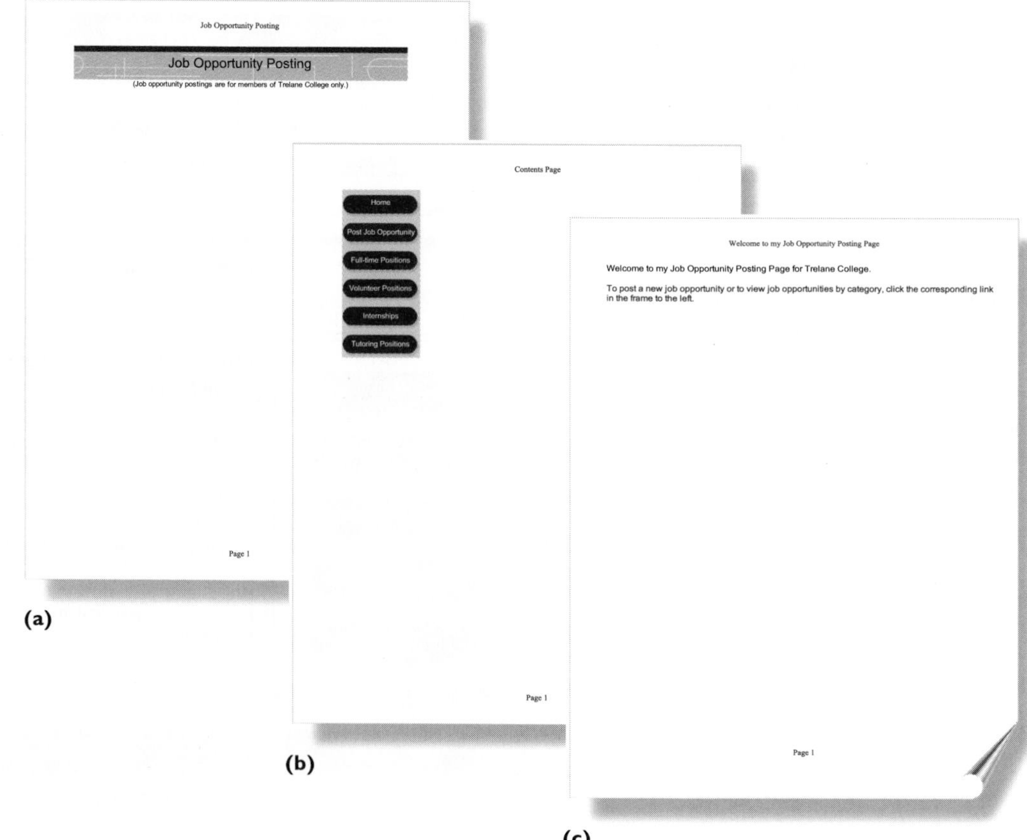

FIGURE 5-69

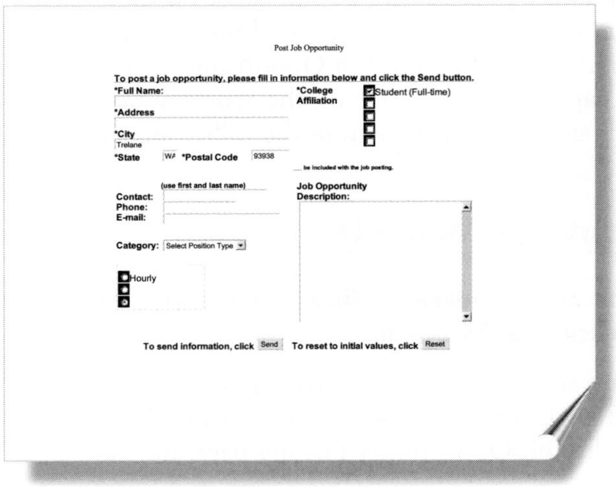

Post Job Opportunity

To post a job opportunity, please fill in information below and click the Send button.

***Full Name:**

***College Affiliation** Student (Full-time)

***Address**

***City**

Trelane

***State** WA ***Postal Code** 93938

be included with the job posting.

(use first and last name)

Contact:
Phone:
E-mail:

Job Opportunity Description:

Category: Select Position Type

Hourly

To send information, click Send **To reset to initial values, click** Reset

(d)

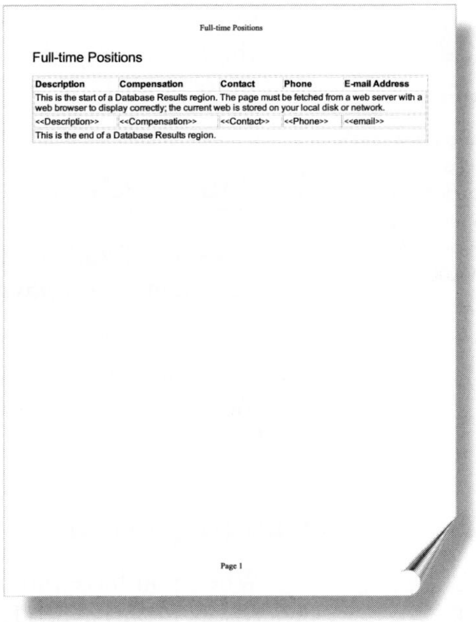

Full-time Positions

Full-time Positions

Description	Compensation	Contact	Phone	E-mail Address
This is the start of a Database Results region. The page must be fetched from a web server with a web browser to display correctly; the current web is stored on your local disk or network.				
<<Description>>	<<Compensation>>	<<Contact>>	<<Phone>>	<<email>>
This is the end of a Database Results region.				

Page 1

(e)

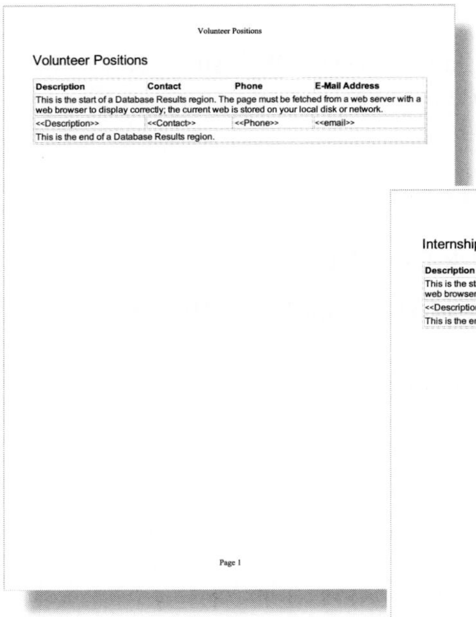

Volunteer Positions

Volunteer Positions

Description	Contact	Phone	E-Mail Address
This is the start of a Database Results region. The page must be fetched from a web server with a web browser to display correctly; the current web is stored on your local disk or network.			
<<Description>>	<<Contact>>	<<Phone>>	<<email>>
This is the end of a Database Results region.			

Page 1

(f)

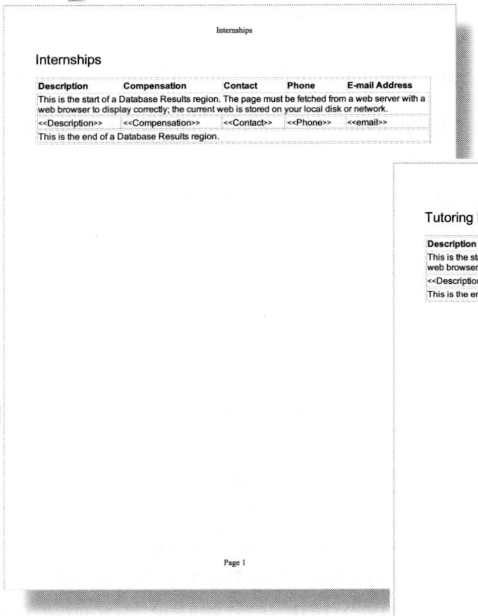

Internships

Internships

Description	Compensation	Contact	Phone	E-mail Address
This is the start of a Database Results region. The page must be fetched from a web server with a web browser to display correctly; the current web is stored on your local disk or network.				
<<Description>>	<<Compensation>>	<<Contact>>	<<Phone>>	<<email>>
This is the end of a Database Results region.				

Page 1

(g)

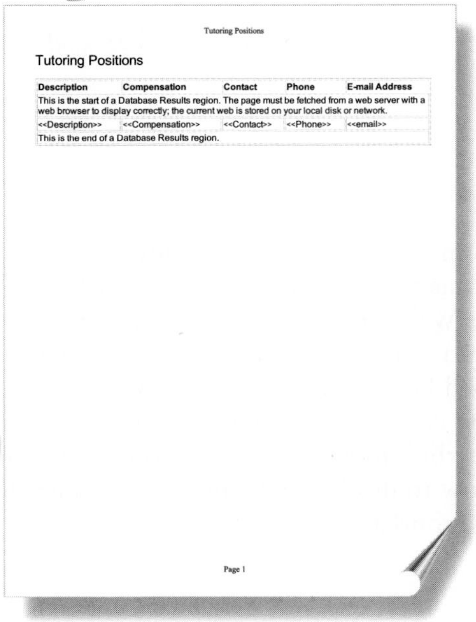

Tutoring Positions

Tutoring Positions

Description	Compensation	Contact	Phone	E-mail Address
This is the start of a Database Results region. The page must be fetched from a web server with a web browser to display correctly; the current web is stored on your local disk or network.				
<<Description>>	<<Compensation>>	<<Contact>>	<<Phone>>	<<email>>
This is the end of a Database Results region.				

Page 1

(h)

FIGURE 5-69

More About

Quick Reference

For more information, see the Quick Reference Summary at the back of this book, or visit the FrontPage 2003 Quick Reference Web page (scsite.com/fp2003/qr).

In this project, you have imported Web pages to the FrontPage Web site, added a frames page, set or created three initial Web pages, and created the Full-time Positions database results page. You also modified the Job Opportunity Posting page and the Home page. For these Web pages to be available on the World Wide Web, you must publish the FrontPage Web site again, as shown in the following step.

To Publish Changes to a FrontPage Web Site

1. **Click the Publish Site button on the Standard toolbar. If necessary, type your user name and password and click the OK button.**

You now can view the changes by entering http://www.trelanecollege.edu/~jkeeler/index.htm (or use your own URL) in any browser and pressing the ENTER key. Be sure to test the hyperlink to the Job Opportunity Posting page and each of the hyperlinks on that page.

Quitting FrontPage

When you have published the changes to James Keeler's Web site, you can quit Microsoft FrontPage. The following steps close the Web site and quit FrontPage.

To Close a Web Site and Quit FrontPage

1. **Click File on the menu bar and then click Close Site.**
2. **Click the Close button on the right side of the FrontPage title bar.**

The FrontPage window closes and the Windows desktop is displayed.

Project Summary

Having completed Project 5, you now are ready to incorporate frames and database results in your own Web pages. In this project, you learned about frames and how you can use them. You imported Web pages into a FrontPage Web site. You learned how to use the Database Results Wizard and to create a custom SQL query to retrieve information from a relational database. The project demonstrated how to use a frames page template. You learned how to set an existing Web page as the initial Web page in a frame and how to modify the size of a frame. You created a new initial Web page for a frame, and then you created hyperlinks to Web pages in frames and a hyperlink to a whole page. You learned how to modify properties of a frame and of a frames page. You learned how to display and edit the no-frames HTML code. Finally, you learned how to print pages within frames in FrontPage.

What You Should Know

Having completed this project, you should be able to perform the tasks below. The tasks are listed in the same order they were presented in this project. For a list of the buttons, menus, toolbars, and commands introduced in this project, see the Quick Reference Summary at the back of this book and refer to the Page Number column.

1. Start FrontPage and Open an Existing Web Site (FP 347)
2. Import Files into an Existing FrontPage Web Site (FP 348)
3. Create a Database Results Region and Custom SQL Query (FP 351)
4. Create a Frames Page Using a Frames Page Template (FP 359)
5. Save the Frames Web Page (FP 361)
6. Set an Existing Web Page as the Initial Page in a Frame (FP 364)
7. Modify the Size of a Frame (FP 367)
8. Save Changes to the Frames Page (FP 367)
9. Create a New Web Page for the Initial Page in a Frame (FP 368)
10. Insert Text in the Initial Page for the Main Frame (FP 368)
11. Save the Initial Page for the Main Frame (FP 369)
12. Create the Initial Page for the Contents Frame (FP 372)
13. Modify the Properties of a Frame (FP 373)
14. Modify the Properties of the Frames Page (FP 374)
15. Create a Link Bar Targeting the Default Frame (FP 378)
16. Insert an Image from the Current Theme (FP 380)
17. Create a Hyperlink to a Whole Page (FP 381)
18. Display the No Frames View (FP 383)
19. Modify a Hyperlink to Link to a Frames Page (FP 384)
20. Print the Web Pages in Frames (FP 386)
21. Publish Changes to a FrontPage Web Site (FP 390)
22. Close a Web Site and Quit FrontPage (FP 390)

Learn It Online

Instructions: To complete the Learn It Online exercises, start your browser, click the Address bar, and then enter the Web address scsite.com/fp2003/learn. When the FrontPage 2003 Learn It Online page is displayed, follow the instructions in the exercises below. Each exercise has instructions for printing your results, either for your own records or for submission to your instructor.

1 Project Reinforcement TF, MC, and SA

Below FrontPage Project 5, click the Project Reinforcement link. Print the quiz by clicking Print on the File menu for each page. Answer each question.

2 Flash Cards

Below FrontPage Project 5, click the Flash Cards link and read the instructions. Type 20 (or a number specified by your instructor) in the Number of playing cards text box, type your name in the Enter your Name text box, and then click the Flip Card button. When the flash card is displayed, read the question and then click the ANSWER box arrow to select an answer. Flip through Flash Cards. If your score is 15 (75%) correct or greater, click Print on the File menu to print your results. If your score is less than 15 (75%) correct, then redo this exercise by clicking the Replay button.

3 Practice Test

Below FrontPage Project 5, click the Practice Test link. Answer each question, enter your first and last name at the bottom of the page, and then click the Grade Test button. When the graded practice test is displayed on your screen, click Print on the File menu to print a hard copy. Continue to take practice tests until you score 80% or better.

4 Who Wants To Be a Computer Genius?

Below FrontPage Project 5, click the Computer Genius link. Read the instructions, enter your first and last name at the bottom of the page, and then click the PLAY button. When your score is displayed, click the PRINT RESULTS link to print a hard copy.

5 Wheel of Terms

Below FrontPage Project 5, click the Wheel of Terms link. Read the instructions, and then enter your first and last name and your school name. Click the PLAY button. When your score is displayed, right-click the score and then click Print on the shortcut menu to print a hard copy.

6 Crossword Puzzle Challenge

Below FrontPage Project 5, click the Crossword Puzzle Challenge link. Read the instructions, and then enter your first and last name. Click the SUBMIT button. Work the crossword puzzle. When you are finished, click the Submit button. When the crossword puzzle is redisplayed, click the Print Puzzle button to print a hard copy.

7 Tips and Tricks

Below FrontPage Project 5, click the Tips and Tricks link. Click a topic that pertains to Project 5. Right-click the information and then click Print on the shortcut menu. Construct a brief example of what the information relates to in FrontPage to confirm you understand how to use the tip or trick.

8 Newsgroups

Below FrontPage Project 5, click the Newsgroups link. Click a topic that pertains to Project 5. Print three comments.

9 Expanding Your Horizons

Below FrontPage Project 5, click the Expanding Your Horizons link. Click a topic that pertains to Project 5. Print the information. Construct a brief example of what the information relates to in FrontPage to confirm you understand the contents of the article.

10 Search Sleuth

Below FrontPage Project 5, click the Search Sleuth link. To search for a term that pertains to this project, select a term below the Project 5 title and then use the Google search engine at google.com (or any major search engine) to display and print two Web pages that present information on the term.

11 FrontPage Online Training

Below FrontPage Project 5, click the FrontPage Online Training link. When your browser displays the Microsoft Office Online Web page, click the FrontPage link. Click one of the FrontPage courses that covers one or more of the objectives listed at the beginning of the project on page FP 340. Print the first page of the course before stepping through it.

12 Office Marketplace

Below FrontPage Project 5, click the Office Marketplace link. When your browser displays the Microsoft Office Online Web page, click the Office Marketplace link. Click a topic that relates to FrontPage. Print the first page.

Apply Your Knowledge

1 Creating a New Frames Page Template

Instructions: Perform the following tasks.

1. Start FrontPage. Click the Create a new normal page button arrow and then click Page on the Create a new normal page menu. When the Page Templates dialog box appears, click the Frames Pages tab. Click the Header, Footer and Contents icon. Click the OK button.
2. A new frames page is displayed with four frames. If the top frame is not the currently selected frame, click that frame to select it.
3. Click Frames on the menu bar and then click Delete Frame. The top frame is deleted and the outline is around the entire outer frame.
4. Click File on the menu bar and then click Save As. When the Save As dialog box appears, click the Save as type box arrow. Click FrontPage Template in the list. Type `footerTOC.tem` in the File name text box. If necessary, change the folder where the template is saved to the Project5 folder on the Data Disk. Click the Save button in the Save As dialog box.
5. When the Save As Template dialog box appears, type `Footer and Contents` in the Title text box. This title is displayed when accessing the template to create a new page.
6. In the Description text box, drag through the text, Type your description here., to select it. Type `Creates a Contents frame on the left which directs hyperlinks to change the main page on the right by default. Hyperlinks in the Footer change the Contents frame by default.` to enter a short description of what this frames page template does. Click the OK button. Close the Web page.
7. Create a new Web page using the template you have just created. The new frames page template should appear as the Footer and Contents template in the Frames Pages sheet, as shown in Figure 5-70. The title you entered should show with a new frames page icon, and the description you typed should show in the Description area. A preview of the frames page should appear.
8. Test the new page to verify that hyperlinks in the contents frame target the contents of the main frame, and that links in the footer frame target the contents frame.
9. Save the Web page as index.htm. Print the Web page, write your name on it, and hand it in to your instructor. Close the Web page and then quit FrontPage.

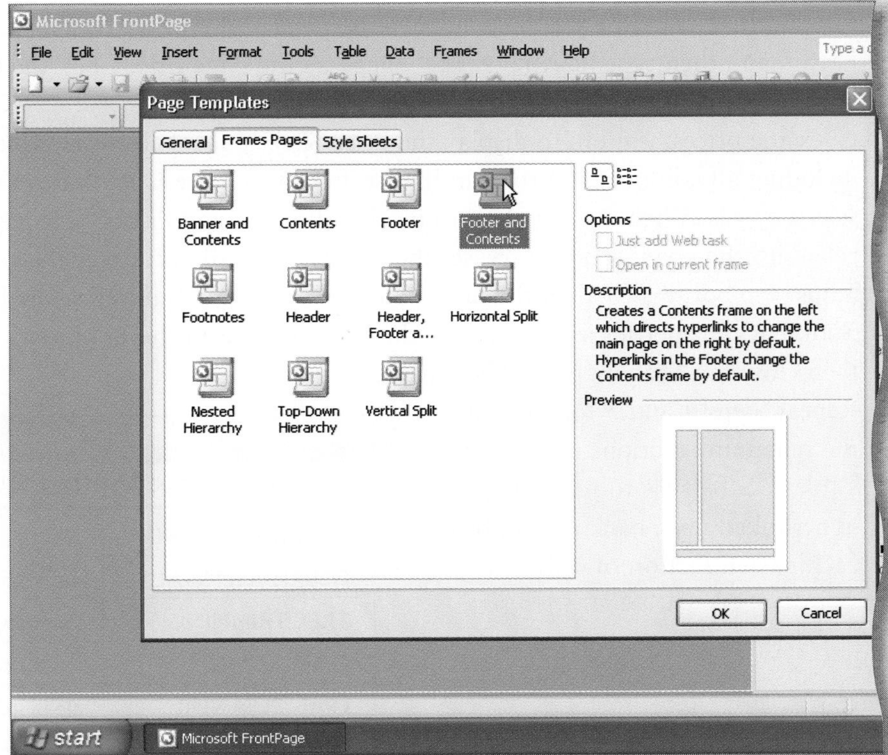

FIGURE 5-70

1 Modify an Existing Web Site to Use Frames

Problem: The price list created earlier for Fairway Lawn Care has all items on one Web page. Different people are responsible for price updates in different categories, so you decide to use frames with separate pages for each service category.

Instructions: Perform the following tasks.

1. Open the Fairway Lawn Care Web site that you modified in Project 4. If you did not complete that exercise for Project 4, see your instructor for a copy of the required files.
2. If necessary, double-click the file, prices.htm, to open the Price Sheet page. Click Page on the Create a new normal page menu. When the Page Templates dialog box appears, click the Frames Pages tab and then, if necessary, click the Banner and Contents icon. Click the OK button. Save the frames page and type `pricesFrames` as the file name. Click the Change title button. When the Set Page Title dialog box appears, type `Price Sheet frames page` as the new title text. Click the OK button in the Set Page Title dialog box. Click the Save button in the Save As dialog box.
3. Click the New Page button in the top (banner) frame. Insert a Page Banner component. Save the banner page and type `pricesBanner` as the file name. Change the page title and type `Price Sheet Banner` as the new title text. In Navigation view, drag and drop the file, pricesFrames.htm, to the left and below the Services icon.
4. In Design view, click the Create a new normal page button. Because this Web site applies shared borders to new pages by default, the shared borders must be removed from the page before using the page in a frame. Right-click the page and then click Page Properties on the shortcut menu. Click the Custom tab in the Page Properties dialog box. In the User variables area, select the name, Microsoft Border. Click the Remove button and then click the OK button. Save the page and type `mowing` as the file name. Click the Change title button and then type `Mowing Price Sheet` as the page title. Click the OK button in the Set Page Title dialog box. Click the Save button in the Save As dialog box.
5. Click the prices.htm tab to display the Price Sheet page. Select the table cells for the MOWING section, including all columns and rows in that section. Click the Copy button on the Standard toolbar to copy the selected cells. Click mowing.htm to display the Mowing Price Sheet page and then paste the copied table cells into the page. If necessary, set the font size for all text except the section title to 3 (12 pt). If necessary, adjust the borders to align the table contents properly. Right-click the bookmarked text, MOWING. Click Bookmark Properties and then click the Clear button in the Bookmark dialog box. Save your changes and then close the Mowing Price Sheet page.
6. Repeat Steps 4 and 5 for each of the remaining sections as listed in Table 5-2. Be sure to remove the hyperlinked text, back to top, from each pasted section of cells.

Table 5-2 Price Sheet File Sections and Titles

SECTION TO COPY	FILE NAME	PAGE TITLE
SHRUB TRIMMING	shrub.htm	Shrub Trimming Price Sheet
DEBRIS REMOVAL	debris.htm	Debris Removal Price Sheet
TREE TRIMMING	trimming.htm	Tree Trimming Price Sheet
FERTILIZING	fertilizing.htm	Fertilizing Price Sheet
LEAF CLEANUP	cleanup.htm	Leaf Cleanup Price Sheet

7. Click the pricesFrames.htm tab. Click the New Page button in the left (contents) frame. Insert a Navigation component based on the navigation structure. Create links to pages at the child level. Save the page, type `pricesTOC` as the file name, and type `Price Sheet Contents` as the page title. In Navigation view, drag and drop the file, pricesFrames.htm, below the Services icon and to the right of the Business Grounds Keeping icon. In Navigation view, drag and drop the file, pricesTOC.htm, below the Price Sheet frames page icon. Drag and drop each of the files listed in Table 5-2 and the mowing.htm Web page below the Price Sheet Contents icon. Modify the page labels as listed in Table 5-3. Drag and drop the file, pricesBanner.htm, to the left and below the Leaf Cleanup icon. In Design view, modify the frame size on the frames page to display the page banner.

Table 5-3 Price Sheet Page Labels

FILE NAME	PAGE LABEL
mowing.htm	Mowing
shrub.htm	Shrub Trimming
debris.htm	Debris Removal
trimming.htm	Tree Trimming
fertilizing.htm	Fertilizing
cleanup.htm	Leaf Cleanup
pricesFrames.htm	Price Sheet

8. Close the prices.htm page and delete the file, prices.htm, from the Web site. Position the insertion point at the top and left of the link bar and then insert the image, chhbs .gif, from the checkers folder within the _themes folder. Using the image, insert a hyperlink to the Home page, using Whole Page as the target. If you cannot access hidden folders, obtain the file from the Project5 folder on the Data Disk. If necessary, adjust the width of the contents frame of the frames page.
9. Click the New Page button in the right (main) frame. Type `Select a category in the left frame to view the corresponding price sheet.` and then save the page. Type `pricesMain` as the file name and type `Price Sheets main page` as the page title.
10. If necessary, save all changes. Print the contents, banner, and initial main frame pages as well as each of the pages linked by the link bar (Figure 5-71 on the next page). Write your name on the pages, and hand them in to your instructor. Close the Web site and then quit FrontPage.

(continued)

Modify an Existing Web Site to Use Frames *(continued)*

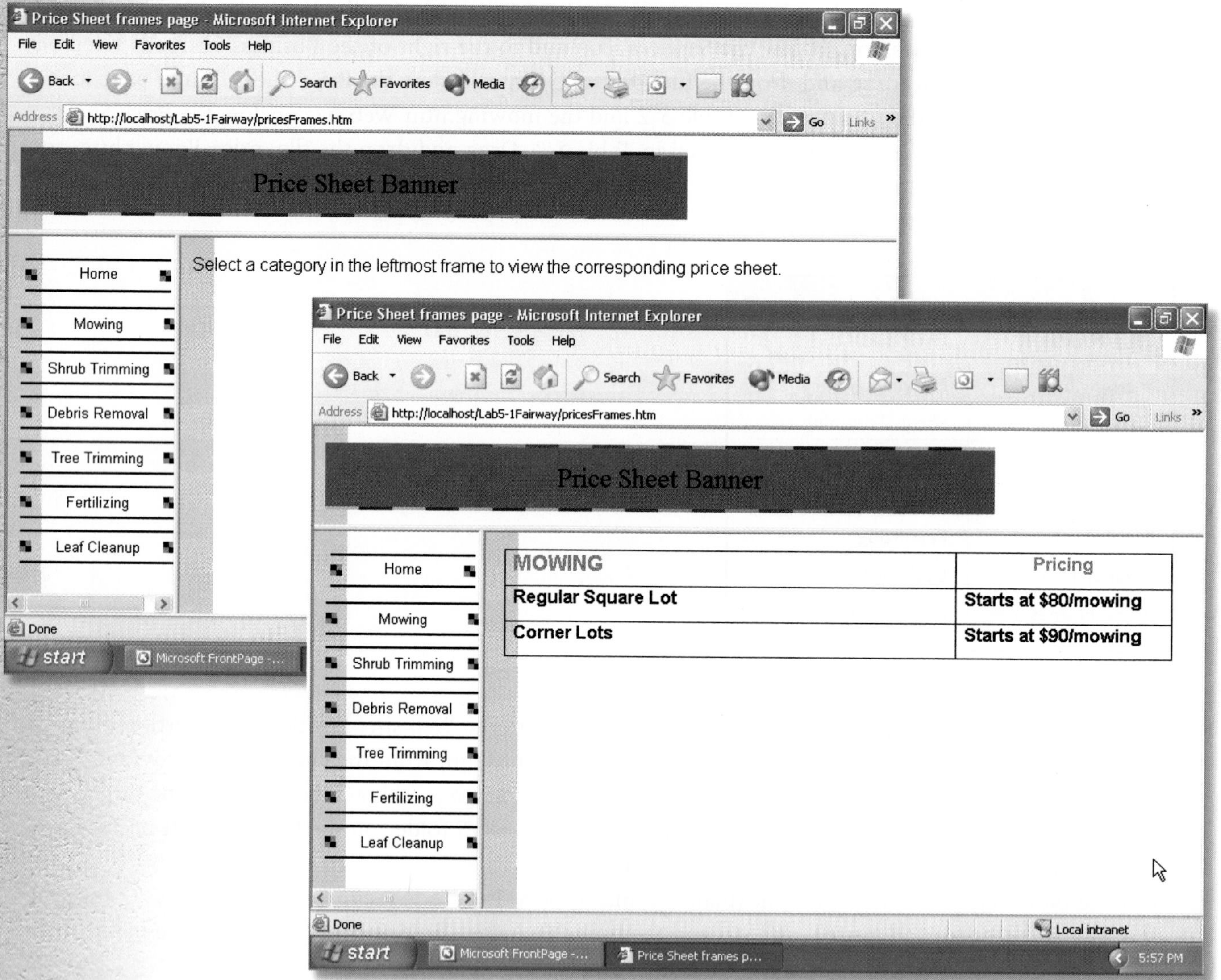

FIGURE 5-71

2 Adding a Database Results Page to a Web Site

Problem: You have a products database created by another process and would like to display information from the database to visitors of your Web site. You decide to incorporate a Database Results region and test it with a smaller sample database of the same format.

Instructions: Perform the following tasks.

1. Open the Web site, Ship-It-Here, that you modified in Project 4. If you did not complete that exercise for Project 4, see your instructor for a copy of the required files.

2. Create a new normal page. On the File menu, click Import. When the Import dialog box appears, add the sample database file, Supplies.mdb, to the Web site.
3. When the Add Database Connection dialog box appears, type `Supplies` in the Name text box and then click the Yes button. Import the resulting database file into the fpdb folder.
4. Using the Database Results Wizard, insert a Database Results region using the existing database connection of Supplies. Select Products in the Record source list.
5. Edit the list of database fields to exclude specific fields. Select and remove all fields except Category, ProductID, Description, and Weight.
6. Click the More Options button. When the More Options dialog box appears, click the Criteria button. When the Criteria dialog box appears, click the Add button to display the Add Criteria dialog box. Click the Field Name box arrow and then click the field name, Category. Select a comparison of Equals. Type `Packing` in the Value text box. Click Use this search form field to remove the selection. Click the OK button and then click the OK button in the Criteria dialog box.
7. When the More Options dialog box again is visible, click the Ordering button. Select ProductID for the Sort order. Display all records together in the results. If necessary, edit the column headings from the defaults. Save the page, type `packing.asp` as the file name, and type `Packing Supplies` as the page title.
8. Edit the page, prod01.htm, and select the text, This paragraph. Type `Packing products` as the replacement text. Select the text and insert a hyperlink to the packing.asp page. Save all changes, publish your page, and test it.
9. Print the results displayed on the Packing products page (Figure 5-72). Write your name on the page and hand it in to your instructor. Close the Web site and then quit FrontPage.

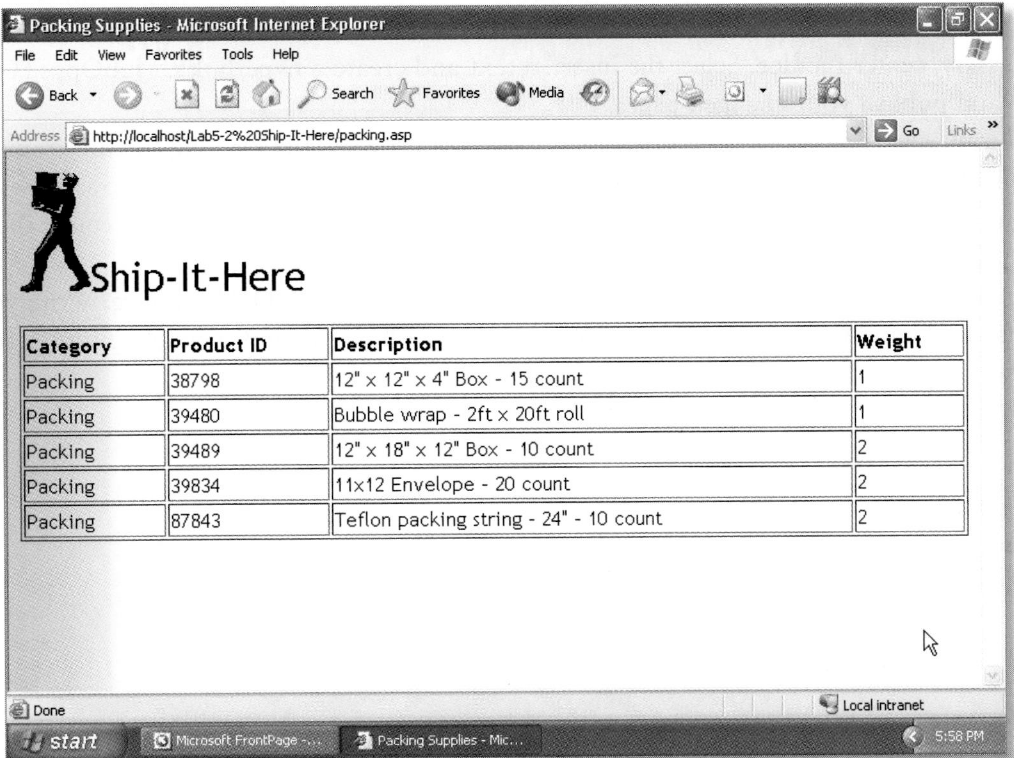

FIGURE 5-72

3 Creating a No-Frames Page

Problem: James Keeler likes the frames used in Project 5, but believes that users should have a choice to not use frames, regardless of the capabilities of their browser. He wants you to add a no-frames version to his Web site.

Instructions: Using James Keeler's Web site from Project 5, perform the following tasks. If you did not complete this exercise in Project 5, see your instructor for a copy of the required files.

1. Open the contents page, JobOppsTOC.htm. Insert a 1 by 3 table at the top of the page. Drag the image hyperlink and link bar and drop them into the left cell. Position the insertion point in the center cell. Hold down the CTRL key and the SHIFT key and then press the SPACEBAR three times to insert three nonbreaking spaces. Position the insertion point in the right cell and then type `To post a new job opportunity or to view job opportunities by category, click the corresponding link in the list to the left.` to enter the cell text. Drag the cell borders to adjust cell widths as needed. Modify the table properties and set the border size to zero. Set the vertical alignment to Top for all of the cells. Save the changes.
2. Open the Job Opportunity Posting main page, JobOppsMain.htm. Right-click the left frame. Click Frame Properties on the shortcut menu. When the Frame Properties dialog box appears, click to deselect Resizable in browser in the Options area. Click the OK button.
3. Click the No Frames button. Position the insertion point after the line that begins, This page uses frames, press the ENTER key, and then type `Use the no-frames version to access the same content.` Select the text, No-frames version, and then insert a hyperlink to JobOppsTOC.htm.
4. Click the Design button. In the index.htm page, position the insertion point below the hyperlink to the Job Opportunity Posting page. Use a font size of 2 (10 pt) and then type `(no-frames version)` to enter the text. If necessary, center the line. Select the inserted text and create a hyperlink to JobOppsTOC.htm. Save all changes and publish your changed pages.
5. Test the no-frames version by viewing the frames page in a browser and clicking the (no-frames version) hyperlink. Each of the hyperlinks should display the corresponding page in a new browser window, except for the Home page link, which returns you to the Home page. Your pages should resemble those shown in Figure 5-73.
6. Print the modified No Frames page, the Home page, and the JobOppsTOC.htm page. Write your name on the printouts, and hand them in to your instructor. Close the Web site and then quit FrontPage.

In the Lab

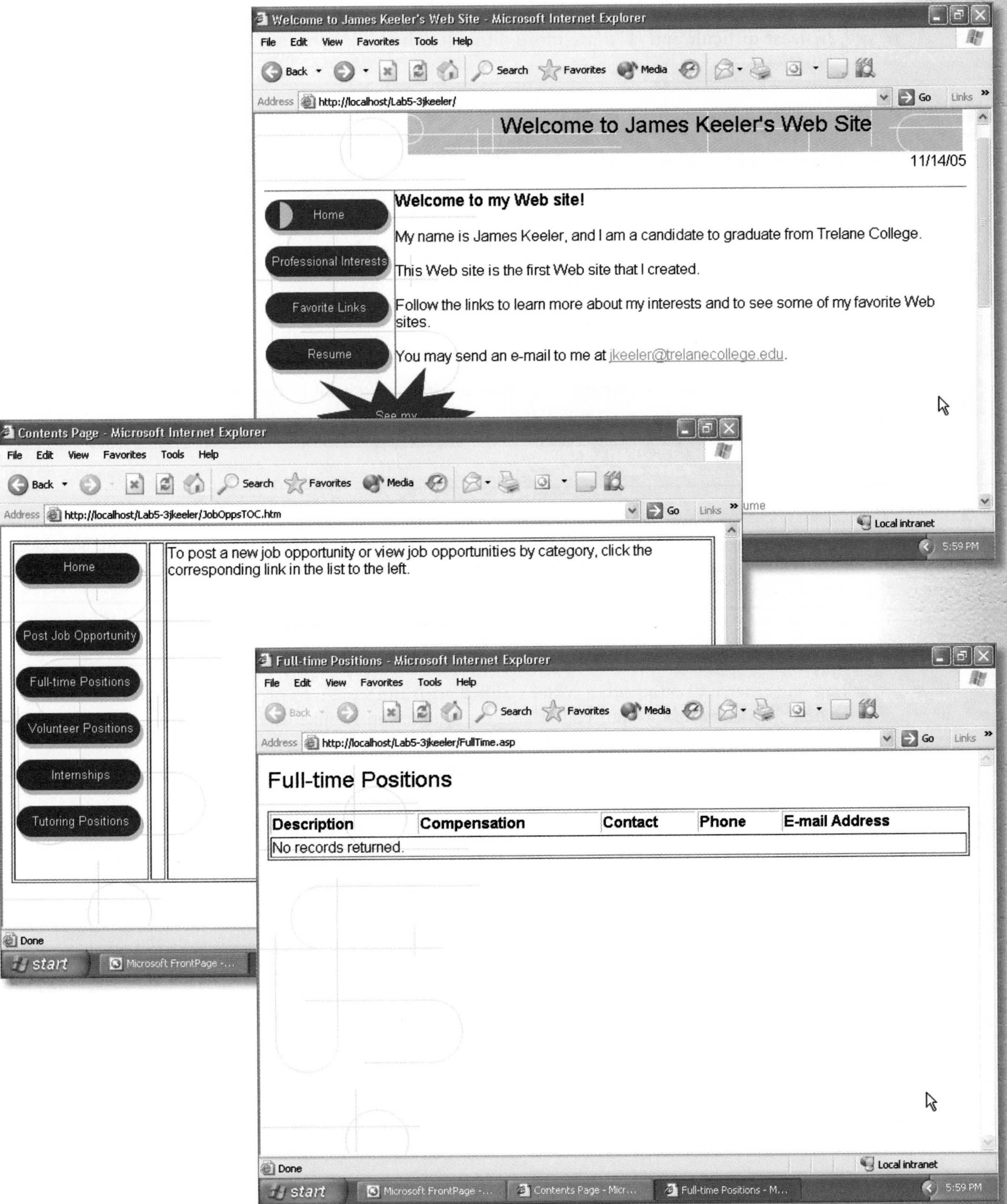

FIGURE 5-73

Cases and Places

The difficulty of these case studies varies:
■ are the least difficult and ■■ are more difficult. The last exercise is a group exercise.

1 ■ Modify your resume page from Project 4 to use frames. Remove the left column with the hyperlinks and place them into a contents frame. Include a hyperlink to the page for suggestions and responses created in the previous project.

2 ■ Modify the Web site for your movie review Web site from Project 4 to use frames for the movie reviews. Remove the shared border from the Web site.

3 ■■ Modify the departmental Web page you created for your school in the previous project to provide results of the instructor evaluations page.

4 ■■ If necessary, create a new frames page template to display a frames page with a main frame, a contents frame, and a footer frame. Incorporate this frames page into your friend's graduation Web site. Add a database results page for the data collected into the database. Include hyperlinks to the pages created in previous projects, as well as the new page.

5 ■■ **Working Together** Create both a frames and a no-frames page to provide access to all forms and pages in the company softball Web page that you updated in Project 4. Create new database results pages to display results previously stored in the database.

MICROSOFT Office FrontPage 2003

Using Subsites, the Database Interface Wizard, and Source Control

PROJECT

CASE PERSPECTIVE

James Keeler is pleased with the success of his Web site. He realizes, however, that some potential problems exist with its construction. James has no way to update or remove outdated or incorrect job opportunity postings without directly manipulating the job opportunity database. Additionally, as the Web site increases in size, the task of managing the site becomes more complex, so James has recruited a friend to help maintain the job opportunity Web pages. James also wants to keep the content from those pages isolated from his personal Web pages.

James asks for your help. You explain that FrontPage has several features to provide solutions. First, he can use a FrontPage wizard to build password-protected Web pages that allow him to add, modify, or delete job opportunity postings stored in the job opportunity database. Next, FrontPage allows for the addition of subsites to an existing Web site, which he can use to organize the job opportunity Web pages to be separate from his personal Web pages. Finally, FrontPage provides source control to ensure that only one person works on a given Web page at a time. James agrees that these are excellent capabilities and asks you to help him incorporate them into his Web site.

As you read through this project, you will learn how to create and manage subsites. You also will learn how to create a new folder in a Web site and convert the folder into a subsite. You will learn how to use Database Editor pages to add, view, update, and delete records in a database. Finally, you will learn how to use source control to protect Web pages as you or others edit the pages.

Using Subsites, the Database Interface Wizard, and Source Control

PROJECT

Objectives

You will have mastered the material in this project when you can:

- Create a new folder in an existing Web site
- Move files and folders into another folder
- Convert a folder to a subsite
- Open a subsite for editing
- Set an existing page as the home page for a Web site
- Use the default page as a hyperlink target
- Use the Database Interface Wizard to create Database Editor pages
- Apply a theme to a subsite
- Publish a Web site and all subsites
- Enable source control for a Web site and subsite
- Check files in and out using source control
- View the Checkout Status report

Introduction

A Web site quickly can grow to include many Web pages and supporting files, such as documents, databases, pictures, and graphics. Effectively managing a Web site can be difficult without some means to organize and update a growing collection of files. Even with a good organizational scheme, if multiple people are maintaining a Web site, changes can be lost if two or more people try to modify the same Web page at the same time.

Managing a Web site with a database also involves making changes to the database to update or delete existing records. The previous two projects demonstrated how to add data to a database and then create Web pages to display selected results, but made no provision for making changes to the database. Web page designers inevitably find that they need to make such changes to add new information or update existing information that is outdated or in error. FrontPage provides several tools and features to help manage a Web site effectively.

Project Six — Using Subsites and the Database Interface Wizard

In this project, folder creation features are presented that show you how to create a folder in an existing FrontPage Web site and then convert the folder into a subsite, named JobOppsSite. A **subsite** is a Web site that is contained within another Web site. A Web site that contains a subsite is called a **parent Web site**. A **root Web site** has no parent Web site and is the default, top-level Web site provided by a Web server. The top-level folder in a root Web site is called a **root folder**. The **home folder** is the top-level folder in a Web site or subsite. Other terms, such as **home directory**, **document root**, and **home root**, as well as root Web site and root folder, often are used interchangeably with the term, home folder.

After the creation of the JobOppsSite subsite, the project illustrates how to organize, edit, and publish a Web site that includes a subsite. This will include setting an existing page as the new home page for the subsite.

You also will learn how to use the Database Interface Wizard to create Web pages for maintaining a database (Figure 6-1). Because it is important to prevent any unauthorized changes to a database, the project demonstrates how to generate a login page to control access by means of a user name and password (Figure 6-1a). Authorized users then can access Web pages to manipulate the data in the database (Figure 6-1b). After adding the Web pages to the subsite using the Database Interface Wizard, applying a theme to the subsite is illustrated. Finally, you will learn how to enable source control for documents, check documents in and out, and view the document Checkout Status report.

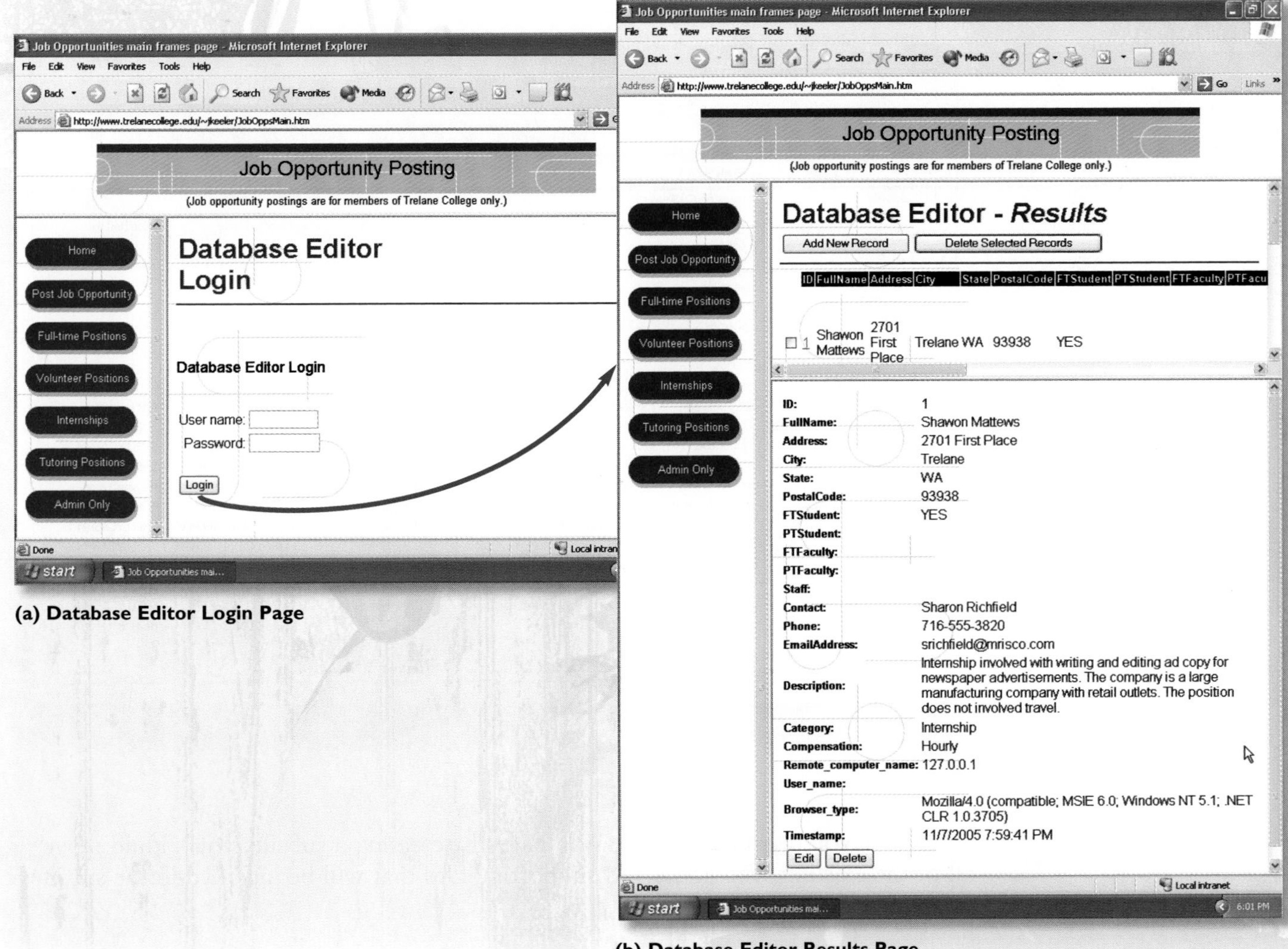

(a) Database Editor Login Page

(b) Database Editor Results Page

FIGURE 6-1

Starting FrontPage and Opening an Existing Web Site

The following steps start FrontPage and then open the FrontPage Web site from Project 5. If you did not complete Project 5, see your instructor for a copy of the Web site.

To Start FrontPage and Open an Existing Web Site

1. **Click the Start button on the taskbar. Point to All Programs on the Start menu.**
2. **Point to Microsoft Office on the All Programs submenu.**
3. **Click Microsoft Office FrontPage 2003 on the Microsoft Office submenu.**
4. **Click the Open button arrow on the Standard toolbar.**
5. **Click Open Site on the Open menu. If necessary, when FrontPage displays the Open Site dialog box, click the Look in box arrow and select the folder location where you stored the Web site for Project 5 (e.g., C:\jkeeler).**
6. **Click the Open button.**

The previously created FrontPage Web site is loaded and is displayed in Folders view (Figure 6-2).

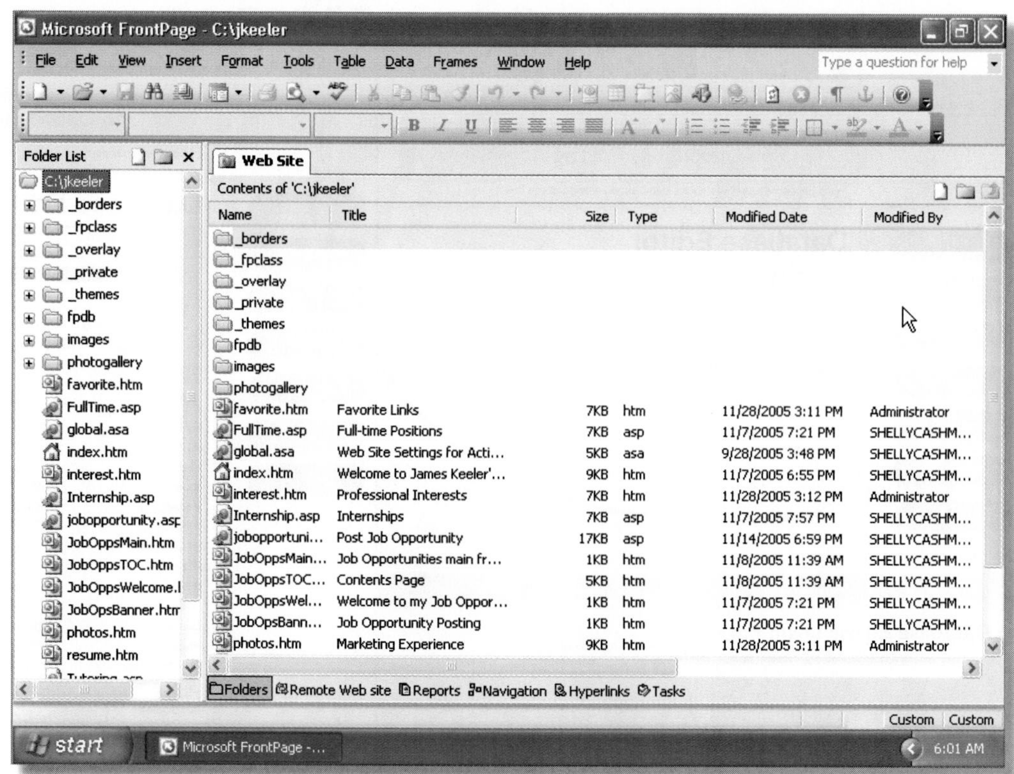

FIGURE 6-2

Before you organize existing Web pages by creating a subsite, you should move all of the existing Web pages and supporting files that will be included in the subsite into a new folder.

Creating a Folder and Converting It to a Subsite

In earlier projects, you organized the FrontPage Web site by placing pictures and graphics into the images folder. You also can organize Web page files by creating folders for related Web pages and files and moving those pages and files into the respective folders.

As a Web site grows, consider reorganizing the files in the Web site into folders or subsites to help manage the relationships between various parts of the Web site.

Creating a Folder in an Existing Web Site

When FrontPage creates a Web site, it creates certain folders, such as the images folder, by default. As your Web site grows to include many Web pages and supporting files, you may want to create new folders to help organize the pages and files in your Web site.

Creating a folder within a FrontPage Web site is similar to creating a folder on your computer using Windows Explorer. Just as with Windows Explorer, creating a new folder in a FrontPage Web site creates a new folder on your hard drive. Although you can add folders to a Web site using Windows Explorer, you should use FrontPage to create and manipulate folders in your Web site to maintain consistency among all folders in the Web site.

In this project, you will create a new folder, named JobOppsSite, in the home folder of the current FrontPage Web site. To create a new folder within an existing folder or Web site, you first must select the existing folder or Web site in which you want to create the new folder.

The following steps create a new folder in an existing FrontPage Web site.

More About

The FrontPage Help System

Need Help? It is no further away than the Type a question for help box on the menu bar in the upper-right corner of the window. Click the box that contains the text, Type a question for help, type `help`, and then press the ENTER key. FrontPage responds with a list of topics you can click to learn about obtaining help on any FrontPage-related topic. To find out what is new in FrontPage 2003, type `what is new in FrontPage` in the Type a question for help box.

To Create a New Folder in an Existing FrontPage Web Site

1

- **With the C:\jkeeler folder selected in the Folder List pane, click the New Folder button in the Folder List pane.**

A new folder is created in the home folder of the current Web site, jkeeler. FrontPage gives the new folder the default name of New_Folder. The new folder name is selected in the Folder List pane (Figure 6-3).

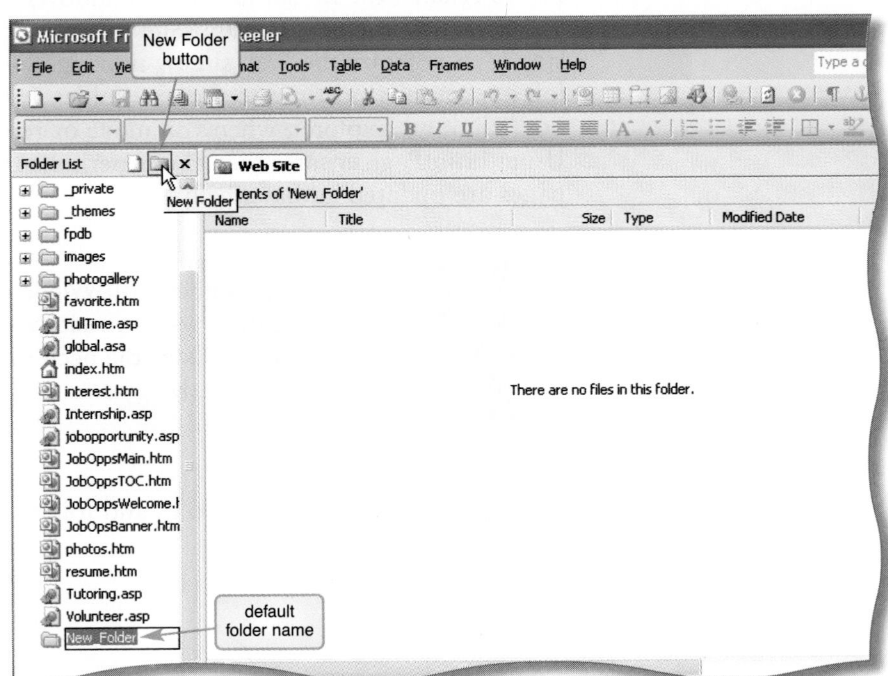

FIGURE 6-3

2

• **Type** JobOppsSite **as the new folder name and then press the ENTER key.**

The new folder is renamed JobOppsSite (Figure 6-4). The JobOppsSite folder is displayed within the home folder of the current Web site, jkeeler.

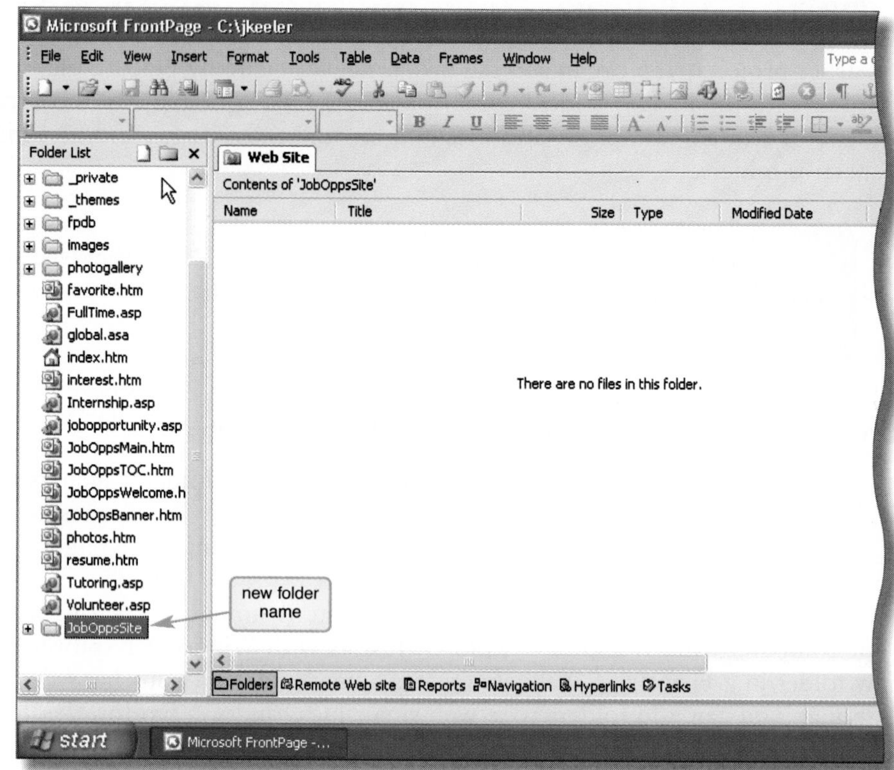

FIGURE 6-4

Other Ways

1. Right-click home folder, click New on shortcut menu, click Folder on New submenu
2. Click the New Folder button at the top of the Folders view pane

When FrontPage creates a new folder, it automatically selects the default folder name so you easily can type a new name to change the name from the default name, New_Folder. If you want to change the folder name again, simply right-click the folder and select Rename on the shortcut menu or select the folder and then press F2. Once the folder name is selected, type the new folder name and then press the ENTER key to rename the folder, just as in Windows Explorer.

Now that the new JobOppsSite folder is created in the existing Web site, the next step is to organize the Web site by moving any files and folders that pertain to the job opportunity postings to the new folder. It is important that you use FrontPage, not Windows Explorer, when you move or rename files or folders in your Web site. Using FrontPage ensures that any hyperlinks that point to the moved or renamed pages are updated automatically.

Design Tip

Use FrontPage, rather than Windows Explorer or other tools, when manipulating the physical structure of the files and folders in a Web site. FrontPage includes the necessary tools to manage links and other relationships properly.

The following steps move files and folders into the new JobOppsSite folder.

To Move Files and Folders to a New Folder

1

- **Click the folder, fpdb, to select it.**
- **Hold down the CTRL key and then click each of the files listed in Table 6-1 on the next page to select them.**

The files and folder to be moved into the JobOppsSite folder are selected (Figure 6-5).

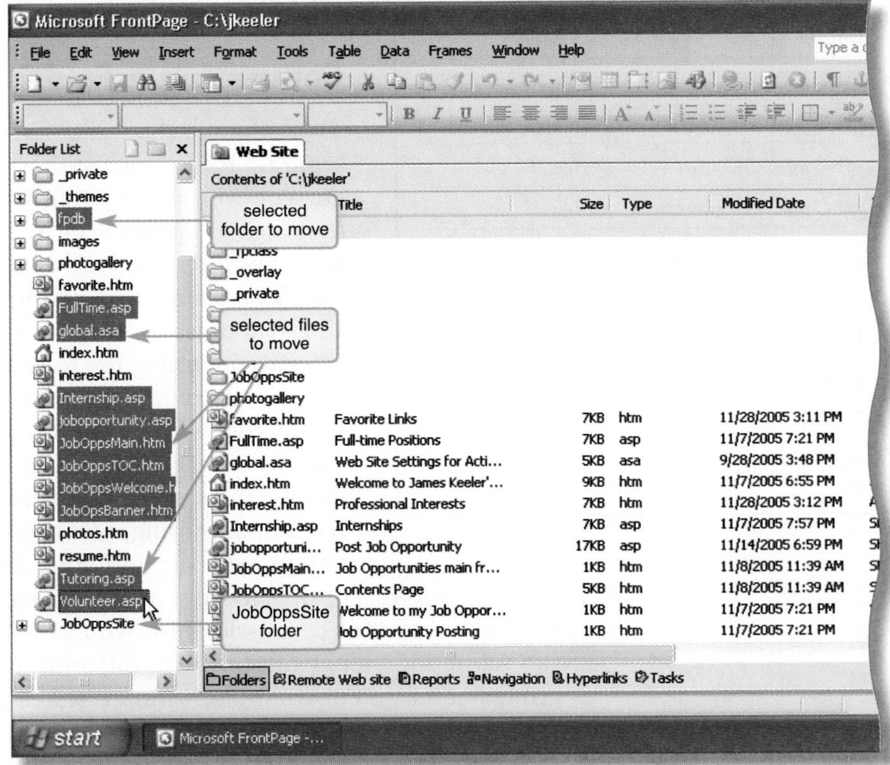

FIGURE 6-5

2

- **Drag the selected files and folder to the JobOppsSite folder.**
- **Release the mouse button.**

The selected files and folder are moved to the JobOppsSite folder (Figure 6-6). As the files and folder are moved, a FrontPage Rename message box is displayed, indicating that FrontPage is renaming them and adjusting any hyperlink references to each file as it is moved.

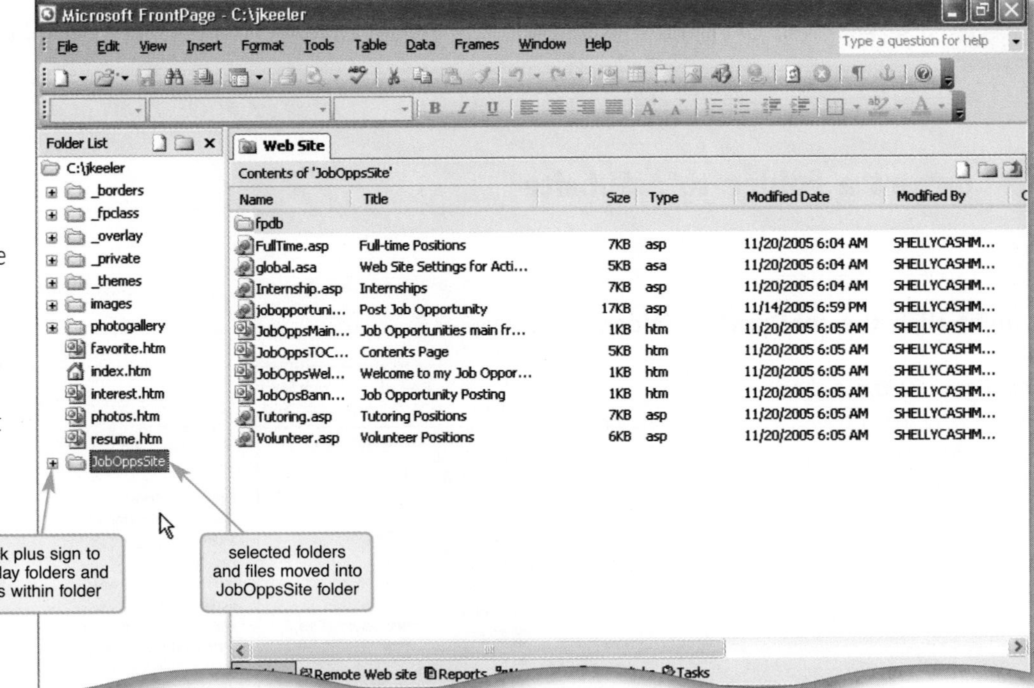

FIGURE 6-6

Table 6-1 Files and Folders to Move to JobOppsSite Folder

NAME	TYPE
fpdb	folder
JobOpsBanner.htm	file
JobOppsMain.htm	file
JobOppsTOC.htm	file
JobOppsWelcome.htm	file
jobopportunity.asp	file
FullTime.asp	file
Internship.asp	file
global.asa	file
Tutoring.asp	file
Volunteer.asp	file

The selected folder and files are moved into the JobOppsSite folder. If you click the plus sign to the left of the JobOppsSite folder icon, the list of folders and files within that folder appears in the Folder List pane.

Converting a Folder to a Subsite

Although the folder and files just moved are located in a separate folder, they still are a part of the original Web site. If the current Web site is published, the JobOppsSite folder and the files in it also are published. Access security for the files in the JobOppsSite folder is the same as it is for any other file in the Web site. To control such attributes separately from the original Web site, you must convert the folder to a subsite.

By converting the folder to a subsite, you change the folder so that it is a completely separate FrontPage Web site within the parent or root Web site. A subsite initially inherits certain site settings, such as security permissions, from its parent Web site. You can change the settings on a subsite so that each subsite has administration, authoring, and browsing permissions independent from the parent Web site and other subsites.

You can use subsites to limit access for security reasons. Because each subsite can have its own set of permissions for who can author, browse, or administer it, you can set up individual subsites with different levels of permissions and different groups of users. For example, within the jkeeler Web site, you can set up the JobOppsSite subsite so that only certain individuals can update the files and folders in the subsite.

The following steps convert the JobOppsSite folder to a subsite.

Design Tip

You can use subsites to limit access for security reasons. Because each subsite can have its own set of permissions for who can author, browse, or administer it, you can set up individual subsites with different levels of permissions and different groups of users.

To Convert a Folder to a Subsite

1

- **Right-click the JobOppsSite folder.**

FrontPage displays a shortcut menu (Figure 6-7). The Convert to Web command tells FrontPage to convert the selected folder to a subsite.

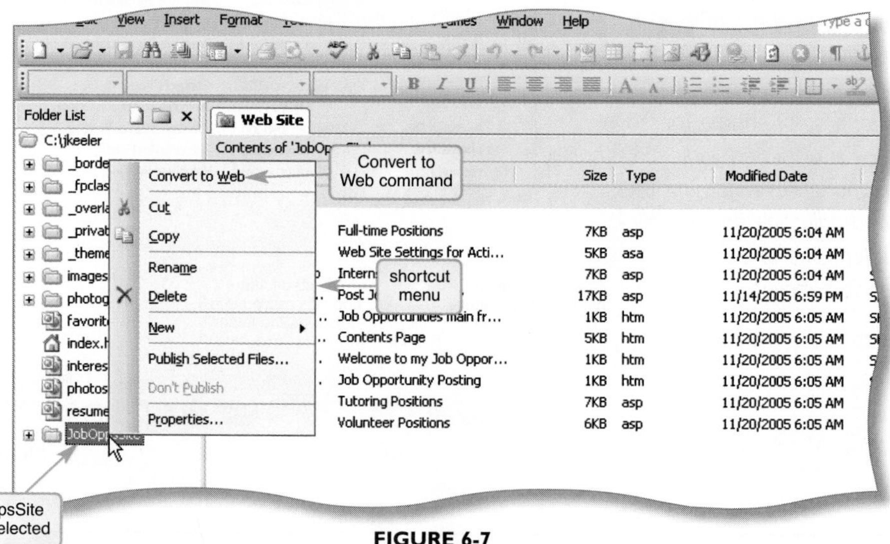

FIGURE 6-7

2

• **Click Convert to Web.**

A Microsoft Office FrontPage dialog box is displayed (Figure 6-8). The dialog box displays information about possible consequences of converting the folder to a subsite and gives you the option to proceed or cancel the conversion.

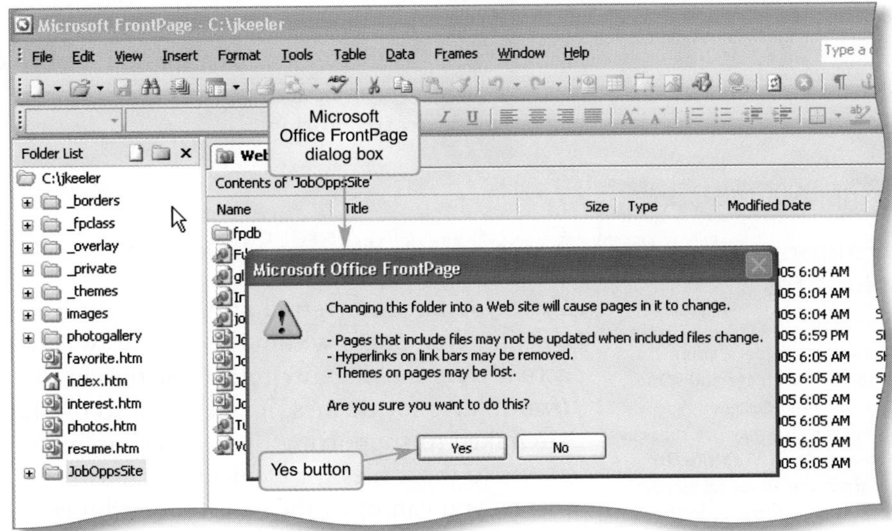

FIGURE 6-8

3

• **Click the Yes button.**

FrontPage displays the new JobOppsSite subsite in the Folder List pane as a folder with a blue globe icon (Figure 6-9).

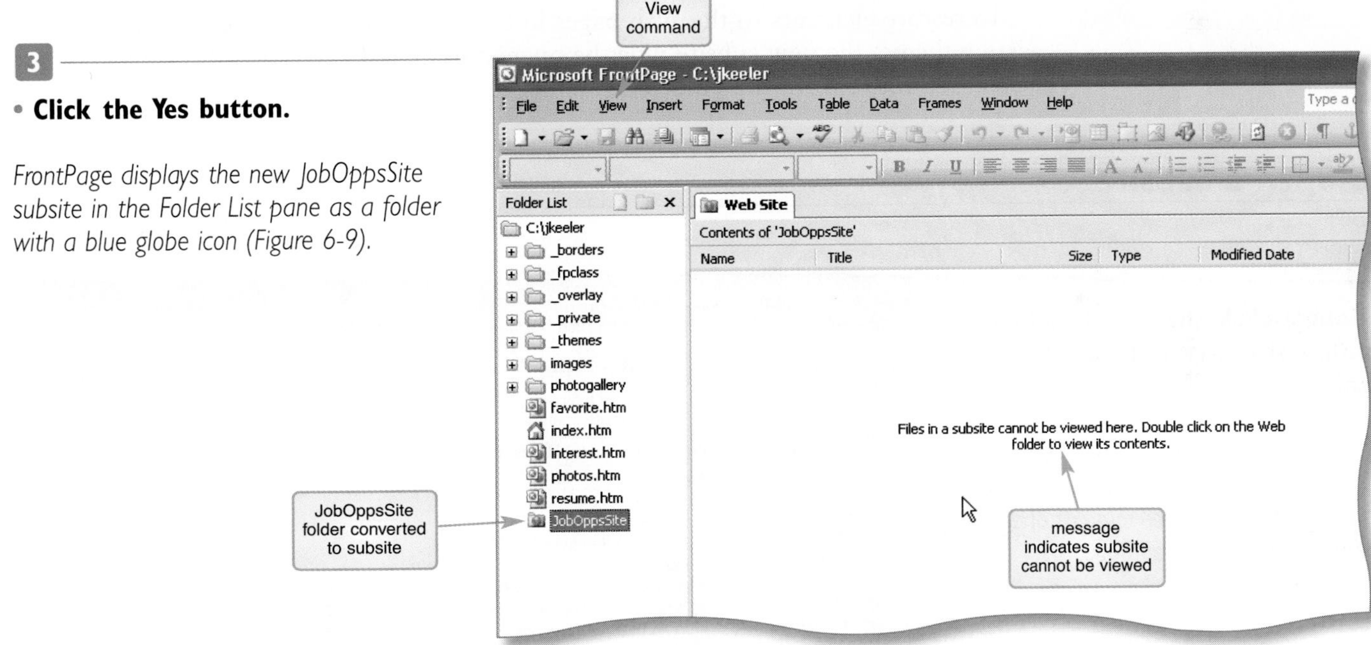

FIGURE 6-9

It is preferable to design the overall organizational structure of your Web site, including subsites, before creating the Web site. Unanticipated growth of a Web site, however, can require some restructuring. Because FrontPage allows you to create a new folder, move folders and files to that folder, and then convert that folder to a subsite, restructuring a Web site can be accomplished with reasonable ease. As you convert a folder to a subsite, be aware that the larger the contents of the folder, the longer it takes to convert the folder to a subsite. For a large folder, this process could take several minutes.

It is preferable to design the overall organizational structure of your Web site, including subsites, before creating the Web site. Unanticipated growth of a Web site, however, can require some restructuring.

More About

Folders and Subsites

A FrontPage Web site may have many folders, some created by FrontPage and some by the Web designer. A designer also may use subsites to organize a Web site. To learn more about folders and subsites, visit the FrontPage 2003 More About Web page (scsite.com/fp2003/more) and then click Folders and Subsites.

Working with Subsites

Once you have converted a folder to a subsite, you may need to update some of the existing Web pages within the subsite. When converting the folder to a subsite, you actually are moving any folders or files in the folder to a new Web site that has its own folders for themes, images, and so on. Because the pages in the new subsite still are linked to supporting files in the parent Web site, the pages in the subsite may lose access to these files for elements such as link bars and themes. To restore such elements, you can open the subsite for editing in FrontPage.

Opening a Subsite for Editing

To restore elements to the Web pages in the new subsite, such as to reapply an existing theme, the new subsite must be opened in FrontPage. The following step opens the subsite from the Folder List pane.

To Open a Subsite

1

• **Double-click the subsite folder, JobOppsSite, in the Folder List pane.**

The subsite, JobOppsSite, opens in a second instance of FrontPage (Figure 6-10). The parent Web site, jkeeler, remains open in the first instance of FrontPage.

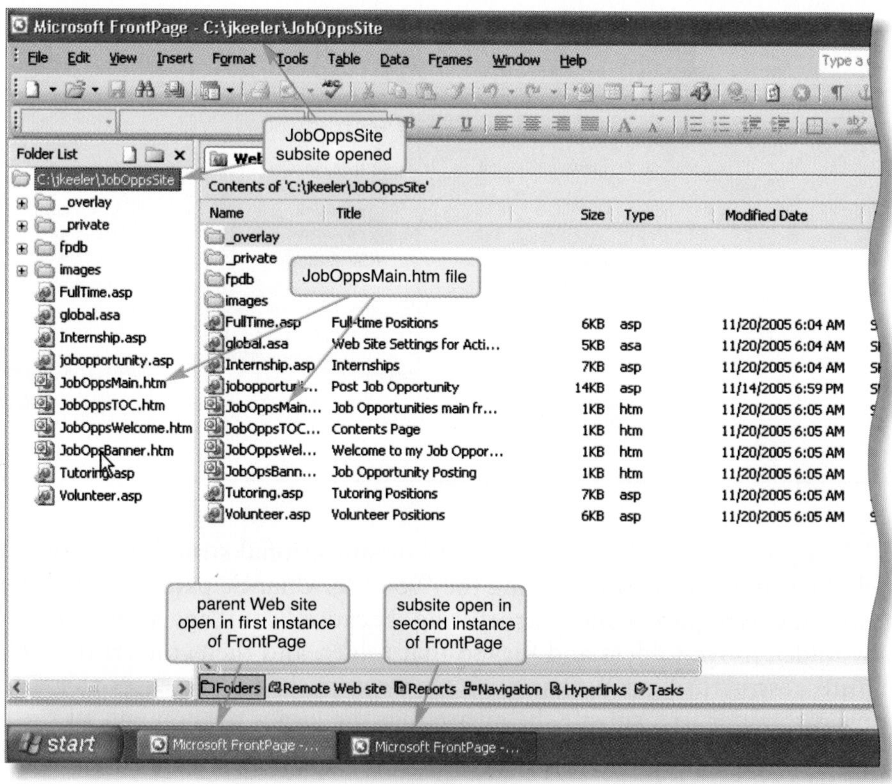

FIGURE 6-10

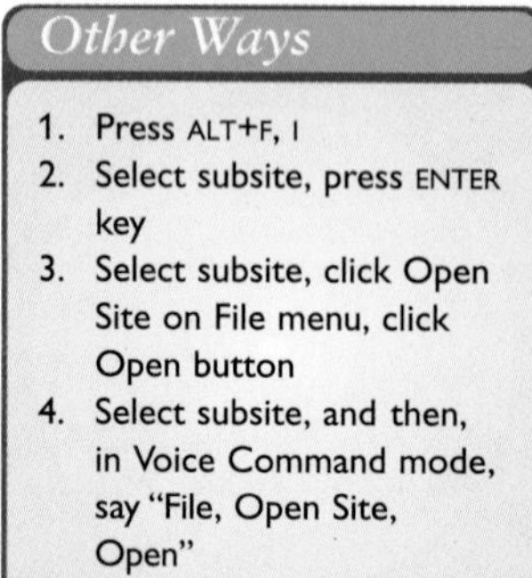

Other Ways

1. Press ALT+F, I
2. Select subsite, press ENTER key
3. Select subsite, click Open Site on File menu, click Open button
4. Select subsite, and then, in Voice Command mode, say "File, Open Site, Open"

Once you have opened a subsite in FrontPage, you can open and edit any of the files in the subsite just as you have edited other files in a Web site.

Setting an Existing Page as the Home Page

As you have learned, every Web site contains a home page, which is the first document users see when they access the Web site. The home page, often named index.htm, serves as an index or table of contents to other documents and files stored on the site. FrontPage automatically created the home page for the parent Web site, jkeeler, when it created the new Web site from the Personal Web template. When the JobOppsSite folder is converted to a subsite, FrontPage does not automatically designate a file as the home page for the subsite.

To create a home page for the subsite, you either can create a new page or can designate an existing page as the home page for the subsite. Because an appropriate page already exists, the following steps set an existing page as the home page for this subsite.

To Set an Existing Page as the Home Page

1

- **Right-click the file, JobOppsMain.htm, in the Folder List pane.**

FrontPage displays a shortcut menu (Figure 6-11).

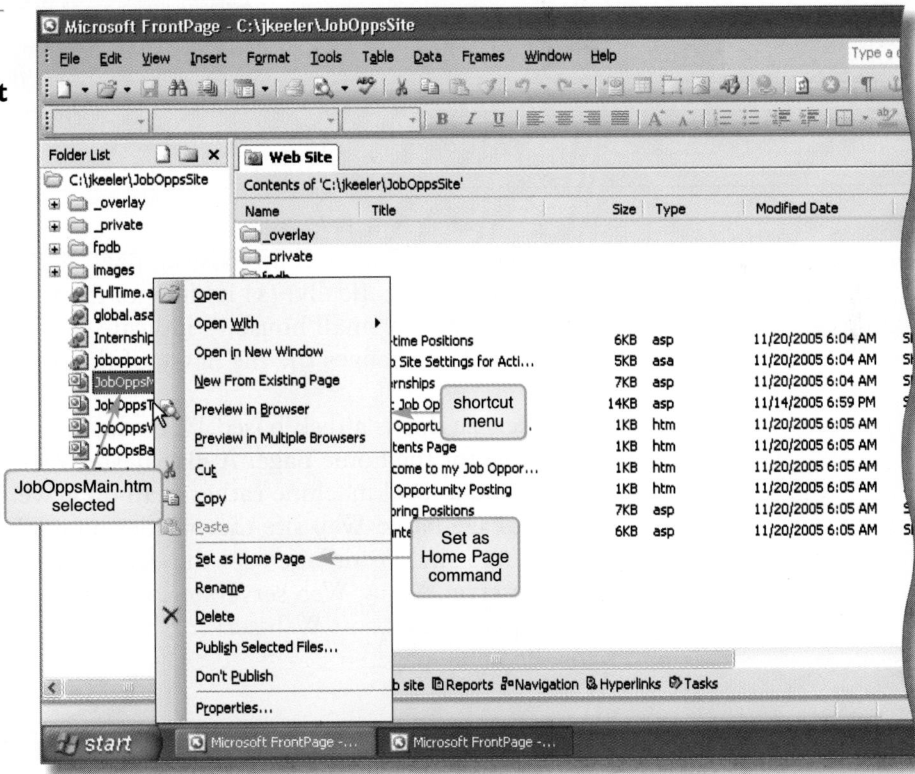

FIGURE 6-11

• **Click Set as Home Page.**

FrontPage renames the file, JobOppsMain.htm, to index.htm and sets it as the home page for the subsite (Figure 6-12). A Rename dialog box is displayed briefly as FrontPage renames the file. The file icon in the Folder List pane changes to a small house to indicate that index.htm is the home page for the subsite.

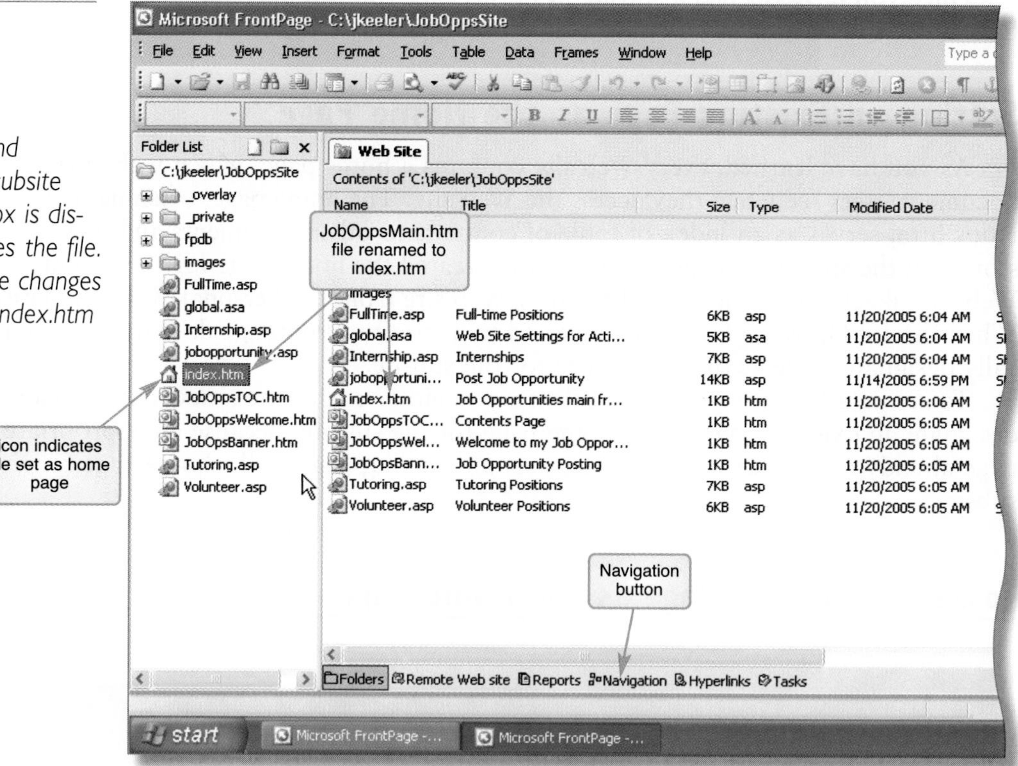

FIGURE 6-12

When FrontPage sets an existing page as the home page for a Web site, it does two things automatically: (1) it changes the file icon in the Folder List pane and Folders view to a small house to indicate that this page is the home page for the Web site, and (2) it changes the file name of the page to the default name for the home page.

Because this is a disk-based Web site, FrontPage uses index.htm as the default file name for the home page. A **disk-based Web site** is a Web site created and opened on a local machine rather than on a Web server. A **server-based Web site** is a FrontPage-based Web site that resides on a Web server. When editing a server-based Web site, FrontPage uses the default file name for the home page as specified by the server. Many Web servers also use index.htm as the default file name for the home page. Microsoft Web servers, however, use default.htm as the default file name for the home page.

Creating a Navigation Structure for a Subsite

A folder or file can be part of only one Web site at a time. Because the folders and files of the JobOppsSite subsite are no longer part of the parent Web site, they are not included in the navigation structure of the parent Web site. Instead, these files and folders must be included in the navigation structure of the JobOppsSite subsite, which is a Web site distinct from the parent Web site, with its own navigation structure.

When a folder is converted to a subsite, FrontPage does not define a navigation structure for the subsite automatically. You can create a navigation structure for the subsite by organizing the pages in Navigation view.

The following steps create a navigation structure for the subsite.

To Create a Navigation Structure for a Subsite

1

• **Click the Navigation command on the View menu.**

FrontPage displays the subsite in Navigation view (Figure 6-13). The home page icon for the Job Opportunities main frames page is displayed in the navigation structure.

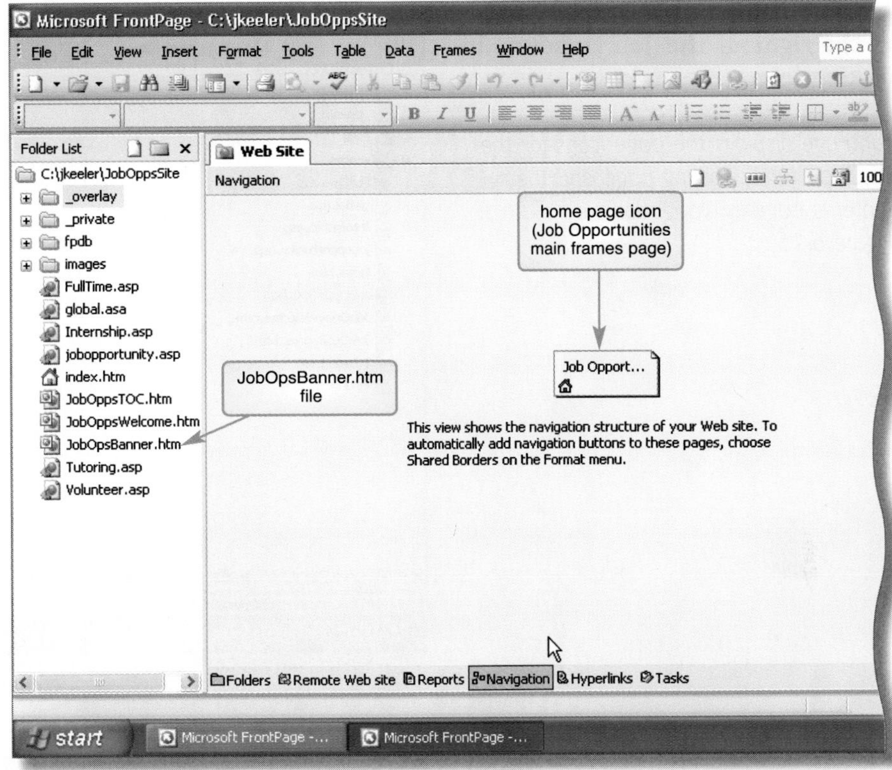

FIGURE 6-13

2

• **Drag the file, JobOpsBanner.htm, from the Folder List pane and drop it below the home page icon in Navigation view.**

FrontPage displays the page icon for the Job Opportunities page in Navigation view below the home page icon (Figure 6-14).

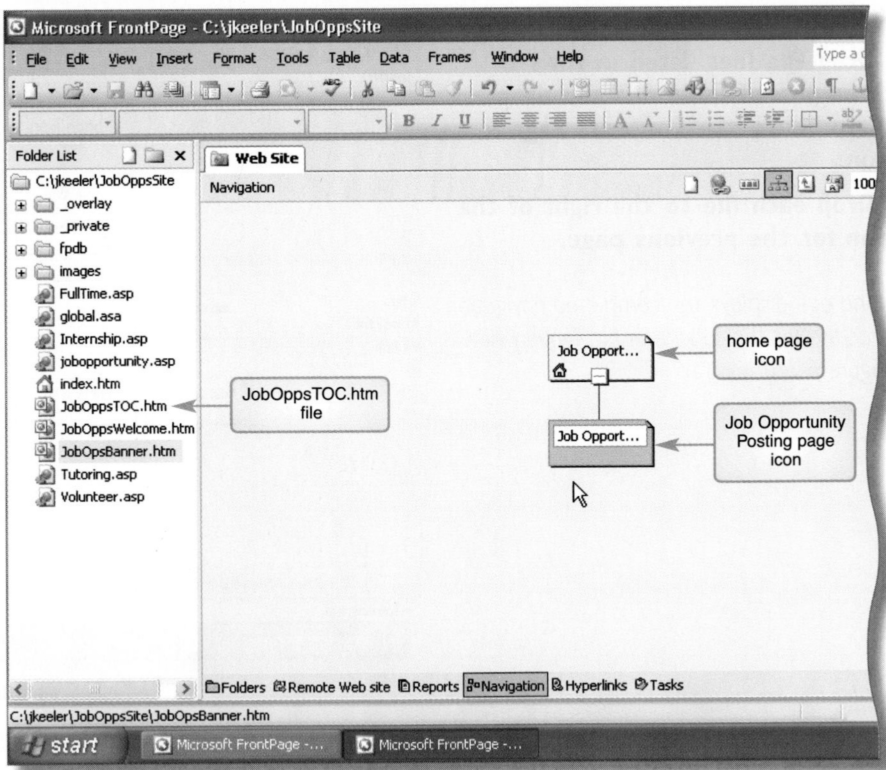

FIGURE 6-14

3

• **Drag the file, JobOppsTOC.htm, from the Folder List pane and drop it below the home page icon and to the right of the Job Opportunity Posting icon.**

FrontPage displays the page icons for the Job Opportunity Posting page and the Contents page in Navigation view (Figure 6-15).

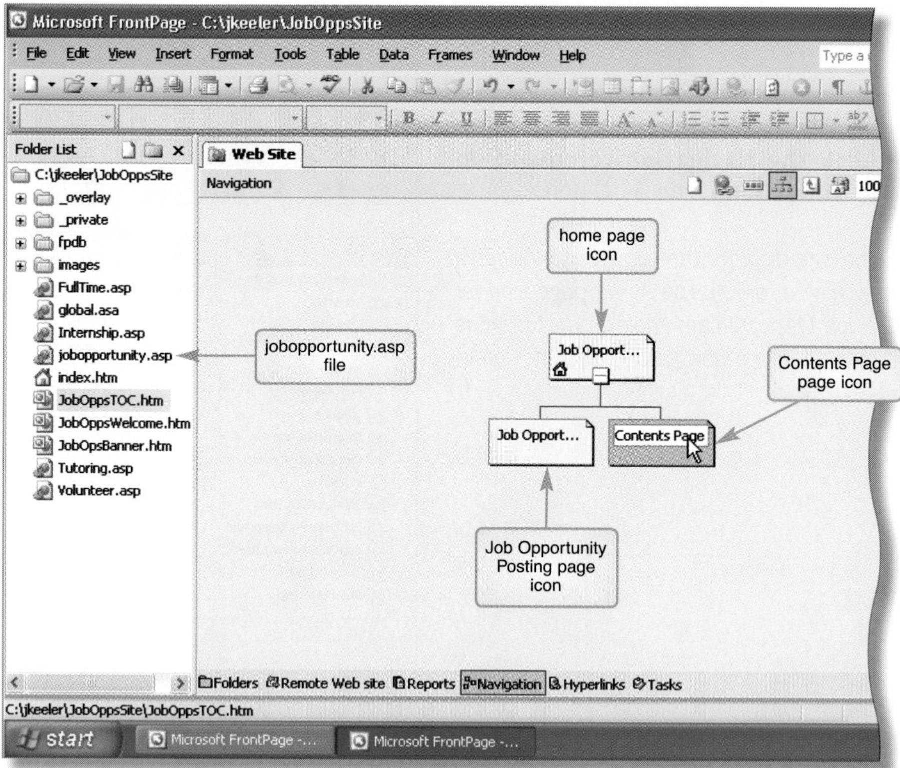

FIGURE 6-15

4

• **Drag the file, jobopportunity.asp, from the Folder List pane and drop it below the Contents Page icon.**

• **Drag the files listed in rows 2 through 5 of Table 6-2 and drop them below the Contents Page icon.**

• **Drop each file to the right of the icon for the previous page.**

FrontPage displays the completed navigation structure for the subsite in Navigation view (Figure 6-16).

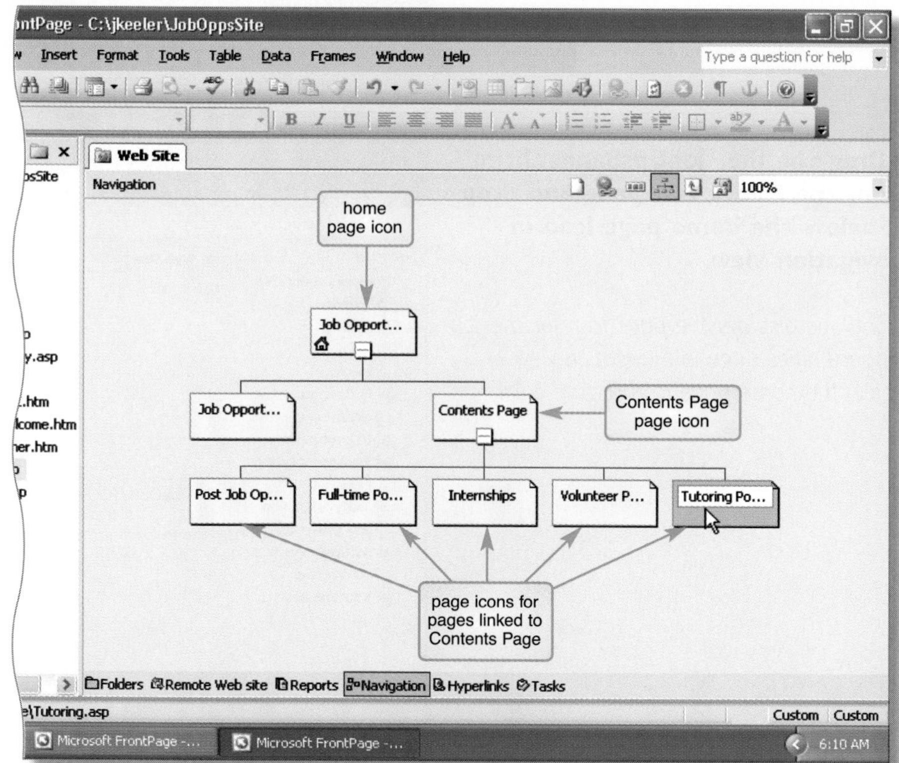

FIGURE 6-16

5

- **Double-click the home page icon.**
- **Right-click the contents frame and then click Frame Properties on the shortcut menu.**
- **Select If needed in the Show scrollbars drop-down box and then click the OK button.**

FrontPage displays the Job Opportunities main frames page in Design view (Figure 6-17). The page includes three frames — banner, contents, and main — each of which displays an initial page. The Home image in the contents frame is a hyperlink to the home page of the parent Web site, jkeeler.

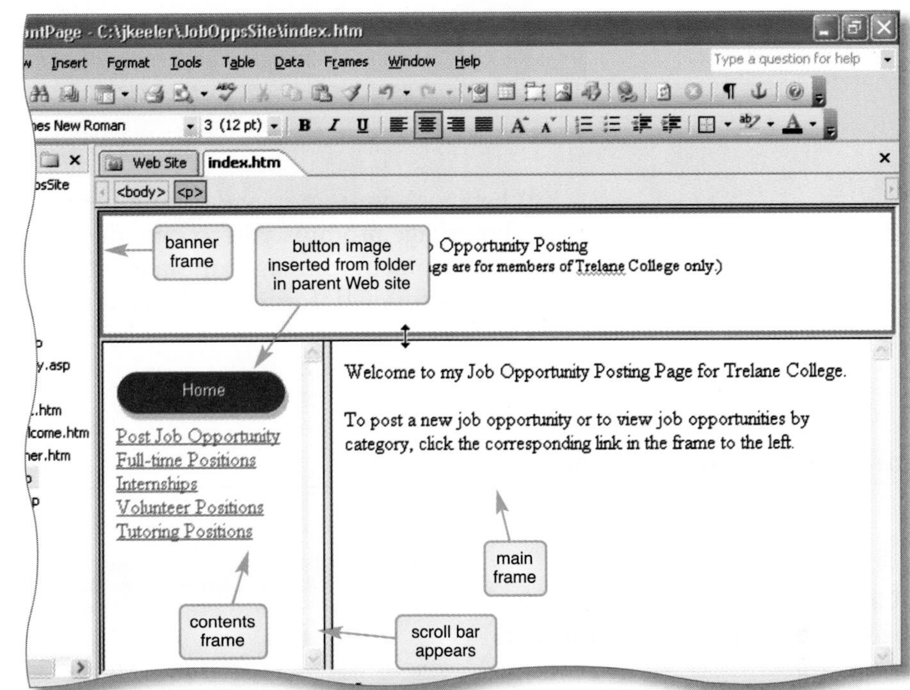

FIGURE 6-17

The navigation structure that the job opportunities pages have in the subsite now is similar to the navigation structure they had in the parent Web site.

Table 6-2 Files below Contents Page in the Subsite Navigation Structure

ORDER	NAME	PAGE NAME
1	jobopportunity.asp	Post Job Opportunity
2	FullTime.asp	Full-time Positions
3	Internship.asp	Internships
4	Volunteer.asp	Volunteer Positions
5	Tutoring.asp	Tutoring Positions

Inserting a New Image from a File

As shown in Figure 6-17, the Capsules theme no longer is applied to the pages in the JobOppsSite subsite. As a result, the framed Web pages are displayed without font colors and styles or background images; the hyperlinks in the Contents page appear as plain text, except for the first hyperlink, which is an image.

As you learned in Project 5, all of the hyperlinks in the Contents page are part of a Link bar Web component, with the exception of the first hyperlink. When you apply a theme to the JobOppsSite subsite, the link bar displays the colors, fonts, and graphics defined for the theme selected for the subsite.

The button image used for the first hyperlink, however, was inserted from a file in a folder in the parent Web site. Recall also that an image is not placed directly into a Web page, only a reference to the image is. The reference to the button image therefore points to a folder in the parent Web site, not the subsite. The button image currently is displayed because this subsite is a disk-based Web site and it references an image file in the parent Web site. Once the parent Web site and subsite are published to a Web server, the image reference will be lost and the button image will not be displayed. Additionally, because the parent Web site and subsite each are complete Web sites in themselves, and because another theme is applied to the subsite, the Contents page should not reference an image in the parent Web site. Rather, it should reference an image stored in the images folder of the subsite.

Design Tip

Eliminate all but the essential references between subsites and the parent Web site. That is, do not reference resources, such as images, from the subsite to the parent Web site.

When you insert an image from a file into a Web page and then save the Web page, FrontPage prompts you to save the image to a folder in the Web site. As it saves the graphic, FrontPage automatically converts any graphic that uses 256 or fewer colors to a GIF format and converts all other graphics to a JPEG format.

The following steps insert a new image from a file and then save the image to the images folder in the subsite.

To Insert a New Image from a File

1

- **Click the button image used for the first hyperlink in the contents frame.**
- **Press the DELETE key.**

FrontPage deletes the original image from the page (Figure 6-18). The Pictures toolbar may appear prior to deletion of the image.

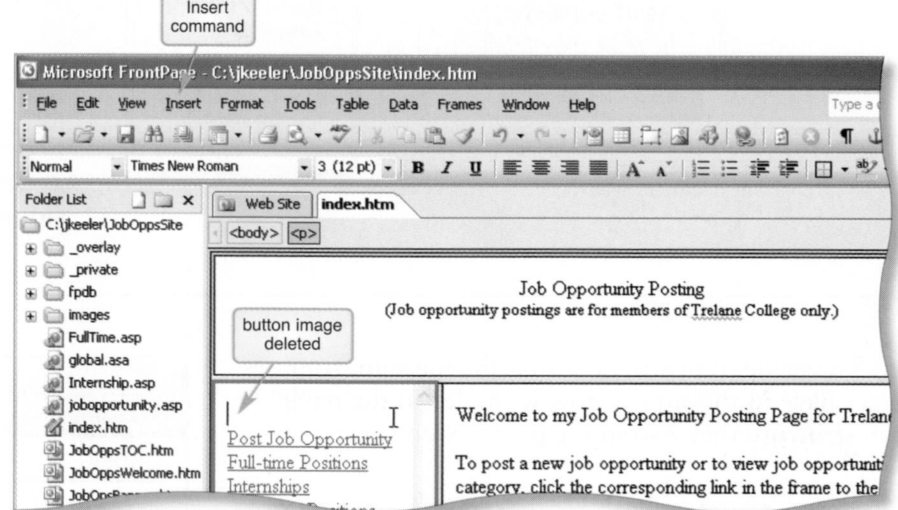

FIGURE 6-18

2

- **Insert the Data Disk in drive A.**
- **Click Insert and then point to Picture.**

FrontPage displays the Insert menu and Picture submenu (Figure 6-19).

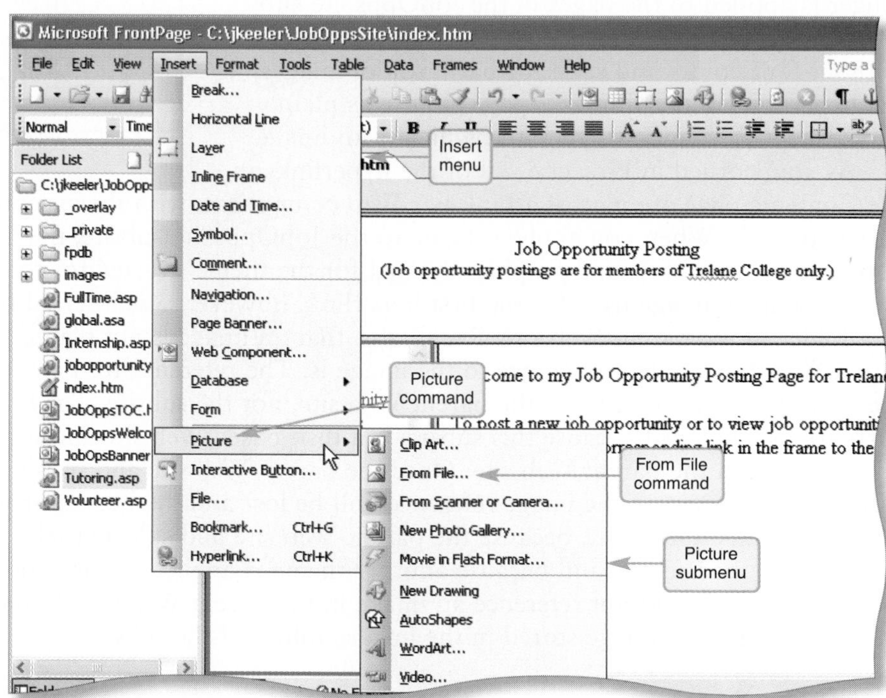

FIGURE 6-19

3

- **Click From File.**
- **If necessary, when FrontPage displays the Picture dialog box, click the Look in box arrow and then click 3½ Floppy (A:).**
- **If necessary, double-click the Project6 folder.**
- **Select the file, HomeButton.**

FrontPage displays the Picture dialog box (Figure 6-20). The file, HomeButton, is selected.

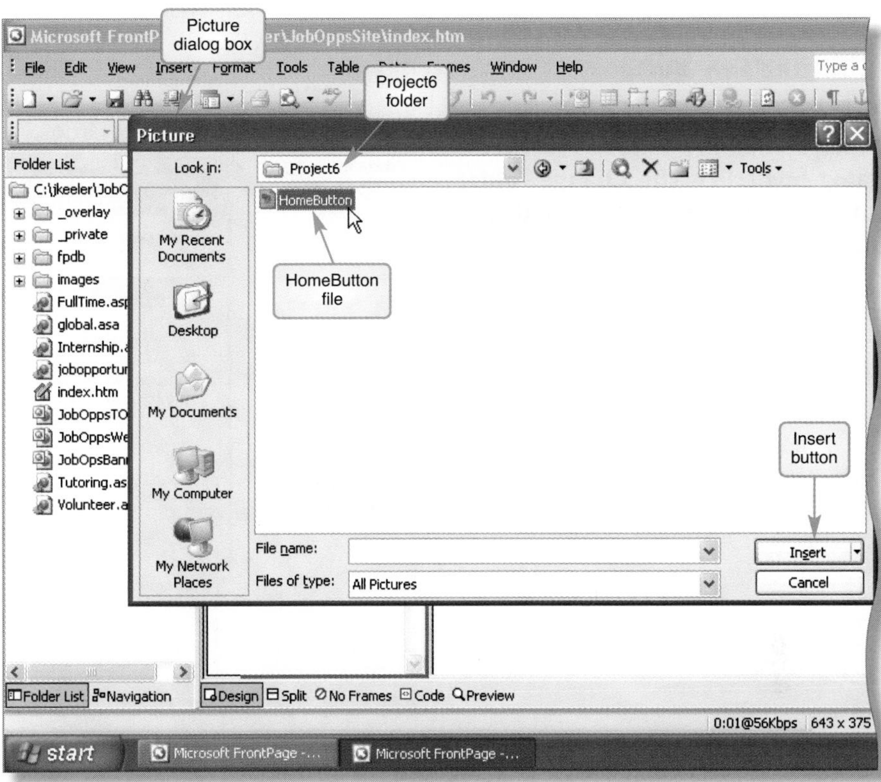

FIGURE 6-20

4

- **Click the Insert button.**

FrontPage displays the Home button image above the link bar (Figure 6-21).

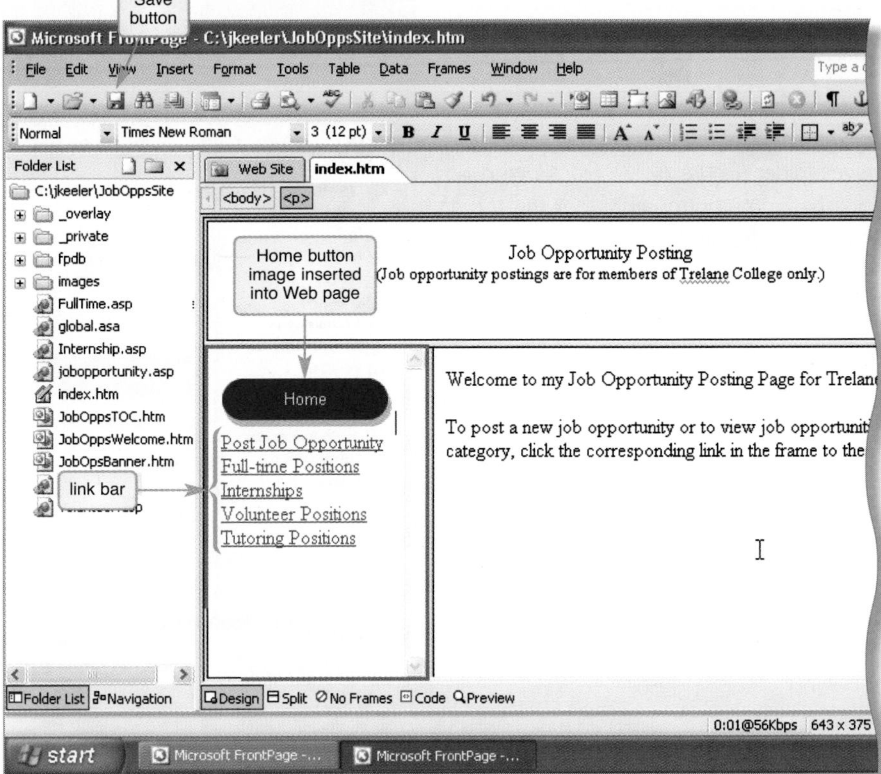

FIGURE 6-21

5

- **Click the Save button.**
- **If necessary, when FrontPage displays the Save Embedded Files dialog box, click the Change Folder button, select the images folder, and then click the OK button.**

FrontPage displays the Save Embedded Files dialog box to prompt you to save the inserted image to a folder in the Web site. (Figure 6-22). A preview of the Home button image is displayed in the Picture preview area.

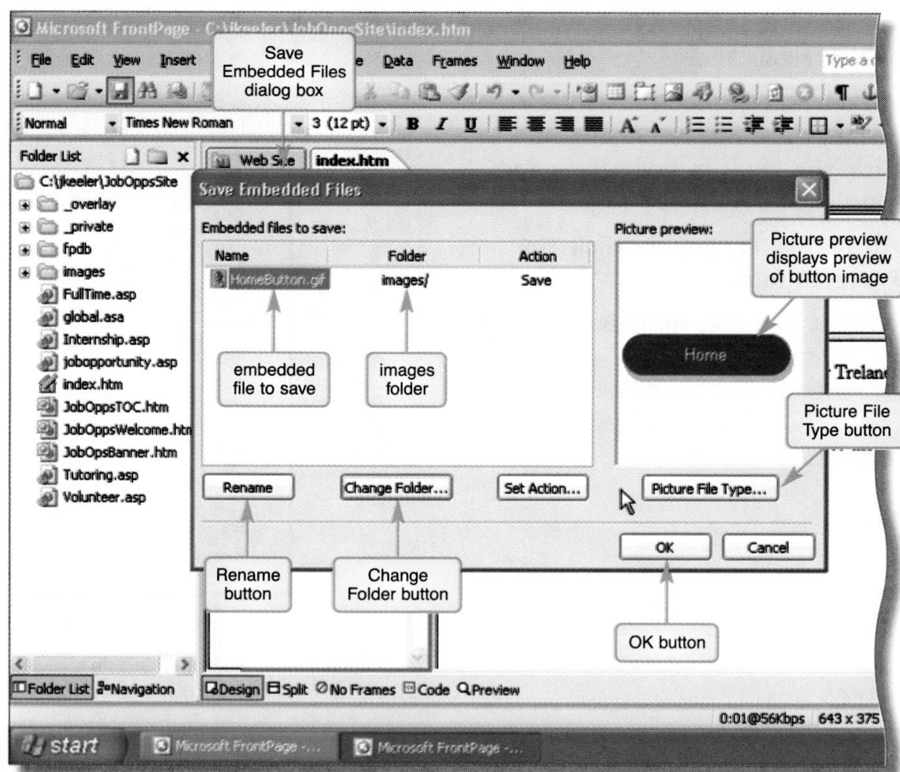

FIGURE 6-22

6

- **Click the OK button.**

The Save Embedded Files dialog box closes and the file, HomeButton, is saved to the images folder (Figure 6-23). FrontPage displays the Home button image at the top of the contents frame.

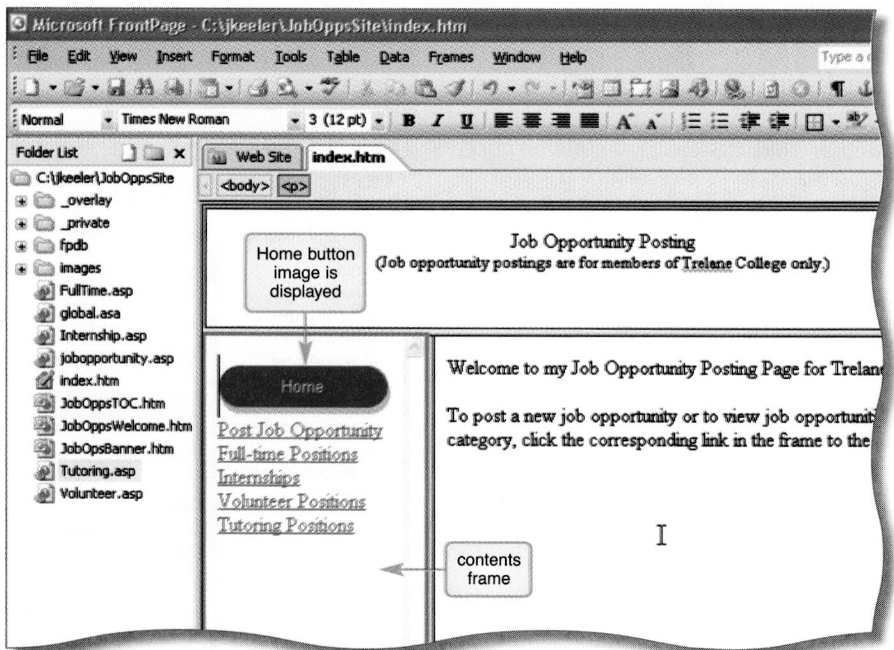

FIGURE 6-23

If you want to rename a file before saving it to a folder, click the Rename button in the Save Embedded Files dialog box and then type the new file name. Clicking the Picture File Type button allows you to set whether the inserted file is saved in a GIF or a JPEG format.

Using the Default Home Page as a Hyperlink Target

When FrontPage publishes a Web site to a server, it changes the name of the published copy of the home page to the default name used on the server, such as default.htm or index.htm. If the file name is the same as the one used on the disk-based, or local, Web site, the references to the home page stay the same. If the name of the default page on the Web server is different from the one on the disk-based Web site, then FrontPage updates all references in the Web site to that page accordingly. Recall that the subsite, although nested within the parent Web site, is an independent Web site. References in the subsite to the home page of the parent Web site are not changed when the parent Web site and subsite are published. Likewise, references in the parent Web site to the home page of the subsite are not changed. To avoid this problem, you can set each hyperlink, respectively, to link to the default page for the referenced Web site, whether its name is default.htm or index.htm.

As you have learned, when a hyperlink references a particular page name, it requests that specific page name from the Web server for a specific URL. If a page by that name does not exist at that URL, then the Web server returns an error to the browser. If the hyperlink reference specifies a URL without a file name, however, then the Web server returns the default page for that location, if one exists. Because the home page is the default page for a given location, the browser displays the home page when its location is referenced, even if the URL does not specify the home page by the specific file name. This solves the problem of having to know the exact file name of the home page when creating the hyperlink.

Design Tip

When linking to a home page within a subsite or parent Web site, be sure to link to a reference to the home page, rather than the file name of the home page itself. Some Web servers require the change of the file name of the home page during the publishing process.

The following steps use the default home page of the parent Web site as the hyperlink target.

More About

Using Images

Images in your Web site can come from a variety of sources - from your own image files, perhaps from your digital camera, from collections supplied with FrontPage, or from collections available on the Web. These and other media files (sound, animation, and video files) are called clips. The Microsoft Clip Organizer can help you organize these clips into collections. On the Insert menu, point to Picture, and then click Clip Art. In the ClipArt task pane, click the Organize links link.

Q&A

Q: Can I customize the behavior of hyperlinks?

A: Yes. You can customize hyperlinks in a variety of ways. You can use different colors for visited versus unvisited links. You can set the target to display the new page in a frame, to replace the current page, or even to open the new page in a new window. To learn more about hyperlinks and hyperlink targets, visit the FrontPage 2003 More About Web page (scsite.com/fp2003/more) and then click Hyperlinks and Hyperlink Targets.

To Create a Hyperlink to the Default Home Page

1

- **Right-click the Home button image in the contents frame.**

FrontPage displays a shortcut menu (Figure 6-24).

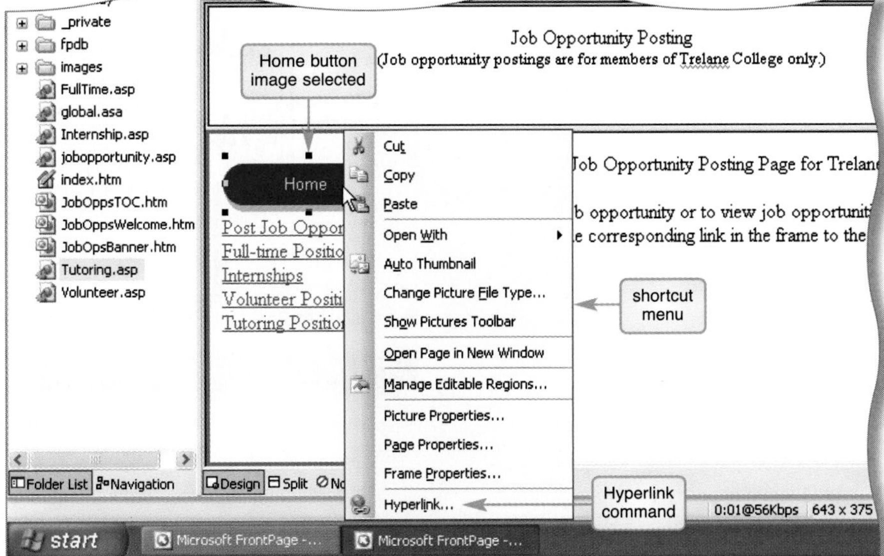

FIGURE 6-24

2

• **Click Hyperlink.**

• **When the Insert Hyperlink dialog box is displayed, type ../ in the Address text box.**

FrontPage displays the address, ../, in the Address text box (Figure 6-25). This address indicates that the hyperlink target page is one level up in the file directory, relative to the location of the current page. It does not, however, specify a particular page or file.

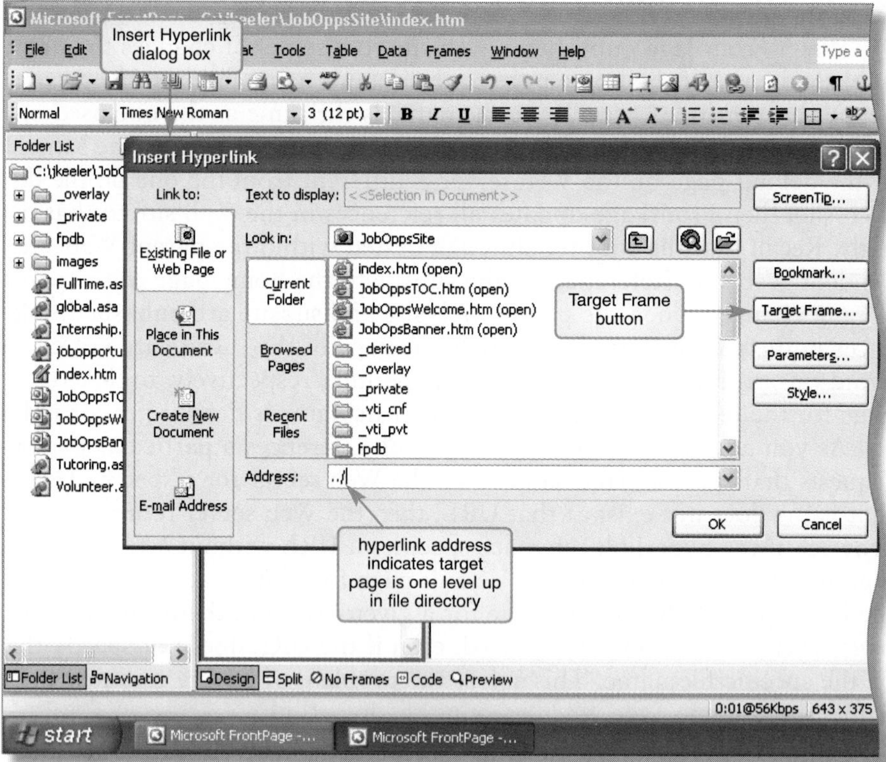

FIGURE 6-25

3

• **Click Target Frame.**

• **When FrontPage displays the Target Frame dialog box, click Whole Page in the Common targets area.**

FrontPage displays the Target Frame dialog box (Figure 6-26). The selection of Whole Page sets the hyperlink to open the target page as a whole page that replaces the frames page, rather than as a page displaying within a frame. When Whole Page is selected, FrontPage automatically changes the Target setting to _top.

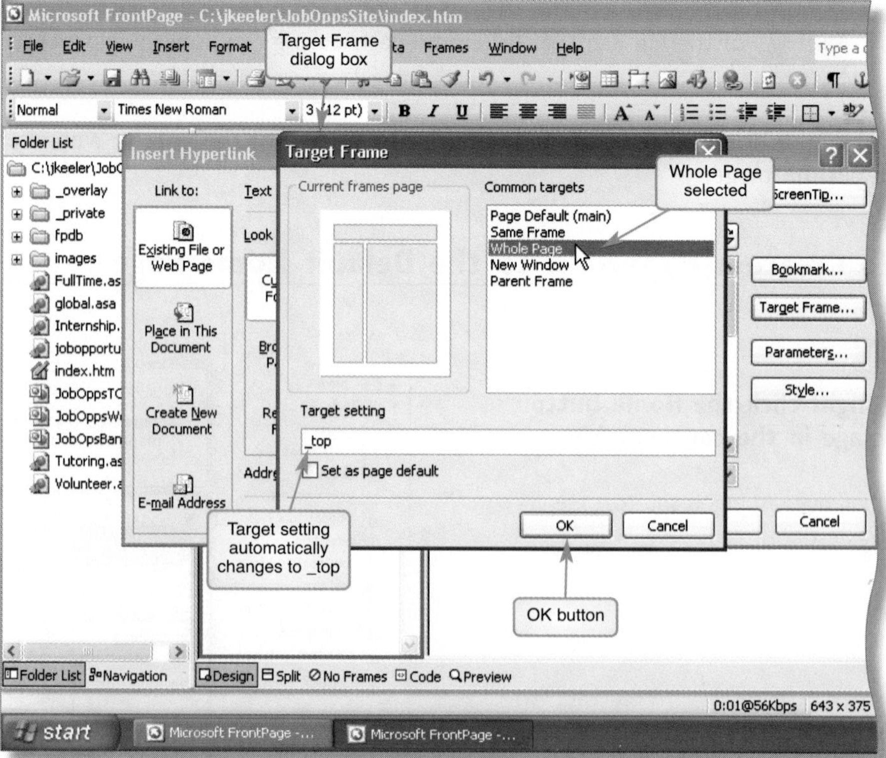

FIGURE 6-26

4

- **Click OK in the Target Frame dialog box.**

The Target Frame dialog box closes (Figure 6-27). FrontPage displays the Target Frame with a value of _top.

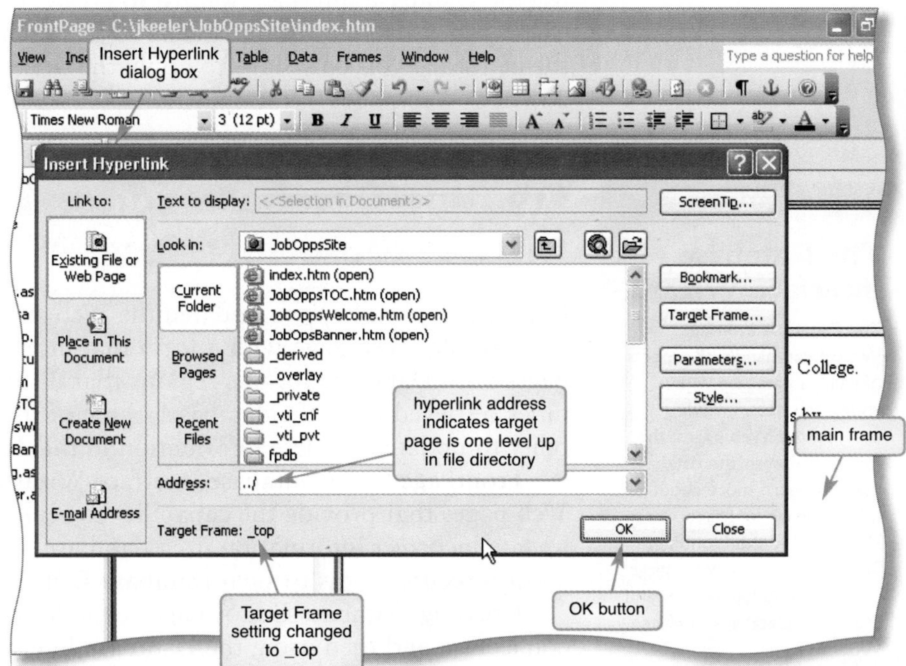

FIGURE 6-27

5

- **Click OK in the Insert Hyperlink dialog box.**
- **When the Insert Hyperlink dialog box closes, click the main frame to deselect the image and then position the mouse pointer over the Home page hyperlink image.**

FrontPage displays a URL of ../ on the status bar (Figure 6-28).

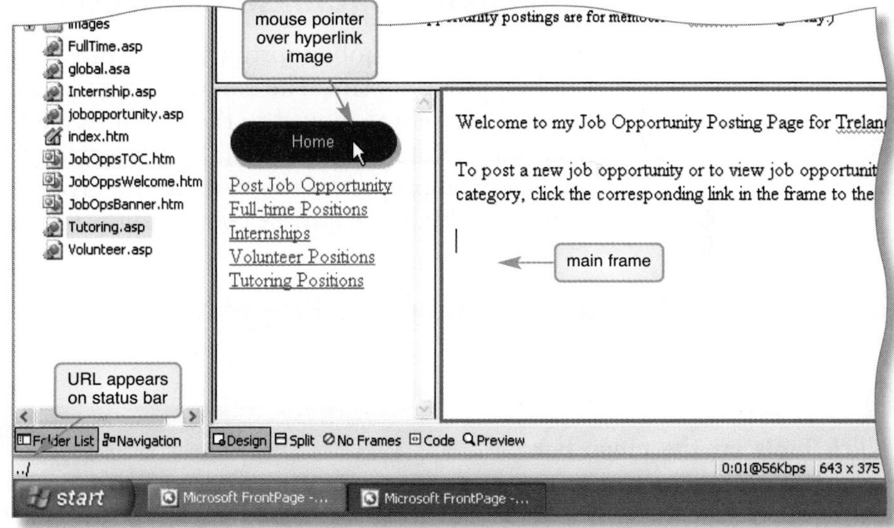

FIGURE 6-28

When the Home button image is clicked, the image hyperlink, ../, tells the browser to request an unnamed target page one level up in the file directory, relative to the current page. Because the parent Web site, jkeeler, is located one folder level higher than the Contents page and because its home page is the default page that is displayed when you view the jkeeler Web site, clicking the Home button image displays the home page for the parent Web site. This means that the hyperlink properly links to the parent Web site home page when the Web site is viewed as a disk-based Web site and also after it is published to a Web server.

The subsite home page still needs to have a FrontPage theme applied so that it is consistent with the rest of the Web site. Before applying the theme, however, you will use the Database Interface Wizard to create Web pages for maintaining a database. These pages also require the theme to be applied; adding them before applying the theme means you only have to apply the theme once to update the home page and any new Web pages in the subsite.

More About

The Database Interface Wizard

The Database Interface Wizard can handle all aspects of using a database within your Web sites, including creating the Web pages, the forms, and even the database itself. To learn more about the Database Interface Wizard, visit the FrontPage 2003 More About Web page (scsite.com/fp2003/more) and then click Database Interface Wizard.

Creating Database Editor Pages Using the Database Interface Wizard

In previous projects, you updated the Web site by adding a database, the Post Job Opportunity Web page with a form that inserts records into the database, and Web pages with Database Results regions that display different views of the job opportunities retrieved from the database. None of these pages, however, provide the capability to update or delete information in the database.

FrontPage has a Database Interface Wizard that helps build Database Editor Web pages that provide the capability to remove outdated information from, and to update incorrect information in, a database, in addition to creating a Web page that ensures secure access to such Database Editor pages.

Creating Database Editor pages includes two key steps: establishing a database connection and then using the Database Interface Wizard to create the pages that allow you to manage database content.

Modifying Database Connection Properties

A database, jobopportunity.mdb, already exists in the fpdb folder of the JobOppsSite subsite. The connection referencing the database is incorrect, because the database was moved to the JobOppsSite folder, which then was converted to a subsite. Before using the Database Interface Wizard, you must update the database connection properties to reference the proper location of the database. The following steps modify the database connection properties.

To Modify the Database Connection Properties

1

- **Click Tools on the menu bar.**

FrontPage displays the Tools menu (Figure 6-29).

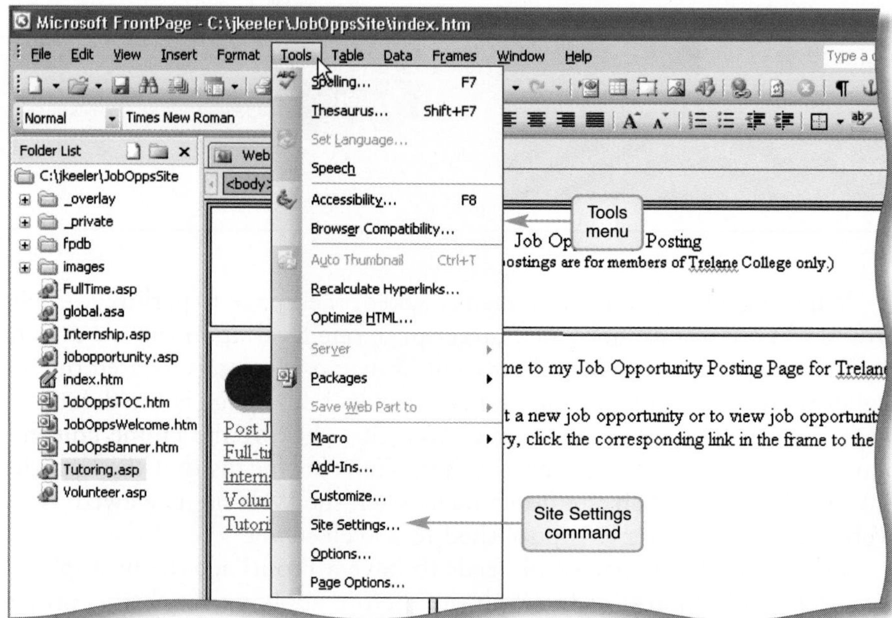

FIGURE 6-29

2

- **Click Site Settings.**
- **When FrontPage displays the Site Settings dialog box, click the Database tab.**

FrontPage displays the Site Settings dialog box (Figure 6-30). The database connection, jobopportunity, is displayed on the Database sheet.

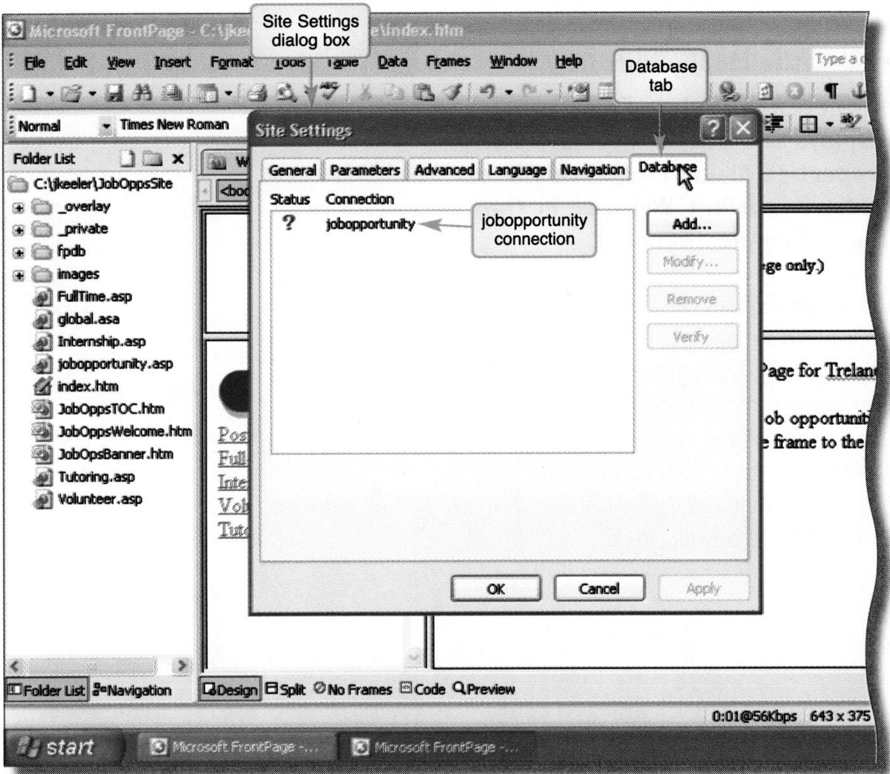

FIGURE 6-30

3

- **Click jobopportunity.**

The connection, jobopportunity, is selected and the Modify button no longer is dimmed (Figure 6-31).

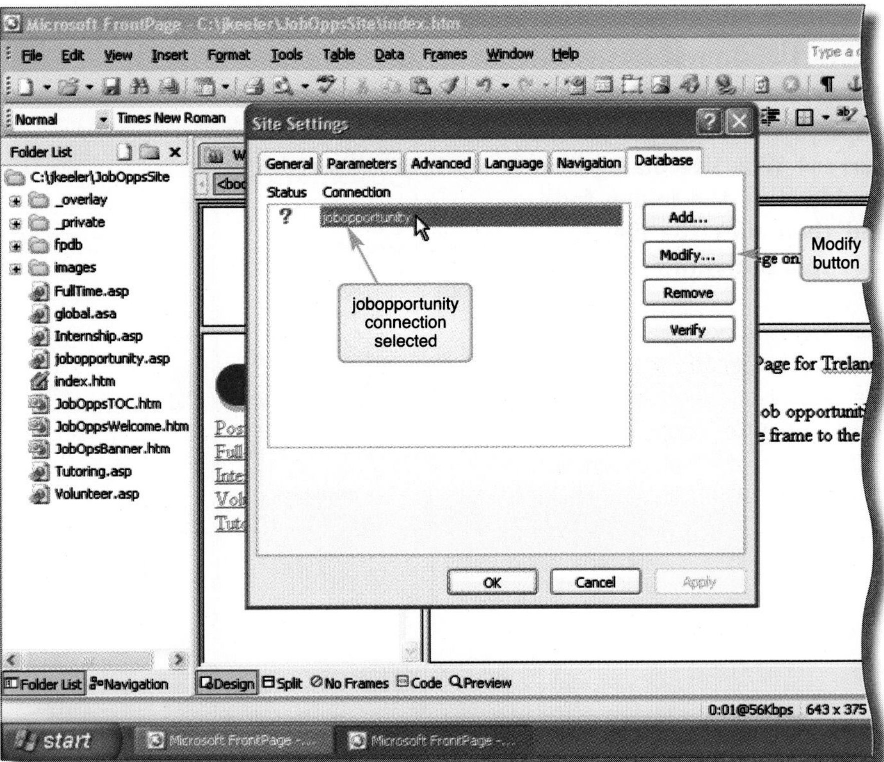

FIGURE 6-31

4

- **Click the Modify button.**
- **If necessary, when FrontPage displays the Database Connection Properties dialog box, click File or folder in current Web site in the Type of connection area.**

FrontPage displays the Database Connection Properties dialog box (Figure 6-32). Database connections of several types can be specified, depending on the location of the database. Because the JobOppsSite folder was converted to a subsite, the current setting for the relative path to the database is incorrect.

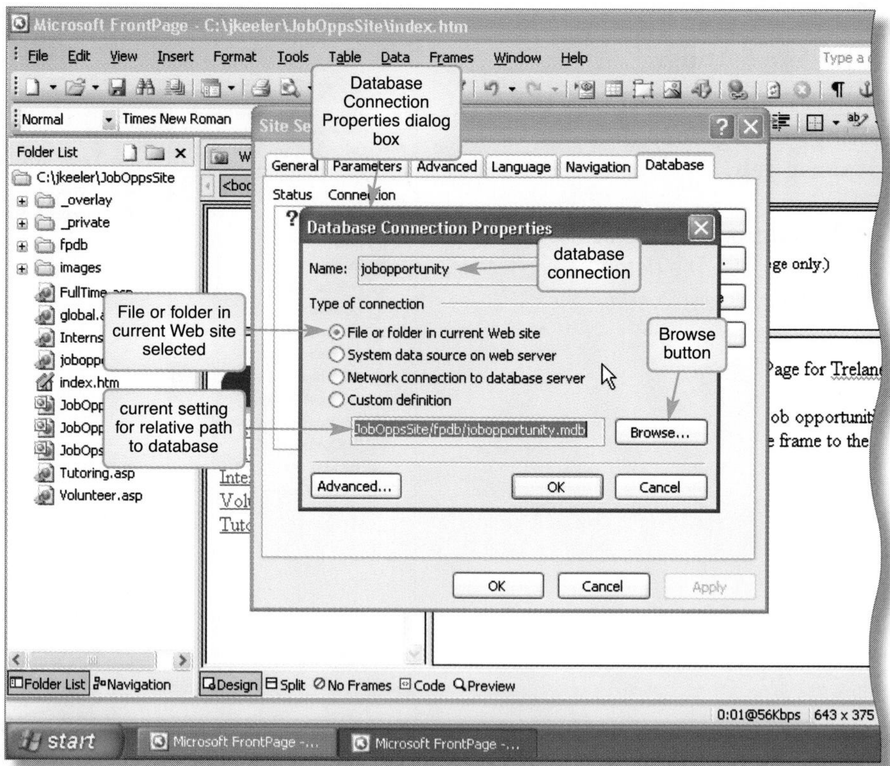

FIGURE 6-32

5

- **Click the Browse button.**
- **If necessary, when FrontPage displays the Database Files In Current Web Site dialog box, double-click the folder, fpdb, and then click the file, jobopportunity.mdb.**

FrontPage displays the Database Files In Current Web Site dialog box (Figure 6-33). The URL for the selected database identifies it as the file, jobopportunity.mdb, in the fpdb folder of the JobOppsSite subsite.

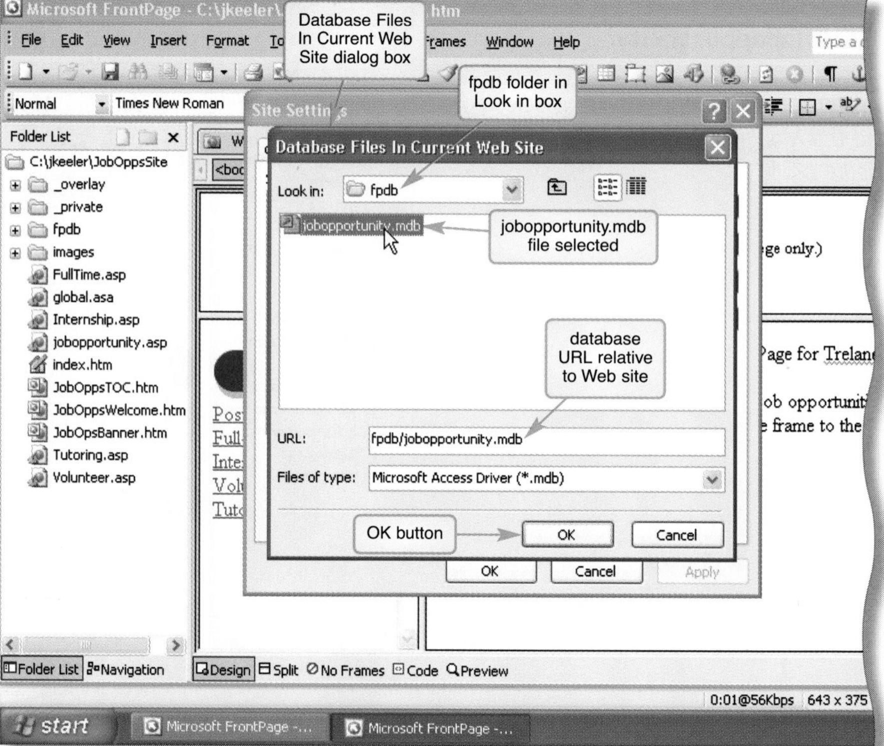

FIGURE 6-33

6

• **Click the OK button in the Database Files In Current Web Site dialog box.**

The setting for the relative path to the database is updated (Figure 6-34).

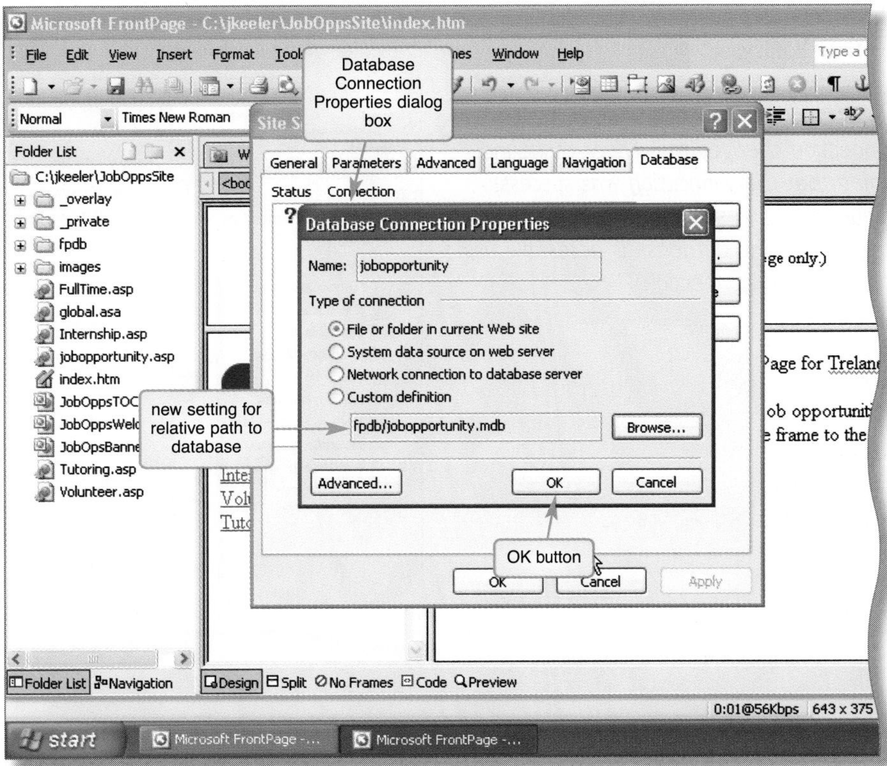

FIGURE 6-34

7

• **Click the OK button in the Database Connection Properties dialog box.**

FrontPage displays the Site Settings dialog box and the jobopportunity database connection with an unknown status, indicated by a question mark (Figure 6-35).

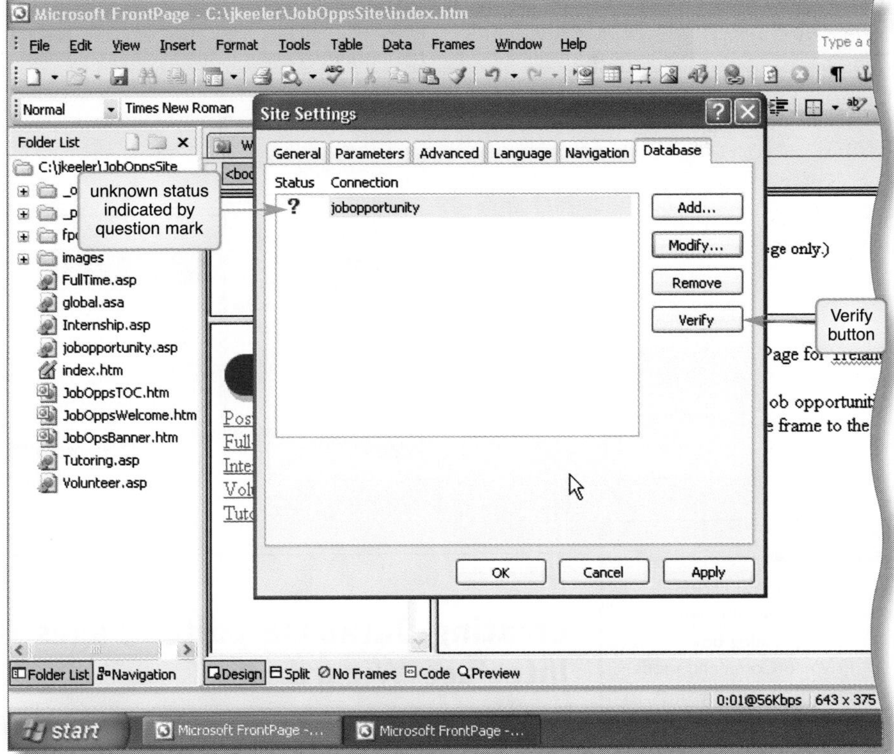

FIGURE 6-35

8

• **Click Verify.**

The status indicator of the database connection changes to a check mark, indicating that the verification was successful (Figure 6-36). A successful verification means that the database is accessible using this database connection.

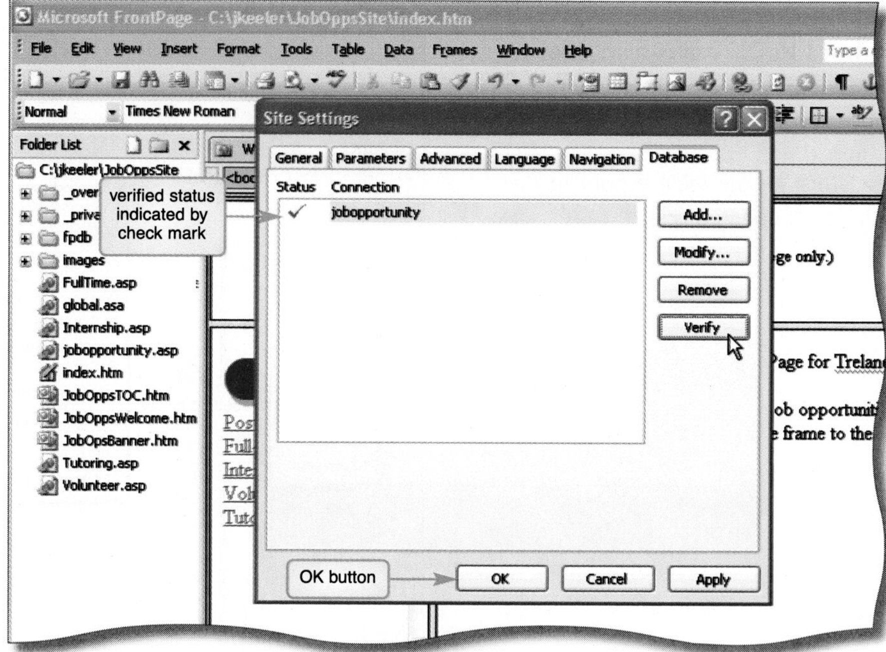

FIGURE 6-36

9

• **Click the OK button.**

The Site Settings dialog box closes (Figure 6-37). FrontPage displays the home page of the JobOppsSite subsite.

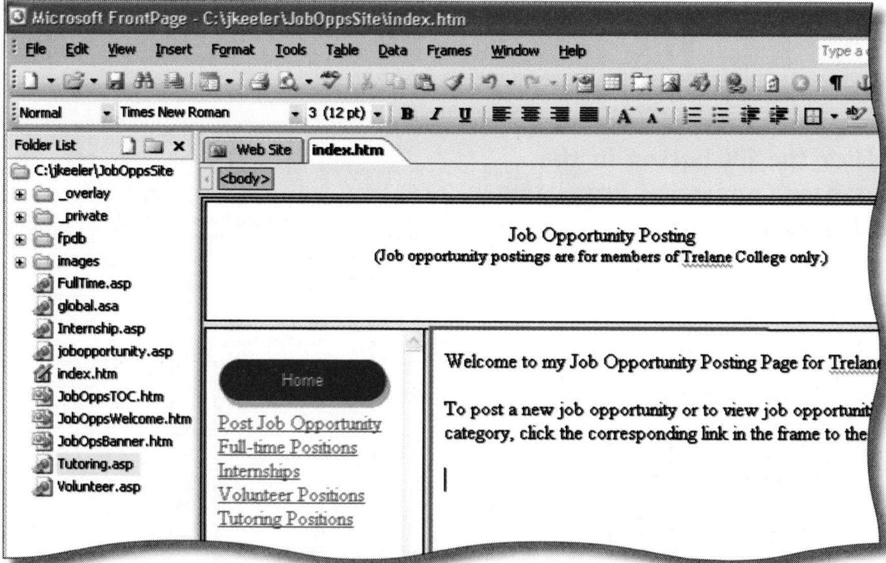

FIGURE 6-37

Other Ways

1. Press ALT+T, I click Database in the Site Settings dialog box
2. In Voice Command mode, say "Tools, Site Settings, Database"

Creating Database Editor Pages Using the Database Interface Wizard

Once the database connection is verified, the Database Interface Wizard can use the connection to locate the database and use information from the database to build the needed Web pages for database maintenance. The Database Interface Wizard guides you through a series of dialog boxes, similar to the Database Results Wizard, to build Database Editor Web pages that allow you to view, update, add, or delete records in the selected database. The Database Interface Wizard allows you to select which pages you want the wizard to build and whether the wizard should add them to the current Web site or create the pages in a new Web site.

In the following steps, the Database Interface Wizard will add a Results folder to the jobopportunity_interface folder, in which to store the new Database Editor pages. The Database Interface Wizard also creates a Database Editor - Results page, with the file name, database_editor.asp, and a Database Editor Login page, with the file name, login.asp.

The following steps use the Database Interface Wizard to create Database Editor pages that provide database maintenance capabilities.

More About

Database Connections

FrontPage needs certain information before it can access a database. This information is stored as a database connection in the file, global.asa. To learn more about database connections, visit the FrontPage 2003 More About Web page (scsite.com/fp2003/more) and then click Database Connections.

To Create Database Editor Pages Using the Database Interface Wizard

1

- **Click the Create a new normal page button arrow on the Standard toolbar.**

FrontPage displays the Create a new normal page menu (Figure 6-38).

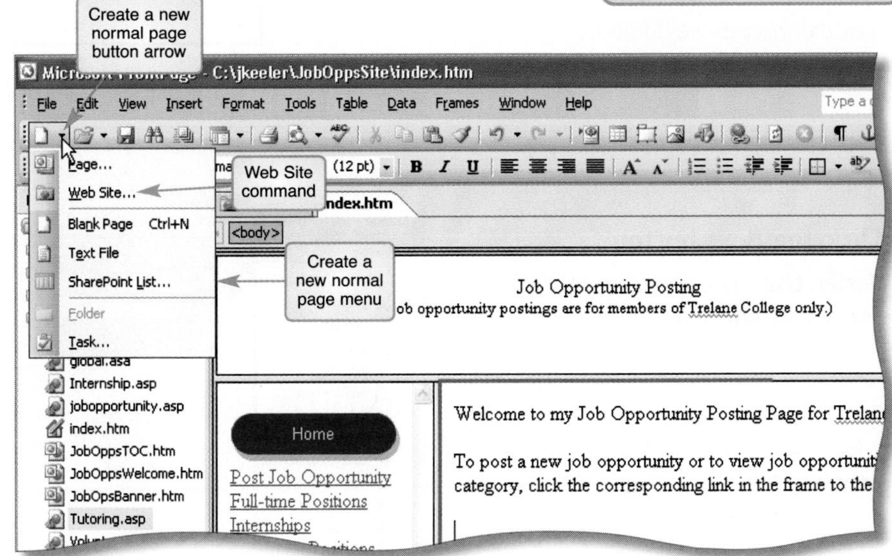

FIGURE 6-38

2

- **Click Web Site.**
- **When FrontPage displays the Web Site Templates dialog box, click the Database Interface Wizard icon.**
- **Click Add to current Web site in the Options area.**

FrontPage displays the Web Site Templates dialog box (Figure 6-39). The Database Interface Wizard icon is selected. Because the Add to current Web site option is selected, the pages created by the Database Interface Wizard will be added to the current Web site.

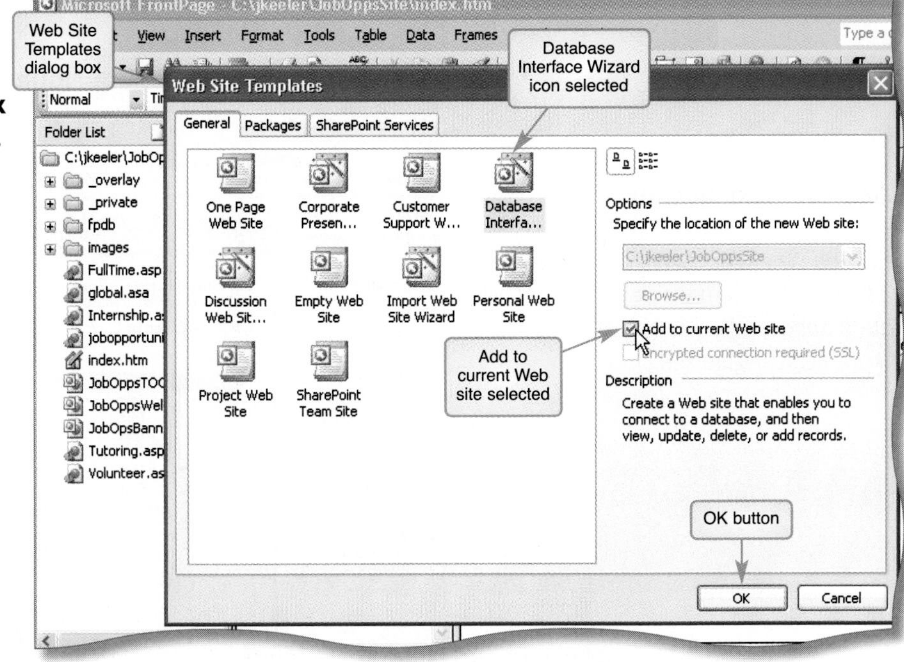

FIGURE 6-39

3

- **Click the OK button.**
- **Click Use an existing database connection.**
- **Verify that jobopportunity is the selected database connection.**

FrontPage displays the Database Interface Wizard dialog box with the Use an existing database connection option selected. The database connection, jobopportunity, is selected (Figure 6-40). The Database Interface Wizard will construct Web pages that access the database, jobopportunity.mdb.

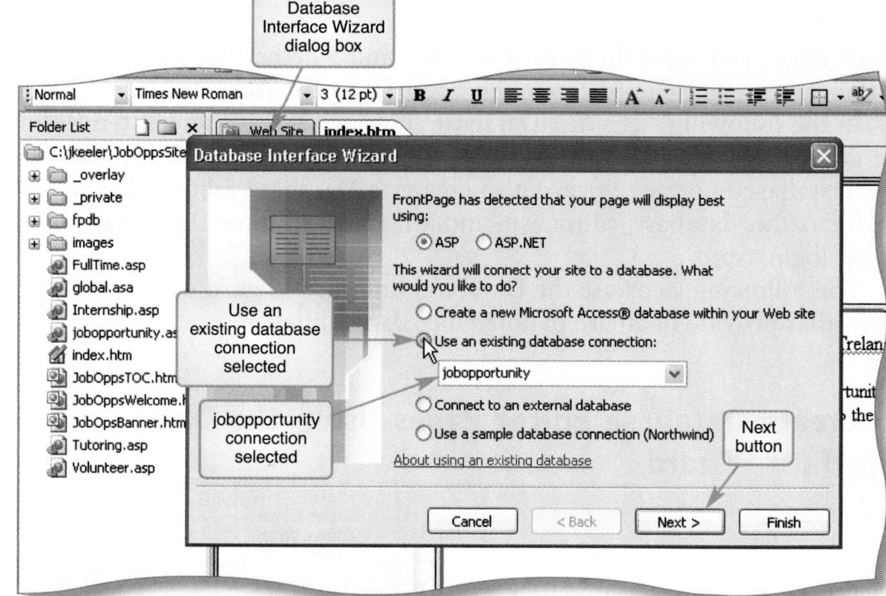

FIGURE 6-40

4

- **Click the Next button.**
- **Verify that the Results table is selected in the list.**

FrontPage displays the Database Interface Wizard with the Results table selected in the list of tables or views to use for this database connection (Figure 6-41).

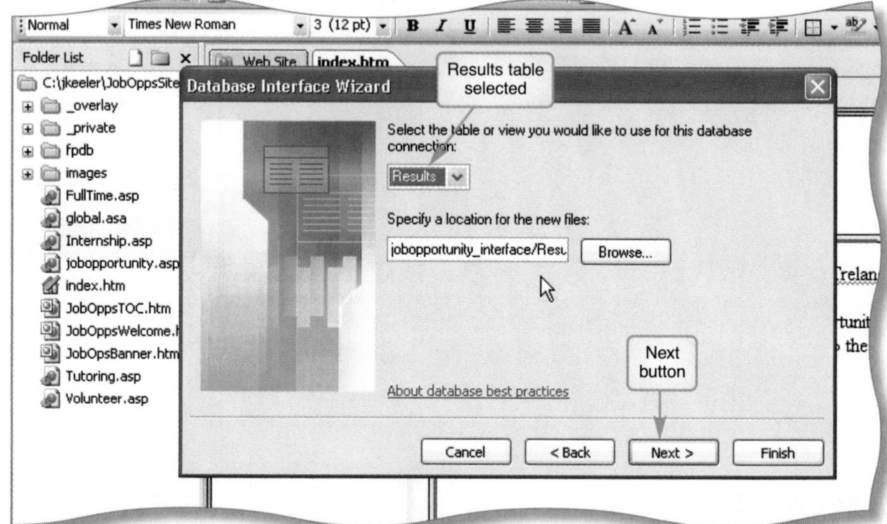

FIGURE 6-41

5

- **Click the Next button.**

The Database Interface Wizard displays a list of form fields from which the wizard will create database columns and submissions for input fields (Figure 6-42).

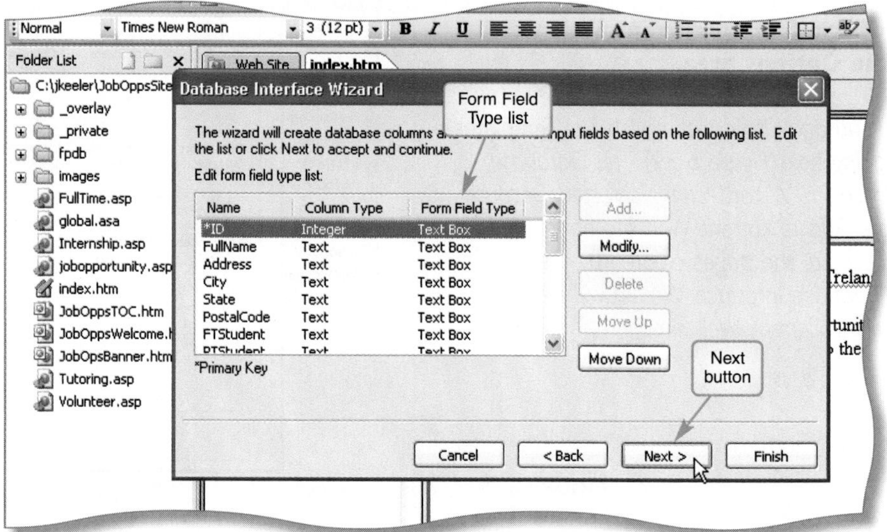

FIGURE 6-42

6

- **Click the Next button.**
- **If necessary, click Results Page and Submission Form to deselect them and then click Database Editor to select it.**

The Database Interface Wizard displays the three types of database interface pages it can create (Figure 6-43). Database Editor is selected. The Results Page and Submission Form pages already exist for this database from previous projects.

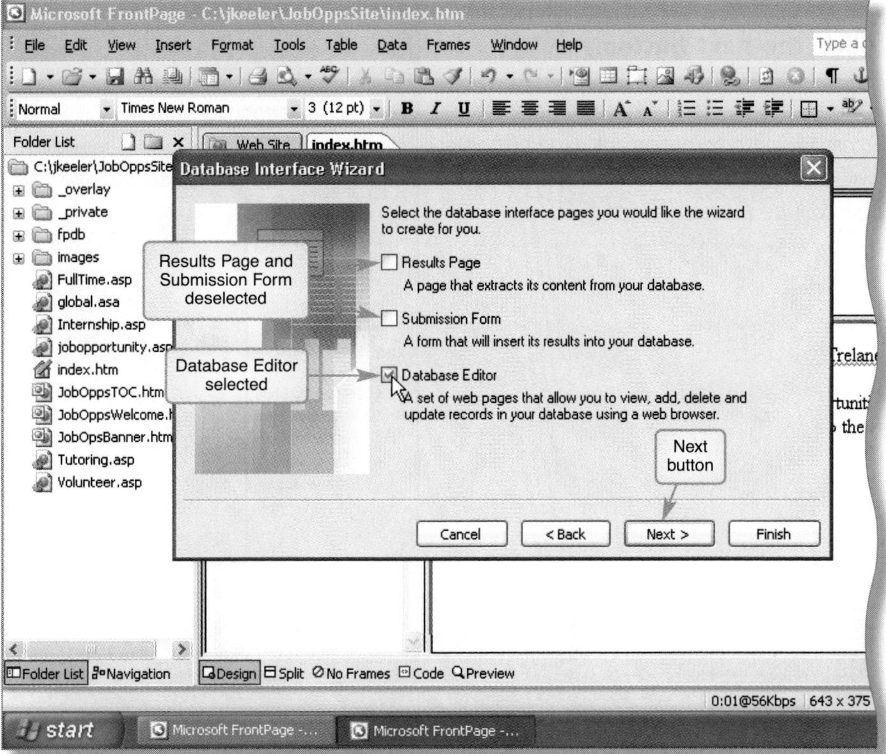

FIGURE 6-43

7

- **Click the Next button.**
- **If necessary, select the default user name, Administrator, and then type** `jkeeler` **(you may substitute your own user name here) in the User name text box.**
- **Type** `James` **(or a password of your choice) in the Password text box.**
- **Again, type** `James` **(or the password you chose) in the Confirm text box.**

FrontPage displays the user name (Figure 6-44). FrontPage displays the password as a series of asterisks for security purposes. FrontPage requires you to type the password again to confirm the selection. Although FrontPage provides an option to not use a user name and password, using them provides basic security to protect access to your database.

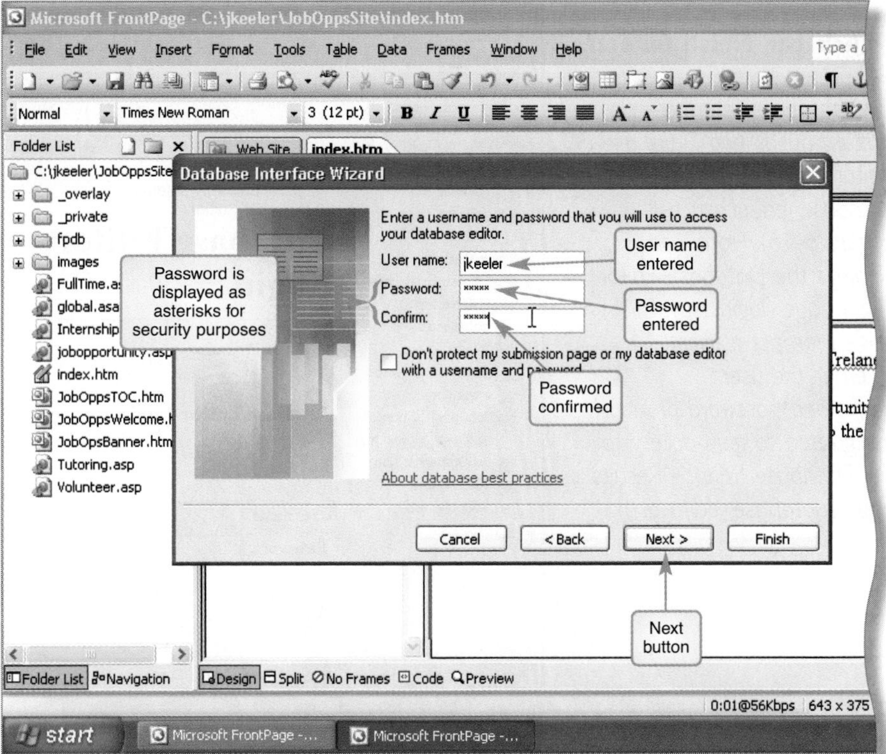

FIGURE 6-44

8

• **Click the Next button.**

FrontPage displays the Database Interface Wizard dialog box, noting the type of pages it will create and the folder in which the pages will be placed (Figure 6-45).

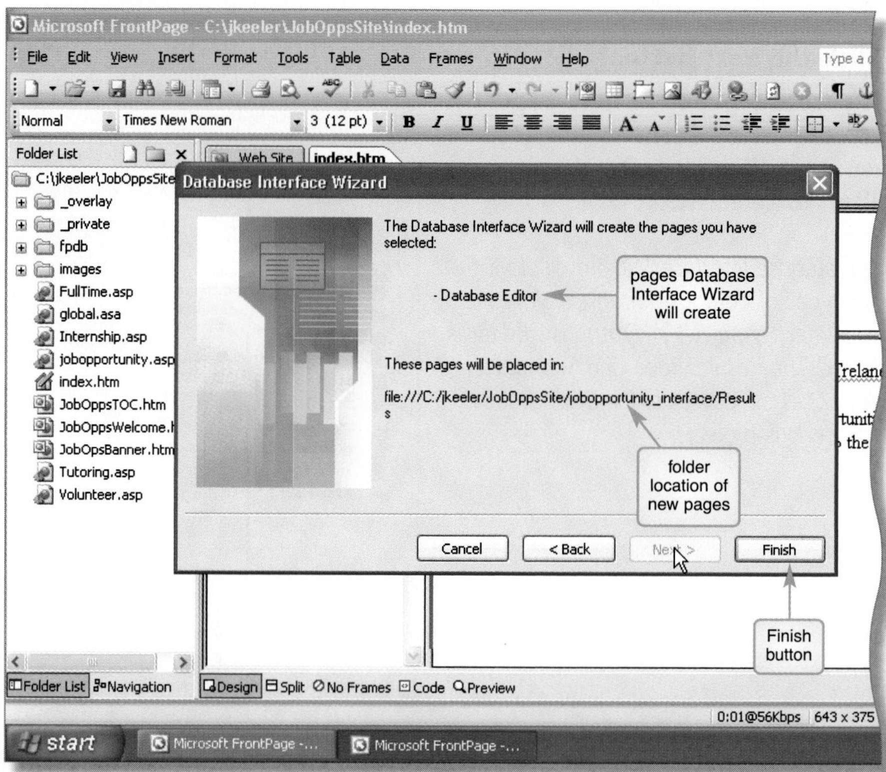

FIGURE 6-45

9

• **Click the Finish button.**

The Database Interface Wizard builds two Database Editor pages, login.asp and database_editor.asp (Figure 6-46). FrontPage displays the Database Editor Login page (login.asp). This page prompts a user to enter the user name and password previously designated to gain access to the Database Editor - Results page (database_editor.asp).

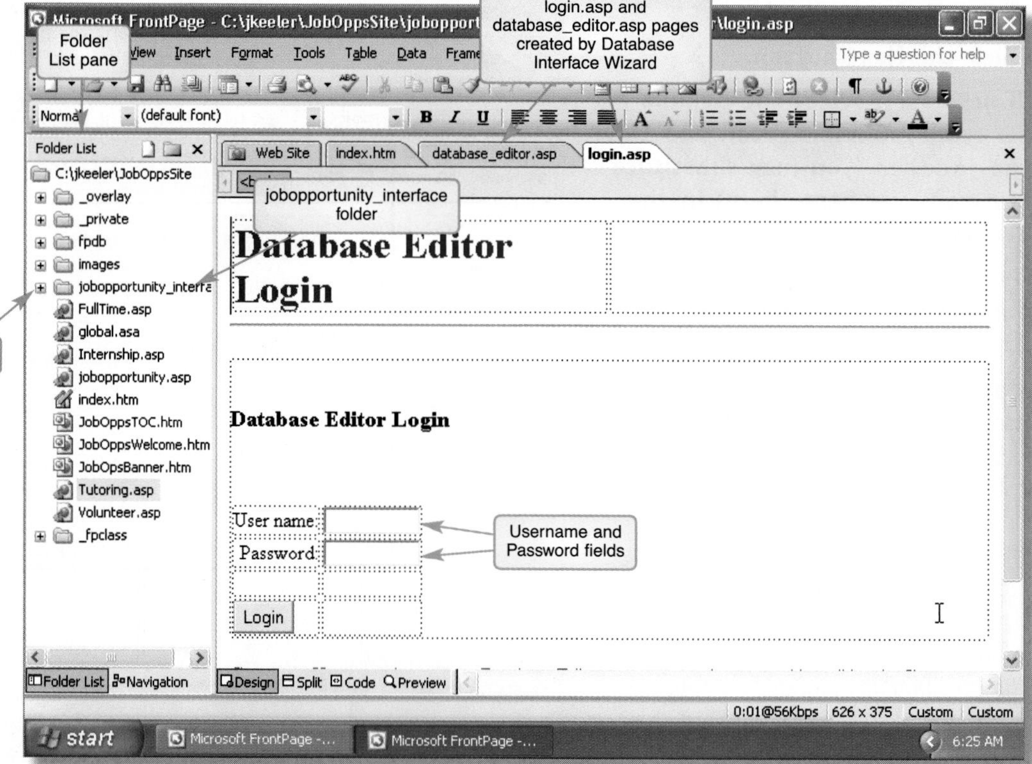

FIGURE 6-46

10

- **Click the plus sign in front of the new folder, jobopportunity_interface, to expand the folder.**
- **Click the plus sign in front of the folder, Results.**
- **When the Results folder expands, click the plus sign in front of the folder, editor.**

The eleven files created by the Database Interface Wizard are placed in the folder, jobopportunity_interface/Results/editor (Figure 6-47).

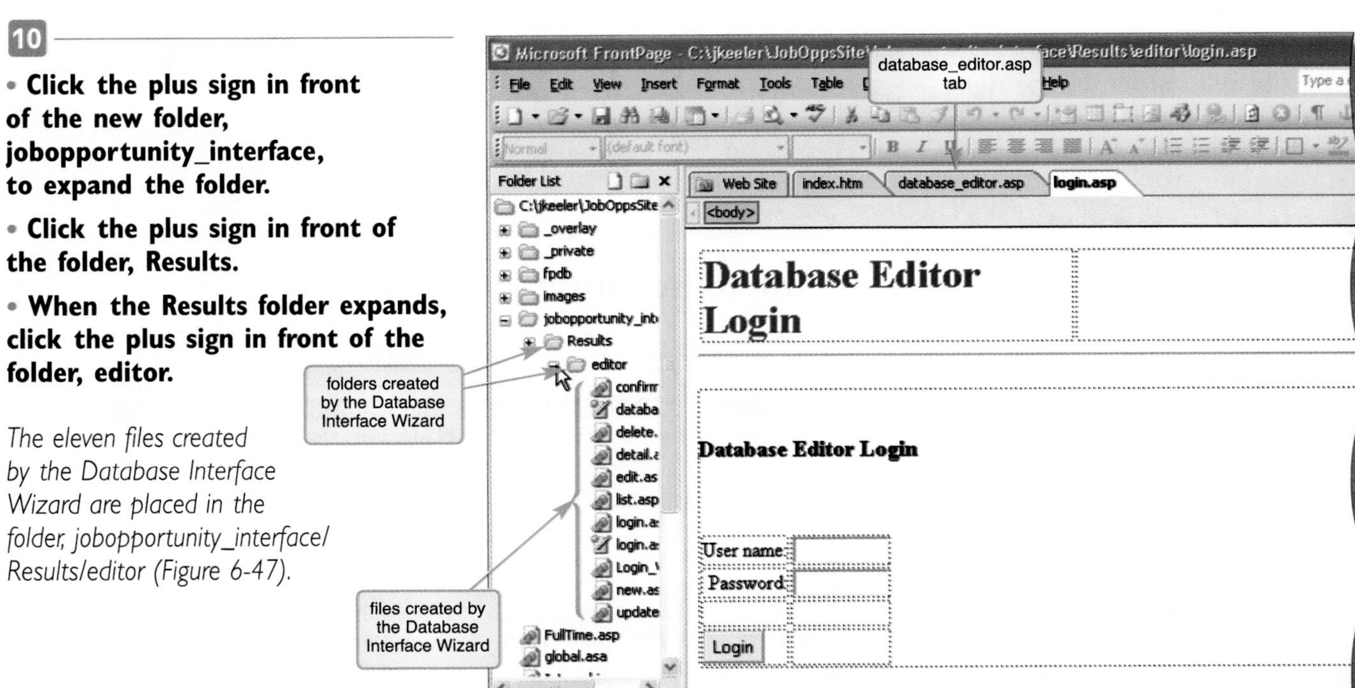

FIGURE 6-47

11

- **Click the database_editor.asp tab.**

FrontPage displays the Database Editor - Results page (Figure 6-48). This page is used to display records and allow users to make changes to the database.

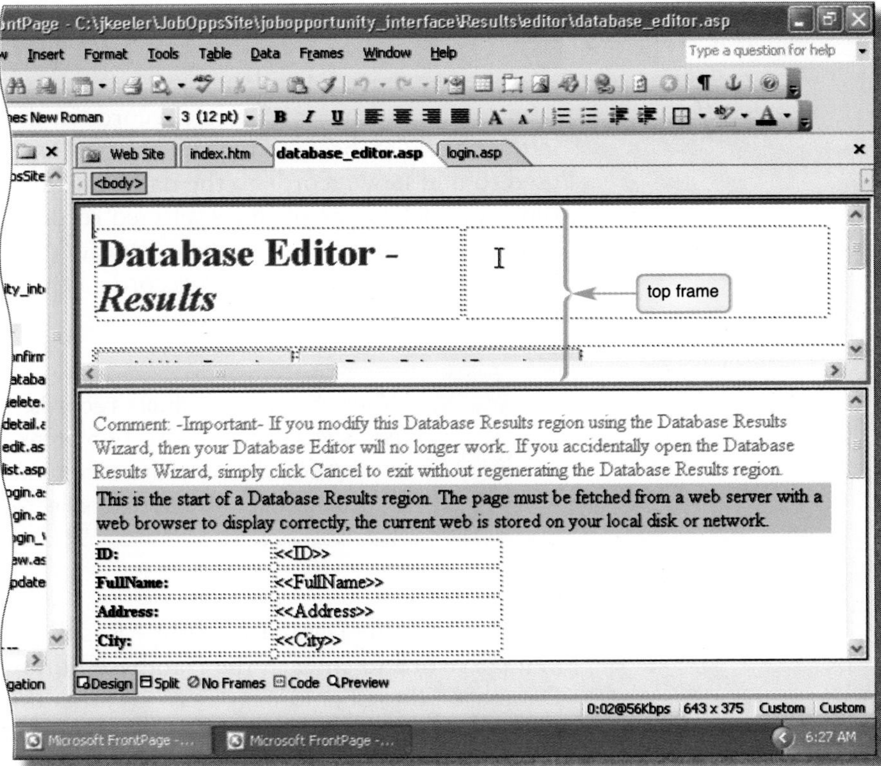

FIGURE 6-48

12

- **Drag the cell border to the right until the title text, Database Editor - Results, is displayed on a single line.**
- **Drag the horizontal border between the top and bottom frames down to display more of the page in the top frame, as shown in Figure 6-49.**

The title text, Database Editor - Results, is displayed on a single line (Figure 6-49). The top frame size is enlarged to display more of the page.

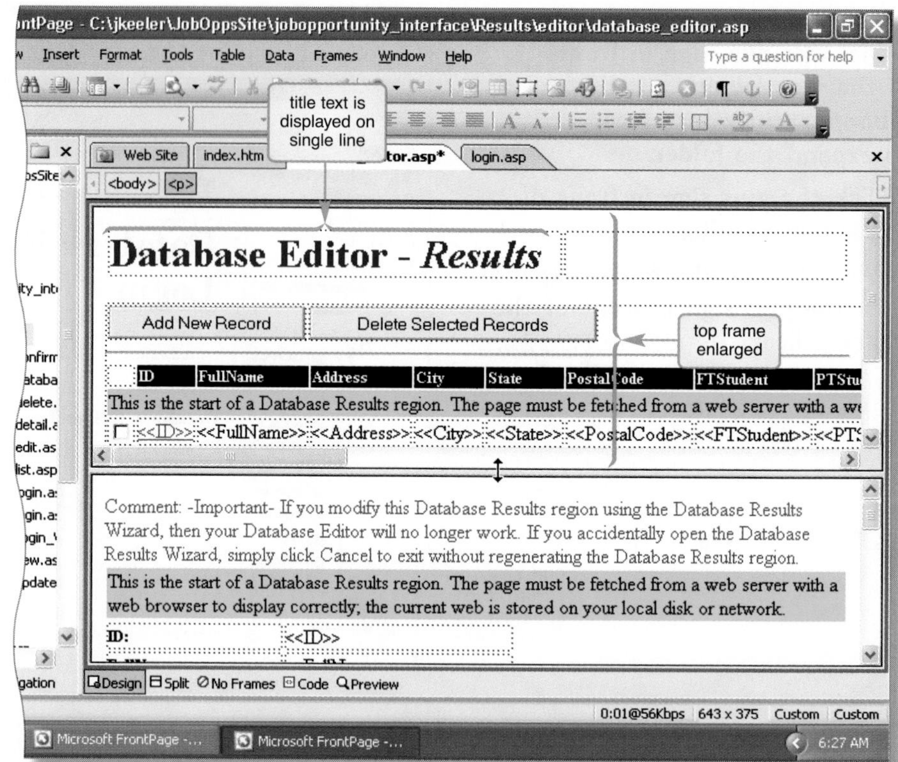

FIGURE 6-49

The Database Editor pages are complete. The Database Editor - Results page is used to add, update, and delete records in the jobopportunity database. Both frames in the page, database_editor.asp, contain Database Results regions. The top frame is used to add new records to the database, display multiple database records at one time, and delete one or more selected records. Clicking the check box next to a record displayed in the Database Results region in the top frame selects the record. Clicking the ID hyperlink in a record causes the record contents to be displayed in the lower frame.

Design Tip

When displaying multiple records, consider using frames to divide the user's viewing area into two areas. The first area contains a listing of all of the records while the second area allows the Web page visitor to view details about a record selected in the first area.

To access the Database Editor - Results page, a user must know the user name and password to enter in the Database Editor Login page. To make access to the Database Editor Login page easy for an authorized user, a hyperlink to the Database Editor Login page can be added to the link bar in the contents frame. Recall that hyperlinks to pages are added automatically to the link bar when the page is added to the navigation structure. The following steps add the Database Editor Login page to the navigation structure of the subsite.

To Add the Database Editor Login Page to the Navigation Structure

1

- **Click the Navigation command on the View menu.**
- **If necessary, scroll the Folder List pane to display the file, login.asp.**

FrontPage displays the Web site in Navigation view (Figure 6-50).

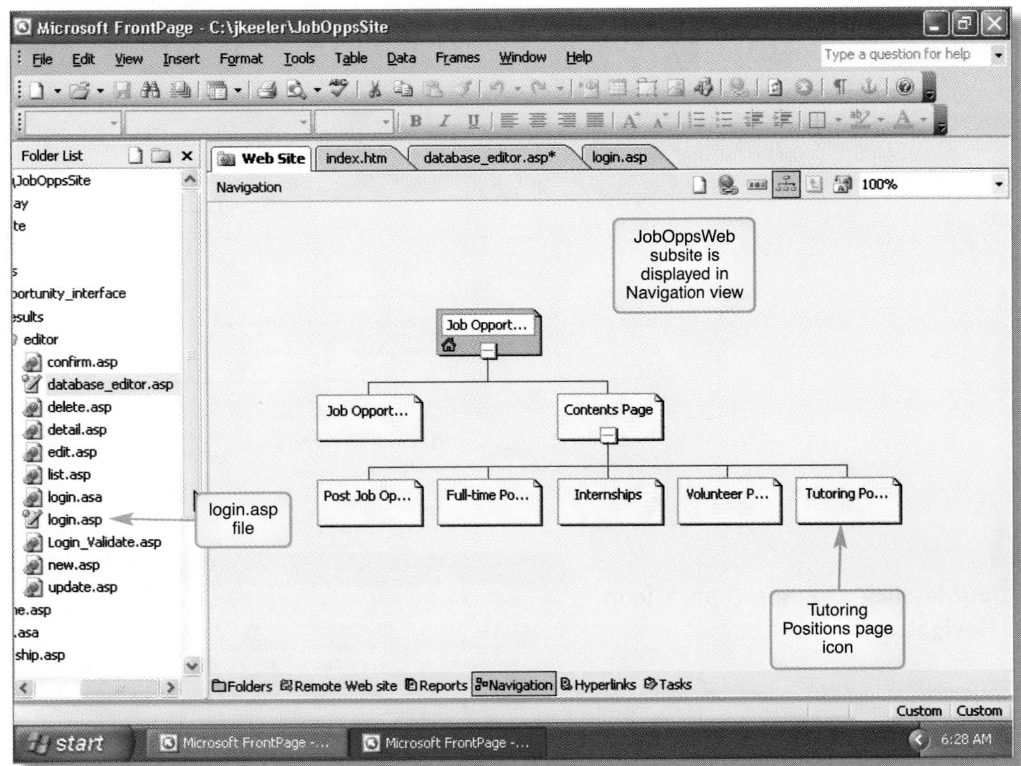

FIGURE 6-50

2

- **Drag the file, login.asp, from the Folder List pane and drop it to the right of the Tutoring Positions page icon in the Navigation pane.**

FrontPage displays the Results -- Login page icon for the file, login.asp, in Navigation view (Figure 6-51). The Database Editor Login page is added to the navigation structure of the JobOppsSite subsite.

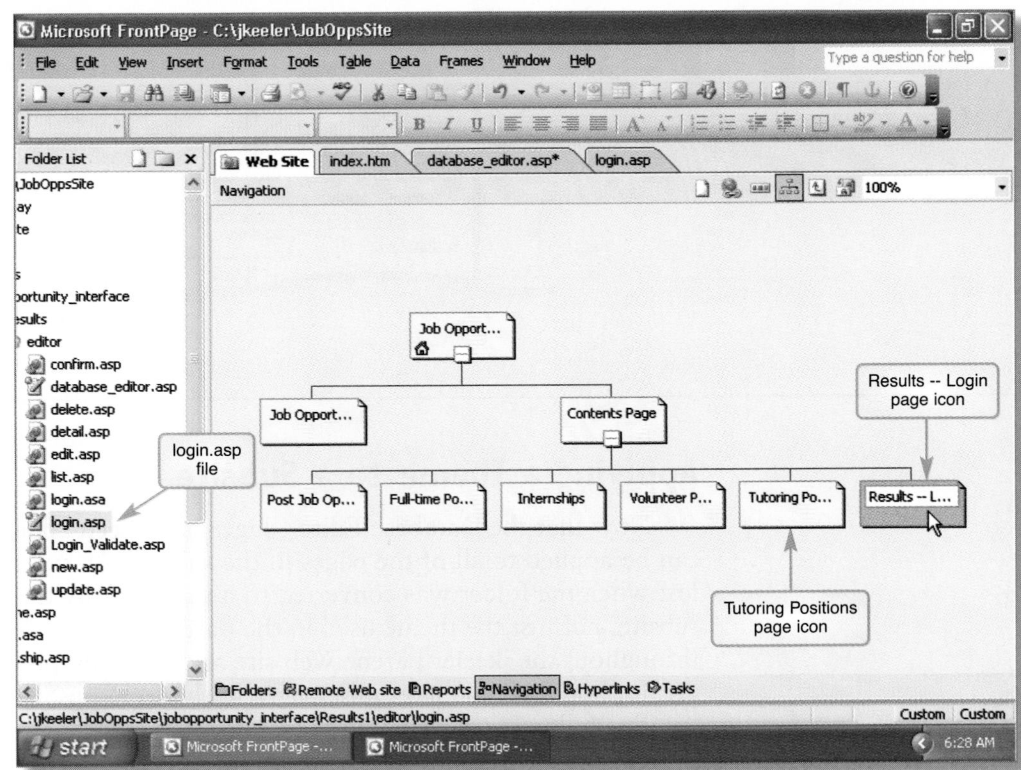

FIGURE 6-51

3

• **Right-click the Results -- Login page icon and then click Rename on the shortcut menu.**

• **Type** `Admin Only` **as the new title and then press the ENTER key.**

FrontPage displays the new title text, Admin Only (Figure 6-52). The title will be displayed on the link bar as the hyperlink name for this page.

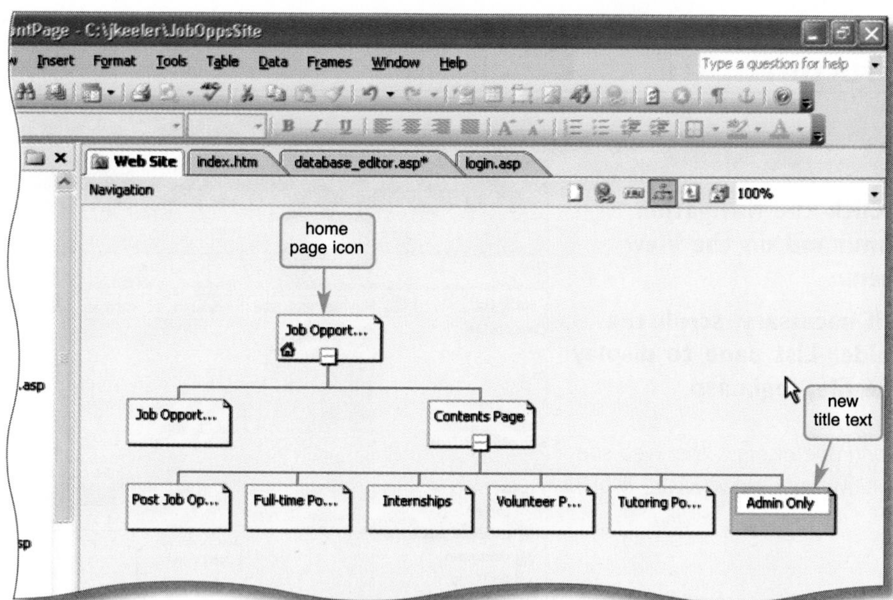

FIGURE 6-52

4

• **Double-click the home page icon in Navigation view.**

FrontPage displays the home page in Design view (Figure 6-53). The Admin Only hyperlink is displayed on the link bar. Clicking the link will display the Database Editor Login page.

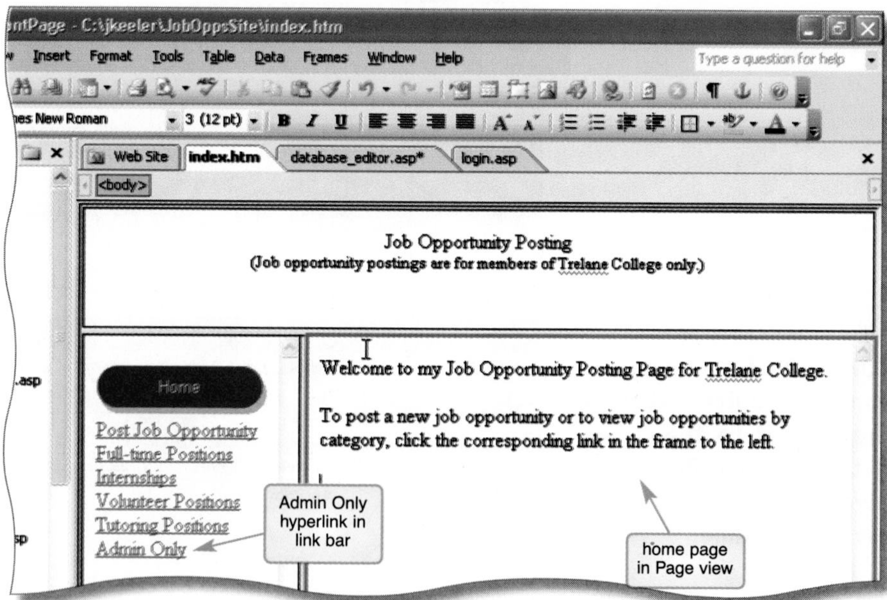

FIGURE 6-53

Applying a Theme to a Subsite

Now that the Database Editor pages have been added to the Web site, a theme can be applied to all of the pages in the subsite. As explained earlier, the theme was lost when the folder was converted to a subsite. Any theme can be applied to the subsite, not just the theme used in the parent Web site. To provide consistency throughout the jkeeler parent Web site and the JobOppsSite subsite, the Capsules theme should be applied to the pages in the JobOppsSite subsite.

The following steps apply the Capsules theme to all of the pages of the subsite.

To Apply a Theme to a Subsite

1

- **Click Format on the menu bar.**

FrontPage displays the Format menu (Figure 6-54).

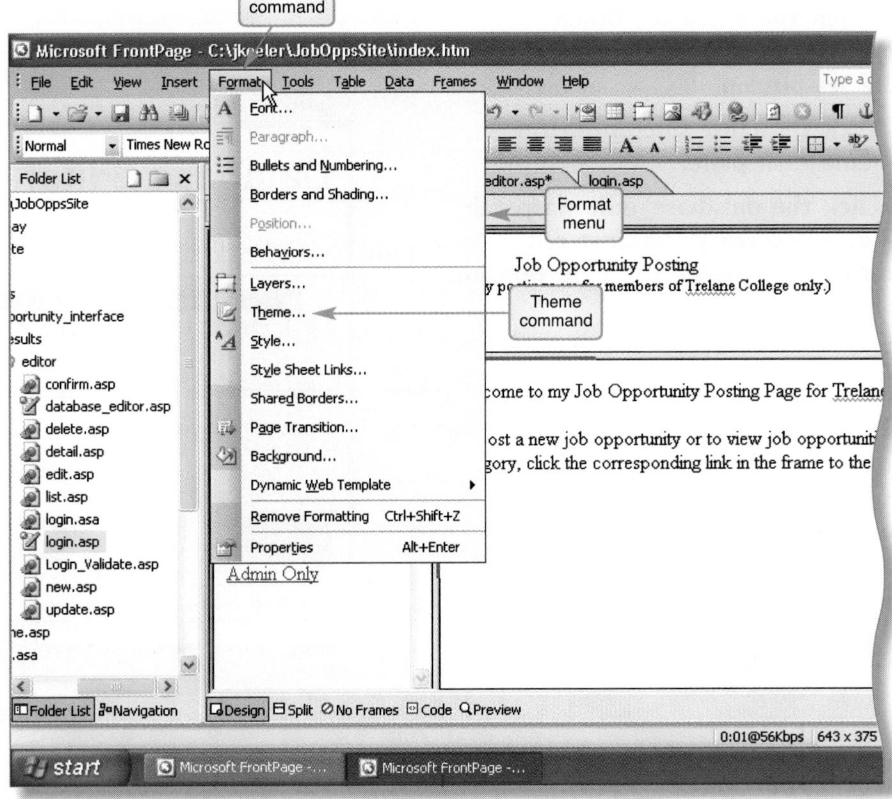

FIGURE 6-54

2

- **Click Theme.**
- **When FrontPage displays the Theme task pane, verify that the parent folder of the subsite is selected in the Folders List pane.**
- **If necessary, click Vivid colors.**
- **Verify that Active graphics and Background picture are selected.**
- **If necessary, scroll down the list of themes and then point to Capsules.**

FrontPage displays the Theme task pane (Figure 6-55). The Capsules theme appears and the Vivid colors, Active graphics, and Background picture options are selected. A sample of the theme is displayed in the Select a theme list.

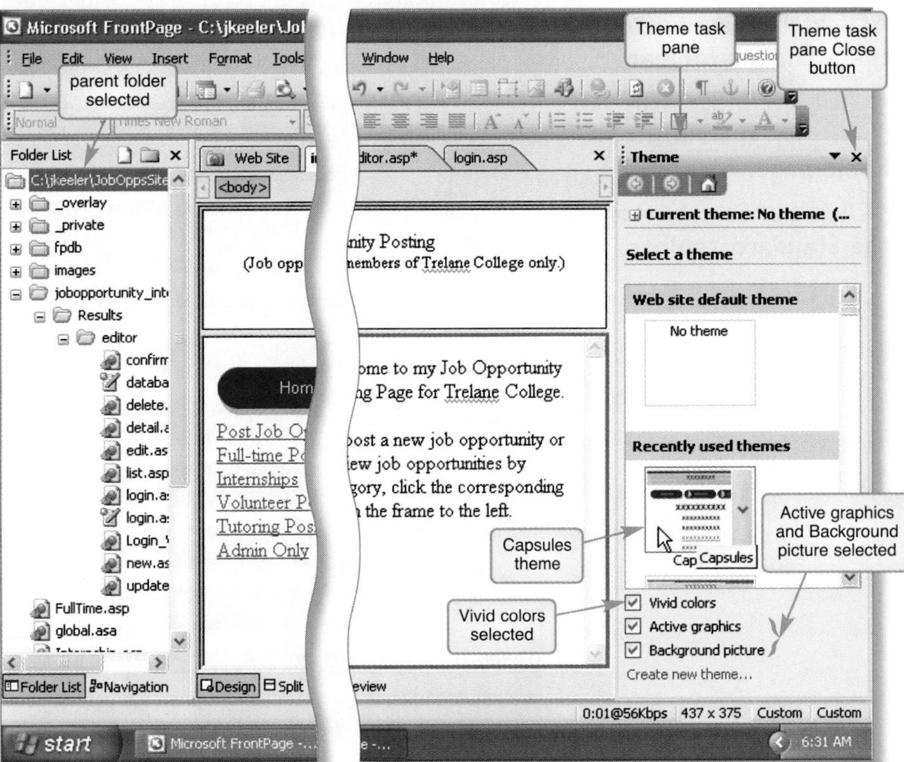

FIGURE 6-55

3

- **Click Capsules.**
- **When the Microsoft Office FrontPage dialog box appears, click the Yes button.**
- **Click the Close button on the Theme task pane.**
- **Click the database_editor.asp tab and, if necessary, readjust cell borders to display the title text on a single line.**

FrontPage displays the Database Editor - Results page. The Capsules theme is applied to all pages in the subsite (Figure 6-56).

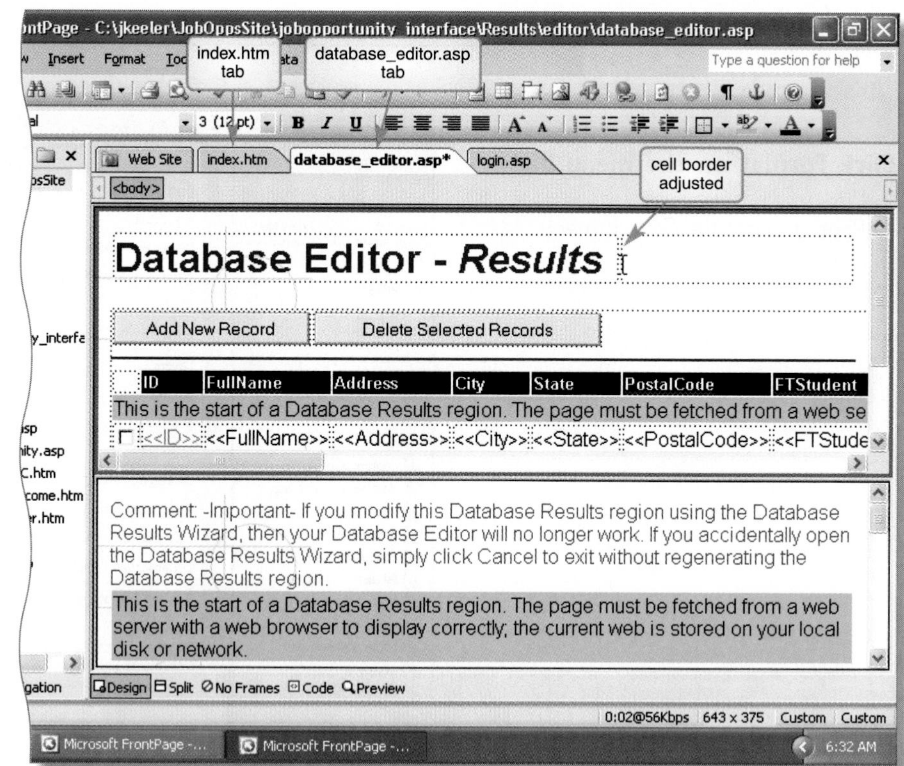

FIGURE 6-56

4

- **Click the Save button on the Standard toolbar.**
- **Click the index.htm tab to display the subsite home page.**
- **Click the Save button on the Standard toolbar.**

With the Capsules theme applied, the Link bar hyperlinks match the Home button image inserted from a file for the home page hyperlink (Figure 6-57).

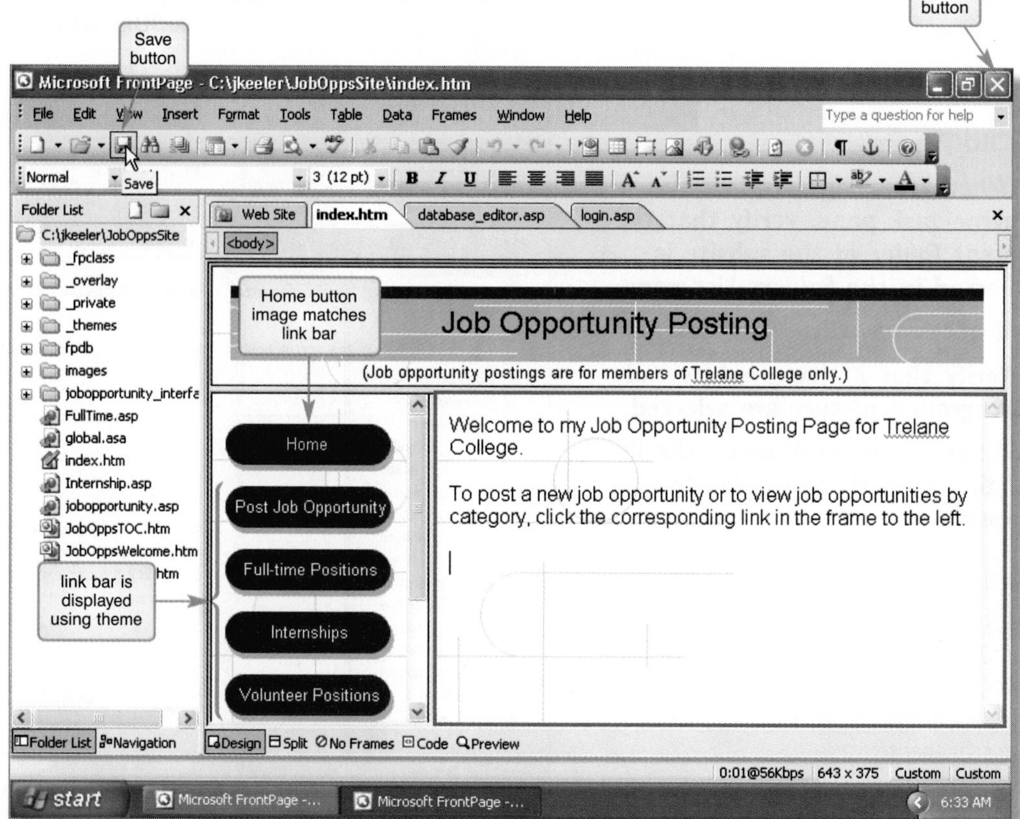

FIGURE 6-57

5

• **Click the Close button on the Microsoft FrontPage title bar.**

The FrontPage window that displayed the JobOppsSite subsite closes. The FrontPage window displaying the parent Web site remains open (Figure 6-58).

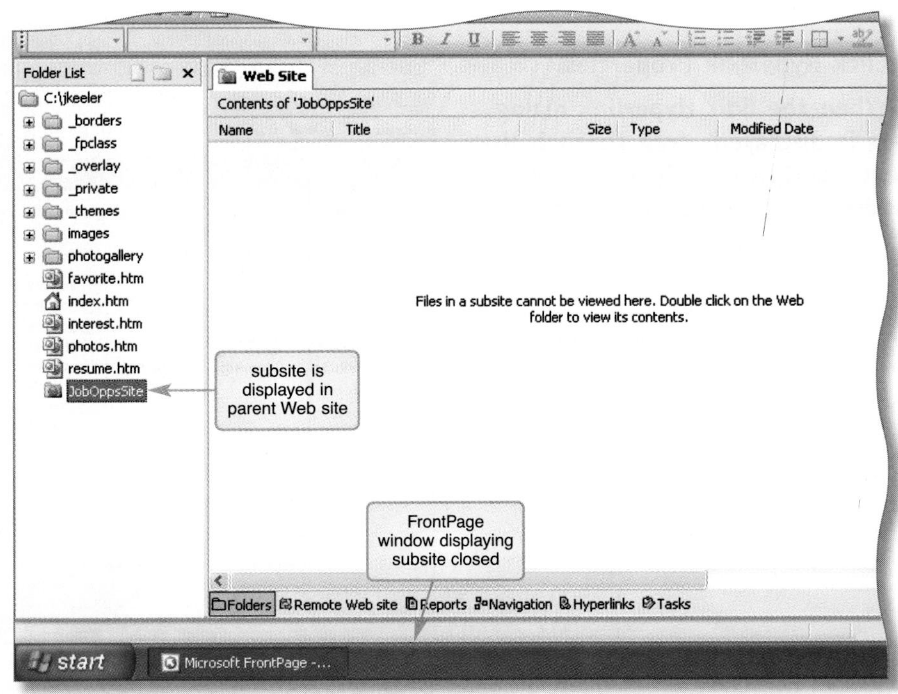

FIGURE 6-58

The changes to the subsite are complete. The Job Opportunities hyperlink on the parent Web site home page, however, uses a specific file name for the subsite home page (JobOppsSite/index.htm). Just as the hyperlink from the subsite to the parent Web site was modified to display the default home page, the Job Opportunities hyperlink must be modified so that it links to the default home page of the subsite (JobOppsSite/). The following steps modify the hyperlink to link to the default home page of the subsite.

To Modify a Hyperlink to Link to the Default Home Page

1

• **Double-click the home page icon in the Folder List pane.**

• **If necessary, scroll the Design view window down until the Job Opportunities link appears.**

• **Right-click the hyperlink text, Job Opportunities.**

FrontPage displays a shortcut menu (Figure 6-59).

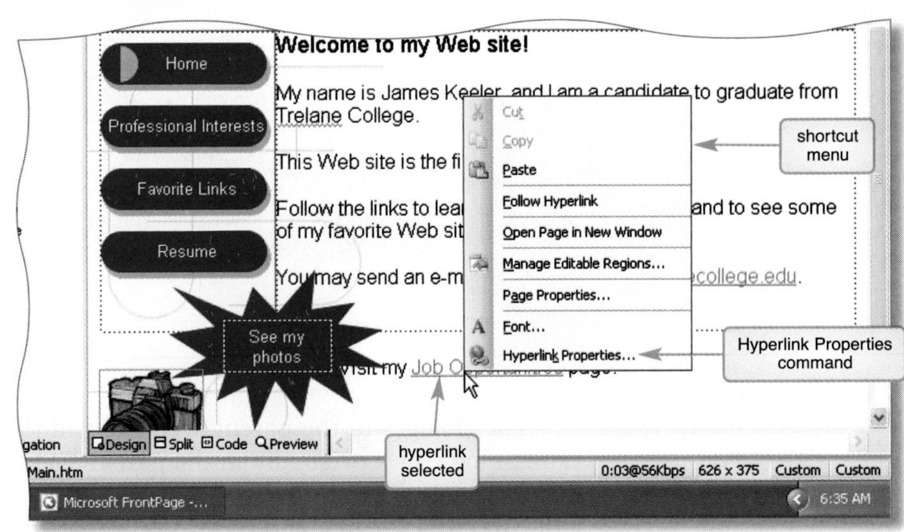

FIGURE 6-59

2

- **Click Hyperlink Properties.**
- **When the Edit Hyperlink dialog box is displayed, drag through the text, JobOppsMain.htm, in the Address text box and then press the DELETE key.**

FrontPage displays the address, JobOppsSite/, in the Address text box (Figure 6-60). This address indicates that the hyperlink target page is the JobOppsSite folder, but does not specify a particular page or file.

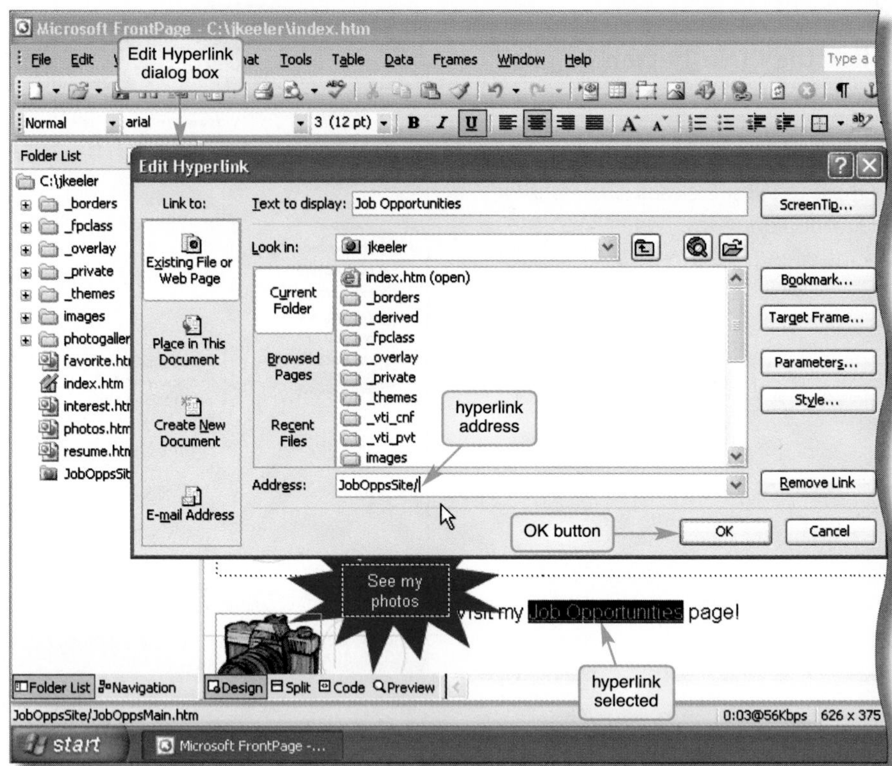

FIGURE 6-60

3

- **Click the OK button.**
- **When the Edit Hyperlink dialog box closes, click the Save button on the Standard toolbar.**
- **Position the mouse pointer over the hyperlinked text.**

FrontPage displays a URL of JobOppsSite/ on the status bar (Figure 6-61). Clicking the hyperlink will request the default home page from this folder location.

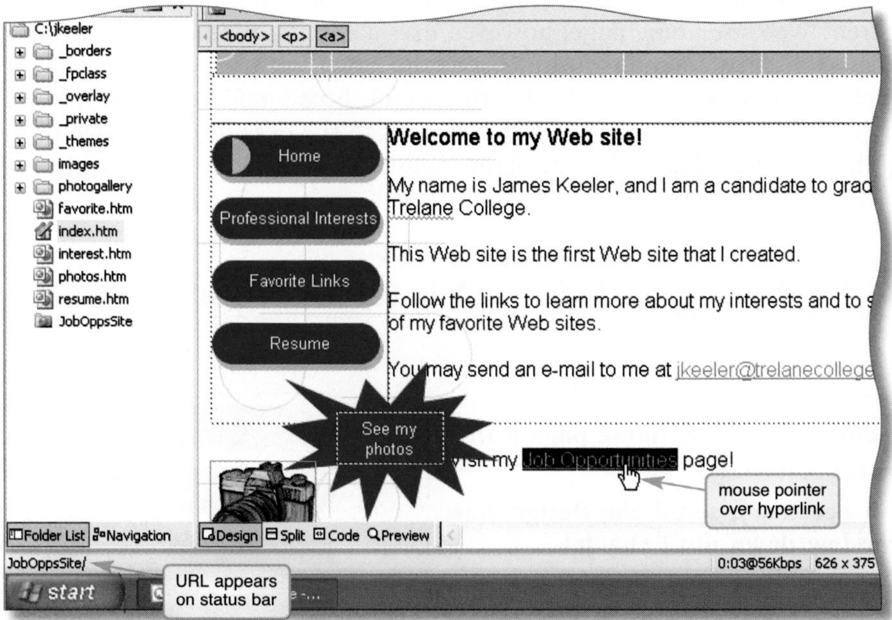

FIGURE 6-61

The changes to the parent Web site and the subsite are complete. The folder containing pages originally in the parent Web site is converted to a subsite and the subsite pages are modified to include Database Editor pages and the correct navigation structure, theme, and hyperlinks. The parent Web site and subsite are ready to be published and tested on a Web server.

Publishing a Web Site and Subsite

Because both the parent Web site and the subsite have changed, you must publish the modified parent Web site and the new subsite. The following steps publish the modified Web site and the new subsite.

To Publish a Parent Web Site and Subsite

1

- **Click the Web Site tab.**
- **Click the Remote Web site button.**

FrontPage displays the Remote Web site view (Figure 6-62).

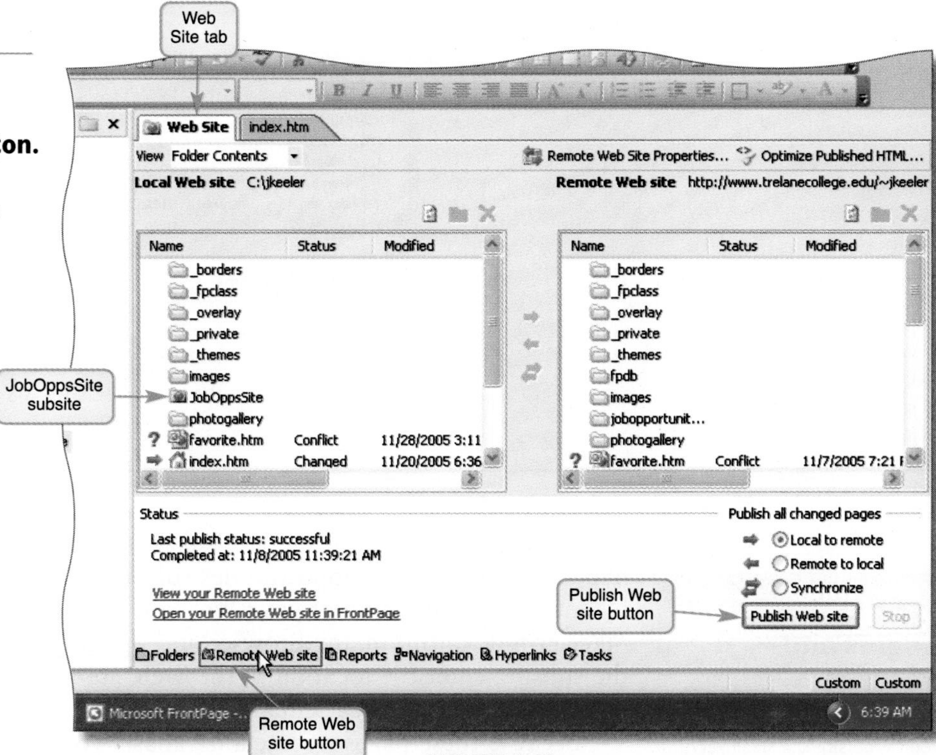

FIGURE 6-62

2

- **If necessary, click the Remote Web Site Properties button and when the Remote Web Site Properties dialog box is displayed, click the Publishing tab and then click the Include subsites check box to select it. Click the OK button to close the Remote Web Site Properties dialog box.**
- **Click the Publish Web site button.**

FrontPage displays the Do you want to remove this file? dialog box (Figure 6-63). The files that previously existed in the parent Web site should be deleted from the remote Web site.

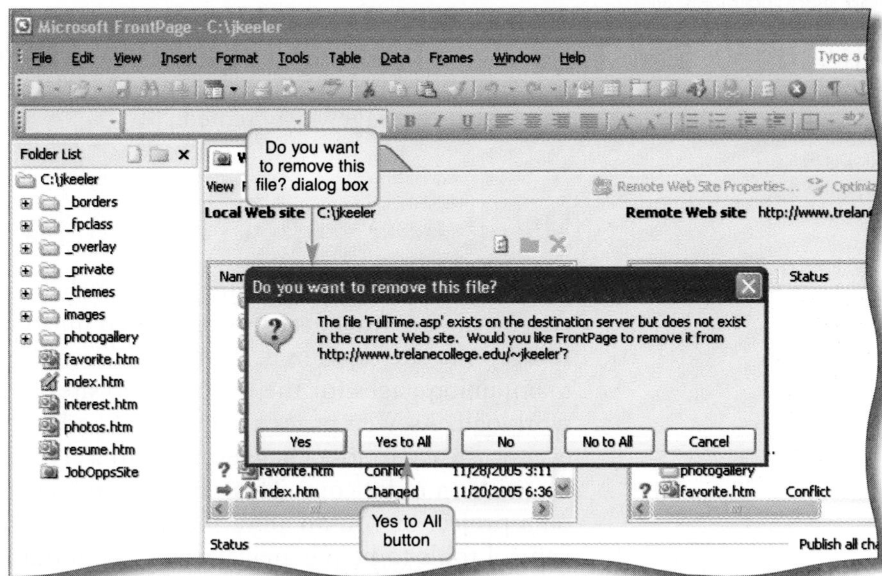

FIGURE 6-63

3

• **Click the Yes to All button.**

FrontPage finishes the publishing process and both the parent Web site and subsite are published to the remote server.

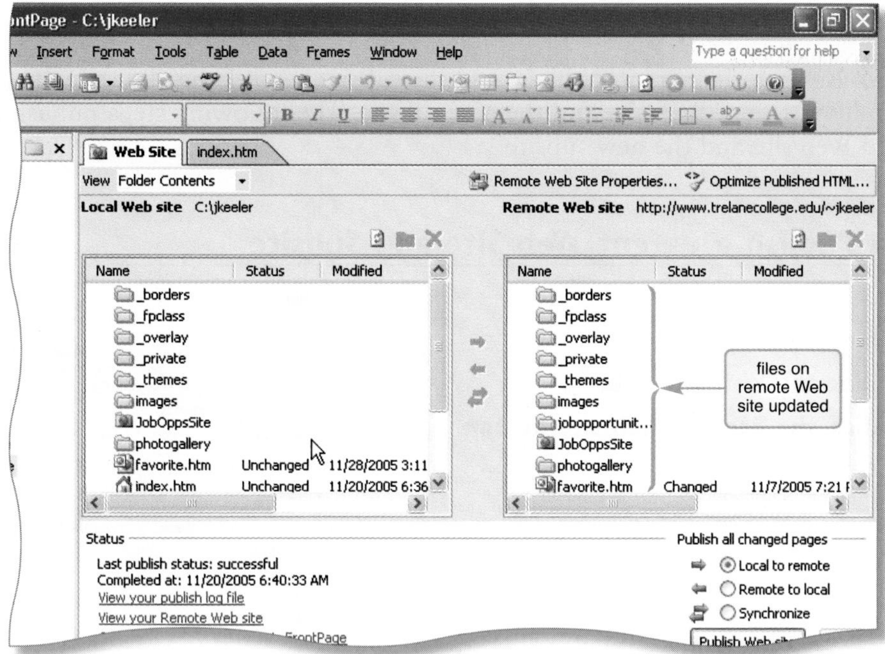

FIGURE 6-64

More About

Logins and Security

Controlling who can log in to your Web site is a small yet important part of providing security for your Web site. To learn more about logins and security, visit the FrontPage 2003 More About Web page (scsite.com/fp2003/more) and then click Logins and Security.

Once the parent Web site and subsite are published, you can view and test the hyperlinks to the Job Opportunities subsite and each of the hyperlinks on that page by entering the location of your Web site (e.g., http://www.trelanecollege.edu/~jkeeler/index.htm) in any browser and pressing the ENTER key. To go directly to the subsite, enter the location of the Web site with the subsite folder specified (e.g., http://www.trelanecollege.edu/~jkeeler/JobOppsSite/index.htm).

Because these pages update a database, you also should test the functionality of the new pages to verify that you actually can update the database. When viewing the Job Opportunities subsite in a browser, click the Admin Only hyperlink to display the Login page. You should test the Login page with an invalid user name and password to verify that this level of security does work. Test the Login page with a valid user name and password and then add, delete, modify, and view records in the database using the pages just created.

Using and Reporting on Source Control

As a Web site grows, maintaining the Web site becomes increasingly complex. As you have learned, separating related information into appropriate subsites helps to keep the site organized. Assigning different individuals the tasks of creating and maintaining pages for the various Web sites and subsites helps to distribute the workload. As Web pages are modified and tested by one or more individuals, however, it is easy to lose changes made to a file by overwriting a newer version of the file with an older copy. This can happen whether you have multiple people working on a project or you do all of the work alone. FrontPage provides built-in source control tools to help manage access and modifications to the files in your Web site.

Decide on using source control during the design process. Use source control when the possibility exists that multiple Web page developers may be able to edit Web pages at the same time.

Enabling Source Control

Source control is the ability to control access to and the updating of files to ensure a file does not get changed improperly. Using source control helps ensure that all developers are using the latest version of a file; that files are not incorrectly moved, deleted, or modified; and that no two people are editing the same file at the same time, resulting in overwritten changes.

Most source control methods use a system of checking files in and out to allow individual Web page developers to update files as needed. If a developer chooses to **check out** a file, that file is marked as being in use by a given developer, and other developers cannot make concurrent modifications to the same file. A file that is checked out may be opened by another developer as **read-only**, a setting that allows a file to be read or copied, but not changed or saved. If you modify a read-only file, you can save any changes only by saving the file with a new file name. When a developer chooses to **check in** a file after editing and saving it, FrontPage releases control of the document so that other developers can check out the file and make modifications. A developer also can choose to **undo a check out**, which means the file is checked in without applying any of the changes that were made since the file was checked out.

Before you can use the FrontPage source control feature for a particular Web site, you must enable it for that Web site. Because the parent Web site and the subsite are both complete Web sites, you must enable the source control feature separately for each. Source control can be enabled for both disk-based Web sites and Web sites published to a Web server. In most cases, as in this project, it is more important to enable source control for the disk-based Web site, because that is where you actually modify pages before publishing them to a Web server. If you do modify files directly on the Web server, however, then you also should enable source control for the Web site published on the Web server.

The steps on the next page enable source control for the JobOppsSite subsite and the parent Web site.

Q&A

Q: What is the difference between source control and version control?

A: Source control is used to prevent multiple developers from making changes to the same file simultaneously. Version control usually means managing multiple versions of the same file. To learn more about source control, visit the FrontPage 2003 More About Web page (scsite.com/fp2003/more) and then click Source Control.

More About

The Quick Reference

For more information, see the Quick Reference Summary at the back of this book, or visit the FrontPage 2003 Quick Reference Web page (scsite.com/fp2003/qr).

To Enable Source Control

1

- **Double-click the subsite, JobOppsSite, to open it in a new FrontPage window.**
- **Close any pages that are open.**

FrontPage displays the subsite (Figure 6-65). All pages in the subsite are closed.

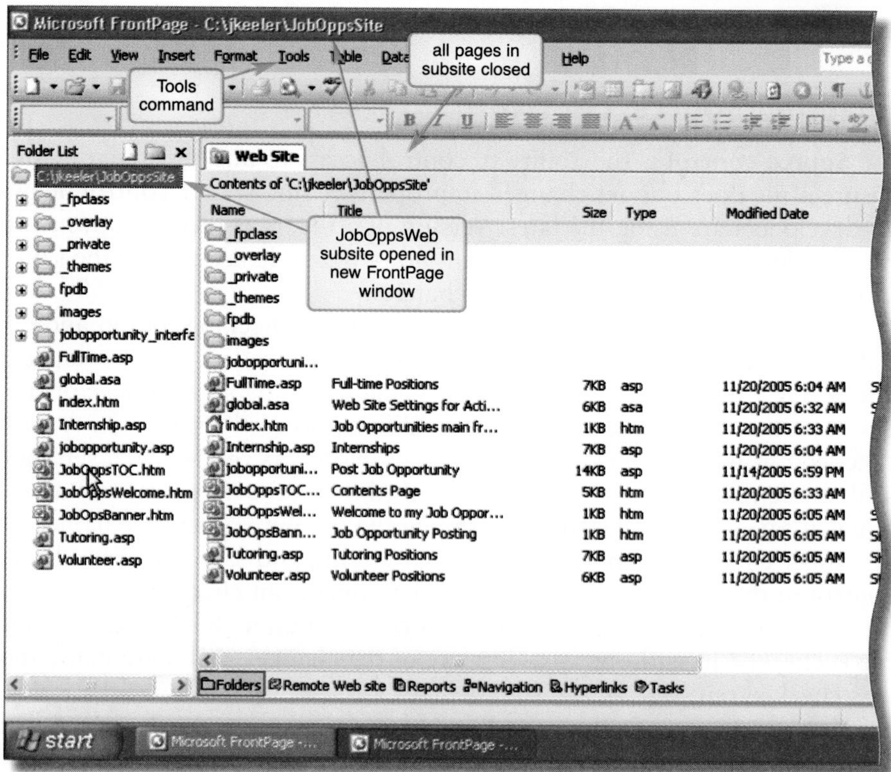

FIGURE 6-65

2

- **Click Tools on the menu bar.**

FrontPage displays the Tools menu (Figure 6-66).

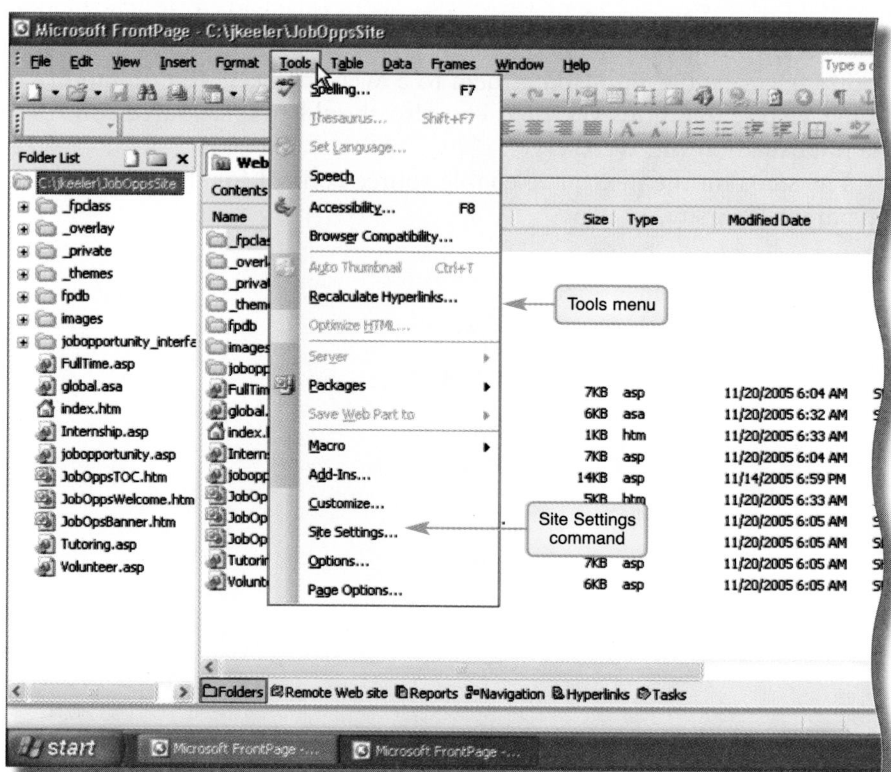

FIGURE 6-66

3

- **Click Site Settings.**
- **If necessary, when FrontPage displays the Site Settings dialog box, click the General tab.**
- **Click Use document check-in and check-out to select it.**

FrontPage displays the Site Settings dialog box (Figure 6-67). Use document check-in and check-out is selected to enable source control for the JobOppsSite subsite. The Check out files from the Local Web Site option is selected.

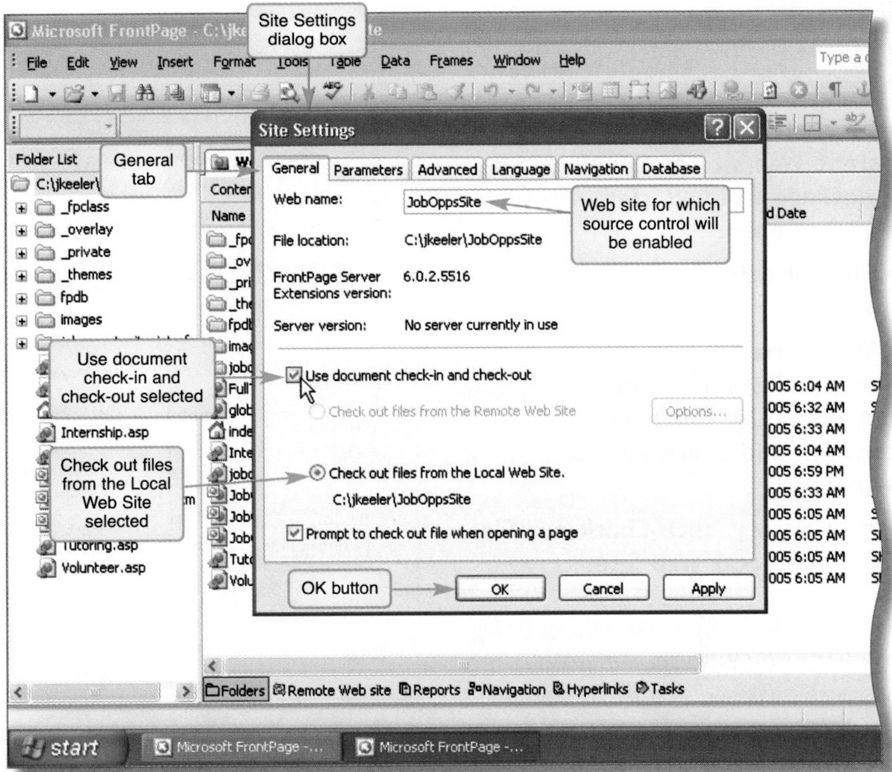

FIGURE 6-67

4

- **Click the OK button.**
- **When the Microsoft Office FrontPage dialog box is displayed, click the Yes button.**

FrontPage displays a dialog box, stating that you have changed the source control for this project and that recalculating the change can take a few minutes. The Web site is displayed in Folders view (Figure 6-68).

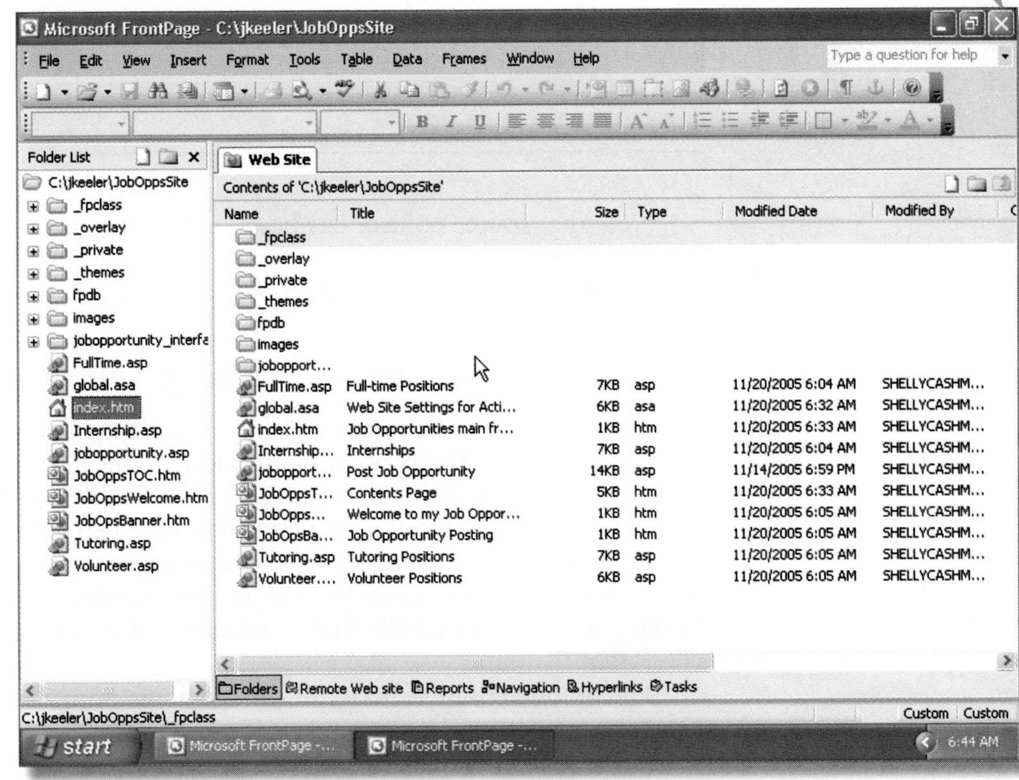

FIGURE 6-68

5

- **Click the Close button on the Microsoft FrontPage window.**
- **When FrontPage displays the parent Web site in the Microsoft FrontPage window, close any pages that are open.**
- **Click Site Settings on the Tools menu.**
- **When FrontPage displays the Site Settings dialog box, Click Use document check-in and check-out to select it.**
- **If necessary, click Check out files from the Local Web Site.**

FrontPage displays the Site Settings dialog box (Figure 6-69). Because the Web site has been published to a remote server, the Check out files from the Remote Web Site option button is available.

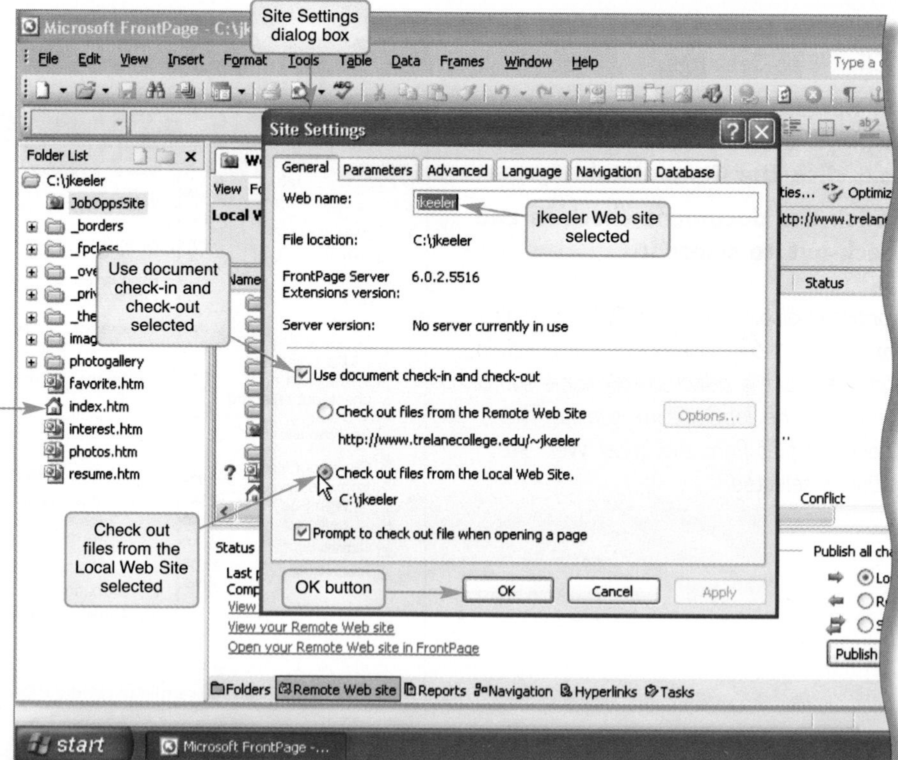

FIGURE 6-69

- **Click the OK button.**
- **When the Microsoft Office FrontPage dialog box is displayed, click the Yes button.**

Other Ways

1. To display the Site Settings dialog box, press ALT+T, I
2. To display the Site Settings dialog box and select the check-in and check-out option, in Voice Command mode, say "Tools, Site Settings, Use document check-in and check-out"

Now that source control has been enabled for the parent Web site and the subsite, developers can check files in and out to make changes. As they do so, individual files are marked as in use (checked out) or available for use by others (checked in).

Checking Files In and Out Using Source Control

Once source control is enabled for a Web site, you have to check out a file before you can modify it. The process for checking out a file is quite simple. First, you should determine if a file is available to check out. FrontPage displays icons next to a file name in the Folder List pane to indicate whether a file is checked out by either you or another developer. A green check mark indicates a file that has been checked out by you; a padlock indicates that another developer has checked out the file. When you try to open a file that is not checked out, FrontPage asks if you want to check that file out.

The following steps check out the file, index.htm, from a Web site with source control enabled.

To Check Out a File Under Source Control

1

• **Double-click the file, index.htm, in the Folder List pane.**

A Microsoft Office FrontPage dialog box is displayed (Figure 6-70). Because the index.htm file is under source control and is available for modification, FrontPage asks if you want to check the file out.

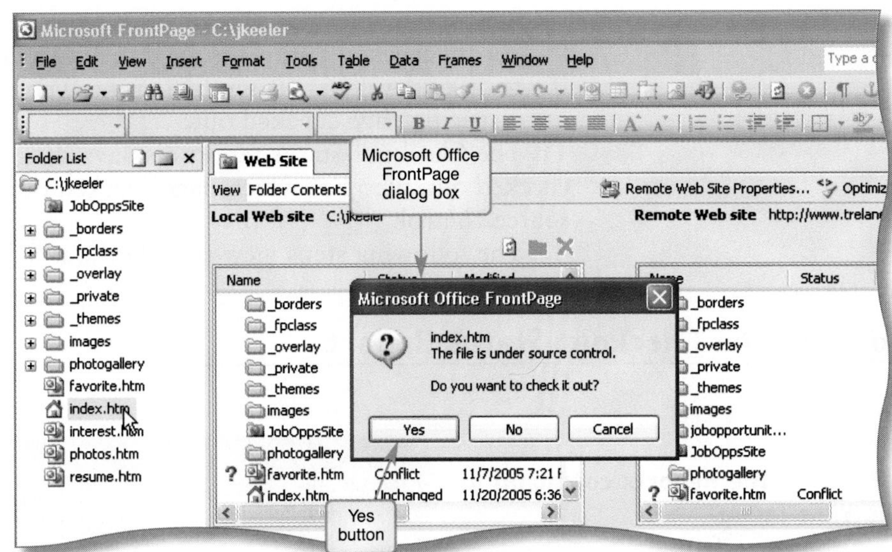

FIGURE 6-70

2

• **Click Yes in the Microsoft Office FrontPage dialog box.**

The Microsoft Office FrontPage dialog box closes and the index.htm file is displayed in Design view (Figure 6-71). Because the file is checked out for editing now, FrontPage displays a green check mark next to the file name in the Folder List pane.

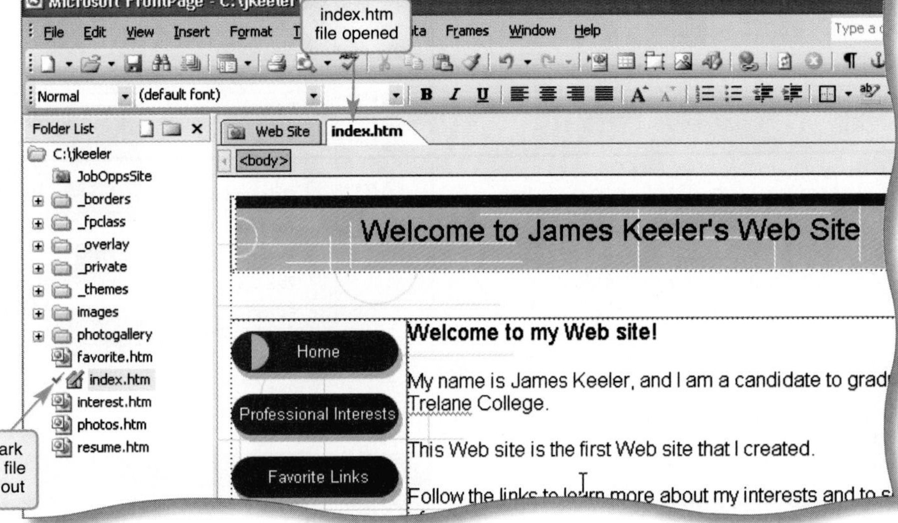

FIGURE 6-71

Other Ways

1. Select file name, click Edit on menu bar, click Check Out
2. Right-click file name, click Check Out on shortcut menu
3. Select file name, press ALT+E, O
4. Select file name, press CTRL+J
5. Select file name and then, in Voice Command mode, say "Edit, Check Out"

You do not have to have a page open to check it out or to check it in. If you plan to modify several related pages in a Web site, you may wish to check out several of those pages at one time so that they are available for use when you need them and so that other developers do not make changes that impact your work. You can check out any number of files at one time, but you should only check out any necessary files, because other developers cannot update the files you have checked out.

When you are finished working with a page, you should always check in that file so that other developers can update the page. If you do not wish to save the changes you have made, you can undo the check out. If you do so, FrontPage does not save your changes and checks in the file for other developers to use.

Viewing the Checkout Status Report

When viewing a small Web site with the Folder List pane displayed, you easily can see that a particular Web page is checked out by looking at the list of files in the Folder List pane. If a large number of pages in a Web site or pages located within folders are checked out, it can be difficult to determine how many pages are in use. If a team of developers is modifying the Web pages, you also may want to know who has a specific page checked out.

The Checkout Status report displays a list of pages that are checked in or checked out, who has which page checked out, and when the page was locked by source control.

The following steps view the Checkout Status report.

To View the Checkout Status Report

1

• **Point to the Reports command on the View menu.**

FrontPage displays the View menu and Reports submenu (Figure 6-72).

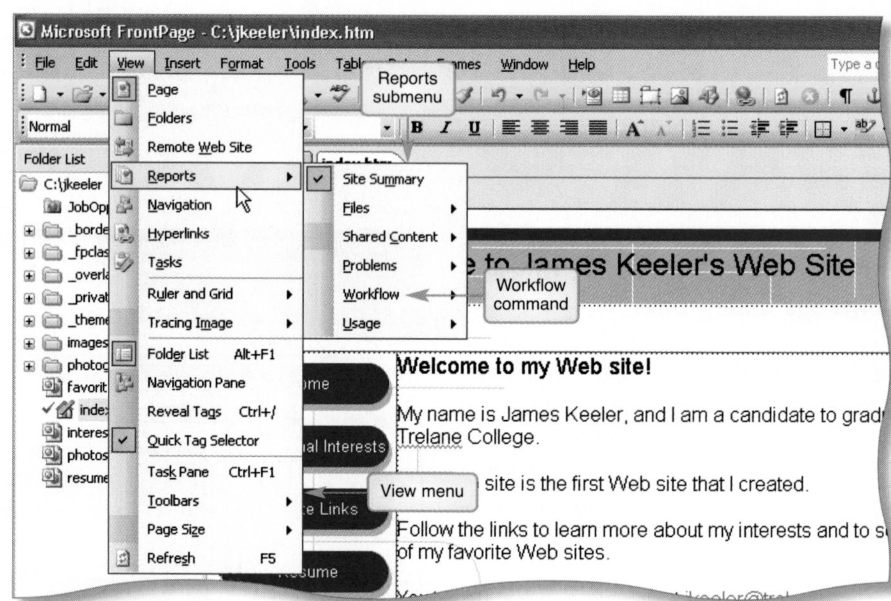

FIGURE 6-72

2

• **Point to Workflow.**

FrontPage displays the Workflow submenu (Figure 6-73). The Workflow submenu lists all Workflow reports available for viewing.

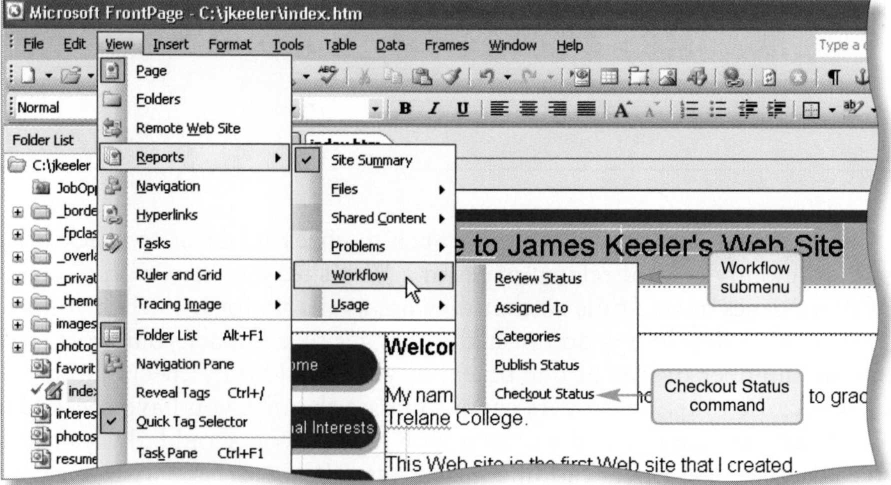

FIGURE 6-73

3

- **Click Checkout Status.**
- **If necessary, scroll down to display the file, index.htm, in the list.**

FrontPage displays the Checkout Status report in Reports view (Figure 6-74). The green check mark next to the file name, index.htm, indicates that you have checked that file out. The Checked Out By column displays the name of the user who checked the file out; the Locked Date displays the date and time you locked the file by checking it out.

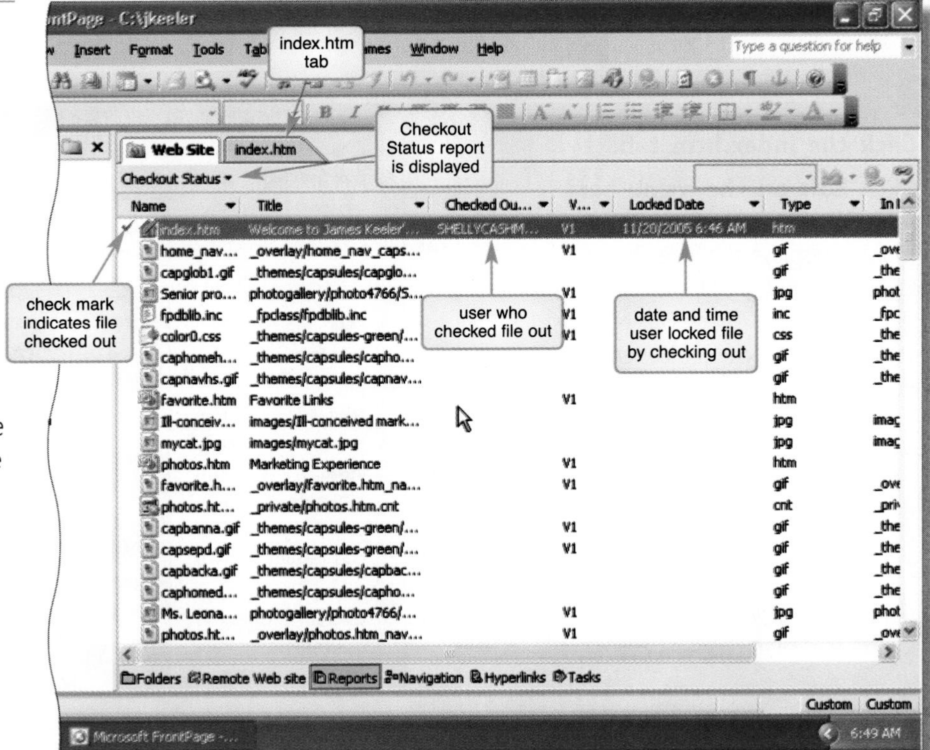

FIGURE 6-74

Other Ways

1. In Reports view, click Workflow on the Reports view menu, click Checkout Status
2. Press ALT+V, R, W, K
3. In Voice Command mode, say "View, Reports, Workflow, Checkout Status"

Checking a File In Under Source Control

Once you have checked out a file, you have locked that file, which means other developers can open a read-only copy of a file and save it with a new file name, but they cannot save a file with the same name as the one that you have locked. When you check the file in, the lock is released and the file is available for checking out and editing.

The steps on the next page check in the file, index.htm, from a Web site with source control enabled.

To Check In a File Under Source Control

1

- **Click the index.htm tab.**
- **Click Edit on the menu bar.**

FrontPage displays the index.htm file in Design view, and displays the Edit menu (Figure 6-75). The Check Out command is dimmed, because the file currently is checked out.

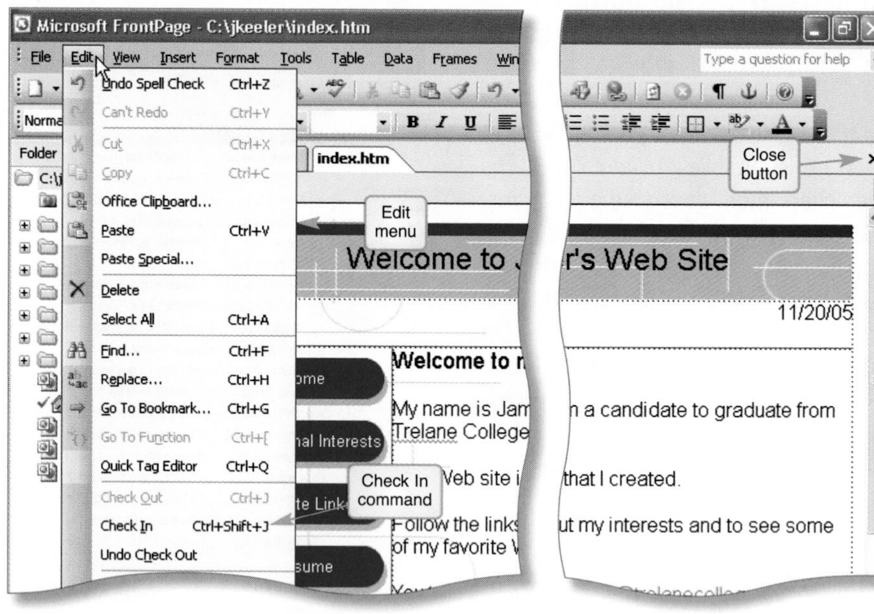

FIGURE 6-75

2

- **Click Check In.**
- **Click the Close button to close the file, index.htm.**

The file is checked in under source control (Figure 6-76). Because the file is checked in now, a green check mark no longer appears next to the file name in the Checkout Status report and Folder List pane and thus indicates that the file is available for use.

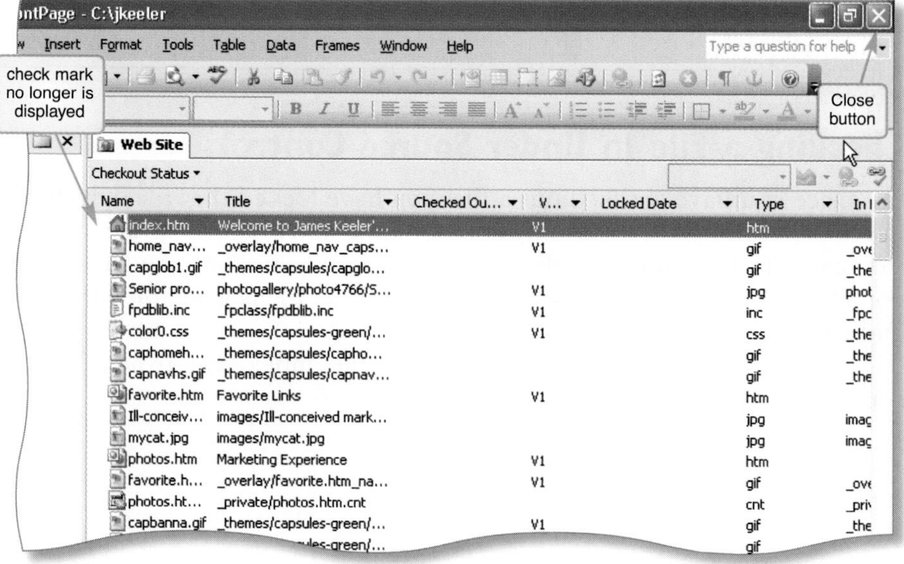

FIGURE 6-76

Other Ways

1. On Edit menu click Check In
2. Right-click file name, click Check In on shortcut menu
3. Press ALT+E, I
4. Press CTRL+SHIFT+J
5. In Voice Command mode, say "Edit, Check In"

When another developer checks out a document, a padlock icon is displayed next to the file name in the Folder List pane and the Checkout Status report. If a second developer tries to check out the locked file, FrontPage displays a dialog box indicating another user has the file checked out and giving the developer the option to open a read-only copy of the file. If the developer edits and then tries to save a copy of the file with the same name as the original file, FrontPage displays a dialog box with an error message and then gives the developer the option to save the file with a different name.

Quitting FrontPage

The modifications to the FrontPage Web site are complete and you can quit Microsoft FrontPage. The following steps quit FrontPage.

To Quit FrontPage

1. **Click File on the menu bar and then click Close Site.**
2. **Click the Close button on the right side of the Microsoft FrontPage title bar.**

The FrontPage window is closed and the Windows desktop is displayed.

Project Summary

With Project 6 completed, you now can use subsites, Database Editor pages, and source control to help manage and maintain a Web site. In this project, you learned about creating a new folder in a Web site and then converting that folder to a subsite. You learned about potential problems when converting folders to subsites and how to correct those problems. You learned how to use the Database Interface Wizard to create Database Editor Web pages for adding, viewing, updating, and deleting records from your database. You also learned how to create a login page to protect access to your database. The project demonstrated how to enable source control for a Web site and subsite and how to check files in and out under source control. Finally, you learned how to generate a report regarding the checkout status of pages in your Web site.

What You Should Know

Having completed this project, you should be able to perform the tasks below. The tasks are listed in the same order they were presented in this project. For a list of the buttons, menus, toolbars, and commands introduced in this project, see the Quick Reference Summary at the back of this book and refer to the Page Number column.

1. Start FrontPage and Open an Existing Web Site (FP 404)
2. Create a New Folder in an Existing FrontPage Web Site (FP 405)
3. Move Files and Folders to a New Folder (FP 407)
4. Convert a Folder to a Subsite (FP 408)
5. Open a Subsite (FP 410)
6. Set an Existing Page as the Home Page (FP 411)
7. Create a Navigation Structure for a Subsite (FP 413)
8. Insert a New Image from a File (FP 416)
9. Create a Hyperlink to the Default Home Page (FP 419)
10. Modify the Database Connection Properties (FP 422)
11. Create Database Editor Pages Using the Database Interface Wizard (FP 427)
12. Add the Database Editor Login Page to the Navigation Structure (FP 433)
13. Apply a Theme to a Subsite (FP 435)
14. Modify a Hyperlink to Link to the Default Home Page (FP 437)
15. Publish a Parent Web Site and Subsite (FP 439)
16. Enable Source Control (FP 442)
17. Check Out a File Under Source Control (FP 445)
18. View the Checkout Status Report (FP 446)
19. Check In a File Under Source Control (FP 448)
20. Quit Microsoft FrontPage (FP 449)

Learn It Online

Instructions: To complete the Learn It Online exercises, start your browser, click the Address bar, and then enter the Web address scsite.com/fp2003/learn. When the FrontPage 2003 Learn It Online page is displayed, follow the instructions in the exercises below. Each exercise has instructions for printing your results, either for your own records or for submission to your instructor.

1 Project Reinforcement TF, MC, and SA

Below FrontPage Project 6, click the Project Reinforcement link. Print the quiz by clicking Print on the File menu for each page. Answer each question.

2 Flash Cards

Below FrontPage Project 6, click the Flash Cards link and read the instructions. Type 20 (or a number specified by your instructor) in the Number of playing cards text box, type your name in the Enter your Name text box, and then click the Flip Card button. When the flash card is displayed, read the question and then click the ANSWER box arrow to select an answer. Flip through Flash Cards. If your score is 15 (75%) correct or greater, click Print on the File menu to print your results. If your score is less than 15 (75%) correct, then redo this exercise by clicking the Replay button.

3 Practice Test

Below FrontPage Project 6, click the Practice Test link. Answer each question, enter your first and last name at the bottom of the page, and then click the Grade Test button. When the graded practice test is displayed on your screen, click Print on the File menu to print a hard copy. Continue to take practice tests until you score 80% or better.

4 Who Wants To Be a Computer Genius?

Below FrontPage Project 6, click the Computer Genius link. Read the instructions, enter your first and last name at the bottom of the page, and then click the PLAY button. When your score is displayed, click the PRINT RESULTS link to print a hard copy.

5 Wheel of Terms

Below FrontPage Project 6, click the Wheel of Terms link. Read the instructions, and then enter your first and last name and your school name. Click the PLAY button. When your score is displayed, right-click the score and then click Print on the shortcut menu to print a hard copy.

6 Crossword Puzzle Challenge

Below FrontPage Project 6, click the Crossword Puzzle Challenge link. Read the instructions, and then enter your first and last name. Click the SUBMIT button. Work the crossword puzzle. When you are finished, click the Submit button. When the crossword puzzle is redisplayed, click the Print Puzzle button to print a hard copy.

7 Tips and Tricks

Below FrontPage Project 6, click the Tips and Tricks link. Click a topic that pertains to Project 6. Right-click the information and then click Print on the shortcut menu. Construct a brief example of what the information relates to in FrontPage to confirm you understand how to use the tip or trick.

8 Newsgroups

Below FrontPage Project 6, click the Newsgroups link. Click a topic that pertains to Project 6. Print three comments.

9 Expanding Your Horizons

Below FrontPage Project 6, click the Expanding Your Horizons link. Click a topic that pertains to Project 6. Print the information. Construct a brief example of what the information relates to in FrontPage to confirm you understand the contents of the article.

10 Search Sleuth

Below FrontPage Project 6, click the Search Sleuth link. To search for a term that pertains to this project, select a term below the Project 6 title and then use the Google search engine at google.com (or any major search engine) to display and print two Web pages that present information on the term.

11 FrontPage Online Training

Below FrontPage Project 6, click the FrontPage Online Training link. When your browser displays the Microsoft Office Online Web page, click the FrontPage link. Click one of the FrontPage courses that covers one or more of the objectives listed at the beginning of the project on page FP 402. Print the first page of the course before stepping through it.

12 Office Marketplace

Below FrontPage Project 6, click the Office Marketplace link. When your browser displays the Microsoft Office Online Web page, click the Office Marketplace link. Click a topic that relates to FrontPage. Print the first page.

Apply Your Knowledge

1 Using the Database Interface Wizard with an Existing Database

Instructions: Start FrontPage and open the Ship-It-Here Web site that you modified in Project 5. If you did not complete that exercise for Project 5, see your instructor for a copy of the required files.

1. Click the Create a new normal page button arrow on the Standard toolbar and then click Web Site on the Create new normal page menu. When the Web Site Templates dialog box is displayed, click the Database Interface Wizard icon. Click Add to current Web site in the Options area. Click the OK button.
2. When the Database Interface Wizard dialog box is displayed, click Use an existing database connection. Verify that the database connection selected is Supplies. Click the Next button.
3. Verify that the table selected for this database connection is Products. Click the Next button.
4. When the list of database column fields is displayed, click the Next button. If a dialog box asking to assign a primary key is displayed, click the No button.
5. When the Database Interface Wizard pages list is displayed, click Results Page and Submission Form to deselect them. Click Database Editor to select it. Click the Next button.
6. If necessary, when the next page of the wizard is displayed, select the default user name, Administrator, and then type `shipithere` (you may substitute your own user name here) in the User name text box. Type `shipping` (or a password of your choice) in the Password text box. Type `shipping` again (or the password you chose) in the Confirm text box, and click the Next button.

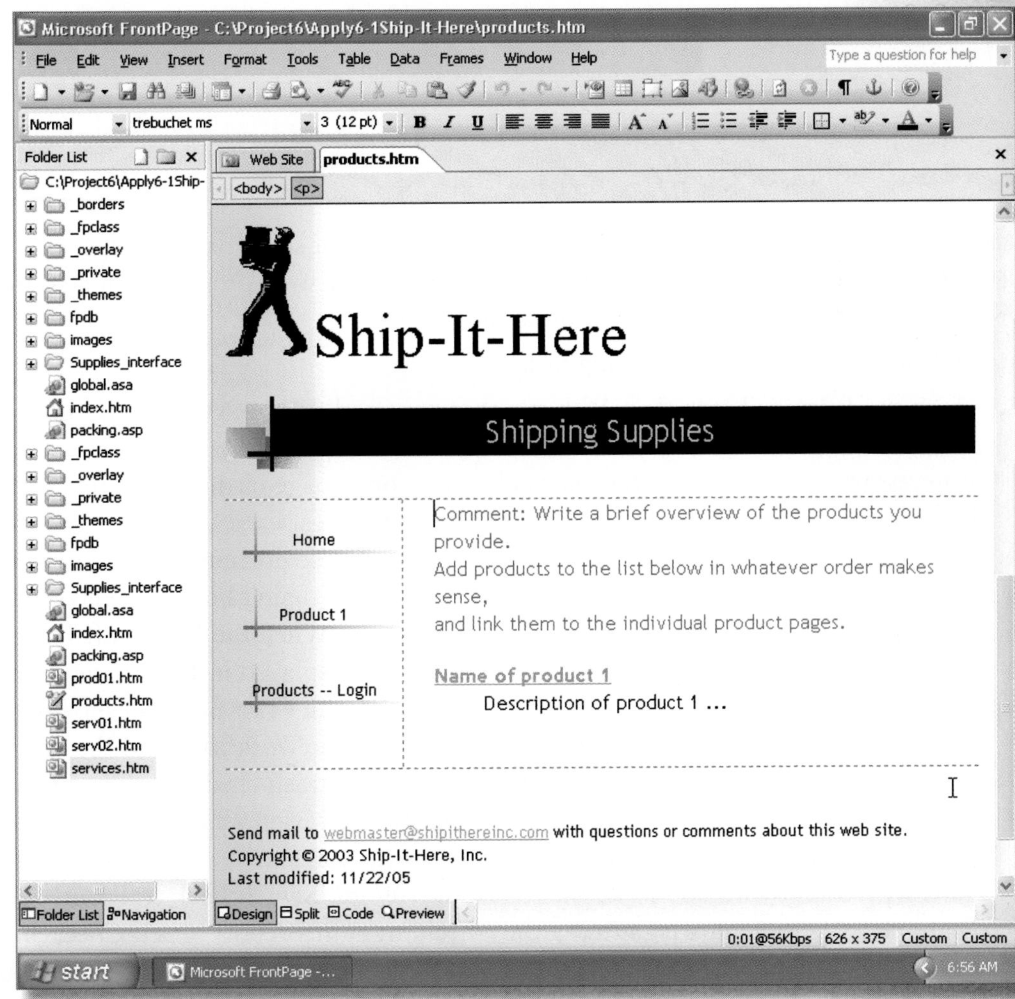

FIGURE 6-77

(continued)

Apply Your Knowledge

Using the Database Interface Wizard with an Existing Database *(continued)*

7. Click the Finish button. Click the Navigation command on the View menu. If necessary, click the plus sign to open the Supplies_interface folder, the Products folder, and then the editor folder in the Folder List pane. Drag the file, login.asp, and drop it to the right of the Product 1 icon, under the icon, Shipping Supplies, in the Navigation pane.
8. Save and then close all open pages. Double-click the file, products.htm, to display the page in Design view. A fourth hyperlink, Products -- Login, should be displayed on the link bar, as shown in Figure 6-77 on the previous page.
9. Publish the Web site. Using your browser, view and then print the new Web pages. Close your browser. Close the Web site and then quit FrontPage. Write your name on the printouts and hand them in to your instructor.

1 Enabling Source Control for a Web Site

Problem: Fairway Lawn Care has experienced the loss of some price changes for various services, apparently due to simultaneous updates of the Web pages. The owner wants to establish a source control procedure for all Web pages to prevent a recurrence of these problems.

Instructions: Perform the following tasks.

1. Open the Fairway Lawn Care Web site that you modified in Project 5. If you did not complete that exercise for Project 5, see your instructor for a copy of the required files.
2. If necessary, click the Close button to close any open page in the Web site.
3. Click Tools on the menu bar and then click Site Settings.
4. When the Site Settings dialog box is displayed, click Use document check-in and check-out to select it. Click the OK button. When the Microsoft Office FrontPage dialog box is displayed, click the Yes button.
5. Double-click the file, mowing.htm, to open the page. When the Microsoft Office FrontPage dialog box is displayed, click Yes. When the file, mowing.htm, is displayed in Design view, verify that a green check mark appears next to the file name, mowing.htm, in the Folder List pane, as shown in Figure 6-78.
6. Click View on the menu bar. Point to Reports, point to Workflow, and then click Checkout Status. When the Checkout Status report is displayed, verify that a green check mark is displayed next to the file name, mowing.htm, to indicate that you checked out the file. Right-click the report header, Checkout Status, at the top of the report. Click Copy Report on the shortcut menu.
7. Start Microsoft Word and paste the report into Word. Switch back to FrontPage.
8. Right-click the file, mowing.htm, in the Checkout Status report. Click Check In on the shortcut menu. Right-click the report header, Checkout Status, at the top of the report. Click Copy Report on the shortcut menu and then switch back to Word.
9. Paste the second report into Word, after the first report. Print the Word document and then save the document with the file name, fairwaycheckoutstatus.doc. Quit Word.

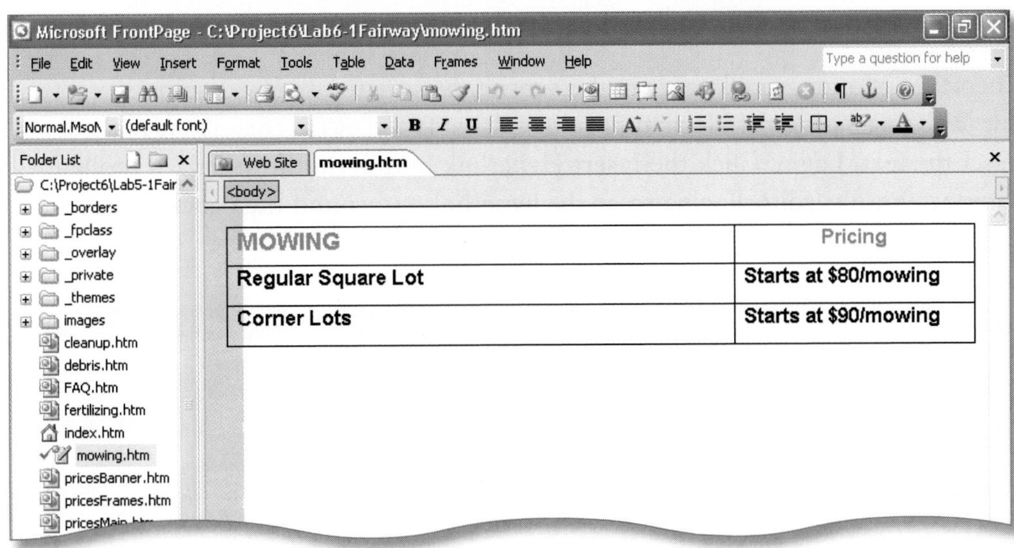

FIGURE 6-78

10. Click the mowing.htm tab. Close the file, mowing.htm, close the Web site, and then quit FrontPage. Write your name on the printout and hand it in to your instructor.

2 Converting Form Results to Database Results in a Subsite

Problem: Your running Web site collects feedback and personal information from your Web site visitors. At this point, however, much of the information is outdated and needs to be updated. You would like to update the Web site so it includes Database Editor pages to allow authorized users to add, edit, and delete e-mail data in the feedback database.

Instructions: Perform the following tasks.

1. Open the Running My Way Web site that you modified in Project 4. If you did not complete that exercise for Project 4, see your instructor for a copy of the required files.
2. Create a new folder, feedback, and then drag and drop the file, feedback.htm, into the feedback folder. Convert the folder, feedback, to a subsite.
3. Open the subsite. If necessary, open the page, feedback.htm, and right-click the form. Click Form Properties on the shortcut menu. When FrontPage displays the Form Properties dialog box, click Send to database and then click Options.
4. If necessary, when the Options for Saving Results to Database dialog box is displayed, click the Database Results tab. Click Create Database. When the Microsoft Office FrontPage dialog box is displayed, click the OK button. Click OK in the Options for Saving Results to Database dialog box, and then click OK in the Form Properties dialog box. When the Microsoft Office FrontPage dialog box is displayed, click OK.
5. Rename the page, feedback.htm, to feedback.asp. If the Microsoft Office FrontPage dialog box is displayed, click Yes. Click the Save button on the Standard toolbar to save the changes.
6. Add a new Web page to the current Web site using the Database Interface Wizard. Use the existing database, feedback, and use all database columns. Use the Database Interface Wizard to create only a Database Editor page, not a Submission Form or a Results Page. Type `Runner` in the User name text box, type `faster` in the Password text box, and then type `faster` again in the Confirm text box. Click Finish and then click OK.

(continued)

Converting Form Results to Database Results in a Subsite *(continued)*

7. Apply the theme, In Motion, to all pages in the subsite. Be sure to use Vivid colors.
8. Create a new Web page using the Normal page template. Type `Login for database administration` and then select the text, Login. Click the Insert Hyperlink button on the Standard toolbar. Click feedback_interface/Results/editor/login.asp as the hyperlink target and then click the OK button. Save the page as index.htm (Figure 6-79).

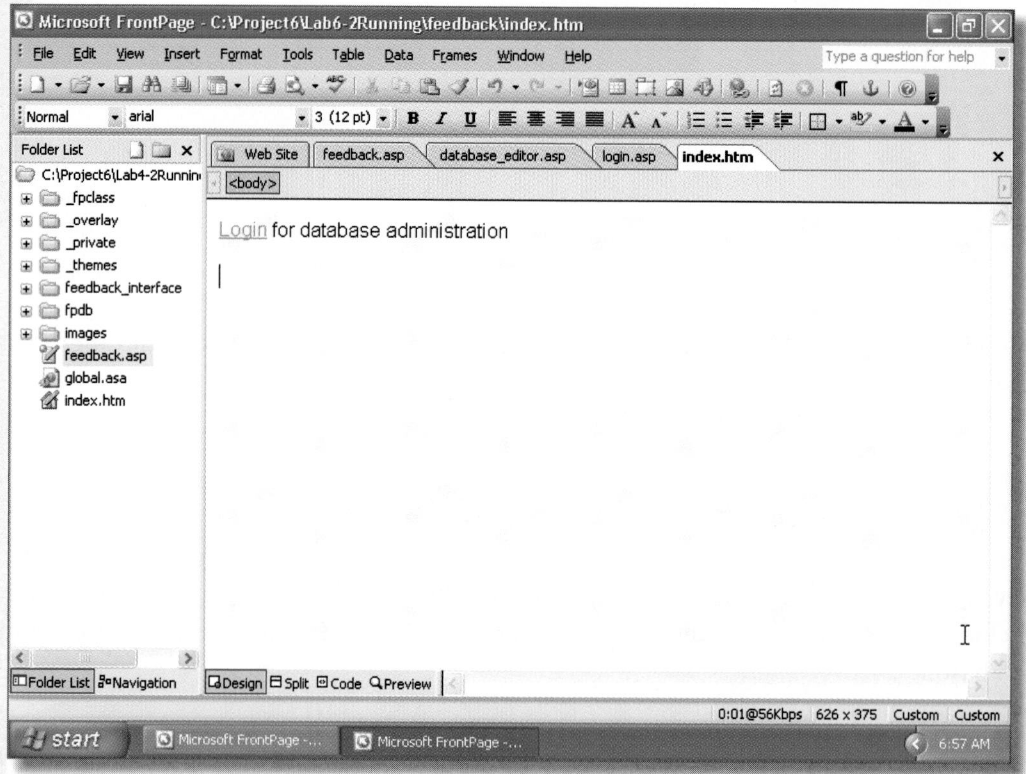

FIGURE 6-79

9. Click the Navigation command on the View menu. Drag and drop the file, feedback.asp, under the home page icon in Navigation view. Double-click the Feedback page icon to open the page in Design view. Delete the link bar on the left side of the page, and in its place type `Home` and then center the new text. Select Home and click the Insert Hyperlink button on the Standard toolbar. Type `../` as the address in the Address text box. Click the OK button. Repeat the process for the link bar at the bottom of the page.
10. Save all changes in both the subsite and the parent Web site, publish both Web sites, and then test them. Print each new page. Write your name on the pages and hand them in to your instructor. Close the Web sites and then quit FrontPage.

3 Creating a New Database with the Database Interface Wizard

Problem: Your company's Information Systems department is exploring options for making available software titles accessible on the Web. You offer to build a simple prototype for demonstration.

In the Lab

Instructions: Perform the following tasks.

1. Start FrontPage and create a new Web site using the Database Interface Wizard Web Site Template. In the Web Site Templates dialog box, type `c:\Project6\Software` as the location of the new Web site. When the Database Interface Wizard dialog box is displayed, select the option to create a new Access database within the Web site and then click the Next button.
2. Type `Software` as the name for the database connection. Click the Next button.
3. Select and delete each of the default database columns except the Key field. Add the new columns listed in Table 6-3. Click the Next button. When the database connection has been established, click the Next button.
4. Select Results Page, Submission Form, and Database Editor. Click the Next button.
5. Type `Infosys` as the User name, type `software` as the password, and again type `software` as the password confirmation. Click the Finish button.
6. Click the results_page.asp tab to display the Results Page in Design view. Double-click the start of the Database Results region. When the Database Results Wizard dialog box is displayed, click the Next button and then click the Next button again. Click the Edit List button. When the Displayed Fields dialog box is displayed, click Key in the Displayed fields area and then click the Remove button. Click the OK button. Click the Next button twice and then click the Finish button. When the Microsoft Office FrontPage dialog box is displayed, click the Yes button to regenerate the Database Results region.
7. Save all changes. Publish the Web site and then test it. Your Results Page should resemble Figure 6-80. Print all of the new pages, write your name on them, and hand them in to your instructor. Close the Web site and then quit FrontPage.

Table 6-3 Books Database Columns

COLUMN NAME	COLUMN TYPE	FORM FIELD INPUT TYPE
Title	Text	Text box
Publisher	Text	Text box
Version	Text	Text box
Available	Boolean	Option button

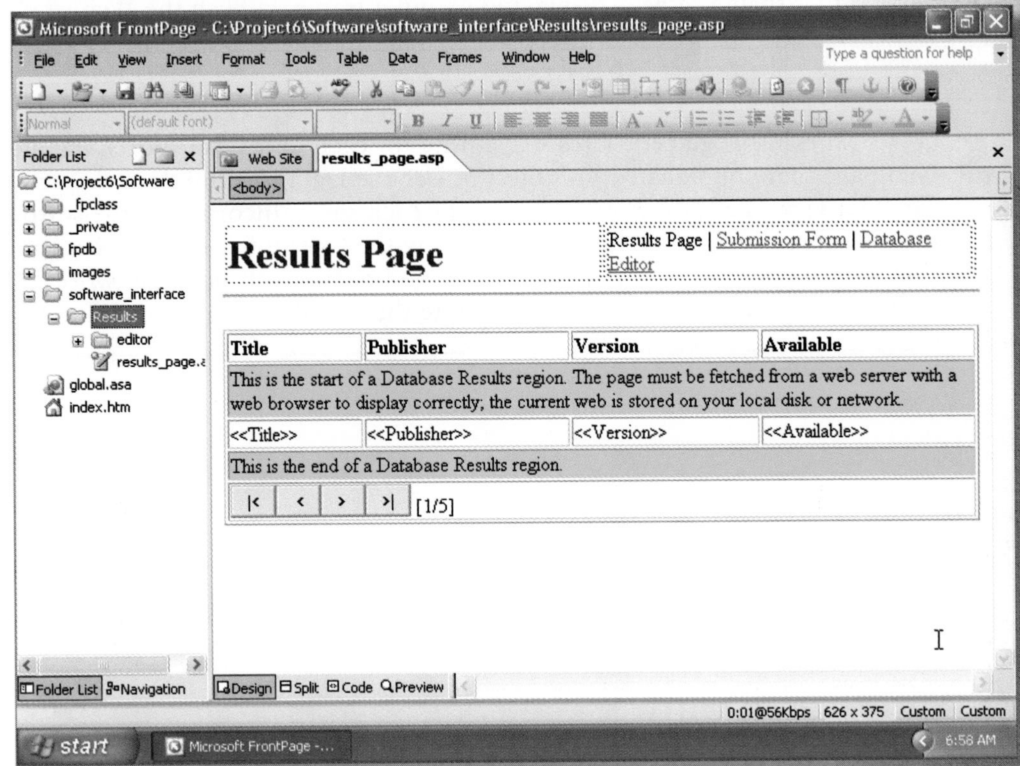

FIGURE 6-80

Cases and Places

The difficulty of these case studies varies:
■ are the least difficult and ■■ are more difficult. The last exercise is a group exercise.

1 ■ Modify your resume page from Project 5 to include a new folder named suggestions. Move the pages for suggestions and responses created earlier to this new folder.

2 ■ Modify the Web site for your movie review Web site from Project 5 to use separate folders for different categories of movie reviews and for the discussion forum.

3 ■■ Create a subsite for the departmental Web page from Project 5 to contain the instructor evaluations page and results. Create hyperlinks from the departmental Web page to the subsite home page and from the subsite home page to the departmental Web page.

4 ■■ Create a subsite for the database functions of your friend's graduation Web site from Project 5. Using the Database Interface Wizard, add Database Editor pages, including a login page, for database maintenance. Include a hyperlink to the login page from the frames page, as well as a hyperlink back to the frames page. Set the hyperlink to open the target page as a whole page that replaces the frames page, rather than as a page displaying within a frame. Publish the Web site.

5 ■■ **Working Together** Create a subsite for each of several sports, including the company softball Web page that you updated in Project 5. Use the Database Interface Wizard to create the necessary database views and maintenance pages for each sport. Incorporate the softball pages created previously. Enable source control for each subsite, using the Checkout Status report to monitor the status of each. Check each page in and out as you make modifications. If possible, work as a team on the different pages, using different login IDs to illustrate the use of source control. Publish all of the subsites.

MICROSOFT Office FrontPage 2003

Using a Tracing Image to Create a Web Page

CASE PERSPECTIVE

As James Keeler's Job Opportunity Web site increases in popularity, the Trelane College Job Placement Center also has taken notice of the Web site. The placement center would like a link from one of its Web pages to James Keeler's Web page. The staff requests that James provide a Web page to serve as a disclaimer before users enter his job opportunity Web site. The Web page provides a disclaimer that his Web site is not officially endorsed by the college or the placement center.

The placement center provides a Web page design for the gateway Web page in the form of an image in JPEG format. The placement center also includes a document with the text for the disclaimer. If the user agrees to the terms provided in the document, then he or she clicks the I Agree button on the Web page to navigate to the Job Opportunity Web page. If the user does not agree, then he or she clicks the I Disagree button to navigate to the Trelane College Home page. You advise James that you will use the JPEG image to create the Web page. You also plan to use an inline frame to display the text to avoid forcing the user to scroll to the end of the Web page through the long text before agreeing to the terms.

As you read through this Layout feature, you will learn how to use a tracing image as a guide when creating a Web page, how to use inline frames to display a Web page within another Web page, and how to use interactive buttons to avoid using a graphics-editing tool to create button images.

Objectives

You will have mastered the material in this feature when you can:

- Use a tracing image as a guide to develop a Web page
- Use an inline frame to display a Web page within a Web page
- Add interactive buttons to a Web page

Introduction

Often when you receive a request for a new Web page, you are provided with a general design for the page in the form of an image created in a graphics-editing program. FrontPage allows you to use such images as guides when creating new pages by using the tracing images feature. The **tracing images** feature allows FrontPage to place the mock-up (tracing image) behind your Web page in Design view and allows the mock-up to serve as a guide while you create the Web page. The image does not appear in the published Web page, but only in Design view behind the Web page. Figure 1a on the next page shows the image used as a guide to develop the job placement disclaimer page. Figure 1b on the next page shows the image behind the Web page under development in Design view.

When a design calls for the embedding of a document or another Web page, an **inline frame** can display the content in a separate box within a Web page. The use of an inline frame does not require a separate frameset Web page, as was developed in Project 5. Instead the inline frame lies within a Web page. Figure 1c on the next page shows an inline frame used to display the disclaimer document from the job placement center.

When working with buttons on a Web page, a graphics-editing program often is required to create button images. FrontPage's **interactive buttons** allow you to create a large variety of graphical buttons, thereby eliminating the need to learn and use a graphics-editing program to create buttons. You can create interactive buttons in a variety of sizes and shapes. FrontPage allows you to assign behaviors to the buttons, such as changing the color of the font or button when the user moves the mouse pointer over the button or clicks the button. Figure 1c shows two interactive buttons on the job placement disclaimer Web page.

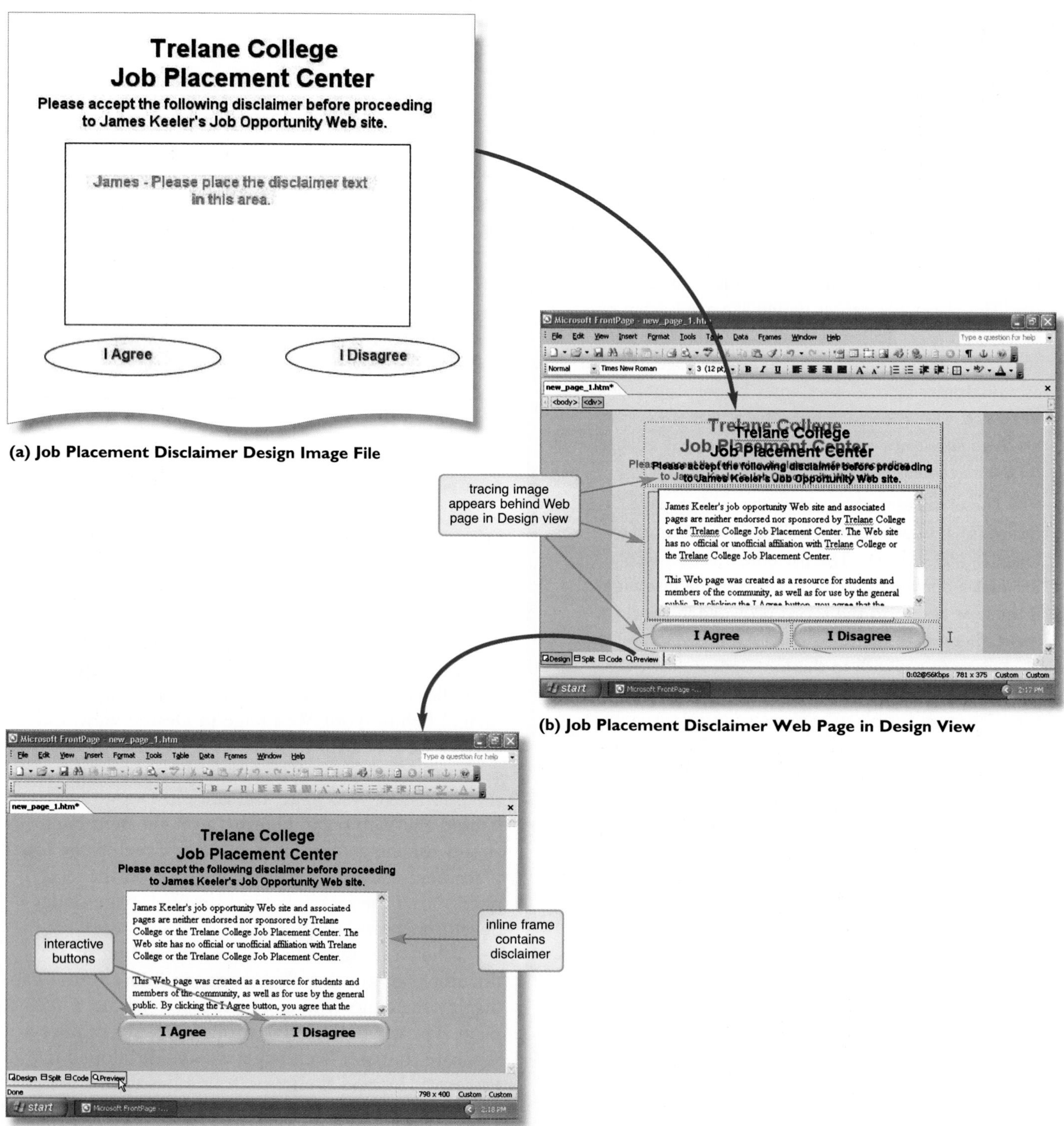

(a) Job Placement Disclaimer Design Image File

(b) Job Placement Disclaimer Web Page in Design View

(c) Job Placement Disclaimer Web Page in Preview View

FIGURE 1

Creating a Web Page with a Tracing Image

The job placement disclaimer Web page should be developed as a Web page, rather than a Web site because it will be added to an already existing Web site with the job placement center. The following steps start FrontPage and create a new Web page.

To Start FrontPage and Create a New Web Page

1. **Click the Start button on the Windows taskbar, point to All Programs on the Start menu, and then point to Microsoft Office on the All Programs submenu.**
2. **Click Microsoft Office FrontPage 2003 on the Microsoft Office submenu.**
3. **If FrontPage opened a previously opened Web site, click File on the menu bar and then click Close Site.**
4. **If a new Web page named new_page_1.htm is not displayed in Design view, click the Create a new normal page button on the Standard toolbar to create a new Web page.**
5. **If a task pane appears, click the Close button in the task pane.**

The FrontPage window opens and an empty page is displayed. The Web Site tab is not displayed because only a Web page is opened in FrontPage.

Q&A

Q: Which image file formats can I use as a tracing image?

A: A tracing image can be in the JPEG, GIF, PNG, or BMP image format. Often, a Web page design is provided as a drawing. In this case, you must scan the image using a scanner or trace the image using a graphics tablet. In either situation, the program used to acquire the image must be able to store the image as one of the four supported image file formats.

Setting a Tracing Image for a Web Page

When you create or are supplied with an image file that contains the design of a Web page, you can place the image behind the design area in Design view as you design the page. FrontPage allows you to modify the location of the image behind the Web page by offsetting the image to the right or down in Design view. You also may change how visible the image is by setting the opacity of the image behind the Web page you are developing. By default, the tracing image appears behind the Web page at 75% opacity.

The steps on the next page set a tracing image for the new_page_1.htm Web page and then set properties for the tracing image so that the image is offset to the right and appears 50% transparent.

To Set a Tracing Image for a Web Page

1

- **Click View on the menu bar.**
- **Point to Tracing Image.**

FrontPage displays the View menu and the Tracing Image submenu (Figure 2).

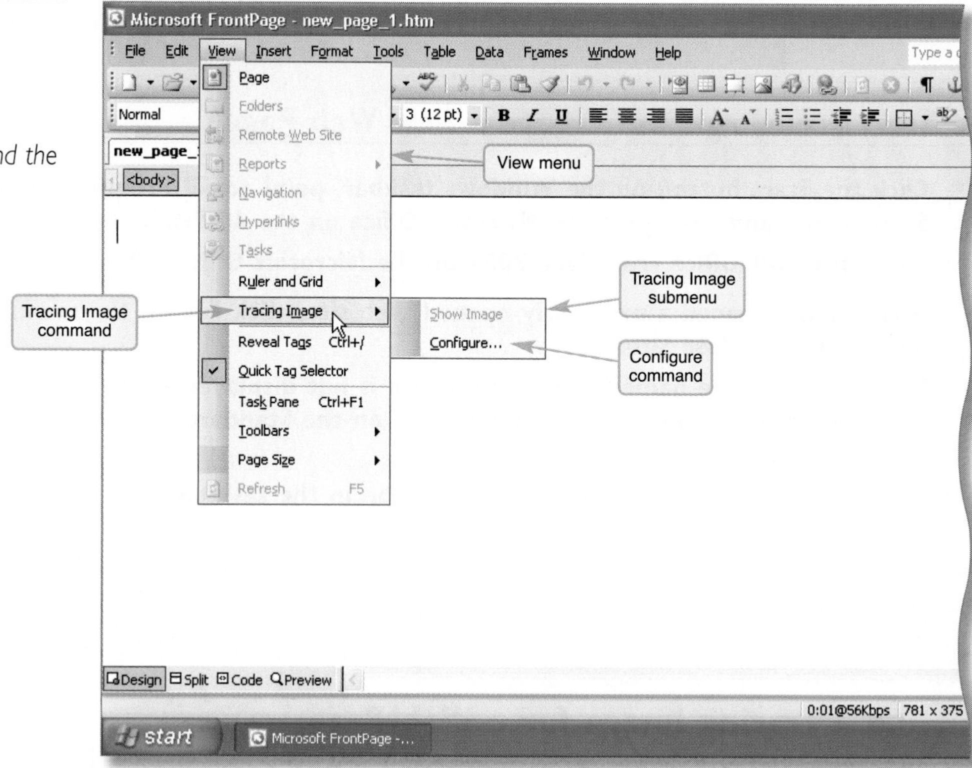

FIGURE 2

2

- **Click Configure.**

FrontPage displays the Tracing Image dialog box (Figure 3).

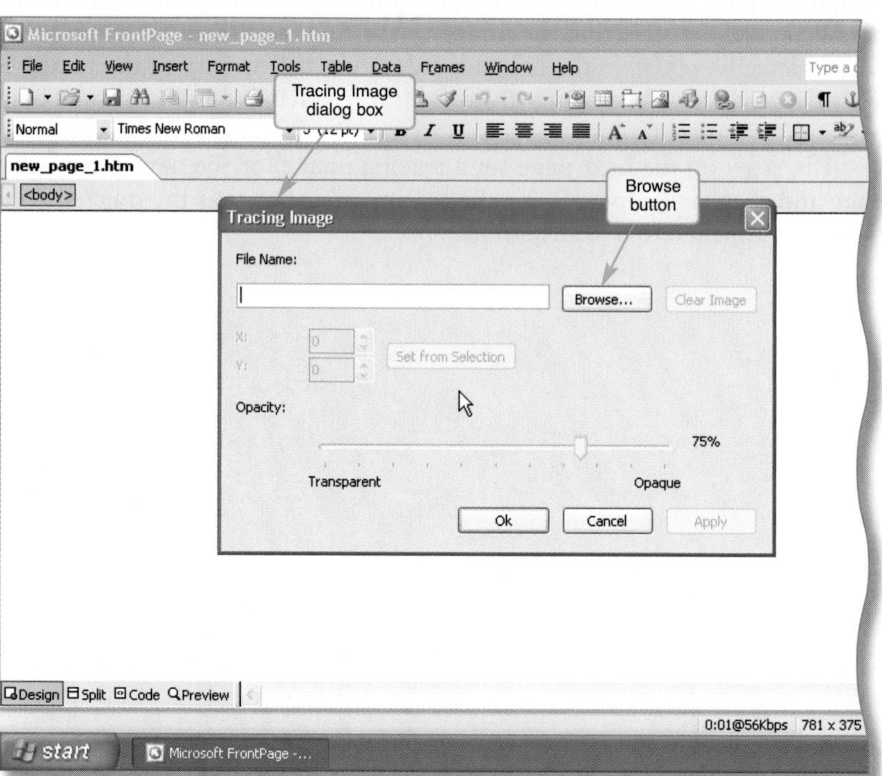

FIGURE 3

3

• **Click the Browse button.**

• **When FrontPage displays the Picture dialog box, click the Look in box arrow and then select the Feature2 folder on the Data Disk.**

FrontPage displays the Picture dialog box (Figure 4).

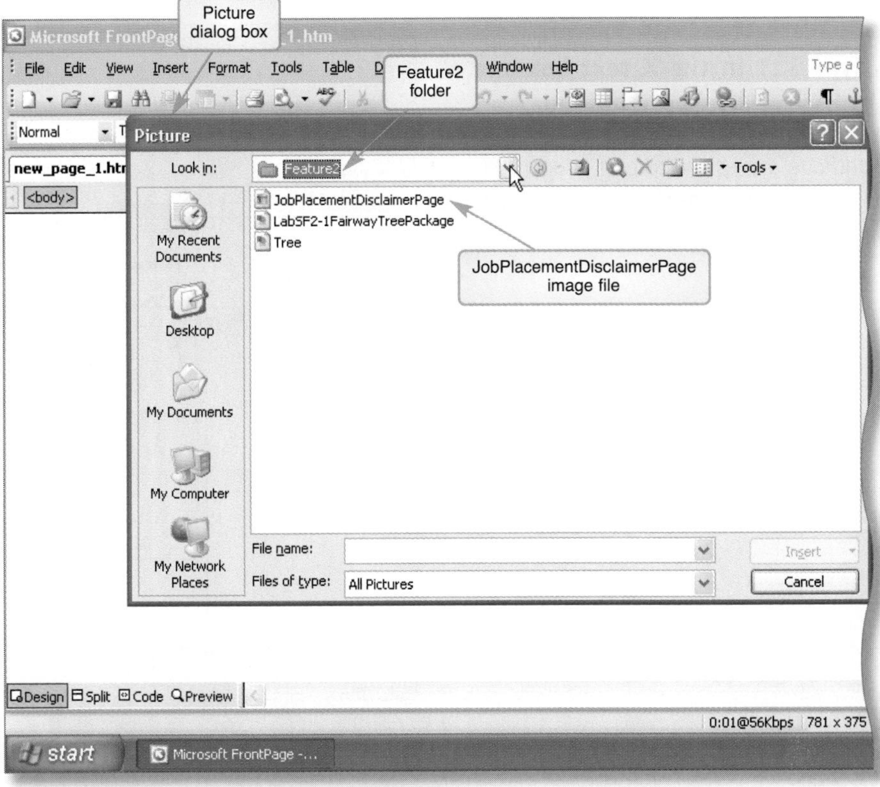

FIGURE 4

4

• **Select the JobPlacementDisclaimerPage image file and then click the Insert button.**

• **When FrontPage closes the Picture dialog box, click the Apply button.**

FrontPage displays the name of the image in the File Name text box and displays the tracing image in the background of the Web page in Design view (Figure 5).

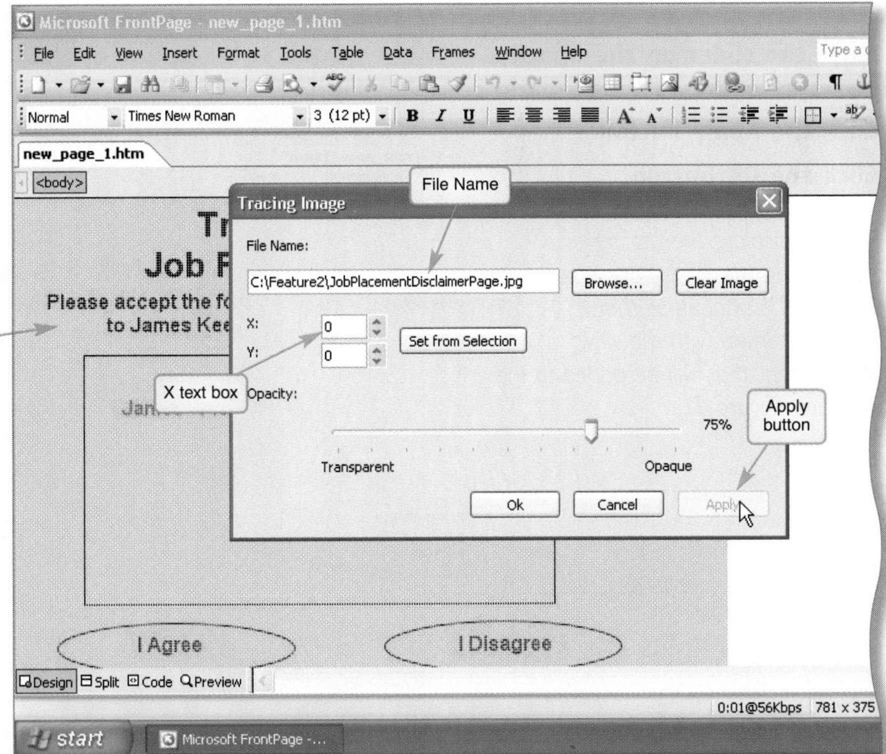

FIGURE 5

5

- **Type** 111 **in the X text box and then click the Apply button.**

FrontPage moves the tracing image 111 pixels to the right behind the Web page (Figure 6).

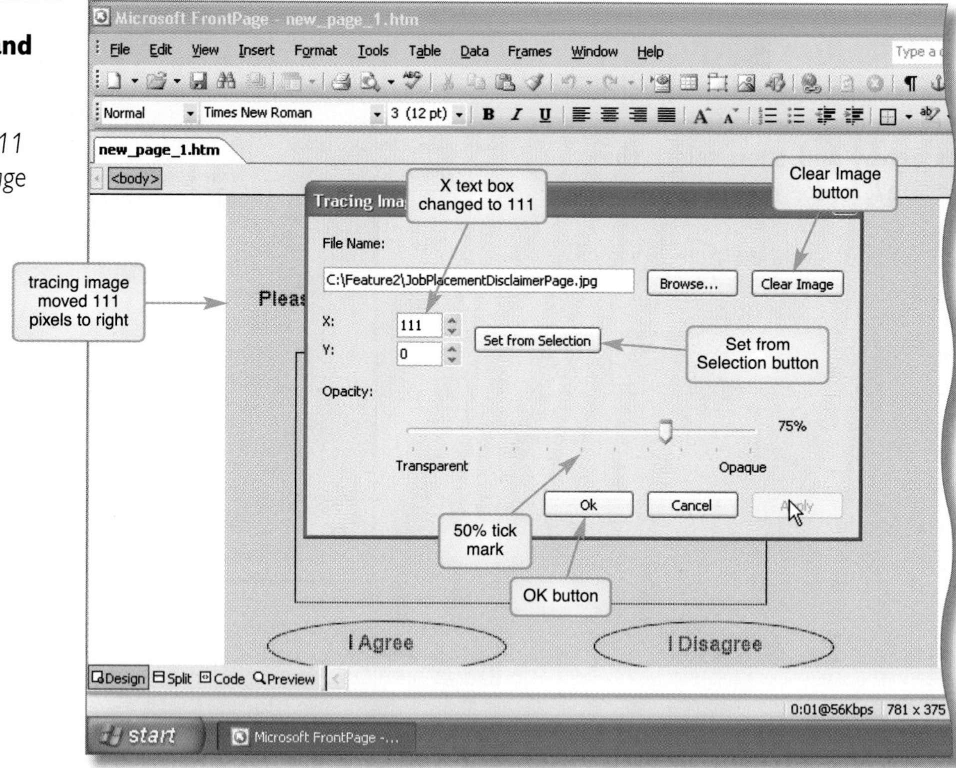

FIGURE 6

6

- **Move the slider on the Opacity slider bar to the 50% tick mark.**
- **Click the Apply button.**
- **Click the OK button.**

FrontPage displays the tracing image behind the Web page; the image is 50% opaque so that it does not interfere with the view of the content that will be added to the Web page (Figure 7).

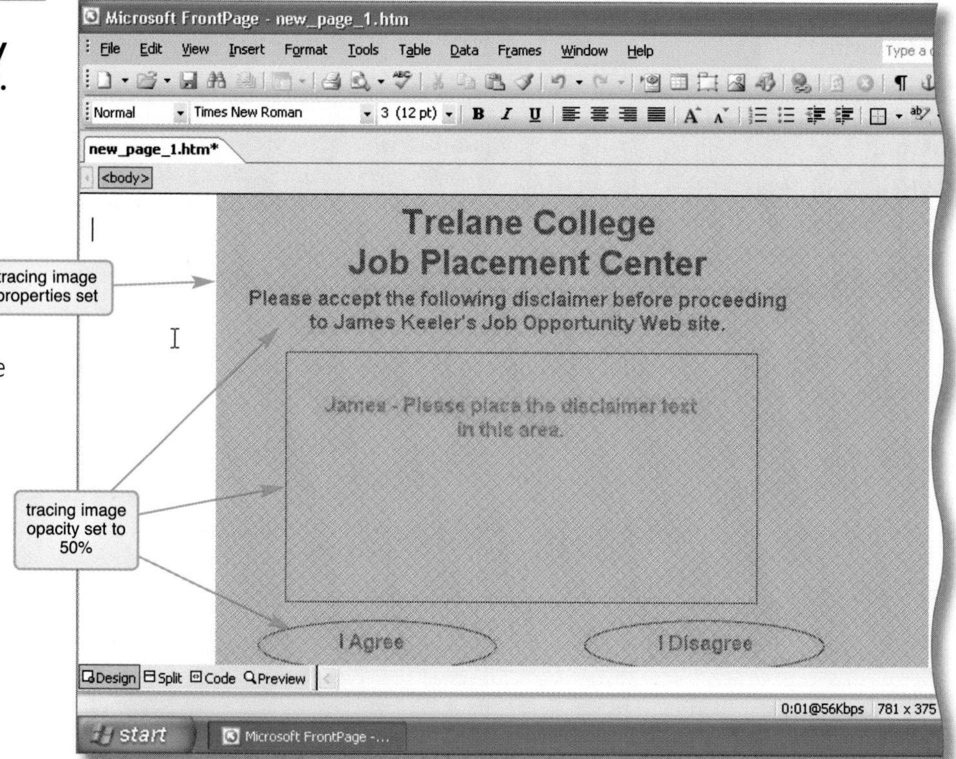

FIGURE 7

With the tracing image in place, it now can be used as a guide to develop the Web page. As the page is developed, the Web page can be viewed without the tracing image either by clicking the Show Image command on the Tracing Image submenu (Figure 2 on page FP 460) or viewing the Web page in Preview view. Clicking the Clear Image button in the Tracing Image dialog box (Figure 6) removes the tracing image from the Web page.

When positioning the tracing image, the X and Y text boxes provide the capability to offset the image from the top-left corner of the Web page. This functionality is useful if the page includes a margin or the design is for only a particular portion of the Web page. Similarly, the Set from Selection button allows the tracing image to be positioned relative to a current selection that has been made in Design mode, such as a table cell or image. When the Set from Selection button is clicked, FrontPage sets the X and Y text boxes based on the area of the Web page that currently is selected.

The opacity of the tracing image can be manipulated to make the image more or less visible. At the start of the layout process, you may find it beneficial to set the opacity to a high value so that the tracing image is very visible. As you develop more of the Web page, you may want to lower the opacity so that the image is more transparent.

Tracing images are stored along with the Web page or Web site. When saving a Web page with a tracing image, FrontPage prompts you for the location in which to store the tracing image. If you set another tracing image for a Web page, the original tracing image is overwritten.

Q&A

Q: What if my tracing image is too large or too small?

A: Often, a tracing image will not be the right size for the Web page you are creating. For example, the image may be a very large representation of the desired Web page. In this case, use an image editing program, such as Microsoft Paint, to stretch the image. The Stretch/Skew command on the Image menu in Microsoft Paint can make the necessary size adjustment.

Laying Out a Web Page Using a Tracing Image

With the tracing image in place, the image can now be used as a guide to ensure that the developed Web page agrees with the intended design of the page. Often, tables or layout tables serve as a good starting point for beginning development of a page. The job placement center disclaimer Web page consists of a header, a content area, and two buttons. A 3-row table can serve as a guide to lay out these elements.

The steps on the next page create a 3-row table, make the table borders invisible, merge cells of the first two rows, and set the header for the Web page in the first row. The tracing image is used as a guide when creating the table and inserting the header.

To Lay Out a Web Page Using a Tracing Image

1

- **Click the Insert Table button on the Standard toolbar and drag through a 3 by 2 table.**
- **Release the mouse button.**
- **When FrontPage displays the new table, right-click anywhere in the table and then click Table Properties on the shortcut menu.**
- **When FrontPage displays the Table Properties dialog box, type** 0 **in the Size box in the Borders area and then click the OK button.**

2

- **Drag through both cells in the first row of the table to select them.**
- **Right-click anywhere in the first row and then click Merge Cells on the shortcut menu.**
- **Drag through both cells in the second row of the table to select them.**
- **Right-click anywhere in the second row and then click Merge Cells on the shortcut menu.**

FrontPage displays the new table (Figure 8). The cell borders are not displayed, and the cells in the first and second rows are merged.

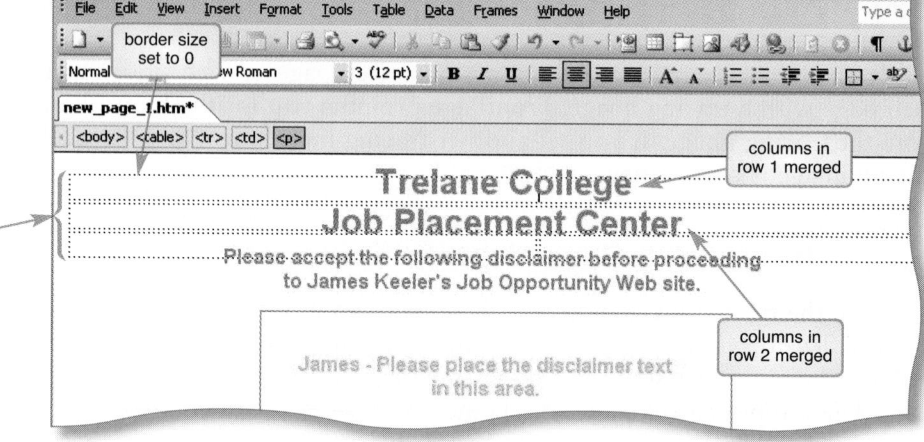

FIGURE 8

3

- **Right-click anywhere outside of the table on the Web page and then click Page Properties on the shortcut menu.**
- **When FrontPage displays the Page Properties dialog box, click the Formatting tab and then click the Background box arrow in the Colors area.**
- **Click More Colors and then select the color with the hex value of {33,CC,FF} as shown in Figure 9.**

FrontPage displays the More Colors dialog box. The light-blue color with a hex value of {33,CC,FF} is selected (Figure 9).

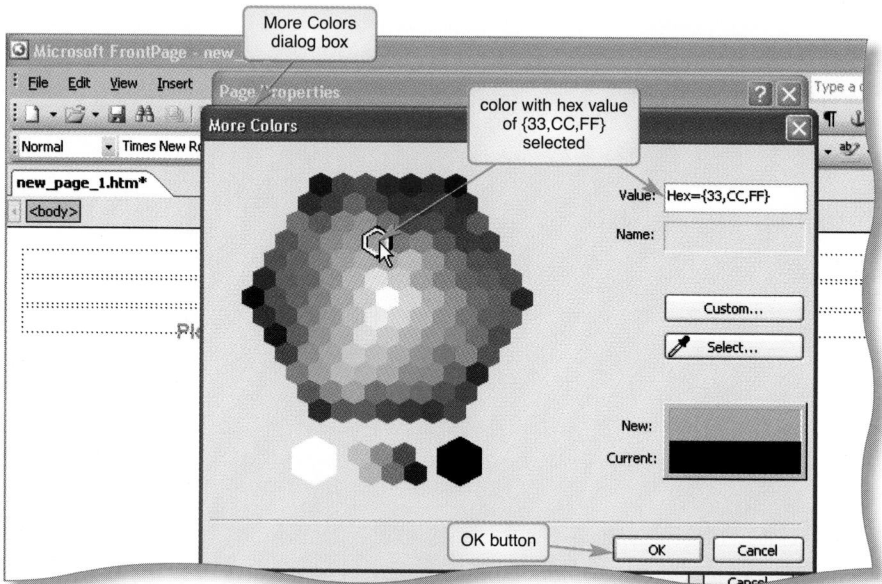

FIGURE 9

• **Click the OK button in the More Colors dialog box.**

• **Click the OK button in the Page Properties dialog box.**

FrontPage displays the Web page with a new background color (Figure 10).

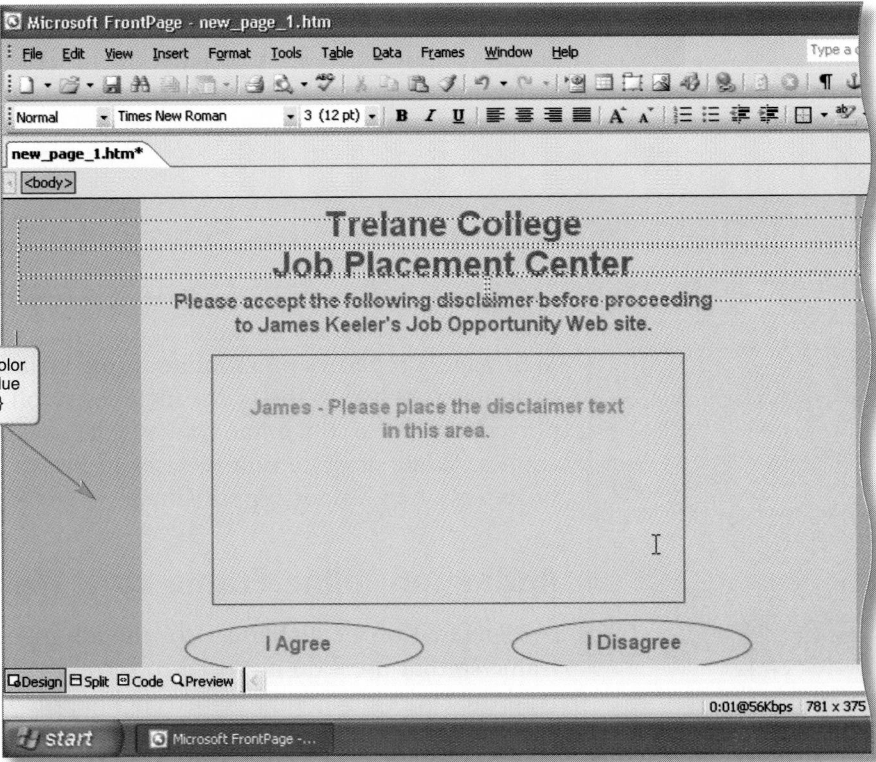

FIGURE 10

• **Click the top cell in the table and then click the Center button on the Formatting toolbar.**

• **Click the Font box arrow and then click Arial in the Font list.**

• **Click the Font Size box arrow on the Formatting toolbar and then click 5 (18 pt) in the Font Size list.**

• **Click the Bold button.**

• **Type** `Trelane College` **and then hold the SHIFT key down and press the ENTER key.**

• **Type** `Job Placement Center` **and then hold the SHIFT key down and press the ENTER key.**

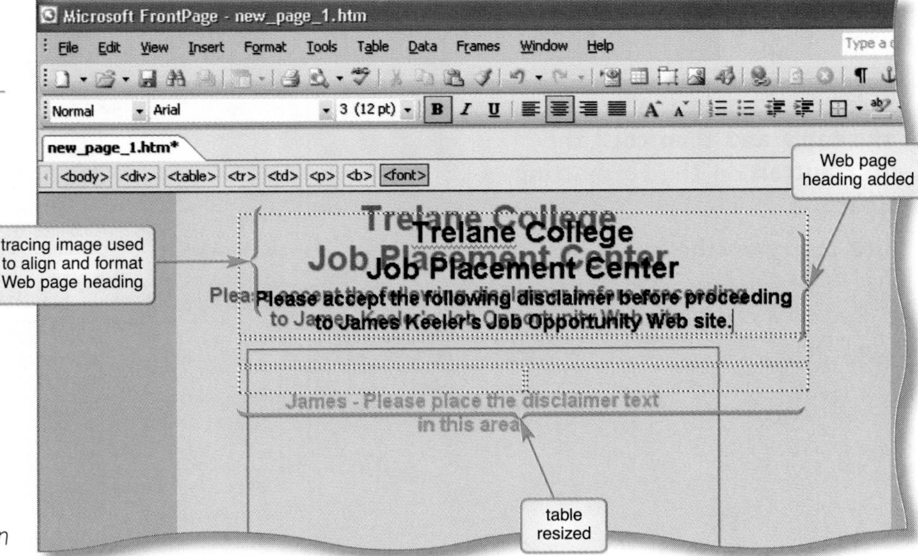

FIGURE 11

• **Click the Font Size box arrow on the Formatting toolbar and then click 3 (12 pt) in the Font Size list.**

• **Type** `Please accept the following disclaimer before proceeding` **and then hold down the SHIFT key and press the ENTER key.**

• **Type** `to James Keeler's Job Opportunity Web site.`

FrontPage displays the Web page header in the first row of the table (Figure 11).

• **Right-click anywhere in the table and then click Table Properties on the shortcut menu.**

• **Type** `61` **in the Specify width text box and make sure that In percent is selected.**

• **Click the OK button.**

As shown in Steps 5 and 6 on the previous page, the tracing image serves to assist in setting the font, font size, and location for the Web page header. With the tracing image set to 50% opacity, the header stands out against the tracing image mock-up. The next step is to insert the job disclaimer text in the middle row of the table.

More About

Inline Frames

An important aspect of inline frames is that the content in an inline frame is a Web page that is completely independent from the page that includes the inline frame. In Design view in FrontPage, this is not obvious. To learn more about inline frames, visit the FrontPage 2003 More About Web page (scsite.com/fp2003/more) and then click Inline Frames.

Using an Inline Frame to Lay Out a Web Page

An inline frame, also called a **floating frame** or **iframe**, is a frame that can appear, or float, anywhere in a Web page. The inline frame displays the contents of another Web page. Properties of an inline frame include width, height, margins, and an indication as to whether the frame includes scroll bars. You also can set text that is displayed in place of the inline frame if the user's browser does not support inline frames. While most current releases of browsers support inline frames, older browsers often do not support them.

Adding an Inline Frame to a Web Page

The text of the disclaimer for the job placement center will be placed in an inline frame so that users do not need to scroll the entire Web page if they do not want to read the entire disclaimer before clicking the I Agree or I Disagree buttons. A new page will be created within the inline frame after the inline frame is added to the Web page. The following steps add an inline frame to the second row of the table and then set properties for the inline frame.

To Add an Inline Frame to a Web Page

1

- **Click anywhere in the second row of the table and then click the Center button on the Formatting toolbar.**
- **Click Insert on the menu bar.**

FrontPage displays the Insert menu (Figure 12).

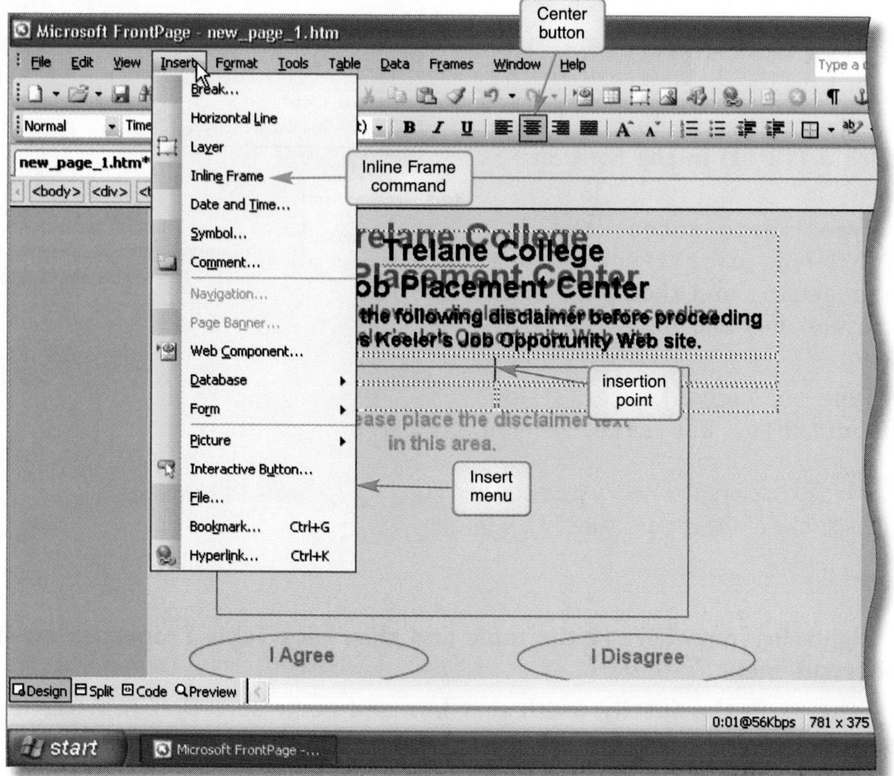

FIGURE 12

2

• **Click Inline Frame.**

FrontPage inserts an inline frame in the table row (Figure 13).

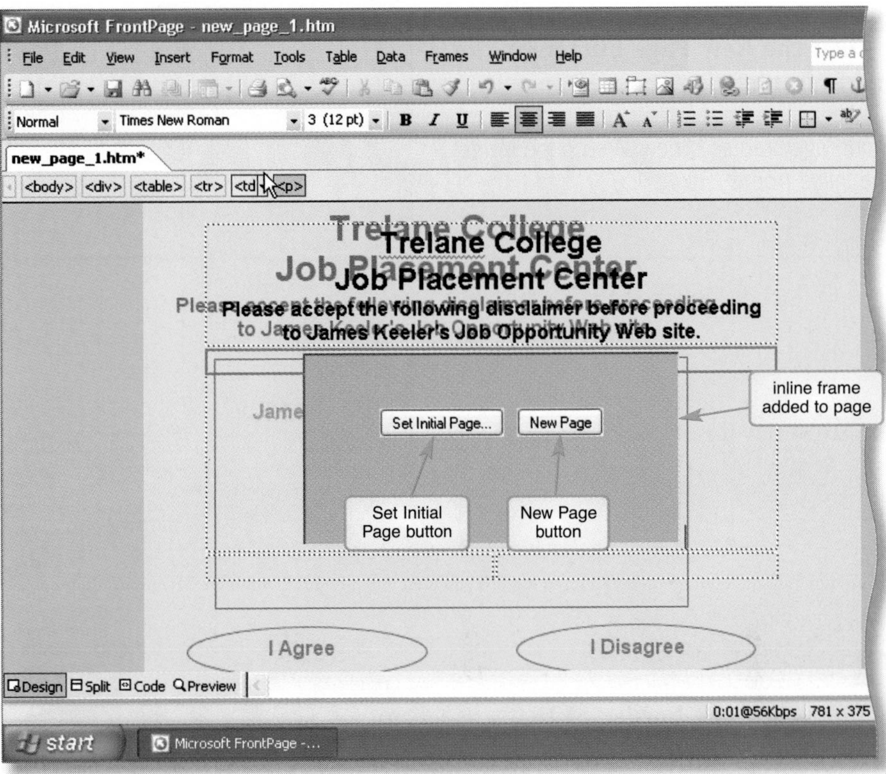

FIGURE 13

3

• **Click the border of the inline frame so that sizing handles are displayed around the inline frame.**

• **Drag the lower-left corner of the inline frame until its size roughly matches that of the box shown in the tracing image.**

The inline frame is resized to match the box in the tracing image (Figure 14).

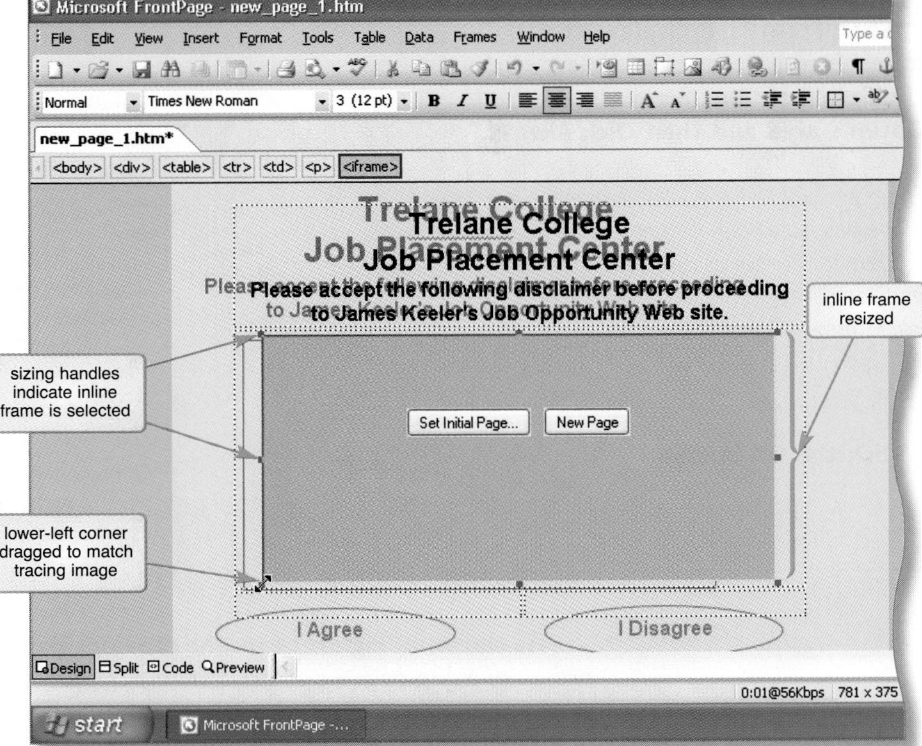

FIGURE 14

4

- **Click the New Page button in the inline frame.**

FrontPage creates a new Web page inside the inline frame (Figure 15).

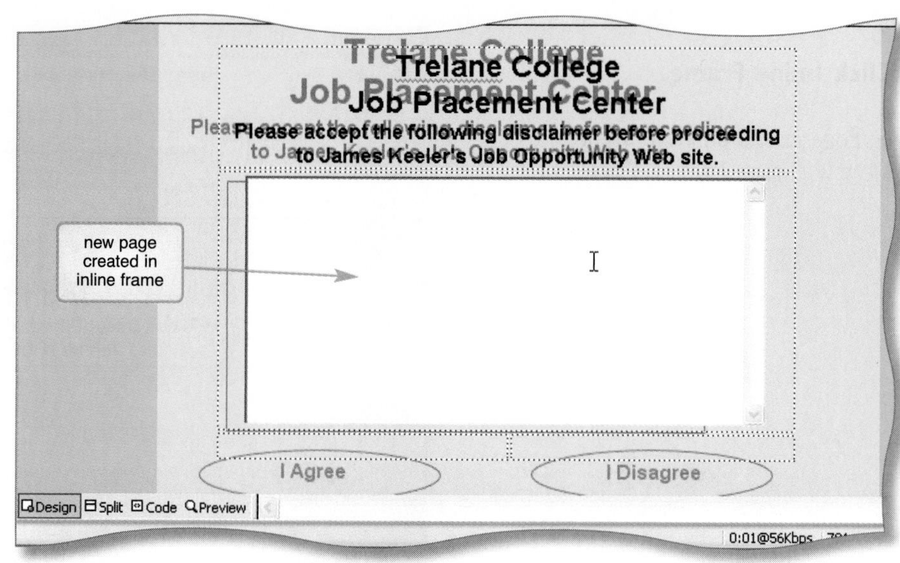

FIGURE 15

5

- **Right-click the border of the inline frame.**
- **When FrontPage displays the shortcut menu, click Inline Frame Properties.**
- **When FrontPage displays the Inline Frame Properties dialog, click the Scrollbars box arrow in the Options area and then click Always.**

FrontPage displays the Inline Frame Properties dialog box. Setting the Scrollbars property to Always causes both horizontal and vertical scrollbars to appear on the inline frame (Figure 16).

6

- **Click the OK button.**

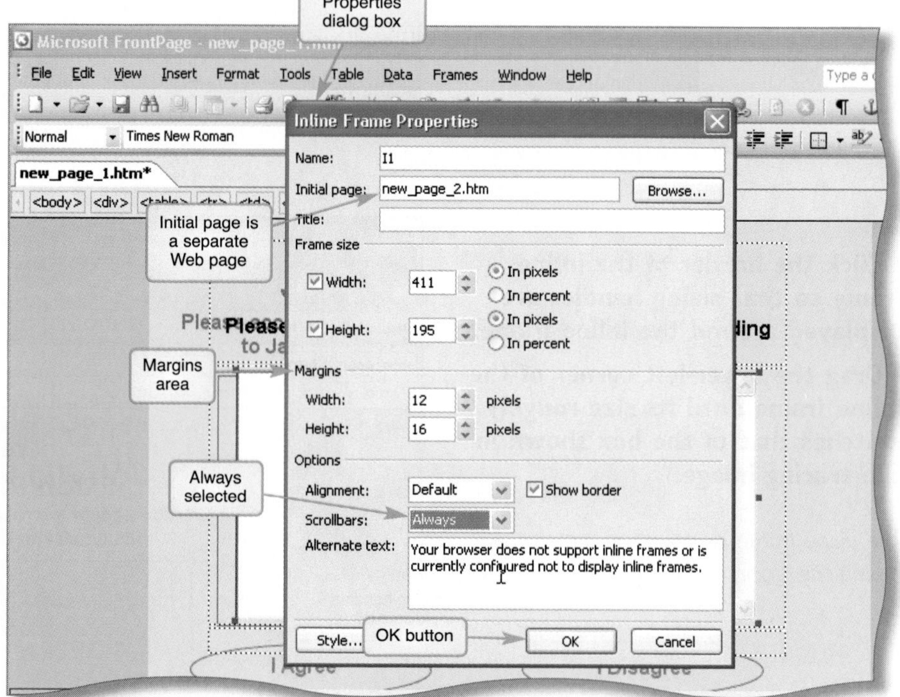

FIGURE 16

As shown in Figure 14 on the previous page, FrontPage allows you to either use an existing page or create a new page for display in the inline frame. Figure 16 shows the properties for the inline frame, including the size, margins, alignment, and the alternate text. The alternate text is displayed when a user's browser does not support inline frames.

The next step is to add the content for the inline frame. A Word document containing the disclaimer is on the Data Disk. The following steps add the content in the disclaimer Word document to the Web page in the inline frame.

To Add Content to an Inline Frame

1

- **Click anywhere inside the inline frame.**
- **Click the Start button on the taskbar.**
- **Point to All Programs on the Start menu.**
- **Point to Microsoft Office on the All Programs submenu.**
- **Click Microsoft Office Word 2003 on the Microsoft Office submenu.**
- **Click the Open button on the Standard toolbar.**
- **When the Open dialog box is displayed, select the file, JobPlacementCenterDisclaimer.doc, from the Feature2 folder on the Data Disk.**

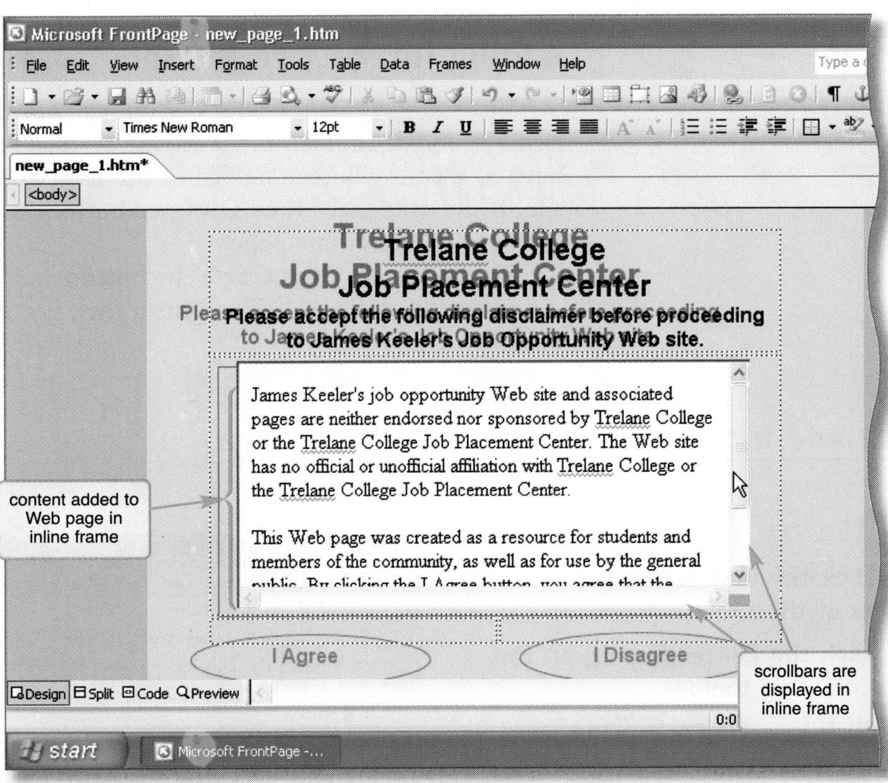

FIGURE 17

2

- **Drag through all of the text in the document to select it and then press CTRL+C to copy it to the Clipboard.**
- **Click the Close button on the Word title bar to quit Word.**
- **With the insertion point in the inline frame, press CTRL+V to paste the text.**
- **If necessary, scroll the inline frame to the top of the inline frame.**

FrontPage displays disclaimer in the inline frame (Figure 17).

When the Web page is saved, FrontPage prompts to save both the new_page_1.htm Web page and the new Web page created in the inline frame. Although FrontPage displays only the new_page_1.htm tab, both the new_page_1.htm and the page in the inline frame are open in Design view. The next step is to add the I Agree and I Disagree buttons to the table.

More About

Interactive Button Formats

FrontPage allows you to save interactive buttons in either the JPEG or the GIF image format. The JPEG format allows for better color effects, such as shading, bevels, and more gradual color variation. If a Web page includes a solid background, the JPEG format is probably the best choice. The GIF format allows for a transparent background, but can include only 256 colors, causing some complex buttons to appear choppy.

Using Interactive Buttons

The use of graphical buttons is a common method to enhance a Web page. Buttons can be made to change their appearance when a user moves the mouse pointer over a button or when a user clicks a button. Creating these effects often requires imaging skills and coding skills. FrontPage's interactive buttons allow you to create buttons with these effects without the previously required imaging or coding skills. You can create buttons in a variety of shapes and sizes with special effects and place text on the buttons using any font style desired.

Adding Interactive Buttons to a Web Page

The job placement center disclaimer Web page requires one button to accept the terms of the disclaimer and a second to reject the terms. If the user clicks the I Agree button, then the button navigates the user to James Keeler's Job Opportunity Web site. If the user clicks the I Disagree button, then the button navigates the user to the Trelane College Home page.

The following steps create the buttons required for the Web page. First, the I Agree button is created. The button then is copied in order to create the I Disagree button.

To Add Interactive Buttons to a Web Page

1

- **Click the first cell in the bottom row of the table.**
- **Click the Center button on the Formatting toolbar.**
- **Click Insert on the menu bar.**

FrontPage displays the Insert menu (Figure 18).

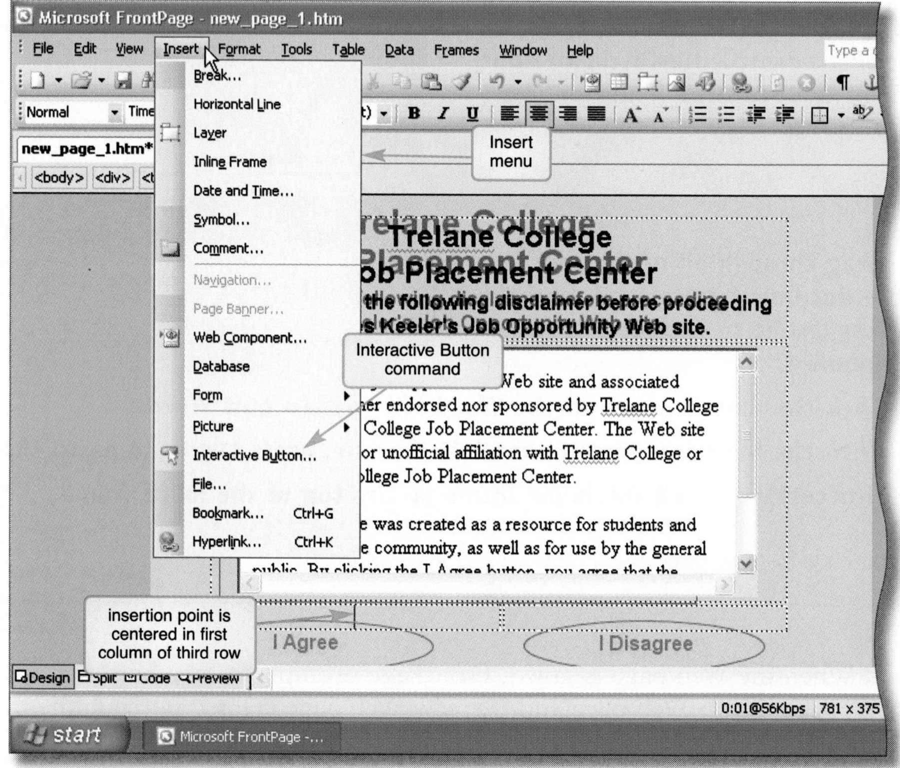

FIGURE 18

2

- **Click Interactive Button.**
- **When FrontPage displays the Interactive Buttons dialog box, scroll as necessary and then select Embossed Capsule 1 in the Buttons list.**
- **Type** `I Agree` **in the Text text box, and then type** `www.trelanecollege.edu/~jkeeler` **(or a URL of your choice) in the Link text box.**

FrontPage displays the Interactive Buttons dialog box. The Preview box displays an image of the button being designed (Figure 19).

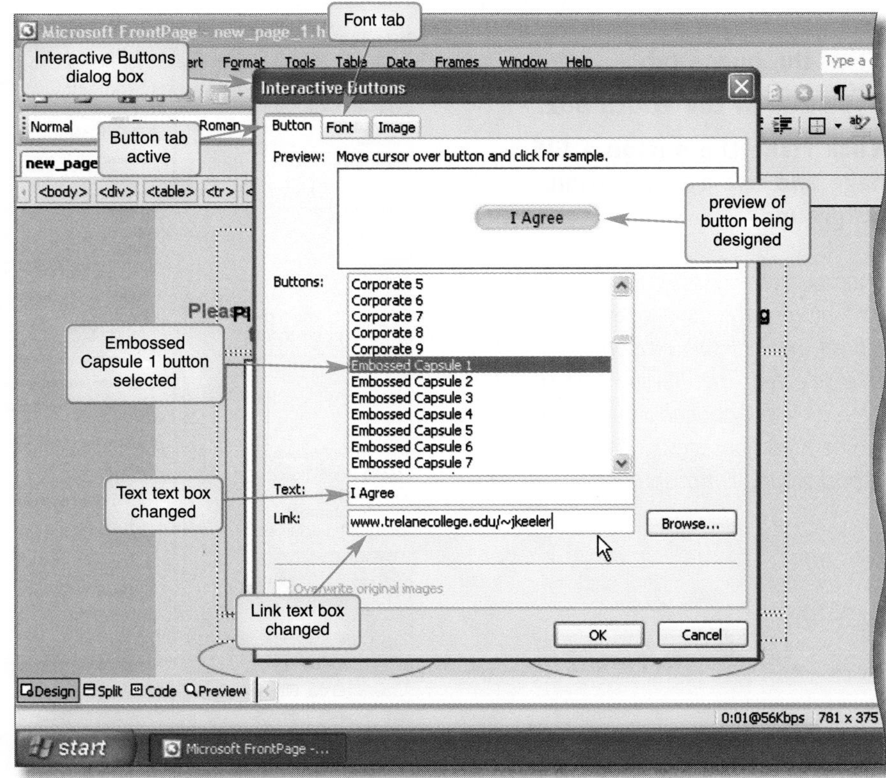

FIGURE 19

3

- **Click the Font tab.**
- **If necessary, click Tahoma in the Font list.**
- **Click Bold in the Font Style list and then click 14 in the Size list.**

FrontPage displays the new font, font style, and size in the Preview area (Figure 20).

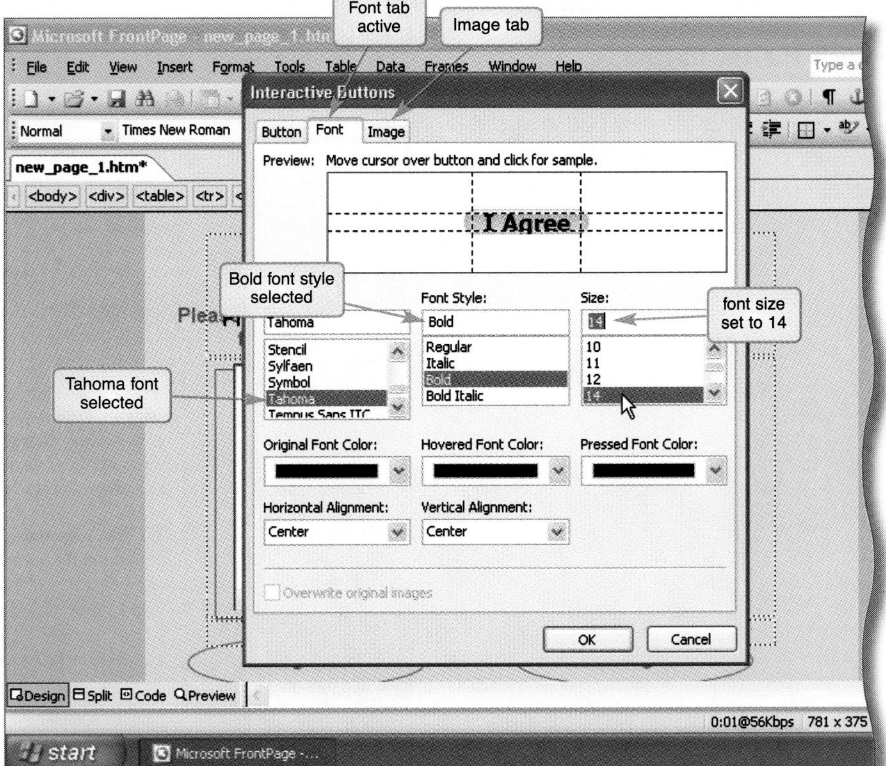

FIGURE 20

4

- **Click the Image tab.**
- **Type** 205 **in the Width box.**
- **Click Make the button a GIF image and use a transparent background.**

FrontPage automatically updates the height of the button when the width is changed because the Maintain proportions check box is selected. The Preview area shows the button as it will appear on the Web page. The checkered background indicates that the background is transparent (Figure 21).

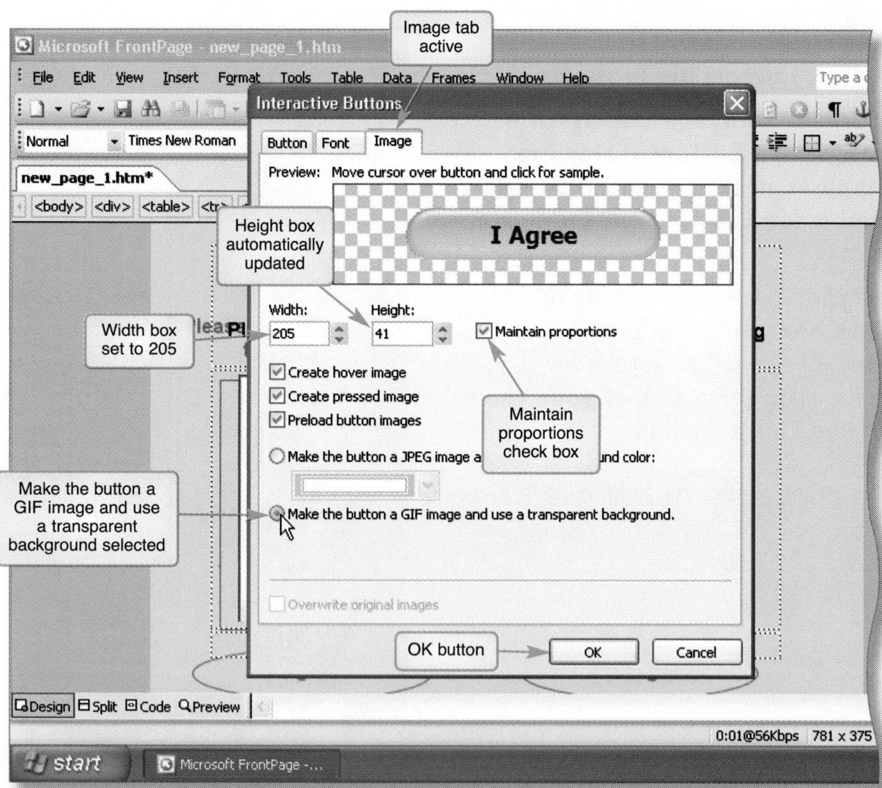

FIGURE 21

5

- **Click the OK button.**

FrontPage displays the new button in the lower-left cell of the table. The button is selected (Figure 22).

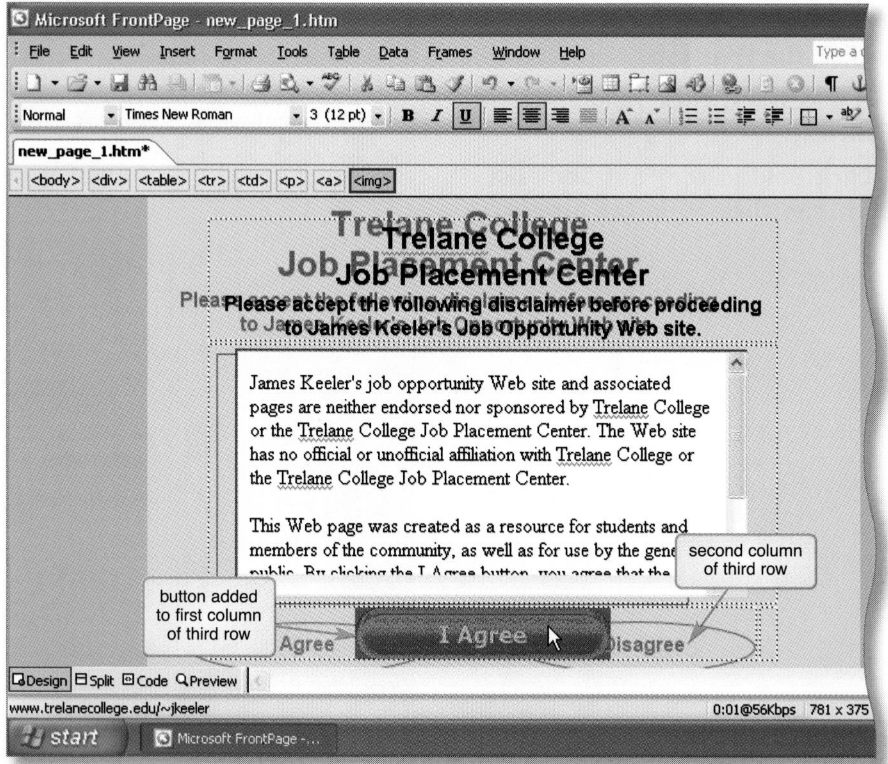

FIGURE 22

6

- **If necessary, click the new button to select it.**
- **Press CTRL+C to copy the button.**
- **Click the lower-right cell of the table and then press CTRL+V to paste a copy of the button in the cell.**

FrontPage copies the button to the lower-right cell (Figure 23).

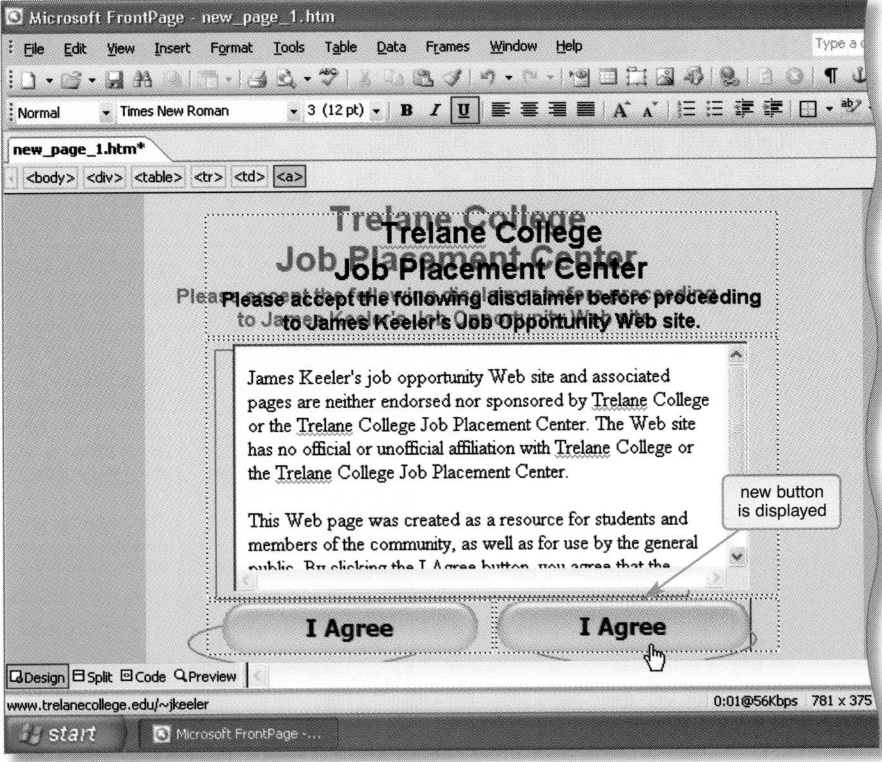

FIGURE 23

7

- **Right-click the new button and then click Button Properties on the shortcut menu.**

8

- **When FrontPage displays the Interactive Buttons dialog box, type** `I Disagree` **in the Text text box and then type** `www.trelanecollege.edu` **in the Link text box.**

FrontPage displays the Interactive Buttons dialog box (Figure 24).

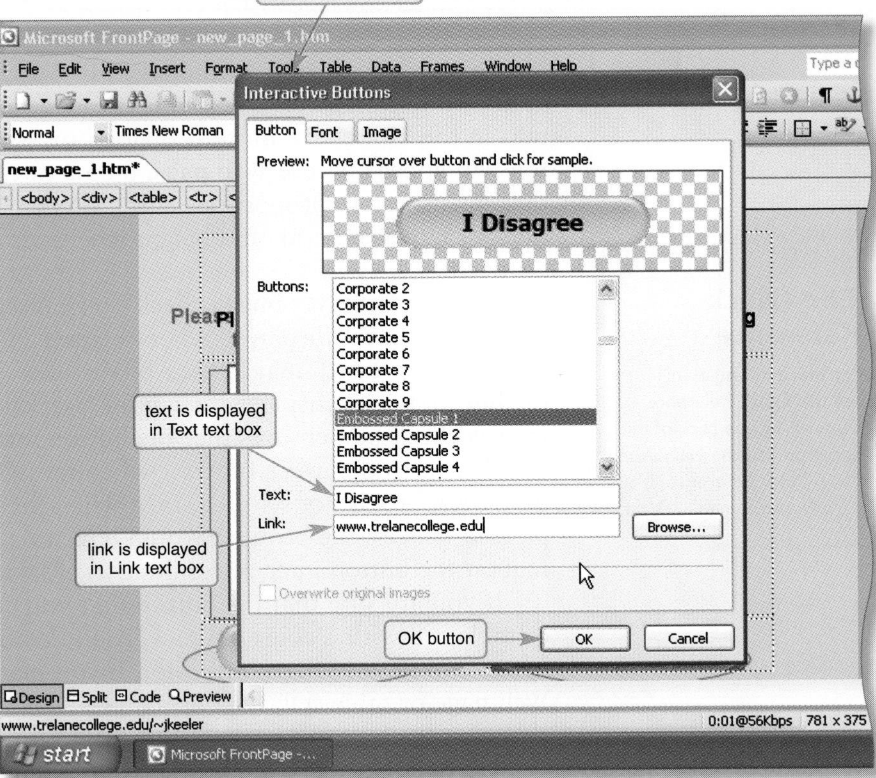

FIGURE 24

8

• **Click the OK button.**

FrontPage displays the I Disagree button in the lower-right cell of the table (Figure 25).

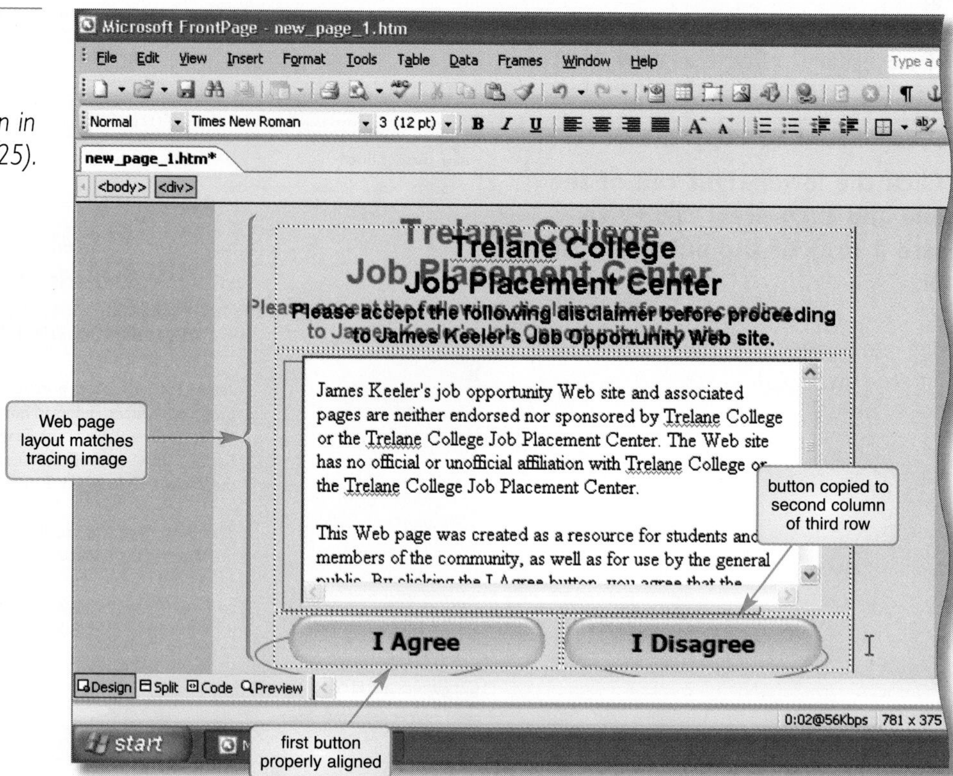

FIGURE 25

As shown in Figure 19 on page FP 471, FrontPage provides a large number of graphical button styles from which to choose. The Preview area exists on all three tabs in the Interactive Buttons dialog box so that you can always view how the button will appear on the Web page. Step 4 in the previous set of steps demonstrates that the Maintain proportions check box causes the button to maintain its proportions in terms of width and height whenever either the width or the height is changed.

The Create hover image check box causes FrontPage to create a special image for the button that is displayed when the user moves the mouse pointer over the button. The Create pressed image check box causes FrontPage to create a special image for the button that is displayed when the user clicks the button. The Preload button images check box ensures that the button image, the hover image, and pressed image are all sent to the user's browser when the Web page loads into the user's browser. If this check box is not selected, then when the Web page needs to display the hover or pressed images, the browser would have to communicate with the Web server to request the button images, resulting in a delay while the special image is retrieved.

If you are sure that the button that you create will always exist on a Web page or table cell with a constant background color, you can save the button as a JPEG image and set a background color. If you may change the background colors of the Web page or table cell, then using a transparent background allows you to avoid changing the button's background color every time you make a change.

The Web page is complete. The next steps are to preview and save the Web pages.

More About

The Quick Reference

For more information, see the Quick Reference Summary at the back of this book, or visit the FrontPage 2003 Quick Reference Web page (scsite.com/fp2003/qr).

Previewing and Saving the Web Page

After you have finished the steps in the project and developed the Web page, you can preview the Web page in Preview view and quit FrontPage. The following steps save the Web page, preview the Web page, and quit FrontPage.

To Save and Preview the Web Page, and Quit FrontPage

1

- **Click the Preview button.**
- **When the Web page appears in Preview view, use the scroll bar to view the content in the inline frame.**

FrontPage displays the completed Web page in Preview view (Figure 26).

2

- **Click the Save button on the Standard toolbar.**
- **When FrontPage displays the Save As dialog box, click the Save in box arrow and then click Local Disk (C:) in the Save in list.**
- **If necessary, click the Create New Folder button and type** `Feature2` **in the Name box in the New Folder dialog box.**
- **Click the OK button.**
- **Type** `JamesKeelerDisclaimer` **in the File name text box and then click the Save button in the Save As dialog box.**

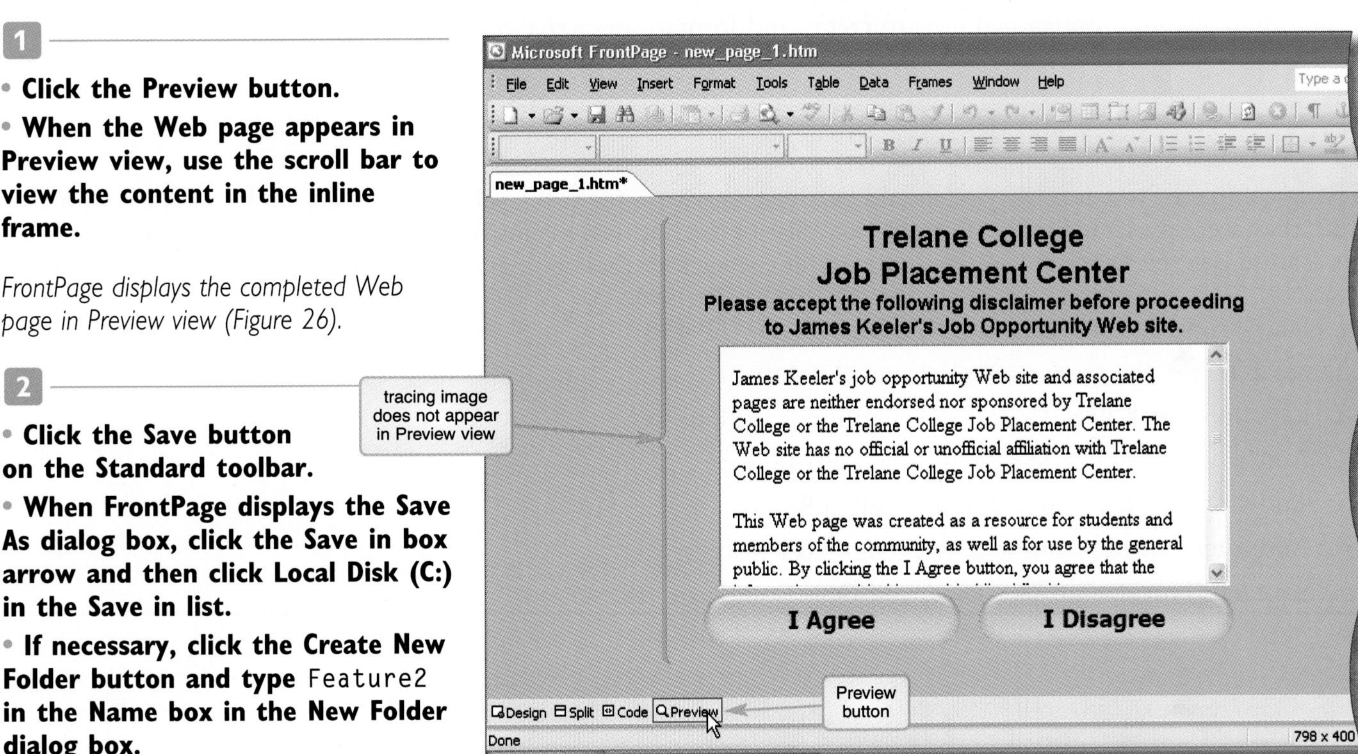

FIGURE 26

3

- **When the Save As dialog box appears to save the inline frame Web page, type** `InlineFrameDisclaimer` **in the File name text box and then click the Save button in the Save As dialog box.**
- **When the Save Embedded Files dialog box appears, click the Change Folder button and select C:\Feature2\images as the folder for the embedded images by clicking the Create New Folder button in the Change Folder dialog box.**
- **Click the OK button on the Save Embedded Files dialog box.**

4

- **Click the Design button to return to Design view.**
- **Click File on the menu bar and then click Close.**
- **Click the Close button on the right side of the FrontPage title bar.**

FrontPage closes the Web page and the FrontPage window closes.

After saving the Web page, the files and folder created with the Web page can be added to a Web site or distributed to the job placement center's Web developer so that he or she can include the Web page in the college's site.

Layout Feature Summary

This Layout feature introduced you to using a tracing image to serve as a guide to positioning content on a Web page. You also learned how to add and format inline frames in a Web page and then how to add content to an inline frame. Finally, you learned how to create and format interactive buttons.

What You Should Know

Having completed this feature, you should be able to perform the tasks below. The tasks are listed in the same order they were presented in this feature. For a list of the buttons, menus, toolbars, and commands introduced in this feature, see the Quick Reference Summary at the back of this book and refer to the Page Number column.

1. Start FrontPage and Create a New Web Page (FP 459)
2. Set a Tracing Image for a Web Page (FP 460)
3. Lay Out a Web Page Using a Tracing Image (FP 464)
4. Add an Inline Frame to a Web Page (FP 466)
5. Add Content to an Inline Frame (FP 469)
6. Add Interactive Buttons to a Web Page (FP 470)
7. Save and Preview the Web Page, and Quit FrontPage (FP 475)

In the Lab

1 Creating a Web Page with a Tracing Image

Problem: Fairway Lawn Care needs a Web page to advertise their Tree Care Package, which includes annual tree trimming and fertilizing. The owner has supplied you with a drawing of the needed Web page. The owner would like you to create the outline of the Web page based on the drawing, and he will fill in the content at a later time.

Instructions: Perform the following tasks.

1. Create a new Web page and apply the Compass theme to the page.
2. Add the file LabSF2-1FairwayTreePackage.gif from the Data Disk as a tracing image to the new Web page. Configure the tracing image with no offset and a transparency of 40%.
3. Create a 3 by 3 table with a border that matches the layout of the tracing image. Combine the cells in the second row to make one cell in the row. Combine the cells in the third row to make one cell in the row. Add a new 2 by 1 table to the second row of the first table. For the second table, set the properties so that the height and width take up 100% of the space available. Set the cell padding and cell spacing to 0, and set the border size to 1.
4. Add the file Tree.gif to the first and third cells of the first row. Size the images appropriately. Add the text as shown in the tracing image, being careful to format the text so that it closely resembles the size and position of that in the tracing image.
5. Preview the Web page in your browser (Figure 27). Save the Web page as LabSF2-1 FairwayTreePackage .htm in a new Feature2\LabSF2-1 FairwayLawnCare folder on the Data Disk or hard disk. Save the embedded images in a new images subfolder.

FIGURE 27

2 Creating a Web Page with Inline Frames and Interactive Buttons

Problem: You decide to update the look of the Running My Way Marathon Training Seminar that you developed in the In the Lab exercise in Feature 1. The new look should include only one column, rather than three (see Figure 23 on page FP 263). The one column should include an inline frame that is updated with session information depending on which button a user clicks. Interactive buttons will allow the user to select one of three sessions, displaying information describing the content of each session in the inline frame.

Instructions: Perform the following tasks.

1. Create a new Web page and apply the Echo theme to the page.
2. Type `Running My Way Marathon Training Seminar` as the page heading, and format the heading with the Heading 2 style. Type `April 4, 2005` as the second line of the heading, and format the line with the Heading 3 style. Center both headers on the page.
3. Start a new line in the Web page, click the Center button on the Formatting toolbar, and then insert an inline frame in the Web page.
4. Create three additional Web pages, each containing the text shown in one of the sessions shown in Figure 23 on page FP 263. Save the Web pages as session1.htm, session2.htm, and session3.htm in the Feature2\Lab2-2RunningMyWay folder on your hard drive. Close the session1.htm, session2.htm, and session3.htm Web pages.
5. Add three interactive buttons below the inline frame using the Embossed Rectangle 1 button style. Set the font of each button to Tahoma with a bold font style and a font size of 12. Change the image width to 135 and the height to 27 for each button. Make the images GIF images with transparent backgrounds.
6. Set the Text properties of the buttons to Session 1, Session 2, and Session 3. Set the Link properties of each button to session1.htm, session2.htm, and session3.htm. Edit the hyperlink properties of each button to target a frame. The frame name to target is I1.
7. Set the initial page for the inline frame to session1.htm.
8. Preview the Web page in your browser (Figure 28) and make sure that the links work as intended. Save the Web page as RunningMyWaySeminar.htm in the Feature2\Lab2-2RunningMyWay folder on your hard drive. Save the embedded images in a new images subfolder.

In the Lab

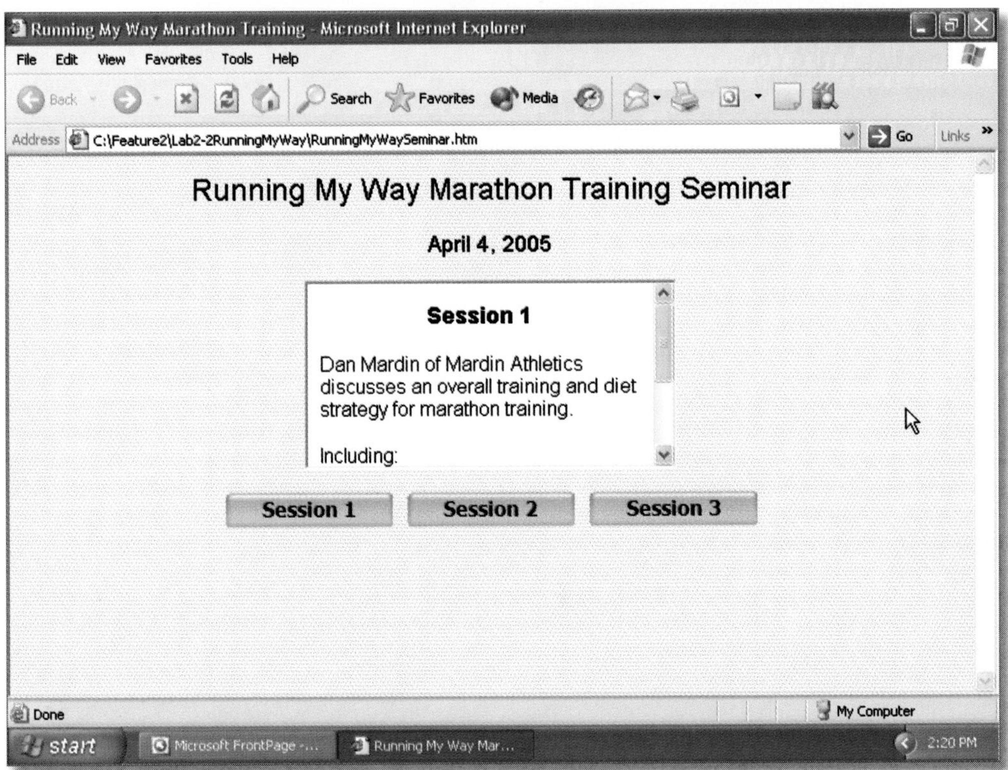
Running My Way Marathon Training - Microsoft Internet Explorer
File Edit View Favorites Tools Help
Back Search Favorites Media
Address C:\Feature2\Lab2-2RunningMyWay\RunningMyWaySeminar.htm
Go Links
Running My Way Marathon Training Seminar
April 4, 2005
Session 1
Dan Mardin of Mardin Athletics discusses an overall training and diet strategy for marathon training.
Including:
Session 1
Session 2
Session 3
Done
My Computer
start
Microsoft FrontPage -...
Running My Way Mar...
2:20 PM

FIGURE 28

MICROSOFT Office FrontPage 2003

Customizing Tables and Searching Web Sites

PROJECT 7

CASE PERSPECTIVE

James Keeler has been asked by the Trelane College Job Placement Center staff to help in the planning of the annual Career Week at Trelane College. During the Career Week events, the center expects an increased number of visitors to the college Web site looking for a list of Career Week events and other college information. James volunteered to build a Career Week - Calendar of Events Web page for the Trelane College Web site. Before publishing the page to the college's Web site, James plans to create and publish a prototype of the page on his Web site for testing. He realizes that a Web page with a table would be appropriate for presenting the calendar. James also wants to add some search capabilities to the Trelane College Web site to help new visitors to the site find information quickly.

After you discuss the possibilities with James, you agree that a table would be good for presenting the calendar of events. FrontPage provides numerous tools that will help James quickly enter text into the table, enhance table format and appearance, as well as add search capabilities to the Web site.

As you read through this project, you will learn how to create and format a table that is part of the visible presentation to the visitor. You will learn to apply one of a number of predetermined table formats to a table, in a manner similar to that of applying a theme to a Web site. You will learn how to make modifications to a table, including adding a caption, filling repetitive text across cells, and using a color or an image as a table cell background. You will learn how to display the Table toolbar, to use the Split Cells button to split cells into two or more cells, and to use the Eraser button to merge cells. Finally, you will learn how to add a search page to a Web site and how to modify the search form properties.

Customizing Tables and Searching Web Sites

PROJECT

7

Objectives

You will have mastered the material in this project when you can:

- Display the Tables toolbar
- Insert a caption for a table
- Fill repetitive information in a table
- Split cells in a table
- Apply the Table AutoFormat feature to an existing table
- Assign a background color to table cells
- Modify properties for a group of cells in a table
- Use the Eraser button to merge table cells
- Use an image as a background for a table cell
- Use the Search Page template to add search capabilities to a Web page
- Modify search form properties

Introduction

In previous projects, the Web pages used tables principally as a means of positioning elements on a Web page, with little concern about using the table itself in the visual presentation. In fact, many times the tables used were made invisible to the Web page visitor. A table can be an important part of a Web page's presentation, however, by using color and other features to help organize and present that information more effectively. This project will utilize several FrontPage features that help simplify the process of creating and adding textual information to a table and enhancing the format and appearance of a table.

As a Web site grows in size, visitors may experience increased difficulty finding relevant information, even on a Web site with clear hyperlinks and a well-organized structure. Most Web site users expect that a Web site of any appreciable size should have some search capability that allows them to locate desired information quickly. In this project, a search page is added to a Web site to allow visitors to search for matching text on pages within the Web site.

Project Seven — Creating the Calendar of Events and Search Web Pages

This project presents the concepts and techniques that illustrate the creation and formatting of a table that is part of the visible presentation to the Web page visitor. A predetermined table format will be applied to a table, in a manner similar to that of applying a theme to a Web site (Figure 7-1a). Modifications will be made to the table, including adding a caption, filling repetitive text across cells, and using a color or an image as a table cell background. Table cells will be split into two or more cells and other cells will be merged. Finally, a search page will be added to the Trelane College Web site (Figure 7-1b on the next page).

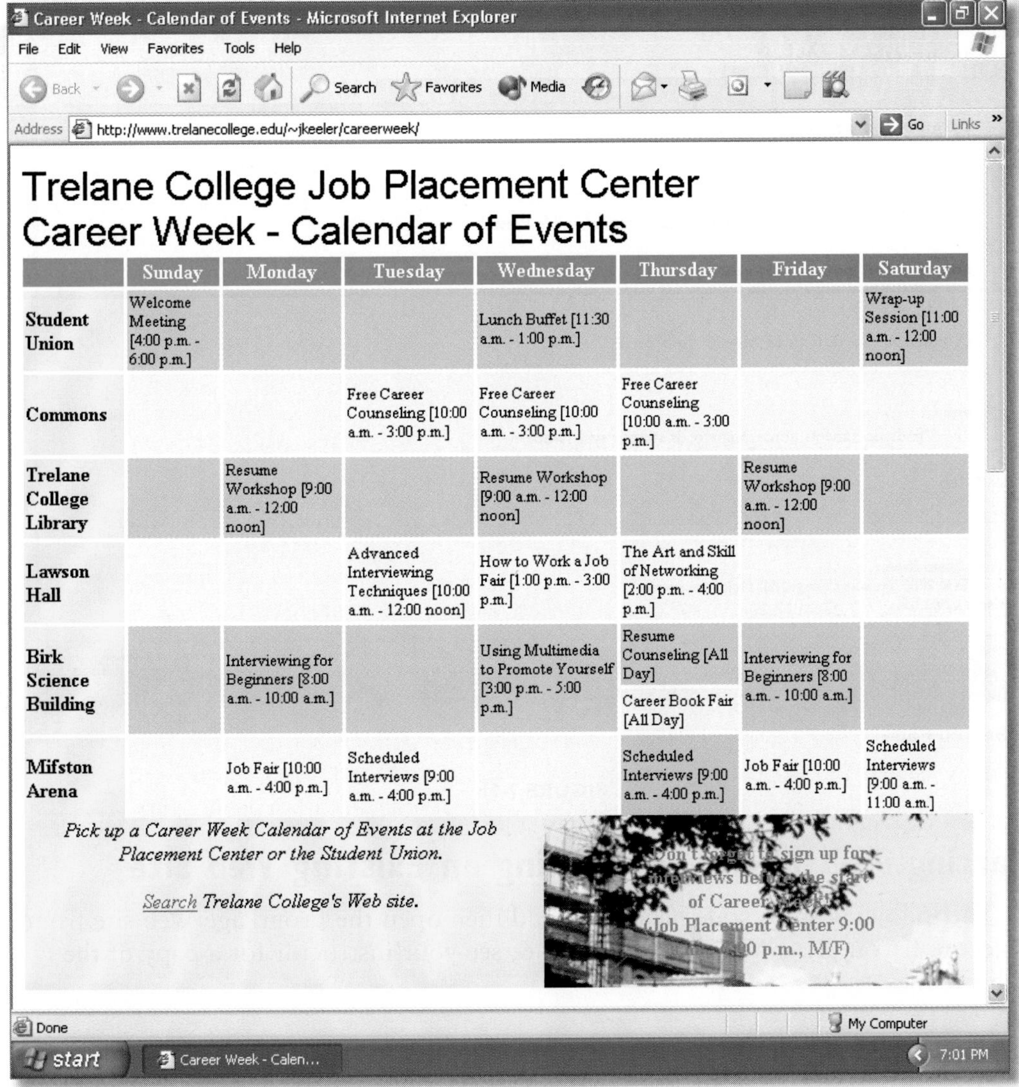

Trelane College Job Placement Center
Career Week - Calendar of Events

	Sunday	Monday	Tuesday	Wednesday	Thursday	Friday	Saturday
Student Union	Welcome Meeting [4:00 p.m. - 6:00 p.m.]			Lunch Buffet [11:30 a.m. - 1:00 p.m.]			Wrap-up Session [11:00 a.m. - 12:00 noon]
Commons			Free Career Counseling [10:00 a.m. - 3:00 p.m.]	Free Career Counseling [10:00 a.m. - 3:00 p.m.]	Free Career Counseling [10:00 a.m. - 3:00 p.m.]		
Trelane College Library		Resume Workshop [9:00 a.m. - 12:00 noon]		Resume Workshop [9:00 a.m. - 12:00 noon]		Resume Workshop [9:00 a.m. - 12:00 noon]	
Lawson Hall			Advanced Interviewing Techniques [10:00 a.m. - 12:00 noon]	How to Work a Job Fair [1:00 p.m. - 3:00 p.m.]	The Art and Skill of Networking [2:00 p.m. - 4:00 p.m.]		
Birk Science Building		Interviewing for Beginners [8:00 a.m. - 10:00 a.m.]		Using Multimedia to Promote Yourself [3:00 p.m. - 5:00 p.m.]	Resume Counseling [All Day] Career Book Fair [All Day]	Interviewing for Beginners [8:00 a.m. - 10:00 a.m.]	
Mifston Arena		Job Fair [10:00 a.m. - 4:00 p.m.]	Scheduled Interviews [9:00 a.m. - 4:00 p.m.]		Scheduled Interviews [9:00 a.m. - 4:00 p.m.]	Job Fair [10:00 a.m. - 4:00 p.m.]	Scheduled Interviews [9:00 a.m. - 11:00 a.m.]

Pick up a Career Week Calendar of Events at the Job Placement Center or the Student Union.

Search Trelane College's Web site.

(a) Calendar Page

FIGURE 7-1a

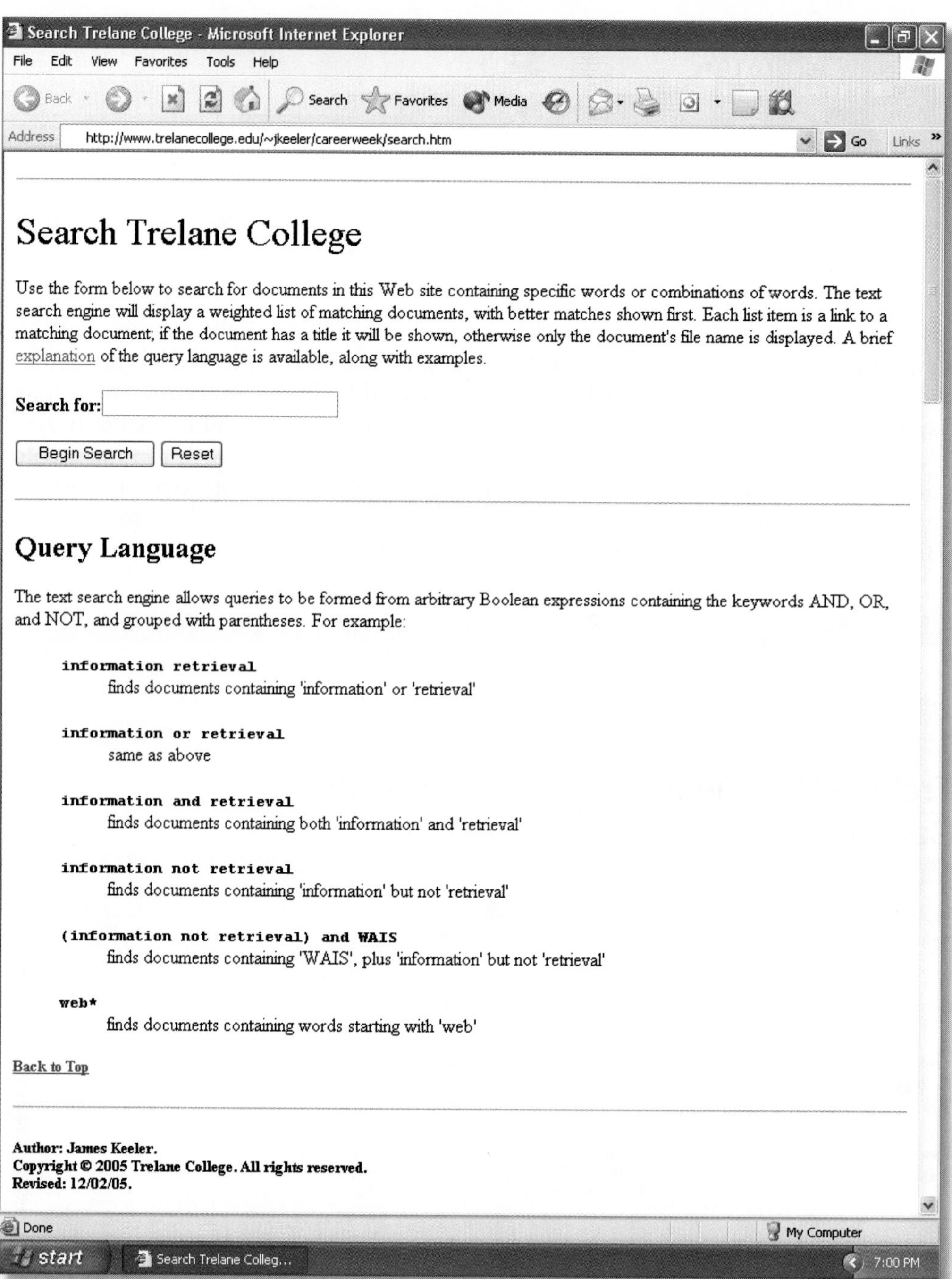

(b) Search Page

FIGURE 7-1b

Starting FrontPage and Opening an Existing Web Site

The following steps start FrontPage and then open the FrontPage Web site from Project 6. If you did not complete Project 6, see your instructor for a copy of the Web site files.

To Start FrontPage and Open an Existing Web Site

1. **Click the Start button on the taskbar. Point to All Programs on the Start menu.**
2. **Click Microsoft Office on the All Programs submenu.**
3. **Point to Microsoft Office FrontPage 2003 on the Microsoft Office submenu.**
4. **Click the Open button arrow on the Standard toolbar.**
5. **Click Open Site on the Open menu. When FrontPage displays the Open Site dialog box, if necessary, click the Look in box arrow and select the folder location where you stored the Web site for Project 6 (e.g., C:\jkeeler).**
6. **Click the Open button.**

The previously created FrontPage Web site is loaded and is displayed in Folders view (Figure 7-2).

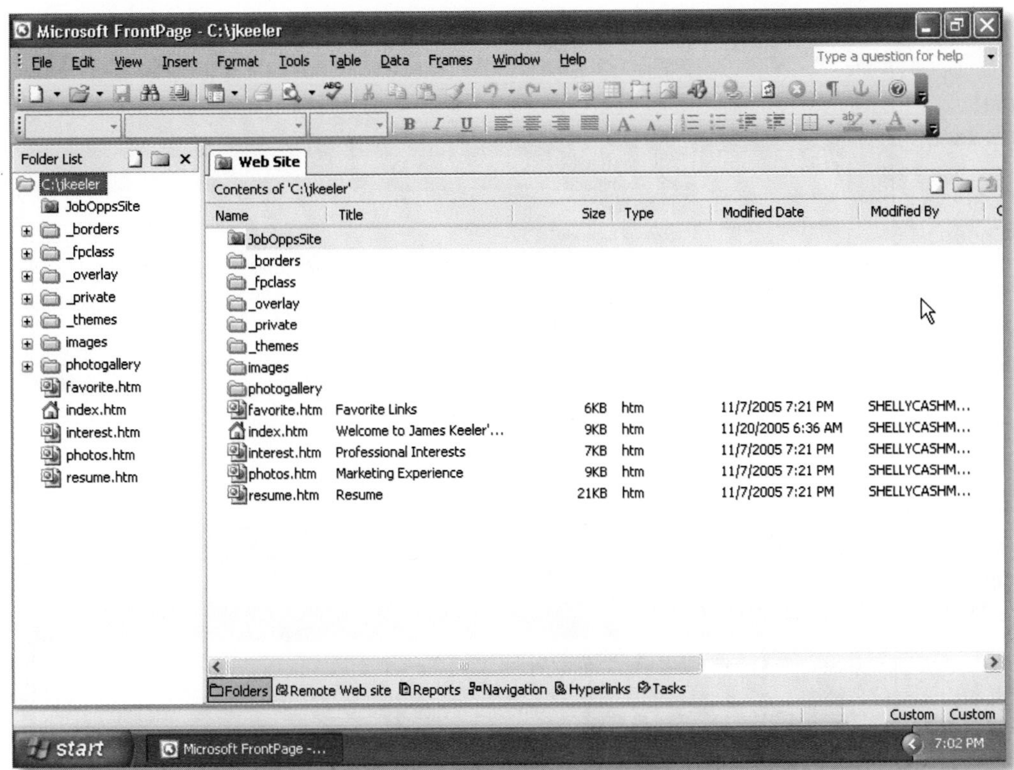

FIGURE 7-2

Customizing Tables in FrontPage

Although it is appropriate to place the finished calendar of events Web page and the search Web page on the official Web site for the college, it is a good idea to review the pages before completing this step to determine if the pages are suitable and ready for public access. It is easier to make any needed changes prior to publishing them to the college Web site. Therefore, in this section, you will create prototype pages for each of the pages in the Web site, within a separate subsite. A **prototype** is an original and usually functional version of a product or design, which serves as a model for a final product or design. By developing a prototype, you can review the pages to ensure they are acceptable before publishing to the college Web site.

> *More About*
>
> **Prototyping**
>
> Prototyping frequently is used in the development of computer applications and particularly is related to the elements a computer will display to users, such as the user interface for a software application. To learn more about prototyping, visit the FrontPage 2003 More About Web page (scsite.com/fp2003/more) and then click Prototyping.

Design Tip

Consider creating a prototype for a new Web site or Web page and testing the site or page in a safe location before incorporating the new site or page into another Web site. By developing a prototype, you and others can review the pages to ensure they are acceptable before publishing to the live Web site.

Creating a Subsite in an Existing Web Site

Before creating the prototype pages, you will create the subsite used to organize the prototype pages. The following steps create a subsite with a blank page in an existing Web site.

To Create a New Subsite in an Existing Web Site

1

• **Click the Create a new normal page button arrow on the Standard toolbar.**

FrontPage displays the Create a new normal page menu (Figure 7-3).

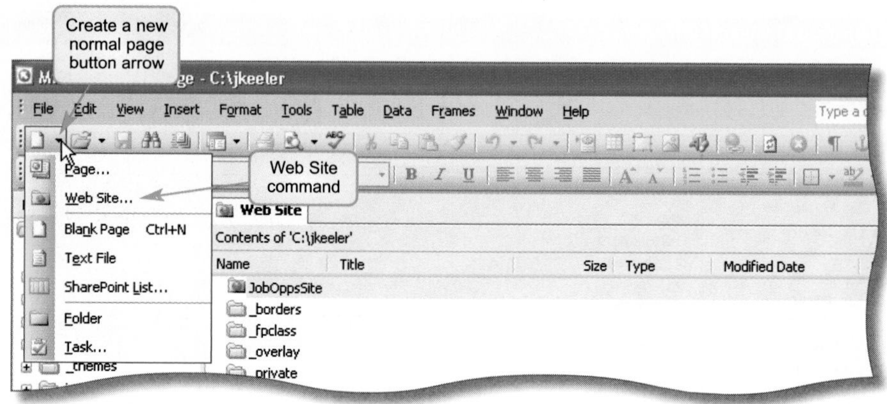

FIGURE 7-3

2

• **Click Web Site.**

• **If necessary, when FrontPage displays the Web Site Templates dialog box, click the One Page Web Site icon.**

• **Drag through the text in the Specify the location of the new Web site text box in the Options area.**

• **Type** `c:\jkeeler\careerweek` **(or the location and name of your current Web site with \careerweek appended).**

FrontPage displays the Web Site Templates dialog box (Figure 7-4). The Specify the location of the new Web site box displays a path to the new Web site, careerweek. Because the location of the new Web site is in an existing Web site, the new Web site will be a subsite.

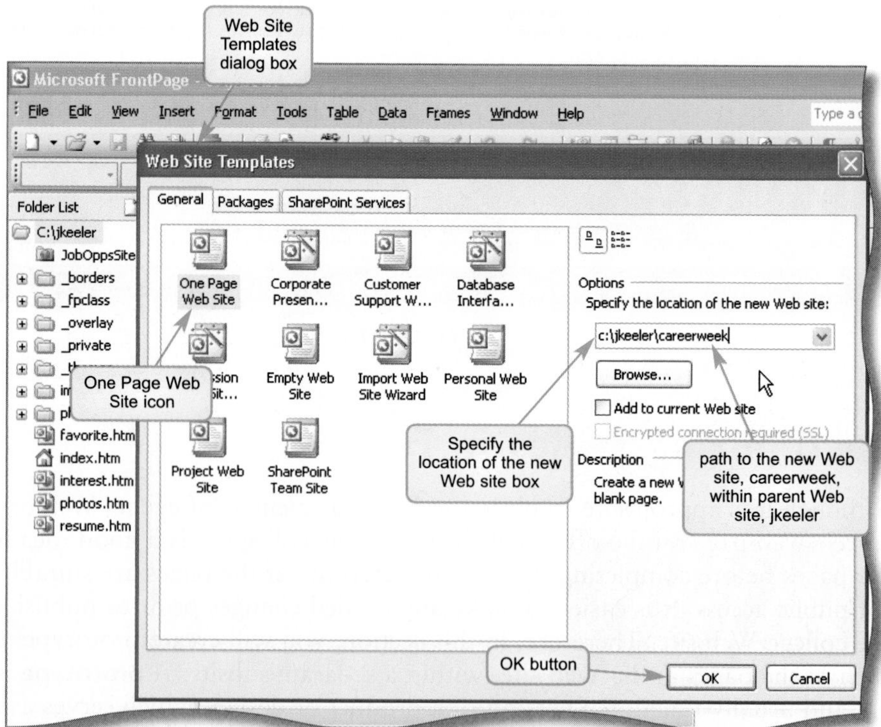

FIGURE 7-4

3

- **Click the OK button.**

The subsite, careerweek, is created and opens in a second instance of FrontPage (Figure 7-5). The parent Web site, jkeeler, remains open in the first instance of FrontPage.

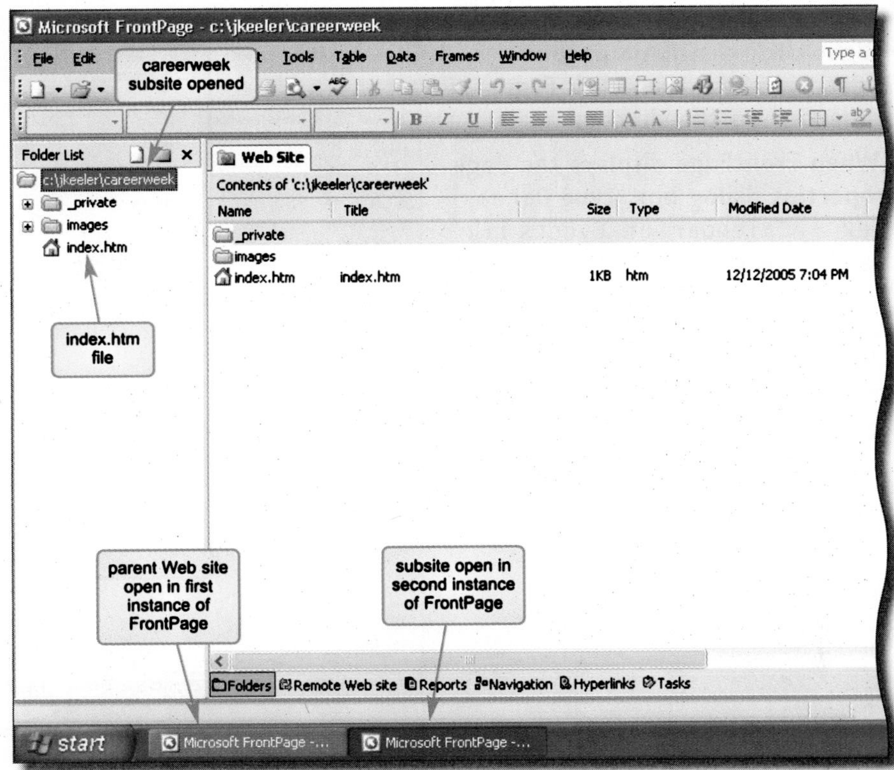

FIGURE 7-5

Setting the Title of a Web Page

The first page to prototype is the calendar page, which uses a table to display events for Career Week. To create the calendar of events page, you will rename the home page for the careerweek subsite and then add and customize a table to display the events. The following steps open and then set the title of the home page.

To Set the Title of a Web Page

1

- **Double-click the file, index.htm, in the Folder List to open the home page for the careerweek subsite.**

FrontPage displays the home page for the careerweek subsite in Design view (Figure 7-6).

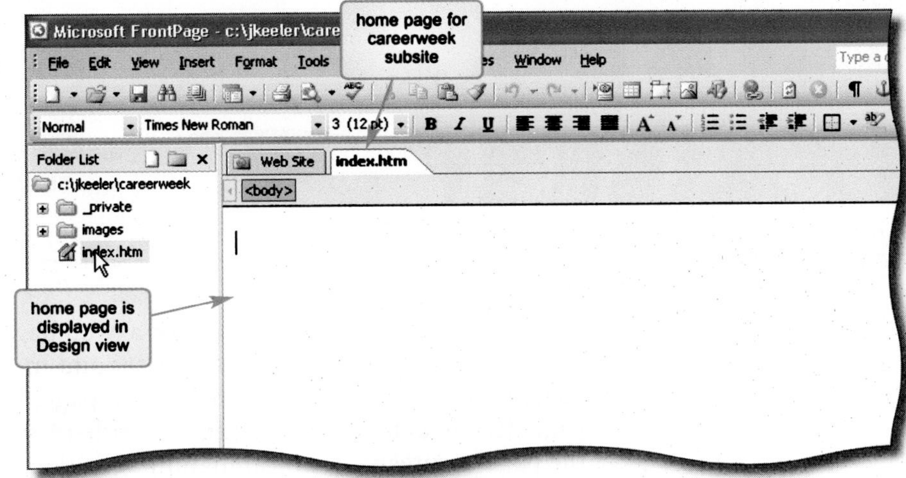

FIGURE 7-6

2

- **Right-click the home page in Design view and then click Page Properties on the shortcut menu.**
- **When FrontPage displays the Page Properties dialog box, type** `Career Week - Calendar of Events` **in the Title text box.**

FrontPage displays the Page Properties dialog box (Figure 7-7). The new page title, Career Week - Calendar of Events, is displayed in the Title text box.

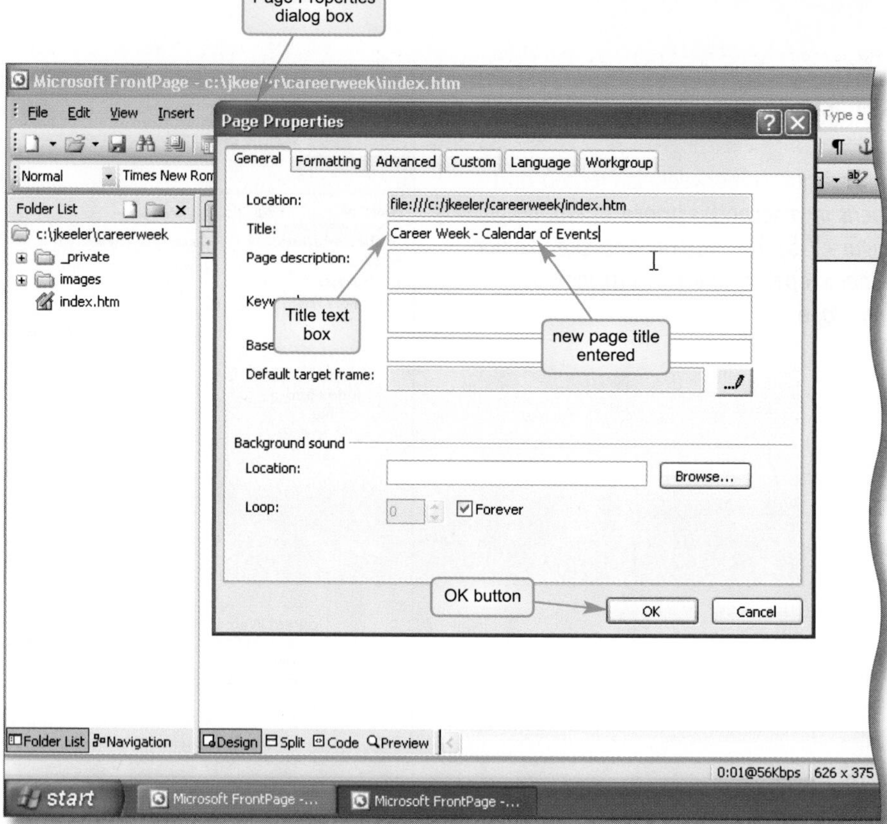

FIGURE 7-7

3

- **Click the OK button.**

FrontPage displays the home page for the careerweek subsite in Design view (Figure 7-8).

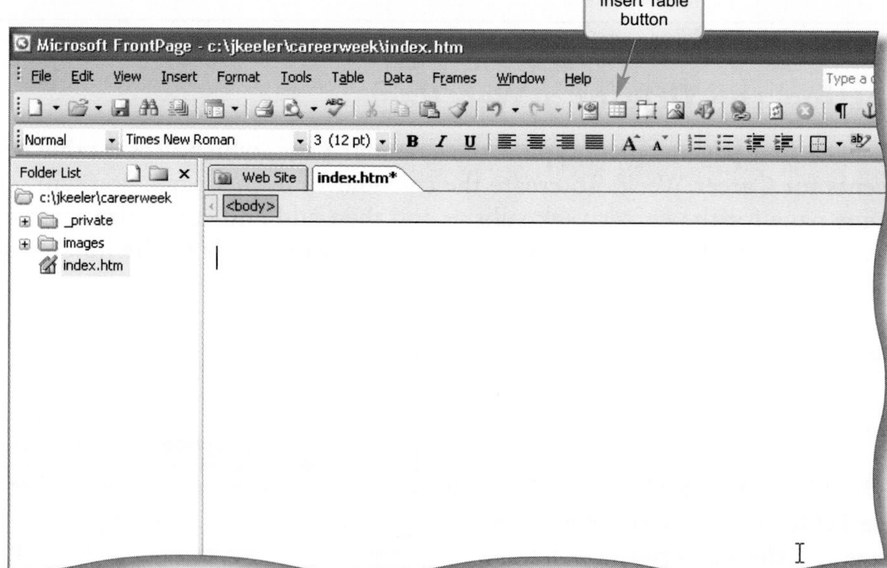

FIGURE 7-8

As you have learned, the title of a Web page is displayed on the title bar when the page is viewed with a Web browser and in any bookmarks or favorites for that page. If you do not set a title for a Web page, the first text on the page becomes the page title by default. Setting the page title to reflect the organization or purpose of the page ensures that a meaningful page title is displayed on the browser title bar and in any bookmarks or favorites.

Inserting Tables and Displaying the Tables Toolbar

With the new title for the home page set, the next task is to create two tables in the home page. Next, the properties of the two tables will be modified and customized to define the structure of the events calendar.

FrontPage provides various ways to manipulate features of a table. The Tables toolbar (Figure 7-9) contains buttons used to execute commands such as inserting rows or columns, aligning text in a cell, and applying a predefined format to a table. The Tables toolbar can be hidden or displayed, or displayed only when the insertion point is in a table. If you click Toolbars on the View menu or right-click any toolbar in the FrontPage window, FrontPage displays a shortcut menu that lists all the available toolbars. Clicking a toolbar name displays that toolbar. A check mark next to a toolbar name indicates that the toolbar currently is displayed in the FrontPage window.

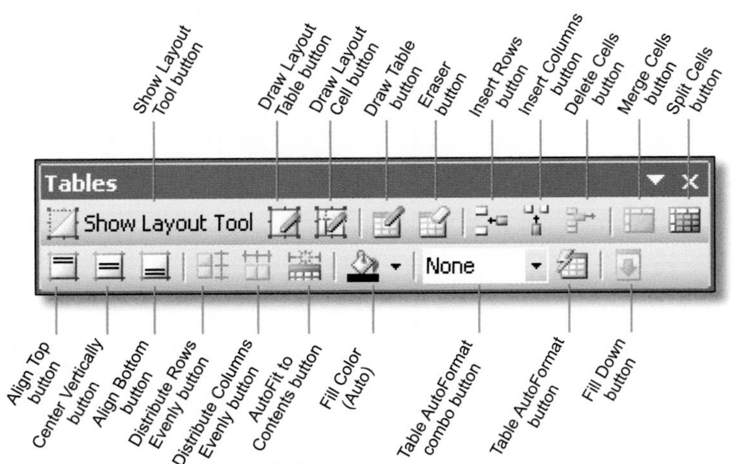

FIGURE 7-9

Tables provide a versatile layout environment. When designing a new Web page, consider beginning the design with a table or multiple tables.

The following steps insert two tables in the subsite home page and then display the Tables toolbar.

To Insert Tables and Display the Tables Toolbar

1

- **Click the Insert Table button on the Standard toolbar and drag to select seven rows and eight columns (7 by 8 table).**

The Insert Table grid displays the cells selected for a seven-row table with eight columns (Figure 7-10). As you learned in Project 2, the grid is a graphical means of displaying the number of rows and columns used in a table.

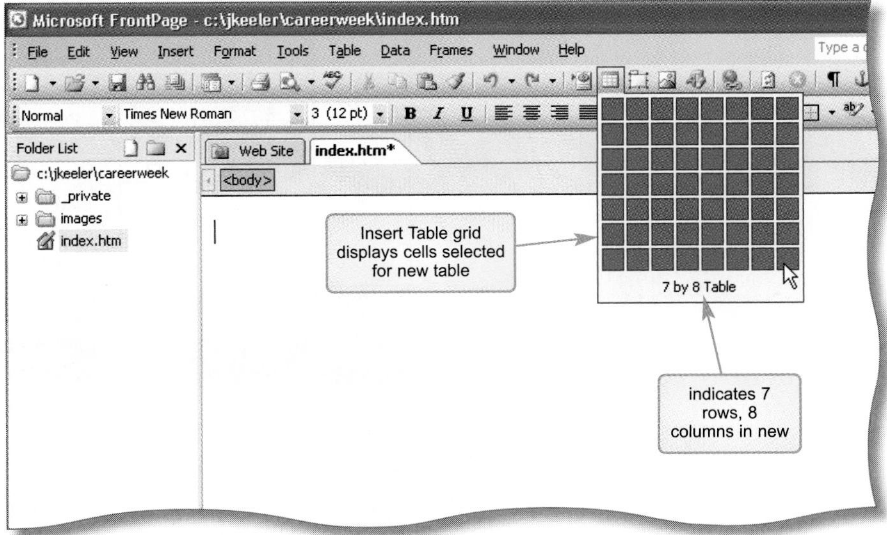

FIGURE 7-10

2

- **Release the mouse button.**
- **If necessary, position the insertion point in the first table cell.**

FrontPage displays a table with seven rows and eight columns in the Web page (Figure 7-11). The insertion point is positioned in the first table cell.

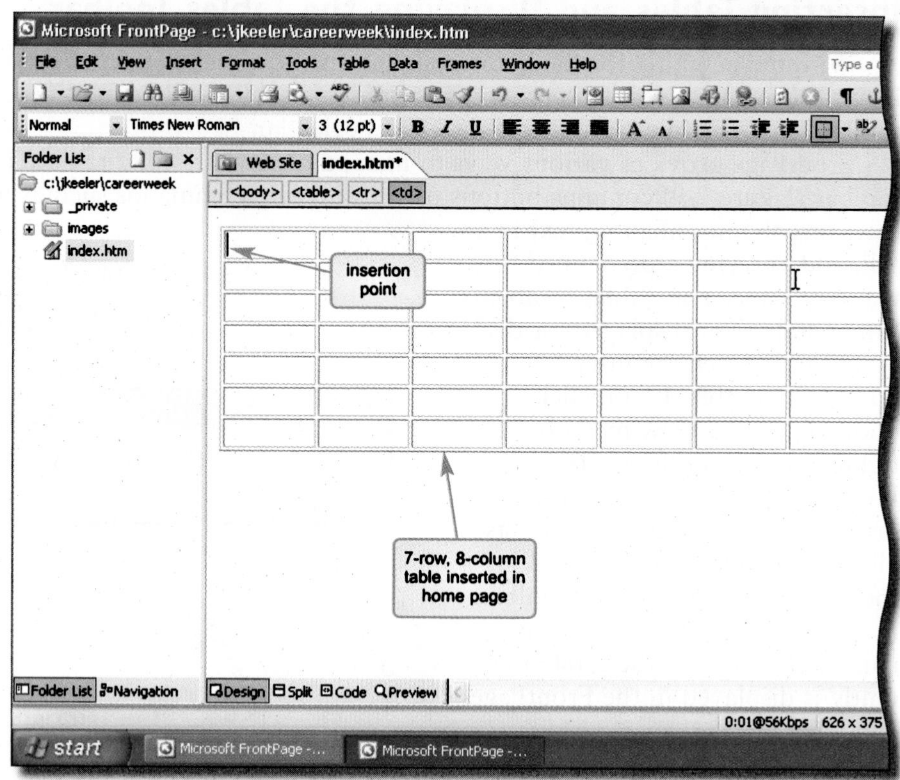

FIGURE 7-11

3

- **Click View on the menu bar and then point to Toolbars.**

FrontPage displays the Toolbars submenu (Figure 7-12). The two check marks indicate toolbars already being displayed in the FrontPage window.

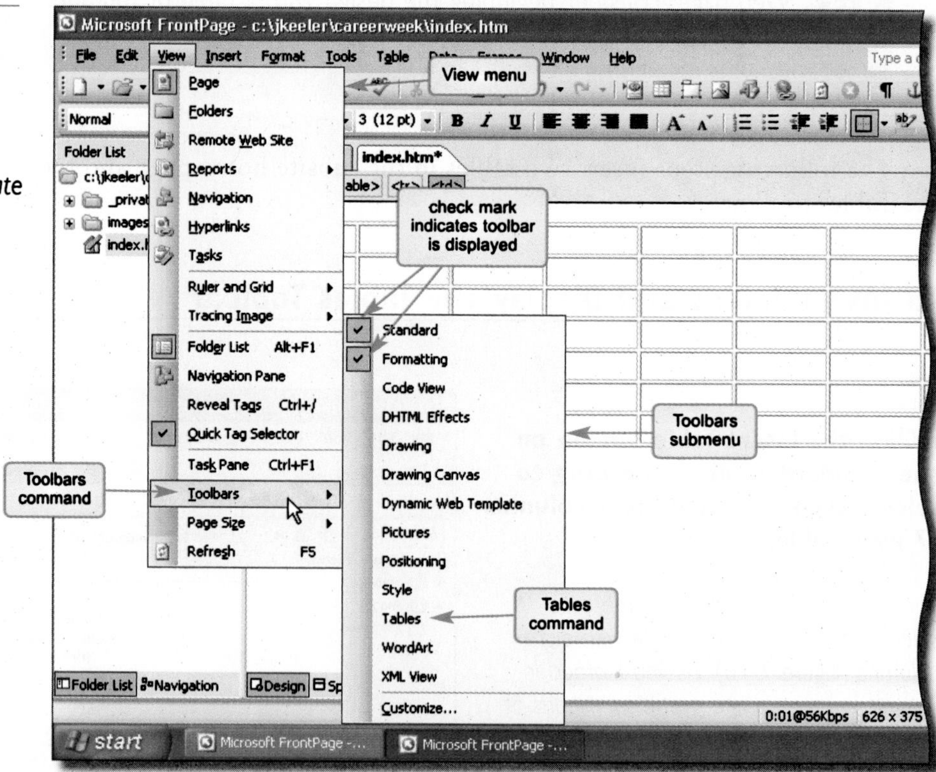

FIGURE 7-12

4

- **Click Tables.**
- **If necessary, drag the Tables toolbar below the table.**

FrontPage displays the Tables toolbar (Figure 7-13).

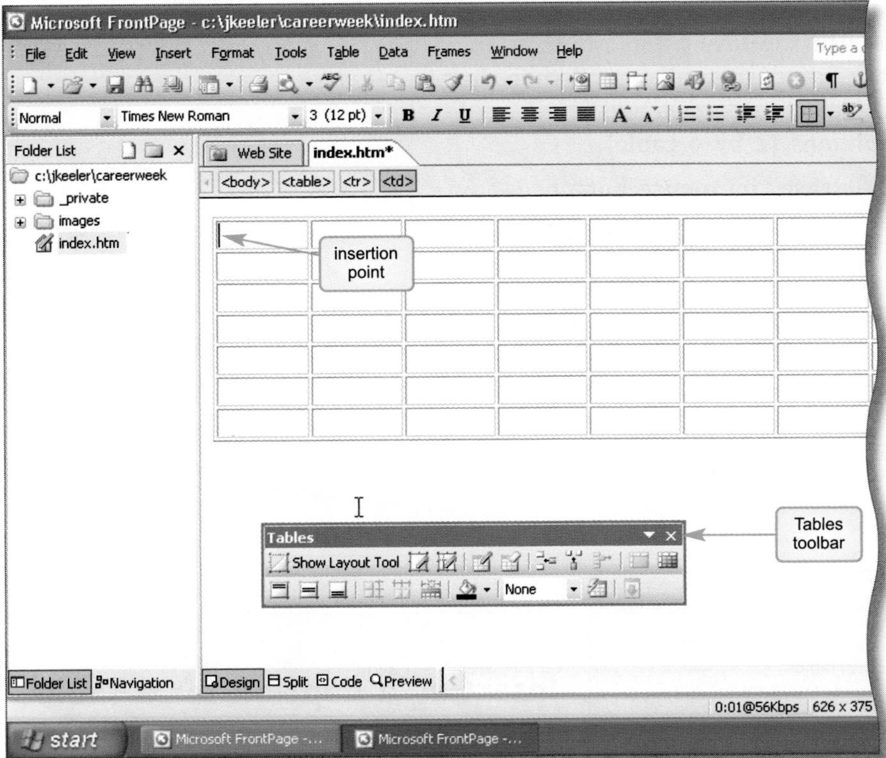

FIGURE 7-13

5

- **Position the insertion point below the table.**

The insertion point is positioned below the table (Figure 7-14).

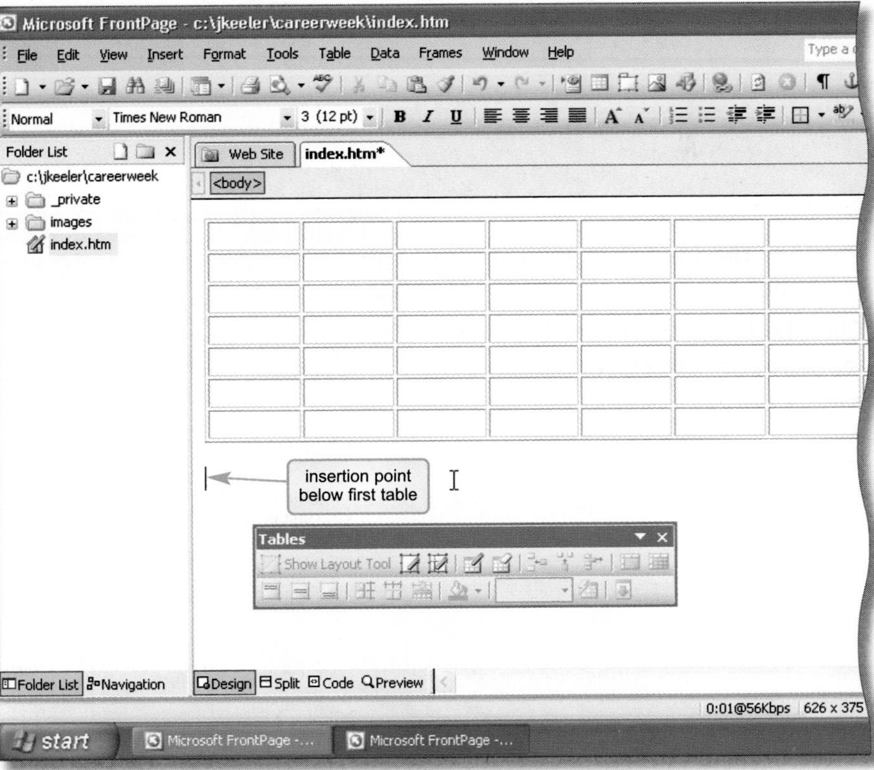

FIGURE 7-14

6

- **Click the Insert Table button on the Standard toolbar and then drag to select two rows and four columns (2 by 4 table).**
- **Release the mouse button.**

FrontPage displays a second table directly beneath the first table. Because the insertion point is positioned in the first cell of the second table, the Tables toolbar again is displayed (Figure 7-15). A thick border visually separates the first table from the second table.

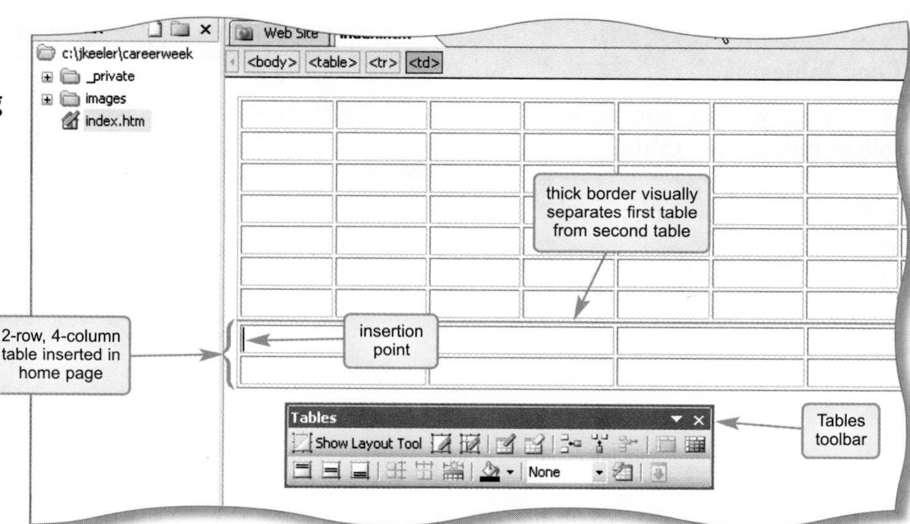

FIGURE 7-15

Other Ways

1. Press ALT+V, T, select Tables
2. In Voice Command mode, say "View, Toolbars, Tables"

Inserting a Caption for a Table

To convey the purpose of a table to a Web page visitor, you can insert a caption for the table. A **caption**, or title, provides a label that summarizes the contents of a table. In this project, a caption will be inserted above the first table to indicate that it lists a calendar of events for Career Week.

The following steps insert a caption for the first table.

To Insert a Caption for a Table

1

- **Position the insertion point in the first table.**
- **Click Table on the menu bar and then point to Insert on the Table menu.**

FrontPage displays the Insert submenu (Figure 7-16).

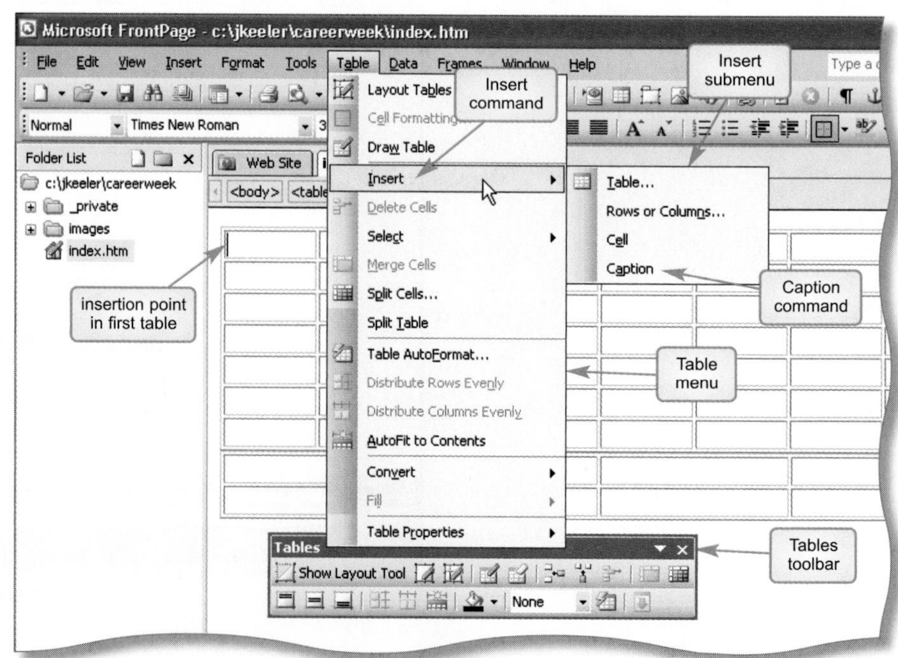

FIGURE 7-16

2

- **Click Caption.**
- **Click the Align Left button on the Formatting toolbar.**

FrontPage positions the insertion point so that the caption will be displayed aligned with the left edge of the table (Figure 7-17).

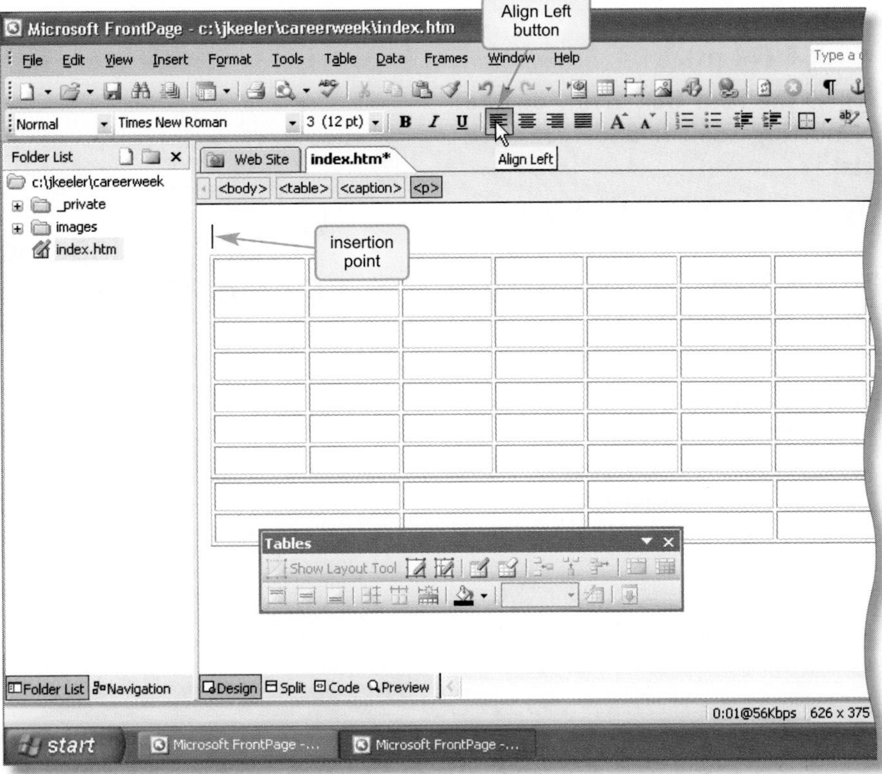

FIGURE 7-17

3

- **Click the Font Size box arrow on the Formatting toolbar.**

FrontPage positions the insertion point to align it with the left edge of the table. The font size, 3 (12 pt), is selected in the Font Size list (Figure 7-18).

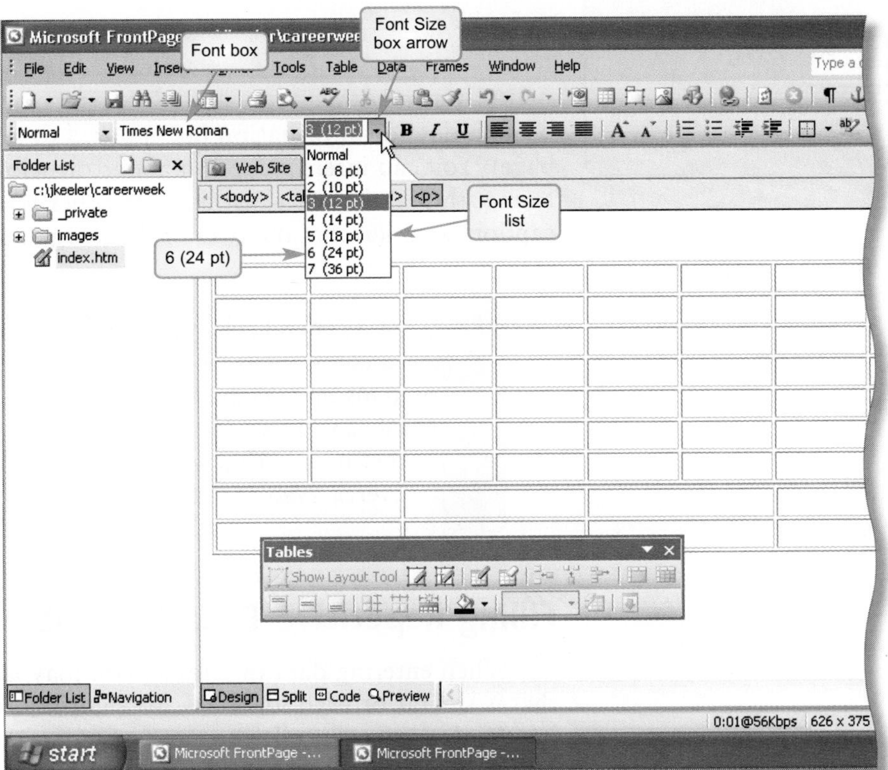

FIGURE 7-18

4

- **Click 6 (24 pt).**
- **Click the Font box arrow on the Formatting toolbar and then click Arial.**
- **Type** `Trelane College Job Placement Center` **as the first line of the caption.**
- **Press SHIFT+ENTER.**
- **Type** `Career Week - Calendar of Events` **as the second line of the caption.**

FrontPage displays the table caption aligned with the left edge of the first table (Figure 7-19).

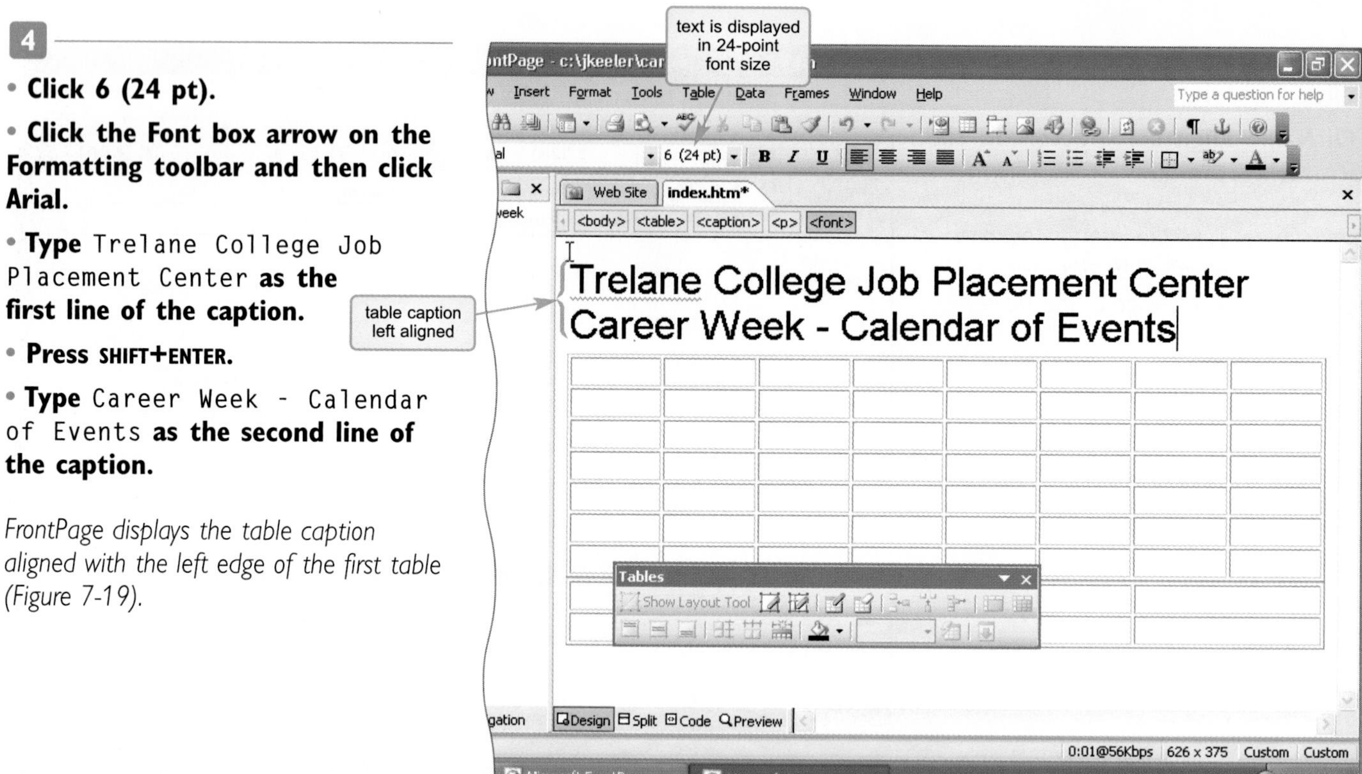

FIGURE 7-19

Other Ways

1. Press ALT+A, I, A
2. In Voice Command mode, say "Table, Insert, Caption"

As a general rule, you should insert a caption for any table that is used to contain data or information (as opposed to a table used to align items on a Web page). You can insert a caption above or below a table; you also can align and format the caption text just like any other text on a Web page, to ensure that the caption complements the overall Web page design.

Design Tip

As a general rule, you should insert a caption for any table that is used to contain data or information (as opposed to a table used to align items on a Web page). You can insert a caption above or below a table; you also can align and format the caption text just like any other text on a Web page, to ensure that the caption complements the overall Web page design.

Filling Repetitive Data in a Table

When entering data in a table, you may find that many of the cells contain data that is similar or even identical. To enter the repetitive data in the table without typing the data in each cell, you can copy and paste data from one cell into another. Depending on the number of cells, however, the copy-and-paste process can be tedious. FrontPage provides a Fill command that allows you to select data from one cell and then fill an adjacent cell or cells with the repetitive data, without having to copy and paste each time. The following steps fill repetitive data from one cell into adjacent table cells across table columns.

To Fill Adjacent Table Columns with Repetitive Data

1

- **Position the insertion point in the table cell in the third row and the fourth column of the first table.**

The insertion point is positioned in the table cell in the third row and the fourth column of the first table (Figure 7-20).

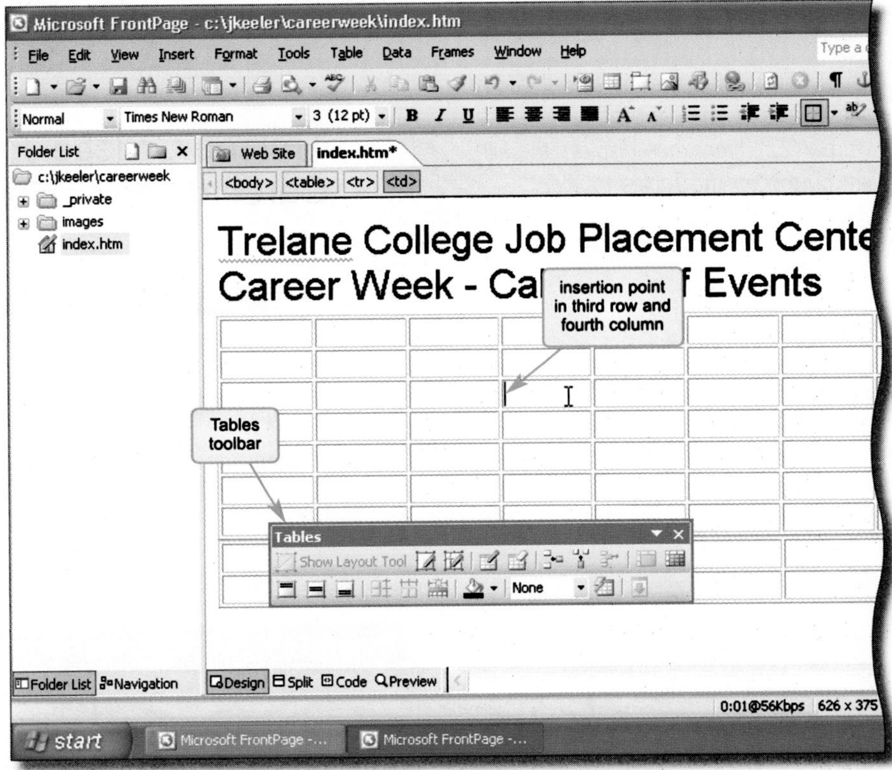

FIGURE 7-20

2

- **Type** `Free Career Counseling [10:00 a.m. - 3:00 p.m.]` **in the table cell.**

FrontPage displays the entered text in the table cell (Figure 7-21).

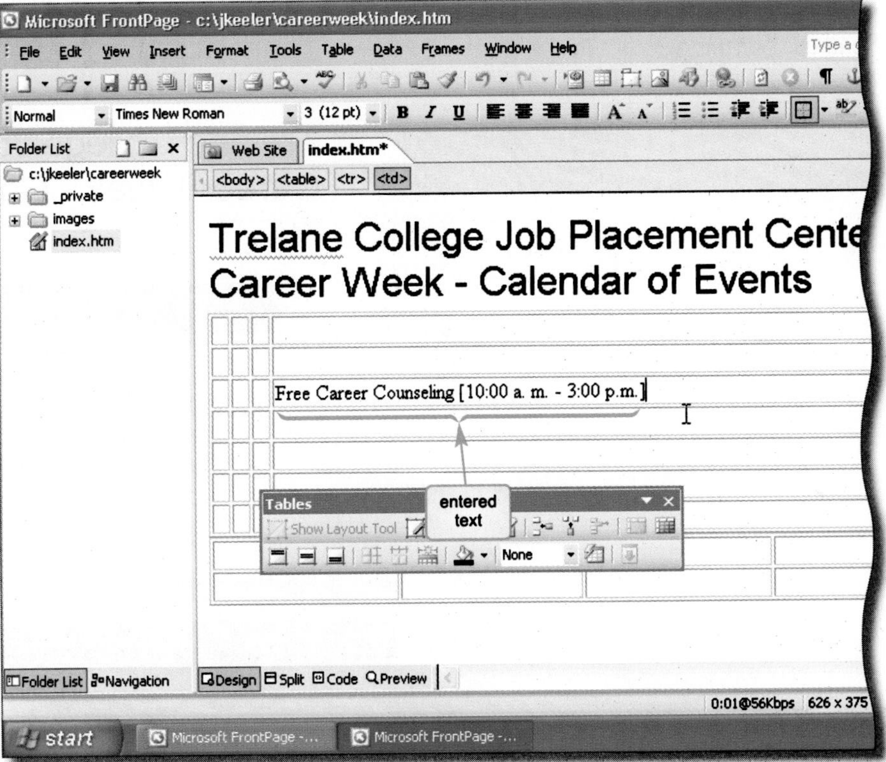

FIGURE 7-21

3

• **Drag to select the text entered in the fourth cell and the two cells to the right of the fourth cell.**

The text entered in the fourth cell and the two cells to the right are selected (Figure 7-22). FrontPage displays the Fill Right button on the Tables toolbar.

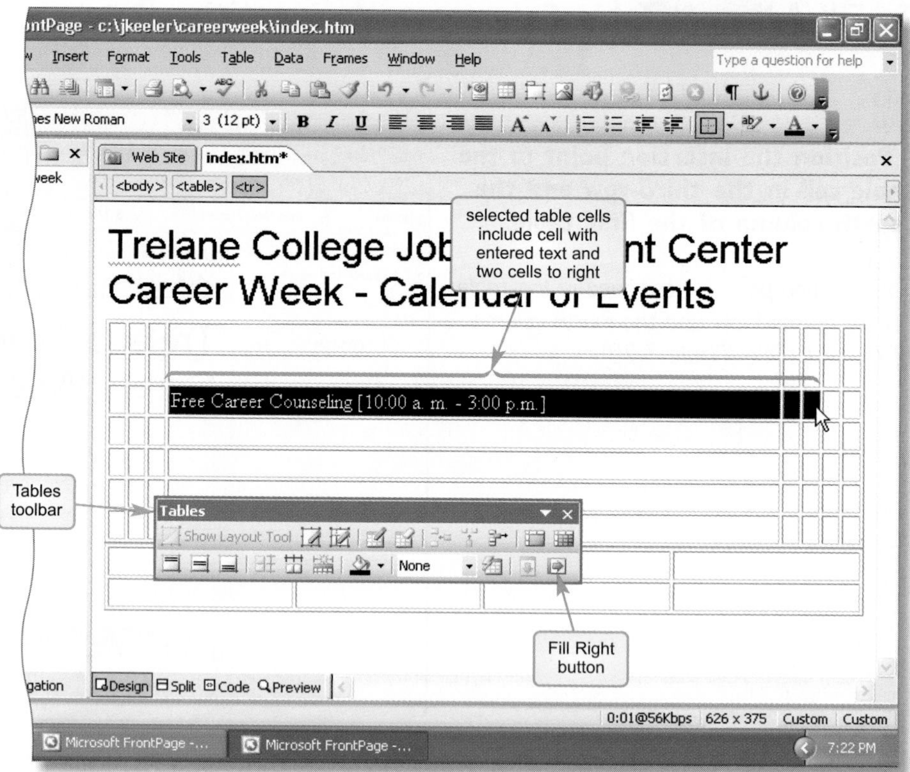

FIGURE 7-22

4

• **Click the Fill Right button on the Tables toolbar.**

FrontPage fills the two cells to the right with the text entered in the fourth cell (Figure 7-23).

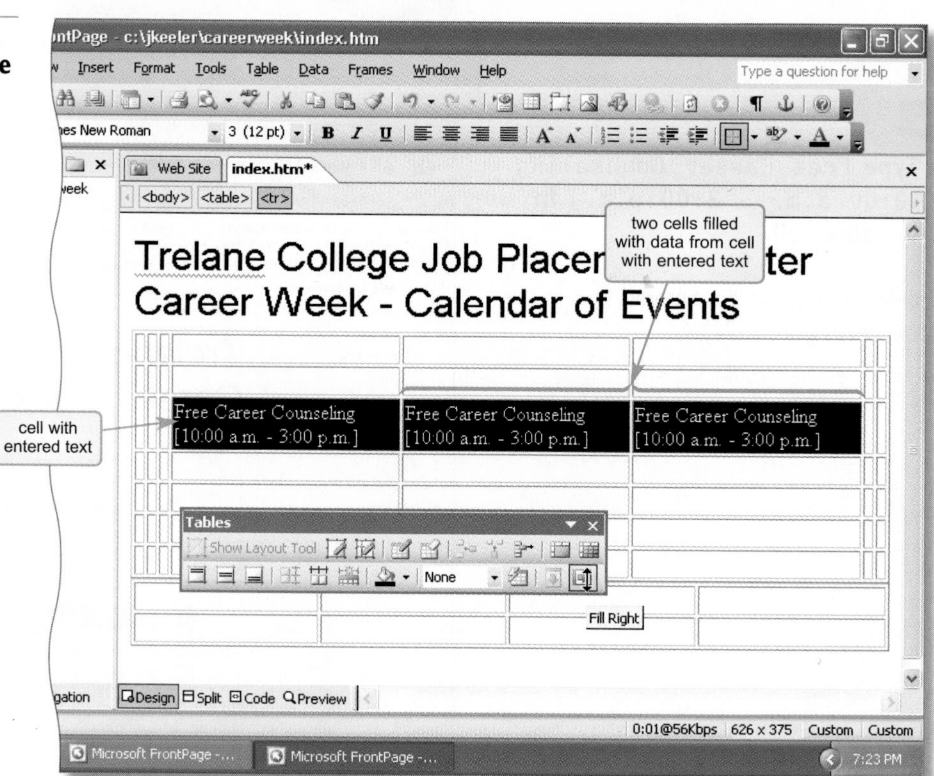

FIGURE 7-23

5

- **Refer to Table 7-1 and finish entering text in the first table, making certain to enter only the text below the header of Table 7-1.**
- **Click the Save button on the Standard toolbar to save the changes.**

FrontPage displays the additional entered text in the table (Figure 7-24). The events for Career Week are entered in the first table. The Tables toolbar automatically moves when necessary to allow typing in the table cells.

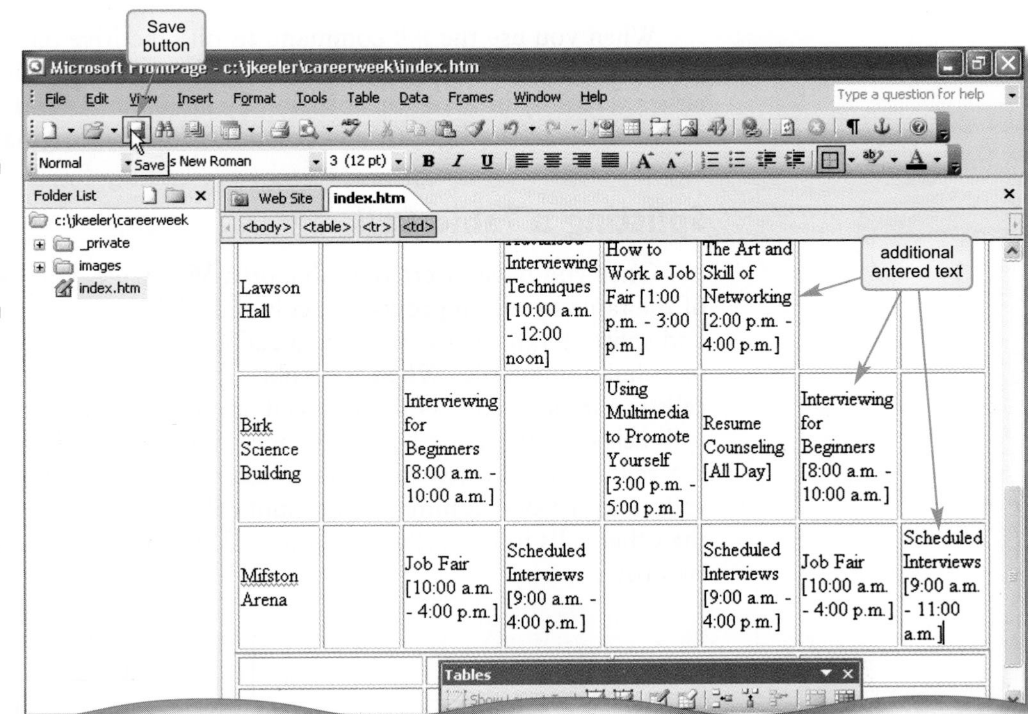

FIGURE 7-24

Other Ways

1. Click Table, click Fill, click Right
2. Press ALT+A, L, R
3. In Voice Command mode, say "Table, Fill, Right"

In addition to filling repetitive data from a cell to an adjacent table column or columns, FrontPage also can fill repetitive data from a cell to an adjacent row or rows. To fill repetitive data from a cell to an adjacent row, you drag to select the cell with the content you want to copy and then select the adjacent cells in a row. Once the cells are selected, click the Fill Down button on the Tables toolbar to fill the repetitive data to the adjacent row or rows.

Table 7-1 Career Week - Calendar of Events

LOCATION	DAY/EVENTS	DAY/EVENTS	DAY/EVENTS	DAY/EVENTS	DAY/EVENTS	DAY/EVENTS	DAY/EVENTS
	Sunday	Monday	Tuesday	Wednesday	Thursday	Friday	Saturday
Student Union	Welcome Meeting [4:00 p.m. - 6:00 p.m.]			Lunch Buffet [11:30 a.m. - 1:00 p.m.]			Wrap-up Session [11:00 a.m. - 12:00 noon]
Commons			Free Career Counseling [10:00 a.m. - 3:00 p.m.]	Free Career Counseling [10:00 a.m. - 3:00 p.m.]	Free Career Counseling [10:00 a.m. - 3:00 p.m.]		
Trelane College Library		Resume Workshop [9:00 a.m. - 12:00 noon]		Resume Workshop [9:00 a.m. – 12:00 noon]		Resume Workshop [9:00 a.m. - 12:00 noon]	
Lawson Hall			Advanced Interviewing Techniques [10:00 a.m. - 12:00 noon]	How to Work a Job Fair [1:00 p.m. - 3:00 p.m.]	The Art and Skill of Networking [2:00 p.m. - 4:00 p.m.]		
Birk Science Building		Interviewing for Beginners [8:00 a.m. - 10:00 a.m.]		Using Multimedia to Promote Yourself [3:00 p.m. - 5:00 p.m.]	Resume Counseling [All Day]	Interviewing for Beginners [8:00 a.m. - 10:00 a.m.]	
Mifston Arena		Job Fair [10:00 a.m. - 4:00 p.m.]	Scheduled Interviews [9:00 a.m. - 4:00 p.m.]		Scheduled Interviews [9:00 a.m. - 4:00 p.m.]	Job Fair [10:00 a.m. - 4:00 p.m.]	Scheduled Interviews [9:00 a.m. - 11:00 a.m.]

When you use the Fill command to fill repetitive data across rows or columns, you must select cells that are adjacent and in a straight line from the original cell, either vertically in rows, or horizontally in columns. You also must select cells that are in a row to the right or in a column below the original cell.

Splitting a Table Cell

Once you have inserted a table on a Web page, you can customize the structure of the table by adding rows and columns, deleting rows and columns, or merging and splitting table cells. Splitting a cell is not the same as inserting an additional row or column in a table. When you split a cell into two rows, for example, the other cells in the same row as the split cell are not split. Combined, the two rows in the split cell span the same height as each of the other cells in the row. The same is true if a cell is split into two or more columns: the other cells in the same column are not split, and the two columns in the split cell combined span the same width as each of the other cells in the column (Figure 7-25). The following steps split a table cell into two rows.

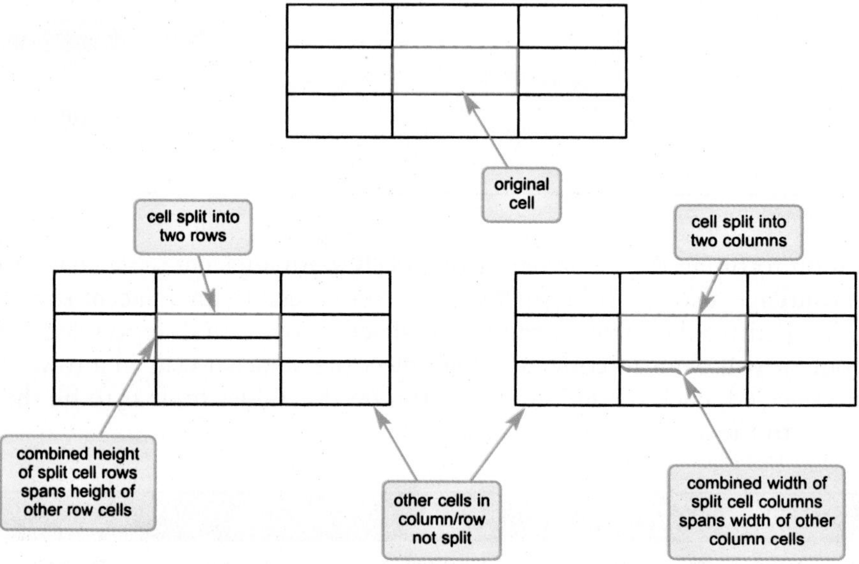

FIGURE 7-25

Design Tip When designing with tables, keep in mind that table cells can be split or combined to accommodate almost any design that includes distinct rectangular areas of the Web page.

To Split a Cell into Rows

1

• **Position the insertion point in the sixth row and the sixth column of the first table.**

FrontPage displays the insertion point in the sixth row and the sixth column of the first table (Figure 7-26).

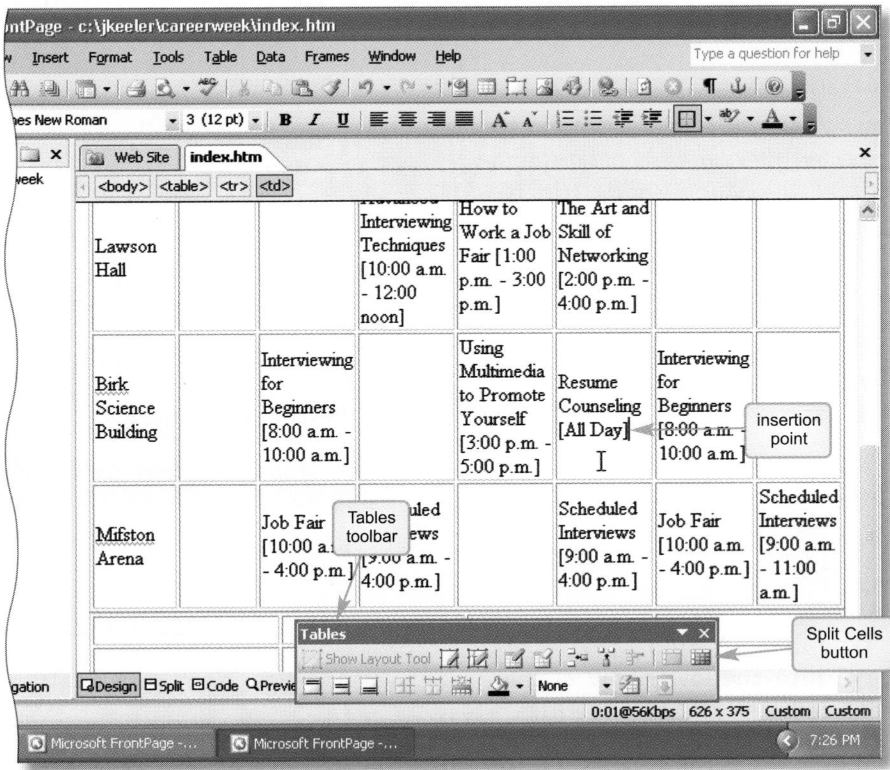

FIGURE 7-26

2

• **Click the Split Cells button on the Tables toolbar.**

• **When FrontPage displays the Split Cells dialog box, click Split into rows.**

• **Verify that the number of rows specified is 2.**

FrontPage displays the Split Cells dialog box (Figure 7-27). Depending on the option selected, the text box label changes to Number of columns or Number of rows, and the dialog box displays a graphic of either two columns or two rows, respectively.

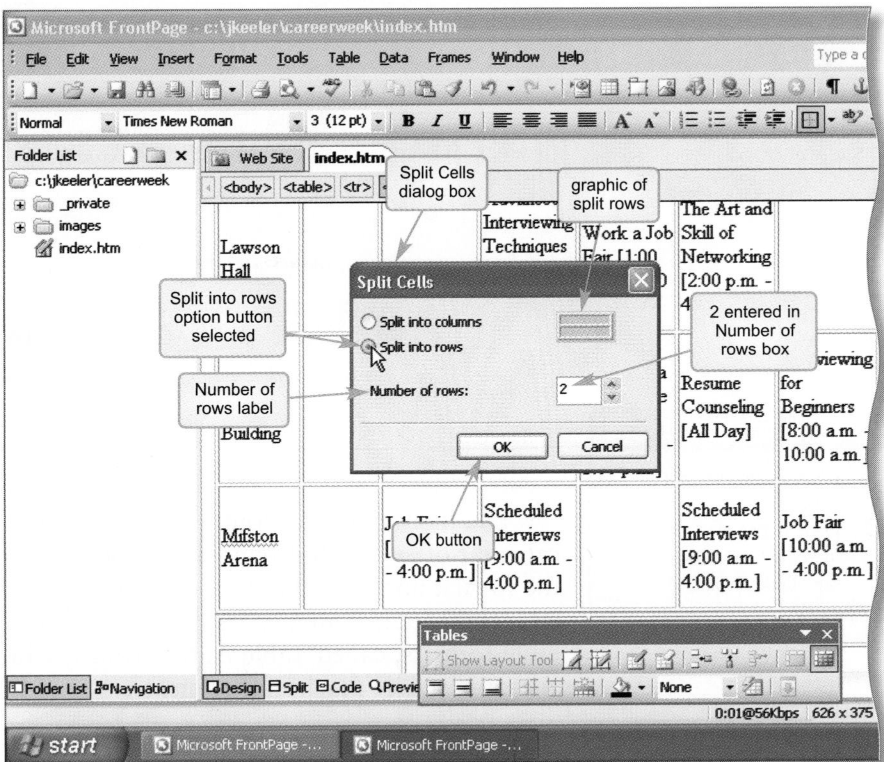

FIGURE 7-27

3

- **Click the OK button.**
- **Position the insertion point in the empty row of the cell.**

The selected cell is split horizontally into two rows (Figure 7-28). FrontPage displays the entered text in the upper row of the split cell. The lower row of the split cell is empty.

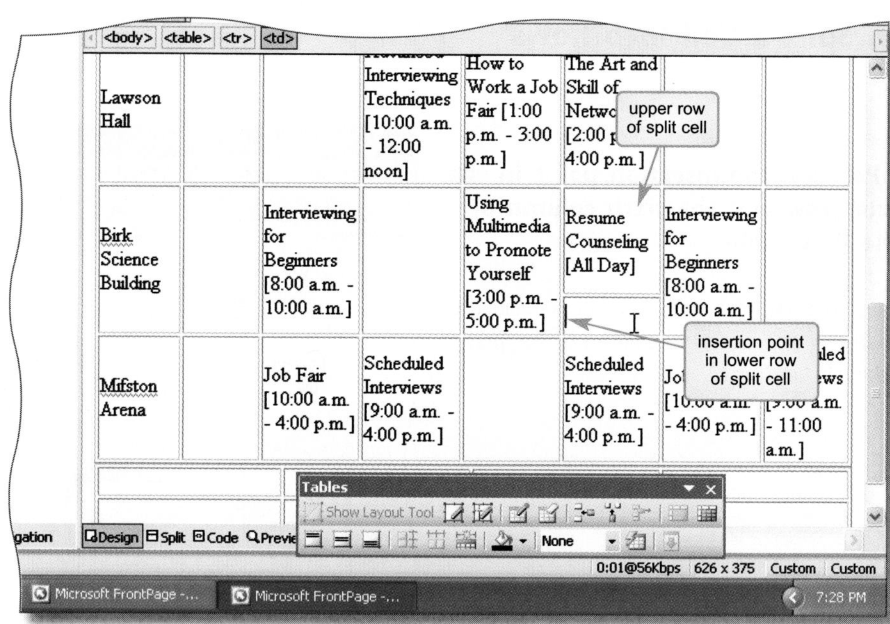

FIGURE 7-28

4

- **Type** `Career Book Fair [All Day]` **into the lower row of the split cell.**

FrontPage displays the entered text in the lower row of the split cell (Figure 7-29). The first table now includes all of the events to be listed in the Career Week - Calendar of Events.

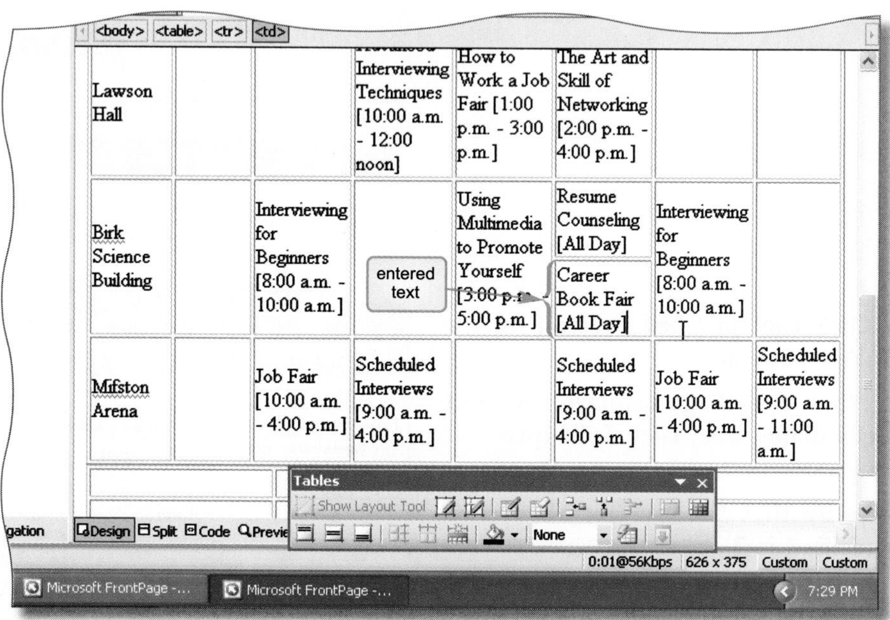

FIGURE 7-29

Other Ways

1. Click Table, click Split Cells
2. Press ALT+A, P
3. In Voice Command mode, say "Table, Split Cells"

The first table now contains all of the required information to complete the calendar of events, but remains simple in its presentation of the events. To modify the format and appearance of the table, you could change any number of table properties individually, in a series of steps. FrontPage provides a number of predefined table formats, called Table AutoFormats, which allow you to update a table's format and appearance much more quickly.

Applying a Table AutoFormat to a Table

A Table AutoFormat is a set of predefined table properties that, when applied to a table, modify at once many of the visible properties of the table, thus yielding a visually pleasing result. The Table AutoFormats modify the table background color, borders, and other properties to produce a well-formatted table that is attractive and easy to read. If desired, you can change each of the table properties later to further customize the format of the table.

Design Tip

Become familiar with FrontPage's predefined Table AutoFormats. AutoFormats provide interesting and visually appealing designs for typically uninteresting tables. After applying an AutoFormat, the table can be further customized to meet your needs.

The following steps apply a Table AutoFormat to an existing table.

To Apply a Table AutoFormat to a Table

1

- **If necessary, scroll the Web page up and position the insertion point in the first table.**

FrontPage displays the Tables toolbar (Figure 7-30).

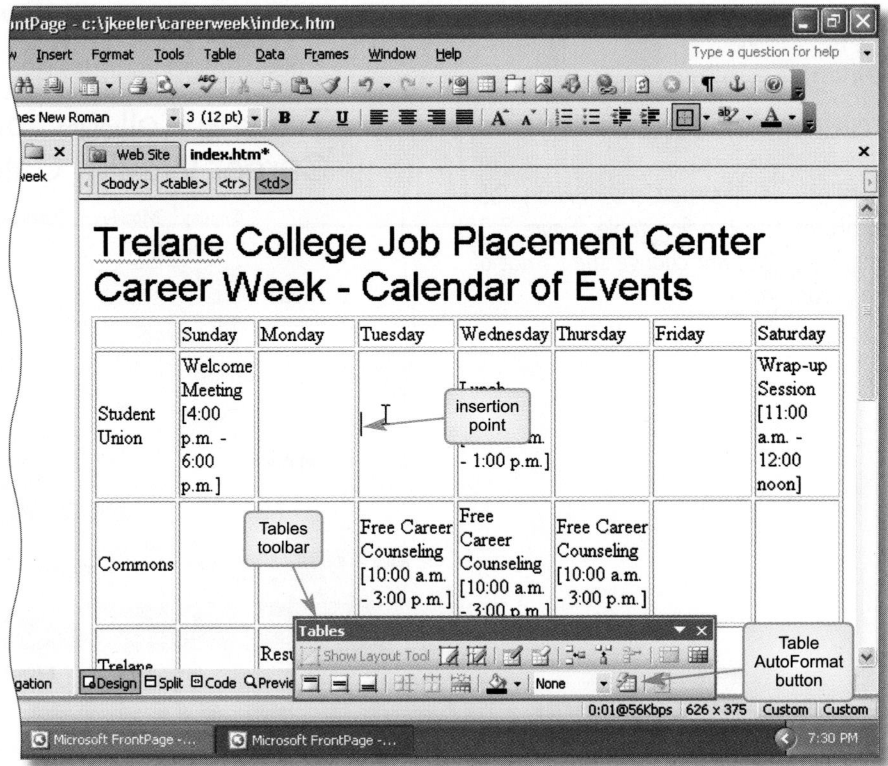

FIGURE 7-30

2

• **Click the Table AutoFormat button on the Tables toolbar.**

• **If necessary, scroll down the Formats list and then click Contemporary.**

FrontPage displays the Table AutoFormat dialog box (Figure 7-31). Contemporary is selected in the Formats list. FrontPage displays a sample preview of the Contemporary Table AutoFormat in the Preview area.

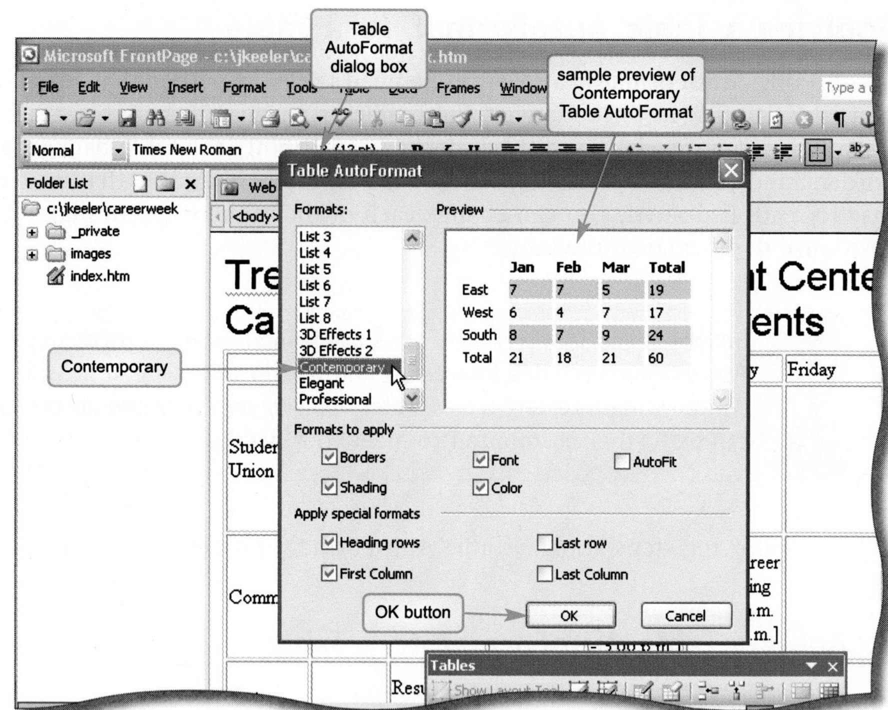

FIGURE 7-31

3

• **Click the OK button.**

FrontPage applies the Contemporary Table AutoFormat to the first table (Figure 7-32). FrontPage does not change the format of the second table.

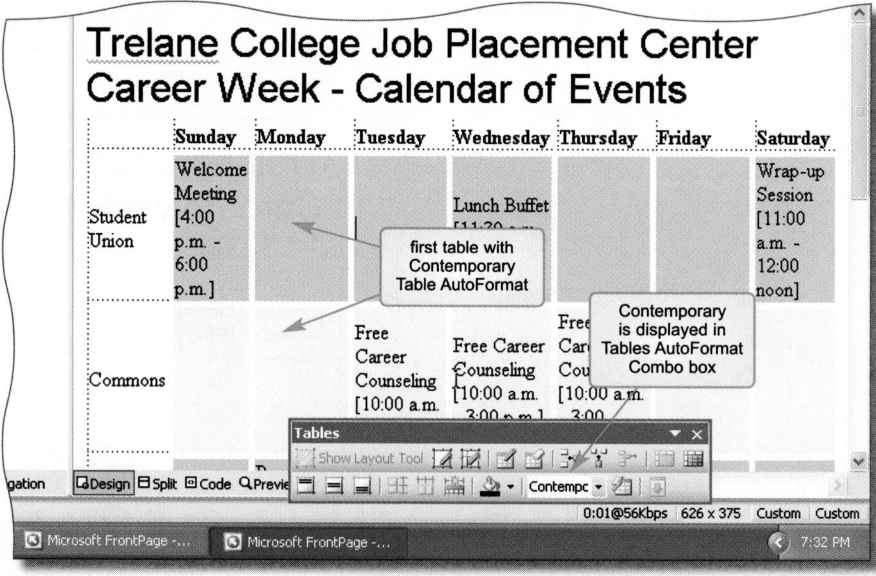

FIGURE 7-32

Other Ways

1. Click Table, click Table AutoFormat
2. Click Table AutoFormat combo arrow button on Tables toolbar
3. Press ALT+A, F
4. In Voice Command mode, say "Table, Table AutoFormat"

As shown in Figure 7-32, applying a Table AutoFormat to a table changes only the format and appearance of the table. The content, such as the text entered in the calendar of events, is not changed. Once you have applied a Table AutoFormat to a table, you may want to make additional modifications to format the appearance of the table. You should apply the Table AutoFormat before further modifying any table properties, such as backgrounds, colors, and fonts. If you reapply a Table AutoFormat after making such modifications, FrontPage overwrites your changes to reset the table properties to the settings predefined in the Table AutoFormat.

Modifying Additional Table Properties

As you have learned in previous projects, a number of table properties affect the format and appearance of a table. For example, you can change the size and color of table borders, use a background picture for the table, or modify the cell padding or the cell spacing.

Cell padding is the number of pixels between the content of a cell and the cell's border. **Cell spacing** is the number of pixels between the borders of adjacent cells. If a cell contains text, the cell padding should be set to allow some space between the text and the cell border, so that the text is easy to read. If a cell contains a graphic, you may want to set cell padding to zero, so that the graphic fills the entire cell.

Design Tip

Keep cell padding and cell spacing in mind when designing tables and cells. If a cell contains text, the cell padding should be set to allow some space between the text and the cell border, so that the text is easy to read. If a cell contains a graphic, you may want to set cell padding to zero, so that the graphic fills the entire cell.

You also can set the properties for the borders of each table cell and the entire table. If the cell borders around the outside of the table appear thicker or darker than the borders of other cells, the table properties likely are set to display both the cell borders and table borders. You can modify a table property to set whether or not to display both cell borders and table borders.

The following steps modify additional table properties.

To Modify Additional Table Properties

1

• **Right-click the first table and then click Table Properties on the shortcut menu.**

FrontPage displays the Table Properties dialog box (Figure 7-33). Cell padding is set to 1.

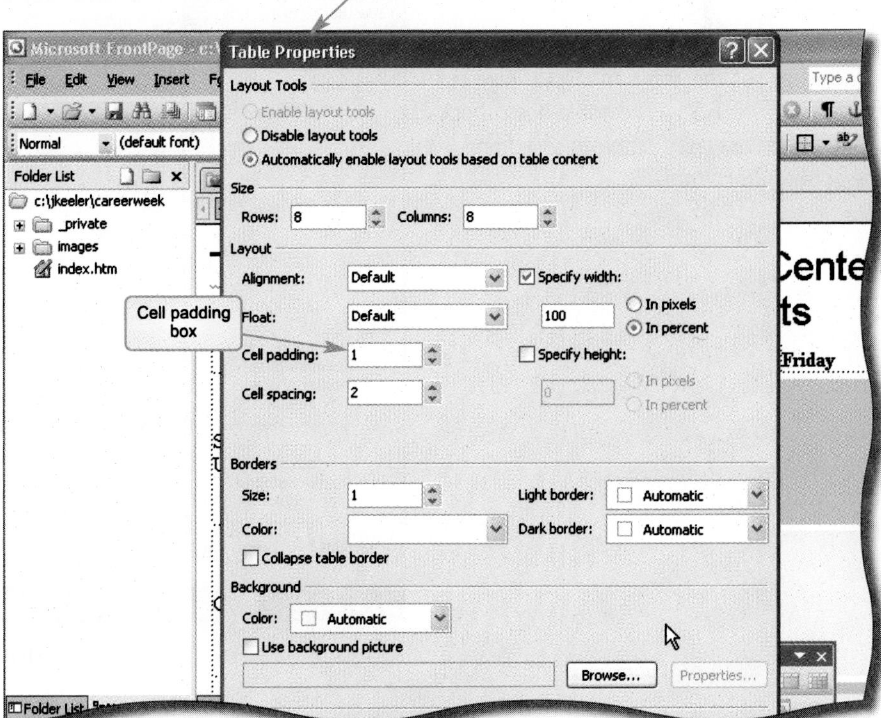

FIGURE 7-33

2

• **Drag through the value in the Cell padding box and then type** 2 **as the new value.**

• **If necessary, drag through the value in the Cell spacing box and then type** 0 **as the new value.**

Cell padding is set to 2 and cell spacing is set to 0 (Figure 7-34). The Collapse table border check box is not selected.

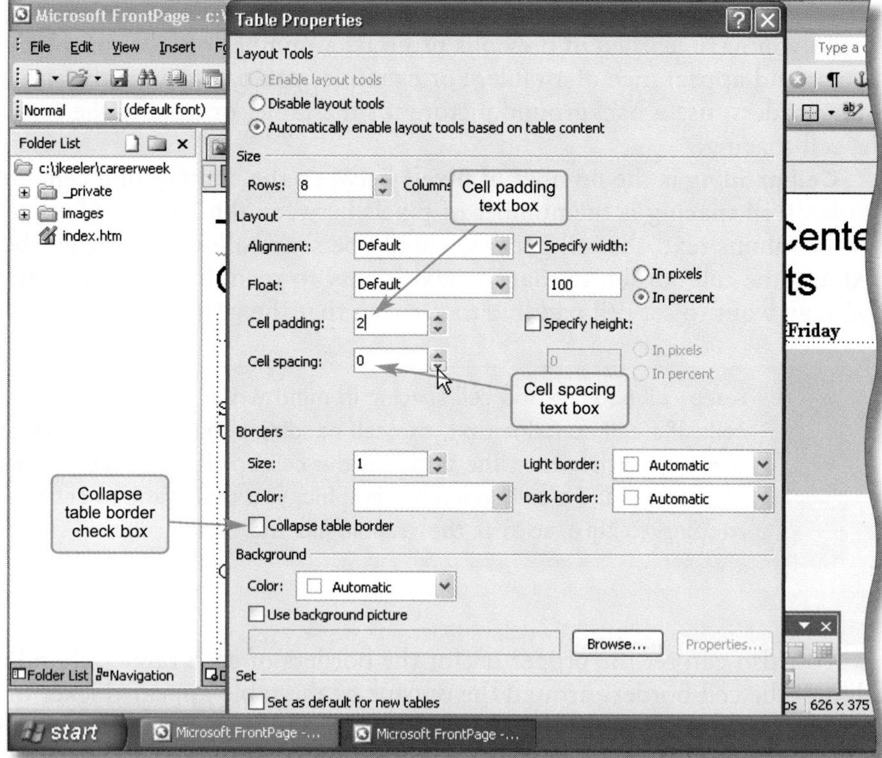

FIGURE 7-34

3

• **If necessary, click Collapse table border in the Borders area to select it.**

The Collapse table border check box is selected to set the table to display only cell borders (Figure 7-35). The table has a background color assigned automatically from the Table AutoFormat.

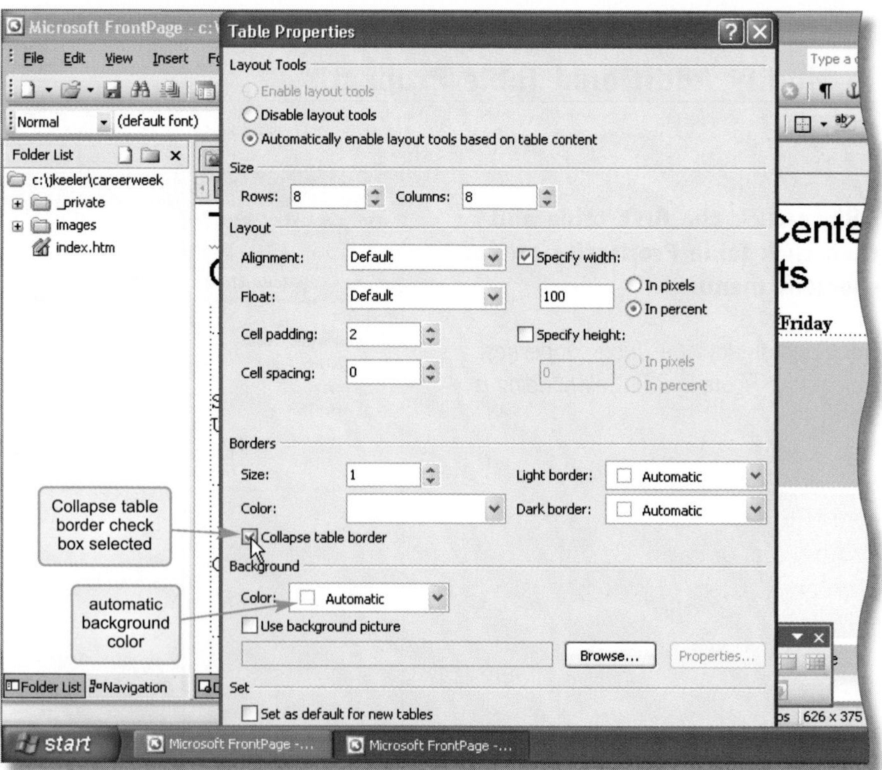

FIGURE 7-35

4

- **Click the OK button.**
- **Position the insertion point in the second table.**

The table displays single borders around cells (Figure 7-36). The cell padding is increased to add space between the cell borders and cell contents. Both changes make the cell contents more readable.

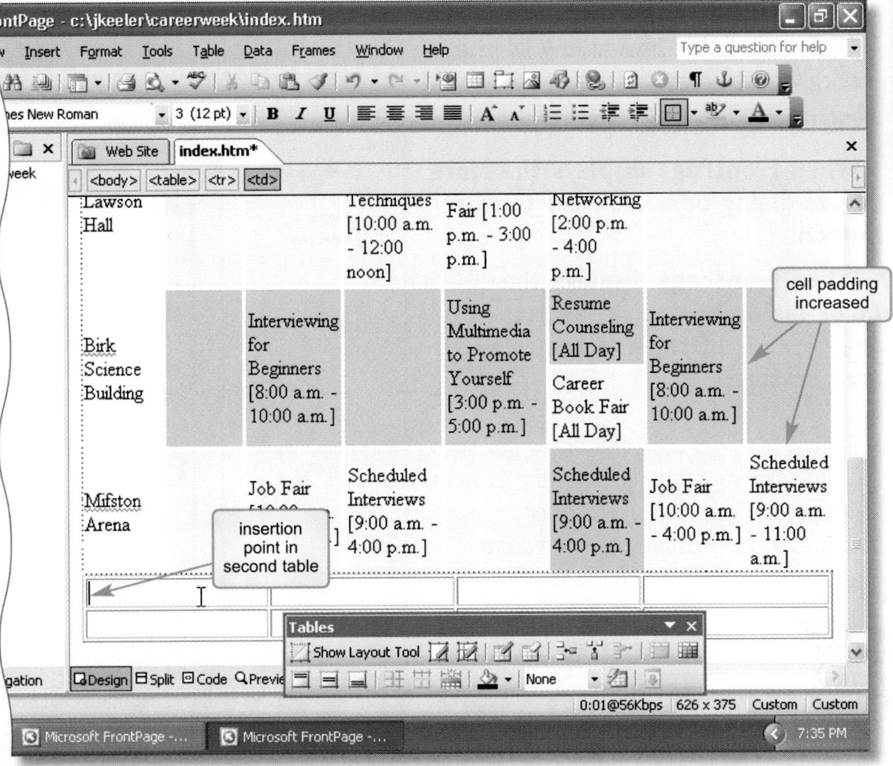

FIGURE 7-36

5

- **Right-click the second table and then click Table Properties on the shortcut menu.**
- **When FrontPage displays the Table Properties dialog box, drag through the value in the Size box in the Borders area and then type** 0 **as the new value.**
- **If necessary, type** 0 **in the Cell padding text box and type** 0 **in the Cell spacing box.**
- **If necessary, click Collapse table border in the Borders area to select it.**

FrontPage displays the Table Properties dialog box for the second table (Figure 7-37). Size is set to 0, so that the table cell borders are not displayed.

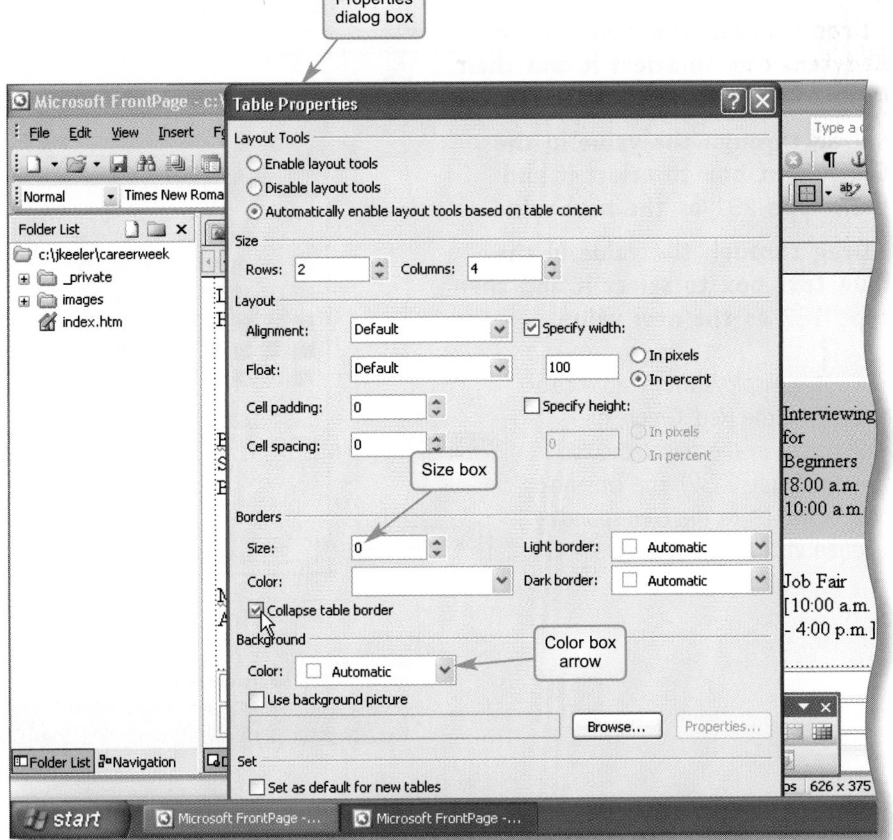

FIGURE 7-37

6

- **Click the Color box arrow in the Background area.**
- **Click More Colors.**
- **When FrontPage displays the More Colors dialog box, click the Custom button.**
- **When FrontPage displays the Color dialog box, click [White] at the top left of the Custom colors area to select it.**

FrontPage displays the Color dialog box with a white color swatch selected in the Custom colors area (Figure 7-38). The color swatches in the Custom colors area are white until set to a custom color.

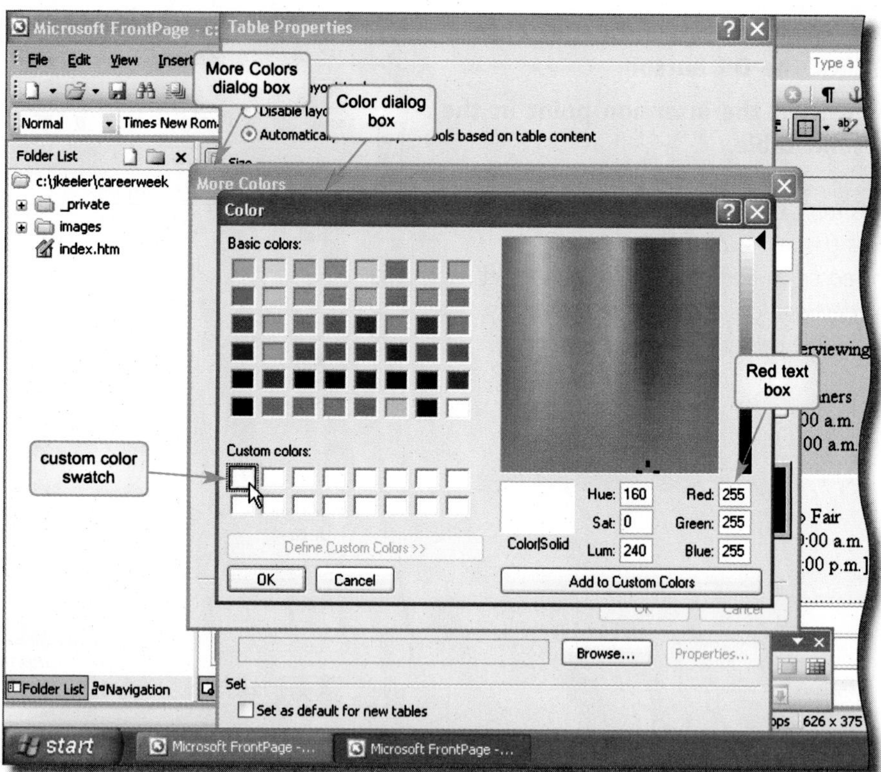

FIGURE 7-38

7

- **Drag through the value in the Red text box to select it and then type** 248 **as the new value.**
- **Drag through the value in the Green text box to select it and then type** 251 **as the new value.**
- **Drag through the value in the Blue text box to select it and then type** 187 **as the new value.**

FrontPage displays the custom color created by the Red, Green, and Blue values in the selected color swatch (Figure 7-39). The crosshair pointer moves to the corresponding location in the color matrix.

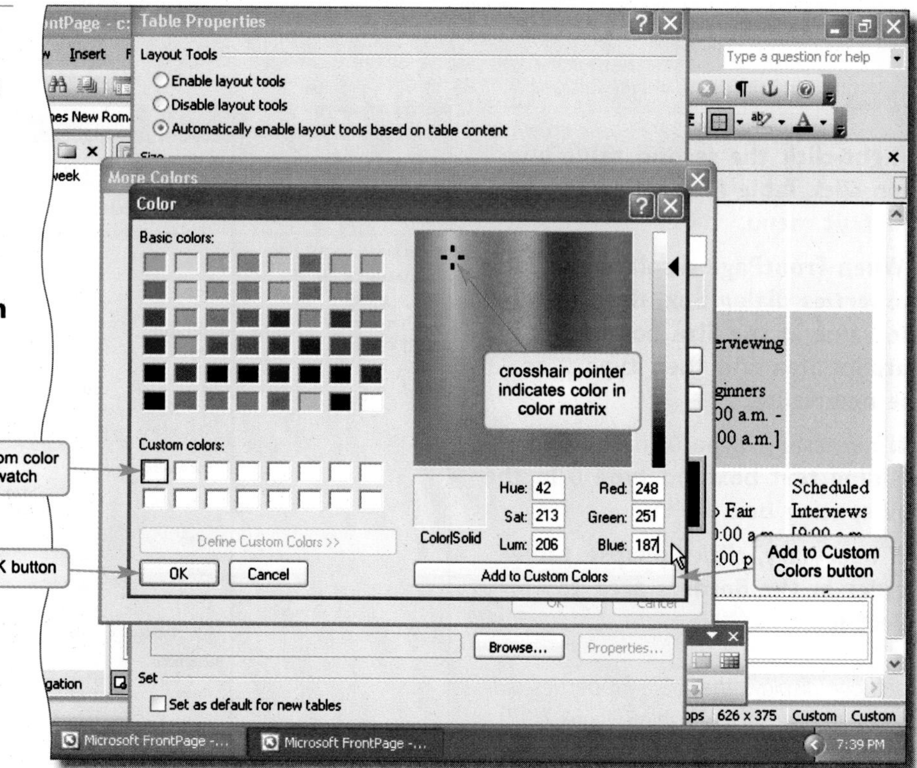

FIGURE 7-39

8

- **Click the Add to Custom Colors button.**
- **Click the OK button in the Color dialog box and then click the OK button in the More Colors dialog box.**
- **Click the OK button in the Table Properties dialog box.**

FrontPage displays the second table with the custom color as the table background and no visible borders, as indicated by the dotted lines (Figure 7-40).

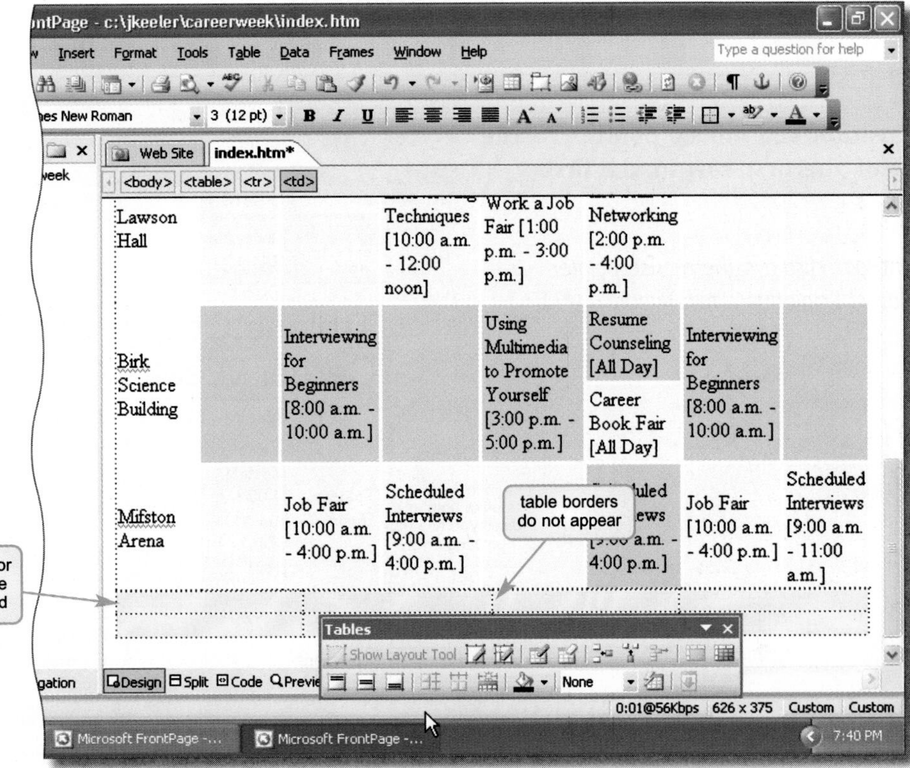

FIGURE 7-40

Other Ways

1. Click Table, click Table Properties, click Table
2. Press ALT+A, R, T
3. In Voice Command mode, say "Table, Table Properties, Table"

As shown in the previous steps, even a small change of one or two properties can make a visible, and sometimes dramatic, difference in the format and appearance of a table.

Modifying Cell Properties for a Group of Cells

Modifying the properties of one or more cells in a table allows you to further modify the format and appearance of a table. Because a single table can contain many cells, it is more efficient to modify a property for a group of adjacent cells, rather than for each individual cell. For example, you can select an entire row, an entire column, or any number of cells, and then modify the property for all of the cells at one time.

The steps on the next page modify cell properties for a group of cells.

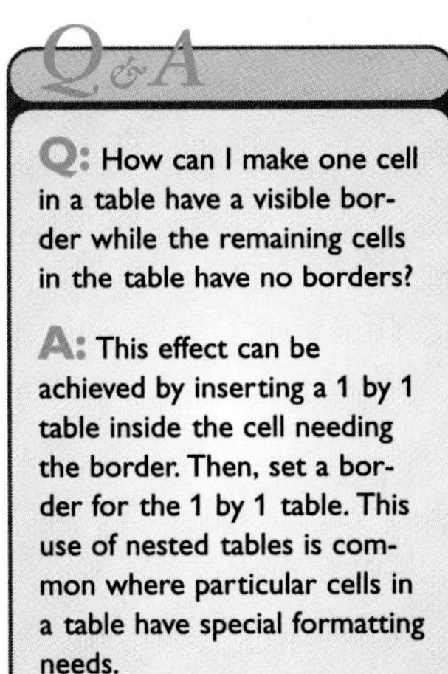

Q&A

Q: How can I make one cell in a table have a visible border while the remaining cells in the table have no borders?

A: This effect can be achieved by inserting a 1 by 1 table inside the cell needing the border. Then, set a border for the 1 by 1 table. This use of nested tables is common where particular cells in a table have special formatting needs.

To Modify Cell Properties for a Group of Cells

1

• **Position the mouse pointer to the left of the first row in the first table.**

FrontPage displays the mouse pointer as a right-pointing arrow (Figure 7-41).

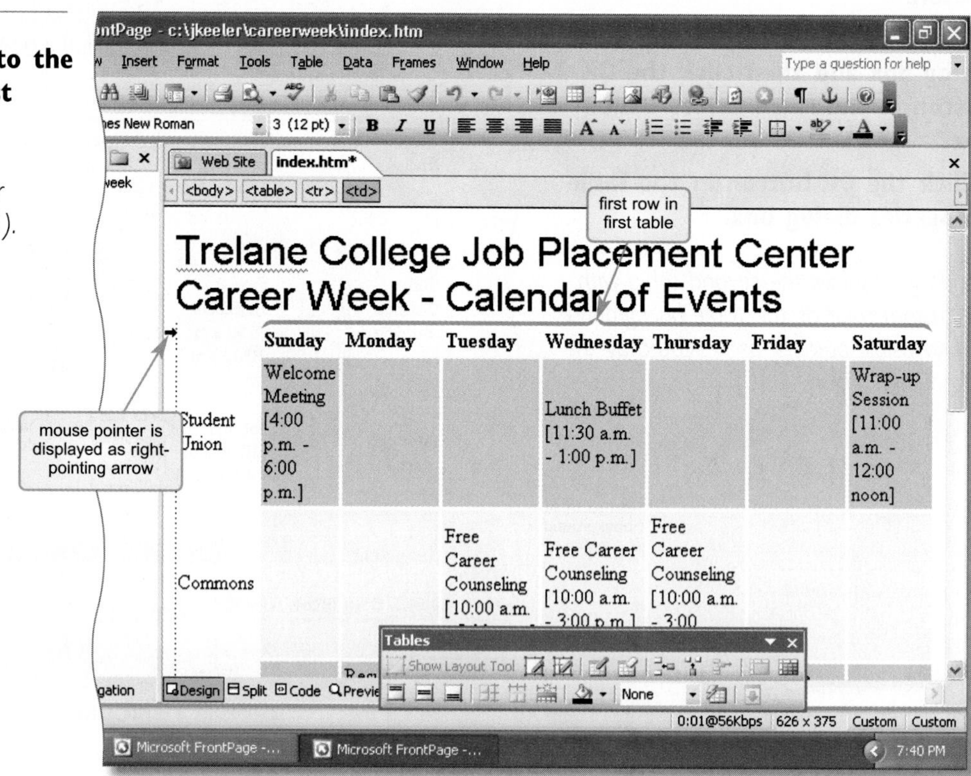

FIGURE 7-41

2

• **Click the mouse button to select the entire first row of the first table.**

The first row of the first table is selected (Figure 7-42).

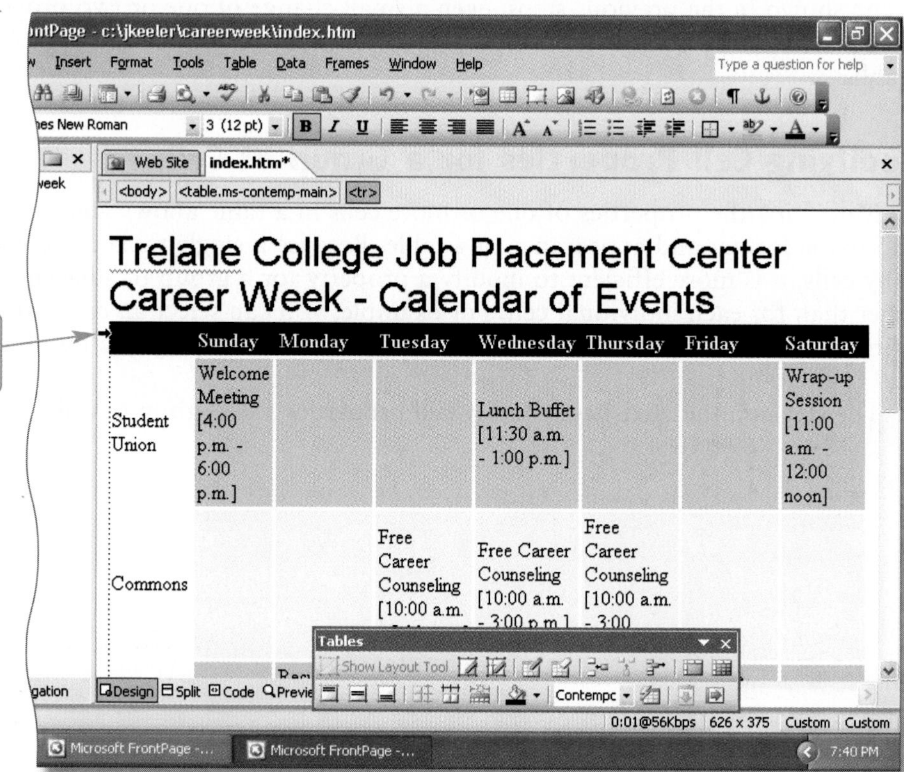

FIGURE 7-42

3

- **Right-click the selected row.**

FrontPage displays the shortcut menu (Figure 7-43).

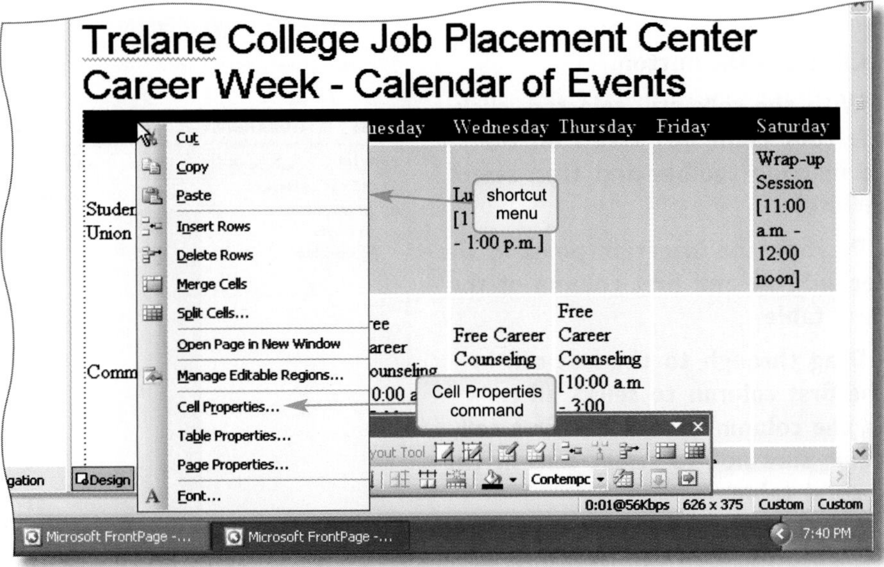

FIGURE 7-43

4

- **Click Cell Properties.**

FrontPage displays the Cell Properties dialog box (Figure 7-44). Any modifications made to cell properties will apply to all of the selected cells.

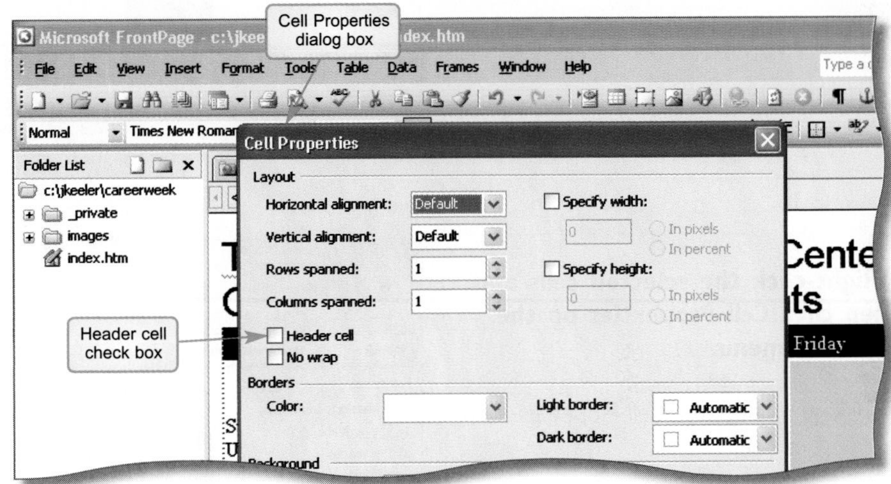

FIGURE 7-44

5

- **Click Header cell to select it.**
- **Click No wrap to select it.**
- **Click the Color box arrow in the Background area and then click [Red].**

The Header cell and No wrap check boxes are selected (Figure 7-45). Selecting Header cell tells the browser to display the header cells emphasized, with bold formatting and center-aligned text. Selecting No wrap prevents browsers from wrapping text in the selected cells.

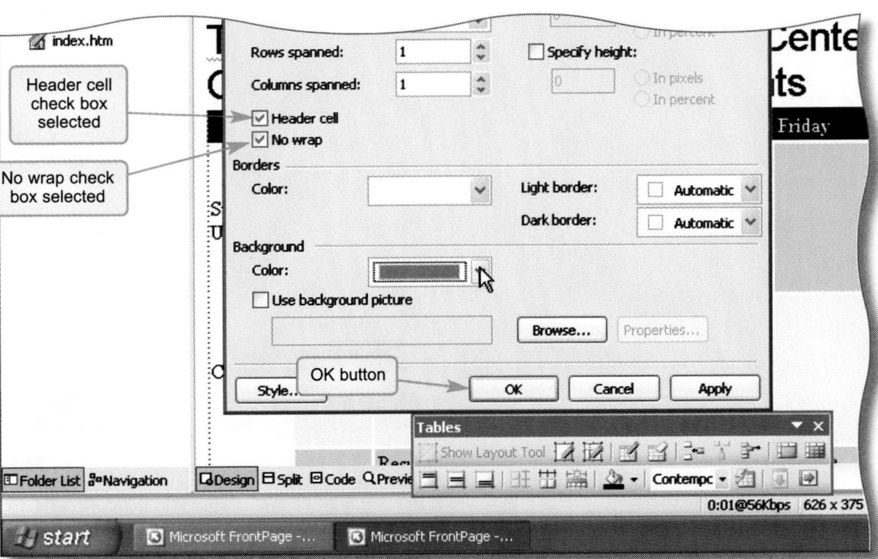

FIGURE 7-45

6

- **Click the OK button.**
- **With the cells still selected, click the Font Color box arrow on the Formatting toolbar and then select [White].**
- **Position the insertion point in the second row and first column of the first table.**
- **Drag through to the last cell in the first column to select all cells in the column except the first cell, being sure not to select cells in the second table.**

FrontPage modifies the cell properties for all cells in the first row. A group of cells in the first column are selected (Figure 7-46).

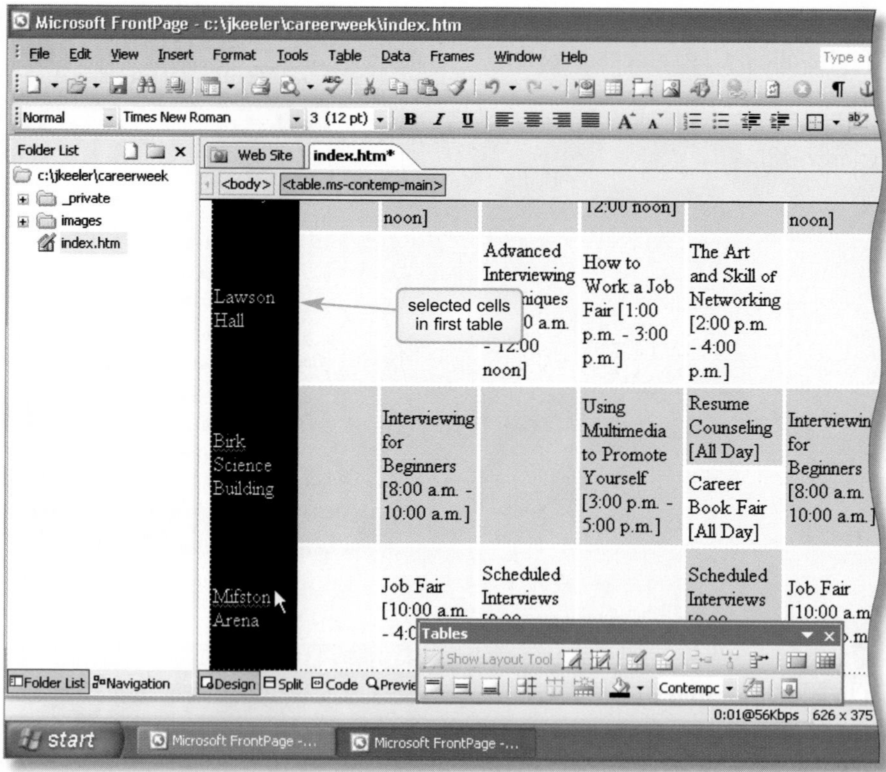

FIGURE 7-46

7

- **Right-click the selected cells and then click Cell Properties on the shortcut menu.**

FrontPage displays the Cell Properties dialog box (Figure 7-47).

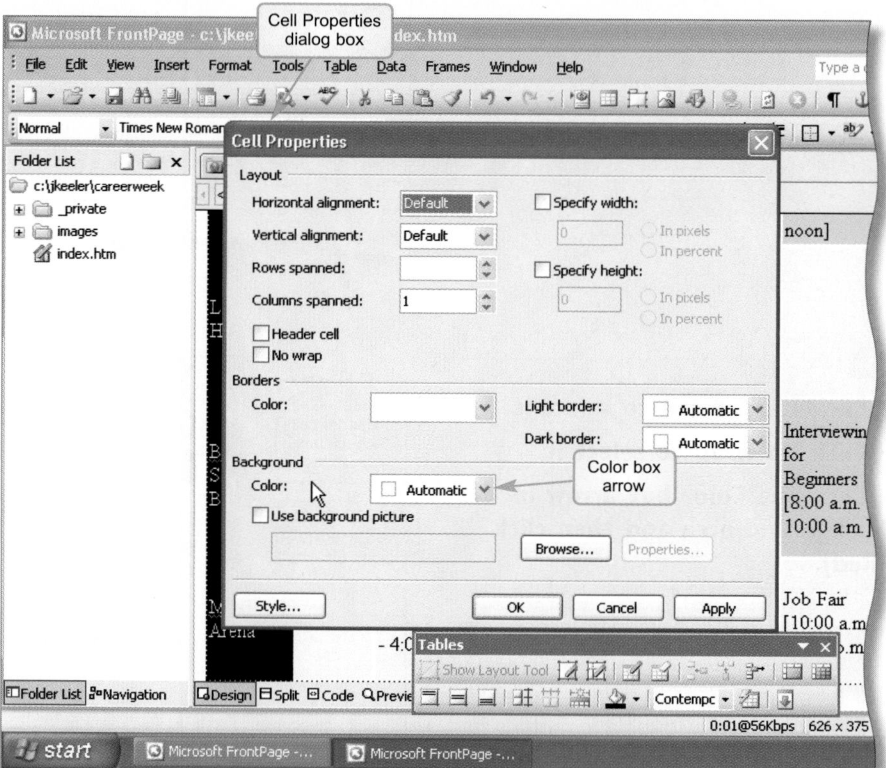

FIGURE 7-47

8

- **Click the Color box arrow in the Background area.**

FrontPage displays the color palette color choices, including saved document colors (Figure 7-48).

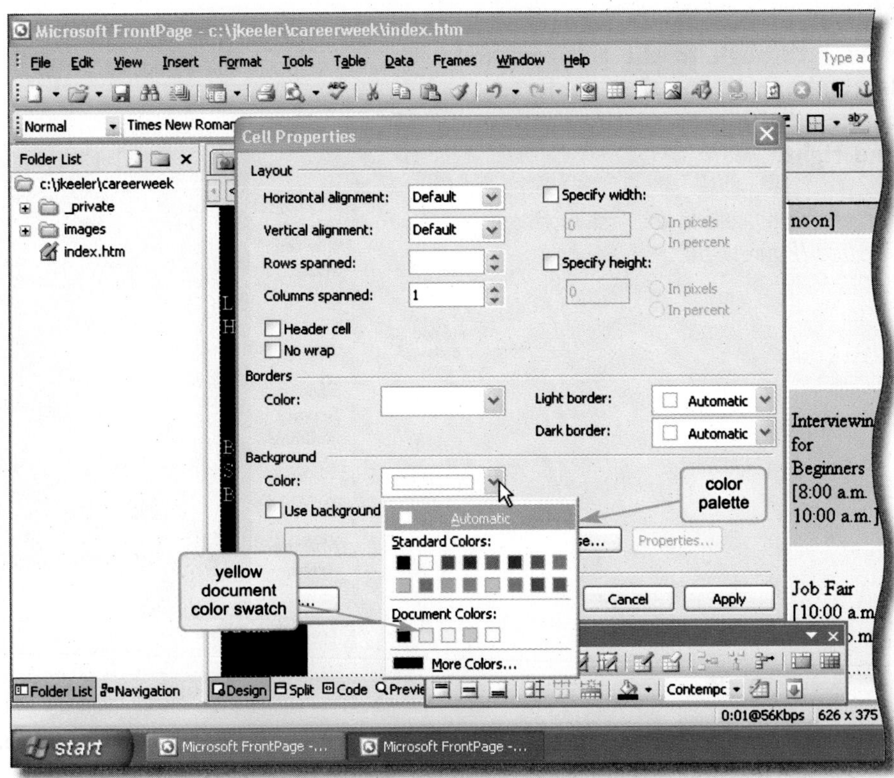

FIGURE 7-48

9

- **Click the yellow document color swatch in the Document Colors area.**
- **Click the OK button in the Cell Properties dialog box.**
- **Click the Bold button on the Formatting toolbar.**
- **Click the cell in the second row and second column of the first table.**

A group of cells in the first column, beginning with the second row, displays bold text and the yellow document color as the background color (Figure 7-49).

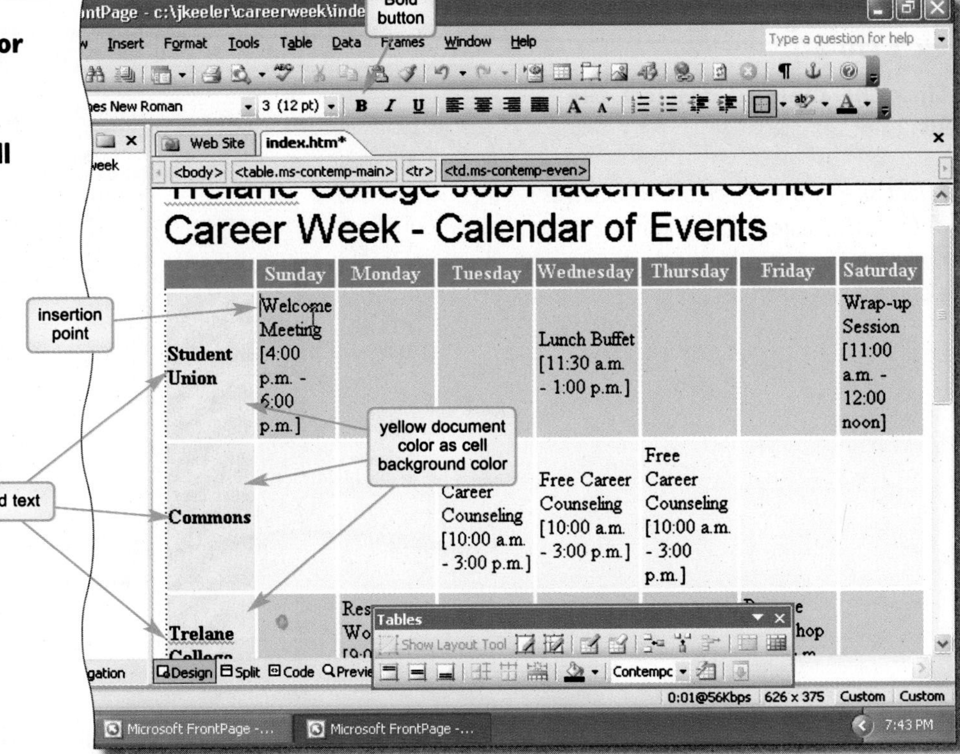

FIGURE 7-49

10

• **Drag through to the last row and last column of the first table to select all the cells to the bottom and right.**

The remaining cells in the first table are selected (Figure 7-50).

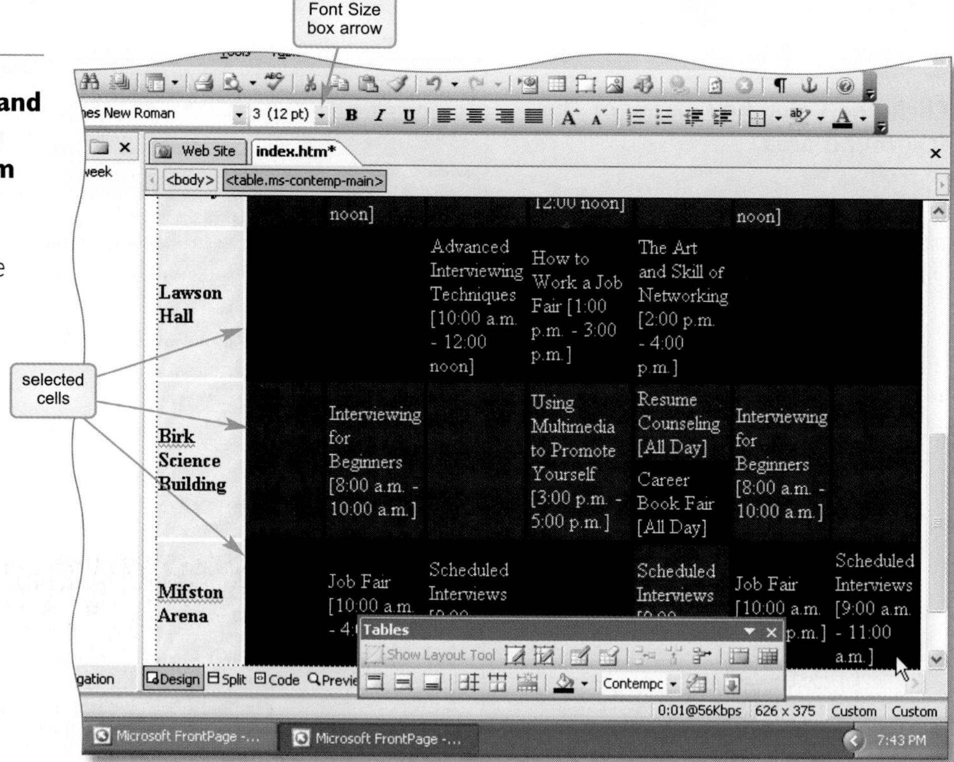

FIGURE 7-50

11

• **Click the Font Size box arrow on the Formatting toolbar and then click 2 (10 pt).**

• **Click the table to deselect the cells.**

The font size in the selected cells changes to 2 (10 pt) (Figure 7-51). The header row and cells in the first column retain the original font size.

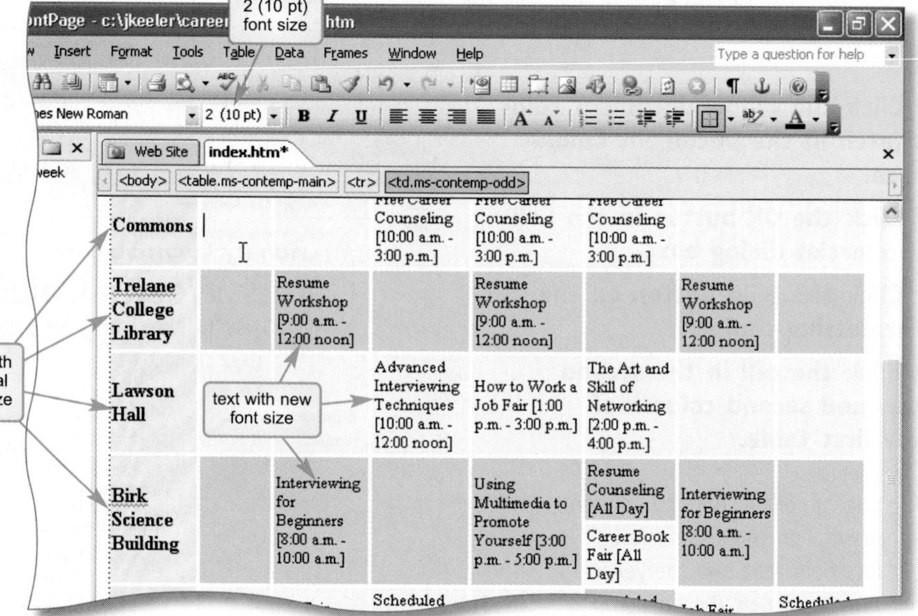

FIGURE 7-51

Using the Eraser Button to Merge Table Cells

In a previous project, you learned how to merge cells using a menu command. The Tables toolbar includes an Eraser button, which allows you to drag through cell borders of cells you want to merge. As you use the Eraser button, the cell borders are removed, much as you might erase lines on a chalkboard.

The following steps use the Eraser tool to merge table cells.

To Use the Eraser Button to Merge Table Cells

1

- **If necessary, position the insertion point in the second table.**

FrontPage displays the Tables toolbar (Figure 7-52).

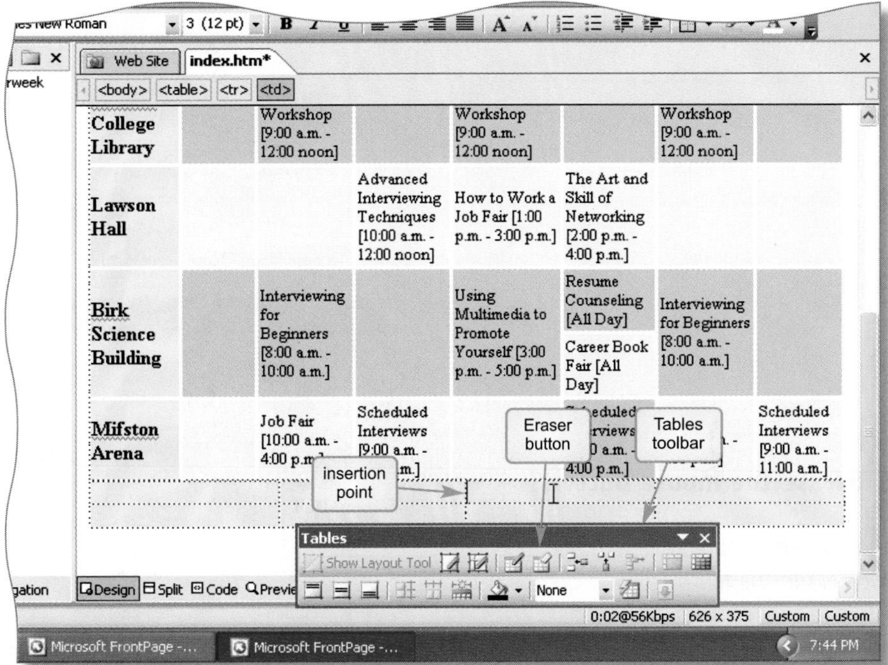

FIGURE 7-52

2

- **Click the Eraser button on the Tables toolbar.**
- **Position the mouse pointer over the cell in the first row and fourth column of the second table.**

The Eraser button is selected and the mouse pointer is displayed as an eraser (Figure 7-53).

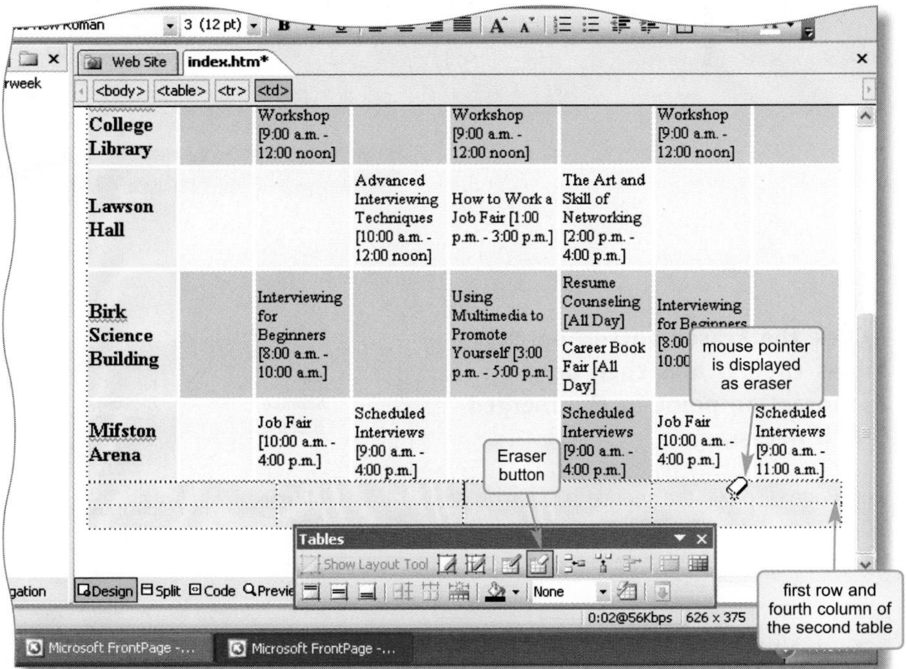

FIGURE 7-53

3

• **Drag through the bottom border of the cell to select it.**

FrontPage displays a red line to indicate that the bottom cell border is selected (Figure 7-54).

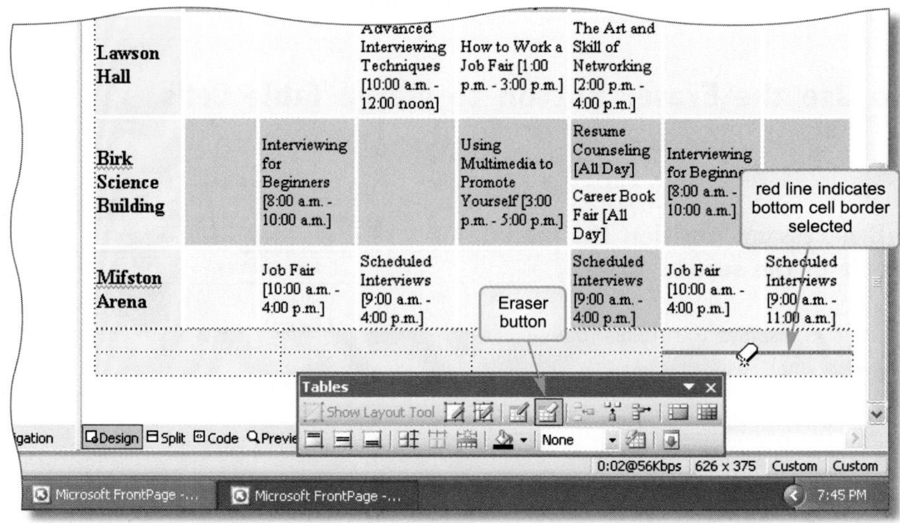

FIGURE 7-54

4

• **Release the mouse button.**

The bottom cell border is removed, and the two cells in the fourth column are merged into one cell (Figure 7-55).

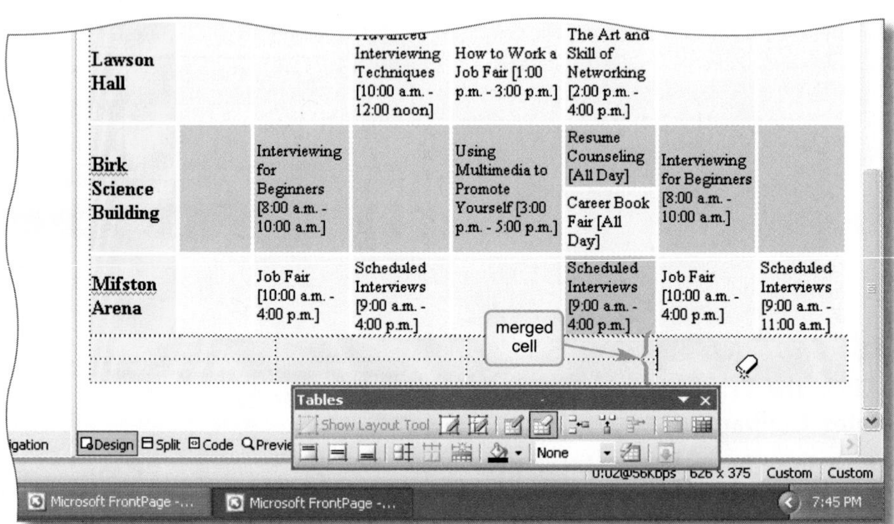

FIGURE 7-55

5

• **Click the Eraser button on the Tables toolbar and then position the insertion point in the merged cell, if necessary.**

FrontPage displays the mouse pointer as an I-beam when the Eraser button is not selected (Figure 7-56).

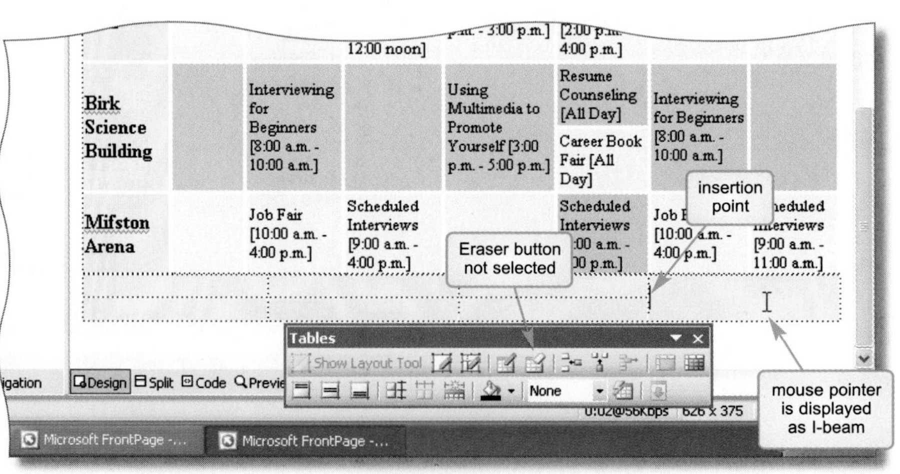

FIGURE 7-56

Other Ways

1. Click Table, click Merge Cells
2. Click Merge Cells button on Tables toolbar
3. Press ALT+A, M
4. In Voice Command mode, say "Table, Merge Cells"

Using an Image as a Table Cell Background

As you have learned, you can modify table and cell properties to set a background color for a table and any cells within a table. FrontPage also allows you to use an image as the background for a table or cell.

Using an image as the background for a table or cell is different than inserting an image in a table cell. As you learned in a previous project, if you insert an image in a cell, the background color of the cell is displayed around the edges of the image, if the image does not fill the cell. Also, if the cell contains any text, then the text wraps around the image. Finally, if the cell is resized, then the image may have to be resized. When an image is used as the background for a cell, the image fills the cell entirely, and text in the cell can overlay the image.

More About

Table and Cell Properties

You can create many different effects by modifying the various properties of tables and table cells. To learn more about table and cell properties, visit the FrontPage 2003 More About Web page (scsite.com/fp2003/more) and then click Table and Cell Properties.

Design Tip

Be careful not to overuse images as cell backgrounds. Consider using images of color gradients or simple clip art rather than pictures to enhance the look of a cell. Images with curved patterns in cells can be used to give the Web page less of a boxy or rectangular feel.

More About

Using Images

You can use images to produce interesting effects, such as rounded corners in tables, and to improve accessibility in your Web site. To learn more about using images, visit the FrontPage 2003 More About Web page (scsite.com/fp2003/more) and then click Using Images.

If the image used for the background is larger than the cell, the browser cuts, or **crops**, the image so that only a portion of the image is displayed in the cell. If the image is smaller than the cell, the browser repeats, or **tiles**, the image, which means that the image is repeated until it fills the cell. Depending on the image used, you may not want FrontPage to crop or tile the background image. In this instance, you can set the background image to remain at a fixed size regardless of the size of the browser window.

The following steps use an image as a cell background.

To Use an Image as a Cell Background

• **Right-click the merged cell and then click Cell Properties on the shortcut menu.**

FrontPage displays the Cell Properties dialog box (Figure 7-57). The Use background picture check box currently is not selected and no file name is displayed in the Use background picture text box.

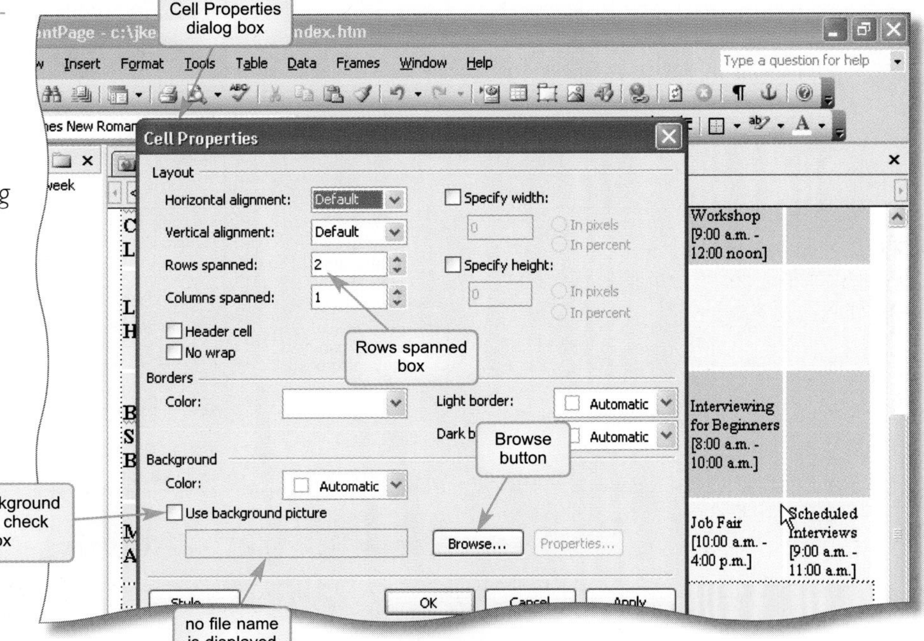

FIGURE 7-57

2

- **Click the Browse button in the Background area, and then, if necessary, insert the Data Disk in drive A.**
- **If necessary, when FrontPage displays the Select Background Picture dialog box, click the Look in box arrow and select the BensonHall file in the Project7 folder.**

FrontPage displays the Select Background Picture dialog box (Figure 7-58). The file, BensonHall, is selected.

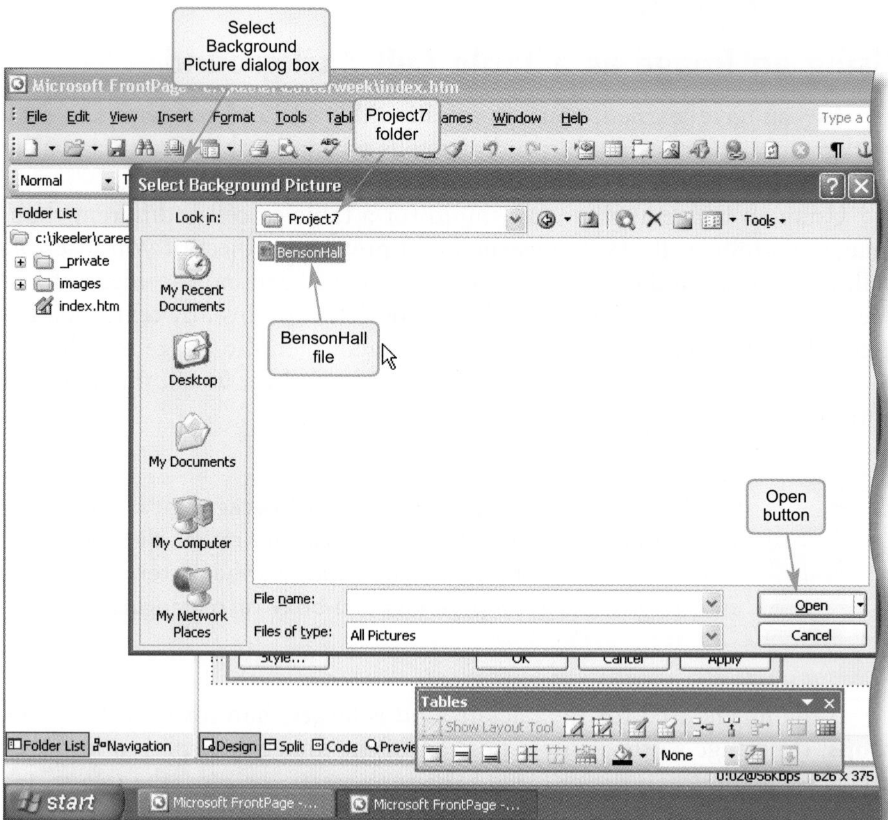

FIGURE 7-58

3

- **Click the Open button in the Select Background Picture dialog box.**

In the Cell Properties dialog box, the Use background picture check box is selected, and the file name is displayed in the Use background picture text box (Figure 7-59).

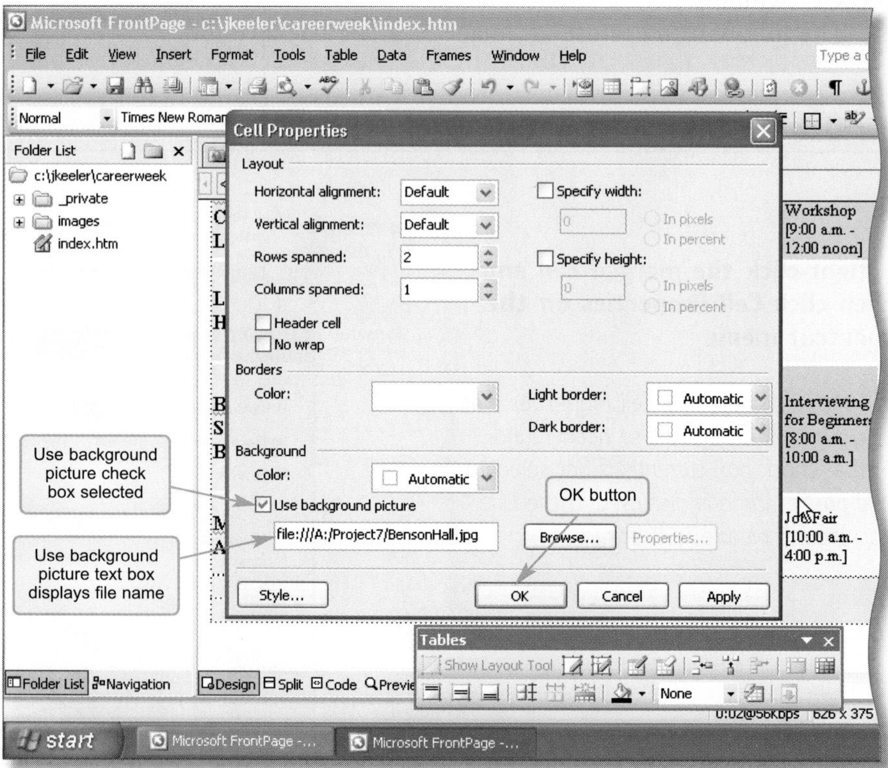

FIGURE 7-59

4

• **Click the OK button.**

• **Position the insertion point in the first row and second column of the current table.**

FrontPage displays the image as a background for the cell (Figure 7-60). The cell is resized to display the full image, without any cropping.

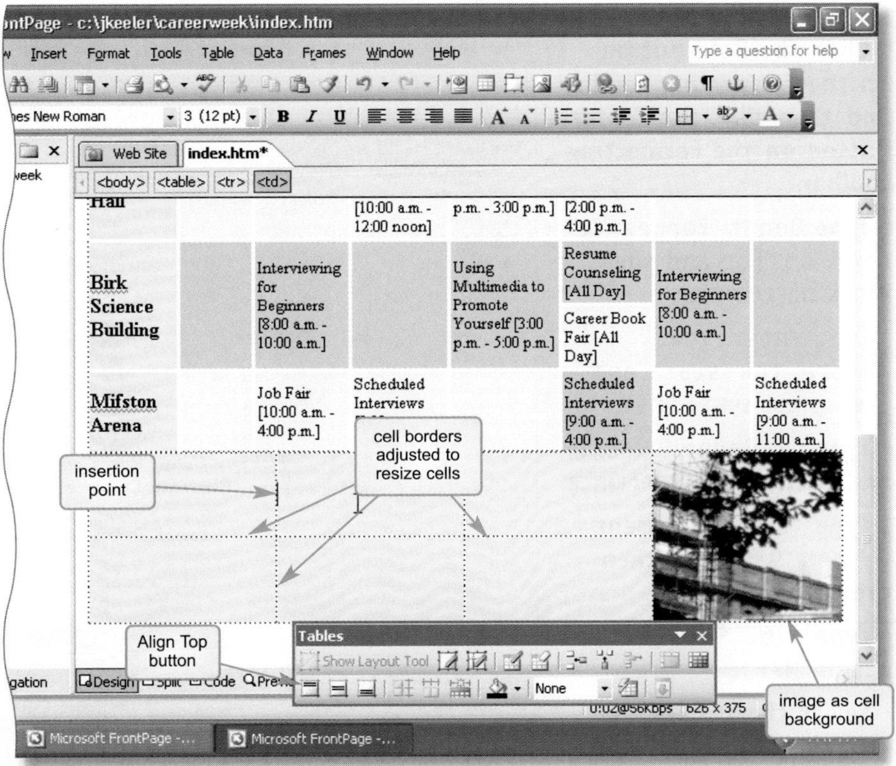

FIGURE 7-60

5

• **Click the Align Top button on the Tables toolbar.**

• **Click the Center button on the Formatting toolbar and then click the Italic button on the Formatting toolbar.**

• **Type** `Pick up a Career Week Calendar of Events at the Job Placement Center or the Student Union.` **and then press the ENTER key.**

• **Type** `Search Trelane College's Web site.`

• **Resize the columns in the table as shown in Figure 7-61 and then position the insertion point in the merged cell with the background image.**

FrontPage displays the entered text in the cell (Figure 7-61). The insertion point is positioned in the merged cell with the background image.

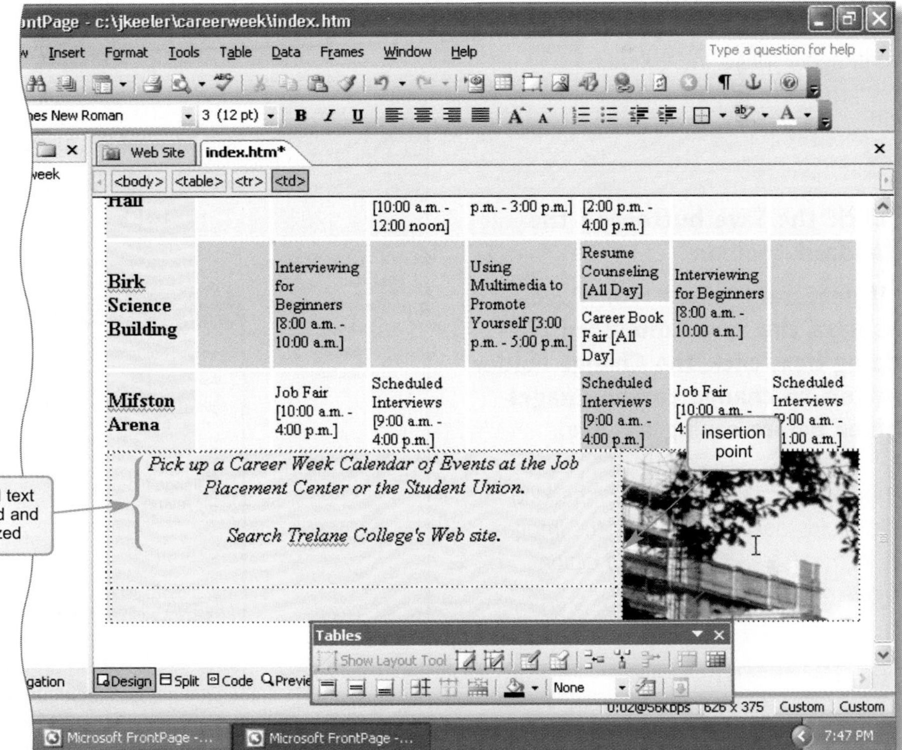

FIGURE 7-61

6

- **Click the Bold button on the Formatting toolbar and then click the Center button on the Formatting toolbar.**
- **Type** `Don't forget to sign up for` **and then press SHIFT+ENTER.**
- **Type** `interviews before the start` **and then press SHIFT+ENTER.**
- **Type** `of Career Week!` **and then press SHIFT+ENTER.**
- **Type** `(Job Placement Center 9:00` **and then press SHIFT+ENTER.**
- **Type** `a.m. - 6:00 p.m., M/F).`
- **Select the text in the cell, click the Font Color arrow on the Formatting toolbar and click [Fuchsia].**

FrontPage displays the entered text in the cell (Figure 7-62).

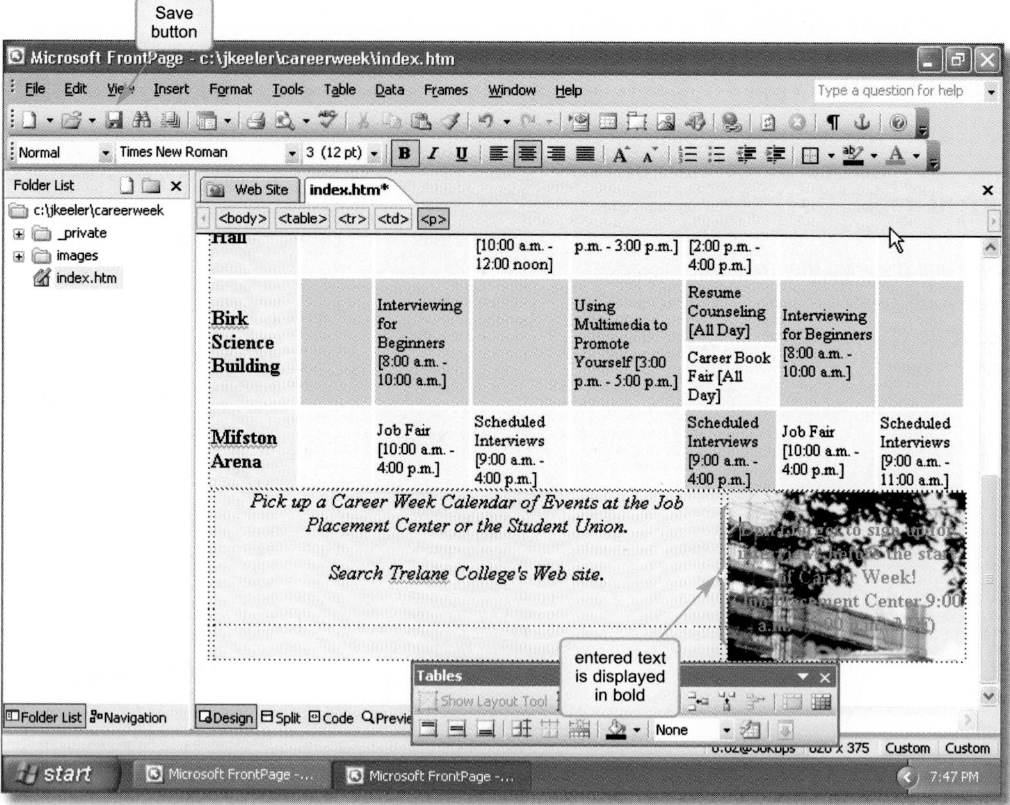

FIGURE 7-62

7

- **Click the Save button on the Standard toolbar.**
- **If necessary, when FrontPage displays the Save Embedded Files dialog box, click the Change Folder button to change to the images folder before saving the file.**

FrontPage displays the Save Embedded Files dialog box, which shows the image file name, folder location, and action (Figure 7-63).

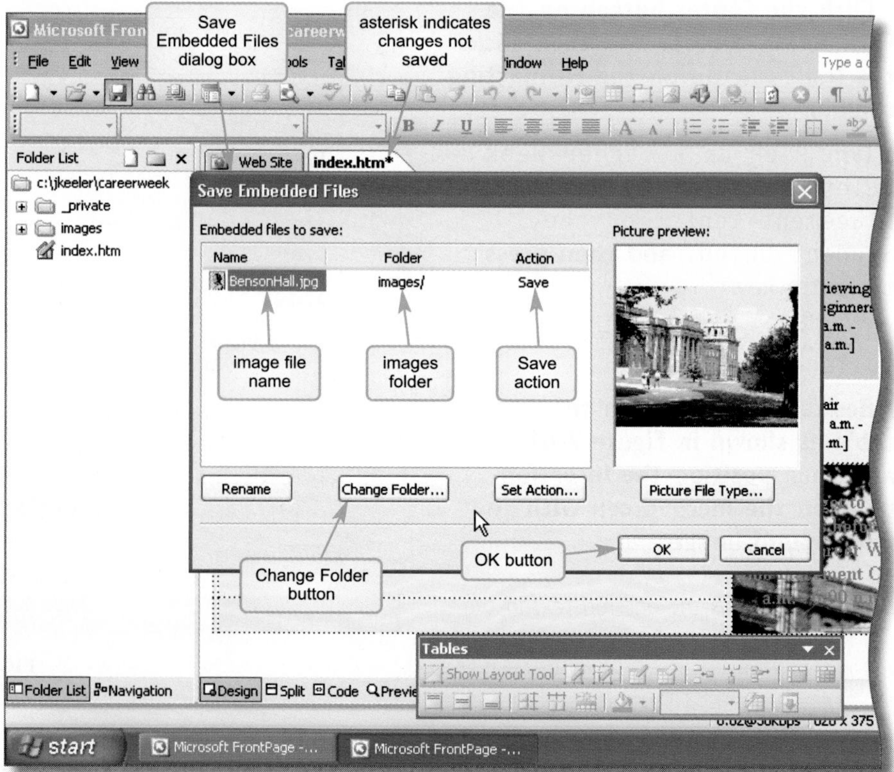

FIGURE 7-63

8

• **Click the OK button.**

FrontPage saves the changes to the Web page and saves the background image file, BensonHall, to the images folder in the Web site (Figure 7-64). The asterisk disappears, indicating all changes are saved.

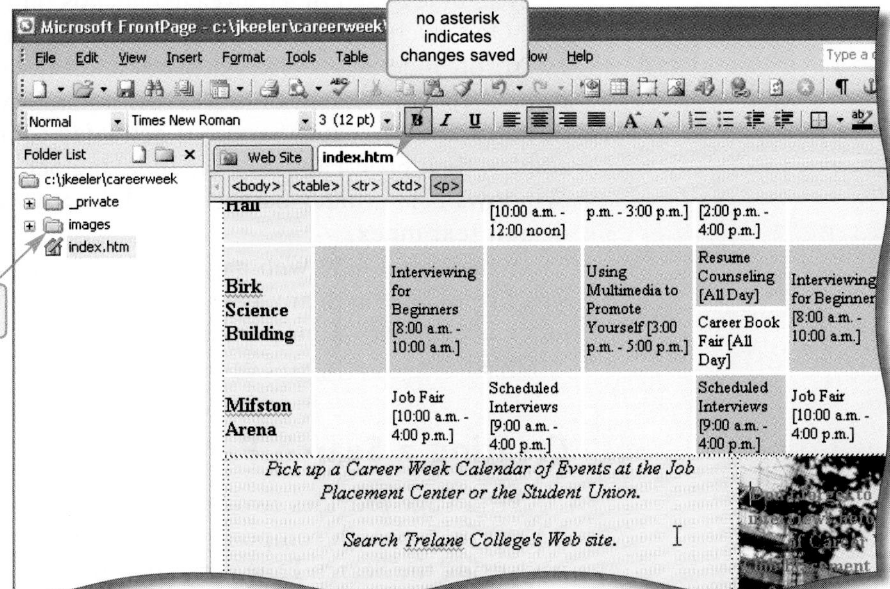

FIGURE 7-64

Other Ways

1. Click Table, click Table Properties, click Cell
2. Press ALT+A, R, E
3. In Voice Command mode, say "Table, Table Properties, Cell"

The last step required to complete the Career Week - Calendar of Events page is to add a hyperlink to a search page that will allow users to search the Trelane College Web site. Once the search page is completed, the hyperlink will be added to the Career Week - Calendar of Events page.

Adding Search Capabilities to a Web Site

Today, many Web sites include search capabilities to help visitors quickly find relevant information on a given site. As a Web site grows more complex, search capabilities become an indispensable tool, allowing users to locate and go directly to the desired information and pages. FrontPage includes templates and tools to simplify the process of adding search capabilities to a Web site.

Using FrontPage, you can create a search form that allows users to search a Web site for specific words or phrases. Scanning every page in a Web site for a specific word each time a user performs a search can be very time-consuming. To alleviate this issue, many Web sites use a **text index**, which lists text on each page in the site and is the means by which a text search engine locates text on a given page. A **text search engine** is a program that searches the index for pages containing matches to the words or phrases entered in the search page. The text search engine returns a weighted search results list of pages with matching words or phrases, along with hyperlinks to those pages. If the page has a title, then the page title typically is displayed in the search results; if the page does not have a title, the file name of the page is displayed in the search results. Typically, the pages with better matches are listed first in the search results.

More About

Search Engines

The Web contains a wide variety of search engines. To learn more about various search engines, how to use them, and how they work, visit the FrontPage 2003 More About Web page (scsite.com/fp2003/more) and then click Search Engines.

Design Tip

A search feature can give visitors the much desired flexibility and control to navigate a Web site in the manner they choose, thus allowing visitors to quickly find the information they need.

The index used by FrontPage depends on the operating environment of the Web site. One mechanism is a server-based index maintained by Microsoft Index Server or Microsoft Indexing Service, depending on the server's operating system. For example, if the Web site is based on a Microsoft Windows 2000 server with Indexing Service installed, and Indexing Service is activated to index the area where the Web site resides, then FrontPage uses the Indexing Service catalog as its text index. With Windows NT 4, Index Server is used. In any other case, FrontPage uses its own default text index.

Whenever a new Web page is saved or hyperlinks are recalculated in the Web site, FrontPage saves any new words to the text index for that Web site. The text index is cumulative, meaning new words are added to the index, but old ones are not removed. As needed, you can create a new text index to remove outdated words.

Creating a Search Page with the Search Page Template

FrontPage provides two ways to add search capabilities to a Web site. You can insert a Web Search component in an existing Web page, or you can create a new page using the Search Page template. In either case, a search form is displayed on the Web page and the search results are displayed below the search form on the same page. Using a Web Search component on an existing page, therefore, causes the search results to be displayed on the existing page. Creating a new page with the Search Page template places both the search form and the search results on a unique page, separate from other Web pages in the site. In general, having a unique search page created using the Search Page template is a clear, easy-to-use way to add search capabilities to a Web site.

The following steps create a search page using the Search Page template.

To Create a Search Page Using the Search Page Template

1

- **Click the Create a new normal page button arrow on the Standard toolbar.**

FrontPage displays the Create a new normal page menu (Figure 7-65).

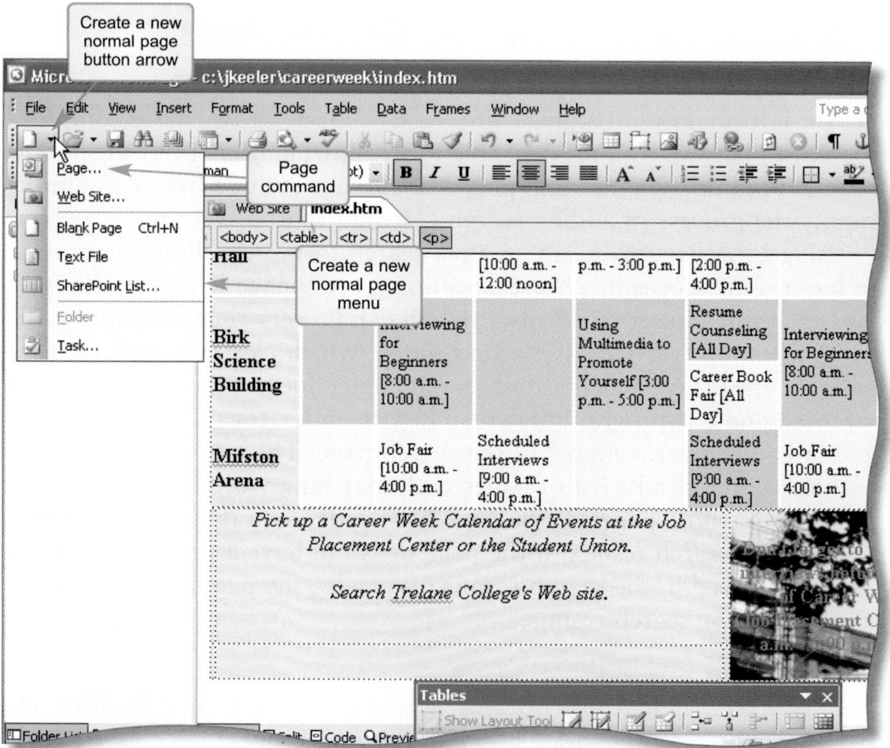

FIGURE 7-65

2

- **Click Page.**
- **If necessary, when FrontPage displays the Page Templates dialog box, click the General tab.**
- **Scroll down as necessary until the Search Page icon is displayed, and then click the Search Page icon.**

FrontPage displays the Page Templates dialog box (Figure 7-66). The Search Page icon is selected. FrontPage displays a description of the Search Page template in the Description area and a preview of the search page is displayed in the Preview area.

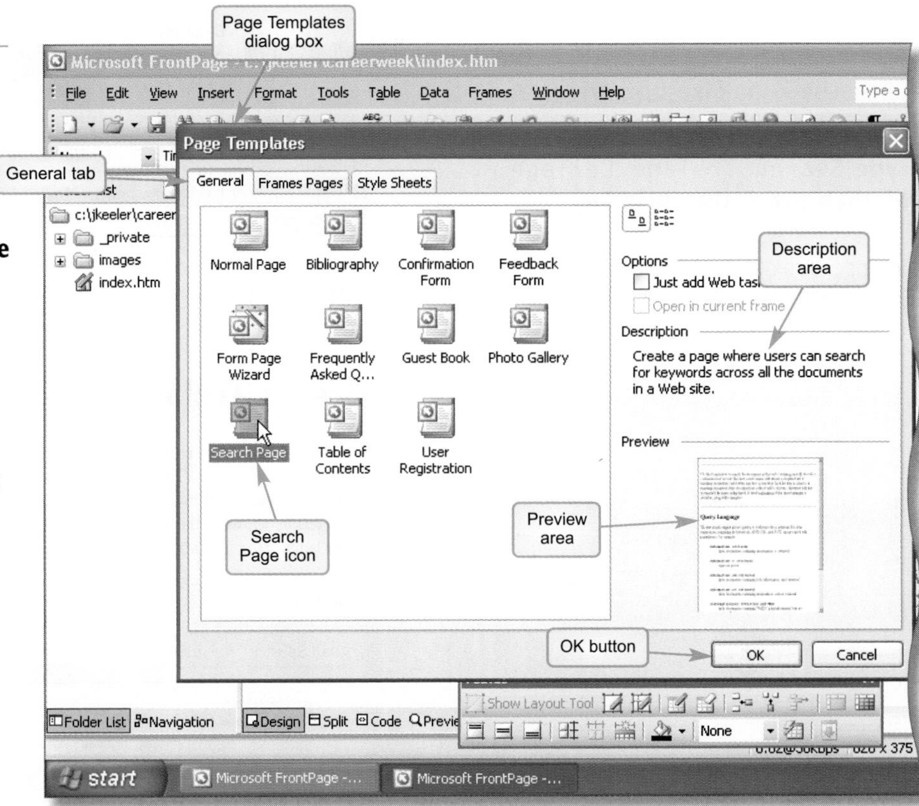

FIGURE 7-66

3

- **Click the OK button.**
- **Position the insertion point to the left of the word, Use, below the first horizontal rule.**

FrontPage creates a default search page with a search form, based on the Search Page template (Figure 7-67).

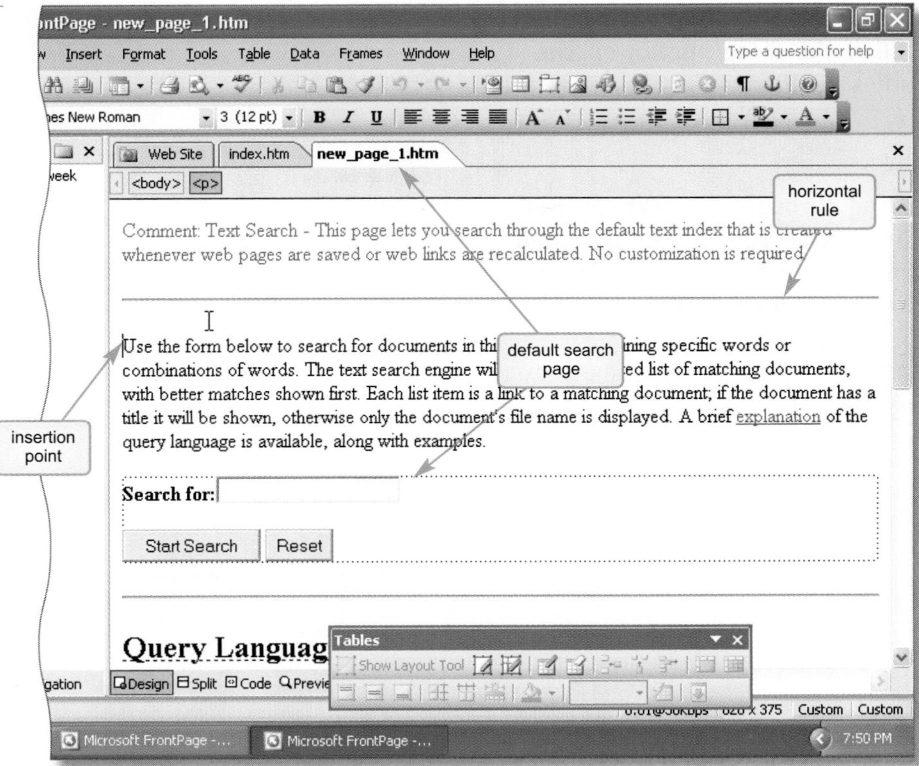

FIGURE 7-67

4

- **Click the Font Size box arrow and then click 6 (24 pt).**
- **Type** `Search Trelane College` **and then press the ENTER key.**

FrontPage displays the entered text (Figure 7-68).

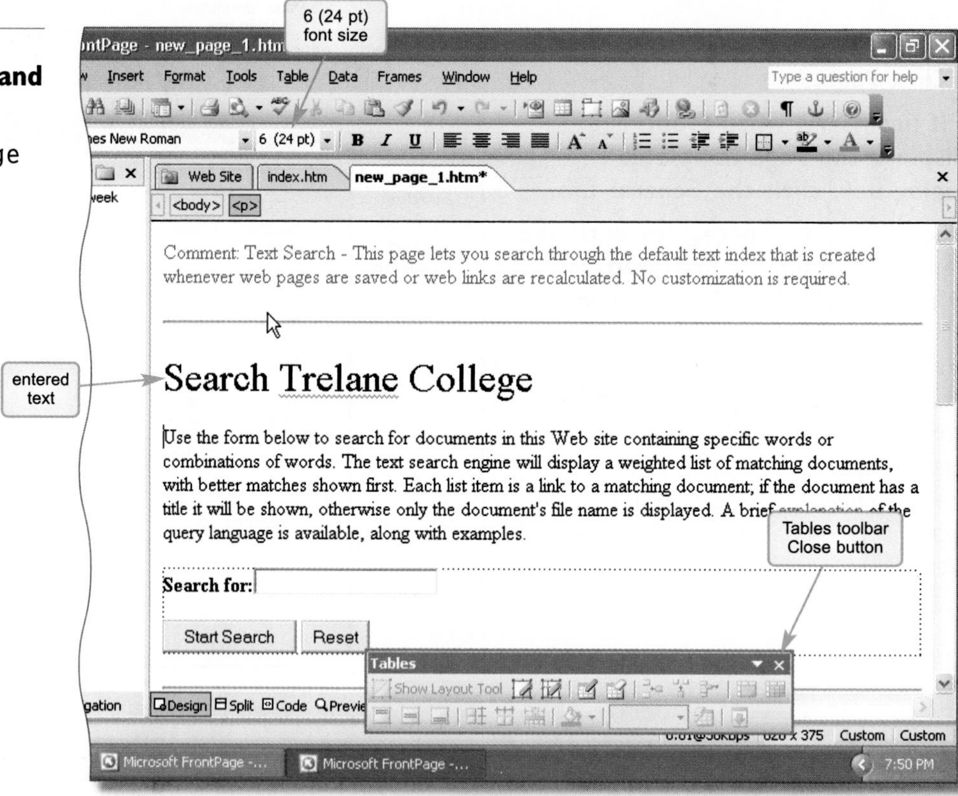

FIGURE 7-68

5

- **Click the Close button on the Tables toolbar.**
- **Scroll down to the bottom of the page.**
- **Drag through the text, Author information goes here., and then type** `Author: James Keeler` **as the replacement text.**

FrontPage displays the replacement text (Figure 7-69).

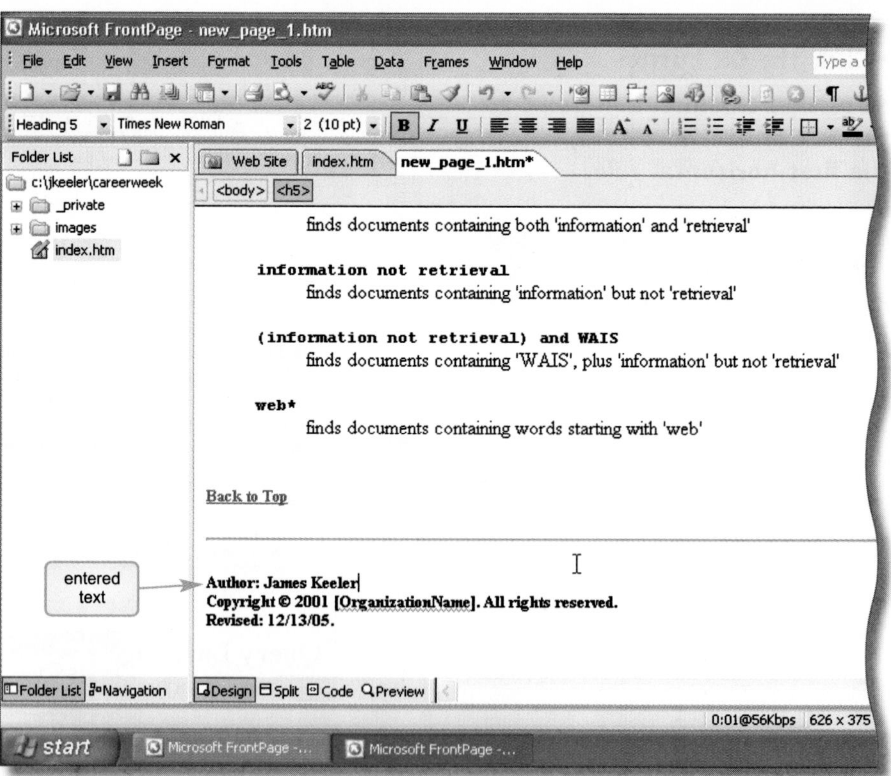

FIGURE 7-69

6

- **In the following line, drag through the text, 2001 [OrganizationName], and then type** `2005 Trelane College` **as the replacement text.**

FrontPage displays the replacement text (Figure 7-70).

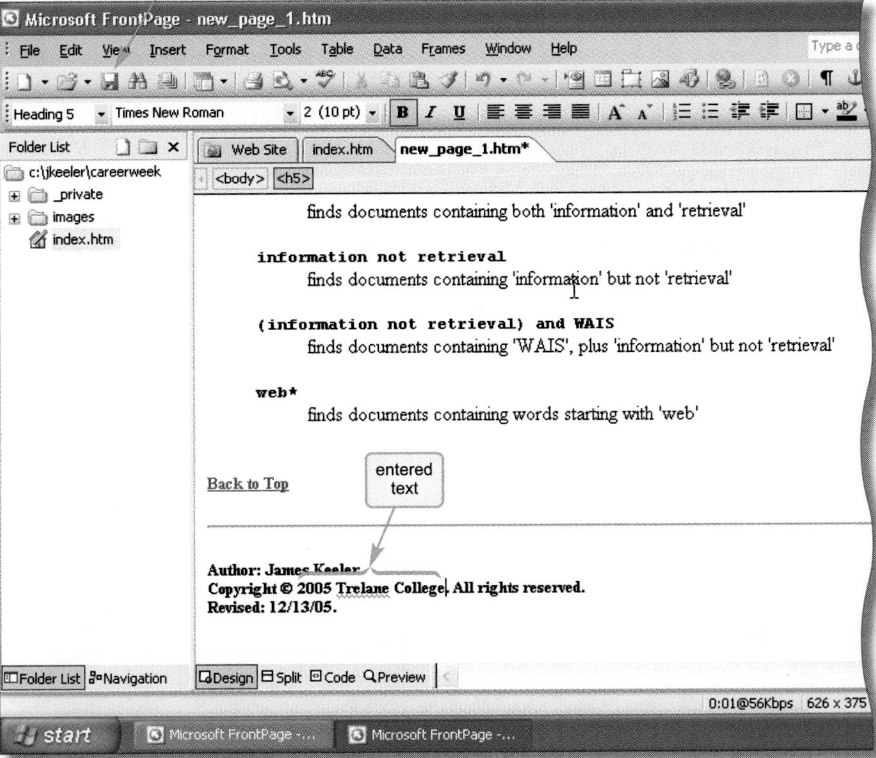

FIGURE 7-70

7

- **Click the Save button on the Standard toolbar.**
- **When FrontPage displays the Save As dialog box, type** `search` **in the File name box.**

FrontPage displays the Save As dialog box with the new file name shown (Figure 7-71). The page title is set by default from the first line of text on the page.

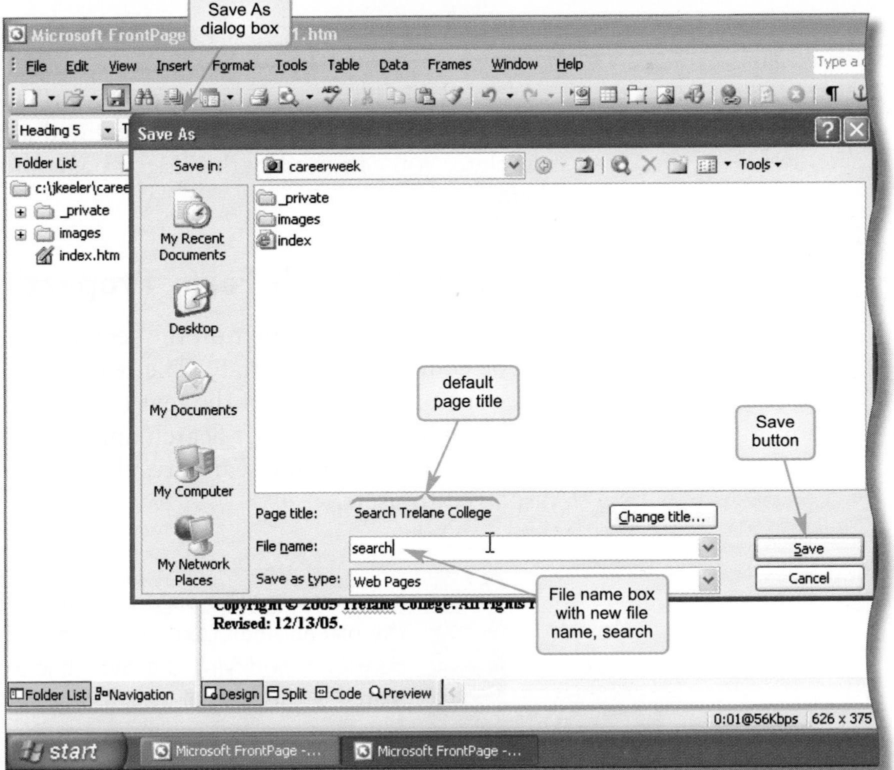

FIGURE 7-71

8

• **Click the Save button in the Save As dialog box.**

The search page is saved as search.htm (Figure 7-72). The mouse pointer changes to a hand holding a page when placed over the search form component.

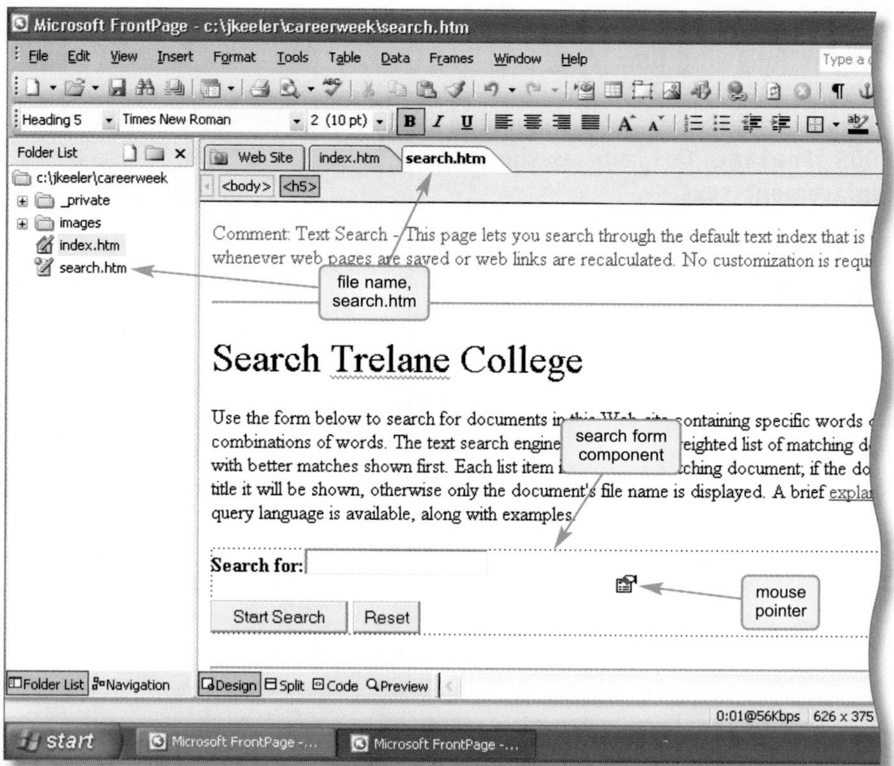

FIGURE 7-72

As shown in the previous steps, FrontPage makes it very easy to create a search page in a Web site. Once you have created a basic search page using the Search Page template, you can modify the search page and search form to further customize them.

Modifying Search Form Properties

Any of the default text on the search page created using the Search Page template can be edited, as appropriate. The search form also can be modified to change properties such as the width of the text box for the search keywords, the text box label, and the labels for the Start Search and Reset buttons. In addition, you can modify certain properties of the search results sheet to customize how search results are displayed to users.

Design Tip

When using Web page templates, be sure to take the time to modify the placeholder text, such as author and date information. Also, consider modifying the overall look of the page so that the page matches the overall design of your Web site.

The following steps modify properties of the search form.

To Modify Search Form Properties

1

- **Double-click the search form component.**
- **If necessary, when FrontPage displays the Search Form Properties dialog box, click the Search Form Properties tab.**

FrontPage displays the Search Form Properties dialog box, with the Search Form Properties sheet selected (Figure 7-73). The Search Form Properties dialog box provides several options to allow you to modify properties of the search form.

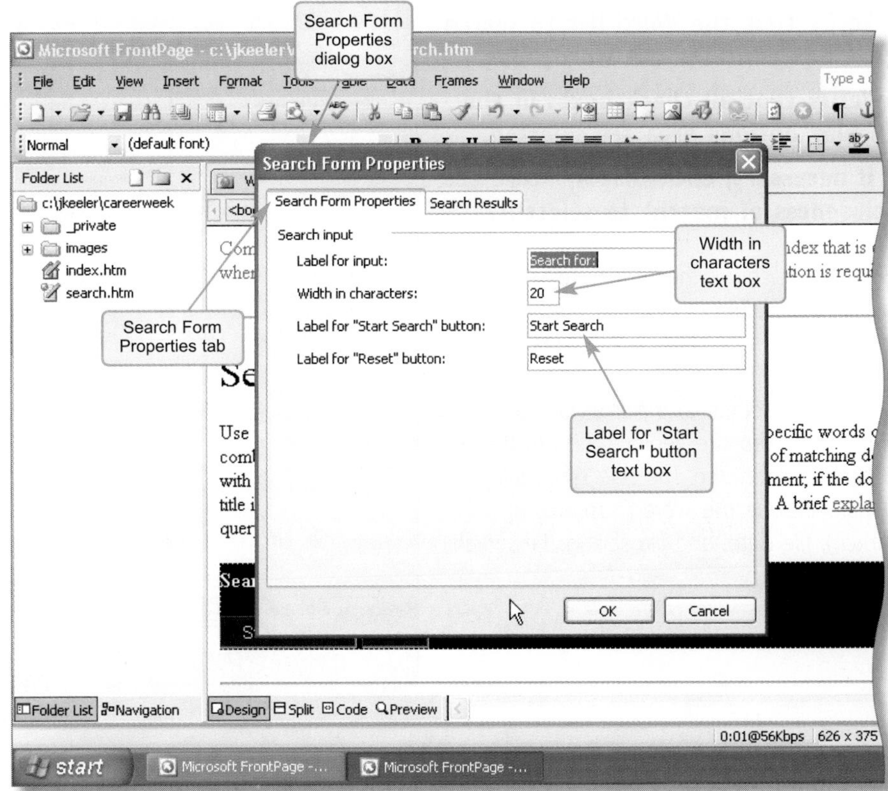

FIGURE 7-73

2

- **Drag through the text in the Width in characters text box and then type** 30 **as the new value.**
- **Drag through the text in the Label for "Start Search" button text box and then type** Begin Search **as the new label.**

FrontPage displays the new property values in the Search Form Properties sheet (Figure 7-74).

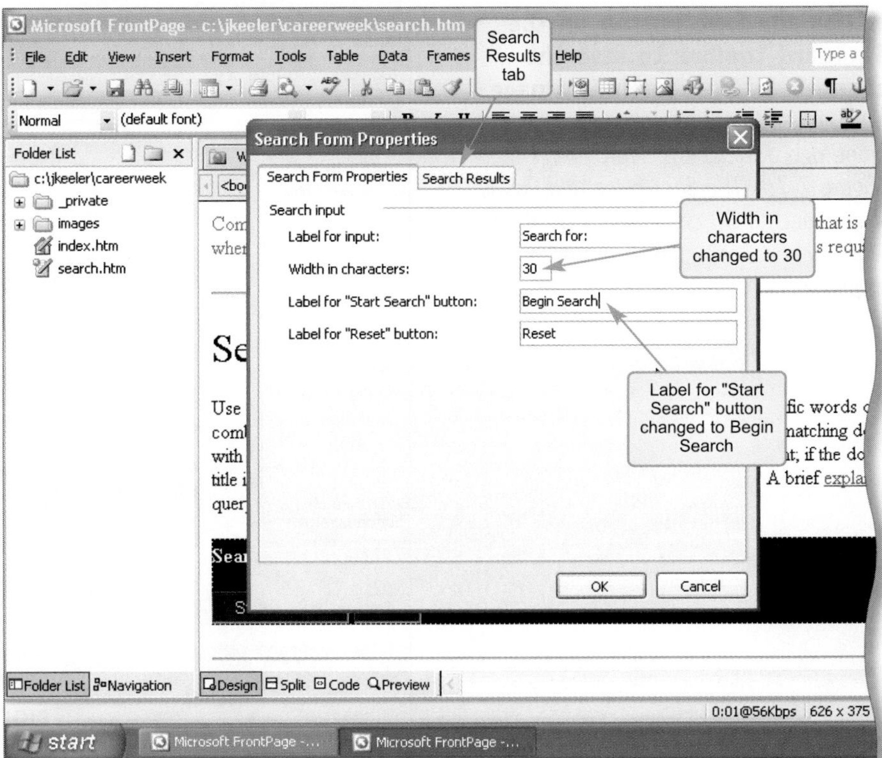

FIGURE 7-74

3

- **Click the Search Results tab.**
- **Verify that the Word list to search text box contains the word, All.**
- **Verify that all check boxes in the Display options area are selected.**
- **If necessary, click Display score (closeness of match) to select it.**

FrontPage displays the Search Results sheet (Figure 7-75). The keyword, All, allows visitors to search all pages in the current Web site, except those pages in hidden folders. To limit the search to a particular folder within the Web site, replace All with the desired folder name. The selected display options include the score (closeness of match), file date, and file size in the search results.

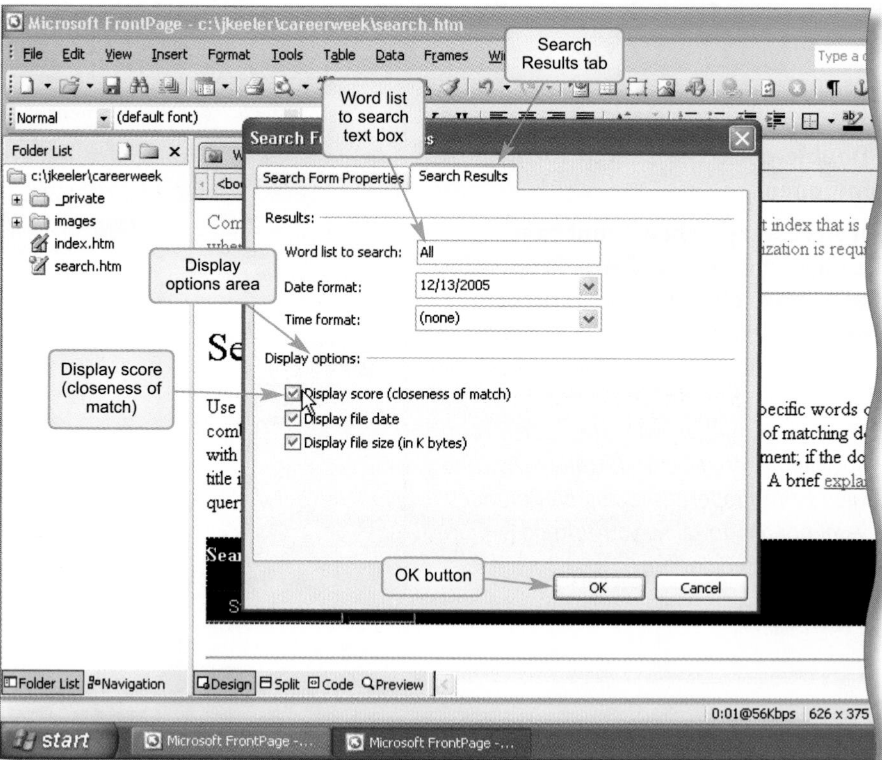

FIGURE 7-75

4

- **Click the OK button.**
- **Click the Save button on the Standard toolbar to save the changes to the search.htm page.**

FrontPage displays the search page (Figure 7-76). The Search for text box is lengthened to 30 characters, and the new label for the Begin Search button is displayed.

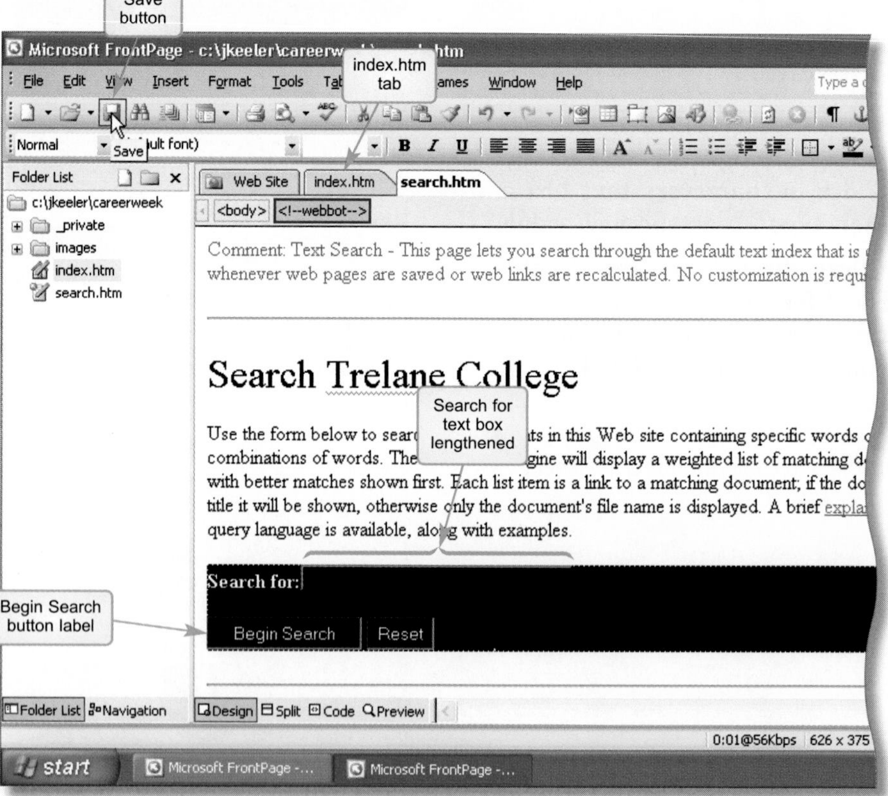

FIGURE 7-76

5

- **Click the index.htm tab.**
- **If necessary, scroll down to the bottom of the page.**
- **Drag through the word, Search.**

FrontPage displays the calendar of events page (Figure 7-77). The word, Search, is selected.

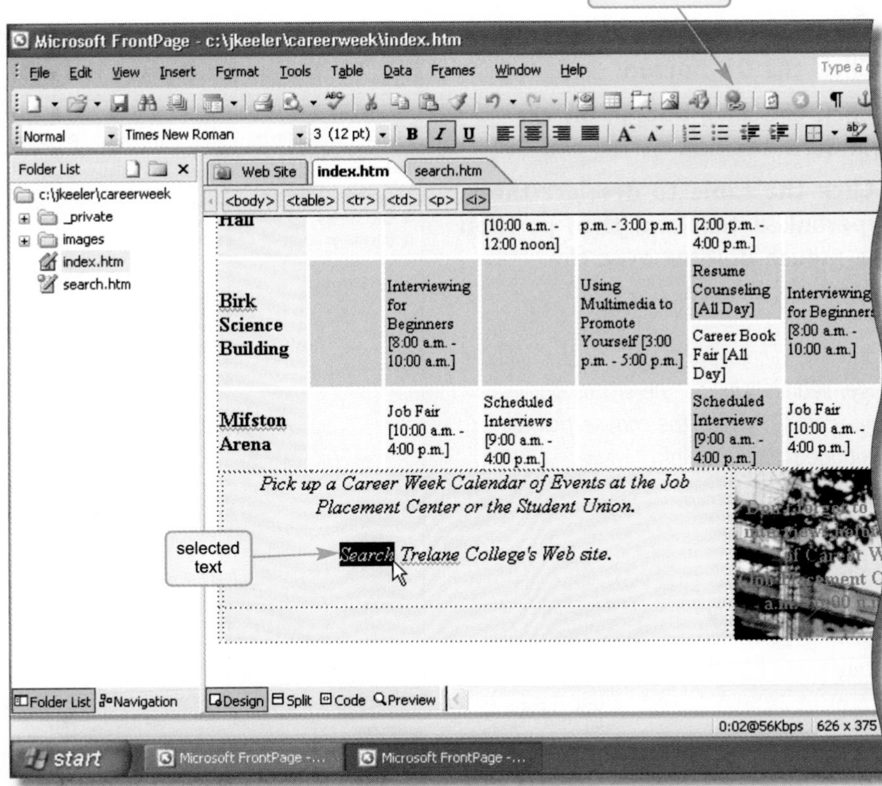

FIGURE 7-77

6

- **Click the Insert Hyperlink button on the Standard toolbar.**
- **When FrontPage displays the Insert Hyperlink dialog box, click search.**

FrontPage displays the Insert Hyperlink dialog box (Figure 7-78). The page to link to, search, is selected.

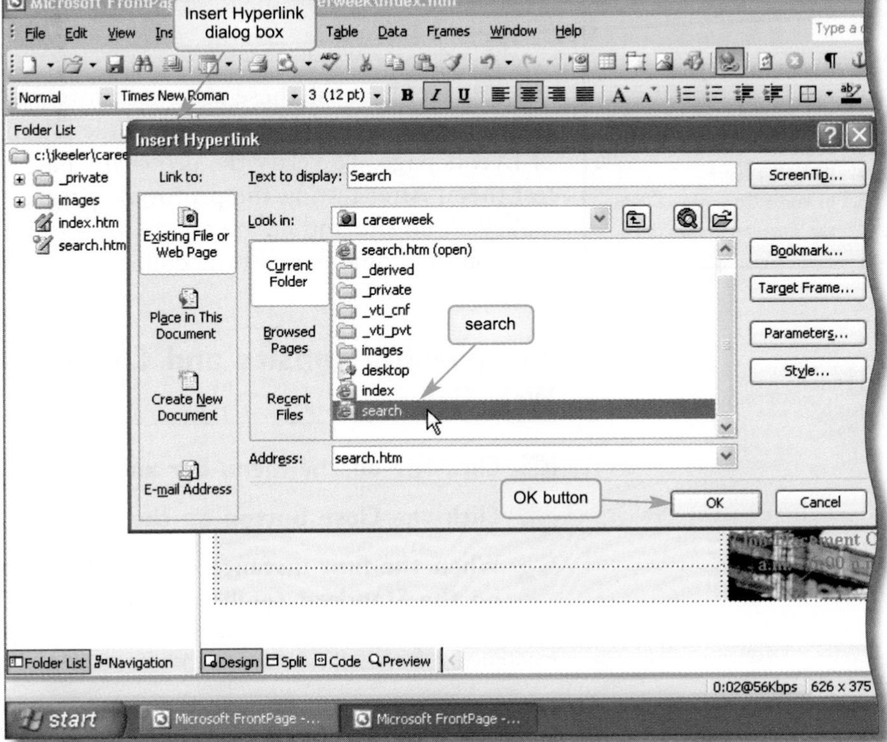

FIGURE 7-78

7

- **Click the OK button.**
- **Click the Save button on the Standard toolbar.**
- **Click the table to deselect the hyperlinked text and then position the mouse pointer over the hyperlink, Search.**

FrontPage displays the URL to the linked page, search.htm, on the status bar (Figure 7-79) when the mouse pointer is positioned over the link.

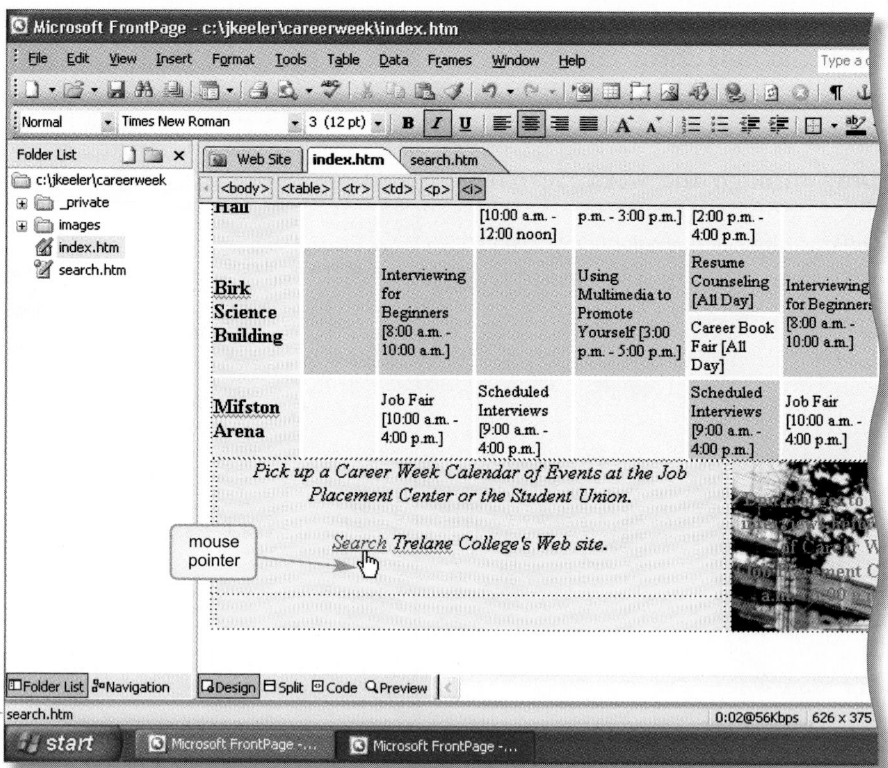

FIGURE 7-79

> **Other Ways**
>
> 1. On Format menu click Properties
> 2. Right-click search form, click Search Form Properties
> 3. Press ALT+ENTER
> 4. Press ALT+O, T
> 5. In Voice Command mode, say "Format, Properties"

The Career Week - Calendar of Events page now includes a hyperlink to the search page. Because these are only prototype Web pages, the home page of the James Keeler Web site does not include a hyperlink to the Career Week - Calendar of Events page. To verify the prototype pages, you will publish the pages and then test them. After testing the prototype pages, you should move them to the Trelane College Web site and create a hyperlink to the Career Week - Calendar of Events page on the home page of the college Web site.

To Publish a Subsite and Changes to an Existing FrontPage Web Site

1. **Click File on the menu bar and then click Close Site.**
2. **Click the Close button on the Microsoft FrontPage title bar.**
3. **When the first instance of FrontPage appears, click the Publish Site button on the Standard toolbar.**

FrontPage publishes the Web site and the subsite.

Once the Web site and subsite are published, you can view and test the prototyped Career Week - Calendar of Events page and the search pages by entering the location of your Web site (e.g., http://www.trelanecollege.edu/~jkeeler/careerweek) in any browser and pressing the ENTER key. Be sure to test the hyperlink to the search page on the Career Week - Calendar of Events page and test the search capabilities added to the Web site by the search form page.

Quitting FrontPage

When you have published and tested the new pages in the Web site, you can quit Microsoft FrontPage. The following steps quit FrontPage.

More About

The Quick Reference

For more information, see the Quick Reference Summary at the back of this book, or visit the FrontPage 2003 Quick Reference Web page (scsite.com/fp2003/qr).

To Quit FrontPage

1. **Click File on the menu bar and then click Close Site.**
2. **Click the Close button on the Microsoft FrontPage title bar.**

The FrontPage window is closed, and the Windows desktop is displayed.

Project Summary

In this project, you learned how to display the Tables toolbar, insert a caption for a table, fill repetitive information in a table, and split table cells into rows or columns. You learned how to apply a Table AutoFormat to a table. You also learned how to assign a background color to cells and how to use an image for a cell background. You learned how to modify properties for a group of adjacent cells and how to merge cells using the Eraser button. Finally, you learned how to add search capabilities to a Web page using the Search Page template and how to modify search form properties.

What You Should Know

Having completed this project, you should be able to perform the tasks below. The tasks are listed in the same order they were presented in this project. For a list of the buttons, menus, toolbars, and commands introduced in this project, see the Quick Reference Summary at the back of this book and refer to the Page Number column.

1. Start FrontPage and Open an Existing Web Site (FP 485)
2. Create a New Subsite in an Existing Web Site (FP 486)
3. Set the Title of a Web Page (FP 487)
4. Insert Tables and Display the Tables Toolbar (FP 489)
5. Insert a Caption for a Table (FP 492)
6. Fill Adjacent Table Columns with Repetitive Data (FP 495)
7. Split a Cell into Rows (FP 499)
8. Apply a Table AutoFormat to a Table (FP 501)
9. Modify Additional Table Properties (FP 503)
10. Modify Cell Properties for a Group of Cells (FP 508)
11. Use the Eraser Button to Merge Table Cells (FP 513)
12. Use an Image as a Cell Background (FP 515)
13. Create a Search Page Using the Search Page Template (FP 520)
14. Modify Search Form Properties (FP 525)
15. Publish a Subsite and Changes to an Existing FrontPage Web Site (FP 528)
16. Quit FrontPage (FP 529)

Learn It Online

Instructions: To complete the Learn It Online exercises, start your browser, click the Address bar, and then enter the Web address scsite.com/fp2003/learn. When the FrontPage 2003 Learn It Online page is displayed, follow the instructions in the exercises below. Each exercise has instructions for printing your results, either for your own records or for submission to your instructor.

1 Project Reinforcement TF, MC, and SA

Below FrontPage Project 7, click the Project Reinforcement link. Print the quiz by clicking Print on the File menu for each page. Answer each question.

2 Flash Cards

Below FrontPage Project 7, click the Flash Cards link and read the instructions. Type 20 (or a number specified by your instructor) in the Number of playing cards text box, type your name in the Enter your Name text box, and then click the Flip Card button. When the flash card is displayed, read the question and then click the ANSWER box arrow to select an answer. Flip through Flash Cards. If your score is 15 (75%) correct or greater, click Print on the File menu to print your results. If your score is less than 15 (75%) correct, then redo this exercise by clicking the Replay button.

3 Practice Test

Below FrontPage Project 7, click the Practice Test link. Answer each question, enter your first and last name at the bottom of the page, and then click the Grade Test button. When the graded practice test is displayed on your screen, click Print on the File menu to print a hard copy. Continue to take practice tests until you score 80% or better.

4 Who Wants To Be a Computer Genius?

Below FrontPage Project 7, click the Computer Genius link. Read the instructions, enter your first and last name at the bottom of the page, and then click the PLAY button. When your score is displayed, click the PRINT RESULTS link to print a hard copy.

5 Wheel of Terms

Below FrontPage Project 7, click the Wheel of Terms link. Read the instructions, and then enter your first and last name and your school name. Click the PLAY button. When your score is displayed, right-click the score and then click Print on the shortcut menu to print a hard copy.

6 Crossword Puzzle Challenge

Below FrontPage Project 7, click the Crossword Puzzle Challenge link. Read the instructions, and then enter your first and last name. Click the SUBMIT button. Work the crossword puzzle. When you are finished, click the Submit button. When the crossword puzzle is redisplayed, click the Print Puzzle button to print a hard copy.

7 Tips and Tricks

Below FrontPage Project 7, click the Tips and Tricks link. Click a topic that pertains to Project 7. Right-click the information and then click Print on the shortcut menu. Construct a brief example of what the information relates to in FrontPage to confirm you understand how to use the tip or trick.

8 Newsgroups

Below FrontPage Project 7, click the Newsgroups link. Click a topic that pertains to Project 7. Print three comments.

9 Expanding Your Horizons

Below FrontPage Project 7, click the Expanding Your Horizons link. Click a topic that pertains to Project 7. Print the information. Construct a brief example of what the information relates to in FrontPage to confirm you understand the contents of the article.

10 Search Sleuth

Below FrontPage Project 7, click the Search Sleuth link. To search for a term that pertains to this project, select a term below the Project 7 title and then use the Google search engine at google.com (or any major search engine) to display and print two Web pages that present information on the term.

11 FrontPage Online Training

Below FrontPage Project 7, click the FrontPage Online Training link. When your browser displays the Microsoft Office Online Web page, click the FrontPage link. Click one of the FrontPage courses that covers one or more of the objectives listed at the beginning of the project on page FP 482. Print the first page of the course before stepping through it.

12 Office Marketplace

Below FrontPage Project 7, click the Office Marketplace link. When your browser displays the Microsoft Office Online Web page, click the Office Marketplace link. Click a topic that relates to FrontPage. Print the first page.

Apply Your Knowledge

1 Apply a Table AutoFormat to a Table

Instructions: Start FrontPage and open the Web site, jkeeler, that you modified in Project 7. If you did not complete Project 7, see your instructor for a copy of the required files.

1. Click the Create a new normal page button on the Standard toolbar. When the new page is displayed, click the Insert Table button on the Standard toolbar and then drag through eight rows and six columns (8 by 6 table).
2. Position the insertion point in the first row and the second column of the table. Type `Monday` and then position the insertion point in the third column of the first row. Type `Tuesday` and then position the insertion point in the fourth column of the first row. Type `Wednesday` as the text for that cell. In the fifth column of the first row, type `Thursday` and then in the far-right column, type `Friday`.
3. If necessary, click Toolbars on the View menu and then click Tables to display the Tables toolbar. If necessary, drag the Tables toolbar below the table. Position the insertion point in the second row and the first column of the table. Click the Font Size box arrow on the Formatting toolbar and then click 1 (8 pt) in the Font Size list. Type `9:00 a.m.` as the text for the cell. Drag through the entered text and down through the remaining cells in this column. Click the Fill Down button on the Tables toolbar. Modify the text in each cell, beginning with the third row, to indicate the next hour (10:00 a.m., 11:00 a.m., etc.) in turn.
4. Position the insertion point in the second row and the second column of the table. Click the Font Size box arrow on the Formatting toolbar and then click 2 (10 pt) in the Font Size list. Type `BUS 126` and then press SHIFT+ENTER. Type `Lawson 351` and do not press the ENTER key. Drag through the entered text and then click the Copy button on the Standard toolbar. Position the insertion point in the second row and the fifth column of the table and then click the Paste button on the Standard toolbar.
5. Position the insertion point in the seventh row and second column of the table. Click the Font Size box arrow on the Formatting toolbar and then click 2 (10 pt) in the Font Size list. Type `BUS 250` and then press SHIFT+ENTER. Type `Birk 135` and do not press the ENTER key. Drag through the entered text and through the remaining cells to the right in this row. Click the Fill Right button on the Tables toolbar.
6. Click Table AutoFormat on the Table menu. When the Table AutoFormat dialog box is displayed, scroll down in the Formats list and then click Column 3. Click AutoFit to select it. Click the OK button.
7. Position the insertion point in the second row and the fourth column of the table. Click the Split Cells button on the Tables toolbar. When the Split Cells dialog box is displayed, select Split into rows and then verify that the number of rows specified is 2. Click the OK button.
8. Position the insertion point in the bottom row of the split cells. Click the Font Size box arrow on the Formatting toolbar and then click 2 (10 pt) in the Font Size list. Type `BUS 110` and then position the insertion point in the cell below the current cell. Click the Font Size box arrow on the Formatting toolbar and then click 2 (10 pt) in the Font Size list. Type `Lawson 351` as the text for the cell. Right-click the cell and then click Cell Properties on the shortcut menu. When the Cell Properties dialog box is displayed, click the Color box arrow in the Background area. When the color palette is displayed, click [White] in the Standard colors area. Click the OK button.

(continued)

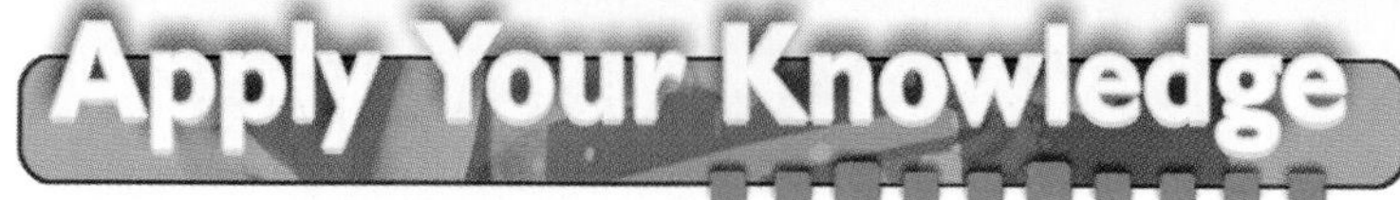

Apply a Table AutoFormat to a Table *(continued)*

9. Click the cell in the second column of the seventh row. Hold down the SHIFT key then click the last cell in the seventh row. Keeping the SHIFT key down, click all the remaining cells in the table that contain text and are not in the first column. Right-click a selected cell and then click Cell Properties on the shortcut menu. When the Cell Properties dialog box is displayed, click the Color box arrow in the Background area. When the color palette is displayed, click [White] in the Standard colors area. Click the OK button.
10. Right-click the table and then click Table Properties on the shortcut menu. When the Table Properties dialog box is displayed, drag through the value in the Cell padding box and then type `3` as the new value. Drag through the value in the Cell spacing box and then type `1` as the new value. Verify that Collapse table border is selected. Click the OK button.
11. Click Insert on the Table menu and then click Caption. Click the Font Size box arrow on the Formatting toolbar and then click 5 (18 pt) in the Font Size list. Type `Introductory Marketing Tutoring Schedule` as the new caption.
12. Click the Save button on the Standard toolbar. When the Save As dialog box is displayed, type `tutoring` in the File name text box and then click the Save button in the Save As dialog box. Close the Tables toolbar.
13. Create a hyperlink on the home page to the Tutoring page, tutoring.htm. You will have to check out the home page.
14. Preview the page in a Web browser, to ensure that it appears as shown in Figure 7-80. Print the two Web pages from FrontPage, write your name on them, and hand them in to your instructor. Close the Web site and then quit FrontPage.

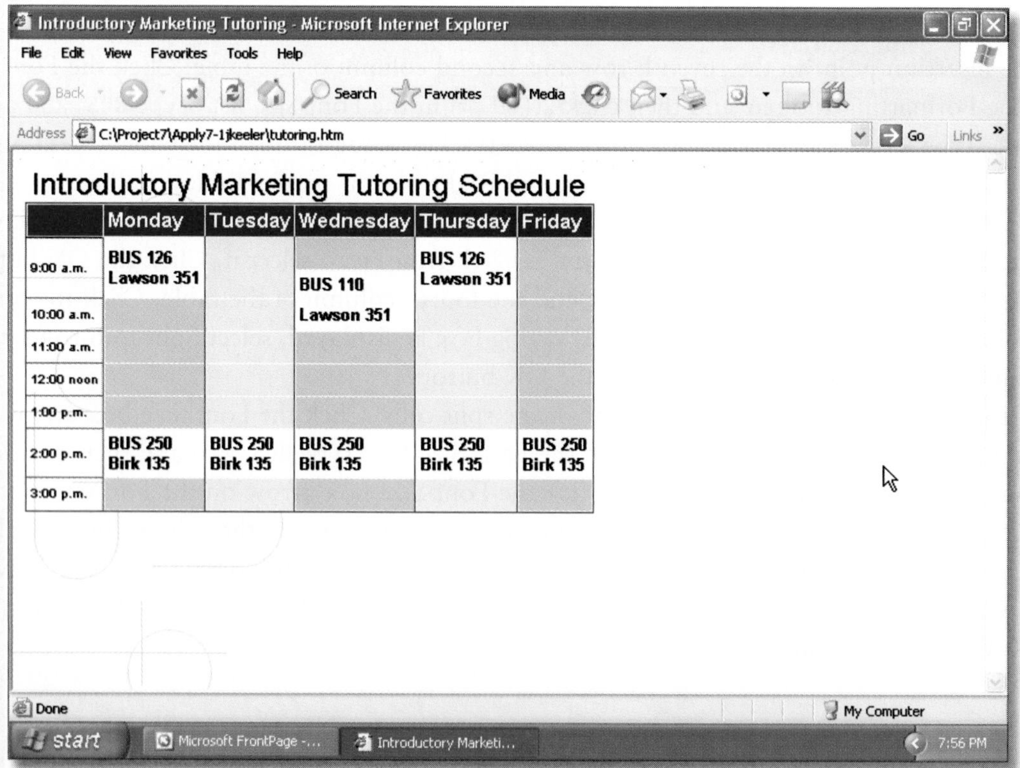

FIGURE 7-80

1 Creating a New Search Page for a Web Site

Problem: Ship-It-Here needs a place where visitors may search the Web site. To avoid the impression that the search applies only to one area of the site, such as Products or Services, the owners of Ship-It-Here ask you to create a new page for the search page.

Instructions: Perform the following tasks.

1. Open the Web site, Ship-It-Here, that you modified in Project 6. If you did not complete that exercise for Project 6, see your instructor for a copy of the required files.
2. Click the Create a new normal page button arrow and then click Page. If necessary, when the Page Templates dialog box is displayed, click the General tab. Scroll down as necessary until the Search Page icon is displayed, and then click the Search Page icon. Click the OK button.
3. When the default search page is displayed, double-click the search form. When the Search Form Properties dialog box is displayed, click the Search Results tab and then click Display score (closeness of match) in the Display options area. Click the OK button.
4. Scroll down and then drag through the three lines of text that begin, Author information goes here. Press the DELETE key.
5. Click the Save button on the Standard toolbar to save the page. When the Save As dialog box is displayed, type `search` in the File name text box. Click the Save button in the Save As dialog box.
6. Click Navigation on the View menu. When the Web site is displayed in Navigation view, drag the file, search.htm, and drop it under the Home page icon and to the right of the Services icon. Click the title of the new icon, type `Search`, and then press the ENTER key. Click the Search tab, right-click anywhere on the page, and then click Properties on the shortcut menu. If necessary, when the Properties dialog box is displayed, click the General tab. If necessary, drag through the text in the Title text box. Type `Search the Ship-It-Here Web Site` in the Title text box and then click the OK button. Save the Web page. Double-click the Home page file in the Folders pane to open the home page in Page view.
7. Click the text that begins, We now ship, and then hold down the SHIFT key. Click the red ribbon AutoShape and each of the yellow star AutoShapes to select them. Drag the selected items down until the top star AutoShape is below the hyperlink for Search. Release the SHIFT key and then click the Save button on the Standard toolbar.
8. Preview the home page and the search page in a Web browser, to ensure that the search page appears as shown in Figure 7-81 on the next page. Publish the Web site and test the search page and the hyperlink from the home page.
9. Print the search page and the home page from the Web browser, write your name on the pages, and hand them in to your instructor. Close the Web site and then quit FrontPage.

(continued)

Creating a New Search Page for a Web Site *(continued)*

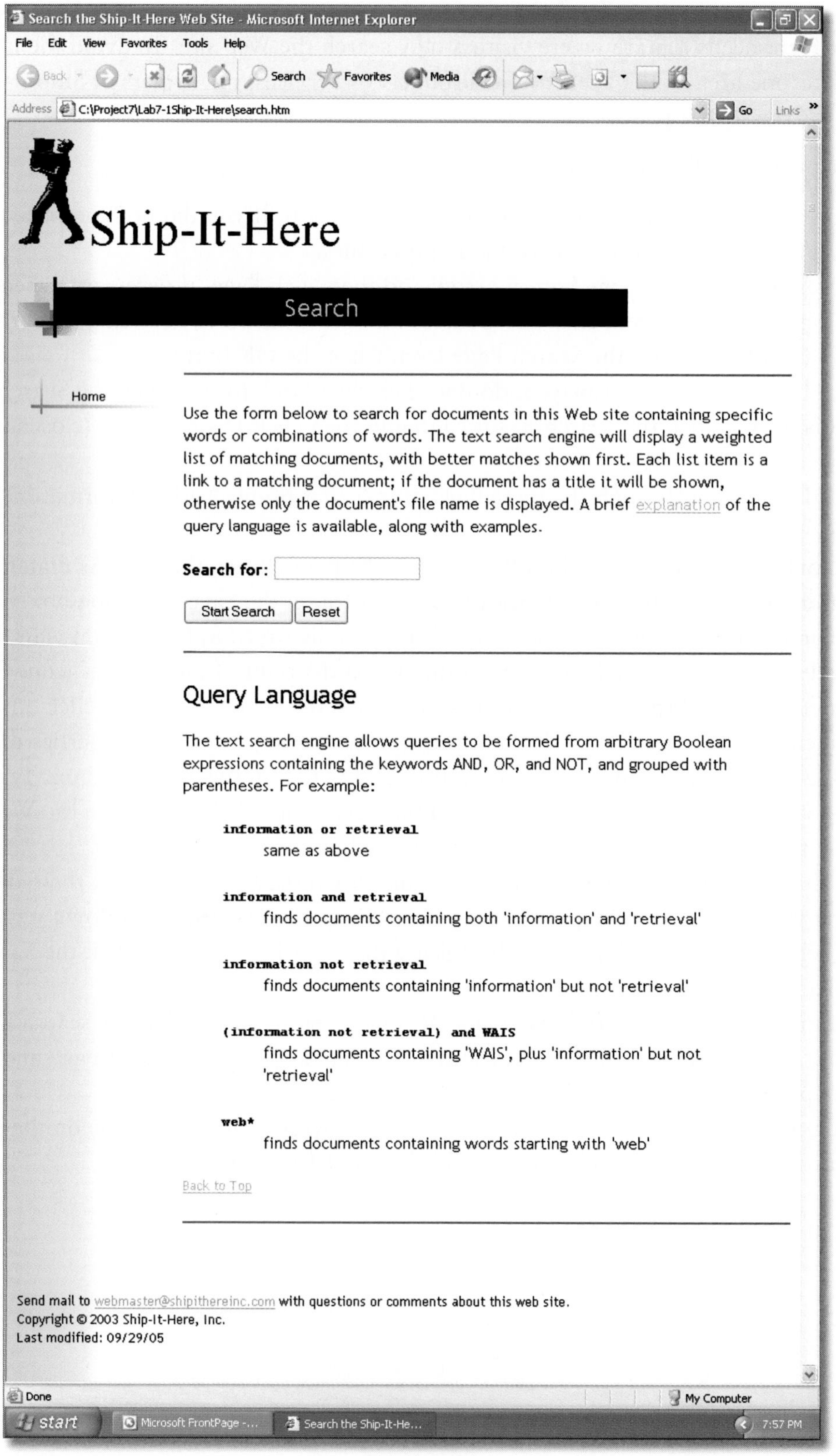

Search the Ship-It-Here Web Site - Microsoft Internet Explorer

File Edit View Favorites Tools Help

Address C:\Project7\Lab7-1Ship-It-Here\search.htm

Ship-It-Here

Search

Home

Use the form below to search for documents in this Web site containing specific words or combinations of words. The text search engine will display a weighted list of matching documents, with better matches shown first. Each list item is a link to a matching document; if the document has a title it will be shown, otherwise only the document's file name is displayed. A brief explanation of the query language is available, along with examples.

Search for:

Start Search | Reset

Query Language

The text search engine allows queries to be formed from arbitrary Boolean expressions containing the keywords AND, OR, and NOT, and grouped with parentheses. For example:

information or retrieval
same as above

information and retrieval
finds documents containing both 'information' and 'retrieval'

information not retrieval
finds documents containing 'information' but not 'retrieval'

(information not retrieval) and WAIS
finds documents containing 'WAIS', plus 'information' but not 'retrieval'

web*
finds documents containing words starting with 'web'

Back to Top

Send mail to webmaster@shipithereinc.com with questions or comments about this web site.
Copyright © 2003 Ship-It-Here, Inc.
Last modified: 09/29/05

Done | My Computer

start | Microsoft FrontPage -... | Search the Ship-It-He... | 7:57 PM

FIGURE 7-81

2 Inserting a Search Component in an Existing Web Page

Problem: The owner of Fairway Lawn Care wants to let visitors to the Web site search for information on services of interest to them. Because the owner does not want an additional page to maintain, you will insert a search component on the Services page, which has the necessary available space.

Instructions: Perform the following tasks.

1. Open the Fairway Lawn Care Web site that you modified in Project 6. If you did not complete that exercise for Project 6, see your instructor for a copy of the required files.
2. If necessary, open the Services page, services.htm, in Design view. You will have to check the page out to open it for editing.
3. Position the insertion point at the end of the paragraph that begins, Select the plan, and then press the ENTER key. Type `Click a link on the left, or search for the service plan you need!` and then press the ENTER key. Change the link bar's style to tabular.
4. Click Web Component on the Insert menu. When the Insert Web Component dialog box is displayed, click Web Search in the Component type list. Verify that Current Web is selected in the Choose a type of search list. Click the Finish button.
5. If necessary, when the Search Form Properties dialog box is displayed, click the Search Form Properties tab. Drag through the value in the Width in characters text box and then type `30` as the new value. Click the Search Results tab. In the Display options area, click Display score (closeness of match), Display file date, and Display file size (in K bytes) to select them. Click the Time format box arrow and then click the last format in the Time format list. Click the OK button.
6. Save the changes and preview the Services page in a Web browser to ensure that it is displayed as shown in Figure 7-82.
7. Print the Products page from the Web browser. Write your name on the page and hand it in to your instructor. Close the Web site and then quit FrontPage.

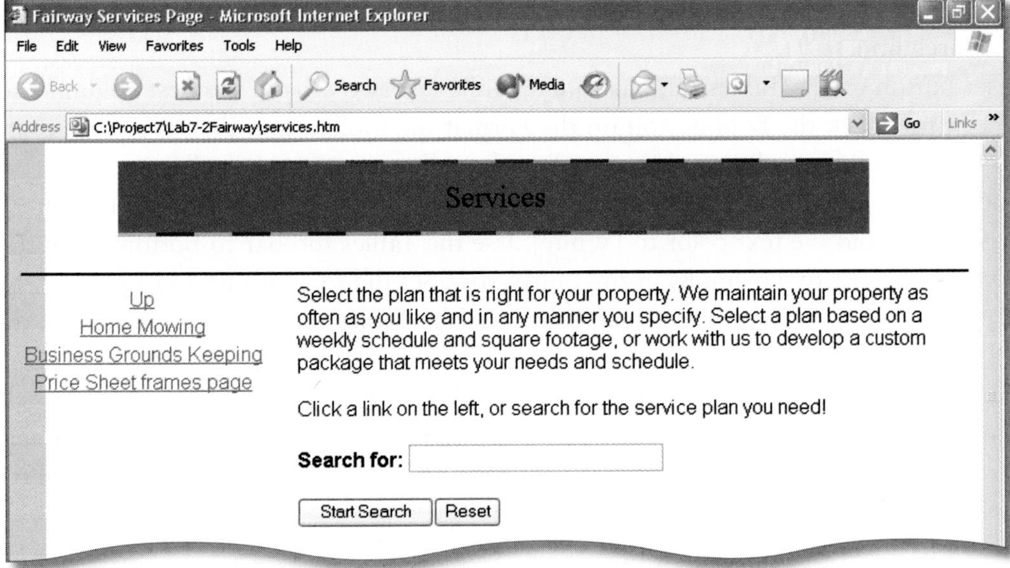

FIGURE 7-82

3 Adding a Customized Table to a Web Page

Problem: Your company's Information Systems department manager liked your prototype for the software database on the company's intranet and has asked you to build a prototype of a home page that would link to the database page. The home page should include such elements as the department's location, hours of operation, a link to a search page, and a link to the department's e-mail address.

Instructions: Perform the following tasks.

1. Start FrontPage and open the Web site, Software, that you modified in Project 6. If you did not complete that exercise for Project 6, see your instructor for a copy of the required files.
2. Create a new normal page and save it with the file name, main. Right-click the file name in the Folder List pane and then click Set as Home Page on the shortcut menu. The file, main.htm, is renamed automatically to index.htm; the file, index.htm, is renamed automatically to index-old.htm. Rename the file, index-old.htm, to search.htm.
3. Verify that the home page (index.htm) is displayed in Design view. Insert a five-row by four-column (5 by 4) table. Modify the table properties to set the table alignment to Center. Modify the table size to a width of 465 pixels and a height of 345 pixels. Set the table border size to zero. Insert the image, CD.JPG, from the Project 7 folder on the Data Disk as the table background. Click the OK button.
4. Display the Tables toolbar. Use the Eraser button on the Tables toolbar to merge the last two columns in the top row. Set the font size to 4 (14 pt) and the font color to [Fuchsia]. Type `Information Systems Department` and then right-align the text in the cell. In the second row and the fourth column, type `5th Floor.` and then right-align the text.
5. Use the Eraser button to merge the first three cells in the first column. Type `Hours of operation:` and then press SHIFT+ENTER. Drag through the text just entered and then click the Underline button on the Formatting toolbar. Below this text, type `7:00 a.m. - 6:00 p.m.` and then press SHIFT+ENTER. Type `Monday - Friday` and then press SHIFT+ENTER. Type `Open Holidays` and do not press the ENTER key.
6. In the third row and fourth column, type `Search software titles` and then right-align the text horizontally in the cell. Align the text to the top of the cell. Drag through the word, Search, and insert a hyperlink to the page, search.htm.
7. Use the Eraser button on the Tables toolbar to merge the last two cells in the first column and then set the font size to 1 (8 pt). Click the Bold button on the Formatting toolbar and then type `Copyright 2005` in the merged cell. Use the Tables toolbar to bottom-align the cell contents in the cell.
8. In the second column and fourth row, type `Stay licensed!` and then drag through the entered text. Set the font size to 5 (18 pt) and the text color to [White]. Use the Tables toolbar to bottom-align the cell contents in the cell. Merge the last two columns in the fourth row. Set the font size to 5 (18 pt) and the text color to [Fuchsia]. Type `Report software theft!` and then use the Tables toolbar to bottom-align the cell contents in the cell.
9. Merge the third and fourth cells in the last row. Set the font size to 2 (10 pt). Use the Tables toolbar to bottom-align the cell contents and then click the Align Right button on the Formatting toolbar to right-align the text. Set the font color to [Fuchsia]. Type `Contact us at infosys@isp.com` and then make the text, infosys@isp.com, a mailto: hyperlink.

In the Lab

10. Verify that the background image is displayed without tiling. Adjust the cell borders to display the home page as shown in Figure 7-83. Save all changes. Print the page and then preview the home page in a Web browser. Print the home page from the Web browser, write your name on the pages, and hand them in to your instructor. Close the Web site and then quit FrontPage.

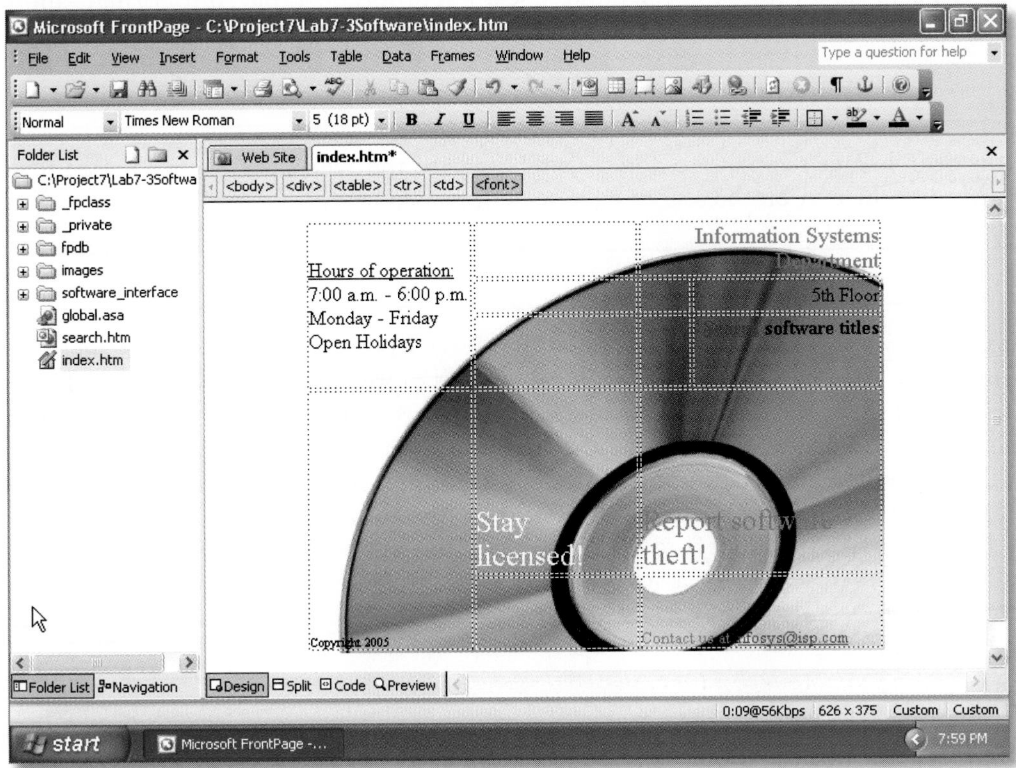

FIGURE 7-83

Cases and Places

The difficulty of these case studies varies:
■ are the least difficult and ■■ are more difficult. The last exercise is a group exercise.

1 ■ Modify your resume page from Project 6 to include a table that lists a summary of your work and school experience. Add a caption to the table. Use an appropriate Table AutoFormat, and modify the table and cell properties as needed.

2 ■ Use the Search Page template to add a search page to the Web site for your movie reviews from Project 6. Modify the text on the search page to reflect its purpose.

3 ■■ Create a new page that lists office hours in a 2 by 7 table for one of the instructors from the departmental Web page from Project 6. Each cell should represent one day of the week. The first row should list days of the week. Include course numbers, hours available, and special circumstances. Use Table AutoFormat Colorful 2 and then modify the table and cell properties, including colors, as desired. Fill in repetitive information using the Fill Right button on the Tables toolbar, and make the hours the same for Wednesday, Thursday, and Friday. Add information for each day of the week, and split cells in at least two of the days to add multiple office hours. Add a Web Search component to the page to allow visitors to search for a specific instructor or course.

4 ■■ Create a table to represent a calendar of events surrounding your friend's graduation and add the new Web page to the graduation Web site from Project 5. Set up the table to represent two weeks of time in early June. Add at least seven events to the table, using various background colors to identify classifications of events, such as personal gatherings or organized school events. Create a second table that serves as a guide to the meaning of each color. Use one or two cells per event, splitting cells when necessary. Add an appropriate table caption.

5 ■■ **Working Together** Create a table for the company sports Web site from Project 6. In the table, include columns for the sports, months that the sports are in progress, and the contact person for each team. In the column for the team name, use a background image that represents the team emblem or sport. In the other table cells, use team colors for the background for each given team. Begin by applying a Table AutoFormat and then modify table and cell properties as needed. Add a search page or Web Search component to an existing page to allow visitors to search the entire company Web site.

MICROSOFT
Office FrontPage 2003

Working with Dynamic Web Templates, Layers, and Behaviors

PROJECT

8

CASE PERSPECTIVE

Having observed the success of James Keeler's Job Opportunity Web site and his work on the Job Placement Center's Career Week event calendar, the Trelane College student government has asked James Keeler to develop a Web page for use in announcing events and meetings for various student and college organizations. Currently, organizations provide event and meeting information in an assortment of Web page formats, resulting in the announcements greatly varying in quality and content. Once developed, the Web page should be used as a standard guideline for all organizations when announcing meetings and events. The student government provides the general design of the Web page and requests some interesting design elements involving motion and other special effects. The student government also requests that the Web pages meet specific criteria for accessibility by people with disabilities.

You tell James that FrontPage includes the development tools to create dynamic Web templates, which allow users of the template to edit only certain regions of a Web page template. Layers and behaviors provide more interesting and dynamic design elements that can be added to a Web page. FrontPage also provides the capability of checking a page to ensure it meets Web page guidelines for accessibility and is accessible to all users.

As you read through this project, you will learn how to add behaviors to elements of a Web page. You will learn how to add layers to a Web page to arrange content. You also will learn how to create, edit, and utilize a dynamic Web template and how to manage the editable and noneditable regions of the template. You will learn how to check that a page is accessible by all users of a Web page. Finally, you will learn how to edit HTML code in Split view.

MICROSOFT Office FrontPage 2003

Working with Dynamic Web Templates, Layers, and Behaviors

PROJECT

Objectives

You will have mastered the material in this project when you can:

- Display page rulers and the page layout grid
- Display the DHTML Effects toolbar
- Add DHTML effects to a Web page
- Add behaviors to elements on a Web page
- Add layers to a Web page
- Modify behaviors of a layer
- Modify the editable regions of a dynamic Web template
- Save a Web page as a dynamic Web template
- Apply a dynamic Web template to a Web page
- Edit a dynamic Web template
- Check the spelling on a Web page
- Test accessibility of a Web page for people with disabilities
- Work with HTML code in Split view

Introduction

Organizations often prefer that Web pages associated with the organization meet certain design guidelines. While templates, shared borders, and themes help to meet much of this need, other Web page developers can alter the template, shared border, or theme, thereby diminishing the goal of a common design. FrontPage's **dynamic Web templates** allow you to create a template and then specify which parts of Web pages created with the template can be modified by other Web page developers. **Editable regions** are those portions of a dynamic Web template that another Web page developer is allowed to modify. **Noneditable regions** are those portions of a dynamic Web template that another Web page developer is not allowed to modify. If you update a dynamic Web template to provide a new look or add new elements to the template, all pages that utilize the template automatically receive the new look.

Like tables, **layers** provide the ability to separate elements of a Web page into distinct regions. Layers often provide more flexibility than tables because layers can be positioned very precisely on the screen, and as their name suggests, they can be layered on top of each other or on top of a Web page. Like tables, layers can contain other layers. Layers also can be transparent. Behaviors often work hand in hand with layers. **Behaviors** are actions that are associated with elements on a Web page, such as text, images, or layers. Behaviors allow a Web page to modify itself without communicating with the Web server.

Layers and behaviors are both part of dynamic HTML. **Dynamic HTML (DHTML)** is a Web standard designed to add interactivity and graphical enhancements to Web pages by providing the capability for the Web pages to change and automatically be updated without communicating with the Web server.

FrontPage provides tools to check that a Web page complies with certain standards for Web page accessibility by people with disabilities. Web page **accessibility** is a measure of how well a Web page is usable for people with one or more disabilities, such as hearing or sight impairments. Several standards exist to measure accessibility, and FrontPage allows you to select specific standards to use when testing for accessibility. After the test is complete, FrontPage provides a report that details the portions of the Web page that are not in compliance with the standards.

Project Eight — Working with Dynamic Web Templates, Layers, and Behaviors

In this project, a dynamic Web template will be created (Figure 8-1a on the next page) and then used to create a new Web page (Figure 8-1b on the next page). A behavior is added to two lines of text below the title of the Web page so that the lines of text fly in to the Web page when the user loads the page. Layers are used to position some of the content on the page. Only certain portions of the template can be modified by developers who use the template. A behavior also is added to a layer so that the layer is displayed only when the user places the mouse pointer over certain text.

After the template is created, the project illustrates how the template is used to create a new Web page. The template then is modified, and the resulting changes are reflected automatically in the created Web page (Figure 8-1b).

This project also illustrates how to check the spelling on a Web page and make corrections. Finally, you will learn how to check the accessibility of the Web page and then adjust the Web page to meet the accessibility criteria. Changes to the HTML will be made using Split view, which allows you to view both the HTML and Web page design simultaneously.

More About

Dynamic Web Templates

Dynamic Web templates include enough power and functionality to replace several other FrontPage features. Dynamic Web templates can be used in place of themes, shared borders, and static templates. In general, dynamic Web templates do a better job than these other features and offer both more flexibility and more control.

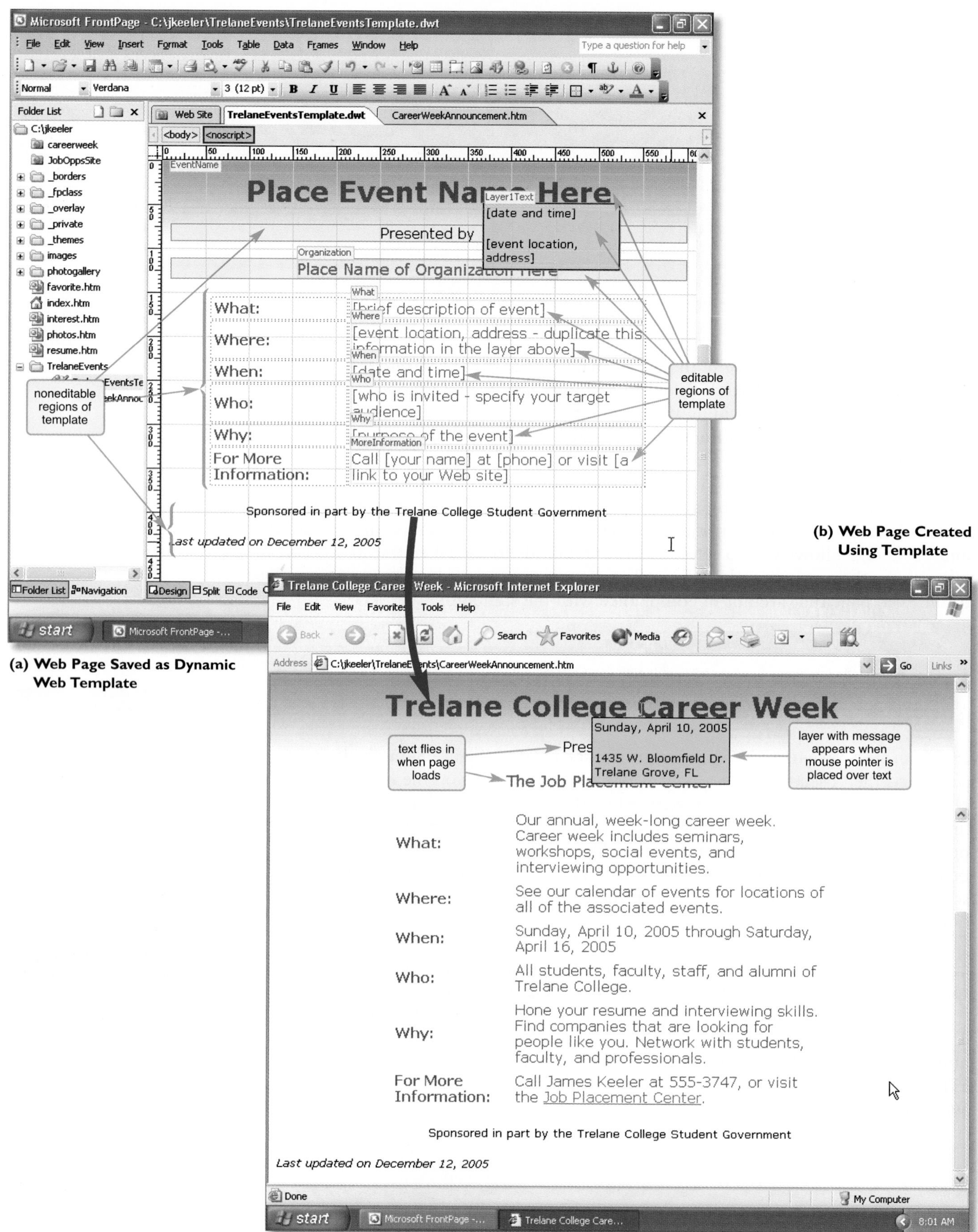

(a) Web Page Saved as Dynamic Web Template

(b) Web Page Created Using Template

FIGURE 8-1

Designing the Dynamic Web Template

A dynamic Web page template is designed in much the same manner as a standard FrontPage template. Two features set apart the dynamic Web template from a standard template. First, a dynamic Web template includes some areas that are not editable by the user of the template. Second, when a dynamic Web page is changed, the changes can be propagated automatically to any Web pages that use the template.

Figure 8-2 shows the design for the Trelane Events template desired by the student government. Two lines of the Web page heading fly in from the left and right sides of the page when the page loads in the browser. Regions that should be editable are marked with notes on the side of the design. The remaining areas of the Web page should not be editable by a user of the template.

> **Design Tip**
> When designing a template, mark those regions of the template that will be editable by the user of the template. Be sure to point out special effects and behaviors.

> *More About*
> **Obtaining Dynamic Web Templates**
> Several companies and Web sites offer pre-built dynamic Web templates for FrontPage. If you need a professional Web site design in a hurry, consider purchasing a dynamic Web template or searching the World Wide Web for free templates.

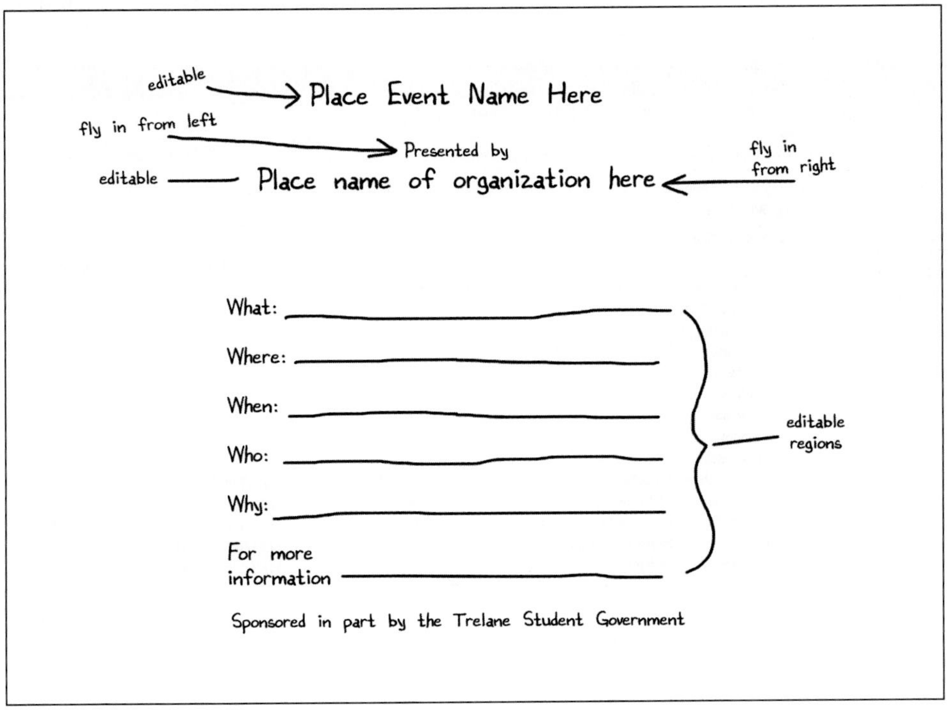

FIGURE 8-2

Using the Rulers and Grid to Lay Out a Web Page

When designing a Web page, you sometimes need to align or place content precisely on the page. FrontPage allows you to display rulers along the sides of the Web page Design view so that you can lay out content precisely. **Rulers** are displayed across the top and left sides of the Web page in Design view and include numbers that designate pixels, inches, centimeters, or points. By default, rulers measure distances in pixels. **Grid lines** also can be displayed on the Web pages at specified intervals. By default, grid lines are displayed both horizontally and vertically every 50 pixels.

> *More About*
> **The Rulers and the Grid**
> The rulers and the grid cannot be displayed when editing a frames page. If you have the rulers or the grid set to display, they will not appear when you edit a frames page. If you require them to lay out the page, edit each individual page within each frame separately in Design view.

Before displaying the rulers and grid, FrontPage must be running. The following steps start FrontPage and then open the FrontPage Web site from Project 7. If you did not complete Project 7, see your instructor for a copy of the Web site.

To Start FrontPage and Open an Existing Web Site

1. **Click the Start button on the taskbar. Point to All Programs on the Start menu.**
2. **Point to Microsoft Office on the Programs submenu.**
3. **Click Microsoft Office FrontPage 2003 on the Microsoft Office submenu.**
4. **Click the Open button arrow on the Standard toolbar.**
5. **Click Open Site on the Open menu. When FrontPage displays the Open Web dialog box, if necessary, click the Look in box arrow and select the folder location where you stored the Web site for Project 7 (e.g., C:\jkeeler).**
6. **Click the Open button in the Open Web Site dialog box.**

The previously created FrontPage Web site is loaded and is displayed in Folders view (Figure 8-3).

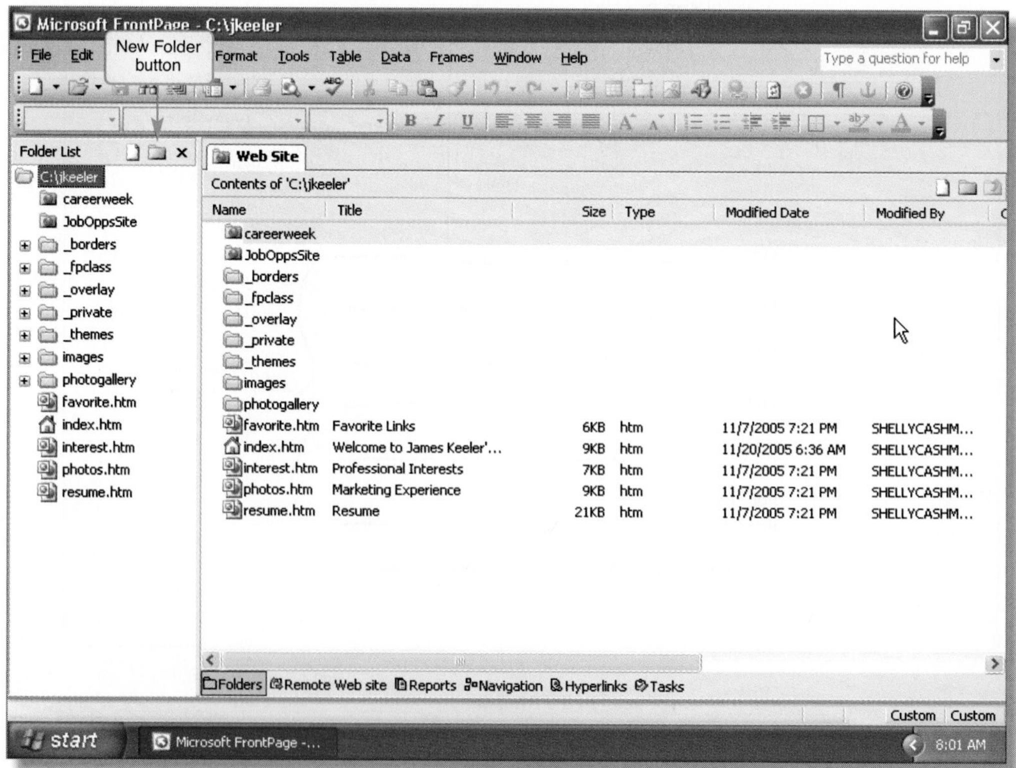

FIGURE 8-3

Displaying the Rulers and Grid

The dynamic Web template will be created in a new folder in James Keeler's Web site. To create a dynamic Web template, you can first design the template by creating and laying out a new Web page. The following steps add a new folder and a new Web page to the new folder and then display the default ruler and grid.

To Display the Ruler and Grid in a New Web Page

1

- **Click the New Folder button at the top of the Folder List pane.**
- **When the new folder appears in the Folder List, type** `TrelaneEvents` **as the new name for the folder and then press the ENTER key.**

FrontPage adds the new folder named TrelaneEvents to the Web site (Figure 8-4).

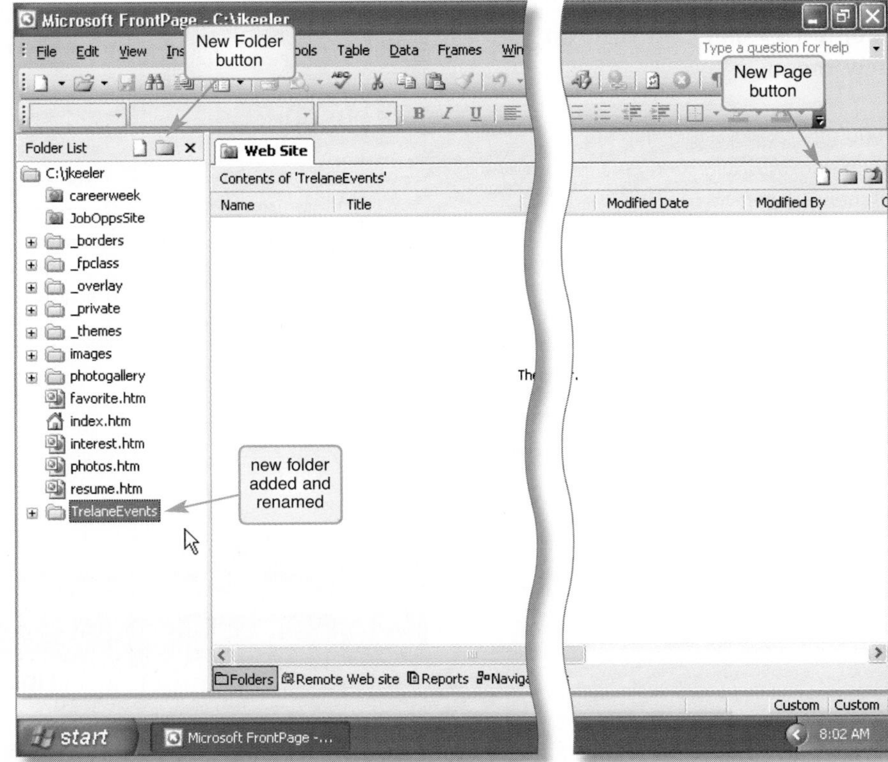

FIGURE 8-4

2

- **Click the New Page button at the top of the Web Site pane.**
- **When FrontPage adds the new page, type** `TrelaneEventsTemplate.htm` **as the page name and press the ENTER key.**
- **Double-click the Web page TrelaneEventsTempate.htm in the Folder List pane.**

FrontPage displays the Microsoft Office FrontPage dialog box indicating that the Web page must be checked out (Figure 8-5).

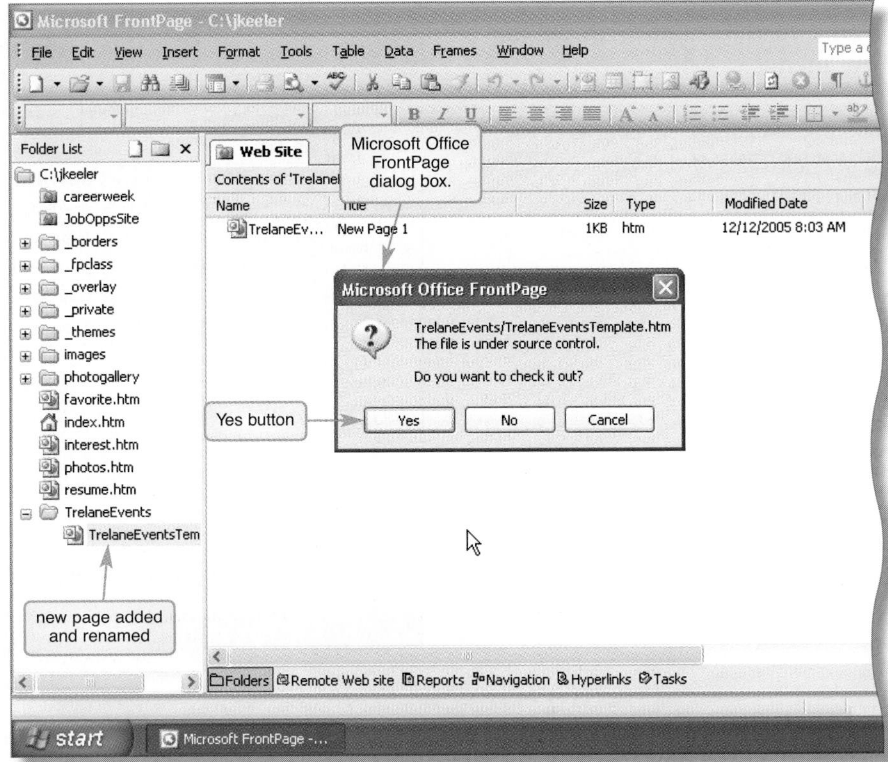

FIGURE 8-5

3

- **Click the Yes button.**
- **Click View on the menu bar.**
- **Point to Ruler and Grid on the View menu.**

FrontPage displays the View menu and the Ruler and Grid submenu (Figure 8-6).

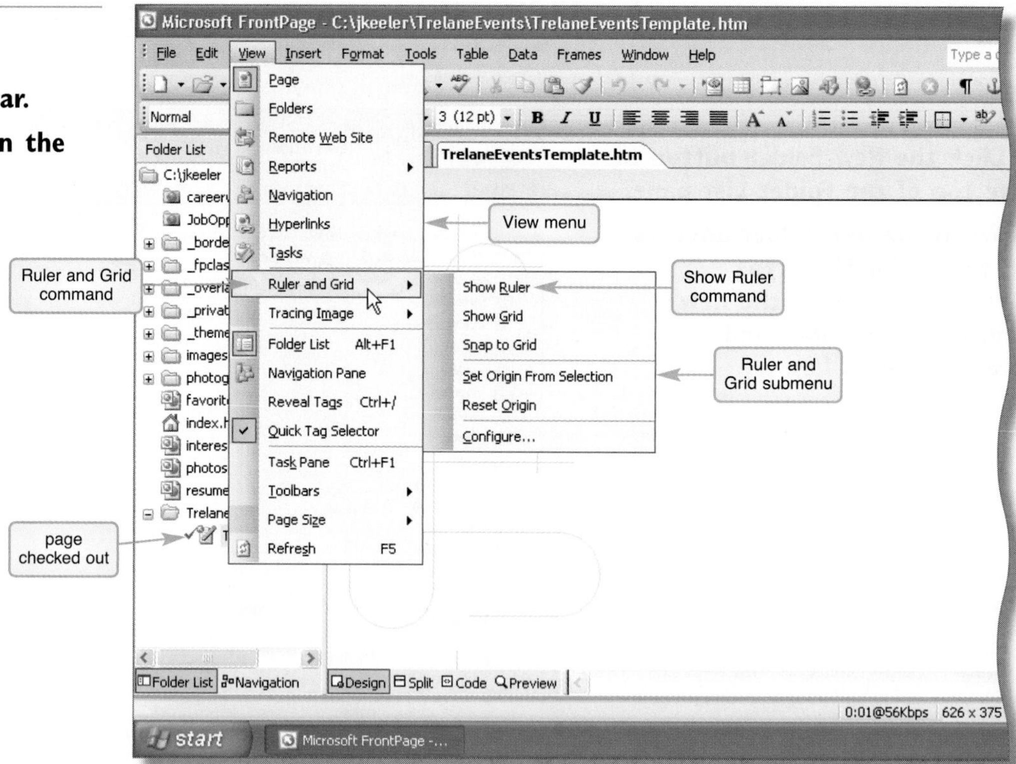

FIGURE 8-6

4

- **Click Show Ruler.**
- **Click View on the menu bar.**
- **Point to Ruler and Grid on the View menu.**

FrontPage displays rulers on the top and left sides of the Web page (Figure 8-7).

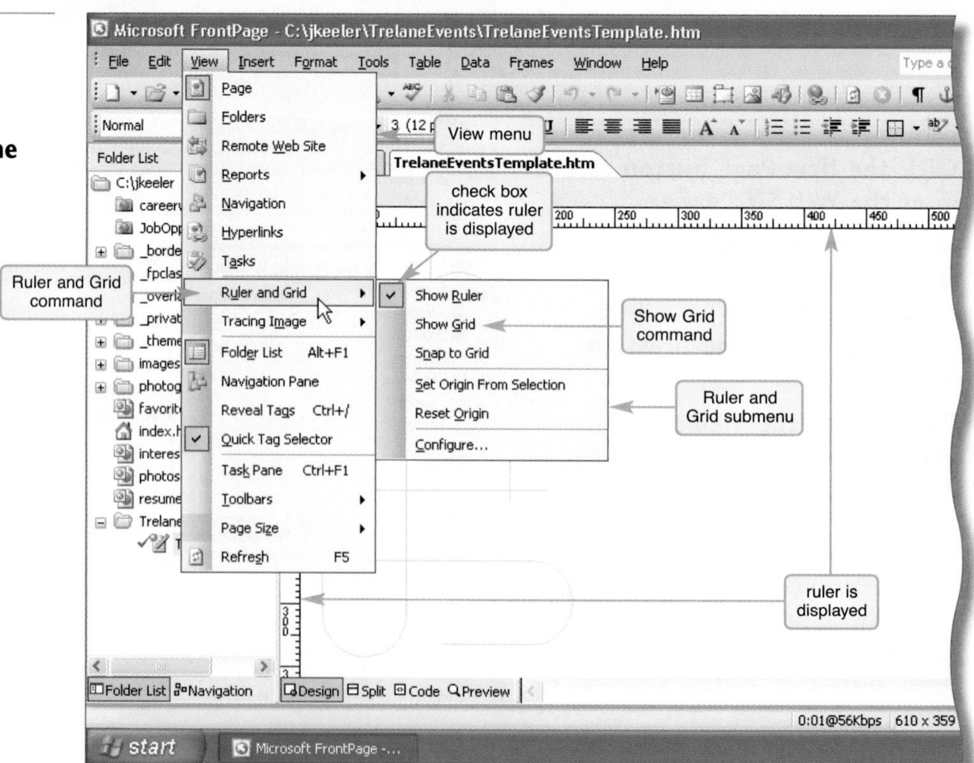

FIGURE 8-7

5

- **Click Show Grid.**

FrontPage displays a grid that can be used to lay out elements of the Web page. By default, the grid lines are displayed every 50 pixels (Figure 8-8).

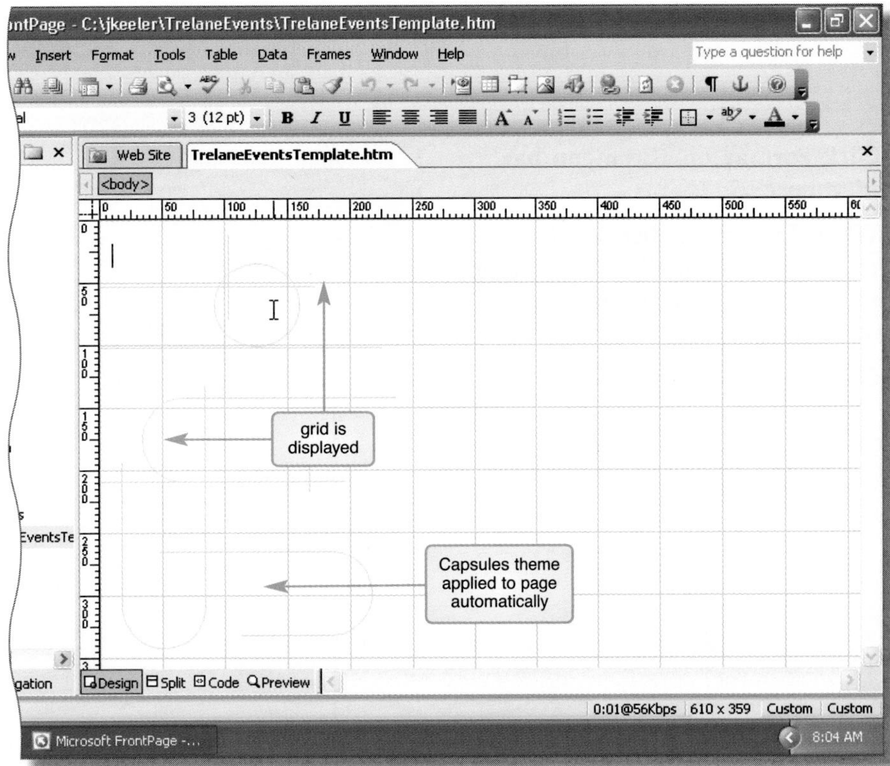

FIGURE 8-8

Properties of the rulers and grid can be modified in the Ruler and Grid sheet in the Page Options dialog box. The Configure command on the Ruler and Grid submenu (Figure 8-7) displays the Ruler and Grid sheet in the Page Options dialog box so that you can configure the ruler and grid. You can make the grid spacing larger or smaller depending on your needs. You also can change the appearance of the lines. For example, you can use a different line color or line style.

If the Snap to Grid command on the Ruler and Grid submenu is checked, then any content that is added to the page automatically is snapped to the nearest grid line. This allows you to line up content on a Web page very precisely.

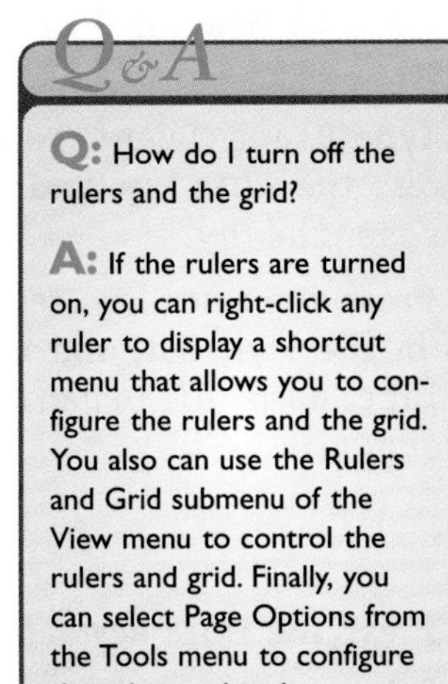
Q&A

Q: How do I turn off the rulers and the grid?

A: If the rulers are turned on, you can right-click any ruler to display a shortcut menu that allows you to configure the rulers and the grid. You also can use the Rulers and Grid submenu of the View menu to control the rulers and grid. Finally, you can select Page Options from the Tools menu to configure the rulers and grid.

Use rulers and grid lines when you need to lay out elements of a Web page very precisely. They are particularly useful when designing Web pages that include a fixed-width layout of the page.

Creating a Web Page Using the Ruler and Grid

The Web page requires a new theme, three lines of heading, a 6 by 2 table that will contain the event information, and text at the bottom of the page that indicates the date the page was last updated.

The steps on the next page lay out the Web page that will become the dynamic Web template.

To Create a Web Page Using the Ruler and Grid

1

- **Click Format on the menu bar and then click Theme.**
- **When FrontPage displays the Theme task pane, click Vivid colors and then scroll to the Iris theme in the Select a theme list.**
- **Click the Iris theme.**

FrontPage applies the Iris theme to the Web page (Figure 8-9).

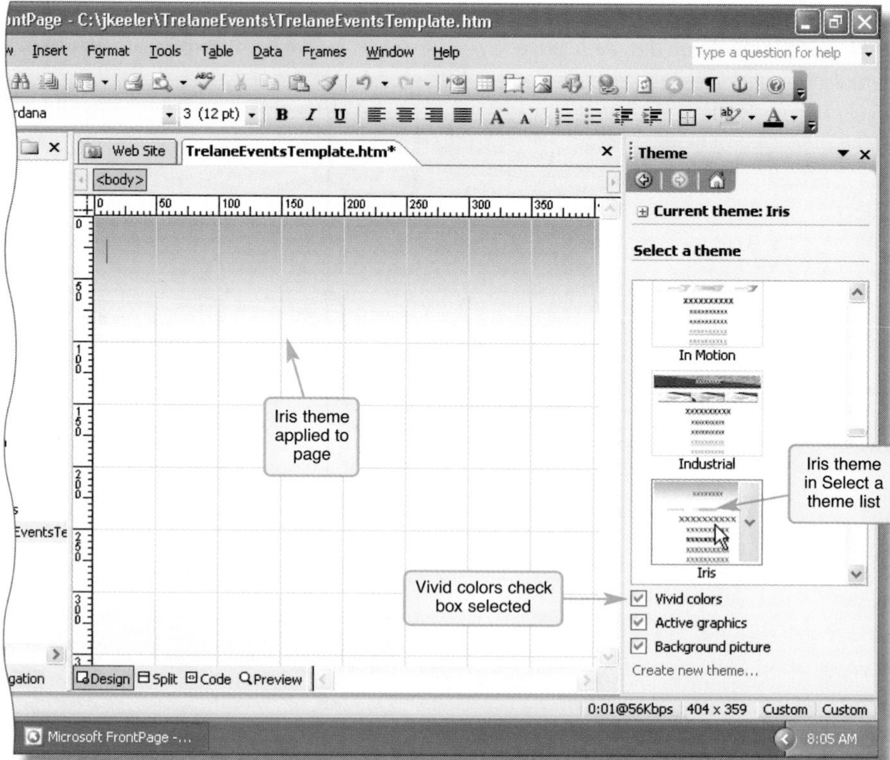

FIGURE 8-9

2

- **Click the Close button in the Theme task pane.**
- **Click the Center button on the Formatting toolbar.**
- **Click the Style box arrow and then click Heading 1 in the Style list.**
- **Type** `Place Event Name Here`, **press the ENTER key, and then type** `Presented by`.
- **Press the ENTER key, select Heading 3 in the Style list, and then type** `Place Name of Organization Here`.

3

- **Press the ENTER key.**
- **Select the text, Place Name of Organization Here, click the Font Color box arrow on the Formatting toolbar, and then click purple in the Theme Colors area ({99,00,FF} hex value).**

Three lines of heading are displayed on the Web page (Figure 8-10).

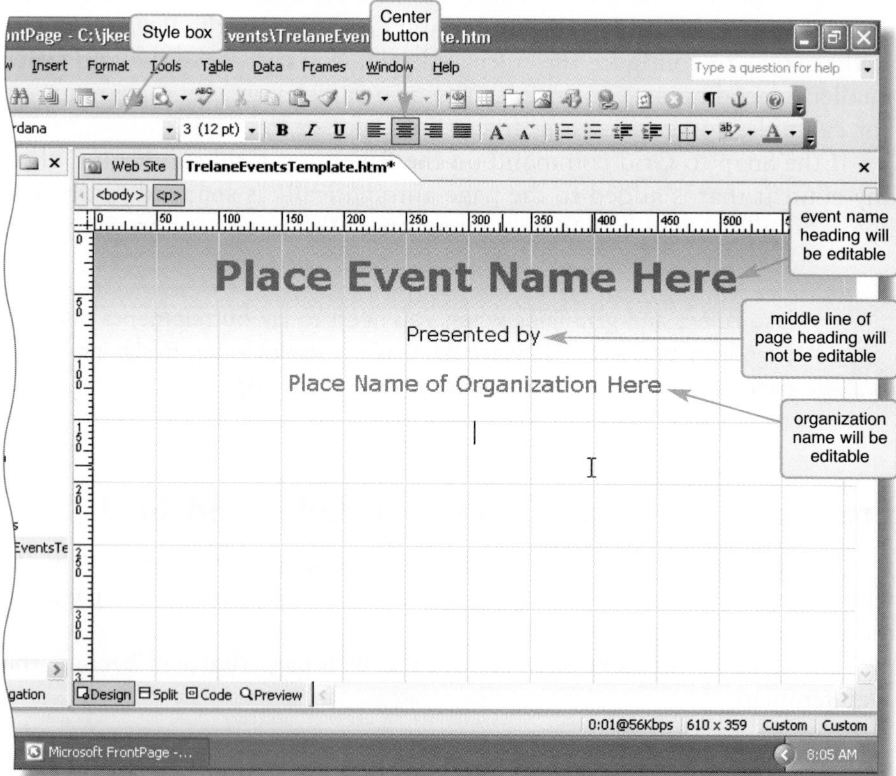

FIGURE 8-10

4

- **Press the DOWN ARROW key.**
- **Click the Insert Table button on the Standard toolbar and insert a 6 by 2 table.**
- **Type the content of the table using the text shown in Table 8-1 on the next page.**
- **Select the content in the first column of the table and then click the Bold button on the Formatting toolbar.**

5

- **Right-click anywhere in the table and then click Table Properties on the shortcut menu.**
- **Set the Alignment to Center, Cell padding to 4, Cell spacing to 1, and border size to 0.**
- **Click In pixels below Specify width in the Layout area and then type** `500` **in the Specify width text box.**
- **Click the OK button.**

FrontPage displays the table with the added content. The borders will not be displayed to a Web page visitor (Figure 8-11).

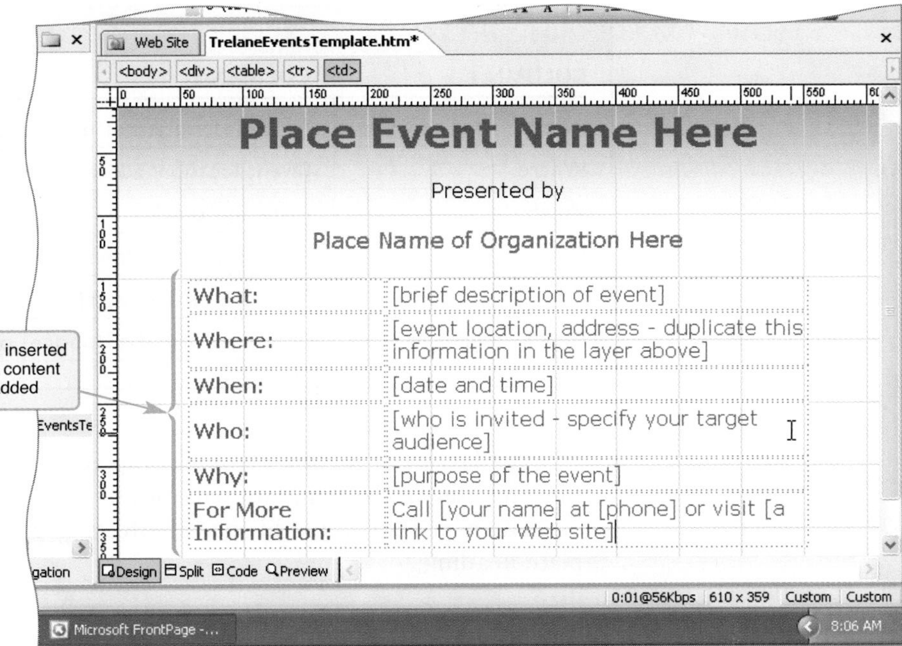

FIGURE 8-11

6

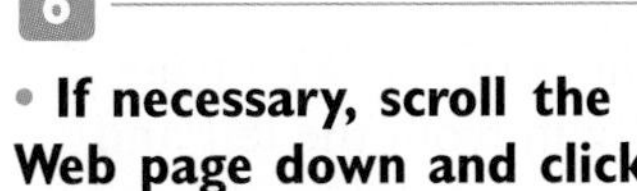

- **If necessary, scroll the Web page down and click below the table.**
- **Click the Font Size box arrow on the Formatting toolbar and then click 2 (10 pt) in the Font Size list.**
- **Click the Italics button on the Formatting toolbar.**
- **Type** `Last Updated on.`

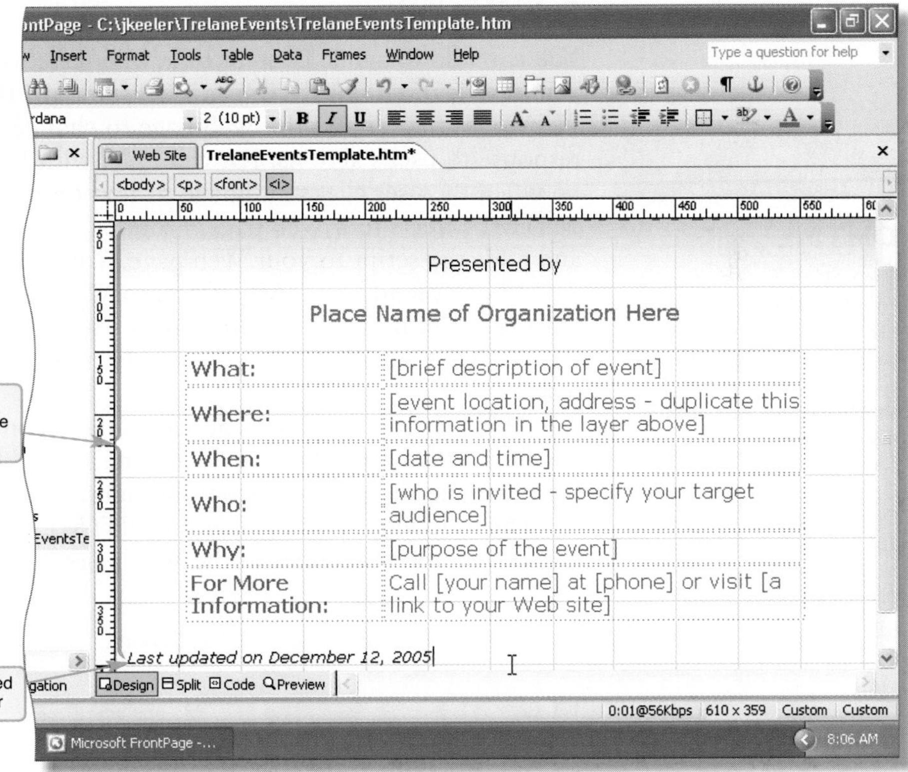

FIGURE 8-12

7

- **Click Insert on the menu bar and then click Date and Time.**
- **Select the third date format in the Date format list to display the date in the format December 12, 2005.**
- **Click the OK button.**

FrontPage displays completed content for the template Web page (Figure 8-12).

Table 8-1 Content for Table

COLUMN 1	COLUMN 2
What:	[brief description of the event]
Where:	[event location, address - duplicate this information in the layer above]
When:	[date and time]
Who:	[who is invited - specify your target audience]
Why:	[purpose of the event]
For More Information:	Call [your name] at [phone] or visit [a link to your Web site]

The layout of the template is complete. Much of the content is placeholder text that the user of the template will modify.

The next step is to add special effects to the second and third lines of the template heading.

Adding Dynamic HTML Effects to Web Page Elements

You can add dynamic content to a Web page using the DHTML Effects toolbar. As you have learned, DHTML is a Web standard that allows you to add script to your Web pages that allows the Web page to change and update itself dynamically in response to user's actions. For example, with DHTML, you can cause a menu to pop up when the user clicks an image or text on the Web page. By default, when you add DHTML effects to a Web page, FrontPage writes script using the JavaScript language and adds the script to your Web page. You can view the script in Code view.

When you add DHTML effects to Web page elements, you specify the event that must occur in order to start the effect. Next, you specify the action, or effect, that should take place. You also can specify more detail about the effect that should take place.

DHTML effects must be added to the second and third lines of the Web page heading. When the Web page loads, the second line should fly in from the left and the third line should fly in from the right.

The following steps display the DHTML Effects toolbar and then add effects to the second and third lines of the Web page heading.

More About

DHTML

The DHTML code that FrontPage adds to your Web site includes a great deal of JavaScript code. The code may appear complex and you should not attempt to edit the code manually unless you have a good understanding of DHTML. To learn more about DHTML, visit the FrontPage 2003 More About Web page (scsite.com/fp2003/more) and then click DHTML.

To Display the DHTML Effects Toolbar and Add Dynamic HTML Effects

1

- **Right-click any toolbar.**
- **Click DHTML Effects on the shortcut menu.**

FrontPage displays the DHTML Effects toolbar (Figure 8-13).

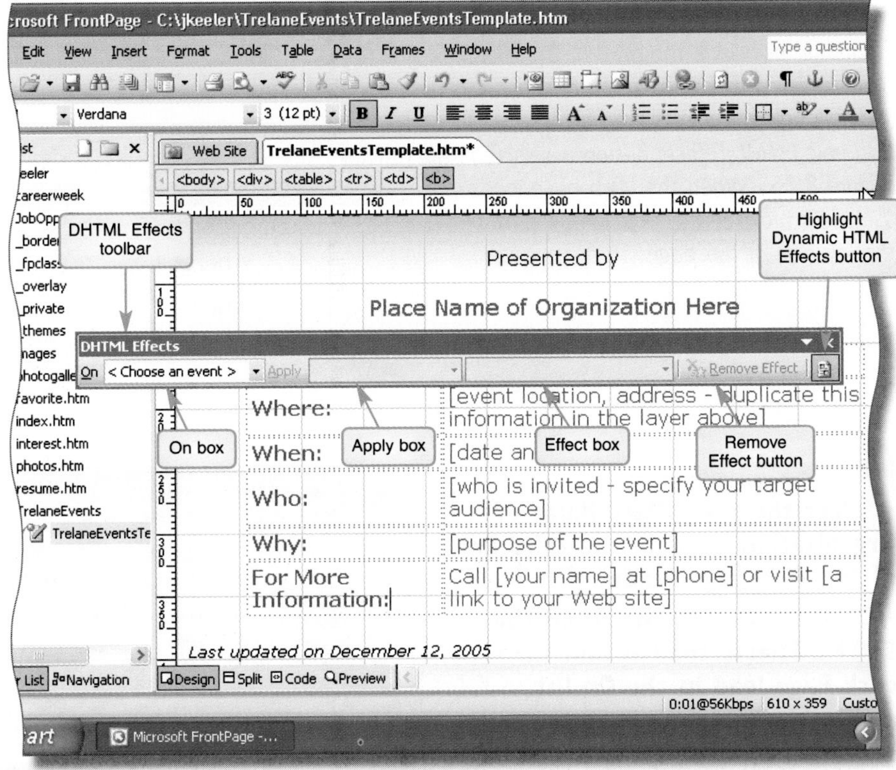

FIGURE 8-13

2

- **Select the text, Presented by, in the second line of the Web page header.**
- **Click the On box arrow on the DHTML Effects toolbar and then click Page load in the On list.**
- **Click the Apply box arrow.**

The text to which the effect will be applied is selected. FrontPage displays the Apply list (Figure 8-14).

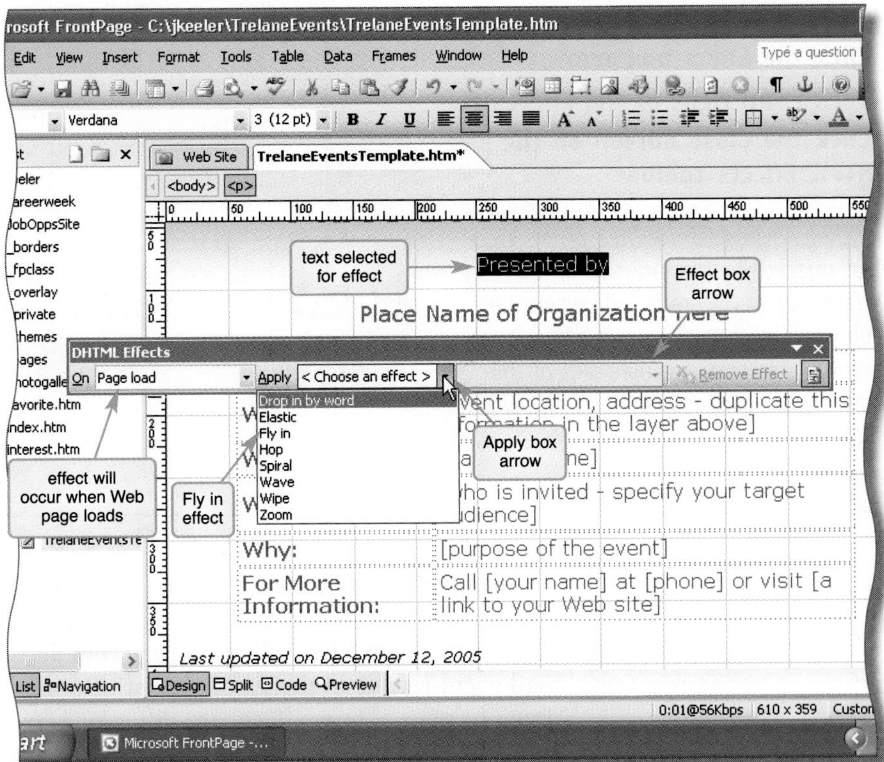

FIGURE 8-14

3

- **Click Fly in in the Apply list.**
- **Click the Effect box arrow.**
- **Click From left in the Effect list.**

FrontPage highlights the area of the Web page affected by the inclusion of the DHTML effect because the Highlight Dynamic HTML Effects button is selected (Figure 8-15). When the Web page loads in the user's browser, the text will fly in from the left side of the page.

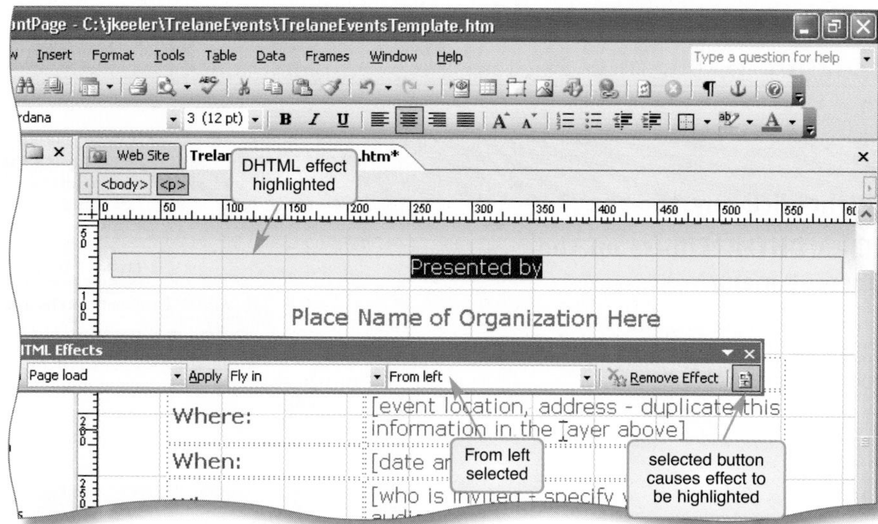

FIGURE 8-15

4

- **Select the text, Place Name of Organization Here, in the third line of the Web page header.**
- **Click the On box arrow on the DHTML Effects toolbar and then click Page load in the On list.**
- **Click the Apply box arrow.**

5

- **Click Fly in in the Apply list.**
- **Click the Effect box arrow.**
- **Click From right in the Effect list.**
- **Click the Close button on the DHTML Effects toolbar.**

FrontPage highlights the area of the Web page affected by the inclusion of the DHTML effect (Figure 8-16). When the Web page loads in the user's browser, the text will fly in from the right side of the page. FrontPage closes the DHTML Effects toolbar.

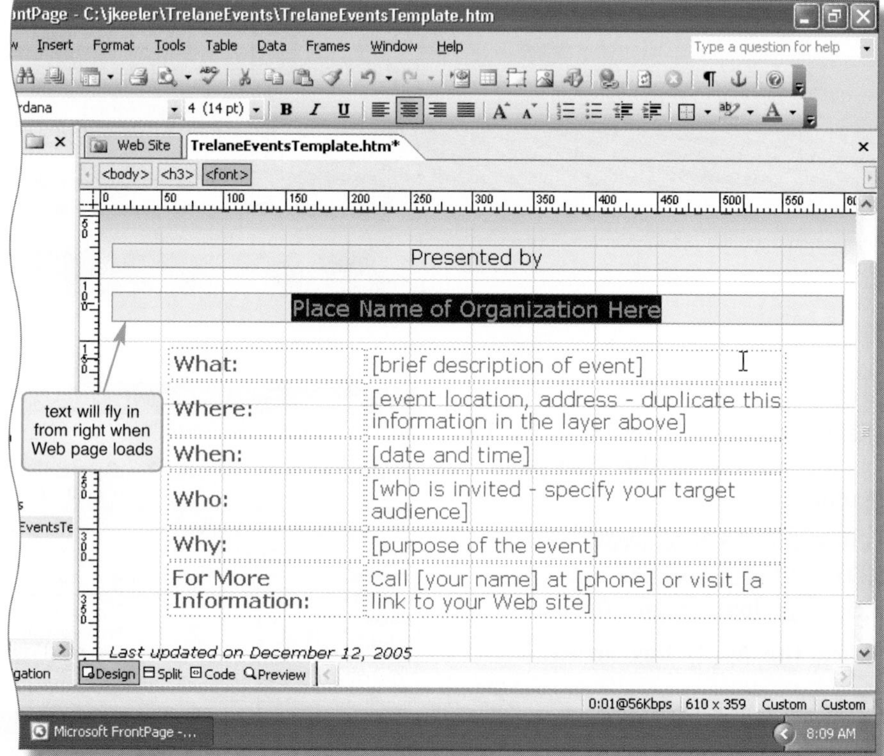

FIGURE 8-16

Other Ways

1. Press ALT+V, T, select DHTML Effects
2. In Voice Command mode, say "View, Toolbars, DHTML Effects"

The On list includes the events for which you can create an effect. These include Click, Double-click, Mouse over, and Page load. The effects listed in the Apply list box are different, depending on the event chosen. For example, selecting the Page load event results in the Apply in list offering the choices shown in Figure 8-14 on the previous page. These effects are different ways in which text or other elements can enter the Web page when the page loads in the user's browser. Similarly, the Effects list box includes different effects, depending on the choice made in the Apply list.

As shown in Figure 8-15, FrontPage places a border and shading around elements that have effects applied to them. To remove the border and shading, click the Highlight Dynamic HTML Effects button on the DHTML Effects toolbar. If you want to remove an effect, click the Remove Effect button on the DHTML Effects toolbar.

More About

DHTML Menus

DHTML commonly is used to create pop-up and drop-down menus on Web pages. Using DHTML, you can create customized menus with a unique look and dynamic content. To learn more about creating DHTML menus, visit the FrontPage 2003 More About Web page (scsite.com/fp2003/more) and then click DHTML Menus.

Design Tip

FrontPage includes the ability to add many types of DHTML effects. Become familiar with the effects in the DHTML Effects toolbar by experimenting with the toolbar. Incorporate effects into your Web page designs by specifying events and actions as notes in your design.

Using Layers and Behaviors in a Web Page

Layers are a type of HTML tag that can overlay a portion of a Web page or another layer and can be made to be either visible or invisible. Layers commonly are used for pop-up menus, pop-up messages, and other special effects. Layers often are used in conjunction with DHTML because DHTML can control the appearance and visibility of a layer. For example, when a user clicks a main menu item, a submenu contained in a layer can be displayed using DHTML. The layer can include hyperlinks that act as commands in the submenu.

Layers can include other layers or any other type of content that a typical Web page can include. You also can control the appearance of a layer, such as positioning, borders, and shading. When combined with behaviors, or DHTML effects, such properties of a layer can be altered dynamically as the user interacts with the Web page.

More About

Positioning of Layers

Absolutely positioned layers are positioned based on the top-left corner of the Web page. Relatively positioned layers are positioned relative to some element on the Web page. You typically should use absolutely positioned content on more complicated Web pages in order to minimize problems involving the browser attempting to reposition content for you. To learn more about the positioning of layers, visit the FrontPage 2003 More About Web page (scsite.com/fp2003/more) and then click Positioning of Layers.

Design Tip

Use layers sparingly in Web page design. Be sure to test pages that include layers in all browsers that your users may use. Also, test layers in a variety of browser window sizes and screen resolutions. Layers may look fine in Design mode on one browser but appear completely different using another browser.

FrontPage's behaviors provide a method to add complex DHTML code to your Web pages without writing programming code. Behaviors allow you to add dynamic effects and interactions to a Web page by using a task pane to assign events and actions to Web page elements. Adding behaviors to elements of a Web page result in DHTML code being added to the Web page.

Adding a Layer to a Web Page

The Trelane events template requires that a pop-up window display a summary of event information when the user moves the mouse pointer over the event name in the heading. A layer will be added to the Web page that includes the summary. Later in this project, the properties of the layer will be modified to change the position, background color, and border for the layer. Behaviors will be added to the elements of the Web page to control when the layer becomes visible or invisible.

The following steps add a layer to the Web page.

To Add a Layer to a Web Page

1

- **If necessary, scroll the Web page so that the first line of the heading is displayed.**
- **Click Format on the menu bar.**

FrontPage displays the Format menu (Figure 8-17).

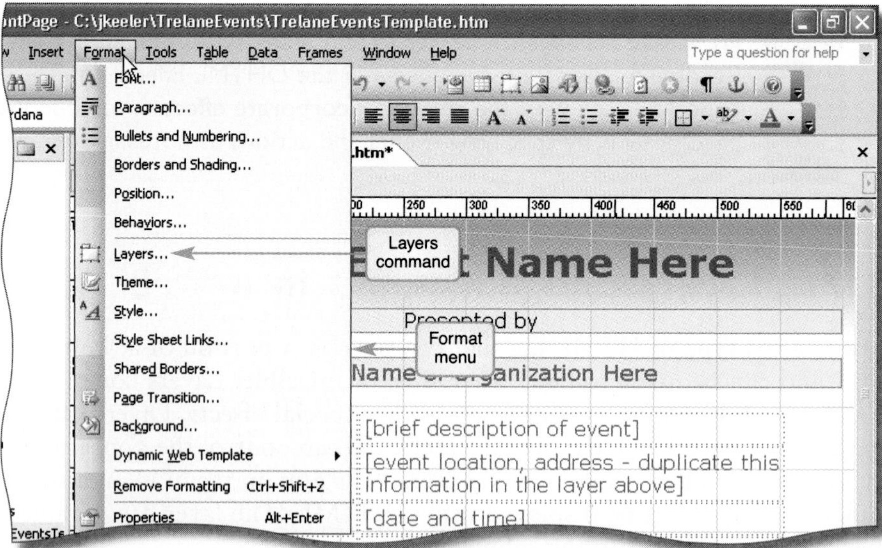

FIGURE 8-17

2

- **Click Layers.**
- **Click after the word, Here, in the first line of the heading.**

FrontPage displays the Layers task pane (Figure 8-18).

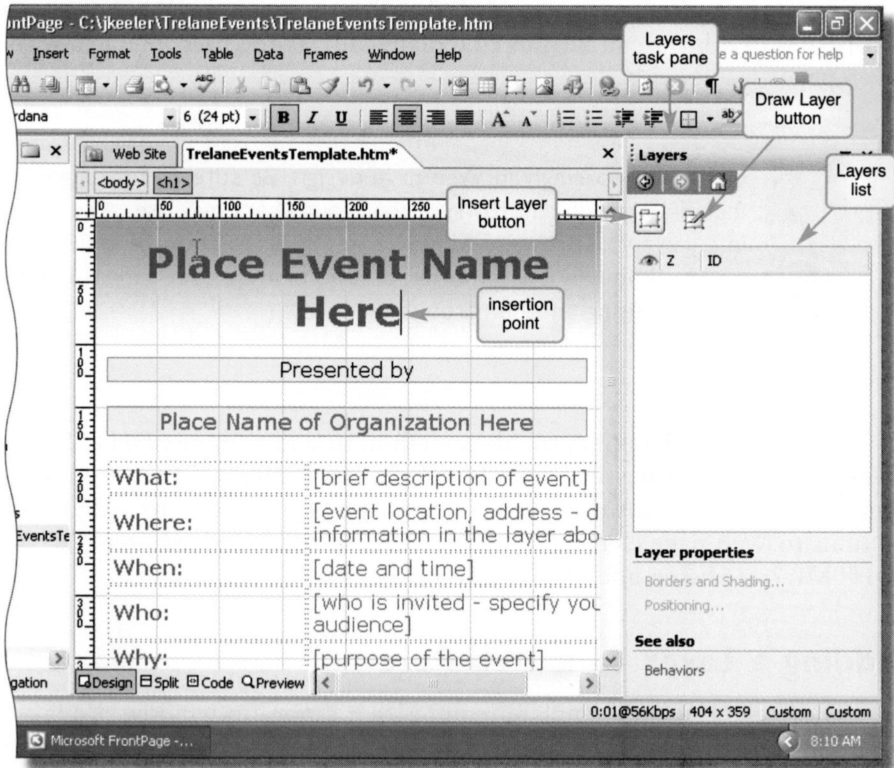

FIGURE 8-18

3

• **Click the Insert Layer button in the Layers task pane.**

FrontPage adds a layer to the Web page and adds the layer to the Layers list in the Layers task pane (Figure 8-19). The layer includes a label and an outline that designates the borders of the layer.

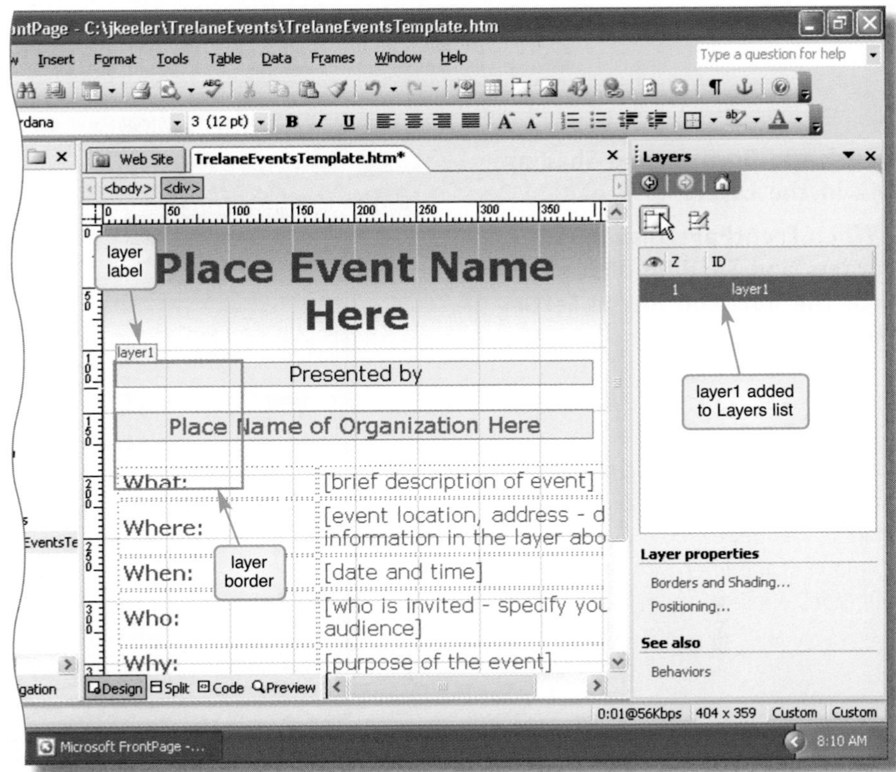

FIGURE 8-19

Other Ways

1. On menu bar click Insert, click Layer
2. Press ALT+I, Y
3. In Voice Command mode, say "Insert, Layer"

While the Layer command on the Insert menu quickly inserts a layer, using the Layers task pane provides the ability quickly to view and manage all of the layers on the Web page. The layer floats above other Web page content as shown in Figure 8-19. Content, such as text, images, tables, and other layers, can be placed in the layer by first selecting the layer and then adding the content. The label at the top of the layer does not appear when the layer is viewed in a browser or when it is not selected in Design view.

The Layers task pane (Figure 8-19) includes the Layers list that lists all of the layers on the current Web page. The first column is the Layer Visibility column and indicates whether the layer is visible when the Web page first loads in the browser. You change the visibility by selecting the layer in the Layers list and then clicking in the first column next to the layer. The eye icon in the column header can be clicked to change simultaneously the visibility of all layers. The Z column is a numeric value that indicates the z-order of the layer. The **z-order** indicates the visual layering of the layers on the browser in terms of depth. A higher z-order indicates that the layer is on top of layers with lower z-order values.

Setting the Properties of a Layer

As you have learned, layers include many of the same properties of other Web page elements, such as tables. These properties include the background color, foreground color, border style, and visibility. Links in the Layers task pane provide quick access to these property values.

The layer1 layer requires a yellow background color and a border. The layer also must be positioned and resized. The steps on the next page set the properties of the layer1 layer.

To Set the Properties of a Layer

1

- **Click the Borders and Shading link in the Layers task pane.**
- **When FrontPage displays the Borders and Shading dialog box, click the Box icon in the Setting area.**

The Borders and Shading dialog box is displayed. The Box setting causes a visible border to appear around the layer when the Web page is displayed in a browser. The Preview area displays a representation of the layer with the selected properties applied (Figure 8-20).

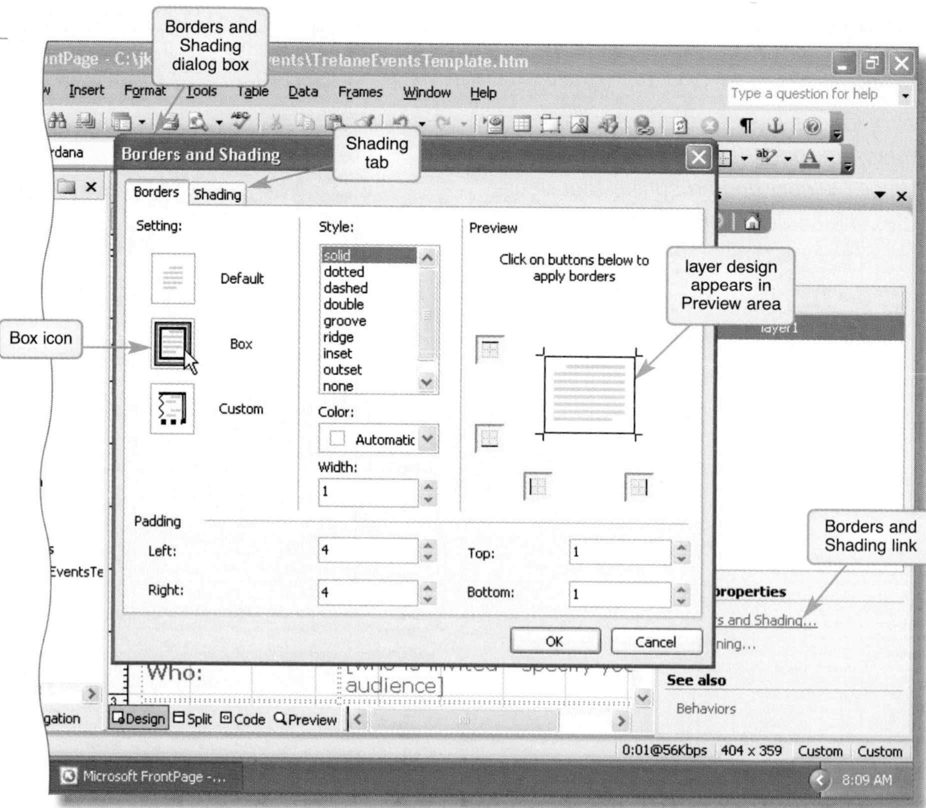

FIGURE 8-20

2

- **Click the Shading tab.**
- **Click the Background color box arrow.**

FrontPage displays the Shading sheet where the background color, foreground color, and background image can be selected (Figure 8-21).

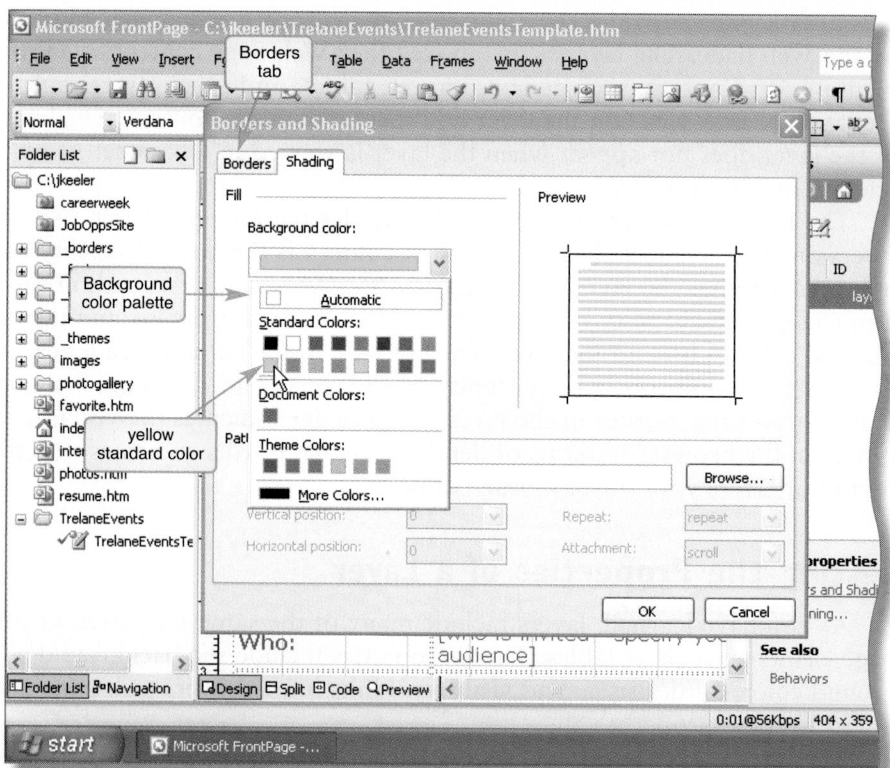

FIGURE 8-21

3

- **Click the yellow color in the Standard Colors area and then click the Borders tab.**
- **When the Borders sheet is displayed, change the Left, Right, Top, and Bottom padding values to 2.**

FrontPage displays the Borders sheet. The Preview area displays a preview of the layer with a yellow background and a border (Figure 8-22).

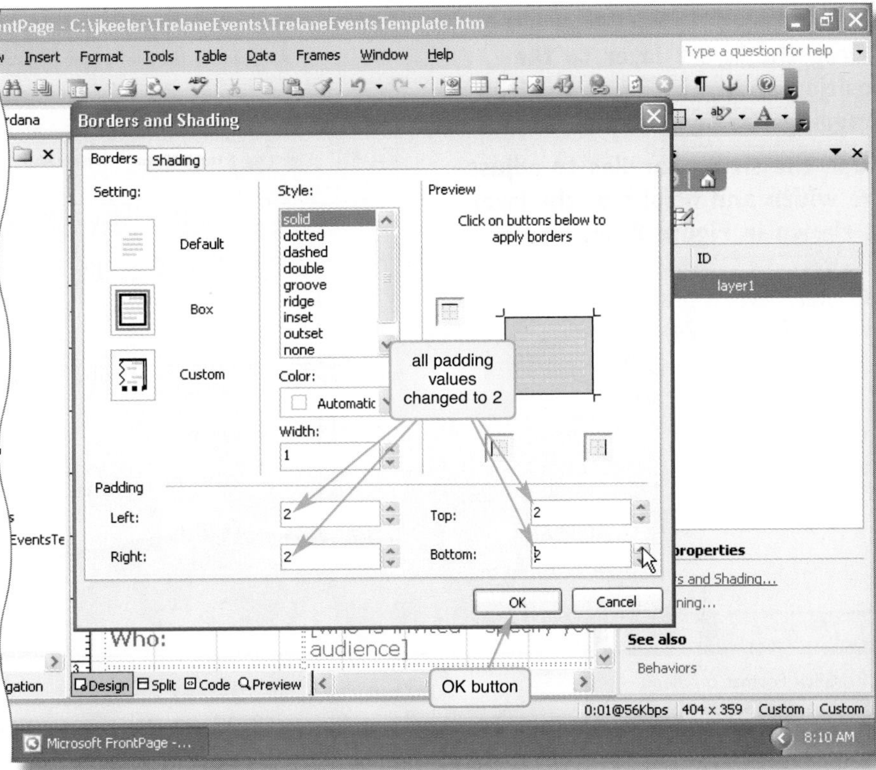

FIGURE 8-22

4

- **Click the OK button.**
- **Click the Close button on the Layers task pane.**

FrontPage closes the Layers task pane and displays the layer1 layer with a yellow background and a border (Figure 8-23).

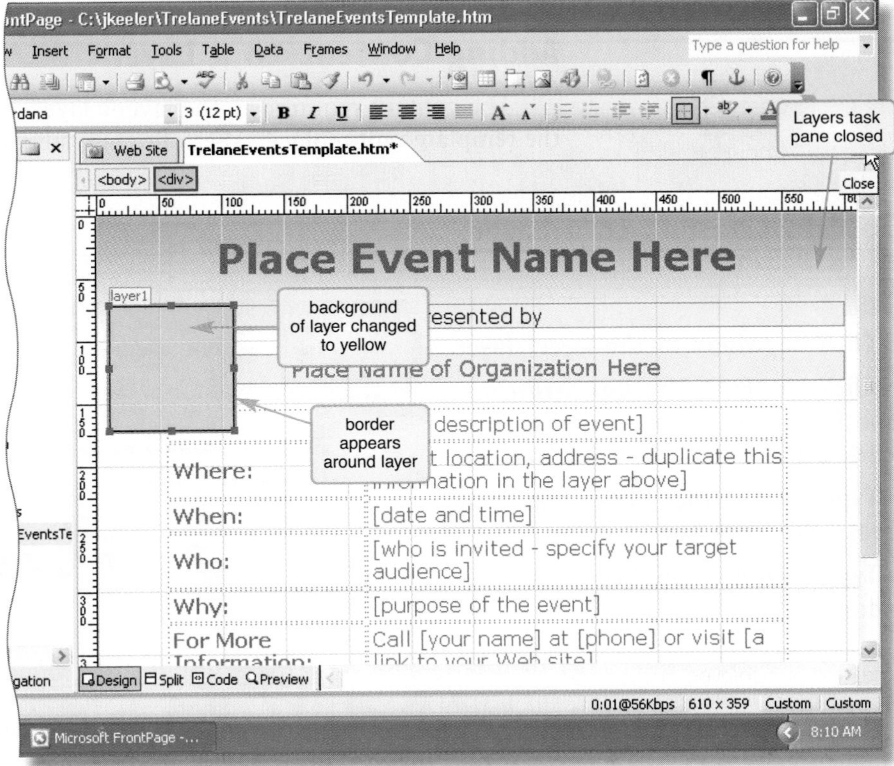

FIGURE 8-23

5

• **Drag the layer1 layer to the position shown in Figure 8-24 by dragging the layer's label.**

• **Use the sizing handles to adjust the width and height of the layer as shown in Figure 8-24.**

The layer1 layer is positioned and sized correctly (Figure 8-24).

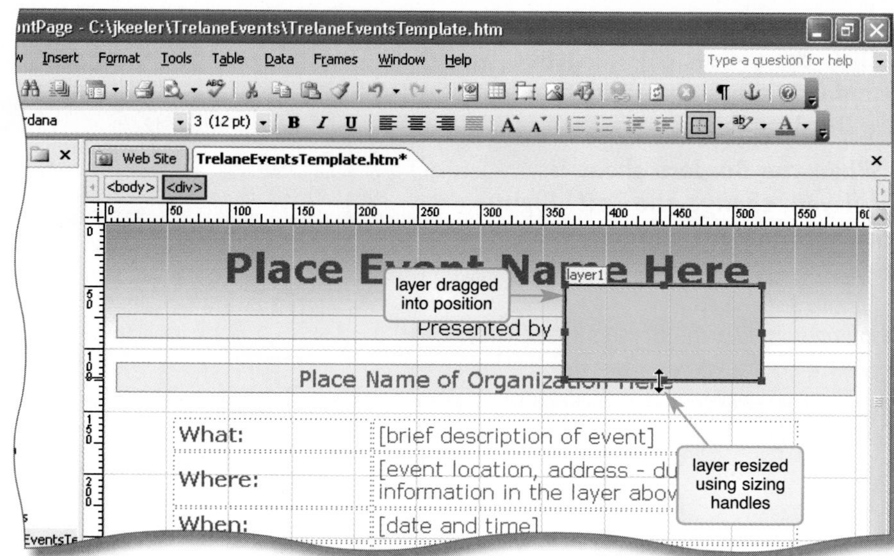

FIGURE 8-24

Other Ways

1. Click Format on menu bar, click Borders and Shading
2. Press ALT+O, B
3. In Voice Command mode, say "Format, Borders and Shading"

As shown in Figure 8-22 on the previous page, padding is added to the layer so that the text in the layer does not touch the border. You may choose to set padding to 0 if the layer contained an image or content that does not require a border. With the properties of the layer set, the next step is to add the text content to the layer.

Adding Content to a Layer

The content required in the layer1 layer includes placeholder text that the user of the template will replace. The following step adds text to the layer1 layer.

To Add Content to a Layer

1

• **Click anywhere in the layer1 layer.**

• **Click the Font Size box arrow on the Formatting toolbar and then click 2 (10 pt) in the Font Size list.**

• **Type** `[date and time]` **and then press the ENTER key.**

• **Type** `[event location, address]`**.**

The text is displayed in the layer (Figure 8-25).

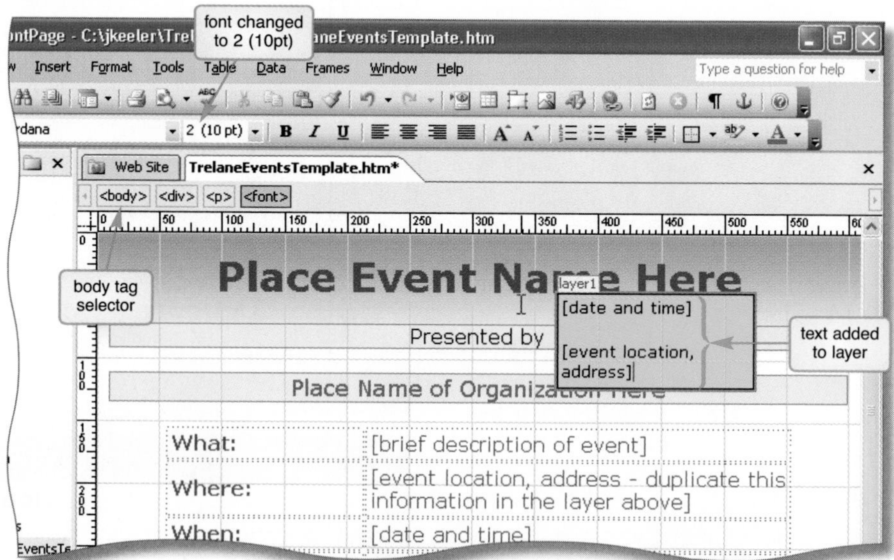

FIGURE 8-25

The new text appears in the layer. The text added in the layer can be formatted in the same manner as text on a Web page. The text will be replaced by the Web page developer who uses the dynamic Web template to create his or her own page. The next step is to hide the layer and the text when the Web page first loads.

Adding Behaviors to a Web Page

When a Web page created with the Trelane events template first loads, the layer1 layer should be hidden. The layer1 layer should appear only when the user moves the mouse pointer over the first line of the Web page heading. A behavior must be added to the Web page that causes the layer1 layer to be hidden when the Web page first loads. Before adding a behavior, the element associated with the behavior first must be selected. In this case, the behavior is associated with the entire Web page. The <body> quick tag selector can be clicked to select the entire Web page. Once the <body> tag is selected, a behavior can be added to the onload event of the Web page. When the page loads, the visibility property of the layer1 layer should be set to the value of hidden.

Events are the result of some action taken by the user. For example, when a Web page loads in a browser, the page's onload event occurs. Any actions associated with that event then execute. Other events include clicking or double-clicking a Web page element, moving the mouse pointer on or off elements, or pressing a key on the keyboard while an element is selected on the Web page.

The following steps set the layer1 visibility property to hidden when the Web page loads.

To Add Behaviors to a Web Page

1

- **Click the <body> tag selector above the Web page.**
- **Click Format on the menu bar.**

The Web page is selected, and FrontPage displays the Format menu (Figure 8-26).

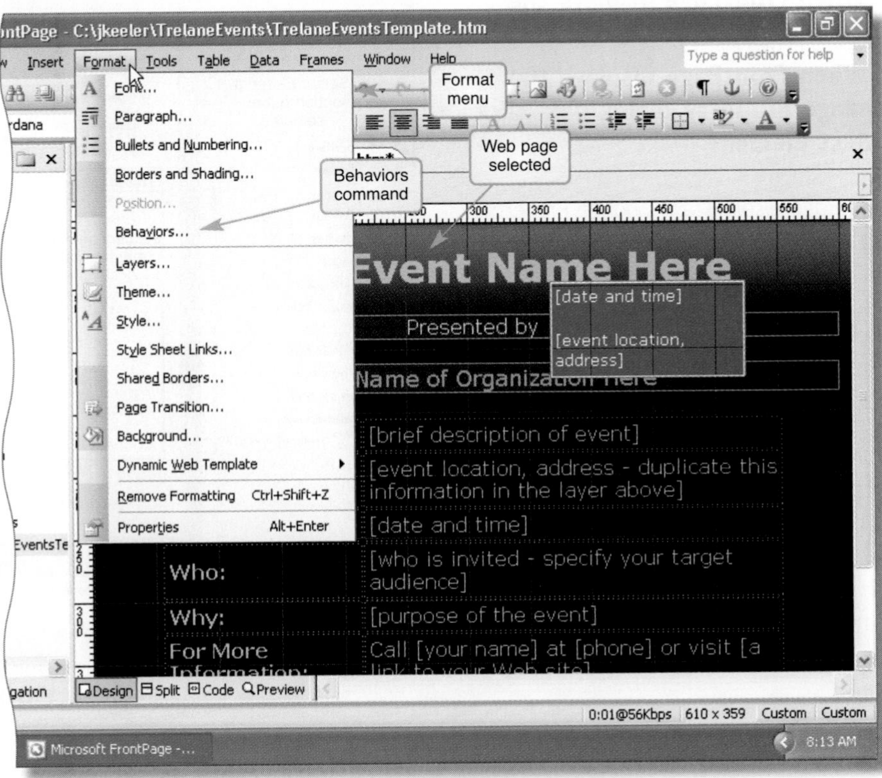

FIGURE 8-26

2

- **Click Behaviors.**

FrontPage displays the Behaviors task pane (Figure 8-27).

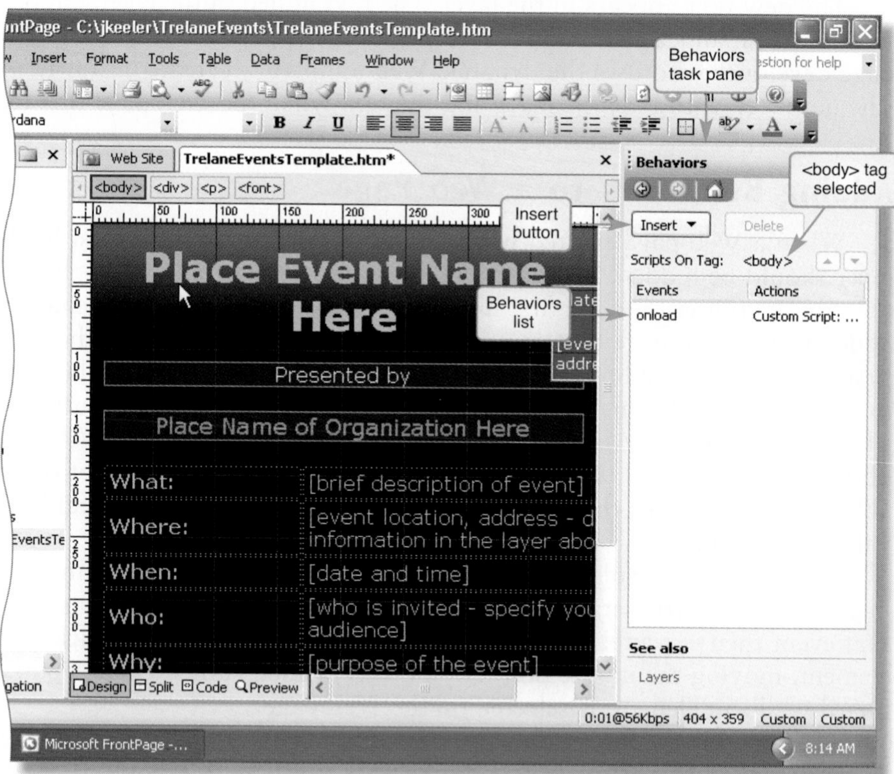

FIGURE 8-27

3

- **Click the Insert button.**
- **When FrontPage displays the Insert menu, click Change Property.**
- **When FrontPage displays the Change Property dialog box, click Select Element.**

FrontPage displays the Change Property dialog box. When Select Element is selected, the layer1 layer automatically is selected in the Element ID box (Figure 8-28).

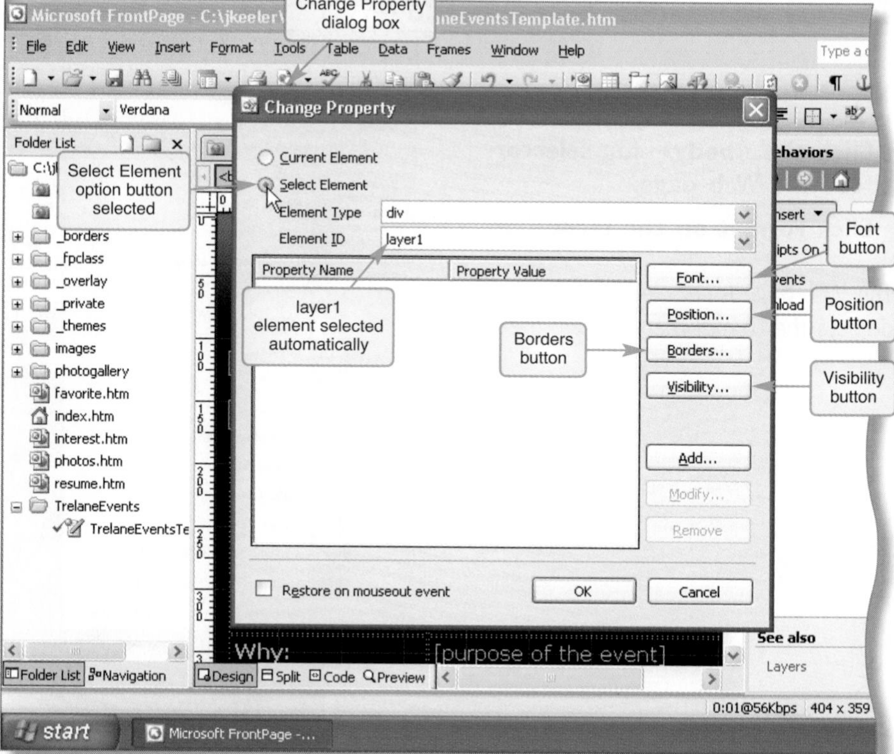

FIGURE 8-28

4

- **Click the Visibility button.**
- **When FrontPage displays the Visibility dialog box, click Hidden.**

FrontPage displays the Visibility dialog box. The layer1 layer will be hidden when the Web page loads in a browser because Hidden is selected (Figure 8-29).

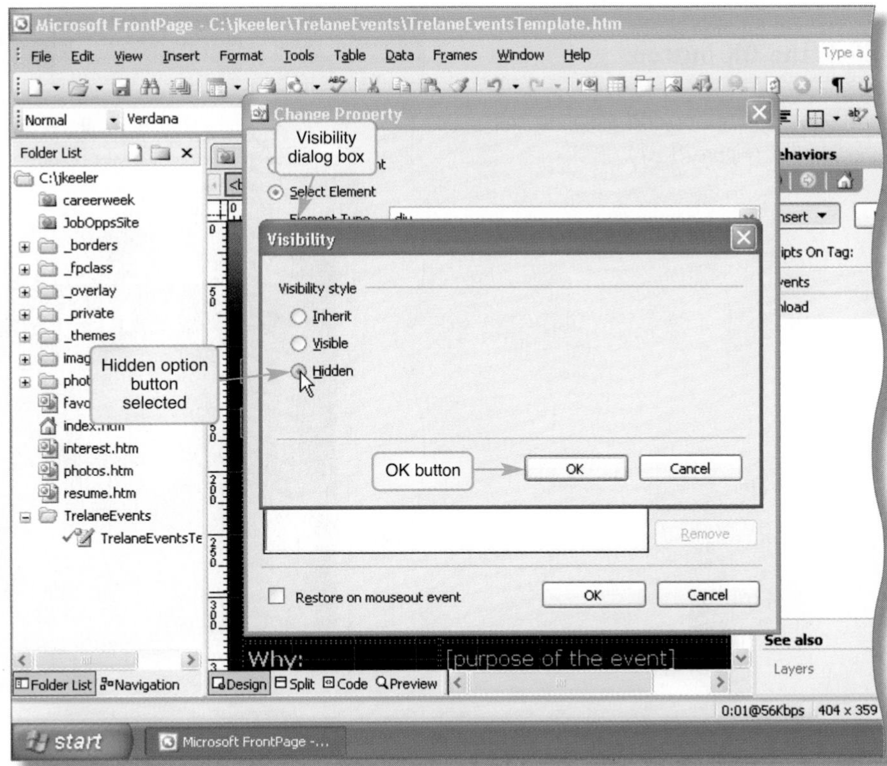

FIGURE 8-29

5

- **Click the OK button.**

FrontPage adds the visibility property and value to the Property list (Figure 8-30).

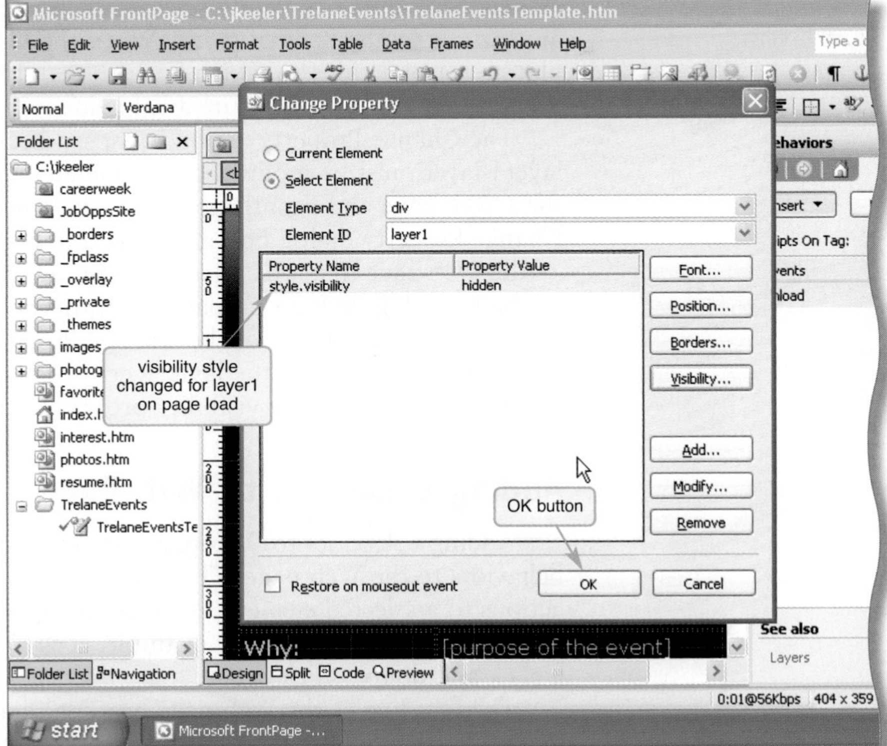

FIGURE 8-30

6

• **Click the OK button.**

FrontPage adds the onload event to the Behaviors list (Figure 8-31).

FIGURE 8-31

Other Ways

1. Click page, click Behaviors link in Layers task pane
2. Press ALT+O, V
3. In Voice Command mode, say "Format, Behaviors"

The Behaviors list in the Behaviors task pane lists those behaviors that are associated with the currently selected Web page element. The selected element's tag appears above the Behaviors list. When the Insert button is clicked, FrontPage displays a list of actions to which an event can be associated. The combination of an event and an action constitute a behavior.

The Change Property action is chosen because the visibility property of the layer1 layer must be modified. The onload event of the Web page is the default event for a Web page and FrontPage inserts the onload event in the Behaviors list. The Change Property dialog box allows you to change a property of the current element — the Web page that was selected — or another event. The layer1 element is selected as shown in Figure 8-28 on page FP 560. The Font, Position, Borders, and Visibility buttons on the right side of the Change Property dialog box indicate the properties that can be changed for the layer when the Web page loads. The only property requiring a change is the visibility property.

Adding Behaviors to Web Page Elements

Adding behaviors to Web page elements requires the same process as adding behaviors to the Web page. The Behaviors task pane is used to add events and actions to a selected element. Multiple actions can be associated with Web pages and elements on a Web page. For example, separate actions can be associated with both a click and double-click event.

The first line of the Web page heading requires actions to be taken when the user moves the mouse pointer either on or off the heading. The text, therefore, requires two behaviors to be added. The actions required include setting the visibility property to visible when the mouse pointer is over the text, and then setting the visibility property to hidden when the mouse pointer no longer is over the text. The following steps add two actions to the first line of the Web page heading.

To Add Behaviors to a Web Page Element

1

- **Select the text in the first line of the Web page heading.**
- **Click the Insert button in the Behaviors task pane.**
- **Click Change Property on the Insert menu.**
- **When the Change Property dialog box is displayed, click Select Element.**
- **Click the Visibility button.**
- **When FrontPage displays the Visibility dialog box, click Visible.**

FrontPage displays the Change Property dialog box and the Visibility dialog box. The Visibility style is set to Visible when the mouse pointer moves over the first line of the Web page heading (Figure 8-32).

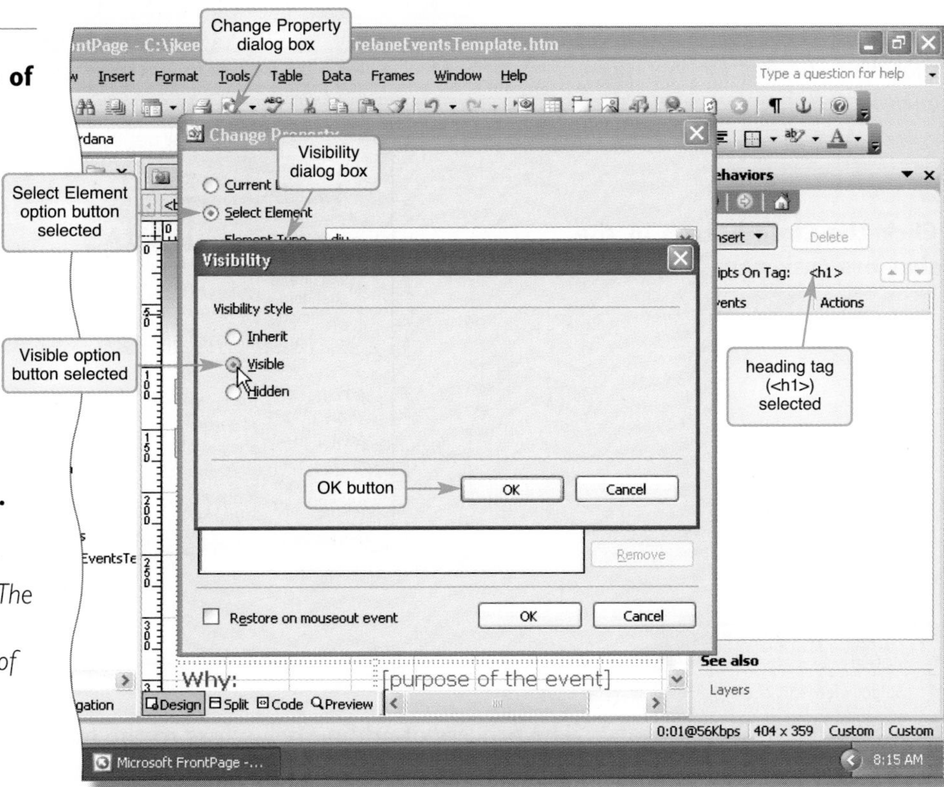

FIGURE 8-32

2

- **Click the OK button.**
- **Click Restore on mouseout event.**

FrontPage adds the visibility style to the Property list. The Restore on mouseout event check box is selected so that the visibility property is set back to the value of hidden when the mouse pointer no longer is over the first line of the Web page heading (Figure 8-33).

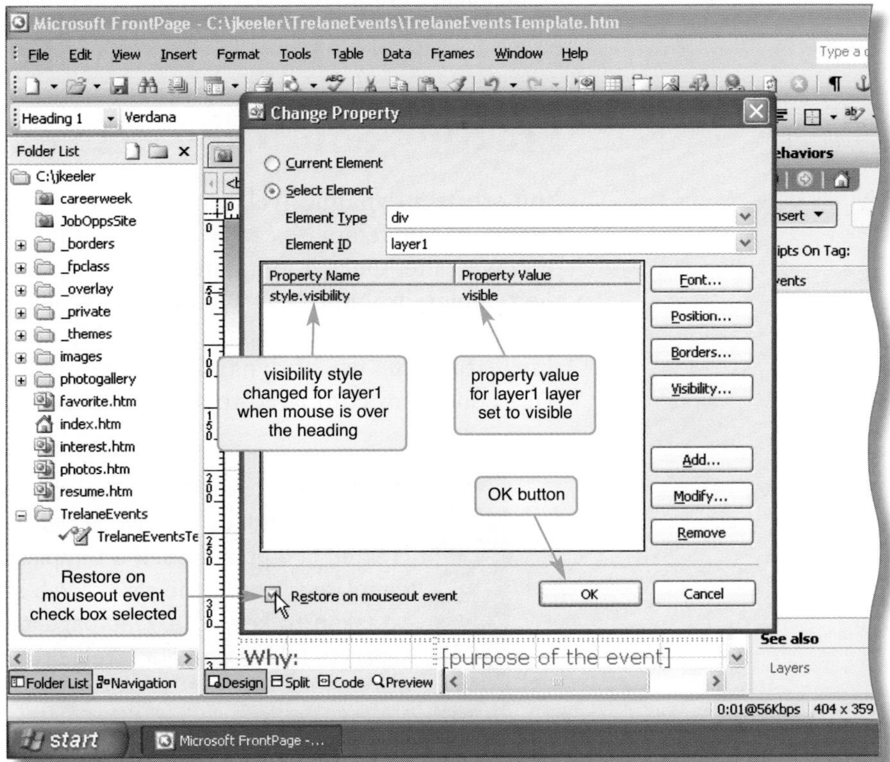

FIGURE 8-33

3

• **Click the OK button.**

FrontPage adds two events to the Behaviors list for the first line of the Web page heading (Figure 8-34).

4

• **Click the Close button in the Behaviors task pane.**

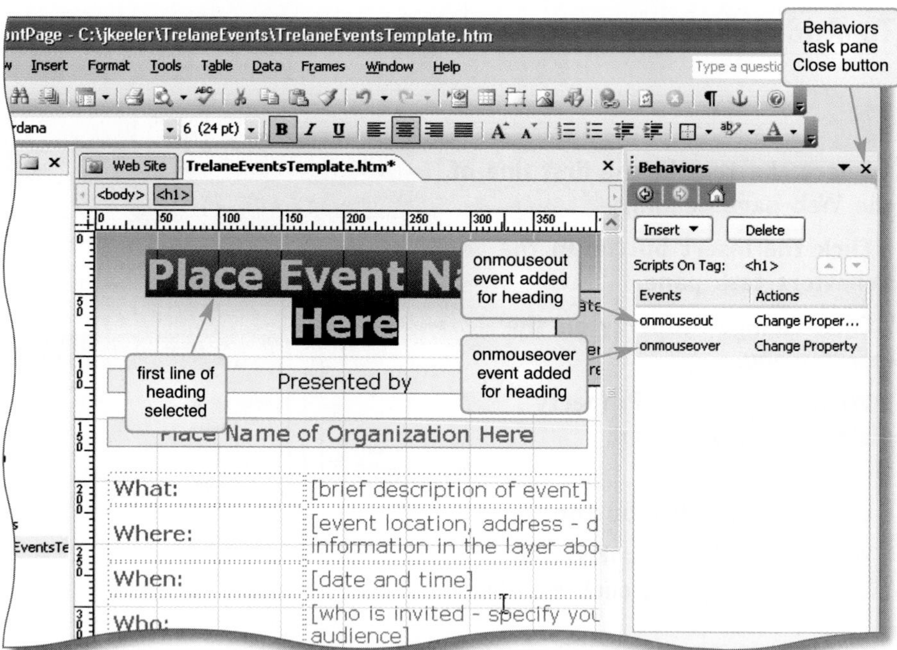

FIGURE 8-34

Other Ways

1. Select element, click Behaviors on Format menu
2. Press ALT+O, V
3. In Voice Command mode, say "Format, Behaviors"

The process of adding behaviors to the heading mimics that of adding behaviors to the Web page. As shown in Figure 8-33 on the previous page, the Restore on mouseout event check box allows you automatically to add two behaviors at once. By selecting the check box, FrontPage restores the visibility property of the layer1 layer back to hidden after the mouse pointer moves off the heading. Figure 8-34 shows the two events in the Behaviors list.

Creating and Using a Dynamic Web Template

You create a dynamic Web template by saving a Web page as a dynamic Web template. The template can be saved within a Web site, or as a separate file outside of a Web site. Once a template is created, anyone with access to the template can use the template to build new Web pages. When you change a dynamic Web template, you automatically can update any Web pages created using the template. Because of this feature, the use of dynamic Web templates is a better solution to common Web page content as compared to shared borders.

Design Tip

Make certain that Web pages that are created using a dynamic Web template continue to have access to the template after the page is created and published. If a template is attached to a Web page and the template is not in the same Web site as the Web page, then care must be taken to keep the Web page and template in sync. Consider using a separate folder on your Web site to contain all the templates you may use.

When you create a dynamic Web template, you indicate which area of the Web page can be changed by the person using the template. A region of the Web page that can be modified by a user of the template is called an **editable region**. A region of the Web page that cannot be modified by a user of the template is called a **noneditable region**. When you change a template and then request FrontPage to update all pages created with the template, FrontPage will not change the editable content of the Web pages, because doing so would destroy the content added by the user of the template.

Saving a Web Page as a Dynamic Web Template

Any Web page can be saved as a dynamic Web template by using the Save As command on the File menu. Once the file is saved as a dynamic Web template, the file extension is changed from htm to dwt. The dwt extension stands for dynamic Web template. The following steps save the Web page as a dynamic Web template.

To Save a Web Page as a Dynamic Web Template

1

- **Click File on the menu bar and then click Save As.**

FrontPage displays the Save As dialog box (Figure 8-35).

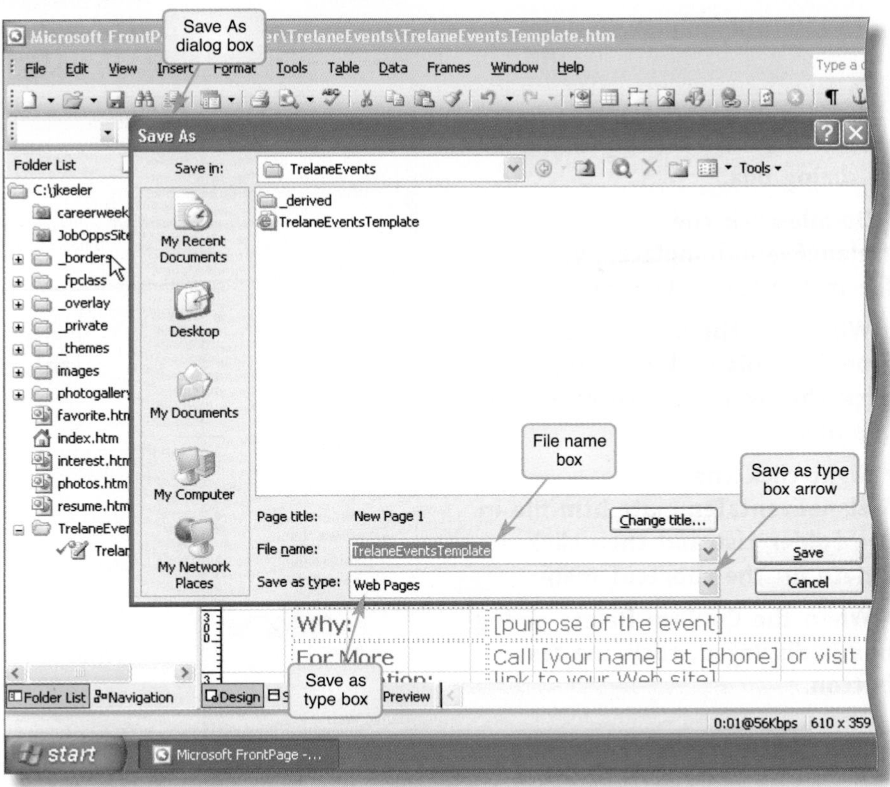

FIGURE 8-35

2

- **Click the Save as type box arrow.**
- **Click Dynamic Web Template in the Save as type list.**

FrontPage changes the Save as type to Dynamic Web Template (Figure 8-36).

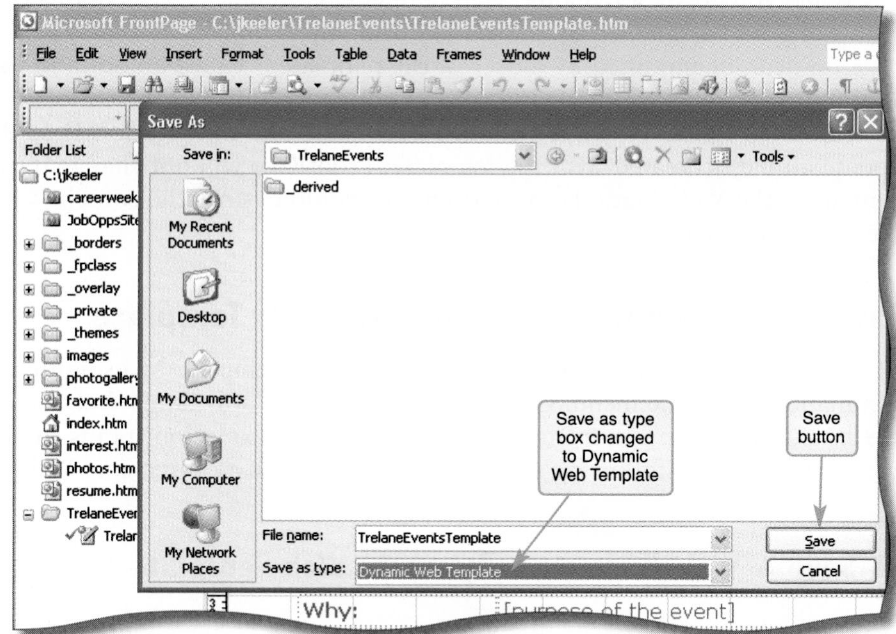

FIGURE 8-36

3

- **Click the Save button in the Save As dialog box.**
- **Double-click the TrelaneEventsTemplate.dwt file in the Folder List pane.**
- **When the Microsoft Office FrontPage dialog box is displayed, click the Yes button to check out the file.**
- **Right-click the TrelaneEventsTemplate.htm file in the Folder List and then click Delete on the shortcut menu.**
- **When the Confirm Delete dialog box is displayed, click the Yes button.**

FrontPage saves the Web page as a dynamic Web template (Figure 8-37). The template is checked out, and the Web page version of the file is removed from the Folder List pane.

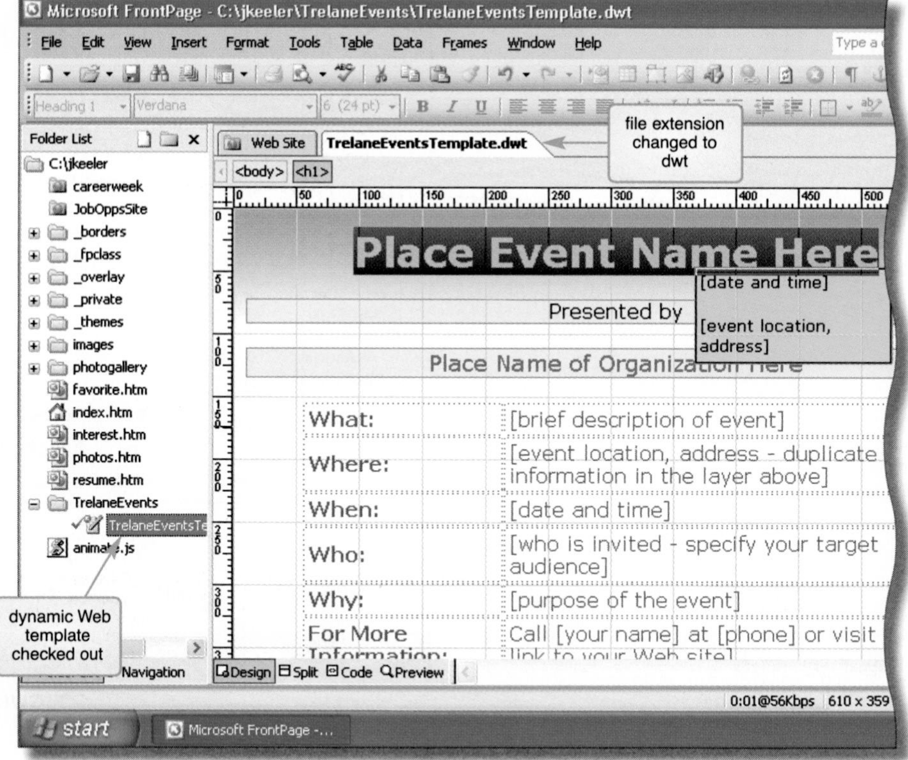

FIGURE 8-37

Other Ways

1. Press ALT+F, A, select Dynamic Web Template in Save as type list
2. In Voice Command mode, say "File, Save As", select Dynamic Web Template in Save as type list

The Web page now is saved as a dynamic Web template and new Web pages can be created using the template. The file for the template is stored in James Keeler's Web site as indicated in the Folder List pane. The next step is to restrict the regions of the template that users of the template are allowed to modify.

Managing Editable Regions of a Dynamic Web Template

The dynamic Web template includes nine areas of placeholder text that the user of the template must modify when creating new Web pages with the template. These areas include the first and third lines of the heading, the text in the layer1 layer, and the six cells of the second column of the table. The remaining portions of the template are off limits to users of the template because the student government wants to maintain a common look to the event Web pages. By default, all areas of a template are noneditable, meaning that a user of the template cannot modify any area of the template. Editable regions specifically must be designated in the template. A **region** can include any amount of selected content on the Web page. The content, however, must include only one element. For example, you cannot select two cells in a table and add the cells as an editable region, because one table cell corresponds to one element in the Web page.

The following steps modify the editable regions of the dynamic Web template.

To Manage Editable Regions of a Dynamic Web Template

1

- **If necessary, select the text in the first line of the Web page heading.**
- **Right-click the selected heading.**

FrontPage displays the shortcut menu (Figure 8-38).

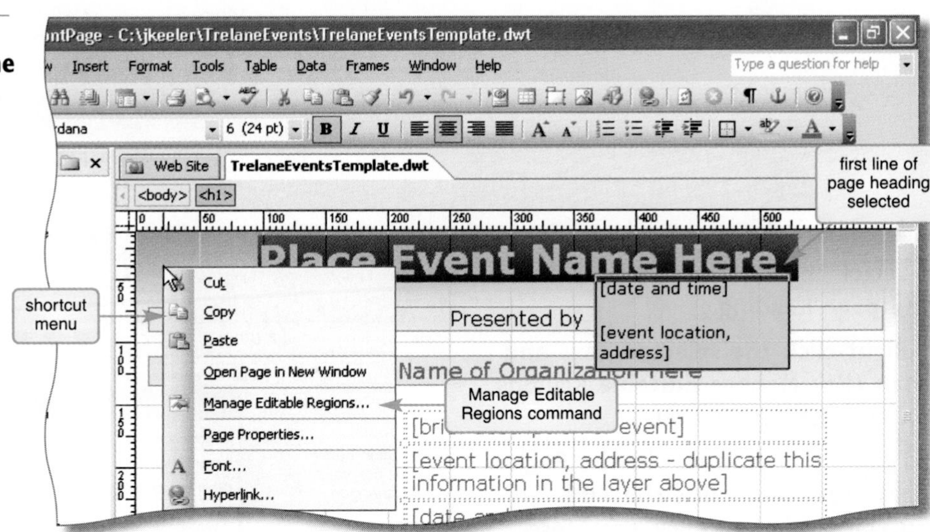

FIGURE 8-38

2

- **Click Manage Editable Regions on the shortcut menu.**
- **When FrontPage displays the Editable Regions dialog box, type** `EventName` **in the Region name text box.**

FrontPage displays the Editable Regions dialog box. The region name is changed to EventName (Figure 8-39).

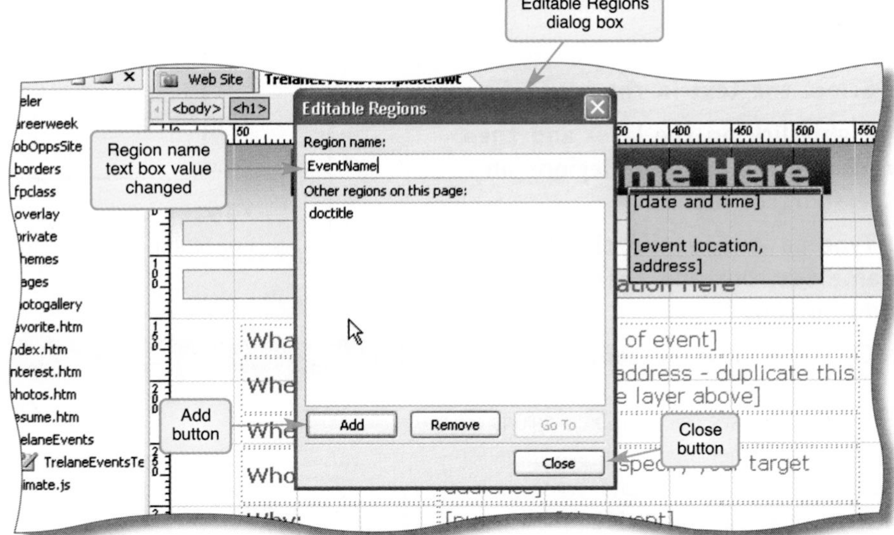

FIGURE 8-39

3

- **Click the Add button.**
- **Click the Close button.**
- **If boxes do not appear around the editable regions, click Page Options on the Tools menu and then click Show Dynamic Web Template region labels.**

FrontPage adds the EventName editable region to the Other regions on this page list. The Editable Regions dialog box is closed, and a label is displayed above the first line of the page heading. A box designating the editable region appears surrounding the editable region (Figure 8-40).

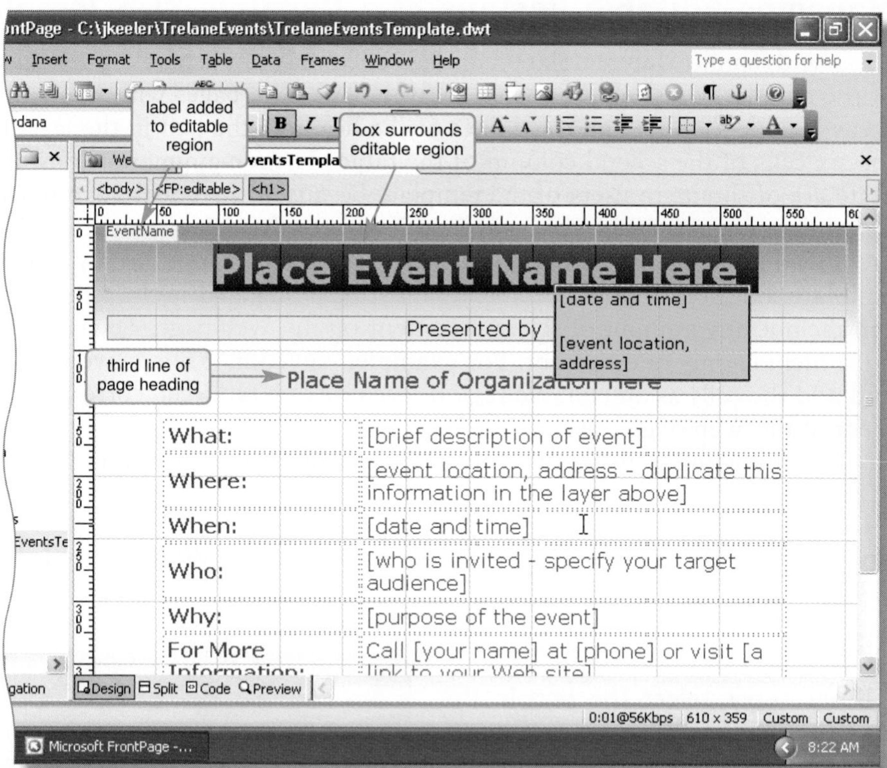

FIGURE 8-40

4

- **Select the text in the third line of the page heading.**
- **Right-click the selected text and then click Manage Editable Regions on the shortcut menu.**
- **Type** `Organization` **in the Region name text box, click the Add button, and then click the Close button.**

5

- **Select the text in the layer1 layer.**
- **Right-click on the layer and then click Manage Editable Regions on the shortcut menu.**
- **Type** `Layer1Text` **in the Region name text box and then click the Add button.**
- **Click the Close button.**

FrontPage displays the Editable Regions dialog box. The Other regions on this page list includes the EventName and Organization editable regions (Figure 8-41).

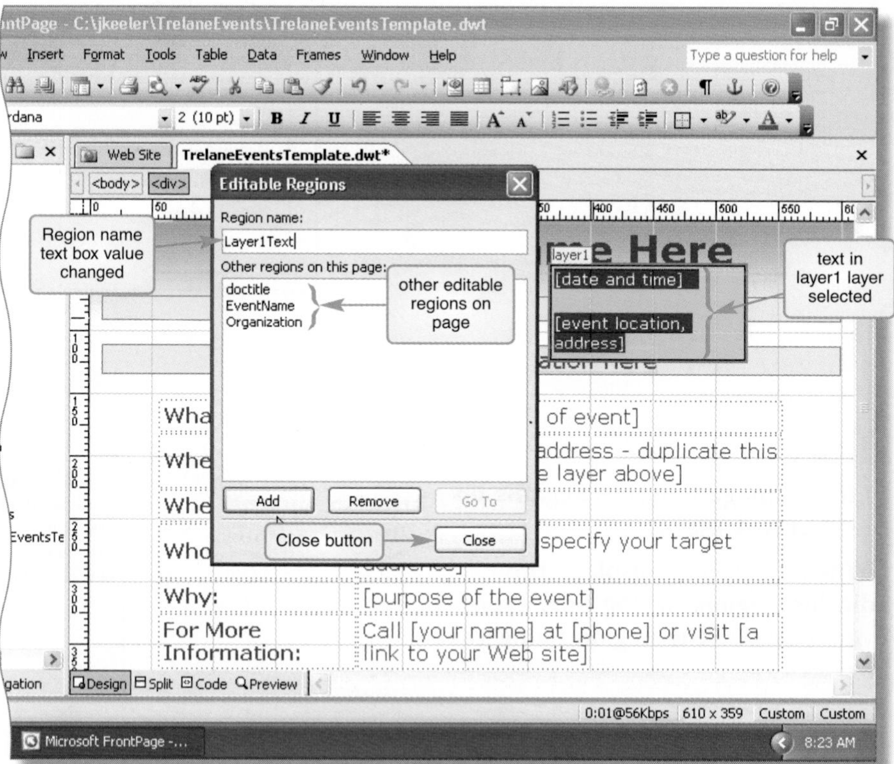

FIGURE 8-41

6

• **Use the instructions in Step 5 to add the six editable regions listed in Table 8-2.**

FrontPage displays labels above the editable regions on the dynamic Web template (Figure 8-42).

7

• **Click the Close button in the Editable Regions dialog box.**

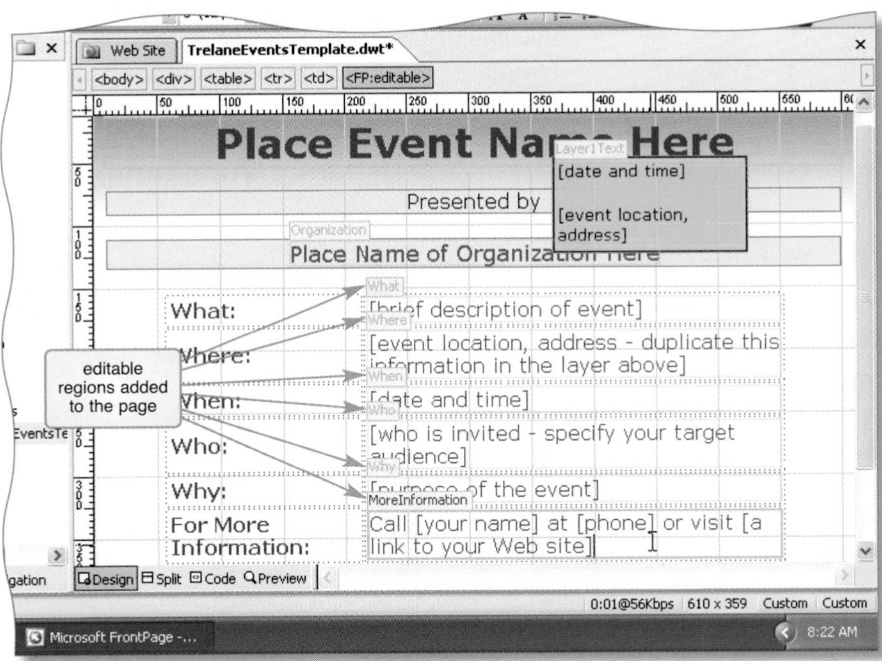

FIGURE 8-42

Other Ways

1. Select element, on Format menu point to Dynamic Web Template, click Manage Editable Regions
2. Select element, press ALT+O, W, M
3. Select element, in Voice Command mode, say "Format, Dynamic Web Template, Manage Editable Regions"

Table 8-2 Editable Regions

NAME OF EDITABLE REGION	TEXT TO SELECT FOR EDITABLE REGION
What	[brief description of event]
Where	[event location, address - duplicate this information in the layer above]
When	[date and time]
Who	[who is invited - specify your target audience]
Why	[purpose of the event]
MoreInformation	Call [your name] at [phone] or visit [a link to your Web site]

The dynamic Web template now includes nine editable regions. As long as other Web page developers use FrontPage when designing Web pages with the template, FrontPage will enforce the editable regions and prohibit any change to noneditable regions. The template is complete. The next step is to create a Web page using the dynamic Web template.

More About

Microsoft Templates

Microsoft provides free dynamic Web templates in addition to a wealth of other free add-ins for FrontPage. To learn more about the downloadable Microsoft templates, visit the FrontPage 2003 More About Web page (scsite.com/fp2003/more) and then click Microsoft Templates.

Creating a Web Page Using a Dynamic Web Template

If the Web page you want to create will be in the same Web site as the dynamic Web template, you can create the Web page from the dynamic Web template so that the Web page initially is displayed in FrontPage with the template applied to the page. You also can attach a dynamic Web template to a Web page after the Web page already is created. In this case, the Web page and dynamic Web template do not need to be in the same Web site. You need access only to the dynamic Web template file.

In order to test the dynamic Web template, a new Web page announcing the Job Placement Center's Career Week will be created using the TrelaneEventsTemplate template. The following steps create a new Web page from a dynamic Web template.

To Create a Web Page Using a Dynamic Web Template

1

- **Click the Save button on the Standard toolbar.**
- **Right-click the TrelaneEventsTemplate dynamic Web template in the Folder List pane.**

FrontPage displays the shortcut menu (Figure 8-43).

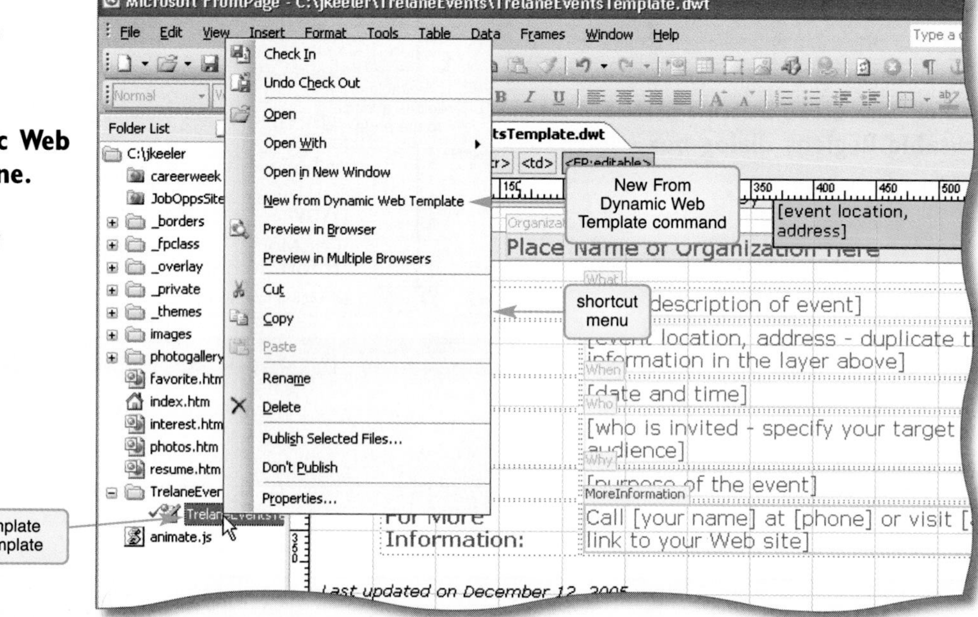

FIGURE 8-43

2

- **Click New From Dynamic Web Template on the shortcut menu.**

FrontPage creates a new Web page, named new_page_1.htm and displays the Microsoft Office FrontPage dialog box (Figure 8-44). The dialog box indicates that one file was updated with the dynamic Web template. The new Web page includes a label at the top of the page indicating the template that is associated with the Web page.

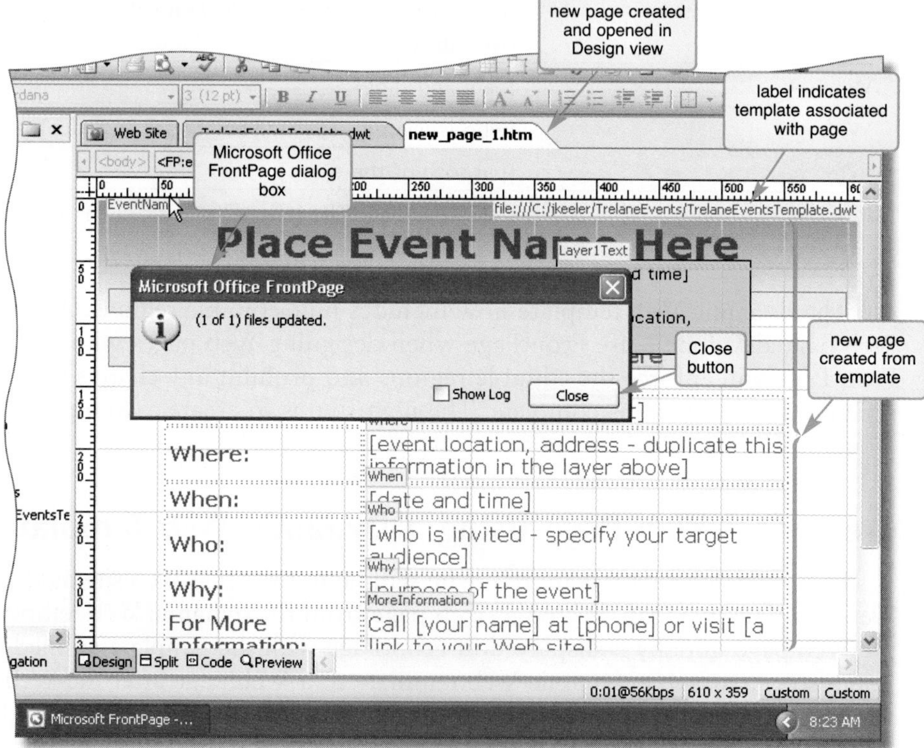

FIGURE 8-44

3

- **Click the Close button in the dialog box.**
- **Select the text in the first line of the Web page heading and then type** `Trelane College Career Week`**.**

The first line of the Web page heading is updated (Figure 8-45).

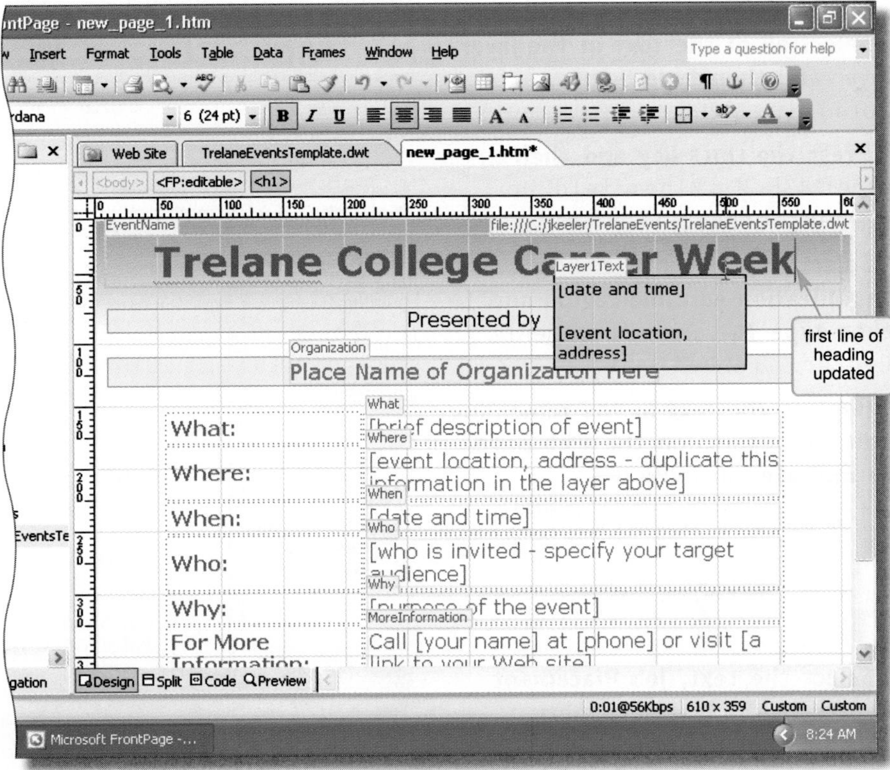

FIGURE 8-45

4

- **Place the mouse pointer over the second line of the Web page heading.**

FrontPage displays a mouse pointer that indicates the second line of the Web page heading is not editable (Figure 8-46).

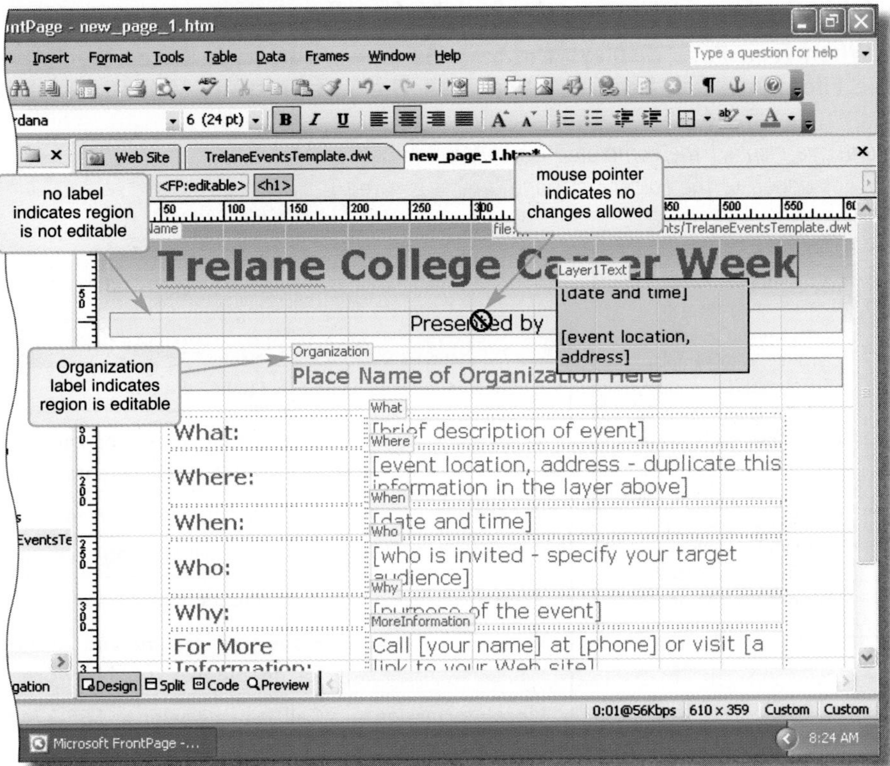

FIGURE 8-46

5

• **Select all of the text in the layer1 layer and then type** Sunday, April 10, 2005.

• **Press the ENTER key and then type** 1435 W. Bloomfield Dr. Trelane Grove, FL.

• **Select the text in the Organization editable region and then type** The Job Placement Center.

• **Replace the text in the remaining editable regions on the Web page as indicated in Table 8-3.**

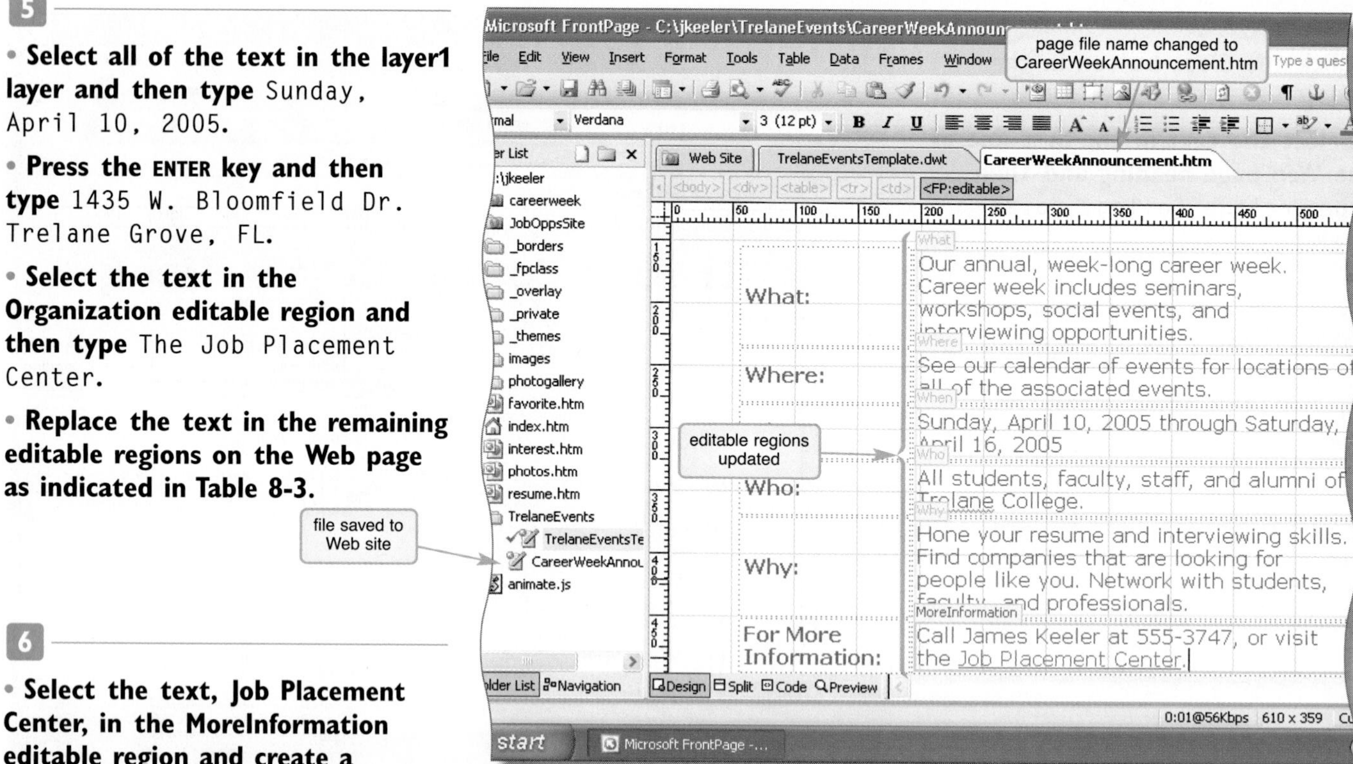

FIGURE 8-47

6

• **Select the text, Job Placement Center, in the MoreInformation editable region and create a hyperlink to the Web page, www.trelanecollege.edu/jobplacementcenter.**

• **Click the Save button on the Standard toolbar.**

• **When FrontPage displays the Save As dialog box, type CareerWeekAnnouncement in the File name text box and then click the Save button in the Save As dialog box.**

FrontPage displays the completed CareerWeekAnnouncement Web page (Figure 8-47). The Web page is added to the Folder List pane after it is saved.

Other Ways

1. Create new page, on Format menu point to Dynamic Web Template, click Attach Dynamic Web Template
2. Create new page, press ALT+O, W, A
3. Create new page, in Voice Command mode, say "Format, Dynamic Web Template, Attach Dynamic Web Template"

Table 8-3 Content for Editable Regions

REGION	CONTENT
What	Our annual week-long career week. Career week includes seminars, workshops, social events, and interviewing opportunities.
Where	See our calendar of events for locations of all the associated events.
When	Sunday, April 10, 2005, through Saturday, April 16, 2005.
Who	All students, faculty, staff, and alumni of Trelane College.
Why	Hone your resume and interviewing skills. Find companies that are looking for people like you. Network with students, faculty, and professionals.
MoreInformation	Call James Keeler at 555-3747, or visit the Job Placement Center.

As shown in Figure 8-43 on page FP 570, the new Web page is created with the same theme and Web page elements as the template. The editable regions are labeled clearly. When the mouse pointer is placed over a noneditable region, the mouse pointer indicates that changes are not allowed (Figure 8-46 on the previous page).

Changing a Dynamic Web Template

An important aspect of a dynamic Web template is that the changes to the template automatically can be propagated to Web pages created using the template. This feature is what makes the template dynamic.

The Trelane College student government would like a credit placed at the bottom of the template indicating that any event created using the template is sanctioned by the student government. The following steps add the credit to the bottom of the template and then automatically update the CareerWeekAnnouncment Web page with the change.

To Change a Dynamic Web Template

1

- **Click the TrelaneEventsTemplate.dwt tab.**
- **Scroll to the bottom of the dynamic Web template and place the insertion point directly to the right of the table.**
- **Press the ENTER key, click the Font Size box arrow on the Formatting toolbar and then click 2 (10 pt) in the Font Size list.**
- **Type** `Sponsored in part by the Trelane College Student Government.`

The new text appears on the dynamic Web page template (Figure 8-48).

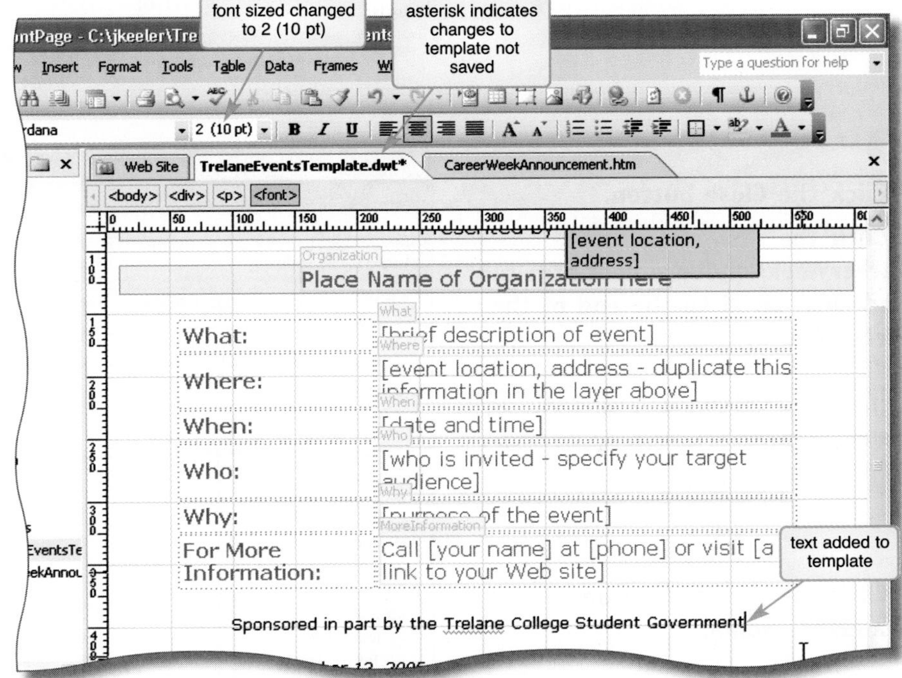

FIGURE 8-48

2

- **Click the Save button on the Standard toolbar.**

FrontPage displays a Microsoft Office FrontPage dialog box. The dialog box indicates that one Web page is associated with the dynamic Web template (Figure 8-49).

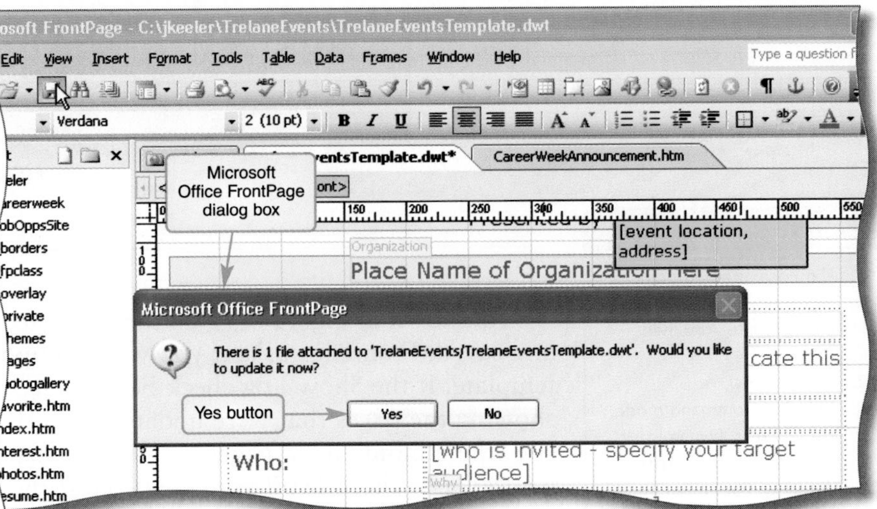

FIGURE 8-49

3

• **Click the Yes button.**

FrontPage displays another Microsoft Office FrontPage dialog box. The dialog box indicates that one Web page was updated with the changes to the dynamic Web template (Figure 8-50).

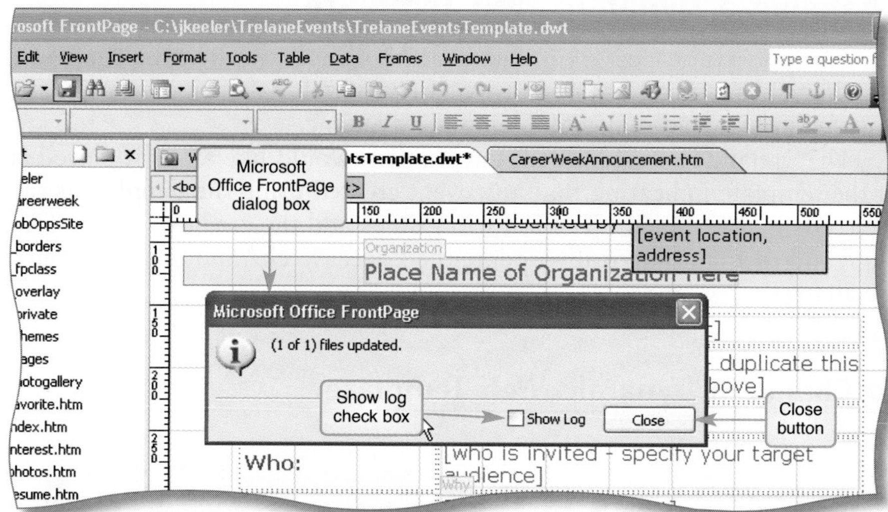

FIGURE 8-50

4

• **Click the Close button.**

• **Click the CareerWeekAnnouncement.htm tab and then scroll to the end of the Web page.**

The text entered on the dynamic Web template automatically is added to the Web page (Figure 8-51).

5

• **Click the Save button on the Standard toolbar.**

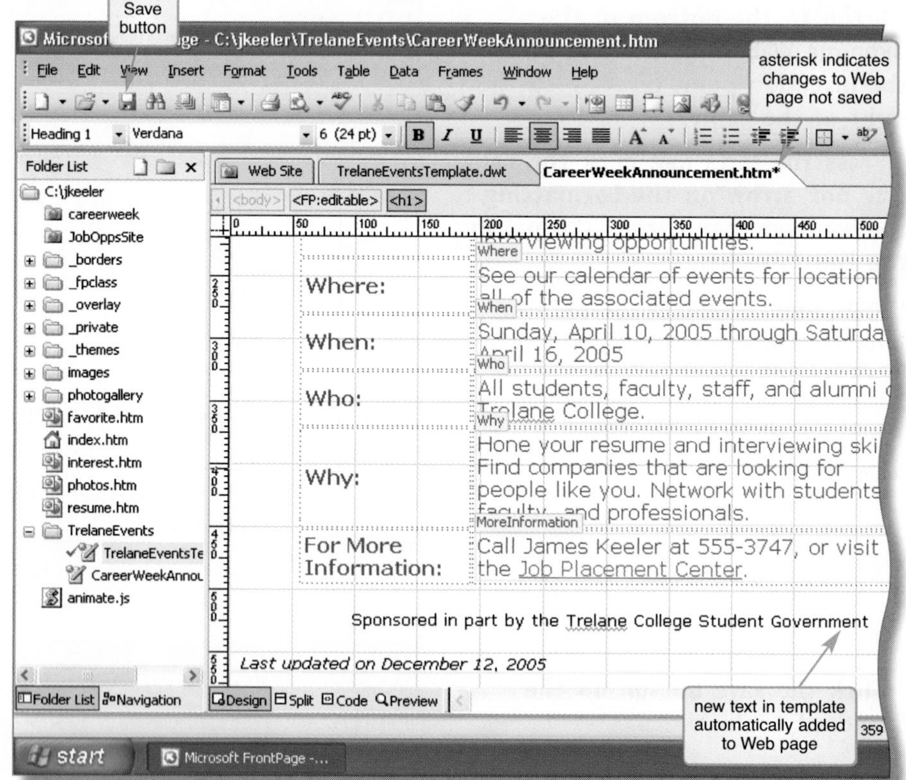

FIGURE 8-51

Other Ways

1. On Format menu point to Dynamic Web Template, click Update Attached Pages
2. Press ALT+O, W, U
3. In Voice Command mode, say "Format, Dynamic Web Template, Update Attached Pages"

As shown in Figure 8-49 on the previous page, whenever the template is updated and saved, FrontPage asks if you want to update the Web pages associated with the template. If the Show Log check box is selected, then FrontPage displays a log file showing the pages that were updated with the template. This is useful in a large Web site where hundreds of pages may be associated with a template. The log file could be used as a check list if you want to test the changes on the updated pages.

Make a habit of creating and saving log files generated when you change a dynamic Web template. Be certain to test all Web pages that were modified as a result of the changed template.

Checking the Spelling of a Web Page

As you have learned, FrontPage includes a **spell checker** that you can use to check a Web page for spelling errors. The spell checker looks for spelling errors by comparing words on the Web page against words contained in its standard dictionary. If you often use specialized terms or proper names that are not in the standard dictionary, you may want to add them to a custom dictionary using the Spelling dialog box.

When the spell checker finds a word that is not in either dictionary, it displays the word in the Spelling dialog box. You then can correct it if it is misspelled.

Design Tip

A good design should include proper grammar and spelling. Always spell check Web pages and templates.

To illustrate how FrontPage responds to a word not in its dictionary, the following steps use the spell checker to check for misspelled words and then add a proper name to the custom dictionary.

Q&A

Q: Can I attach a dynamic Web template to an existing Web page?

A: Yes. Click Attach Dynamic Web Template on the Dynamic Web Template submenu of the Format menu. You may have to tweak the page to account for editable and noneditable regions. You also can detach a dynamic Web template from a Web page by clicking Detach Dynamic Web Template on the Dynamic Web Template submenu of the Format menu.

To Check the Spelling of a Web Page

- **Click Tools on the menu bar.**

FrontPage displays the Tools menu (Figure 8-52).

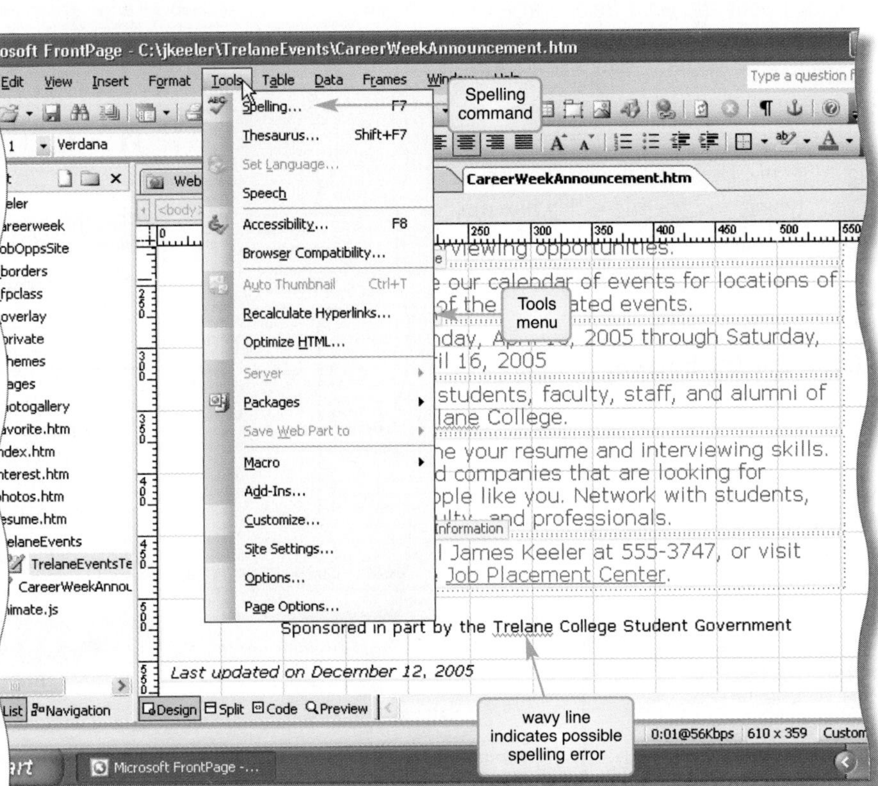

FIGURE 8-52

2

• **Click Spelling.**

FrontPage displays the Spelling dialog box. The Not in Dictionary text box indicates that FrontPage found a possible spelling error. The Change To text box suggests a possible correct spelling for the apparent spelling error. The Suggestions list indicates other possible correct spellings for the apparent spelling error (Figure 8-53).

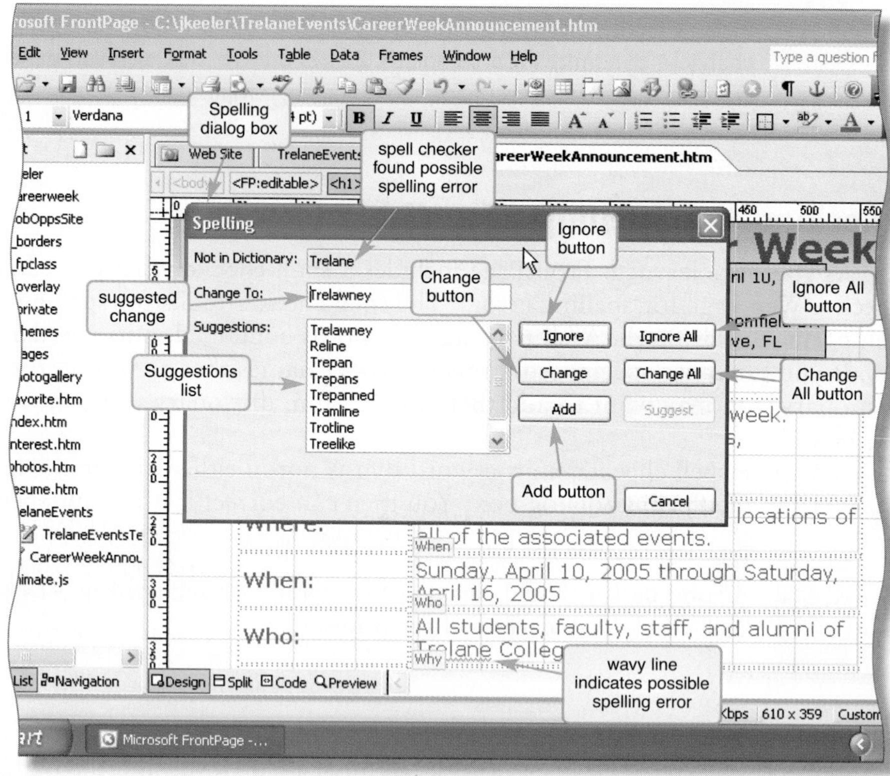

FIGURE 8-53

3

• **Click the Add button.**

FrontPage adds the word Trelane to the dictionary and closes the Spelling dialog box because no other possible spelling errors were found. FrontPage removes the wavy line from all occurrences of the word Trelane (Figure 8-54). Depending upon the accuracy of your typing, the Spelling dialog box may display additional errors.

4

• **Click the OK button.**

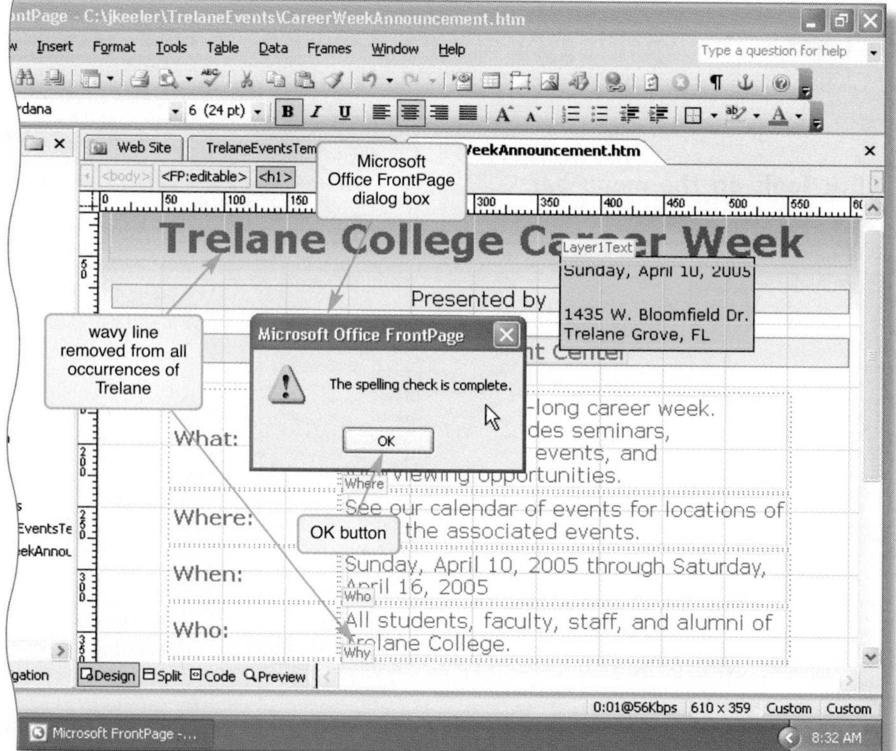

FIGURE 8-54

Other Ways

1. Press F7
2. Press ALT+T, S
3. In Voice Command mode, say "Tools, Spelling"

When the spell checker identifies a word not in its standard or custom dictionary, it selects the word and displays the Spelling dialog box. The Spelling dialog box (Figure 8-53) lists the word not found in the dictionary, a suggested correction, and a list of alternative suggestions. If one of the words in the Suggestions list is correct, click it and then click the Change button. If none of the suggestions is correct, type the correct word in the Not in Dictionary text box and then click the Change button. To change the word throughout the Web page, click the Change All button instead of the Change button. To skip correcting the word, click the Ignore button. To have FrontPage ignore the word for the remainder of the Web page, click the Ignore All button.

In the previous example, the word, Trelane, is a proper name that should be added to the custom dictionary. As shown in the previous set of steps, clicking the Add button adds the word to the custom dictionary and no longer considers the word to be a spelling error. The wavy lines below the word Trelane are removed throughout the Web page.

Q&A

Q: Can I rely on the spell checker to find every misspelling?

A: While FrontPage's spell checker is a valuable tool, it is not infallible. You should proofread your Web pages carefully. Consider asking a friend or coworker to assist you in this endeavor, or take a break from the Web page for a day or two and then go back and read it. Nothing undermines a good impression more than a professional-looking Web page with misspelled words.

Checking the Accessibility of a Web Page

FrontPage provides the ability to check a Web page or several Web pages to make sure that the pages are accessible by people with special needs, such as vision or hearing impairment. Several standards exist for determining how accessible a Web page is for people with special needs. Table 8-4 lists the three standards supported by FrontPage's accessibility checking feature.

Table 8-4 Accessibility Standards Supported by FrontPage

STANDARD	DESCRIPTION
WCAG Priority 1 (Web Content Accessibility Guidelines)	Provides a list of checkpoints that a Web page must satisfy in order to be accessible by all groups. If a checkpoint is not satisfied, one or more groups will find the site to be impossible to use.
WCAG Priority 2 (Web Content Accessibility Guidelines)	Provides a list of checkpoints that a Web site should satisfy. If a checkpoint is not satisfied, one or more groups may find the site difficult to use.
Access Board Section 508	Refers to the Rehabilitation Act of 1973. Many of the checkpoints correspond to WCAG Priority 1 checkpoints. The standard applies to Federal agencies purchasing electronic and information technology.

Each of the standards includes a list of checkpoints. **Checkpoints** are specific rules against which you can check elements of a Web page. You can use the checkpoints in the standards as a checklist when manually checking a Web page. The WCAG standard also includes a Priority 3 standard. FrontPage, however, does not provide the ability to check Priority 3 checkpoints, which include guidelines that a Web page developer optionally may address in addition to Priority 1 and Priority 2 checkpoints.

Design Tip

If you work with or for a government agency, make sure that you adhere to any accessibility guidelines. Many government agencies, including state government agencies, are required to adhere to the Section 508 accessibility guidelines.

More About

Accessibility Guidelines

The W3C sets standards and guidelines for the Web and has taken the initiative to formulate accessibility guidelines. To learn more about accessibility guidelines, visit the FrontPage 2003 More About Web page (scsite.com/fp2003/more) and then click Accessibility Guidelines.

More About

Section 508

Section 508 refers to the law enacted by Congress in 1998 that requires federal agencies to make electronic and information technology more accessible to people with special needs. To learn more about Section 508, visit the FrontPage 2003 More About Web page (scsite.com/fp2003/more) and then click Section 508.

Checking the Accessibility of the Current Web Page

When checking the accessibility of a Web page, FrontPage allows you to choose which accessibility standards to use in the check. You also can check either the current Web page or many pages at once. Finally, FrontPage allows you to check only for errors, warnings, or a manual checklist. Errors are considered to be those parts of the Web page that violate the guidelines. Warnings are those parts of a Web page that may violate the guidelines, and include general suggestions to improve accessibility. A manual checklist includes questionable accessibility warnings that require manual checking to verify that the item listed is an accessibility problem.

The student government would like the Trelane events template checked for WCAG Priority 1 and Access Board Section 508 errors and warnings. The following steps perform the accessibility check on the TrelaneEventsTemplate dynamic Web page template.

To Check the Accessibility of the Current Web Page

1

- **Click Tools on the menu bar.**

FrontPage displays the Tools menu (Figure 8-55).

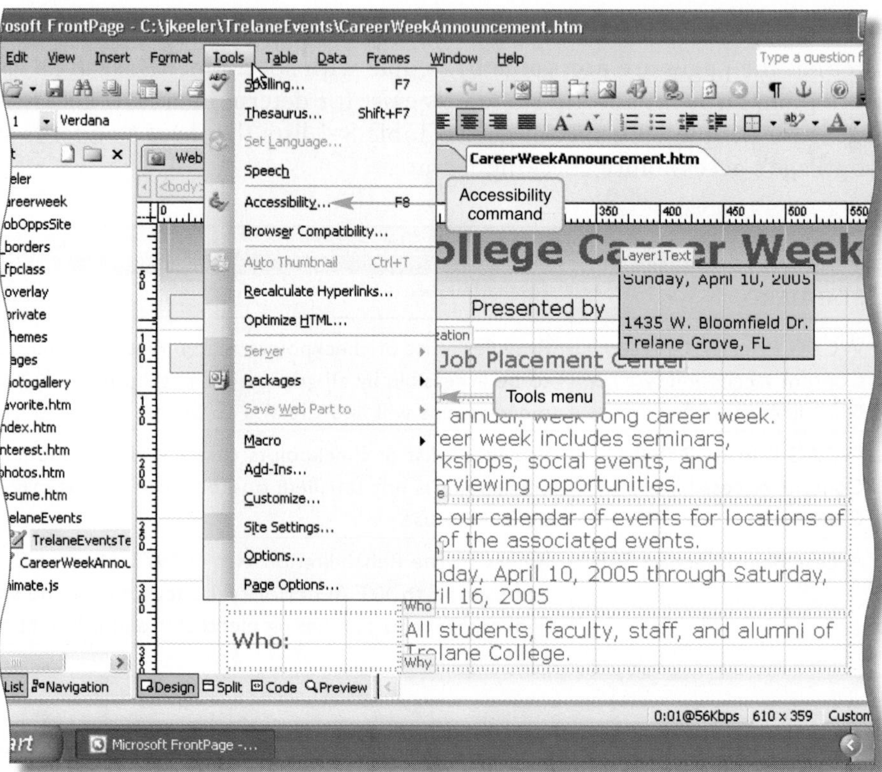

FIGURE 8-55

2

- **Click Accessibility.**

FrontPage displays the Accessibility dialog box with the default options selected (Figure 8-56).

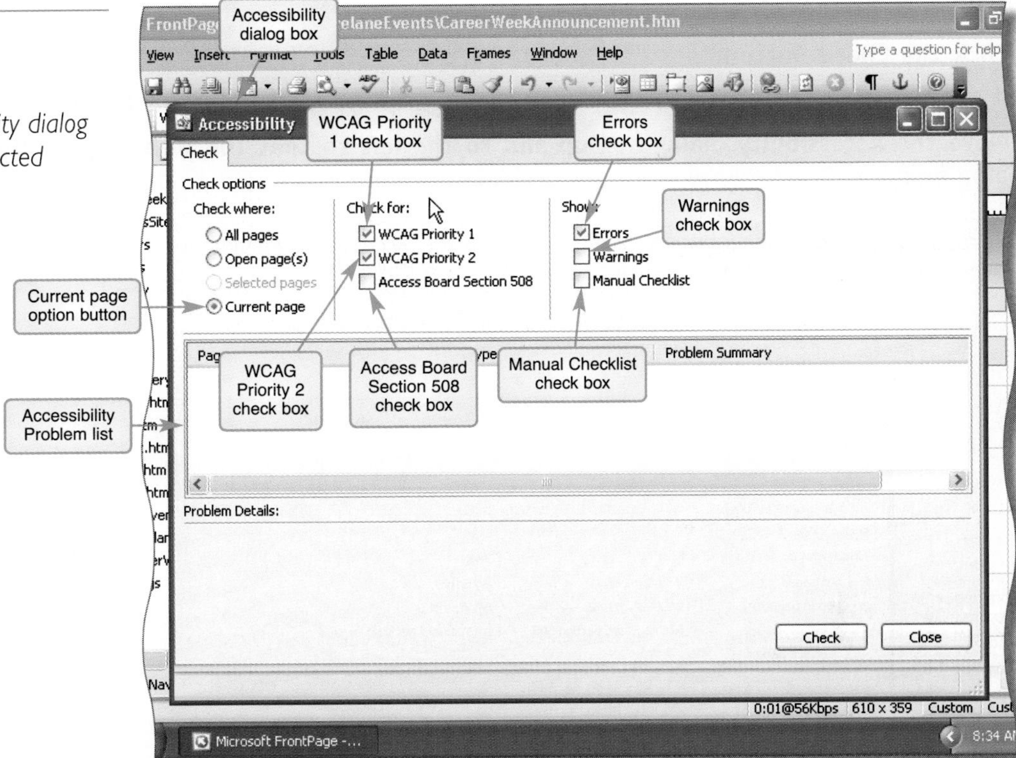

FIGURE 8-56

3

- **If necessary, click Current page to select it.**
- **Click WCAG Priority 2 to remove the check mark.**
- **Click Access Board Section 508 to select it.**
- **Click Warnings to select it.**

The Check options area includes the options desired for the accessibility check (Figure 8-57).

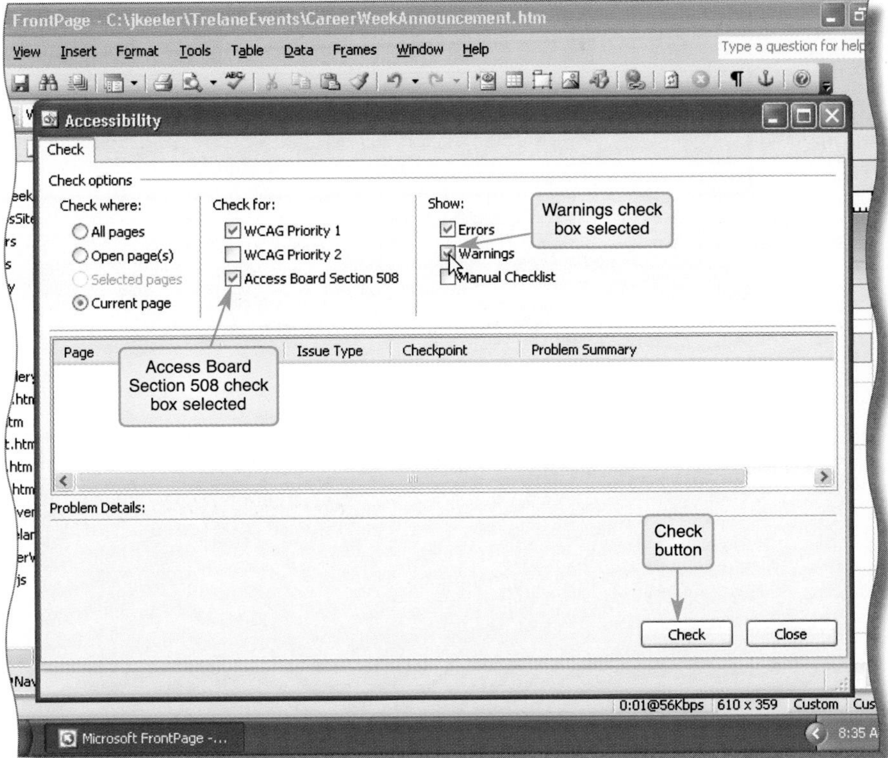

FIGURE 8-57

4

- **Click the Check button.**
- **If the Microsoft Office FrontPage dialog box is displayed, click the OK button.**
- **Move the Accessibility dialog box up and to the left so that the Web page is displayed behind the dialog box.**

FrontPage lists several potential accessibility problems in the Accessibility Problem list. The Web page changes to Split view so that both the Web page and HTML code are viewable (Figure 8-58).

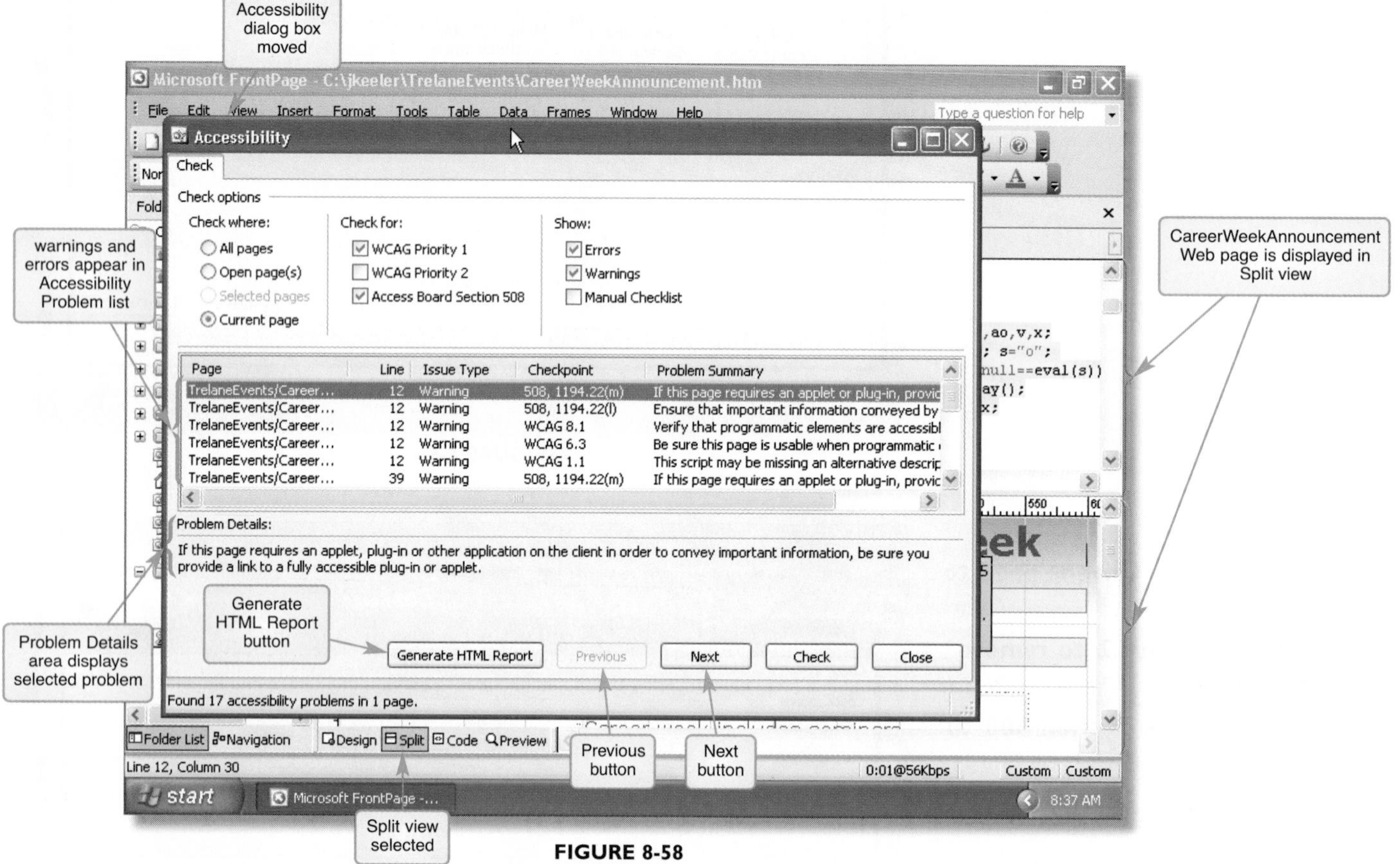

FIGURE 8-58

5

- **Scroll through the Accessibility Problem list until the bottom of the list is displayed.**
- **Click the second to the last problem in the Accessibility Problem list.**

FrontPage highlights the selected problem and highlights the HTML code containing the problem in the top window of Split view (Figure 8-59).

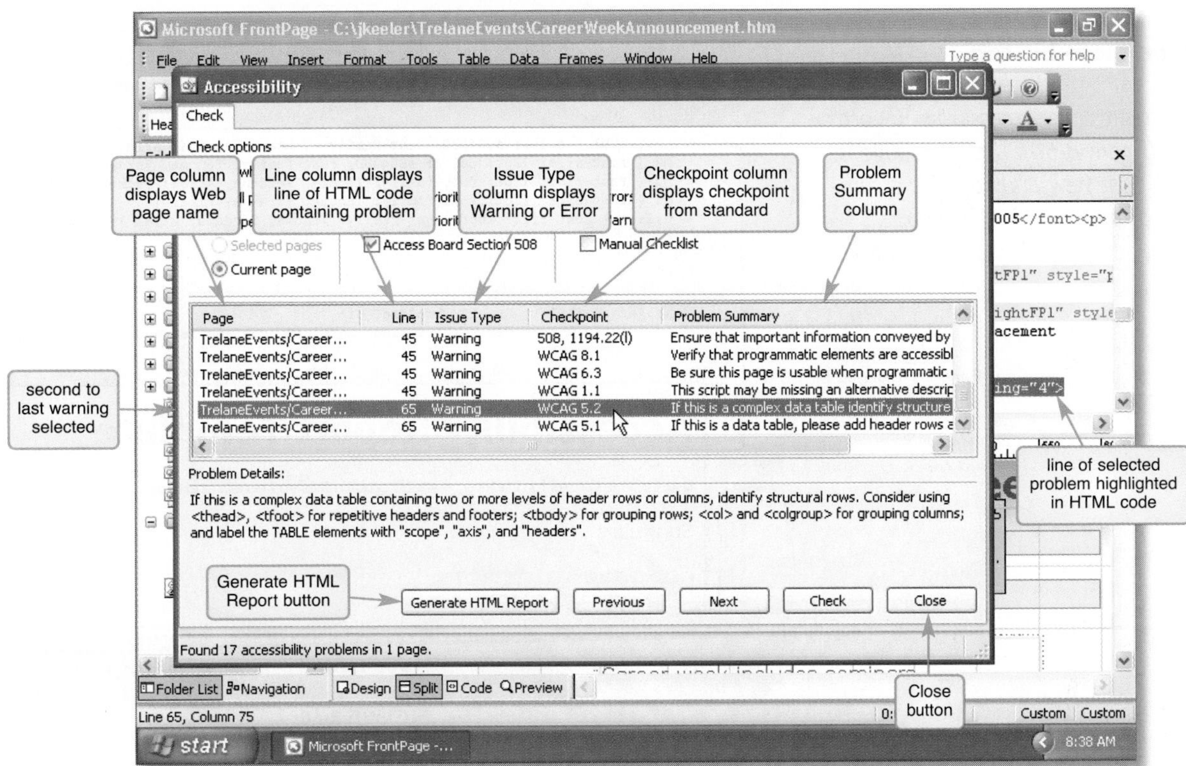

FIGURE 8-59

Other Ways

1. Press F8
2. Press ALT+T, Y
3. In Voice Command mode, say "Tools, Accessibility"

The Accessibility Problem list contains 17 warnings (Figure 8-58). The list notes the line number and the checkpoint related to the warning. Clicking an individual problem causes FrontPage to display more information about the problem in the Problem Details area. Warnings generally include items that require a judgment call, and the warning may not be a problem about which you need to be concerned. For example, the problem selected in Figure 8-59 indicates that if the table is a data table, some corrective action may be needed. Because the table does not meet those criteria, however, no action is required.

Creating an Accessibility Report

FrontPage allows you to create a Web page report that lists the accessibility problems found in an accessibility check. The report can be published to a Web site and then used as a checklist while fixing the problems. The report includes a summary of the problems and then lists individual problems grouped by checkpoints.

The following steps create an accessibility report.

To Create an Accessibility Report

1

- **Click the Generate HTML Report button.**
- **Click the Close button.**

FrontPage creates the Accessibility Report Web page (Figure 8-60). The Web page is displayed in Split view and contains a summary of all of the possible Accessibility problems found by the Accessibility check.

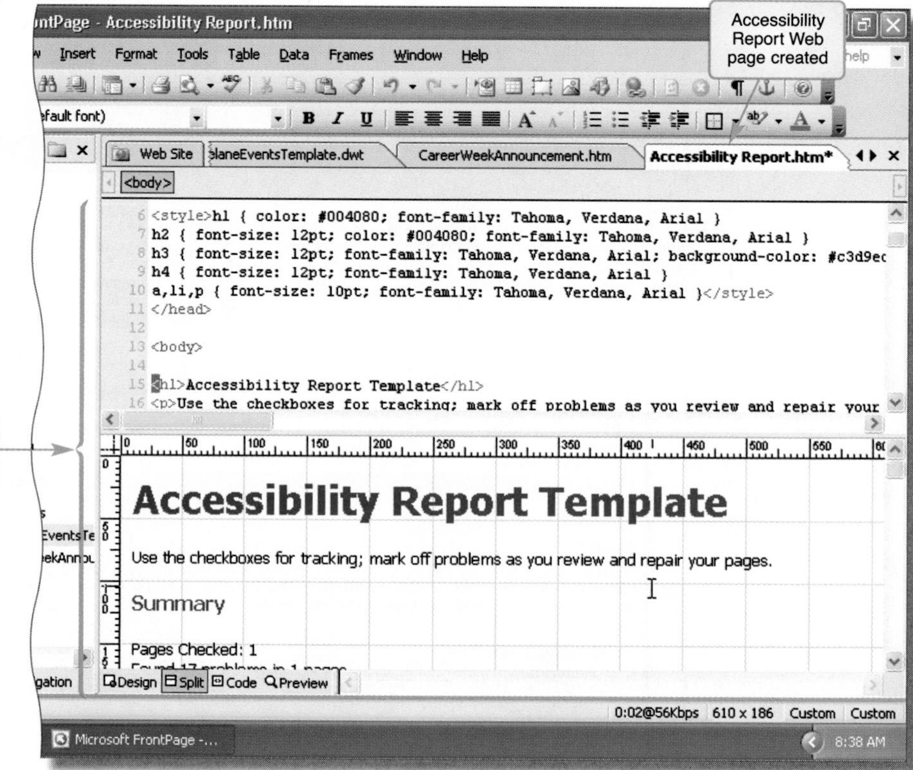

FIGURE 8-60

2

- **Click the Design button.**

FrontPage displays the Accessibility Report Web page in Design view. The top of the report contains a summary of the entire report followed by a summary of the first page checked in the report (Figure 8-61).

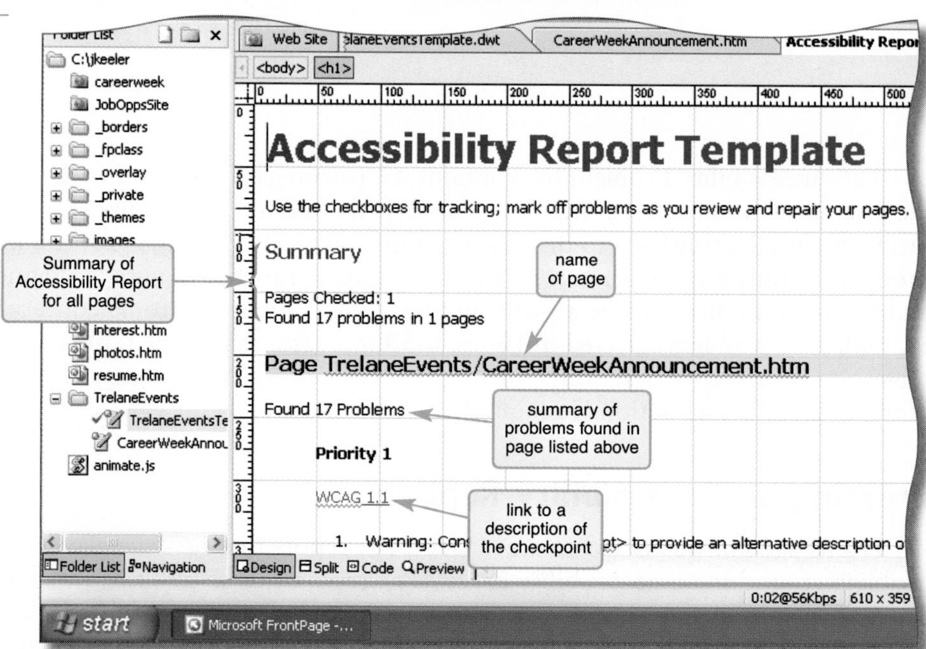

FIGURE 8-61

3

• **Scroll to the bottom of the Accessibility Report Web page.**

The bottom of the Accessibility Report Web page is displayed (Figure 8-62). The report contains problems grouped by checkpoints. Check boxes allow you to track the problems that you have corrected or will disregard. Some of the checkpoints include a link to a description of the checkpoint.

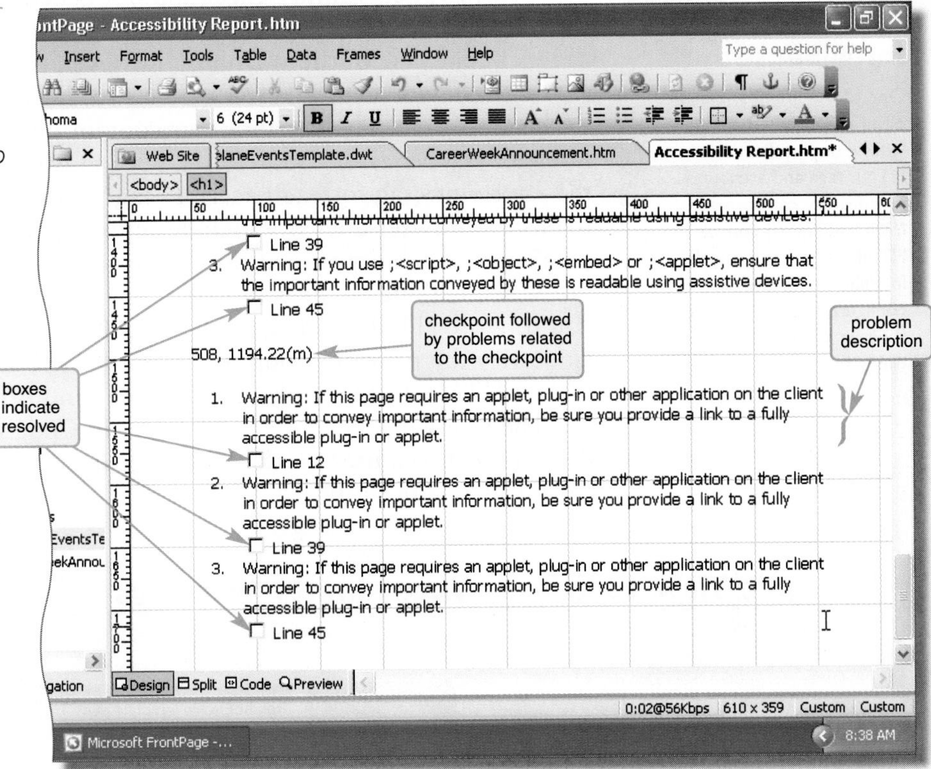

FIGURE 8-62

Figure 8-61 shows the summary of the report at the top of the report Web page. If multiple Web pages were checked for problems, then the summary would list the number of pages checked. Several of the checkpoints are hyperlinks that link to external Web pages that include information about the particular checkpoint. As shown in Figure 8-62, check boxes allow you to track progress on fixing or researching each problem.

Using Split View

The accessibility check automatically places the current Web page in Split view. FrontPage's **Split view** combines both Design view and Code view by placing the Code view above the Design view. The two views are coordinated so that selecting a Web page element in Design view automatically navigates the Code view to the corresponding code. Similarly, selecting code in the Code view automatically navigates the Design view to the corresponding Web page element. Code view allows you to quickly find the HTML code associated with an element on the Web page.

Design Tip

When using Split view, your screen may become cluttered with windows, task panes, and toolbars. Consider using as high a screen resolution and as large a monitor as you can when working with FrontPage. Split view also offers you a chance to learn the HTML generated by FrontPage behind the scenes.

More About

Split View

If you make changes in the Design view pane of Split view, the changes are reflected automatically in the Code view pane of Split view. If you make changes in the Code view pane in Split view, however, the changes are not reflected automatically in the Design view pane. You must press F5 or click the Design view pane to cause the updates to transfer from the Code view pane to the Design view pane.

More About

IntelliSense

One of the greatest benefits of IntelliSense is that it provides a pop-up list of valid HTML tags and attributes. This feature can save you from needing to consult HTML reference manuals. IntelliSense features can be configured in the IntelliSense sheet in the Page Options dialog box.

While the accessibility check did not generate any errors, it did generate several warnings. Covering all of the warning and possible corrections is beyond the scope of this book. One of the warnings, however, is common and easily can be corrected. Adding behaviors and DHTML effects to the Web page added several <script> tags to the Web page. The <script> tags contain JavaScript code that contains the instructions for the behaviors and effects. Several warnings indicate that you should include the <noscript> tag for each <script> tag in order to display something to the user if the user's browser does not include support for JavaScript or if the user has JavaScript capability turned off on the browser.

When making changes in Code view, FrontPage provides IntelliSense that helps you to write HTML code quickly. **IntelliSense** assists you in adding HTML to the Code view by providing pop-up lists of HTML tags as you type, automatically adding HTML to the Code view for you, and offering other helpful assistance.

The following steps use IntelliSense in Code view to add a <noscript> tag that displays text to a user on the Web page if the user's browser does not have the capability to run script.

To Use Split View to Correct Accessibility Warnings

1

- **Click the TrelaneEventsTemplate.dwt tab.**
- **Click the Split button.**
- **Click after the last end bracket (]) in the layer1 layer in the lower panel of Split view.**
- **Click the end of line 55 or the line near line 55 that contains the <!--#EndEditable></div> tags in the top panel of Split view to place the insertion point at the end of the line.**

FrontPage displays the dynamic Web template in Split view (Figure 8-63). When an element is selected in the lower panel, the code panel on top of Split view automatically is moved to the location in the HTML code corresponding to the selected element.

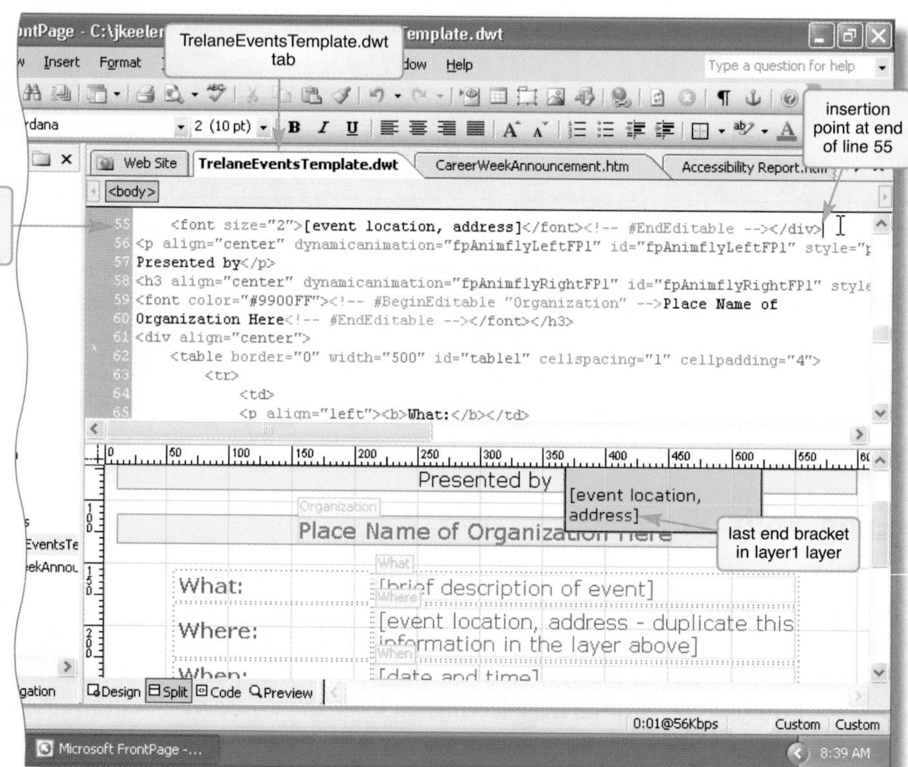

FIGURE 8-63

2

- **Press the ENTER key.**
- **Type < (less than symbol).**

FrontPage displays the IntelliSense pop-up list in the code panel of Split view under the just-typed code element (Figure 8-64).

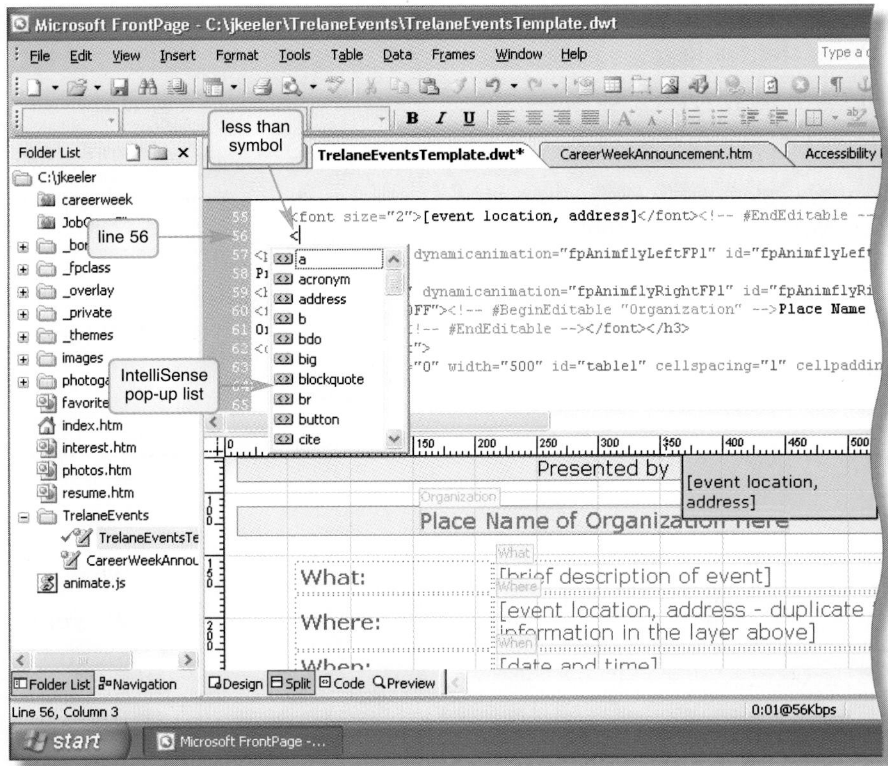

FIGURE 8-64

3

- **Type** nos.

FrontPage automatically scrolls the IntelliSense pop-up list to the noscript HTML tag (Figure 8-65).

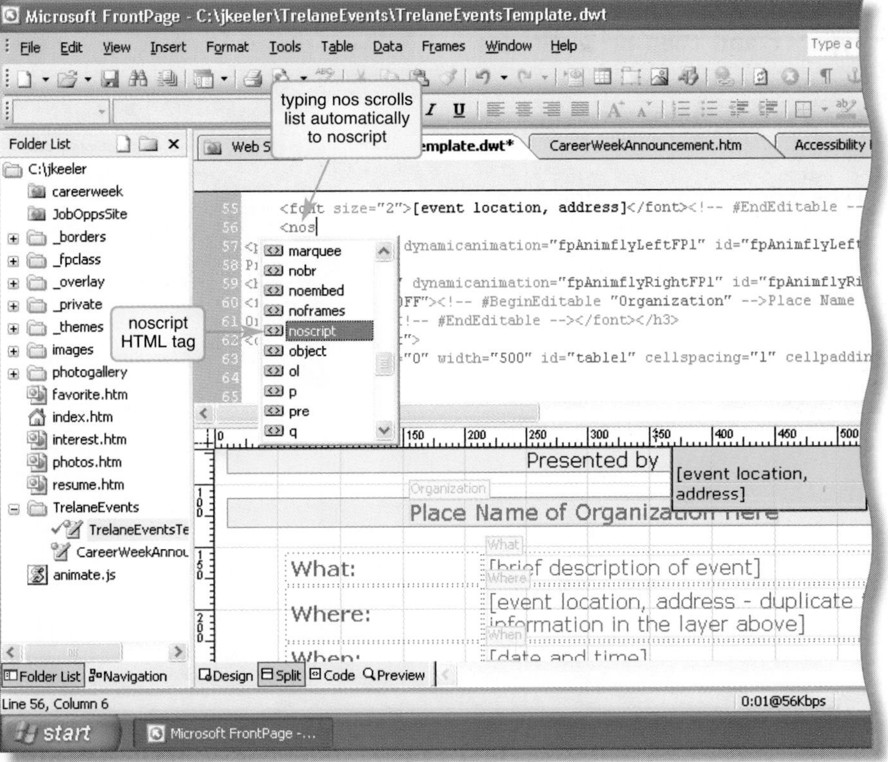

FIGURE 8-65

4

- **Press the TAB key.**
- **If necessary, type > to close the HTML tag.**

FrontPage automatically inserts the remaining characters of the <noscript> HTML tag. The </noscript> ending tag also is inserted. FrontPage places the insertion point between the start and end tags (Figure 8-66).

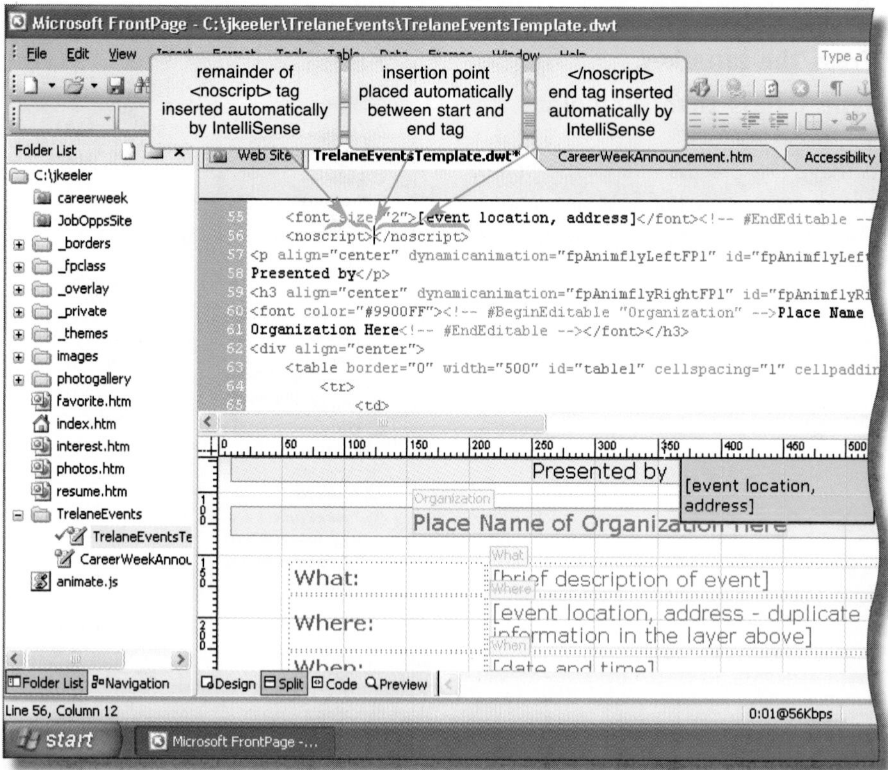

FIGURE 8-66

5

- **Type <i and then press the TAB key.**
- **If necessary, type > to close the HTML tag.**
- **Type** `Your browser does not support JavaScript. Some nonessential content may not appear properly.`

FrontPage automatically inserts the italics HTML tags <i> and </i>. The <noscript> text appears in line 56 (Figure 8-67).

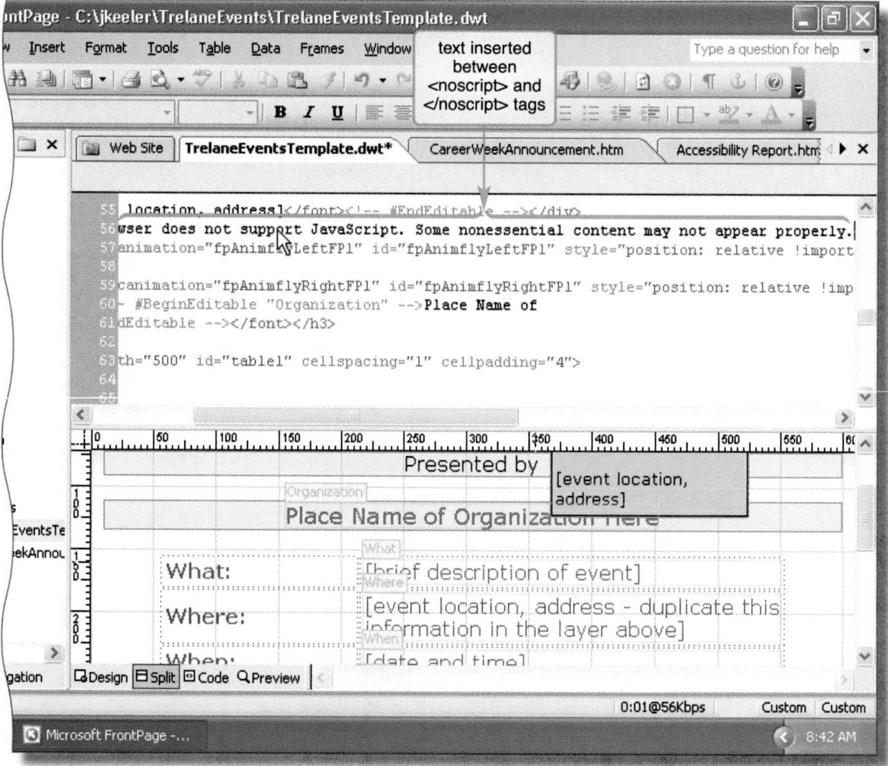

FIGURE 8-67

6

- **Click the Design button.**

FrontPage closes Split view and displays the dynamic Web template in Design view (Figure 8-68).

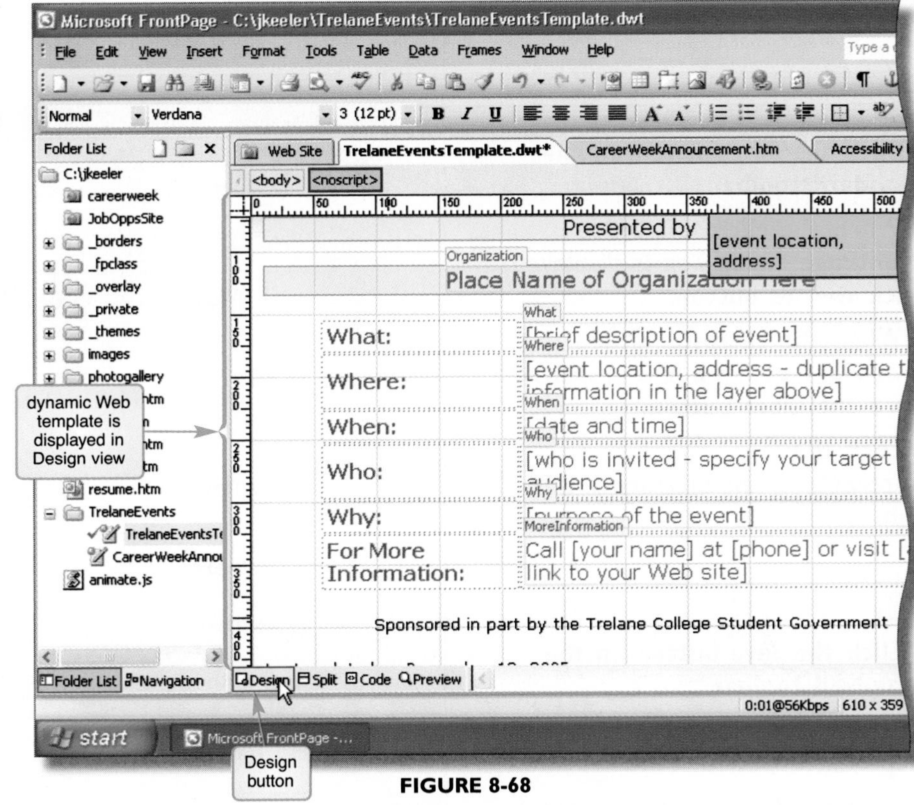

FIGURE 8-68

As shown in Step 1, clicking an element in Design view automatically navigates Code view to the corresponding HTML code. Figure 8-64 on page FP 585 shows an IntelliSense pop-up list that contains a list of all possible HTML tags. As you type, IntelliSense navigates to the closest tag that matches what you have typed (Figure 8-65). The text entered between the <i> and </i> tags appears on the Web page if the user's browser does not support JavaScript. The <i> tag causes the text to appear italicized.

Saving and Testing the Web Page

The template and Web page are complete. The next step is to save and test the template and Web page. Because the template was modified, the changes to the template must be propagated to the Web page. The steps on the next page save the template and Web page, then use the Preview in Browser command to preview the CareerWeekAnnouncement Web page in Internet Explorer.

To Save and Test the Web Page

1

- **Click the Save button on the Standard toolbar.**
- **When the Microsoft Office FrontPage dialog box is displayed, click the Yes button.**
- **When the Microsoft Office FrontPage dialog box is displayed, click the Close button.**
- **Click the CareerWeekAnnouncement.htm* tab.**

2

- **Click the Save button on the Standard toolbar.**
- **Click the Accessibility Report.htm* tab.**
- **Click the Close button to the right of the tab to close the page.**
- **When the Microsoft Office FrontPage dialog box is displayed, click the No button.**

3

- **Click File on the menu bar and then point to Preview in Browser.**
- **Click Microsoft Internet Explorer 6.0.**

FrontPage opens Internet Explorer and displays the Web page. Two lines of the Web page heading fly in to the Web page (Figure 8-69).

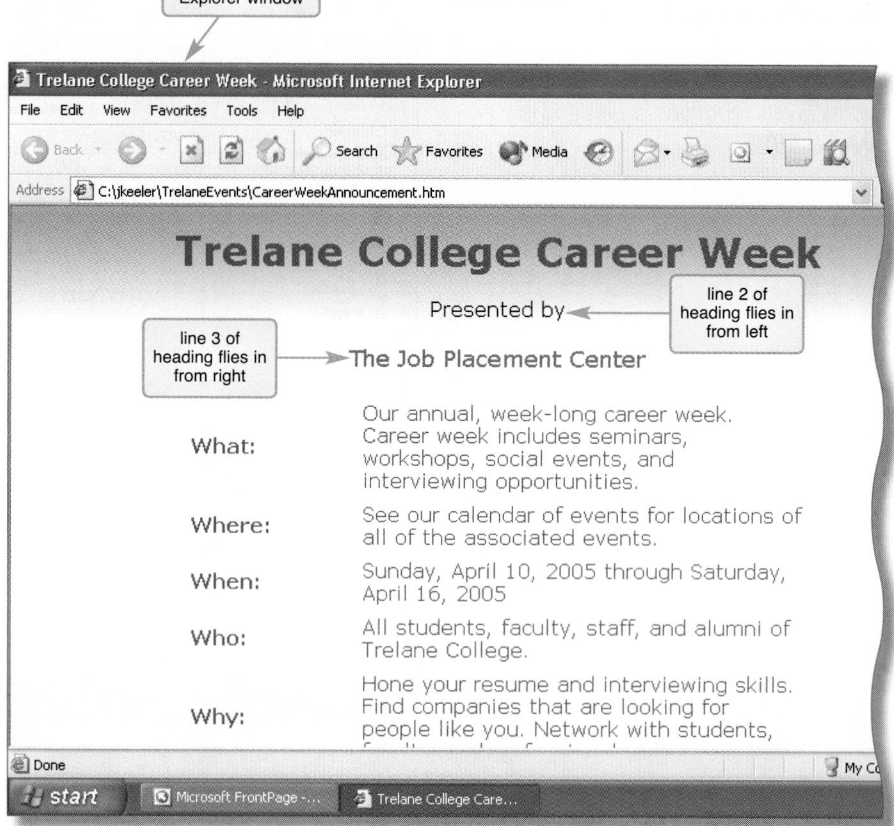

FIGURE 8-69

4

• **Place the mouse pointer over the first line of the Web page heading.**

The layer1 layer appears on the Web page (Figure 8-70).

5

• **Click the Close button in the Microsoft Internet Explorer window.**

• **Right-click the TrelaneEventsTemplate.dwt file in the Folders List pane and then click Check In on the shortcut menu.**

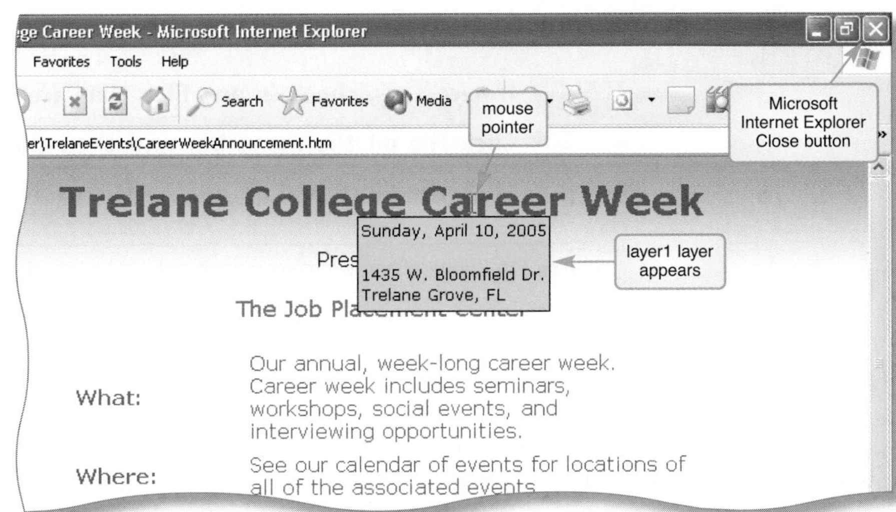

FIGURE 8-70

The second and third lines of the Web page heading fly in from the left and right. The layer1 layer appears when the mouse pointer is placed over the first line of the heading. The next step is to publish the new pages to the Web server. The following steps republish James Keeler's Web site.

To Publish a Subsite and Changes to an Existing FrontPage Web Site

1. **Click the Publish Site button on the Standard toolbar. When the Publish Web dialog box is displayed, click Include subsites. Because this Web site was published previously, FrontPage assumes that you will publish to the same location and does not display the Publish Destination dialog box. Click the Publish button.**
2. **If necessary, type your user name and password. Click the OK button.**
3. **When the Microsoft Office FrontPage dialog box indicates that the Web site has been published successfully, click the Done button.**

Once the Web and subsite are published, you can view and test the Career Week Announcement Web page by entering the location of your Web site (e.g., http://www.trelanecollege.edu/~jkeeler/TrelaneEvents/CareerWeekAnnouncement.htm) in any browser and pressing the ENTER key.

More About

The Quick Reference

For more information, see the Quick Reference Summary at the back of this book, or visit the FrontPage 2003 Quick Reference Web page (scsite.com/fp2003/qr).

Quitting FrontPage

When you have published and tested the new pages in the Web site, you can quit Microsoft FrontPage. The steps on the next page quit FrontPage.

To Quit FrontPage

1. **If necessary, check in any files that are checked out.**
2. **Click File on the menu bar and then click Close Site.**
3. **Click the Close button on the Microsoft FrontPage title bar.**

The FrontPage window is closed, and the Windows desktop is displayed.

Project Summary

In this project, you learned how to display the ruler and grid to assist you in laying out a Web page. You learned how to display the DHTML Effects toolbar and add DHTML effects to elements of a Web page. Next, you learned how to add a layer to a Web page, set properties for the layer, and add content to the layer. You learned how to add behaviors to a Web page and to elements of a Web page. You learned how to create a dynamic Web template, modify the editable regions of the template, and then use the template to create a new Web page. You also learned how to change a dynamic Web template and then apply those changes to pages that were created using the dynamic Web template. You learned how to check the spelling of the content of a Web page and how to check the accessibility of a Web page. Finally, you learned how to modify HTML code in Split view and use IntelliSense to write HTML code.

What You Should Know

Having completed this project, you should be able to perform the tasks below. The tasks are listed in the same order they were presented in this project. For a list of the buttons, menus, toolbars, and commands introduced in this project, see the Quick Reference Summary at the back of this book and refer to the Page Number column.

1. Start FrontPage and Open an Existing Web Site (FP 544)
2. Display the Ruler and Grid in a New Web Page (FP 545)
3. Create a Web Page Using the Ruler and Grid (FP 548)
4. Display the DHTML Effects Toolbar and Add Dynamic HTML Effects (FP 551)
5. Add a Layer to a Web Page (FP 554)
6. Set the Properties of a Layer (FP 556)
7. Add Content to a Layer (FP 558)
8. Add Behaviors to a Web Page (FP 559)
9. Add Behaviors to a Web Page Element (FP 563)
10. Save a Web Page as a Dynamic Web Template (FP 565)
11. Manage Editable Regions of a Dynamic Web Template (FP 567)
12. Create a Web Page Using a Dynamic Web Template (FP 570)
13. Change a Dynamic Web Template (FP 573)
14. Check the Spelling of a Web Page (FP 575)
15. Check the Accessibility of the Current Web Page (FP 578)
16. Create an Accessibility Report (FP 582)
17. Use Split View to Correct Accessibility Warnings (FP 584)
18. Save and Test the Web Page (FP 588)
19. Publish a Subsite and Changes to an Existing FrontPage Web Site (FP 589)
20. Quit FrontPage (FP 590)

Learn It Online

Instructions: To complete the Learn It Online exercises, start your browser, click the Address bar, and then enter the Web address `scsite.com/fp2003/learn`. When the FrontPage 2003 Learn It Online page is displayed, follow the instructions in the exercises below. Each exercise has instructions for printing your results, either for your own records or for submission to your instructor.

1 Project Reinforcement TF, MC, and SA

Below FrontPage Project 8, click the Project Reinforcement link. Print the quiz by clicking Print on the File menu for each page. Answer each question.

2 Flash Cards

Below FrontPage Project 8, click the Flash Cards link and read the instructions. Type 20 (or a number specified by your instructor) in the Number of playing cards text box, type your name in the Enter your Name text box, and then click the Flip Card button. When the flash card is displayed, read the question and then click the ANSWER box arrow to select an answer. Flip through Flash Cards. If your score is 15 (75%) correct or greater, click Print on the File menu to print your results. If your score is less than 15 (75%) correct, then redo this exercise by clicking the Replay button.

3 Practice Test

Below FrontPage Project 8, click the Practice Test link. Answer each question, enter your first and last name at the bottom of the page, and then click the Grade Test button. When the graded practice test is displayed on your screen, click Print on the File menu to print a hard copy. Continue to take practice tests until you score 80% or better.

4 Who Wants To Be a Computer Genius?

Below FrontPage Project 8, click the Computer Genius link. Read the instructions, enter your first and last name at the bottom of the page, and then click the PLAY button. When your score is displayed, click the PRINT RESULTS link to print a hard copy.

5 Wheel of Terms

Below FrontPage Project 8, click the Wheel of Terms link. Read the instructions, and then enter your first and last name and your school name. Click the PLAY button. When your score is displayed, right-click the score and then click Print on the shortcut menu to print a hard copy.

6 Crossword Puzzle Challenge

Below FrontPage Project 8, click the Crossword Puzzle Challenge link. Read the instructions, and then enter your first and last name. Click the SUBMIT button. Work the crossword puzzle. When you are finished, click the Submit button. When the crossword puzzle is redisplayed, click the Print Puzzle button to print a hard copy.

7 Tips and Tricks

Below FrontPage Project 8, click the Tips and Tricks link. Click a topic that pertains to Project 8. Right-click the information and then click Print on the shortcut menu. Construct a brief example of what the information relates to in FrontPage to confirm you understand how to use the tip or trick.

8 Newsgroups

Below FrontPage Project 8, click the Newsgroups link. Click a topic that pertains to Project 8. Print three comments.

9 Expanding Your Horizons

Below FrontPage Project 8, click the Expanding Your Horizons link. Click a topic that pertains to Project 8. Print the information. Construct a brief example of what the information relates to in FrontPage to confirm you understand the contents of the article.

10 Search Sleuth

Below FrontPage Project 8, click the Search Sleuth link. To search for a term that pertains to this project, select a term below the Project 8 title and then use the Google search engine at google.com (or any major search engine) to display and print two Web pages that present information on the term.

11 FrontPage Online Training

Below FrontPage Project 8, click the FrontPage Online Training link. When your browser displays the Microsoft Office Online Web page, click the FrontPage link. Click one of the FrontPage courses that covers one or more of the objectives listed at the beginning of the project on page FP 540. Print the first page of the course before stepping through it.

12 Office Marketplace

Below FrontPage Project 8, click the Office Marketplace link. When your browser displays the Microsoft Office Online Web page, click the Office Marketplace link. Click a topic that relates to FrontPage. Print the first page.

Apply Your Knowledge

1 Creating and Using a Dynamic Web Template

Instructions: Start FrontPage and open the Web site, jkeeler, that you modified in the Apply Your Knowledge exercise in Project 7. If you did not complete this exercise, see your instructor for a copy of the required files.

1. Check out and open the tutoring.htm Web page. Save the Web page as a dynamic Web template. Undo the check out on the tutoring.htm file. Delete the tutoring.htm file from the Web site.
2. Delete the content from all of the cells in the table that include scheduling information. Leave the column and row headers in place. Select the text, Introductory Marketing, in the heading and then type `Course Name` to replace the text.
3. Select the text, Course Name, in the heading. Right-click the text and then click the Manage Editable Regions on the shortcut menu. Add a region named CourseName.
4. Except for the column and row headings, one by one, select each cell in the table and make each cell an editable region. Use a naming convention for each cell such as Monday9 for the cell that indicates the Monday at 9:00 a.m. time slot. Figure 8-71a shows all of the editable regions in the template.
5. Save the template. Right-click the template in the Folder List pane and then create a new page from the template. Type `Accounting 101 Tutoring Schedule` in the CourseName editable region. Populate cells in the table with scheduling information as shown in Figure 8-71b.
6. Save the new Web page as accounting_101_tutoring_schedule.htm.
7. Spell check the Web page and correct any spelling errors. Add any abbreviations or proper names to the custom dictionary. Save the Web page.
8. Preview the page in a Web browser to ensure that it appears as shown in Figure 8-71b. Print the Web page from FrontPage, write your name on it, and hand it in to your instructor. Check in the Web page and template. Close the Web site and then close FrontPage.

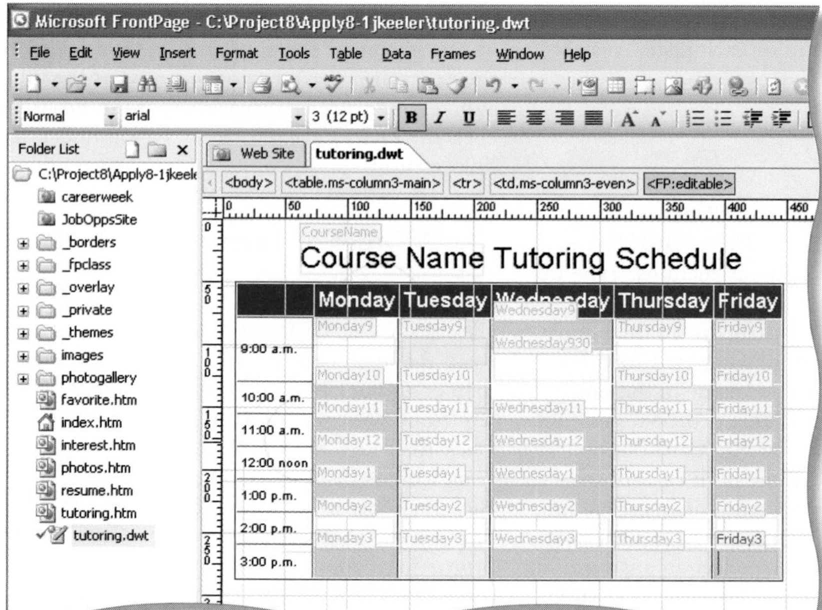

(a)

Accounting 101 Tutoring Schedule - Microsoft Internet Explorer

File Edit View Favorites Tools Help

Address C:\Project8\Apply8-1jkeeler\accounting_101__tutoring_schedule.htm

Accounting 101 Tutoring Schedule

	Monday	Tuesday	Wednesday	Thursday	Friday
9:00 a.m.	Birk 133			Birk 135	
10:00 a.m.					
11:00 a.m.					
12:00 noon					
1:00 p.m.	BUS220		BUS 220		BUS 220
2:00 p.m.					
3:00 p.m.					

(b)

FIGURE 8-71

1 Working with DHTML Effects and Layers

Problem: The owner of Fairway Lawn Care would like the FAQ to be easier to read. Instead of requiring users to navigate to each question, the answer to the question in the FAQ should pop up when the user places the mouse pointer over the question. The FAQ title should also include a special effect that draws attention to the FAQ.

Instructions: Perform the following tasks.

1. Open the Fairway Lawn Care Web site that you modified in Project 7. If you did not complete that exercise for Project 7, see your instructor for a copy of the required files.
2. Check out and open the FAQ.htm Web page. Select the text, Frequently Asked Questions. Open the DHTML Effects toolbar. Select the Page load event in the On list and then select the Hop effect in the Apply list.
3. Close the DHTML Effects toolbar.
4. Open the Layers task pane and insert a layer to the left of the list of questions. Add a box border style and set the background color to green. Click the Visibility column next to the layer1 layer in the Layers list until the visibility is set to hidden. The layer no longer is visible in Design view when the layer is not selected.
5. Scroll down to the answer to the first question on the Web page. Select the answer and copy the answer to the Clipboard. Scroll up to the link to the first question and select the question. Open the Behaviors task pane. Click the Insert button and then point to Set Text. Click the Set Text of Layer command. Paste the answer to Question 1 in the HTML text area. Click the OK button on the Set Text of Layer dialog box.
6. Change the event for the Set Text of Layer action to onmouseover.
7. Insert another onmouseover action for the same selected text and select the Change Property action. If necessary, select Select Element in the Change Property dialog box, select div in the Element Type list, and then select layer1 in the Element ID list. Set the property of the layer1 layer to visible for the onmouseover event. Select the Restore on mouseout event.
8. Repeat Steps 5 through 7 for the remaining questions. You do not need to add additional layers because the text of the layer changes depending over which question the user places the mouse pointer.
9. Preview the FAQ page in a Web browser to ensure that the effect and layer appear as shown in Figure 8-72 on the next page. Publish the Web site and test the FAQ page.
10. Make the layer visible and then print the FAQ page from Design view, write your name on the pages, and hand them in to your instructor. Check in the Web page, close the Web site, and then quit FrontPage.

(continued)

Working with DHTML Effects and Layers *(continued)*

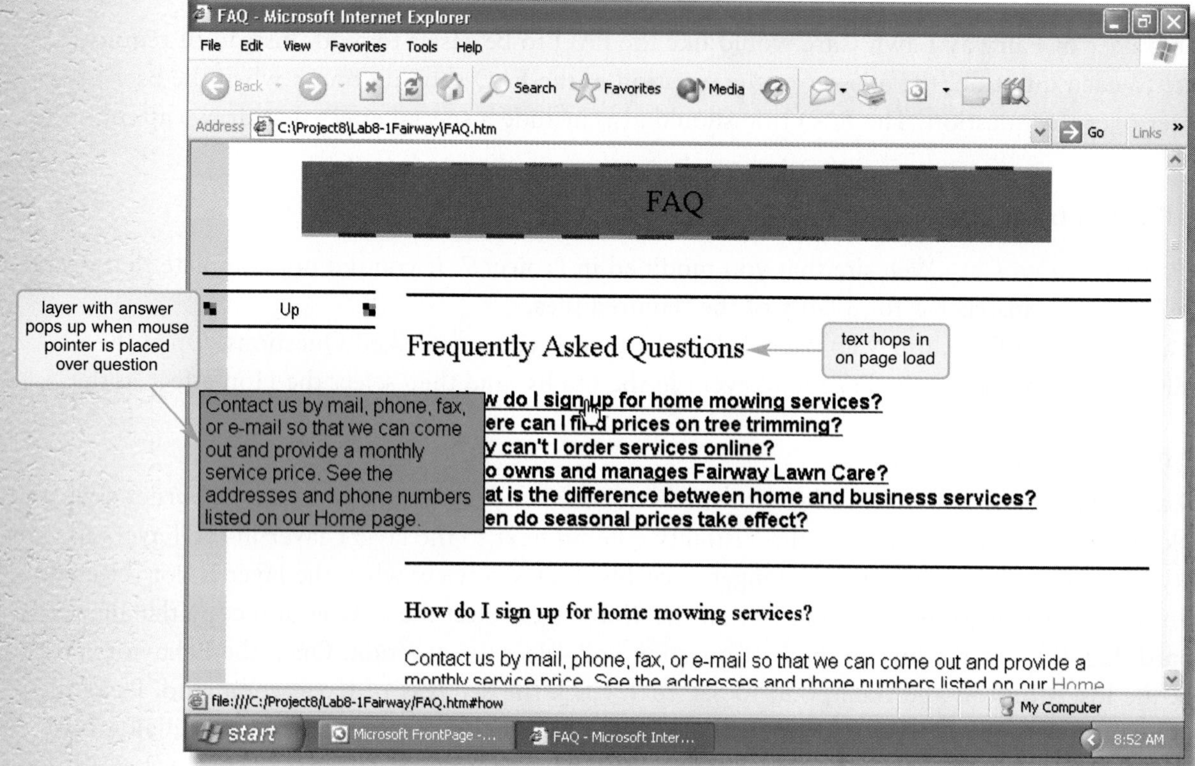

FIGURE 8-72

2 Using a Layer and Behaviors to Create a Pop-up Menu

Problem: Pop-up menus are a common means of navigating a Web page. Using pop-up menus saves on valuable screen space and provides users with a familiar interface. A pop-up menu will be added to the Ship-It-Here home page to demonstrate how to create a pop-up menu.

Instructions: Perform the following tasks.

1. Open the Ship-It-Here Web site that you modified in Project 7. If you did not complete that exercise for Project 7, see your instructor for a copy of the required files.
2. Open the index.htm Web page in Design view. Place the insertion point just before the first horizontal line below the heading, and press the ENTER key. Type `Menu`.
3. Add a layer to the page and position and size the layer as shown in Figure 8-73. Set the background color of the layer to blue and do not place a border on the layer. Click the visibility column next to the layer1 layer until the Hidden icon appears next to the layer1 layer.
4. Select the layer and then type `Home` followed by 17 space characters and press the ENTER key. Type `Shipping Supplies` and then press the ENTER key. Type `Services` followed by 13 space characters and then press the ENTER key. Type `Search` followed by 16 space characters and then press the ENTER key. Select all of the new text and set the font to the color white.

5. Add two separate behaviors to the text that reads Menu. The first behavior should make the layer1 layer visible when the mouse pointer is placed over the word Menu. And the second should make the layer1 layer hidden when the mouse pointer moves out of the layer. Add the same two behaviors to the layer itself.
6. Click the Shipping Supplies text in the layer1 layer. Click the Split button to enter Split view. Above the selected text in the code portion of Split view, find the text that reads <id="id1" and change the 1 to a 2 so that it reads <id="id2". Repeat the process for the Services text, changing the number from 1 to 3. Repeat the process for the Search text, changing the number from 1 to 4. By changing the id of each menu item, properties of the individual text can be changed by using behaviors.
7. Return to Design view. Select the text, Home, and the spaces that follow it in the layer1 layer. Add an onclick event that causes the Go To URL event to execute. Set the URL to index.htm for the action. Add two additional events to the text. The first should cause the background color to change to red on the mouseover event (Note: click the Borders button in the Change Property dialog box). The second event should cause the background color to change back to blue on the mouseout event.
8. Repeat Steps 6 and 7 for the other three links. In the Change Property dialog box, select id1 for the Home link, id2 for the Shipping Supplies link, id3 for the Services link, and id4 for the Search link. Add appropriate URLs for each.
9. Save the changes to the Web page. Preview the page in a Web browser to ensure that it appears as shown in Figure 8-73, and that the menu items link to appropriate pages. The links will not work in Preview view. Use the Preview in Browser submenu on the File menu to test the Web page.
10. Make the layer visible in Design view and then print the page in Design view. Write your name on the page and hand it in to your instructor. Make the layer invisible again and save the changes to the Web page. Close the Web site and then quit FrontPage.

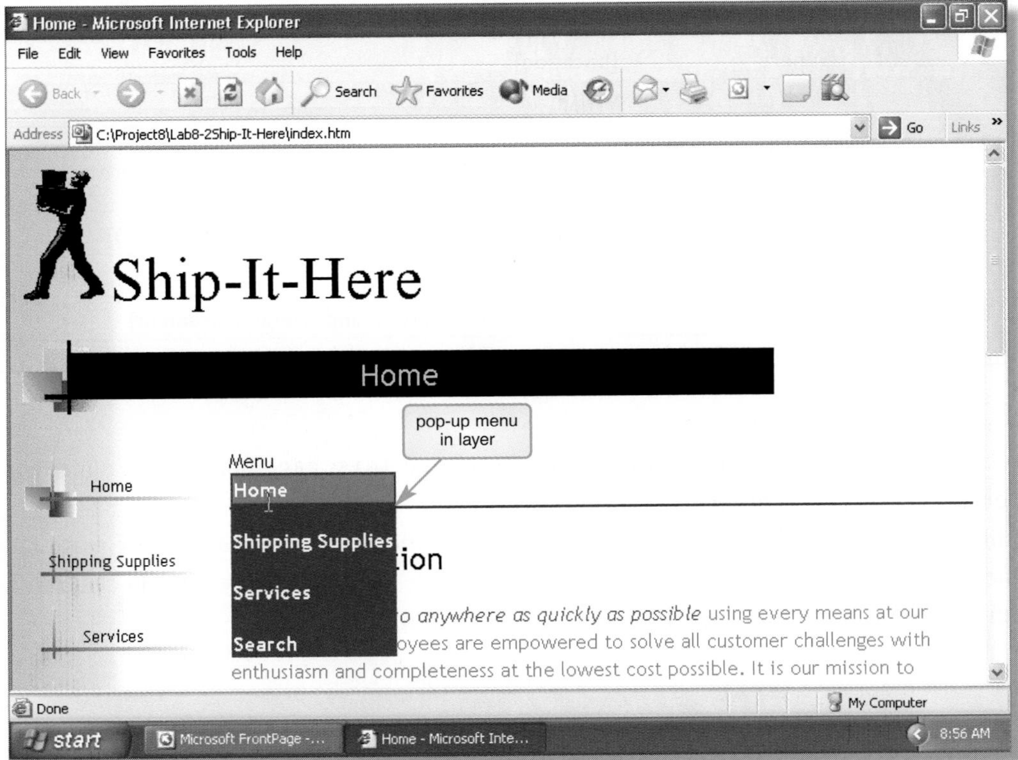

FIGURE 8-73

3 Creating a Dynamic Web Template and Checking Web Page Accessibility

Problem: You would like to start logging the races in which you compete on your running Web site. You need a template that you can use to create a new Web page for each race.

Instructions: Perform the following tasks.

1. Start FrontPage and open the Running Web site that you modified in Project 6. If you did not complete that exercise for Project 6, see your instructor for a copy of the required files.
2. Create a new Web page in the Web site. Remove the shared border from the Web site. Save the new Web page as a dynamic Web template with the name RaceSummaryTemplate.
3. Add four lines of heading to the Web site as shown in Figure 8-74a. Use the styles Heading 1 for the first line, Heading 3 for the second line, Normal for the third line, and Heading 2 for the fourth line. Add a 2 by 5 table to the Web page and drag the shoes2.gif image from the images folder to the cell in the upper-left corner of the table.
4. Add text to the table as shown in the last column of Table 8-5. Format the last four rows of the table as bold.

Table 8-5 Text for Table in Running Summary Template

ROW	COLUMN	EDITABLE REGION NAME	TEXT
1	2	RaceDescription	[Place a general overview of the race here. Include a description of the competition, any injuries, and other interesting notes.] [Place a picture from the race to the left if one is available.]
2	1		Where:
2	2	Where	[Location]
3	1		When:
3	2	When	[Date and time]
4	1		Conditions:
4	2	Conditions	[Weather and the type of course (i.e., hills, etc.)]
5	1		Placement:
5	2	Placement	[Placement in age group and overall placement]

5. Below the table, using a font size of 2 (10 pt) and italics, type `This page was last updated on`. Insert a date using the Date and Time command on the Insert menu.
6. Create an editable region for the fourth line of the heading and name it RaceName. Create an editable region for the image and name it RacePicture. Create editable regions for the cells in column 2 of the table using the region names in column 3 of Table 8-5. Save the template.

7. Perform an accessibility check on the template using all the three standards, listing errors and warnings. Save the report as an HTML page with the name accessibility_report1. View the report. One error on the page indicates that the image requires an alternate tag. Right-click the image on the template and then click Picture Properties on the shortcut menu. Click the General tab and then click Text in the Alternative representations area. Type `Running Image` in the Text text box. Close the dialog box.
8. Save the template and perform another accessibility check using the same options as noted in Step 7. Generate the HTML report and name the Web page accessibility_report2. Correct any warnings that you want to correct.
9. Create a new Web page using the template and save the Web page (Figure 8-74b on the next page). Save the Web page as HalloweenFunRun2005.htm.
10. Print the template page created from the template and print the accessibility reports. Write your name on the pages and hand them in to your instructor. Close the Web site and then close FrontPage.

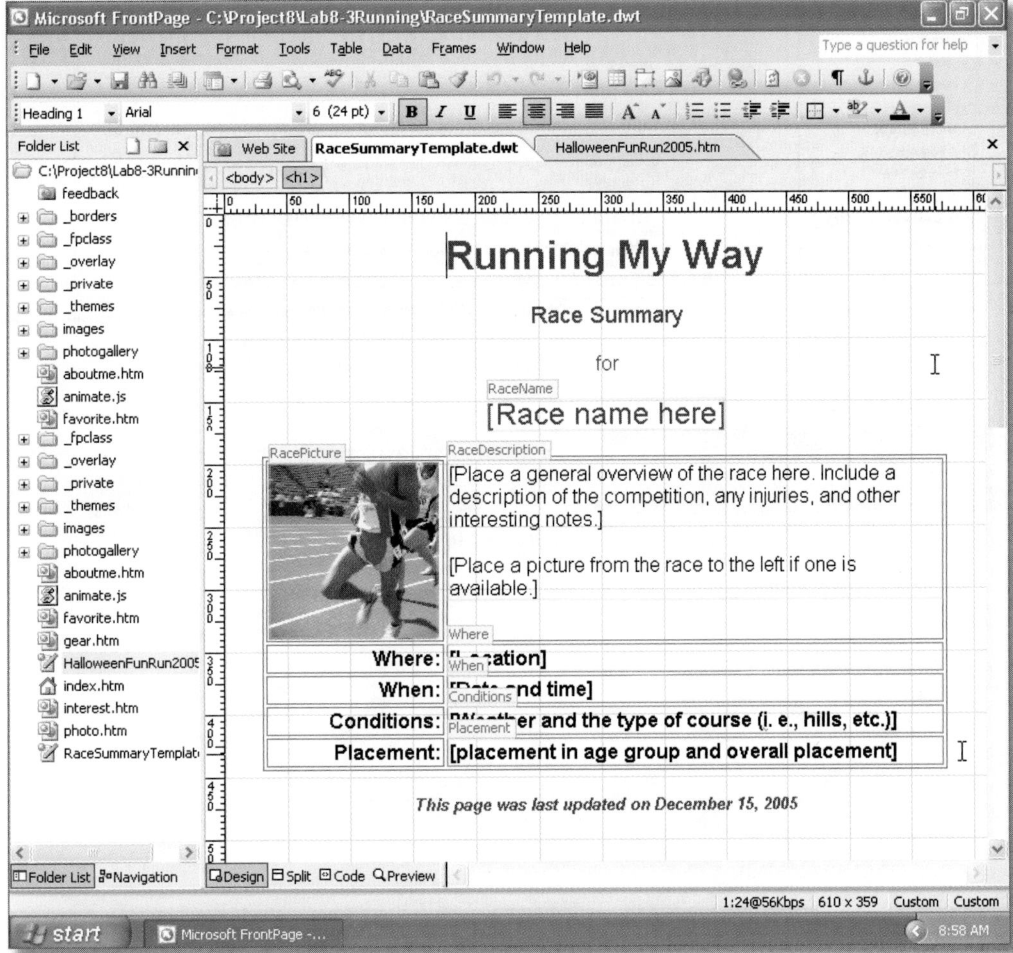

FIGURE 8-74a

(continued)

Creating a Dynamic Web Template and Checking Web Page Accessibility *(continued)*

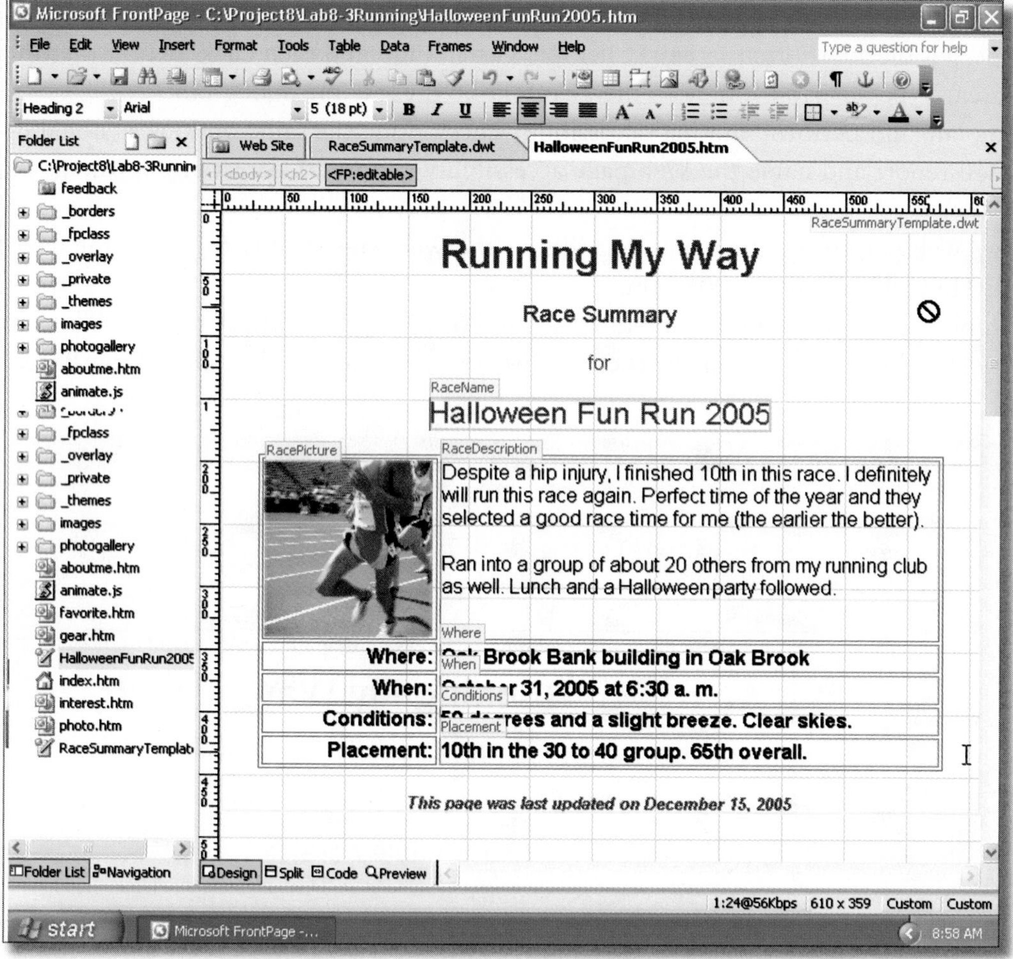

FIGURE 8-74b

Cases and Places

The difficulty of these case studies varies:
■ are the least difficult and ■■ are more difficult. The last exercise is a group exercise.

1 ■ Open your resume Web site from Project 7 and check the accessibility of the Web site. Check for errors on all pages. Generate an HTML report for the pages and print the report. Using Split view, fix the problems in the Web site that violate the WCAG Priority 1 recommendations and run the accessibility check again. Generate the HTML report for the pages and print the report. Hand in both reports to your instructor.

2 ■ Create a dynamic Web template for your movie review Web site. The template should include standard headings at the top of the page, a noneditable footer, and noneditable section headings for movie name, director, release year, and studio. Use at least three different DHTML effects to add headings, links, or a footer to the page when the page loads. Check the page for spelling errors.

3 ■■ Add a layer to the main frame page of your friend's graduation Web site. The layer should include a border, and the entire layer should include an image of your friend. The image should pop-up at the top of the Web page whenever the user places the mouse pointer over your friend's name on the Web page. Add DHTML effects so that each line of the table of contents flies in from the left when the page loads.

4 ■■ Check the office hours Web page in the departmental Web page from Project 7 for accessibility. Use the WCAG Priority 1 and Access Board Section 508 standards and check for errors and warnings. Fix all of the errors and as many warnings as possible using Split view. For items requiring an alternate description, right-click the item and then change its properties. Generate the HTML report for accessibility both before and after you fix the page. Print the HTML reports and hand them in to your instructor.

5 ■■ **Working Together** Create a template for the company sports Web site from Project 7. Apply a new theme to the template. Make sure that the background image that represents the team is in an editable region. Add a noneditable heading and footer to the page, including the date the page was last modified. Add a layer to the template that includes editable content. The layer should display the time, date, and location of the team's next game and should appear when the user places the mouse pointer over the team name, which should be on the second line of the heading.

MICROSOFT Office FrontPage 2003

Managing Web Sites on a Server

PROJECT 9

CASE PERSPECTIVE

James Keeler's Web site has gained recognition and popularity, and James is satisfied with all that he has learned about FrontPage, although he still has several questions. He is concerned about the recently added features to his Web site, including the Database Editor and search form pages, which must be published to a server in order to test them. He would like to be able to test the features and verify that they are working properly before publishing pages containing them on the World Wide Web. Trelane College provides only one Web server for student Web pages, however, and that is the live server accessible from the World Wide Web. Because he has another person helping him maintain the JobOppsSite subsite in his site, James also wants to know if he can manage permissions for a subsite separate from the parent Web site and track the pages that are new or have been modified recently. Finally, James wants to manage his Web site better by tracking the usage of each page on the site.

You assure James that FrontPage and other software typically provided with his operating system can help address his concerns and provide tools to help him manage his Web site on a server.

As you read through this project, you will learn the fundamentals of managing a Web site using the Internet Information Services administration tools. You will learn how to open a Web site on a local host and publish a Web site to a local host. You also will learn about roles and permissions on a Web site and how they help to secure a Web site. You will learn how to optimize the HTML published to a Web site. Finally, you will learn how to view usage reports for a Web site.

MICROSOFT Office FrontPage 2003

Managing Web Sites on a Server

PROJECT

Objectives

You will have mastered the material in this project when you can:

- Describe roles and permissions for a Web site
- Use Internet Information Services (IIS) administration tools to start a local Web server
- Set server options for a Web server
- Publish a Web site to multiple locations
- Set publishing options for a Web site
- Publish and open a Web site to the local host
- Manage permissions for Web sites and subsites
- Access the Web site Administration page
- Add a custom role
- Add a new user to a subsite and assign a custom role
- Enable source control for a subsite and recalculate a Web site
- Optimize the HTML published to a Web server
- Report file status for a Web site
- Report Web site usage in summary and detailed views

Introduction

Creating disk-based Web sites and then publishing them to a server on the World Wide Web is one of the many activities for which FrontPage commonly is used. As a Web site grows, however, you may need to perform certain management tasks associated with a server-based Web site, such as setting permissions for a Web site or subsite or running usage reports.

FrontPage provides many features to help simplify these tasks and help with testing a Web site. For example, you can use FrontPage to publish the same Web site to more than one server. This means that you could publish a Web site to a Web server running on the same computer where you developed your Web site, test it, and then publish the Web site to a server available on the World Wide Web. This facilitates testing the functionality of the Web site before making it available on the World Wide Web.

FrontPage also provides features for Web site management tasks, such as setting permissions for a Web site or subsite and tracking new and changed file status. FrontPage provides tools to optimize the HTML that is published to a Web site so that the Web pages in the Web site load faster for a user. Finally, FrontPage can produce usage reports that allow you to determine the activity of pages on your Web site.

Using these FrontPage capabilities requires access to a Web server. When you install Windows XP, you also can install Internet Information Services (IIS) and a set of administrative tools to manage the Web server. This software, along with the FrontPage Server Extensions 2002, provides a local Web server to which you can publish and test a Web site and run reports.

Project Nine — Web Site Administration on a Local Server

In this project, you will learn the different types of permissions on a Web site for users of that site. You will learn how to use the Internet Information Services administration tools to start and stop a Web server running on the local computer, and how to publish a Web site to that Web server. You will learn how to administer a Web site, including managing user accounts and roles; this will include creating a custom role and then assigning that role to a user. You will learn to manage subsites and how to grant access to a subsite without granting access to the parent Web site. You will learn how to publish a Web site to multiple locations and how to optimize the published Web pages. Finally, you will learn how to report the status of new and changed files and of Web page usage (Figure 9-1 on the next two pages).

Permissions and Roles for a Web Site

FrontPage provides administrative tools that let you set permissions and roles for a Web site. **Permissions**, or rights, allow the owner of a Web site to control who has access to a published Web site and the type of access permitted. With FrontPage, a user can have one of three types of hierarchical permissions — browse, author, and administer. **Browse permissions**, the lowest level of permissions, allow a user to open, or view, pages on the Web site. **Author permissions** include browsing and add the ability to create and edit the pages of a Web site. **Administer permissions** allow browsing and authoring, as well as the ability to manage other users.

More About

Permissions and Roles

The use of permissions and roles to implement Web security sometimes can be confusing. To learn more about permissions and roles, visit the FrontPage 2003 More About Web page (scsite.com/fp2003/more) and then click Permissions and Roles.

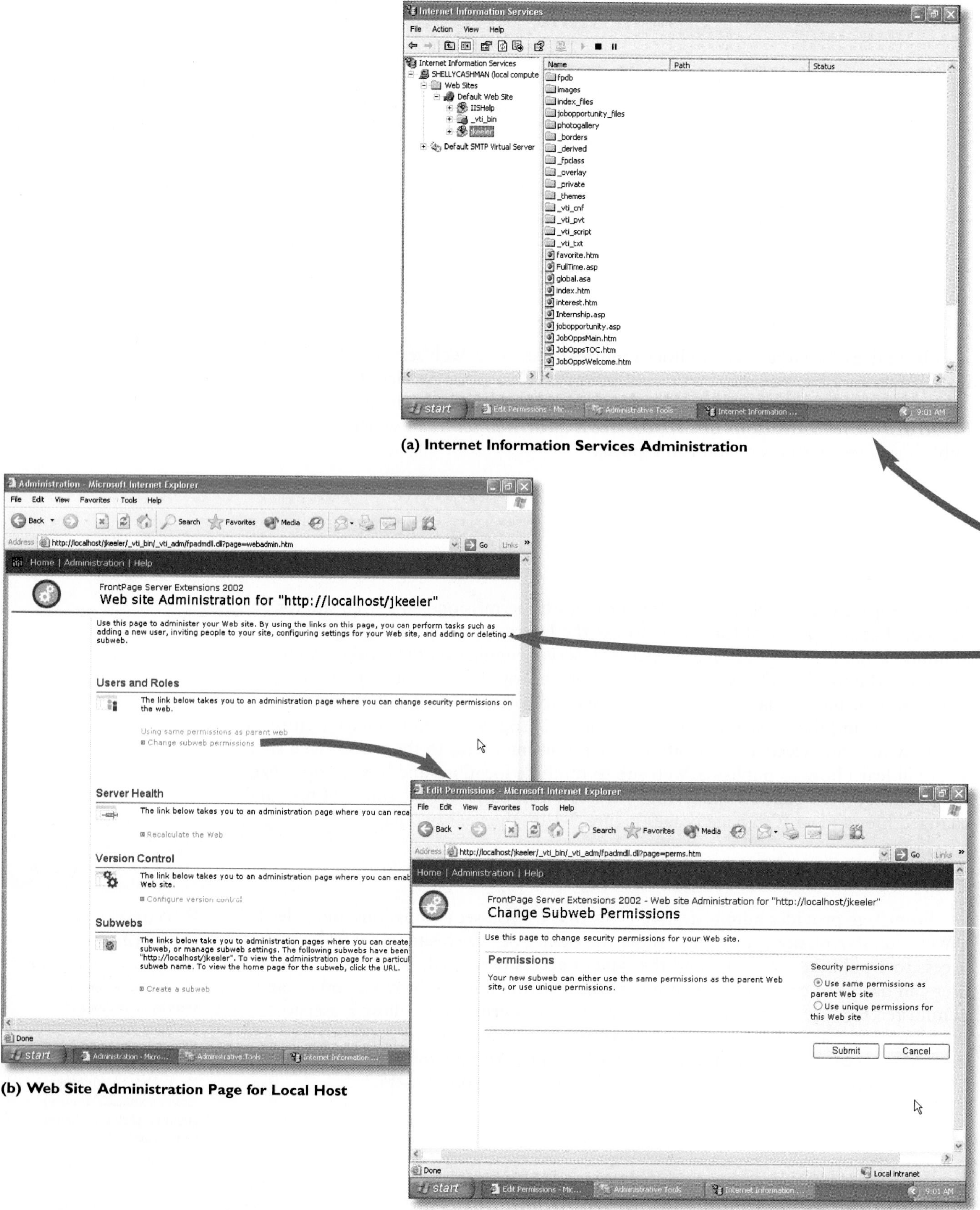

(a) Internet Information Services Administration

(b) Web Site Administration Page for Local Host

(c) Change Subweb Permissions Page

FIGURE 9-1

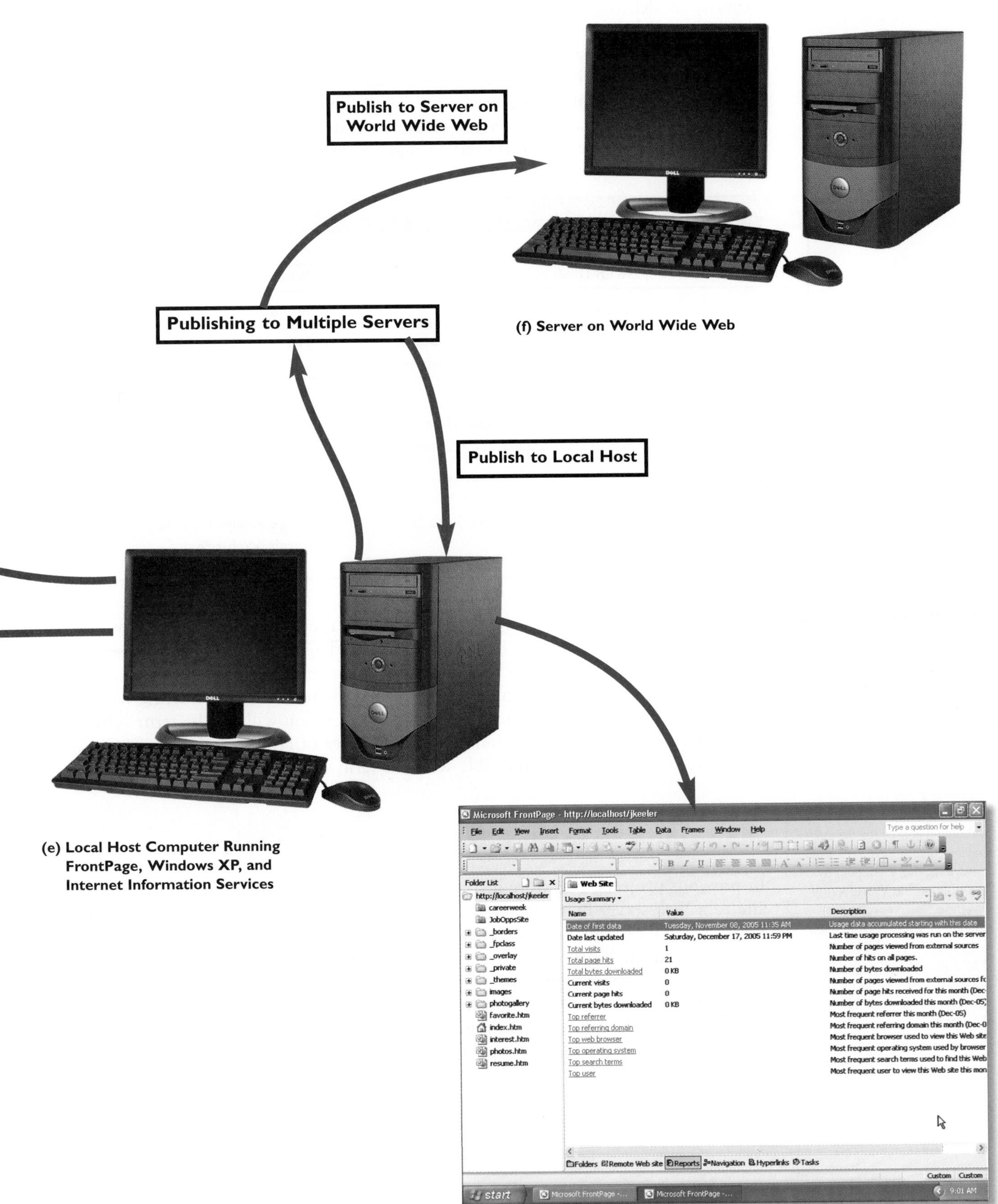

(f) Server on World Wide Web

(e) Local Host Computer Running FrontPage, Windows XP, and Internet Information Services

(d) Usage Reporting

In addition to these broad types of permissions, FrontPage uses a role-based security model to control user access or permission based on specific tasks. A role is a set of granted permissions for specific tasks that can be assigned to a user or group of users. Users are assigned one or more roles, each of which gives them specific permissions. Table 9-1 lists the default roles and the permissions available for a FrontPage Web site published on a server with the FrontPage Server Extensions 2002 installed. FrontPage also allows you to define custom roles, in which you select the specific permissions granted to users in that custom role.

Table 9-1 Default Roles and Permissions

ROLE	PERMISSIONS OR RIGHTS GRANTED	
	WEB DESIGN RIGHTS	WEB ADMINISTRATION RIGHTS
Browser	Browse	None
Contributor	Browse, View, and contribute to discussions (SharePoint Web sites only)	None
Author	Author Pages, Browse	None
Advanced Author	Author Pages, Browse, Theme Web, Border Web, Link Style Sheets	Recalc Web site
Administrator	Author Pages, Browse, Set Source Control, Theme Web, Border Web site, Link Style Sheets	Configure Access, Create Accounts, Manage Server Health, Manage Usage Analysis, Manage Subweb, Recalc Web site

More About

Internet Information Services

Using Internet Information Services on your computer provides an easy and convenient way to control a Web server. IIS is an especially valuable resource for developing and testing new Web sites before making them publicly available on the World Wide Web. To learn more about Internet Information Services, visit the FrontPage 2003 More About Web page (scsite.com/fp2003/more) and then click Internet Information Services.

Note that the term subweb is used in some of the administrative functions of FrontPage Server Extensions. The version of FrontPage Server Extensions used in this book is version 2002. Prior to FrontPage 2003, the term **subweb** was used rather than the term subsite. The term subsite replaced the term subweb starting with FrontPage 2003. Therefore, throughout this project, you will see the term subweb when discussing some of the administrative features of FrontPage Server Extensions. The term subweb is interchangeable with the term subsite.

Managing Internet Information Services

In previous projects, you were instructed to publish your disk-based FrontPage Web site to a Web server by replacing the URL, http://www.trelanecollege.edu/~jkeeler with the URL of your Web server. Most likely, that Web server was located at a URL accessible via the World Wide Web and was managed by someone at your school, workplace, or service provider.

In this project, you will publish your disk-based FrontPage Web site to a Web server running on your own computer, which is referred to as the local host or local server. Unlike a server on the World Wide Web, you can manage the local host directly.

You must have Web server software executing before you can publish to or manage the local host. Windows XP Professional and Windows 2000 also provide all of the required software to install and run a Web server on your computer so it can work as a local host. The Windows XP and Windows 2000 installation processes allow you to install Internet Information Services (IIS) Web server software, which provides a simple interface for starting, stopping, and managing the Web server. By default, IIS is not installed with Windows XP Professional or Windows 2000. IIS must be installed after Windows XP Professional or Windows 2000 is installed by going to Add or Remove Programs in the Control Panel and clicking Add/Remove Windows Components. While it is beyond the scope of this book to discuss the installation of this software, you will need access to a computer with Windows XP Professional or Windows 2000 and IIS installed to complete Project 9. If you are using an earlier version of Windows, see your instructor for instructions. You also must have FrontPage Server Extensions 2002 installed, although FrontPage Server Extensions 2000 will provide much of the needed functionality.

Running an IIS Web server is a task that should not be performed lightly. The risks of running an IIS Web server cannot be underestimated from a security standpoint. Ask your system administrator for any assistance in properly securing an IIS Web server. Make sure that all recent patches and updates have been applied to the server and that all unnecessary services have been turned off. For example, by default, IIS starts a mail server. If this functionality is not required, it should be turned off. Run the server only when necessary. Turn off the server after you have finished your development or testing work for the day.

Q&A

Q: Should I use a software- or hardware-based firewall?

A: While Windows XP provides a software-based firewall, you should consider obtaining a hardware-based firewall for production servers. Software-based firewalls can take much needed resources from the computer and can have a detrimental effect on performance. Many hardware-based firewalls provide more flexibility and often are relatively inexpensive. Whether you choose to use a hardware- or a software-based firewall, firewalls are a vital part of any Web server.

Design Tip

When using IIS as a local host, take the time to properly secure your computer with a firewall. Windows XP includes firewall functionality that is configured easily. Make sure that your computer includes up-to-date patches for Windows and any other software.

Using Internet Information Services to Start a Local Web Server

Before you can publish a disk-based Web site to a local host server, the IIS Web server installed on your computer must be running. IIS provides tools that allow you to start and stop the IIS Web server. The steps on the next page start the IIS Web server from Control Panel.

More About

The IIS Lockdown Tool

Microsoft provides a free tool to assist you in securing an IIS server — the IIS Lockdown tool. The IIS Lockdown tool includes a wizard that helps to set many security options in IIS automatically. To learn more about the IIS Lockdown tool, visit the FrontPage 2003 More About Web page (scsite.com/fp2003/more) and then click IIS Lockdown Tool.

To Use Internet Information Services to Start a Local Web Server

1

- **Click the Start button on the Windows taskbar.**

Windows displays the Start menu (Figure 9-2).

FIGURE 9-2

2

- **Click Control Panel.**

The Control Panel window opens (Figure 9-3).

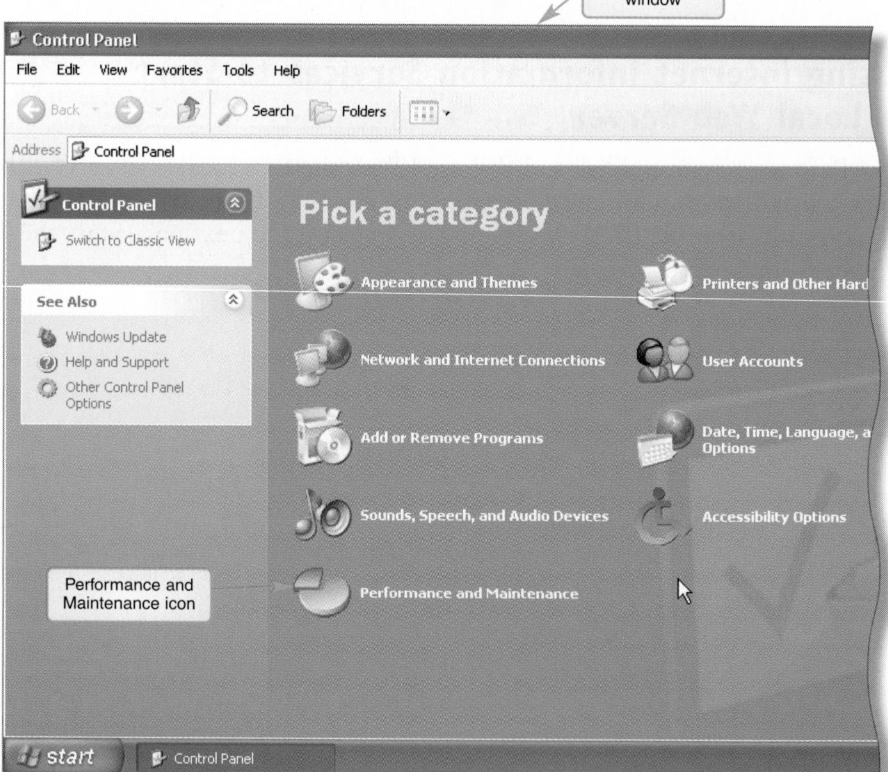

FIGURE 9-3

3

- **Click the Performance and Maintenance icon.**
- **When the Performance and Maintenance window opens, click the Administrative Tools icon.**

The Administrative Tools window opens (Figure 9-4). Administrative Tools configure administrative settings for your computer. The list of tools on your computer may vary.

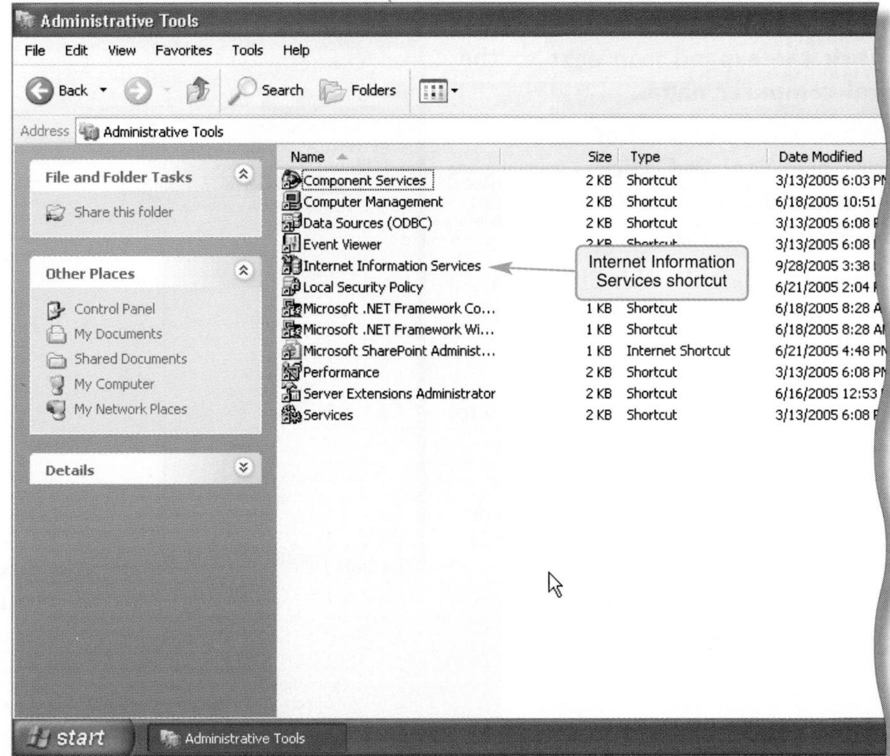

FIGURE 9-4

4

- **Double-click Internet Information Services.**

The Internet Information Services window opens (Figure 9-5).

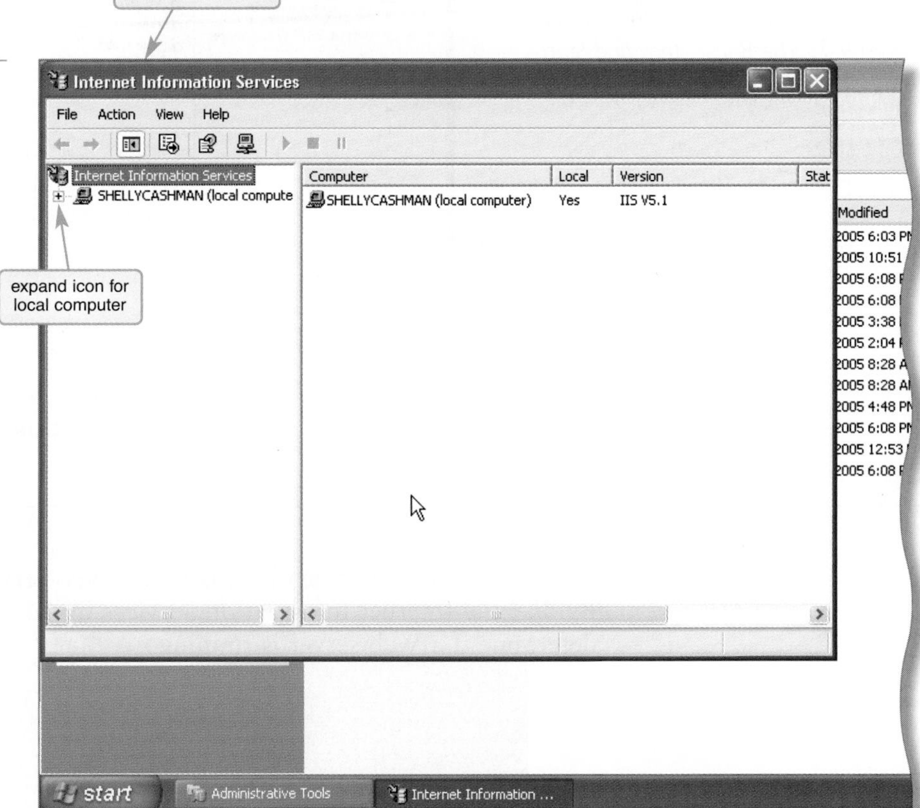

FIGURE 9-5

5

- **Click the expand icon next to the local computer name.**
- **When the next level of icons are displayed, click the expand icon next to the Web Sites folder.**
- **Click the Default Web Site item and hold the mouse pointer over the item.**

The current subsites in the default Web site are displayed in the right side pane. The Default Web Site item indicates that the Web site is stopped. Your IIS server already may be started (Figure 9-6).

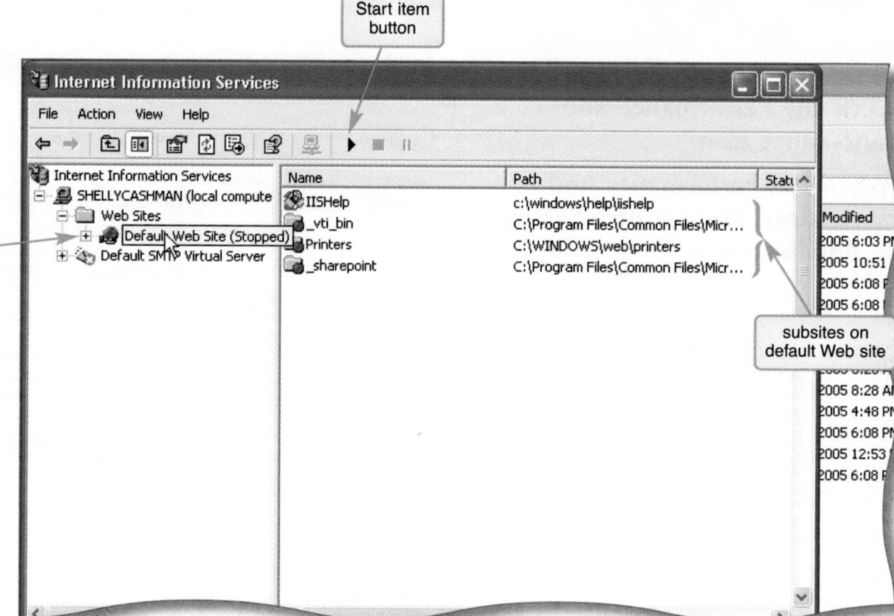

FIGURE 9-6

6

- **If necessary, click the Start item button on the toolbar.**

The Web server is started. The Start item button changes to a Stop button (Figure 9-7). The Pause item and Stop item buttons become enabled.

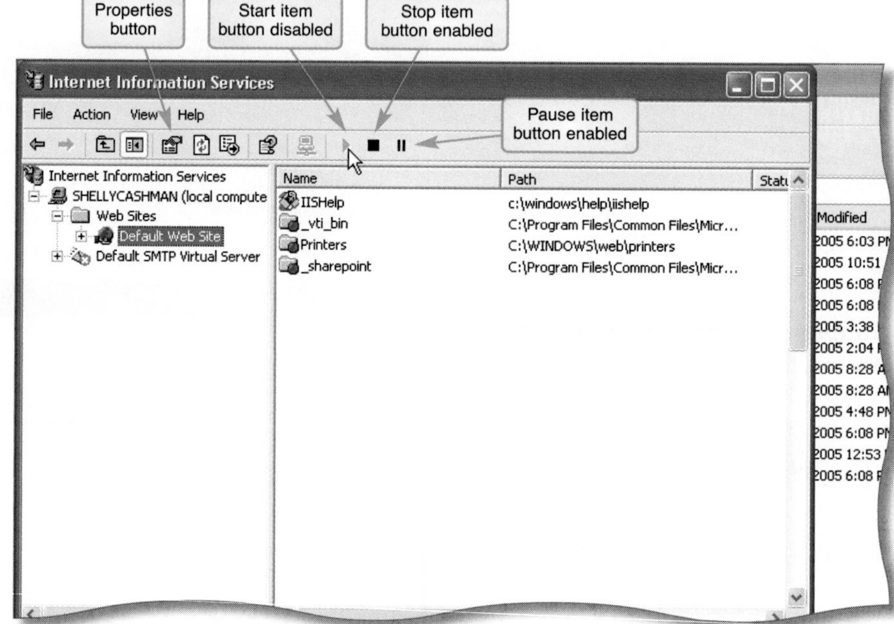

FIGURE 9-7

Often, it may not be obvious that a Web server is running on the local computer. By opening Internet Information Services in Administrative Tools, you quickly can determine if a Web server is running.

Setting Server Options for a Web Server

In addition to allowing you to start and stop the Web server, IIS provides an interface to configure the server by setting a number of options. This includes creating virtual directories, setting their access permissions, and setting multiple default document names. A **virtual directory** is a directory that is not necessarily contained in the server root directory and yet appears to client browsers as though it were. As shown in Table 9-2, a virtual directory has an alias that is mapped to the physical location of the content on a server. When you access a Web page in a virtual directory, the browser appends the alias to the URL of the root directory, so that it appears to be contained within the root directory.

More About

Virtual Directories

Virtual directories add another layer of security to your Web site, because visitors do not see the actual location of a given directory, only an alias. To learn more about virtual directories, visit the FrontPage 2003 More About Web page (scsite.com/fp2003/more) and then click Virtual Directories.

Table 9-2 Virtual Directories and Mappings

PHYSICAL LOCATION OF DIRECTORY	ALIAS	URL VIEWED IN BROWSER
C:\Inetpub\wwwroot	(none) root directory	http://sales
C:\Inetpub\wwwroot\products	(none)	http://sales/products
\\server2\orderupdates	orders	http://sales/orders
D:\marketing\news	news	http://sales/news

A **default document** is the document IIS tries to open when no document name is supplied in the URL. For example, as you saw in previous projects, if a user types http://www.trelanecollege.edu/~jkeeler in the Address bar of a browser, IIS opens the default document, index.htm. With IIS, you can specify multiple default documents. If a user does not supply a document name in the URL, IIS will try to open each document in turn.

Design Tip

While designing your site, begin considering where and how your site will be published to a server. Decide on a virtual directory structure and begin the process of configuring the server. If your server is managed by a third party, contact the server administrator and begin to discuss your requirements.

Most likely, the default settings for the server are appropriate, so you will not need to change them. You may want to examine them and confirm this, however. You easily can check the Web server options using IIS. IIS includes sophisticated Web site management tools that allow you to configure many aspects of a Web site. Make sure that you are familiar with the meanings of a feature before you attempt to change any settings.

The steps on the next page examine and set server options for the Web server using IIS.

To Set Web Server Options for Internet Information Services

1

- **Click the Properties button on the toolbar.**

The Default Web Site Properties dialog box is displayed (Figure 9-8). The Web Site sheet displays technical information about the Web site.

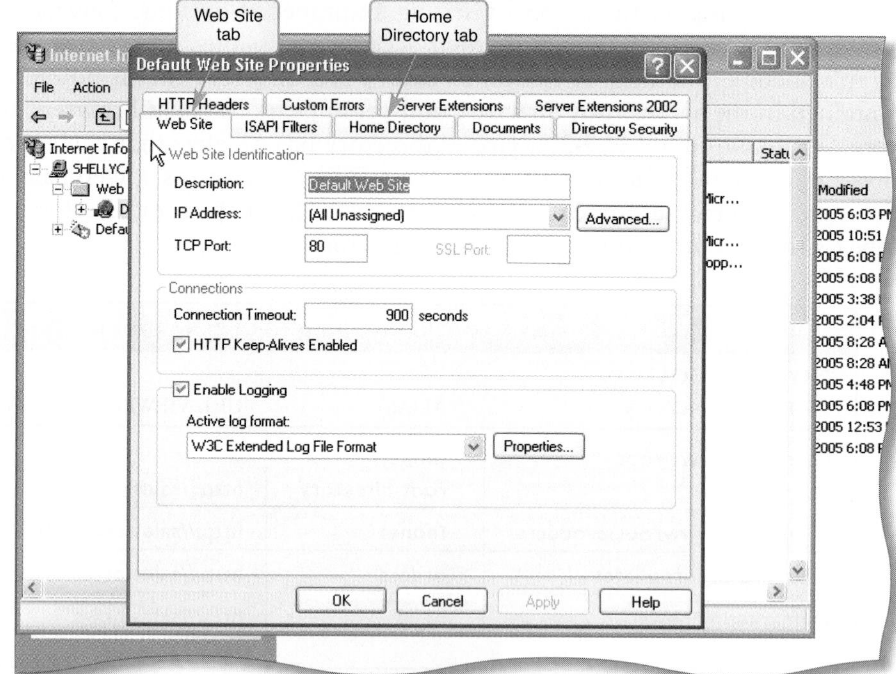

FIGURE 9-8

2

- **Click the Home Directory tab.**
- **When the Home Directory sheet is displayed, in the Local Path area verify that Read is selected and that Write, Script source access, and Directory browsing are not selected.**

The Home Directory sheet is displayed with the Read check box selected (Figure 9-9).

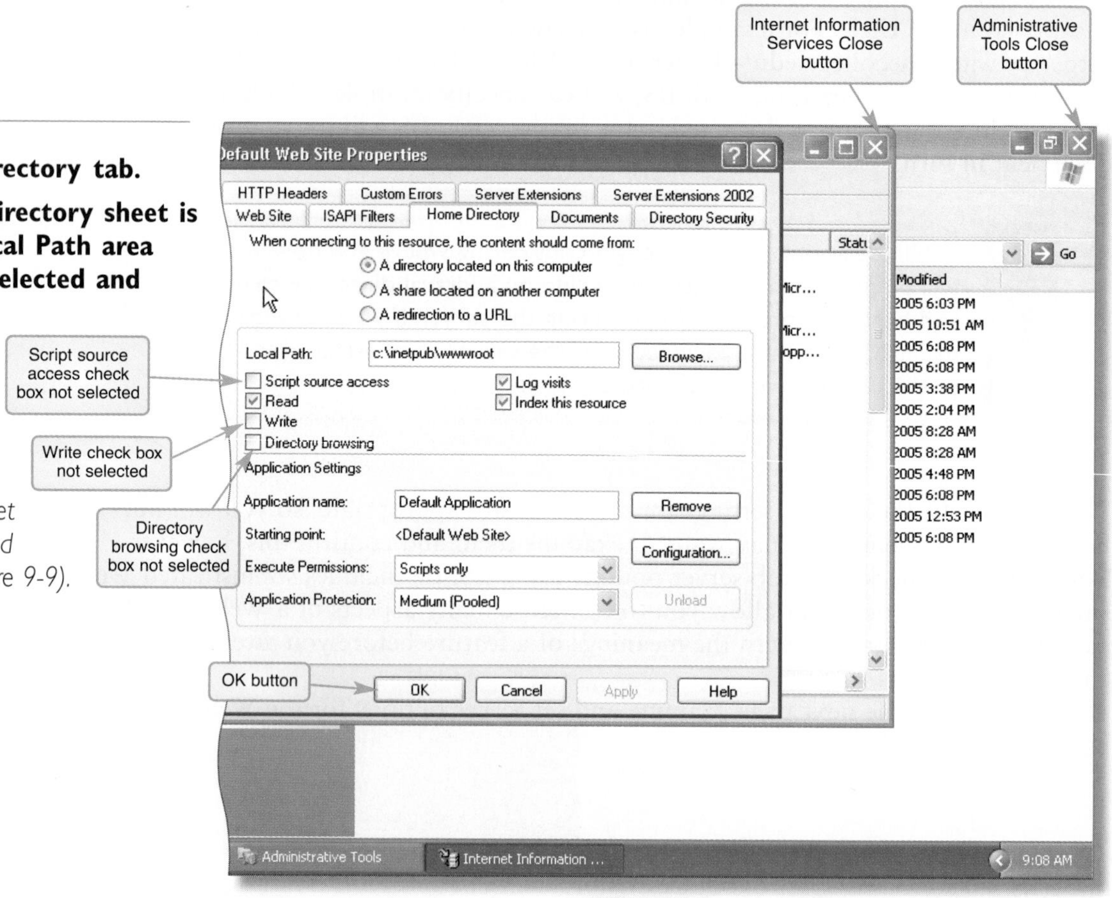

Internet Information Services Close button

Administrative Tools Close button

Script source access check box not selected

Write check box not selected

Directory browsing check box not selected

OK button

FIGURE 9-9

3

- **Click the OK button.**
- **Click the Close button on the title bar of the Internet Information Services window.**
- **Click the Close button on the title bar of the Administrative Tools window and the Control Panel window.**

The windows are closed, and the Windows Desktop is displayed (Figure 9-10).

FIGURE 9-10

The Web server now is running, so you can publish a Web site to the local host. The Read check box selected in the Home Directory sheet in the Default Web Site Properties dialog box allows users to read or download files or folders from the root directory. Because the Write check box was not selected, users cannot upload or change files in the root directory. Because the Script source access check box was not selected, users cannot access the source HTML code of pages in the root directory.

Starting FrontPage and Opening an Existing Web Site

The following steps start FrontPage and then open the FrontPage Web site from Project 8. If you did not complete Project 8, see your instructor for a copy of the required files.

To Start FrontPage and Open an Existing Web Site

1. **Click the Start button on the taskbar. Point to All Programs on the Start menu.**
2. **Point to Microsoft Office on the All Programs submenu.**
3. **Click Microsoft Office FrontPage 2003 on the Microsoft Office submenu.**
4. **Click the Open button arrow on the Standard toolbar.**

5 **Click Open Site on the Open menu. When FrontPage displays the Open Site dialog box, if necessary, click the Look in box arrow and select the folder location where you stored the Web site for Project 8 (e.g., C:\jkeeler).**

6 **Click the Open button in the Open Site dialog box.**

The previously created FrontPage Web site is loaded and is displayed in Folders view (Figure 9-11).

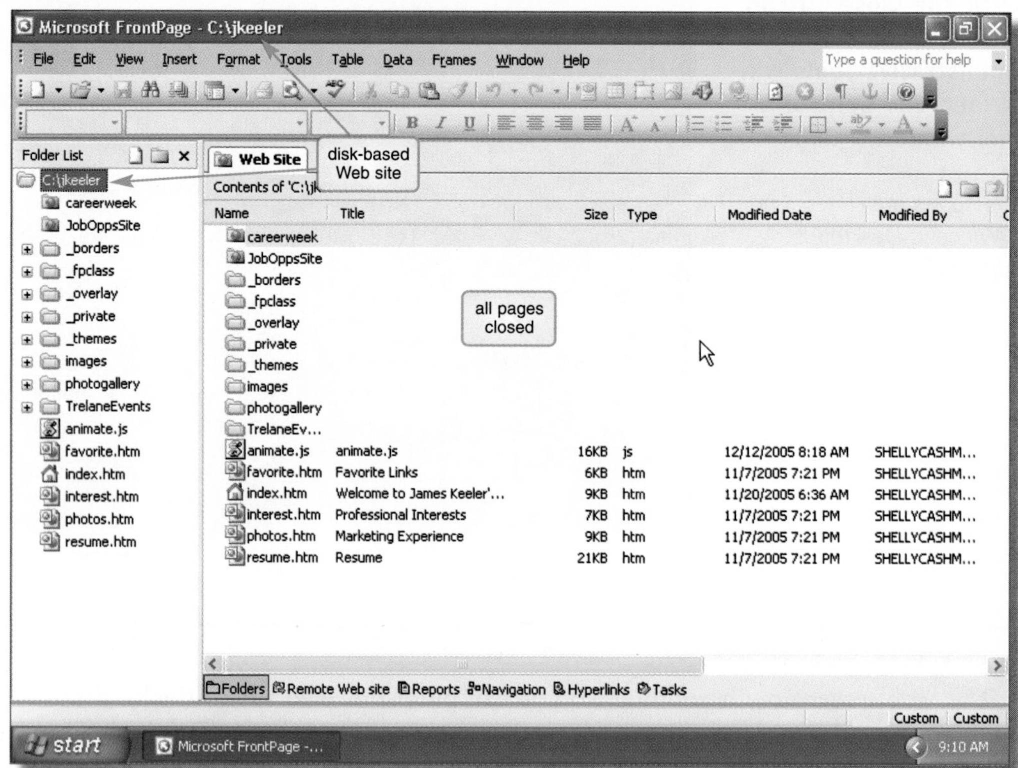

FIGURE 9-11

Publishing a Web Site to Multiple Locations

In a previous project, you learned the difference between a disk-based Web site and a server-based Web site. The jkeeler Web site currently open in FrontPage is a disk-based Web site. The Web site management functions covered in this project, however, are focused on managing a server-based Web site.

If you have authorization to do so, you can open pages in a Web site directly from the server you published in previous projects. In general, however, it is good development practice to make and test changes on a test site published to a different server. The server where you develop and test your Web pages often is called a **test server**, sometimes called a **staging server**. You also can develop your pages locally or on a shared development server that is different from a test server. Once the pages are tested, you can publish the Web site from the test server to the publicly available Web server or **production server**. This process of first publishing to a test server and then to the production server is accomplished easily by using the local host as the test server. **Migration** is the process of moving a Web site from one location to another after it has passed through some approval process.

More About

Web Packages

FrontPage allows you to gather up all or some of the files and folders in a Web site and store them in a single file called a Web package. The Web package then can be moved to another computer and the Web site can be recreated. Web packages also offer a convenient storage mechanism for backing up Web sites. The Import and Export commands on the Packages submenu on the Tools menu provide the capability to create and utilize Web packages.

Design Tip

The migration and management of development, test, and production servers should be done in a controlled and careful manner. Include plans to go back to a previous version of a Web site if the deployment of a new version does not work out. The methods in which you perform a migration should be documented and well understood by your team and the server administrators.

Setting Publishing Options for a Web Site Using FrontPage

FrontPage provides tools that allow you to set publishing options for a Web site, before you publish it to a server. When you publish to the local host as a test server, you may want to set different publishing options than you would with a production Web site. For example, when publishing over the Web site to a production server, you may want to publish only the pages that have changed, thus minimizing the amount of data sent over the network. Or, you may want to optimize the HTML code that is published to the production Web site. When publishing to your local host, this is not an issue, so you may want to publish all pages and overwrite pages that already exist. So that you can track changes made to the pages on any server, FrontPage includes an option that creates a log file of changes made to the destination Web site during publishing.

The following steps use FrontPage to set publishing options for the current Web site.

To Set Publishing Options for a Web Site Using FrontPage

1

- **Click the Remote Web site button.**

FrontPage displays the Web site in Remote Web site view (Figure 9-12).

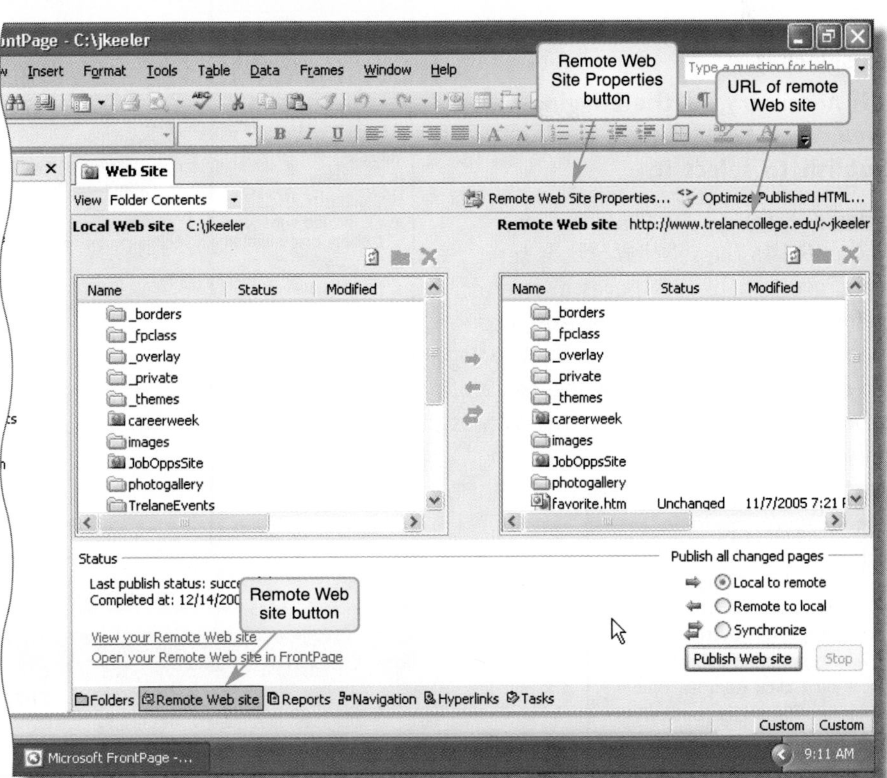

FIGURE 9-12

2

• **Click the Remote Web Site Properties button.**

FrontPage displays the Remote Web Site Properties dialog box (Figure 9-13).

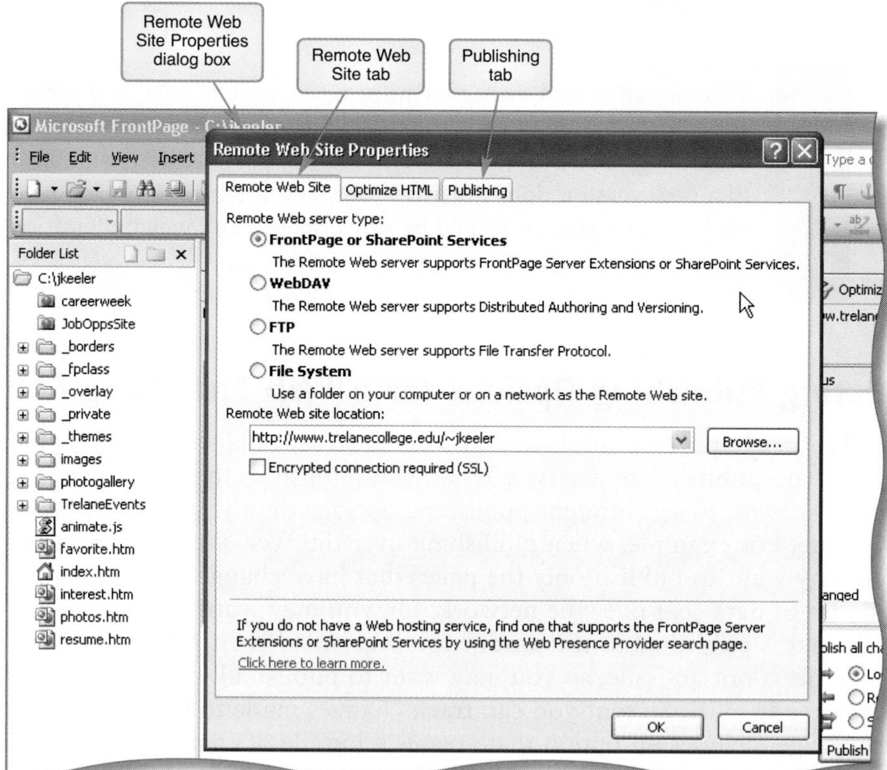

FIGURE 9-13

3

• **Click the Publishing tab.**

• **In the General area, click All pages, overwriting pages already on destination to select it.**

• **If necessary, click Include subsites to select it.**

• **If necessary, in the Logging area, click Log changes during publish to select it.**

FrontPage displays the Publishing sheet (Figure 9-14). The selected options set FrontPage to publish all pages to a server, overwriting pages that already exist, and track the changes in a log file. The View log file button allows you to view the log file of changes made when the Web site last was published.

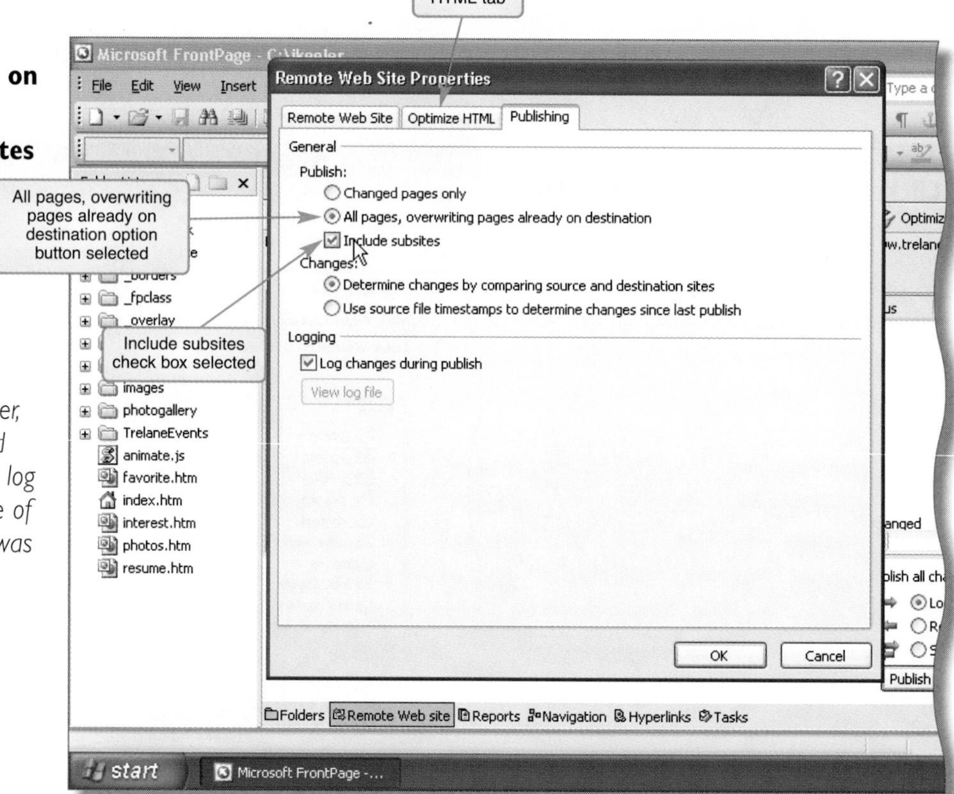

FIGURE 9-14

Other Ways

1. On File menu click Publish Site, if necessary, click Remote Web Site Properties button
2. Press ALT+F, U; if necessary, click Remote Web Site Properties button
3. In Voice Command mode, say "File, Publish Site"; if necessary, click Remote Web Site Properties button

As shown in Figure 9-14, the General area of the Publishing sheet includes two Changes options that define how FrontPage determines which pages have been changed. One option is to compare source file timestamps — the date and time the files last were modified — to determine changes made since the Web site was last published. This option is fast, but can be inaccurate if multiple developers are modifying files on the server. The other option compares source and destination Web sites, which requires downloading a directory listing from the server. Although this may take more time because of the download, it is more accurate.

Optimizing HTML

When you publish a Web site to a production server, you may want to optimize the HTML code that is published. **Optimizing** the HTML results in smaller Web page file sizes and, therefore, faster Web page downloads for users of your Web site. The file sizes are reduced in a variety of ways. FrontPage provides several options for optimizing HTML when publishing or designing Web sites. To optimize a page that you are developing in Design view, use the Optimize HTML command on the Tools menu. This command optimizes the Web page that you currently have open in Design view. Optionally, you can choose to optimize the HTML only when it is published to the Web server. In this case, the HTML of the published Web pages will differ from the Web pages that you keep on the disk-based Web site.

The following steps set the options to optimize the HTML that is published to the remote Web site.

More About

Optimizing HTML

When working on a Web site, either you can open and change the disk-based version of the site or you can open and change the remote Web site. Make a habit of always working on the disk-based version of the site and then publishing your changes with optimized HTML. If you open and change the remote Web site, the site will contain the optimized HTML rather than the full HTML, and the full HTML may contain important comments and may be easier to read.

To Set Options to Optimize Published HTML

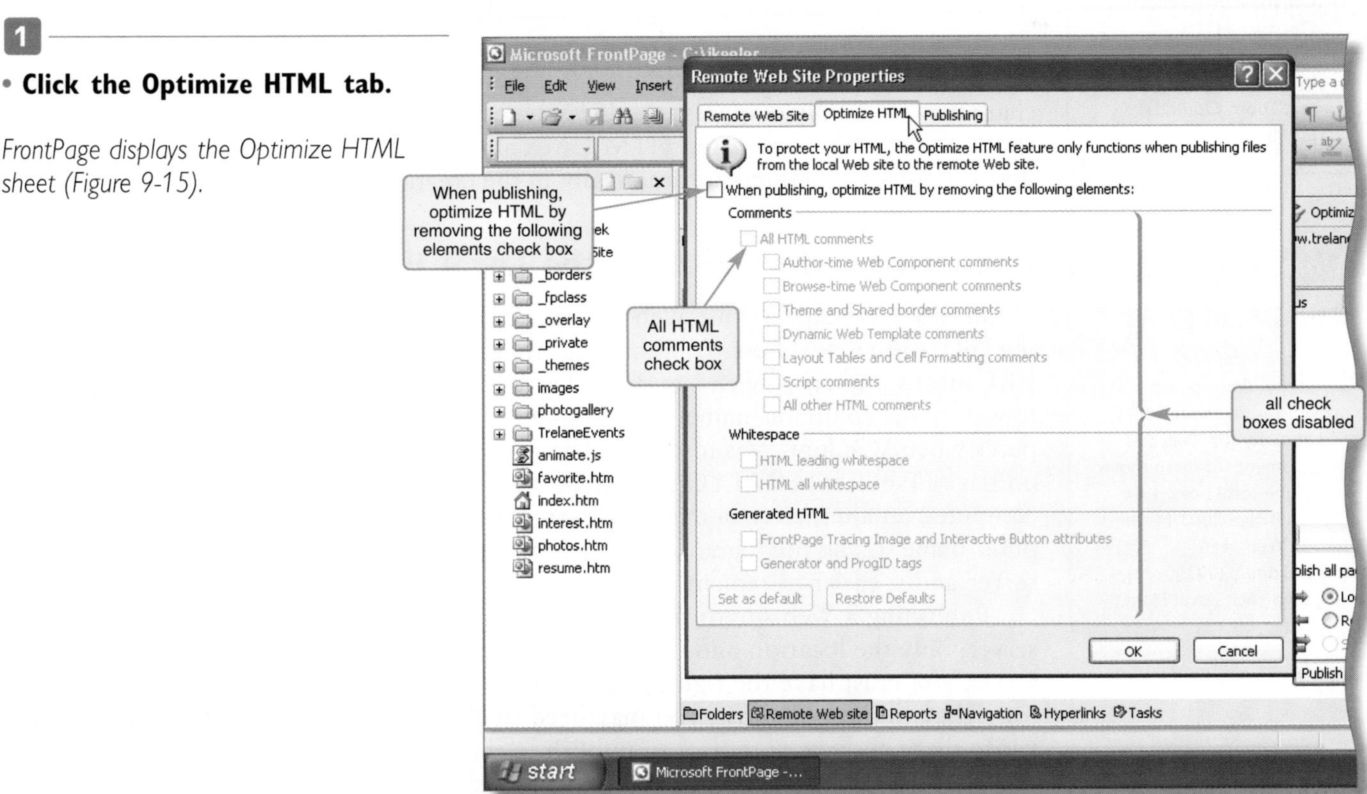

FIGURE 9-15

2

- **Click When publishing, optimize HTML by removing the following elements.**
- **Click All HTML comments.**
- **Click HTML leading whitespace.**
- **Click HTML all whitespace.**

FrontPage displays the Optimize HTML sheet with the selected options (Figure 9-16). The Set as default button allows you to use these settings for all Web sites that you publish. The Restore Defaults button restores the options to the original settings.

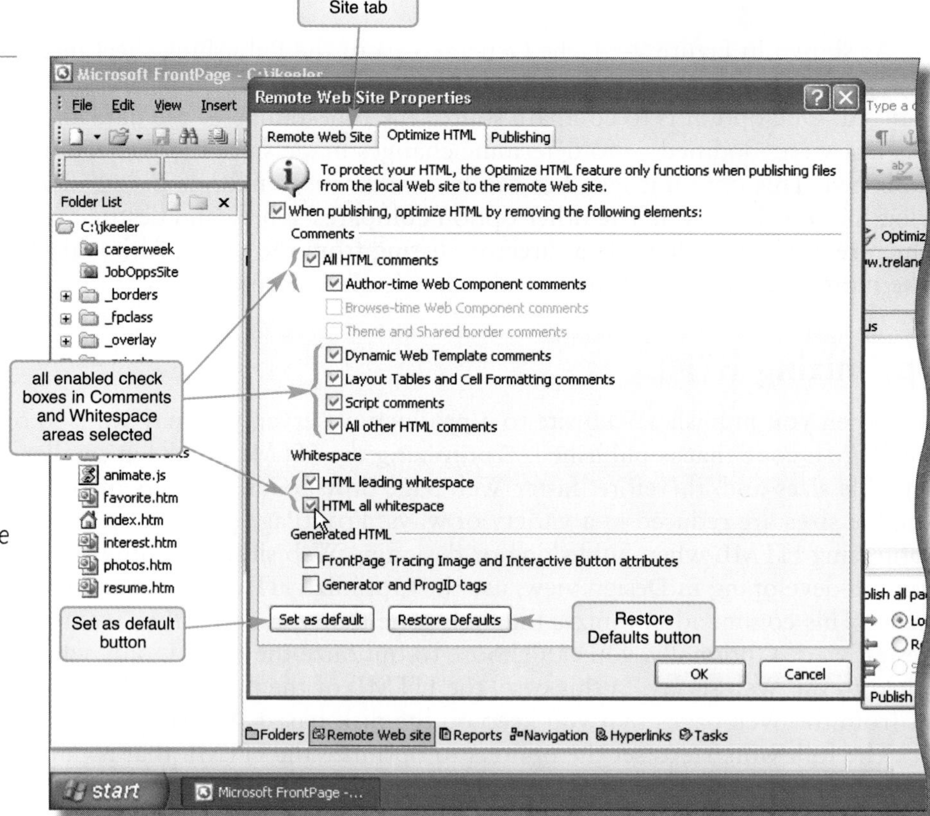

FIGURE 9-16

Other Ways

1. On Tools menu click Optimize HTML
2. Press ALT+T, H
3. In Voice Command mode, say "Tools, Optimize HTML"

As shown in Figure 9-16, FrontPage provides several methods for optimizing HTML. Removal of comments and whitespace — such as tab characters and space characters — simply compress the HTML code and publish only necessary code. The check boxes in the Generated HTML area allow you to remove special HTML code that FrontPage generated automatically in the creation of the Web page.

More About

The Local Host

Using the local host to support a Web server provides both convenience and security for Web site development. To learn more about the local host, visit the FrontPage 2003 More About Web page (scsite.com/fp2003/more) and then click Local Host.

Publishing a Web Site to the Local Host

In order to publish your Web site to the local host or server, you need to know the URL of the local host. A Web server that runs locally on your computer has a URL just as any other Web site does. The URL consists of the HTTP protocol followed by the computer name. The computer name is the name assigned to the computer when Windows was installed. The **computer name** shown in Figure 9-5 on page FP 609 is SHELLYCASHMAN. Because the computer name varies for each computer, an alternative name, **localhost**, often is used in place of the actual computer name. Using the name localhost provides the same result for any local host server and is easier to remember.

Publishing a Web site to the local host is much like publishing it to any other server; only the location and URL of the server are different. As with any other server, you must have the rights to publish to the server. Unless you have administrator rights on the local host, you may need to check with the system administrator to verify that you have authority to publish to the server.

The following steps publish an existing disk-based Web site to the local host.

To Publish a Web Site to the Local Host

1

• **Click the Remote Web Site tab.**

FrontPage displays the Remote Web site sheet, indicating the site where this Web site previously was published (Figure 9-17).

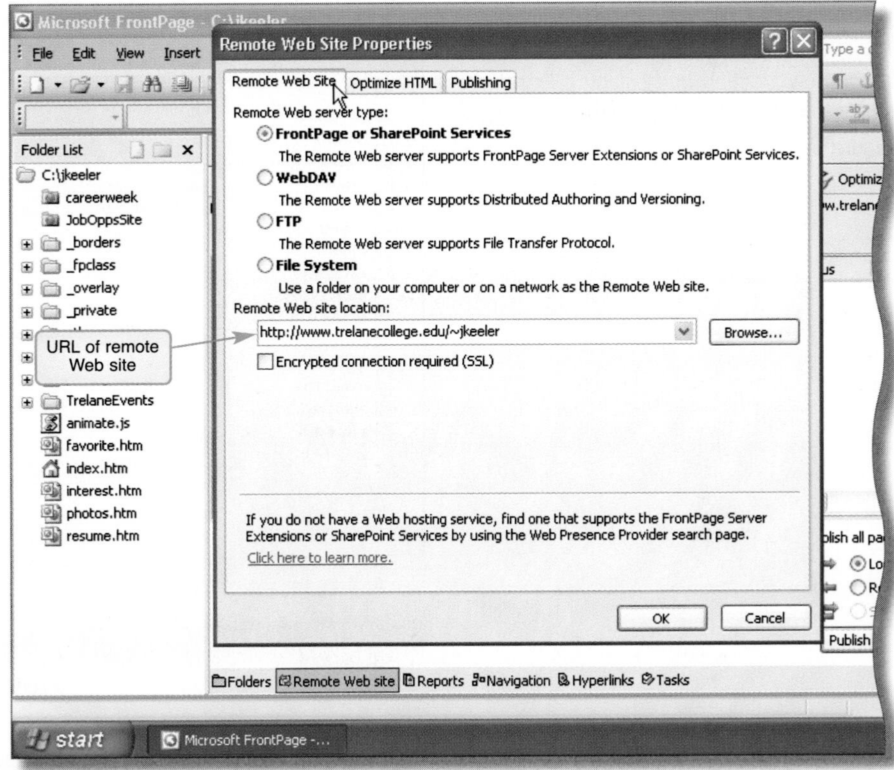

FIGURE 9-17

• **If necessary, click the FrontPage or SharePoint Services option button to select it.**

• **Type** `http://localhost/jkeeler` **in the Remote Web site location box.**

FrontPage displays the URL for the new publish destination, which is the local host (Figure 9-18).

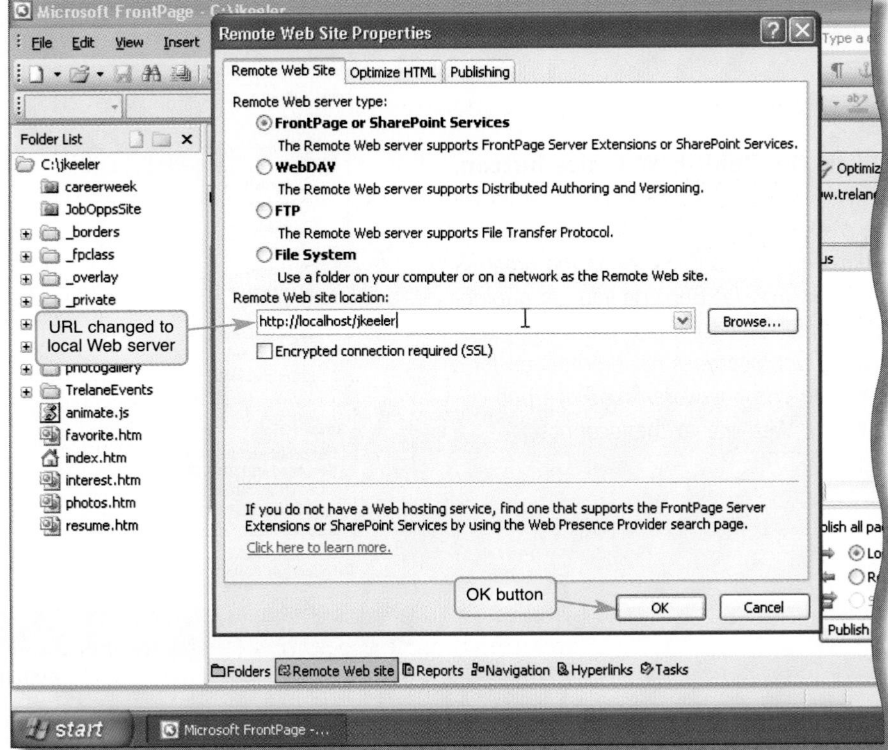

FIGURE 9-18

3

• **Click the OK button.**

The Microsoft Office FrontPage dialog box is displayed, indicating that no Web site exists at the new location and asking if FrontPage should create a Web site at that location (Figure 9-19).

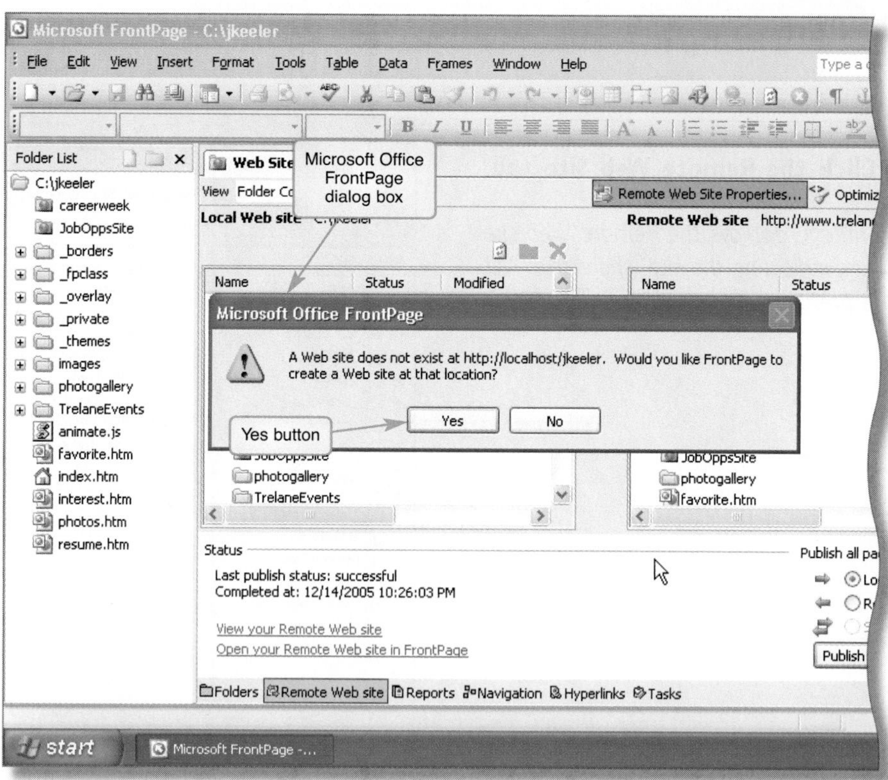

FIGURE 9-19

4

• **Click the Yes button.**

FrontPage creates a new Web site on the local host.

5

• **Click the Publish Web site button.**

The Microsoft Office FrontPage dialog box displays a status bar indicating the progress of the file transfer. Because you are publishing to the local host where you already are a user, FrontPage does not prompt you for a username and password. FrontPage publishes the Web site to the local host (Figure 9-20).

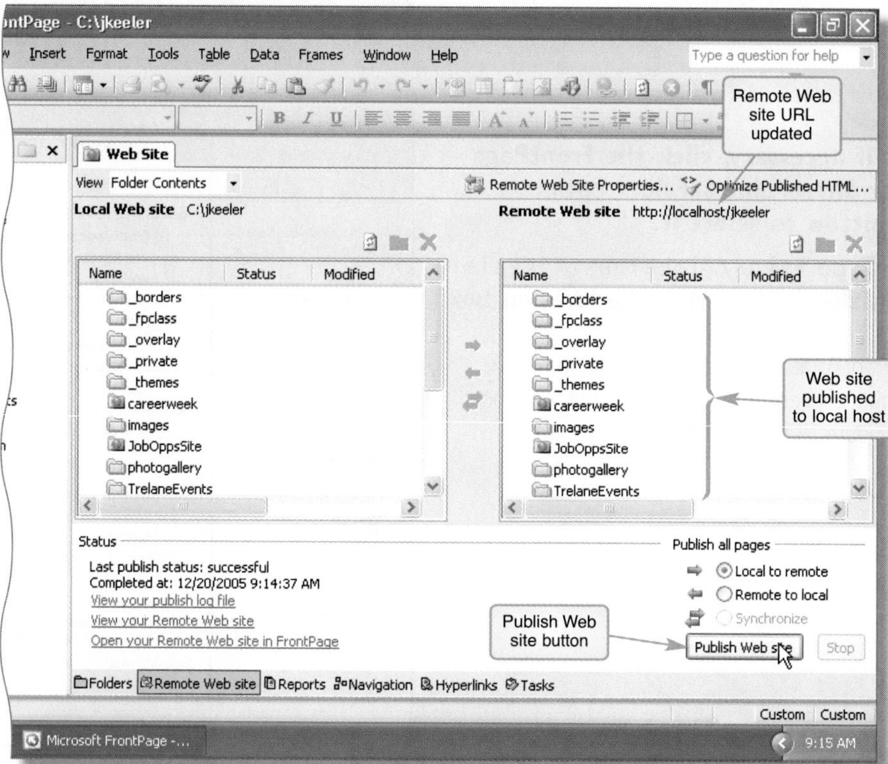

FIGURE 9-20

Opening a Web Site on the Local Host

The disk-based Web site now has been published to the local host. To use the server management features of FrontPage for a Web site, the Web site must be opened on a server. Opening a Web site on a server is similar to opening a disk-based Web site. Before the server-based Web site can be opened, the server must be started. Because the Web server was started using IIS in Control Panel, the server is running on the computer, and because the Web site has been published to the local host, the Web site now can be opened on the local host.

The following step opens an existing server-based Web site on the local host.

To Open a Web Site on the Local Host

1

• **Click the Open your Remote Web site in FrontPage link in the lower-left portion of Remote Web site view.**

FrontPage opens the server-based Web site, jkeeler, on the local host (Figure 9-21). Document source control is not enabled, even though it was applied to the disk-based Web site. To use source control for the server-based Web site, source control must be applied specifically to the server-based Web site, independent of the disk-based Web site.

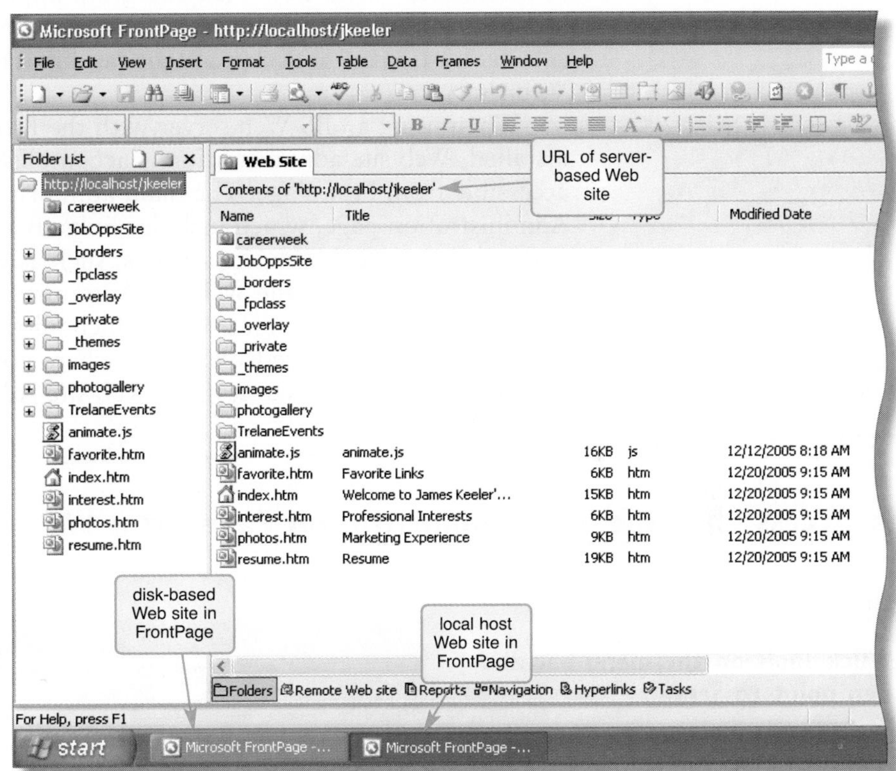

FIGURE 9-21

Managing a Web Site on the Local Web Server

Using your computer as a local host when running IIS with Windows XP Professional or Windows 2000, you can use FrontPage and Windows features to manage various server options. You can use Windows features, for example, to add and maintain users and groups. FrontPage provides features that allow you to set permissions for a Web site or subsite.

More About

FrontPage Server Extensions 2002

FrontPage Server Extensions 2002 are required for many of the advanced features available in FrontPage 2003. To learn more about the FrontPage Server Extensions 2002, visit the FrontPage 2003 More About Web page (scsite.com/fp2003/more) and then click FrontPage Server Extensions 2002.

Managing Permissions for Web Sites and Subsites

As you have seen in previous projects, the process of working with a Web site and a subsite essentially is the same. When managing Web sites and subsites, however, you must have permission to manage the given Web site or subsite. By default, a subsite uses the same permissions as the parent Web site. Similarly, a parent Web site uses the same permissions as the root Web site of the server. When managing the Web site, you can change these permissions to restrict access to a Web site or subsite.

In this Web site, another user (Doreen Maris) will be given access to manage the Job Opportunities subsite. This user also will be able to perform many authoring and administration tasks, but not all of the tasks allowed for an administrator role. The new user will not have access to the James Keeler personal Web site. Because the default roles inherited from the parent Web site do not provide the desired level of access permissions, you will create a custom role for the subsite, add a user account to the subsite for the new user, and grant appropriate access permissions to the account by assigning it the custom role. Before a custom role can be created, the subsite must be set to accept unique permissions rather than use those of the parent Web site.

When using an IIS Web server with the FrontPage Server Extensions 2002 installed, Web site administration is accomplished through a series of Web pages accessible from FrontPage. The main administration page is the Web site Administration page, which includes links to pages that allow you to access and update server-based Web site settings, such as users and roles, source control, and subsites. For example, the Web site Administration page includes a link to the Change Subweb Permissions page, which allows you to define permissions for subsites and the Manage Roles page, where you can add, delete, or edit roles.

The following steps access the Web site Administration page for the current Web site.

To Access the Web Site Administration Page for a Web Site

1

- **Click Tools on the menu bar and then point to Server.**

FrontPage displays the Tools menu and the Server submenu (Figure 9-22).

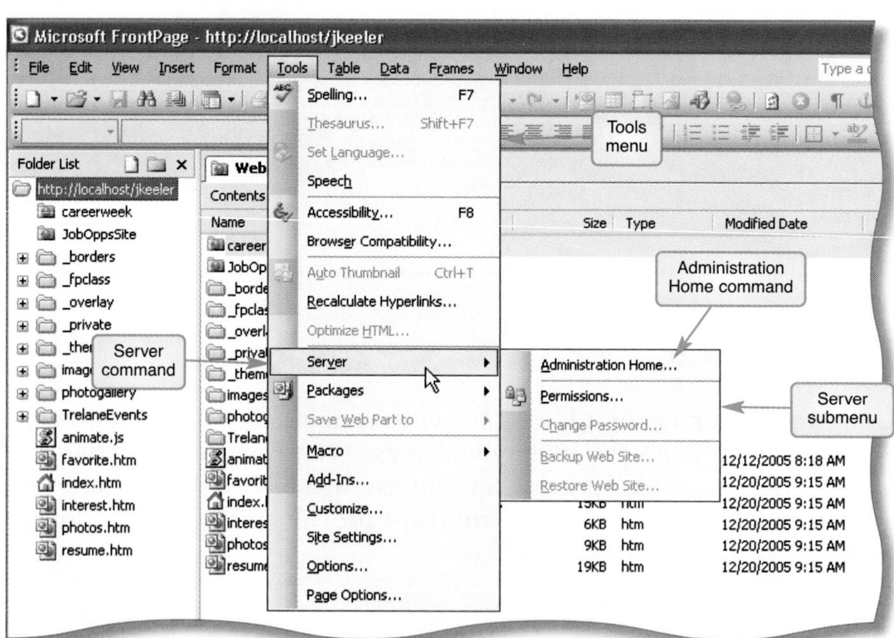

FIGURE 9-22

2

- **Click Administration Home.**

The Web site Administration page for the Web site opens in a Web browser (Figure 9-23). The Web site Administration page contains a variety of links to Web site management functions. At the top of the page is a navigation bar with links to the Home page of the current Web site, the Administration page (the current page), and Help.

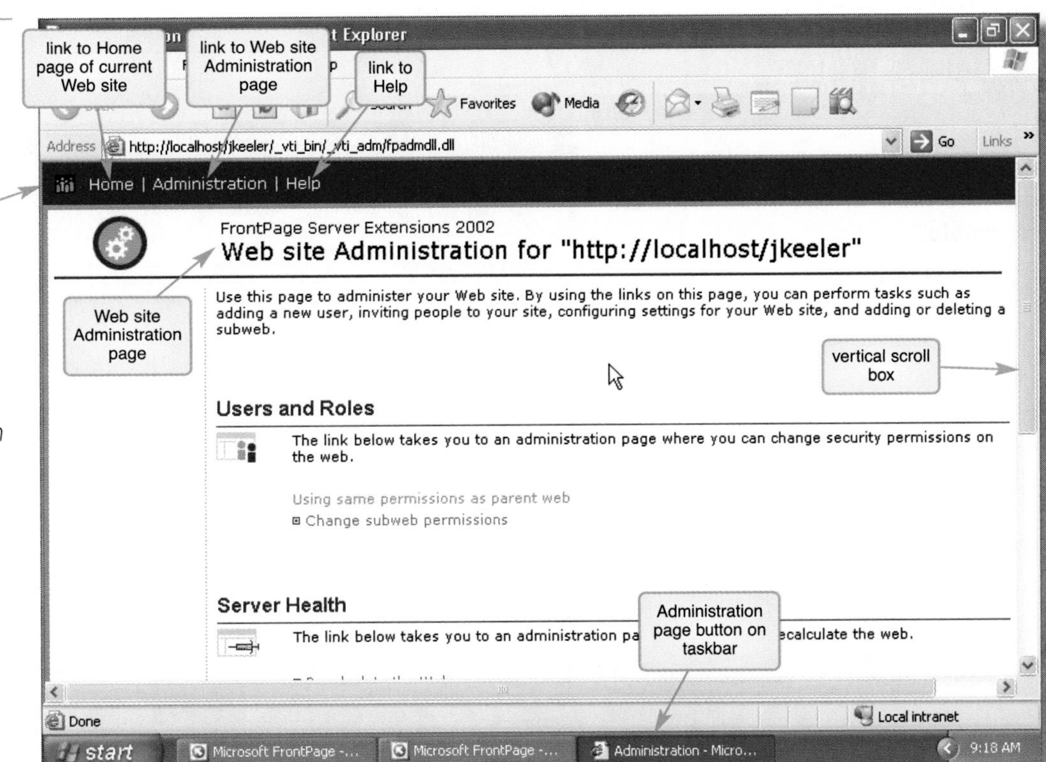

FIGURE 9-23

Recall that the new user will be able to perform authoring and administration tasks in the subsite, but not access the personal Web site, which is the parent and root Web site. With FrontPage, if you open the parent Web site and then access the Web site Administration page, you can access all functionality for the Web site and any subsites it contains. If you open the subsite in FrontPage and then access either of these pages, you cannot access the parent Web site. The process of Web site administration and managing permissions, however, is the same for both a parent Web site and a subsite. The steps on the next page manage permissions for a subsite from the parent Web site Administration page.

Other Ways

1. Press ALT+T, V, A
2. In Voice Command mode, say "Tools, Server, Administration Home"

More About

IIS Security

Managing and securing an IIS Web server can be a full-time job. Several simple steps can be taken, however, to combat the most common security problems. To learn more about IIS security, visit the FrontPage 2003 More About Web page (scsite.com/fp2003/more) and then click IIS Security.

To Manage Permissions for a Subsite

1

- **Drag the vertical scroll box down until the links in the Subwebs area are visible.**

The Subwebs area is displayed (Figure 9-24).

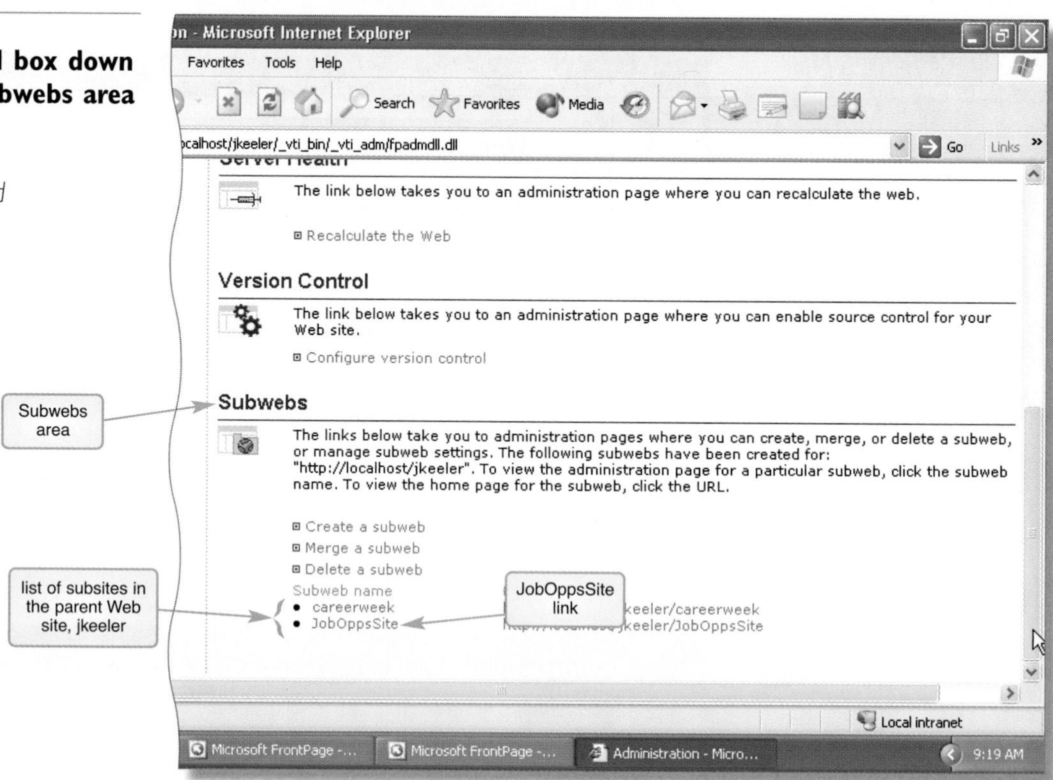

FIGURE 9-24

2

- **Click the JobOppsSite link.**
- **If necessary, click the Maximize button to maximize the new browser window.**

The Web site Administration page for the subsite, JobOppsSite, is displayed in a Web browser (Figure 9-25). The page indicates that the subsite currently uses the same permissions as the parent Web site.

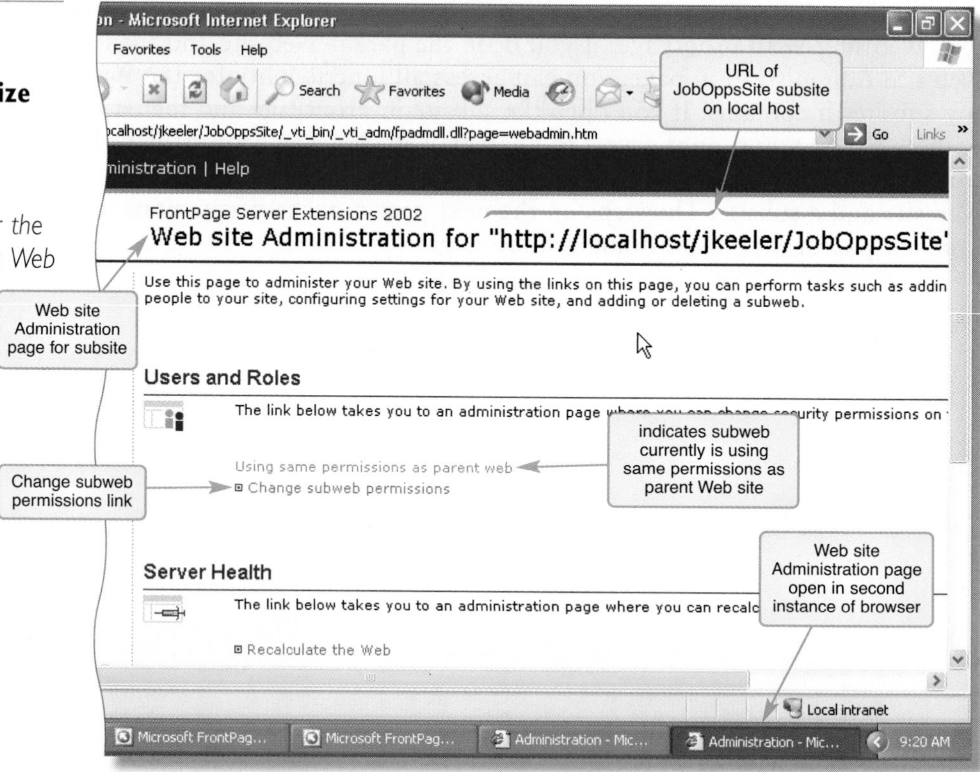

FIGURE 9-25

3

- **Click the Change subweb permissions link.**
- **When the Change Subweb Permissions page is displayed, if necessary, scroll to the right.**
- **Click Use unique permissions for this Web site.**

The Change Subweb Permissions page for the subsite, JobOppsSite, is displayed (Figure 9-26).

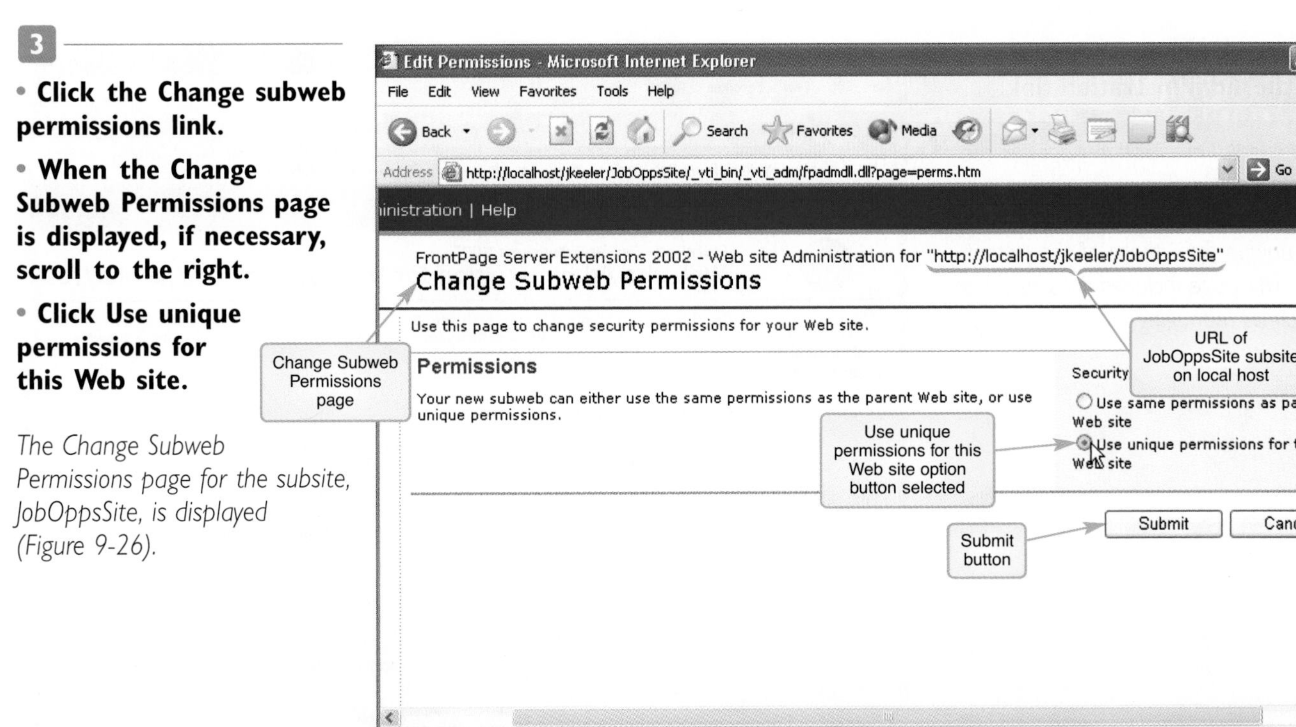

FIGURE 9-26

4

- **Click the Submit button.**

While the Web server is making the indicated changes to the subsite, the Operations Results Web page is displayed briefly. Once the changes are complete, the Change Subweb Permissions page is displayed, with the option to use unique permissions selected (Figure 9-27).

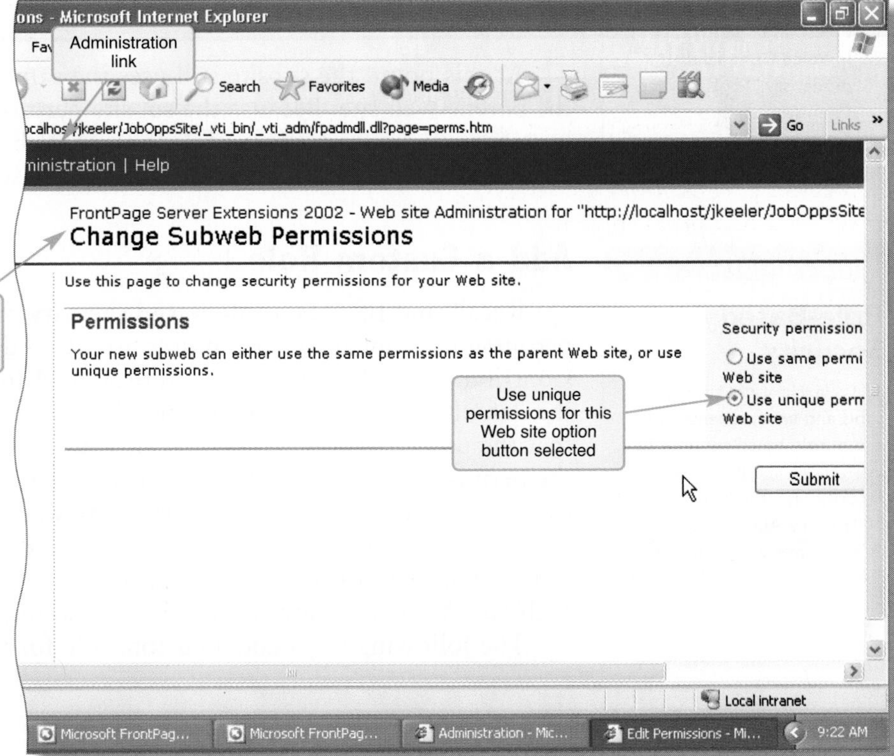

FIGURE 9-27

5

• **Click the Administration link.**

The Web site Administration page for the subsite is displayed (Figure 9-28). The page indicates that the subsite now can use permissions unique from those of the parent Web site. The page includes links to other tasks, such as managing users and roles.

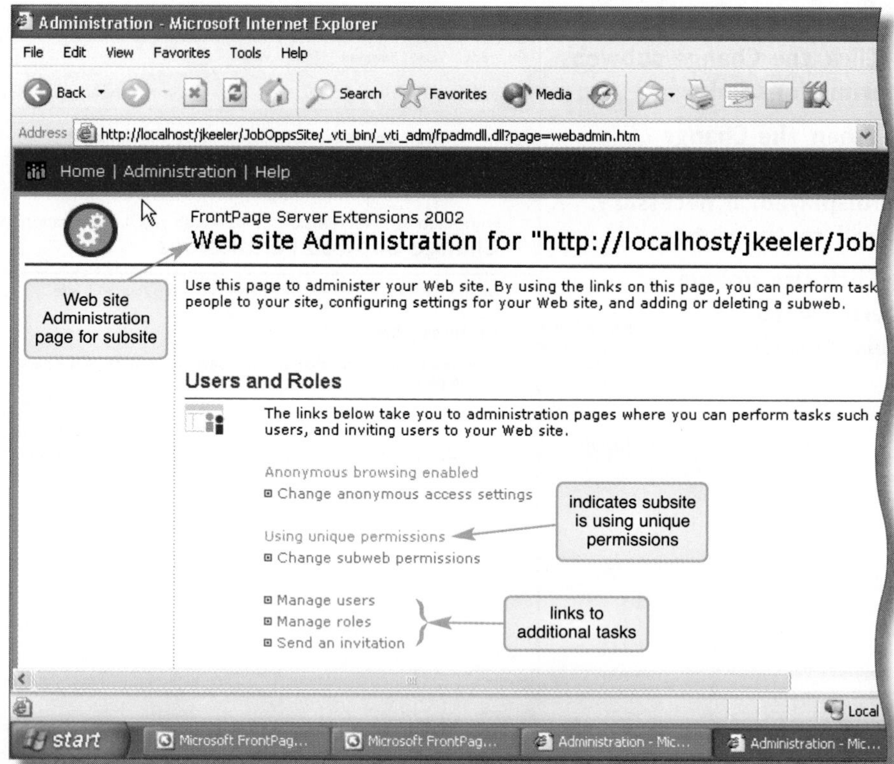

FIGURE 9-28

Other Ways

1. Press ALT+T, V, P
2. In Voice Command mode, say "Tools, Server, Permissions"

At this point, the subsite still uses the same set of permissions it inherited from the parent Web site. Because the subsite permissions have been changed to allow permissions unique from those of the parent Web site, however, you now can set unique permissions for the user roles defined for the subsite.

More About

Role-Based Security

Today, a variety of software tools and environments make use of role-based security. To learn more about role-based security, visit the FrontPage 2003 More About Web page (scsite.com/fp2003/more) and then click Role-Based Security.

Add a Custom Role

Recall that IIS uses a **role-based security model**, meaning that the specific permissions granted to a given user are derived from the standard role — Browser, Contributor, Author, Advanced Author, or Administrator — assigned to that user. If the default roles do not provide permissions for the particular combination of tasks that the user needs to complete, then you can create a new, custom role with exactly the permissions necessary for the custom role. Once a custom role is created, you can assign the role to users as you would any standard roles.

Next, you will create a custom role called Subsite Manager. The Subsite Manager role will have all of the Web Design Rights, except Set Source Control, and all of the Web Site Administration Rights, except Configure Access and Create Accounts.

The following steps add a custom role for the subsite.

To Add a Custom Role

1

- **Point to the Manage roles link in the Users and Roles area on the Web site Administration page for the subsite.**

The Users and Roles area of the Web site Administration page for the subsite is displayed (Figure 9-29). The mouse pointer changes to a pointing hand when positioned on the Manage roles link.

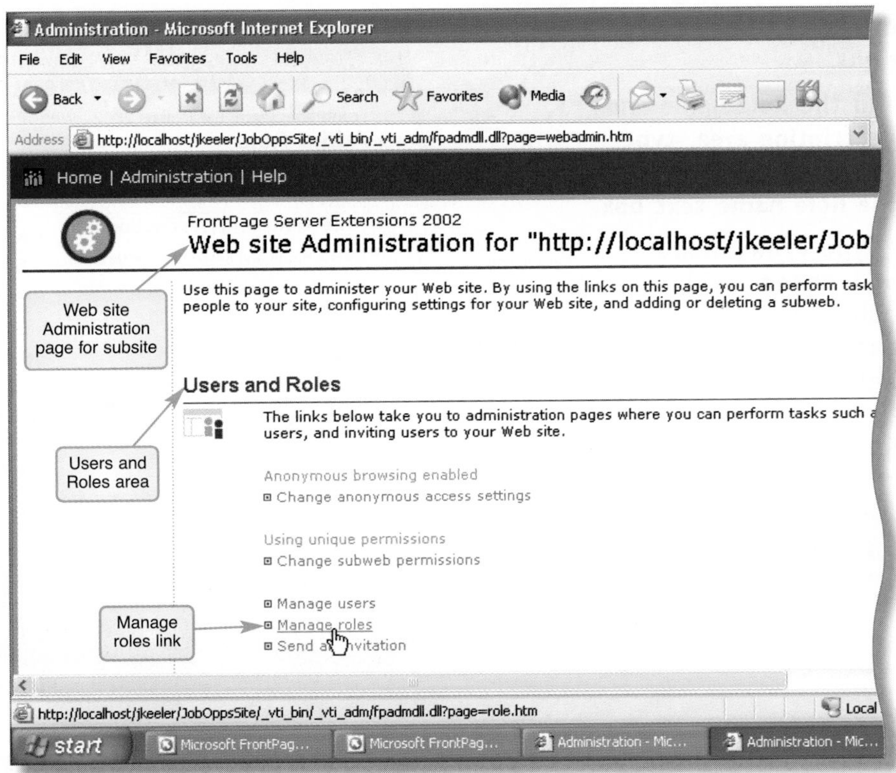

FIGURE 9-29

2

- **Click the Manage roles link.**

The Manage Roles page for the subsite is displayed (Figure 9-30). The standard roles inherited from the parent Web site are shown with their descriptions.

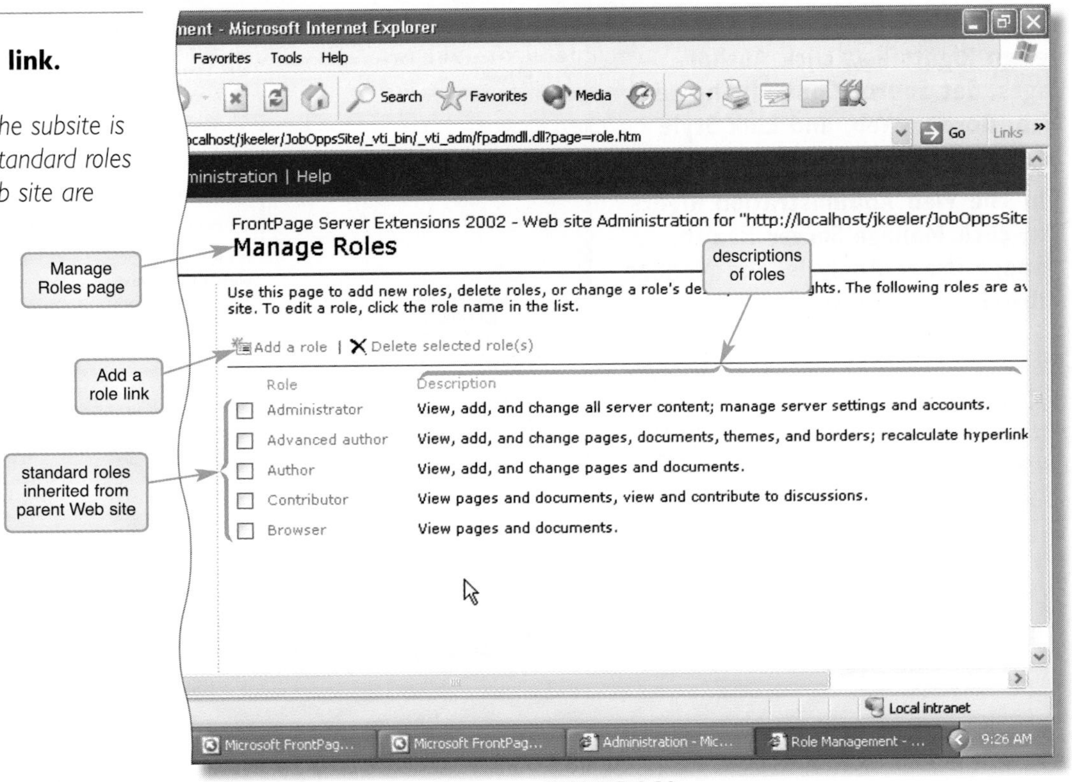

FIGURE 9-30

3

- **Click the Add a role link.**
- **When the Add a Role page is displayed, if necessary, scroll to the right.**
- **In the Role name and Description area, type** `Subsite Manager` **in the Role name text box.**
- **Type** `View, add, and change all subsite content; manage subsite settings; cannot create accounts or configure access.` **in the Description text box.**

The Add a Role page is displayed (Figure 9-31). The Add a Role page provides options for defining a role name, description, and access rights (permissions) for a new, custom role.

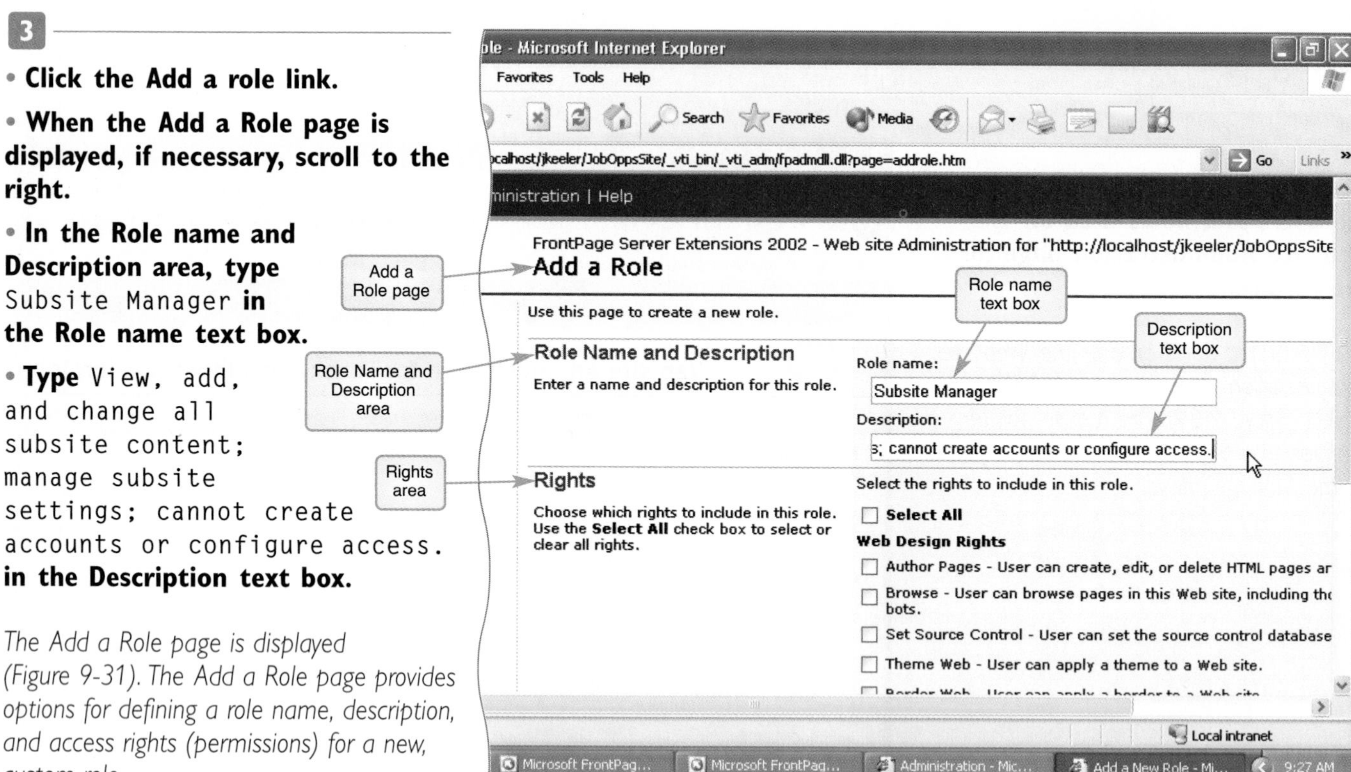

FIGURE 9-31

4

- **Scroll down the page and then, if necessary, scroll right.**
- **In the Rights area, in the Web Design Rights list, click Author Pages, Set Source Control, Theme Web, Border Web, and Link Style Sheets to select them.**
- **In the Web Administration Rights list, click Manage Server Health, Manage Usage Analysis, and Manage Subweb to select them.**

The selected rights for the Subsite Manager custom role are displayed (Figure 9-32). Browse and Recalc Web were selected automatically based on other rights selected.

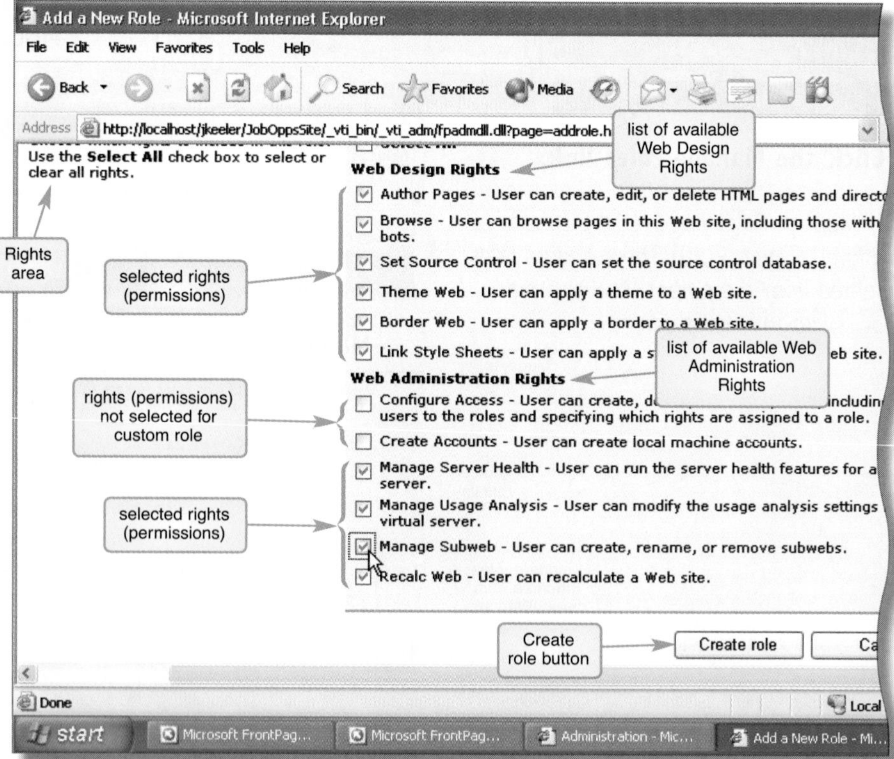

FIGURE 9-32

5

- **Click the Create role button.**
- **When the Manage Roles page is displayed, if necessary, scroll right to view the new Subsite Manager custom role and description.**

While the Web server is adding the new role to the Web site, the Operations Results Web page is displayed briefly. The Manage Roles page displays the list of roles available for this Web site, including the new Subsite Manager custom role and its description (Figure 9-33).

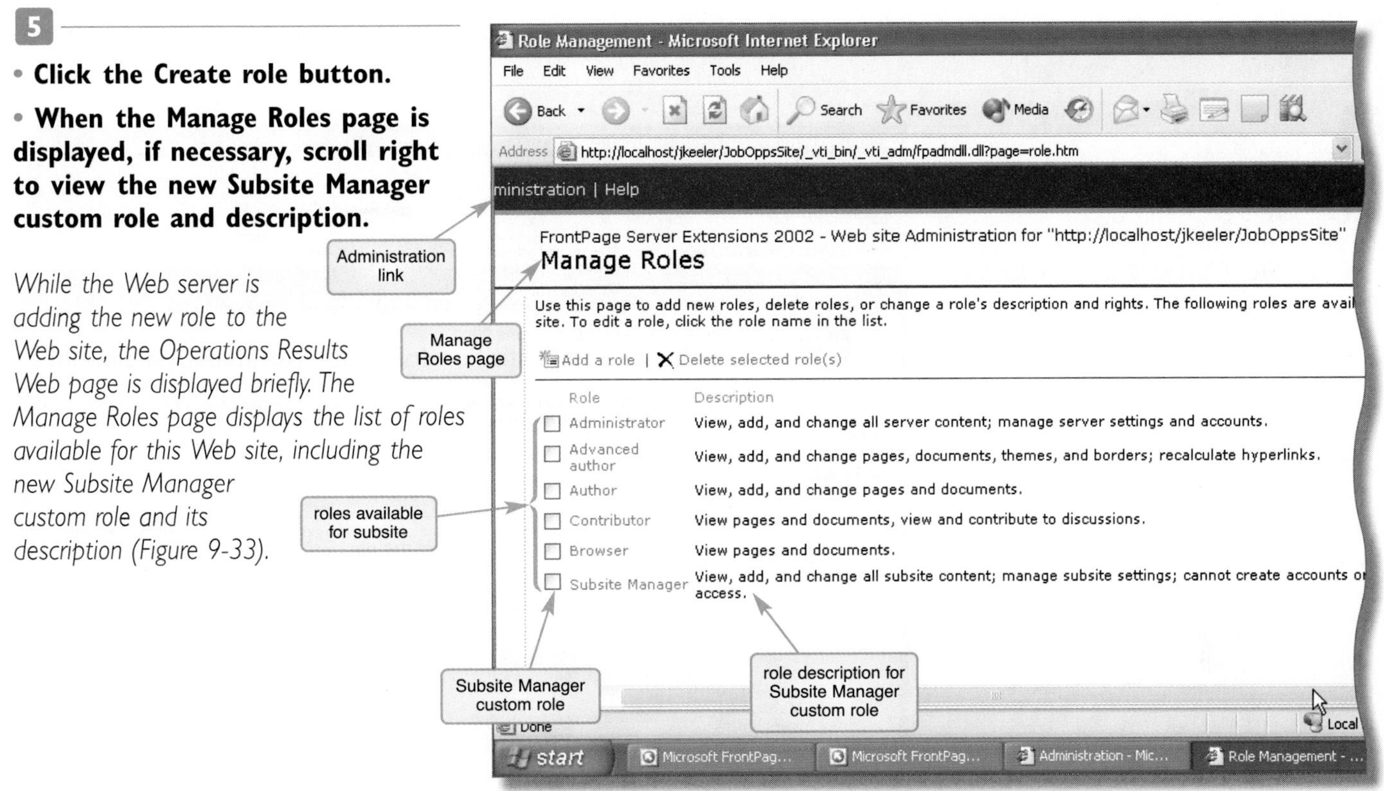

FIGURE 9-33

Add a New User to a Subsite and Assign a Custom Role

Once a role with the desired permissions exists, a user account can be added to the Web site and then assigned to this role. To be added to a Web site, the user must have an existing network or system account to a FrontPage Web site. Adding a new user to a server-based Web site running on IIS creates a local system account for the user. For the user to access files, however, the system administrator may need to set additional permissions for that account on the computer.

Plan the roles for your Web site administration carefully. Too often, everyone in a group receives full authority. Limit all users to the bare essential roles, adding new privileges only after careful consideration.

The next step is to create a new user account for the user named Doreen Maris (dmaris) and then assign to it the custom role of Subsite Manager. The steps on the next page add a new user account to a subsite and then assign it to a custom role.

To Add a New User to a Subsite and Assign a Custom Role

1

- **Click the Administration link on the navigation bar.**

The Web site Administration page for the subsite is displayed (Figure 9-34).

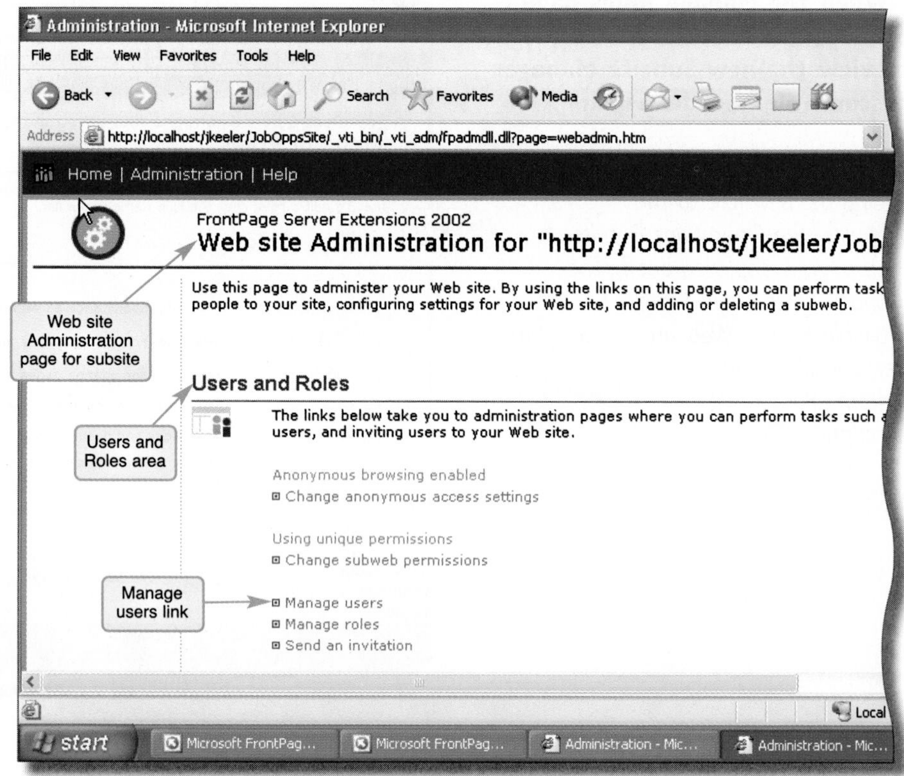

FIGURE 9-34

2

- **Click the Manage users link.**

The Manage Users page for the subsite is displayed (Figure 9-35). The page lists all current users for the subsite with their respective roles. The list of users shown on your computer will vary from the list shown in Figure 9-35.

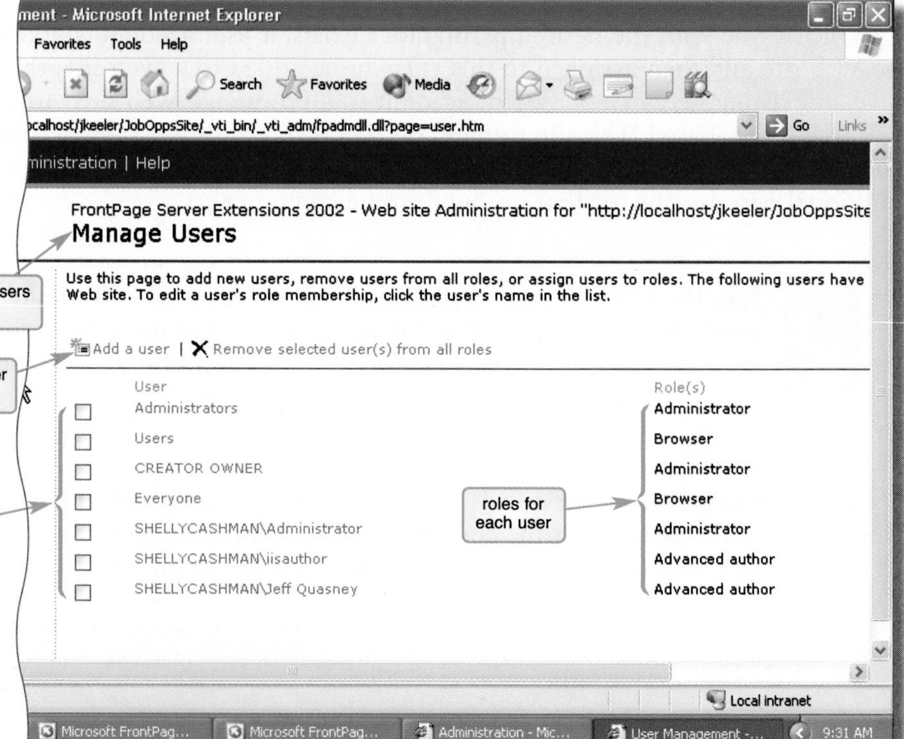

FIGURE 9-35

3

- **Click the Add a user link.**
- **When the Add a User page is displayed, if necessary, scroll to the right.**
- **In the User area, confirm that Add a new user with the following information is selected.**

4

- **Type** dmaris **(or a user name of your choice) in the User name text box.**
- **Type** lopez2 **(or a password of your choice) in the Password text box.**
- **Type** lopez2 **(or the password entered previously) in the Confirm password text box.**

The Add a User page is displayed (Figure 9-36). The Add a new user with the following information option button is selected automatically. The new user name is entered. The entered password is displayed as bullets for security purposes and is entered and then confirmed to reduce the chance of a typographical error.

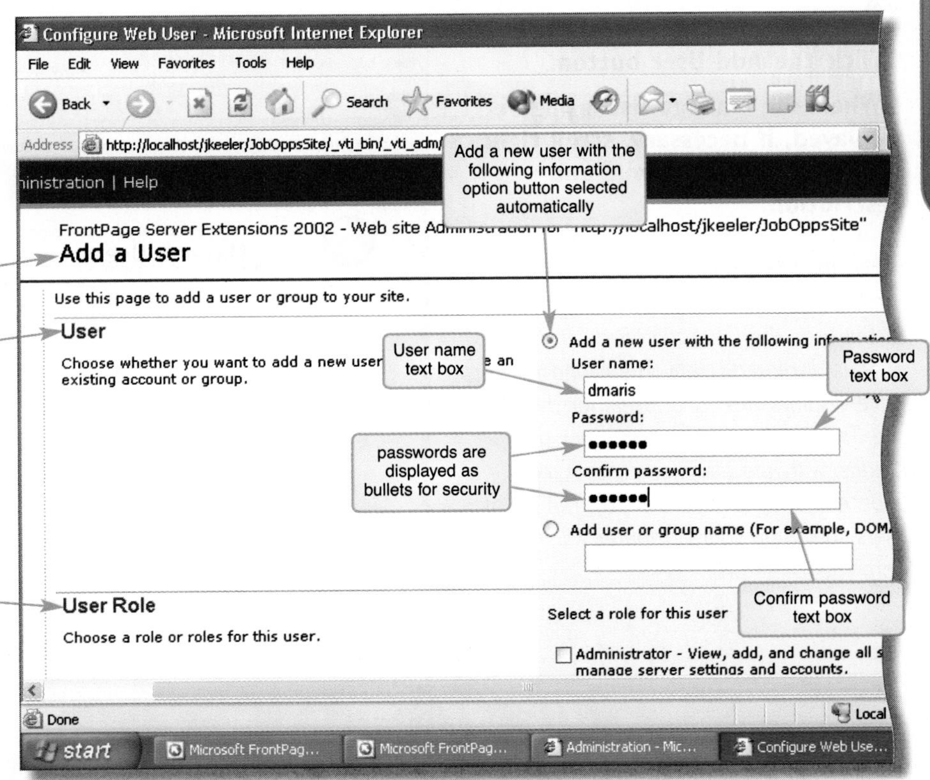

FIGURE 9-36

5

- **Scroll down and then, if necessary, scroll right.**
- **In the User Role area, click Subsite Manager to select it.**

The Subsite Manager check box is selected as the role for the user, dmaris (Figure 9-37). The selected role is the custom Subsite Manager role added in previous steps.

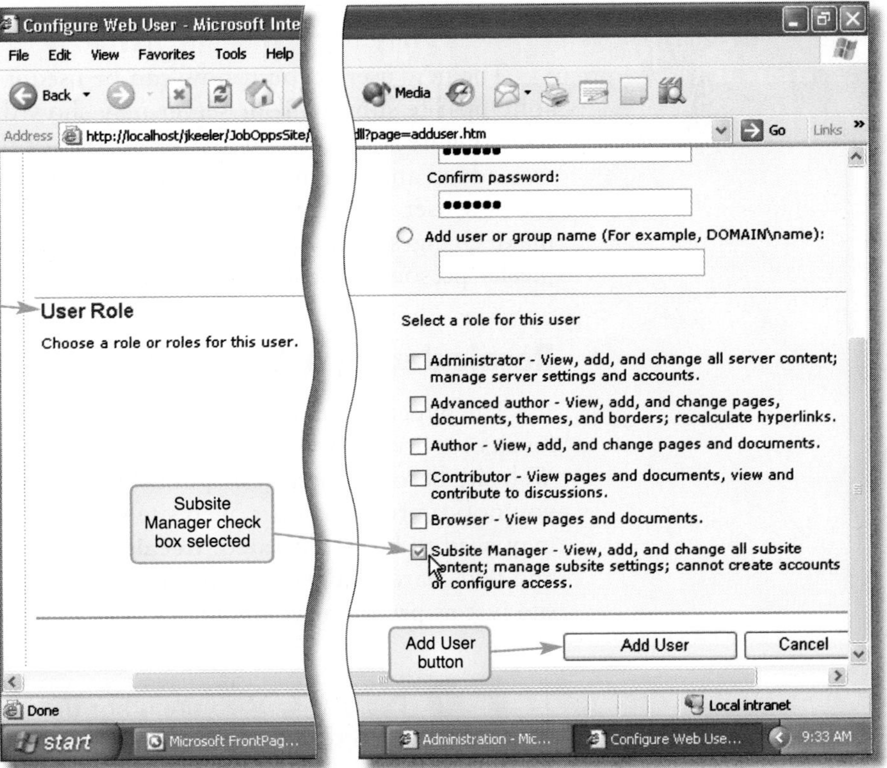

FIGURE 9-37

6

• **Click the Add User button.**

• **When the Manage Users page is displayed, if necessary, scroll right to view the custom role and description.**

While the Web server adds the new user to the Web site and assigns the custom role to the user, the Operation Results Web page is displayed briefly. The Manage Users page displays the list of users for this Web site. The list now includes the new user, dmaris, with the assigned custom role, Subsite Manager (Figure 9-38). The list of users shown on your computer will vary from the list shown.

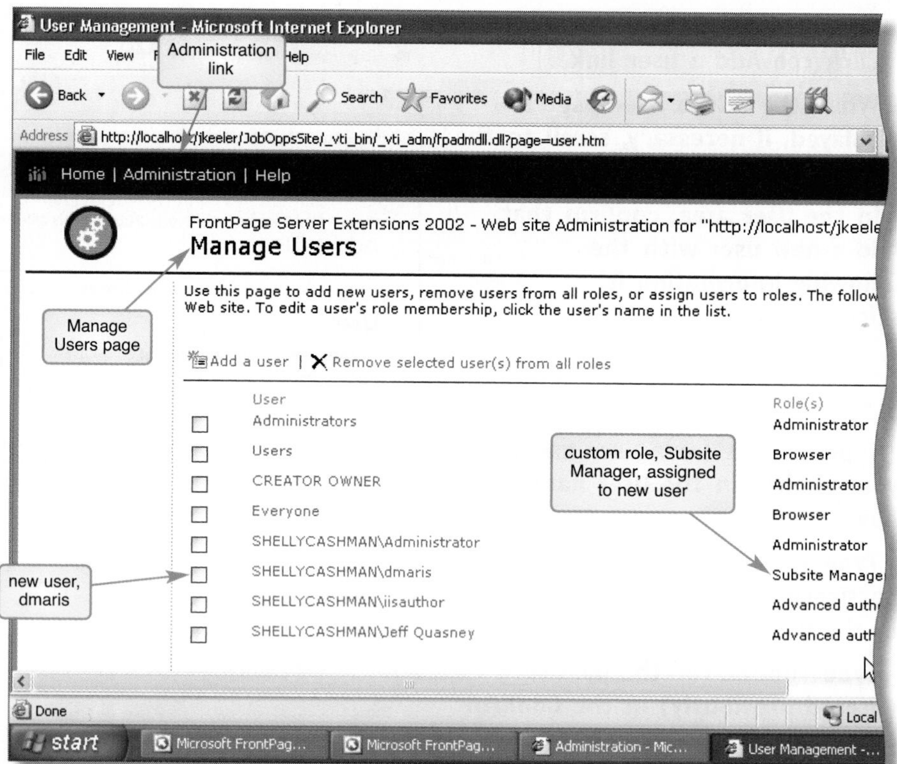

FIGURE 9-38

The new user account now can be used in the role of Subsite Manager for the JobOppsSite subsite. Your server may show different Users on the Manage Users page (Figure 9-38). If you are the creator of the subsite, your account automatically was added and assigned the Administrator role when the subsite was created. With the new user and custom role added for dmaris, both users (you and dmaris) can make changes to the JobOppsSite subsite. Only you, however, can maintain the jkeeler personal Web site, which is the parent Web site.

Recalculating a Web Site

The hyperlinks and searching capabilities of Web sites may produce erroneous results for a variety of reasons. Sometimes, the hyperlinks and searching features of a Web site become corrupt or publishing the Web site results in broken hyperlinks. If you notice problems on a Web site with broken links or searches, then the Web site may need to be recalculated. **Recalculating** a Web site updates all of the hyperlinks and text search indexes. From time to time, you may want to recalculate your Web site just as preventative maintenance.

Publishing a Web site is not the final step in the development of a Web site. A Web site requires ongoing troubleshooting and preventive maintenance. Consider recalculating your Web site from time to time.

The following steps recalculate the JobOppsSite subsite.

To Recalculate a Web Site

1

- **Click the Administration link on the navigation bar.**
- **Scroll down to the Recalculate the Web link in the Server Health area.**

The Server Health area of the Web site Administration page for the subsite is displayed (Figure 9-39).

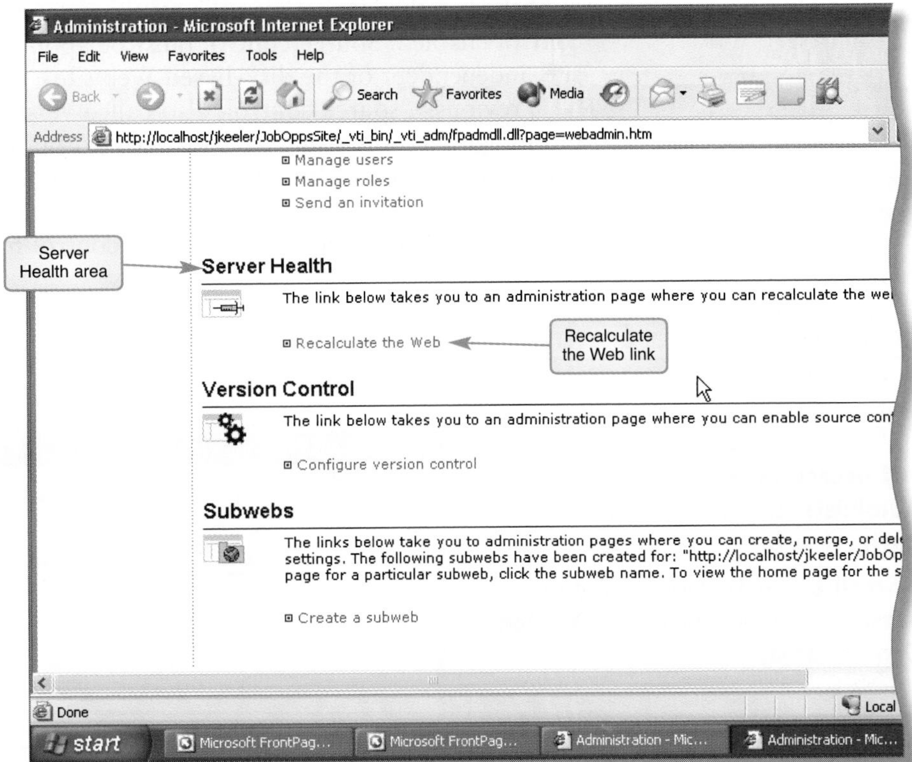

FIGURE 9-39

2

- **Click the Recalculate the Web link.**
- **The Recalculate the Web page is displayed (Figure 9-40).**

3

- **Click the Recalculate button.**

While the Web server is recalculating the subsite, the Operation Results Web page is displayed briefly. The Web site Administration page for the subsite is displayed. Larger Web sites can take a long time to recalculate. The subsite now is recalculated.

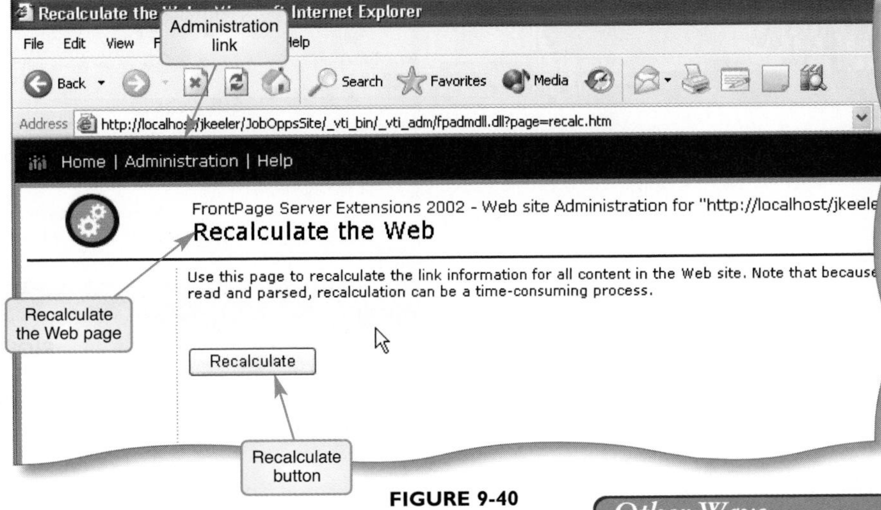

FIGURE 9-40

Other Ways

1. On the Tools menu click Recalculate Hyperlinks
2. Press ALT+T, R
3. In Voice Command mode, say "Tools, Recalculate Hyperlinks"

Enabling Source Control for a Subsite

As you learned in Project 7, problems can arise when multiple users try to make changes to the same Web pages. FrontPage, however, provides built-in source control tools to help manage access and modifications to the files in your Web site and reduce these problems. When a disk-based Web site, with source control in effect, is published to the local server, the resulting server-based Web site does not have source control enabled. Source control must be applied specifically to the server-based Web site, independent of the disk-based Web site.

Previously, source control, also called version control, was applied to a FrontPage Web site using tools directly within FrontPage. You also can enable source control from the Configure Version Control page, which is accessible via the Web site Administration page.

The following steps enable source control for the subsite.

To Enable Source Control for a Subsite

1

- **If necessary, click the Administration link on the navigation bar.**
- **Scroll down to the Configure version control link in the Version Control area.**

The Version Control area of the Web site Administration page for the subsite is displayed (Figure 9-41).

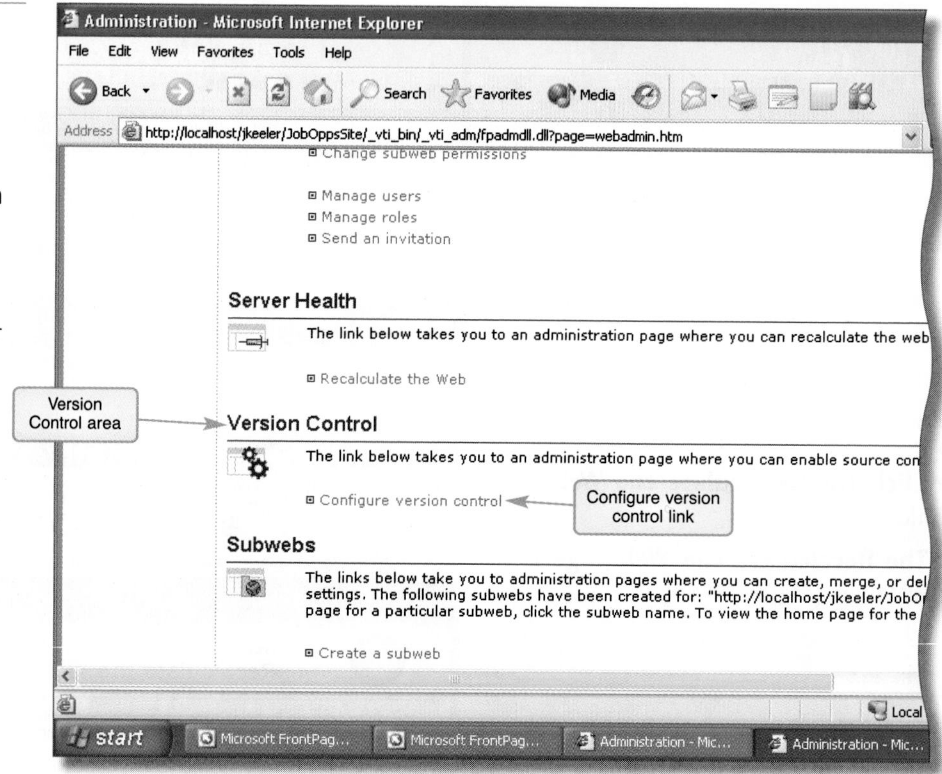

FIGURE 9-41

2

- **Click the Configure version control link.**
- **When the Configure Version Control page is displayed, if necessary, scroll right.**
- **Click Use built-in version control in the Version Control area to select it.**

The Configure Version Control page for the subsite is displayed (Figure 9-42). The Use built-in version control option button is selected.

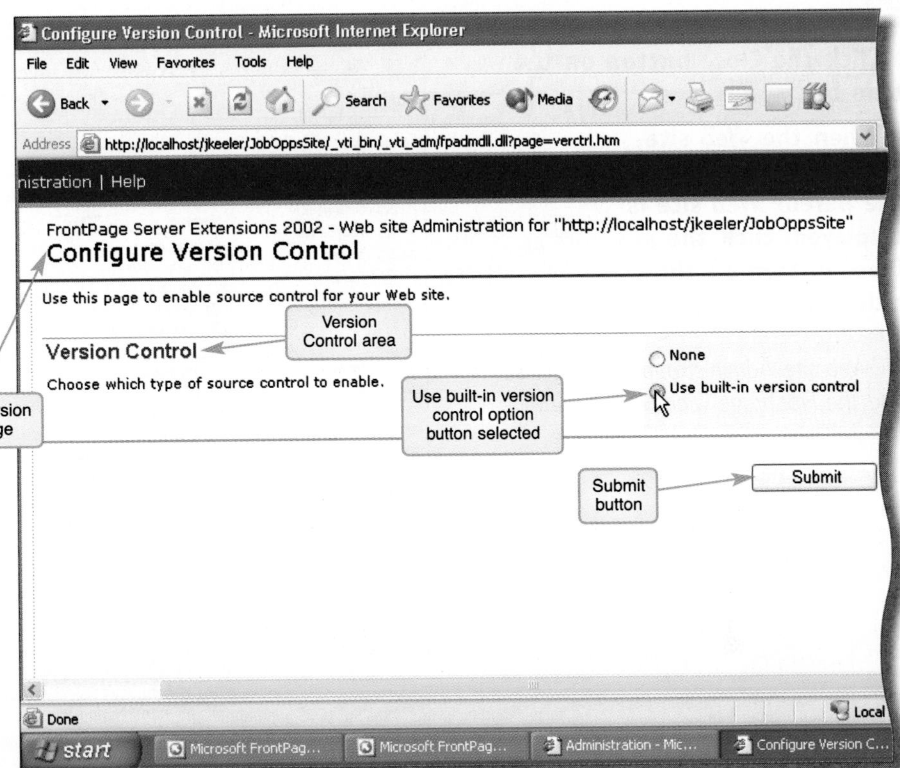

FIGURE 9-42

3

- **Click the Submit button.**

While the Web server is configuring source control for the subsite, the Operation Results Web page is displayed briefly. The Web site Administration page for the subsite is displayed (Figure 9-43). Source control now is enabled for the subsite.

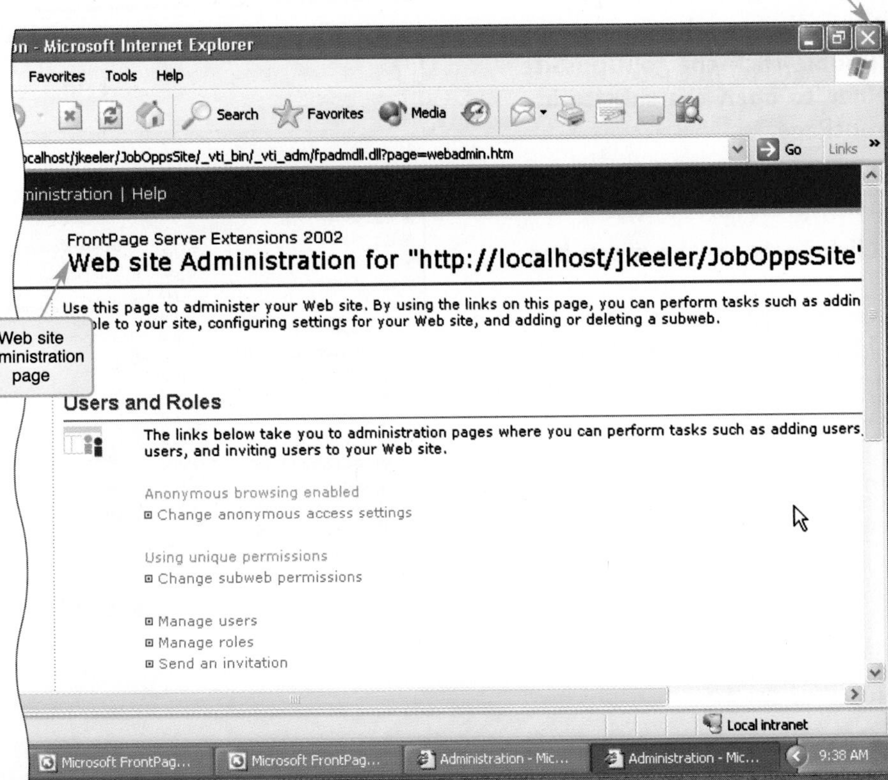

FIGURE 9-43

4

- **Click the Close button on the title bar.**
- **When the Web site Administration page for the parent Web site is displayed, click the Close button on the title bar.**

All Web site Administration pages close, and the FrontPage window is displayed (Figure 9-44).

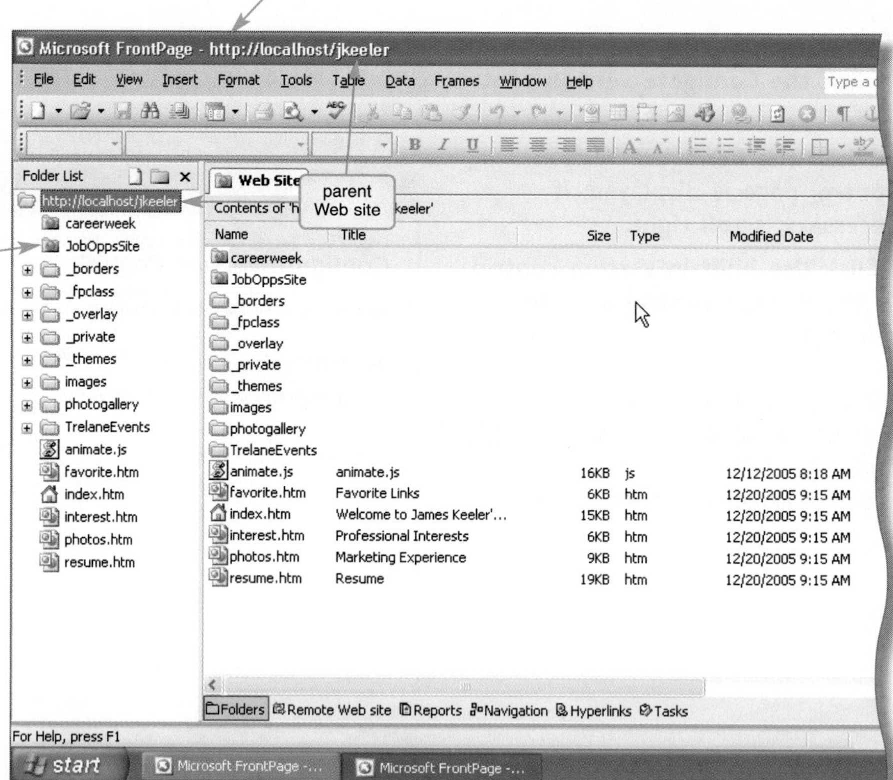

FIGURE 9-44

5

- **Double-click the JobOppsSite folder to open the subsite in FrontPage.**
- **When the JobOppsSite subsite opens, press the F5 key.**
- **Click Tools on the menu bar.**

The subsite, JobOppsSite, is displayed in a third instance of FrontPage (Figure 9-45). Pressing the F5 key refreshes the current view.

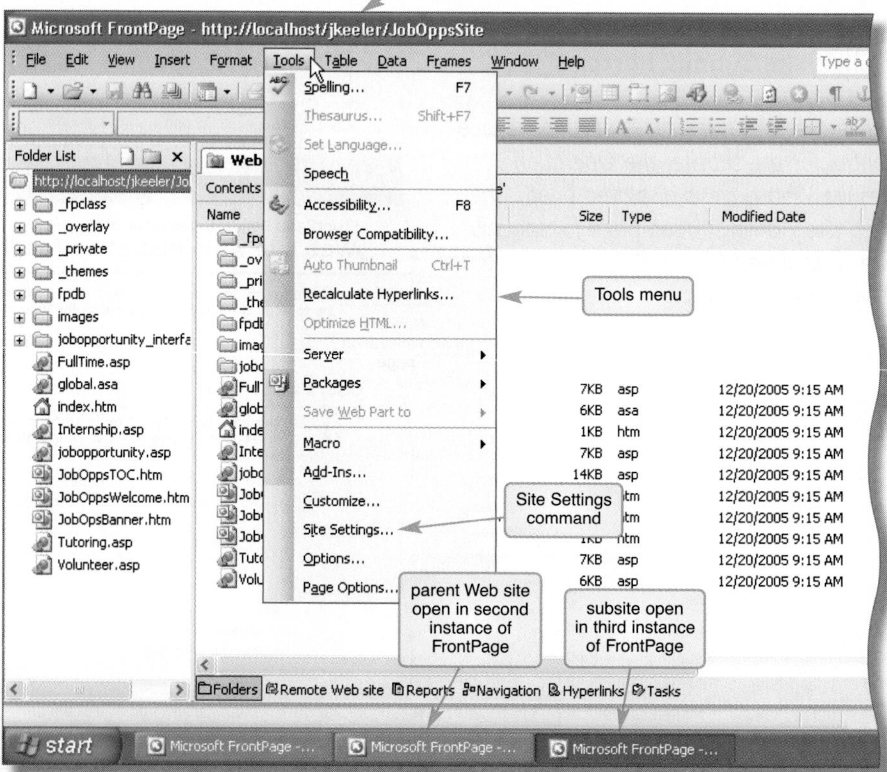

FIGURE 9-45

6

• **Click Site Settings.**

FrontPage displays the Site Settings dialog box (Figure 9-46). Because this is a server-based Web site, the General sheet displays information about the server, such as the Web server URL, FrontPage Server Extensions version, server software name and version number, along with the Web site name. Because source control was enabled, the Use document check-in and check-out check box is selected.

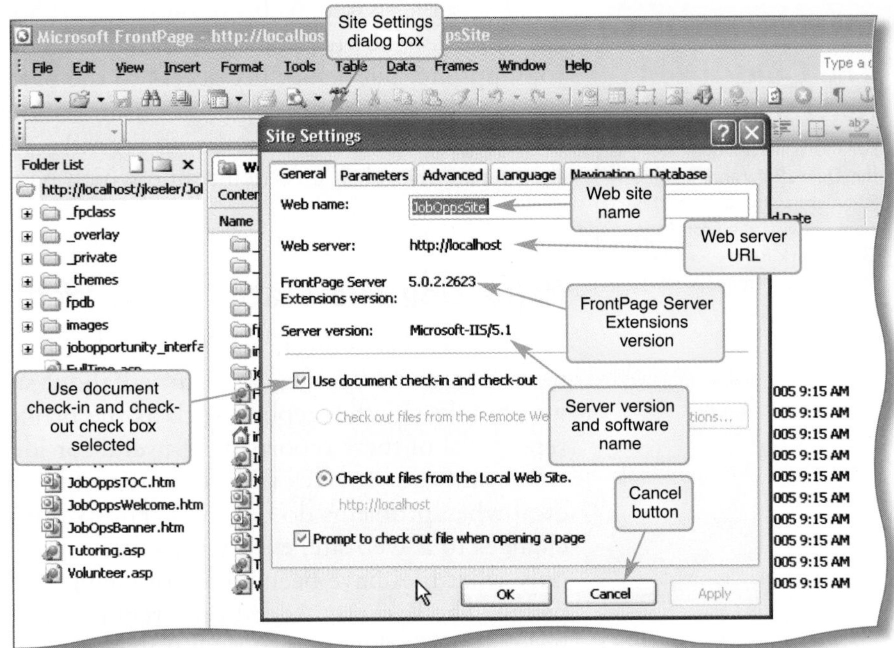

FIGURE 9-46

7

• **Click the Cancel button.**

• **Click the Close button on the title bar to close the subsite.**

The JobOppsSite subsite is closed, and the parent Web site is displayed in the FrontPage window (Figure 9-47).

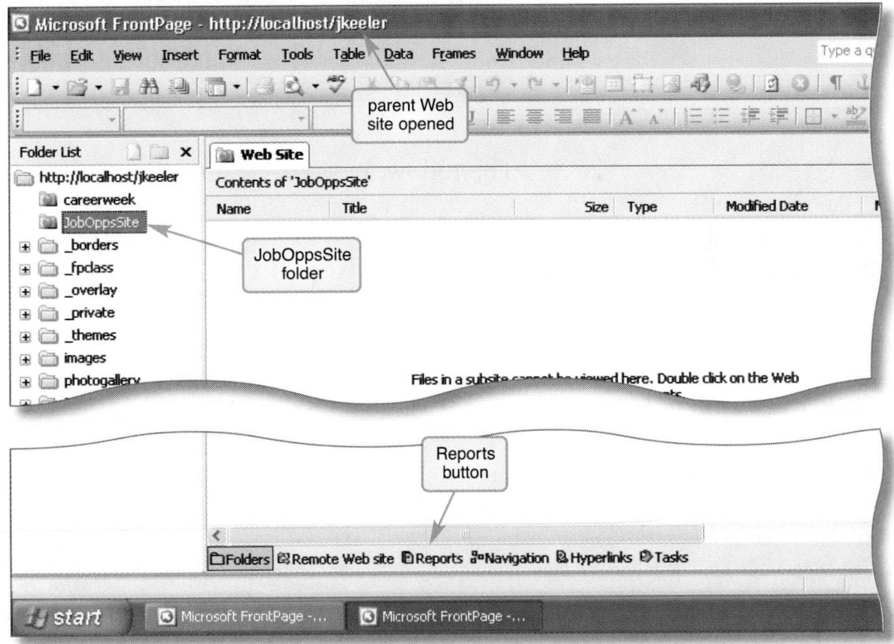

FIGURE 9-47

As shown in the previous steps, enabling source control (version control) using the Web site Administration pages has the same result as selecting the Use document check-in and check-out option button in the Site Settings dialog box in FrontPage. Whether you use FrontPage or the Web site Administration pages, enabling source control for a subsite does not affect source control for the parent Web site, because they are two different Web sites with independent source control settings.

More About

The Quick Reference

For more information, see the Quick Reference Summary at the back of this book, or visit the FrontPage 2003 Quick Reference Web page (scsite.com/fp2003/qr).

The server-based Web site on the local host is complete. A new account and custom role, Subweb Manager, allows the new user, dmaris, to access the subsite, JobOppsSite, but denies her access to the parent Web site. Source control for the subsite is enabled to ensure that both users cannot mistakenly make changes to the same Web page at the same time. Using FrontPage reporting features, they also can track the status of each file to determine which pages are new, which have been modified recently, and so on.

Reporting File Status for a Web Site

In an earlier project, you learned that FrontPage provides various reports to help in managing a Web site. You learned about such reports as the Site Summary report, which links to other reports such as the Broken Hyperlinks report and Unlinked Files report. All of these reports were useful for identifying problems in the Web site.

FrontPage provides additional reports to help with Web site management tasks, even when problems do not exist. For example, when multiple users are making changes to a Web site, even with source control enabled, it is useful to know not only what files have been added or changed, but also when these actions were completed. The Recently Added Files report lists files in the Web site or subsite that have been added within a given time frame, in various increments from 1 day to 365 days.

Design Tip

File status reports can serve as a security mechanism. By running these reports weekly or monthly, you can determine if anyone is changing or adding files without your knowledge.

The following steps view the Recently Added Files report for the Web site.

To View the Recently Added Files Report

1

- **Click the Reports button.**

The Web site is displayed in Reports view (Figure 9-48). The Site Summary report is displayed (your displayed report may be different, depending on the report last viewed).

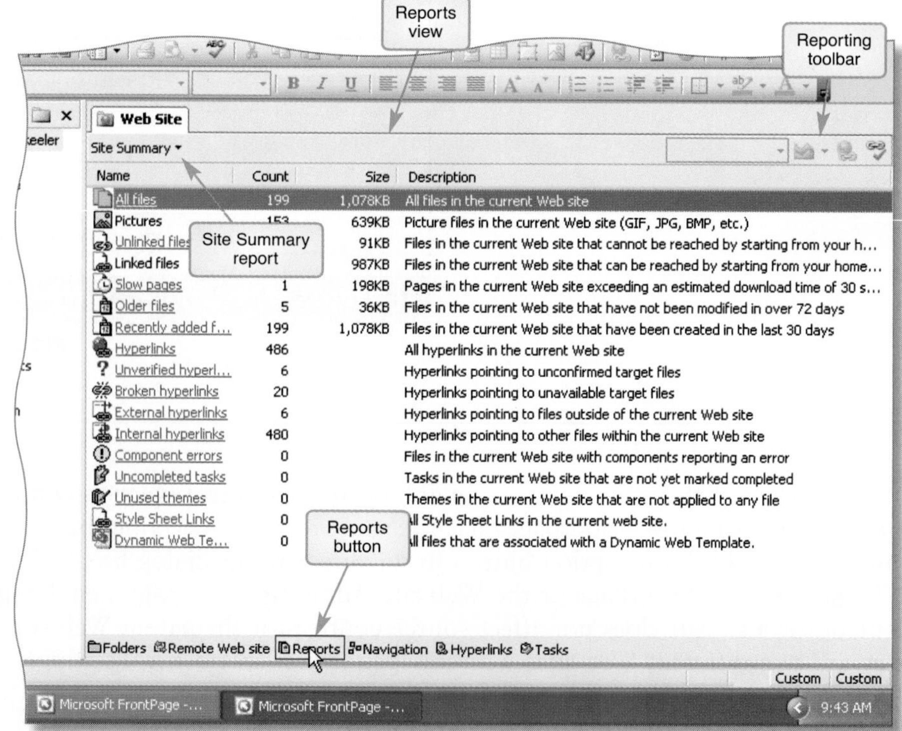

FIGURE 9-48

2

- **Click the Site Summary button.**
- **Point to Files.**

FrontPage displays the Reports menu and the Files submenu (Figure 9-49).

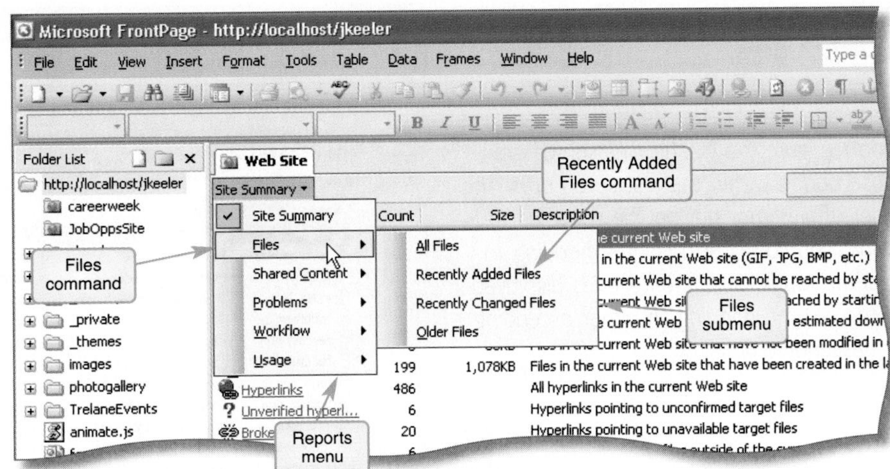

FIGURE 9-49

3

- **Click Recently Added Files.**

FrontPage displays the Recently Added Files report (Figure 9-50). The Report Setting box displays an increment of 30 days, or one month. Your increment may be different. The Site Summary button's caption changes to reflect the name of the currently selected report.

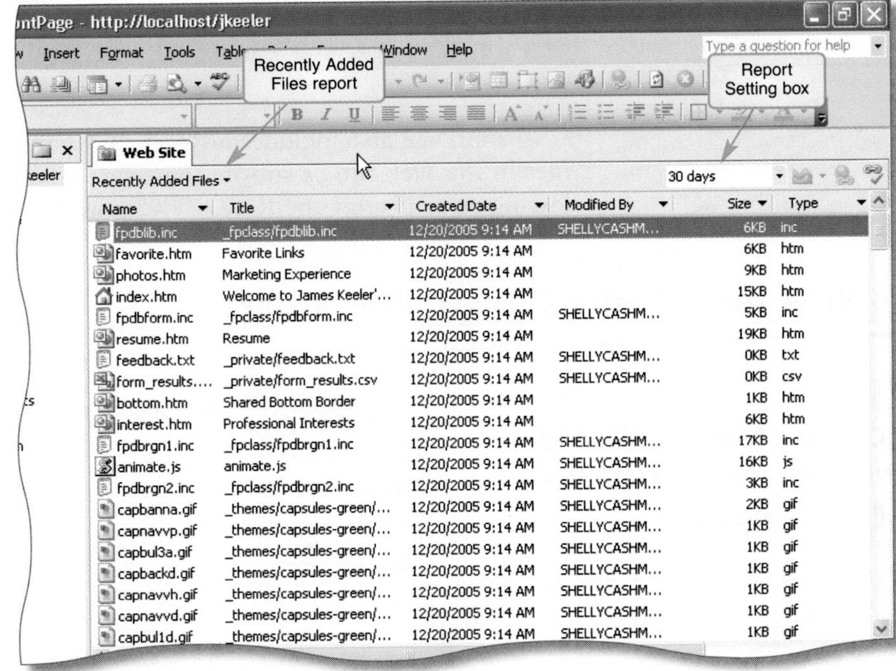

FIGURE 9-50

4

- **Click the Report Setting box arrow.**

FrontPage displays the Report Setting list (Figure 9-51). The setting selections for report time frames range from 1 to 365 days. The report determines the range of dates to display, based on the current day.

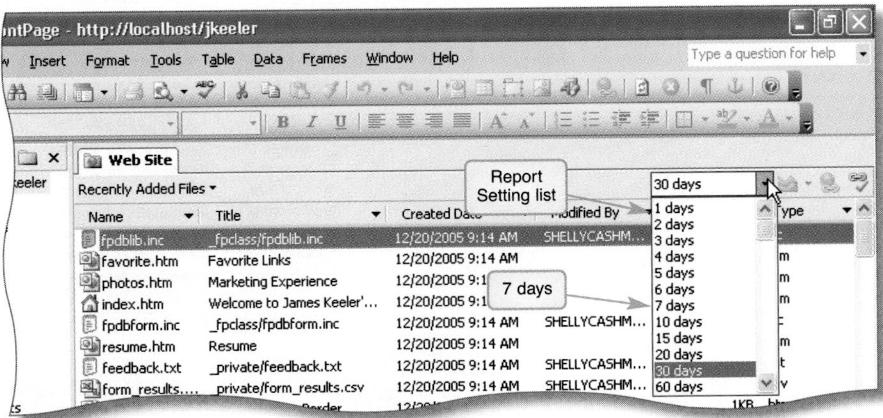

FIGURE 9-51

5

• **Click 7 days.**

FrontPage displays the Recently Added Files report (Figure 9-52). The files shown are those added within the last seven days. The order of files may not be the same as your report. You can click a column heading to sort the report by the categories displayed in the column heading, in either ascending or descending order.

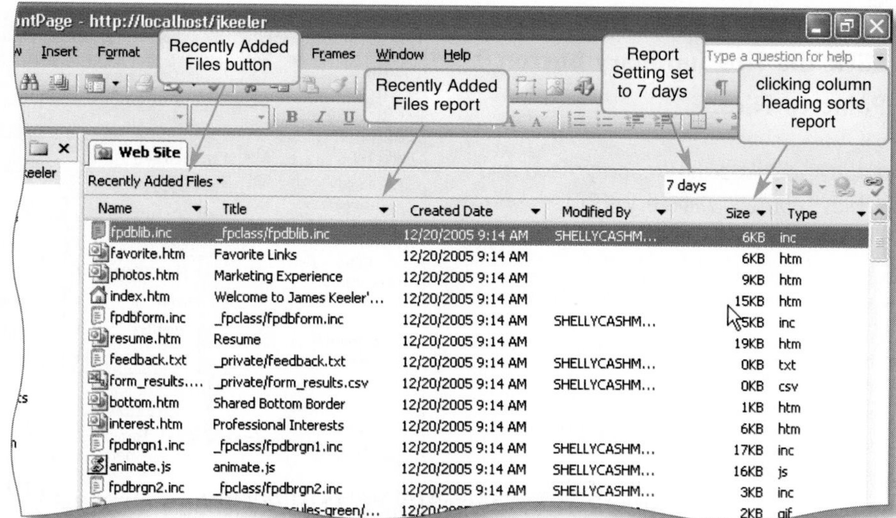

FIGURE 9-52

FrontPage also includes a Recently Changed Files report that displays a list of files in the Web site or subsite that were changed within a given time frame. The following steps display the Recently Changed Files report for the Web site.

To View the Recently Changed Files Report

1

• **Click the Recently Added Files button on the Reporting toolbar.**

• **Point to Files.**

FrontPage displays the Reports menu and the Files submenu (Figure 9-53).

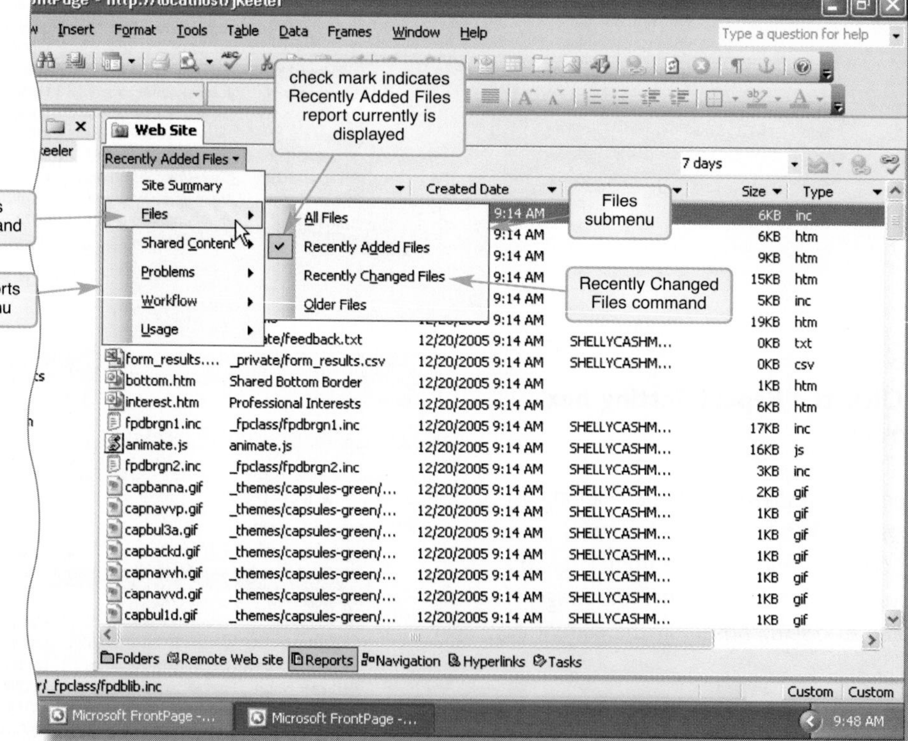

FIGURE 9-53

2

• **Click Recently Changed Files.**

FrontPage displays the Recently Changed Files report (Figure 9-54). By default, FrontPage uses the time frame selection used for the previous report. The setting can be changed using the Report Settings box on the Reporting toolbar. Your report may be different.

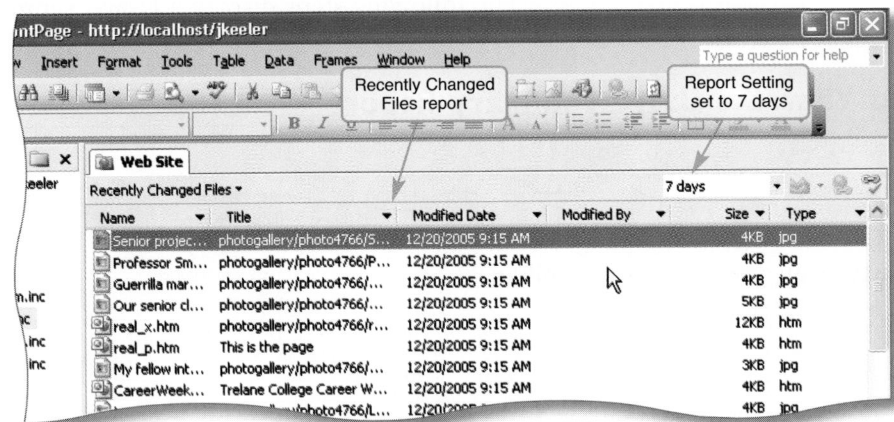

FIGURE 9-54

Reporting Usage for a Web Site

When a Web site is published to a server, FrontPage provides additional reports on a variety of usage statistics for the server-based Web site. Usage statistics reported in various FrontPage reports include the number of visitors to a Web site, the top (most frequently used) browser, the top operating system, and total page hits, along with others. A **page hit** is a single file request from the server. Many of these reports are available in both a detailed and a summary form.

To compile the usage statistics, FrontPage relies on the processing of log files located on the server. By default, the server is configured to run and process log files every Sunday at midnight. The Web server administrator also can change these settings to run and process log files daily, weekly, or monthly, at any given time of day or night.

More About

Usage Analysis

Usage analysis provides Web authors with a variety of useful statistics, which are compiled from log files on the server. The compilation process may run daily, weekly, monthly, or on demand by the Web administrator. To learn more about usage analysis, how it works, how to configure it, and what data is collected, visit the FrontPage 2003 More About Web page (scsite.com/fp2003/more) and then click Usage Analysis.

While designing a Web site, consider the types of usage reports that you would like to see. Determine which Web pages you would like to particularly observe. Make sure that you turn on the options on the server to gather your Web page statistics.

In general, usage reporting is more useful on the production Web server, because Web site traffic to the local host test server is usually low. Reviewing these reports on the test server, however, is useful in helping you to understand the reports, how to control traffic to the Web site, and what activities affect the reports. After publishing the Web site from the test server to the production server, you then can report on actual usage, provided the server is set to collect statistics in a log file and they are available to you.

Note: If you plan to step through the steps in this feature and want to run the usage reports, you may need to force IIS to generate the statistics using a command-line utility. If the usage reports generated in the following steps show no usage, close the Web site, open a browser, and browse to the Web site. Visit a number of pages and then close the browser. Wait for the log file of usage statistics to run on the server. If you have the proper level of security permission to run usage processing manually, then open a command-prompt window. Change to the directory C:\Program Files\Common Files\Microsoft Shared\web server extensions\50\bin and then type `owsadm.exe -o usage` to start the process. You may need to restart your computer after running the process in order to generate the statistics.

The following steps display a Usage Summary report.

To View the Usage Summary Report

1

- **Click the Recently Changed Files button on the Reporting toolbar.**
- **Point to Usage.**

FrontPage displays the Reports menu and the Usage submenu (Figure 9-55).

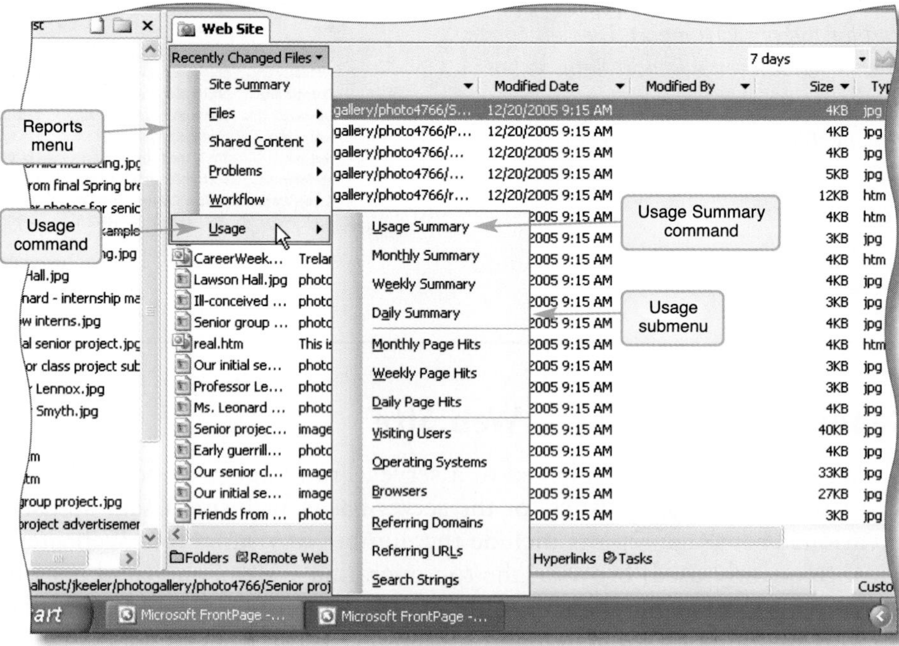

FIGURE 9-55

2

- **Click Usage Summary.**

FrontPage displays the Usage Summary report (Figure 9-56). Links to other monthly usage reports are displayed as links on the Usage Summary report.

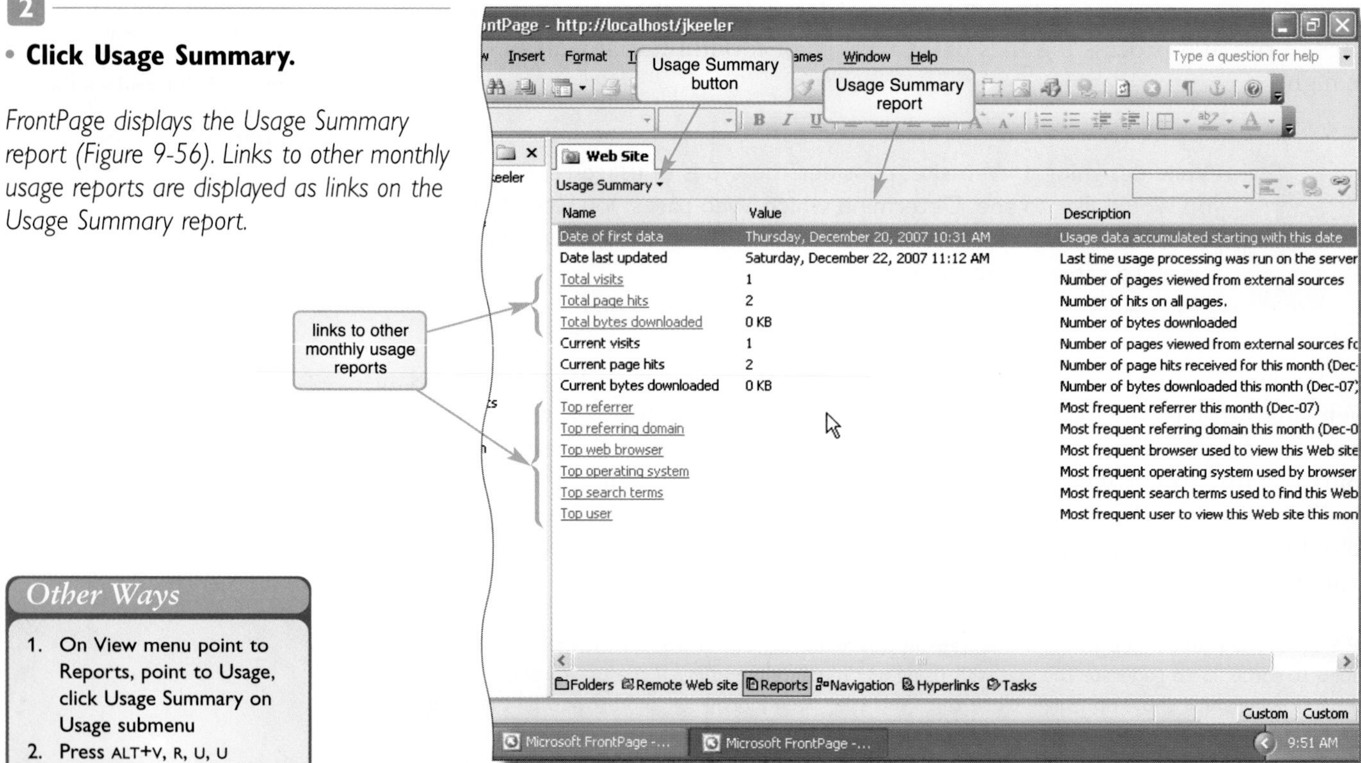

FIGURE 9-56

Other Ways

1. On View menu point to Reports, point to Usage, click Usage Summary on Usage submenu
2. Press ALT+V, R, U, U
3. In Voice Command mode, say "View, Reports, Usage, Usage Summary"

FrontPage also provides a more detailed report, such as the Daily Page Hits report, in addition to a summary. The following steps display the Daily Page Hits report.

To View the Daily Page Hits Report

1

- **Click the Usage Summary button on the Reporting toolbar.**
- **Point to Usage.**

FrontPage displays the Reports menu and the Usage submenu (Figure 9-57).

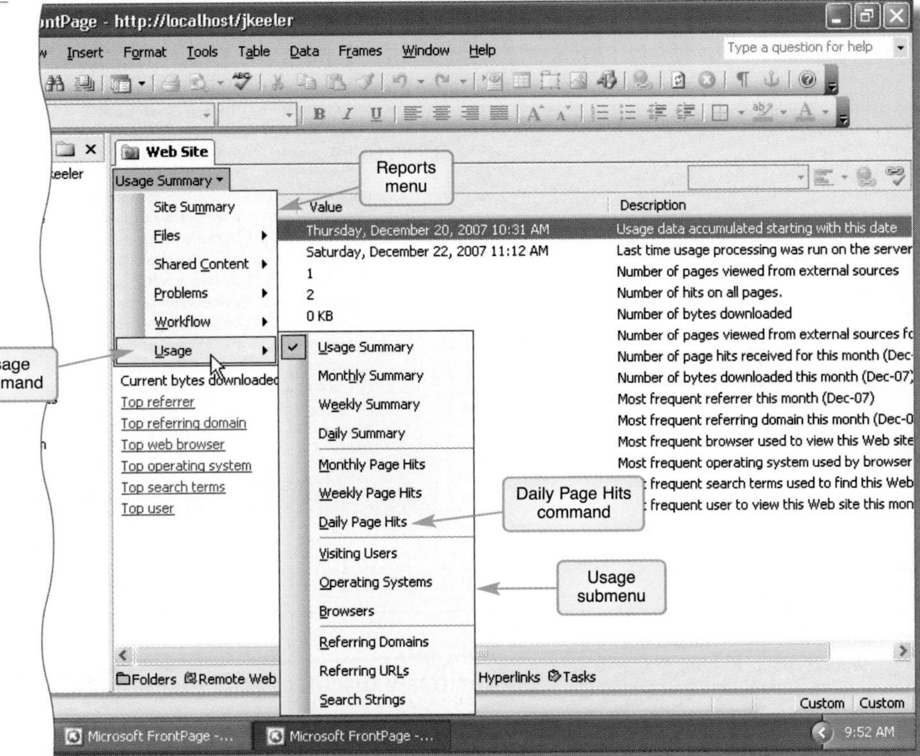

FIGURE 9-57

2

- **Click Daily Page Hits.**

FrontPage displays the Daily Page Hits report (Figure 9-58). You can scroll to the right to see the hits for each file for each day of the last week.

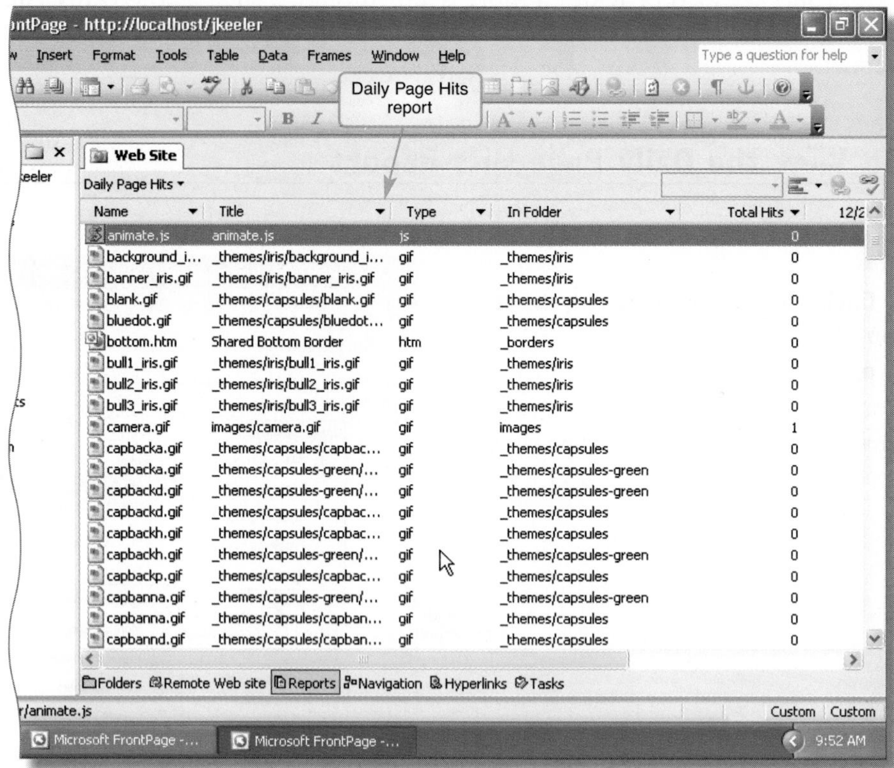

FIGURE 9-58

Other Ways

1. On View menu point to Reports, point to Usage, click Daily Page Hits on Usage submenu
2. Press ALT+V, R, U, D
3. In Voice Command mode, say "View, Reports, Usage, Daily Page Hits"

As previously discussed, the logging and subsequent reporting of some usage information may require changes to settings on the server. You should check with your site administrator to determine what usage information is being logged by the server.

Once you are familiar with the usage reports available in FrontPage, you should publish the Web site from the local host test server to the production server. Remember, however, that the Subsite Manager user was added to the local host test server and not to the production server. A user in the Subsite Manager role thus will not be able to publish the subsite independently of the parent Web site, unless he or she has an appropriate account on the production server.

Quitting FrontPage

The following steps quit FrontPage.

To Quit FrontPage

1. **Click File on the menu bar and then click Close Site.**
2. **Click the Close button on the FrontPage title bar.**
3. **Repeat Steps 1 and 2 above for the second instance of FrontPage.**

The FrontPage windows close, and the Windows desktop is displayed.

Project Summary

In this project, you learned how to use Internet Information Services to start a local Web server and how to set server options and publishing options for a Web site. In addition, you learned how to optimize the published HTML for a Web site and open a Web site on a local host. You also learned about roles and permissions on a Web site and how they help make a Web site more secure. You learned how to create a custom role, add a new user to a Web site, assign a custom role to a user, manage permissions for Web sites, and report on recently added or changed files for a Web site. Finally, you learned how to view usage reports for a Web site.

What You Should Know

Having completed this project, you should be able to perform the tasks below. The tasks are listed in the same order they were presented in this project. For a list of the buttons, menus, toolbars, and commands introduced in this project, see the Quick Reference Summary at the back of this book and refer to the Page Number column.

1. Use Internet Information Services to Start a Local Web Server (FP 608)
2. Set Web Server Options for Internet Information Services (FP 612)
3. Start FrontPage and Open an Existing Web Site (FP 613)
4. Set Publishing Options for a Web Site Using FrontPage (FP 615)
5. Set Options to Optimize Published HTML (FP 617)
6. Publish a Web Site to the Local Host (FP 619)
7. Open a Web Site on the Local Host (FP 621)
8. Access the Web Site Administration Page for a Web Site (FP 622)
9. Manage Permissions for a Subsite (FP 624)
10. Add a Custom Role (FP 627)
11. Add a New User to a Subsite and Assign a Custom Role (FP 630)
12. Recalculate a Web Site (FP 633)
13. Enable Source Control for a Subsite (FP 634)
14. View the Recently Added Files Report (FP 638)
15. View the Recently Changed Files Report (FP 640)
16. View the Usage Summary Report (FP 642)
17. View the Daily Page Hits Report (FP 643)
18. Quit FrontPage (FP 644)

Learn It Online

Instructions: To complete the Learn It Online exercises, start your browser, click the Address bar, and then enter the Web address scsite.com/fp2003/learn. When the FrontPage 2003 Learn It Online page is displayed, follow the instructions in the exercises below. Each exercise has instructions for printing your results, either for your own records or for submission to your instructor.

1 Project Reinforcement TF, MC, and SA

Below FrontPage Project 9, click the Project Reinforcement link. Print the quiz by clicking Print on the File menu for each page. Answer each question.

2 Flash Cards

Below FrontPage Project 9, click the Flash Cards link and read the instructions. Type 20 (or a number specified by your instructor) in the Number of playing cards text box, type your name in the Enter your Name text box, and then click the Flip Card button. When the flash card is displayed, read the question and then click the ANSWER box arrow to select an answer. Flip through Flash Cards. If your score is 15 (75%) correct or greater, click Print on the File menu to print your results. If your score is less than 15 (75%) correct, then redo this exercise by clicking the Replay button.

3 Practice Test

Below FrontPage Project 9, click the Practice Test link. Answer each question, enter your first and last name at the bottom of the page, and then click the Grade Test button. When the graded practice test is displayed on your screen, click Print on the File menu to print a hard copy. Continue to take practice tests until you score 80% or better.

4 Who Wants To Be a Computer Genius?

Below FrontPage Project 9, click the Computer Genius link. Read the instructions, enter your first and last name at the bottom of the page, and then click the PLAY button. When your score is displayed, click the PRINT RESULTS link to print a hard copy.

5 Wheel of Terms

Below FrontPage Project 9, click the Wheel of Terms link. Read the instructions, and then enter your first and last name and your school name. Click the PLAY button. When your score is displayed, right-click the score and then click Print on the shortcut menu to print a hard copy.

6 Crossword Puzzle Challenge

Below FrontPage Project 9, click the Crossword Puzzle Challenge link. Read the instructions, and then enter your first and last name. Click the SUBMIT button. Work the crossword puzzle. When you are finished, click the Submit button. When the crossword puzzle is redisplayed, click the Print Puzzle button to print a hard copy.

7 Tips and Tricks

Below FrontPage Project 9, click the Tips and Tricks link. Click a topic that pertains to Project 9. Right-click the information and then click Print on the shortcut menu. Construct a brief example of what the information relates to in FrontPage to confirm you understand how to use the tip or trick.

8 Newsgroups

Below FrontPage Project 9, click the Newsgroups link. Click a topic that pertains to Project 9. Print three comments.

9 Expanding Your Horizons

Below FrontPage Project 9, click the Expanding Your Horizons link. Click a topic that pertains to Project 9. Print the information. Construct a brief example of what the information relates to in FrontPage to confirm you understand the contents of the article.

10 Search Sleuth

Below FrontPage Project 9, click the Search Sleuth link. To search for a term that pertains to this project, select a term below the Project 9 title and then use the Google search engine at google.com (or any major search engine) to display and print two Web pages that present information on the term.

11 FrontPage Online Training

Below FrontPage Project 9, click the FrontPage Online Training link. When your browser displays the Microsoft Office Online Web page, click the FrontPage link. Click one of the FrontPage courses that covers one or more of the objectives listed at the beginning of the project on page FP 602. Print the first page of the course before stepping through it.

12 Office Marketplace

Below FrontPage Project 9, click the Office Marketplace link. When your browser displays the Microsoft Office Online Web page, click the Office Marketplace link. Click a topic that relates to FrontPage. Print the first page.

Apply Your Knowledge

1 Publish a Web Site to the Local Host

Instructions: Start FrontPage and open the Whalen Metal support Web site that you modified in Project 4. If you did not complete Project 4, see your instructor for a copy of the required files.

1. Open Control Panel. When the Control Panel window opens, click the Performance and Maintenance icon. When the Performance and Maintenance window opens, click the Administrative Tools icon.
2. When the Administrative Tools window opens, double-click the Internet Information Services icon. When the Internet Information Services window opens, determine if the Web server is started. If not, navigate to the local Web server and then click the Start item button to start the Web server. Click the Close button on the title bar of the Internet Information Services window. Click the Close button in the Administrative Tools window.
3. In the FrontPage window, click File on the menu bar and then click Publish Site. If the Remote Web Site Properties dialog box is displayed, then click the Browse button. Otherwise, click the Remote Web Site Properties button and then click the Browse button.
4. In the New Publish Location dialog box, type `http://localhost/Apply9-1Whalen` in the Site name text box. Click the Open button.
5. If the Microsoft Office FrontPage dialog box is displayed, click the OK button. Click the Remote Web Site Properties button at the top of the Remote Web Site view.
6. When the Remote Web Site Properties dialog box is displayed, click the Publishing tab. If necessary, in the General area, click All pages, overwriting pages already on destination to select it. If necessary, in the Logging area, click Log changes during publish to select it.
7. Click the Optimize HTML tab. Select all options for optimizing the HTML for the Web site. Click the OK button. Click the Publish Web Site button.
8. When the Web site is published successfully, click the View your publish log file link. When the browser opens, print the Publish Log and then close the browser.
9. Click the Open your Remote Web site in FrontPage link at the bottom of the Remote Web site view.
10. Click Tools on the menu bar and then click Site Settings. The Site Settings dialog box is displayed, as shown in Figure 9-59. Record your server URL, FrontPage Server Extensions version, server software name and version number on paper or in a word-processing document, along with your name, and hand it in to your instructor.

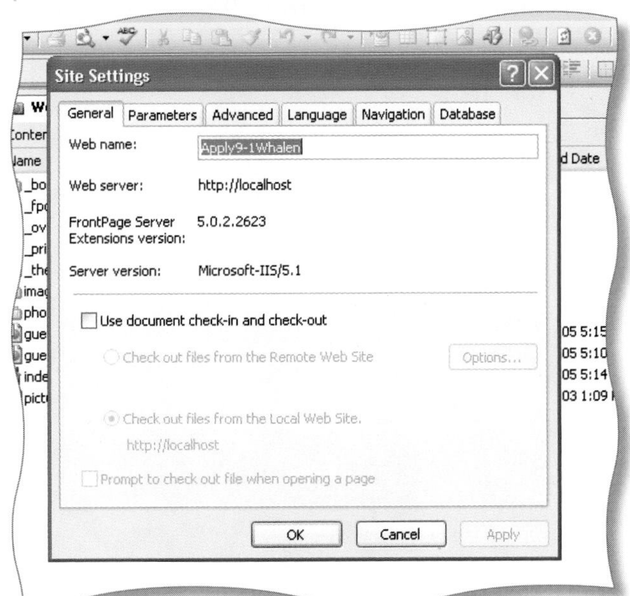

FIGURE 9-59

1 Viewing Web Usage Reports

Problem: The owner of Fairway Lawn Care wants to know how he can determine what services are of interest to visitors of the Web site. Although not an accurate indicator, he believes that knowing the number of page hits on various services pages can give him some idea of their popularity. He wants you to show him how to get this information.

Instructions: Perform the following tasks.

1. Open the Fairway Lawn Care Web site that you modified in Project 8. If you did not complete that exercise for Project 8, see your instructor for a copy of the required files.
2. If necessary, publish the Web site to a server, either a server on the World Wide Web or a local host.
3. Navigate to Remote Web site view and then click the Open your Remote Web site in FrontPage link to open the server-based Web site.
4. Click the Reports button at the bottom of the Web Site view. When the Web site is displayed in Reports view, click the Site Summary button, point to Usage, and then click Monthly Page Hits on the Usage submenu.
5. If no files have hits greater than zero, close the Web site, start a browser, and browse to the Web site. Visit a number of pages and then close the browser. Wait for the log file of usage statistics to run on the server. If you have the proper level of security permission to run usage processing manually, then open a command-prompt window. Change to the directory C:\Program Files\Common Files\Microsoft Shared\web server extensions\50\bin and then type `owsadm.exe -o usage` to start the process. You may need to restart your computer after running the process in order to generate the statistics. Open the server-based Web site and again display the Monthly Page Hits report.
6. Click the column heading, Total Hits, to sort the report in descending order by total number of page hits (Figure 9-60).
7. Right-click the report and then click Copy Report on the shortcut menu. Start Word and paste the report into a new document. Print the report from Word, write your name on the report, and hand it in to your instructor.

In the Lab

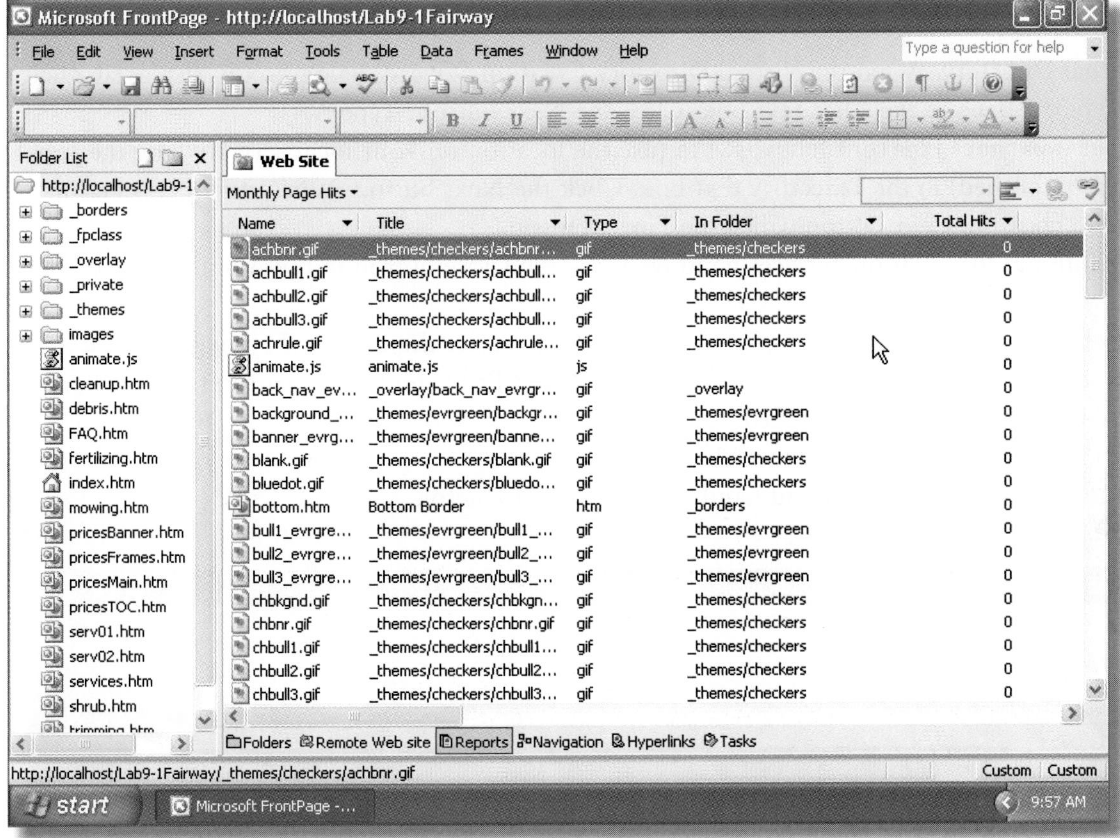

FIGURE 9-60

2 Setting Server Options to Create a New Virtual Directory

Problem: James Keeler would like visitors to have access to the Job Opportunities Web site without the address showing that it is located within his personal Web site. To do so, he must set the server options on the local host to create a virtual directory and an alias for the Job Opportunities Web site.

Instructions: Perform the following tasks.

1. Open Control Panel. When the Control Panel window opens, click the Performance and Maintenance icon. When the Performance and Maintenance window opens, click the Administrative Tools icon.
2. When the Administrative Tools window opens, double-click the Internet Information Services icon. When the Internet Information Services window opens, navigate to the local host Web site and determine if the Web server is started. If not, click the Start item button to start the Web server.
3. Right-click the Default Web Site (localhost) icon. Point to New on the shortcut menu.

(continued)

Setting Server Options to Create a New Virtual Directory *(continued)*

4. Click Virtual Directory. When the Virtual Directory Creation Wizard dialog box is displayed, click the Next button. Type `JobOpps` in the Alias text box. Click the Next button. Type `C:\Inetpub\wwwroot\jkeeler\JobOppsSite` (use the location on your local server where the JobOppsSite subsite was published) in the Directory text box. Click the Next button. When the Access Permission page is displayed, click the Next button. Click the Finish button.
5. Close the Internet Information Services window. Click the Close button in the Administrative Tools window.
6. Start a Web browser and drag through the Address bar to select the default Web page URL, if any. Type `http://localhost/JobOpps` and then press the ENTER key. Print the Job Opportunities home page when it is displayed in the browser (Figure 9-61).
7. Click the Close button on the browser title bar.
8. Write your name on the printout and hand it in to your instructor.

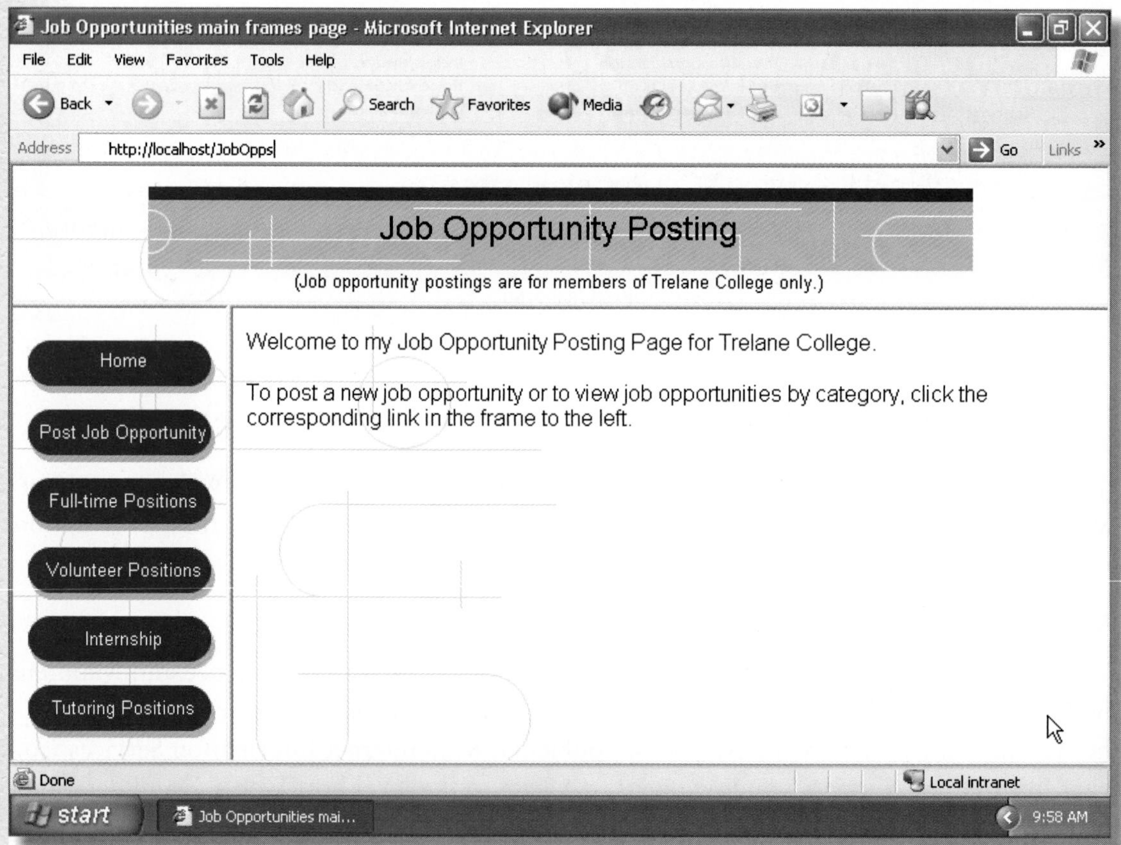

FIGURE 9-61

3 Adding a User to a Web Site

Problem: After viewing your prototypes for the software Web pages, the Information Systems departmental manager wants to begin construction of a production Web site as soon as possible. He already has assigned Rhonda Washington, a new staff member, to maintain the pages. For security purposes, you suggest adding a new user account for Rhonda, with permissions limited to authoring Web pages, leaving site administration to a more experienced person. You demonstrate this on a computer's local host.

Instructions: Perform the following tasks.

1. Start FrontPage and open the Web site, Software, that you modified in Project 7. If you did not complete that exercise for Project 7, see your instructor for a copy of the required files.
2. If necessary, start the Web server using Internet Information Services and then publish the disk-based Web site to the local host.
3. Click the Open your Remote Web site in FrontPage link at the bottom of the Remote Web site view.
4. Click Tools on the menu bar and then point to Server. Click Administration Home on the Server submenu to open the Web site Administration page for the Web site.
5. If necessary, change the subsite permissions to Use unique permissions for this Web site. Return to the Web site Administration page when completed.
6. Click the Manage users link and then click Add a user. Type `author1` in the User name text box, type `itdepartment31` in the Password text box and then type `itdepartment31` in the Confirm password text box. Select the role of Advanced author for the new user. Click the Add User button to add the new user.
7. Verify that the Manage Users page displays the new user and the proper role, as shown in Figure 9-62 on the next page. Print the Web page, write your name on it, and hand it in to your instructor.
8. Click the Administration link at the top of the page. Scroll to the Server Health area and then click the Recalculate the Web link. Recalculate the Web site.
9. Close the Web browser. Close the server-based Web site and then quit FrontPage. Close the disk-based Web site and then close FrontPage.

(continued)

Adding a User to a Web Site *(continued)*

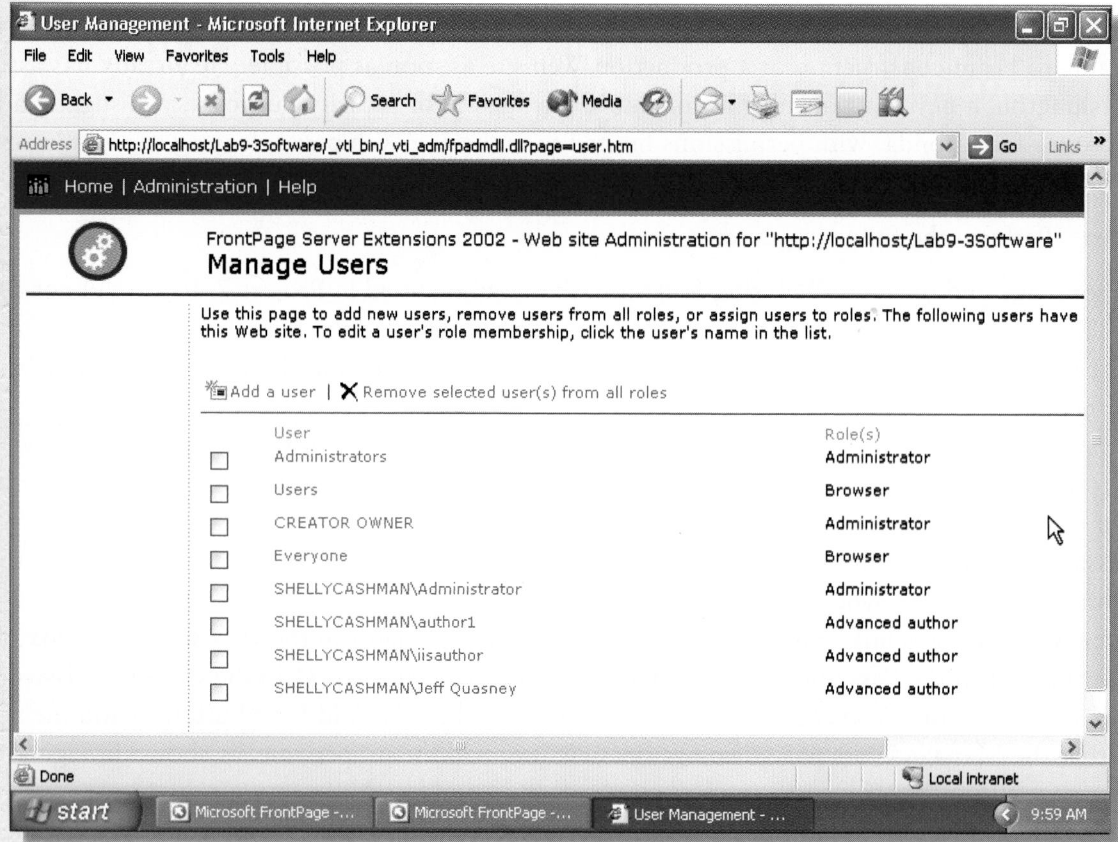

FIGURE 9-62

Cases and Places

The difficulty of these case studies varies:
■ are the least difficult and ■■ are more difficult. The last exercise is a group exercise.

1 ■ Open your resume page from Project 8. Use the Reports view to report recently added files and recently changed files for the previous 30 days. Add a graphic to the page from the Clip Art task pane and run the report again.

2 ■ If necessary, publish the Web site for your movie reviews from Project 8. Optimize the HTML for the Web site. Open the Web site on the server and then enable source control by using the Web site Administration page.

3 ■■ Start a Web server on the local host. Open the departmental Web site from Project 8. Set publishing options to publish all pages. Publish the Web site to the local host.

4 ■■ If necessary, publish your friend's graduation Web site using optimized HTML. Open the Web site on the server and examine the server option settings. View reports for recently changed files and usage of the Web site, including the Site Summary. If necessary, start a Web server on the local host and publish the Web site to the local host.

5 ■■ **Working Together** On the server for the company sports Web site from Project 8, add a new custom role with permissions that allow a user to manage a subsite but not create accounts. Add a new user to each of the subsites for each sport that you created in Project 7. Assign the custom role to each new user. Verify that source control is enabled for each of the subsites. If possible, work as a team on the different pages, using different login IDs to illustrate the use of user accounts and roles. View reports for files added and changed within the last month, as well as usage reports for number of visits, browser used, and operating systems used by the visitors to the Web site.

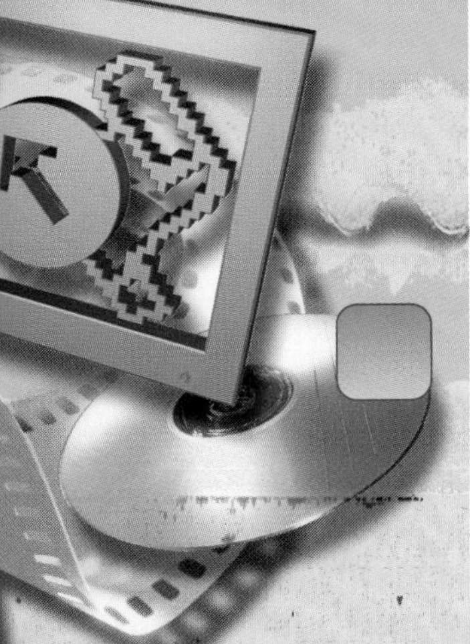

MICROSOFT Office FrontPage 2003

Working with Multimedia Content in Web Pages

CASE PERSPECTIVE

As James Keeler approaches his graduation from Trelane College, he wants to use his Web site to showcase some of the work he has done during his years at the college. While he already has posted his resume on the Web site, he feels that offering the results of some of his other Web design and marketing projects would provide potential employers a unique perspective on his experience.

James has a Web page in mind that includes multimedia content that he developed in his capstone multimedia advertising course in his senior year. For these projects, James developed various multimedia advertising pieces that promote Trelane College to potential students. The content includes a Macromedia Flash movie, a short video that includes an audio track, and an audio radio advertisement.

James will utilize FrontPage's capability of importing multimedia content into Web pages and managing the content. In addition, he will set properties to size and place the media elements and allow Web page visitors to play each element when they want. You offer to help James create the page and educate him on the potential to stream video content across the Internet.

As you read through this Multimedia feature, you will learn how to insert multimedia content into Web pages, including Macromedia Flash content, video, and audio. You also will learn how to set properties for the multimedia elements. Finally you will learn about streaming multimedia content to a browser.

Objectives

You will have mastered the material in this feature when you can:

- Add a Macromedia Flash movie to a Web page
- Add video to a Web page
- Add audio to a Web page
- Understand multimedia formats and streaming

Introduction

FrontPage allows you to include a variety of multimedia content in a Web page. **Multimedia** elements include sound, graphics, animation, and video. One of the more popular multimedia file formats in use on the Web is Macromedia Flash. **Flash** is a graphic animation technology used to produce movies, animations, or presentations. Flash is commonly used for banner advertisements on Web pages and can include images and sounds. Flash files are created using a software application capable of creating Flash files, such as Macromedia Producer.

Video and audio can be included in a Web page by embedding a file in a Web page or providing a link to the video or audio content. In either case, the video or audio can be streamed to the user so that the Web page visitor does not need to download the entire file before the content begins to play in the user's browser or media player.

FrontPage supports a variety of popular video and audio formats and provides the ability to modify how the content appears in the browser. For example, you can set the height and width of the video and determine whether the video plays automatically when the Web page loads or plays when the user moves the mouse pointer over the video.

In James Keeler's Multimedia Showcase Web page, the three multimedia elements — the Macromedia Flash animation, the video, and the audio — are displayed in separate table cells (Figure 1). Descriptions and instructions appear next to each item. The Web page visitor must take an action to play each element.

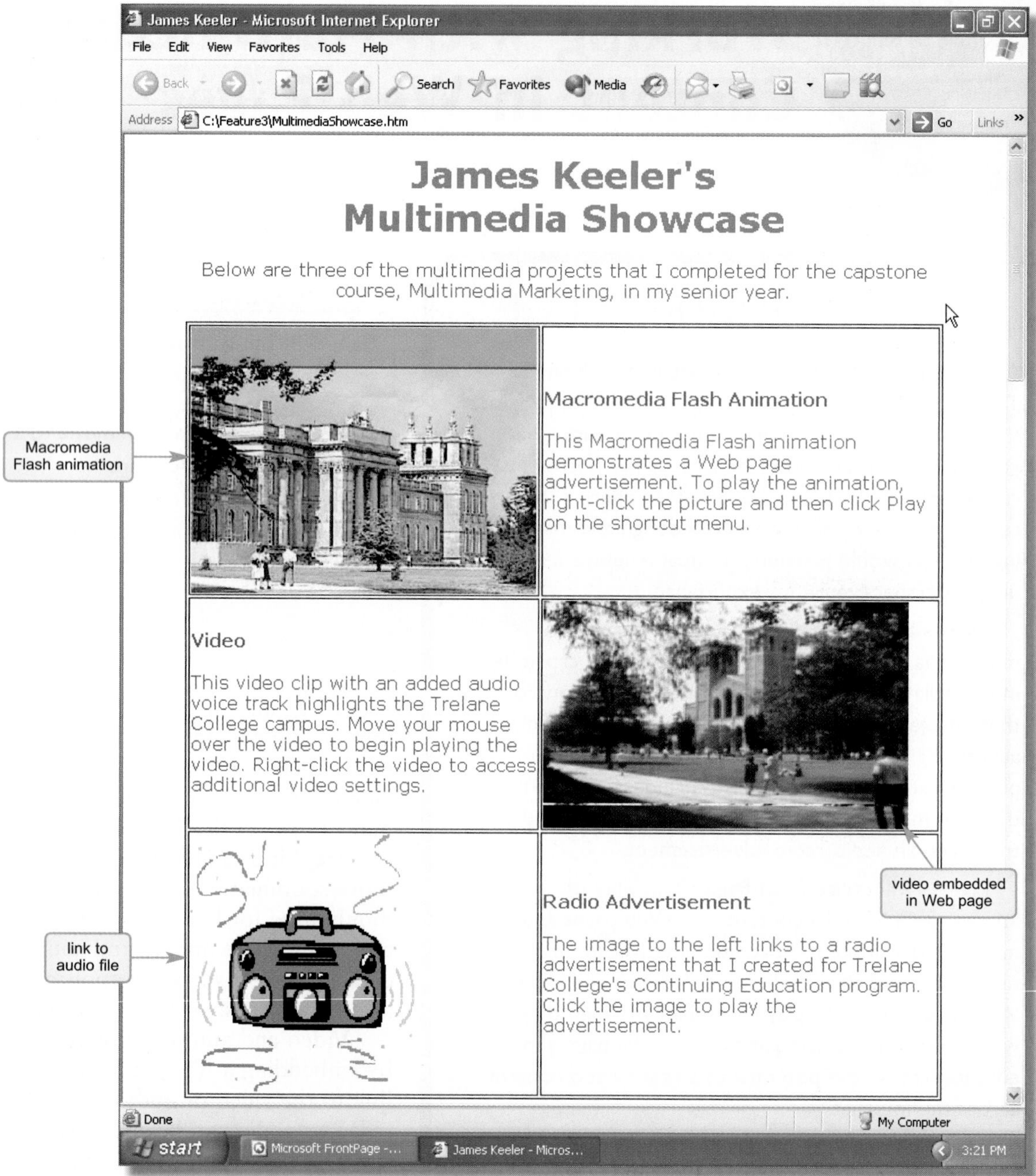

FIGURE 1

Adding a Macromedia Flash Animation to a Web Page

The Multimedia Showcase Web page should be created as a stand-alone Web page so that it can be added to a Web site a later time. The following steps start FrontPage and create a new Web page.

Note: If you plan to complete the steps in this feature, the data files must be placed on your hard drive or accessible network drive because the multimedia files are too large for the capacity of a floppy disk.

More About

Macromedia Flash

Before you can play Macromedia Flash movies in Preview view or in your browser, you will need to install the Macromedia Flash plug-in. To learn more about the Macromedia Flash plug-in, visit the FrontPage 2003 More About Web page (scsite.com/fp2003/more) and then click Flash Movies.

To Start FrontPage and Create a New Web Page

1. **Click the Start button on the Windows taskbar, point to All Programs on the Start menu, and then point to Microsoft Office on the All Programs submenu.**
2. **Click Microsoft Office FrontPage 2003 on the Microsoft Office submenu.**
3. **If FrontPage opened a previously opened Web site, click File on the menu bar and then click Close Site.**
4. **If a new Web page named new_page_1.htm is not displayed in Design view, click the Create a new normal page button on the Standard toolbar to create a new Web page.**
5. **If a task pane appears, click the Close button on the task pane.**
6. **Apply the Ice theme with vivid colors to the Web page.**

The FrontPage window opens and an empty page is displayed. The Web Site tab is not displayed because only a Web page is opened in FrontPage.

Before adding the multimedia content to the new Web page, two lines of heading must be added to the page. Also, a table including the descriptions of the multimedia elements must be added. A 3 by 2 table allows a description to accompany each multimedia element by placing a description in one column of a row and the multimedia element in the other.

The steps on the next page create the layout for the Web page by add two lines of headings, a table, and descriptions of the multimedia elements.

More About

Creating Flash Movies

Several Web sites allow you to use their free wizards to create Flash movies, so you do not need to purchase a tool to create the movies. Such free wizards are useful for creating simple Flash movies, such as Web site introductory pages. To learn more about free Flash movies, visit the FrontPage 2003 More About Web page (scsite.com/fp2003/more) and then click Free Flash Movies.

To Create the Layout for the Web Page

1

- **Click the Center button on the Formatting toolbar.**
- **Click the Style box arrow on the Formatting toolbar and then click Heading 1 in the Style list.**
- **Click the Font Color box arrow on the Formatting toolbar and then click red.**
- **Type** `James Keeler's` **and then press SHIFT+ENTER.**

2

- **Type** `Multimedia Showcase` **and then press the ENTER key.**
- **If necessary, click the Style box arrow on the Formatting toolbar and then click Normal in the Style list.**
- **Type** `Below are three of the multimedia projects that I completed for the capstone` **and then press SHIFT+ENTER.**
- **Type** `course, Multimedia Marketing, in my senior year.` **and then press the ENTER key.**

FrontPage displays the two lines of heading in Design view (Figure 2).

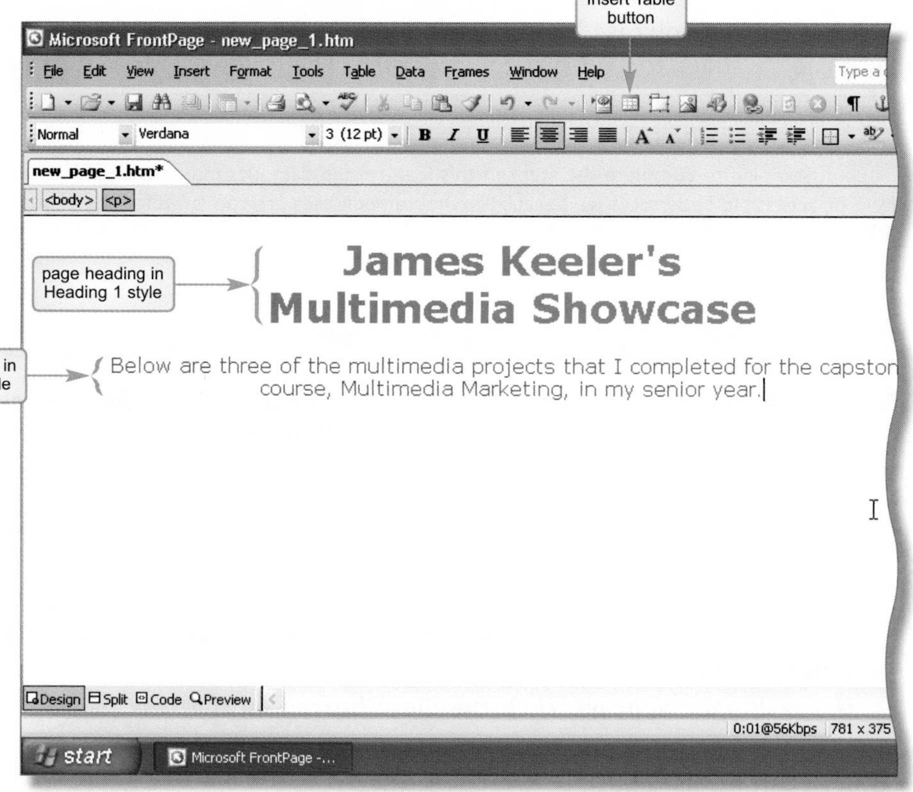

FIGURE 2

3

- **Click the Insert Table button on the Standard toolbar and then drag through the grid to create a 3 by 2 table.**
- **Release the mouse button.**
- **Type the descriptions of the multimedia content in the cells of the table as shown in Table 1.**

4

- **Select the first line of each cell with the newly added text and then click the Bold button on the Formatting toolbar.**

FrontPage displays the table with the added descriptions (Figure 3).

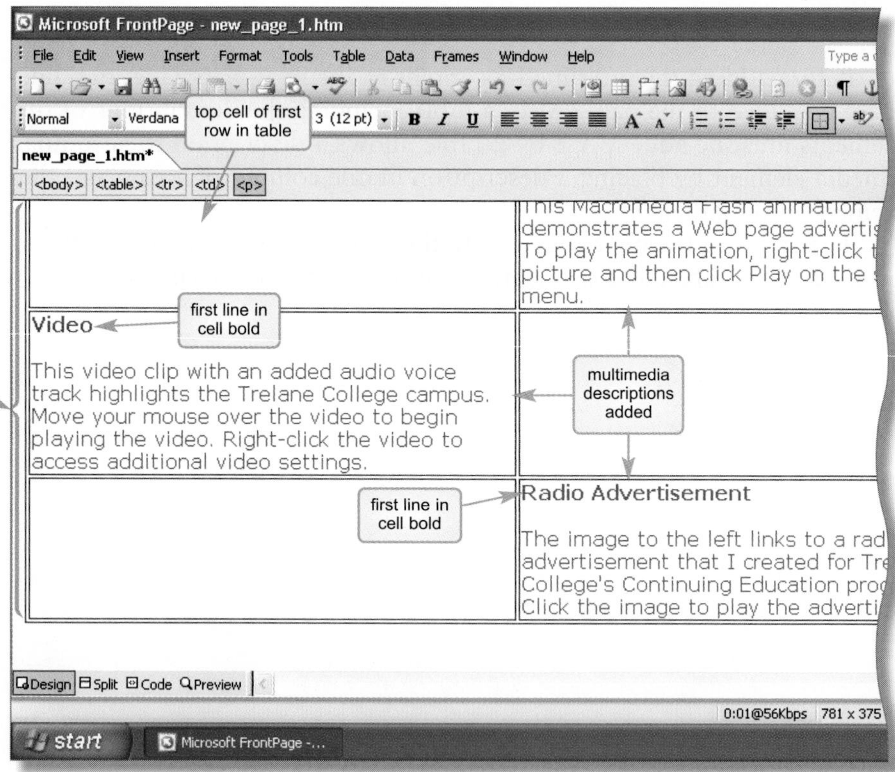

FIGURE 3

Table 1 Contents of Table in Web Page

ROW	COLUMN	TEXT
1	2	Macromedia Flash Animation This Macromedia Flash animation demonstrates a Web page advertisement. Right-click the picture and then click Play on the shortcut menu to play the animation.
2	1	Video This short video clip with an added audio voice track highlights the Trelane College campus. Move your mouse pointer over the video to begin playing the video. Right-click the video to access additional video settings.
3	2	Radio Advertisement The image to the left links to a radio advertisement that I created for Trelane College's Continuing Education program. Click the image to play the advertisement.

As shown in Figure 3, the descriptions of the multimedia items alternate columns to create a more visually appealing appearance. The descriptions explain to the user how to cause each multimedia element to play.

The next step is to add the Macromedia Flash movie to the top-left cell of the table.

Adding a Macromedia Flash Animation to a Web Page

Q: Where can I find plug-ins?

A: A variety of plug-ins exist for most Web browsers, and most plug-ins are free. Several Web sites provide central repositories of plug-ins for you to download. To learn more about popular plug-ins, visit the FrontPage 2003 More About Web page (scsite.com/fp2003/more) and then click Plug-ins.

Macromedia Flash movies commonly are used for Web-based advertisements or short animations. Special software, such as Macromedia Flash MX, is required to create Flash movies. Macromedia Flash movies usually have the file extensions of .spl (Macromedia Splash), .swf (Macromedia Shockwave Flash), or .swt (Macromedia Shockwave Template). Before a Web page visitor can view a Flash movie, the user must have the Macromedia Flash plug-in installed with the browser. A **plug-in** is a software program that is installed alongside a browser and adds additional functionality to the browser, such as the ability to view or interact with files that the browser typically does not understand. If the user does not have the Macromedia Flash plug-in, the browser prompts the user to install the plug-in and provides a link to the Web site where the plug-in can be obtained for free.

When you add a Flash movie to a Web page in FrontPage, the movie appears as a placeholder that indicates where the movie will play when a user views the Web page. The steps on the next page add a Macromedia Flash movie from the Data Disk to the Web page.

To Add a Macromedia Flash Animation to a Web Page

1

- **Click anywhere in the top-left cell of the table.**
- **Click Insert on the menu bar and then point to Picture.**

FrontPage displays the Insert menu and the Picture submenu (Figure 4).

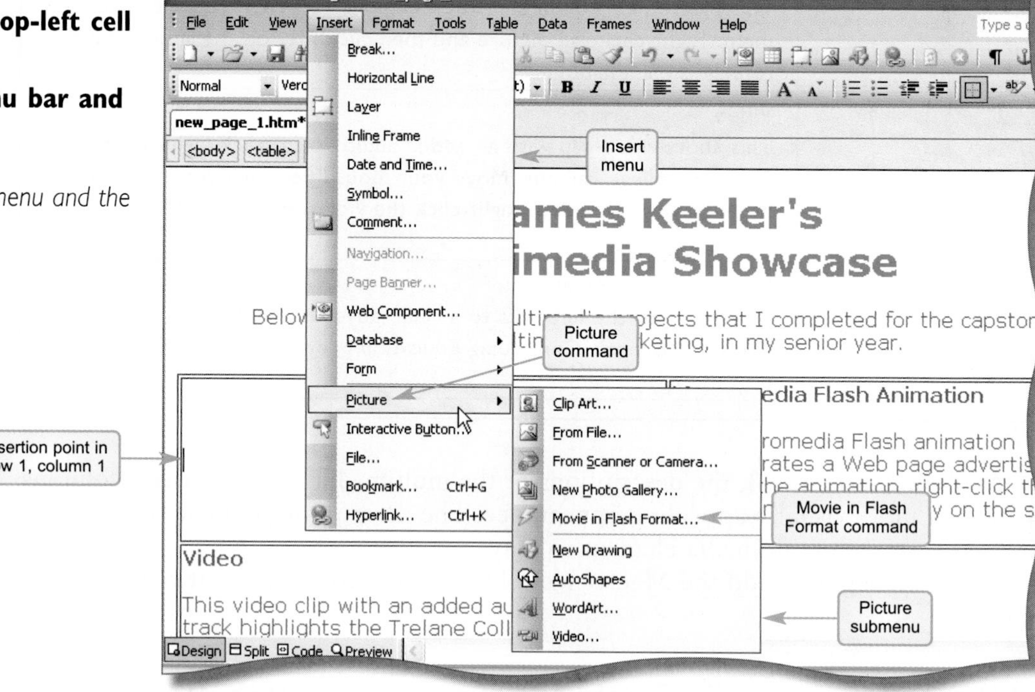

FIGURE 4

2

- **Click Movie in Flash Format.**
- **When the Select File dialog box is displayed, navigate to the Feature3 folder on the hard disk and then click TrelaneCollegeBannerAd.**

FrontPage displays the files available in the Feature3 folder on the Data Disk (Figure 5).

- **Click the Insert button.**

FrontPage inserts a placeholder for the Macromedia Flash movie in the top-left cell of the table.

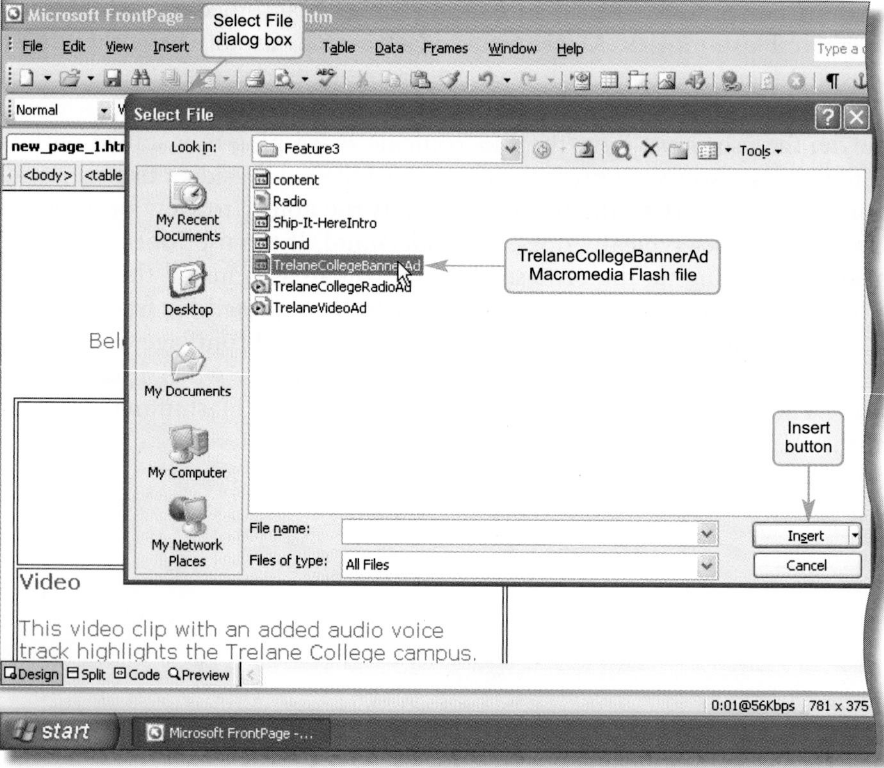

FIGURE 5

Other Ways

1. Press ALT+I, P, L
2. Drag the movie from Windows Explorer into the Web page
3. In Voice Command mode, say "Insert, Picture, Movie in Flash Format"

FrontPage displays the Macromedia Flash movie as a placeholder. The movie can be previewed in Preview view or previewed in a browser. The next step is to set properties of the movie so that it properly plays in the user's browser.

Setting Properties of a Macromedia Flash Movie

By default, Macromedia Flash movies automatically play at the highest quality when the Web page loads in a browser. In the Multimedia Showcase Web page, the movie should not play until the user wants to play the movie. Also, when the movie is set to play at high quality, the movie briefly may pause while it plays in order for the browser to download more of the movie if the movie does not download from the Web server fast enough to keep up with the playback.

Table 2 shows the options for the movie quality available with a Macromedia Flash movie. Macromedia Flash movies include the ability automatically to lower or raise the visual quality of the movie as it plays. The quality can depend on whether the browser has downloaded the entire movie. That is, the quality may be reduced as you view the movie if the browser still is waiting for more of the movie from the Web server.

Table 2 Macromedia Flash Movie Quality Settings

SETTING	MEANING
Low	Always favor playback speed over quality.
Auto Low	Start playback at low quality, but increase quality if more data arrives in time.
Auto High	Start the movie at the highest speed and quality as possible, but adjust the speed as the need arises.
Medium	A setting between the Low and High settings.
High	Always favor quality over speed.
Best	Always favor quality over speed. Pauses the movie when necessary to get all of the data possible in order to generate the highest quality.

The steps on the next page set the movie quality to Auto High and turn off the option that causes the movie to play automatically when the Web page loads in the browser.

More About

Flash Quality Settings

A Flash movie is a series of pictures. The quality of the movie depends on the quality of the pictures used to create the movie. The quality of the playback that a user sees depends on the user's connection speed, the Web site's speed, and the performance of the user's computer. Take all of these factors into account when deciding which quality setting to use. Consider providing users with multiple links to the same Flash movie, but at different quality settings. This allows users to decide how they will view the movie, based on their own situations.

To Set Properties of a Macromedia Flash Movie

1

- **Right-click the Macromedia Flash movie placeholder.**

FrontPage displays a shortcut menu (Figure 6).

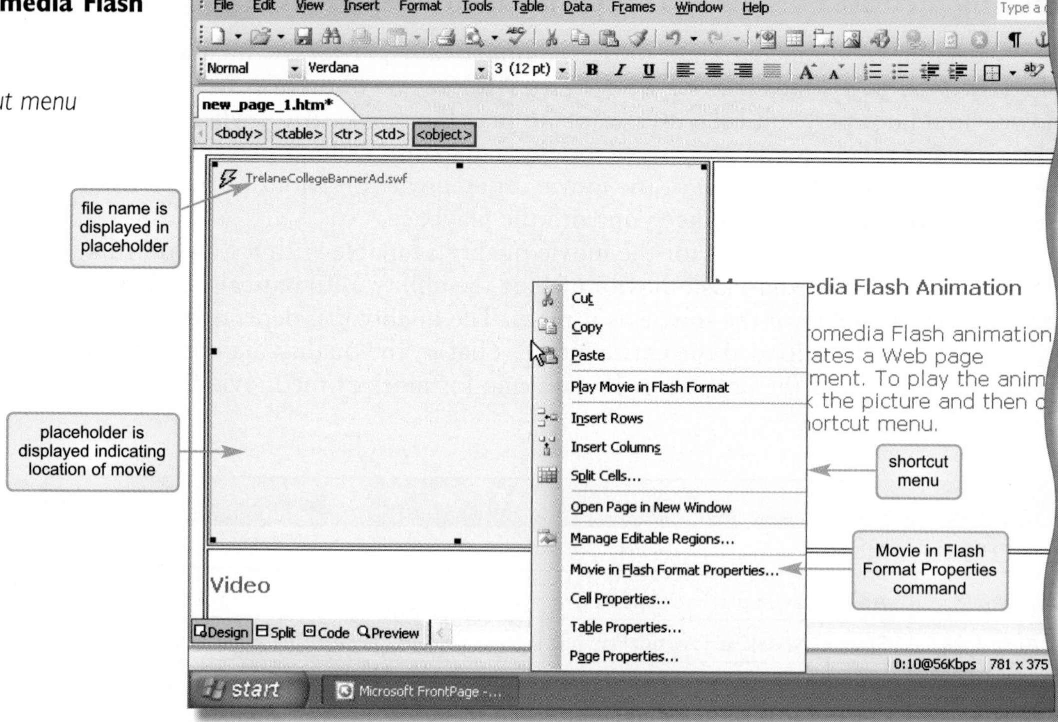

FIGURE 6

2

- **Click Movie in Flash Format Properties.**
- **When FrontPage displays the Movie in Flash Format Properties dialog box, click the Quality box arrow and then click Auto High in the Quality list.**

FrontPage displays the Movie in Flash Format Properties dialog box. The Quality is set to Auto High, ensuring that the movie plays back smoothly at the highest quality possible (Figure 7).

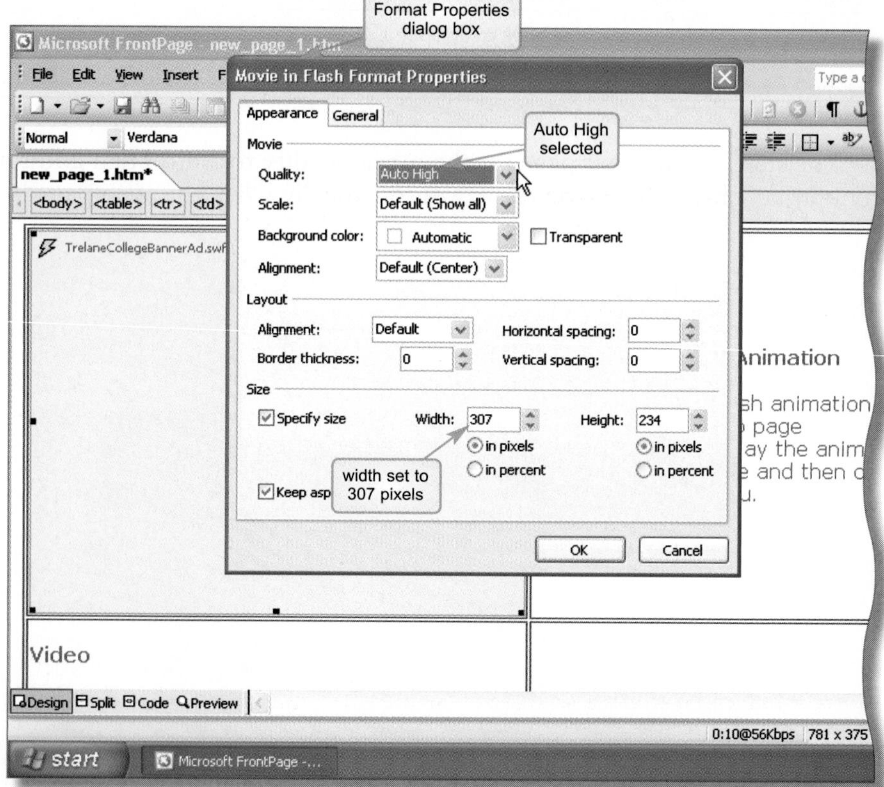

FIGURE 7

3

- **Click the General tab.**
- **If necessary, deselect Auto play in the Playback area.**

FrontPage displays the General sheet (Figure 8). The Auto play check box is deselected so that the movie does not play as soon as the Web page loads in the browser.

4

- **Click the OK button.**
- **Click the movie to select it.**
- **Use the sizing handles to change the size of the movie placeholder to approximately one third the width of the Web page.**
- **Drag the vertical cell border between the column until the size of the top-left cell of the table matches that of the movie.**

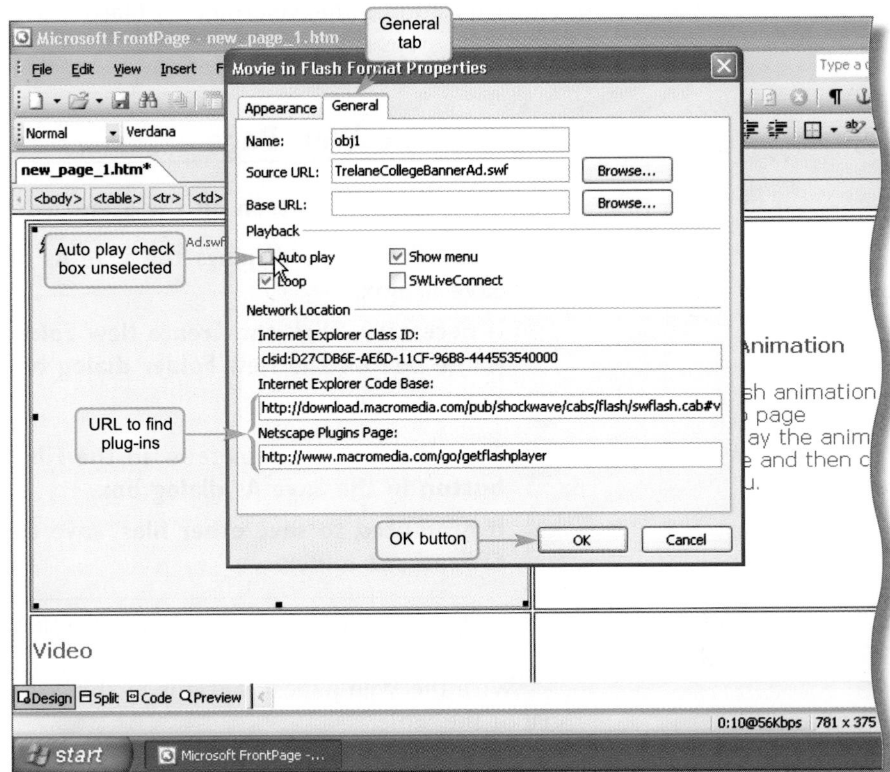

FIGURE 8

The Appearance sheet in the Movie in Flash Format Properties dialog box shows the many properties available for Flash movies. The Scale box allows you to either show the entire movie using the Default (Show all) setting, with a border around the movie, or as an exact fit based on the Size settings in the Size area. You also can set a background color for the movie and optionally set the background color to be optional, thereby allowing the background of the Web page to show through the movie. This option is useful if you do not want the movie to be seen as a rectangle, but as some other shape. You can place the movie in a layer and then set a transparent color to allow the movie to play on top of the contents of a Web page.

The General sheet in the Movie in Flash Format Properties dialog box allows you to set playback options, such as Auto play and Loop. Select the Auto play check box if you want the movie to play automatically when the Web page loads. Select the Loop check box if you want the movie to play continuously after it starts playing.

The Network Location area in the General sheet indicates where the user can download the proper plug-ins for the browser if the browser does not have the Macromedia Flash plug-in installed. By default, these are set to locations on the World Wide Web from which the plug-ins can be downloaded. You can, however, change these to a location on your computer or a location elsewhere on your network.

More About

Flash Movie Properties

Flash movies offer several configuration options for you, as shown in Figure 7 and Figure 8. To learn more about popular Flash movie configuration options and properties, visit the FrontPage 2003 More About Web page (scsite.com/fp2003/more) and then click Flash Properties.

After adding the Macromedia Flash movie, the Web page should be saved. The following steps save the Web page.

To Save the Web Page

1. **Click the Save button on the Standard toolbar.**
2. **When FrontPage displays the Save As dialog box, select Local Disk (C:) in the Save in box.**
3. **If necessary, click the Create New Folder button and type** `Feature3` **in the Name box on the New Folder dialog box.**
4. **Click the OK button.**
5. **Type** `MultimediaShowcase` **in the File name box and then click the Save button in the Save As dialog box.**
6. **If prompted to save other files, save the files in an images subfolder of the C:\Feature3 folder.**

FrontPage saves the Web page and changes the file name on the Design view tab.

With the Web page saved, the next step is to add the video to the middle-right cell of the table.

Adding Video to a Web Page

Several methods exist for adding video or audio to a Web page, and the techniques for both video and audio are similar. Video and audio can be embedded, linked, or streamed in a Web page. **Embedded** content is displayed in the Web page and is downloaded along with the Web page. **Linking** to content causes the audio or video to play in the user's audio or video player when the user clicks a link to the content. In this case, the content is downloaded only when the user clicks the link. Streaming content requires special Web server software. **Streaming** involves sending the audio or video as the player needs the audio or video. The content is sent to either a plug-in in the user's browser or to the user's audio or video player.

FrontPage provides two methods of embedding video content. First, the content can be inserted as a picture. In this case, FrontPage uses the **dynsrc** attribute of the <img> HTML tag to show a placeholder image for the video. Some browsers do not support the dynsrc attribute. Second, a plug-in can be used to show the video. In this case, the browser typically includes controls around the video that can be used by the Web page visitor to play, pause, or stop the video. The plug-in approach should be used when possible to avoid the incompatibility problems of the dynsrc attribute.

Table 3 lists the common video formats used on the World Wide Web, the file extensions used for each format, and a short description for each one.

Q&A

Q: How should I decide how to provide multimedia content on a Web page?

A: Consider carefully the method that you will use to provide multimedia content over the Web. Think about the potential number of visitors to your page, the size of the content files, and the amount of bandwidth that your ISP allows you to use. For larger content that may be accessed heavily, consider obtaining server add-ons that provide streaming capability. Some Web site hosting companies provide streaming services, such as Real Server from Real Networks.

Table 3 Common Video Formats

FORMAT	EXTENSION	DESCRIPTION
AVI (Audio Video Interleaved)	.avi	Supported by most versions of Windows, but not always supported by non-Windows computers.
MPEG (Moving Pictures Experts Group)	.mpg, .mpeg	This cross-platform format is the most popular format on the Internet. Typically, most users do not have to download special software to play it.
QuickTime	.qt, .mov	Developed by Apple, this format requires that the user install the QuickTime software.
RealVideo	.rm, .ram	Developed by Real Networks, this format requires the RealPlayer software. The format is very popular for streaming video.
Windows Media Format	.wmv, .wvx	Microsoft's popular format for Windows-based computers commonly is used for video streaming.
Shockwave (Flash)	.swf	Developed by Macromedia, Shockwave movies require the Macromedia Flash player.

Adding Video to a Web Page

The Multimedia Showcase Web page requires a video to be inserted in the second cell in the second row of the table. While FrontPage offers several methods of adding video to a Web page, the simplest way to add a short video clip to a Web page is to insert the video in the same manner that you insert pictures, clip art, or Macromedia Flash movies on a Web page. The Picture submenu includes a Video command to add video files to a Web page.

The following steps embed a video in AVI format into a Web page.

To Add Video to a Web Page

1

- **If necessary, scroll down to the second row of the table and then click the right cell in the second row of the table.**
- **Click Insert on the menu bar and then point to Picture.**

FrontPage displays the Insert menu and the Picture submenu (Figure 9).

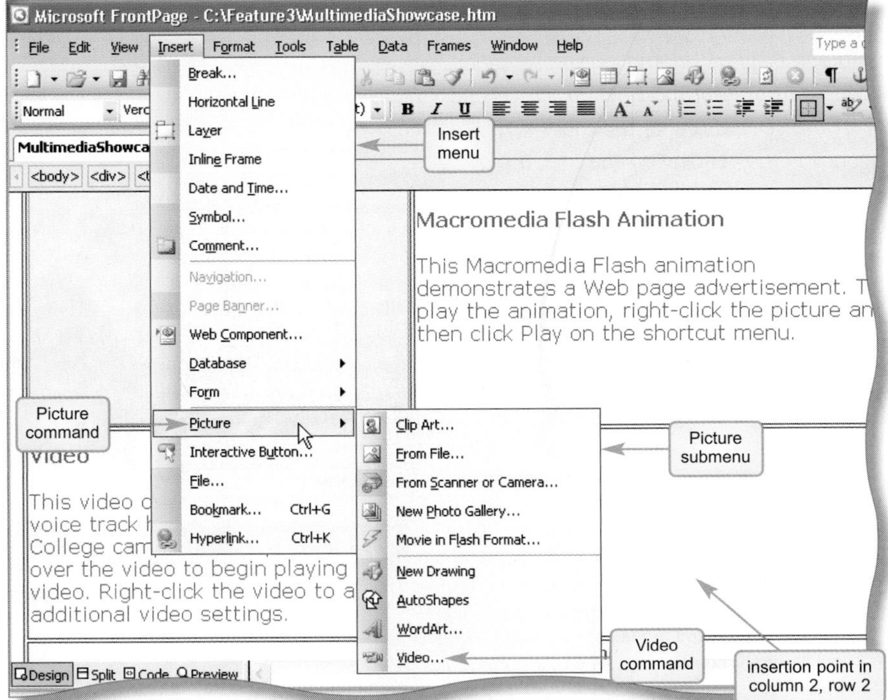

FIGURE 9

2

- **Click Video.**
- **When FrontPage displays the Video dialog box, navigate to the Feature3 folder on the Data Disk.**
- **Click the TrelaneVideoAd file.**

FrontPage displays the Video dialog box (Figure 10).

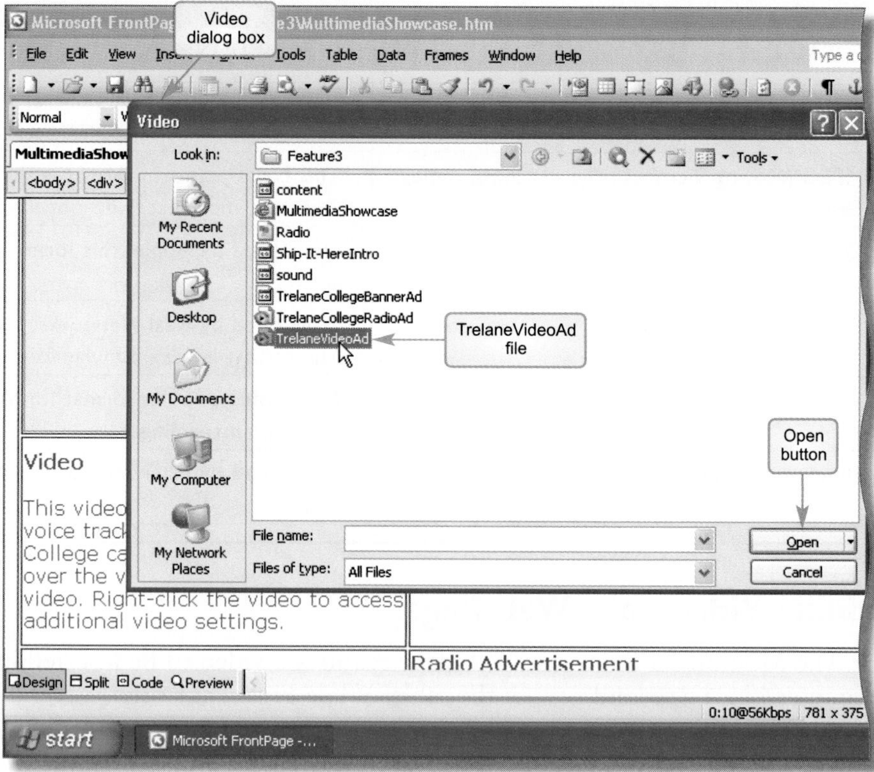

FIGURE 10

3

- **Click the Open button in the Video dialog box.**
- **If necessary, click the video and use the sizing handles to resize the video as shown in Figure 11.**

FrontPage displays an image representation of the first frame of the video in the second cell of the second row of the table (Figure 11). Depending on the media players and codecs installed on your computer, a placeholder may appear instead.

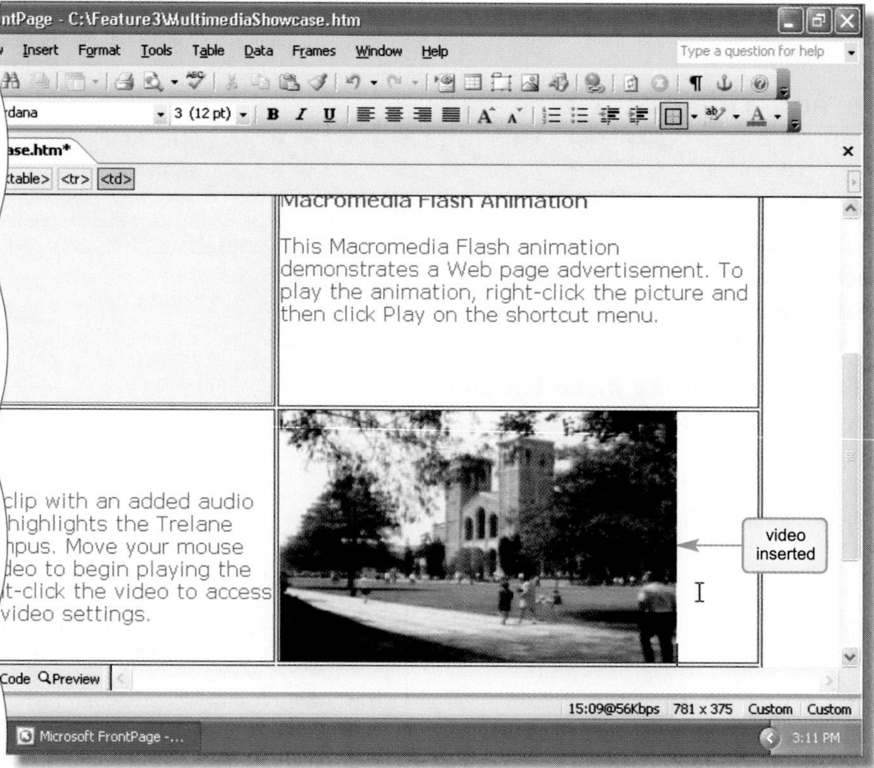

FIGURE 11

Other Ways

1. Press ALT+I, P, V
2. In Voice Command mode, say "Insert, Picture, Video"

As shown in Figure 11, FrontPage displays an image representation of the first frame of the video in Design view. Depending on the format of the video file, FrontPage may not be capable of displaying the image. The video, however, still will be available and in place when the Web page is viewed in a browser.

More About

Video

In addition to the wealth of file formats available for video, video within the files also can be encoded using a number of different video encoding algorithms. The quality of your video, the file's size, and the frame rate are all important factors to consider when encoding a video for the Web. To experiment with different video encoding algorithms, use Microsoft Windows Movie Maker to create video for the Web. To learn more about Microsoft Windows Movie Maker, visit the FrontPage 2003 More About Web page (scsite.com/fp2003/more) and then click Windows Movie Maker.

Setting Properties of a Video

The video currently appears in Design view as a representation of the first frame of the video. By default, the browser plays the video as soon as the user loads the Web page. In the case of the Multimedia Showcase Web page, the video should play only when the user places the mouse pointer over the video.

If a browser is not capable of playing the video, the browser may either display only an image representation of the first frame of the video, or the browser may display only alternative text. For the Multimedia Showcase Web page, alternative text should be added to the video image so that a message is displayed if the user's browser cannot play the video.

The following steps set properties to play the video when the mouse pointer is placed over the video and to display alternative text if the user's browser cannot play the video.

To Set Properties of a Video

1

- **Right-click the image representation of the video.**
- **When FrontPage displays the shortcut menu, click Picture Properties.**
- **When FrontPage displays the Picture Properties dialog box, if necessary, click the Video tab.**
- **Click On mouse over in the Start area.**

FrontPage displays the Picture Properties dialog box (Figure 12). The On mouse over property causes the video to play when the mouse pointer moves over the image representation of the video.

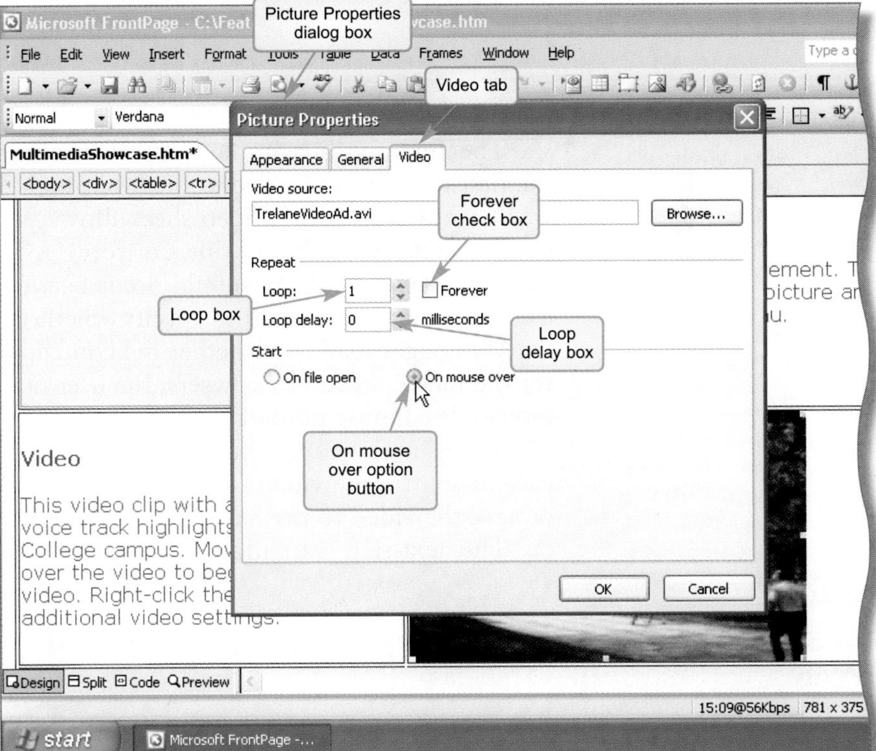

FIGURE 12

2

- **Click the General tab.**
- **Click the Text check box.**
- **Type** `Your browser is not capable of playing this video.` **in the Text text box.**

FrontPage displays the General sheet in the Picture Properties dialog box (Figure 13).

3

- **Click the OK button.**

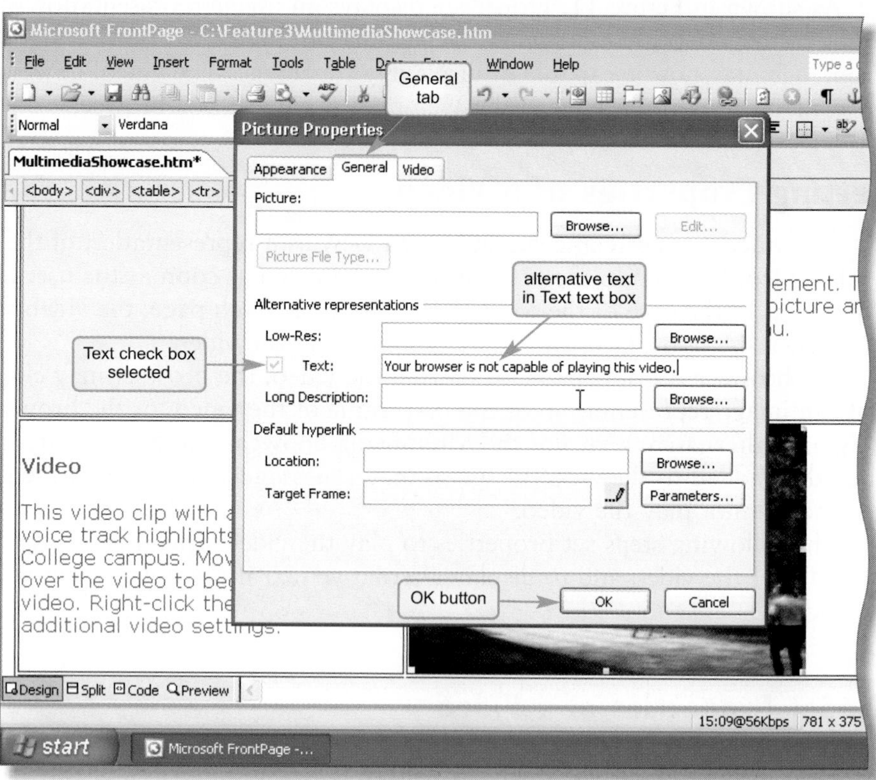

FIGURE 13

The Text text box in the General sheet indicates the text that appears in place of the first frame of the video in the event that the user's browser cannot play the video. The Repeat area in the Video sheet allows you to specify whether the video repeats either a certain number of times or forever. The Loop delay box allows you to specify how much of a delay should occur between successive playbacks of the content. The Start area allows you to specify whether the content automatically plays when the Web pages loads or whether the content should play during the mouse over event for the image. In some browsers, the user may have to click the image in addition to moving the mouse pointer over the image.

The user also can right-click the video to access a shortcut menu that allows the user to control the video. The user can play the video, stop the video if it is playing, or save the video to the hard drive.

The next step is to add the audio content to the Web page.

> *More About*
>
> **Audio on the Web**
>
> When you embed audio in a Web page, you can set the audio to play once, loop a certain number of times, or loop forever. To learn more about audio on the Web, visit the FrontPage 2003 More About Web page (scsite.com/fp2003/more) and then click Audio.

Adding Audio to a Web Page

Just as with video, several audio formats exist, and FrontPage includes several methods of providing audio content on Web pages. Audio can be embedded, linked, or streamed, just as it can with video. Table 4 lists the most popular audio formats, the file extensions typically associated with the format, and whether the format is capable of streaming. Like video streaming, audio streaming requires special software on the Web server that is capable of streaming the audio.

Table 4 Common Audio Formats

FORMAT	EXTENSION	USED FOR STREAMING?	DESCRIPTION
WAV	.wav	Rarely	The default audio format for Windows-based computers.
MP3	.mp3	Yes	The most popular format for digital music.
AIFF	.aif, .aiff	No	Apple's original audio format is popular on Macintosh computers.
QuickTime	.qt	Yes	Apple's QuickTime format is widely used on the Web, although more so for video streaming. Requires that the user's computer has the QuickTime player installed.
Windows Media Audio	.wma	Yes	Includes more features than WAV files and commonly is used on portable music players.
RealAudio	.rm, .ram	Yes	Real Networks proprietary audio format is used by many Web sites, including Internet radio stations and news Web sites. Requires that the user's computer has the RealPlayer installed.

Adding Audio to a Web Page

Before adding the audio content to the Web page, an image of a radio needs to be added to the bottom-left cell of the table. After the image is added, properties of the image must be modified to cause audio to play when the Web page visitor places the mouse pointer over the image or clicks the image. The audio will be embedded in the Web page.

The following steps add an image of a radio to the bottom-left cell of the table.

To Add an Image to a Web Page

1

- **Click in the bottom-left cell in the table.**
- **Click Insert on the menu bar and then point to Picture.**

FrontPage displays the Insert menu and the Picture submenu (Figure 14).

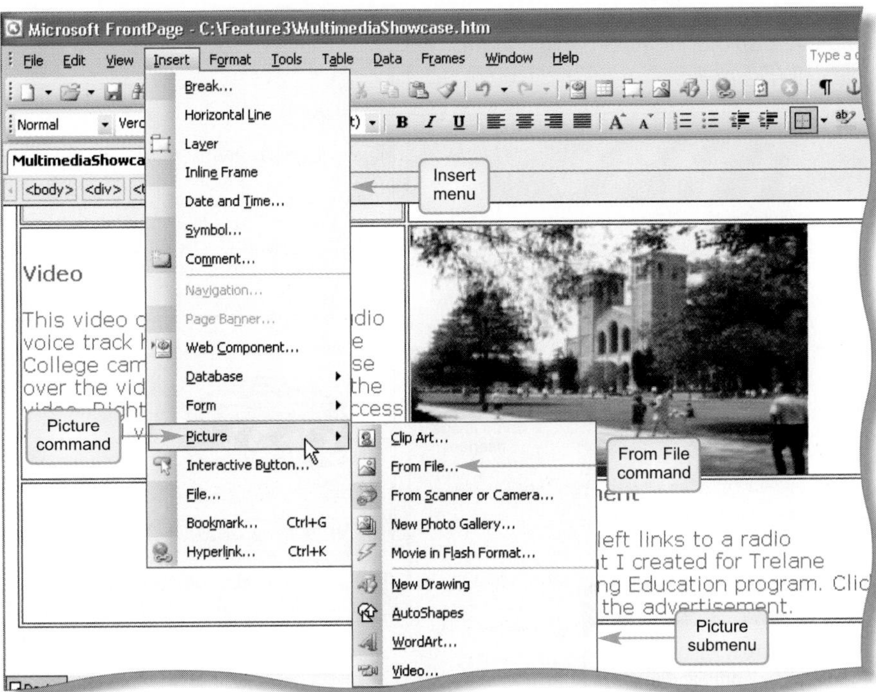

FIGURE 14

2

- **Click From File.**
- **When FrontPage displays the Picture dialog box, if necessary, navigate to the Feature3 folder on the Data Disk.**
- **Click the Radio file.**

FrontPage displays the Picture dialog box. The Radio image file is selected (Figure 15).

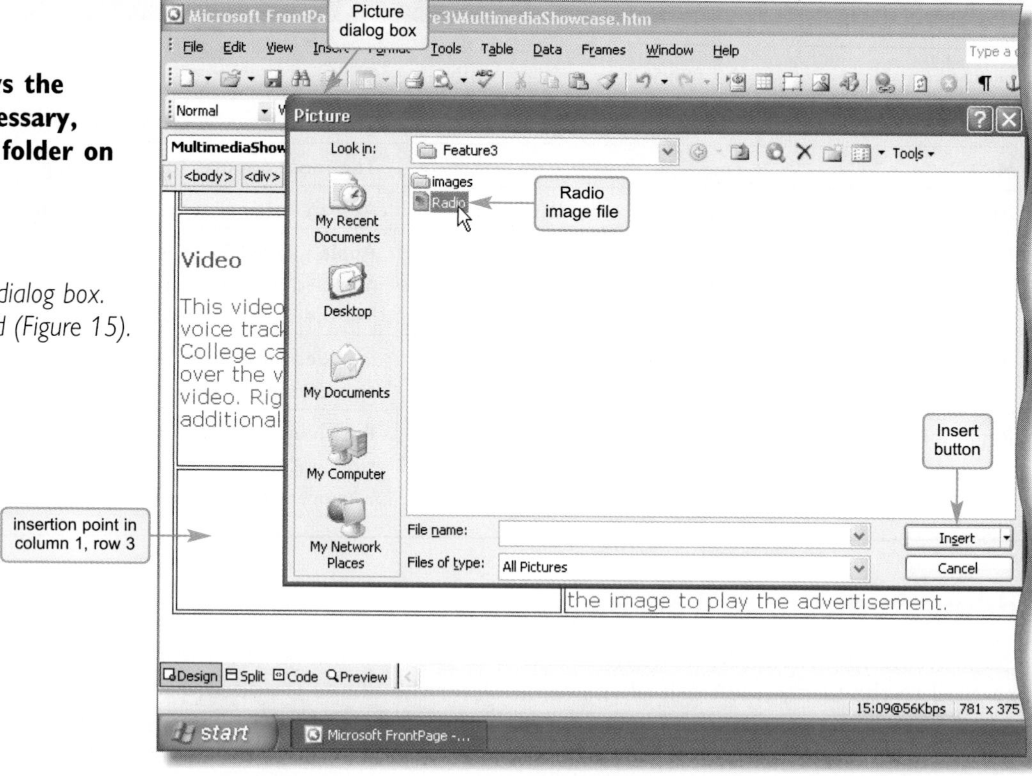

FIGURE 15

3

- **Click the Insert button.**
- **If necessary, resize the new image as shown in Figure 16.**

FrontPage displays the Radio image in the table cell (Figure 16).

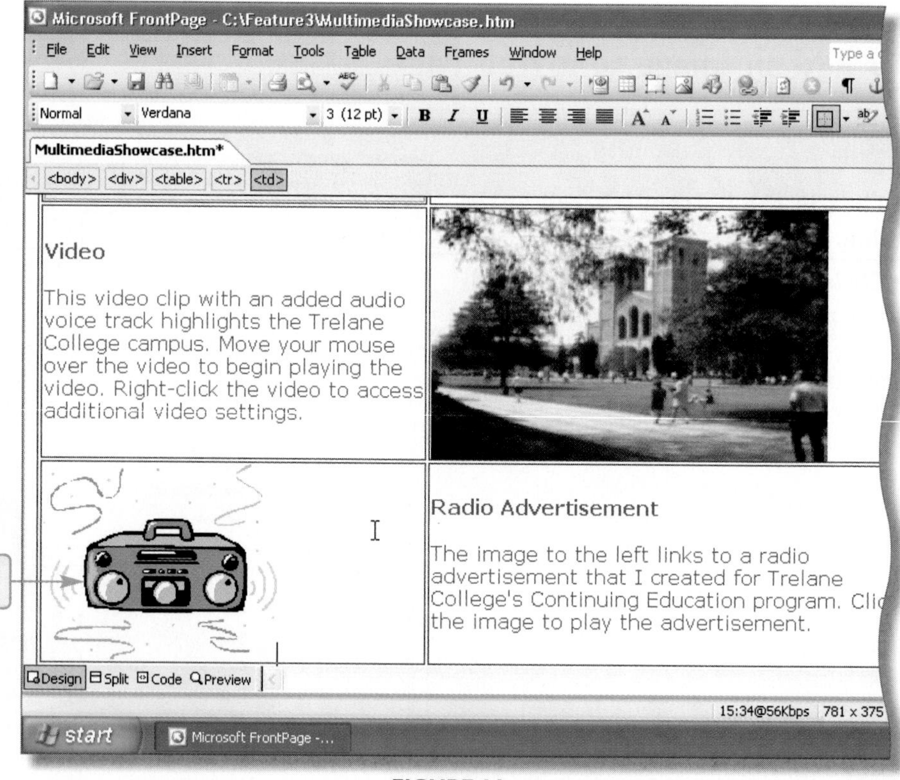

FIGURE 16

Other Ways

1. Press ALT+I, P, F
2. In Voice Command mode, say "Insert, Picture, From File"

The previous set of steps did not add the audio to the Web page. Rather, an image was added. Next, properties of the image will be modified so that the audio plays when the user places the mouse pointer over the image or clicks the image.

Setting Properties of Audio Content

Any image in a Web page can have an audio or video file associated with it. The multimedia content plays either when the page is loaded or when the user moves the mouse pointer over the image. This method of adding audio or video to a Web page is ideal for smaller multimedia files.

The audio for the Multimedia Showcase Web page is included on the Data Disk as a WAV file. The WAV format is a popular audio format and is the default audio format for the Windows operating system. You are assured, therefore, that most of the visitors to a Web site will be able to hear the audio if the WAV format is used.

The following steps associate an audio file with the radio image and set properties of the audio content.

To Set Properties of Audio Content

1

- **Right-click the radio image.**
- **When FrontPage displays the shortcut menu, click Picture Properties.**
- **If necessary, when the Picture Properties dialog box is displayed, click the Video tab.**

FrontPage displays the Video sheet in the Picture Properties dialog box (Figure 17). The Video sheet allows you to add either audio or video content to the image.

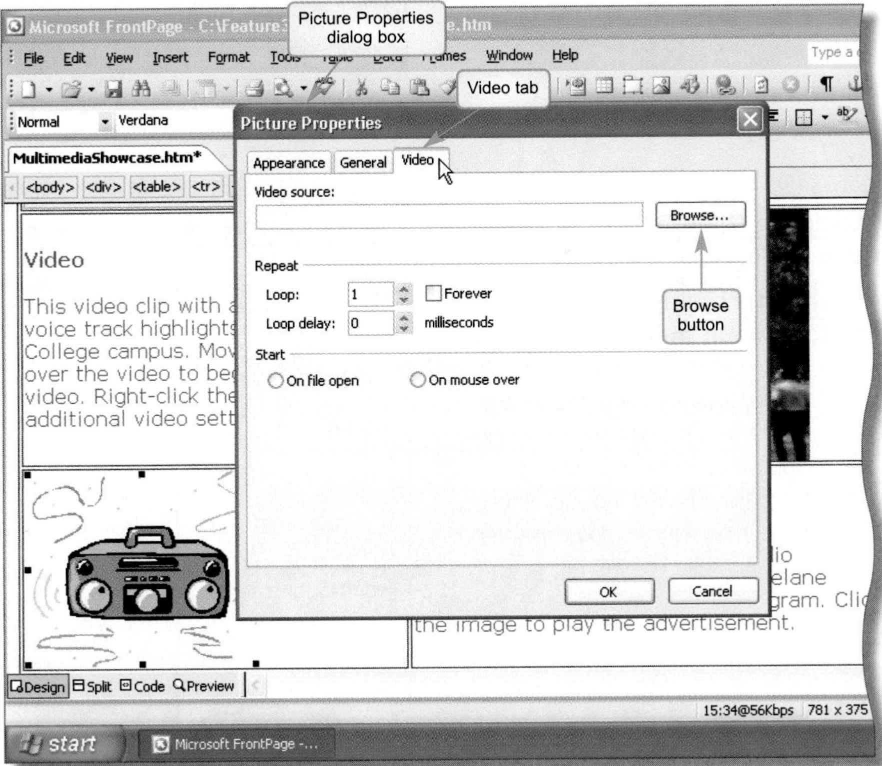

FIGURE 17

2

- **Click the Browse button.**
- **When FrontPage displays the Video dialog box, navigate to the Feature3 folder of the Data Disk and then click the TrelaneCollegeRadioAd file.**

FrontPage displays the Video dialog box and the TrelaneCollegeRadioAd file is selected (Figure 18). The Video dialog box allows you to select either audio or video content.

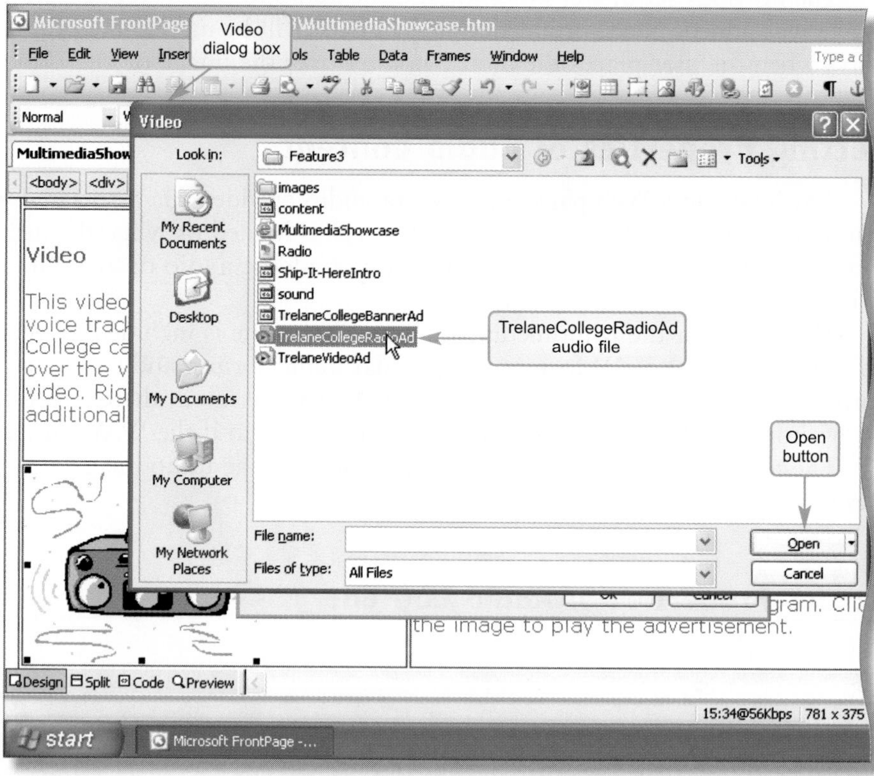

FIGURE 18

3

- **Click the Open button in the Video dialog box.**
- **In the Start area in the Video sheet, click On mouse over.**

FrontPage displays the file name for the audio content in the Video source text box. The On mouse over option button is selected, meaning that the audio plays when the user moves the mouse pointer over the radio image (Figure 19).

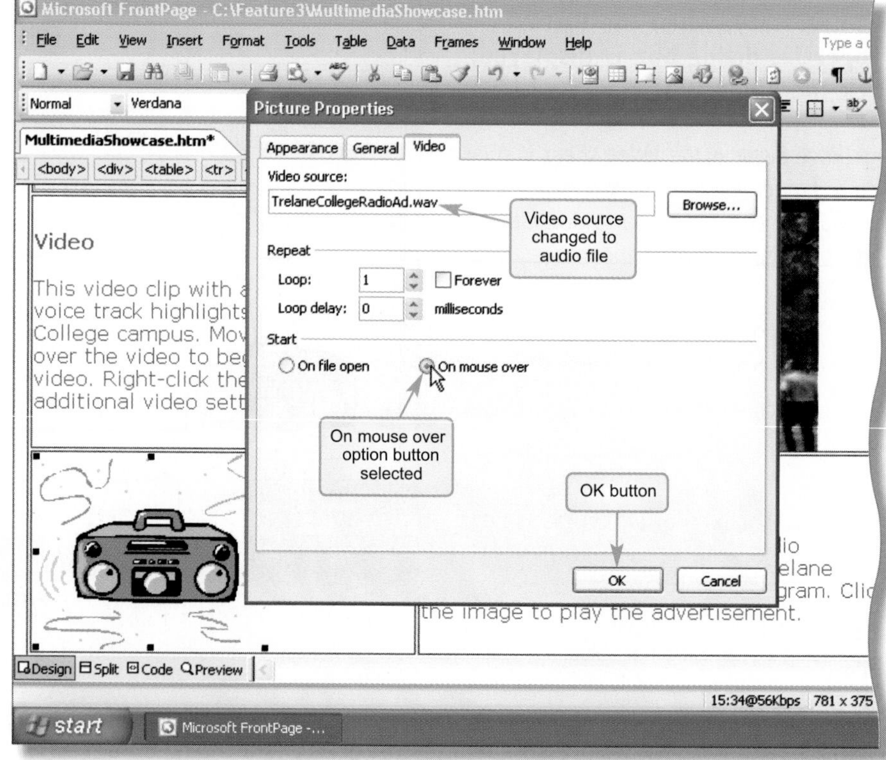

FIGURE 19

4

• **Click the OK button.**

FrontPage displays the radio image at a much smaller size as a result of setting properties (Figure 20).

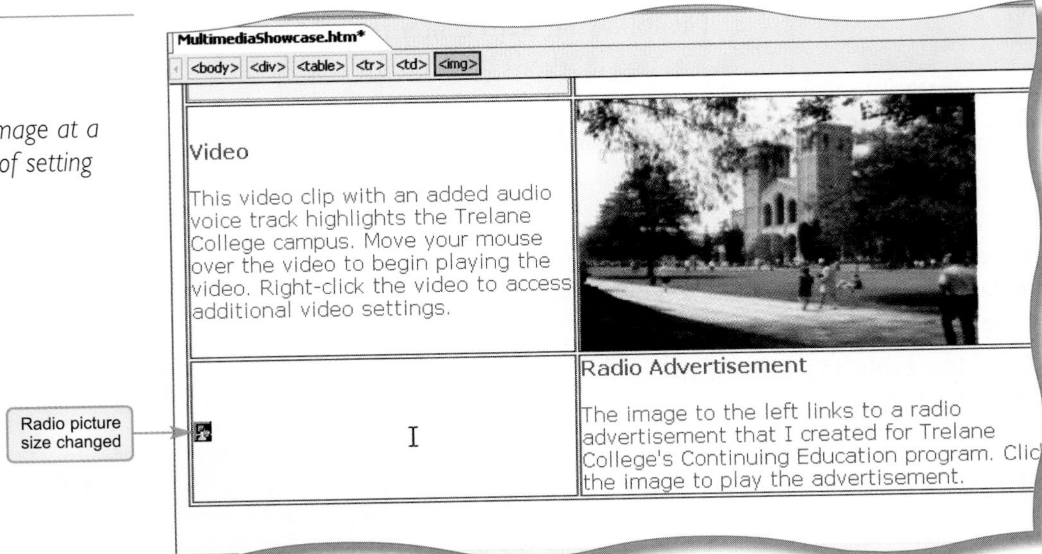

FIGURE 20

5

• **Use the sizing handles on the radio image to resize the image as shown in Figure 21.**

FrontPage displays a placeholder for the radio image at the proper location and size (Figure 21).

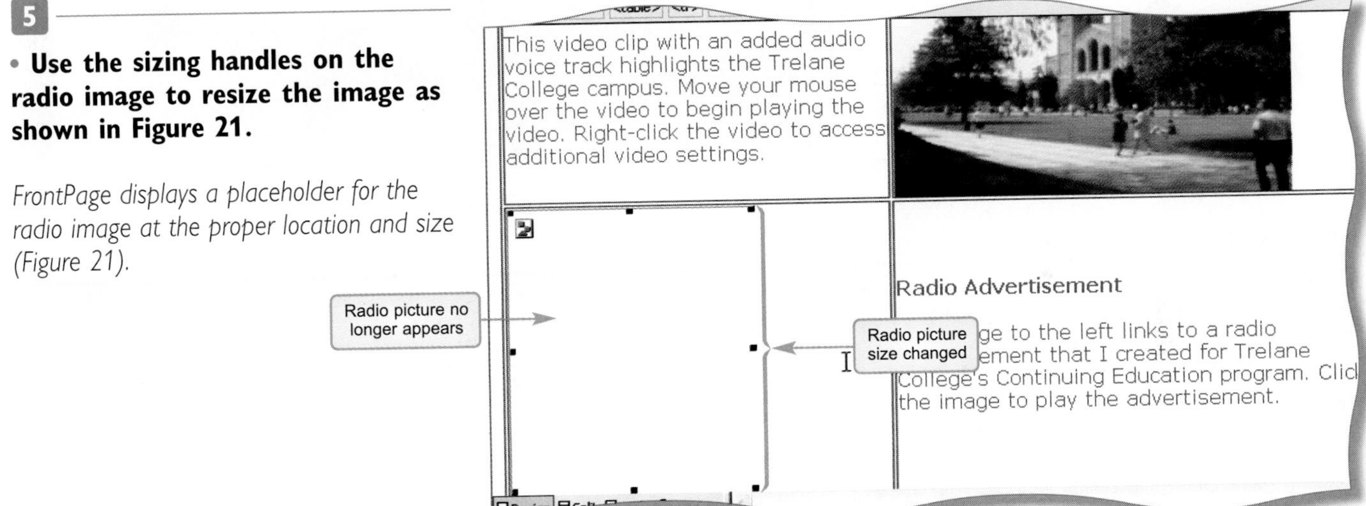

FIGURE 21

Audio or video multimedia content can be associated with any image on a Web page. The process of setting the properties mimics that of setting the properties of the video earlier in this feature. Although the Picture Properties dialog box labels the content as video (Figure 19), both audio and video may be added. Just as with the video content, the user also can right-click the radio image to access a shortcut menu that allows the user to control the audio.

You also can associate an audio file with a Web page and have the audio play as a background sound while a user visits the Web page. The General sheet in the Page Properties dialog box includes a Background sound area where you can set the location of the audio file to play when the page loads.

With the multimedia content added to the table, the table now can be formatted. The following steps center the table on the Web page and resize the table.

To Complete the Web Page Layout

1

- **If necessary, scroll to the top of the table and then click anywhere in the table.**
- **Click the table tag button to select the table.**
- **Click the Center button on the Formatting toolbar.**

The table is selected and centered on the Web page (Figure 22).

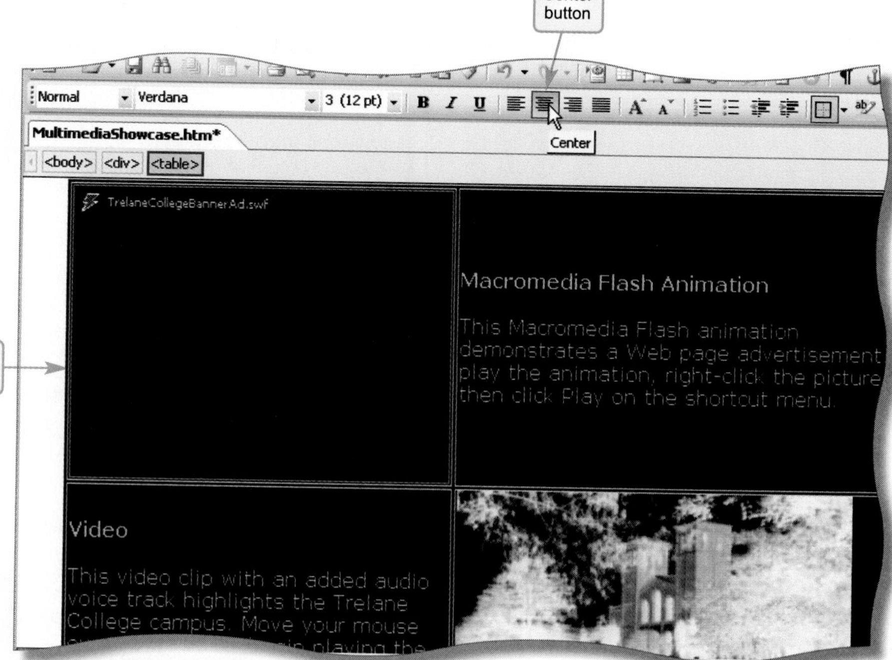

FIGURE 22

2

- **Drag the right border of the table until the right border is aligned approximately with the end of the text in the first line of the second heading.**

The table is resized, and the text in the table rewraps in the table cells (Figure 23).

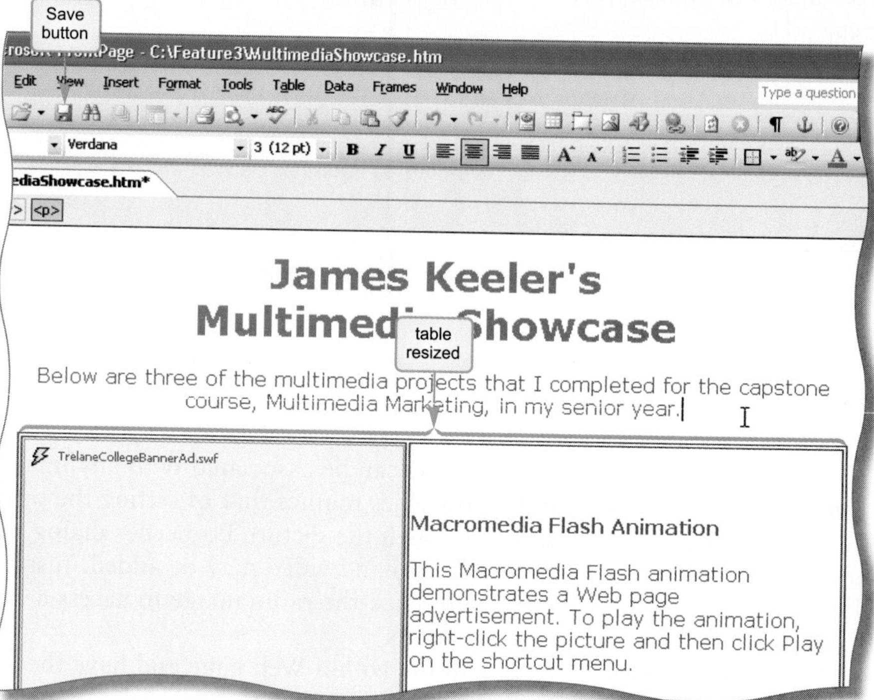

FIGURE 23

The Web page is complete. The next steps are to preview and save the Web pages.

More About

The Quick Reference

For more information, see the Quick Reference Summary at the back of this book, or visit the FrontPage 2003 Quick Reference Web page (scsite.com/fp2003/qr).

Previewing and Saving the Web Page

After you have finished the steps in the project and developed the Web page, you can preview the Web page in your browser and quit FrontPage. The best method to test a Web page that includes multimedia content is to test it in the browser, rather than in Preview view. Preview view may not include all the features that your browser supports.

The following steps save the Web page, preview the Web page, and quit FrontPage.

Note: You may need to install the Macromedia Flash plug-in for your browser when you attempt to play the Macromedia Flash movie. If this is the case, then follow the instructions given to you by your browser or see your instructor for assistance.

To Save the Web Page, Preview the Web Page, and Quit FrontPage

1

- **Click the Save button on the Standard toolbar.**
- **Click File on the menu bar and then point to Preview in Browser.**

FrontPage displays the File menu and the Preview in Browser submenu. The Preview in Browser submenu may appear differently on your computer depending on the browsers installed on the computer (Figure 24).

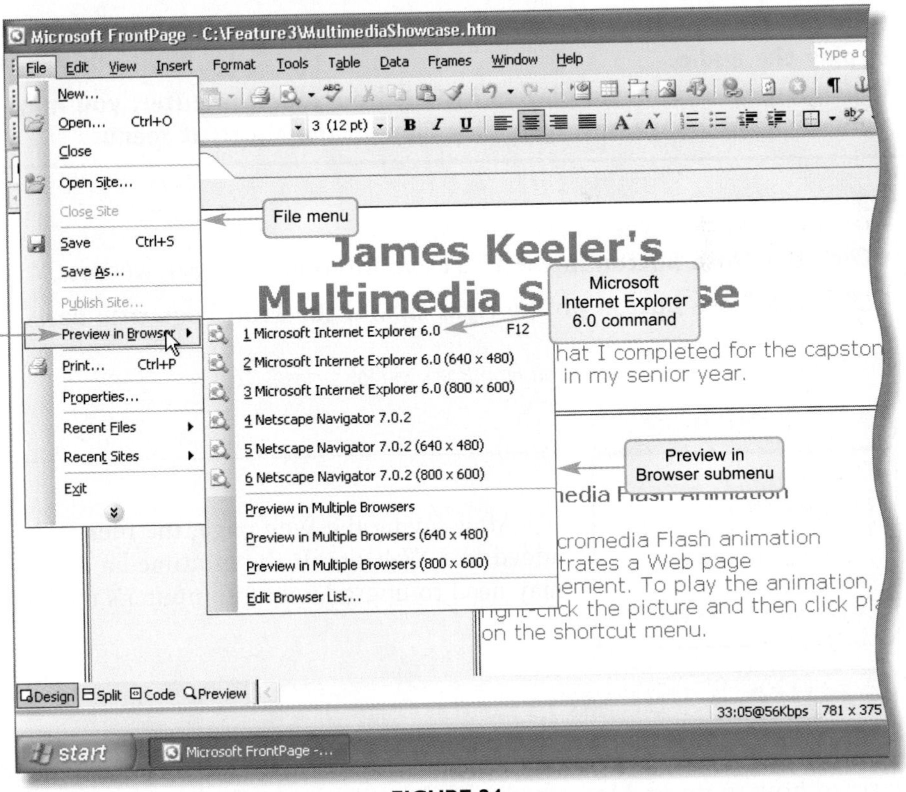

FIGURE 24

2

• **Click 1 Microsoft Internet Explorer 6.0.**

FrontPage displays the Multimedia Showcase Web page in the browser (Figure 25).

3

• **Right-click the Macromedia Flash movie and then click Play on the shortcut menu.**

• **When the movie is finished playing, click the video or move the mouse pointer over the video to play the video.**

• **When the video is finished playing, scroll to the radio picture and click the radio picture to play the audio. Depending on the media players installed on your computer, you may need to right-click the image and then click Play on the shortcut menu.**

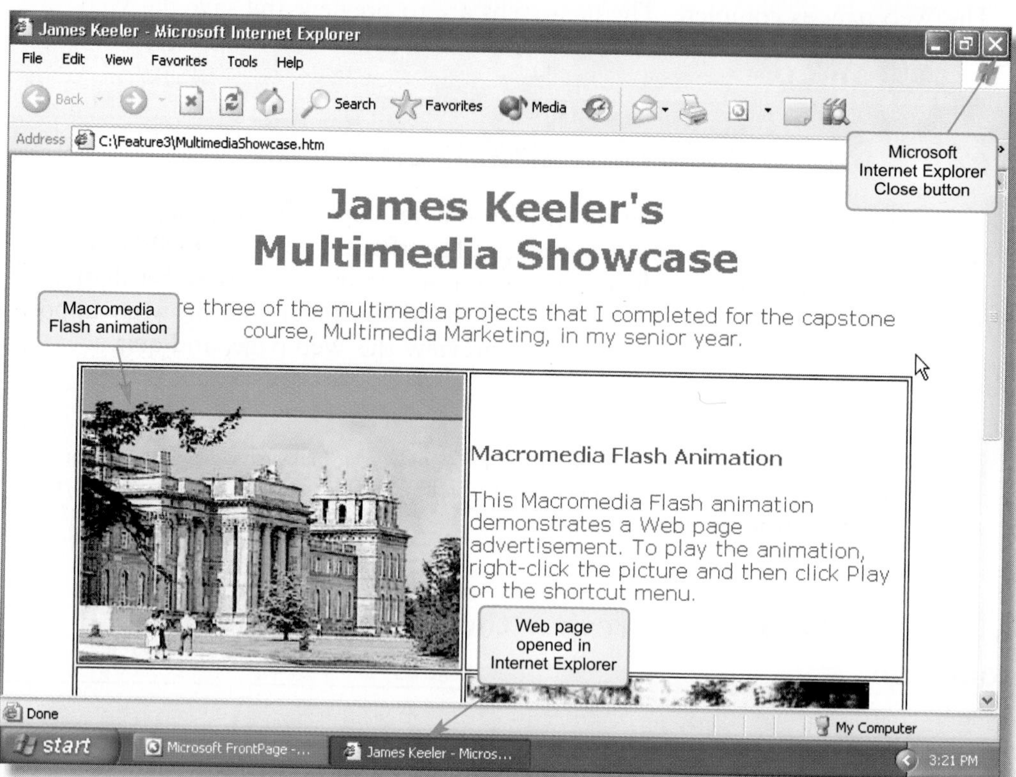

FIGURE 25

4

• **Click the Close button in the Microsoft Internet Explorer window.**

• **Click the Close button on the right side of the FrontPage title bar.**

The Microsoft Internet Explorer and FrontPage windows close.

Other Ways

1. Press F12
2. Press ALT+F, B, 1
3. In Voice Command mode, say "File, Preview in Browser, Microsoft Internet Explorer 6"

After saving the Web page, the files and folder created with the Web page can be added to a Web site. If the multimedia content does not play in your browser, you may need to upgrade your computer's media player or browser.

Feature Summary

This Multimedia feature introduced you to adding three types of multimedia elements to a Web page. You learned how to insert Macromedia Flash content on a Web page and set properties for the animation. You also learned how to add video content to a Web page and set properties for the video. Finally, you learned how to add audio content to a Web page.

What You Should Know

Having completed this feature, you should be able to perform the tasks below. The tasks are listed in the same order they were presented in this feature. For a list of the buttons, menus, toolbars, and commands introduced in this feature, see the Quick Reference Summary at the back of this book and refer to the Page Number column.

1. Start FrontPage and Create a New Web Page (FP 657)
2. Create the Layout for the Web Page (FP 658)
3. Add a Macromedia Flash Animation to a Web Page (FP 660)
4. Set Properties of a Macromedia Flash Movie (FP 662)
5. Save the Web Page (FP 664)
6. Add Video to a Web Page (FP 665)
7. Set Properties of a Video (FP 667)
8. Add an Image to a Web Page (FP 669)
9. Set Properties of Audio Content (FP 671)
10. Complete the Web Page Layout (FP 674)
11. Save the Web Page, Preview the Web Page, and Quit FrontPage (FP 675)

1 Using a Plug-in to Play Video and Audio Files

Problem: A second method for inserting media is to use plug-ins to play the media. Plug-ins can operate as applications that are embedded in a Web page. For example, adding a video or audio plug-in to a Web page displays audio and video controls on the Web page.

Instructions: Perform the following tasks.

1. Create a new Web page and apply the Iris theme to the page. Add a heading using the Heading 1 style as shown in Figure 26 on the next page.
2. Create a 2 by 2 table and enter instructions in the top-left and lower-right cells as shown in Figure 26.
3. Select the top cell in the second column. Click Insert on the menu bar and then click Web Component. When the Insert Web Component dialog box is displayed, scroll down in the Component type list and click Advanced Controls. Click Plug-In in the Choose a control list and then click the Finish button. When the Plug-In Properties dialog box is displayed, click the Browse button and select the file, TrelaneVideoAd. Type a message in the Message for browsers without plug-in support text box to let users know that they cannot view the content if their browser does not support plug-ins.
4. Repeat Step 3 to add the TrelaneCollegeRadioAd audio file to the bottom cell in the first column. Size both plug-in placeholders as shown in Figure 26.
5. Save the Web page as LabSF3-1MultimediaPlugins.htm in a new LabSF3-1MultimediaPlugins folder in the Feature3 folder on the Data Disk or your hard drive. Save the embedded images in a new images subfolder. Preview the Web page in your browser and make sure that the media plays as intended (Figure 26). Your browser may need to download and install the proper plug-in to play the files.

(continued)

In the Lab

Using a Plug-in to Play Video and Audio Files *(continued)*

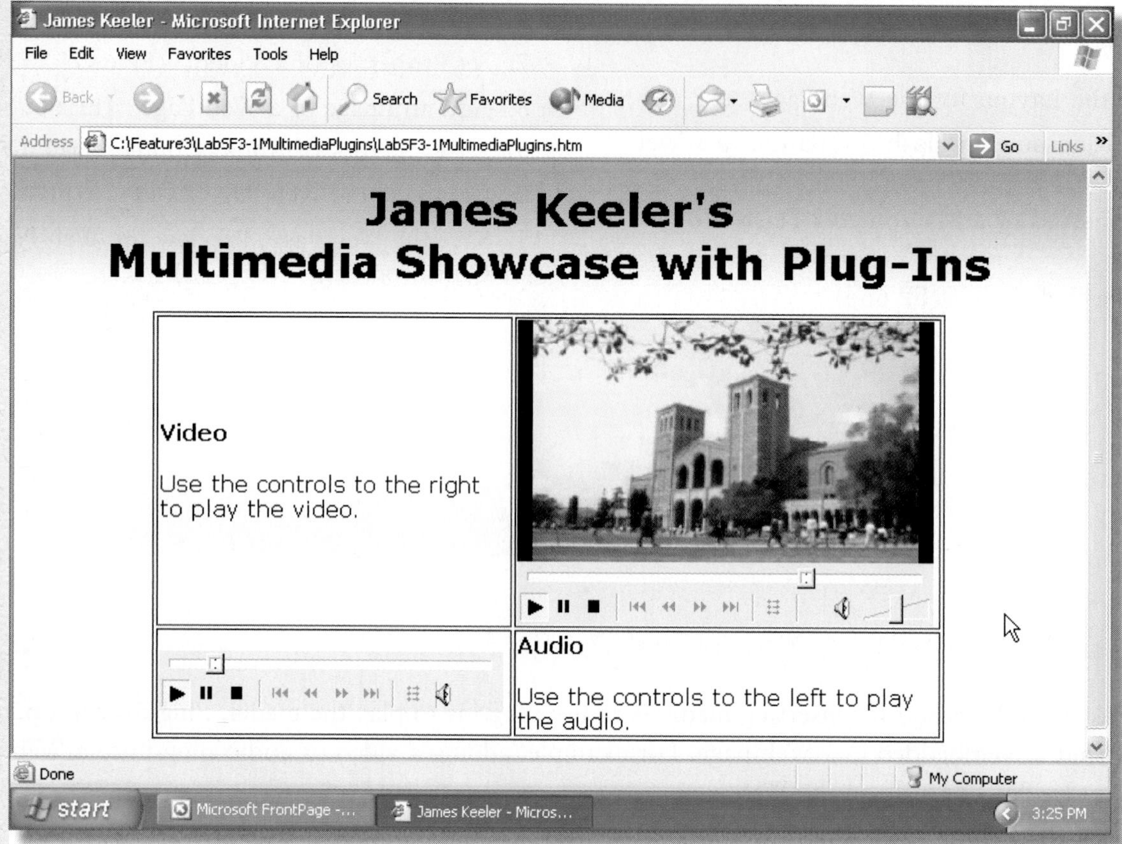

FIGURE 26

2 Using a Macromedia Flash Movie as a Web Site Introduction

Problem: The Ship-It-Here Web site administrator would like a Macromedia Flash movie to be used as the introduction to the Ship-It-Here Web site. She has supplied you with the Flash movie. The movie should be displayed on a stand-alone Web page and play the movie one time.

Instructions: Perform the following tasks.

1. Create a new Web page and insert the Flash movie, Ship-It-HereIntro, from the Data Disk.
2. Use the sizing handles on the movie to change the size of the movie so that it fits in the Design view window. Click the Center button on the Formatting toolbar. Change the page title to Ship-It-Here Introduction.
3. Right-click the movie and then click Movie in Flash Format Properties. When the Movie in Flash Format Properties dialog box is displayed, in the Appearance sheet, select Auto High in the Quality list in the Movie area. Change the Scale to Exact fit. Change the Border thickness to 5.

4. Click the General tab. Click Loop to deselect it. Click Show menu to deselect it. When the user navigates to the Web page, the movie will play automatically and then navigate to a Web site specified in the Flash movie.
5. Save the Web page as LabSF3-2Ship-It-HereIntro, in a new LabSF3-2Ship-It-HereIntro folder in the Feature3 folder. If necessary, open Windows Explorer and copy the files content.swf and sound.swf to the location where you stored the Web page.
6. Preview the Web page in your browser (Figure 27). If necessary, save the embedded files in a new images subfolder under the LabSF3-2Ship-It-HereIntro folder.

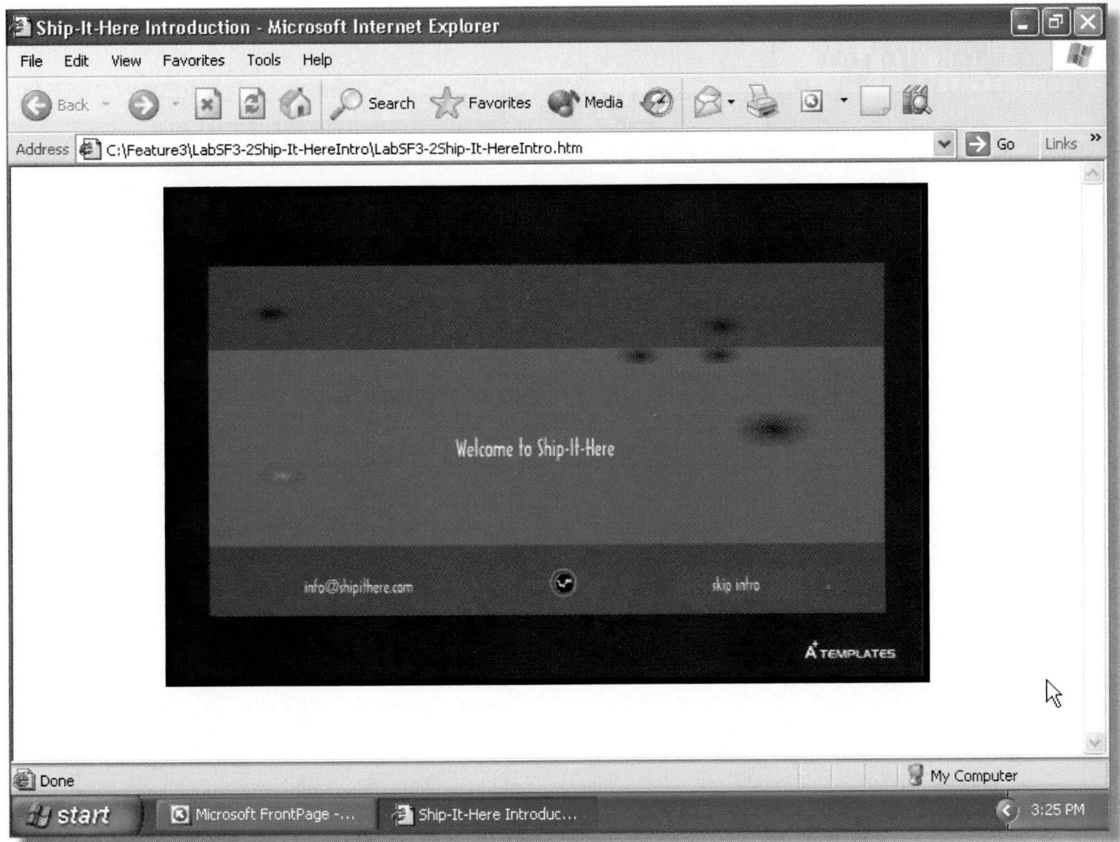

FIGURE 27

Appendix A

Microsoft Office FrontPage Help System

Using the FrontPage Help System

This appendix shows you how to use the FrontPage Help system. At anytime while you are using FrontPage, you can interact with its Help system and display information on any FrontPage topic. It is a complete reference manual at your fingertips.

As shown in Figure A-1, five methods for accessing the FrontPage Help system are available:

1. Microsoft Office FrontPage Help button on the Standard toolbar
2. Microsoft Office FrontPage Help command on the Help menu
3. Function key F1 on the keyboard
4. Type a question for help box on the menu bar
5. Office Assistant

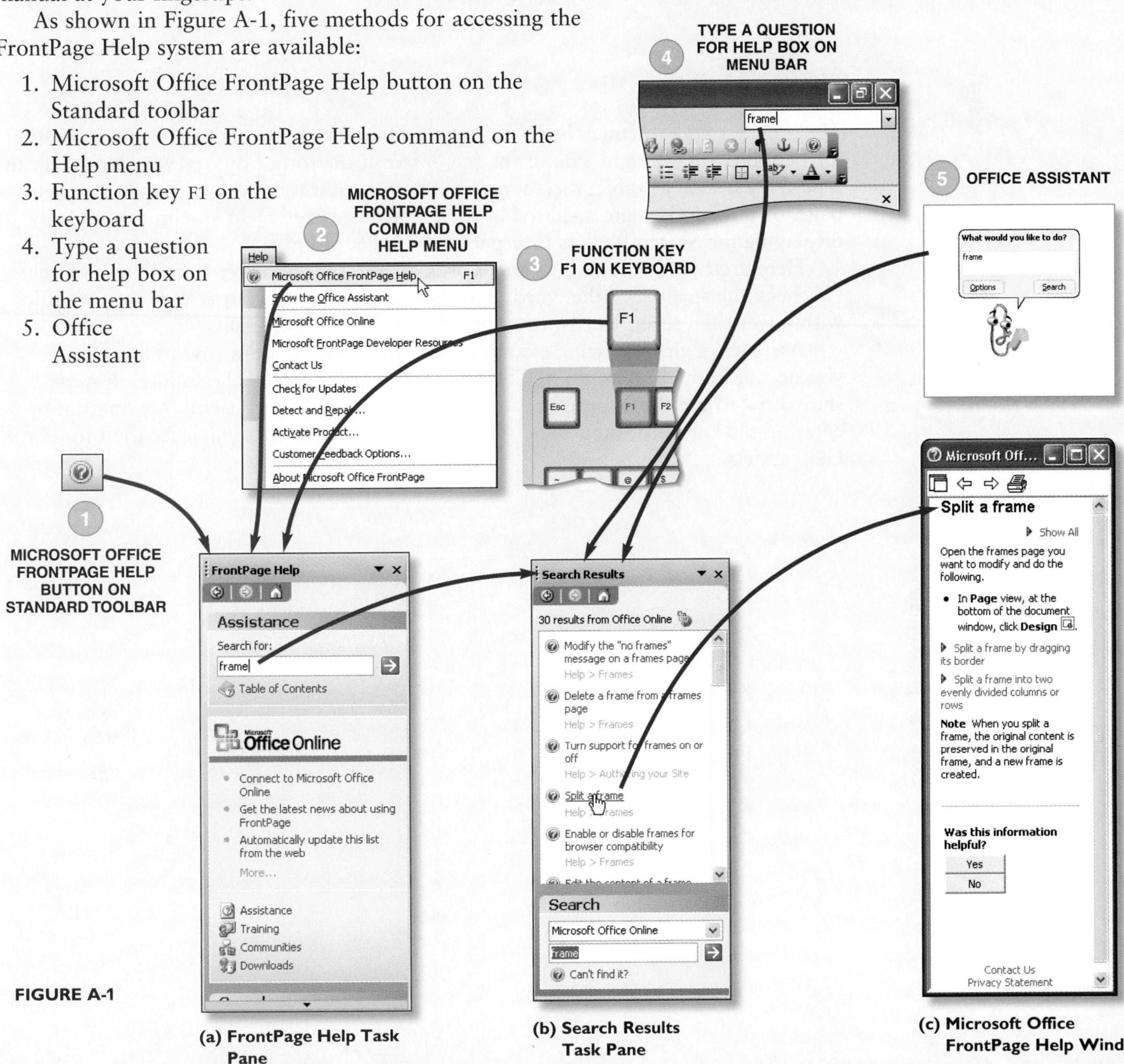

FIGURE A-1

(a) FrontPage Help Task Pane

(b) Search Results Task Pane

(c) Microsoft Office FrontPage Help Window

All five methods result in the FrontPage Help system displaying a task pane on the right side of the FrontPage window. The first three methods cause the **FrontPage Help task pane** to appear (Figure A-1a on the previous page). This task pane includes a Search for text box in which you can enter a word or phrase on which you want help. Once you enter the word or phrase, the FrontPage Help system displays the Search Results task pane (Figure A-1b on the previous page). With the Search Results task pane displayed, you can select specific Help topics.

As shown in Figure A-1, methods 4 and 5 bypass the FrontPage Help task pane and immediately display the **Search Results task pane** (Figure A-1b) with a list of links that pertain to the selected topic. Thus, the result of any of the five methods for accessing the FrontPage Help system is the Search Results task pane. Once the FrontPage Help system displays this task pane, you can choose links that relate to the word or phrase on which you searched. In Figure A-1, for example, frame was the searched topic (Split a frame), which resulted in the FrontPage Help system displaying the Microsoft Office FrontPage Help window with information about splitting a frame (Figure A-1c on the previous page).

Navigating the FrontPage Help System

The quickest way to enter the FrontPage Help system is through the Type a question for help box on the right side of the menu bar at the top of the screen. Here you can type words, such as table, theme, or stylesheet, or phrases, such as preview a Web page, or how do I create a shared border. The FrontPage Help system responds by displaying the Search Results task pane with a list of links.

Here are two tips regarding the words or phrases you enter to initiate a search: (1) check the spelling of the word or phrase; and (2) keep your search very specific, with fewer than seven words, to return the most accurate results.

Assume for the following example that you want to add a row to a table, and you do not know how to do it. The likely keyword is table. The following steps show how to use the Type a question for help box to obtain useful information by entering the keyword, table. The steps also show you how to navigate the FrontPage Help system.

To Obtain Help Using the Type a Question for Help Box

1

- **Click the Type a question for help box on the right side of the menu bar, type `table`, and then press the ENTER key.**

The FrontPage Help system displays the Search Results task pane on the right side of the window. The Search Results task pane includes 30 resulting links (Figure A-2). If you do not find what you are looking for, you can modify or refine the search in the Search area at the bottom of the Search Results task pane. The results returned in your Search Results task pane may be different.

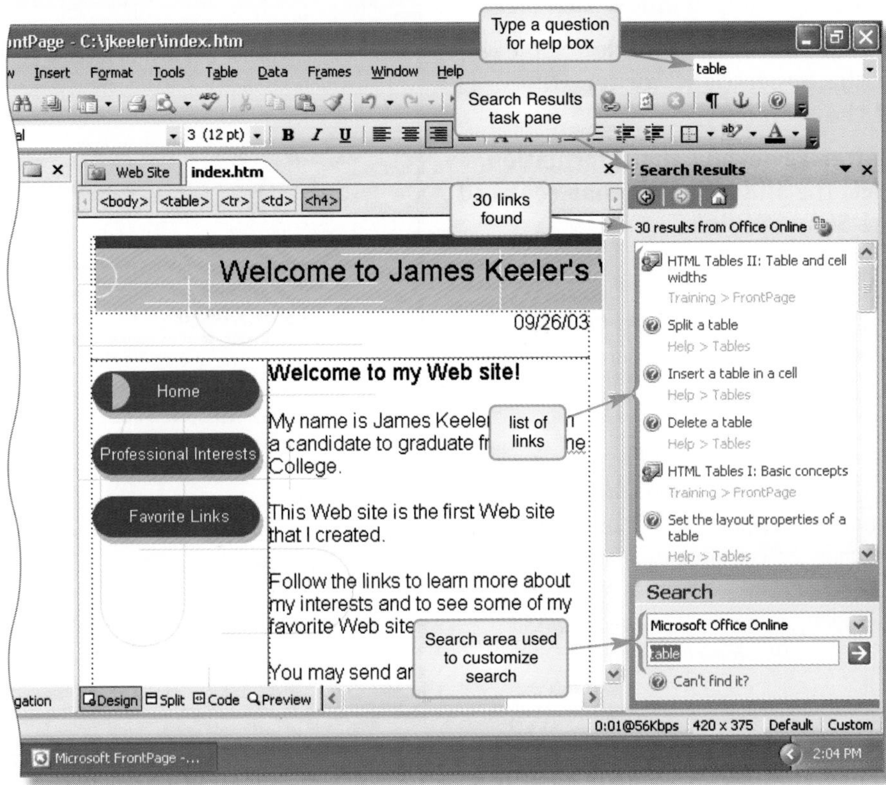

FIGURE A-2

2

- **Scroll down to the bottom of the list of links in the Search Results task pane and then click the Add a cell, row, or column to a table link.**
- **If necessary, when FrontPage displays the Microsoft Office FrontPage Help window, click its Auto Tile button in the upper-right corner of the window (Figure A-4 on the next page) to tile the windows.**

FrontPage displays the Microsoft Office FrontPage Help window with the desired information (Figure A-3). With the Microsoft Office FrontPage Help window and Microsoft FrontPage window tiled, you can read the information in one window and complete the task in the other window.

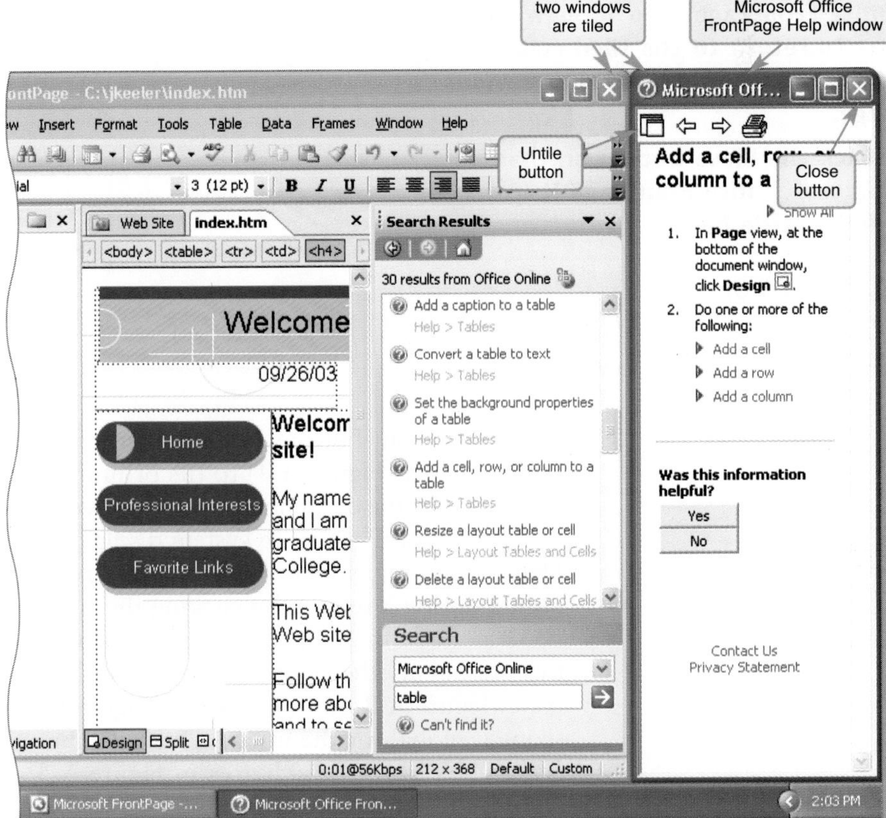

FIGURE A-3

3

- **Double-click the Microsoft Office FrontPage Help window title bar.**
- **Click the Show All link in the upper-right corner of the window.**
- **After reviewing the information, click the Hide All link that replaced the Show All link.**

The Microsoft Office FrontPage Help window is maximized so it fills the entire screen (Figure A-4). If you are connected to the Internet, you can give Microsoft your opinion as to whether the information was helpful by clicking the Yes or No button at the bottom of the page. The Show All link expands the coverage of information and the Hide All link condenses the information displayed on the topic in the Microsoft Office FrontPage Help window.

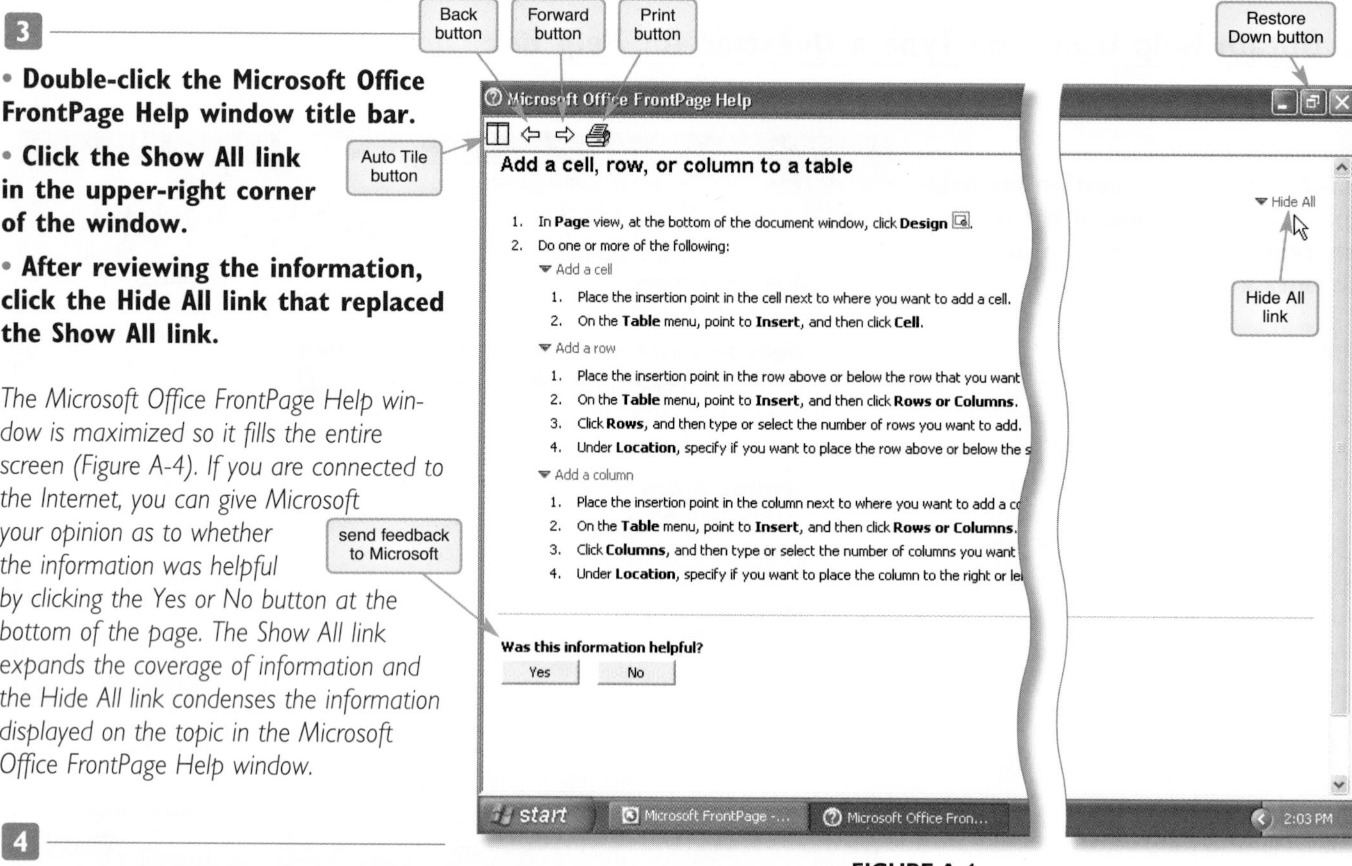

FIGURE A-4

4

- **Click the Restore Down button on the right side of the Microsoft Office FrontPage Help window title bar to return to the tiled state shown in Figure A-3 on the previous page.**
- **Click the Close button on the Microsoft Office FrontPage Help window title bar.**

The Microsoft Office FrontPage Help window is closed and the Web page is active.

Use the four buttons in the upper-left corner of the Microsoft Office FrontPage Help window (Figure A-4) to tile or untile windows, navigate through the Help system, or print the contents of the window. As you click links in the Search Results task pane, the FrontPage Help system displays new pages of information. The FrontPage Help system remembers the links you visited and allows you to redisplay the pages visited during a session by clicking the Back and Forward buttons (Figure A-4).

If none of the links presents the information you want, you can refine the search by entering another word or phrase in the Search text box in the Search Results task pane (Figure A-2 on the previous page). If you have access to the Web, then the scope is global for the initial search. **Global** means all the categories listed in the Search box of the Search area in Figure A-5 are searched. For example, you can restrict the scope to **Offline Help**, which results in a search of related links only on your hard disk.

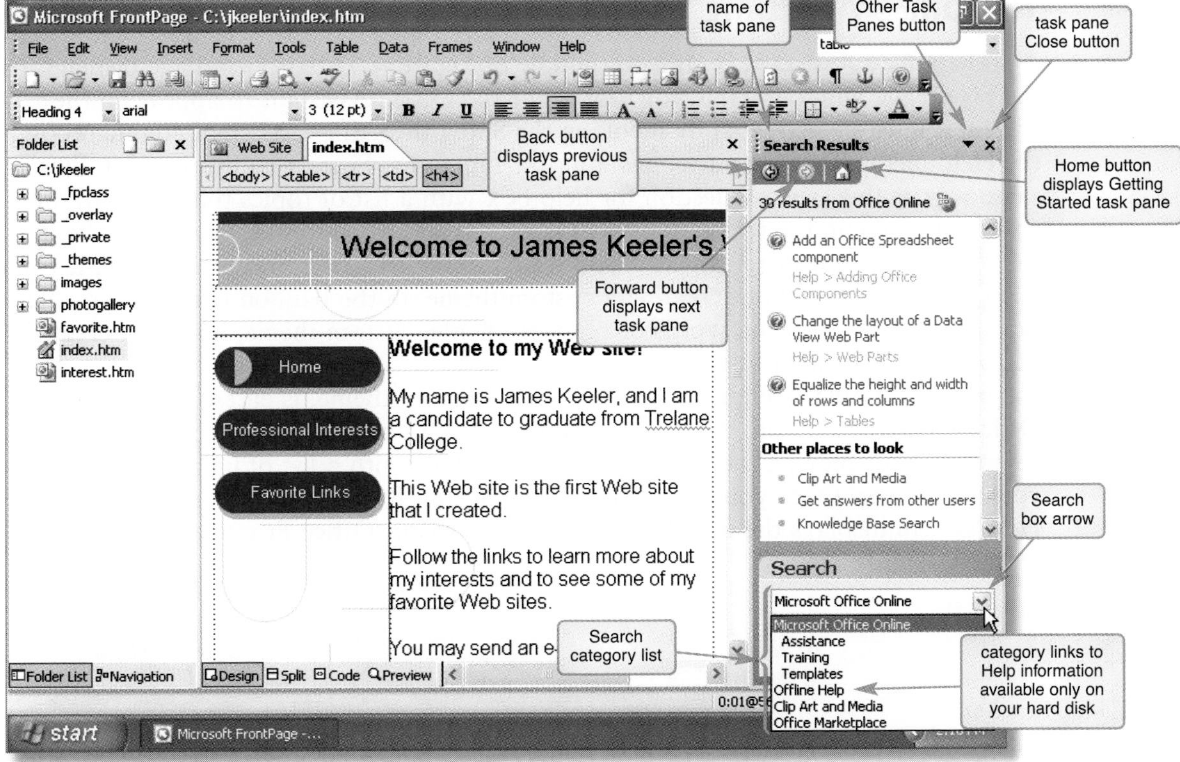

FIGURE A-5

Figure A-5 shows several additional features of the Search Results task pane with which you should be familiar. The buttons immediately below the name of the task pane allow you to navigate between task panes. The Other Task Panes button and the Close button on the Search Results task pane title bar let you change task panes and close the active task pane.

As you enter questions and terms in the Type a question for help box, the FrontPage Help system adds them to its list. Thus, if you click the Type a question for help box arrow, a list of previously used words and phrases is displayed (Figure A-6).

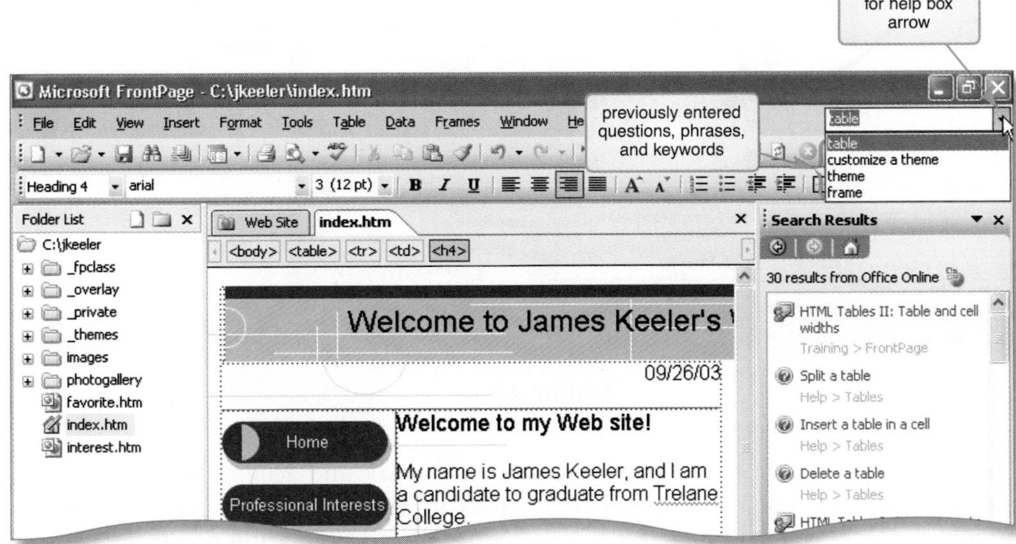

FIGURE A-6

The Office Assistant

The **Office Assistant** is an icon (middle of Figure A-7) that FrontPage displays in the FrontPage window while you work. For the Office Assistant to appear on the screen, it must be activated by invoking the Show the Office Assistant command on the Help menu. This Help tool has multiple functions. First, it will respond in the same way as the Type a question for help box with a list of topics that relate to the entry you make in the text box in the Office Assistant balloon. The entry can be in the form of a word or phrase as if you were talking to a person. For example, if you want to learn more about creating a custom theme, in the balloon text box, you can type any of the following words or phrases: theme, custom theme, how do I create a custom theme, or anything similar.

In the example in Figure A-7, the phrase, custom theme, is entered into the Office Assistant balloon. After you click the Search button, the Office Assistant responds by displaying the Search Results task pane with a list of links from which you can choose. Once you click a link in the Search Results task pane, the FrontPage Help system displays the information in the Microsoft Office FrontPage Help window (Figure A-7).

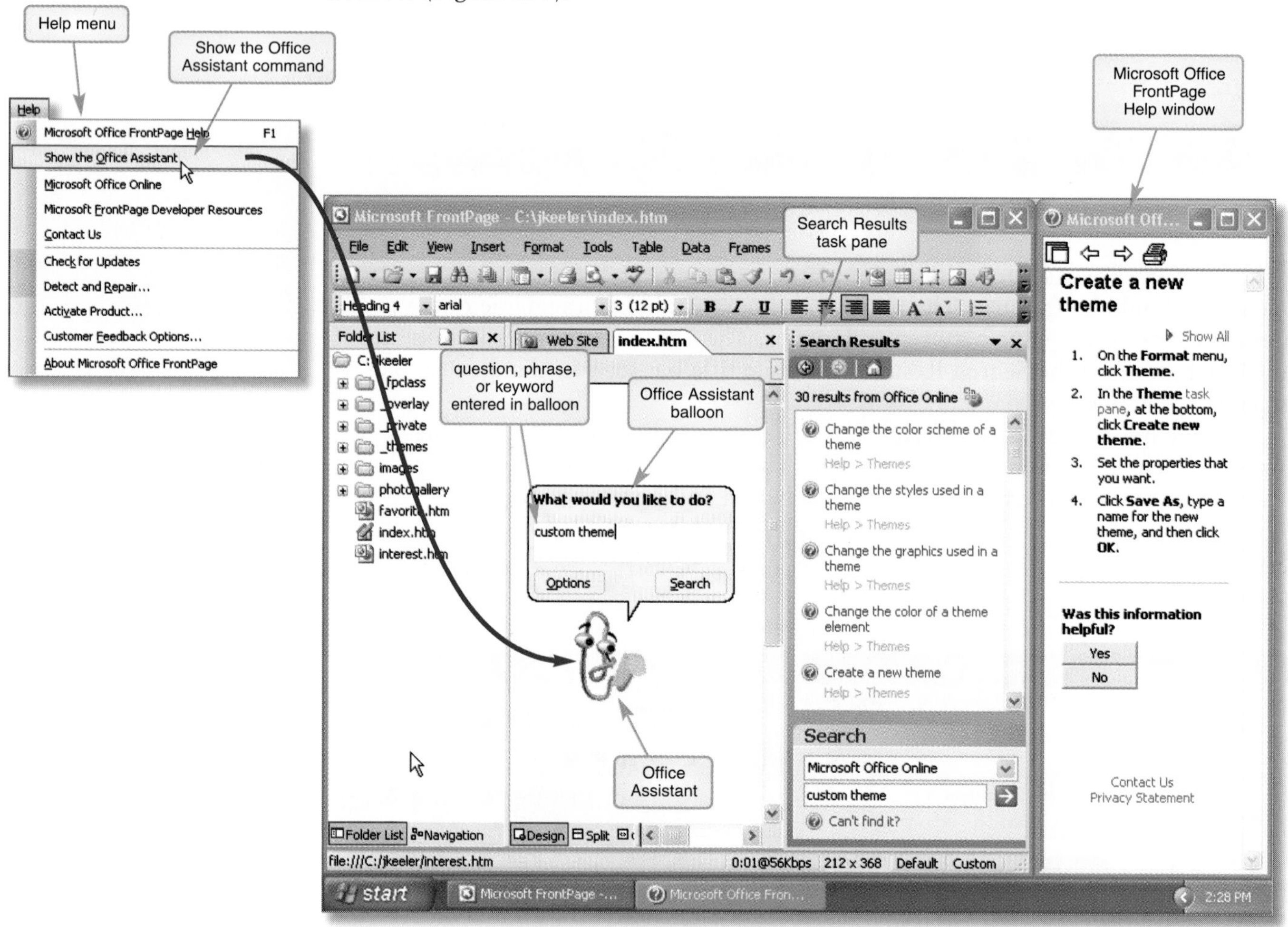

FIGURE A-7

In addition, the Office Assistant monitors your work and accumulates tips during a session on how you might increase your productivity and efficiency. The accumulation of tips must be enabled. You enable the accumulation of tips by right-clicking the Office Assistant, clicking Options on the shortcut menu, and then selecting the types of tips you want accumulated. You can view the tips at anytime. The accumulated tips appear when you activate the Office Assistant balloon. Also, if at anytime you see a light bulb above the Office Assistant, click it to display the most recent tip. If the Office Assistant is hidden, then the light bulb shows on the Microsoft Office FrontPage Help button on the Standard toolbar.

You hide the Office Assistant by invoking the Hide the Office Assistant command on the Help menu or by right-clicking the Office Assistant and then clicking Hide on the shortcut menu. The Hide the Office Assistant command shows on the Help menu only when the Office Assistant is active in the FrontPage window. If the Office Assistant begins showing up on your screen without you instructing it to show, then right-click the Office Assistant, click Options on the shortcut menu, click the Use the Office Assistant check box to remove the check mark, and then click the OK button.

If the Office Assistant is active in the FrontPage window, then FrontPage displays all program and system messages in the Office Assistant balloon.

You may or may not want the Office Assistant to display on the screen at all times. As indicated earlier, you can hide it and then show it later through the Help menu. For more information about the Office Assistant, type `office assistant` in the Type a question for help box and then click the links in the Search Results task pane.

Help Buttons in Dialog Boxes and Subsystem Windows

As you invoke commands that display dialog boxes or other windows, such as the Print Preview window, you will see buttons and links that offer helpful information. Figure A-8 shows the types of Help buttons and links you will see as you work with FrontPage.

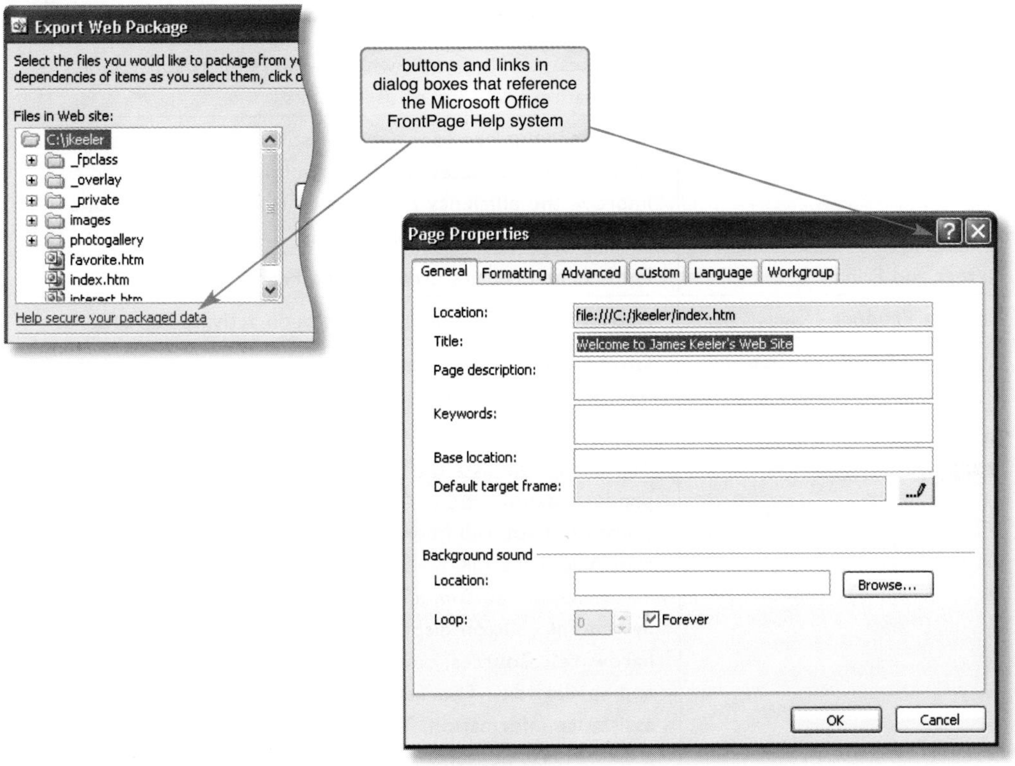

FIGURE A-8

Other Help Commands on the Help Menu

Thus far, this appendix has discussed the first two commands on the Help menu: (1) the Microsoft Office FrontPage Help command (Figure A-1 on page APP 1) and (2) the Show the Office Assistant command (Figure A-7 on page APP 6). Several additional commands are available on the Help menu, as shown in Figure A-9. Table A-1 summarizes these commands.

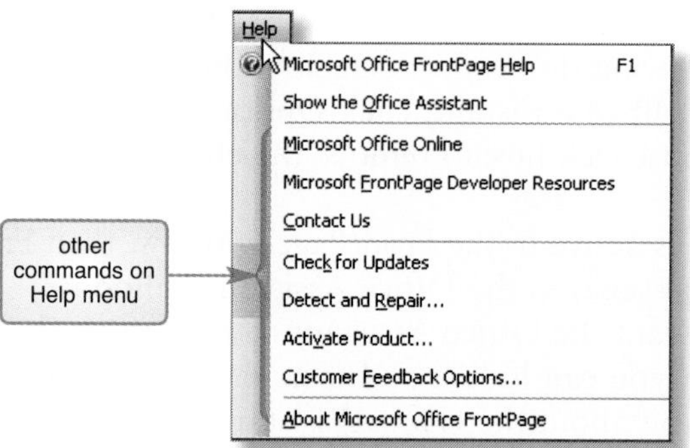

FIGURE A-9

Table A-1 Summary of Other Help Commands on the Help Menu

COMMAND ON HELP MENU	FUNCTION
Microsoft Office Online	Activates your browser, which displays the Microsoft Office Online Home page. The Microsoft Office Online Home page contains links that can improve your Office productivity.
Contact Us	Activates your browser, which displays Microsoft contact information and a list of useful links.
Check for Updates	Activates your browser, which displays a list of updates to Office. These updates can be downloaded and installed to improve the efficiency of Office or to fix an error in one or more of the Office applications.
Detect and Repair	Detects and repairs errors in the FrontPage program.
Activate Product	Activates FrontPage if it has not been activated already.
Customer Feedback Options	Gives or denies Microsoft permission to collect anonymous information about your hardware.
About Microsoft Office FrontPage	Displays the About Microsoft Office FrontPage dialog box. The dialog box lists the owner of the software and the product identification. You need to know the product identification if you call Microsoft for assistance. The three buttons below the OK button are the System Info button, the Tech Support button, and the Disabled Items button. The System Info button displays system information, including hardware resources, components, software environment, and applications. The Tech Support button displays technical assistance information. The Disabled Items button displays a list of disabled items that prevent FrontPage from functioning properly.

1 Using the Type a Question for Help Box

Instructions: Perform the following tasks using the FrontPage Help system.

1. Use the Type a question for help box on the menu bar to get help on inserting pictures.
2. Click About WordArt in the list of links in the Search Results task pane. Tile the windows. Double-click the Microsoft Office FrontPage Help window title bar to maximize it. Click the Show All button. Read and print the information. At the top of the printout, write down the number of links the FrontPage Help system found.
3. One at a time, click two additional links in the Search Results task pane and print the information. Hand in the printouts to your instructor. Use the Back and Forward buttons to return to the original page.
4. Use the Type a question for help box to search for information on stylesheets. Click the Apply a style link in the Search Results task pane. When the Microsoft Office FrontPage Help window is displayed, maximize the window. Read and print the information. One at a time, click the links on the page and print the information for any new page that is displayed. Close the Microsoft Office FrontPage Help window.
5. For each of the following words and phrases, click one link in the Search Results task pane, click the Show All link, and then print the page: text; layer; background; borders and shading; reveal tags; task pane; and bookmarks.

2 Expanding on the FrontPage Help System Basics

Instructions: Use the FrontPage Help system to understand the topics better and answer the questions listed below. Answer the questions on your own paper, or hand in the printed Help information to your instructor.

1. Show the Office Assistant. Right-click the Office Assistant and then click Animate! on the shortcut menu. Repeat invoking the Animate command to see various animations. Right-click the Office Assistant, click Options on the shortcut menu, click the Reset my tips button, and then click the OK button. Click the light bulb above the Office Assistant if it appears. When you see the light bulb, it indicates that the Office Assistant has a tip to share with you.
2. Use the Office Assistant to find help on undoing tasks. Print the Help information for three links in the Search Results task pane. Close the Microsoft Office FrontPage Help window. Hand in the printouts to your instructor. Hide the Office Assistant.
3. Press the F1 key. Search for information on Help. Click the first two links in the Search Results task pane. Read and print the information for both.
4. One at a time, invoke the first three commands in Table A-1. Print each page. Click two links on one of the pages and print the information. Hand in the printouts to your instructor.
5. Click About Microsoft Office FrontPage on the Help menu. Click the Tech Support button and print the resulting page. Click the System Info button. Below the Components category, print the CD-ROM and Display information. Hand in the printouts to your instructor.

Appendix B

Speech and Handwriting Recognition

Introduction

This appendix discusses the Office capability that allows users to create and modify worksheets using its alternative input technologies available through **text services**. Office provides a variety of text services, which enable you to speak commands and enter text in an application. The most common text service is the keyboard. Other text services include speech recognition and handwriting recognition.

The Language Bar

The **Language bar** allows you to use text services in the Office applications. You can utilize the Language bar in one of three states: (1) in a restored state as a floating toolbar in the FrontPage window (Figure B-1a or Figure B-1b if Text Labels are enabled); (2) in a minimized state docked next to the notification area on the Windows taskbar (Figure B-1c); or (3) hidden (temporarily closed and out of the way). If the Language bar is hidden, you can activate it by right-clicking the Windows taskbar, pointing to Toolbars on the shortcut menu (Figure B-1d), and clicking Language bar on the Toolbars submenu. If you want to close the Language bar, right-click the Language bar and then click Close the Language bar on the shortcut menu (Figure B-1e).

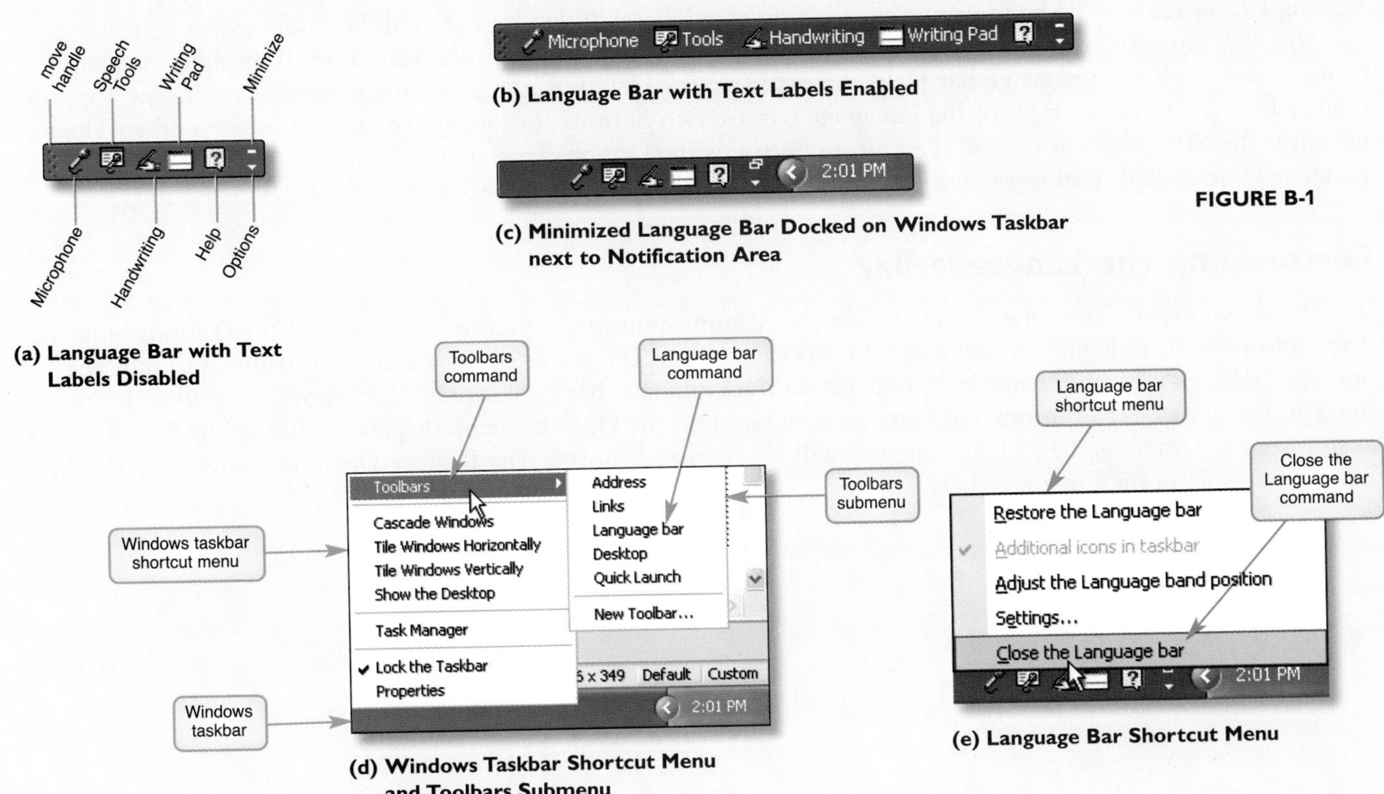

(a) Language Bar with Text Labels Disabled

(b) Language Bar with Text Labels Enabled

(c) Minimized Language Bar Docked on Windows Taskbar next to Notification Area

(d) Windows Taskbar Shortcut Menu and Toolbars Submenu

(e) Language Bar Shortcut Menu

FIGURE B-1

When Windows was installed on your computer, the installer specified a default language. For example, most users in the United States select English (United States) as the default language. You can add more than 90 additional languages and varying dialects such as Basque, English (Zimbabwe), French (France), French (Canada), German (Germany), German (Austria), and Swahili. With multiple languages available, you can switch from one language to another while working in FrontPage. If you change the language or dialect, then text services may change the functions of the keys on the keyboard, adjust speech recognition, and alter handwriting recognition. If a second language is activated, then a Language icon appears immediately to the right of the move handle on the Language bar. This appendix assumes that English (United States) is the only language installed. Thus, the Language icon does not appear in the examples in Figure B-1 on the previous page.

Buttons on the Language Bar

The Language bar shown in Figure B-2a contains seven buttons. The number of buttons on your Language bar may be different. These buttons are used to select the language, customize the Language bar, control the microphone, control handwriting, and obtain help.

The first button on the left is the Microphone button, which enables and disables the microphone. When the microphone is enabled, text services adds two buttons and a balloon to the Language bar (Figure B-2b). These additional buttons and the balloon will be discussed shortly.

The second button from the left is the Speech Tools button. The Speech Tools button displays a menu of commands (Figure B-2c) that allow you to hide or show the balloon on the Language bar; train the Speech Recognition service so that it can interpret your voice better; add and delete words from its dictionary, such as names and other words not understood easily; and change the user profile so more than one person can use the microphone on the same computer.

The third button from the left on the Language bar is the Handwriting button. The Handwriting button displays the Handwriting menu (Figure B-2d), which lets you choose the Writing Pad (Figure B-2e), Write Anywhere (Figure B-2f), or the on-screen keyboard (Figure B-2g). The On-Screen Symbol Keyboard command on the Handwriting menu displays an on-screen keyboard that allows you to enter special symbols that are not available on a standard keyboard. You can choose only one form of handwriting at a time.

The fourth button indicates which one of the handwriting forms is active. For example, in Figure B-2a, the Writing Pad is active. The handwriting recognition capabilities of text services will be discussed shortly.

The fifth button from the left on the Language bar is the Help button. The Help button displays the Help menu. If you click the Language Bar Help command on the Help menu, the Language Bar Help window appears (Figure B-2h). On the far right of the Language bar are two buttons stacked above and below each other. The top button is the Minimize button and the bottom button is the Options button. The Minimize button minimizes the Language bar so that it appears on the Windows taskbar. The next section discusses the Options button.

Customizing the Language Bar

The down arrow icon immediately below the Minimize button in Figure B-2a is called the Options button. The Options button displays a menu of text services options (Figure B-2i). You can use this menu to hide the Speech Tools, Handwriting, and Help buttons on the Language bar by clicking their names to remove the check mark to the left of each button. The Settings command on the Options menu displays a dialog box that lets you customize the Language bar. This command will be discussed shortly. The Restore Defaults command redisplays hidden buttons on the Language bar.

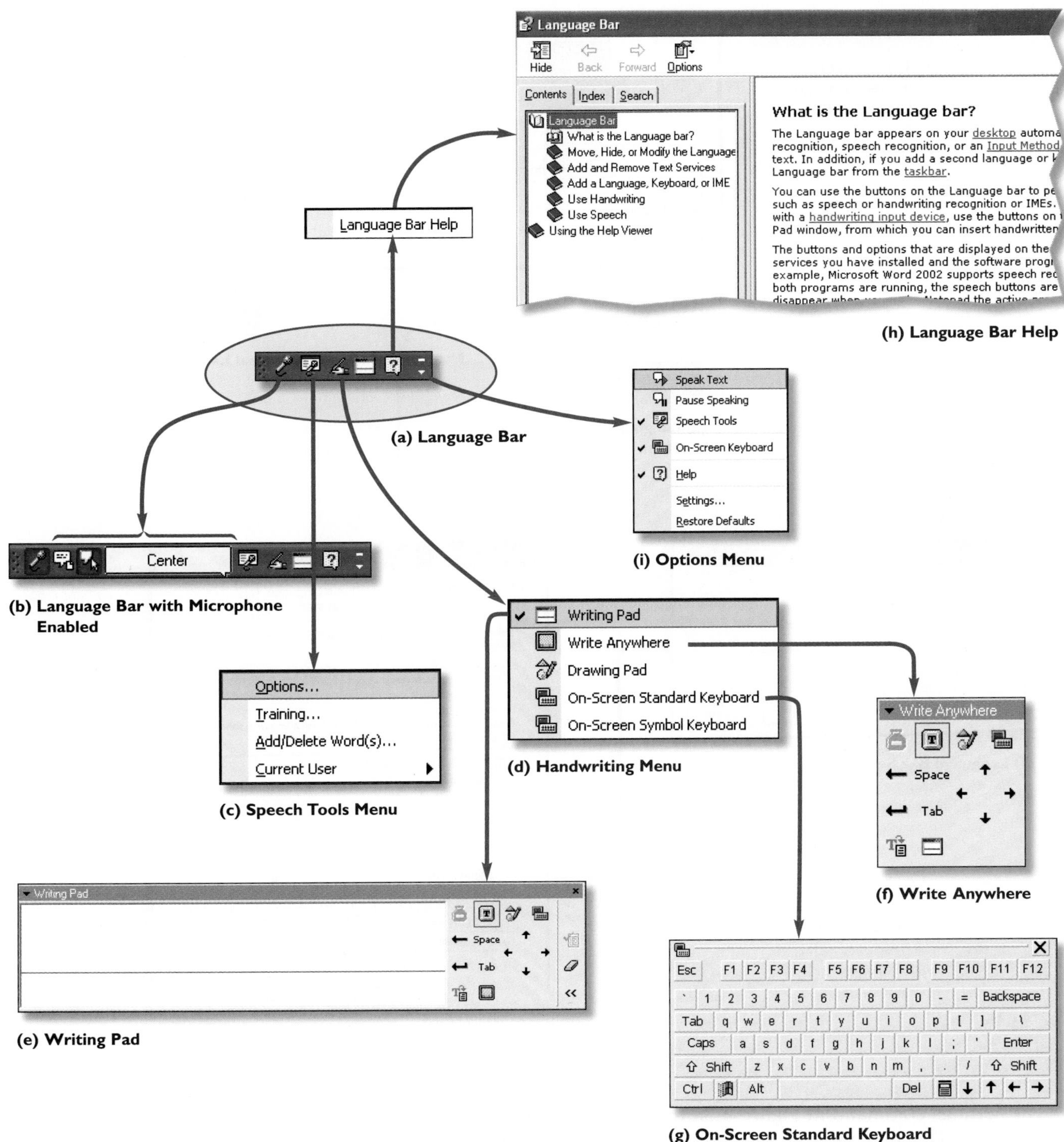

(a) Language Bar

(b) Language Bar with Microphone Enabled

(c) Speech Tools Menu

(d) Handwriting Menu

(e) Writing Pad

(f) Write Anywhere

(g) On-Screen Standard Keyboard

(h) Language Bar Help

(i) Options Menu

FIGURE B-2

If you right-click the Language bar, a shortcut menu appears (Figure B-3a on the next page). This shortcut menu lets you further customize the Language bar. The Minimize command on the shortcut menu docks the Language bar on the Windows taskbar. The Transparency command in Figure B-3a toggles the Language bar between being solid and transparent. You can see through a transparent Language bar (Figure B-3b). The Text Labels command toggles on text labels on the Language bar (Figure B-3c) and off (Figure B-3b).

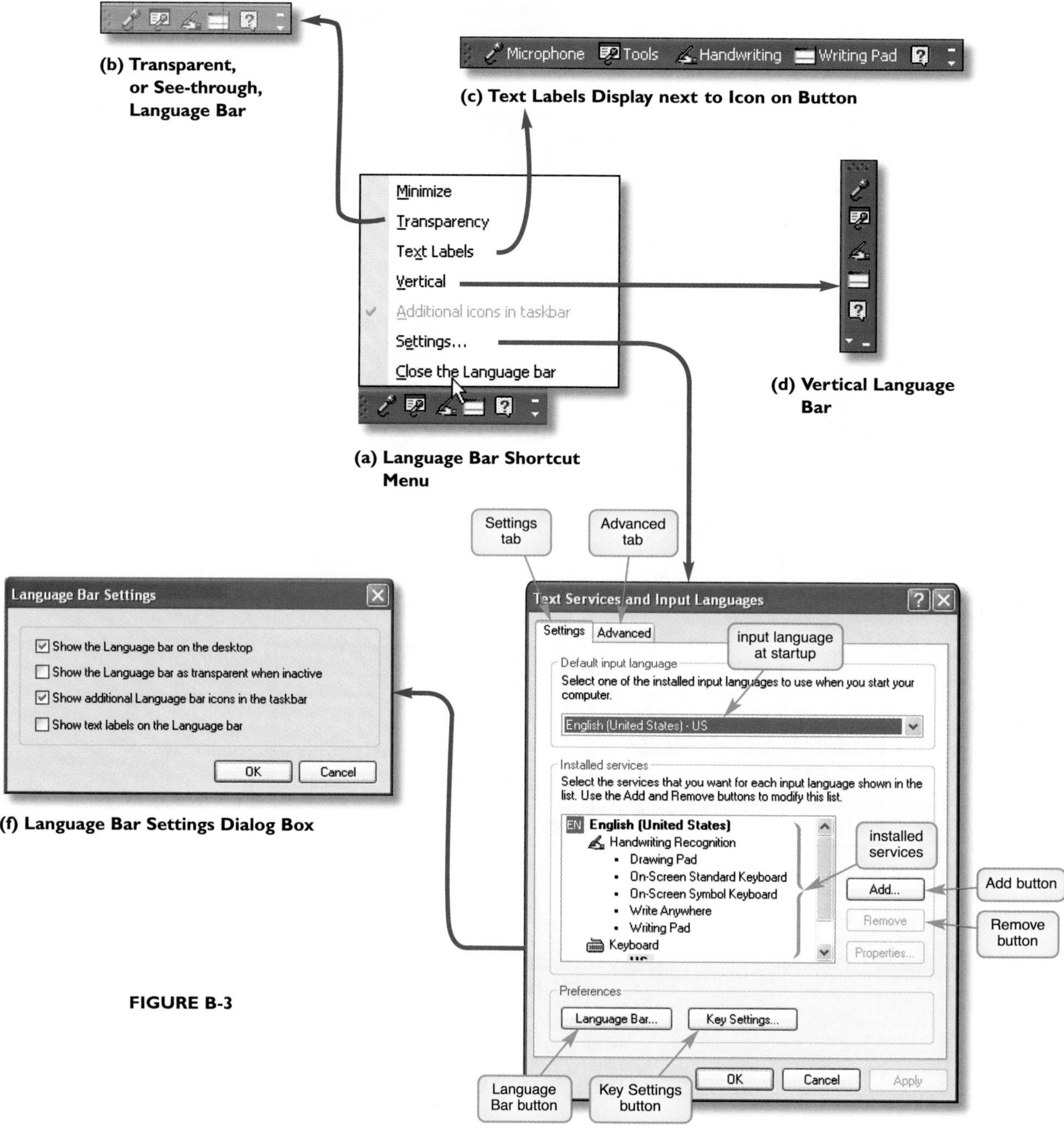

FIGURE B-3

The Settings command in Figure B-3a displays the Text Services and Input Languages dialog box (Figure B-3e). The Text Services and Input Languages dialog box allows you to add additional languages, add and remove text services, modify keys on the keyboard, modify the Language bar, and extend support of advanced text services to all programs, including Notepad and other programs that normally do not support text services (through the Advanced tab). If you want to remove any one of the services in the Installed services list, select the service, and then click the Remove button. If you want to add a service, click the Add button. The Key Settings button allows you to modify the keyboard. If you click the Language Bar button in the Text Services and Input Languages dialog box, the Language Bar Settings dialog box appears (Figure B-3f). This dialog box contains Language bar options, some of which are the same as the commands on the Language bar shortcut menu shown in Figure B-3a.

The Close the Language bar command on the shortcut menu shown in Figure B-3a closes or hides the Language bar. If you close the Language bar and want to redisplay it, see Figure B-1d on page APP 11.

Speech Recognition

The **Speech Recognition service** available with Office enables your computer to recognize human speech through a microphone. The microphone has two modes: Dictation and Voice Command (Figure B-4). You switch between the two modes by clicking the Dictation button and the Voice Command button on the Language bar. These buttons appear only when you turn on Speech Recognition by clicking the Microphone button on the Language bar (Figure B-5a on the next page). If you are using the Microphone button for the very first time in FrontPage, it will require that you check your microphone settings and step through voice training before activating the Speech Recognition service.

The Dictation button places the microphone in Dictation mode. In **Dictation mode**, whatever you speak is entered as text. The Voice Command button places the microphone in Voice Command mode. In **Voice Command mode**, whatever you speak is interpreted as a command. If you want to turn off the microphone, click Microphone button on the Language bar or in Voice Command mode, say "Mic off" (pronounced mike off). It is important to remember that minimizing the Language bar does not turn off the microphone.

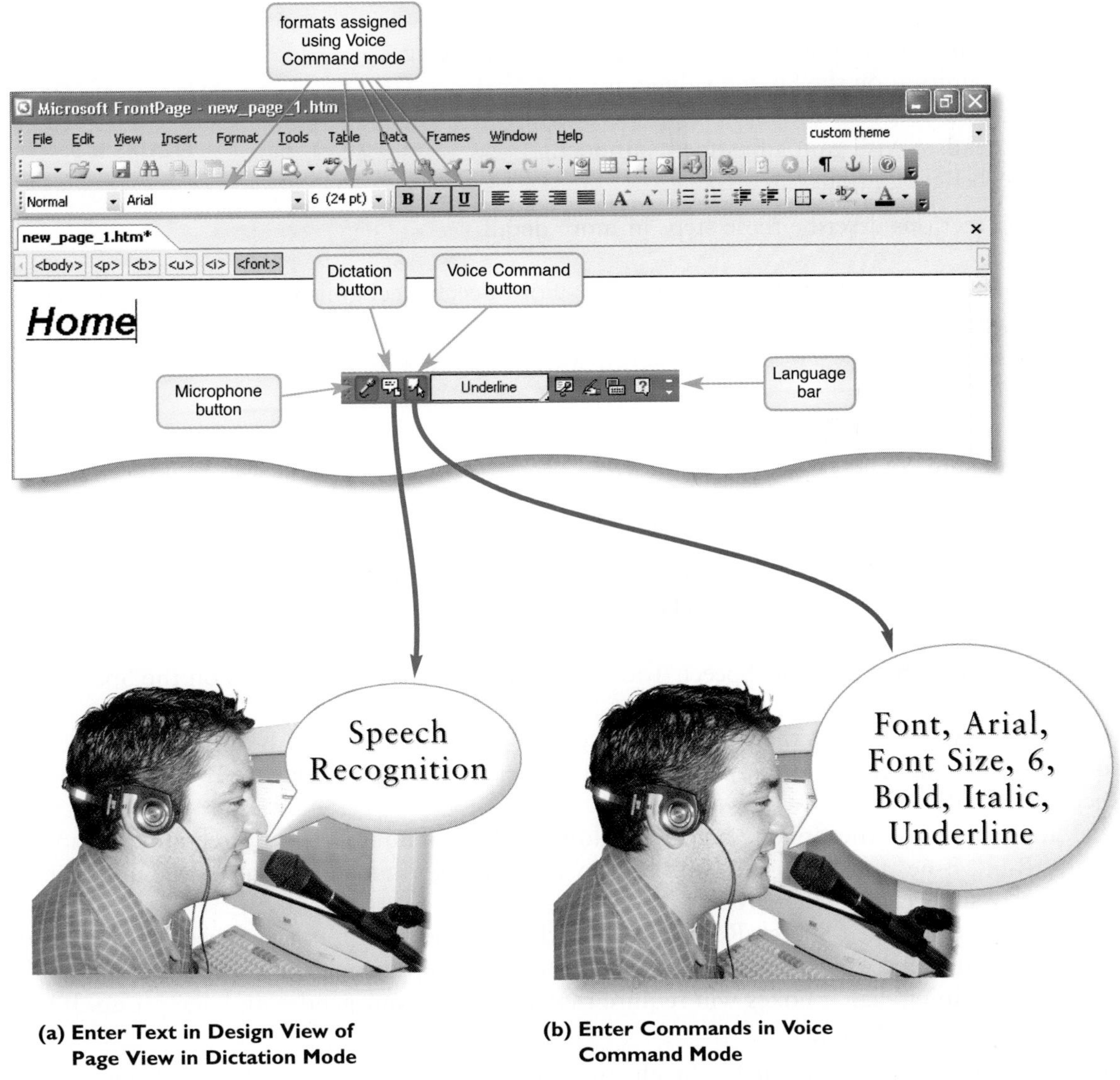

(a) Enter Text in Design View of Page View in Dictation Mode

(b) Enter Commands in Voice Command Mode

FIGURE B-4

The Language bar speech message balloon shown in Figure B-5b displays messages that may offer help or hints. In Voice Command mode, the name of the last recognized command you said appears. If you use the mouse or keyboard instead of the microphone, a message will appear in the Language bar speech message balloon indicating the word you could say. In Dictation mode, the message, Dictating, usually appears. The Speech Recognition service, however, will display messages to inform you that you are talking too soft, too loud, too fast, or to ask you to repeat what you said by displaying, What was that?

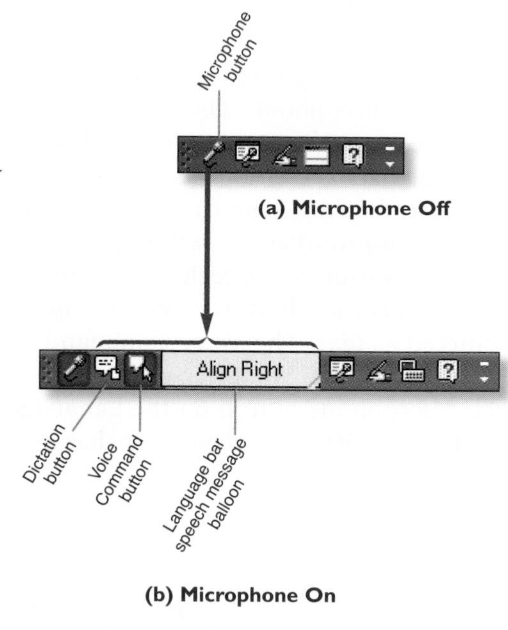

FIGURE B-5

Getting Started with Speech Recognition

For the microphone to function properly, you should follow these steps:

1. Make sure your computer meets the minimum requirements.
2. Start FrontPage. Activate Speech Recognition by clicking Tools on the menu bar, pointing to Speech, and then clicking Speech Recognition on the Speech submenu.
3. Set up and position your microphone, preferably a close-talk headset with gain adjustment support.
4. Train Speech Recognition.

The following sections describe these steps in more detail.

SPEECH RECOGNITION SYSTEM REQUIREMENTS For Speech Recognition to work on your computer, it needs the following:

1. Microsoft Windows 98 or later or Microsoft Windows NT 4.0 or later
2. At least 128 MB RAM
3. 400 MHz or faster processor
4. Microphone and sound card

SET UP AND POSITION YOUR MICROPHONE Set up your microphone as follows:

1. Connect your microphone to the sound card in the back of the computer.
2. Position the microphone approximately one inch out from and to the side of your mouth. Position it so you are not breathing into it.
3. On the Language bar, click the Speech Tools button, and then click Options on the Speech Tools menu (Figure B-6a).
4. When text services displays the Speech input settings dialog box (Figure B-6b), click the Advanced Speech button. When text services displays the Speech Properties dialog box (Figure B-6c), click the Speech Recognition tab.
5. Click the Configure Microphone button. Follow the Microphone Wizard directions as shown in Figures B-6d, B-6e, and B-6f. The Next button will remain dimmed in Figure B-6e until the volume meter consistently stays in the green area.
6. If someone else installed Speech Recognition, click the New button in the Speech Properties dialog box and enter your name. Click the Train Profile button and step through the Voice Training dialog boxes. The Voice Training dialog boxes will require that you enter your gender and age group. It then will step you through voice training.

You can adjust the microphone further by clicking the Settings button in the Speech Properties dialog box (Figure B-6c). The Settings button displays the Recognition Profile Settings dialog box that allows you to adjust the pronunciation sensitivity and accuracy versus recognition response time.

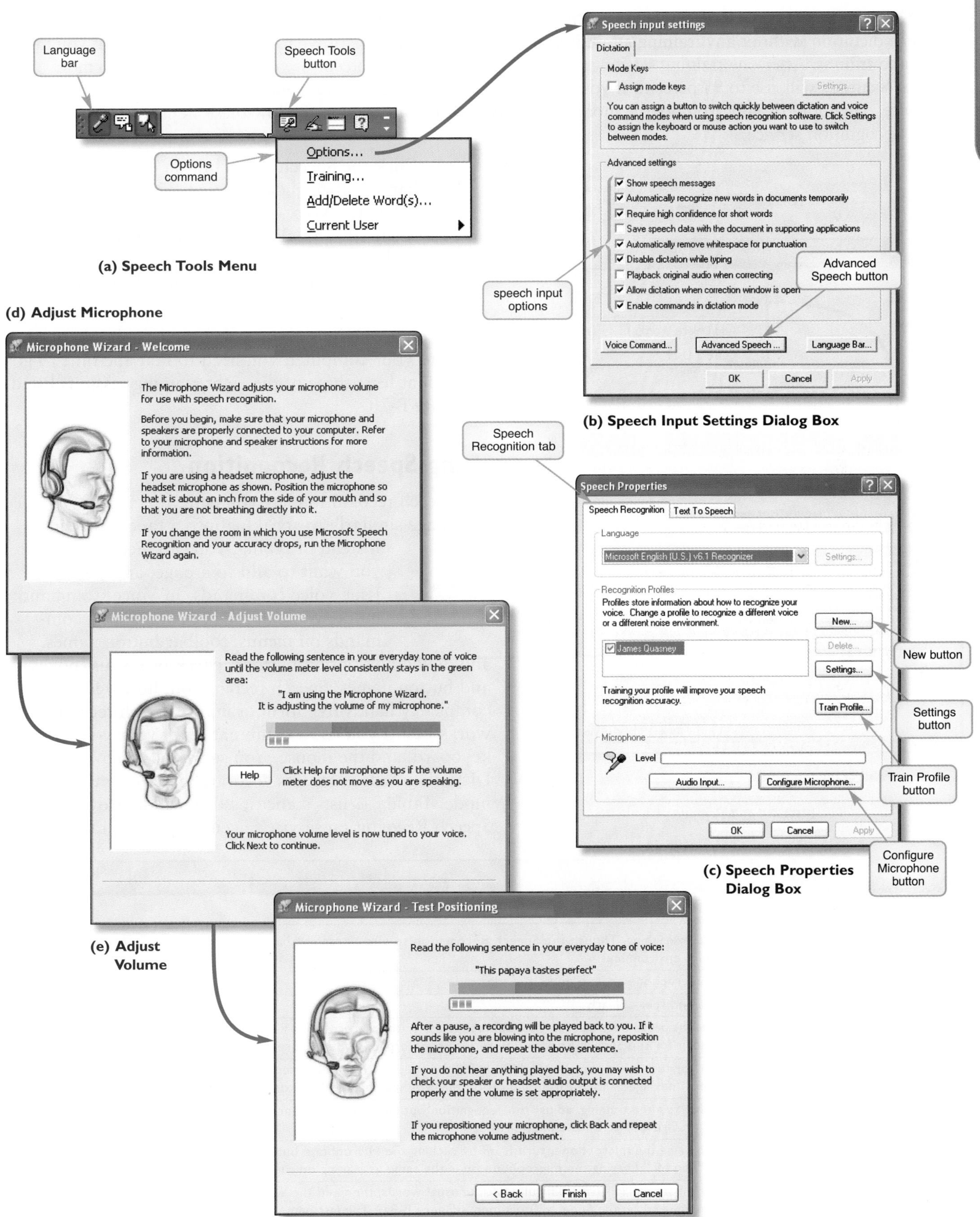
Language bar
Speech Tools button
Options command
Options...
Training...
Add/Delete Word(s)...
Current User
(a) Speech Tools Menu
Speech input settings
Dictation
Mode Keys
Assign mode keys
Settings...
You can assign a button to switch quickly between dictation and voice command modes when using speech recognition software. Click Settings to assign the keyboard or mouse action you want to use to switch between modes.
Advanced settings
Show speech messages
Automatically recognize new words in documents temporarily
Require high confidence for short words
Save speech data with the document in supporting applications
Automatically remove whitespace for punctuation
Disable dictation while typing
Playback original audio when correcting
Allow dictation when correction window is open
Enable commands in dictation mode
speech input options
Advanced Speech button
Voice Command...
Advanced Speech...
Language Bar...
OK
Cancel
Apply
(b) Speech Input Settings Dialog Box
(d) Adjust Microphone
Microphone Wizard - Welcome
The Microphone Wizard adjusts your microphone volume for use with speech recognition.
Before you begin, make sure that your microphone and speakers are properly connected to your computer. Refer to your microphone and speaker instructions for more information.
If you are using a headset microphone, adjust the headset microphone as shown. Position the microphone so that it is about an inch from the side of your mouth and so that you are not breathing directly into it.
If you change the room in which you use Microsoft Speech Recognition and your accuracy drops, run the Microphone Wizard again.
Speech Recognition tab
Speech Properties
Speech Recognition
Text To Speech
Language
Microsoft English (U.S.) v6.1 Recognizer
Settings...
Recognition Profiles
Profiles store information about how to recognize your voice. Change a profile to recognize a different voice or a different noise environment.
New...
James Quasney
Delete...
Settings...
Training your profile will improve your speech recognition accuracy.
Train Profile...
Microphone
Level
Audio Input...
Configure Microphone...
OK
Cancel
Apply
New button
Settings button
Train Profile button
Configure Microphone button
(c) Speech Properties Dialog Box
Microphone Wizard - Adjust Volume
Read the following sentence in your everyday tone of voice until the volume meter level consistently stays in the green area:
"I am using the Microphone Wizard. It is adjusting the volume of my microphone."
Help
Click Help for microphone tips if the volume meter does not move as you are speaking.
Your microphone volume level is now tuned to your voice. Click Next to continue.
(e) Adjust Volume
Microphone Wizard - Test Positioning
Read the following sentence in your everyday tone of voice:
"This papaya tastes perfect"
After a pause, a recording will be played back to you. If it sounds like you are blowing into the microphone, reposition the microphone, and repeat the above sentence.
If you do not hear anything played back, you may wish to check your speaker or headset audio output is connected properly and the volume is set appropriately.
If you repositioned your microphone, click Back and repeat the microphone volume adjustment.
< Back
Finish
Cancel
(f) Test Microphone

FIGURE B-6

TRAIN THE SPEECH RECOGNITION SERVICE The Speech Recognition service will understand most commands and some dictation without any training at all. It will recognize much more of what you speak, however, if you take the time to train it. After one training session, it will recognize 85 to 90 percent of your words. As you do more training, accuracy will rise to 95 percent. If you feel that too many mistakes are being made, then continue to train the service. The more training you do, the more accurately it will work for you. Follow these steps to train the Speech Recognition service:

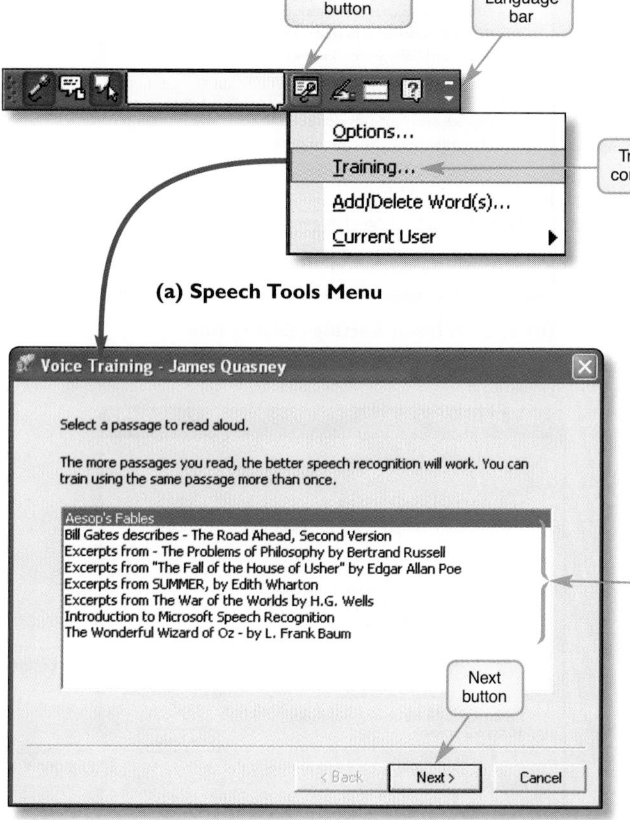

(a) Speech Tools Menu

(b) Voice Training Dialog Box

FIGURE B-7

1. Click the Speech Tools button on the Language bar and then click Training (Figure B-7a).
2. When the Voice Training dialog box appears (Figure B-7b), click one of the sessions and then click the Next button.
3. Complete the training session, which should take less than 15 minutes.

If you are serious about using a microphone to speak to your computer, you need to take the time to go through at least three of the eight training sessions listed in Figure B-7b.

Using Speech Recognition

Speech recognition lets you enter text into a Web page similarly to speaking into a tape recorder. Instead of typing, you can dictate text that you want to add to a page, and you can issue voice commands. In Voice Command mode, you can speak menu names, commands on menus, toolbar button names, and dialog box option buttons, check boxes, list boxes, and button names. Speech recognition, however, is not a completely hands-free form of input. Speech recognition works best if you use a combination of your voice, the keyboard, and the mouse. You soon will discover that Dictation mode is far less accurate than Voice Command mode. Table B-1 lists some tips that will improve the Speech Recognition service's accuracy considerably.

Table B-1 Tips to Improve Speech Recognition

NUMBER	TIP
1	The microphone hears everything. Though the Speech Recognition service filters out background noise, it is recommended that you work in a quiet environment.
2	Try not to move the microphone around once it is adjusted.
3	Speak in a steady tone and speak clearly.
4	In Dictation mode, do not pause between words. A phrase is easier to interpret than a word. Sounding out syllables in a word will make it more difficult for the Speech Recognition service to interpret what you are saying.
5	If you speak too loudly or too softly, it makes it difficult for the Speech Recognition service to interpret what you said. Check the Language bar speech message balloon for an indication that you may be speaking too loudly or too softly.
6	If you experience problems after training, adjust the recognition options that control accuracy and rejection by clicking the Settings button shown in Figure B-6c on the previous page.
7	When you are finished using the microphone, turn it off by clicking the Microphone button on the Language bar or in Voice Command mode, say "Mic off." Leaving the microphone on is the same as leaning on the keyboard.
8	If the Speech Recognition service is having difficulty with unusual words, then add the words to its dictionary by using the Add/Delete Word(s) command on the Speech Tools menu (Figure B-8a). The last names of individuals and the names of companies are good examples of the types of words you should add to the dictionary.
9	Training will improve accuracy; practice will improve confidence.

The last command on the Speech Tools menu is the Current User command (Figure B-8a). The Current User command is useful for multiple users who share a computer. It allows them to configure their own individual profiles, and then switch between users as they use the computer.

For additional information on the Speech Recognition service, enter `speech recognition` in the Type a question for help box on the menu bar.

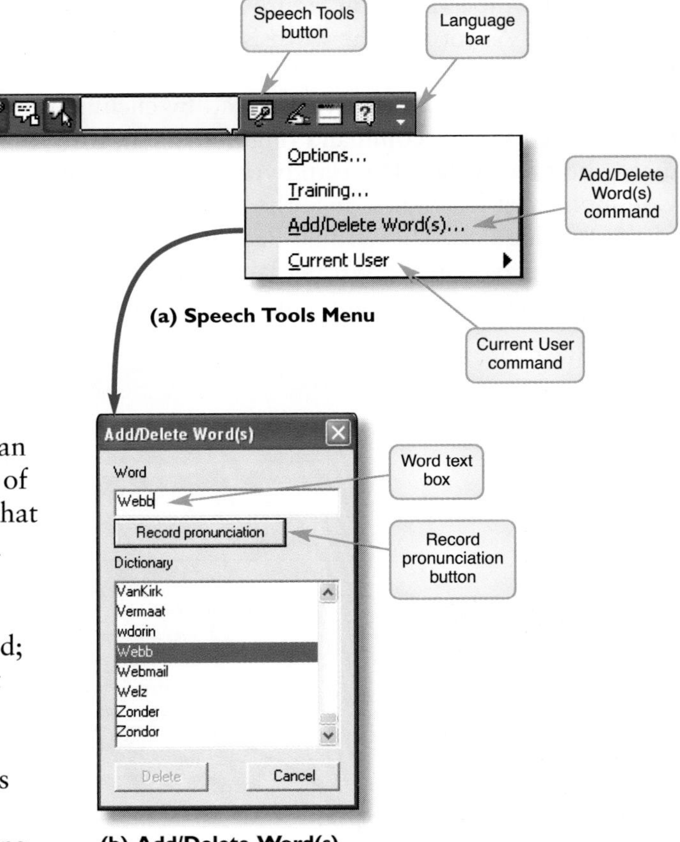

FIGURE B-8

Handwriting Recognition

Using the Office **Handwriting Recognition service**, you can enter text and numbers into FrontPage by writing instead of typing. You can write using a special handwriting device that connects to your computer or you can write on the screen using your mouse. Four basic methods of handwriting are available by clicking the Handwriting button on the Language bar: Writing Pad; Write Anywhere; Drawing Pad; and On-Screen Keyboard. The Drawing Pad button is not available in FrontPage. Although the on-screen keyboard does not involve handwriting recognition, it is part of the Handwriting menu and, therefore, will be discussed in this section.

If your Language bar does not include the Handwriting button, then, for installation instructions, enter `install handwriting recognition` in the Type a question for help box on the menu bar.

Writing Pad

To display the Writing Pad, click the Handwriting button on the Language bar and then click Writing Pad (Figure B-9). The **Writing Pad** resembles a notepad with one or more lines on which you can use freehand to print or write in cursive. With the Text button enabled, you can form letters on the line by moving the mouse while holding down the mouse button. To the right of the notepad is a rectangular toolbar. Use the buttons on this toolbar to adjust the Writing Pad, make selections, and activate other handwriting applications.

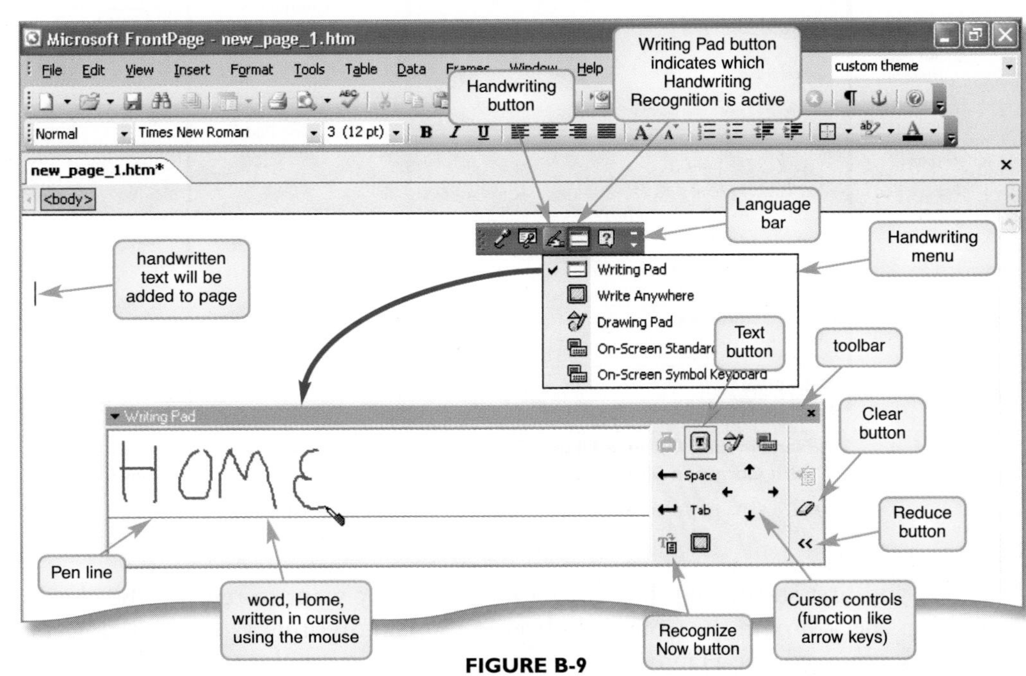

FIGURE B-9

Consider the example in Figure B-9 on the previous page. Home is written in cursive on the **Pen line** in the Writing Pad. As soon as the word is complete, the Handwriting Recognition service automatically places the word on the page.

You can customize the Writing Pad by clicking the Options button on the left side of the title bar and then clicking the Options command (Figure B-10a). Invoking the Options command causes the Handwriting Options dialog box to display. The Handwriting Options dialog box contains two sheets: Common and Writing Pad. The Common sheet lets you change the pen color and pen width, adjust recognition, and customize the toolbar area of the Writing Pad. The Writing Pad sheet allows you to change the background color and the number of lines that are displayed in the Writing Pad. Both sheets contain a Restore Default button to restore the settings to what they were when the software was installed initially.

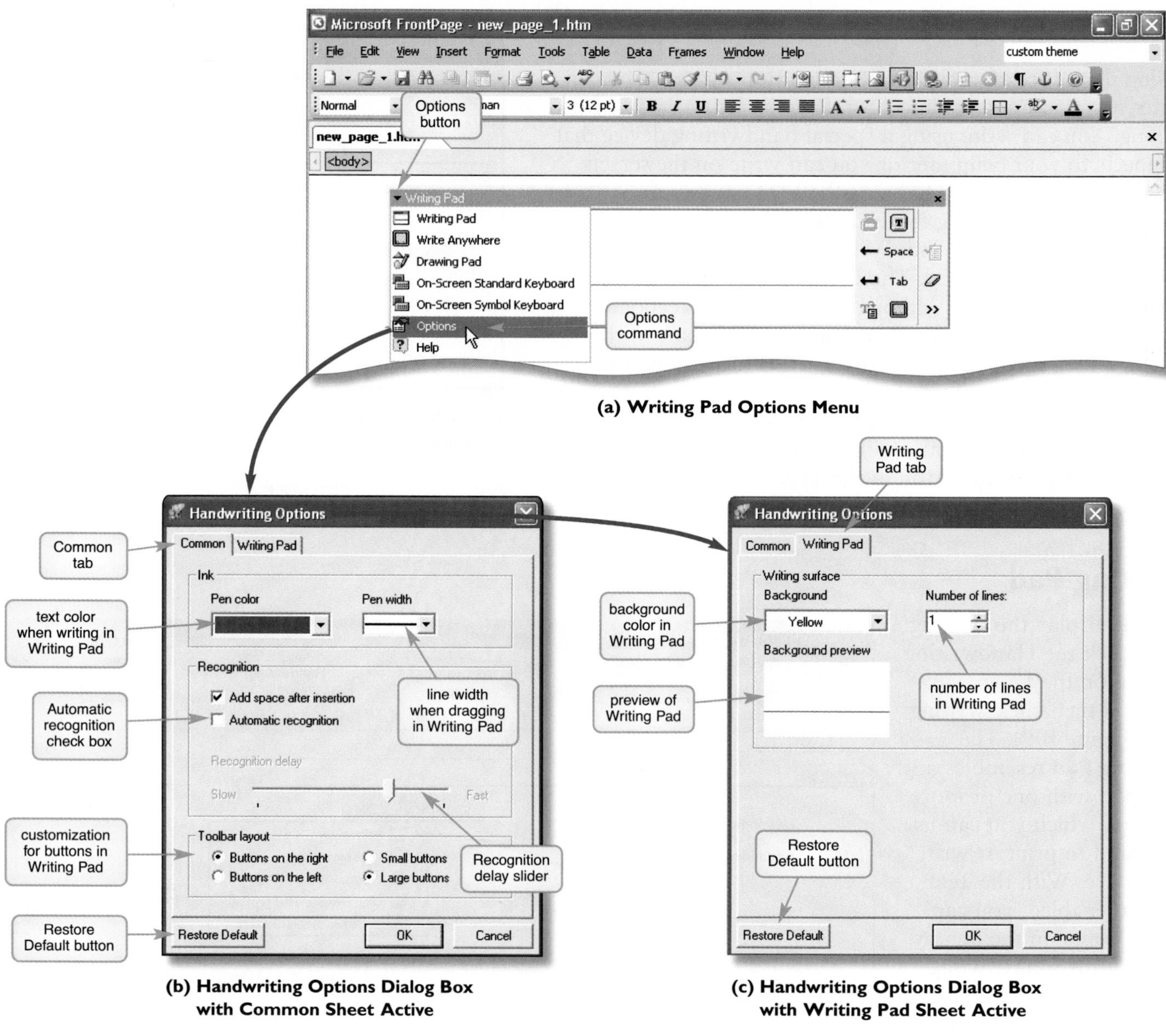

(a) Writing Pad Options Menu

(b) Handwriting Options Dialog Box with Common Sheet Active

(c) Handwriting Options Dialog Box with Writing Pad Sheet Active

FIGURE B-10

When you first start using the Writing Pad, you may want to remove the check mark from the Automatic recognition check box in the Common sheet in the Handwriting Options dialog box (Figure B-10b). With the check mark removed, the Handwriting Recognition service will not interpret what you write in the Writing Pad until you click the Recognize Now button on the toolbar (Figure B-9 on the previous page). This allows you to pause and adjust your writing.

The best way to learn how to use the Writing Pad is to practice with it. Also, for more information, enter `handwriting recognition` in the Type a question for help box on the menu bar.

Write Anywhere

Rather than use Writing Pad, you can write anywhere on the screen by invoking the Write Anywhere command on the Handwriting menu (Figure B-11) that appears when you click the Handwriting button on the Language bar. In this case, the entire window is your writing pad.

In Figure B-11, the word, Home, is written in cursive using the mouse button. Shortly after the word is written, the Handwriting Recognition service interprets it, adds it to the Web page, and erases what was written.

It is recommended that when you first start using the Writing Anywhere service that you remove the check mark from the Automatic recognition check box in the Common sheet in the Handwriting Options dialog box (Figure B-10b). With the check mark removed, the Handwriting Recognition service will not interpret what you write on the screen until you click the Recognize Now button on the toolbar (Figure B-11).

Write Anywhere is more difficult to use than the Writing Pad, because when you click the mouse button, FrontPage may interpret the action as selecting a table cell rather than starting to write. For this reason, it is recommended that you use the Writing Pad.

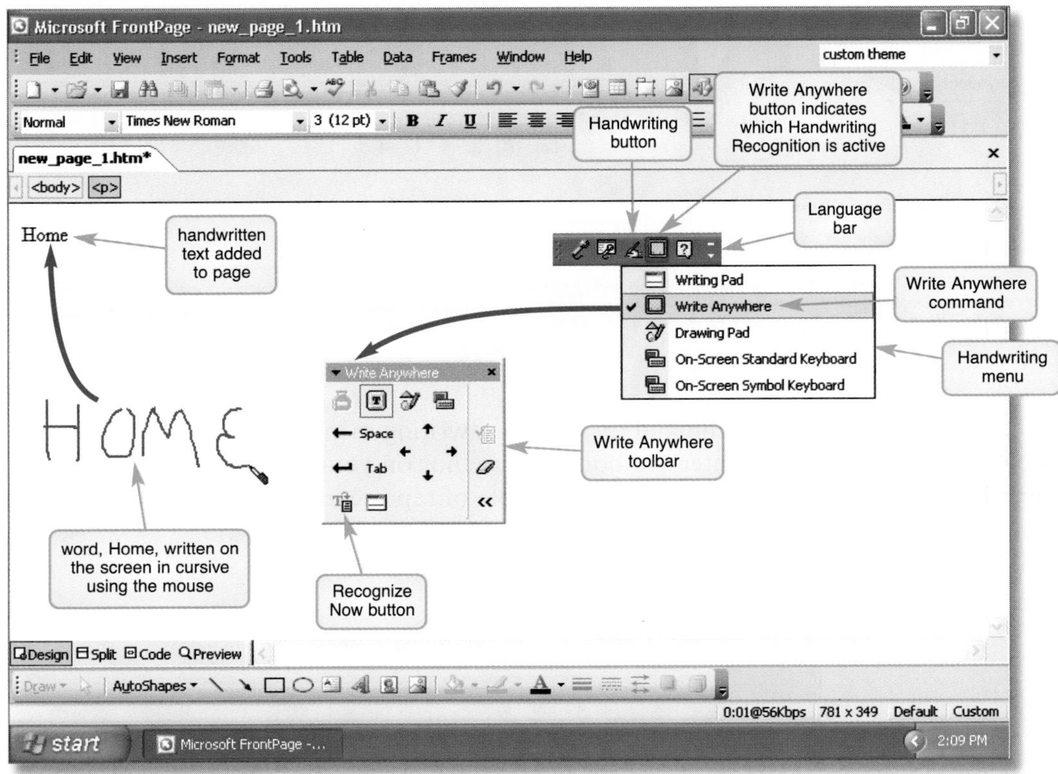

FIGURE B-11

On-Screen Keyboard

The On-Screen Standard Keyboard command on the Handwriting menu (Figure B-12) displays an on-screen keyboard. The **on-screen keyboard** lets you enter data into a cell by using your mouse to click the keys. The on-screen keyboard is similar to the type found on handheld computers.

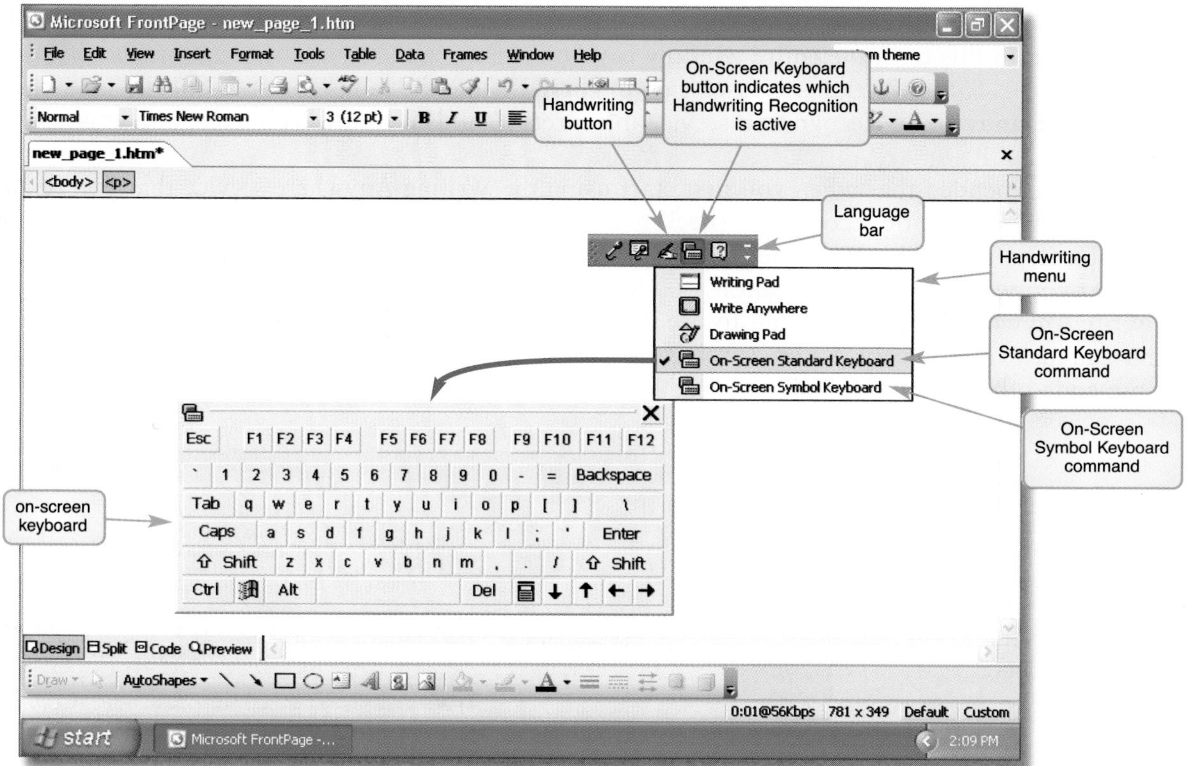

FIGURE B-12

The On-Screen Symbol Keyboard command on the Handwriting menu (Figure B-12) displays a special on-screen keyboard that allows you to enter symbols that are not on your keyboard, as well as Unicode characters. **Unicode characters** use a coding scheme capable of representing all the world's current languages.

Appendix C

Publishing FrontPage Web Sites to a File System

If you do not have access to a Web server for publishing the Web sites developed in this book, you can publish the sites to a file system. A **file system** is a folder on a hard drive or a network drive. This appendix lists the steps necessary to publish a Web site to a file system. When a Web site is published to a file system, the site does not have access to FrontPage Server Extensions. Some functionality of the Web sites developed in this book do not work without FrontPage Server Extensions. For example, Web components, such as counters, cannot work when a Web site is published to a file system. By publishing to a file system, however, you will be able to use a browser to navigate to the Web site.

The Remote Web Site view allows you to select an existing folder or create a new folder to which to publish a site. You must have access rights to the folder that allow you to write files to the folder. Table C-1 explains how to publish a Web site to a folder on drive C. After publishing the site to a folder, you can click the View your Remote Web site link in Remote Web Site view to view the site. Table C-2 explains how to use your browser to navigate to a Web site that has been published to a file system.

Table C-1 Publishing to a File System

1. Click View on the menu bar. When the View menu is displayed, click Remote Web Site. When the Remote Web Site view appears, click the Remote Web Site Properties button.
2. Click the File System button and then click the Browse button.
3. When the New Publish Location dialog box is displayed, use the Look in box to select the location to which to publish the site. If necessary, use the Create New Folder button to create a new folder.
4. Click the Open button on the New Publish Location dialog box and then click the OK button on the Remote Web Site Properties dialog box. When the Microsoft Office FrontPage dialog box appears, click the Yes button.
5. Click the Publish Web site button in the Publish all changed pages area.

Table C-2 Navigating to a Web Site on a File System

1. Open Microsoft Internet Explorer.
2. Click File on the menu bar and then click Open. When the Open dialog box is displayed, click the Browse button.
3. When the Microsoft Internet Explorer dialog box is displayed, use the Look in box to navigate to the folder to which you published the Web site. Select the index.htm file in the folder.
4. Click the Open button. Click the OK button in the Open dialog box.

Appendix D

Changing Screen Resolution and Resetting the FrontPage Toolbars and Menus

This appendix explains how to change your screen resolution in Windows to the resolution used in this book. It also describes how to reset the FrontPage toolbars and menus to their installation settings.

Changing Screen Resolution

The **screen resolution** indicates the number of pixels (dots) that your system uses to display the letters, numbers, graphics, and background you see on your screen. The screen resolution usually is stated as the product of two numbers, such as 800 × 600. An 800 × 600 screen resolution results in a display of 800 distinct pixels on each of 600 lines, or about 480,000 pixels. The figures in this book were created using a screen resolution of 800 × 600.

The screen resolutions most commonly used today are 800 × 600 and 1024 × 768, although some Office specialists operate their computers at a much higher screen resolution, such as 2048 × 1536. The following steps show how to change the screen resolution from 1024 × 768 to 800 × 600.

To Change the Screen Resolution

1

- **If necessary, minimize all applications so that the Windows desktop appears.**
- **Right-click the Windows desktop.**

Windows displays the Windows desktop shortcut menu (Figure D-1).

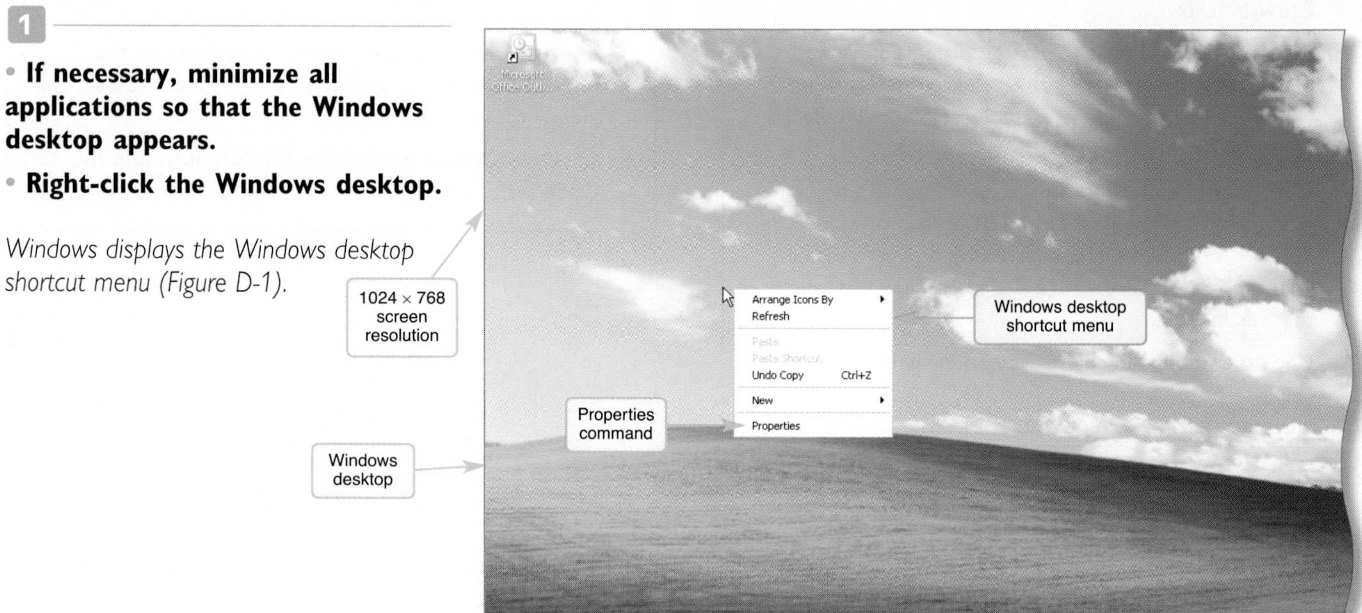

FIGURE D-1

2

• **Click Properties on the shortcut menu.**

• **When Windows displays the Display Properties dialog box, click the Settings tab.**

Windows displays the Settings sheet in the Display Properties dialog box (Figure D-2). The Settings sheet shows a preview of the Windows desktop using the current screen resolution (1024 × 768). The Settings sheet also shows the screen resolution and the color quality settings.

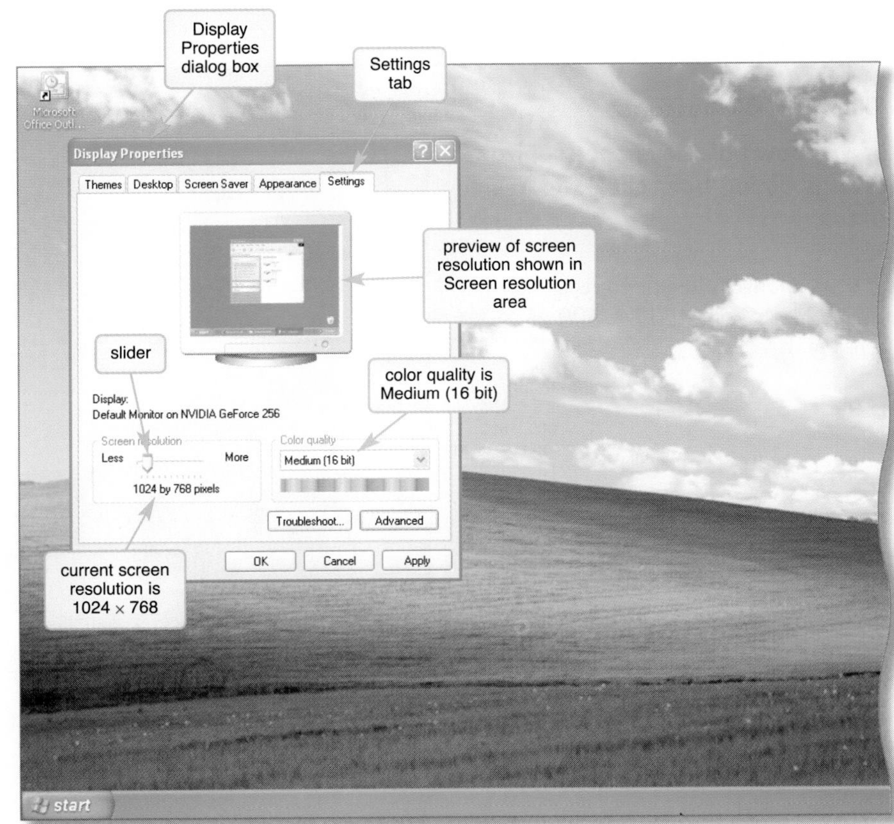

FIGURE D-2

3

• **Drag the slider in the Screen resolution area to the left so that the screen resolution changes to 800 × 600.**

The screen resolution in the Screen resolution area changes to 800 × 600 (Figure D-3). The Settings sheet shows a preview of the Windows desktop using the new screen resolution (800 × 600).

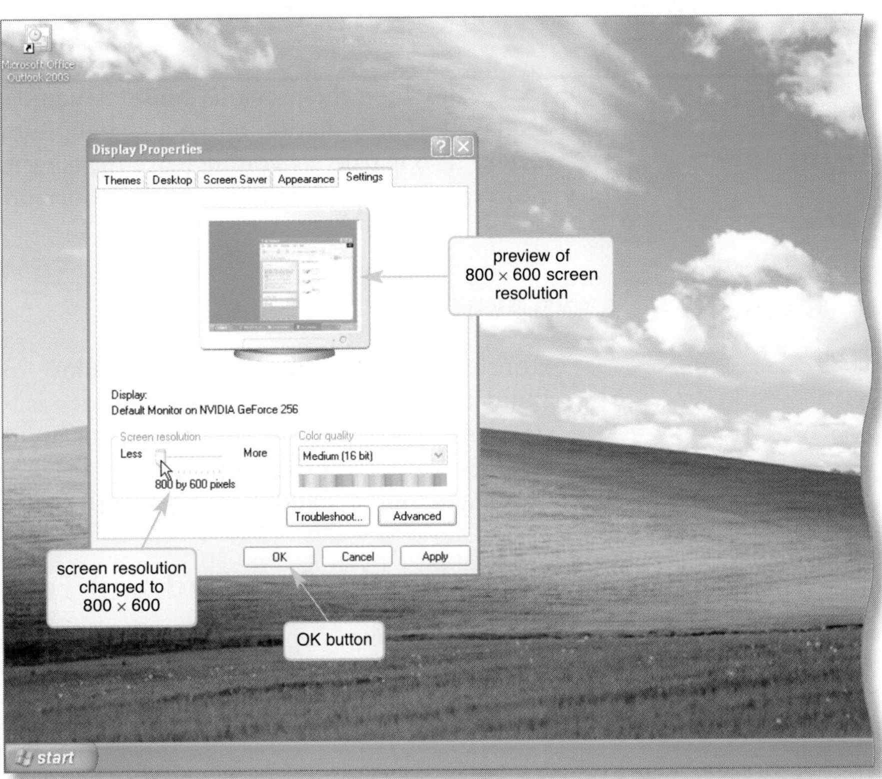

FIGURE D-3

4

- **Click the OK button.**
- **If Windows displays the Monitor Settings dialog box, click the Yes button.**

Windows changes the screen resolution from 1024 × 768 to 800 × 600 (Figure D-4).

FIGURE D-4

As shown in the previous steps, as you decrease the screen resolution, Windows displays less information on your screen, but the information increases in size. The reverse also is true: as you increase the screen resolution, Windows displays more information on your screen, but the information decreases in size.

Resetting the FrontPage Toolbars and Menus

FrontPage customization capabilities allow you to create custom toolbars by adding and deleting buttons and personalize menus based on their usage. Each time you start FrontPage, the toolbars and menus are displayed using the same settings as the last time you used FrontPage. The figures in this book were created with the FrontPage toolbars and menus set to the original, or installation, settings.

Resetting the Standard and Formatting Toolbars

The following steps show how to reset the Standard and Formatting toolbars.

To Reset the Standard and Formatting Toolbars

1

- **Start FrontPage following the steps outlined at the beginning of Project 1 on page FP 14.**
- **Click the Toolbar Options button on the Standard toolbar and then point to Add or Remove Buttons on the Toolbar Options menu.**

FrontPage displays the Toolbar Options menu and the Add or Remove Buttons submenu (Figure D-5).

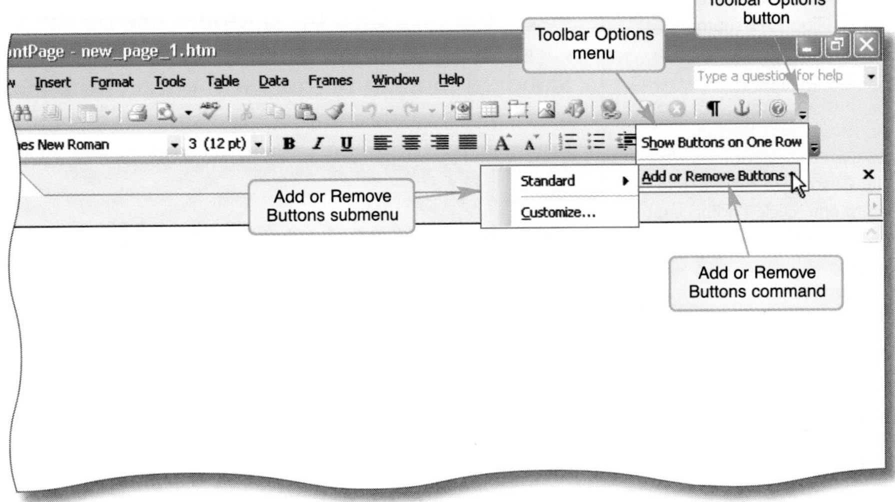

FIGURE D-5

2

- **Point to Standard on the Add or Remove Buttons submenu.**
- **Scroll down and then point to Reset Toolbar on the Standard submenu.**

FrontPage displays the Standard submenu indicating the buttons and boxes that appear on the Standard toolbar (Figure D-6). To remove a button from the Standard toolbar, click a button name with a check mark to the left of the name to remove the check mark.

3

- **Click Reset Toolbar.**
- **If FrontPage displays the Microsoft Office FrontPage dialog box, click the Yes button.**

FrontPage resets the Standard toolbar to its original settings.

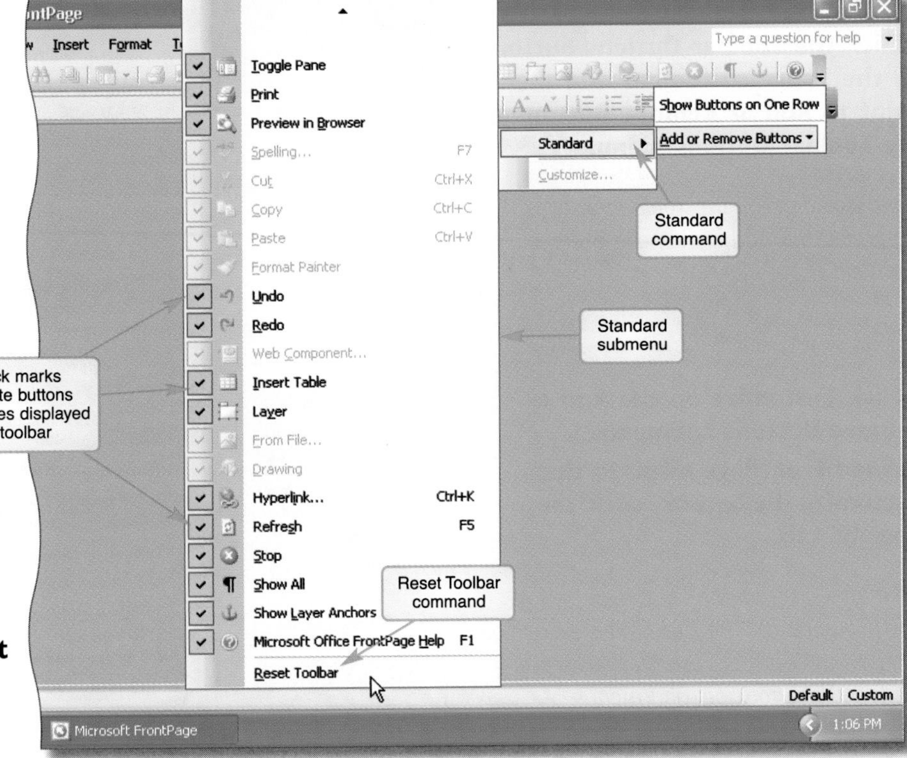

FIGURE D-6

4

- **Reset the Formatting toolbar by following Steps 1 through 3 and replacing any reference to the Standard toolbar with the Formatting toolbar.**

Other Ways

1. On View menu point to Toolbars, click Customize on Toolbars submenu, click Toolbars tab, click toolbar name, click Reset button, click OK button, click Close button
2. Right-click toolbar, click Customize on shortcut menu, click Toolbars tab, click toolbar name, click Reset button, click OK button, click Close button
3. In Voice Command mode, say "View, Toolbars, Customize, Toolbars, [desired toolbar name], Reset, OK, Close"

Not only can you use the Standard submenu shown in Figure D-6 on the previous page to reset the Standard toolbar to its original settings, but you also can use it to customize the Standard toolbar by adding and deleting buttons. To add or delete buttons, click the button name on the Standard submenu to add or remove the check mark. Buttons with a check mark to the left currently are displayed on the Standard toolbar; buttons without a check mark are not displayed on the Standard toolbar. You can complete the same tasks for the Formatting toolbar, using the Formatting submenu to add to and delete buttons from the Formatting toolbar.

Resetting the FrontPage Menus

The following steps show how to reset the FrontPage menus to their original settings.

To Reset the FrontPage Menus

1

- **Click the Toolbar Options button on the Standard toolbar and then point to Add or Remove Buttons on the Toolbar Options menu.**

FrontPage displays the Toolbar Options menu and the Add or Remove Buttons submenu (Figure D-7).

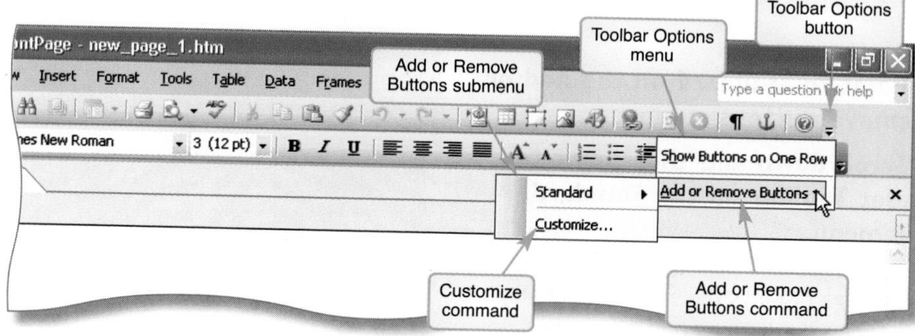

FIGURE D-7

2

- **Click Customize on the Add or Remove Buttons submenu.**
- **When FrontPage displays the Customize dialog box, click the Options tab.**

FrontPage displays the Customize dialog box (Figure D-8). The Customize dialog box contains three sheets used for customizing the FrontPage toolbars and menus.

3

- **Click the Reset menu and toolbar usage data button. When FrontPage displays the Microsoft Office FrontPage dialog box, click the Yes button. Click the Close button in the Customize dialog box.**

FrontPage resets the menus to the original settings.

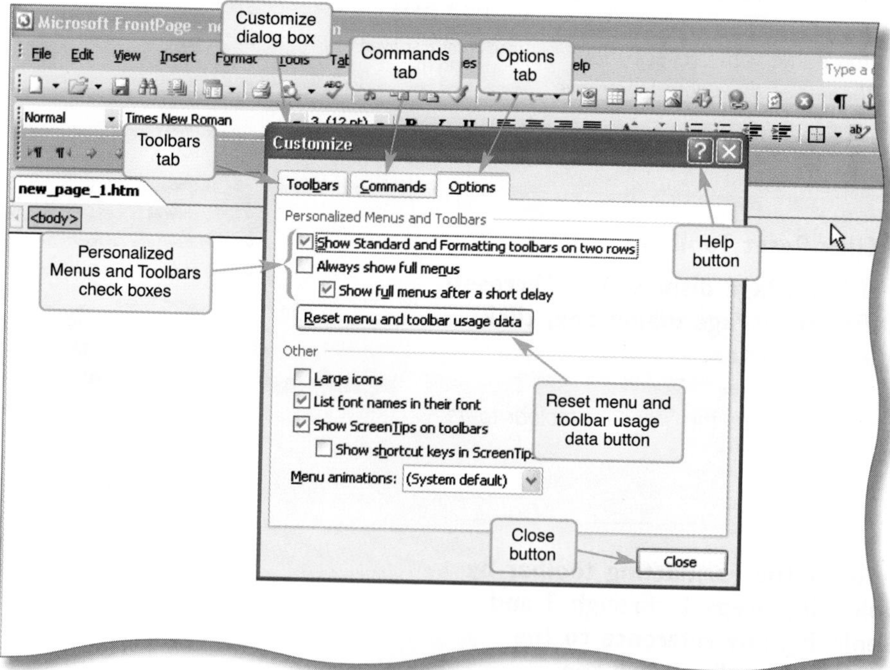

FIGURE D-8

Using the Options sheet in the Customize dialog box, as shown in Figure D-8, you can select options to personalize menus and toolbars. For example, you can select or deselect a check mark that instructs FrontPage to display the Standard and Formatting toolbars on two rows. You also can select whether FrontPage always displays full menus or displays short menus followed by full menus, after a short delay. Other options available in the Options sheet include settings to instruct FrontPage to display toolbars with large icons; to use the appropriate font to display font names in the Font list; and to display a ScreenTip when a user points to a toolbar button. Clicking the Help button immediately to the left of the Close button on the Customize dialog box's title bar (Figure D-8) instructs FrontPage to display topics that will assist you in customizing toolbars and menus.

Using the Commands sheet in the Customize dialog box, you can add buttons to toolbars and commands to menus. Recall that the menu bar at the top of the FrontPage window is a special toolbar. To add buttons to a toolbar, click a category name in the Categories list and then drag the command name in the Commands list to a toolbar. To add commands to a menu, click a category name in the Categories list, drag the command name in the Commands list to a menu name on the menu bar, and then, when the menu appears, drag the command to the desired location in the list of menu commands.

Using the Toolbars sheet in the Customize dialog box, you can add new toolbars and reset existing toolbars and the menus. To add a new toolbar, click the New button, enter a toolbar name in the New Toolbar dialog box, and then click the OK button. After you create the new toolbar, you can use the Commands sheet to add or remove buttons, as you would with any other toolbar. If you add one or more buttons to an existing toolbar and want to reset the toolbar to its original settings, click the toolbar name in the Toolbars list so a check mark displays to the left of the name and then click the Reset button. If you add commands to one or more menus and want to reset the menus to their default settings, click Menu Bar in the Toolbars list on the Toolbars sheet so a check mark displays to the left of the name and then click the Reset button. When you have finished, click the Close button to close the Customize dialog box.

Other Ways

1. On View menu point to Toolbars, click Customize on Toolbars submenu, click Options tab, click Reset menu and toolbar usage data button, click Yes button, click Close button
2. Right-click toolbar, click Customize on shortcut menu, click Options tab, click Reset menu and toolbar usage data button, click Yes button, click Close button
3. In Voice Command mode, say "View, Toolbars, Customize, Options, Reset menu and toolbar usage data, Yes, Close"

Appendix E

FrontPage Web Design Tips

This appendix lists in project sequence the Design Tips boxed throughout this book. The first column contains the page number on which the corresponding Design Tip in the second column is presented. Use this page number to focus on the circumstances surrounding the development of the Design Tip. Use the second column as a quick overview of the Design Tips and as preparation for examinations.

Project 1 Design Tips

PAGE NUMBER	DESIGN TIP
FP 9	As you develop a Web site, test the Web pages in as many browsers as your audience might use.
FP 11	Many Web pages use common elements to which users are accustomed. When designing your page, consider using standard design elements such as a title, page banners, and link bars.
FP 13	Plan to publish your Web site on a regular basis to keep content up to date after your Web site is up and running. Do not allow your content to become stale, or out of date.
FP 19	Before creating a Web site from scratch, lay out the navigation structure of your Web site and consider a template to alleviate a great deal of manual work when creating the Web site.
FP 23	If your Web site's navigation structure is both well-designed and focused on your users, your visitors will be able to move to different locations on a page or to other pages in your Web site to find usable information quickly and easily.
FP 25	Generate a sense of unity or familiarity within your Web site by utilizing a common graphic theme and a common color theme.
FP 31	If the main content for your Web page is not already in a word-processing document, consider first placing all of your content in one. You and other contributors can manage the content much easier in a common file format. When the content is ready to be made available on the Web, simply copy and paste the content from the document into the Web page in FrontPage.
FP 47	Consider adding hyperlinks from key terms or phrases in the content on your page to other Web pages or external Web sites that include more information about the topic than you are willing to provide on your Web page.
FP 48	If your Web page contains a link to external Web sites, periodically check the link to be sure that the external Web site still exists or has not changed location. One of the more important elements of the World Wide Web is the ease of navigation to other sites through the use of hyperlinks.
FP 52	Build into your Web pages simple and convenient ways for Web site visitors to interact with you or your organization.

Project 2 Design Tips

PAGE NUMBER	DESIGN TIP
FP 85	Each individual Web page should have one purpose or present one concept. Avoid splitting one concept into two parts simply to reduce the size of a page. Likewise, refrain from combining two unrelated ideas just to make a Web page larger. If information is designed to be read online, limit the pages to two screens, and provide links to additional information.
FP 85	Use the criteria outlined in Table 2-1 on page FP 84 as a guide for designing Web pages.
FP 86	Begin your Web page design with a single purpose in mind. If something appears on the Web page, then it should serve some purpose. If something serves no purpose, then it should not be on the Web page. Choose content that adds value, that is, content that is relative, informative, timely, accurate, and usable.
FP 92	Use descriptive names for file names and maintain a standard for naming files. Over time and as your site includes more pages, a well-maintained organizational structure for the files in the Web site can decrease the amount of time spent on maintenance.
FP 95	Browser title bars display approximately 80 to 90 characters, so keep this limitation in mind when designing Web page titles.
FP 98	Generate a sense of oneness within your Web site by utilizing consistent alignment, a common graphic theme, and a common color theme. Be judicious about whether a page properly fits within the chosen scheme.
FP 103	Before you create any table, sketch it on paper. Determine the number of rows and columns and the content that you will place in the cells. Calculate the overall width of the table and necessary width for each column.
FP 107	When you design a Web page, do not limit your creativity to the print environment. Where appropriate, include color, photographs, animation, video, and sound clips.
FP 109	Before downloading photos or other media from the Web, ensure that they have no copyright restrictions or royalty charges that you cannot or will not pay. Royalty charges are fees to be paid to the creator/owner of the art for its use.
FP 110	Using images with a transparent background allows the color or image used in a Web page background to show through the background of the inserted image, thus hiding the rectangular shape of the image. Cropping an image can eliminate distracting background elements and establish the focal point of the image. Discarding unwanted portions of an image also reduces its file size.
FP 120	Use common fonts in your Web pages to increase the chances of overriding default font settings and allowing the visitor to view the page in the manner in which it was designed. Type that is 10 points or smaller may not be readable to many Web page visitors.
FP 122	It is customary to separate logical sections of Web pages, such as the header and body, using dividing elements called horizontal lines, or horizontal rules. Use headers and footers on pages that comprise the main navigational structure of your site. Secondary pages need not fit a rigid design structure.

Project 3 Design Tips

PAGE NUMBER	DESIGN TIP
FP 157	GIF files are best suited for solid-colored images such as logos and illustrations. The 256-color limitation of GIF files makes them inappropriate for displaying photographs.
FP 157	Each time a JPEG image is edited and saved, the image is compressed and decompressed, which degrades the image quality. You should make a copy of the original source image file and never alter the original image.
FP 170	Use shared borders when multiple pages in a Web site contain identical information in the same location on the page.
FP 181	Copy and paste text from other documents into your Web page when the source application of the document cannot save the document in a suitable Web page format. Be sure to keep the Web page updated with any changes to the original document.
FP 191	If there are a number of links to relatively short pieces of information, and the user is likely to go back and forth from one page to another visiting these links, it may be better to place all of the information on a single Web page and use bookmarks to navigate to the short pieces of information.
FP 199	To hide the rectangular shape common to all images, use images that have the same background color as the Web page, or use images that have a transparent background. Using images with a transparent background allows the color or graphic used in a Web page background to show through the background of the image, thus hiding the rectangular shape of the image.
FP 201	To make an image transparent, select one of the colors in the image to be the transparent color. The transparent color is replaced by the background color, background design, or image of the page. An image can have only one transparent color.
FP 203	When working with large image files, resample the images after adding the image to the page if the image is resized on the page. The resulting smaller file size allows the page to download faster.
FP 205	When designing a Web page that contains elements that are positioned absolutely, be sure to test the page with all browsers that Web page visitors use.
FP 213	When creating an image map, the use of a motif, or metaphor, for the images helps to guide the user. Consider image maps as a replacement for related text hyperlinks.
FP 216	Avoid broken hyperlinks by testing the Web site before publishing the Web site, after publishing the Web site, and on a regular basis once the Web site is published.

Project 4 Design Tips

PAGE NUMBER	DESIGN TIP
FP 261	Use caution when using multiple forms in a Web page. In general, develop a design in such as manner that the main area of the Web page contains only one form.
FP 263	In general, the Post method is the preferred method to handle forms. Use the Get method when you want to use special features provided by the Get method.
FP 264	When designing a form for a Web page, typically you lay out the input fields in the order you would read a book - from left to right and top to bottom. You can use tables to organize and control the spacing of the form fields in the Web page.
FP 274	Although not required, insert a new form into a table in order to control positioning of the form on the Web page.
FP 275	Although not required, inserting a new table into a form allows you to control positioning of the elements of the form, such as text and form fields.

Project 4 Design Tips

PAGE NUMBER	DESIGN TIP
FP 278	Label each form field appropriately and associate labels with their form fields to make navigation of the Web page easier.
FP 278	Use a text box form field when the user needs to enter only one line of text. Use a text area form field when the user may enter multiple lines of text.
FP 293	Before working with nested tables, sketch out the design on paper to be sure you have a good idea of how to draw the table in Design view. Calculate the necessary widths and heights of the columns and rows and the size of the overall table.
FP 294	While you can use spaces to separate labels from form fields, consider using table cells to separate the items. By adjusting the position of the cell borders, you can obtain the required alignment.
FP 294	Use a drop-down list when you need to provide the user with a variety of choices. Use option buttons for a variety of choices when the user has only a few choices.
FP 303	Always place option buttons in a group box. Use option buttons when the user must choose one option from among a small set of mutually exclusive options.
FP 321	Include meta tags as part of your design. Choose targeted meta tags that succinctly describe the use and content of the Web page. The use of common words in meta tags decreases the chance that a Web user will find your page using a search engine.

Project 5 Design Tips

PAGE NUMBER	DESIGN TIP
FP 341	With frames, a Web page designer has greater flexibility in page design. Frames allow the designer to display several Web pages in the same browser window, with each Web page being displayed in its own frame. With frames, you can create a Web page to display the common links in one frame and display the linked target Web pages in another frame.
FP 342	Although most Web browsers support frames, some users of your site may have browsers that do not support frames or may prefer a no-frames version. When designing with frames, consider the creation of an alternative set of pages without frames to display to those users.
FP 351	If you do not understand the structure of a database or do not have access to the structure of a database, work with a database administrator (DBA) or a developer familiar with the database structure when designing the queries used to gather data from the database.
FP 358	Use FrontPage's built-in frames templates when designing a Web page with frames. If you cannot find a template to match your intended design, then choose the closest template to the design you have in mind and alter the frames in the Web page.
FP 364	Use an existing Web page as the initial page in a frame to provide flexibility in the design process. Using this technique, you can assign different individuals or work groups to develop the Web pages simultaneously, thus reducing the time it takes to implement complex frames pages.
FP 373	Carefully consider the set of features that you add to each frame, such as whether the user can resize the frame, the initial size of the frame, and whether the frame includes scroll bars. Take into consideration your user's browser and screen resolution when making these decisions.
FP 376	Carefully consider the behavior of each hyperlink in a frame. Hyperlinks may target a default frame, the same frame as the hyperlink, the entire page, a new browser window, or the parent frame. Consider whether targeting a link to another frame may cause unwanted behavior, such as the nesting of one framed page within another.
FP 385	FrontPage and most browsers do not support printing multiple frames at the same time. For this reason, when designing a Web page with frames, try to combine a region of information that a user may want to print within a single frame, rather than requiring that a user print multiple frames.

Project 6 Design Tips

PAGE NUMBER	DESIGN TIP
FP 405	As a Web site grows, consider reorganizing the files in the Web site into folders or subsites to help manage the relationships between various parts of the Web site.
FP 406	Use FrontPage, rather than Windows Explorer or other tools, when manipulating the physical structure of the files and folders in a Web site. FrontPage includes the necessary tools to manage links and other relationships properly.
FP 408	You can use subsites to limit access for security reasons. Because each subsite can have its own set of permissions for who can author, browse, or administer it, you can set up individual subsites with different levels of permissions and different groups of users.
FP 410	It is preferable to design the overall organizational structure of your Web site, including subsites, before creating the Web site. Unanticipated growth of a Web site, however, can require some restructuring.
FP 416	Eliminate all but the essential references between subsites and the parent Web site. That is, do not reference resources, such as images, from the subsite to the parent Web site.
FP 419	When linking to a home page within a subsite or parent Web site, be sure to link to a reference to the home page, rather than the file name of the home page itself. Some Web servers require the change of the file name of the home page during the publishing process.
FP 432	When displaying multiple records, consider using frames to divide the user's viewing area into two areas. The first area contains a listing of all of the records while the second area allows the Web page visitor to view details about a record selected in the first area.
FP 441	Decide on using source control during the design process. Use source control when the possibility exists that multiple Web page developers may be able to edit Web pages at the same time.

Project 7 Design Tips

PAGE NUMBER	DESIGN TIP
FP 486	Consider creating a prototype for a new Web site or Web page and testing the site or page in a safe location before incorporating the new site or page into another Web site. By developing a prototype, you and others can review the pages to ensure they are acceptable before publishing to the live Web site.
FP 489	Tables provide a versatile layout environment. When designing a new Web page, consider beginning the design with a table or multiple tables.
FP 494	As a general rule, you should insert a caption for any table that is used to contain data or information (as opposed to a table used to align items on a Web page). You can insert a caption above or below a table; you also can align and format the caption text just like any other text on a Web page, to ensure that the caption complements the overall Web page design.
FP 498	When designing with tables, keep in mind that table cells can be split or combined to accommodate almost any design that includes distinct rectangular areas of the Web page.
FP 501	Become familiar with FrontPage's predefined Table AutoFormats. AutoFormats provide interesting and visually appealing designs for typically uninteresting tables. After applying an AutoFormat, the table can be further customized to meet your needs.
FP 503	Keep cell padding and cell spacing in mind when designing tables and cells. If a cell contains text, the cell padding should be set to allow some space between the text and the cell border, so that the text is easy to read. If a cell contains a graphic, you may want to set cell padding to zero, so that the graphic fills the entire cell.
FP 515	Be careful not to overuse images as cell backgrounds. Consider using images of color gradients or simple clip art rather than pictures to enhance the look of a cell. Images with curved patterns in cells can be used to give the Web page less of a boxy or rectangular feel.

Project 7 Design Tips

PAGE NUMBER	DESIGN TIP
FP 519	A search feature can give visitors the much desired flexibility and control to navigate a Web site in the manner they choose, thus allowing visitors to quickly find the information they need.
FP 524	When using Web page templates, be sure to take the time to modify the placeholder text, such as author and date information. Also, consider modifying the overall look of the page so that the page matches the overall design of your Web site.

Project 8 Design Tips

PAGE NUMBER	DESIGN TIP
FP 543	When designing a template, mark those regions of the template that will be editable by the user of the template. Be sure to point out special effects and behaviors.
FP 547	Use rulers and grid lines when you need to lay out elements of a Web page very precisely. They are particularly useful when designing Web pages that include a fixed-width layout of the page.
FP 553	FrontPage includes the ability to add many types of DHTML effects. Become familiar with the effects in the DHTML Effects toolbar by experimenting with the toolbar. Incorporate effects into your Web page designs by specifying events and actions as notes in your design.
FP 553	Use layers sparingly in Web page design. Be sure to test pages that include layers in all browsers that your users may use. Also, test layers in a variety of browser window sizes and screen resolutions. Layers may look fine in Design mode on one browser but appear completely different using another browser.
FP 564	Make certain that Web pages that are created using a dynamic Web template continue to have access to the template after the page is created and published. If a template is attached to a Web page and the template is not in the same Web site as the Web page, then care must be taken to keep the Web page and template in sync. Consider using a separate folder on your Web site to contain all the templates you may use.
FP 575	Make a habit of creating and saving log files generated when you change a dynamic Web template. Be certain to test all Web pages that were modified as a result of the changed template.
FP 575	A good design should include proper grammar and spelling. Always spell check Web pages and templates.
FP 577	If you work with or for a government agency, make sure that you adhere to any accessibility guidelines. Many government agencies, including state government agencies, are required to adhere to the Section 508 accessibility guidelines.
FP 583	When using Split view, your screen may become cluttered with windows, task panes, and toolbars. Consider using as high a screen resolution and as large a monitor as you can when working with FrontPage. Split view also offers you a chance to learn the HTML generated by FrontPage behind the scenes.

Project 9 Design Tips

PAGE NUMBER	DESIGN TIP
FP 607	When using IIS as a local host, take the time to properly secure your computer with a firewall. Windows XP includes firewall functionality that is configured easily. Make sure that your computer includes up-to-date patches for Windows and any other software.
FP 611	While designing your site, begin considering where and how your site will be published to a server. Decide on a virtual directory structure and begin the process of configuring the server. If your server is managed by a third party, contact the server administrator and begin to discuss your requirements.
FP 615	The migration and management of development, test, and production servers should be done in a controlled and careful manner. Include plans to go back to a previous version of a Web site if the deployment of a new version does not work out. The methods in which you perform a migration should be documented and well understood by your team and the server administrators.
FP 629	Plan the roles for your Web site administration carefully. Too often, everyone in a group receives full authority. Limit all users to the bare essential roles, adding new privileges only after careful consideration.
FP 632	Publishing a Web site is not the final step in the development of a Web site. A Web site requires ongoing troubleshooting and preventive maintenance. Consider recalculating your Web site from time to time.
FP 638	File status reports can serve as a security mechanism. By running these reports weekly or monthly, you can determine if anyone is changing or adding files without your knowledge.
FP 641	While designing a Web site, consider the types of usage reports that you would like to see. Determine which Web pages you would like to particularly observe. Make sure that you turn on the options on the server to gather your Web page statistics.

Index

MICROSOFT

Office FrontPage 2003

Quick Reference Summary

In Microsoft Office FrontPage 2003, you can accomplish a task in a number of ways. The following table provides a quick reference to each task presented in this textbook. The first column identifies the task. The second column indicates the page number on which the task is discussed in the book. The subsequent four columns list the different ways the task in column one can be carried out. You can invoke the commands listed in the MOUSE, MENU BAR, and SHORTCUT MENU columns using Voice commands.

Microsoft Office FrontPage 2003 Quick Reference Summary

TASK	PAGE NUMBER	MOUSE	MENU BAR	SHORTCUT MENU	KEYBOARD SHORTCUT
Accessibility, Check	FP 578		Tools | Accessibility		F8
Align Left	FP 114	Align Left button on Formatting toolbar	Format | Paragraph | Indents and Spacing tab	Paragraph | Indents and Spacing tab	CTRL+L
Align Right	FP 114	Align Right button on Formatting toolbar	Format | Paragraph | Indents and Spacing tab	Paragraph | Indents and Spacing tab	CTRL+R
AutoShape, Add	FP 206	AutoShapes button on Drawing toolbar	Insert | Picture | AutoShapes		ALT+U
AutoShape, Insert	FP 291	AutoShapes button on Drawing toolbar			ALT+U
Background Color, Modify	FP 99		Format | Background | Background tab	Page Properties | Background tab	ALT+O | K
Behavior, Add	FP 559		Format | Behaviors		ALT+O | V
Bold	FP 120	Bold button on Formatting toolbar	Format | Font | Font tab	Font | Font tab	CTRL+B or ALT+ENTER
Bookmark, Create	FP 190	Insert Hyperlink button on Standard toolbar	Insert | Bookmark	Hyperlink	CTRL+G
Center	FP 114	Center button on Formatting toolbar	Format | Paragraph | Indents and Spacing tab	Paragraph | Indents and Spacing tab	CTRL+E
Checkout Status Report, View	FP 446	Reports button on Reporting toolbar	View | Reports | Workflow | Checkout Status		ALT+V | R | W | K
Clip Art, Insert	FP 107	Insert Picture From File button on Standard toolbar	Insert | Picture | Clip Art; Insert | Picture | From File		
Clip Art, Replace	FP 110	Insert Picture From File button on Pictures toolbar	Insert | Picture | Clip Art; Insert | Picture | From File	Picture Properties | General tab | Browse	
Color Characters	FP 122	Font Color button arrow on Formatting toolbar	Format | Font | Font tab	Font | Font tab	ALT+ENTER
Copy	FP 112	Copy button on Standard toolbar	Edit | Copy	Copy	CTRL+C
Create Web Site, Template or Wizard	FP 20	New Page button arrow on Standard toolbar, Web Site	File | New		
Daily Page Hits Report, View	FP 643	Reports button on Reporting toolbar, Usage, Daily Page Hits	View | Reports | Usage | Daily Page Hits		ALT+V | R | U | D
Data, Fill Down	FP 496	Fill Down button on Tables toolbar	Table | Fill | Down		ALT+A | L | D
Data, Fill Right	FP 497	Fill Right button on Tables toolbar	Table | Fill | Right		ALT+A | L | R

Microsoft Office FrontPage 2003 Quick Reference Summary *(continued)*

TASK	PAGE NUMBER	MOUSE	MENU BAR	SHORTCUT MENU	KEYBOARD SHORTCUT
Database Editor Pages, Create with Database Interface Wizard	FP 427		File | New | More Web site templates		ALT+F | N
Database Results, Insert	FP 351		Insert | Database | Results		ALT+I | D | R
Delete Page	FP 44		Edit | Delete	Right-click file name in Folder List pane, Delete	DELETE
Delete Text	FP 31	Cut button on Standard toolbar	Edit | Cut or Edit | Delete	Cut	DELETE or BACKSPACE
Design View	FP 24	Design button			
DHTML Effects toolbar, Display	FP 551		View | Toolbars | DHTML Effects		ALT+V | T | DHTML Effects
Dynamic Web Template, Create	FP 565		File | Save As | Dynamic Web Template in Save as type box		ALT+F | A Dynamic Web Template in Save as type box
Editable Region, Create	FP 567		Format | Dynamic Web Template | Manage Editable Regions	Manage Editable Regions	ALT+O | W | M
File, Check In under Source Control	FP 448		Edit | Check In	Check In	ALT+E | I CTRL+SHIFT+J
File, Check Out under Source Control	FP 445		Edit | Check Out	Check Out	ALT+E | O CTRL+J
File, Import	FP 348		File | Import		
File, Set as Home Page	FP 411			Set as Home Page	
File, Rename	FP 92			Right-click file name in Folder List, Rename	
Flash Movie, Set Properties	FP 662		Format | Properties	Movie in Flash Format Properties	ALT+ENTER
Folder, Convert to Web site	FP 408			Convert to Web	
Folder, Create	FP 405			Right-click home folder, New | Folder	
Folders View	FP 265	Folders button	View | Folders		ALT+V | F
Font	FP 120	Font box arrow on Formatting toolbar	Format | Font | Font tab	Font | Font tab	ALT+ENTER
Font Size	FP 126	Font Size box arrow on Formatting toolbar	Format | Font | Font tab	Font | Font tab	ALT+ENTER
Form, Insert	FP 274		Insert | Form | Form		ALT+I | F | F
Form, Modify Properties	FP 314		Insert | Form | Form Properties	Form Properties	ALT+I | R | R
Form Field, Assign Label	FP 287		Insert | Form | Label		ALT+I | R | A
Form Field, Insert Check Box	FP 285		Insert | Form | Checkbox		ALT+I | R | C
Form Field, Insert Drop-Down List Box	FP 297		Insert | Form | Drop-Down Box		ALT+I | R | D
Form Field, Insert Group Box	FP 303		Insert | Form | Group Box		ALT+I | R | G
Form Field, Insert Option Button	FP 305		Insert | Form | Option Button		ALT+I | R | O
Form Field, Insert Text Area	FP 311		Insert | Form | Text Area		ALT+I | R | E

Microsoft Office FrontPage 2003 Quick Reference Summary

TASK	PAGE NUMBER	MOUSE	MENU BAR	SHORTCUT MENU	KEYBOARD SHORTCUT
Form Field, Insert Textbox	FP 279		Insert | Form | Textbox		ALT+I | R | T
Form Field, Modify Properties	FP 280		Format | Properties	Form Field Properties	ALT+ENTER
Form Handler	FP 317		Insert | Form | Form Properties	Form Properties	ALT+I | R | R
Frame, Modify Properties	FP 373		Frames | Frame Properties	Frame Properties	
Frame, Resize	FP 367	Drag frame border	Frames | Frame Properties	Frame Properties	ALT+R | P
Frames Page, Modify Properties	FP 374		Click frame border, then File | Properties | Frames tab	Frame Properties | Frames Page button	ALT+F | I
Full Menu	FP 17	Double-click menu name or click menu name, wait a few seconds	Tools | Customize | Options tab		
Grid, Display	FP 546		View | Ruler and Grid | Show Grid		ALT+V | U | G
Help	FP 63 and Appendix A	Microsoft Office FrontPage Help button on Standard toolbar	Help | Microsoft Office FrontPage Help		F1
HTML, Optimize	FP 617	Remote Web Site Properties button in Remote Web Site view, Optimize HTML tab	File | Publish Site | Optimize HTML tab		
Horizontal Rule, Insert	FP 123		Insert | Horizontal Line		ALT+I | L
Hotspot, Add Polygonal	FP 213	Polygonal Hotspot button on Pictures toolbar			
Hotspots, Highlight	FP 213	Highlight Hotspots button on Pictures toolbar			
HTML, Modify or View	FP 322	Code button or Split button			
Hyperlink, Create	FP 52	Hyperlink button on Standard toolbar	Insert | Hyperlink	Hyperlink	CTRL+K
Hyperlink, Edit	FP 52	Hyperlink button on Standard toolbar		Hyperlink Properties	CTRL+K
Hyperlinks, Display	FP 215	Hyperlinks icon on Views bar	View | Hyperlinks		ALT+V | H
Hyperlinks, Verify	FP 218	Verify Hyperlinks button on Reporting toolbar	View | Toolbars | Reporting, Verify Hyperlinks button	Reporting	
Image, Insert from File	FP 106	Insert Picture From File button on Standard toolbar	Insert | Picture | From File		
Image, Resample	FP 203	Resample button on Pictures toolbar			
Image, Resize	FP 203	Drag sizing handles	Format | Properties	Picture Properties | Appearance	
Image, Select	FP 112	Click graphic			Position insertion point before image, CTRL+SHIFT+ RIGHT ARROW
Image, Transparent	FP 201	Set Transparent Color button on Pictures toolbar			
Inline Frame, Add	FP 466		Insert | Inline Frame		ALT+I | E
Interactive Button, Insert	FP 470		Insert | Interactive Button		ALT+I | U
Italicize	FP 120	Italic button on Formatting toolbar	Format | Font | Font tab	Font | Font tab	CTRL+I or ALT+ENTER
Language Bar	FP 19 and Appendix B	Language indicator button in tray	Tools | Speech		ALT+T | H

Microsoft Office FrontPage 2003 Quick Reference Summary *(continued)*

TASK	PAGE NUMBER	MOUSE	MENU BAR	SHORTCUT MENU	KEYBOARD SHORTCUT
Layer, Add	FP 554	Insert Layer button in Layers task pane	Insert | Layer		ALT+I | L
Layer, Modify Properties	FP 556		Format | Properties	Layer Properties	ALT+O | T
Layout cell, Properties	FP 249			Cell Properties	
Layout cell, resize	FP 246	Drag sizing handles		Cell Properties	
Layout table, add	FP 243		Table | Layout Tables and Cells		ALT+T | B
Modify Component	FP 42	Double-click component		<component name> Properties	
Movie in Flash Format, Add	FP 660		Insert | Picture | Movie in Flash Format		ALT+I | P | L
Movie, Insert	FP 665		Insert | Picture | Video		ALT+P | V
Movie, Set Properties	FP 667		Format | Properties	Picture Properties	ALT+ENTER
Navigation Structure, Add Page	FP 433	On Web Site tab, click Navigation	View | Navigation icon on Views bar, drag and drop		ALT+V | N
Navigation Structure, Create	FP 413	On Web Site tab, click Navigation button, drag and drop	View | Navigation		ALT+V | N
Navigation View	FP 44	Navigation icon on Views bar	View | Navigation		
No Frames View, Display	FP 383	No Frames button			
Page, Edit	FP 97	Double-click page icon in Navigation pane			
Page in Web Site, Open	FP 24	Double-click file name in Folder List pane	File | Open	Right-click Folder List pane, Open	CTRL+O
Page Label, Change	FP 96	Click page icon in Navigation view, click text box		Right-click page icon in Navigation view, Rename	
Page, New	FP 89	Create a new normal page button on Standard toolbar	File | New		CTRL+N
Page, New from Dynamic Web Template	FP 570			New from Dynamic Web Template	
Page Title, Change	FP 94		File | Properties	Right-click page icon in Navigation view, click Properties, click General tab; right-click file name, click Properties, click General tab; right-click Page, click Page Properties, click General tab	
Page, View	FP 97		View | Page		
Paste	FP 112	Paste button on Standard toolbar	Edit | Paste	Paste	CTRL+V
Preview Page	FP 41	Preview tab			CTRL+PAGE UP, CTRL+PAGE DOWN
Preview Page in Browser	FP 41	Preview in Browser button on Standard toolbar	File | Preview in Browser		
Print Page	FP 54	Print button on Standard toolbar	File | Print		CTRL+P
Print Preview	FP 137		File | Print Preview		ALT+F | V
Publish Web Site	FP 56	Publish Web button on Standard toolbar	File | Publish Web		

Microsoft Office FrontPage 2003 Quick Reference Summary

TASK	PAGE NUMBER	MOUSE	MENU BAR	SHORTCUT MENU	KEYBOARD SHORTCUT
Publishing Options, Set	FP 616	Remote Web Site Properties button in Remote Web Site view, Publishing tab	File | Publish Site | Publishing tab		
Quit FrontPage	FP 65	Close button on title bar	File | Exit		ALT+F4
Recently Added Files Report, View	FP 638	Reports button on Reporting toolbar	View | Reports | Files | Recently Added Files		ALT+V | R | F | D
Recently Changed Files Report, View	FP 640	Reports button on Reporting toolbar	View | Reports | Files | Recently Changed Files		ALT+V | R | F | H
Redo	FP 106	Redo button on Standard toolbar	Edit | Redo		CTRL+Y
Reports, View Site Summary Report	FP 218	Report box arrow on Reporting toolbar, Site Summary	View | Reports | Site Summary		ALT+V | R | M
Rulers, Display	FP 546		View | Ruler and Grid | Show Ruler		ALT+V | U | R
Save Page - Same Name	FP 39	Save button on Standard toolbar	File | Save		CTRL+S
Save Web - Embedded Files	FP 139	Save button on Standard toolbar	File | Save		CTRL+S
Search Form, Modify Properties	FP 525		Format | Properties	Search Form Properties	ALT+O | T ALT+ENTER
Search Page, Create	FP 520		File | New | More Page Templates link | General tab		
Shared Border, Add	FP 169		Format | Shared Borders		ALT+O | D
Shortcut menu	FP 33	Right-click object			SHIFT+F10
Source Control, Enable or Disable	FP 442, FP 634	Tools | Site Settings | General tab | Use document check-in and check-out			ALT+T | W
Spell Check	FP 575	Spelling button on Standard toolbar	Tools | Spelling		F7
Start FrontPage	FP 13	Start button on taskbar, All Programs, Microsoft Office, Microsoft Office FrontPage 2003			
Style, Modify Paragraph	FP 121	Style box arrow on Formatting toolbar			
Subsite, Open	FP 410	Double-click subsite folder	File | Open Site		ALT+F | I
Subsite Permissions, Manage	FP 626		Tools | Server | Permissions		ALT+T | V | P
Table, Adjust Cell Borders	FP 115	Drag cell border	Table | Table Properties | Cell	Cell Properties	ALT+A | R | E
Table, Autoformat	FP 502	Table AutoFormat button on Tables toolbar	Table | Table AutoFormat		ALT+A | F
Table Caption, Insert	FP 492		Table | Insert | Caption		ALT+A | I | A
Table Cell, Modify Properties	FP 506		Table | Table Properties | Cell	Cell Properties	ALT+A | R | E
Table Cell, Split	FP 499	Split Cells button on Tables toolbar	Table | Split Cells	Split Cells	ALT+A | P
Table Cells, Align	FP 125		Table | Table Properties | Cell	Cell Properties	ALT+A | R | E
Table Cells, Delete	FP 33		Table | Delete Cells	Delete Cells	ALT+A | D
Table Cells, Merge	FP 105, FP 513	Eraser button on Tables toolbar, drag through cell border	Table | Merge Cells	Merge Cells	ALT+A | M

Microsoft Office FrontPage 2003 Quick Reference Summary *(continued)*

TASK	PAGE NUMBER	MOUSE	MENU BAR	SHORTCUT MENU	KEYBOARD SHORTCUT
Table Cells, Select	FP 32	Click first cell, hold SHIFT key, click last cell	Table | Select | Cell		ALT+A | C | E
Table, Create	FP 103	Insert Table button on Standard toolbar	Table | Insert | Table		ALT+A | I | T
Table, Hide Borders	FP 119		Table | Table Properties | Table	Table Properties	
Table, Insert Column	FP 165		Table | Insert | Rows or Columns	Insert Columns	ALT+A | I | N
Table, Insert Row	FP 165		Table | Insert | Rows or Columns	Insert Rows	ALT+A | I | N
Table, Modify Properties	FP 117		Table | Table Properties | Table	Table Properties	
Table, Select	FP 32	Drag through table	Table | Select | Table		
Tables Toolbar, View	FP 490		View | Toolbars | Tables		ALT+V | T | Tables
Task Pane	FP 15		View | Task Pane		ALT+V | K
Template, Frames	FP 359		File | New, click More page templates | Frames tab		ALT+F | N
Text, Add to Image	FP 207	Text button on Pictures toolbar		Add text	
Text, Select	FP 29	Drag through text			
Theme, Apply	FP 25		Format | Theme		ALT+O | H
Toolbar, Customize	FP 18	Toolbar Options button on toolbar, Add or Remove Buttons, click Customize		Customize	
Toolbar, Dock	FP 18	Drag toolbar to dock			
Toolbar, Reset	FP 18 and Appendix D	Toolbar Options, Add or Remove Buttons, Customize, Toolbars tab		Customize | Toolbars tab	ALT+V | T | C | T
Tracing Image, Set	FP 460		View | Tracing Image | Configure		ALT+V | I | C
Underline	FP 120	Underline button on Formatting toolbar	Format | Font | Font tab	Font | Font tab	CTRL+U or ALT+ENTER
Undo	FP 106	Undo button on Standard toolbar	Edit | Undo		CTRL+Z
Usage Summary Report, View	FP 642	Reports button on Reporting toolbar, Usage, Usage Summary	View | Reports | Usage | Usage Summary		ALT+V | R | U | U
Web Component, Insert Hit Counter	FP 167	Web component button arrow on Standard toolbar, Hit Counter	Insert | Web Component | Hit Counter		ALT+I | W
Web Component, Insert Link bar	FP 133	Web component button arrow on Standard toolbar, Link Bars	Insert | Web Component | Link Bars		ALT+I | W
Web Component, Insert Photo Gallery	FP 128	Web component button arrow on Standard toolbar, Photo Gallery	Insert | Web Component | Photo Gallery		ALT+I | W
Web Component, Insert Web Search	FP 520	Web Component button on Standard toolbar, Web Search	Insert | Web Component | Web Search type		ALT+I | W
Web Page, Set Title	FP 487		File | Properties | General tab	Page Properties | General tab	ALT+F | I
Web Site Administration Page, Access	FP 622		Tools | Server | Administration Home		ALT+T | V | A
Web Site, Open Site	FP 88	Open Site button arrow on Standard toolbar, Open Site	File | Open Site		ALT+F | I